ENCYCLOPEDIA

THE

BEATLES

ENCYCLOPEDIA

BILL HARRY

I dedicate this book to my two lost friends, John Lennon and Stuart Sutcliffe, remembering the days when we vowed to make Liverpool famous. John and I were to see that happen, but Stuart never did. John's work will always live – but I am especially pleased to see that Stuart's work is at last receiving recognition.

This edition first published in 2000 by
Virgin Publishing Ltd
Thames Wharf Studios
Rainville Road
London W6 9HA

First published in Great Britain in 1992 by
Virgin Publishing Ltd

A catalogue record for this title is available from the British Library

ISBN 0 7535 0481 2

Typeset by Phoenix Photosetting
Printed and bound in Great Britain

ACKNOWLEDGEMENTS

Material in this book began to be gathered in 1961 when I founded the *Mersey Beat* newspaper in Liverpool and became the first person to write about the Beatles on a regular basis.

I have used quotes and background material from interviews and conversations I have conducted personally with John Lennon, Paul McCartney, George Harrison, Ringo Starr, Pete Best, Stuart Sutcliffe, Brian Epstein, Bob Wooler, Allan Williams, Ray McFall, Rory Storm, Milli Sutcliffe, Brian Casser, Johnny Hutchinson, Johnny 'Guitar' Byrne, Pat Delaney, Brian Kelly, Sam Leach, Joe Flannery, Neil Aspinall, Mal Evans, Clive Epstein, Alistair Taylor, Derek Taylor, Gerry Marsden, Jackie Lomax, Cilla Black, Kingsize Taylor, Jim McCartney, Mike McCartney, Billy J. Kramer, Elsie Greaves, Iris Caldwell, Jonathan Hague, Les Chadwick, Cynthia Lennon, Pete Shotton, Rod Davis, Tony Bramwell, Peter Brown, Beryl Marsden, Ray Connolly, Ray Coleman, Chris Hutchins, Mike Berry, Steve Aldo, Mitch Murray, Arthur Ballard, Cliff Bennett, Frieda Kelly, Howie Casey, Eddie Amoo, the Beach Boys, Terry Doran, Bob Dylan, Manfred Weissleder, Horst Fascher, the Fourmost, Paul Murphy, Jim Gretty, Johnny Hamp, Dezo Hoffman, the Hollies, Peter Jones, Bert Kaempfert, Rod Murray, Alun Owen, P. J. Proby, Little Richard, Norman Rossington, Dick Rowe, Tony Sheridan, Mimi Smith, Brian Sommerville, Tony Barrow, Henry Henriod, Sounds Incorporated, Alvin Stardust, the Swinging Bluejeans, Lu Walters, Mary Wells, Kenny Lynch and many others.

I have also researched from my vast library of over 500 Beatles books and 500 fan magazines, and my collection of newspaper clippings and various other magazines. In addition, I have corresponded with dozens of other contacts associated with the Beatles story and used research I have compiled in the hundreds of Beatles articles I have written over the past 38 years in newspapers, magazines and Beatles fanzines.

I would also like to thank the many Beatles fans who contacted me with items of useful information, including Rolf-Peter Schmitz, Erich Weber, Michael Turner, Carmen Salmon, Harry Prytherch, Connie Krauth, Ian Forsyth and Rene Van Haarlem.

Thanks to everyone at Virgin Publishing who helped to put the book together: Peter Darvill-Evans, Ian Gittins and Kirstie Addis.

I must also acknowledge the help and support of my wife

Virginia, who was as much a part of the whole scene as I was myself, from the time in 1960 when she began to aid me in planning *Mersey Beat*. Her constant companionship through those years led people to call us 'Mr & Mrs Mersey Beat'. Incredibly, songwriter John Schroeder wanted to write a musical about the two of us! He was intrigued as to how an impecunious young couple, with hardly any experience of the world, helped to keep a whole scene going – and one which was eventually to change the entire international music industry.

Bill Harry, London, 1999

Abbey Road (Album)

The Beatles' twelfth British album and the last one that the group recorded in the studio – *Let It Be* had been recorded earlier, when sessions had been organised using the title 'Get Back'.

Abbey Road was issued in Britain on Parlophone PCS 7088 on 26 September 1969 and went straight to No. 1 in Britain within a week. It was issued in America on SO 383 on 1 October 1969, where it also topped the charts.

Originally, there was some conflict as to the approach to the album. John wanted a rock 'n' roll style album and Paul plumped for a pop symphony, or pop opera, with the songs segued into each other to produce one long medley. A compromise was achieved with Side One following along the lines of John's wish for individual tracks and Side Two satisfied Paul with tracks so close together they basically formed a sixteen-minute medley.

Abbey Road became the best-selling Beatles album with sales of approximately ten million during the decade after release. It was also the first Beatles album to be issued solely in stereo and it won a Grammy Award as best Engineered Non-Classical Recording.

The tracks were: Side One: 'Come Together', 'Something', 'Maxwell's Silver Hammer', 'Oh Darling', 'Octopus's Garden', 'I Want You (She's So Heavy)'. Side Two: 'Here Comes The Sun', 'Because', 'You Never Give Me Your Money', 'Sun King', 'Mean Mr Mustard', 'Polythene Pam', 'She Came In Through The Bathroom Window', 'Golden Slumbers', 'Carry That Weight', 'The End', 'Her Majesty'.

The cover was striking and comprised a colour photograph, bled off on all sides with no title or text. The photograph was taken by Iain Macmillan at 10.00 a.m. on 8 August 1969. He was given ten minutes to take the shot outside the Abbey Road Studios. He balanced on a stepladder and took six shots of the four walking across the zebra crossing. It was Paul who selected the cover shot from the pictures taken by Macmillan. Paul had, in fact, come up with the original idea for the sleeve and had presented Macmillan with a sketch for it. Many people can see Paul's hand in *Abbey Road* and the individual tracks written by him were: 'Maxwell's Silver Hammer', 'Oh Darling', 'You Never Give Me Your Money', 'She Came In Through The Bathroom Window', 'Golden Slumbers', 'Carry That Weight', 'The End' and 'Her Majesty'.

A bizarre affair grew from the photograph. From America, a few weeks after *Abbey Road* was issued, a 'Paul Is Dead!' movement got underway. Disc jockey Russ Gibbs, on the Detroit radio station WKNR-FM, suggested that Paul had an argument with the other members of the Beatles at Abbey Road Studios on 9 (or 10) November 1966 and had stormed out of the session, driven away in his Aston-Martin and been decapitated in a crash. Brian Epstein had hushed up the death and replaced Paul with a lookalike. Gibbs said clues could be found on subsequent Beatles albums, including *Abbey Road*. It was pointed out that Paul was barefoot in the picture, which indicated a Mafia (or Grecian) sign of death. A Michigan journalist, Fred LaBour, reviewing the album, claimed that the group was leaving a cemetery and that John was dressed as a minister. Ringo as an undertaker and George as a gravedigger, and pointed out that Paul was out of step with the others, which apparently meant that it was in fact either his corpse, or, more popularly, a substitute who'd had plastic surgery. According to the rumours, proof positive of the imposter theory was the fact that Paul was holding a cigarette in his right hand and everyone knew the real Paul McCartney was left-handed.

Photographer Iain Macmillan pointed out, 'Paul turned up in his Oxfam suit and sandals and because it was a hot day he decided to do some shots with sandals on and some with sandals off. Paul checked all the pictures with a magnifying glass. I don't think the other three were particularly bothered. He chose the nearest shot with the legs stretched in almost uniform style and it was pure coincidence that it happened to be the one with his sandals off. I got the job through John but it was Paul's idea and I was given ten minutes around lunchtime to do it.'

Paul himself told disc jockey Paul Gambaccini, 'I just turned up at the photo session. It was a really nice hot day and I think I wore sandals. I only had to walk around the corner to the crossing because I lived pretty nearby. I had me sandals off and on for the session. Of course, when it comes out people start looking at it and they say. "Why has he got no shoes on? He's never done that before." Okay, you've never seen me do it before but in actual fact it's just me with me shoes off. Turns out to be some old Mafia sign of death or something.'

But 'Paul Is Dead!' fanatics were not deterred. In the course of their study of the *Abbey Road* cover they discovered that the registration number – 28IF – of a Volkswagen car in the background, indicated that Paul would have been 28 IF he had lived.

In fact Paul was 27. Macmillan had been aware of the car, which belonged to a man who lived in the block of flats next door to the studios, and had tried to get the car moved for the photo session but the police pick-up truck was not able to get there in time. For years afterwards the man's number plates were stolen on numerous occasions and the car, with the plates (LMW 28IF) was eventually sold at auction at Sotheby's in 1986.

A photograph on the reverse of the sleeve shows the Abbey Road street sign. There is a crack in it – which theorists claimed was a mystical omen of the split in the group following Paul's death!

Abbey Road Studios, 3 Abbey Road, St John's Wood, London NW8

Due to its association with the Beatles, Abbey Road is recognised as the most famous recording studio in the world; but in fact this EMI recording complex has always been the home of hit records, producing a stream of No. 1 recordings since charts first appeared in 1952. In fact, in the first 30 years of the charts, between 1952 and 1982, Abbey Road Studios accounted for a total of 74 No. 1 records, fifteen of them by the Beatles.

The building was first erected as a detached residence in 1830 with nine bedrooms, five reception rooms, two servants' rooms, a wine cellar and a large garden area.

It was purchased by the Gramophone Company Limited in December 1929 for £16,500 and converted into recording studios. By the time it was officially opened on 12 November 1931, the Gramophone Company had merged with Columbia Records to become EMI.

The studio complex has four Studios known as One, Two, Three and Four. The largest is Studio One, which is mainly used for orchestral and opera recording. The Beatles mainly used Studio Two, which was generally referred to as the 'pop studio', although they did use some of the other studios from time to time.

The Beatles first entered Abbey Road Studios for their original recording audition on Wednesday, 6 June 1962, and became regular users over a period of seven years. The Beatles were half an hour late for their recording audition and George Martin and Ron Richards were producing, with Norman Smith as engineer, Chris Neal as second engineer. Another member of the Abbey Road staff who decided to stay behind that summer's evening to work on the audition was Ken Townsend, later to become general manager of the studios.

Reports from some of those present indicate that it was the personalities of the individual Beatles and not the numbers they recorded which really convinced George Martin to sign them up. Pete Best was the band's drummer, but had been replaced by Ringo Starr by the time the group next arrived at the studios on Tuesday, 4 September 1962, to record 'Love Me Do' and 'How Do You Do It' in Studio Two, which was to become almost a second home for them.

As time went by the Beatles' productions became more intricate and many musicians, orchestras and choirs were eventually to appear on their records. Almost all of their Abbey Road sessions were produced by George Martin and among the host of people at Abbey Road who participated in Beatles recordings, mainly as engineers, or second engineers, at one time or another were: Norman Smith, Chris Neal, Richard Langham, Stuart Eltham, Geoff Emerick, Jacques Esmenjaud, David Lloyd, Ken Scott, Ron Pender, Hugh Davies, Mike Stone, Jerry Boys, Malcolm Davies, Vic Gann, Phil McDonald, Pete Abbott, Graham Platt, Richard Lush, Peter Vince, Graham Kirkby, Mike Sheady, Peter Bown, John Smith, Dave Harries, Jeff Jarratt, Glyn Johns, Tony Clark, Alan Parsons, Martin Benge, Nick Webb, Chris Black, Neil Richmond and John Kurlander.

Abbey Road is a busy recording studio and does not offer access to visitors. Beatles enthusiasts have to make do with taking photographs of the exterior, while a few yards from the studio gates is the most photographed zebra-crossing in the world, as immortalized on the cover of the *Abbey Road* album. However, between 18 July and 11 September 1983, Abbey Road Studios were opened to the public at a special multi-media event called 'The Beatles At Abbey Road', which took place in Studio Two, and during this time presented a special compilation video of the Beatles' recording career and provided visitors with souvenirs.

Interestingly enough, one of the first Beatles-related auctions took place at the studios. The auctioneers Phillips, Son & Neale presented their 'Sale Of The Century' at Abbey Road Studios on

Thursday, 16 October 1980. Among the items for sale were: a pair of Studer J37 4-track tape recorders used by the Beatles on *Sgt Pepper*; the loudspeaker used on the Beatles EMI audition by Paul McCartney; a Mellotron tape organ used by the Beatles on various recordings, with original tapes; metal positive ('silver disc') with original Beatles signatures; a standing brass ashtray used by Ringo Starr on EMI sessions and a roll of loo paper stamped 'EMI Ltd', the last one of a batch rejected by the Beatles.

The entire history of the studio has been documented in *Abbey Road* by Brian Southall (Patrick Stephens Ltd).

Abbotsfield Park, Chassen Road, Urmston, Lancashire

The site which hosted the annual 'Urmston Show'. During the 1963 Urmston Show, Kennedy Street Enterprises, a Manchester-based agency, promoted a special music carnival in a marquee on Monday, 5 August. The show itself commenced at 11.30 a.m., but the 'Pop Carnival' actually started at 7.30 p.m.

Advertised as a *'Twist & Dance Show'*, it starred the Beatles, with Brian Poole & the Tremeloes, the Dennisons and Johnny Martin & the Tremors in support. Compere for the event was David Hamilton.

The Dennisons had their new single 'Be My Girl' approaching the Top 30 – and the audience that night were entertained with two versions of 'Twist And Shout', one by Brian Poole & the Tremeloes, the other by the Beatles.

When the Beatles were due to go on, Ringo's drum kit had already been set up. A van arrived at the back of the tent and the boys got out, carrying their guitars, with Ringo carrying drumsticks. They went straight on stage, dressed in their collarless Pierre Cardin suits, and the crowd rushed forward – there were no seats provided; the inside of the marquee was in a dance hall format. After their performance the Beatles rushed back into their van and were driven away.

Hamilton was to comment:

My job was to introduce the acts and fill in the bits where one set of equipment was being carried off and another set brought on. By the time the Beatles arrived, the atmosphere was white hot.

The boys were smuggled in in a van. They jumped out and leapt on stage and started to play. I watched from the back of the marquee as screaming girls rushed the stage, trying to get hold of their idols. Huge bouncers threw them back. Many girls fainted, others were trampled on. If they'd managed to reach one of the Beatles, I'm sure he would have been torn limb from limb. There also seemed a great danger of the whole marquee collapsing.

At the end of the evening I collected my cheque for ten guineas, scant reward for what was certainly a hard day's night.

ABC Theatre, Blackpool, Lancashire

The Beatles made their debut at this venue on Sunday, 14 July 1963 and next appeared there the following month on Sunday, 11 August and Sunday, 25 August. Their final appearance in 1963 took place on Sunday, 8 September when the Sons of the Piltdown Men, Terry Young, Jack Douglas, Lee Leslie, the Countrymen and Chas McDevitt and Shirley Douglas were also on the bill.

Their Sunday, 19 July 1964 appearance at the venue was for a live broadcast of ABC TV's 'Blackpool Night Out'. *Mersey Beat* covered the event and the report read:

When we arrived at the ABC Theatre, Blackpool, at the invitation of Nems Enterprises recently, the Beatles were in the middle of rehearsals on stage and Paul was belting out 'Long Tall Sally' – in fine form.

Seated around the vast, luxurious theatre were members of the cast – Mike and Bernie Winters, Jimmy Edwards, Lionel Blair and also Brian Epstein, Neil Aspinall, Mal Evans and Johnny Hackett.

For almost an hour the boys were on stage performing – 'I wish we could have mimed during rehearsals,' John told us later – and soon after they joined us they were called back on stage.

'We've been rehearsing for hours,' John said, when he rejoined us, and in another half hour he was on stage again.

During the whole time, on stage or off, the boys were clowning around and having quite a laugh.

When one of the production team called for silence and gave instructions to the cast he was greeted with applause from John, George, Paul and Ringo, and when there was a delay during dress rehearsals George was shouting 'Come 'ead' and John, 'I'm going home!'

'The rehearsals for the TV show 'Blackpool Night Out' were proving to be even more hilarious than the programme that was screened, as Jimmy Edwards and Frank Berry kept coming out with jokes that weren't in the script.

'They'll use different jokes on the actual programme because they want to keep the musicians in the pit laughing,' John explained.

Apart from singing several numbers including 'A Hard Day's Night' and 'Long Tall Sally', the Beatles appeared in several sketches.

Ringo really looked picturesque as a patient in a brightly coloured smock and patterned pyjamas during the first sketch and all four were certainly dressed for the part when they took the stage as dustmen.

The boys are certainly branching out, having emerged as personalities and comedians and we look forward to seeing them on a similar variety programme.

In fact, the four were back at the ABC for another 'Blackpool Night Out' show hosted by Mike and Bernie on Sunday, 1 August 1965. Also on the bill were Teddy Johnson and Pearl Carr, Johnny Hart and the Lionel Blair Dancers. The songs performed by the Beatles were 'I Feel Fine', 'I'm Down', 'Act Naturally', 'Ticket to Ride', 'Yesterday' and 'Help!'.

ABC Cinema, Warwick Road, Carlisle, Cumberland

The Beatles first appeared at this venue as part of the Helen Shapiro tour on Friday, 8 February 1963. An unfortunate incident at their hotel, the Crown and Mitre, later that night during which they were refused entrance to a function because of their leather jackets, resulted in an anti-Beatles report in the *Daily Express*.

Their second and final appearance at the cinema took place on the group's autumn tour of Britain on Thursday, 21 November 1963. John Lennon was quite delighted with the reception the Beatles received at this gig and said, 'There was even a bit of screaming for us. We'd had that in clubs, but in a big hall like the ABC, there it was a marvellous experience.'

ABC Cinema, London Road, West Croydon, Surrey

The Beatles appeared at this venue only once, during the Tommy Roe/Chris Montez Tour, on Thursday, 21 March 1963.

ABC Cinema, Lothian Road, Edinburgh, Midlothian, Scotland

The Beatles' debut appearance at this cinema was on Wednesday, 29 April 1964. Brian Epstein and Albert Bonici jointly promoted the event. Radio reporter Bill Aitkenhead interviewed the Beatles in their dressing room at the venue and it was broadcast later that evening on the Scottish Home Service. The group next appeared at the cinema on Monday, 19 October 1964.

ABC Cinema, London Inn Square, Exeter, Devon

The Beatles made their debut here on Thursday, 28 March 1963 as part of the Tommy Roe/Chris Montez Tour. They returned to the venue later the same year during their Autumn Tour on Thursday, 14 November and their final appearance at the cinema took place on Wednesday, 28 October 1964.

ABC Cinema, Great Yarmouth, Suffolk

The Beatles appeared at this cinema in the seaside resort of Great Yarmouth only once. The occasion was a concert on Sunday, 28 July 1963.

ABC Cinema, Market Street, Huddersfield, Yorkshire

The Beatles appeared at this venue only once, on a concert which took place on Friday, 29 November 1963. Between shows Gordon Kaye interviewed them in their dressing room for the Huddersfield Tape Recording Society. In the 1980s Kaye, who'd become an actor, rose to fame in Britain as Rene, in the popular sitcom ''Allo 'Allo!'.

ABC Cinema, Ferensway, Hull, Yorkshire

The Beatles made their debut at this venue on Sunday, 24 November 1963. Their second and final appearance at the cinema took place on Friday, 16 October 1964.

ABC Cinema, Saltergate, Lincoln, Lincolnshire

The Beatles appeared here once, on Thursday, 28 November 1963. At a press conference before the show Ringo developed earache. A doctor was called and, because she was female, was delayed by guards and it took her twenty minutes to get by them and examine her patient. They went to the local hospital for a further examination and one of the nurses commented that it was an occupational hazard for a Beatle with the hair getting into their ears.

Ringo was rushed back in time for the show and as soon as they finished their performance they whizzed away to the nearest police station, still in their stage clothes and make-up. After they'd changed and were ready to leave in their car, which had been surrounded by twenty policemen, the police chief insisted they sign autographs for his daughters.

ABC Cinema, Abington Square, Northampton, Northamptonshire

Both appearances by the Beatles at this cinema took place in 1963. The first was as part of the Tommy Roe/Chris Montez Tour on Wednesday, 27 March and the second was during the group's own Autumn Tour on Wednesday, 6 November.

ABC Cinema, George Street, Plymouth, Devon

The Beatles appeared in concert on two occasions at this venue. The first appearance took place on 13 November 1963 and the second on 29 October 1964.

ABC Cinema, South Street, Romford, Essex

The Beatles only appeared at this venue once, as part of the Tommy Roe/Chris Montez Tour on Wednesday, 20 March 1963.

ABC Cinema, Station Road, Wigan, Lancashire

The Beatles made a single appearance at this venue on their only British tour of 1964 on Tuesday, 13 October.

The ABC manager Neville Ward had been making arrangements for some weeks and in addition to the 40 members of the St John Ambulance Brigade who were on call, his six members of staff were aided by six volunteers from the Wigan Amateur Operatic Society.

There was a capacity audience of 2,000 and the acts who preceded the Beatles were the Rustiks, Michael Haslam, Sounds Incorporated, Mary Wells and Tommy Quickly. Compere for the show was Bob Bain.

Abergavenny Town Hall Ballroom, Abergavenny, Monmouthshire, Wales

The Beatles appeared here on 22 June 1963. Paul, George, Ringo and Neil Aspinall travelled to the gig in the group van, while John remained in London to record a 'Juke Box Jury' appearance. Brian Epstein booked a helicopter to fly John to Wales at a cost of £100. He landed at Peny Pound football ground and rushed to the Town Hall where the show was to start at 9.50 p.m.

There were approximately 500 people at the gig, and afterwards the Beatles were invited to a small reception by Lord Mayor Jack Thurston. A local singer Bryn Yemm was one of the selected guests and since everyone seemed to know him, Paul asked: 'Who are you?' 'I'm only a local kid,' he replied and Paul laughed and said, 'I like that.' Later, Brian Epstein had a chat with Bryn and asked him to come up and see him in London. 'But I didn't have any money, so I couldn't do it,' he said. However, Bryn Yemm and the Yemmen recorded for EMI Columbia and their first single was called 'Black Is The Night'. Bryn was later to team up with his wife Ann and promote his own career, which resulted in four albums in the British charts in a single year and an entry in *The Guinness Book of Records*.

Academy Of Meditation, Shankaracharya Nagar, India

The Maharishi Mahesh Yogi's ashram in the Himalayas. He invited the Beatles and their party to take part in a three-month course of Transcendental Meditation with him at the ashram (a holy place where people study and meditate), set on a plateau 150 feet above the River Ganges, half a mile south of the mountain town of Rishikesh.

On Friday, 15 February 1968 John and Cynthia Lennon, George and Pattie Harrison, Jennie Boyd and a number of friends flew out from London airport to Delhi. Also on the flight were some representatives of the press, including Don Short of the *Daily Mirror* and Robin Turner of the *Daily Express*. After a 20-hour flight they arrived at Delhi at 8.15 a.m. Mia Farrow was at the airport to meet them. Three cars were needed to drive them to Rishikesh, 150 miles away. It was a cold, wet day and when they arrived they were met by the Maharishi, had some tea, then went to bed.

Paul McCartney and Jane Asher and Ringo and Maureen Starkey flew out from London on 19 February.

There were approximately 70 students at the ashram for the course, ranging from the young to the old and from America, Britain, Finland, Denmark, Sweden and Germany. They included a German Lufthansa pilot, a British Rail signalman with his mother, a Hollywood actor named Tom, a hairdresser from Canada and a German physicist. Among the friends of the Beatles were Mia and Prudence Farrow, Donovan and Gypsy Dave, Mike Love of the Beach Boys, Neil Aspinall, Mal Evans, Alexis Mardas and jazz musician Paul Horn.

The Academy was extremely luxurious for an ashram. There was a lecture hall and two dining halls. One dining room was covered, the other had no roof. A new swimming pool was being built beside the lecture hall. The accommodation was very comfortable and comprised five-room stone-built cottages, newly furnished, which had twin beds or four-poster beds, new rugs on the walls and floors, dressing tables, shelves and cupboards and a bathroom, toilet and shower, plus electric heating. The ashram employed a full-time staff of 40, which included cooks, cleaning staff and printers at the Academy's printing works.

Breakfast was served outdoors at 7.00 a.m. It consisted of corn-flakes, puffed wheat or porridge, fruit juice, tea or coffee, toast, marmalade or jam. The students then meditated before they had a vegetarian lunch and dinner, which comprised soup, lots of salads, rice and potatoes, which they ate from long, plastic-covered tables. For the Beatles and their party, Mal Evans often travelled all the way to Delhi to obtain eggs. The Maharishi didn't take meals with his students.

There were two 90-minute lectures each day at 3.30 p.m. and 8.30 p.m. The students meditated alone and had notices for their rooms which read: 'Meditating: Do Not Disturb'. George and John were most enthusiastic students and meditated between seven and nine hours a day.

During the party's stay, there were celebrations for three birth-days. George was 25 on 25 February and was presented with a cake with white icing and pink flowers which had the greeting 'Jai Guru Deva' in gold letters. Pattie was 23 on 17 March. A boy from Lancaster, called Mike, who with his mate Paul had hitch-hiked to India on their way to Australia and were paying for their course by working in the kitchens, celebrated his 21st birthday.

Ringo, who had been troubled so much by stomach ailments since he was a child, couldn't adapt to the food and Maureen couldn't stand the insects, so the couple decided to leave Rishikesh much earlier than planned, on 1 March. On their return, Ringo compared the ashram to a Butlin's holiday camp. Paul and Jane managed to remain for six weeks, but left before the three-month course was over on 26 March. When asked if they were disillusioned, Paul replied, 'No, just a little homesick.'

On 31 March, there was an announcement by the Beach Boys that they would embark on a concert tour with the Maharishi called 'World Peace I' and they hinted that the Beatles would be involved.

Alexis Mardas didn't like the ashram because be felt that it was too materialistic and not spiritual enough. The Academy was surrounded by barbed wire, there was a helicopter pad, and he was appalled at the idea of an ashram with four-poster beds, masseurs and servants bringing water – and accountants. He suspected that the presence of full-time accountants indicated an overriding interest in money. He discovered that some of the Swedish ladies on the course had left all their money to the Maharishi and he also heard that the Maharishi expected the Beatles to donate 10–25 per cent of their annual income to a Swiss account in his name.

An example of the Maharishi's business sense occurred during discussions about Apple financing a film about the Maharishi with the proceeds going to a Transcendental Meditation University in London. The Maharishi kept haggling over the finances and Neil Aspinall made a special trip to discuss the film with him – the Maharishi had an accountant at his side throughout the meeting and kept insisting that he be paid an additional 2.5 per cent.

Magic Alex decided to discover if he could expose the Maharishi to the Beatles. He began to smuggle wine into the compound to give to some of the women, particularly a blonde nurse from California. She revealed that she'd had several private meetings in the Maharishi's cottage, during which he'd provided her with chicken for dinner, despite the fact that it was a vegetarian community. The girl also alleged that at one of her private consultations, the Maharishi had made sexual advances. Alex set a trap for the Maharishi and then confronted John and George with what he'd discovered. George didn't believe it at first and was angry with Alex. Then they began to discuss it and decided to leave the next morning. When morning came, John told the Maharishi that they were leaving. When he asked why, John told him, 'You're the cosmic one, you should know.'

The Maharishi was a powerful figure in the area and the group began to worry about how they were going to get home. Alex sent to Deradoon to fetch taxis, but the word was out and they couldn't hire any. Eventually they rented two old cars and paid the drivers to take them to Delhi. The cars broke down and the party had to flag down a saloon car and hitch a lift to their destination.

Despite the disappointing conclusion to their adventure, the period at the ashram had done them well, particularly in the case of John. There were no drugs or alcohol allowed at the ashram and as a result John was weaned off the drugs he had been taking. Both he and Paul wrote a large number of songs, approximately fifteen each, and Cynthia was to comment: 'He [John] went so deeply within himself through meditation that he separated himself from everything.'

Across The Universe

The inspiration for the song came when John woke up at 7 o'clock one morning with the words 'pools of sorrow, waves of joy' spinning around in his head. He couldn't get back to sleep and began writing the number.

Evidence of the influence of the Maharishi Mahesh Yogi is contained in the chorus phrase '*Jai Guru De Va Om*' which refers to the Maharishi's teacher Guru Deva. The first version of the song was produced by George Martin on 4 February 1968.

During the session it was decided that some female voices were needed to sing the line, 'Nothing's going to change my world'.

Paul found two girls standing in the rain outside the studio and brought them in on the session. There was sixteen-year-old Lizzie Bravo from Brazil, who was staying in nearby Maida Vale and had ambitions of becoming an actress, and seventeen-year-old Gayleen Pease from Stoke Newington, London N16, who was studying for her A levels.

The two were asked to sing the line over and over again.

The number was originally considered as the A side of a Beatles' single, but 'Lady Madonna' was chosen instead and the track lay on the shelf for some time.

Comedian Spike Milligan had suggested to the World Wildlife Fund that they issue an album, with the proceeds going to their charity, and 'Across The Universe' was donated by the Beatles.

The album was called *No One's Gonna Change Our World* and it was issued on EMI Star Line SRS 5013 (LP) on 12 December 1969. Other artists featured on the album included Cilla Black; Rolf Harris; the Hollies; Spike Milligan; the Bee Gees; Lulu; Dave, Dee, Dozy, Beaky, Mick and Tich; Cliff Richard & the Shadows; Bruce Forsyth and Harry Secombe.

When Phil Spector was called in to work on a number of Beatles tapes, he completely altered 'Across The Universe', removing the vocals by Paul and the two girls and introducing his 'wall of sound' and the famous 'Spector overkill'. This was the version which wound up on the *Let It Be* album.

The number also appeared on *The Beatles 1967–1970* and the *Rarities* compilations and in the boxed set of albums *The Beatles Box*.

David Bowie featured the number on his *Young Americans* album and John played on the track with him. The song was also performed by the Beatles in the film *Let It Be*. A version was included on the *Past Masters Volume Two* CD and on the Beatles' *Anthology 2* CD.

Act Naturally

Country music fan Ringo Starr got a chance to air his vocals on live shows and on record with this song, composed by Johnny Russell and Voni Morrison, which was a hit for Buck Owens in 1963. Ringo performed it on the group's American and British tours in 1965.

The number appears on the British *Help!* album and the American *Yesterday ... And Today* LP. It is also found on the British EP *Yesterday* and was issued in the States as the flipside to 'Yesterday' on Capitol 5498 on 13 September 1965. It's also to be found on *The Beatles Box* and *The Beatles Collection* sets.

It was also a TV highlight for Ringo and he played the number on 'The Ed Sullivan Show' in 1965, the 'Cilla' show in 1965 and his own 'Ringo' TV special in 1978. In 1989 he re-recorded the number at Abbey Road Studios with Buck Owens.

Adams, Beryl

Brian Epstein's original secretary, who was 26 years old when she began to work for him following his transference to the Whitechapel branch of NEMS. When Brian began to manage the Beatles, she also had to deal with a number of their affairs, including preparing their weekly pay packets.

When Brian moved to London she remained in Liverpool and married disc jockey Bob Wooler. For a time she managed the local band the Kirkbys, then divorced Bob and later remarried.

Adelphi Cinema, Middle Abbey Street, Dublin, Eire

Venue where the Beatles made their first-ever appearance in Ireland on 7 November 1963. On landing at Dublin Airport they were interviewed by Frank Hall of Radio Telefis Eireann, the television station, during which there was mention of their Irish backgrounds. Paul commented, 'I think we've all got a bit, except "limey" on the end here' – pointing to Ringo. John, Paul and George all had Irish ancestry and George's mother Louise was at the airport, having come over to Ireland to visit her numerous relations. Paul was to bring up the link again at their show when he told the audience, 'It's nice to be back home.'

Compere for the concert was Frank Barry and the Beatles opened with 'I Saw Her Standing There' and finished with 'Twist and Shout'. They were hustled out of the stage door into an *Evening Herald* van and on to the Gresham Hotel, where they were staying.

When the concert ended there was a riot by a mob of screaming teenagers during which windows were smashed, cars overturned, a hundred people injured and twelve of the rioters arrested.

Adelphi Hotel, Ranelagh Street, Liverpool L1

The most famous hotel in Liverpool. Extremely popular in the days when the luxury liners ploughed their way across the Atlantic and headed for the seaport, it was once described as 'a great Cunard liner stuck in the middle of the city'.

Before setting off for the registry office to get married, Freddie Lennon and Julia Stanley met on the Adelphi steps on 3 December 1938, and after the ceremony were treated to lunch by Fred's brother Stanley at the large public house, nicknamed 'the big house', at the side of the Adelphi.

On 6 March 1964 the hotel was the setting for the annual ball organised by the Hospital Wing Aid Committee of the Home for Aged Jews. The dinner was in honour of Brian Epstein, who attended, along with Alma Cogan, Lionel Bart, Gerry Marsden and Bernard Delfont.

The hotel, now known as the Britannia Adelphi, has become the venue for the annual Beatles convention held in Liverpool each August bank holiday.

Adelphi Theatre, Bath Road, Slough, Berkshire

Venue where the Beatles commenced their third British tour on 18 May 1963 on a bill with Roy Orbison and Gerry & the Pacemakers. Initially, Roy Orbison topped the bill to the show, but within a short time the Beatles were officially announced as headliners.

Their repertoire comprised: 'Some Other Guy', 'Do You Want To Know A Secret', 'Love Me Do', 'From Me To You', 'Please Please Me', 'I Saw Her Standing There' and 'Twist and Shout'.

Prior to the actual show on the opening night, Gerry Marsden, leader of Gerry & the Pacemakers, presented them with a silver disc for 'From Me To You'.

The group also appeared at the theatre on their following tour on 5 November 1963 with the Brook Brothers and the Kestrels.

On 16 November 1965 Paul McCartney visited the cinema to see the Gene Pitney package show, primarily to watch Peter and Gordon, who were on the bill. From behind the curtain he made an announcement over the microphone: 'Arthur Howes presents ... the Gene Pitney Show! And to start the show in swinging style – the Mike Cotton Sound!' The audience, of course, had no idea that a member of the Beatles was making the announcement.

Adelphi Ballroom, New Street, West Bromwich, Birmingham

The Beatles appeared at this venue only once, on the evening of 19 November 1962, following an earlier lunchtime session at the Cavern.

Ad Lib Club, The

Trendy 'Swinging London' venue. Situated at 7 Leicester Place, which originally opened on Friday, 13 December 1963. It was one of the first discotheques that boasted an exclusive celebrity membership list and was a watering hole for stars such as the Beatles, The Rolling Stones and the Hollies. In fact, it was the first London club the Beatles began to frequent.

Brian Morris managed it.

The Ad Lib was the venue where Ringo proposed to his Liverpool girlfriend Maureen Cox.

John and Cynthia and George and Pattie experienced their first psychedelic trip one night at the club. Earlier that evening they had attended a dinner party in Bayswater, hosted by the Beatles' London dentist. He lined up four sugar cubes on his mantel and then put them in their coffee. After they'd drunk their coffee he informed them that the cubes contained LSD.

Cynthia and Pattie were frightened. The four made their excuses and left, first stopping at the Pickwick Club to look in on their friends, the group Paddy, Klaus & Gibson. They then arrived at the Ad Lib Club. John was to say that they were out of their heads. The club was on the fourth floor of the building and had to be reached by a lift. John said, 'When we finally got in the lift we all thought there was a fire, but it was just a little red light. We were all hot and hysterical, and when we arrived on the floor, the lift stopped and the door opened, and we were all screaming.'

Rock artist Guy Peellaert executed a painting of the Ad Lib Club interior that was featured in his 1974 book *Rock Dreams*. In the painting the Beatles are depicted holding court. Other Ad Lib regulars in the painting are Keith Richard, Anita Pallenberg, Brian Jones, Jeff Beck, Keith Relf, Scott Walker, Alan Price, Eric Burdon, Keith Moon, Charlie Watts, Mick Jagger, Marianne Faithfull, P. J. Proby, Sandie Shaw, Zoot Money and Georgie Fame.

The Ad Lib was destroyed by fire in 1966.

Aintree Institute, Longmoor Lane, Aintree, Liverpool L9

In August 1961 Bob Wooler noticed two girls dancing in rhythm at the Aintree Institute. He considered them so good he invited them to dance on stage and suggested they form an act. Bob coined the name 'Shimmy Shimmy Queens' for them and with specially made dresses and the addition of another girl dancer, they made their debut at Litherland Town Hall. Further appearances followed at venues such as the Aintree Institute and Hambleton Hall. The girls' names were Marie Williams, Joan Pratt and Maureen O'Donnell. They appeared on the same bill as the Beatles at the Aintree Institute on 19 August 1961.

The Beatles made a total of 31 appearances at the venue after making their debut there on 7 January 1961. All but one of their appearances, their last, took place in 1961. They were: 13, 14, 18, 21, 27, 28 January; 8, 10, 15, 18, 22 February; 1, 4, 8, 11 March; 21, 28 July; 4, 12, 18, 19, 26 August; 2, 9, 16, 23, 28 October; and 11 November.

When they appeared there on 27 January 1962, Brian Kelly paid their fifteen pounds fee in coins. Brian Epstein was furious and described the incident in *A Cellarful of Noise* when they were paid '... in sixpences and florins and even halfpennies and I kicked up an awful fuss, not because £15 isn't £15 in any currency, but because I thought it was disrespectful to the Beatles.' Epstein ensured that they never appeared at the Aintree Institute again.

The venue featured non-stop jiving every Thursday, Friday and Saturday and posters announced 'Take a bus to the Black Bull – we're next door.'

The promotions by Brian Kelly were usually compered by Bob Wooler and generally featured three bands a night. The promotions ceased early in 1962 when the building was sold to a local church and it became a church social club.

Ain't She Sweet

A number originally penned in the twenties by Jack Yellen and Milton Ager. A rock 'n' roll interpretation of the song was recorded by Gene Vincent in 1956 and included on his album *Bluejean Bop*.

It was the only number recorded during the May 1961 recording sessions in Hamburg on which John Lennon sang lead vocals. From that session this was a pure Beatle track, with no Tony Sheridan participation.

Strangely enough, it wasn't the first of the Polydor numbers to be issued as a single in either Britain or the United States, though it must have been the most obvious track from the entire recordings to capitalise on the Beatles' success. Which is how it turned out when it was issued in Britain on Polydor NH 52-317 on 29 May 1964 with 'If You Love Me Baby' on the flipside. The previous Polydor releases by the Beatles, 'My Bonnie', 'Sweet Georgia Brown' and 'Why' had all failed to chart, but 'Ain't She Sweet' reached No. 24 in the *New Musical Express* charts. The same pattern followed in America. Atco had a flop with 'Sweet Georgia Brown' but when 'Ain't She Sweet' was issued on ATCO 6308 on 6 July 1964 with 'Nobody's Child' on the flip it reached No. 19 in *Billboard*, No. 14 in *Cash Box* and No. 13 in *Record World*.

Ain't She Sweet was also the title of an album issued by Atco on Atco SD 33-169 on 5 October 1964, in an attempt to cash in on the

Top Twenty success of the 'Ain't She Sweet' single. It contained the title track, plus three other numbers recorded by Tony Sheridan and the Beatles in Hamburg in 1961: 'Sweet Georgia Brown' 'Take Out Some Insurance On Me Baby' and 'Nobody's Child'. The sleeve featured the caption: 'Ain't She Sweet. The Beatles & Other Great Group Sounds From England'. The 'other great group sounds from England' were by an unknown group called the Swallows, who were unlikely to be an English group. The Swallows performed eight numbers: 'I Wanna Be Your Man', 'She Loves You', 'How Do You Do It', 'Please Please Me', 'I'll Keep You Satisfied', 'I'm Telling You Now', 'I Want To Hold Your Hand' and 'From Me To You'.

The American record buyers were now cottoning on to the fact that old tracks were being recycled and this was reflected in poor sales and the lack of any chart position.

This album minus the tracks 'How Do You Do It' and 'I'll Keep You Satisfied', was re-released on Clarion 601 on 17 October 1966 under the title *The Amazing Beatles And Other Great English Group Sounds*. The version recorded with Tony Sheridan was included on the Beatles *Anthology 1* CD and a different version arising from a jam session at Abbey Road studios surfaced on *Anthology 3*.

Akustik Studio, Kirchenalle 57, Hamburg, Germany

A small recording booth on the fifth floor of a building to the rear of Hamburg's main railway station.

On Saturday, 15 October 1960, Allan Williams decided to have a record cut in what was basically a record-your-voice booth for sending greetings to relatives and such. Williams had booked two groups appearing in Hamburg at the time – the Beatles and Rory Storm & the Hurricanes – but he was most impressed with the voice of Lu Walters, a singer/guitarist with the Hurricanes.

Rory Storm was the lead vocalist with the Hurricanes, but Lu Walters sang on numbers such as 'Fever' and 'Summertime', and Williams was particularly impressed by his voice and wanted to record him. He also got the idea of bringing in the three frontline Beatles for the harmonising. So he kept Ringo Starr as the drummer, because he played 'Fever' and 'Summertime' with Walters all the time. They considered 'Fever' to be one of those numbers that you need to be familiar with to play. He didn't bother with Stuart Sutcliffe as Walters also played bass. The session proved to be the first time that John, Paul, George and Ringo played together. They backed Lu on a version of George Gershwin's 'Summertime'. Two other members of the Hurricanes, Ty Brien and Johnny 'Guitar' Byrne, then joined Lu and Ringo on two further tracks, 'Fever' and 'September Song'.

The Beatles asked Williams if they could cut a record themselves, but he wasn't willing to pay the extra money.

The discs cost three marks each, but only six of the 78rpm acetates were bought. No one seems to know what happened to them. Rory Storm had one, Lu gave one to his ex-wife and Williams left his copy behind him in a London pub several years later. Ty Brien had also bought one, but it couldn't be traced after his death. Johnny Guitar also recalls that John and Paul bought a copy each, but they have never mentioned doing so.

Albany Cinema, Northway, Maghull, Liverpool L31

A three-hour charity variety show to raise funds for an ambulance for the local St John Ambulance Brigade, organized by Jim Gretty, saw comedian Ken Dodd topping the bill on 15 October 1961. The Beatles were an odd choice for this Sunday afternoon concert which featured light operatic arias, songs from *Carousel*, trad jazz and country music. Other acts on the bill were Les Arnold, Joe Cordova, Dave Dunn, Jim Markey, Lennie Rens, Bert King and the Eltones, Denis Smerdon, Edna Bell and Jackie Owen and the Joe Royal Trio. Country music was performed by Hank Walters & the Dusty Road Ramblers and Walters was to say, many years later, that Lennon had come up to him and said, 'I don't go much on your music, lad, but give us your hat.' Walters told Lennon that he didn't think much of the Beatles' music and they'd never get anywhere unless they got with it and played country music.

Ken Dodd also thought their music was terrible and made a complaint to the organisers. When one of them came into his dressing room and said they'd been told that if they gave him their card he might be able to get them some bookings, he threw the card away. He was reminded of it years later when Paul McCartney mentioned that they'd worked with him before. 'No, you've never worked with me, lad,' Dodd told him. When Paul mentioned it had been at the Albany, Dodd said, 'That noise wasn't you, was it?' 'Yeah, we were rubbish, weren't we?' 'You certainly were,' said Dodd. 'I had you thrown off.'

The Beatles closed the show with a ten-minute spot.

Album Sleeves

The cover of *Sgt Pepper's Lonely Hearts Club Band* is arguably the most famous album cover of all time and the *Abbey Road* sleeve the most parodied, although these feats shouldn't conceal the fact that the entire series of Beatles album covers was innovative for their time and changed the entire approach to album sleeve presentation and design.

Prior to the consideration, care and creativity which went into the design of a Beatles album cover, the covers of albums were usually very basic and static, generally consisting of a photograph of the artist/artists concerned and a piece of lettering with the album title and artist's name. The field of album cover design was never the same after the release of *Sgt Pepper's Lonely Hearts Club Band*.

The Beatles' first album was at one time to be called 'Off The Beatle Track' and Paul McCartney designed a cover for it – a head-and-shoulders sketch of each of the four members of the band, two on top, two below, with the lettering in between, and the 'B' in 'Beatle' sporting antennae. This plan was abandoned and the album was called *Please Please Me* while the cover featured a photograph by veteran theatrical/ film photographer Angus McBean of the Beatles looking down from the stairwell at EMI House. An interesting shot, although the sleeve wasn't particularly trendsetting. The sleeve notes were by Beatles Press Officer Tony Barrow.

The next album cover was taken by photographer Robert Freeman. Called *With The Beatles*, the sleeve featured a black and white shot of the heads of the four Beatles, wearing turtleneck sweaters, presenting the faces in a half-light, a technique pioneered by American photographer Richard Avedon and used to effect by Astrid Kirchherr in her Hamburg photographs of the Beatles. It was Freeman who conceived the idea of a black and white photograph, and although EMI initially resisted the idea, Brian Epstein and George Martin pressed for its use. The image has since become one of the most potent images of the Beatles and has been utilised by artists in paintings (e.g. David Oxtoby's *Yesterdays*) and parodied by other bands (e.g. the 1974 EP *With The Roogalator*). Sleeve notes were by Tony Barrow.

Robert Freeman was also responsible for the cover of the *A Hard Day's Night* album, which was done in the style of a photostrip, Polyphoto or photo kiosk strip – five square shaped head shots of each member of the group stretched across the cover in a total of twenty images, similar to the images Freeman designed for the *A Hard Day's Night* film, also displaying the half-light technique.

Brian Epstein and the Beatles were using Freeman regularly and he was once again commissioned to produce an album sleeve, this time for *Beatles For Sale*, for which he featured a colour portrait of the group, in the open air, unsmiling. It was a gatefold sleeve and an

inner photograph consists of a collage of the group standing against
a background of photographs of film stills – including images of
Albert Finney, Jayne Mansfield, Ian Carmichael and Victor Mature
– perhaps a hint at the *Sgt Pepper* sleeve to come? The back cover
featured another colour shot of the four by Freeman (which was
used as the cover of the American *The Early Beatles* album) and
sleeve notes were by Derek Taylor.

The cover of *Help!* shows the four in their costumes from the
Alpine sequences in the film, against a stark white background.
Each of the four is posed miming a letter in semaphore. This is said
to spell out the name of the film H-E-L-P. On the American album,
which is more like the cover of the film poster, the figures of John
and Paul have been transposed, which would make any planned
semaphore message gobbledegook.

The photograph on the cover of *Rubber Soul* was the last album
cover to be taken by Robert Freeman. The shot was taken in the
garden of John's house in Weybridge, Surrey, and an intriguing
distorted effect has been produced. Freeman explained it by saying,
'The distorted effect in the photo was a reflection of the changing
shape of their lives. They had begun their careers as musicians, but
the wide range of people and ideas they had encountered, their
financial success, and the new privacy of their homes encouraged
them to take up more varied and personal interests.' There is also a
selection of seven black and white Freeman shots on the back cover.

The Beatles asked their friend Klaus Voormann to design the
cover of their *Revolver* album. It comprises some fine line drawings
of the heads of the individual Beatles surrounding a collage of
photographs. The impressive image, with its delicate draughtsman-
ship, brought Voormann a Grammy Award.

A cover painting by David Christian was displayed on the cover
of the compilation album *A Collection of Beatles' Oldies (But
Goldies)*, which was a colourful and decorous design of a male
dressed in 'Swinging London' fashions sitting on a drum-like shape
with a drawing of the Beatles surrounding a vintage car in the background. The back cover featured a photograph by Robert
Whitaker. This was probably put together by EMI without consul-
tation with the Beatles, as it was not an album of new material.

The cover of *Sgt Pepper's Lonely Hearts Club Band* was the most
expensive and elaborate front cover design ever produced up to that
time and the first to print the complete song lyrics contained in the
album.

In stark contrast to the intricate detail of the *Sgt Pepper* sleeve,
the cover of *The Beatles* double album was in plain white, with the
name 'The Beatles' written in small letters on it. This was a concept

by artist Richard Hamilton and the sleeve package also contained some poster collages and a set of colour prints of photographs taken by John Kelly. As with the *Sgt Pepper* album, the Beatles had sought advice on the cover design from Robert Fraser, who'd recommended artist Peter Blake for *Sgt Pepper* and suggested Hamilton for the double album which, because of its design, has come to be known as the 'white' album. It is indicative of the fact that the Beatles seriously approached the subject of their album covers – apart from ones they were not really involved in, such as the compilations and *Yellow Submarine* – and their interest in the appearance of their album covers led to other groups taking an active part in how theirs were designed.

The *Yellow Submarine* cover was an illustration of the cartoon Beatles as featured in the animated cartoon.

The cover of *Abbey Road* is, next to *Sgt Pepper*, their most famous cover and the most imitated – how many album sleeves have since featured artists traversing a zebra crossing? The cover photograph was taken on the morning of 8 August 1969 by Iain Macmillan and the actual design of the sleeve was simple with only two photographs used and no title on the front cover – a bold move in itself.

Originally, the cover of the next sleeve, initially called 'Get Back', was to be taken on the same spot on the EMI stairwell as the *Please Please Me* album cover and taken by the same photographer, Angus McBean (a reference to them 'getting back' to their roots). This shot was taken, but not used until the double-album compilations *The Beatles 1962–1966* and *The Beatles 1967–1970*. The *Let It Be* (as the album was re-titled) sleeve featured four close-up shots of the individual members of the band, taken by Ethan Russell during the filming, placed in a square on a black background.

The Beatles had no real say in further sleeves. John Lennon's request to design the cover of their *Rock 'n' Roll* compilation was turned down by EMI and a cover painting by Roy Kohara, which the Beatles hated, was used.

It was Capitol Records who generally controlled the look of their American sleeves, which didn't display the imagination of the British releases in which the Beatles were involved. The one sleeve in which they took active participation, for *Yesterday ... And Today*, was actually withdrawn by Capitol and a different cover pasted over it.

However, in the field of album cover design the Beatles, once again, had proved to be innovators, and the covers of albums of popular music have benefited and evolved into an art form in their own right as a result.

Aldo, Steve

One of Liverpool's leading black vocalists, Steve originally began singing at the age of thirteen in *The Backyard Kids* at the Pavilion, Lodge Lane. When he was fourteen he sang at Holyoake Hall, and on holiday in the Isle of Man he sang with the Ivy Benson Band. Later, he appeared occasionally with Howie Casey & the Seniors, before moving to Cardiff to become a ladies' hairdresser. He worked at Raymonde's (Mr Teasy Weasy) in London, then went to sea for a year. He returned to Liverpool and fronted the Challengers, then moved to Germany and sang occasionally with the Dominoes. On his return to Liverpool he joined the Nocturnes for a short while, before becoming a member of the Griff-Parry Five.

At one time Spencer Lloyd Mason managed him and made his recording debut with 'Can I Get A Witness' in December 1964. He later recorded for Parlophone.

Steve appeared with the Beatles on their last British tour in 1964 which, with only nine appearances, became their shortest theatre tour of Britain.

He later became a publican.

Alexander, Arthur

A rhythm and blues singer, born on 10 May 1940 in Florence, Alabama.

Alexander first made an impact in 1961/2 with songs such as 'Anna', 'Soldier Of Love', 'A Shot Of Rhythm And Blues', 'You Better Move On' and 'Go Home Girl'. In fact, his use of the word 'girl' in his songs became common lyrical parlance and had an influence on John Lennon's lyrics.

In 1962, John introduced four songs popularised by Alexander into the Beatles act, and sang lead vocals on all of them: 'Anna (Go To Him)', 'A Shot Of Rhythm And Blues', 'Soldier Of Love (Lay Down Your Arms)' and 'Where Have You Been All My Life?'.

The Beatles recorded 'Anna', which was included on their debut album *Please Please Me,* and 'Where Have you Been All My Life?' is to be found on the Star Club albums. The group performed 'A Shot Of Rhythm And Blues' and 'Soldier Of Love' on their BBC Radio appearances.

The Rolling Stones recorded 'You Better Move On'.

Alexander died on 9 June 1993, age 53, of heart troubles and respiratory problems.

Alexandra Hall, College Road, Crosby, Liverpool L23

A hall where promoter Brian Kelly ran promotions. He booked the Beatles here only once, on 19 January 1961.

It was at halls like this where rock 'n' roll prospered and thrived on Merseyside, in the days when the events were referred to as 'jive' and lots of the venues were called 'jive hives'.

Brian Kelly was one of the handful of promoters who provided work for the growing army of Mersey bands after launching his first jive session in May 1959. Apart from Alexandra Hall he ran promotions at Lathom Hall, Litherland Town Hall and the Aintree Institute.

Ali, Muhammad (Cassius Clay)

When the Beatles travelled to Miami in February 1964 to stay at the Deauville Hotel to record 'The Ed Sullivan Show', they were asked to visit the training camp of Cassius Clay on Tuesday, 18 February.

Harold Conrad, who was promoting the world heavyweight championship bout between Sonny Liston and Clay, had asked Brian Epstein if the Beatles would like to visit Clay's camp, but the offer was rejected. Following their televised show at the Mau Mau Lounge, Conrad asked Ed Sullivan if he could meet the Beatles and Sullivan took him to their room and introduced him. Paul said, 'I think Clay is going to win.' Conrad mentioned that the visit to Clay's camp had been turned down, but they said they'd go and John commented, 'Don't worry about Brian, we'll handle him.'

The boxer and the Beatles clowned it up for the assembled photographers, with shots of Clay standing over a supine group of Beatles on the canvas. The 'Louisville Lip' told the press that although the Beatles were the prettiest, he was the greatest. He made up a poem: 'When Liston reads about the Beatles visiting me, he'll get so mad, I'll knock him out in three.' He also commented, 'They were regular, friendly, everyday fellows. Success hasn't gone to their heads.' A few days later he won the heavyweight title for the first time.

Clay was to change his name to Muhammad Ali and he won the world heavyweight championship title three times.

On hearing Ringo play drums, he joked, 'My dog plays better drums!'

Allen, Dave

Popular Irish comedian who has enjoyed success for many years with his own series of comedy shows on British television. He was compere of the Helen Shapiro Tour on which the Beatles appeared in 1963 and commented, 'They gradually took over as stars of the show. They were very dynamic and even at that early date I saw something special in them.' He then appeared on the same bill as the Beatles on the TV show 'Sunday Night At The London

Palladium' on Sunday, 12 January 1964. His scene as a drunk was hilarious and brought the house down. He was to claim that he received more laughs than the Beatles, but qualified it by commenting, 'but that's because they're singers. I still don't know whether they're good singers or not because you can't hear them for all the girls' screaming.'

Later that same year he toured Australia with them. During the tour he was one of the judges, together with Derek Taylor and the editor of the Sydney *Sunday Mirror*, of a competition organised by that paper offering the winners an invitation to Paul's 22nd birthday party at the Sheraton Hotel. There were over 10,000 entrants and seventeen girls won the opportunity of meeting the Beatles at the party.

Dave and his wife Judith are neighbours of the Harrisons at Henley.

All I've Got To Do

A John Lennon composition featured on the *With The Beatles* album. The group recorded the song on Wednesday, 11 September 1963. It was also included on Capitol's American album, *Meet The Beatles*.

All My Loving

A song which first appeared on the *With The Beatles* album in November 1963.

Paul originally conceived the number one day while he was having a shave. He said of it, 'I wrote "All My Loving" like a piece of poetry and then, I think, I put a song to it later.'

In February 1964 the number was the title track of an EP release (GEP 8891) and reached No. 13 in the British charts.

The other numbers on the EP were 'Ask Me Why', 'Money (That's What I Want)' and 'P.S. I Love You'. It was also featured on the Capitol Records EP *Four By The Beatles*, issued in America in May 1964.

The song has been featured on several albums, including the American *Meet The Beatles*, *The Beatles 1962–1966* compilation, the live *The Beatles At The Hollywood Bowl* in 1977, *The Beatles Collection* in 1978 and the mammoth World Records' *The Beatles Box* and *The Beatles' Ballads* in 1980.

The group also featured the number on various TV shows including 'Sunday Night At The London Palladium', 'The Ed Sullivan Show' and 'With The Beatles' and on two of their 'Saturday Club' and two of their 'From Us To You' radio recordings.

'All My Loving' has been recorded by almost 100 different artists including the Trends, Count Basie, the Chipmunks, Herb Alpert and the George Martin Orchestra. On the version by the George Martin Orchestra, Beatles publisher Dick James sang part of the number. Foreign language versions included 'Toi l'ami', the French version by Richard Anthony, 'Con todo mi amor', a Spanish version by the Sandpipers, 'Feche os olhos', a Portuguese version by Renato & his Blue Caps and 'Gyts a gras', a Welsh version by Beti Williams.

All My Loving (EP)

The Beatles' fourth EP. As usual, Parlophone took two tracks from the latest Beatles album release, *With The Beatles*, together with two tracks from their *Please Please Me* album, which had previously been released as the flipsides of the group's first two singles.

All My Loving was issued on Parlophone GEP 8891 on 7 February 1964 and contained the tracks 'All My Loving', 'Ask Me Why', 'Money (That's What I Want)' and 'P.S. I Love You'. The EP reached No. 13 in the British charts. One of their radio recordings of the number was included on the *Beatles Live At the BBC* CDs while an alternative version was included on *Anthology 1*.

All Shook Up

Elvis Presley's first British No. 1 hit. It was also his only No. 1 on the HMV label when it reached the charts in July 1957, and the composition was credited to Otis Blackwell/Elvis Presley.

The Quarry Men included it in their repertoire soon after the Presley record hit the charts, with Paul on lead vocals.

All Things Must Pass

Tuesday, 25 February 1969, was George Harrison's 26th birthday and he went to Abbey Road and, in the absence of the other members of the Beatles, recorded three of his own compositions: 'Old Brown Shoe', 'Something' and 'All Things Must Pass'.

'All Things Must Pass' had been inspired by American group the Band and George had considered it might be suitable for the *Let It Be* album. It wasn't included on that release and George recorded it again with a set of musicians, including Eric Clapton, at Trident Studios and it was issued as the title track of his *All Things Must Pass* album. The track from the *Let It Be* sessions, recorded on George's 26th birthday was included on the Beatles' *Anthology 3* CDs.

All Together Now

This song was recorded on Friday, 12 May 1967 for the *Yellow Submarine* album. The number was mainly written by Paul, with a little help from John. All four Beatles come in to repeat 'All Together Now' approximately 50 times and the sequence of the Beatles singing the number was used in the live footage at the end of the *Yellow Submarine* film.

All You Need Is Love

The song which John and Paul wrote specially for the 'Our World' programme, beamed to 400 million viewers on Sunday, 25 June 1967.

They only had a short time to write a number which was suitable for the occasion and recording for the backing track began at Olympic Sound Studios on Wednesday, 14 June, and continued at Abbey Road in the large Number One studio, where the orchestra began recording on Friday, 23 June. The following day the Beatles attended a press call at the studio and on Sunday, 25 June performed the number live before the satellite audience on five continents.

Only 25 hours before it went on the air, the decision was taken to issue 'All You Need Is Love' as the group's fifteenth single.

The single was issued in Britain on Friday, 7 July on Parlophone R 5620 and went straight to the No. 1 position where it remained for four weeks. It was issued in America on Capitol 5964 on 17 July, where it also went to No. 1. The flipside was 'Baby You're A Rich Man'.

'All You Need Is Love' was also used as the title of the television documentary series by Tony Palmer and an album of that title was issued by Theatre Projects Records (9199 995) in February 1978 with the Beatles number as the first track. The song was also included on the *Yellow Submarine* album in January 1969, *The Beatles 1967–1970* in April 1973; the *Magical Mystery Tour* album in November 1976 and *Reel Music* in March 1982.

American Bandstand

An ABC Television show in the United States which first interviewed the Beatles by telephone on 15 February 1964 and also on 18 April. An entire edition of the show was devoted to the Beatles on 25 July 1964. It included a short, behind-the-scenes film of the making of *A Hard Day's Night*, in addition to clips from the film itself. Another programme with a Beatles theme was broadcast on 10 October and included a filmed interview with the group. In May 1965 the programme screened excerpts of the Beatles performing at the *New Musical Express* Poll Winner's Concert at Wembley, although there was no soundtrack to the clip.

And I Love Her

Jane Asher was the inspiration for this ballad by Paul, although John gave him a hand with the lyrics.

It first appeared on the *A Hard Day's Night* album in August 1964, followed by the British EP *Extracts From The Film 'A Hard Day's Night'* and the American Capitol EP *Four By The Beatles*. The track was also included on the American album *Something New*, the compilations *The Beatles 1962–1966*, *Love Songs* and *The Beatles' Ballads*, and the American *The Beatles Rarities* in 1980 and *Reel Music* in 1982.

The group also performed the number on their 'Top Gear' radio show on 16 July 1964.

One of the most popular of the Beatles' love ballads, it has been recorded by over 300 different artists, covering a range of styles and moods, including Ray Davies, Julie London, Smokey Robinson, Georgie Fame and Connie Francis. An alternative track of the song was used on the Beatles' *Anthology 1* CDs.

And Your Bird Can Sing

A John Lennon composition recorded in April 1965 and featured on the *Revolver* album. A version of the number was used on the Beatles' *Anthology 2* CDs.

Anello and Davide

Specialist shoemakers, based in Charing Cross Road, London WC2, who made footwear for the entertainment fraternity, ranging from ballet shoes to boots for movies, dancers and show business personalities.

When John and Paul returned from a fortnight's holiday in Paris in October 1961, they passed through London and saw some footwear which impressed them in the window of the shop. The black boots were of a narrow-toed, high-Cuban-heeled, elastic-sided, ankle-length Flamenco style. They went into the store and bought a pair each. When they returned to Liverpool, George and Pete were also struck by the boots and both ordered a pair for themselves from Anello and Davide.

This company was later to make the special 'Beatle boots' for the group, including those worn on the American tour of 1964.

Anna (Go To Him)

Number composed by Arthur Alexander and released by him on the Dot label on 17 September 1962. It was a particular favourite with John Lennon who sang lead vocal on the Beatles' interpretation.

The group recorded it for their *Please Please Me* album and on two BBC radio 'Pop Go The Beatles' shows. It was included on their *The Beatles (No. 1)* EP and on *The Beatles Collection*. In America it was issued on the EP *Souvenir of Their Visit: The Beatles* and on the album *Introducing The Beatles, The Beatles Versus The Four Seasons, Songs, Pictures and Stories Of The Fabulous Beatles* and *The Early Beatles*.

Ann-Margret

Following the Beatles' initial success in America, the media was 100 per cent behind them. However, the scandal magazine *Confidential*, true to its image, produced an issue with the Beatles' picture on the cover and the cover-lines 'Psst! Who Hushed Up These Stories About The BEATLES? * Their Wild antics in a Hamburg Sex Cellar. * The Nite Two Beatles went in Jail. * How Ringo Flipped for Ann-Margret. * The Marriage Nobody Talks About. * Their Secret Love Life.'

The magazine hinted that Ringo and Ann-Margret were having a romance and commented that Ringo had 'bent her shell-pink ears with an hour of long-distance oggly-googling, all in a special Teddy Boy lingo that left little Annie limp.'

There were other reports that the two were linked romantically, which Ringo had to dent at press interviews during their second American tour.

Ann-Margret, a stunning singer/actress/dancer, born in Stockholm, was to co-star with Elvis Presley in *Viva Las Vegas*, which brought her the nickname 'the female Elvis'. Her name was also linked romantically with 'the king'.

She'd lived in America from the age of five and found success as both a singer and film actress. In fact, the Beatles introduced her current hit 'I Just Don't Understand' into their repertoire in 1961 with John Lennon on lead vocal. They also recorded it on their 'Pop Go The Beatles' radio show.

The number was Ann-Margret's only US hit and it reached No. 17 in the American charts in August 1961. Interestingly enough, Delbert McLinton played harmonica on her record. 'I Just Don't Understand' was covered by Freddie & the Dreamers in September 1964 and by Jerry Reed in 1973.

Another Girl

Number penned by Paul and recorded on Monday, 15 February 1965 for inclusion on the *Help!* album.

Another Hard Day's Night

Title of one of the orchestral tracks performed by the George Martin Orchestra on the soundtrack of the film *Help!* The instrumental version of 'A Hard Day's Night' is heard in the background of a scene set in an Indian restaurant.

Although the track wasn't included on the British *Help!* album, Capitol included it among six orchestral tracks on the American album version of *Help!* issued in August 1965.

Antonioni, Michaelangelo

Italian director of films such as *L'Aventura* and *La Notte*. When he was in England making *Blow Up* in 1966, Paul made his acquaintance and gave him a screening of his own avant garde films such as *The Defeat Of The Dog* and *The Next Spring Then*. Antonioni was announced as the director of the projected third Beatles feature *Shades Of A Personality* which was due to commence filming in Spain in September 1967, but the project fell through.

Antrobus Arms, Amesbury, Wiltshire

A public house where the Beatles lodged for three days from 3 May 1965, during the filming of the Salisbury Plain sequences in *Help!* During the evening they were able to relax in the pub's lounge where, on several occasions, Paul and Ringo played poker with actor Leo McKern.

Any Time At All

A number penned by John Lennon and recorded in June 1964 for the *A Hard Day's Night* album. It was also included on the *Extracts From The Album 'A Hard Day's Night'* EP, the *Rock 'n' Roll Music* compilation and the Capitol album *Something New*.

Apache

A British No. 1 and a million-seller for the Shadows in 1960. Britain's leading group at the time, they were also the backing band for Cliff Richard and during their March 1960 tour, Jerry Lordan, a singer on the bill, played them an instrumental he had written called 'Apache'. It became the group's first hit. The Beatles included it in their repertoire in 1960, although they dropped it by the following year.

Apollo Theatre, Stockport Road, Ardwick Green, Ardwick, Manchester

Also known as the ABC Cinema. The Beatles appeared at this venue three times.

Their Apollo debut took place on 20 November 1963 when three of the numbers they performed were filmed by Pathe News, and, together with backstage scenes, released as an eight-minute colour short for cinema release for the week of 22 December.

The film was called *The Beatles Come To Town* and the three numbers were 'From Me To You', 'She Loves You' and 'Twist And Shout'.

Their second appearance at the venue, on 14 October 1964, received the following report in *Mersey Beat*:

The audience went completely wild when the Beatles took the stage at Ardwick's Apollo Theatre last week, and although the screams, yells and shrieks continued almost unabated throughout the whole of their 28-minute spot, the boys could still be heard above the din. Attendants tried to keep the audience seated, but virtually everyone in the theatre was standing on a seat seeking a better view of the four lads who, with this tour, have proved once and for all that they remain the biggest and most talented show-biz phenomenon this country has ever produced.

The show opened with the Rustiks, who also backed the second act on the bill, Bolton vocalist Michael Haslam, who received a great ovation.

Sounds Incorporated were the next to take the stage and their act has improved tremendously during the last few months. Stage presentation is original and entertaining and their choice of material (ranging from 'Maria' to the 'William Tell Overture') was greeted with wholesale enthusiastic response.

Sounds remained on stage to back Mary Wells, who was accompanied by her own guitarist Melvin Turrell. Looking exceptionally glamorous in a full-length silver dress, Mary sang many of her big hits, including 'Two Lovers' and 'My Guy'. Although her performances proved she is one of the world's leading songstresses, the young audience didn't seem to appreciate her talents, although her reception was warm. Her rendition of 'Time After Time', although excellent, would have been more suitable in cabaret.

The Remo Four opened the second half of the show and were joined by Tommy Quickly who had the girls in the audience screaming continually as he strode, walked, pranced and danced across the stage, full of bounce and verve. Despite the fact that he was directly before the Beatles' act, no one seemed impatient and he made quite an impact. Perhaps this tour can help to sell Tommy's current release, 'The Wild Side of Life'.

When the Beatles appeared to perform their old favourites, including 'Money', 'Twist and Shout' and many others – that was it!

Brian Epstein, who was standing at the side of the stage, could well be proud of the best value-for-money tour of the year.

Their last appearance at the venue took place on 7 December 1965.

Apple Boutique, 94 Baker Street, London W1

In the nineteenth century when it had been built, it was a four-storey house. Over the years it evolved into a shop and offices in a busy shopping area of the capital. Situated at the corner of Baker Street and Paddington Street, it became the first of the Beatles' Apple ventures to open.

Three Dutch designers, one male (Simon Posthuma) and two female (Josje Leeger and Marijke Koger), had set up a fashionable boutique called the Trend in Amsterdam, which, after an apparently successful start, soon developed financial troubles and had to close. Simon and Marijke wandered around Europe for a time and then settled in London where they met Simon Hayes and Barry Finch, partners in a public relations firm. Hayes became their business manager, Josje joined them from Amsterdam and Finch became the fourth member of the Fool.

They created a number of psychedelic-style designs for the Beatles, painting a Rolls-Royce for John, a fireplace for George and sundry other colourful tasks. Suddenly, it seemed they had talked the Beatles into launching a boutique, Pattie Harrison, who wore some of their designs, was to comment: 'I don't know how we met them. They just appeared one day.' And Neil Aspinall said: 'They crept up on us.'

Whatever the case, the Beatles gave the Fool £100,000 in September 1967 to design and stock the boutique. They immediately engaged a few dozen art students to paint a huge psychedelic mural across the entire front and side of the building. It was an exciting visual display but brought a torrent of complaints from local traders. Eventually, the complaints were so vociferous that the mural had to be erased.

The idea for the Apple Boutique was to be, as Paul was to comment, 'A beautiful place where you could buy beautiful things'. Pete Shotton was called down from his Hayling Island Supermarket to manage the store and among the shop assistants was Pattie Harrison's sister Jennie.

Invitations to the Gala party on 5 December 1967 read: 'Come at

7.46. Fashion Show at 8.16.' and the star-studded assembly discovered that the single drink available was apple juice. John and George were in attendance, but Ringo was filming in Rome and Paul had retreated to his farm in Scotland.

The venture lasted barely eight months. It was a financial disaster with a great amount of pilfering, together with overspending by the Fool. Pete Shotton wanted out and John Lydon was brought in as head of Apple Retail, but couldn't sort out the problems. It was decided to close down the venture.

On Tuesday morning, 30 July 1968, the staff were told they could give everything away. The Beatles and their girlfriends had been around the previous evening selecting their pick of the stock. Paul commented: 'We went along, chose all the stock we wanted – I got a smashing overcoat – then told our friends. Now everything that's left is for the public.' Ringo was to say, 'I couldn't find anything that fitted me.'

Their first customer that morning was actor Michael J. Pollard who, when he'd completed his shopping, was told to keep his wallet in his pocket.

Not much publicity had been given to the fact that Apple were to give away the entire £10,000 worth of stock because Paul didn't want traders from Carnaby Street to turn up and take it away in handcarts. It was a gift to the ordinary punter and by word of mouth, telephone calls, and the staff going on to the street to bring passers-by into the store, the stock began to go, people began to gather and the police were called in to handle the crowds.

Paul, with the help of Derek Taylor, prepared a press statement, which read:

'We decided to close down our Baker Street shop yesterday and instead of putting up a sign saying "Business will be resumed as soon as possible" and then auction off the goods, we decided to give them away. The shops were doing fine and making a nice profit on turnover. So far, the biggest loss is in giving the things away but we did that deliberately . . . We're giving them away – rather than selling them to barrow boys – because we wanted to give rather than sell.

'We came into shops by the tradesman's entrance but we're leaving by the front door. Originally, the shops were intended to be something else, but they just became like all the boutiques in London. They just weren't our thingy. The staff will get three weeks' pay but if they wish they'll be absorbed into the rest of Apple. Everyone will be cared for. The Kings Road shop, which is known as Apple Tailoring, isn't going to be part of Apple any more but it isn't closing down and we are leaving our investment there

because we have a moral and personal obligation to our partner
John Crittle who is now in sole control. All that's happened is that
we've closed our shop in which we feel we shouldn't, in the first
place, have been involved.

'Our main business is entertainment – communication. Apple is
mainly concerned with fun not with frocks. We want to devote all
our energies to records, films and our electronics adventures. We
had to re-focus. We had to zoom in on what we really enjoy, and we
enjoy being alive, and we enjoy being Beatles.

'It's 1968: already, it's 1968. Time is short. I suppose really what
we're doing is spring cleaning in mid-summer. The amazing thing is
our giving things away. Well, the answer is that it was much funnier
to give things away.

'Well, it's just that the Beatles are the Beatles are the mop tops are
the Beatles are the mop tops ... are whatever you see them to be,
whatever you see us to be. Create and preserve the image of your
choice. We are yours with love.'

Apple Corps

By 1967 the Beatles were advised that they were in a financial position in which any further money they earned could be instantly
taken in tax – and that they had £2 million to play around with
which, if they didn't invest, would be taken by the taxman. They
decided to create a company with a number of divisions and, in
January 1968, changed their company Beatles Ltd to Apple Corps
Ltd. Paul McCartney commented: 'It's a pun – apple core – see?'

All four Beatles became company Presidents. Neil Aspinall was
appointed Managing Director, Alistair Taylor, General Manager, and
Peter Brown and Harry Pinsker (head of the accountancy firm Bryce
Hanmer) became Directors. As the company grew Peter Asher became
A&R man, Malcolm Evans was made assistant Managing Director,
Derek Taylor became Director of Public Relations, Alexis Mardas
became their electronics ace, Dennis O'Dell, manager of films, Ron
Kass, Head of the Record Division, Jeremy Banks, Art Director, and
Tony Bramwell, Assistant to the Film Division and record plugger to
Apple Records. The actual divisions were Apple Electronics, Apple
Films Ltd, Apple Music Publishing, Apple Wholesale, Apple Retail,
Apple Television and Apple Records. Arrangements were made for
Capitol Records to be the distributor for America, Canada and
Mexico, while EMI handled the rest of the world.

Offices were found at 95 Wigmore Street, London W1 and then
at 3 Savile Row, London W1. The first venture was the television
presentation of Magical Mystery Tour, followed by the Apple
Boutique at 94 Baker Street, London W1.

Initially, there was great euphoria over the Apple concept, which was to provide an opportunity for creative people without 'the men in suits' inhibiting them.

Paul said, 'We want to help other people but without doing it like charity and without seeming like patrons of the arts. We always had to go to the big man on our knees, touch our forelocks and say, "Please can we do so and so?" And most of those companies are so big, and so out of touch with people like us who just want to sing or make films, that everyone has a bad time. We are just trying to set up a good organisation, not some great fat institution that doesn't care. We don't want people to say yessir, nossir.'

John Lennon commented, 'The aim of the company isn't a stack of gold teeth in the bank. We've done that bit. It's more of a trick to see if we can get artistic freedom within a business structure; to see if we can create things and sell them without charging three times our cost.'

Unfortunately, it didn't take long for the dream to go sour and the Apple Boutique closed within ten months. The only division which seemed to be making money was Apple Records, primarily because of the Beatles' releases. The staff indulged in extravagances – with orders of champagne and caviare among the daily supplies ordered; office furniture and equipment regularly disappeared; company expenses were used to buy cars, while lavish expense accounts soon began to cause financial problems. Their accountant warned the Beatles that they would encounter severe problems unless they brought someone in to sort out the mess.

They discussed hiring various business experts, such as Lord Beeching, and Paul suggested that they hire the New York law firm, Eastman and Eastman, to run their business affairs. Although the other members of the group were aware that the company was run by the relatives of Paul's girlfriend Linda, they were brought in as financial advisers. The group were also approached by Allen Klein and with John, George and Ringo voting for him, he was appointed to take charge of Apple. He immediately began sacking people and put an end to the extravagances. The experienced Ron Kass went and an inexperienced Jack Oliver was appointed to take his place. The tea ladies were sacked – and no one could get a cup of tea!

Apart from personnel sacked by Klein, others resigned and the Beatles' original dream faded until, by 1970, the only function of the company seemed to be the collection of Beatles royalties.

Apple Electronics

A division of Apple Corps set up specially for Alexis Mardas to develop and market the various electronic gadgets he created.

Mardas had been introduced to John Lennon who was intrigued by the series of electronic gadgets which Mardas, who became known as 'Magic Alex', had shown him. The previous 'electronics genius' in the life of the Beatles had been Adrian Barber who had designed the 'coffins' (amplifiers) for them and the sound system for the Star Club. In Liverpool, Adrian had also made gadgets before their time, putting radios inside coke cans and such.

Magic Alex dazzled the Beatles with his claims, some of which were quite extraordinary, yet the Beatles provided him with the finance and told him to develop the gadgets and market them for Apple.

The major brief he had was to build a studio for the Beatles at Apple, and he told them he would construct a 72-track studio.

Alexis filed one hundred patent applications – but none of them was accepted. Not a single item was completed or marketed for Apple Electronics, a division which actually didn't produce anything, and when Allen Klein appeared on the horizon, Apple Electronics ceased to exist.

Apple Films Limited

One of several companies formed by Apple Corps. Apple Films operated between 1967 and 1974. Dennis O'Dell was appointed to run the company and Tony Bramwell assisted. They only completed one film, *Magical Mystery Tour.* Apple Films announced the making of three movie projects – *Walkabout, Gorgeous Accident* and *The Jam* – but didn't make any of them. *Walkabout* was eventually filmed by another company and was directed by Nicolas Roeg, with Jenny Agguter starring. *Yellow Submarine* and *Let It Be,* although credited as 'presented' by Apple, were actually made by United Artists. The last project Apple Films participated in was *Little Malcolm & his Struggle Against the Eunuchs.* Based on the David Halliwell play, it starred John Hurt and John McEnery. Unfortunately, they were unable to find a distributor for the film.

Applejacks, The

A group from Solihull in Birmingham who comprised Al Jackson (vocals), Martin Baggott (lead guitar), Phil Cash (rhythm guitar), Don Gould (organ), Megan Davies (bass guitar) and Gary Freeman (drums).

Their first single 'Tell Me When' reached No. 7 in the British charts and their follow-up was the Lennon & McCartney composition 'Like Dreamers Do', which was issued in Britain on Decca FII916 on 5 June 1964, and in America on London 9681 on 6 July. Paul McCartney wrote the number for the group.

The record reached No. 20 in the British charts.

Apple Records

Of the several different companies launched by the Beatles' Apple Corps, Apple Records seemed to be the one with the most potential, particularly as an agreement was made for future Beatles products to be issued on the Apple label. However, EMI's Parlophone label still maintained its catalogue numbers and continued to handle distribution.

The company was launched in August 1968, with 33-year-old American Ron Kass, former head of Liberty's International Division, as Managing Director; 23-year-old Peter Asher as the company's A&R man and 23-year-old Tony Bramwell in charge of promoting the products.

Advertisements and posters announcing the venture had brought in hundreds of tapes to Apple's HQ, but most were left unheard and the main signings came from personal preferences of the individual directors.

The very first artist signed to Apple was James Taylor, discovered by Peter Asher. He only found fame after leaving the label. He cited the main complaint made by the artists about Apple – that they felt that the company did not handle the promotion of their signings very well. The artists also complained that they found themselves being neglected due to the internal financial disputes at Apple.

'Our First Four' was a specially promoted package conceived by an advertising agency, Wolff Olins, to promote the first four releases by the Beatles, Mary Hopkin, Jackie Lomax and the Black Dyke Mills Band.

Apple Records basically lasted from August 1968 to May 1976 and, apart from the success of records by the Beatles as a group and individually, the company did not do very well commercially and only achieved two non-Beatles Gold Discs.

When Apple Records was being wound down late in 1975 there was consideration given to the idea of releasing a double album of the best of the non-Beatle Apple artists, but it went the way of other Apple Records ideas – nowhere.

Despite the lack of success of the Apple artists, apart from the initial chart action of acts such as Mary Hopkin and Badfinger, there were some excellent artists and releases. Over the years there has grown a keen collector's market for Apple products and in 1991, the first Apple CDs were eventually released.

APPLE DISCOGRAPHY – SINGLES (in chronological order)

'HEY JUDE' c/w 'REVOLUTION', THE BEATLES.
Released in Britian on Apple R 5722 on 30 August 1968 and in America on Apple 2276 on 26 August 1968.

'THOSE WERE THE DAYS' c/w 'TURN, TURN, TURN', MARY HOPKIN.
Released in Britain on Apple 2 on 30 August 1968 and in America
on 26 August 1968. The number was an old song, penned by Gene
Raskin, which Paul McCartney had discovered and liked and had
once tried to interest the Moody Blues in recording. The single was
also produced by Paul and the same instrumental backing track was
used while Mary sang new vocal tracks for the Italian, French,
German and Spanish markets. A multi-million seller internationally
and a No. 1 hit in Britain and No. 2 in America.

'SOUR MILK SEA' c/w 'THE EAGLE LAUGHS AT YOU', JACKIE LOMAX.
Released in Britain on Apple 3 on 6 September 1968 and in
America on Apple 1802 on 26 August 1968. Produced by George
Harrison, this single failed to register, even though the musicians
playing on the track included George Harrison and Jackie Lomax
on rhythm guitars, Paul McCartney on bass, Eric Clapton on lead
guitar, Ringo Starr on drums and Nicky Hopkins on piano.

'THINGUMYBOB' 'YELLOW SUBMARINE', BLACK DYKE MILLS BRASS
BAND.
Issued in Britain on Apple 4 on 6 September 1968 and in America
on Apple 1800 on 26 August 1968. Paul McCartney produced this
record of the instrumental theme he composed for the television
series 'Thingumybob'. Unfortunately, the record wasn't a hit and
the Brass Band didn't record for Apple again.

'QUELLI ERAND GIORNI' c/w 'TURN, TURN, TURN', MARY HOPKIN.
Issued in Europe on Apple 2 on 25 October 1968.

'MAYBE TOMORROW' c/w 'AND HER DADDY'S A MILLIONAIRE', THE
IVEYS.
Issued in Britain on Apple 5 on 15 November 1968 and in America
on Apple 1803 on 27 January 1969.

'ROAD TO NOWHERE' c/w 'ILLUSIONS', TRASH.
Issued in Britain on Apple 6 on 24 January 1969 and in America on
Apple 1804 on 3 March 1969. Originally a group from Glasgow
called the Pathfinders, discovered by Tony Meehan who brought
them to Apple's attention. They changed their name to White Trash,
which proved to be a burden – the name was banned by the BBC –
and shortened it to Trash. Their next projected album wasn't
released, they had one more single from Apple and were then dropped
from the label.

'LONTANO DAGLI OCCHI' c/w 'THE GAME', MARY HOPKIN.
Issued in Italy on Apple 7 on 7 March 1969.

'PRINCE EN AVIGNON' c/w 'THE GAME', MARY HOPKIN.
Issued in France on Apple 9 on 7 March 1969.

'CAROLINA ON MY MIND' c/w 'TAKING IT IN', JAMES TAYLOR.
Issued in America on Apple 1805 on 17 March 1969. The single

was produced by Peter Asher and Paul McCartney played bass on the title track, but the single failed to register in the charts.

'GOODBYE' c/w 'SPARROW', MARY HOPKIN.

Issued in Britain on Apple 10 on 28 March 1969 and in America on Apple 1806 on 7 April 1969. The record reached the No. 2 position in the British charts and No. 13 in the American.

'GET BACK' c/w 'DON'T LET ME DOWN', THE BEATLES WITH BILLY PRESTON.

Issued in Britain on Apple R 5777 on 11 April 1969 and in America on Apple 2490 on 5 May 1969.

'NEW DAY' c/w 'I FALL INSIDE YOUR EYES', JACKIE LOMAX.

Issued in Britain on Apple 11 on 9 May 1969. The 'A' side was produced by Jackie Lomax and Mal Evans and the flipside by George Harrison. None of Jackie's Apple records made any impact on the charts.

'KING OF FUH' c/w 'NOBODY KNOWS', BRUTE FORCE.

Issued in Britain on Apple 8 on 16 May 1969. Brute Force was the pseudonym of a 20-year-old New York songwriter, Steven Friedland, who penned and produced this fantasy story. EMI refused to press or distribute the record, so Apple tried to take on the task themselves, but the record received no airplay, poor distribution – and vanished. The single was eventually issued in America in 1971 on Brute Force Records.

'THE BALLAD OF JOHN AND YOKO' c/w 'OLD BROWN SHOE', THE BEATLES.

Issued in Britain on Apple R 5786 on 30 May 1969 and in America on Apple 2531 on 7 June 1969.

'NEW DAY' c/w 'THUMBIN' A RIDE', JACKIE LOMAX.

Issued in America on Apple 1807 on 2 June 1969. The flipside of this single, a Jerry Leiber/Mike Stoller composition, was produced by Paul McCartney on the eve of his wedding to Linda.

'THAT'S THE WAY GOD PLANNED IT' c/w 'WHAT ABOUT YOU', BILLY PRESTON.

Issued in Britain on Apple 12 on 27 June 1969 and in America on Apple 1808 on 7 July 1969. The Beatles bought Preston's contract from Vee Jay Records in America and he was with Apple for three years. This single achieved a No. 11 position in the British charts.

'GIVE PEACE A CHANCE' c/w 'REMEMBER LOVE', THE PLASTIC ONO BAND.

Issued in Britain on Apple 13 on 4 July 1969 and in America on Apple 1809 on 7 July 1969. The number which has become a peace anthem was recorded at John and Yoko's second 'Bed In' at the Queen Elizabeth Hotel in Montreal, Canada, with backing vocals provided by a number of their celebrity visitors. John and Yoko had embarked on their recording partnership and used the name Plastic Ono Band and its variations. The flipside was a Yoko composition, also recorded at the hotel. The single reached No. 2 in the British charts and No. 14 in the American.

'NO ESCAPING YOUR LOVE' c/w 'DEAR ANGIE', THE IVEYS.

Issued in Europe on Apple 14 on 18 July 1969.

'STORM IN A TEACUP', THE IVEYS. 'SOMETHING'S WRONG', JAMES TAYLOR. 'LITTLE YELLOW PILLS', JACKIE LOMAX. 'HAPPINESS RUNS', MARY HOPKIN.

Issued on CT2 on 18 July 1969. This was a special promotional EP produced by Apple for Wall's Ice Cream and available only for a limited period of time at various outlets in London's West End which sold Wall's Ice Cream.

'HARE KRISHNA MANTRA' c/w 'PRAYER TO THE SPIRITUAL MASTERS', RADHA KRISHNA TEMPLE.

Issued in Britain on Apple 15 on 29 August 1969 and in America on Apple 1810 on 22 August 1969. The record reached No. 12 in the British charts, but failed to make the American charts.

'QUE SERA SERA' c/w 'FIELDS OF ST ETIENNE', MARY HOPKIN.

Issued in Britain on Apple 16 on 19 September 1969 and in America on Apple 1823 on 15 June 1970.

'GOLDEN SLUMBERS'/'CARRY THAT WEIGHT' c/w 'TRASH CAN', TRASH.

Issued in Britain on Apple 17 on 3 October 1969 and in America on Apple 1811 on 15 October 1969. A modest hit which only reached No. 35 in the British charts. It was the last release on Apple for Trash.

'GIVE PEACE A CHANCE' c/w 'LIVING WITHOUT TOMORROW', HOT CHOCOLATE BAND.

Issued in Britain on Apple 18 on 10 October 1969 and in America on 17 October 1969. Errol Brown and Tony Wilson approached Apple for permission to change the lyrics of 'Give Peace A Chance' for a reggae version they wanted to record. John Lennon liked the idea and they recorded it for Apple, with Tony Meehan producing. It failed to register and they didn't make another Apple single, but went on to be one of the most successful chart artists in Britain for the next two decades.

'EVERYTHING'S ALL RIGHT' c/w 'I WANT TO THANK YOU', BILLY PRESTON.

Issued on Apple 19 on 17 October 1969 and in America on Apple 1814 on 20 October 1969. The 'A' side was produced by George Harrison.

'COLD TURKEY' c/w 'DON'T WORRY KYOKO', THE PLASTIC ONO BAND.

Issued in Britain on Apple R 1001 on 24 October 1969 and in America on Apple 1813 on 20 October 1969. Paul McCartney refused to record this song as a Beatles single, so John decided to collect together some musicians in another incarnation of the Plastic Ono Band. They included himself on guitar/vocals, Eric Clapton on lead guitar, Klaus Voormann on bass guitar, Ringo Starr on drums and Yoko Ono on backing vocals. John also decided to dispense with the Lennon & McCartney composing credit and the song is simply credited to John Lennon. The flipside is a song Yoko wrote to her daughter Kyoko. The single reached No. 13 in the British charts and No. 30 in the American.

'SOMETHING' C/W 'COME TOGETHER', THE BEATLES.
Issued in Britain on Apple R 5814 on 31 October 1969 and in America on Apple 2654 on 6 October 1969.

'YOU KNOW MY NAME' C/W 'WHAT'S THE NEWS MARY JANE', THE PLASTIC ONO BAND.
This was an Apple single scheduled to be issued on Apple 1002 on 5 December 1969, but it was never released.

'COME AND GET IT' C/W 'ROCK OF ALL AGES', BADFINGER.
Issued in Britain on Apple 20 on 5 December 1969 and in America on Apple 1816 on 29 January 1970. The first of three British hit singles for Badfinger. This title track of Ringo Starr's movie *The Magic Christian* was penned by Paul McCartney and reached No. 4 in the charts. It did even better in America where it topped the charts.

'TEMMA HARBOUR' C/W '*LONTANO DAGLI OCCHI*', MARY HOPKIN.
Issued in Britain on Apple 22 on 16 January 1970 and in America on Apple 1816 on 29 January 1970. A No. 6 chart hit in Britain which reached the position of No. 39 in America. Mickie Most produced the 'A' side, Paul McCartney the flipside.

'ALL THAT I'VE GOT' C/W 'AS I GET OLDER', BILLY PRESTON.
Issued in Britain on Apple 21 on 30 January 1970 and in America on Apple 1817 on 16 February 1970.

'HOW THE WEB WAS WOVEN' C/W 'THUMBIN' A RIDE', JACKIE LOMAX.
Issued in Britain on Apple 23 on 6 February 1970. The single was produced by George Harrison, but Jackie's career with Apple was coming to a close.

'INSTANT KARMA' C/W 'WHO HAS SEEN THE WIND', JOHN/ YOKO WITH THE PLASTIC ONO BAND.
Issued in Britain on Apple R 1003 on 6 February 1970 and in America on Apple 1818 on 20 February 1970. John wrote this number, Phil Spector produced and the Plastic Ono line-up this time was John Lennon (vocal/guitar/electric piano), George Harrison

(guitar/grand piano), Klaus Voormann (bass guitar/electric piano), Alan White (drums/grand piano), Billy Preston (organ), Mal Evans (chimes), Yoko Ono (vocals). The chanting was provided by a group of people who were brought in from a nearby late-night club, Hatchetts in Piccadilly. John produced the flipside which was written and sung by Yoko. The single reached No. 5 in Britain and No. 3 in America.

'AIN'T THAT CUTE' c/w 'VAYA CON DIOS', DORIS TROY.
Issued in Britain on Apple 24 on 13 February 1970 and in America on Apple 1820 on 16 March 1970. R&B singer Doris signed with Apple in 1970 after recording and co-writing some songs with Billy Preston. George Harrison produced the title track.

'GOVINDA' c/w 'GOVINDA JAI JAI', RADHA KRISHNA TEMPLE.
Issued in Britain on Apple 25 on 6 March 1970 and in America on Apple 1821 on 24 March 1970. The second and last single on Apple by this vocal/instrumental assembly who reached No. 23 in the British charts with this track, produced by George Harrison.

'LET IT BE' c/w 'YOU KNOW MY NAME', THE BEATLES.
Issued in Britain on Apple R 5833 on 6 March 1970 and in America on Apple 2764 on 11 March 1970.

'HOW THE WEB WAS WOVEN' c/w 'I FALL INSIDE YOUR EYES', JACKIE LOMAX.
Issued in America on Apple 1819 on 9 March 1970.

'KNOCK KNOCK WHO'S THERE' c/w 'I'M GOING TO FALL IN LOVE AGAIN', MARY HOPKIN.
Issued in Britain on Apple 26 on 20 March 1970. A No. 2 chart hit for Mary in Britain.

'THE LONG AND WINDING ROAD' c/w 'FOR YOU BLUE', THE BEATLES.
Issued in America on Apple R 2832 on 11 May 1970.

'JACOB'S LADDER' c/w 'GET BACK', DORIS TROY.
Issued in Britain on Apple 28 on 28 August 1970 and in America on Apple 1824 on 21 September 1970. Although she'd had some chart hits on Atlantic early in the sixties, Doris wasn't to find any chart success with her Apple releases.

'MY SWEET LORD' c/w 'LONG AS I GOT MY BABY', BILLY PRESTON.
Issued in Britain on Apple 29 on 4 September 1970. The George Harrison composition, co-produced by George and Billy.

'BEAUCOUPS OF BLUES' c/w 'COOCHY-COOCHY', RINGO STARR.
Issued in America on Apple R 2969 on 5 October 1970. No British release for this single, which reached No. 87 in the American charts.

'NO MATTER WHAT' c/w 'CARRY ON TILL TOMORROW', BADFINGER.
Issued in America on Apple 1822 on 10 December 1970, where it reached No. 8 in the charts.

'THINK ABOUT YOUR CHILDREN' c/w 'HERITAGE', MARY HOPKIN.
Issued in Britain on Apple 30 on 16 October 1970 and in America on Apple 1825 on 18 October, 1970. Written by Errol Brown and Tony Wilson, who had recorded for Apple as the Hot Chocolate Band. Mary reached No. 19 in the British charts with the number.

'CAROLINA ON MY MIND' c/w 'SOMETHING'S WRONG', JAMES TAYLOR.
Issued in Britain on Apple 32 on 6 November 1970 and in America on Apple 1805 on 26 October 1970.

'NO MATTER WHAT' c/w 'BETTER DAYS', BADFINGER.
Issued in Britain on Apple 31 on 6 November 1970. A No. 5 hit in the British charts.

'MY SWEET LORD' c/w 'ISN'T IT A PITY', GEORGE HARRISON.
Issued in America on Apple 2995 on 23 November 1970. A No. 1 hit in America.

'MY SWEET LORD' c/w 'LITTLE GIRL', BILLY PRESTON.
Issued in America on Apple 1826 on 3 December 1970.

'MOTHER' c/w 'WHY', JOHN/YOKO WITH THE PLASTIC ONO BAND.
Issued in America on Apple 1827 on 28 December 1970.

'MY SWEET LORD' c/w 'WHAT IS LIFE', GEORGE HARRISON.
Issued in Britain on Apple R 5884 on 15 January 1971. It was George's first solo single and gave him a No. 1 hit. Apart from topping the British charts, the single was No. 1 in various countries around the world, including Australia, Austria, Brazil, France, Germany, Mexico, Norway, Singapore, Spain, Sweden and Switzerland. Among the backing musicians were Ringo Starr on drums, Klaus Voormann on bass guitar, Gary Wright on piano, George Harrison and Badfinger on guitars, Peter Drake on steel guitar. The number also proved controversial when George was sued for plagiarising the Chiffons' hit 'He's So Fine', and he paid compensation a few years later.

'WHAT IS LIFE' c/w 'APPLE SCRUFFS', GEORGE HARRISON.
Issued in America on Apple 1828 on 15 February 1971. Another track from the *All Things Must Pass* album, released only in America and reaching No. 10 in the charts.

'ANOTHER DAY' c/w 'OH WOMAN OH WHY', PAUL MCCARTNEY.
Issued in Britain on Apple R 5889 on 19 February 1971 and in America on Apple 1829 on 22 February 1971. First solo single from Paul, which brought him a No. 1 in Britain and a No. 5 position in the American charts. This was the song credited to Paul and Linda McCartney, which caused Sir Lew Grade to sue – but the dispute was settled when Paul agreed to appear in a TV special for Grade.

'POWER TO THE PEOPLE' c/w 'OPEN YOUR BOX', JOHN/YOKO WITH THE PLASTIC ONO BAND.
Issued in Britain on Apple R 5892 on 12 March 1971. John and Yoko produced both tracks with Phil Spector. Another political

message from John which reached No. 6 in the British charts.

'POWER TO THE PEOPLE' c/w 'TOUCH ME', JOHN/YOKO WITH THE PLASTIC ONO BAND.
Issued in America on Apple 1830 on 22 March 1971 where it reached the No. 11 position. Capitol insisted on changing the flipside as they were concerned about the lyrics to 'Open Your Box'.

'IT DON'T COME EASY' c/w 'EARLY 1970', RINGO STARR.
Issued in Britain on Apple R 5898 on 9 April 1971 and in America on Apple 1831 on 19 April 1971. Ringo's first solo single which reached No. 5 in the British charts. It was his second American single and reached No. 4 in the charts there. Ringo penned the number himself and George Harrison and Steve Stills are featured on guitars, Klaus Voormann on bass guitar and Ron Cattermole on saxophone and trumpet. The flipside, also written by Ringo, was a tribute to his fellow Beatles.

'TRY SOME, BUY SOME' c/w 'TANDOORI CHICKEN', RONNIE SPECTOR.
Issued in Britain on Apple 33 on 16 April 1971 and in America on Apple 1832 on 19 April 1971. George Harrison and Phil Spector got together on this single to try to find a hit for Spector's wife. George also wrote the song, which only reached No. 77 in the American charts.

'LET MY NAME BE SORROW' c/w 'KEW GARDENS', MARY HOPKIN.
Issued in Britain on Apple 34 on 18 June 1971. This single was produced by Tony Visconti, whom she married. After their divorce, Visconti married John Lennon's former lover May Pang. The single reached No. 46 in the British charts.

'SOUR MILK SEA' c/w 'I FALL INSIDE YOUR EYES', JACKIE LOMAX.
Issued in America on Apple 1834 on 21 June 1971.

'GOD SAVE US' c/w 'DO THE OZ', BILL ELLIOTT AND THE ELASTIC OZ BAND.
Issued in Britain on Apple 36 on 16 July 1971 and in America on Apple 1836 on 7 July 1971. When the alternative magazine *Oz* was taken to court over its notorious 'Schoolkids' issue, John decided to record this number to raise money for the defence. It was written by Yoko, recorded at their studio in Tittenhurst Park and produced by John, Yoko, Phil Spector and Mal Evans. Newcastle vocalist Bill Elliott was featured, while John Lennon provided lead vocals on the flipside of the record. It had no chart success.

'BANGLADESH' c/w 'DEEP BLUE', GEORGE HARRISON.
Issued in Britain on Apple R 5912 on 30 July 1971 and in America on Apple 1836 on 28 July 1971. The title song was written as part of George's efforts to bring relief to the troubled country of Bangladesh. The flipside was composed immediately after George's mother Louise had died of a terminal illness. The

number reached No. 10 in the British charts and No. 23 in the American.

'UNCLE ALBERT/ADMIRAL HALSEY' c/w 'TOO MANY PEOPLE', PAUL AND LINDA MCCARTNEY.

Issued in America on Apple 1837 on 2 August 1971. The single reached No. 1 in the American charts and received a Grammy Award.

'BACK SEAT OF MY CAR' c/w 'HEART OF THE COUNTRY', PAUL AND LINDA MCCARTNEY.

Issued in Britain on Apple R 5914 on 13 August 1971. A track from the *Ram* album which eventually reached No. 39 in the British charts.

'JOI BANGLA/OH BHAUGOWAN' c/w 'RAGA MISHRA-JHINJHOTI', RAVI SHANKAR AND CHORUS.

Issued in Britain on Apple 37 on 27 August 1971 and in America on 9 August 1971. Produced by George Harrison.

'MRS LENNON' c/w 'MIDSUMMER NEW YORK', YOKO ONO WITH THE PLASTIC ONO BAND.

Issued in Britain on Apple 38 on 29 October 1971 and in America on Apple 1839 on 29 September 1971. The first solo single from Yoko, comprising two numbers from her forthcoming album *Fly*.

'IMAGINE' c/w 'IT'S SO HARD', JOHN LENNON WITH THE PLASTIC ONO BAND.

Issued in America on Apple 1840 on 11 October 1971. The number reached No. 3 in the American charts.

'DAY AFTER DAY' c/w 'MONEY', BADFINGER.

Issued in America on Apple 1841 on 10 November 1971, where it reached No. 4 in the charts.

'HAPPY XMAS (WAR IS OVER)' c/w 'LISTEN, THE SNOW IS FALLING', JOHN/YOKO WITH THE PLASTIC ONO BAND AND THE HARLEM COMMUNITY CHOIR.

Issued in Britain on Apple R 5970 on 24 November 1972 and in America on Apple 1842 on 1 December 1971. The single reached No. 2 in Britain. It had been released in America the year previously, but didn't chart, although it has since become a Christmas classic and is regularly re-released. John did not feature the Apple logo on the single.

'WATER PAPER AND CLAY' c/w 'JEFFERSON', MARY HOPKIN.

Issued in Britain on Apple 39 on 3 December 1971. The record didn't register in the charts.

'DAY AFTER DAY' c/w 'SWEET TUESDAY MORNING', BADFINGER.

Issued in Britain on Apple 40 on 14 January 1972. Third and final British chart hit for Badfinger – it reached the No. 5 position.

'MIND TRAIN' c/w 'LISTEN, THE SNOW IS FALLING', YOKO ONO WITH THE PLASTIC ONO BAND.

Issued in Britain on Apple 41 on 21 January 1972.

'GIVE IRELAND BACK TO THE IRISH' c/w 'GIVE IRELAND BACK TO THE IRISH (INSTRUMENTAL VERSION)', WINGS.
Issued in Britain on Apple R 5936 on 25 February 1972 and in America on Apple 1847 on 28 February 1972. The single reached No. 13 in the British charts and No. 21 in the American. Paul and Linda wrote the song regarding the Bloody Sunday incident in Ireland on 3 January 1972. Due to the political nature of the song it was banned in Britain by both the BBC and the IBA.

'SWEET MUSIC' c/w 'SONG OF SONGS', LON AND DERREK VAN EATON.
Issued in America on Apple 1845 on 6 March 1972. A tape of these two brothers performing was sent to several record companies. Apple A&R man Tony King liked their tape and took it to George Harrison. George liked it, and so did Ringo and John, so the group were signed to Apple and flew to London to record their debut album. The 'A' side of this single was produced by George Harrison and Ringo Starr was one of the drummers on the track. The flipside was produced by Klaus Voormann.

'BABY BLUE' c/w 'FLYING', BADFINGER.
Issued in Britain on Apple 42 on 10 March 1972 and in America on Apple 1844 on 6 March 1972. It was their final American hit, reaching No. 14 in the charts.

'BACK OFF BOOGALOO' c/w 'BLINDMAN', RINGO STARR.
Issued in Britain on Apple R 5944 on 17 March 1972 and in America on Apple 1849 on 20 March 1972. The single reached No. 2 in Britain and No. 9 in America. Ringo wrote the song and George Harrison produced the session. The backing musicians included George Harrison on guitar, Klaus Voormann on bass guitar, Ringo on drums and vocals, Gary Wright on keyboards and Lesley Duncan, Madeline Bell and Jean Gilbert on backing vocals.

'F IS NOT A DIRTY WORD' c/w 'THE BALLAD OF NEW YORK CITY/ JOHN LENNON–YOKO ONO', DAVID PEEL AND THE LOWER EAST SIDE.
Originally scheduled for release in America on Apple 6498/ 6499 on 20 April 1972, but only promotional copies were sent out to disc jockeys. John and Yoko discovered the controversial singer in New York in 1971.

'WOMAN IS THE NIGGER OF THE WORLD' c/w 'SISTERS O SISTERS', JOHN/YOKO WITH ELEPHANT'S MEMORY.
Issued in Britain on Apple 5953 on 12 May 1972 and in America on Apple 1848 on 24 April 1972.

'MARY HAD A LITTLE LAMB' c/w 'LITTLE WOMAN LOVE', WINGS.
Issued in Britain on Apple R 5949 on 12 May 1972 and in America on Apple 1851 on 29 May 1972. Number penned by Paul and Linda for their daughter Mary which reached No. 6 in the British charts and No. 28 in the American.

'WE'RE ON OUR WAY' C/W 'SUPERSOUL', CHRIS HODGE.
Issued in Britain on Apple 43 on 9 June 1972 and in America on
Apple 1850 on 3 May 1972. This first Apple single by Hodge
reached No. 44 in the American charts. His second single failed to
register and he moved to RCA Records.
'HIPPY FROM NEW YORK CITY' C/W 'THE BALLAD OF NEW YORK
CITY/JOHN LENNON–YOKO ONO', DAVID PEEL AND THE LOWER EAST
SIDE.
Originally scheduled for release in America on Apple 6545/
6546 on 16 June 1972, but only promotional copies were sent out
to disc jockeys.
'KNOCK KNOCK WHO'S THERE' C/W 'INTERNATIONAL', MARY
HOPKIN.
Issued in America on Apple 1855 on 8 November 1972.
'NOW OR NEVER' C/W 'MOVE ON FAST', YOKO ONO WITH
ELEPHANT'S MEMORY.
Issued in America on Apple 1853 on 13 November 1972. Two tracks
from Yoko's *Approximate Infinite Universe* album.
'SATURDAY NIGHT SPECIAL' C/W 'VALSE DE SOLEIL COUCHER',
SUNDOWN PLAYBOYS.
Issued in Britain on Apple 44 on 24 November 1972 and in
America on Apple 1852 on 26 September 1972. The only Apple
release for this group of Cajun-style players.
'HI, HI, HI' C/W 'C MOON', WINGS.
Issued in Britain on Apple 5972 on 1 December 1972 and in
America on Apple 1857 on 4 December 1972. Paul produced the
single which became the second Wings single to be banned by the
BBC – they cited suggestive lyrics. It reached No. 3 in the British
charts and No. 10 in the American.
'WATER PAPER AND CLAY' C/W 'STREET OF LONDON', MARY HOPKIN.
Issued in America on Apple 1843 on 1 December 1972.
'POWER BOOGIE' C/W 'LIBERATION SPECIAL', ELEPHANT'S MEMORY.
Issued in Britain on Apple 45 on 8 December 1972 and in America
on Apple 1854 on 4 December 1972. A group John Lennon and
Yoko Ono discovered in New York and hired to provide backing on
some records and gigs.
'GOODBYE SWEET LORRAINE' C/W 'CONTACT LOVE', CHRIS HODGE.
Issued in America on Apple 1858 on 22 January 1973. This second
and final release on Apple for Hodge was unsuccessful and he left
the label.
'DEATH OF SAMANTHA' C/W 'YANG YANG', YOKO ONO WITH
ELEPHANT'S MEMORY.
Issued in Britain on Apple 47 on 4 May 1973 and in America on
Apple 1859 on 26 February 1973.

'WARM WOMAN' c/w 'MORE THAN WORDS', LON AND DERREK VAN EATON.

Issued in Britain on Apple 46 on 9 March 1973. Last Apple single from the brothers. By this time it was obvious that the majority of artists signed to Apple weren't achieving chart success, despite the fact that there had been some talented acts, such as Jackie Lomax, Doris Troy and James Taylor; and the hits by artists such as Mary Hopkin and Badfinger seemed to have dried up. From then on, the Apple singles were basically solo releases from the individual Beatles and Yoko Ono.

'MY LOVE' c/w 'THE MESS', PAUL MCCARTNEY AND WINGS.

Issued in Britain on Apple R 5985 on 23 March 1973 and in America on Apple 1861 on 9 April 1973. The 'A' side was recorded during the *Red Rose Speedway* album sessions and the flipside was recorded during a Wings concert in Holland. The single reached No. 7 in Britain and hit the No. 1 spot in America.

'GIVE ME LOVE' c/w 'MISS O'DELL', GEORGE HARRISON.

Issued in Britain on Apple 5988 on 25 May 1973 and in America on Apple 1862 on 7 May 1973. George's last hit single for some time, it reached No. 8 in the British charts and No. 1 in the American.

'LIVE AND LET DIE' c/w 'I LIE AROUND', WINGS.

Issued in Britain on Apple R 5987 on 1 June 1973 and in America on Apple 1863 on 18 June 1973. The number which Paul composed for the eighth Bond film, although he insisted that he record the number himself. On the flipside, Denny Laine takes over on lead vocal for the first and only time on a Wings single. The number reached No. 7 in the British charts and No. 2 in the American.

'PHOTOGRAPH' c/w 'DOWN AND OUT', RINGO STARR.

Issued in Britain on Apple R 5992 on 10 October 1973 and in America on Apple 1865 on 24 September 1973. Ringo co-wrote the title number with George Harrison. The musicians include Ringo and Jim Keltner on drums, George Harrison on twelve string guitar, Nicky Hopkins on piano, Klaus Voorman on bass guitar, Vini Poncia and Jimmy Calvert on acoustic guitars, Lon and Derrek Van Eaton on percussion and Bobby Keyes on tenor sax. The single reached No. 4 in the British charts and No. 1 in the American.

'WOMAN POWER' c/w 'MEN, MEN, MEN', YOKO ONO.

Issued in America on Apple 1867 on 24 September 1973.

'HELEN WHEELS' c/w 'COUNTRY DREAMER', PAUL MCCARTNEY AND WINGS.

Issued in Britain on Apple R 5993 on 26 October 1973 and in America on Apple 1869 on 12 November 1973. The name in the title refers to Paul's Land-Rover. The single reached No. 12 in Britain and No. 10 in America.

'RUN, RUN, RUN' c/w 'MEN, MEN, MEN', YOKO ONO.

Issued in Britain on Apple 48 on 9 November 1973.

'MIND GAMES' c/w 'MEAT CITY', JOHN LENNON.

Issued in Britain on Apple R 5994 on 16 November 1973 and in America on Apple 1868 on 29 October 1973. John dropped the Plastic Ono credit and began recording again under his own name – he also finished his producing collaboration with Phil Spector and only worked with him again on the *Rock 'n' Roll* album. The single reached No. 19 in the British charts and No. 9 in the American.

'JET' c/w 'MAMUNIA', PAUL McCARTNEY AND WINGS.

Issued in America on Apple 1871 on 28 January 1974. A few weeks after this American release, Capitol Records changed the flipside to 'Jet' and reissued it on 18 February, with the same catalogue number. It reached No. 7 in the American charts.

'YOU'RE SIXTEEN' c/w 'DEVIL WOMAN', RINGO STARR.

Issued in Britain on Apple R 5995 on 8 February 1974 and in America on Apple 1870 on 3 December 1973. Another American No. 1 single for Ringo and a No. 4 position in Britain.

'OH MY MY' c/w 'STEP LIGHTLY', RINGO STARR.

Issued in America on Apple 1872 on 18 February 1974. Ringo's fifth American Top Ten hit, reaching No. 5 in the charts.

'APPLE OF MY EYE' c/w 'BLIND OWL', BADFINGER.

Issued in Britain on Apple 49 on 8 March 1974 and in America on Apple 1864 on 17 December 1973.

'BAND ON THE RUN' c/w 'NINETEEN HUNDRED EIGHTY FIVE', PAUL McCARTNEY AND WINGS.

Issued in America on Apple 1873 on 8 April 1974. The single reached No. 1 in the American charts and won a Grammy Award.

'WHATEVER GETS YOU THRU THE NIGHT' c/w 'BEEF JERKY', JOHN LENNON.

Issued in Britain on Apple R 5998 on 4 October 1974 and in America on Apple 1874 on 23 September 1974. Among the musicians backing John on this single are Elton John (organ/piano), Jim Keltner (drums), Eddie Mottau (acoustic guitar), Jessie Ed Davis (guitar), Arthur Jenkins (percussion) and Bobby Keyes (tenor saxophone). John uses the pseudonym the Hon. John St John Johnson for his guitar credit. The single reached No. 24 in the British charts and provided him with his first No. 1 in America as a solo artist. Elton John had predicted he'd top the charts with the number and, following a promise, he appeared on stage at Elton's Madison Square Garden concert.

'JUNIOR'S FARM' C/W 'SALLY G', PAUL MCCARTNEY AND WINGS.
Issued in Britain on Apple R 5999 on 25 October 1974 and in
America on Apple 1875 on 4 November 1974. More tracks from
the *Band On The Run* album. The single reached No. 16 in the British
charts and No. 3 in the American. It was Paul's last single for Apple.
'ONLY YOU' C/W 'CALL ME', RINGO STARR.
Issued in Britain on Apple R 6000 on 15 November 1974 and in
America on Apple 1876 on 11 November 1974. John Lennon
suggested that Ringo should cover this old Platters song and he also
played acoustic guitar on the session. Ringo shared drumming
honours with Jim Keltner, Billy Preston played electric piano, Jesse
Ed Davis and Steve Cropper were on electric guitars and Harry
Nilsson provided backing vocal support. The single reached No. 25
in the British charts and No. 6 in the American.
'DARK HORSE' C/W 'I DON'T CARE ANYMORE', GEORGE HARRISON.
Was due to be issued in Britain on Apple 6001 on 22 November
1974, but wasn't. It was issued in America on Apple 1877 on 18
November 1974. It reached No. 15 in the American charts.
'DING DONG DING DONG' C/W 'I DON'T CARE ANYMORE', GEORGE
HARRISON.
Issued in Britain on Apple R 6002 on 6 December 1974. It only
managed to scrape into the British charts at No. 38. The song is
said to have been inspired by the engravings on the walls of
George's home, Friar Park.
'DING DONG DING DONG' C/W 'HARI'S ON TOUR (EXPRESS)', GEORGE
HARRISON.
Issued in America on Apple 1879 on 23 December 1974. The single
only reached No. 36 in the American charts.
'NO NO SONG' C/W 'SNOOKEROO', RINGO STARR.
Issued in America on Apple 1880 on 27 January 1975. The flipside
was an Elton John/Bernie Taupin composition. The single wasn't a
chart success for Ringo.
'NO 9 DREAM' C/W 'WHAT YOU GOT', JOHN LENNON.
Issued in Britain on Apple R 6003 on 31 January 1975 and in
America on Apple 1878 on 16 December 1974. Another track from
Walls and Bridges, which only reached No. 23 in the British charts
and No. 9 in the American.
'SNOOKEROO' C/W 'OO-WEE', RINGO STARR.
Issued in Britain on Apple R 6004 on 21 February 1975. Ringo's run
of chart success seemed to have ended – and so did his releases on
Apple. This was his last British Apple single.
'DARK HOUSE' C/W 'HARI'S ON TOUR (EXPRESS)', GEORGE HARRISON.
Issued in Britain on Apple R 6001 on 28 February 1975. Not a
chart entry.

'STAND BY ME' C/W 'MOVE OVER MS L', JOHN LENNON.
Issued in Britain on Apple R 6005 on 18 April 1975 and in America on Apple 1881 on 10 March 1975. A track from the *Rock 'n' Roll* album which reached No. 27 in the British charts and No. 20 in the American. John had originally written the flipside for Keith Moon's album *Two Sides Of The Moon*.
'IT'S ALL DOWN TO GOODNIGHT VIENNA' C/W 'OW-WEE', RINGO STARR.
Issued in America on Apple 1882 on 2 June 1975. Another track from the *Goodnight Vienna* album which achieved a modest position of No. 31 in the American charts – this was Ringo's first single not to reach the Top 30.
'SLIPPIN' AND SLIDIN'' C/W 'AIN'T THAT A SHAME', JOHN LENNON.
Plans were in preparation for this second single from the *Rock 'n' Roll* album to be issued in America on Apple 1883 on 2 June 1975, but the plan was dropped.
'YOU' C/W 'WORLD OF STONE', GEORGE HARRISON.
Issued in Britain on Apple R 6007 on 12 September 1975, and in America on Apple 1884 on 15 September 1975. Taken from the *Extra Texture* album, it only reached No. 38 in the British charts, and No. 20 in the American charts.
'IMAGINE' C/W 'WORKING CLASS HERO', JOHN LENNON.
Issued in Britain on Apple 6009 on 24 October 1975.
'THIS GUITAR' C/W 'MAYA LOVE', GEORGE HARRISON.
Issued in America on Apple 1885 on 8 December 1975 and in Britain on Apple 6012 on 6 February 1976. George Harrison's last single on the Apple label and also the last solo Beatle single to be issued on Apple. It did not reach either the British or American charts.

APPLE DISCOGRAPHY – ALBUMS
WONDERWALL MUSIC, GEORGE HARRISON.
Issued in Britain on SAPCOR 1 on 1 November 1968 and in America on Apple ST 3350 ON 2 December 1968.
THE BEATLES, THE BEATLES.
Issued in Britain on Apple PCS 7067/8 on 22 November 1968 and in America on Apple SWBO 101 on 25 November 1968.
TWO VIRGINS, JOHN LENNON AND YOKO ONO.
Issued in Britain on SAPCOR 2 on 29 November 1968 and in America on Apple T 5001 on 11 November 1968.
JAMES TAYLOR, JAMES TAYLOR.
Issued in Britain on SAPCOR 3 on 6 December 1968 and in America on Apple SKAO 3352 on 17 February 1969. The tracks were, Side One: 'Don't Talk Now', 'Something's Wrong', 'Knocking 'Round The Zoo', 'Sunshine Sunshine', 'Taking It In', 'Something

In The Way She Moves'. Side Two: 'Carolina On My Mind', 'Brighten Your Night With My Day', 'Night Owl', 'Rainy Day Man', 'Circle 'Round The Sun', 'Blues Is Just A Bad Dream'. Taylor was discovered by Peter Asher and moved to England to record for Apple. He had no success with the label and felt that he was not being given adequate promotion. He left Apple in 1969 and later found success with Warner Brothers Records, while retaining Peter Asher as his producer. Taylor later married Carly Simon and both Paul and Linda McCartney contributed vocals to albums by both singers.

UNDER THE JASMINE TREE, THE MODERN JAZZ QUARTET.
Issued in Britain on SAPCOR 4 on 6 December 1968 and in America on Apple ST 3353 on 17 February 1969. The tracks were, Side One: 'Blue Necklace', 'Three Little Feelings'. Side Two: 'Exposure', 'Jasmine Tree'. This well-established jazz outfit only signed with Apple for a specifically limited period, during which they issued two albums.

YELLOW SUBMARINE, THE BEATLES.
Issued in Britain on Apple PCS 7070 on 17 January 1969 and in America on Apple SW 153 on 13 January 1969.

POST CARD, MARY HOPKIN.
Issued in Britain on SAPCOR 5 on 21 February 1969 and in America on Apple ST 3351 on 3 March 1969. Paul McCartney produced this album which contained a selection of songs from various songwriters including Donovan, Nilsson, Gershwin and Irving Berlin. The tracks were, Side One: 'Lord Of The Reedy River', 'Happiness Runs (Pebble And The Man)', 'Love Is The Sweetest Thing', 'Y Blodwyn Gwyn', 'The Honeymoon Song', 'The Puppy Song', 'Inchworm'. Side Two: 'Voyage Of The Moon', 'Lullaby Of The Leaves', 'Young Love', 'Someone To Watch Over Me', 'Prince En Avignon', 'The Game', 'There's No Business Like Show Business'. For the American release, 'Those Were The Days' replaced 'Someone To Watch Over Me'. The album reached the No. 3 position in Britain.

IS THAT WHAT YOU WANT, JACKIE LOMAX.
Issued in Britain on SAPCOR 6 on 21 March 1969 and in America on Apple ST 3354 on 19 May 1969. Lomax's only album for Apple, produced by George Harrison. The tracks were, Side One: 'Speak To Me', 'Is This What You Want', 'How Can You Say Goodbye', 'Sunset', 'Sour Milk Sea', 'I Fall Inside Your Eyes'. Side Two: 'Little Yellow Pills', 'Take My Word', 'The Eagle Laughs At You', 'Baby You're A Lover', 'You've Got Me Thinking', 'I Just Don't Know'. For the American release 'How Can You Say Goodbye' was replaced by 'New Day'.

LIFE WITH THE LIONS, JOHN LENNON AND YOKO ONO.
Issued in Britain on Zapple 01 on 9 May 1969 and in America on Zapple ST 3357 on 26 May 1969.
ELECTRONIC SOUND, GEORGE HARRISON.
Issued in Britain on Zapple 02 on 9 May 1969 and in America on Zapple ST 3358 on 26 May 1969.
LISTENING TO RICHARD BRAUTIGAN, RICHARD BRAUTIGAN.
Originally scheduled to become Zapple 03 and to be issued on 23 May 1969, but the project was dropped.
ACCEPT NO SUBSTITUTE, DELANEY AND BONNIE.
Originally due to be issued in Britain on SAPCOR 7 on 30 May 1969, but the project was dropped and the LP was issued on the Elektra label the following month.
WHITE TRASH, TRASH.
The debut album by Trash was given the catalogue number SAPCOR 7 and the release date in Britain on 20 June 1969, but it was never issued.
MAYBE TOMORROW, THE IVEYS.
Issued in Europe (but not Britain) on SAPCOR 8 on 4 July 1969 while a projected American release on Apple ST 3355 on 14 July 1969 was withdrawn. The album, produced by Tony Visconti and Mal Evans, was also available in Japan. At the time of this release the Iveys comprised Tom Evans (rhythm guitar), Pete Ham (lead guitar), Ron Griffith (bass guitar) and Mike Gibbons (drums). They later decided to drop the name Iveys and call themselves Badfinger. The tracks were, Side One: 'Maybe Tomorrow', 'See-Saw Grampa', 'Beautiful And Blue', 'Dear Angie', 'Think About The Good Times', 'Yesterday Ain't Coming Back'. Side Two: 'Fisherman', 'Sali Bloo', 'Angelique', 'I'm In Love', 'Knocking Down Our Home', 'I've Been Waiting'.
THAT'S THE WAY GOD PLANNED IT, BILLY PRESTON.
Issued in Britain on SAPCOR 9 on 22 August 1969 and in America on 10 September 1969. The tracks were, Side One: 'Do What You Want', 'I Want To Thank You', 'Everything's All Right', 'She Belongs To Me', 'It Doesn't Matter', 'Morning Star'. Side Two: 'Hey Brother', 'What About You', 'Let Us Get Together Right Now', 'This Is It', 'Keep To Yourself', 'That's The Way God Planned It'.
ABBEY ROAD, THE BEATLES.
Issued in Britain on PCS 7088 on 26 September 1969 and in America on Apple SO 383 on 1 October 1969.
WEDDING ALBUM, JOHN LENNON AND YOKO ONO.
Issued in Britain on SAPCOR 11 on 24 October 1969 and in America on Apple SMAX 3361.

SPACE, THE MODERN JAZZ QUARTET.
Issued in Britain on SAPCOR 10 on 24 October 1969 and in America on 10 November 1969. The tracks were, Side One: 'Visitor From Venus', 'Visitor From Mars', 'Here's That Rainy Day'. Side Two: 'Dilemma', 'Adagio From Concierto De Aranjuez'.

LIVE PEACE IN TORONTO, PLASTIC ONO BAND.
Issued in Britain on Apple CORE 2001 on 12 December 1969 and in America on Apple SW 3362 on 12 December 1969. The tracks were, Side One: 'Blue Suede Shoes', 'Money', 'Dizzy Miss Lizzy', 'Yer Blues', 'Cold Turkey', 'Give Peace A Chance'. Side Two: 'Don't Worry Kyoko (Mummy's Only Looking For A Hand In The Snow)', 'John John (Let's Hope For Peace)'. An appearance at the Toronto Rock 'n' Roll Revival Concert in September 1969 resulted in this album with John backed by Eric Clapton on guitar. Alan White on drums and Klaus Voormann on bass guitar. The second side of the album featured two numbers written by Yoko. The album didn't chart in Britain, but it reached No. 10 in America.

MAGIC CHRISTIAN MUSIC, BADFINGER.
Issued in Britain on SAPCOR 12 on 9 January 1970 and in America on Apple ST 3364 on 16 February 1970. The tracks were, Side One: 'Come And Get It', 'Crimson Ship', 'Dear Angie', 'Fisherman', 'Midnight Sun', 'Beautiful And Blue', 'Rock Of All Ages'. Side Two: 'Carry On 'Til Tomorrow', 'I'm In Love', 'Walk Out In The Rain', 'Angelique', 'Knocking Down Our Home', 'Give It A Try', 'Maybe Tomorrow'. For the American release, the tracks 'Angelique' and 'Give It A Try' were not included.

MCCARTNEY, PAUL MCCARTNEY.
Issued in Britain on Apple PCS 7102 on 17 April 1970 and in America on Apple STAO 3363 on 20 April 1970. Paul's first solo album, produced by himself, on which he also plays all the instruments. The tracks were, Side One: 'The Lovely Linda', 'That Would Be Something', 'Valentine Day', 'Every Night', 'Hot As Sun', 'Glasses', 'Junk', 'Man We Was Lonely'. Side Two: 'Op You', 'Momma Miss America', 'Teddy Boy', 'Singalong Junk', 'Maybe I'm Amazed', 'Kreen-Akrore'. The album reached No. 2 in Britain and No. 1 in America.

LET IT BE, THE BEATLES.
Issued in Britain on Apple PXS 1 on 8 May 1970 and in America on Apple AR 34001 on 18 May 1970.

DORIS TROY, DORIS TROY.
Issued in Britain on SAPCOR 13 on 11 September 1970 and in America on Apple ST 3370 on 9 November 1970. The singer produced this album herself and among the artists performing on it are George Harrison, Ringo Starr, Jackie Lomax, Klaus Voormann

and Steve Stills. The tracks were, Side One: 'Ain't That Cute', 'Give Me Back My Dynamite', 'You Tore Me Up Inside', 'Games People Play', 'Gonna Get My Baby Back', 'I've Got To Be Strong'. Side Two: 'Hurry', 'So Far', 'Exactly Like You', 'You Give Me Joy Joy', 'Don't Call Me No More', 'Jacob's Ladder'.

ENCOURAGING WORDS, BILLY PRESTON.
Issued in Britain on SAPCOR 14 on 11 September 1970 and in America on Apple ST 3370 on 9 November 1970. Billy's second and final album for Apple, produced by himself and George Harrison. The tracks were, Side One: 'Right Now', 'Little Girl', 'Use What You Got', 'My Sweet Lord', 'Let The Music Play', 'The Same Thing Again'. Side Two: 'I've Got A Feeling', 'Sing One For The Lord', 'When You Are Mine', 'I Don't Want You To Pretend', 'Encouraging Words', 'All Things Must Pass', 'You've Been Acting Strange'.

THE WHALE, JOHN TAVENER.
Issued in Britain on SAPCOR 15 on 25 September 1970 and in America on Apple SMAS 3369 on 9 November, 1970. The tracks were, Side One: 'The Whale' (Part One). Side Two: 'The Whale' (Concluded). Tavener was a British classical composer/conductor who had studied at the Royal Academy of Music. His composition *The Whale* was first performed in 1966. The Apple recording was made at the Church of St John the Evangelist in London with a host of musicians, including the London Sinfonietta and Chorus, with Tavener playing Hammond organ.

BEAUCOUPS OF BLUES, RINGO STARR.
Issued in Britain on Apple PAS 10002 on 25 September 1970 and in America on Apple SMAS 3368 on 28 September 1970. Recorded in Nashville. The tracks were, Side One: '*Beaucoups* Of Blues', 'Love Don't Last Long', 'Fastest Growing Heartache In The West', 'Without Her', 'Woman Of The Night', 'I'd Be Talking All The Time'. Side Two: '$15 Draw', 'Wine, Women And Loud Happy Songs', 'I Wouldn't Have You Any Other Way', 'Loser's Lounge', 'Waiting', 'Silent Homecoming'. The album reached No. 65 in America.

NO DICE, BADFINGER.
Issued in Britain on SAPCOR 16 on 27 November 1970 and in America on Apple ST 3367 on 9 November 1970. The tracks were, Side One: 'I Can't Take It', 'I Don't Mind', 'Love Me Do,' 'Midnight Caller', 'No Matter What', 'Without You'. Side Two: 'Blodwyn', 'Better Days', 'It Had To Be', 'Waterford John', 'Believe Me', 'We're For The Dark'.

ALL THINGS MUST PASS, GEORGE HARRISON.
Issued in Britain on Apple STCH 639 on 30 November 1970 and in America on Apple STCH 639 on 27 November 1970. The tracks

were, Side One: 'I'd Have You Anytime', 'My Sweet Lord', 'Wah-Wah', 'Isn't It A Pity'. Side Two: 'What Is Life', 'If Not For You', 'Behind That Locked Door', 'Let It Down', 'Run Of The Mill'. Side Three: 'Beware Of Darkness', 'Apple Scruffs', 'Ballad of Sir Frankie Crisp (Let It Roll)', 'Awaiting On You All', 'All Things Must Pass'. Side Four: 'I Dig Love', 'Art Of Dying', 'Isn't It A Pity' (second version), 'Hear Me Lord'. Side Five: 'Out Of The Blue', 'It's Johnny's Birthday', 'Plug Me In'. Side Six: 'I Remember Jeep', 'Thanks For The Pepperoni'. The album rose to No. 1 in both the British and American charts.

PLASTIC ONO BAND, JOHN LENNON.
Issued in Britain on Apple PCS 7124 on 11 December 1970 and in America on Apple SW 3372 on 11 December 1970. Often nicknamed 'The Primal Scream' album. The tracks were, Side One: 'Mother', 'Hold On', 'I Found Out', 'Working Class Hero', 'Isolation'. Side Two: 'Remember', 'Love', 'Well Well Well', 'Look At Me', 'God', 'Mummy's Dead'. The album reached No. 13 in the British charts and No. 6 in the American.

PLASTIC ONO BAND, YOKO ONO.
Issued in Britain on SAPCOR 17 on 11 December 1970 and in America on Apple SW 3373 on 11 December 1970. A six-track album, with all songs composed by Yoko. As this was her first real solo album, John does not receive the usual co-credit. The tracks were, Side One: 'Why', 'Why Not', 'Greenfield Morning I Pushed An Empty Baby Carriage All Over The City'. Side Two: 'AOS', 'Touch Me', 'Paper Shoes'.

FROM THEN TO US; THE BEATLES CHRISTMAS ALBUM, THE BEATLES.
Issued in Britain on LYN 2154 on 18 December 1970 and in America on SBC 100 on 18 December 1970 – although only to members of the Beatles' fan clubs in both countries and not to the general public.

RAM, PAUL AND LINDA MCCARTNEY.
Issued in Britain on Apple PAS 1003 on 28 May 1971 and in America on Apple SMAS 3375 on 17 May 1971. The tracks were, Side One: 'Too Many People', '3 Legs', 'Ram On', 'Dear Boy', 'Uncle Albert/Admiral Halsey', 'Smile Away'. Side Two: 'Heart Of The Country', 'Monkberry Moon Delight', 'Eat At Home', 'Long Haired Lady', 'Ram On', 'The Back Seat Of My Car'. The album reached No. 1 in the UK and No. 2 in America.

RADHA KRISHNA TEMPLE, RADHA KRISHNA TEMPLE.
Issued in Britain on SAPCOR 18 on 28 May 1971 and in America on Apple SKAO 3376 on 21 May 1971. Members of the London branch of the Radha Krishna Temple, whom George Harrison took into the Apple studios. He produced this album, which came in a

package with the lyrics to the chants, a biography of Krsna and other material relevant to the temple. The tracks were, Side One: 'Govinda', 'Sri Gurvastakam', 'Bhaja Bhakata/Arati', 'Hare Krishna Mantra'. Side Two: 'Sri Isopanisad', 'Bhaja Hunre Mana', 'Govinda Jaya Jaya'.

CELTIC REQUIEM, JOHN TAVENER.
Issued in Britain on SAPCOR 20 on 2 July 1971. The tracks were, Side One: 'Celtic Requiem'. Side Two: 'Coplas', 'Nomine Jesu'. The final Apple album from this classical composer. All three compositions were recorded at the Church of St John the Evangelist in London.

COME TOGETHER, STELVIO CIPRIONI.
Issued in America on Apple SW 3377 on 17 September 1971. The tracks were, Side One: 'Games People Play', 'Come Together (Arrival in Rome)', 'Love Is Blue', 'Fascinum', 'Monument To Love', 'Love Is Blue'. Side Two: 'Love Is Blue' 'I Can Sing A Rainbow', 'Come Together', 'Love Is Blue'/'Bas Vibrations', 'Come Together'/'Get Together'. A soundtrack album for the film, which Allen Klein added to the Apple catalogue.

FLY, YOKO ONO.
Issued in Britain on SAPCOR 21 on 1 October 1971 and in America on Apple SVBB 3380 on 20 September 1971. The full album credit was: By Yoko Ono and the Plastic Ono Band with Joe Jones Tone Deaf Music Co. The tracks were, Side One: 'Midsummer New York', 'Mind Train', Side Two: 'Mind Holes', 'Don't Worry Kyoko', 'Mrs Lennon', 'Hirake', 'Toiler Piece'/'Unknown', 'O Wind (Body Is The Scar Of Your Mind)'. Side Three: 'Airmale', 'Don't Count The Waves', 'You'. Side Four: 'Fly', 'Telephone Piece'.

EARTH SONG – OCEAN SONG, MARY HOPKIN.
Issued in Britain on SAPCOR 21 on 1 October 1971 and in America on Apple SMAS 3381 on 3 November 1971. The tracks were, Side One: 'Earth Song', 'Ocean Song', 'International', 'How Come The Sun', 'There's Got To Be More'. Side Two: 'Silver Birch And Weeping Willow', 'Martha', 'Streets Of London', 'Wind, Water, Paper And Clay'.

IMAGINE, JOHN LENNON AND THE PLASTIC ONO BAND, WITH THE FLUX FIDDLERS.
Issued in Britain on Apple PAS 10004 on 8 October 1971 and in America on Apple SW 3379 on 9 September 1971. The tracks were, Side One: 'Imagine', 'Crippled Inside', 'Jealous Guy', 'It's So Hard', 'I Don't Want To Be A Soldier Mama, I Don't Want To Die'. Side Two: 'Give Me Some Truth', 'Oh My Love', 'How Do You Sleep?', 'How?', 'Oh Yoko'. The album reached No. 1 in both the British and American charts.

RAGA, RAVI SHANKAR.
Issued in America on SWAO 3384 on 7 December 1971. The tracks were, Side One: 'Dawn To Dust', 'Vedic Hymns', 'Baba Teaching', 'Birth To Death', 'Vinus House', 'Gurur Bramha', 'United Nations'. Side Two: (Medley) 'Raga Parameshwari'/'Rangeswhart', 'Banaras Ghat', 'Bombay Studio', 'Kinnara School', 'Frenzy And Distortion', 'Raga Desh'. This was the soundtrack album to the film *Raga*.
WILD LIFE, WINGS.
Issued in Britain on PCS 7142 on 7 December 1971 and in America on Apple SW 3386 on 7 December 1971. First album from Paul and Linda McCartney's new band, Wings, which reached No. 11 in the British charts and No. 10 in the American. The tracks were, Side One: 'Mumbo', 'Bip Bop', 'Love Is Strange', 'Wild Life'. Side Two: 'Some People Never Know', 'I Am Your Singer', 'Tomorrow', 'Dear Friend'.
EL TOPO, ALEXANDRO JODOROWSKY.
Issued in America on SWAO 3388 on 27 December 1971. The tracks were Side One: 'Entiero Del Primer Juguete', 'Bajo Tierra', 'La Cathedral De Los Puerlos', 'Los Mendigos Sagrados', 'La Muerte Es Un Nacimiento', 'Curios Mexicano', 'Valas Fatasma'. Side Two: 'El Alma Nace En La Sangre', 'Topo Triste', 'Los Dioses De Azucar', 'Las Flores Nacen En El Barro', 'El Infierno De Las Angeleses Prostitutos', 'Marcha De Los O Jos En El Trianqulos', 'La Mieldel Dolor', '300 Conejos', 'Conocimiento A Traves De La Musica', 'La Primera Flor Despues Del Diluvio'. An unusual release for Apple – the soundtrack for a metaphysical Western movie produced by cult director Jodorowsky.
THE CONCERT FOR BANGLADESH, GEORGE HARRISON AND FRIENDS.
Issued in Britain on STCX 3385 on 10 January 1972 and in America on STCX 3385 on 20 December 1971.
STRAIGHT UP, BADFINGER.
Issued in Britain on SAPCOR 19 on 11 February 1972 and in America on Apple SW 3387 on 13 December 1971. The tracks were, Side One: 'Take It All', 'Baby Blue', 'Money', Flying', 'I'd Die, Babe', 'Name Of The Game'. Side Two: 'Suitcase', 'Sweet Tuesday Morning', 'Day After Day', 'Sometimes', 'Perfection', 'It's Over'. Album produced by Todd Rundgren, excepting four tracks produced by George Harrison: 'I'd Die, Babe', 'Name Of The Game', 'Suitcase' and 'Day After Day'.
THE POPE SMOKES DOPE, DAVID PEEL.
Issued in America on SW 3391 on 28 April 1972. The tracks were, Side One: 'I'm A Runaway', 'Everybody's Smoking Marijuana', 'F Is Not A Dirty Word', 'The Hippie From New York City', 'McDonald's Farm', 'The Ballad Of New York City'. Side Two:

'The Ballad Of Bob Dylan', 'The Chicago Conspiracy', 'The Hip Generation', 'I'm Gonna Start Another Riot', 'The Birth Control Blues', 'The Pope Smokes Dope'. The album was produced by John Lennon and Yoko Ono.

SOME TIME IN NEW YORK CITY, JOHN LENNON AND YOKO ONO AND THE PLASTIC ONO BAND WITH ELEPHANT'S MEMORY PLUS INVISIBLE STRINGS.

Issued in Britain on Apple PCSP 716 on 15 September 1972 and in America on Apple SVBB 3392 on 12 June 1972. The tracks were, Side One: 'Woman Is The Nigger Of The World', 'Sisters, O Sisters', 'Attica State', 'Born In A Prison', 'New York City'. Side Two: 'Sunday Bloody Sunday', 'The Luck Of The Irish', 'John Sinclair', 'Angela', 'We're All Water'. The album reached No. 19 in the British charts and No. 48 in the American.

ELEPHANT'S MEMORY, ELEPHANT'S MEMORY.

Issued in Britain on SAPCOR 22 on 10 November 1972 and in America on SMAS 3389 on 18 September 1972. The band who backed John Lennon and Yoko Ono on some American gigs. They were originally going to tour with John, but he cancelled it. However, he agreed to produce an album with the band, together with Yoko. The tracks were, Side One: 'Liberation Special', 'Baddest Of The Mean', 'Cryin' Blacksheep Blues', 'Chuck 'n' Bo'. Side Two: 'Gypsy Wolf', 'Madness', 'Wind Ridge', 'Power Boogie', 'Local Plastic Ono Band'.

THOSE WERE THE DAYS, MARY HOPKIN.

Issued in Britain on SAPCOR 23 on 24 November 1972 and in America on SW 3395 on 25 September 1972. The tracks were, Side One: 'Those Were The Days', 'Que Sera Sera', 'Fields Of St Etienne', 'Kew Gardens', 'Temma Harbour', 'Think About Your Children'. Side Two: 'Knock Knock, Who's There', 'Heritage', 'Sparrow', 'Lontano Dagli Occhi', 'Goodbye'.

PHIL SPECTOR'S CHRISTMAS ALBUM, VARIOUS ARTISTS.

Issued in Britain on SAPCOR 24 on 8 December 1972 and in America on SW 3400 on 11 December 1972. The tracks were, Side One: 'White Christmas', 'Frosty The Snowman', 'Bells Of St Mary', 'Santa Claus Is Coming To Town'. 'Sleigh Ride', 'It's A Marshmallow World'. Side Two: 'I Saw Mummy Kissing Santa Claus', 'Rudolph, The Red Nosed Reindeer', 'Winter Wonderland', 'Parade Of The Wooden Soldiers', 'Christmas (Baby Please Come Home)', 'Here Comes Santa Claus', 'Silent Night'. An album which Spector had originally produced several years earlier with a range of artists from his original Phillies record label: Darlene Love, the Ronettes and Bob B Soxx & the Blue Jeans.

BROTHER, LON AND DERREK VAN EATON.
Issued in Britain on SAPCOR 25 on 9 February 1973 and in America on SMAS 3390 on 22 September 1972. The tracks were, Side One: 'Warm Woman', 'Sun Song', 'More Than Words', 'Hear My Cry', 'Without The Lord', 'Sweet Music'. Side Two: 'Help Us All', 'Maybe There's Another', 'Ring', 'Sunshine', 'Another Thought'. The only Apple album from the brothers. It was produced by Klaus Voormann with the exception of 'Sweet Music', which was produced by George Harrison.

APPROXIMATELY INFINITE UNIVERSE, YOKO ONO.
Issued in Britain on SAPDO 1001 on 16 February 1973 and in America on SVBB 3399 on 8 January 1973, with the credit: By Yoko Ono and the Plastic Ono Band with Elephant's Memory, Endless Strings and Choir Boys. Yoko's second double album. The tracks were, Side One: 'Yang Yang', 'Death Of Samantha', 'I Want My Love To Rest Tonight', 'What Did I Do!', 'Have You Seen A Horizon Lately'. Side Two: 'Approximately Infinite Universe', 'Peter The Dealer', 'Song For John', 'Catman (The Roses Are Coming)', 'What A Bastard The World Is', 'Waiting For The Sunrise'. Side Three: 'I Felt Like Smashing My Face In A Clear Glass Window', 'Winter Song', 'Kite Song', 'What A Mess', 'Shiranakatta (I Didn't Know)', 'Air Talk'. Side Four: 'I Have a Woman Inside My Soul', 'Move On Fast', 'Now Or Never', 'Is Winter Here To Stay?', 'Looking Over From My Hotel Window.'

IN CONCERT 1972, RAVI SHANKAR AND ALI AKBAR KHAN.
Issued in Britain on SAPDO 1002 on 13 April 1973 and in America on SVBB 3396 on 22 January 1973. The tracks were, Side One: 'Raga – Hem Bihag'. Side Two: 'Raga – Manj Khamaj (Part One)'. Side Three: 'Raga – Manj Khamaj (Part Two)'. Side Four: 'Raga – Sandhi Bhairabi'. The album was produced by George Harrison, Zakir Hussein and Phil McDonald.

THE BEATLES 1962–1966, THE BEATLES.
Issued in Britain on PCSP 717 on 20 April 1973 and in America on SKBO 3403 on 2 April 1973.

THE BEATLES 1967–1970, THE BEATLES.
Issued in Britain on PCSP 718 on 20 April 1973 and in America on SKBO 3404 on 2 April 1973.

RED ROSE SPEEDWAY, PAUL MCCARTNEY AND WINGS.
Issued in Britain on Apple PCTC 251 on 4 May 1973 and in America on Apple SMAL 3409 on 30 April 1973. The tracks were, Side One: 'Big Barn Bed', 'My Love', 'Get On The Right Thing', 'One More Kiss', 'Little Lamb Dragonfly'. Side Two: 'Single Pigeon', 'When The Night', 'Loup (1st Indian On The Moon)', 'Hold Me Tight', 'Lazy Dynamite', 'Hands Of Love', 'Power Cut'. The album reached No. 4 in Britain and No. 1 in America.

LIVING IN THE MATERIAL WORLD, GEORGE HARRISON.

Issued in Britain on Apple PAS 10006 on 22 June 1973 and in America on Apple SMAS 3410 on 30 May 1973. The tracks were, Side One: 'Give Me Love (Give Me Peace On Earth)', 'Sue Me Sue You Blues', 'The Light That Has Lighted The World', 'Don't Let Me Wait Too Long', 'Who Can See It', 'Living In The Material World'. Side Two: 'The Lord Loves The One (That Loves The Lord)', 'Be Here Now', 'Try Some Buy Some', 'The Day The World Gets Round', 'That Is All'. The album reached No. 3 in Britain and No. 1 in America.

RINGO, RINGO STARR.

Issued in Britain on Apple PCTC 252 on 9 November 1973 and in America on Apple SWAL 3413 on 2 November 1973. The tracks were, Side One: 'I'm The Greatest', 'Have You Seen My Baby', 'Photograph', 'Sunshine Life For Me (Sail Away Raymond)', 'You're Sixteen'. Side Two: 'Oh My My', 'Step Lightly', 'Six O'Clock', 'Devil Woman', 'You And Me (Babe)'. The album reached No. 6 in the British charts and No. 2 in the American.

MIND GAMES, JOHN LENNON WITH THE PLASTIC U.F. ONO BAND.

Issued in Britain on Apple PCS 7165 on 16 November 1973 and in America on Apple SW 3414 on 2 November 1973. The tracks were, Side One: 'Mind Games', 'Tight A$', 'One Day (At A Time)', 'Bring On The Lucie (Freda Peeple)', 'Nutopian International Anthem'. Side Two: 'Intuition', 'Out Of The Blue', 'Only People', 'I Know (I Know)', 'You Are Here', 'Meat City'. The album reached No. 9 in the British charts and No. 18 in the American.

FEELING THE SPACE, YOKO ONO.

Issued in Britain on SAPCOR 26 on 23 November 1973 and in America on SW 3412 on 2 November 1973. The tracks were, Side One: 'Growing Pain', 'Yellow Girl (Stand By For Life)', 'Coffin Car', 'Woman Of Salem', 'Run, Run, Run', 'If Only'. Side Two: 'A Thousand Times Yes', 'Straight Talk', 'Angry Young Woman', 'She Hits Back', 'Woman Power', 'Men, Men, Men'.

BAND ON THE RUN, PAUL MCCARTNEY AND WINGS.

Issued in Britain on Apple PAS 10007 on 30 November 1973 and in America on Apple SO 3415 on 5 December 1973. The tracks were, Side One: 'Band On The Run', 'Jet', 'Bluebird', 'Mrs Vandebilt', 'Let Me Roll It'. Side Two: 'Mamunia', 'No Words', 'Picasso's Last Words (Drink To Me)', 'Nineteen Hundred And Eighty Five'. The album reached No. 1 in both Britain and America.

ASS, BADFINGER.

Issued in Britain on SAPCOR 27 on 8 March 1974 and in America on 26 November 1973. The tracks were, Side One: 'Apple Of My Eye', 'Get Away', 'Icicles', 'The Winner', 'Blind Owl'. Side Two:

'Constitution', 'When I Say', 'Cowboy', 'I Can Love You', 'Timeless'.

WALLS AND BRIDGES, JOHN LENNON WITH THE PLASTIC ONO NUCLEAR BAND.

Issued in Britain on Apple PCTC 253 on 4 October 1974 and in America on Apple SW 3416 on 26 September 1974. The tracks were, Side One: 'Going Down On Love', 'Whatever Gets You Thru The Night', 'Old Dirt Road', 'What You Got', 'Bless You', 'Scared'. Side Two: 'No. 9 Dream', 'Surprise Surprise (Sweet Bird Of Paradox)', 'Steel And Glass', 'Beef Jerky', 'Nobody Loves You (When You're Down And Out)'. The album reached No. 5 in the British charts and reached No. 1 in America.

GOODNIGHT VIENNA, RINGO STARR.

Issued in Britain on Apple PCS 7168 on 15 November 1974 and in America on Apple SW 3417 on 18 November 1974. The tracks were, Side One: 'Goodnight Vienna', 'Occapella', 'Oo-Wee', 'Husbands And Wives', 'Snookeroo'. Side Two: 'All By Myself', 'Call Me', 'No No Song', 'Only You', 'Easy For Me', 'Goodnight Vienna'. The album reached No. 24 in Britain and No. 8 in America.

DARK HORSE, GEORGE HARRISON.

Issued in Britain on Apple PAS 10008 on 20 December 1974 and in America on Apple SMAS 3418 on 9 December 1974. The tracks were, Side One: 'Hari's On Tour (Express)', 'Simply Shady', 'So Sad', 'Bye Bye Love', 'Maya Love'. Side Two: 'Ding Dong Ding Dong', 'Dark Horse', 'Far East Man', 'It Is "He"'. The album didn't reach the British charts but reached No. 4 in America.

ROCK 'N' ROLL, JOHN LENNON.

Issued in Britain on Apple PCS 7169 on 21 February 1975 and in America on Apple SMAS 3418 on 17 February 1975. The tracks were, Side One: 'Be-Bop-A-Lula', 'Stand By Me', 'Rip It Up'/'Ready Teddy', 'You Can't Catch Me', 'Ain't That A Shame', 'Do You Wanna Dance', 'Sweet Little Sixteen'. Side Two: 'Slippin' And Slidin'', 'Peggy Sue', 'Bring It On Home To Me'/'Send Me Some Lovin'', 'Bony Moronie', 'Ya Ya', 'Just Because'. The album reached No. 10 in the British charts and No. 6 in the American.

EXTRA TEXTURE, GEORGE HARRISON.

Issued in Britain on Apple PAS 10009 on 3 October 1975 and in America on Apple SW 3420 on 22 September 1975. The tracks were, Side One: 'You', 'The Answer's At The End', 'The Guitar (Can't Keep From Crying)', 'Ooh Baby (I Know That I Love You)', 'World Of Stone'. Side Two: 'A Bit More Of You', 'Can't Stop Thinking About You', 'Tired Of Midnight Blue', 'Grey Cloudy Lies', 'His Name Is Legs (Ladies and Gentlemen)'. The album reached No. 22 in the British charts and No. 8 in the American.

SHAVED FISH, JOHN LENNON.
Issued in Britain on Apple PCS 7173 on 24 October 1975 and in
America on Apple SW 3421 on 24 October 1975. The tracks were,
Side One: 'Give Peace A Chance', 'Cold Turkey', 'Instant Karma',
'Power To The People', 'Mother', 'Woman Is The Nigger Of The
World'. Side Two: 'Imagine', 'Whatever Gets You Thru The Night',
'Mind Games', 'No. 9 Dream', 'Happy Xmas (War Is Over)', 'Give
Peace A Chance'. It reached No. 6 in the British charts and reached
No. 12 in the American.
BLAST FROM YOUR PAST, RINGO STARR.
Issued in Britain on Apple PCS 7170 on 12 December 1975 and in
America on Apple SW 3422 on 20 November 1975. The tracks
were, Side One: 'You're Sixteen', 'No No Song', 'It Don't Come
Easy', 'Photograph', 'Back Off Boogaloo'. Side Two: 'Only You
(And You Alone)', '*Beaucoups* Of Blues', 'Oh My My', 'Early
1970', 'I'm The Greatest'.
In 1975 Paul McCartney's releases began to be issued by EMI in
Britain and Capitol in America. In 1976 George Harrison's records
began to be issued by his own label, Dark Horse. Although Ringo
Starr also formed his own record label, Ring O' Records, his own
releases were issued by different labels, including Atlantic, Portrait,
Capitol and Boardwalk. John Lennon moved to Capitol and then to
Geffen Records.

Apple School

In 1968 it was decided to establish an Apple School in which Julian
Lennon, Zak Starkey and the children of Apple employees such as
Derek Taylor, could be educated. There were to be between fifteen
to twenty children, including any children of friends such as Bob
Dylan, and the school would introduce some exciting new educational ideas – which is why Ivor Cutler, who appeared as Buster
Bloodvessel in *Magical Mystery Tour*, was hired as consultant – he
had some interesting theories on what could be achieved. The head
of the school was to be Ivan Vaughan, the friend who had introduced John and Paul to each other.

These are the minutes of a meeting held at Apple to discuss the
school on 9 May 1968. Those present were John Lennon, Ringo
Starr, Ivan Vaughan, Alexis Mardas and Derek Taylor:

Administration.
1. (Ministry of Education) regulations concerning required
amenities e.g. lavatories, fire escape, open space, size of accommodation, concerning quality of staff, if aim is to get the school
approved by the Ministry at a future date.

It was decided to leave the regulations for the school in the hands of Ivan who would be aided by Professor Doris M. Lee.

2. Accommodation: Suitability in terms of proximity to the homes of the prospective pupils.

A decision cannot yet be made concerning a suitable site for the school until new homes have been found by the people concerned.

(Note 1. Full account to be taken of proposed moves in the near future on the part of a number of the interested families).

Suitability in terms of ease of conversion to meet both the [Ministry's] regulations and also to meet requirements on educational grounds.

Finance.

Immediate: A. Initial funds required to pay for the time of professional people engaged in a consultative capacity during the initial planning stages.

It was agreed to discuss the matter of finance with Stephen Maltz who would advise which would be the best company to supply the funds necessary.

B. Salary of Ivan Vaughan – to begin investigations and consultations as soon as possible.

As from today Ivan will receive £50 per week, being the average wage for a Headmaster.

Future: A. Accommodation: Cost of initial purchase
Cost of conversion
Cost of equipment and
books

Ivan promises to set out a list for the above requirements listing prices.

B. Salary of permanent staff.

C. Funds for professional and other visitors invited to contribute to the school in one way or another.

4. What overall policy to adopt with regard to payment of fees.

No decision was finalised with regard to future finance, and a further meeting in approximately three weeks time was decided upon.

Appointment of Staff

A. Ivan Vaughan

B. Two additional members of staff on a permanent basis (both female, male or one male and one female?)

C. One secretary on a permanent/part-time basis. John stressed the need for a permanent secretary.

D. Other contributions to the school to be invited as necessary on a casual basis.

Enrolment of Pupils.

What overall policy with regard to their number and to their background.

John stated there should be no discrimination regarding background.

Questions for discussion at a future date. Interested people are invited to give thought to them during the coming weeks.

Curriculum: What examinations, if any, to be allowed to influence the curriculum:? A flexible approach to be the guideline to follow in all respects. At the same time, how far should content of traditional state schools be taught? i.e. Reading, writing, mathematics, science, etc. What importance to be attached to other activities? i.e. music, astrology, art, history, archaeology, drama, one foreign language (French?) electronics, etc.

John requested that all arts including music, dancing, theatre, films should be in the school timetable. The art of propaganda in the advertising field must also be taught.

With regard to religious teaching, all aspects must be dealt with e.g. gods of other countries.

Games and physical exercises will be encouraged but not enforced. Aids to learning: T.V. tape, film, programmed learning.

Discipline:

No physical discipline of any kind.

Every attempt will be made to deal with any difficulties of a disciplinary nature during school time. If necessary, consultations will be held with the parents concerned. The aim of the school is for the children concerned to enjoy it so much they would prefer it to home.

Duration of school times:

Terms to follow (strictly?) those already adopted by state schools. Length of the school day? Normal school times were decided upon.

The school will accommodate children from the age of 2 to 40 which means they will remain at one school.

John stated that all attempts should be made to open the school by September.

As it turned out, the venture never got off the ground. Pete Shotton pointed out that the original idea for the school had been John's. John had wanted the children of Beatles and Apple employees to have an alternative to the traditional system of education that he had hated as a child and thought that a more enlightened, alternative system could be developed. He felt that with enlightened teachers such as Ivan Vaughan, the right atmosphere could be created for the children, so that they could really enjoy learning.

Ivan was persuaded to leave his studies in educational psychiatry to join the project, although he was sensible enough to request a guarantee – and £10,000 was deposited in his account.

It was Neil Aspinall and Pete Shotton who finally persuaded John that the project was too ambitious and costly to undertake until the other Apple subsidiaries began showing a profit.

Apple Scruffs

The name a group of the Beatles' most dedicated fans began to call themselves.

A number of the girls, mainly from Britain and America, left their homes to move to London in order to follow the Beatles around, spending endless hours waiting outside recording studios, houses and the Apple building itself, hoping for a glimpse of their idols.

What made this act of dedication so unusual was that the girls didn't just hang around for a few days or weeks or months, but spent a few years devoting their time to Beatles-watching.

They regarded themselves as an extra special group and included Margo Stevens, Nancy Allen, Wendy Sutcliffe, Gill Pritchard, Sue-John, Chris, Di, Kathy, Virginia, Dani, Lucy, and two boys – Tommy and Jimmy.

After they'd got to know each other from sitting around on the steps of 3 Savile Row, the girls decided to officially call themselves Apple Scruffs. Tommy was the only boy they would allow to join the group at the time, although they later admitted Jimmy.

Tommy and Jimmy, both gay, hailed from New York. One day they saw John Lennon emerging from Apple and asked if they could take his photograph. Imitating comedian Dick Emery, he said 'Ohhh, you are awful, but you know every man loves a sailor. Only for you, mind . . . I wouldn't do this for just anyone.'

The American Scruffs came from Houston, New York, Chicago and Cleveland.

Margo was the leader of the Scruffs and in 1970 they launched their own *Apple Scruffs* magazine. This contained so much information about Beatles activities that even members of the Apple staff read it to find out what was going on and the Beatles themselves also received copies. Margo was to become employed at Apple as a tea girl.

A group of rogue Apple Scruffs broke into Paul McCartney's house in Cavendish Avenue one day by climbing up a ladder and entering through an open bathroom window. They stole clothes and photographs. Some of the photographs were important to Paul and he told Margo about them, and she managed to get them back for him. As a result, Paul wrote the song 'She Came In Through The Bathroom Window'.

When the girls were waiting outside the Abbey Road Studios one night while George had been recording, he suddenly came out and invited them into the studio where he played them a song he'd written specially for them, 'Apple Scruffs', which was included on his *All Things Must Pass* album.

The Apple Scruffs eventually disbanded in December 1973, after the Savile Row building was no longer occupied, and as the members of the Beatles had gone their separate ways. They occasionally gathered together for reunions. One of the girls, Carol Bedford, wrote a book about the Scruffs and called it *Waiting For The Beatles*. One of the boys, Jimmy Lyford, died of an AIDS-related disease in San Francisco in October 1988. Gill went to work at Abbey Road Studios and Lucy became George Harrison's assistant.

Apple Studios, 3 Savile Row, London W1

The Beatles' own recording studio in the basement of the Apple building. The entire story of the studio was something of a fiasco. Naturally, since they had such a building, the Beatles felt they should have a studio of their own and they turned to 'Magic' Alex Mardas, head of Apple Electronics, who promised them that he would not only build them a studio but construct the most modern recording studio in the world. While Abbey Road had been using a four-track machine and had recently acquired an eight-track, Alex promised the Beatles that he would provide them with a 72-track, built by himself. He would also erect a sonic screen, an invisible wall of ultra-high-frequency beams which would surround Ringo in place of the usual heavy screens which blocked his view of what was going on.

When the Beatles were becoming disenchanted with working on the 'Get Back' project at Twickenham Film Studios, they decided to continue filming and recording at their own studios and on 20 January 1969, moved to the Apple Studios. It was impossible to record there.

The mixing console Alex had been building was a crude affair which didn't work – and was sold to an electronics shop in Edgware Road for five pounds. Alex had even forgotten to install an intercom system between the studio and the control booth. The basement also contained the heating and ventilation units for the entire building and was continually making hissing sounds.

The Beatles appealed to George Martin who arranged for two four-track machines to be sent down from the Abbey Road Studios and brought in some engineers and staff to set up the mobile unit and prepare the basement for recording.

Two days later, on 22 January, the Beatles were able to return and continued recording for the rest of that month with George Martin producing, assisted by Glyn Johns and Alan Parsons.

Archer, Jeffrey

Author of bestselling novels such as *Kane and Abel* and erstwhile MP. While at Oxford in 1963 he offered his services to Oxfam and suggested that the Beatles become involved in the charity's new campaign to raise £1 million.

Archer sent a telegram to Brian Epstein requesting an interview and signed it on behalf of 8,000 students at Oxford. However, Epstein was reluctant for the Beatles to become involved as he believed it would result in requests from other charities.

Knowing that Epstein was unsure of how he should deal with the situation, Beatles press officer Brian Somerville suggested to Archer that he attend a Beatles concert in Liverpool. Together with Nicholas Lloyd, editor of the University magazine *Cherwell*, Archer travelled to Liverpool, armed with Oxfam posters and collecting tins, managed to get backstage and had photos taken of the Beatles putting money into the tins. The Beatles also liked the idea of associating their name with Oxfam.

Pat Davidson, Oxfam's press officer, phoned to apologise to Epstein over an announcement that had been made without his consent. She said that Epstein 'was spitting blood about it. He didn't want to speak to anyone from Oxfam. He was furious.'

A meeting was arranged between Epstein, Davidson and the *Daily Mail* and it was formally agreed that the Beatles would lend their name to the campaign, although they couldn't do much more than that.

Archer had pulled off the coup by explaining to Epstein and Somerville that it would look bad if the Beatles withdrew.

Archer also helped to organise a Beatles charity performance in aid of the NSPCC at the Grafton Ballroom, Liverpool, on Wednesday, 12 June 1963.

He then organised a dinner for the Beatles at Brasenose College, Oxford, on Thursday, 5 March 1964 to celebrate their fund-raising efforts.

12 Arnold Grove, Wavertree, Liverpool L17

Birthplace of George Harrison. In common with terraced houses of its type, it had no bathroom and no indoor toilet. The outdoor toilet was situated in a paved backyard. Thirty-three-year-old Louise Harrison (née French) gave birth to her fourth and final child at 12.10 p.m. on 25 February 1943.

His father, George Harold Harrison, was to say, 'I vaguely remember tiptoeing up the stairs to see him after he was born. A tiny, squalling, miniature replica of myself.' The new arrival, a boy, was named George after King George VI.

George spent the first six years of his life at Arnold Grove and as a baby was bathed in the kitchen sink and later, like the rest of the family, graduated to a zinc tub which was brought in from the backyard at bathtime. George was to recall that the downstairs rooms were extremely cold in the winter, with the only heating consisting of a single coal fire.

The Harrisons had spent eighteen years on the Council Housing List and were finally allocated a brand new Council house in Speke, Liverpool. As soon as they heard, they packed their belongings and moved from Arnold Grove on 2 January 1950.

During the six years that George lived in the Arnold Grove two-up, two-down house, the rent was ten shillings (50p) a week.

Around the Beatles

The British television company Associated-Rediffusion had expressed interest in a Beatles television special and, when Brian Epstein was in New York with the Beatles in February 1964, he had a meeting with Jack Good and suggested that Good produce the show.

During negotiations with Vyvienne Moynihan of Rediffusion, Epstein insisted that Good be the producer. He also demanded that his own artists Cilla Black and Sounds Incorporated be included in the show, that Murray The K be hired as compere, that NEMS would retain world distribution rights and that he would be credited and co-producer.

John Lennon talked Brian out of having Murray The K in the show.

Rediffusion agreed to all his terms and the sixty-minute special, provisionally called 'John, Paul, George and Ringo', then had a name change to 'Around the Beatles' – possibly a reference to the fact that the audience sat in a semi-circle around the Beatles as they performed.

The special was filmed at Rediffusion's Studio 5 in Wembley over a two day period on 27 and 28 April 1964, and networked a week later on Wednesday, 6 May. It was repeated the following month on Monday, 8 June and ABC TV in America screened excerpts from the show on Sunday, 24 May.

The Beatles performed 'She Loves You', 'I Want To Hold Your Hand', 'Can't Buy Me Love', 'Twist And Shout', 'Roll Over Beethoven', 'I Wanna Be Your Man', 'Long Tall Sally' and 'Shout'. They also sang a medley of 'Love Me Do', 'Please Please Me' and 'From Me To You' and presented an excerpt from Shakespeare's *A Midsummer Night's Dream*.

Jack Good was to comment, 'The boys will be seen in the play-within-the-play that Bottom and his friends perform'. This amusing sketch, in which the group appeared in costume, featured John as Thisbe, Paul as Pyramus, George as Moonshine and Ringo as the Lion, although the group were at first reluctant to appear in the sketch. Trevor Peacock also joined them as Wall. Peacock's biggest claim to fame was to come some years later as a cast member of the popular TV series 'Are You Being Served?'

In addition to Cilla and Sounds Incorporated, the show also featured Long John Baldry, P. J. Proby, The Vernons Girls, Millie and an American dance group the Jets.

Asher, Jane

Actress, born in London on 5 April 1946.

Her father, Dr Richard Asher, was a consultant in blood and mental diseases at Central Middlesex Hospital in Acton, London, in addition to being a writer and broadcaster. Her mother Margaret Asher was a Professor of Classical Music at the Guildhall School of Music and Drama and had taught George Martin to play the oboe – she was also to teach Paul McCartney to play the recorder. Jane had a brother Peter, who was two years older, and a sister Claire, who was two years younger. All three Asher children had the distinctive Titian-red hair.

Jane was educated at Queen's College, Harley Street. At the age of five she made her film debut in *Mandy* (1952). Her interest in acting began when her parents took their three children to a theatrical agency, thinking it would be fun for them to learn to act.

Her other screen appearances over the years have included *Third Party Risk* (1953); *Dance Little Lady, Adventure In The Hopfields* (1954); *The Quatermass Xperiment* (1955); *Charley Moon, The Greengage Summer* (1956); *The Prince And The Pauper* (1962); *Girl In The Headlines* (1963); *The Masque Of The Red Death* (1964); *Alfie* (1966); *The Winter's Tale* (1967); *The Buttercup Chain, Deep End* (1970); *Henry VIII And His Six Wives* (1972); *Runners* (1983) and *Success Is The Best Revenge* (1984).

Her television appearances are numerous and a brief selection included 'The Cold Equations' episode of 'Out Of This World' (1962); Nigel Kneale's 'The Stone Tape' (1972); 'Brideshead Revisited' (1981); 'A Voyage Round My Father' (1982); 'The Mistress' (1987); 'Wish Me Luck' (1990); and 'Murder Most Horrid' (1991). This is in addition to appearances in various series such as 'The Adventures of Robin Hood', 'The Adventurer', 'The Saint' and 'The Buccaneers', plus prestigious productions including the part of 'Lisle in The Brothers Karamazov' and Maggie Tulliver in 'The Mill on the Floss'.

At the age of twelve she made her stage debut as Alice in *Alice In Wonderland* at the Oxford Playhouse. In 1960, Jane became the youngest actress to play Wendy in a West End stage version of *Peter Pan*. Her stage roles included the Broadway production of *The Philanthropist*, playing Perdita in *A Winter's Tale* and Cassandra in *The Trojan Women*. She also featured in various productions for the Bristol Old Vic, including the title role in *Cleo* by Frank Marcus, the part of Ellen Terry in *Sixty Thousand Nights* and Eliza in *Pygmalion*.

She was seventeen when she first met the Beatles on Thursday, 18 April 1963. They were appearing on the BBC radio broadcast 'Swingin' Sound' at the Royal Albert Hall. Jane went along to pose for *Radio Times* photographer Tony Aspler who pictured her screaming in the audience. The article appeared in the 2 May 1963 edition of the *Radio Times* with Jane commenting, 'Now these I could scream for.'

Jane then approached them while they were having a snack in the Royal Court Hotel in Sloane Square, where they were staying. She mentioned to them that she had been asked to write about them in the *Radio Times*. They were aware of her as she'd been a guest panellist on the TV show 'Juke Box Jury' and they were all charmed by her.

Brian Epstein returned to his own hotel and Ringo stayed behind to have an early night. Singer Shane Fenton, who'd also been on the concert bill that day, drove John, Paul, George and Jane to journalist Chris Hutchens' flat, situated on the top floor of Kings House on the Kings Road. Initially, it was George who seemed to engage most of her attention. During the course of the next few hours, Paul began to show his interest in Jane and the others left him to talk to her alone. Later, he escorted her home and arranged to meet her again.

The romance became public when they were snapped by a photographer as they left the Prince of Wales Theatre after attending Neil Simon's play *Never Too Late*.

Paul moved into the Asher family home at 57 Wimpole Street, a five-storey terraced house. It happened shortly after Paul had missed his last train home to Liverpool following a date with Jane and stayed the night. Margaret Asher suggested that he regard the house as his London home, thus saving on hotel bills. He moved into the top floor, where there were two rooms and a bathroom – the second room was Peter's bedroom. Jane and Claire had the two rooms below.

This relationship with an upper-middle-class family broadened his cultural horizons. There were stimulating discussions around the Asher family dinner table and the two of them attended musicals, classical concerts, plays and exhibitions and went on holidays together to exotic places. Paul even opened an account at Coutts, the Queen's bankers, and ordered Jane's birthday cake from Maxim's in Paris, while Jane helped Paul select his new car, a midnight-blue Aston Martin DB6.

The young actress became the inspiration for a number of his songs, initially purely love songs, which changed as the relationship entered stormy patches – primarily because she refused to give up her career. 'She Loves You' was written in the music room at Wimpole Street. Songs inspired by Jane included 'And I Love Her', 'Every Little Thing', 'We Can Work It Out', 'You Won't See Me', 'I'm Looking Through You' and 'Here, There And Everywhere'.

The crisis in their relationship arose from the fact that Jane had a successful career which she was determined to pursue. Paul wanted his girlfriend to dedicate herself to him in the type of relationship common between men and women in working-class Liverpool. However, Jane came from a different world and had her own strong opinions; extending her own horizons as an actress didn't include becoming a subservient woman and sacrificing her career for 'her man'. At one point she refused to answer his telephone calls, which inspired 'You Won't See Me'. Jane was appearing in *Great Expectations* at the Theatre Royal, Bristol, when he recorded the number.

He obviously tried to give messages to her through his songs and told Beatles' biographer Hunter Davies: 'I knew I was selfish, it caused a few rows. Jane went off and said, "OK, then, leave. I'll find someone else." It was shattering to be without her. That was when I wrote "I'm Looking Through You".'

Jane was appearing at the Bristol Old Vic, as Barbara Cahoun in John Dighton's *The Happiest Days of Your Life*, when Paul visited Bristol to see her. While there he noticed the name on a shop, *Rigby & Evans Ltd, Wine & Spirit Shippers,* which he says, gave him the surname for the song 'Eleanor Rigby'.

Jane helped Paul to find the five-storey Victorian ⌐
Cavendish Avenue, St John's Wood, which they moved into in 1.
Jane decorated the house and always kept it in tip-top condition.
Unfortunately, during a spring-cleaning session a number of original
early Lennon and McCartney songs were lost forever when she
threw away a notebook full of lyrics while emptying a cupboard.

It was Jane who, in June 1966, persuaded Paul to buy High
Farm, a 183-acre farm in Machrihanish, Campbeltown, suggesting
it would be a good idea for them to have a remote retreat to which
they could escape from the pressures of being constantly in the
public eye.

She embarked on a five-month tour of America in 1967,
appearing with the Bristol Old Vic in *Romeo and Juliet* in Boston,
Washington and Philadelphia. Paul flew over to America to celebrate her 21st birthday, which took place during the tour. It was
during this trip that he conceived the idea of *Magical Mystery Tour*.

On her return, Jane said: 'Paul had changed so much. He was on
LSD, which I knew nothing about. The house had changed and it
was full of stuff I didn't know about.'

The two decided to get married and during an interview in the
Daily Express in 1967 she said: 'I love Paul. I love him very deeply,
and he feels the same. I don't think either of us has looked at
anyone else since we first met.' She was to add: 'I want to get
married, probably this year, and have lots and lots of babies. I
certainly would be surprised indeed if I married anyone but Paul.'

On New Year's Day 1968 he proposed, gave her a diamond and
emerald ring and they travelled up north to Rembrandt to tell Paul's
father.

But the five-year romance came to an abrupt end, despite the fact
that they obviously loved each other. Jane had been a virgin when
they met and fidelity to a partner obviously meant a great deal to
her. On the other hand, Paul had always been a womaniser. During
her absences when touring, he had been dating other girls and
began an affair with an American, Francie Schwartz.

Jane arrived home unexpectedly when Paul was in bed with
Schwartz. She walked out on him and sent her mother to Cavendish
Avenue to collect her belongings. On the 20 July edition of the BBC
Television show 'Dee Time', she announced officially that their
engagement was off.

The couple did meet once or twice after the Schwartz incident,
but the split was final, although Jane was to say: 'I know it sounds
corny, but we still see each other and love each other, but it hasn't
worked out. Perhaps we'll be childhood sweethearts and meet again
and get married when we're about 70.'

artoonist Gerald Scarfe at the tenth anniver-
e Eye. The two fell in love and their first child
n 17 April 1974.

d in further acting parts, including a TV production
id Juliet. After the birth of Katie, she curtailed her
act... er for a while, but appeared in the stage version of
Whos... ife Is It Anyway?

Two more children were born, including a son Alexander, and
she and Gerald were eventually married in 1981 and settled in
Chelsea.

She returned to acting in the 1980s with many television appearances. They included the part of Celia Rider opposite Jeremy Irons
in 'Brideshead Revisited'; with James Fox in 'Love Is Old, Love Is
New', a drama about a couple obsessed with the 1960s which
featured a lot of Beatles music; and with Laurence Olivier in John
Mortimer's 'A Voyage Round My Father'.

Other TV appearances included the costume drama 'Hawkmoor'
and an episode of 'Tales of the Unexpected'. She teamed up with
James Fox once again for the film *Runners,* and in 1985 with Ian
Holm and Coral Browne in *Dreamchild.*

Jane has written ten books on entertaining, fancy dress and
ornate cake decoration, and in 1995 launched her own national
publication *Jane Asher's Magazine,* at a time when she was regularly featured on television commercials.

The 1990s was the most successful decade of her career. She had
her various cake products sold in the supermarkets, her kitchen
items in the do-it-yourself stores, a regular TV show of her own,
and her own weekly column in a national newspaper. In 1998 she
had her first two novels published, *The Longing* and *The Question.*

Tragically, her father died of an overdose of barbiturates and
alcohol. His body was discovered on 26 April 1969.

Jane met Paul again in 1994 for the first time in more than twenty
years.

Asher, Peter

Jane's elder brother, born 22 June 1944. At the age of eight he
appeared in the film *The Planter's Wife* and the stage play *Isn't Life
Wonderful*. He became a day boy at Westminster School where he
met Gordon Waller and in 1962 the two formed a folk duo called
Gordon And Peter.

Peter got to know Paul McCartney very well when Paul lived at
the Asher family house in Wimpole Street, London WI.

He became a member of MENSA and also had a short-lived relationship with Millie Small, who sang 'My Boy Lollipop'. The duo

changed their name to Peter & Gordon and Peter asked Paul if he could provide them with a number to record. He gave them 'World Without Love', a number which Billy J Kramer had rejected, which took Peter & Gordon to the top of the British charts and established them in America. They had several further hits before they disbanded in 1967.

In the meantime, he'd also entered partnership with John Dunbar and Barry Miles in launching a bookshop-cum-gallery called Indica, which also had support from Paul. A company had been formed called MAD Ltd (Miles, Asher, Dunbar), with Peter lending £600 each to Dunbar and Miles and forking out £600 himself.

Peter then joined Apple Records as head of A&R and his first discovery was the American singer/songwriter James Taylor.

On Monday, 22 July 1968, following Jane Asher's declaration on Saturday, 20 July on the TV show 'Dee Time' that her romance with Paul was over, Paul allegedly stormed into Apple and demanded that Peter be sacked. Ron Kass talked him out of this course of action, although it has been suggested that Asher's productions were no longer to receive any priority or strong promotion.

When Allen Klein entered the scene he sacked the principals of Apple Records, the only part of the company that was making any money. In 1969, Tony King replaced Peter at Apple Records as head of A&R. Ron Kass went to MGM Records and Peter joined him in the A&R department. James Taylor asked Peter to become his manager and continue to produce his records. Peter then left for America where he enjoyed great success with Taylor and also became manager of Linda Rondstadt.

Ask Me Why

A number which was written in the spring of 1962. The Beatles immediately included it in their repertoire. Paul recalls that they were influenced in writing the number by the works of Smokey Robinson and the Miracles.

John performs lead vocal on the track, which was issued as the 'B' side of their 'Please Please Me' single on Friday, 11 January 1963. It was also one of the tracks on their debut album *Please Please Me,* issued in March of that year, and was also included on the *All My Loving* EP in February 1964.

Vee Jay Records in America utilised it on their re-release of *Introducing The Beatles, Beatles Vs the Four Seasons* and *Songs, Pictures And Stories Of The Fabulous Beatles* albums and *Souvenir Of Their Visit To America (The Beatles)* EP. Capitol Records also issued it as a track on their *The Early Beatles* album. The group performed it live on stage at Hamburg's Star Club and it is included on *The Beatles Live At The Star Club In Hamburg, Germany, 1962* album.

The Beatles performed the number during their Parlophone recording audition on Wednesday, 6 June 1962, but recorded the song on Monday, 26 November 1962, when there was a dispute about how the composition should be credited on release: to McCartney–Lennon or Lennon–McCartney. The credit was finally resolved, some months later, in John's favour.

They performed the number on the BBC radio programme 'Teenager's Turn' on Monday, 11 June 1962, the first time a Lennon & McCartney number had been broadcast on the radio.

Aspinall, Neil

Neil was born in Prestatyn, North Wales, on 13 October 1942. His mother had been evacuated there during the blitz on Liverpool and his father was at sea with the Royal Navy. Neil and his mother returned to Liverpool in 1942 when the bombing had ceased and he attended West Derby School, where he passed his eleven-plus exams. He next went to Liverpool Institute in Mount Street where he shared the same class as Paul McCartney for English and Art lessons.

George Harrison also attended the school but was in the class one year behind Paul and Neil. Neil was to comment,

> My first encounter with George was behind the school's air-raid shelters. This great mass of shaggy hair loomed up and an out-of-breath voice requested a quick drag of my Woodbine. It was one of the first cigarettes either of us had smoked. We spluttered our way through it bravely but gleefully. After that the three of us did lots of ridiculous things together. By the time we were ready to take the GCE exams we'd added John Lennon to our 'Mad Lad' gang. He was doing his first term at Liverpool College of Art which overlooks the Institute playground and we all got together in a students' coffee bar at lunchtime.

Neil took nine GCEs and gained eight, failing to pass in French. He left the Institute in July 1959 to study accountancy and remained with a local firm for two years, receiving a wage of fifty shillings (£2.50) per week as a trainee accountant. At the time he was living as a lodger in Pete Best's house and it was through the Best connection that he became involved with the Beatles. Pete had joined the group and travelled to Germany with them. On their return they were booked at the Casbah Club and Mona Best asked Neil to make some posters announcing 'The Return Of The Beatles'.

The group had relied on public transport to get them to local gigs, but by February 1961 it was obvious that they could no longer rely on that method of rushing from hall to hall. They'd tried a spell hiring Frank Garner to drive them to gigs, but he was the bouncer at the Casbah Club and found he couldn't keep the two jobs going at the same time.

Pete decided to approach Neil and ask him to drive them to their gigs. Pete suggested that he buy a van and commented, 'He bought a battered old grey and maroon model for fifteen pounds (other sources say he bought a second-hand van for £80), but at least it went, which was the main consideration. So Neil entered enthusiastically the world of showbusiness as our first roadie.' He charged each of them five shillings (25p) per man, per gig.

By July 1962, on the group's return from their second trip to Germany, Neil decided to take the plunge and become their official road manager, as he was now earning more money driving them around than as an accountant. He was also helping Mrs Best to run the Casbah Club.

Neil and Pete Best were the closest of friends and when Brian Epstein called Pete in for a meeting and then announced that he had been sacked, Neil was waiting for him downstairs in the NEMS shop. Neil was furious when he heard. He phoned Mona to tell her what had happened, then joined Pete for a few beers at the Grapes pub. Disgusted with the situation, Neil told Pete he'd quit – but Pete told him he must stay, that the Beatles were going places.

When Neil turned up at the group's next gig, Brian Epstein asked him why Pete hadn't turned up. 'Well, what did you expect,' he told him. Neil asked Paul and John what had happened and was told, 'It's got nothing to do with you. You're only the driver.'

Pete's prediction that the Beatles were going places was exceeded beyond expectations ... and wherever the Beatles went, Neil was with them. Mal Evans was brought in to help out as assistant road manager and Neil became much more of a personal assistant to the group.

Paul McCartney dubbed him 'Nell', and the Beatles always called him Nell rather than Neil.

When the Beatles launched their Apple Corps company, they appointed Neil as managing director.

On 30 August 1968, he married Suzy Ornstein at Chelsea Registry Office. Paul, Ringo and Maureen attended, and Alexis Mardas was best man.

Neil survived the appearance of Allen Klein in the Beatles' affairs and, after the Apple building in Savile Row was sold, he continued to administer their affairs from offices in Mayfair, a post that he still holds.

There has probably been no one closer to the Beatles than Nell and no one privy to the most private aspects of their lives. He has always been discreet, utterly loyal, and would keep everything in complete confidence. If ever he wrote a book about his experiences, he has mused, he would arrange for it to be published after his death.

Neil remains the managing director of Apple Corps, although he and his American wife Suzy are the sole directors of Standby Films Ltd, which is based in their large house in Twickenham, Middlesex. In 1994, Apple paid Standby £408,000, from which Neil paid himself a salary of £62,000, and he and his wife are able to enjoy the trappings of their success, including transportation by Rolls Royce.

Incidentally, Suzy is the daughter of Bud Ornstein, who was responsible for the launch of the Beatles' United Artists film career.

Following a heart attack, Neil had to restrict his attendances at the Apple offices in Ovington Square to three days a week. However, 1995 finally saw the release of 'The Beatles Anthology', a television series on the Beatles, which Neil had first started working on in 1969, when he had called it 'The Long And Winding Road'.

Assembly Hall, High Street, Mold, Flintshire, Wales

The Beatles only appeared at this venue once, on Thursday, 24 January 1963.

Assembly Rooms, Corporation Street, Tamworth, Staffordshire

This gig took place on Friday, 1 February 1963, on the eve of their first major British tour with Helen Shapiro. It was a double booking and they also appeared in nearby Sutton Coldfield.

Astoria Ballroom, King Street, Oldham, Greater Manchester

The Beatles only appeared at this venue once, on Tuesday, 12 February 1963. They'd previously appeared in Sheffield, Yorkshire, earlier the same evening.

The Astoria originally opened on 24 December 1908 as the Grand Theatre. On 14 June 1937 it became a cinema, the

Gaumont, and on 14 November 1962 it became a Top Rank Ballroom. In subsequent years it continued as a dance venue under several different names – Bailey's Butterflys, Romeo & Juliet's and Nix Nightclub.

When the Beatles appeared at the Astoria the venue had a capacity of 1,250. However, the police had requested that only 840 be allowed into the venue for fears there would be problems of overcrowding, then agreed to a figure of 1,000 – although an audience of only 800 was allowed in on the night.

The Beatles performed two half-hour spots.

Astoria Ballroom, Wilson Street, Middlesborough, Yorkshire

The Beatles only appeared at this venue once, on Tuesday, 25 June 1963. The group had originally been provisionally booked to appear there on Tuesday, 29 January 1963, but the booking had not been confirmed and Eden Kane appeared that night.

Astoria Cinema, 232–6 Seven Sisters Road, Finsbury Park, London N4

Site of *The Beatles Christmas Show* which ran from 24–31 December 1963. There were two performances each evening, with the exception of 24 and 31 December. There were also no performances on 25 and 29 December.

Brian Epstein engaged Peter Yolland to produce the show on the recommendation of agent Joe Collins (father of Joan and Jackie). Peter, who had been producing traditional pantomimes for several years, devised a spectacular opening.

The houselights were dimmed and the theatre was in semi-darkness when two spotlights trained on the curtain, which opened to display a small screen, which flickered images of a silent movie car chase, a channel swimmer and an ancient aircraft as a commentator was announcing, 'By land ... by sea ... by air ... Yes, by land, by sea, and by air come the stars of Brian Epstein's fabulous Beatles Christmas Show.'

A dummy helicopter landed. 'And here's your pilot for the evening, Rolf Harris' introduced the voice, and Rolf came down the steps, holding his clipboard with the passenger list. One by one the guest artists appeared and after Cilla Black had been introduced, Rolf said that the entire cast had been assembled. In pantomime style the audience contradicted him and he had to call back the helicopter and say, 'And now ladies and gentlemen, boys and girls . . .' but the 'copter began to move away again. He called it to land and the Beatles emerged to a raucous welcome from the audience. A backcloth then hid them as the Barron Knights rostrum drew them on to the stage as they played 'Big Girls Don't Cry'. When the Barron Knights finished their set the rostrum moved back and Tommy Quickly emerged from the wings. As he finished his set with 'Kiss Me Now', there was no sign of another act. A small screen appeared with the words 'Three out of four doctors . . .' and a spotlight picked out the Beatles, huddled together in conversation, dressed in white coats like doctors. 'Yes, three out of four doctors . . .' came the words on the screen, to be replaced by '. . . leaves one doctor'. Ringo, Paul and George had moved away and the lone John suddenly disappeared as the spotlight turned off. The Fourmost were on stage and began playing 'Hello Little Girl'. After their performance the small screen appeared with the announcement, 'Beatlerama Productions present, in breathtakingly colourful black and white Beatlescope, "What A Night".'

The Beatles then appeared in a sketch with John as Sir John Jasper, Paul as the Signalman, Ringo as a snowman and George as Ermyntrude.

The comedy melodrama over, Billy J. Kramer & the Dakotas next appeared. There was a ten-minute interval and then the Barron Knights opened the second half, followed by Cilla Black, who had an eight-minute spot which ended with her singing 'Love Of The Loved'. She was followed by Rolf Harris, who had altered the lyrics to his two hits 'Tie Me Kangaroo Down Sport' and 'English Country Garden' to fit the spirit of the occasion. Then the Beatles appeared to perform 'Roll Over Beethoven', 'All My Loving', 'This Boy', 'I Wanna Hold Your Hand', 'Money' and 'Twist And Shout'.

The Astoria could seat over 3,000 per show and 100,000 tickets for the 30 shows were sold in advance.

The Beatles were to appear at the venue two further times as part of their UK concert tours. They performed there on 1 November 1964 as part of their only British concert tour that year and their final appearance at the venue took place on 11 December 1965.

The cinema was later transformed into the Rainbow Theatre, a venue exclusively for rock concerts.

ATC Club, Birkdale, Lancashire

A venue where the Beatles appeared only once, early in 1961. The club was close to the seaside resort of Southport, and they were said to have received only one pound and ten shillings between them for their appearance.

Atlanta Stadium, Atlanta, Georgia

Almost 36,000 fans turned out to see the Beatles at this 55,000-seater baseball stadium, newly built for the Braves, on Wednesday, 18 August 1965.

The group arrived at the airport in a private Lockheed Electra at around 2.00 p.m. and they and their entourage were transported in three limousines which took them to the stadium. Their 5.00 p.m. press conference at the venue began ten minutes late and they were introduced by local DJ Paul Drew who acted as master of ceremonies to the assembly of 150 journalists, the majority of them editors of high school papers. The *Atlanta Journal* had called Drew 'the fifth Beatle', because the DJ from the local radio station WQXI had visited the Beatles in London and travelled with them in the US in 1964. He'd also visited them in Nassau and New York. Apart from acting as master of ceremonies at the press conference, he was to introduce the group on stage at the stadium. Drew had also written a piece called 'How to get along with the Beatles' in the local paper. Members of the 457-strong local fan club were at the conference to present the Beatles with gifts and Mayor Ivan Allen Jr. attended and presented the group with the key to the city. The Mayor had said that their appearance in Atlanta had stirred up as much excitement as the 'Gone With The Wind' premiere in 1939. The press conference took fifteen minutes and was held in a locker room of the stadium.

The show was preceded at 7.30 by 'London Look', a fashion show, with a local group the Atlanta Vibrations providing background music, having won the honour in a 'Battle of Beatle Bands' competition.

The show itself began at 8.15 with King Curtis, the Discotheque Dancers, Cannibal & the Headhunters, Brenda Holloway and Sounds Incorporated. The Beatles appeared on stage at 9.37 p.m. wearing dark blue suits. They performed 'Twist and Shout', 'She's A Woman', during which Paul's mike fell over, 'I Feel Fine', 'Dizzy Miss Lizzy', 'Ticket To Ride', 'Everybody's Trying To Be My Baby', in which George performed lead vocal, 'Can't Buy Me Love', 'Baby's In Black', 'I Wanna Be Your Man', with Ringo performing lead vocal, 'A Hard Day's Night', 'Help!' and 'I'm Down'.

The group were then driven directly to Atlanta Airport.

Australia House, The Strand, London WC2

Prior to their trip to Australia, the Beatles were invited to a special reception at Australia House during the last week in April 1964. They were the guests of the Rt Hon. Sir Eric Harrison, the Australian High Commissioner, who had left a reception at

Downing Street hosted by Prime Minister Alec Douglas-Home, to preside at the function.

The Strand was crowded with fans and inside the building the Beatles held a press reception. Among the 700 guests were celebrities such as actress Jessie Matthews and actors Dick Van Dyke and Wilfred Brambell.

Sir Eric told the press, 'There has never been a reception quite like this in Australia House and I hope there will never be another one. I guess I am what you would call a square but those photographers were just too much. They climbed all over the chairs and then when we went inside an enclosed office they were thrusting their cameras through the windows and rapping on the glass. I threatened to draw the blinds unless they could comport themselves.'

Avedon, Richard

Innovative American photographer, born in 1923, who changed the face of fashion photography in the late 1940s. He was also a noted portraitist and one of his distinctive traits, of having a subject's face in half-shadow, inspired Astrid Kirchherr when she took her famous portraits of the Beatles in Hamburg. The style was also used to good effect by Robert Freeman on his famous *With The Beatles* album cover.

Look magazine commissioned him to photograph the Beatles for their front cover. The picture was also published as a poster the same year and was later to be used on the cover and gatefold of *Love Songs,* a 1977 compilation, although the positions of Paul and Ringo were changed on the album sleeve.

Avedon's most famous pictures of the Beatles were a series of portraits in an almost psychedelic style, which he shot in January 1968.

During a trip to London, Avedon told how he was drawn to the Beatles and related an anecdote to journalist Pete Clark:

Ringo loved photography. He said he would pose for me if he could photograph me at the same time. His idea was we'd do it like a western movie. We'd each have a scotch, then take a picture. Another drink, another picture . . . until the last man took the last picture. We went on until we were both nearly unconscious. I took the last picture before he passed out, and that was of his toe – it looked like an interesting art photograph. Then Ringo slid off the chair. The next thing I remember was vomiting in the bathroom and the tiles felt nice and cold, and I looked out of the door and two women were carrying Ringo off into the night. I never saw him again.

Azena Ballroom, White Lane, Gleadless, Sheffield, South Yorkshire

During a break in their tour with Helen Shapiro, the Beatles appeared at this venue on 12 February 1963. The promoter who had booked the group was Peter Stringfellow. Originally, he'd booked them to appear at St Aidan's Church Hall, where he usually held his dances. However, due to the growing popularity of the Beatles, the police advised Stringfellow to alter the venue and select larger premises so he transferred the dance to the Azena.

Baby, The

Nickname which the 'Exis' (Existentialists) gave to Paul McCartney during the Beatles' first trip to Hamburg. The 'Exis' were the students who attended their gigs and included Astrid Kirchherr. They called George 'The Beautiful One' and John 'The Sidie Man'.

Baby It's You

A number composed by Burt Bacharach, Hal David and Barney Williams, which was originally a hit for the Shirelles in December 1961. The Beatles immediately included it in their repertoire, with John Lennon on lead vocals, and continued to perform it until late in 1963.

They recorded the number on Monday, 11 February 1963 during their marathon recording session for the *Please Please Me* album. The number was also included on Vee Jay's American albums *Introducing The Beatles and Songs, Pictures And Stories of the Fabulous Beatles*. It was also included on Capitol's *The Early Beatles* album.

The Beatles performed 'Baby It's You' on two of their BBC radio programmes, 'Side By Side' and 'Pop Go The Beatles'. The 'Pop Go The Beatles' version was included on *The Beatles Live At The BBC* CD on Wednesday, 30 November 1994.

'Baby It's You' was also issued as the Beatles official 27th single on Monday, March 6 1996, with 'I'll Follow the Sun', 'Devil in Her Heart' and 'Boys', all taken from BBC shows. The single entered the Music Week chart at No. 7 on Saturday, 1 April, the same day as a promo of 'Baby It's You' was featured on the ITV programme 'The Chart Show'. The video included previously unscreened colour home movie of the Beatles, taken outside the BBC's Paris studios in 1963.

Baby's In Black

Some sources have claimed that this number was penned solely by John, others claim that it was a true Lennon & McCartney collaboration in a room during one songwriting bout. Paul actually recalls that the song was written when he visited John at his home in Kenwood and the two wrote it together.

Neither mentioned who inspired them to write the song, but the speculation in Liverpool at the time, from Millie Sutcliffe, Stu Sutcliffe's mother, was that Astrid Kirchherr, who had been mourning Stuart's death, had inspired it.

The number was the first song recorded for the *Beatles For Sale* album on Tuesday, 11 August 1964.

The track was also included on the *Beatles For Sale (No 2)* EP and the *Beatles '65* album in America.

It was one of the songs which the Beatles performed regularly in concert and they generally included it as the third number in their set, with Paul announcing 'and now for something different . . .' They included it in their 1964 Christmas show, on their European and British tours in 1965 and on their world tour in 1966.

Their version recorded at the Hollywood Bowl was included on the *Anthology 2* CD.

Baby You're A Rich Man

Recorded at Olympic Sound Studios in Barnes, London SW13, a studio which the Rolling Stones had been using. In fact, Mick Jagger was present at this session and it was rumoured that he joined in on backing vocals. Brian Jones of the Rolling Stones played oboe on the track. At the beginning of the song John played a clavioline and both he and Paul played pianos. Keith Grant was the engineer for the session and the second engineer, Eddie Kramer, played vibraphone.

As the number was also mixed at Olympic it became the first Beatles record to be recorded and mixed outside of Abbey Road since they began recording with EMI.

The song was the amalgamation of two songs, one written by Paul, the other by John, and the original title had been 'One Of The Beautiful People'. They'd recorded the song specially for the animated film *Yellow Submarine*, but it was used as the 'B' side of 'All You Need Is Love'. Although the number wasn't used on the

Yellow Submarine soundtrack album, it was used in the actual film. The recording session took place on Thursday, 11 May 1967.

Bach, Barbara

Ringo Starr's second wife. Barbara was born in New York City in 1947. She and her sister Margarite were raised in a predominantly Jewish area of Queens. Barbara was educated at an all-girls school in Long Island and left school at the age of sixteen to become a model, shortening her surname from Goldbach. She married an Italian industrialist Augusto Gregorini and moved to Rome where her European origins (Rumanian grandmother, Irish mother and Austrian father) helped her secure roles in several international films.

Her daughter, Francesca, was born in 1969 and her son, Gianni, four years later. Barbara lived in Italy for ten years, appearing in TV commercials and movies.

While in Rome she divorced her first husband. Her most famous role was as the glamorous Russian spy Anya Amasova opposite Roger Moore in the James Bond spectacular *The Spy Who Loved Me*. She featured as the evil Lady Agatha in the Italian science-fiction epic *The Humanoid*. Other movies included *Force Ten From Navaronne, Black Belly Of The Tarantula, Stateline Motel, Screamers, The Great Alligator, The Jaguar Lives, The Volcanic Island* and *The Unseen*.

Barbara also posed for a nude picture spread for *Playboy* magazine.

She'd become estranged from her husband and while filming *The Unseen* she began a romance with cinematographer Roberto Quezada.

She first met Ringo when she co-starred with him as Lana, a prehistoric beauty, in the film *Caveman*. Barbara was to say: 'It wasn't love at first sight. It began to grow within days of meeting each other.'

Ringo then shed his current girlfriend Nancy Andrews and Barbara bade farewell to Roberto.

The couple were married on Monday, 27 April 1981 at Marylebone Register Office in London. Wedding guests included George and Olivia Harrison and Paul and Linda McCartney. Sixty guests and their relatives then celebrated at the London club Rags.

Barbara wore a cream satin suit made by David and Elizabeth Emanuel, who designed the famous wedding dress for Diana, Princess of Wales. Registrar Joseph Jevons, who had also performed the marriage ceremony for Paul and Linda at the same venue, conducted the ceremony.

Ringo and Barbara had originally intended marrying in America, but the murder of John Lennon no doubt had an influence on their deciding to return to England to live. They settled at Tittenhurst Park.

In 1983 they were almost killed when their car collided with a lorry.

They appeared together in the TV mini-series 'Princess Daisy' as a jet-set couple and in 'Give My Regards To Broad Street', but by the mid-1980s their film careers seemed to be over.

During the decade there were rumours of fierce arguments and they both took to the bottle. Their alcoholism reached such a state that they checked into a rehabilitation centre in Arizona in October 1988 for five weeks.

Incidentally, Barbara's sister Marjorie married Lord Alexander Rufus Isaacs in Cornwell, Gloucestershire, in 1994 – Ringo and Barbara were present at the wedding.

Back In The USSR

A parody of the Beach Boys style and one of the many compositions which Paul McCartney wrote during his sojourn at Rishikesh. Beach Boy Mike Love was also at the ashram and it has been suggested that he helped Paul on some of the verses. Paul's brother Mike even suggested that the Beatles should get the Beach Boys to sing the middle section of the song on the record, but they didn't.

Twiggy, a friend of Paul's, claims that Paul wrote the song specially for a projected documentary of a visit she was making to Russia, but the trip was cancelled.

When the group began recording the number in August 1968, they were even experiencing tensions during their recording sessions and Ringo became so fed up that he walked out of the recording. Paul took over on drums and 'Back In The USSR' became one of the few Beatles records on which Ringo was absent. A few days later he returned – and found the studio festooned with flowers, including lots of flowers around his drum kit, with the message, 'Welcome Back Ringo'.

The number was included on *The Beatles* double album and was also featured on the compilation *The Beatles 1967–1970*.

In 1976, when it was included on a double album, *Rock 'n' Roll Music*, it was decided to issue the number as a single to help to promote the album. 'Back In The USSR' coupled with 'Twist And Shout' was issued in Britain on Parlophone R 6016 on 25 June 1976.

Bad Boy

On Monday, 10 May 1965, during their sessions for *Help!* the Beatles recorded two Larry Williams numbers, 'Dizzy Miss Lizzy' and 'Bad Boy'. 'Bad Boy' had been released by Williams in 1959, although it hadn't been a big hit for him, and the Beatles had included it in their repertoire in 1960, with John on lead vocals.

The day after the session the tapes were sent to Capitol Records in America and 'Bad Boy' was used on the *Beatles VI* release in June 1965. 'Dizzy Miss Lizzy' turned up on the *Help!* album.

'Bad Boy' wasn't issued in Britain until it appeared on the compilation album *A Collection Of Beatles Oldies (But Goldies)*, although it hadn't been a goldie or an oldie for them. It was also to be included on the *Rock 'n' Roll Music* and *Rarities* compilations. The number was included on the CD compilation *Past Masters Volume One*.

Badfinger

Group comprising two members from Liverpool and two from Wales. The two Mersey Beat bands the members came from were the Masterminds and the Calderstones. Under the name the Iveys they were managed by Bill Collins and for a while they provided backing for Liverpool singer David Garrick.

Mal Evans, who recommended them to Paul McCartney, spotted the group at the Marquee Club in London. Their line-up at the time comprised Pete Ham, guitarist, pianist, vocalist, who was born in Swansea, South Wales, on 27 April 1947; rhythm guitarist Tom Evans, who was born in Liverpool on 21 June 1947; Mike Gibbons on bass; and Rob Griffiths on drums.

They were to become Apple's most successful group, apart from the Beatles themselves, and made their recording debut with 'Maybe Tomorrow' in November 1968. It was Paul McCartney who suggested the name change from Iveys to Badfinger, recalling his working title for 'With A Little Help From My Friends', which was 'Badfinger Boogie'.

Gibbons left the band and Evans took over on bass guitar, with Liverpool guitarist Joey Molland taking over on rhythm.

Paul also penned their biggest hit, 'Come And Get It', which was used on the soundtrack of the Ringo Starr movie *The Magic Christian*. They had several other hits, including 'No Matter What', 'Day After Day' and 'Baby Blue'.

Ham and Evans wrote the number 'Without You', which provided a chart-topper for Harry Nilsson.

The group also appeared on *The Concert For Bangladesh* and played on John Lennon's *Imagine* album and George Harrison's *All Things Must Pass*.

After they left Apple the band suffered financial difficulties and Ham hanged himself on 23 April 1975. He was 28 years old. He left a note blaming the group's American manager. Joey Molland and Tom Evans worked for a couple of years as labourers. Evans, who had co-written 'Without You', which was a million seller, was plagued by financial troubles and a lengthy and unsuccessful battle to receive his fair royalty for 'Without You'. He hanged himself on Saturday, 19 November 1983. He was 36 years old, married with a young son.

Molland formed another band, also called Badfinger, and they've been performing in America, enjoying a mini-revival from 1995. During that year, an Apple CD, *The Best Of Badfinger,* was released, there was an official Badfinger fan club, and a Badfinger documentary went into production, produced by Gary Katz, which included interviews with Joey and Katie Molland, Mike Gibbons and Marianne Evans. In Los Angeles the surviving members, Mike Gibbons and Joey Molland, together with Marianne and Stephen Evans and original manager Bill Collins, received an ASCAP (the American Society of Composers, Authors and Publishers) award for 'Without You'.

Badge

A number George Harrison co-wrote with Eric Clapton. It was recorded by Cream and entered the British Top Twenty following its release in April 1969. It reached No. 60 in the American charts. An instrumental section of the number is to be found in the middle of Harrison's number 'Here Comes The Sun'.

George and Eric performed the number on stage together during a concert at London's Rainbow Theatre in 1971.

Bad To Me

A song John Lennon penned while on holiday in Spain. It was written for Billy J. Kramer as a follow-up to his debut disc 'Do You Want To Know A Secret!' and was issued in Britain on Parlophone R 5049 on 26 July 1963, and in the States on Liberty 55626 on 23 September 1963. The single provided Billy with his second British chart topper, reached No. 9 in the American charts and eventually sold more than a million copies.

Although John made a demo disc of the song for George Martin to work from, the Beatles themselves never recorded the number.

Bag O' Nails Club, 9 Kingly Street, London W1

A basement night-club, situated in a narrow street parallel to Carnaby Street, which was originally opened on 24 November 1966 by John Gunnell and Lawrie Leslie. Gunnell, together with his brother Rick, had previously run clubs such as the Whiskey A Go Go and the Flamingo. It became a regular haunt for members of the Beatles, particularly after Abbey Road recording sessions. Paul was the Beatle who frequented the club most regularly as he reckoned it to be his favourite London nightspot and he even had his own reserved table there. On 15 May 1967, Paul was sitting with Chas Chandler, watching Georgie Fame and the Blue Flames, when he met Linda Eastman. They began chatting and he then invited her to accompany him to another nearby club, the Speakeasy.

Ballad Of John And Yoko, The

The 'Get Back' single was still No. 1 in the charts when 'The Ballad Of John And Yoko' was issued on Parlophone R 5786 on 30 May 1969. John had considered holding up the release until 'Get Back' had started to slip down the charts, but felt that the single might date as it was a 'newsy' tale of John's recent marriage to Yoko Ono and their trips to Paris and Amsterdam, with references to his 'Bigger Than Christ' newspaper story and the attitude of journalists to the couple.

When the number was recorded on 14 April 1969, only John and Paul performed on the session as George was out of the country and Ringo was filming *The Magic Christian*. Paul played piano, bass and drums on the track.

When the single was issued in America on Apple 2531 on 4 June 1969 'Get Back' was also in the No. 1 position. Although 'The Ballad Of John And Yoko' reached No. 1 in Britain, it only reached No. 8 in the American charts. This is probably due to the reaction in America against John's use of the name 'Christ' in the lyrics. There was initially a deal of pressure exerted to have the word bleeped out, but Apple refused. Some radio stations censored the record themselves, others played the flipside, George Harrison's 'Old Brown Shoe', others simply banned it.

John once referred to the track as 'Johnny B. Paperback Writer'.

The record reached No. 1 in Germany, Austria, Holland, Norway, Spain, Belgium, Denmark and Malaysia.

The track was included on *The Beatles 1967–1970* compilation, the *Hey Jude* album and the 1982 compilation *20 Greatest Hits*. The number was included on the CD compilation *Past Masters Volume Two*.

Ballard, Arthur

Painter and teacher, born in Liverpool in 1915, who initially won a scholarship to Liverpool College of Art in 1930. He was to spend most of his life in the city and taught at the college from 1947 to 1980.

His paintings attracted great interest in the late 1950s and early 1960s and were bought by the likes of Aldous Huxley, J. B. Priestley and Sam Wanamaker. However, his changing style and determination to remain in Liverpool impeded his chances of major success.

In 1957 he left for Paris for a short time to paint and study, and in 1958 had an exhibtition at the New Shakespeare Gallery in Liverpool. His work was exhibited in the John Moore exhibitions at the Walker Art Gallery in 1950 and 1961.

Commenting about Arthur in his book *Art In A City*, art critic John Willet wrote: 'He has great faith in Liverpool's individuality, which he thinks will assert itself in art sooner or later: we'll see something "better than the Beatles." He's proud of the efforts he's made to support individuals in the college, e.g. precisely, Lennon of the Beatles, whom the graphic design department were reluctant to accept. "The boy was no good as an artist," he claims, "and an intolerable, rebellious nuisance. But he had character."'

As a teacher, he took a personal interest in the fortunes of his pupils and aided them when in difficulties. His most talented student was Stuart Sutcliffe, who was to share Arthur's passion for the works of Nicholas da Stael.

Due to Stuart's reluctance to attend various classes at college, Arthur took it on himself to provide him with one-to-one tuition at Stu's flat in nearby Percy Street. He also took an interest in John Lennon and at one time prevented his expulsion from the college. Arthur also used to meet students for discussions in the 'War Office' of Ye Cracke pub in Rice Street.

Arthur was married twice, the second time to Carol, one of his students. He had two sons and a daughter. On his retirement he moved to London for a while to live with his daughter, before settling down with one of his sons and his family in Wales. He died in Corwen Clyd on 25 November 1994.

His biographer, art critic Peter Davies, prepared a touring exhibition of Arthur's work in 1996.

Baltimore Civic Center, West Baltimore, Maryland

There were two performances at the Civic Center on Sunday, 13 September 1964, each one drawing more than 13,000 people. Seventy-one police were stationed in the auditorium. There was the obligatory press conference and when Ringo was asked what he thought of American television, he replied, 'It's great – you get eighteen stations, but you can't get a good picture on any of them.'

Bambi Kino, 33 Paul-Roosen Strasse, St Pauli, Hamburg, Germany

The Bambi Filmkunsttheatre was a cinema run by Bruno Koschmider. When the Beatles first arrived in Hamburg on 17 August 1960 they were taken to the Bambi Kino (as it was more popularly known) and told that they were to sleep there. Along a gloomy little hallway were some small, windowless rooms, which Paul was to call 'dungeons'. They were next to the Bambi's toilets, where the Beatles were expected to wash and shave, using cold water from the urinals.

The first room they were taken to had one light bulb, two beds, and an old sofa. John and Stuart Sutcliffe immediately commandeered the beds and George took over the sofa. There were only two other rooms, so tiny, measuring 5 ft × 6 ft, that there was only space to fit in a bed. Paul and Pete took one each.

These were their uncomfortable quarters for the next four months, although there was some respite at night due to the number of girls who came to share their beds with them, some buying tickets to the cinema and making their way to their rooms through a connecting door.

Some weeks later they made friends with a group of students; one of them, Astrid Kirchherr, arranged for Stuart to move out and stay in the attic room of her parents' home. George took his bed over.

Due to complaints about noise the Indra was closed and the Beatles were moved to the Kaiserkeller club on 4 October, although they were to remain billeted in the Bambi. By this time the boys were acutely aware of their low pay and approached Koschmider for a rise. He refused. They received an offer from a rival club, the Top Ten, and agreed to take it up when their Kaiserkeller contract lapsed in December. Koschmider's spies reported their intentions to him and he threatened them and then reported to the police that George was only seventeen and under-age for the St Pauli area. He was deported. The group decided to continue at the Top Ten Club as a quartet and John Lennon was the first to remove his personal belongings to the new club, where they were to share a large top-floor room with Tony Sheridan. When Paul and Pete went to the Bambi to collect their possessions, the absence of light in their rooms caused them to take an unusual step in providing light of their own. They attached four rubber contraceptives to some old tapestry covering on the wall and lit them. By the time they'd burned out, Pete and Paul had gathered their belongings and left, the contraceptives having left some scorch marks on the wall.

They were settled in at their new billet when, in the middle of the night, the police arrived and took Pete and Paul away to the local police station where they were charged with attempting to cause a fire at the Bambi Kino. Their explanations were ignored and they were taken to prison and put in cells. A few hours later the police took them to the airport and deported them, having obtained their passports from their belongings – but leaving the rest of their possessions in Hamburg.

Banks, Jeremy

Silver-haired photographic co-ordinator at Apple, who joined the Beatles' employ in 1968. He was 33 years old at the time and was also engaged as photographic co-ordinator for the Beatles and worked with Derek Taylor in the Apple press office.

Taylor had first met Jeremy on 3 November 1966 in Arthur Howes' office. Taylor had brought his clients, the Beach Boys, there and Banks was handling special features for the *Daily Star* newspaper and covered the Beach Boys story with photographer John Kelly.

He joined Apple and was part of the organisation until December 1969. He would arrange photographic sessions, deal directly with photo agencies to obtain a commission for Apple, advise on sleeve design and think up publicity gimmicks – one of which was to send Apple's first four releases to Her Majesty The Queen, which resulted in a thank-you letter from Buckingham Palace.

Barber, Adrian

A Yorkshire-born musician who moved to Liverpool and became a founder-member of Cass & the Cassanovas, who formed in December 1959. The group became the Big Three in January 1961.

Barber played lead guitar, Johnny 'Gus' Gustafson was on bass and Johnny 'Hutch' Hutchinson on drums.

Adrian was regarded as an electronics wizard and surprised friends at the Jacaranda Club, one of his haunts, with his little gimmicks, such as putting a radio in a Coke can. His most impressive contribution to the local sound was his development of huge amplifiers, nicknamed 'coffins', which gave the trio a powerful stage sound. Other groups were impressed and Adrian was asked to make some 'coffins' for the Beatles.

Mersey Beat columnist 'Onlooker' wrote in the 30 November 1961 issue: 'A good night at the OPB last Saturday with the Big Three. I wonder who carried their coffins upstairs. The Undertakers probably – they were there as well. These enormous amplifiers on wheels always intrigue me. They must have quite a job getting them on some stages I've seen.'

Johnny Gustafson commented: 'Our speakers were five feet high by one and a half to two feet wide. Adrian Barber was a bit of an electronics wiz – he concocted these things. He got two Goodmans 15-inch speakers and made up this great big amp – it was only 50 watts but he acoustically designed the cabinets to give it the most oomph, and they did sound very, very loud.'

When Brian Epstein showed an interest in the group, Adrian

decided to leave and was replaced by Brian Griffiths in July 1962. Adrian then became stage manager at the Star Club in Hamburg.

Star Club owner Manfred Weissleder wanted to start a Star Club record label and record the acts on stage, so he engaged Adrian to develop a special sound system.

While Adrian was fitting in the system he was also testing it out by recording various groups, including the Beatles and Kingsize Taylor & the Dominoes.

He had been experimenting with a domestic tape recorder to check out the acoustics. With a single mike fixed in the right spot, he found he could get good results recording the Beatles on stage, complete with the dialogue between the group and the audience, the repartee, the jokes and even a laugh and a bit of a song from Horst Fascher.

Adrian completed his recordings on Monday, 31 December 1962 and was approached by Taylor for the tapes of the Dominoes. The Beatles' recordings from their first and final engagement at the Star Club were also on the tapes and these were the ones that eventually emerged as the double album *The Beatles Live! At the Star Club in Hamburg, Germany: 1962*.

When Joey Dee and the Starliters appeared at the Star Club, Dee was so impressed by the sound system Adrian had devised that he invited him to New York to design and install a sound system in the Peppermint Lounge.

Adrian went to live in America, fitted the Peppermint Lounge with a sound system, became a recording manager at Atlantic Records and managed a group called the New York Rock & Roll Ensemble. During the years he became recording manager for a number of prominent acts, including the Allman Brothers Band and Aerosmith.

Currently he lives in Hawaii.

Bardot, Brigitte

All four Beatles saw Brigitte Bardot as an ideal, but John Lennon, in particular, was fascinated by her. It then seemed odd that when they filled in their personal lifelines for the *New Musical Express* in 1963 Paul, George and Ringo all cited Brigitte as their favourite actress while John named Juliet Greco and Sophia Loren.

John had a lifesize poster of Bardot pasted on his bedroom ceiling in Mendips and insisted that his girlfriend Cynthia alter her appearance to look like Bardot. She was to comment, 'John's perfect image of a woman was Brigitte Bardot. I found myself fast becoming moulded into her style of dress and haircut.' John also called Astrid Kirchherr 'the German Brigitte Bardot'. Paul bought a leather skirt for his girlfriend Dot Rhone and told her to grow her hair long to look like Brigitte. He was later to say, 'John and I lusted after Brigitte Bardot in our teen years and tried to make our girlfriends look like her.'

When they made their first trip to Paris in January 1964, the Beatles made a special request that they would like to meet up with Bardot. Unfortunately, she was out of the country filming at the time.

In 1968, when Bardot came to London, she requested a meeting with the Beatles. The only one to turn up was John. He was so nervous he took LSD and didn't know what to say to her.

When Paul originally worked on some sketches for the *Sgt Pepper* album sleeve he included a large pin-up picture of Brigitte, ten times the size of any other character. Oddly enough, the Beatles' favourite actress never appeared on the finished cover – although Diana Dors, a British sex symbol, did.

Barron Knights, The

A comedy/rock group from Leighton Buzzard comprising Duke D'mond, vocals; Paul Longford, guitar; Butch Baker, guitar; Barron Anthony, bass; and Dave Balinger, drums. The group had a series of record hits with comic medleys of hits by other groups, including 'Call Up The Groups', 'Come To The Dance', 'Pop Go The Workers' and 'Merry Guitar Pops'.

The group were booked to appear on the *Beatles Christmas Show* in December 1963/January 1964 at the Gaumont, Bradford, the Liverpool Empire and the Finsbury Park Astoria, London.

In those days there were high jinks between the groups. The Beatles' act on the *Christmas Show* began when they stood on a blacked-out stage and a small spotlight picked out each of their heads in turn, ending with John Lennon's. One night some members of the Barron Knights grabbed John in the wings and held him so that when the spotlight turned to where John should have been, there was nothing there.

Barrow, Tony

At the age of seventeen, when he was still a sixth form student at Merchant Taylor's College in Crosby, Merseyside, Tony Barrow was appointed record reviewer for the *Liverpool Echo*. Under the name 'Disker', he reviewed the latest record releases and also included a small local chart of the top-selling singles.

He moved to London in 1954 to work at Decca Records where he became the only full-time writer of album sleeve notes in Britain, while still retaining his *Echo* column.

Brian Epstein sent a letter to Disker requesting a mention of the
Beatles. The letter was passed on to Barrow who contacted Epstein
and told him that he only wrote about actual recording acts. He
suggested that Epstein contact a colleague on the *Echo*, columnist
George Harrison. Having discovered that Tony worked for Decca,
Brian once again contacted him requesting help with contacts at
Decca. Barrow passed over the message and the Beatles auditioned
for the company. When Barrow asked Mike Smith how the audition
went, Smith was very positive and in his Disker column, Barrow
wrote: 'Latest episode in the success story of Liverpool's instrumental group the Beatles. Commenting upon the outfit's recent
recording test, Decca disc producer Mike Smith tells me that he
thinks the Beatles are great. He has a tape of their audition which
runs over thirty minutes and is convinced his label will be able to
put the Beatles to good use. I'll keep you posted.'

However, Decca gave the Beatles the thumbs down. After Brian
succeeded in gaining a Parlophone contract for the band, he
approached Barrow for advice again. Tony pointed out that it would
be sensible if he paid for independent public relations to plug the
record and Brian offered him twenty pounds to produce a publicity
kit for 'Love Me Do'. As he couldn't send out all the kits from his
office at Decca, Tony noted that Tony Calder, who used to work in
the same office at Decca, had left to set up a PR company with
Andrew Loog Oldham. He contacted them and they were hired by
Epstein to send out the press releases and arrange press interviews.

With the release of 'Love Me Do', Barrow wrote in his Disker
column: 'John Lennon and Paul McCartney chant out their self-
written lyrics of "Love Me Do", an infectious medium-paced ballad
with an exceptionally haunting harmonica accompaniment. There's
nothing startlingly distinguished about the simple, repetitive lyrics
but "Love Me Do" relies more upon punchy ear-catching presentation. There's a refreshing do-it-yourself approach to the single.'

Epstein had offered the Beatles' PR account to Oldham, who
turned it down. He asked Barrow if he would take on the task.
Barrow also turned it down. He had a secure job at Decca and a
steady girlfriend, Corinne, whom he married. He didn't want to
take the chance of giving it all up for what seemed a risky venture.
Brian then took him to lunch at the popular seafood restaurant
Wheelers and offered him £32 per week, twice the amount he was
getting at Decca – and he took up the offer.

Epstein asked him to find a London office for NEMS where he
could handle the press work and he found premises at Service
House, 13 Monmouth Street. Eventually hiring an assistant, Jo
Berman, and a secretary, Valerie Sumpter.

As the organisation grew he graduated to plush offices in Argyle Street, next to the London Palladium, and as the Beatles were more or less a full-time account, he concentrated on the other NEMS artists while Brian employed various people such as Brian Somerville and Derek Taylor to look after the Beatles' press personally, although Tony did continue to handle their press activities from time to time.

He also managed to write prolifically: a series of souvenir magazines about the Beatles, the Cavern and other beat artists, record sleeve notes for the early Beatles albums and regular features about the Beatles' activities for *Beatles Monthly*. In many cases he had to use a pseudonym. Although he wasn't earning a fortune from NEMS Enterprises, his contract stated that any proceeds from freelance writing under his own name would have to be shared with the company, therefore Tony used the name Alistair Griffin for his books and Frederick James for his *Beatles Monthly* articles.

It was Tony who came up with the suggestion for the Beatles' Christmas records for fan club members.

After Brian Epstein's death he set up his own PR company, Tony Barrow International, retaining artists such as Cilla Black and expanding his activities until he had a roster of star names. Unfortunately, ill health caused him to retire in the late seventies and he moved to Morecambe on the north-west coast.

In 1980 he had recovered sufficiently to begin freelance writing and by 1981 had become prolific in his output with regular features in *Beatles Monthly* (this time under his own name) and syndicated columns in provincial publications, in addition to numerous commissions for record sleeves. He also sought out personalities with former Beatles associations in order to ghost their 'stories' for the national press. Angie McCartney was the subject of one of his series in the *Daily Star*, her daughter Ruth was another (in *19* magazine). In 1982 he penned *P.S. We Love You* for Mirror Books.

Tony's features for *Beatles Monthly* are of tremendous interest to readers due to the fact that Tony travelled quite extensively with the group. He was present on their American trips, their trip to the far east (and the harrowing experience in Manila), attended their meeting with Elvis Presley and, at the request of Paul, taped their final concert at Candlestick Park.

Bart, Lionel
A major British composer of hit songs and musicals, particularly in the 1960s. Born in London's East End on 1 August 1930, his songs helped launch the careers of Cliff Richard and Tommy Steele.

He began to write musicals and was intrigued by the Liverpool folk song 'Maggie May' to such an extent that he decided to work on a 'folk opera set in Liverpool' based around the legendary Liverpool tart, asking writer Alun Owen to work on it with him. For a time Bart moved up to Liverpool to soak in the local atmosphere. In his book *Bart*, David Roper reports Lionel Bart as saying:

> At that time I was very thick with Brian Epstein and all of the Beatles. They really took off in a big way as I was writing 'Maggie May' and John Lennon phoned me once saying, 'Can I have a lend of your scriptwriter, we're going to do this film.' So I downed tools for a couple of months, and Alun went off to write the screenplay for *A Hard Day's Night*.

Bart became a very close friend of Brian Epstein, and the Beatles regularly dropped by Bart's flat, where he held 'open house'.

A story he often related concerns 'Eleanor Rigby'. He says that he helped Paul rethink the lyrics, recalling that Paul came to visit him to seek his approval for a song he'd written. The two of them were walking Bart's Alsatians Simon and Garfunkel in Wimbledon Common cemetery when they noticed a family headstone for Ann and Eleanor Bygraves. Bart says: 'But when he sat down at my clavichord and sang it, I wasn't too happy about Max Bygraves at the time – and made him change it to Rigby.'

Paul himself believes he used the name Eleanor because of Eleanor Bron and has said that Rigby came from the Bristol firm of wine and spirits shippers whose sign he saw when visiting Jane Asher once. Others claim that Paul may have subconsciously remembered the gravestone of Eleanor Rigby in St Peter's graveyard in Liverpool.

Bart's biggest success was the musical *Oliver!*

Lionel died of cancer on Saturday, 3 April 1999. He was 68 years old.

Bayerischer Hof Hotel, Munich, Germany

Hotel where the Beatles stayed on Thursday, 23 June, 1966 during their short German tour. They arrived late in the afternoon and moved into their fifth-floor suite. Later, on their way to a press conference at the hotel, they were jammed in a lift for ten minutes as there were fifteen people crammed inside. Once freed, they attended their conference, during which they were presented with a Golden Otto Award by *Bravo* magazine. They returned to their rooms where they carried out preliminary rehearsals for their concert the following day as they hadn't performed for several weeks. During the following evening they relaxed by taking a dip in the hotel pool.

Beach Ballroom, Sea Beach, Aberdeen, Aberdeenshire, Scotland

Setting for the Beatles' final appearance of their short Scottish tour, on Sunday, 6 January 1963.

Beach Boys, The

Californian group famous for their 'surf sound', who were one of the leading American bands when the Beatles first arrived in the States in February 1964. That was the month in which the group reached No. 5 in the charts with 'Fun, Fun, Fun' and later the same year they topped the American charts for the first time with 'I Get Around'. They shared the same record label as the Beatles in America, Capitol Records, and because both their names began with 'Bea', they were bedfellows in the record bins at record stores.

The following year they appeared in the film *The Girls On The Beach*, with the Crickets and Leslie Gore. The plot concerned kids at a school hop who think they have booked the Beatles, but get the Beach Boys instead.

In fact, a fierce competitiveness was generated when the Beatles became successful in America, particularly in the mind of Brian Wilson. Brian was the creative fire behind the group, which also comprised his brothers Carl and Dennis, his cousin Mike Love and friend Al Jardine.

Brian's output following the appearance of the Beatles was so stimulated that the group had a huge string of hits and became the biggest-selling band on Capitol Records next to the Beatles. Brian, at times, seemed obsessed with the Beatles' success and once, when the Beach Boys were stranded at Shannon Airport in Ireland on their way to London, they shared the VIP lounge with Brian Epstein. Brian Wilson was keen to ask him when the Beatles were next appearing in America and when Brian told him it would be in almost a year's time, Brian seemed visibly relieved.

Brian Wilson turned his concentration increasingly to the production and writing of music, and ceased touring. He was replaced for a while on the road by Glen Campbell and then by Bruce Johnson.

After hearing the *Rubber Soul* album in 1965, Brian was so impressed that he was determined to outshine it and said, 'I was sitting around a table with friends, making a joint when we heard "Rubber Soul" for the first time, and I'm smoking and I'm getting high, and the album blew my mind because it was a whole album with all good stuff.' He then stated that he would produce the greatest rock 'n' roll album ever made and set to work on *Pet*

Sounds. It was well received critically in Britain, but was something of a failure in America where Capitol rush-released *The Best Of The Beach Boys* compilation several weeks later, which sold better and went Gold.

Still determined to outshine the Beatles, Brian invited lyricist Van Dyke Parks to join him in producing a rock 'n' roll album which would be his masterpiece, initially to be called *Dumb Angel*, then *Smiley Smile*.

During the making of the album, the Beatles' *Sgt Pepper's Lonely Hearts Club Band* was released and it was suggested that this had such an effect on Brian that he scrapped his project and merely issued a few of the tracks on an album called *Smile*.

Later, when the Beach Boys decided not to appear at the Monterey Rock Festival, Jan Wenner, editor of *Rolling Stone*, was to write in his publication: 'The Beach Boys are just one prominent example of a group that has gotten hung up in trying to catch the Beatles.'

The Beatles and the Beach Boys actually became quite good friends. Carl Wilson and Mike Love visited the Beatles backstage at their Portland Coliseum concert on 22 August 1965, and when the Beach Boys toured England, the Beatles rang them up at their hotel, individually.

Paul McCartney also attended a Beach Boys recording session on 10 April 1967. Rumours were spread that Paul either produced or sang on one of the numbers recorded, 'Vegetables', although it seems unlikely.

The Beatles also praised the Beach Boys back home in England, which helped to increase the group's popularity. In fact, the Beach Boys employed Derek Taylor, the Beatles' former press officer, as their own publicist.

He was to comment: 'I lived in Hollywood then but my British links were strong and with *Pet Sounds* out and the Beatles increasingly flattering about the Beach Boys and with *Good Vibrations* on the way, we started to pump information into England about this tremendous band.'

In fact, Paul said at the time that he regarded 'God Only Knows' as the best song ever written.

In 1967 Mike Love and Bruce Johnson performed at the Beatles' party held to celebrate their *Magical Mystery Tour* film. Mike Love was also to join the Beatles at the Maharishi's ashram in Rishikesh in India where it was rumoured that he helped Paul in composing 'Back In The USSR'.

Paul and Linda McCartney attended the group's concert at Anaheim, California, in 1976.

Beat Brothers, The

A generic name created for the various musicians who backed Tony Sheridan on stage and record.

The first group to actually back him on record were the Beatles, who cut the tracks 'My Bonnie', 'The Saints', 'Why (Can't You Love Me Again)?', 'Sweet Georgia Brown', 'Nobody's Child' and 'Take Out Some Insurance On Me Baby' (also known as 'If You Love Me Baby') with him in Hamburg in June 1961.

They were paid a session fee rather than a royalty deal, and recording man Bert Kaempfert decided to use the name Beat Brothers on the actual record, although only Tony Sheridan is mentioned on the picture sleeve.

It was alleged that Kaempfert decided not to use the name Beatles because he thought it sounded like 'Peedles', a German slang word for the male sex organ.

The Beatles recorded no more tracks with Sheridan, although other musicians did. Since the name the Beat Brothers was consistent on a number of Sheridan's releases, people were originally confused, mistakenly believing the Beatles had recorded more tracks than they did. During 1961 and 1962 there were 27 recordings made on eight different occasions with Tony Sheridan and Bert Kaempfert using different personnel as the Beat Brothers.

Other musicians who recorded under the name the Beat Brothers included organist Roy Young, bass guitarist Colin Milander, tenor saxophonist Rikki Barnes and drummer Johnny Watson. In 1995, Tony Sheridan reformed the Beat Brothers with Howie Casey and Roy Young, but the outfit was short-lived.

Beatlemania (Term)

A term which came into existence following the Beatles' appearance on 'Sunday Night At The London Palladium', on 13 October 1963. The group appeared live before an audience of 15,000,000 viewers nationwide that evening, performing a twelve-minute act. For the first time ever, the stars of the show were seen briefly at the beginning of the evening, albeit only for a few seconds. Compere Bruce Forsyth announced, 'If you want to see them again, they'll be back in 42 minutes.' The crowds of fans had begun to build up during the day and when the Beatles attempted to escape the theatre via the front entrance in Argyle Street, they were swamped by fans – and the cameras of the national newspapers. Despite Philip Norman in *Shout!* implying that there were only a handful of fans and photographer Dezo Hoffman saying that there were only about eight fans, photographs and eye witnesses disprove their claims. The headlines of the national newspapers were full of reports of the group's spectacular success and the *Daily Mirror* coined the phrase 'Beatlemania!' which was taken up by all the other newspapers. It then became an established term throughout the world, which is still in use today.

The group's press officer Tony Barrow was to tell Hunter Davies, 'From that day on, everything changed. My job was never the same again. From spending six months ringing up newspapers and getting "No", I now had every national reporter and feature writer chasing me.'

With tedious regularity ever since, any new pop group who creates a sensation is generally labelled to be 'as big as the Beatles' and a variation of the word is used – Monkeemania, Rollermania, and so on.

The word 'Beatlemania' was once considered as the title of their debut film and it was eventually used as the title of a Broadway show, based on the Beatles, which opened in 1977.

Beatles, The

Inspired by the skiffle boom, a pupil at Quarry Bank School in Liverpool named John Lennon decided to form a skiffle group in 1957 and laid the foundation of what was to become the most famous rock band of all time. His initial name the Blackjacks only lasted a week and the school became the inspiration for the new name when John dubbed the group the Quarry Men in March 1957. John sang and played guitar and he was accompanied by Colin Hanton on drums, Eric Griffiths on guitar, Pete Shotton on washboard, Rod Davis on banjo and Bill Smith on tea-chest bass; the latter was soon replaced by Ivan Vaughan, who alternated on the instrument with Nigel Whalley.

The band's main inspiration was skiffle music, as performed by artists such as Lonnie Donegan and bands such as the Vipers. Numbers in their repertoire included: 'Freight Train', 'Maggie May', 'Midnight Special', 'Railroad Bill', 'Come Go With Me' and 'Worried Man Blues'. Such a repertoire was appropriate for the type of cheap instruments they could afford. One of the advantages of skiffle music was that the basic instruments were not costly, enabling thousands of youngsters throughout Britain to emulate the skiffle sounds of the hit artists.

At the same time, John, inspired by 'Heartbreak Hotel', was a fan of American rock 'n' roll music and continued to introduce numbers into their repertoire which had been hits for Buddy Holly, Carl Perkins, the Coasters, Elvis, Jerry Lee Lewis and Gene Vincent. Between June and July 1957, there was a six-man line-up for the group with Len Garry on tea-chest bass.

On 6 July 1957, Ivan Vaughan invited Paul McCartney, one of his friends from the Liverpool Institute, along to their gig at Woolton Parish Church. The fifteen-year-old McCartney and the sixteen-year-old Lennon were introduced and a unique songwriting partnership was to flourish.

The line-up of the Quarry Men increased to seven with the inclusion of Paul on guitar and vocals. John Lowe on piano and George Harrison on guitar and vocals from February 1958. Harrison was a friend of Paul's from the Liverpool Institute whom he'd met on the bus journeys to school. By the middle of 1958 Garry and Griffiths had left, leaving a five-man outfit.

The group appeared in several local talent contests, but had few gigs. By January 1959 they weren't operating as a group, although John and Paul kept in touch with their mutual interest in songwriting. George joined a group called the Les Stewart Quartet.

That might have been the end of the Quarry Men saga, but for a stroke of good fortune. The Les Stewart Quartet had been booked as a resident band at a new cellar club in Liverpool called the Casbah. Situated in the West Derby area of Liverpool, it was run by Mrs Mona Best, primarily for the benefit of her sons Pete and Rory. Stewart, upset because of the time his guitarist Ken Brown had spent on decorating the club, refused to play there. George Harrison and Brown walked out of the group, George contacted his friends John and Paul and the Quarry Men were reunited as a quartet. After seven gigs at the club Ken Brown left the group following a disagreement about money and he encouraged Pete Best to form a group with him called the Blackjacks. Between October 1959 and January 1960 John, Paul and George continued as a trio, calling themselves Johnny & the Moondogs for some Carroll Levis auditions.

John Lennon was, by this time, a student at Liverpool College of Art. Conscious of their need for a bass guitarist, he approached two other students, independently of each other, and offered them the job if they could obtain a guitar. The two were Stuart Sutcliffe and Rod Murray. Both were unable to afford a guitar, so Rod began to make one by hand. Then Stuart sold a painting at an exhibition and he was able to buy a bass guitar and joined the group in January 1960, when they called themselves the Beatals. The quartet continued together until May, when they were joined by drummer Tommy Moore and called themselves the Silver Beetles. The 36-year-old Moore was only with them for a short time, during which they auditioned for pop impresario Larry Parnes and appeared on a short tour of Scotland backing singer Johnny Gentle. In July 1960 they had another drummer, Norman Chapman, but his tenure lasted barely weeks.

Chapman was called up for National Service and the group
urgently needed another drummer. They had been booked for a
short season in Hamburg. The gig had come about via a local coffee
bar owner, Allan Williams, who had already sent another band,
Derry & the Seniors to Hamburg. He'd used the re-spelled Silver
Beatles at his Jacaranda Club, a short-lived strip club, and the New
Cabaret Artistes Club and had obtained a few local bookings for
them at venues such as the Grosvenor Ballroom. By his own admission, he only used them because they were cheap and he did not
reckon them to be in the same class as many of the other local
bands.

Liverpool by this time, was literally swarming with rock 'n' roll
groups who, like the Silver Beatles, had continued playing music
long after the skiffle boom had faded.

McCartney contacted Pete Best and offered him the drum seat. He
took it. The group decided to call themselves the Beatles as from
August 1960 and their first trip to Hamburg. When Sutcliffe joined,
and they'd briefly used the name Beatals, they strove for a better
title. As their main rock 'n' roll inspiration at the time was Buddy
Holly, Stuart thought they should have a name similar to that of
Holly's back band the Crickets and thought up Beetles. This was
changed to the Silver Beetles, but then it was truncated again, John
Lennon added the 'a', making it Beatles, George Harrison's assumption that the name might have been inspired by a motorcycle gang
called the Beetles in the film *The Wild One* is wrong; the film was
barred from British screens until the late sixties and they couldn't
possibly have seen the film at the time of their name change.

When the Beatles left for Hamburg in 1960, they weren't
regarded as a leading band in Liverpool and, in some cases, were
looked down on by some of the other groups. It was their stint in
Hamburg which pulled the band together musically, a 'baptism of
fire' which transformed them from an average band into a dynamic
outfit. This was caused by the fact that they had to play such long
hours and were bullied by the clubowner Bruno Koschmider to
'make a show', which resulted in their act becoming much tighter
musically. Oddly, this transformation didn't seem to happen to the
many other Liverpool acts who appeared in Hamburg.

However, it wasn't Hamburg alone which made the Beatles
something special. The fact that Liverpool had so many venues for
local acts to play at, coupled with the rivalry between more than
300 Merseyside groups, continued to forge the Beatles until they
were to be regarded as Liverpool's top band, a fact confirmed by the
poll published by the music paper *Mersey Beat* on 4 January 1962.

At the time Pete Best was regarded as the most potent symbol in the band. Following their stint in Hamburg, bass guitarist Stuart Sutcliffe had left them and they were a four-man outfit. John Lennon, Paul McCartney and George Harrison were the three front-line guitarists and they alternated as lead singers and also performed vocal harmony with either Paul and John or all three. Pete Best played drums and occasionally sang one song, although he had developed a distinctive drum sound during his spell in Hamburg which became known as 'the atom beat', which was copied by other drummers.

Intrigued by the growing interest in the Beatles, a local record retailer, Brian Epstein, signed them up and they initially auditioned for Decca Records on New Year's Day, 1962. They weren't successful, but Epstein managed to secure a contract with Parlophone Records and George Martin became their A&R Man. In August of that year Pete Best was sacked and replaced by Ringo Starr, a drummer from Liverpool group Rory Storm & the Hurricanes, whom the Beatles had appeared with in Hamburg.

Their first single 'Love Me Do' was issued on 5 October 1962, and was a modest hit.

1963 and 1964 proved to be the most important years in their careers. During 1963 they created a sensation in Britain and 'Beatlemania' was born. Within months they had graduated from being a support act at concerts to starring in the Royal Variety Show and the highest rating TV show 'Sunday Night At The London Palladium'.

There were various reasons for their success. National Service in Britain had ended and young men no longer had their lives disrupted for two years, while they were seconded for compulsory army training. The post-war bulge (later known as the 'baby boom'), in which an unprecedented number of babies were born immediately at the end of the war as returning servicemen were reunited with their wives, caused the largest explosion in the birth rate up to that time and those babies were now teenagers – the largest number of teenagers Britain had ever known. In addition, these teenagers had money to spend. The youngsters were also demanding more freedom than their parents had experienced in their youth and were eager to create their own sounds and fashions. The media had also developed to the extent that it was possible to create an overnight sensation – with television, radio and the prolif-eration of newspapers and magazines, it no longer required years performing at theatres throughout the country to achieve fame.

1964 was the most important year of all for it was the year in which the Beatles conquered the biggest record market in the world – America.

It took a combination of talent and luck – and the group also became symbols. America was mourning the death of President John F. Kennedy and the Beatles appeared on the scene to bring them fun and excitement and end their mourning. They also brought rock 'n' roll back to its homeland. Rock 'n' roll had been created in America in the fifties, but had waned to an extent because the major rock artists had faded from the public eye. After Elvis Presley's army service, he lost much of his early rebelliousness. Jerry Lee Lewis and Chuck Berry had been the subject of scandals and their careers had suffered. Buddy Holly, the Big Bopper and Ritchie Valens had been killed in an air crash, and the American media had promoted music of a more sanitised nature, performed by good-looking young singers who were acceptable to the parents of teenagers – Frankie Avalon, Tab Hunter, Ricky Nelson, Bobby Vee, James Darren and so on.

Being in the right place at the right time seemed to favour the Beatles. They were hanging around the Jacaranda when Allan Williams was seeking a group to go to Hamburg. Ed Sullivan happened to be at London Airport when the Beatles arrived back from Sweden to a tumultuous welcome, which resulted in them appearing on the top-rating 'Ed Sullivan Show'. Lucky instances were frequent in their career. If Brian Epstein hadn't dropped into the HMV store in London to have some acetates cut they might never have secured a recording contract.

At some contrast to the luck was the fact that they initially weren't regarded highly in various quarters. Derry & the Seniors didn't want them to go to Hamburg as they believed the Beatles would ruin the scene for other groups. When they appeared at Litherland Town Hall in Liverpool, part of the audience believed they were a German group. All three pop labels of EMI turned them down and didn't think they had anything new to offer. Several parties approached by Epstein wouldn't invest in the group because they believed the Beatles didn't have a future. Capitol Records rejected them on three occasions and their initial record releases in America in 1963 only sold in the hundreds of copies.

During the sixties, the Beatles not only became a musical phenomenon, they affected the styles and fashions of the decade. Apart from being musically innovative, they changed almost every aspect of the record industry, from bringing about the restructure of royalties for artists and producers to influencing the designs of album sleeves. They revolutionised music tours, popularised the Pop promo and transformed studio recording.

The Beatles officially split on 31 December 1970, when Paul McCartney took out a lawsuit in the High Court to dissolve their partnership, resulting in an official receiver being appointed to handle the group's affairs.

After more than a decade together, they were like four young men ready to leave the family nest. All four were married, although it was the wives of John and Paul who were most active in their husbands' careers. John had become more interested in his collaborations with Yoko Ono than with Paul and the other Beatles, and Paul was ready to embark on solo ventures with his wife Linda. George was also loath to continue being a Beatle. They had abandoned touring in 1966 and the succeeding years were known as their 'studio years', when they mainly gathered together to record. George had developed as a songwriter in his own right and his recorded efforts with the Beatles were almost George Harrison solo works.

It was Paul who had mainly kept the group together after Brian Epstein had died, egging them on to make *Magical Mystery Tour* and constantly eager for the Beatles to go on the road again. They had been drifting apart for some time, but the main bone of contention seemed to be when John, George and Ringo officially appointed Allen Klein to represent them. Paul insisted on John Eastman as his representative and the scene was set for the dissolution of the group.

On Tuesday, 27 April 1971 John, George and Ringo decided to drop their appeal against the High Court order placing their affairs in the hands of a receiver. They faced legal costs of £100,000. Mr James Douglas Spooner was immediately appointed as receiver and manager of the group's business and the saga of the Beatles had finally come to an end.

Beatles, The (Album)

The Beatles was the simple title of the group's first double album which, when released, became the biggest-selling double album of all time. It reached the No.1 position in various international charts, including those in Britain and America, selling more than six and a half million copies within the first two years of issue. It sold nearly two million units during the first week of its release in America alone.

The cover of *The Beatles* was in marked contrast to the elaborate sleeve of *Sgt. Pepper's Lonely Hearts Club Band*. Richard Hamilton, the artist who was brought in to advise the Beatles on the sleeve design by Robert Fraser, suggested a plain white cover, individually numbered in the style of a limited edition. He also suggested a collage of images of the Beatles should be enclosed on the poster. His ideas were adopted, with Gordon Howes designing the package which included four colour prints of portraits of the individual Beatles by John Kelly, together with a poster montage of shots of the Beatles which also contained the lyrics to the songs on the reverse side.

Jeremy Banks, Neil Aspinall and Mal Evans assembled the montage of photographs for the poster and there was some controversy because they included a 'nude' shot of Paul. Oddly enough, there was a larger photograph of John Lennon in the nude that passed without comment.

Due to the starkness of the sleeve, the album became commonly known as the White Album. Incidentally, it had originally gone by the working title 'A Doll's House', but it was pointed out that Family had just released an album called *Music In A Doll's House*.

The Beatles was the first Beatles album to be issued on Apple's own label, and Paul McCartney asked Derek Taylor to arrange for an advertising agency to develop a major publicity and advertising campaign for the release. A meeting was arranged between a senior director of J. Walter Thompson, the advertising agency, and after a preliminary discussion, a second meeting was held a week later. There were several representatives from J. Walter Thompson present, plus Paul McCartney, Derek Taylor, Ron Kass, Jeremy Banks, Peter Asher, Neil Aspinall and Jack Oliver. The agency suggested that there be television adverts, with Paul McCartney appearing in them – the cost of the TV commercials would be £50,000. Thompsons also suggested six London buses be painted white with 'Beatles bus' written on the side of the windows. Paul didn't like the idea and the proposed massive campaign was dropped.

The album took five months to record and the sessions began on Thursday, 30 May 1968 at Abbey Road Studios and ended on Thursday, 17 October 1968, during which time a staggering 32 tracks had been recorded, 30 of which found their way on to the double album. One of the tracks recorded but not issued was 'What's The New Mary Jane'. The other was the George Harrison composition 'Not Guilty' – however, George was to have an unprecedented four tracks on the album.

The sessions had not been entirely happy ones and at one period Ringo walked out following a criticism by Paul, and didn't return for two weeks. John Lennon had become disillusioned with the group and had wanted to leave. Since they'd recorded their previous album there had been other changes, apart from the creation of Apple – the death of Brian Epstein and the emergence of Yoko.

The majority of the thirty tracks had been written while the

Beatles were studying at the ashram in Rishikesh. The diversity of the music ranged from the eight-minute 'Revolution 9' by John with the help of his partner Yoko to the Beach Boys influenced 'Back In The USSR'. George Martin felt that the number of songs should be pared down and the best selected for a strong single two-sided album. But the group, who were all manoeuvring for their own particular numbers, overruled him. There was a certain amount of rancour during the making of the album, with John annoyed that he'd not been asked to perform on Paul's 'Why Don't We Do It In The Road' and with the other members not too happy about the avant garde 'Revolution 9' experiment of John's.

There was so much tension during the period of recording that engineer Geoff Emerick decided to quit. Ringo also left the group for a two-week period during the sessions saying he felt 'unloved and unappreciated.' There was also a deal of stress caused by the constant presence of Yoko Ono at the sessions.

The tracks were, Side One: 'Back In The USSR', 'Dear Prudence', 'Glass Onion', 'Ob-La-Di Ob-La-Da', 'Wild Honey Pie', 'The Continuing Story Of Bungalow Bill', 'While My Guitar Gently Weeps', 'Happiness Is A Warm Gun'. Side Two: 'Martha My Dear', 'I'm So Tired', 'Blackbird', 'Piggies', 'Rocky Raccoon', 'Don't Pass Me By', 'Why Don't We Do It In The Road', 'I Will', 'Julia'. Side Three: 'Birthday', 'Yer Blues', 'Mother Nature's Son', 'Everybody's Got Something To Hide Except Me And My Monkey', 'Sexy Sadie', 'Helter Skelter', 'Long Long Long'. Side Four: 'Revolution 1', 'Honey Pie', 'Savoy Truffle', 'Cry Baby Cry', 'Revolution 9', 'Goodnight.'

Although this was the first Beatles album on the Apple label, EMI still retained the Beatles and the releases went out using the Parlophone catalogue numbers. *The Beatles* was issued in Britain on Parlophone 7067-8 on 22 November 1968, and went straight to No. 1 in the charts.

The album was issued in America on Capitol SWBO 101 on 25 November 1968 with advance orders of almost two million and went straight to No. 1 in the charts.

On 23 November 1998, to celebrate the 30th anniversary of the original release, EMI issued a 'White Album' CD in a limited edition. There was a gatefold wallet in a slipcase, individually numbered. The package also included miniature replicas of the poster and four postcards from the original release.

Beatles Abroad, The

A 45-minute radio programme transmitted on the Light Programme on 30 August 1965. The show was hosted by Brian

Matthew who had recorded interviews with the group which were included in the broadcast.

Beatles Anthology, The (The TV Series)

A five-part six-hour TV version of the group's official history screened in November 1995, which was sold to more than 110 countries. The first instalment was screened in America on ABC TV on Sunday, 19 November and in Britain on ITV on Sunday, 26 November 1995. The original concept was mooted in the late 1960s by Neil Aspinall, who began to gather archive footage for a visual history which he dubbed 'The Long And Winding Road' and initially planned to be available at Christmas 1970.

A press release from Apple Corps Ltd and the American ABC TV was issued on Wednesday, 10 May 1995. It was headed: 'Definitive History Of The Beatles Will Be Told In The Band's Own Words In A Five-Hour Special Which Will Air Over Two Nights In November, 1995, On The ABC Television Network.'

The release read:

The definitive history of the Beatles, the most significant band in the annuls of popular music, will finally be told in the band's own words, in a five-hour television special which will air on the ABC Television Network over two nights in November 1995. The special, featuring the world premier of two songs – the first new Beatles recordings in 25 years – was announced jointly by the ABC entertainment president Ted Harbert, and Apple Corps Ltd.

The unprecedented musical event will feature John, Paul, George and Ringo, with the latter three bringing additional instrumentation, voices and arrangements to two unreleased John Lennon songs on which he sings and plays.

'The Beatles story will be an extraordinary event on ABC,' Harbert said. 'The five-hour special is designed to provide a comprehensive look at the lives and sound of the band that changed the culture of a generation.'

The surviving Beatles will tell their own stories in exclusive interviews, and the special will incorporate a rich archive of interviews on audio and video tape left by the late John Lennon. Together the four recall the group's formation in Liverpool and its meteoric rise, along with seminal moments from their career – such as the first trip to the United States, the making of their films, and inside stories behind specific record releases.

The special will also reveal the impact of these developments on their private lives, including reminiscences by other key players in the Beatles' story. There will also be never-before-seen footage of the legendary musicians in their youth through home movies, film outtakes and other rarities.

The new Beatles songs featured on the special, 'Free As a Bird' and 'Real Love', will be released by Apple Records.

The making of the television special and associated video series has been the responsibility of Apple Productions Ltd, a company owned by the surviving Beatles and the estate of John Lennon, administered by his widow, Yoko Ono Lennon. The executive producer is Neil Aspinall, the producer is Chips Chipperfield and the director is Geoffrey Wonfor.

It was estimated that throughout the world there were 400 million people who watched the television series.

Beatles Anthology, The (Video)

An eight-volume video set with a running time of 9 hours 51 minutes 54 seconds, almost double the length of the TV Anthology series. When the video box set was issued in the States on Thursday, 5 September 1996, it was decided not to sell individual tapes. This was due to the problems Turner Home Entertainment had when they issued the series *Baseball* and *The Civil War* on video. Former Turner executive Steve Chamberlain, who was spearheading the *Beatles Video Anthology*, explained it as a matter of logistics. 'It is a logistical nightmare to offer the tapes on an individual basis', he said. 'You've got to deal with returns and reorders and 95 per cent of the sales on *Baseball* were for the whole set anyway.'

It was released in Britain on Monday, 7 October 1996.

Beatles Anthology, The, Volume 1

The two-CD package was issued simultaneously around the world on Tuesday, 21 November 1995 on Apple 7243 83444525. It was kept off the No. 1 spot in Britain by the album *Robson & Jerome*.

The tracks were: Disc One: 'Free As A Bird'. 'We Were Four Guys (an excerpt from a interview with John Lennon)', 'That'll Be The Day', In Spite Of All The Danger', 'Sometimes I'd Borrow (reminiscences from Paul)', 'Hallelujah, I Love Her So', 'You'll Be Mine', 'Cayenne', 'First Of All (Paul discussing My Bonnie)', 'My Bonnie', 'Ain't She Sweet', 'Cry For A Shadow', 'Brian Was A Beautiful Guy (John discussing their late manager)', 'I Secured Them (short speech by Brian Epstein)', 'Searchin'', 'Three Cool Cats', 'The Sheik Of Araby', 'Like Dreamers Do', 'Hello Little Girl', 'Well, The Recording Test (another speech track)', 'Besame Mucho', 'Love Me

Do', 'How Do You Do It', 'Please Please Me', 'One After 909', 'Lend Me Your Comb', 'I'll Get You', 'We Were Performers (another John Lennon short speech)', 'I Saw Her Standing There', ' From Me To You', 'Money (That's What I Want)', 'You Really Got A Hold On Me', 'Roll Over Beethoven'.

Disc Two: 'She Loves You', 'Till There Was You', 'Twist And Shout', 'This Boy', 'I Want To Hold Your Hand', 'Boys, What I Was Thinking (comedian Ernie Wise)', 'Moonlight Bay', 'Can't Buy Me Love', 'All My Loving', 'You Can't Do That', 'And I Love Her', 'A Hard Day's Night', 'I Wanna Be Your Man', 'Long Tall Sally', 'Boys', 'Shout', 'I'll Be Back', 'You Know What To Do', 'No Reply', 'Mr Moonlight', 'Leave My Kitten Alone', 'No Reply', ' Eight Days A Week', 'Kansas City/Hey Hey Hey'.

Beatles Anthology, The, Volume 2

The 45-track two-CD release was issued simultaneously around the world on Monday, 18 March 1996. It covered the years 1965–8. The Anthology 2 immediately topped both the American and British charts, achieving for the Beatles their seventeenth American No. 1 album.

The tracks were: Disc One: 'Real Love', 'Yes It Is', 'I'm Down', 'You've Got To Hide Your Love Away', 'If You've Got Trouble', 'That Means A Lot', 'Yesterday', 'It's Only Love', 'I Feel Fine', 'Ticket To Ride', 'Yesterday [different version]', 'Help!', 'Everybody's Trying To Be My Baby', 'Norwegian Wood (This Bird Has Flown)', 'I'm Looking Through You', '12-Bar Original', 'Tomorrow Never Knows', 'Got To Get You Into My Life', 'And Your Bird Can Sing', 'Taxman', 'Eleanor Rigby', 'I'm Only Sleeping', 'Rock And Roll Music', 'She's A Woman'. Disc Two: 'Strawberry Fields Forever', 'Penny Lane', 'A Day In The Life', 'Good Morning, Good Morning', 'Only A Northern Song', 'Being For The Benefit Of Mr Kite', 'Lucy In The Sky With Diamonds', 'Within You, Without You', 'Sgt Pepper's Lonely Hearts Club Band (Reprise)', 'You Know My Name (Look Up The Number)', 'I Am The Walrus', 'The Fool On The Hill', 'Hello, Goodbye', 'Lady Madonna', 'Across The Universe'.

Beatles Anthology, The, Volume 3

The two-CD set was issued simultaneously around the world on Monday, 21 October 1996 on Apple 7243 83445127. In America it entered the charts at No. 1, becoming their third consecutive American chart topper that year. Another record was created when it became the Beatles' eighteenth US chart-topper. In Britain it reached No. 2, being kept off the top spot by the Boyzone album *A Different Beat*.

However, there was no single issued to promote it, although there were rumours that the Threatles had discussed working on another John Lennon track 'Grow Old With Me' to issue as a single to tie in with the final *Anthology* CDs. However, it's suspected that because the other two *Anthology* singles releases, 'Real Love' and 'Free As A Bird', disappointed by not topping the charts, they decided not to issue another single.

This release basically covered the years 1968–70.

The tracks were: Disc One: 'A Beginning' (a short George Martin instrumental piece intended as a preface to Ringo's 'Don't Pass Me By')', 'Happiness Is A Warm Gun', 'Helter Skelter', 'Mean Mr Mustard', 'Polythene Pam', 'Glass Onion', 'Junk', 'Piggies', 'Honey Pie', 'Don't Pass Me By', 'Ob-La-Di, Ob-La-Da', 'Good Night', 'Cry Baby Cry', 'Blackbird', 'Sexy Sadie', 'While My Guitar Gently Weeps', 'Hey Jude', 'Not Guilty', 'Mother Nature's Son', 'Glass Onion', 'Rocky Raccoon', 'What's The New, Mary Jane', 'Step Inside Love', 'Los Paranoias', 'I'm So Tired', 'I Will', 'Why Don't We Do It In The Road', 'Julia'.

Disc Two: 'I've Got A Feeling', 'She Came In Through The Bathroom Window', 'Dig A Pony', 'Two Of Us', 'For You Blue', 'Teddy Boy', 'Medley: Rip It Up/Shake, Rattle & Roll/Blue Suede Shoes', 'The Long And Winding Road', 'Oh! Darling', 'All Things Must Pass', 'Mailman, Bring Me No More Blues', 'Get Back', 'Old Brown Shoe', 'Octopus's Garden', 'Maxwell's Silver Hammer', 'Something', 'Come Together', 'Come And Get It', 'Ain't She Sweet', 'Because', 'Let It Be', 'I Me Mine', 'The End'.

Beatles, The, 1962–1966 (The Red Album)

Released on Parlophone BEACD 2511 in the UK on Monday, 20 September 1993 and in America on Tuesday, 5 October. It was one of two double albums of 'greatest hits' issued by EMI on CD despite the reluctance of the Beatles to sanction them. Apple did, however, insist that they be produced as two double CDs, which caused a degree of controversy due to the fact that the total number of tracks could have fitted happily on to two CDs and would have cost the fans half the price. In fact, the two CDs on the Red Album lasted for a total of only 65 minutes, which could well have been included on a single CD.

It contained five tracks in stereo which appeared on CD for the first time – 'All My Loving', 'Can't Buy Me Love', 'And I Love Her', 'A Hard Day's Night' and 'Eight Days A Week'.

Beatles, The, 1967–1970 (The Blue Album)

EMI's second double CD release of the Beatles' 'greatest hits' issued on Monday, 20 September 1993 on Parlophone BEACD 2512.

Beatles At Shea Stadium, The

A documentary of the concert, also known as 'Live at Shea Stadium'. This one-hour TV special was filmed at Shea Stadium in Flushing, New York, on 15 August 1965, when the Beatles appeared before an audience of 55,600 fans.

There were lots of behind-the-scenes incidents in the film: George chatting with Brian Epstein; images of the four preparing for their entrance; shots of some of the other bands, such as Sounds Incorporated, performing; Brian Epstein proudly watching from the wings, with introductions by Ed Sullivan and Murray the K.

The group performed: 'I'm Down', 'Twist And Shout', 'I Feel Fine', 'Dizzy Miss Lizzie', 'Ticket To Ride', 'Act Naturally', 'Can't Buy Me Love', 'Baby's In Black' and 'A Hard Day's Night'.

The show was first screened in Britain on BBC TV on 1 March 1966, and in America on 10 January 1967.

Beatles At The Hollywood Bowl, The

The Beatles concerts at the Hollywood Bowl were both recorded by Capitol Records and produced by Voyle Gilmore. The engineer on the 1964 concert was Hugh Davies, and Pete Abbott engineered the concert the following year.

It was decided that the tapes were not of sufficiently high standard to release. Over twelve years later Capitol asked George Martin to use the latest technical advances to enhance the original tapes and, together with engineer Geoff Emerick, he succeeded.

The Beatles At The Hollywood Bowl was issued in Britain on EMTV 4 on 6 May 1977 and reached No. 1; Capitol issued it on SMAS 11638 on 4 May 1977 and the album reached No. 2.

The tracks were: Side One: 'Twist And Shout', 'She's A Woman', 'Dizzy Miss Lizzy', 'Ticket To Ride', 'Can't Buy Me Love', 'Things We Said Today', 'Roll Over Beethoven'. Side Two: 'Boys', 'A Hard Day's Night', 'Help!', 'All My Loving', 'She Loves You', 'Long Tall Sally'.

Beatles Ballads – The 20 Original Tracks

An EMI compilation issued on PCS 7214 on 20 October 1980. This first Beatles album of the eighties was also the first twenty-track album of Beatles music, although ten of the tracks had already been contained on a previous compilation, *Love Songs*. The album was released without promotion or advertising and initially didn't warrant enough sales to enter the charts. Then came the tragic death of John Lennon and sales increased, with the result that it reached No. 21 in the *New Musical Express* charts.

The cover featured a painting by John Patrick Byrne which had previously been featured in the book *The Beatles Illustrated Lyrics*. In a style not unlike that of the French primitive painter Henri Rousseau, it depicted the Beatles in a garden surrounded by animals.

The tracks on the album were Side One: 'Yesterday', 'Norwegian Wood (This Bird Has Flown)', 'Do You Want To Know A Secret?', 'For No One', 'Michelle', 'Nowhere Man', 'You've Got To Hide Your Love Away', 'Across The Universe', 'All My Loving', 'Hey Jude'. Side Two: 'Something', 'The Fool On The Hill', 'Till There Was You', 'The Long And Winding Road', 'Here Comes The Sun', 'Blackbird', 'And I Love Her', 'She's Leaving Home', 'Here, There And Everywhere', 'Let It Be'.

Beatles Box, The

A boxed set of eight Beatles albums which first became available via World Records, the mail-order arm of EMI Records in December 1980 on SM 701–SM 708. Although packaged for the UK market only, import copies found their way to various record stores in America the following year.

The albums comprised variations of songs which were different from the original releases and each album had a completely new sleeve design by Frank Watkin. Sleeve notes were compiled by Hugh Marshall and the selection of 125 tracks in chronological order was compiled by Simon Sinclair.

The set comprised:

Album One, Side One: 'Love Me Do', 'P.S. I Love You', 'I Saw Her Standing There', 'Please Please Me', 'Misery', 'Do You Want To Know A Secret?', 'A Taste Of Honey', 'Twist And Shout'. Side Two: 'From Me To You', 'Thank You Girl', 'She Loves You', 'It Won't Be Long', 'Please Mr Postman', 'All My Loving', 'Roll Over Beethoven', 'Money (That's What I Want)'.

Album Two, Side One: 'I Want To Hold Your Hand', 'This Boy', 'Can't Buy Me Love', 'You Can't Do That', 'A Hard Day's Night', 'I Should Have Known Better', 'If I Fell', 'And I Love Her'. Side Two: 'Things We Said Today', 'I'll Be Back', 'Long Tall Sally', 'I Call Your Name', 'Matchbox', 'Slow Down', 'She's A Woman', 'I Feel Fine'.

Album Three, Side One: 'Eight Days A Week', 'No Reply', 'I'm A Loser', 'I'll Follow The Sun', 'Mr Moonlight', 'Every Little Thing', 'I Don't Want To Spoil The Party', 'Kansas City/Hey Hey Hey'. Side Two: 'Ticket To Ride', 'I'm Down', 'Help!', 'The Night Before', 'You've Got To Hide Your Love Away', 'I Need You', 'Another Girl', 'You're Going To Lose That Girl'.

Album Four, Side One: 'Yesterday', 'Act Naturally', 'Tell Me What You See', 'It's Only Love', 'You Like Me Too Much', 'I've Just Seen A Face', 'Day Tripper', 'We Can Work It Out'. Side Two: 'Michelle', 'Drive My Car', 'Norwegian Wood (This Bird Has Flown)', 'You Won't See Me', 'Nowhere Man', 'Girl', 'I'm Looking Through You', 'In My Life'.

Album Five, Side One: 'Paperback Writer', 'Rain', 'Here, There And Everywhere', 'Taxman', 'I'm Only Sleeping', 'Good Day Sunshine', 'Yellow Submarine'. Side Two: 'Eleanor Rigby', 'And Your Bird Can Sing', 'For No One', 'Dr Robert', 'Got To Get You Into My Life', 'Penny Lane', 'Strawberry Fields Forever'.

Album Six, Side One: 'Sgt Pepper's Lonely Hearts Club Band', 'With A Little Help From My Friends', 'Lucy In The Sky With Diamonds', 'Fixing A Hole', 'She's Leaving Home', 'Being For The Benefit Of Mr Kite', 'A Day In The Life'. Side Two: 'When I'm Sixty-four', 'Lovely Rita', 'All You Need Is Love', 'Baby You're A Rich Man', 'Magical Mystery Tour', 'Your Mother Should Know', 'The Fool On The Hill', 'I Am The Walrus'.

Album Seven, Side One: 'Hello Goodbye', 'Lady Madonna', 'Hey Jude', 'Revolution', 'Back In The USSR', 'Ob-La-Di Ob-La-Da', 'While My Guitar Gently Weeps'. Side Two: 'The Continuing Story of Bungalow Bill', 'Happiness Is A Warm Gun', 'Martha My Dear', 'I'm So Tired', 'Piggies', 'Don't Pass Me By', 'Julia', 'All Together Now'.

Album Eight, Side One: 'Get Back', 'Don't Let Me Down', 'The Ballad Of John And Yoko', 'Across The Universe', 'For You Blue', 'Two Of Us', 'The Long And Winding Road', 'Let It Be'. Side Two: 'Come Together', 'Something', 'Maxwell's Silver Hammer', 'Octopus's Garden', 'Here Comes The Sun', 'Because', 'Golden Slumbers', 'Golden Slumbers/Carry That Weight', 'The End', 'Her Majesty'.

Beatles Cartoon Series, The

King Features, the major American agency for cartoon strips in newspapers and animated shorts for television, obtained the rights to make a series of cartoon films featuring the Beatles and their songs.

Al Brodax, who later became involved in the Beatles' animated feature film *Yellow Submarine*, was the executive producer of the series.

The majority of the shorts were animated abroad by Canawest of Vancouver, Canada, and the Artransa Studio in Sydney, Australia. Twenty-six were also commissioned from a British company, George Dunning's TV Cartoons Studio.

Paul Frees, an American 'voice-over' professional, who had worked on 'voices' for several Hollywood firms, was contracted to provide the voices of John Lennon and George Harrison. The English actor who dubbed the voices of Paul McCartney and Ringo Starr preferred to remain anonymous, although it was later suggested that Lance Percival provided the voice-overs. The voices were quite unlike those of the Beatles themselves and no attempt was made to mimic a 'Scouse' accent as it was considered to be too difficult for American youngsters to understand.

The basic idea of the series was that the Beatles would always be harassed by a group of fans, the novelty being that the fans could materialise in all manner of inventive disguises.

The 67-episode series was first screened on ABC TV in the US on 25 September 1965. The weekly half-hour series was screened by ABC TV each Saturday from 10.30–11.00 a.m. until 7 September 1969. It has since appeared in syndication in the latter part of the seventies. The series was shown in England on Granada Television, but not networked.

The series was stylistically typical of American children's cartoons and owed nothing to either the Beatles' real personalities or their lives, though an attempt was made to capture their visual appearance.

There were no Liverpool-based adventures – even the 'Penny Lane' episode was set in London. The group became involved in adventures with various characters, including vampires, leprechauns, mad scientists and bullfighters in locations ranging from Africa, Mexico and Hawaii to Spain, London and Hollywood. Each episode used a title from a well-known Beatles recording and they ranged from 'A Hard Day's Night' to 'You've Really Got A Hold On Me'.

Beatles Christmas Records, The

Beatles press officer Tony Barrow first came up with the idea of a special Beatles recorded message for their fans in 1963. He was a bit concerned that due to the swelling membership of the official fan club, there had been inevitable delays in the processing of the large number of membership applications and Barrow considered a bonus gift would act as a sweetener. The Beatles agreed and promptly insisted that he write the script of their personal message. It was decided to issue a 33⅓ rpm flexidisc, manufactured by Lyntone Recordings.

The record was posted out with the fan club's second national newsletter, dated Christmas 1963, part of which read:

Dear Beatle People,

    With this Newsletter comes your own special Christmas gift from John, Paul, George and Ringo – a copy of THE BEATLES' CHRISTMAS RECORD. This record is exclusive to our Club and will not be made available elsewhere – it has exceptional souvenir value too because only 25,000 copies of the disc have been pressed. Just enough to supply every existing Club member with a free copy in time for Christmas. We hope you enjoy it and that you'll be able to make your non-member friends just a little bit jealous by playing it to them over the holiday!

The recording had been made at Studio Two in Abbey Road on 17 October, following the sessions for 'I Want To Hold Your Hand' and 'This Boy'. George Martin produced and the single-sided flexi-disc lasted for five minutes and ten seconds, issued on LYN 492 on 6 December 1963.

    The order of tracks was: 'Good King Wenceslas', 'John Talking', 'Paul Talking', 'Good King Wenceslas, Ringo', 'George Talking', 'Good King Wenceslas, George' and 'Rudolph The Red Nosed Ringo'.

    The Christmas record proved to be such a success that it was decided to make it an annual gift to fan club members and the second disc was recorded with George Martin between 26–28 October 1964 at Studio Two in Abbey Road. Membership had now increased to a massive 65,000 and the flexidisc, called 'Another Beatles Christmas Record', was issued on LYN 757 on 18 December 1964. It was four minutes and five seconds long and comprised: 'Jingle Bells', 'Paul Talking', 'John Talking', 'George Talking', 'Ringo Talking', 'Can You Wash Your Father's Shirts?' and 'Happy Christmas'.

    'The Beatles Third Christmas Record' was recorded in October 1965 at Abbey Road's Studio Two with George Martin after they'd completed some *Rubber Soul* recordings. The cover was a photograph which Roger Whitaker had taken at Granada Studios in Manchester during the filming of 'The Music Of Lennon & McCartney' special. It was issued on 17 December 1965, on LYN 948. It was six minutes and twenty-six seconds long and comprised: 'Yesterday', sung out of tune; 'All Talking'; 'Happy Christmas', John; 'Auld Lang Syne'; 'All Talking'; 'Same Old Song', John; 'All Talking'; 'Auld Lang Syne'; and 'All Talking'.

    The 1966 fan club release was a more structured production because, possibly on a suggestion by Paul, it was decided to make it into a mini-pantomime and was called 'The Beatles Fourth

Christmas Record – Pantomime: Everywhere It's Christmas'. George Martin produced, as usual, but this year the disc was recorded in the basement studios of Dick James Music at Dick James House, 71/75 New Oxford Street, London WC1, on Friday, 25 November 1966. It was also the Beatles' first double-sided Christmas record. It was issued on LYN 1145 on 16 December 1966, was six minutes and thirty-eight seconds long and comprised, A Side: 'Everywhere It's Christmas', all singing; 'Orowanyna', intro by Paul, all singing; 'A Rare Cheese', intro by Ringo; George and John; 'The Feast', all; 'The Loyal Toast', intro by George; 'Toast', Ringo. B Side: 'Podgy The Bear & Jasper', intro by Paul; 'Podgy' by John; 'Jasper' by George; 'Felpin Mansions' with John as the Count and Ringo as the Butler; 'Please Don't Bring Your Banjo Back', Paul, all singing; 'Everywhere It's Christmas', all singing.

Their next flexi, 'The Beatles Fifth Christmas Record – Christmas Time (Is Here Again)', was another pantomime. It was recorded on Tuesday, 28 November 1967 at EMI's Studio Two and was the last time George Martin presided over the recordings. It was also the last time the Beatles recorded a Christmas message together. The applause used was recorded on location in Dublin. The front cover was designed by John and Ringo and there was a back-cover painting by Julian Lennon. The Beatles wrote a song specially for the disc, 'Christmas Time (Is Here Again)', which was attributed to Lennon/McCartney/Harrison/Starr. The group also brought in a guest artist, Victor Spinetti. The single-sided flexidisc was issued on LYN 1369 on 15 December 1967. It was six minutes and nine seconds long and the tracks were: 'Christmas Time (Is Here Again)', intro by John, with all singing; 'The Boys Arrive At BBC House', Victor Spinetti as the BBC Wise One; 'An Audition', John; 'Tap Dancing', Ringo and Victor Spinetti; 'Are you 13 Amp', Mal Evans; 'Get One Of Those For Your Trousers', John; 'Sir Gerald', Paul; 'Sir Gerald', John; 'Christmas Time (Is Here Again), Onto The Next Round And Introduction', by George; 'Plenty Of Jam Jars'; 'Quiz Show', John as Quizmaster; 'Prizewinner', George; 'Get One Of Those For Your Trousers'; 'Theatre Hour', Ringo; 'Christmas Time (Is Here Again)'; 'They'd Like To Thank You . . .', George Martin and all; 'When Christmas Time Is O'er', George Martin on organ, John as Scottish Poet.

The next release, 'The Beatles Sixth Christmas Record', was recorded separately in November 1968. John and Paul were recorded at their London homes and Ringo in Surrey. George recorded his excerpt in America with Mal Evans and Tiny Tim and some of the musical links were made during rehearsals for *The Beatles* white album at George's home in Esher. Disc jockey Kenny

Everett became involved in the recording and editing of the flexi, on which each of the four gave separate Christmas greetings. The disc was issued on LYN 1743/1744 on 20 December 1968. It was another double-sided flexi, lasting a total of seven minutes and fifty-five seconds. The track listings were: A Side: 'Ob-La-Di', Ringo; 'Happy Christmas, Happy New Year', Paul; 'Helter Skelter'; 'Yok And Jono', a poem by John; 'George from America', with Mal Evans. B Side: 'Ringo Starr'; introduction by Ringo Starr; 'Happy Christmas, Happy New Year', Paul; 'Once Upon A Pool Table', poem by John; 'George and Tiny Tim'; 'Nowhere Man', Tiny Tim; Ending.

The final release, 'The Beatles Seventh Christmas Record', was recorded separately during the autumn of 1969 with John and Yoko recording their pieces at Tittenhurst Park, Ringo from his home in Surrey, Paul from his Cavendish Avenue house and George at Apple in Savile Row.

Once again, Kenny Everett was in charge of producing the record and he receives credit under his real name of Maurice Cole.

Ringo took the photograph used on the cover of the record and the back cover sported a drawing by Ringo's son, Zak. The flexidisc was issued on LYN 1970/1 on 19 December 1969. The double-sided record lasted seven minutes and forty seconds. The track listings were, A Side: 'Happy Christmas', Ringo; 'John and Yoko Talking'; 'Wonderful Christmas', George; 'Ringo Talking'; 'John and Yoko Talking'; 'This Is To Wish You All A Merry, Merry Christmas', Paul; 'Paul Talking'; 'This Is To Wish You A Merry, Merry Christmas', reprise. B Side: 'John and Yoko Talking'; 'Happy Christmas', John and Yoko; 'Happy Christmas'/'Magic Christian', Ringo; 'Ringo Talking'; 'John and Yoko Talking'.

As there was no specially recorded Christmas disc the following year, the fan club decided to issue a twelve-inch album containing all seven previous Christmas messages. This was issued on Apple LYN 2154 on 18 December 1970 under the title *From Them To You – The Beatles Christmas Record 1970*.

The album was also issued in America. As the flexidiscs hadn't been previously released there, the American album was issued with a different sleeve than the British one, which had pictures of all the previous covers of the Christmas flexis. The album was issued in America on Apple SBC 100 on 18 December 1970, and was simply called *The Beatles Christmas Album*.

Beatles Collection, The

To capitalise on the Christmas market, EMI decided to issue a special de luxe limited edition boxed set of Beatles albums. The package was called *The Beatles Collection* and it was issued on Parlophone/Apple BC 13 on 2 December 1978.

A set of twelve British Beatles albums, previously released between the years 1962 and 1970 was issued in a dark blue box which had the title and individual signature of the Beatles printed in gold on the front. The package also contained a bonus album called *Rarities*, which had seventeen tracks considered 'rare', which were a combination of 'B' sides of records, foreign releases and EP tracks. It was announced that the *Rarities* album would only be available with the boxed set and would not be issued separately – however, this was not to be the case.

The albums contained in the boxed set were; *Please Please Me, With The Beatles, A Hard Day's Night, Beatles For Sale, Help!, Rubber Soul, Sgt Pepper's Lonely Hearts Club Band, The Beatles, Yellow Submarine, Abbey Road, Let It Be* and *Rarities*. This was not actually a 'complete' collection of all recordings between 1962–1970 as a number of albums such as *A Collection of Beatles Oldies (But Goldies), Magical Mystery Tour, Hey Jude* and *The Beatles At the Hollywood Bowl* were excluded.

The Beatles Collection was also issued in America on Capitol BC 14 on 1 December 1978. The American set, however, was to become much more of a collector's item because Capitol only produced 3,000 sets – and they were all numbered. It was said that 3,050 sets had actually been pressed with the first 50 sets going to Capitol executives and prominent record industry figures. The American *Rarities* album was also slightly different from the British one. With the catalogue number Capitol SPRO 8969, *Rarities* substituted the English versions of 'She Loves You' and 'I Want To Hold Your Hand' for the German language versions which were on the British release. The set was of obvious interest to American collectors as it comprised the original British versions of the albums, which differed from the individual Capitol album releases which generally included fewer tracks.

Beatles Come To Town, The

An eight-minute film of the Beatles, screened in British cinemas during the week commencing 22 December 1963 as an item of Pathe News.

This was a weekly cinema newsreel which ran for decades, but finally succumbed to the competition from television news in the mid-sixties.

The new team filmed the Beatles performing three numbers at the Apollo Theatre, Ardwick, Manchester on 20 November 1963. The newsreel showed them performing two of the numbers, 'She Loves You' and 'Twist And Shout', amid much audience hysteria.

Pathe shot the film in both black and white and colour and the performance was also used in the film *Pop Gear* in 1965.

Beatles EPs Collection, The

After EMI had released collections of Beatles singles and albums, they decided to release the EP collection, presented in a matching box to that of *The Beatles Collection* of albums, with the title and the Beatles' autographs in gold on the cover of the box.

The collection comprised the original twelve British Beatles EPs, together with the *Magical Mystery Tour* double EP and a special bonus EP of four songs, previously unavailable in stereo.

This bonus EP was simply called *The Beatles* and it featured the same picture sleeve as that used on the cover of the 'Penny Lane' single, issued in 1967. The tracks were: 'The Inner Light', 'Baby You're A Rich Man', 'She's A Woman' and 'This Boy'.

The Beatles EPs Collection was issued on Parlophone BEP 14 on 7 December 1971, once again aimed at the Christmas market and comprised: *The Beatles' Hits, Twist And Shout, The Beatles No. 1, All My Loving, Long Tall Sally, Extracts From The Film A Hard Day's Night, Extracts From The Album A Hard Day's Night, Beatles For Sale, Beatles For Sale No. 2, The Beatles' Million Sellers, Yesterday, Nowhere Man, Magical Mystery Tour* and *The Beatles*.

Beatles For Sale (Album)

Their fourth album release, which took them two and a half months to record. It was issued in Britain on Parlophone PCS 3062 on 4 December 1964 where it topped the charts immediately on release, simultaneously entering the Top 30 singles charts at No. 28. Tracks were: Side One: 'No Reply', 'I'm A Loser', 'Baby's In Black', 'Rock And Roll Music', 'I'll Follow The Sun', 'Mr. Moonlight', 'Kansas City/Hey! Hey! Hey!', Side Two: 'Eight Days A Week', 'Words Of Love', 'Honey Don't', 'Every Little Thing', 'I Don't Want To Spoil The Party', 'What You're Doing', 'Everybody's Trying To Be My Baby'.

It featured a cover by Robert Freeman and sleeve notes written by Derek Taylor. There have been numerous comments regarding the expressions of the four on the cover, remarking that the pace of the hectic lifestyle was reflected in their strained and weary faces.

Only eight of the fourteen tracks were compiled by the Beatles, probably due to the pressure of constant touring. The influence of Bob Dylan can be detected in the writing of some of the numbers, and though the American wordsmith had influenced both Paul and John, it was John, in particular, who was most excited by Dylan's lyrics.

There was an advance order for 750,000, the highest advance for an album ever recorded in Britain. Sales in the UK were to exceed one million

The American version of the album was titled *Beatles '65*.

Beatles For Sale (EP)

An EP with the same title as that of their most recent album release. Three of the four titles had once been considered as possible singles. The EP was issued on Parlophone GEP 8931 on 6 April 1965 and contained the tracks: 'No Reply', 'I'm A Loser', 'Rock And Roll Music' and 'Eight Days A Week'. The cover of the EP was the same Bob Freeman shot used on the cover of the album.

Beatles For Sale (No. 2)

The second collection of tracks from the *Beatles for Sale* album to be issued on an EP in Britain. This was the Beatles' ninth EP release in the UK and was issued on Parlophone GEP 8938 on 4 June 1965. The tracks were: 'I'll Follow The Sun', 'Baby's In Black', 'Words Of Love' and 'I Don't Want To Spoil The Party'.

Beatles' Hits, The

The second Beatles EP to be issued by Parlophone. *The Beatles' Hits* featured a front cover by Angus McBean and, as with the first EP, sleeve notes by Beatles Press Officer Tony Barrow. It was issued on Parlophone GEP 8882 on 6 September 1963 and reached the position of No. 17 in the British charts. The tracks were the first three Beatles singles, together with one former 'B' side. They were: 'From Me To You', 'Thank You Girl', 'Please Please Me' and 'Love Me Do'.

Beatles Invite You To Take A Ticket To Ride, The

A Bank Holiday radio special which took place on Monday, 7 June 1965, between 10.00 a.m. and 12.00 noon. Produced by Keith Bateson and presented by Denny Piercey, it had been recorded on 26 May at the Piccadilly Theatre studios in London.

All previous Bank Holiday specials had been called 'From Us To You', but this title had been dropped. The BBC radio programme was the very last appearance by the Beatles in which they performed songs on the radio. Times were changing with the appearance of the pirate ship Radio Caroline, to be followed by other ships such as Radio London which brought competition. The system of groups performing live or recording specially for radio had arisen because of restrictions on the number of records which could be played. A wind of change was blowing through the world of British radio which was to provide a wider range and much wider choice for listeners.

On this, their final BBC radio recording, they performed 'Everybody's Trying To Be My Baby', 'I'm A Loser', 'Honey Don't', 'She's A Woman', 'Ticket To Ride', 'The Night Before' and 'Dizzy Miss Lizzy'. Their special guests were the Hollies and the Ivy League. The Ivy League comprised John Carter on vocals and bass guitar, Ken Lewis on vocals and keyboards and Perry Ford on vocals, keyboards and alto. Under their previous name of Carter-Lewis & The Southerners, they had been special guests on two of the 'Pop Go The Beatles' programmes.

Beatles Live! The, At The Star Club In Hamburg, Germany, 1962

When Adrian Barber left The Big Three to become stage manager at the Star Club in Hamburg, he developed a completely new sound system for the club. Initially, testing the sound, he decided to record the various bands who performed there. Adrian used a tape recorder and strapped a mike to the centre mike stand on stage – there were three stage mikes at the time.

Over a period of time he recorded numerous bands and some of the recordings, including ones of Jerry Lee Lewis and Cliff Bennett & the Rebel Rousers, were released in Hamburg on the Hanseatic label.

In December 1962 he recorded the Beatles. One of the Liverpool bands appearing at the club at the time were Kingsize Taylor & The Dominoes and leader Ted Taylor asked Adrian if he could have the tapes. Adrian gave them to him and they were forgotten about for ten years, until there was a Mersey Beat revival show in Liverpool promoted by Allan Williams and Ted Taylor was on the bill. He mentioned the tapes to Williams, who eagerly told him they could make a fortune from them. Taylor remembered he'd given them to a local recording engineer years previously and they set off to find him. Fortunately, they were able to obtain the tapes.

Williams contacted Bill Harry in London and asked him if he could sell them to a record company. Harry took a number of record executives on trips to Taylor's butcher shop in Southport, but they weren't enthusiastic. One main problem was that 'bootleg' records were now outlawed in Britain by an act of Parliament and since EMI had signed the group at the time of the recordings, the tapes would be illegal. Williams insisted that the recordings had taken place before they'd signed with EMI, but Harry pointed out to him that Ringo was on drums and therefore the tapes were recorded in December 1962 when the EMI contract had been in force for three months. Williams suggested that they concoct a story that it was an earlier gig when Pete Best was a member, that at the time of the recordings he was ill and replaced by Ringo. Harry rejected this suggestion.

Most record companies were concerned about the legal can of worms which could be opened by such a release. However, one entrepreneur introduced to Williams by Harry did arrange a deal with a major record company who were willing to spend a great deal of money enhancing the quality of the tapes and were prepared to advertise the album on television. Their lawyers had concluded that they might be able to fight off an injunction by a defence based on the recordings being of historical interest. This deal would probably have made Williams and Taylor wealthy men.

They suddenly announced they'd done a deal with Paul Murphy of Buk Records. Murphy was a former singer from Liverpool who had worked as a recording manager for Polydor in Hamburg. The tapes were cleaned and enhanced and initially issued in Germany on the Bellaphon label on 8 April 1977 as a double album. The Beatles' lawyers attempted to prevent the release in Britain, but the judge concluded that they were of historic interest – the lawyers did not point out to him that the recent law in Parliament relating to bootlegs made release of the records illegal. These recordings have been released throughout the world on a number of occasions and a great deal of money has been made – but certainly not by Williams and Taylor. Adrian Barber, who made the original recordings in the first place, has never received a cent.

The British release on Lingasong LNL 1 on 25 May 1977 reached No. 27 in the *New Musical Express* album chart. It was issued in America on Atlantic/Lingasong LS-2-7001 on 13 June 1977. It reached No. 111 in *Billboard*, No. 183 in *Cash Box* and No. 165 in *Record World*. It has since been issued on a variety of different labels every few years.

The tracks on the album are: 'I Saw Her Standing There', 'Roll Over Beethoven', 'Hippy Hippy Shake', 'Sweet Little Sixteen', 'Lend Me Your Comb', 'Your Feet's Too Big', 'Twist And Shout', 'Mr Moonlight', 'A Taste Of Honey', 'Besame Mucho', 'Reminiscing', 'Kansas City/Hey Hey Hey', 'Nothin' Shakin' (But The Leaves On The Trees)', 'To Know Her Is To Love Her', 'Little Queenie', 'Falling In Love Again', 'Ask Me Why', 'Be-Bop-A-Lula', 'Hallelujah, I Love Her So', 'Red Sails In The Sunset', 'Everybody's Trying To Be My Baby', 'Matchbox', 'I'm Talking About You', 'Shimmy Shimmy', 'Long Tall Sally' and 'I Remember You'.

The original tapes and the albums included dialogue between the numbers when the Beatles made announcements and the audience responded. When Paul announced 'a request for the Scottish lady', he was referring to Scots singer Isabelle Bond, who was appearing at the Top Ten Club at the time and whose favourite number performed by the Beatles was 'A Taste Of Honey'. Horst Fascher can also be heard making an introduction and the mention of Bettina refers to Bettina Derlin, the 23-stone Star Club Barfrau who was one of Lennon's many German girlfriends.

Beatles' Million Sellers, The

At the time of the Beatles' tenth British EP release, the group had achieved a total of five million-selling singles and EMI decided to include four of them on this EP and issue it in time to capitalise on the Christmas market.

It was issued on Parlophone GEP 8946 on 6 December 1965 and the tracks were: 'She Loves You', 'I Want To Hold Your Hand', 'Can't Buy Me Love' and 'I Feel Fine'.

Beatles' Movie Medley, The

In 1981 a medley of Beatles songs by a number of session musicians from Holland was issued as a single called 'Stars On 45'. It topped the American charts and reached No. 2 in the British charts in 1981.

As a result, Capitol Records in the US decided to issue something similar – a medley of songs by the Beatles themselves. John Palladino edited together seven tracks and segued them together, using extracts from 'Magical Mystery Tour', 'All You Need Is Love', 'You've Got To Hide Your Love Away', 'I Should Have Known Better', 'A Hard Day's Night', 'Ticket To Ride' and 'Get Back'. Consideration was given to including a 'B' side which would feature a Beatles interview called 'Fab Four On Film' which had been recorded during the filming of *A Hard Day's Night*. This was dropped in favour of the track 'I'm Happy Just To Dance With You'.

The single was issued in America on Capitol B-5107 on 15 March 1982, but didn't fare as well as the Dutch medley and only reached No. 12 in the *Billboard* charts. EMI Records in Britain did not want to issue the single, but due to demand and the fact that imports of the American single began to trickle over, they issued it two months later on Parlophone R6055 on 24 May 1982 and the record reached the position of No. 10 in the charts.

In some way, the medley single acted as a promotional booster to *Reel Music*, an album of Beatles film tracks, issued the week following the single's release in America.

Beatles 1962–1966, The

The release of a four-album bootleg Beatles set in America called *The Beatles Alpha Omega* is said to have inspired EMI to release two double albums of Beatles material, *The Beatles 1962–1966*, and *The Beatles 1967–1970*.

The two double albums were issued on the same day in America, 2 April 1973, and in Britain on 19 April 1973. The British album was released on Parlophone PCSP 717 and reached No. 1 in the charts. The American album was released on Capitol SKBO 3403 and reached No. 3 in the charts.

In both countries the covers were the same. The front cover sported a photograph of the Beatles on the EMI House stairwell, taken at the *Please Please Me* photo session, and the reverse featured a photograph taken in the same place and position a few years later.

The tracks on the album are, Record One/Side One: 'Love Me Do', 'Please Please Me', 'From Me To You', 'She Loves You', 'I Want To Hold Your Hand', 'All My Loving', 'Can't Buy Me Love'. Record One/Side Two: 'A Hard Day's Night', 'And I Love Her', 'Eight Days A Week', 'I Feel Fine', 'Ticket To Ride', 'Yesterday'. Record Two/Side One: 'Help!', 'You've Got To Hide Your Love Away', 'We Can Work It Out', 'Day Tripper', 'Drive My Car', 'Norwegian Wood (This Bird Has Flown)'. Record Two/Side Two: 'Nowhere Man', 'Michelle', 'In My Life', 'Girl', 'Paperback Writer', 'Eleanor Rigby', 'Yellow Submarine'.

Beatles 1967–1970, The

A double album issued in Britain on Parlophone PCSP 718 on 19 April 1973 where it reached No. 1 in the charts for one week. It was issued in America on Capitol SKBO 3404 on 2 April 1973 where it was No. 1 for one week.

The sleeves on the British and American releases were identical: a photograph of the Beatles looking down from a stairwell at EMI House in a similar style to the shot on the cover of the *Please Please Me* album, but taken a few years later.

The album was issued simultaneously with *The Beatles 1962–1966* and the cover of that double album is featured on the reverse side of this.

The tracks on the album are, Record One/Side One: 'Strawberry Fields Forever', 'Sgt Pepper's Lonely Hearts Club Band', 'With A Little Help From My Friends', 'Lucy In The Sky With Diamonds', 'A Day In The Life', 'All You Need Is Love'. Record One/Side Two: 'I Am The Walrus', 'Hello Goodbye', 'The Fool On The Hill',

'Magical Mystery Tour', 'Lady Madonna', 'Hey Jude', 'Revolution'. Record Two/Side One: 'Back In The USSR', 'While My Guitar Gently Weeps', 'Ob-La-Di Ob-La-Da', 'Get Back', 'Don't Let Me Down', 'The Ballad Of John And Yoko', 'Old Brown Shoe'. Record Two/Side Two: 'Here Comes The Sun', 'Come Together', 'Something', 'Octopus's Garden', 'Let It Be', 'Across The Universe', 'The Long And Winding Road'.

Beatles '65

An American album issued on Capitol ST 2228 on 15 December 1964.

It is the US version of the *Beatles For Sale* album and includes eight of the tracks from the British LP, plus 'I'll Be Back', a track from the British album *A Hard Day's Night*, and two tracks from a single release, 'I Feel Fine' and 'She's A Woman'.

Beatles '65 sold over three million copies within six weeks and was the fastest-selling American album of the year, rushing into the No. 1 spot less than ten days after its release.

The tracks on the album are, Side One: 'No Reply', 'I'm A Loser', 'Baby's In Black', 'Rock And Roll Music', 'I'll Follow The Sun', 'Mr Moonlight'. Side Two: 'Honey Don't', 'I'll Be Back', 'She's A Woman', 'I Feel Fine', 'Everybody's Trying To Be My Baby'.

Beatles (No. 1), The

The third Beatles EP which only reached the No. 24 position in the charts, although it entered the charts on four different occasions.

The EP was issued on Parlophone GEP 8883 on 1 November 1963 and contained four tracks from the *Please Please Me* album, which was still No. 1 in the charts. The EP cover was the EMI stair-well shot by Angus McBean and sleeve notes were by Tony Barrow. The tracks were: 'I Saw Her Standing There', 'Misery', 'Anna (Go To Him)' and 'Chains'.

Beatles Official Fan Club

The first Beatles fan club was formed by a Liverpool fan, Bernard Boyle, in September 1961 prior to Brian Epstein managing the group and several months before an official fan club was sanctioned.

Bernard was president, Jennifer Dawes treasurers and Maureen O'Shea secretary.

In 1962 the first official club was run by Roberta 'Bobbie' Brown from her house in Buchanan Road, Wallasey. Shortly after forming the club she was aided by a friend, Frieda Kelly, and when she became engaged to be married the club was placed in Frieda's capable hands. By that time Frieda was working at NEMS and funds were provided by Brian Epstein on behalf of the Beatles.

It was the Beatles' press agent Tony Barrow who, in June 1963, proposed that the club should have a National Secretary and be run from London. The official club was now run from 13 Monmouth Street, London, while Frieda continued as its Northern Secretary, operating from Liverpool.

Barrow created a fictitious name for the head of the London office, Anne Collingham. Due to the vast amount of mail which had to be dealt with, several full-time workers were employed: Michael Crowther-Smith, Tony Catchpole, Yvonne Sainsbury, Monica Stringer and Mary Cockram.

Sean O'Mahoney agreed to an official fan club section each month in the *Beatles Book* and NEMS employees Maureen Payne and Valerie Sumpter posed for the photographs which 'identified' them as Bettina Rose and Anne Collingham.

The fan club thrived with 80,000 paid-up members in 1965, one of the largest fan clubs ever. Despite subscriptions, it was not a profitable venture and had to be subsidised throughout its existence.

Apart from the membership cards, newsletters and special offers, members of the club were given a unique treat – a series of special Beatles Christmas records, made specially for the club. This was an idea originated by Tony Barrow, which the Beatles were enthusiastic about.

In October 1966 Freda was appointed Joint National Secretary and later the London office was closed and Frieda was running the entire operation again from Liverpool, which she continued to do until the club was officially closed in March 1972.

Beatles Second Album, The

With a montage of photographs on the cover and the subtitle *Electrifying big-beat performances by England's Paul McCartney, John Lennon, George Harrison and Ringo Starr*, Capitol Records' second Beatles album was issued on Capitol ST 2080 on 10 April 1964.

The album contained the five tracks from the British *With The Beatles* album which weren't included on *Meet The Beatles*, together with four tracks from singles already released in America and two tracks from *Long Tall Sally*, the British EP, previously unreleased in America.

The album became Capitol Records' fastest-selling album ever, up to that date, with over 250,000 copies sold on the first day of release. It swiftly reached No. 1 in the charts and sold over a million copies.

The tracks were, Side One: 'Long Tall Sally', 'I Call Your Name', 'Please Mr Postman', 'I'll Get You', 'She Loves You'. Side Two: 'Roll Over Beethoven', 'Thank You Girl', 'You Really Got A Hold On Me', 'Devil In Her Heart', 'Money (That's What I Want)', 'You Can't Do That'.

On 2 May 1964 *The Beatles Second Album* was No. 1 in the chart, followed by *Meet The Beatles* at No. 2 and *Introducing The Beatles* at No. 4.

Beatles Sing For Shell, The
A film of the Beatles' performance at the opening night of their concerts at the Festival Hall, Melbourne on Monday, 15 June 1964.

The concerts were filmed by the Nine Television network and edited into a film called *The Beatles Sing For Shell*, which was televised throughout Australia.

Beatles VI
Issued on Capitol ST 2358 on 14 June 1965, *Beatles VI* contained the six tracks from *Beatles For Sale* which weren't used on the *Beatles '65* album, together with three tracks from the forthcoming British album *Help!* and two further tracks.

The tracks were, Side One: 'Kansas City'/'Hey! Hey! Hey!', 'Eight Days A Week', 'You Like Me Too Much', 'Bad Boy', 'I Don't Want To Spoil The Party', 'Words Of Love'. Side Two: 'What You're Doing', 'Yes It Is', 'Dizzy Miss Lizzy', 'Tell Me What You See', 'Every Little Thing'.

The album topped the charts in *Billboard*, *Cash Box* and *Record World*.

Beatles Story, The
A double-album issued in America on Capitol STBO 2222 on 23 November 1964 to celebrate the first anniversary of the label issuing 'I Want To Hold Your Hand'.

The album included a medley of Beatles numbers, a brief excerpt from a concert and various interviews in what was a musical biography of the group's career. It sold a million copies and reached No. 7 in the American charts. Written and narrated by John Babcock, Al Wiman and Roger Christian, the album contained interviews with all the Beatles, plus Brian Epstein and George Martin.

The tracks were, Side One: 'On Stage With The Beatles', 'How Beatlemania Began', 'Beatlemania In Action', 'Man Behind The Beatles – Brian Epstein' and 'John Lennon – Who's a Millionaire?' Side Two: 'Beatles Will Be Beatles', 'Man Behind Their Music – George Martin' and 'George Harrison'. Side Three: 'A Hard Day's

Night – Their First Movie', 'Paul McCartney', and 'Sneaky Haircuts And More About Paul'. Side Four: A live performance of 'Twist And Shout' from the 23 August 1964 performance at the Hollywood Bowl, 'The Beatles Look at Life', 'A Beatles Medley', 'Things We Said Today', 'I'm Happy Just To Dance With You', 'Little Child', 'Long Tall Sally', 'She Loves You', 'Ringo Starr' and 'Liverpool And All The World'.

Beatles Today, The
An hour-long BBC Radio One special, transmitted on 30 March 1970, which included music from the *Get Back* (before the name was changed to *Let It Be*) album sessions. George Harrison was interviewed for the programme on 11 March.

Beatles vs The Four Seasons, The
After Capitol Records had secured the rights to issue all further Beatles product in America, Vee Jay Records continued to exploit the limited material they had, using various packaging ideas. One of these was a two-album set *The Beatles vs The Four Seasons*, containing all the tracks Vee Jay had previously issued on the *Introducing The Beatles* album, together with a set of twelve numbers from a Four Seasons album. Despite its subtitle *The International Battle Of The Century*, the album failed to register in either the *Cash Box* or *Record World* charts and only reached No. 142 in *Billboard* after it was issued on Vee Jay DX-30 on 1 October 1964.

The album came with: 'Scorecards, biographies, pictures, stories of all the contestants plus: free bonus 8″ × 15″ full colour Beatles picture suitable for framing'.

The Beatles tracks were: 'I Saw Her Standing There', 'Misery', 'Anna', 'Chains', 'Boys', 'Ask Me Why', 'Please Please Me', 'Baby It's You', 'Do You Want To Know A Secret?', 'A Taste Of Honey', 'There's A Place' and 'Twist And Shout'.

The Four Seasons numbers were: 'Sherry', 'I've Cried Before', 'Marlena', 'Soon', 'Ain't That A Shame', 'Walk Like A Man', 'Connie-O', 'Big Girls Don't Cry', 'Star Maker', 'Candy Girl', 'Silver Wings' and 'Peanuts'.

The Four Seasons comprised Frankie Valli (vocals), Gerry Polci (vocals/drums), Don Ciccone (bass), Lee Shapiro (keyboards) and John Paiva (guitar).

This basic idea was heavily exploited by a series of bootleg albums in the States, several of them lampooning *The Beatles vs The Four Seasons* album cover. Among the numerous bootleg LPs in this vein were *Beatles vs Chuck Berry*, *Beatles vs Don Ho*,

Beatles vs Buddy Holly And The Isley Brothers, Beatles vs Little Richard And Larry Williams and *Beatles vs Carl Perkins*.

Beatle Talk: Red Robinson Interviews The Beatles

Interview album, issued in America by Great Northwest Music Co. on GWC 4007 on 15 November 1978.

The album contained excerpts from interviews with the Beatles taken at press conferences in Vancouver, Canada, in 1964 and Seattle in 1966, and ran for approximately 20 minutes, with narration from disc jockey Red Robinson. It failed to make the charts.

With a different cover and title, it was issued in Britain as *The Beatles Interviews* on Everest Records CBR 1008 on 25 June 1982, with the addition of further material including John Lennon's comments about 'the Beatles are bigger than Jesus' remarks.

Beat Show, The

A BBC radio programme, broadcast from Manchester. The show was presented by Gay Byrne, produced by Geoff Lawrence and featured the Northern Dance Orchestra. 'The Beat Show' was broadcast from 1.00 to 1.30 p.m. each Thursday and the Beatles made a single appearance on 4 July 1963 when they performed 'From Me To You', 'A Taste Of Honey' and 'Twist And Shout'.

Beautiful Dreamer

A song originally written by Stephen Foster at the end of the last century, but very popular in this one. A number which had been recorded over the years by many major artists, including Al Jolson and Bing Crosby. Slim Whitman recorded a popular version in 1954 and at the beginning of the sixties several Liverpool bands began to perform it at gigs, including the Searchers, Rory Storm & the Hurricanes and Billy J. Kramer. The Beatles included it in their repertoire in 1962 and performed it on BBC radio's 'Saturday Club' on 26 June 1963.

Be-Bop-A-Lula

A rock classic which provided Gene Vincent with his first million-seller in 1956. Penned by Vincent and Tex Davis, Vincent and the Blue Caps performed it in the film *The Girl Can't Help It*. The film influenced the Quarry Men who included the number in their repertoire. The group still performed the song, with John as lead vocalist, when they became the Beatles and it was one of the numbers they performed at Hamburg's Star Club and is subsequently to be found on the Star Club album releases.

Because

John Lennon composition featured on the *Abbey Road* album. John was writing a number about himself and Yoko one day when he heard Yoko at the piano playing some Beethoven chords. It was the 'Moonlight Sonata' (Beethoven's piano sonata in C sharp minor, opus 27 No. 2). John was inspired to reverse the chords and then wrote 'Because' around them. John, Paul and George are featured on the track performing three-part vocal harmony. A version was included on the Beatles' *Anthology 3* CDs.

Beecher-Stevens, Sydney A.

In 1961 when he was marketing manager at Decca records, he received a call from Tony Barrow who informed him that an influential record retailer, Brian Epstein, was seeking a record company for his group. Epstein talked to Beecher-Stevens and a meeting was arranged, supposedly to discuss retail percentages. When Beecher-Stevens and his assistant Colin Borland invited Epstein up for lunch in the executive club at Decca's embankment offices, the topic soon turned to the Beatles. Brian showed them a copy of *Mersey Beat* in which the group were prominently featured and later they listened to 'My Bonnie'. Beecher-Stevens contacted Dick Rowe who arranged for his assistant Mike Smith to see the group in Liverpool.

Beecher-Stevens and Dick Rowe met Epstein for lunch in the executive club once again on 6 February 1962, but this time to say that Decca was not interested in his band.

Beecher-Stevens died at his Home in Hove, Sussex, in 1987 at the age of 79.

Beeching, Dr Richard

A former executive of ICI, born in Sheerness, Kent, on 21 April 1913. He was appointed by British Railways in 1961 to reorganise the nationalised company, which was a huge loss-maker. Within seven years he had streamlined the entire system, with a loss of 150,000 jobs, the axing of 5,000 miles of track and the closing of 2,363 stations.

When the Beatles were having financial difficulties with the Apple organisation and needed a tough businessman to sort out the mess, they reputedly approached him. He turned them down, but gave them a straightforward piece of advice: 'Get back to making records.'

The Queen knighted him.

Begin The Beguine

Famous Cole Porter composition. The Beatles introduced the number into their repertoire for a short time during 1960.

Being For The Benefit Of Mr Kite

A John Lennon composition from the *Sgt Pepper* album. John was to comment, 'It was from this old poster I'd bought at an antique shop. We'd been down to Surrey, or somewhere, filming a TV piece to go with "Strawberry Fields Forever". There was a break and I went into this shop and bought an old poster advertising a variety show which starred Mister Kite. It said the Hendersons would also be there, late of Pablois Fanques Fair. There were hoops and horses and someone going through a hogshead of real fire. Then there was Henry the Horse. The band would start at ten to six. All at Bishopsgate.

'I hardly made up a word, just connecting lines together word for word really. I wasn't very proud of that. There was no real work. I was just going through the motions because we needed a new song for *Sgt Pepper* at that time.'

The antique shop where John purchased the poster on 31 January 1967 was actually located in Sevenoaks, Kent, and it referred to a fair which took place near Rochdale in Lancashire in February 1843.

In 1980, John was to add: 'The whole song is from a Victorian poster which I bought in a junk shop. It is so cosmically beautiful. It's a poster for a fair that must have happened in the 1880s. Everything in the song is from that poster, except the horse wasn't called Henry'.

The sound effects on the record were quite elaborate, John had told George Martin that he wanted to capture the genuine sensation of a circus and Martin suggested that they use a calliope, an instrument of steam whistles played through a keyboard. They weren't able to hire such an instrument but Martin managed to obtain a tape of a calliope playing Sousa marches. The tape was cut up into pieces and thrown into the air, so that the pieces could all be mixed up and reassembled. More effects were included on overdubs with Ringo, George, Mal Evans and Neil Aspinall playing harmonicas, George Martin playing Wurlitzer organ and John playing Hammond organ. A version was included on the Beatles' *Anthology 2* CDs.

2850 Benedict Canyon, Bel Air, California

The Beatles rented a house at this address for nine days in August 1965 when they were on the West Coast. Rented on Monday, 23 August, it had a mountainside view and swimming pool. While they relaxed at the house they had several visitors. On Tuesday, 24 August, Eleanor Bron was one of the first of their guests and sat talking to John by the swimming pool. Other visitors included Joan Baez, members of the Byrds and Maureen Payne, a former NEMS Enterprises receptionist who was now living in LA.

The house was guarded by a dozen policemen and members of the Burns Agency, and was protected by a five-bar wooden gate. On Wednesday, 25 August, a group of four fans, Paula, Mikki, Sue and Kay hired a single-seater helicopter and each of them in turn flew over the house to wave at the Beatles.

The Beatles' presence in the area was well publicised and local radio stations broadcast the address. There were lots of sightseers and fans gathering on hillsides with binoculars.

It was during this sojourn that they were hosted to a Capitol Records party on Tuesday, 24 August, whose guests included Julie Andrews, Gene Barry, Tony Bennett, Jack Benny, Richard Chamberlain, Eddie Fisher, Jane Fonda, Rock Hudson, Gene Kelly, Henry Mancini, Groucho Marx, Steve McQueen, Hayley and Juliet Mills, Edward G. Robinson, James Stewart and Dick Van Dyke. On Friday, 27 August they visited Elvis Presley. George and Paul also dropped into the recording studios to see the Byrds, who were recording 'The Times They Are A-Changing'.

During their stay the temperature soared over 90 degrees and they made full use of the pool.

On Monday, 30 August, the group held a farewell party at the poolside for the media.

Bennett, Kim

A publisher at Ardmore and Beechwood, EMI's music publishing arm.

Bennett was assistant to Sid Coleman who was enthusiastic about the Beatles and wanted to publish their material at a time when no one else in the industry was interested. Even the individual pop labels of EMI had turned Epstein down. After Coleman had arranged the meeting between Epstein and George Martin, his company was to promote the Beatles' first release, 'Love Me Do'.

With the amount of new records released each week, the number of established artists with new products and the rigid attitudes of people in the industry, the promotion of this unusual record by an unknown northern group was not an easy task. Yet Kim Bennett was enthusiastic and began approaching the various disc jockeys. He didn't have much success. Jack Jackson, a prominent disc jockey, was to say, 'I've seen pictures of them (the Beatles) and my first reaction was that there was something wrong with my eyesight.' This was a typical attitude.

Bennett managed to get 'Love Me Do' its first BBC radio play on

'Twelve O'Clock Spin'. The man who gave the record its first BBC plug was an ex-Radio Luxembourg disc jockey, Ted King, who commented on his meeting with Bennett. He said, 'We met one lunchtime in a Tin Pan Alley pub. I knew a little about the Beatles, of course, but I wasn't mad about the disc. But Kim was so enthusiastic over it all that I decided if you can't beat 'em, then you have to join 'em. And I must say now that I'm mighty glad I did so.'

King was also to say, 'EMI bullied me into taking a chance on it, but I honestly don't think the song was strong enough to do anything. Most of the people who heard the programme told me they thought I was barking up the wrong tree supporting the Beatles.'

It's ironic that the two people who were so enthusiastic about the Beatles and helped to get them with EMI in the first place were to have George Martin shut the door in their face by suggesting to Brian Epstein that he see Dick James about being their publisher. For one thing, it was Coleman who, after talking to Brian, realised that the only A&R man at EMI who hadn't rejected the Beatles was George Martin. Apparently, Coleman had a hard job persuading Martin to see Epstein. Even then, Martin wasn't initially impressed by their sound. He only agreed to a test session at EMI's No. 3 studio four weeks later, then another three months elapsed before the release of their first single. EMI and Martin weren't even confident enough to give the Beatles a plug rating. Artists such as Cliff Richard received an 'A' plug on EMI's Radio Luxembourg shows. The lowest rating was 'B2'. The Beatles weren't even given this low plug, EMI gave 'Love Me Do' a nil rating.

So Bennett had a hard job pushing the record without EMI using their clout. As a result, Epstein refused Ardmore & Beechwood the future Beatles publishing. Had he done so, the Beatles might have retained the rights to their own songs and Coleman might have received some acknowledgement from Martin for having placed the Beatles into his hands in the first place.

Bennett, Peter

An independent American record promotions man, hired by the Beatles to promote Apple Records in the States from 1967. This included promotion of the Beatles' records, including a number of their solo releases and discs by James Taylor, Mary Hopkin and Billy Preston.

Bennett worked hard on promoting all the discs, including ones he was unhappy about, such as John and Yoko's 'Woman Is the Nigger Of The World'. He set up a television coup by arranging for John and Yoko to co-host the 'Mike Douglas Show' on TV for a week and he also took George Harrison backstage at Madison

Square Garden to meet Elvis Presley and renew their acquaintance-ship. He was with John during his 'long weekend' in Los Angeles, following the break-up with Yoko. Bennett, who also worked for Allen Klein, became a government witness against Klein in a tax-evasion trial in 1978.

Bernstein, Sid

In 1963, Sid Bernstein, a former student at Columbia University and an ex-ballroom manager who had also acted as an independent promoter/agent, was 38 years old and earning $200 a week working for General Artists Corporation (GAC), the largest theatrical agency in America.

During the evenings, Sid was taking a night-school course under Dr Max Lerner at the New School for Social Research in New York. He'd begun the course in 1962 and in October of that year, as part of the course, he was required to read English newspapers each week. By the time his course had finished in February 1963 he had noted the rise of an obscure group from Liverpool who had begun to dominate the British press with headlines of 'Beatlemania'.

He had a hunch that the Beatles were unique, but couldn't convince anyone at GAC, so he decided to strike out on his own.

He sought out and found Brian Epstein's phone number in Liverpool and called him in February 1963. Sid had decided on promoting them independently in New York and suggested to Epstein that he would like to book them to appear at Carnegie Hall. Epstein was impressed with the idea of such a prestigious venue, but was still cautious. Bernstein was thinking of booking them in four months' time, but Epstein pointed out that they didn't have an American audience and there was no airplay in the States and so such a concert would be premature.

Sid asked Brian how much the Beatles were being paid for an appearance. It was the equivalent of $2,000 a night. Bernstein offered him $6,500 for two concerts on the one day at Carnegie Hall. He suggested that the appearance should take place the following year on Lincoln's birthday, 12 February 1964. Epstein agreed on the condition that the deal would become null and void if the Beatles didn't have a hit in the American charts by the end of 1963.

Fortunately for Bernstein, his gamble paid off when it was announced that Ed Sullivan had booked them for his TV show shortly prior to the Carnegie Hall appearance.

Booking the Beatles for Carnegie Hall was no simple matter. No pop group had ever appeared at the world-famous concert hall and Bernstein knew he'd be turned down if it were discovered exactly who the Beatles were. When he phoned to make the booking, a

Polish lady asked him who the Beatles were. He told her they were a phenomenon. 'Oh, that's all right, then,' she said.

Bernstein, who came from the East Bronx and only had a low income, had to borrow the $500 required for the deposit. He'd taken a gamble on his hunch because he had booked them without even hearing one of their records and he had no idea what they sounded like.

The shows at Carnegie Hall were presented at 2.30 and 7.30 p.m. on Wednesday, 12 February 1964, and there were 20,000 people milling about outside, trying to get a glimpse of the 'phenomenon'. All 2,870 seats at each show had been sold out in advance and Bernstein had to obtain permission to place 150 chairs on the stage.

After the second show, Bernstein walked with Epstein across to the 17,000-seater Madison Square Garden and told him that the huge venue wanted to present the Beatles and he could have the tickets printed up and on sale within 24 hours. He offered Epstein £25,000 for the booking and said he would pay an additional $5,000 to the British Cancer Fund. Brian pondered for a moment, then said, 'Sid, let's leave it for the next time.'

As it turned out, 'the next time' became an even bigger event – the largest-ever live entertainment presentation up to that time. The box office manager of Carnegie Hall had told Sid that they could have sold 250,000 tickets if they had them – Bernstein then lost interest in Madison Square Garden and began to think in terms of the biggest venue in New York – Shea Stadium, the 55,600-seater baseball park.

He phoned Brian Epstein with the proposal. Epstein demurred. Bernstein told him he was so convinced it would be a success that he'd pay Brian for every empty seat. 'Let's do it, Sid,' said Epstein.

As with the Carnegie Hall gig and all dealings between Bernstein and Epstein, there were no written contracts. Everything was settled by gentleman's agreement over the phone. Bernstein offered $100,000 in advance against 60 per cent of gross receipts. Epstein told him to send $50,000 immediately and pay the balance before the concert.

Bernstein didn't have the money; in fact, he had lost everything on a recent stage tour of 'Shindig'. He told Brian that his money was tied up and asked if he could be given a few months' grace. Brian said he'd be in New York in two months' time, on 10 April, at the Waldorf Towers, and Sid could give him the deposit then and pay the balance on 10 June. Sid asked him if he could begin to advertise the event and Epstein said 'no'. He asked if he could mention the fact that he was presenting the show, without actually advertising the fact, and Epstein said he had no objection to Sid talking about it.

Bernstein was in financial straits at the time. His wife Gerry had just given birth to Adam, the first of their six children, they owed rent on their home in the East Bronx, money on grocery bills and had no way of raising a loan. Sid began to tell friends that he was promoting the Beatles at Shea Stadium in August 1965 and that deposits for tickets should be sent to him at PO Box 21. Sid had hoped to get thirty or forty deposits in advance, which could help his perilous financial state. When he went to the post office three weeks later there were more than three sacks of mail. The concert had sold out within three weeks. When Sid went to see Brian at the Waldorf, he was able to give him a cheque for $100,000.

The Shea Stadium concert proved to be a sensation, although it cost Sid a lot of money to stage. He brought in a team of detectives and hundreds of security men and paid Lloyd's of London $25,000 for insurance cover. The receipts totalled more than $300,000. He was able to give the Beatles a cheque for a further $80,000 for their 28-minute performance, but his costs had been such that he only made a profit of $6,500. However, his association with the Beatles transformed his life and he became manager of the Rascals, Laura Nyro and numerous other acts over the years and even launched his own independent record label.

Commenting on the Beatles, Sid said, 'I found Paul just warm and very kind. I found John kind of satirical and very clever, Ringo rather quiet, funny but quiet. George was very serious, sober and sombre in his attitude, and meditative. I liked them so much individually.'

He set up a deal for another Shea Stadium appearance for Tuesday, 23 August 1966, with the Beatles receiving 65 per cent of the gate. The concert grossed $282,000 and the Beatles received $183,000. It wasn't as successful as the first concert as there were 11,000 seats unsold and tickets were given away free.

Bernstein travelled to Britain with the Rascals in October 1966 and met Brian Epstein over dinner. He offered him one million pounds for the Beatles to appear at Shea Stadium in 1967, to include world television rights. Brian told him that he couldn't make any plans for live appearances by the group at that time.

The last time that Bernstein saw Brian Epstein was in April 1967. Brian had called him to a meeting at the Waldorf Astoria in New York, together with Nat Weiss. Epstein proposed that Sid should join himself and Weiss in a management partnership. Bernstein would bring in his groups the Rascals and the Blues Project and Epstein would offer all his artists with the exception of the Beatles. Bernstein and Weiss would run the American operation and Epstein and Robert Stigwood would run the London end of the business. As the Bee Gees and Cream were still relatively unknown and as Cilla Black had failed to penetrate the American market, Bernstein turned the offer down.

In 1979, Bernstein wanted the Beatles to reunite for a special concert in aid of the Vietnamese Boat People. He believed that the Beatles' name and the concert, recording and television rights of the event could raise $500 million around the world. However, as he was always closer to Epstein than the Beatles and because Brian was now dead, he just couldn't reach any of the former members of the Beatles individually. He decided to go over the heads of their advisers, agents, lawyers and so on by reaching them through advertising. He took out a full-page advertisement in the *New York Times* outlining his plan for a benefit in aid of the Boat People. The only response was an enquiry on behalf of John. Bernstein placed all the information in writing and took it over to the Dakota building where the doorman took the package. That was the last Sid heard of the matter, apart from a comment from George Harrison who told a journalist, 'It was cute the way the ad in the (New York) *Times* tried to put the responsibility for saving the world on our shoulders.'

Sid was to admit that he'd tried to do something similar a few years earlier, in 1976. He placed an ad in the *European Herald Tribune* and the *Sunday Times* in England suggesting that the Beatles get together for a concert in aid of either the victims of a recent major earthquake in Italy or the homeless and parentless children of Biafra. He received no response, but noticed that Paul McCartney later held a benefit concert to raise money to save the city of Venice from sinking.

In 1981, Sid teamed up with Clive Epstein to manage a Liverpool band called Motion Pictures. Unfortunately, Clive died before they could develop their partnership. Later on, with the help of his wife Gerry, Sid began to write his memoirs.

Berry, Chuck

One of the seminal influences on the Beatles and one of their favourite musicians. Berry and artists like him should have been featured on the cover of the *Sgt Pepper* album rather than the boxers, film stars and West Coast painters selected by Peter Blake and Robert Fraser and would have reflected the Beatles' idols and heroes more accurately.

During the period 1957–66, the Beatles were to perform more songs penned by Chuck Berry than by any other artist. Paul McCartney sang 'Little Queenie', but the other Berry numbers were mainly sung by John Lennon and included 'Roll Over Beethoven',

'Johnny B. Goode', 'Rock And Roll Music', 'Sweet Little Sixteen', 'Maybellene', 'Almost Grown', 'Carol', 'Memphis Tennessee', 'Reelin' and Rockin'', 'Too Much Monkey Business', 'I'm Talking About You', 'I Got To Find My Baby', 'Thirty Days' and 'Vacation Time'.

Their number 'Back In The USSR' was no doubt influenced by his 1959 hit 'Back In The USA' and Paul McCartney claimed that he borrowed the bass riff from Berry's 'I'm Talking About You' for 'I Saw Her Standing There'.

Born Charles Berry in San Jose, California, on 18 October 1926, he formed his first trio in 1952 while he worked by day as a hair-dresser and beautician. He signed with Chess Records in 1955 and his first release was 'Maybellene'.

In 1962 he was convicted of violating the Mann Act by bringing an under-age girl over a state line (this occurred in 1959) and jailed for two years.

On his release in 1964, his career received a boost when the Beatles recorded 'Roll Over Beethoven' on their second album. He was so pleased at how rock 'n' roll had been revived in Liverpool that he recorded the album St Louis To Liverpool and penned the number 'Liverpool Drive'.

On 13 September 1969 he appeared at the Toronto Rock 'n' Roll Revival Concert on a bill which included John Lennon's Plastic Ono Band. John, the main Berry fan in the group, used to introduce a Berry song at the Cavern with the words, 'This is a record by Chuck Berry, a Liverpool-born white singer with bandy legs and no hair.'

In 1975, Berry's publisher Morris Levy claimed that John had plagiarised Berry's 'You Can't Catch Me' when writing 'Come Together'. John maintained that it was not a plagiarism, merely a tribute, and agreed to settle the matter by recording two Berry numbers for his album *Rock 'n' Roll*.

John eventually managed to perform with Berry when he was hosting The Mike Douglas Show on American TV in February 1972. He selected Berry as a guest and the two of them performed 'Johnny B. Goode' and 'Memphis Tennessee' together.

Berry's autobiography was published in 1988 to coincide with a film of his 1988 birthday concert, *Hail! Hail! Rock 'n' Roll*, during which he was joined on stage by Julian Lennon.

Berry, Mike (Singer)

Real name Michael Bourne, born in Hackney, east London, in 1943. Independent record producer Joe Meek gave him his stage name and produced his hit 'Don't You Think It's Time'.

Mike, who had established himself initially in Britain with his 'Tribute To Buddy Holly' single, was to appear regularly at the Cavern, initially with Mike Berry and the Outlaws for a week from Monday, 21 to Friday, 25 May 1962, during which he plugged his new record. Among the members of the Outlaws were two musicians who were later to find fame in their own right, Ritchie Blackmore and Chas Hodges (of Chas & Dave).

Brian Epstein and the Beatles saw him perform during that week and Epstein, who had watched Berry on the TV programme 'Thank Your Lucky Stars' the previous week promoting his latest release 'Don't You Think It's Time', was introduced to him by compere Bob Wooler. Epstein invited the nineteen-year-old singer back to his flat in Faulkner Street, where he played him a demo tape of the Beatles. Hodges accompanied Mike. Brian told Berry that if he could arrange a television appearance for the group, he'd see to it that Berry was given a lot of work in the Merseyside area. He also invited Mike to NEMS' store and arranged for Paul McCartney to give him a lift home from the Cavern one night.

Three months later, Mike was back again, leading Mike Berry and the Phantoms. They appeared on the same bill as the Beatles on Sunday, 26 August. He returned to the Cavern the following year with Mike Berry & the Marauders.

He was booked to appear with the Beatles on their short tour of Scotland, which opened at the Concert Hall, Glasgow, on 6 October 1963, and he also joined the Beatles on their very first tour abroad, a five-date mini-tour of Sweden, commencing on 25 October 1963.

A few years later Mike didn't have a manager and asked his brother, actor Peter Bourne (who was one of Epstein's boyfriends), if he'd mention to Epstein that he was looking for a manager. Brian said he couldn't do anything for Mike at the time and Mike thought he'd be on the scrap heap at the age of 22.

Berry's last hit of the 1960s was 'My Little Baby' in April 1963 and he vanished from the pop scene for more than a decade, to reappear much later as a television actor in series such as 'Are You Being Served?' and 'Wurzel Gummidge'.

Interestingly enough, his biggest hit was 'The Sunshine Of Your Smile' in 1980, produced by Chas Hodges, which topped the British charts. He had the self-penned number 'I'm As Old As Paul McCartney' on the flip. He was to have two further hits, 'If I Could Only Make You Care' and 'Memories'. With the growth of the retro rock scene in Britain in the late 1980s, he reformed the Outlaws and began appearing live on stage once more.

Besame Mucho

A song written in 1943 by Consuelo Valazquez and Selig Shaftel which has been recorded by over a hundred different artists, ranging from Mario Lanza to the Coasters. It was the Coasters' version in 1960 which led it to being added to the repertoire of rock groups and the Beatles began performing it in 1962. Paul took the lead vocal honours and the group can be heard performing the number on *The Beatles Live! At The Star Club In Hamburg, Germany, 1962* album. They also recorded it during their Decca audition on 1 January 1962 and on the BBC radio show 'Here We Go', transmitted on 14 June 1962. The group are also seen performing the number in their *Let It Be* movie. A version of the number was included on the Beatles *Anthology 1* CDs.

Best, Mona

Arguably, the first Merseyside promoter to give the Beatles regular support.

Born of English parents in India, she worked for the Red Cross in Delhi, where she met and married John Best, an army officer. The couple had two sons, Peter and Rory. In 1945 the family returned to England and lived in a flat in Casey Street, Liverpool, for two years. Then they settled in a large Victorian house at 8 Haymans Green in the West Derby area of Liverpool.

The huge house had a large complex of cellars and when Pete was sixteen, Mona had noticed the number of young friends visiting him at the house and decided to turn part of the cellar area into a private club for him. But word got out and more ambitious plans developed, which resulted in a club for young people with live groups. It became one of the first cellar clubs to present rock 'n' roll exclusively when it opened in August 1959. And 'Mo', as she was called, decided to call it the Casbah Club. This was because her favourite film at the time was *Algiers*, which starred Charles Boyer, who, people asserted, said 'Come with me to the Casbah', although that line of dialogue isn't actually in the film.

The resident group became the Quarry Men, who had re-formed specially for the club's opening on Saturday, 29 August 1959. George Harrison, who was in another band, the Les Stewart Quartet, quit the outfit, along with Ken Brown, and sought out John and Paul to join them. The Quarry Men had been inactive for several months and had more or less disbanded. If Mo hadn't opened the Casbah, the Beatles might never have existed!

In some ways, the Casbah has more right to be called 'the birth-place of the Beatles' than the Cavern, which didn't book them

until two years later, when they had already become established
locally.

After her son Pete joined the group as drummer in August 1960,
Mo began to take an active role in their career. For a time she
arranged for the Casbah doorman Frank Garner to become the
Beatles' road manager, and then presented them with a permanent
roadie in the form of her lover, Neil Aspinall. Mona also bought the
Beatles their first van.

When the Beatles returned from their first trip to Hamburg they
appeared at the Casbah and Mo, in an effort to keep them in work,
began a series of independent promotions at St John's Hall,
Tuebrook, and booked the Beatles for eleven gigs there. She also
booked them on shows at Knotty Ash Village Hall, in addition to
their Casbah work. On the first of the Beatles' bookings at St John's
Hall, Mona paid them £20 – a large increase on the £5 she used to
pay for the Casbah bookings. These gigs, plus the Casbah appearances and the gigs Pete was lining up, proved a lifeline for the
Beatles during the early months of 1961.

Mona was championing the group, obviously because of her
son's part in it, and even wrote off to Granada Television in an
attempt to get them on the 'People and Places' show. Producer
David Plowright wrote back to her on Thursday, 21 September
1961.

Dear Mrs Best,
Thank you for your letter telling me about the Beatles. I will
certainly bear them in mind and will contact you again if it is
possible to invite them to take part in our programme People
and Places at any time.

Ironically, the Beatles were to make their television debut on that
very show.

Once Brian Epstein entered the picture, he took over the reins of
management, although Mrs Best was still obviously keen to
promote the group in which her son was a member.

Mo was furious when her son was sacked without explanation
and set out to find the reason why. Epstein wouldn't answer her
calls, but she managed to contact George Martin, who told her that
he was completely surprised by the decision as he regarded Pete as
a valuable member of the group.

Mo was to tell Beatles biographer Hunter Davies: 'He'd (Pete)
been their manager before Brian (Epstein)) arrived, did the bookings and collected the money. I'd looked upon them as friends. I'd
helped them so much, got them bookings, lending them money. I

fed them when they were hungry. I was far more interested in them than their own parents.'

It was felt by various people in Liverpool who were associated with the local scene that perhaps the Beatles had resented Mo's efforts on their behalf – a situation which may have been one of the elements involved in Pete's dismissal.

Sadly, Mo died in hospital on 9 September 1988 following a heart attack after a long illness.

Best On Record, The

Title of the annual 'Grammy Awards' shows presented on American television by NBC TV.

The Beatles received many awards and the presentations were featured in several video clips. The segment screened on 18 May 1965 showed a film of Peter Sellers presenting the Beatles with their Grammy awards on the set of *Help!* Also screened was a scene from *A Hard Day's Night* and film of the boys performing 'I'm Happy Just To Dance With You'.

On 24 May 1967, Liberace introduced an excerpt from their 'Strawberry Fields' promotional film. They were featured again on the show on 5 May 1969. John Lennon appeared as a guest presenter on 1 March 1975 and Ringo Starr and Harry Nilsson were guest presenters on 19 February 1977.

Best, Pete

Drummer with the Beatles from 1960–2 and, at one point, the most popular member of the group among the majority of Liverpool fans. In fact, in 1962, *Mersey Beat* was to observe that he was: 'a figure with mystique, darkly good-looking and seemingly the one likely to emerge as the most popular Beatle'.

He was born Peter Randolph Best in Madras, India, on 24 November 1941. His English parents were stationed in India at the time, where his father, John, was an army physical training instructor and his mother, Mona, a nurse in the Red Cross.

Following the birth of Pete's brother, Rory, in 1944, the family sailed to England, moving to Liverpool and initially settling into a flat in Casey Street. Two years later they moved to 8 Haymans Green, a fifteen-room Victorian house in the West Derby district of the city.

When, at the age of 16, Pete began to take an interest in skiffle and rock 'n' roll music, he was encouraged by his parents. As so many friends were dropping in to see Pete and Rory, their mother suggested a novel idea – they could have a meeting place of their own by utilising the seven adjoining basement rooms. The idea developed until they decided to turn the basement into a coffee-bar-style venue, which was similar to Lowlands, a nearby club.

Mona (generally known to everyone as 'Mo') and her sons, together with about ten friends, began work on converting the basement. They had decided to open during the week as a coffee bar – where youngsters could dance to jukebox music – but would hire live groups for the weekend.

One of their helpers was Ruth Morrison, the girlfriend of George Harrison, who suggested that the Les Stewart Quartet, of which George was a member, could play at the club. They were currently appearing at the Lowlands Club, which was situated on the opposite side of the street, fifty yards down from the Bests' home.

As a result, George and Ken Brown, another member of the quartet, went round to see Mo.

However, group leader Les Stewart didn't want to appear in the new coffee club, which Mo called the Casbah, and he had an argument with Brown. Brown left the group and George followed.

George then turned up with John Lennon and Paul McCartney and they teamed up with Brown as a quartet, assuming the former name of John's skiffle group, the Quarry Men, to begin their residency. The group didn't use a drummer at the time.

The club officially opened on Saturday, 29 August 1959 and within a year they enrolled 1,000 members.

On Saturday, 10 October 1959 there was a dispute because Brown was unable to play, yet Mrs Best still paid him a share of the group's fee. As a result, John, George and Paul walked out on their residency and sacked Brown.

Ken then encouraged Pete to form a new outfit with him and to take over a residency at the club. They called themselves the Blackjacks (the original name of Lennon's first group). Brown played rhythm, Charles Newby played lead, Bill Barlow played bass and Pete became the group's drummer.

Mo bought Pete a drum kit from Blackler's store (where George Harrison was to work for a time) and the group repertoire comprised numbers from rock 'n' roll acts such as Little Richard, Jerry Lee Lewis, Chuck Berry and Carl Perkins.

In the meantime, the Quarry Men underwent a number of name changes ranging from Johnny & the Moondogs to the Beatals to the Silver Beetles, and enlisted the services of drummer Tommy Moore. As the Silver Beetles, they toured Scotland, backing Johnny Gentle, and then began appearing in Liverpool, mainly at the Jacaranda Coffee Club, the Grosvenor Ballroom, Liscard and the Institute, Neston. By this time they had changed their name to the Beatles.

On 6 August 1959 their Grosvenor gig was cancelled when the

Wallasey Corporation withdrew promoter Les Dodd's licence to operate there, and that evening they dropped into the Casbah Club, where they saw Pete perform with the Blackjacks. His new blue mother-of-pearl drum kit particularly impressed them.

At that time they had accepted their first Hamburg booking, which was to commence on 13 August. However, they were without a drummer as Tommy Moore had just left them.

One afternoon Paul phoned Pete at home and asked: 'How'd you like to come to Hamburg with the Beatles?'

Aware that the Blackjacks were on the point of disbanding and excited by the prospect of foreign climes, Pete accepted and successfully auditioned for the band at the Wyvern Club. After playing together for twenty minutes on numbers such as 'Shakin' All Over', they told him, 'You're in!'

The line-up of the Beatles now comprised John Lennon (rhythm/vocals), Paul McCartney (rhythm/vocals), George Harrison (lead/vocals), Stuart Sutcliffe (bass/vocals) and Pete Best (drums).

Arriving in Hamburg they discovered they were not playing at the Kaiserkeller as they had assumed, but at a smaller club called the Indra, which was further down, at the seedier end of the Grosse Freiheit.

After several weeks at the Indra, they then played at the Kaiserkeller, and when their season was coming to an end they had intended to move on to the Top Ten Club in the nearby Reeperbahn.

The group's sleeping quarters were cramped ones at the rear of the Bambi Kino, owned by Bruno Koschmider, who ran the Kaiserkeller. Stu Sutcliffe moved out to live in Astrid Kirchherr's house and, when Koschmider found the group intended to move on to the rival Top Ten, George was deported for being under age.

John, Paul and Pete moved into the dormitory of the Top Ten, intending to play for a season at the club as a quartet with Stuart.

As Pete and Paul needed to collect the rest of their belongings from the Bambi Kino, they crept along there one night to pack. In the windowless rooms, there was no light so some lateral thinking had them pinning condoms into a frayed tapestry in the hall and then lighting them. The condoms singed the tapestry and that evening the police came and arrested the two of them for allegedly trying to set fire to the premises.

Pete and Paul left their equipment behind and John remained in Hamburg for a further week, while Stuart decided to stay on with Astrid. Mona Best phoned Peter Eckhorn, who sent their kit over by ship, and the group then intended to take up a residency at Williams' new club, the Top Ten. Unfortunately, it burned to the ground and the Beatles were left with few bookings. Mo got to work, offering them several gigs at the Casbah, setting up some promotions of her own to keep them in work, and Pete and Mo began to take over the bookings for the group. They were, in effect, managing the Beatles at the time.

Through Bob Wooler, the group were booked by Brian Kelly for Litherland Town Hall on 27 December 1960 – a highlight in their local career. Their baptism of fire in Hamburg had made them an exceptionally dynamic outfit.

When recalling this time to Beatles' biographer, Hunter Davies, Pete said: 'When we came back from Germany I was playing using my bass drum very loud and laying down a very solid beat. This was unheard of at the time in Liverpool as all the groups were playing in the Shadows' style. Even Ringo in Rory's group copied our beat and it wasn't long before most drummers in Liverpool were playing the same style. This way of drumming had a great deal to do with the big sound we were producing.'

This style of playing (which Pete had developed in Germany) earned the tag 'the Atom Beat', and Pete was regarded as one of the 'Pool's leading drummers.

Issue No. 2 of *Mersey Beat,* published on 20 July 1961, devoted its entire front page to the story of the Beatles' Hamburg recording and Brian Epstein ordered 144 copies of that particular issue.

When Bob Wooler wrote his report on the Beatles' impact locally (in *Mersey Beat* on 31 August 1961), the only Beatle he named was Pete, describing the group as 'musically authoritative and physically magnetic, example the mean, moody magnificence of drummer Pete Best – a sort of teenage Jeff Chandler'.

It was due to pressure from Mo and Bob Wooler that Ray McFall eventually decided to book the Beatles at the Cavern, and their rise to local fame continued at a meteoric pace. Pete and Mo continued to act as unofficial managers and agents for the group, arranging all their gigs and negotiating the fees.

Pete Best was emerging as the most popular Beatle among the fans. Bob Wooler considered him the Beatles' biggest asset and said that it was principally Best who was the attraction at the Aintree Institute and Litherland Town Hall gigs.

Due to his popularity, he was encouraged to introduce his own singing spot, 'Peppermint Twist', into the act. Next, Bob Wooler suggested something unprecedented – place Pete in front of the other three members of the group. This unusual line-up was presented only once – at the St Valentine's Dance on 14 February 1961 at Litherland Town Hall – because the stage was mobbed when the girls surged forward and almost pulled him off.

Reports in *Mersey Beat* and comments by people involved in the local scene confirm Best's huge local appeal. One story related how girls slept in his garden overnight just to be near him!

Promoter Ron Appleby was to comment: 'He was definitely the big attraction with the group and did much to establish their popularity during their early career.'

In 1963, the Cavern doorman, Paddy Delaney, was to recall:

> Before the Beatles recorded, Pete was inclined to be more popular with the girls than any other member of the group. There were several reasons why I believe he was so popular. Girls were attracted by the fact that he wouldn't smile, even though they tried to make him. They also tried to attract his attention on stage, but he wouldn't look at them. When he left the Beatles there were exclamations of surprise – 'the Beatles will never be the same without him' . . . ' He *was* the Beatles' . . . 'They've taken away the vital part', were comments I heard.

When Brian Epstein took over the management reins, it was Pete who discussed gigs and fees with him. The two men had an amicable relationship, although Pete was to point out that Brian once attempted to seduce him and had asked if he would come to a hotel and stay with him overnight. Pete politely told him to forget it – and nothing further was said.

1961 was an event-packed year, in which the group's Cavern bookings increased. They went on another trip to Hamburg, during which Stuart Sutcliffe left the band. The Beatles also recorded in Hamburg with Tony Sheridan and Bert Kaempfert. Astrid Kirchherr fashioned Stuart's hair in a style that was developed by Jurgen Vollmer for John and Paul in Paris and later became known as the 'moptop'. Astrid never offered to style Pete's hair and no one ever asked him to adopt the hairstyle.

They began 1962 with a Decca recording audition and were confirmed as Liverpool's No.1 group in a January issue of *Mersey Beat*. On 7 March 1962 they made their broadcasting debut on 'Teenager's Turn' in Manchester. When they recorded their second radio appearance on 11 June, Pete was mobbed by the Manchester girls, while John, Paul and George managed to make their way to the coach. When Pete finally managed to break free and join the others, he was reprimanded by Paul's father, who accused him of hogging the limelight.

That month, Pete learned by accident that Decca had rejected the group. The other members knew about it, but no one had bothered to inform Pete. He said: 'I was hurt because I was the last to know about it. The others knew a couple of weeks earlier. They let it slip out in a casual conversation one day.'

Pete was also to comment: 'When I did eventually learn our fate, their lame excuse was that they had all thought I would take the result extremely badly.'

When news of the Parlophone deal came through, *Mersey Beat* ran the story on the front page, featuring a photograph of Pete Best with the caption: 'Congratulations to Pete, Paul, John and George.'

The Beatles were now on the brink of success, but a number of incidents hinted at a covert plan to get rid of Pete. Apart from the fact that the others had not immediately informed him of the Decca audition result, a similar situation occurred regarding the Parlophone contract – they just didn't bother to tell him.

When Pete was chatting with Paul and mentioned he was considering buying a Ford Capri, Paul told him: 'If you take my advice you won't buy it, that's all. You'd be better saving your money.'

On Wednesday, 15 August 1962, following their lunchtime gig at the Cavern, Pete asked John what time he and Neil Aspinall would collect him for the customary lift in the van the next day. John said: 'No, don't bother. I've got other arrangements,' and rushed away.

Brian was still in the Cavern and asked Pete if he could come and see him at the office the next morning. Pete saw nothing unusual in this – he was the one who met with Brian regularly to discuss forthcoming gigs. He arrived at NEMS the next day, driven by Neil, and went to meet Brian in his office.

The manager seemed unusually flustered and blurted out: 'The boys want you out and Ringo in. They don't think you're a good enough drummer, Pete. And George Martin doesn't think you're a good enough drummer.'

When Pete asked him: 'Does Ringo know yet?' Brian told him that he was joining the band on the coming Saturday. Then the phone rang – it was someone asking if Pete had been given the news. Brian asked Pete if he could fulfil the remaining three bookings until Ringo replaced him.

Stunned, Pete said 'Yes', then left, in somewhat of a daze.

When Pete rejoined Neil downstairs, he told him the news and the two retreated to the Grapes to discuss it over a drink. Neil was furious and threatened to resign as the Beatles' road manager, but Pete told him to stay with the group as they were about to become successful.

When Neil phoned Mo, she was furious and spent the afternoon trying to contact Epstein by phone – in vain. She then managed to talk to George Martin on the phone and he denied that he had ever suggested sacking Pete. All he would say was that he would prefer having a session drummer that he was familiar with in a recording studio. In fact, this was confirmed when he used a session drummer even after Ringo had joined the group.

Martin actually told Mo:

I never suggested that Pete Best must go. All I said was that for the purposes of the Beatles' first record I would rather use a session man. I never thought that Brian Epstein would let him go. He seemed to be the most saleable commodity as far as looks went. It was a surprise when I learned that they had dropped Pete. The drums were important to me for a record, but they didn't matter much otherwise. Fans don't pay particular attention to the quality of the drumming.

At that point in time it was not uncommon for A&R men to use session drummers. Ringo was to experience something similar when he arrived at the recording studios on Tuesday, 11 September 1962. A session drummer, Andy White, was present. White also played drums on 'P.S. I Love You', while Ringo was handed a pair of maracas.

Martin told Beatles' biographer, Hunter Davies: 'He (Ringo) couldn't do a roll – and still can't – though he's improved a lot since. Andy was the kind of drummer I needed. Ringo was only used to ballrooms. It was obviously best to use someone with experience.'

Ringo himself was to tell Davies how shocked he was to arrive at the session and find another drummer there: 'I thought, "that's the end", they're doing a Pete Best on me.'

The decision to sack Pete was not a sudden one. It had been claimed that Paul and George had been overheard talking to Bob Wooler in the Grapes about sacking Pete, once they had John's approval. Their next step was to approach Epstein and tell him.

Epstein then considered Johnny Hutchinson as the best replacement and contacted Hutchinson to offer him the job. Hutchinson turned him down – he didn't have a good opinion of the group.

Years later, Hutchinson was to tell broadcaster Spencer Leigh: 'Brian asked me to join the Beatles and I said, "I wouldn't join the Beatles for a gold clock. There's only one group as far as I'm concerned and that's the Big Three. The Beatles can't make a better sound than that, and Pete Best is a very good friend of mine. I couldn't do the dirty on him." '

On the evening of Best's sacking, Epstein was surprised to find that Pete didn't turn up for the gig at the Riverpark Ballroom. Neil told him: 'What do you expect?' Brian got Hutchinson to fill in the three bookings until Ringo was able to join. That evening when

Neil questioned Paul and John about it all, he was told: 'It's got
nothing to you with you. You're only the driver.'

The story in *Mersey Beat* read:

BEATLES CHANGE DRUMMER!

Ringo Starr (former drummer with Rory Storm & the
Hurricanes) has joined the Beatles, replacing Pete Best on
drums. Ringo has admired the Beatles for years and is
delighted with his new engagement. Naturally he is tremendously excited about the future.

The Beatles comment, 'Pete left the group by mutual agreement. There were no arguments or difficulties, and this has
been an entirely amicable decision.'

On Tuesday September 4th, the Beatles will fly to London
to make recordings at EMI Studios. They will be recording
numbers that have been specially written for the group, which
they have received from their recording manager, George
Martin.

The Beatles' comment, issued by Brian Epstein, was false. Pete
was to tell *Mersey Beat*: 'The news came as a big surprise to me as
I had had no hint that it could happen and didn't even have the
opportunity of discussing it with the rest of the group.'

Local fans went wild with fury and hundreds of letters and peti-
tions of protest were sent to *Mersey Beat*. When the Beatles were
due to appear at the Cavern with Ringo on Sunday, 19 August
1962, the Best fans were out in force. Ray McFall arranged for
Brian Epstein to have a bodyguard and, during scuffles, George
Harrison was given a black eye. Fans were chanting 'Peter for
ever, Ringo never' and 'Pete is Best.'

However, the protests didn't last long. George was to write to a
fan: 'Ringo is a much better drummer and he can smile – which is a
bit more than Pete could do. It will seem different for a few weeks,
but I think that the majority of our fans will soon be taking Ringo
for granted.' To his credit, John Lennon was later to say: 'We were
cowards when we sacked him.'

Added to the devastating news for Pete Best that after two years'
unblemished service with the band, he was unceremoniously sacked
when they were finally about to achieve success, was the fact that
his name was tarnished.

Epstein attempted to soften the harshness of the group's decision
by implying that Pete wasn't a good enough drummer. The fellow-
Merseyside musicians disputed this as did fans who actually heard
him play. He genuinely contributed to the Beatles' success and was

an integral part of them as they established themselves as the number one band on Merseyside. There had never been a single complaint about his drumming and he had developed the 'Atom Beat', which other drummers had copied.

In 1984, Geoff Nugent of the Undertakers was to tell Spencer Leigh: 'Pete Best put the Beatles on the map. You'd see two or three girls around Paul and George and John, but you'd see fifty around Pete. I very rarely saw him smile and yet he was always pleasant. If you look at any of the Beatles photographs with Pete Best, the first face you're drawn to is Pete's. I don't care if you're a man or woman.'

Instead of seeking to investigate the real motives behind the sacking of Best, writers have merely continued to perpetuate the lie that 'he was not a good enough drummer'. If a lie is repeated enough, people will assume it is the truth.

Pete was to say, 'I wouldn't rate Ringo as a better drummer than me – I'm adamant about that – and when it happened I felt like putting a stone around my neck and jumping off the Pier Head.'

Mo told Epstein, quite frankly, that she believed the reason Pete was sacked was due to the fact that he was so popular locally and would probably have become the most popular Beatle when they achieved success. She put it down to jealousy by the other members of the group – particularly since a lot of people in Liverpool had been calling the group 'Pete Best and the Beatles'.

She said to Hunter Davies:

They were jealous and they wanted him out. Pete hadn't realised what a following he had till he left. He was always so very shy and quiet, never shot his mouth off, like some people I could mention.

He'd been their manager before Brian arrived, did the bookings and collected the money. I'd looked upon them as friends. I'd helped them so much, got them bookings, lending them money. I fed them when they were hungry. I was far more interested in them than their own parents.

In some quarters of Liverpool at the time, people suspected that the Beatles wanted to get rid of Pete because his mother was such a strong personality that she would continue to make her presence felt, even though Epstein was now managing the band.

Another reason was that Pete just never quite fitted in personality wise with the other three members of the group. He was taciturn and didn't have the same wacky sense of humour. He didn't even adopt their hairstyle, although he says they never asked him to and he would have done so, if requested. The truth probably lies in a combination of these theories.

Still upset by the turn of events Epstein, who had had a sleepless night prior to sacking Pete, then told him that he wanted to continue managing him and would place him with another band – the Mersey Beats. Pete didn't want to remain with Epstein after what had happened and certainly didn't want to start at the beginning again with an unknown group.

Behind the scenes, Epstein arranged for Joe Flannery to approach Pete about joining Lee Curtis and the All Stars. Pete had had numerous offers to join other bands, but decided to give the All Stars a shot and made his debut with them at the Majestic Ballroom, Birkenhead, on Monday, 10 September 1962. On Saturday, 24 November, Pete was again appearing at the Majestic with the All Stars and also celebrating his 21st birthday. Compering the show, Bob Wooler read out a telegram that had arrived for Pete: 'Congratulations. Many happy returns. All the best, John, Paul, George, Ringo and Brian.'

Epstein probably sent this as the relationship between Pete and his former colleagues was now a difficult one. Pete commented: 'We played on the same bill as the Beatles on two occasions. One was at the Cavern when we were second on the bill to the Beatles. The other was in the *Mersey Beat* Pollwinners' concert. On both occasions we were on just prior to the Beatles, and we had to pass one another face-to-face, yet nothing was said.'

In fact, Lee Curtis and the All Stars were voted into second place in the second *Mersey Beat* Popularity poll – and this was entirely due to the fact that Pete had joined them.

Lee Curtis and the All Stars comprised Lee Curtis (vocals), Tony Waddington (rhythm), Wayne Bickerton (bass), Frank Bowen (lead) and Pete Best (drums).

Pete began to pick up the pieces of his life and in August 1963 he married his girlfriend Kathy.

Lee Curtis signed with Decca, but recorded without the band. Decca then offered the group a separate deal. Pete said: 'Decca suggested we push my name, so we became the Pete Best Four.' Ironically, Mike Smith, who had recorded the Beatles' original audition for Decca, produced their debut record.

The single, 'I'm Gonna Knock On Your Door', was released in June 1964, but it didn't register and Decca dropped the band.

On Monday, 30 March 1964, Pete appeared as a guest on the American TV show, 'I've Got A Secret'.

Pete was to say, 'Magazines, both in Britain and across the Atlantic, have been printing far-fetched stories that I had quit the

Beatles because of illness and that Ringo was called in only because I was too sick to play.'

In fact, this sort of falsification of the facts came to a head when a Beatles interview in *Playboy* magazine in February 1963 had a quote from John saying: 'Ringo used to fill in sometimes if our drummer was ill, with his periodic illness.' Ringo commented, 'He took little pills to make him ill.' Pete sued and a few years later an out-of-court settlement was eventually reached.

To counter the accusations that he was always taking time off due to illness, Pete confirmed that during the entire two years he was with the group, he was only off on two occasions and had given the group an advance warning. Other members of the group had spent as much time away from the band with illnesses.

Pete and his wife Kathy were living in Haymans Green, but one night when Kathy was visiting his mother, Pete became terribly depressed and attempted to gas himself. His brother Rory smelled the gas, battered down the door and, together with Mo, spent several hours reviving him.

Mo became manager of the group and they appeared in Hamburg and recorded with Joe Meek – although the Meek recordings were never released.

They were offered the opportunity of recording in America by an independent A&R man, Bob Gallo. By this time, Tommy McGurk had replaced Bowen, but McGurk left before their American trip. The band added two sax players – Trevor and Bill – and, as a quintet known as the Pete Best Combo, they flew to the States, along with the Undertakers.

The Pete Best Combo appeared on television, toured Canada with Roy Orbison and cut almost forty numbers in the recording studios. The American producers attempted to capitalise on the Beatles association and some of the releases included 'Best Of the Beatles', 'The Beatle That Time Forgot' and 'My Three Years (sic) As A Beatle'.

Tony Waddington revealed to *Record Collector* magazine: 'In the summer of 1965, we were due to audition for the Monkees TV show – Pete Best could have been a Monkee! We'd been told what sort of show it was going to be and what it was all about, and we were going to fly out to Hollywood. By then, we'd split with the Gallo camp and we had a manager called Chick Petri, who was wealthy and influential.'

However, it wasn't to be. They had been in America so long that they either had to return to England and re-apply for a work permit, or become American citizens. If they became citizens, they would be eligible to be drafted for Vietnam, although it seemed an unlikely prospect. They returned home in July 1966 to appear at the Cavern and disbanded soon after that. By 1969, Pete had left the world of music and settled down to become a civil servant for the employment service in Liverpool.

In 1978, Dick Clark invited him to appear on a television reunion with various other veteran musicians. Then Clark invited him to be the technical adviser on a TV movie called *The Birth of the Beatles*, although the producers reportedly ignored the advice of Pete and other Mersey Beat veterans, such as Bob Wooler.

In 1984 his autobiography, written in collaboration with Pat Doncaster, was published. In 1990, together with Billy Kinsley, a former member of the Mersey Beats, he recorded a Rick Wakeman song, 'Heaven'. He also formed a new band and recorded a live album of their appearance at the Beatles convention in Liverpool in 1991. Pete's younger brother Rory also plays drums with the band.

Pete was then invited to tour cities throughout Japan and became a guest at several international Beatles conventions. He took early retirement in 1994 and resumed his musical career with his outfit, the Pete Best Band. His CD of rock 'n' roll favourites from the early Beatles repertoire, released in 1993, was called *Back To The Beat* and the same year, he set out on a year-long world tour of twenty countries, which included Britain, America, Belgium, South Africa, Russia and Dubai.

Pete then received an unexpected piece of good fortune when it was revealed that the Beatles new *Anthology* double CD, set for release in November, would contain several tracks on which Pete made an appearance. These included the Bert Kaempfert Hamburg recordings, tracks from the Decca audition and the initial Parlophone audition recordings. His reward, reputedly, was for an undisclosed seven-figure sum.

Bibliography

There have been more books published about the Beatles than any other twentieth-century icons. There is such an extensive bibliography of Beatles books that, treated in any detail, they would need to be contained in a separate volume. In fact, there have been two books published on the subject – *Paperback Writers: The History Of the Beatles In Print* (Virgin, 1984) and *Here, There & Everywhere: The First International Beatles Bibliography: 1962–1982* (Pierian Press, 1985).

There are more books being published about the Beatles at the present time than there were during the Beatles' heyday.

Almost every aspect of their personal lives, careers and music has been put to detailed scrutiny in more than 1,000 books. These days there are two most interesting trends. The first is the examination in detail of a particular aspect of the group. For example, *The Beatles In The Netherlands 1964–1993* (which closely examines every nook and cranny concerning associations with the Netherlands), echoed in *The Beatles In Holland, The Beatles In New Zealand, The Beatles In Canada, The Beatles In Tokyo*, etc., together with individual books on a particular album, film or event. The research and scholarship that goes behind the compiling of such books is admirable, in particular *From Cavern To Star Club* by Hans Olof Gottfridsson and *It Was All In The Mind: The Co-Creation Of The Beatles Yellow Submarine* by Dr Robert Hieronimus.

The second trend is the self-publishing of their own books by Beatles enthusiasts, such as *It Won't Be Long: The Beatles in Oldham And Middleton,* by Michael Turner, and *Destined For Greatness: The Beatles and Me* by Connie Krauth.

A basic list of most of the books follows, in the chronological sequence in which they were published, year by year.

1964
The True Story of the Beatles, Billy Shepherd, Beat Publications.
All About the Beatles, Edward De Blasio, MacFadden-Bartell.
The Beatles Up To Date, uncredited, Lancer Books.
The Beatle Book, Dezo Hoffmann, Lancer Books.
Here Come The Beatles, Charles Hamblett, Four Square Books.
Out of the Mouths of Beatles, Adam Blessing, Bell Books.
Beatles Ltd, Robert Freeman, George Newnes.
Ringo's Photo Album, Ringo Starr, Jamie Publishers.
Love Me Do: The Beatles Progress, Michael Braun, Penguin Books.
A Hard Day's Night, John Burke, Pan Books (UK) Dell Books (USA).
A Cellarful of Noise, Brian Epstein, Souvenir Press.
The Beatles, Norman Parkinson and Maureen Cleave, Hutchinson.
The Beatles Quiz Book, Jack House, William Collins & Sons Ltd.
Love Letters to the Beatles, selected by Bill Adler, Putnam & Sons.
Dear Beatles, selected by Bill Adler, Grosset & Dunlap.
In His Own Write, John Lennon, Jonathan Cape.
Die Beatles Kommen, Dennis Bow, Fahrplan Einer Weltsensation.
Grapefruit, Yoko Ono, Wunternaum.

1965
Help!, Al Hine, Dell Books.
Help!, Random House.
A Spaniard in the Works, John Lennon, Jonathan Cape.
Communism, Hypnotism, and the Beatles, The Reverend David A. Noebel, Christian Crusade.

Die Beatles: Fabelwesen Unswerer Zeit, Christine Ehrhardt, Wolf Frhr Von Tucker.
The Beatles Diary, Beat Publications.

1966
The Penguin John Lennon, John Lennon, Penguin Books.
Up the Beatles' Family Tree, Cecil R. Humphrey-Smith, Michael G. Heenan, Jennifer Mount, Achievements Ltd.
Murray the K Tells It Like It Is, Baby, Murray Kaufman, Holt, Rinehart & Winston.

1967
John Lennon, In His Own Write & A Spaniard In The Works, Signet Books.
The Writing Beatle: John Lennon, Signet Books.
The Golden Beatles, Northern Songs.
Art & The City, John Willett, Methuen.

1968
The Beatles: The Authorised Biography, Hunter Davies, Heinemann.
The Beatles: the Real Story, Julius Fast, Putnam & Sons.
The Beatles, Anthony Scaduto, Signet Books.
The Beatles: a Study in Sex, Drugs and Revolution, The Reverend David A. Noebel, Christian Crusade.
The Beatles in Yellow Submarine, Max Wilk, Signet Books.
The Yellow Submarine Gift Book, World Distributors.
The Beatles: Words Without Music, Rick Friedman, Grosset & Dunlap.
The Beatles Book, edited by Edward E. Davis, Cowles Educational Corporation.
In His Own Write: the Lennon Play, Adrienne Kennedy, Victor Spinetti, John Lennon, Jonathan Cape.
Beatles & Co, Juan Carlos Kreimer, Editorial Galerma.

1969
The Beatles Illustrated Lyrics, edited by Alan Aldridge, Macdonald Unit 75.

1970
The Beatles Get Back, photographs: Ethan Russell. text: Jonathan Cott, David Dalton.
The Girl Who Sang With The Beatles, Robert Hemenway, Alfred A. Knopf.

1971
We Love You Beatles, Margaret Sutton, Doubleday.
The Beatles Illustrated Lyrics: Volume Two, edited by Alan Aldridge, BCI Publishing Ltd.

The Beatles, Aram Saroyan, Barn Dream Press.
Lennon Remembers, Jann Wenner, Straight Arrow.

1972
Apple to the Core, Peter McCabe & Robert D. Shonfeld, Pocket Books.
The Lennon Factor, Paul Young, Stein & Day.
The Longest Cocktail Party, Richard DiLello, Charisma Books.
Body Count, Francie Schwartz, Straight Arrow.
Les Beatles, Alain Dister, Albin Michel.
Beowulf to Beatles and Beyond, edited by David R. Pichaske, Macmillan.
The Beatles Years, edited by Ray Connolly, Macmillan.

1973
As Time Goes By, Derek Taylor, Straight Arrow.
Twilight of the God: The Beatles in Retrospect, Wilfred Mellors, Viking Press.

1974
The Beatles: Yesterday . . . Today . . . Tomorrow, Rochelle Larkin, Scholastic Book Services.
The Beatles, Patricia Parmangton, Creative Education.
The Beatles Lyrics Complete, Futura Books.

1975
The Paul McCartney Story, George Tremlett, Futura Books.
The Beatles: The Fabulous Story of John, Paul, George & Ringo, compiled by Robert Burt, edited by Jeremy Pascall, Octopus Books in association with Phoebus Publishing Company.
The Beatles Lyrics Complete, Futura Books.
The Beatles Story, edited by Rob Burt, Phoebus.
The Beatles Lyrics Illustrated, Dell Books.
The Beatles Illustrated Record, Roy Carr & Tony Tyler, New English Library.
The Beatles Collection, City of Liverpool Public Relations Department.
The Beatles, Dezo Hoffmann, Shinko Music Co.
The Beatles, Shinko Music Co.
The Man Who Gave the Beatles Away, Allan Williams & Bill Marshall, Elm Tree Books.
The John Lennon Story, George Tremlett, Futura Books.
The Complete Beatles Quiz Book, Edwin Goodgold & Dan Carlinsky, Warner Books.

1976
Linda's Pictures, Linda McCartney, Alfred A. Knopf.
All Together Now, Harry Castleman & Walter J. Podrazik.

Beatles Discography, Arno Guzek, privately published.
Paul McCartney in His Own Words, Paul Gambaccini, Omnibus Press.
Beatles A–Z, John Neville Leppert, privately published.
Growing Up With the Beatles, Ron Shaumburg, Pyramid Books.
John Lennon: One Day at a Time, Anthony Fawcett, Grove Press.
On Stage: The Beatles, Debra Keenan, Creative Education.
The Beatles, George Zanderbergen, Crestwood House.
Los Beatles, Alistair Simms, Ediciones Technical Press.
All You Need is Love, Tony Palmer, Weidenfeld & Nicolson.

1977
The Facts About a Pop Group Featuring Wings, Dave Gelly, André Deutsch.
Paul McCartney & Wings, Tony Jasper, Octopus Books.
Paul McCartney & Wings, Jeremy Pascall, Hamlyn.
George Harrison: Yesterday & Today, Ross Michaels, Flash Books.
Paul McCartney: A Biography in Words and Pictures, John Mendelsohn, Sire Books/Chappell Music Ltd.
Wings, Rock Fun.
A Hard Day's Night, edited by Philip DiFranco, Chelsea House.
Yesterday Seems So Far Away: The Beatles Yesterday and Today, John Swenson, Zebra Books.
The Beatles Again?, Harry Castleman & Walter Podrazik, Pieron Press.
1000 Beatles Facts (And a Little Hearsay), ed Nibbervoll and Evan Thorburn, J. Albert.
Mersey Beat: The Beginning of the Beatles, Bill Harry, Omnibus Press.

1978
The Beatles: The Authorised Biography, Hunter Davies, William Heinemann.
The Beatles: An Illustrated Record, Roy Carr & Tony Tyler, English Library.
Behind the Beatles Songs, Philip Cowan, Polytantric Press,
Paperback Writer, Mark Shipper, Grosset & Dunlap.
The Beatles in Their Own Words, Miles, Omnibus Press.
Hands Across the Water: Wings Tour USA, Hipgnosis, Paper Tiger.
26 Days that Rocked the World, O'Brien Publishing.
Beatle Madness, Martin A. Grove, Manor Books.
The Beatles Trivia Quiz Book, Helen Rosenbaum, New American Library.
Paul McCartney: Beatle with Wings, Martin A. Grove, Manor Books.

The Official Sgt Pepper's Lonely Hearts Club Band Scrapbook, Robert Stigwood and Dee Anthony, Guild & Western.
Sgt Pepper's Lonely Hearts Club Band, Henry Edwards, Pocket Books.
A Twist of Lennon, Cynthia Lennon, Star Books.
The Beatles Forever, Nicholas Schaffner, McGraw-Hill.

1979
Pocket Beatles Complete, Wise Publications.
The Beatles Concert-ed Efforts, Jan Van de Bunt & Friends.
Every Little Thing: The Beatles on Record, Mitchell McGeary and William McCoy, privately published.
Beatles Movie Catalog, Toru Matahira.
Up Against It: A Screenplay For the Beatles, Joe Orton, Eyre Methuen.
All You Need Is Ears, George Martin, Macmillan.
Elvis Presley – The Beatles, Stella H. Alicio, Pendulum Press.
Il Viaggio Dei Cuori: Un Libro Sui Beatles, Roberto Antoni, Il Formichiere.

1980
Things We Said Today, Colin Campbell and Allan Murphy, Pierian Press.
The Beatles: A Day In The Life, compiled by Tom Schultheiss.
Strawberry Fields Forever: John Lennon Remembered, Vic Garbarini, Brian Cullman, Barbara Graustark. Delilah/Bantam.
Across The Universe, Arno Guzek, privately published.
The Boys From Liverpool: John, Paul, George, Ringo, Nicholas Schaffner, Methuen.
The Beatles Illustrated Lyrics, Volumes One and Two, edited by Alan Aldridge, Macdonald Futura.
John Lennon 1940-80: One Day at a Time, Anthony Fawcett, New English Library.
John Lennon: Death of a Dream, George Carpozi Jr, Manor Books.
I, Me, Mine, George Harrison, Genesis Publications.
The Beatles A to Z, Goldie Friede, Robin Titone, Sue Weiner, Eyre Methuen.
In His Own Write/A Spaniard in the Works, John Lennon, New American Library.
The Beatles, Geoffrey Stokes, Rolling Stone/W. H. Allen/ Omnibus Press.
The Writings of John Lennon, John Lennon, Simon & Schuster.
Lennon: What Happened!, edited by Timothy Green Beckley, Sunshine Publications.
Lennon: Up Close & Personal, edited by Timothy Green Beckley, Sunshine Publications.

Paul McCartney Und Wings, Klaus Dewes & Rudi Oertel, Bergisch Gladbach.

1981
John Lennon in His Own Words, compiled by Miles, Omnibus Press.
In The Footsteps of the Beatles, Mike Evans and Ron Jones, Merseyside County Council.
Rock 'N' Roll Times, Jurgen Vollmer, Google Plex Books.
The Compleat Beatles, Delilah/ATV/Bantam.
Paul McCartney Composer/Artist, Pavilion Books.
All You Needed Was Love: The Beatles After the Beatles, John Blake, Hamlyn.
Shout! The True Story of the Beatles, Philip Norman, Elm Tree Books.
Lennon & McCartney, Malcolm Doney, Midas Books.
The Beatles Apart, Bob Woffinden, Proteus Books.
John Lennon & the Beatles Forever, Ed Naha, Tower Books.
You Can't Do That: Beatles Bootlegs & Novelty Discs, Charles Reinhart, Pierian Press.
John Lennon 4 Ever, Conrad Snell, Crown Summit Books.
The John Lennon Story, John Swenson, Leisure Books.
The Beatles, Alan Clark, Alan Clark Productions.
Lennon '69: Search for Liberation, edited by Jeff Long, The Bhaktivedanta Book Trust.
A Tribute to John Lennon 1940–1980, edited by Lyn Belanger, Michael Brecher, Jo Kearns, Nicolas Locke and Mike Shatzkin, Proteus Books.
A Cellarful of Noise, Brian Epstein, New English Library.
The Beatles For the Record, Stafford Pemberton Publishing.
The Lennon Tapes, Andy Peebles, BBC Publications.
John Lennon: 1940–1980, compiled by Ernest E. Schworck, ESE.
John Lennon: A Personal Pictorial Diary, Sportomatic Ltd.
John Lennon 1940–1980, Ray Connolly, Fontana.
Thank U Very Much, Mike McCartney, Arthur Baker.
The Beatles at the Beeb, Kevin Howlett, BBC Publications.
Pour John Lennon, Maurice Achard, Alain Moreau.

1982
Liverpool 8, John Cornelius, John Murray.
Das Album Der Beatles, Michael Jurgs, Hans Heinrich Ziemann and Willi Braam.
The Beatles Forever, Helen Spence, Colour Library Books.
The Beatles Album File & Complete Discography, Jeff Russell, Blandford Press.

The Beatles On Record, Mark Wallgren, Simon & Schuster.

The Long & Winding Road, Neville Stannard, Virgin Books.

Lots of Liverpool, Beatles Unlimited Special.

The Beatles' England, David Bacon and Norman Maslov, Columbus Books.

John Lennon's Secret, David Stuart Ryan, Kosmik Press.

The Legacy of John Lennon: Charming or Harming A Generation, The Reverend David A. Noebel, Thomas Nelson Publishers.

As I Write This Letter, Marc A. Catone, Greenfield Books.

The Beatles: A Collection, Robin and Cindy DelBuno, Robcin Associates.

Collecting the Beatles, Barb Fenick, Pierion Press.

The Complete Beatles Lyrics, Omnibus Press.

The 1975 John Lennon Interview, Lavinia Van Driver, privately published.

The Playboy Interviews With John Lennon & Yoko Ono, David Sheff, Playboy Press.

The Ballad of John & Yoko, the Editors of Rolling Stone, Rolling Stone Press.

Photographs, Linda McCartney, MPL Communications.

Abbey Road, Brian Southall, Patrick Stephens Limited.

The Beatles Down Under, Glenn A. Baker, Wild & Wooley Press.

P.S. We Love You, Tony Barrow, Mirror Books.

The Beatles' Who's Who, Bill Harry, Aurum Press.

With the Beatles, Dezo Hoffmann, Omnibus Press.

The Beatles For the Record, Don Mills, Collins.

Remember: Recollections and Photographs of the Beatles, Mike McCartney, Henry Holt & Co.

The Beatles on Record, Jeff Russell, Charles Scribner's.

1983

The Ocean View, Humphrey Ocean, MPL Communications/ Plexus Books.

Loving John, May Pang and Henry Edwards, Warner Books.

Dakota Days, John Green, St Martin's Press.

John Lennon: Summer of 1980, Perigee Books.

The Beatles: 24 Posters, Colour Library Books.

John Lennon: A Family Album, photographs by Nishi F. Saimaru.

The Complete Beatles U.S. Record Price Guide, Perry Cox and Joe Lindsay, O'Sullivan Woodside & Co.

Let's Go Down the Cavern, Spencer Leigh, Royal Life Insurance.

Working Class Heroes, Neville Stannard, Virgin Books.

Yesterday: Photographs of the Beatles, Robert Freeman, Weidenfeld & Nicolson.

Paul McCartney, Alan Hamilton, Hamish Hamilton.
The Literary Lennon, Dr James Sauceda, Pierian Press.
The Beatles: An Illustrated Diary, Har van Fulpen, Plexus Books.
Follow the Merseybeat Road, Sam Leach, Eden Publications.
John Lennon: In My Life, Pete Shotton and Nicholas Schaffner, Stein & Day.
The Beatles Records in Australia, Bruce Hamlin, privately published.
The Beatles: The Fab Four Who Dominated Pop Music For a Decade, Robert Burt, Jeremy Pascall, Treasure Press.
The Beatles, Colour Library Books.
Liverpool – the 60s, Brunnings.
The Mersey Sound, Adrian Henri, Roger McGough and Brian Patten, Penguin.
New Volume, Adrian Henri, Roger McGough and Brian Patten, Penguin.
Stardust Memories, Ray Connolly, Pavilion Books.
The Love You Make: An Insider's Story of the Beatles, Peter Brown and Stephen Gaines, McGraw-Hill.
The Beatles: A Musical Evolution, Terence O'Grady, Twayne Publishers.
Give Peace a Chance: Music and the Struggle For Peace, Marianne Philbin, Chicago Review Press.

1984
The Beatles: It Was 20 Years Ago, Michael Press.
The Music of the Beatles, Martin E. Horn, Big Eye Publications.
The Beatles Reader, Charles P. Meises, Pierian Press.
A Cellarful of Noise, Brian Epstein, Pierian Press.
The Longest Cocktail Party, Richard DiLello, Pierian Press.
Waiting For the Beatles, Carol Bedford, Blandford Press.
As Time Goes By, Derek Taylor, Pierian Press.
The Beatles at the BEEB, Kevin Howlett, Pierian Press.
The Book of Lennon, Bill Harry, Aurum Press.
The Day the Music Died, various authors, Plexus Books.
The Beatles, Bill Harry, Beatle City.
The Art of the Beatles, Mike Evans, Anthony Blond (UK), William Morrow (USA).
John Lennon: For The Record, Peter McCabe and Robert D. Schonfeld, Bantam Books.
Give My Regards to Broad Street, Andrew Harvey with George Perry, MPL Communications.
The Beatles, John Tobler, W. H. Smith (UK). Exeter Books (USA).
Come Together: John Lennon in His Time, Jon Wiener, Random House.

The Beatles' Labels, Howard Kramer, privately published.

The Beatles Conquer America, Dezo Hoffmann, Virgin Books.

Lennon: A Liverpool Echo Tribute, The Liverpool Echo.

Paul McCartney: The Definitive Biography, Chris Welch, Proteus Books.

John Winston Lennon 1940–1966, Ray Coleman, Sidgwick & Jackson.

John Ono Lennon 1967–1980, Ray Coleman, Sidgwick & Jackson.

Beatles, Musketeers and Supermen: The Films of Dick Lester, Neil Sinyard, Croom Helm.

Fifty Years Adrift (In An Open-Necked Shirt), Derek Taylor, Genesis Books.

John Lennon: An Illustrated Biography, Richard Wootton, Hodder & Stoughton.

Beatlemania: A History of the Beatles on Film, Bill Harry, Virgin Books (UK), Avon Books (USA).

Paperback Writers: An Illustrated Bibliography, Bill Harry, Virgin Books (UK), Avon Books (USA).

June 1964: De Bietels Tussen de Bollen (The Beatles Amongst The Tulips), MMM Magazines.

1985

Beatle! The Pete Best Story, Pat Doncaster and Pete Best, Plexus (UK), Dell (USA).

Collecting the Beatles: Volume Two, Barb Fenick, Pierian Press.

Julian Lennon, Yolande Flesch, Running Press.

Listen to These Pictures: Photographs of John Lennon, Bob Gruen, William Morrow.

Ask Me Why: The Beatles Quizbook, Bill Harry, Javelin Books.

The Book of Beatles Lists, Bill Harry, Javelin Books.

The Book of Beatles Lists, Charles F. Reinhart, Contemporary Books.

Here, There & Everywhere: The First International Beatles Bibliography 1962–1982, Carol D. Terry, Pierian Press.

The Beatles, Orbis.

Dear Mr Fantasy, Ethan Russell, Houghton Mifflin Co.

The Beatles Authorised Biography: Second Revised Edition, Hunter Davies, McGraw-Hill.

John Lennon Conversations, Linda Deer Domnitz, Coleman Publishing.

Step Inside, Cilla Black, J. M. Dent.

The Beatles: Untold Tales, Howard A. DeWitt, Horizon Books.

Yesterday . . . Came Suddenly, Bob Cepicon and Waleed Ali, Timbre Books/Arbor House.

Beatles For Sale: The Beatles Merchandising Guide, Bill Harry, Virgin Books.
John Lennon, Dezo Hoffmann, Columbus Press.
Beatlefan Volumes One and Two, Pierian Press.
The Beatles: Their Greatest Hits, edited by Joyce Robins, St Michael.
Lennon, Ray Coleman, McGraw-Hill.

1986
McCartney: Songwriter, Howard Elson, Comet Books.
The McCartney File, Bill Harry, Virgin Books.
McCartney: The Definitive Biography, Chris Salewicz, St. Martin's Press.
The Beatles: A Recording History, Allen J. Wiener, McFarland (USA), Bailey Brothers and Swinfen (UK).
The Faces of John Lennon, Dezo Hoffmann, McGraw-Hill.
The Beatles Live!, Mark Lewisohn, Pavilion Books.
Julian Lennon, Kalia Lulow, Ballantine.
John Lennon/Julian Lennon, Nancie S. Martin, Avon Superstars.
Songs of George Harrison, Genesis Publications.
Mike Mac's Black and Whites Plus One Colour, Mike McCartney, Aurum Press (UK), Viking Penguin (USA).
Skywriting By Word of Mouth, John Lennon, Pan Books (UK), Harper & Row (USA).
The Beatles Price and Reference Guide For American Records, Perry Cox and Michael Miller, Cox–Miller Publications.
Beatlefan: Volumes 3 and 4, Pierian Press.
Four Ever – 25 Jahre Beatles, Peter Schuster, Belser Verlag.
In His Own Youth. In My Own Words, Julia Baird, River Women Press.
The Beatles: A Celebration, Geoffrey Giuliano, St Martin's Press.
The Beatles Down Under: The 1964 Australian and New Zealand Tour, Glenn A. Baker and Roger Dilernia, Pierian Press.
The Beatles in Tokyo, Jam Publishing Co.

1987
It Was 20 Years Ago Today, Derek Taylor, Simon & Schuster (UK), Bantam (USA).
Come Together: John Lennon in His Time, Jon Wiener, Faber.
Sgt Pepper's Lonely Hearts Club Band, Bill Harry, Atalanta Press.
Yoko Ono, Jerry Hopkins, Macmillan.
Alles Was Du Brauchst Is Liebe, Andreas Peglau, Zentralhaus Publikation.
Bob Dylan and the Beatles, Tino Markworth, Hobo Press.
The Beatles Last Concert, Eric Lefcowitz, Terra Firma Press.
The Beatles Book, Omnibus Press.

Music and Maiden Overs: My Showbusiness Life, Vic Lewis, Chatto & Windus.

The Lennon Companion, edited by Elizabeth Thomson and David Gutman, Macmillan (UK), Schirmer Books (USA).

McCartney, Chet Flippo, Doubleday (USA), Sidgwick & Jackson (UK).

Lennon, Carole Lynn Corbin, Franklin Watts Ltd.

30 Years of Beatles Music – A Chronicle, Kurt Erlemann, Er-Ro Publications.

The Beatles in Liverpool, Peter Kaye, Starlit Liverpool Ltd.

Les Beatles, Pierre Merle and Jacques Volcouve, Solar.

Paul Ist Schuld, Corinne Ullrich Crox, Phantom Verlag.

John Lennon, Alan Posener, Rowohlt Taschenbuch Verlag.

Beatle People: In Words and Pictures, The Walrus, privately published.

1988
Yesterday: The Unauthorised Biography of Paul McCartney, Chet Flippo, Doubleday.

The Lives of John Lennon, Albert Goldman, William Morrow.

The Beatles Recording Sessions, Mark Lewisohn, Harmony Books (USA).

Tell Me Why: A Beatles Commentary, Tim Riley, Alfred A. Knopf.

Imagine: John Lennon, Andrew Solt and Sam Egan, Macmillan.

1989
Who Killed John Lennon?, Fenton Bresler, St Martin's Press.

The Beatles, Bill Yenne, Gallery Books.

Sweet Beatle Dreams: The Diary of Mary Mack Conger, Mary Mack Conger, Andrews & McMeel.

1990
John Lennon: Vicendo Cantando, Racconti, Arcana Editrice SRL.

John Lennon: Lennon Sense, Arcana Editrice SRI.

John Lennon: Gimme Some Truth, The Complete John Lennon Songbook, Pendragon Verlag.

1991
Paul McCartney, Jurgen Siebold, Moewig.

The Beatles Myth, Michael Bryan Kelly, McFarland.

The Last Days of John Lennon, Fred Seaman, Citadel Press.

The Unseen Beatles, Bob Whitaker and Martin Harrison, Collins Publishers.

Forever Beatles, John Alvarez Taylor, Bison Books.

The Revolver Sessions, photography Robert Freeman, text Brian Hogg, UFO Books.

Illegal Beatles: Archival Back Issues 1986–1988, Doug Sulpy, Storyteller Productions.

1992

Getting Sober . . . and Loving It, Joan and Derek Taylor.

Mach Shau: Die Beatles Im Hamburg, Thomas Rehwagen and Thorsten Schmidt, Einsfallsreich.

Sixties: Portrait of an Era, Linda McCartney, Reed Books.

The Immortal John Lennon, Michael Heatley, Octopus International.

The Beatles, Mike Clifford, Smithmark Publishers.

Paul McCartney, Carola Deurwaarder, De Geillustreerde Pers.

AI: Japan Through John Lennon's Eyes, Yoko Ono, Cadence Books.

Mike McCartney's Merseyside, Cornerhouse Publications.

Yesterday, The Beatles Die 60er. Haus Der Jugend, Ludwig Hafen.

Stars, Mythen & Legenden, John Alvarex Taylor, Lechner Verlag.

Paul McCartney: From Liverpool to Let It Be, Howard A. DeWitt, Horizon Books.

Paul McCartney, Dominique Grandfils, Zelie.

McCartney: 50 Ans, Francois Jouffa, Michel Lafon.

Beatles Dictionary, Jordi Sierra I Fabra, Plaza y Janes.

Paul McCartney – Im Gesprach Fur Europa, Christian Frietsch, Radio Victoria.

Beatles Tutti I Testi, 1962–1970, Arcana Editrice.

Beatles and Lennon: Marmalade and Dynamite, Nicolas, Ediciones Casser S.L.

Ringo Starr; Straight Man or Joker?, Alan Clayson, Paragon House.

The Beatles: A Celebration, Geoffrey Giuliano, Wellfleet Press.

The Ultimate Beatles Encyclopedia, Bill Harry, Virgin Books (UK), Hyperion (USA).

1993

The Unseen Beatles, photographs by Bob Whitaker, Conran Octopus.

Linda McCartney's Sixties, Mitchell Beazley.

The Beatles: A Private View, Robert Freeman, Mitchell Beazley.

Beatles: A Tear-Out Photo Book, Oliver Books.

Getting Sober . . . and Loving It, Joan and Derek Taylor, Vermillion.

John Lennon, Myths and Reality. V. V. Bokaryov, Klyon. Moscow.

Tony Sheridan. E Ein Leben Fur Die Musik and Mit Der Musik, Edmund Thielow.

The Beatles in New Zealand, Bruce Renwick, B. Tell Publications.

The Colour of Your Dreams, The Beatles Psychedelic Music, Stuart Madow and Jeff Sobul, Dorrance Publications.
The Anthology of Rock Music. John Lennon, Nikolay Emelyanov, Klion Books.
Let Me Take You Down: Inside the Mind of MDS, the Man Who Shot John Lennon. Jack Jones, Villard.
The Beatles Music Index 1958–1990, Michael Todd, B. Tell Publications.
Candles For Lennon: Philosophical Reflections on the Vision of a Pop Icon, Ralph Synning, Aardvark Books.
The Beatles – A Reference and Value Guide, Michael Stern, Barbara Crawford and Hollis Lamon, Collector Books.
Beatles For Sale, Michael Todd, AMV Entertainment.
John Lennon in Heaven – Crossing the Borderlines of Being, Linda Keen, Pan Publishing.
Beatles I Sverige, Artillo Bercholtz and Carl Hallberg.

1994
Liverpool Days, Max Scheler and Astrid Kirchherr, Genesis.
The Beatles Japanese Record Guide, Jason Anjoorian, Jason Press.
The Beatles, Theresa Celsi, Ariel books.
The Beatles – The Early Years, Yarden Uriel, Uriel.
The Beatles I Norge, Knut Uller and Roger Stormo, Norwegian Wood.
The Beatles CD Guide, John Ewing, Orion Books.
I Read the News Today: The Social Drama of John Lennon's Death, Fred Logo, Littlefields Adams Quality Paperbacks.
Meet the Beatles, Shinko Music.
The Maharishi: The Biography of the Man Who Gave Transcendental Meditation to the West, Paul Masin, Element.
Ole, Beatles, Javier de Castro Fresnadillo and Enrique Sanches Romero, Pages Editors.
The Beatles, John Alvarez Taylor, J. G. Press.

1995
Destined For Greatness: The Beatles and Me, Connie Krauth, Say The Word.
The Beatles: The Art of the Yellow Submarine, Max Wilke, UFO Books.
Beatles Story, Elmar Horigs, Eichborn/SWF-3.
The Beatles, El Libro, Maurillo De Miguel, Luca Editorial S.A.
John Lennon, Miquel Martinez and Vicente Escudero, Jucar.
John Lennon: Young Rock Star, Laurence Santrey, Troll Associates.
Die Beatles Und Ich, Gunther Butkus.
El Joven Lennon, Jordi Sierra I Fabra, Ediciuones S.M.

John Lennon, Zeichnungen, Performance, Film, Wulf Herzogen Rath and Dorothea Hansen, Cantz Verlag.

Los Beatles, Alain Dister, Jugar.

Die Beatles Und Ich, Gunther Butkus, Pendragon.

The Beatles – Baby It's You: A Visual Record, Andy Neill, Vinyl Experience.

Cancelled! The Beatles Unreleased Recordings, Mr Kite, Soundbit Verlag.

Things We Said Today, Phil Bowen, Stride.

Servus Beatles, Fandly, Leopold, Planiger and Zechmeister, Lowenedition.

The Beatles. Yeah! Yeah! Yeah!, Y. Kabluchko, O. Chernienko and V. Avilov, T/O Dialog.

They Died Too Young: John Lennon, Tom Stockdale, Parragon.

The Big Klaus Beyer Beatles Book, Frank Behnke, Martin Schmitz Verlag.

Raimonds Traum, Ein Beatles Roman, Elmar Hoerig, Eichborn Verlag.

The Beatles, Una Filmografia Musical, Alejeandro Iranzo de Riguier and Magi Crussells Valeta, Royal Books.

The McCartney Interviews: After the Breakup, Paul Gambaccini, Omnibus Press.

The Beatles, Hunter Davies, W. W. Norton.

The Beatles: Free As a Bird, Giles Coren and David Sinclair, UFO Music.

The Beatles With Lacan: Rock 'N' Roll as Requiem For the Modern Age, Henry W. Sullivan, Peter Lang.

1996

Imagine: A Celebration of John Lennon, Penguin Books.

The Beatles in Tokyo, Peter Brum, The Japan Times Ltd.

Help!, Ray Coleman.

Beatles at the BBC, Kevin Howlett.

The Beatles BBC Sessions, Fujieda and Nakada, Ginka-sha.

Golden Dreams, Astrid Kirchherr and Max Scheler, Genesis Publications.

The Beatles and the Sixties, Michka Assayas and Claude Meunier, Henry Holt.

Stuart: The Life of Stuart Sutcliffe, Pauline Sutcliffe and Kay Williams, Genesis Publications.

The Definitive Visual Guide – USA Feb 1964, Keith Badman and Terry Rawlings, Best Buy Record Shops.

Beatles Beatles, Carl Magnus Palm, Tiden Childrens' Books.

Beatles in Germany, Gunter Zint, Tracks.

Who Was Eleanor Rigby?, Brandon Toropove, Harper Reference.

John Lennon – Lonely Heart, Satokuni Ishigamore, Shinpusha.
Sociology of the Beatles, Asahi Shimbun.
The Making of the Beatles Sgt Pepper, Belmo, Collectors Guide Publishing.
The Walrus Was Paul – The Great Beatles Death Clues of 1969, R. Gary Patterson, Dowling Press.
Beatles Recordings Decoder, Dynamo House.
The Beatles Exhibition, Raul Blisniuk, Produccio Graficas Integradas SRL.
The Summer of 1968: The Mad Day Out, Peter Doggett, Tracks.
The 910's Guide to the Solo Beatles Outtakes, Doug Sulpy and Chip Madinger, 910.
Die Beatles – Blitztournee, Uwe Blaschke, Thorsten Schmidt and Mathias Hoelings, Kultur Buch Bremen.
Made in Holland: The Dutch Beatles Discography, Ed Dieckmann, Franck Leenheer Records.
The Presence of Astrid K, Narumi Kamatsu, Sekai Bunkasha.
The Beatles: Collecting the Original UK Pressings, Mitch Scharoff.
Beatlesmania Made in the Deutsche Demokratische Republik, Edmund Thielow, Sgt Pepper's Club.
The Beatles: The Way Up, Yarden Uriel, Uriel.
The Quiet One, Alan Clayson, Sanctuary Publishing.
Straight Man or Joker?, Alan Clayson, Sanctuary Publishing.
The Encyclopedia of Beatles People, Bill Harry, Blandford Press.
The Beatles: An Encyclopedic Reference Book, Andrey Ponomarenko and Nikolay Kiozlov, Bibliopolis Publishing House.
Roadworks, Linda McCartney, Little, Brown & Co.
Can You Dig It, Kent O Shinzaki, Cranberry Hills Productions.
The Beatles in Belgium, Johan Ral and Jos Bijnews.
Beatles Unseen, John Howard, Penguin Books.

1997
The Beatles and Some Other Guys: Rock Family Trees of the Early 60s, Pete Frame, Omnibus Press.
The Beatles Fun Trivia Quiz Book, Keith Badman, UCI.
Without You: The Tragic Story of Badfinger, Dan Matovina, Omnibus Press.
We All Shine On, Paul du Noyer, Carlton Books.
The Great Beatles Death Clues, R. Gary Petterson, Robson Books.
Paul McCartney: Many Years From Now, Barry Miles, Secker and Warburg (UK), Henry Holt and Co (USA).
The Beatles Fab Four CD & Book Set.
The Beatles First Tour of America, Terry Rawlings and Keith Badman.

Beatles Story, Elmar Horig, SWF3 Buch von Eich Born Verlag.

Les Dictionaire Des Beatles, Jean-Louis Poland and Francois Jouffa, Michel Lafan.

The Complete Guide to the Music of John Lennon, Johnny Rogan, Omnibus Press.

The Beatles: A Collector's Guide to Beatles Memorabilia, Yesterday and Tomorrow, Courtney McWilliams, A. Schiffer.

John, Paul & Me: Before the Beatles, Len Garry, Hot Wacks Press.

She Loves You: A Curious Tale Concerning A Miraculous Intervention, Elaine Segal, Simon and Schuster.

All You Need Is Love: The Beatles Dress Rehearsal, David Magnus, Tracks.

Selections From the Beatles Anthology, Volume 3, Hal Leonard Corp.

The Beatles: From Cavern to Star Club, Olof Gottridsson, Premier Publishing.

Big Beatles in Germany, Astrid Kirchherr, Gunter Zint and Peter Bruchmann, Genesis Publications.

Sir Paul McCartney, Tracks.

Epic Moments and Secrets: John Lennon and the Beatles, At the Mirror of Man's Destiny. The Beatles Trilogy, Part One, The Last Concerts, Richard Warren Lipack, Barrister Publishers.

The Lost Lennon Interviews, Geoffrey and Brenda Giuliano, Adams Media Corporation.

The Beatles 1965/1966/1967, Koh Hasebe, Shinko Music.

The Beatles, Tony Burrows, Carlton Books.

The Beatles Not For Sale, Belmo, Hot Wacks Press.

Sir Paul McCartney, Liverpool Echo.

Abbey Road, Brian Southall, Peter Vince and Allan Rouse, Omnibus Press.

From Hamburg to Hollywood, Jurgen Vollmer, Genesis Publications.

Made in Holland Two, Ed Dieckmann, Franck Leenheer Records.

Record Sgt Pepper, Johnny Black, Tracks.

Classic Rock Albums: Abbey Road/Let It Be/The Beatles, Pete Doggett, Schirmer Books.

Hamburg: The Cradle of British Rock, Alan Clayson, Sanctuary.

The Beatles – The Summer of 1968, Peter Doggett, Tracks.

Not For Sale: The Beatles Music Legacy, Belmo, Hot Wacks Press.

1998

The Complete Idiot's Guide to the Beatles, Richard Buskin, Alpha Books.

Paul McCartney: The Standing Stone Premier, Harriet Perry, Tracks.

The Beatles Undercover, Kristofer K. Engelhardt.

The Beatles TV Performances, Shu Fujieda and Masotoshi Nakada, Ginkasha.

The Beatles Sgt Pepper's Lonely Hearts Club Band, Allan F. Moore, Cambridge Music Handbooks.

A Complete Discography of Norwegian Beatles Records, Hans Petter Nesseth, Nesseth.

Recording Sgt Pepper's, Johnny Black, Tracks.

The Beatles: A Diary, Barry Miles, Omnibus Press.

The Beatles Illustrated Lyrics, Alan Aldridge, Little & Brown.

Drummed Out: The Sacking of Pete Best, Spencer Leigh, Northdown.

The Beatles Book of Lists, Stephen J. Spignesi, Citadel Press Book.

The Beatles, Pitkin Guides.

The Beatles: An Oral History, David Pritchard and Alan Lysaght, Hyperion.

Het Geluid Van De Beatles, Ger Tillekens, Het spinhuis Oudezijds Achterburgwal.

Revolution Les Beatles, Jacques Volcouve and Pierre Merle, Fayard.

Love Is All You Need, Regina Burch, The Chapel Hill Press.

The Beatles (Vol 2), Patrick Humphries, Omnibus Press.

In My Life: Encounters With The Beatles, Robert Cording, Shelli Jankowski and E.J. Miller, Laino Fromm International Publishing.

Beatlemania: An Unauthorised Collector's Guide, Courtney McWilliams.

The Beatles Undercover, Kristopher Engelhardt, Collectors Guide Publishing Ltd.

The Beatles Now and Then, Harry Benson.

The Importance of the Beatles, Adam Wood.

The Beatles: The Music Was Never the Same.

The Beatles Files, Andy Davis, Bramley Books.

Beatles–Beatles, Carl Magnus Palm, Tiden.

The Beatles, John Macilwain, Pitkin Guides.

The Beatles Invasion of Canada: Our Hearts Went Boom, Brian Kendal, Viking/Penguin Books.

The Beatles in Nederland 1964–1993, Azing Moltmaker, SBF.

1999

It Won't Be Long: The Beatles in Oldham and Middleton, Michael Turner, Marjensor Productions.

Wide Open, Linda McCartney, Little Brown.

Magical Mystery Tour, Tony Barrow, Omnibus Press.

The Mourning of John Lennon, Anthony Elliott, The University of California Press.

The Beatles' Mixes, Holger Schoeler and Thorsten Schmidt, Kultur Buch Bremen Verlag.

Body Count, Francie Schwartz.

The Beatles in New Zealand, B. Tell Publications.

The Beatles, Getting to Know the World's Greatest Composers, Mike Venezia, Children's Press.

Beatlemania: A Collector's Guide, Courtney McWilliams, Schiffer.

Every Little Thing, Maxwell MacKenzie, Avon Music Books.

Head to Toe and Up Against It, Joe Orton, De Capo Press.

Schwarze Seiten '99, Thorsten Schmidt, Kultur Buch Bremen.

The Importance of the Beatles, Adam Woog, Lucent Books.

The Beatles US LPs: Where They Came From and How They Charted, Kenneth D. Westover, Cliff Canyon Publishing.

The Beatles Undercover, Kristofer Engelhardt, Collectors Guide Publishing.

In My Life: Encounters With the Beatles, edited by Robert Landing, Shelli Jankowski-Smith and E. J. Miller Laino, Fromm International Publishers.

The History of the World in Nine Guitars, Eric Osenna and Thierry Arnoult, Welcome Rain Press.

Ticket To Ride, Alasdair Ferguson and Alf Bicknell, Glitter Books.

The Rocking City, Sam Leach, Pharoah Books.

The Beatles as Musicians: Revolver Through the Anthology, Walter Everett, Oxford University Press.

The Beatles, Popular Music and Society: A Thousand Voices, Ian Inglis, St Martin's Press.

Glass Onion: The Beatles in Their Own Words, Geoffrey Giuliano and Vrnda Devi, Da Capo Press.

She Came In Through The Kitchen Window: Recipes Inspired by the Beatles and Their Music, Stephen J. Spignesi.

The Early Days of the Beatles, David Richter, Cimino Publishing Group.

A Hard Day's Write, Steve Turner, Carlton Books.

Have You Seen the Horizon Lately?, Yoko Ono, Museum Villa Stuck.

Ticket To Ride (The Ultimate Beatles Tour Diary), Alasdair Ferguson and Alf Bicknell, Glitter Books.

John Lennon, The Beatles and Beyond, David K. Wright, Enslow Publishers.

A Grateful Heart, Daily Blessings For the Evening Meal From Buddha to the Beatles, edited by M. J. Ryan, Conari Press.

Paul McCartney 1942–1966, Gerrit Wijnne, AO BV.

Paul McCartney Paintings, Wolfgang Suttner and Nicola van Velsen, Kultur Verlag.

Real Love, The Drawings for Sean, John Lennon, Random House.
The Original Baby, You Can Drive My Car, Garry Marsh, Number 9 Books.
Paul McCartney, Arturo Blay, Editorial La Mascara.
The Beatles In Holland, Henk van Gelder and Lucas Ligtenberg, Loeb.
Classic Beatles. The Beatles 1958–1964, Azing Moltmaker, SBF.
World Stars. The Beatles 1964–1966, Azing Moltmaker, SBF.
The Brian Epstein Story, Faber.
Hamburg Days, Klaus Voormann and Astrid Kirchherr, Genesis Publications.
The Beatles After the Break-Up. 1970–2000, Keith Badman, Omnibus Press.
Beatletoons: The Real Story Behind the Cartoon Beatles, Mitchell Axelrod, Wynn Publishing.
Act Naturally, Shawn Huff, Chasdon.
Days in the Life: The Lost Beatles Archives, edited by R. E. Robinson, text by Richard Buskin.
The Official Price Guide to the Beatles: Records and Memorabilia (Second Edition), Perry Cox, House of Collectibles.
The 910's Guide to the Beatles Outtakes (Third Edition), Doug Sulpy, Poptomes.

2000
It Was All In the Mind: The Co-Creation of the Beatles Yellow Submarine, Dr Robert Hieronimus.
The Beatles' Anthology, Genesis Publications/Pavilion Books.
The Beatles' Story on Capitol Records, Bruce Spizer.
The Beatles Encyclopedia, Bill Harry, Virgin Publishing.
The John Lennon Encyclopedia, Bill Harry, Virgin Publishing.

Bicknell, Alf
Chauffeur to the Beatles whose memoirs, *Baby, You Can Drive My Car*, were published in 1989.

Born on 28 October 1928, Alf spent most of his working life as chauffeur to a host of famous names. He joined the Beatles' team during their British tour, late in 1964, and it was while he was driving the group to Salisbury Plain during the filming of *Help!* that John Lennon asked him if he'd like to travel to America with them.

While in the States he recalls, 'I remember attending a party with the Beatles, thrown by Capitol Records boss Alan Livingston. The guest list was incredible: there was Gene Barry, Tony Bennett, Richard Chamberlain, Jane Fonda, Rock Hudson, Dean Martin, Groucho Marx, Hayley and Juliet Mills and James Stewart. I knew

James Stewart from before, and him and his missus invited me back, but Brian [Epstein] wouldn't let me go.'

Alf also joined the Beatles on Friday, 27 August 1965, when they met Elvis Presley. 'He shook my hand and called me "Sir",' he recalls.

He also accompanied the group on their trips to Germany, the Philippines and Tokyo and during the recording of 'Yellow Submarine' he even joined in the singing on the chorus.

He was present at their last concert at Candlestick Park in San Francisco and, with their touring days over, Alf found himself returning to his old job, but with unique and exciting memories of four years of travelling with the Beatles.

In 1989, No. 9 Books in Britain published Alf's memoirs, *Baby, You Can Drive My Car*, which was co-written by Garry Marsh and included an introduction by George Harrison.

Also in 1989, Alf, who had settled down in Ruthin, North Wales, put up five Beatles tapes for auction at Sotheby's in London. The tapes had been given to him by John Lennon when Alf was still the group's driver. One tape has John making several attempts at a demo recording of 'If I Fell'. In the recording he experiments with different keys and guitar patterns.

Another tape has George Harrison composing his first song, while a third has the Beatles assuming comic voices to read passages from the Bible and sing their favourite hymns.

Alf had expected to raise £60,000 at the auction, but three of the tapes unfortunately failed to reach their reserve price, although he did sell two of them for a total of £12,000.

Big Three, The

A group who evolved from Cass & the Cassanovas, a four-piece band formed in the late 1950s, and was, for a time, regarded as the top group on Merseyside. They even ran their own club, the Cassanova Club, in Fraser Street. Brian Casser, the leader, also used the names Casey Valence and Casey Jones. He was a dynamic personality, adept at organisation.

They were a trio in 1959, comprising Casey Jones, Adrian Barber and Johnny Hutchinson, when Hutchinson brought Johnny Gustafson to see the group as they needed a bass guitarist. He was asked to join them, but didn't have a guitar and couldn't play. Adrian converted a Hoyer Acoustic for him and put bass strings on it. He joined them and was commonly known as Johnny Bass, but later on was referred to as Johnny Gus.

Leader and rhythm guitarist Cass left for London at the end of 1960, missing out on the entire Mersey success scene, although it has been suggested that the other members pushed him out.

The three remaining members of the Cassanovas stayed together and in January 1961 emerged as the Big Three. They were the first Merseyside group to play Ray Charles numbers and had a raw edge to their sound.

Despite the fact that they were a trio, they were one of the loudest bands on Merseyside, due to Adrian's electronic wizardry. He made giant amps, standing over five feet high, which were nicknamed 'coffins'. They were in big demand and the Beatles and other groups asked Adrian to make 'coffins' for them.

The Big Three's reputation locally was very high and, after the Beatles had signed with Epstein, Brian wanted the group in his 'stable'. He initially tried them out by putting them on a shared bill with the Beatles at Southport. When he signed the Big Three, he sent them over to Hamburg.

Adrian Barber had never been happy with the idea of Epstein managing the group and when he said that for the German season they had to be a four-piece – and he added Brian Griffiths to the line-up – Adrian decided it was time to leave. 'After all, we were supposed to be the big three, not the Big Four,' he said.

Barber's suspicions about Epstein's capabilities proved correct. Brian arranged for them to audition for Decca and they recorded 'Some Other Guy'. Gus was able to tell broadcaster Spencer Leigh: 'This was actually a demo tape for Decca. My voice was completely gone. We'd come back from Hamburg that very morning and were thrown into Decca's No. 2 studio in the basement. It was horrible. We were croaking like old frogs. Eppy wouldn't let us do it again and we went berserk. The bass sound was non-existent and the drum sound was awful.'

The group were appalled when they were told that Decca would be releasing their test recording and wouldn't allow them a proper recording session to perform 'Some Other Guy' the way they wished it to be played.

Instead of understanding why the Big Three were so popular – because of their aggressive sound, their wildness, their casual appearance on stage – Brian also forced them to wear uniform suits and began to dilute their sound, choosing lightweight pop numbers and insisting, against their wishes, that they record them.

He had them record Mitch Murray numbers, which were totally unsuitable for the group. Commenting to Leigh on the Decca recordings, Gus said: 'It was arms up the back. "Do it, boys, or it's all over." We didn't like it but we tried our best. We hated 'By The Way' and 'I'm With You' because they were pop songs: poppy, horrible, three-chord Gerry-and-the-Pacemakers type songs.'

In 1963 their A&R man Noel Walker recorded them live at the

Cavern. Decca engineers had spent three days experimenting with microphone positions and the recording took ten hours because of technical problems.

The Big Three and Epstein officially came to a parting of the ways on Saturday, 20 July 1963, but the damage had been done. Before their EP *The Big Three At The Cavern* was released on Friday, 22 November 1963, there was dissension in the group. Johnny Hutch insisted he was leaving. Gus and Griff replaced him with Ian Broad, drummer with Rory Storm & the Hurricanes, and decided to call themselves the Seniors. They left for Germany, where they appeared at the Tanz Club, Hamburg.

Hutch approached Faron and Paddy Chambers of Faron's Flamingos and asked them to join him.

Letters poured into the *Mersey Beat* office from Flamingos and Big Three fans, upset at the split. Hutch was being so heavily criticised that he phoned *Mersey Beat* to comment: 'Because I now have two members of the Flamingos with me a number of people presume that I broke up the group. This is not the case. I'd known for some time that there were internal disagreements among the Flamingos and I heard they were breaking up, otherwise I would not have approached them.'

In the meantime, Billy Kinsley had left the Mersey Beats, and their manager, Alan Cheetham, and members of the band flew to Germany to offer Johnny Gus the job. They also paid compensation to Griff and Broad.

The Big Three At The Cavern featured an introduction by Bob Wooler and the tracks 'What'd I Say?' 'Don't Start Running Around', 'Zip-a-Dee-Doo-Dah' and 'Reelin' And A Rockin''.

The Big Three had signed with Kennedy Street Enterprises but didn't find success on record again. They recorded an EP at the Oasis Club, Manchester. Titles were 'Money Honey', 'Cruel Cruel World', 'New Orleans' and 'Whole Lotta Shakin''. In June 1964, 'If You Ever Change Your Mind' was issued.

The days of the Big Three were numbered. Paddy Chambers left, to be replaced by Paul Pilnick of the All Stars, and the group recorded 'Bring It On Home To Me'. In August 1964, Paul was asked to join Tony Jackson's new band and Hutch had an offer to join Kingsize Taylor, although he decided to hang up his drumsticks instead.

In 1973 there was an attempt at reviving the band with Gus, Griff and Elton John's drummer Nigel Ollsen. Tony Bramwell produced an album called *Resurrection*, comprising numbers previously recorded by the band, which was issued by Polydor.

Adrian Barber now lives in Hawaii, Brian Griffiths is in Canada,

Johnny Gustafson in London and Johnny Hutchinson remains in Liverpool.

The Big Three appeared on numerous bills with the Beatles. In 1961 they included the Valentine's night 'Rock Ball' at the Cassanova Club on Tuesday, 14 February and an appearance at St John's Hall, Bootle, the same month. They also appeared on the 'Rock Around The Clock' all-night session at the Liverpool Jazz Society on Saturday, 11 March.

In 1962 they included the 'A Night To Remember' at the Tower Ballroom, New Brighton, on Friday, 6 April; the 'Star Show' at the Tower on Thursday, 21 June; the Plaza Ballroom, St Helens, on Monday, 25 June; Heswall Jazz Club on Saturday, 30 June; the Tower Ballroom on Friday, 27 July; 'The Beatles Show' at the Rialto Ballroom on Thursday, 6 September; the Cavern on Wednesday, 19 September; and the 'Little Richard Show' at the Tower on Friday, 12 October.

During 1963, Brian Epstein had the idea of presenting a series of shows featuring his stable of acts: the Beatles, Gerry & the Pacemakers, Billy J. Kramer with the Dakotas and the Big Three. With permission from Bill Harry, he called the series of concerts Mersey Beat Showcase. The first one took place on Thursday, 7 March at the Elizabethan Ballroom in Nottingham. Other dates included the King's Hall, Stoke-on-Trent, on Friday, 29 March; the Majestic Ballroom, Finsbury Park, London, on Wednesday, 24 April; the Fairfield Hall, Croydon, on Thursday, 25 April; the Tower Ballroom, New Brighton, on Friday, 14 June; and the Odeon, Romford, on Sunday, 16 June.

There are three tracks by the classic Big Three personnel which have never been released: 'Fortune Teller', 'Long Tall Sally' and 'Walkin' The Dog'.

Bilk, Acker – and his Paramount Jazz Band

Somerset-born Bernard Stanley Bilk ('Acker' is slang for 'mate') was the first British artist to go to No. 1 in the American charts – twenty months before the Beatles led the 'British Invasion' – with his single 'Stranger On The Shore', which also reached No. 2 in Britain.

Bilk was one of Britain's leading proponents of 'trad jazz', which became a popular fad in the late fifties and early sixties.

He appeared a number of times at the Cavern Club in Liverpool and shared the bill with the Beatles on a 'Riverboat Shuffle' on the MV Royal Iris on Friday, 25 August 1961. The ferry boat left Liverpool landing stage at 7.45 p.m. and sailed along the Mersey providing entertainment for the fans, before returning to the pier head at 11.00 p.m.

The Beatles were once again teamed up with Acker and his Paramount Jazz Band when the two attractions appeared at the Queens Hall, Leeds on 28 June 1963.

Bill Black Combo, The

Born in Memphis on 17 September 1926, Bill Black was the bass player on most of Elvis Presley's early records. Black quit as a Presley backing musician when Presley hit the big time as Elvis only paid his band $200 a week each. Black formed his own band with Carl McVay (piano), Martin Willis (sax), Reggie Young (guitar) and Jerry Arnold (drums).

With his new group he had eight American chart hits between 1959 and 1962. His biggest being the No. 9 chart entry 'White Silver Sands'.

When the Beatles arranged their first American tour, which was to be 31 concerts in 24 cities, Nat Weiss of the General Artists Corporation drew up a list of possible acts who would be available to tour. The Bill Black Combo was one of the acts which the Beatles and Brian Epstein chose to appear with them.

Possibly, they decided on Black because of his association with Presley, although only the combo and not Black himself were to appear on the tour.

The musicians were booked on a weekly basis. The Bill Black Combo was the opening act and was paid $1,500 per week.

Bill Black suffered from a brain tumour and died during the operation to remove it on Thursday, 21 October 1965.

Birthday

Song recorded for *The Beatles* white album on Wednesday, 18 September 1968. That evening BBC 2 were screening a 1956 rock 'n' roll film *The Girl Can't Help It* for the first time on British TV and the Beatles wanted to nip around to Paul's nearby house to see the movie in between their session.

Paul arrived in the studio early and had almost completed writing when the others arrived. With a little help from his friends, mainly John, the song was completed and the backing track recorded in time for them to see the film.

They then returned to Abbey Road and completed the recording.

Yoko Ono and Pattie Harrison were in the studio and joined in the singing of the 'Birthday' chorus, while Mal Evans helped out with handclaps. Paul sang lead vocals, with John joining in, and Paul also played piano on the track, although the instrument had been adjusted to sound like an electric harpsichord.

Black, Cilla

Liverpool's most famous female vocalist singer, born Priscilla Maria
Veronica White in Stanley Hospital on 27 May 1943. She had a
younger brother, Alan.

She was working as a dictaphone typist at BICC, the cable
company, when she first started singing with local groups. It all
began when she went to the Iron Door Club with her friend Pauline
Behan, who was going steady with George Harrison at the time and
was later to marry Gerry Marsden of Gerry & the Pacemakers.

The group on stage was Rory Storm & the Hurricanes and
Pauline asked them if Cilla could get up with them and sing 'Fever'.
As a result she made several further appearances with the band.

Rory's drummer was Ritchie Starkey, whom Rory had dubbed
Ringo Starr. Rory had also given him his own five-minute spot in
the show called 'Starrtime' and he generally sang one song per
performance.

'Boys', the song popularised by the Shirelles, was the number he
usually performed, but when Cilla began to sing with the band it
was also the number that she preferred. There was a bit of a dispute
about this, which was resolved when they performed it as a duet.

Commenting on the compromise, Cilla said: 'We did it as a duet,
and even then he didn't concede anything. He had a microphone
over the drums and I used to have to sing it bent over his kit.'

Ringo also took to calling her 'Swinging Cyril'.

While still working as a secretary, Cilla began to sing with the Big
Three at the Zodiac Club – and was paid for it! She also sang with
Kingsize Taylor & the Dominoes, the group led by Ted Taylor,
Cilla's then boyfriend.

The numbers in her small repertoire were 'Fever', 'Always',
'Boys' and 'Summertime'.

On 6 July 1961, in the first issue of *Mersey Beat*, Bill Harry ran a
feature called 'Swinging Cilla'. It began: 'Cilla Black is a Liverpool
girl who is starting on the road to fame.' The name was a mistake.
He'd been rushing to complete the first issue and his mind had gone
blank when writing about Cilla, although he remembered her
surname related to a colour and he decided to plump for 'Cilla Black'.

When the issue hit the streets, Cilla White was pleased with the
article and said that she liked the sound of the new name and would
use it in future.

In 1963, when Cilla was being launched, her press officer
concocted a story that Brian Epstein had thought of the name
change. He was probably unaware that the proof lay in the issue of
Mersey Beat published almost two years before Brian was even
aware of her existence.

In her autobiography, *Step Inside,* Cilla wrote: 'Not all the changes in my life met with the approval of me Dad. Although he was generally happy for me, he didn't approve of the change of name from White to Black, which began as a misprint in *Mersey Beat.*'

In an interview in the book *Secret Lives,* she said: 'The Black bit came when a local paper, called the *Mersey Beat,* had a misprint. They knew my surname was a colour and guessed wrong!'

As the Mersey scene began to thrive locally, Cilla's ambitions grew. She was still performing as a semi-pro and a guy called Terry McGrath was pressing her to make him her manager.

She often dropped into the *Mersey Beat* office suggesting to Bill Harry that he become her manager, but he was too occupied with producing the newspaper. During one of her visits he took her to the nearby coffee bar, the Coffee Pot, where she described the career she had in mind. Peggy Lee was her idol and she wanted to become a jazz singer. She asked him if he could fix up for her to have a jazz trio backing her.

This situation lasted for some time, until one evening early in 1963 at the Blue Angel Club. Harry noticed Brian Epstein huddled in conversation with Andrew Loog Oldham. He took Cilla over to Epstein, introduced her and asked him if he would listen to her sing. Then he arranged for Cilla to join the group on stage and sing the number 'Boys'. Then he brought her back to Epstein's table and left her to it. She then told him that Epstein had arranged a meeting for her at his office the next day and she became the first female artist in his stable.

Epstein realised that he could express his creative talents in the management of Cilla. He had no real grasp of the music of the Mersey Beat scene but had displayed an interest in the theatre and he set about developing Cilla's image, even designing dresses for her to wear. Managing a female artist enabled Epstein to express part of his own personality.

'Love Of The Loved' didn't prove to be the right song for her and was only a minor hit, reaching No. 35 in the British charts following its release on 27 September 1963.

Initial 1963 publicity described her as 'The Gal with the Bright Red Hair and the Jet Black Voice', and she made her concert debut at the Odeon, Southport, in a show with the Beatles on 30 August. She then appeared with the Beatles on the all-Merseyside edition of the 'Thank Your Lucky Stars' TV show and was booked for the Beatles Christmas Show at the Finsbury Park Astoria in north London from 24 December.

Not unnaturally, Brian exploited the Beatles association in the building of Cilla and his other artists – and also placed her with the Beatles' recording manager, George Martin.

Her career changed direction with a number Epstein picked for her, 'Anyone Who Had A Heart', which had been a big hit for Dionne Warwick in America. He heard the number while on a trip to the States and brought the record back with him, taking it to George Martin as a song for Cilla to record. George said it would be perfect for another of his artists, Shirley Bassey, and told Epstein that Cilla couldn't cope with such a song and wouldn't have a chance with it. Sticking to his guns, Epstein insisted and Cilla's version of the song topped the British charts.

Brian was delighted at the opportunity of moulding a female artist and was able to continue placing her in concerts and TV shows with his other acts. She toured with Gerry & the Pacemakers and Billy J. Kramer, appeared on 'Around The Beatles' and 'The Music of Lennon and McCartney' TV specials and featured in the Pacemakers' film *Ferry 'Cross The Mersey*.

Gradually, however, her image was directed away from beat music towards the conventional world of traditional show business, with appearances at the London Palladium, the Royal Variety Show and in cabaret and pantomime.

By 1965, using his prestige and contacts, Epstein attempted to break the 22-year-old Cilla in America. She made her debut on the 'Ed Sullivan Show' on 4 April and her American cabaret debut at the Persian Room in the Plaza Hotel, New York, from 26 July. However, American success was to elude her and her sole chart entry there was 'You're My World', which reached No. 26 in the *Billboard* charts in July 1964.

Success on record in Britain continued throughout the decade. She followed 'Anyone Who Had A Heart' with her second consecutive No. 1, 'You're My World', an adaptation of an Italian tune.

A Lennon and McCartney composition, 'It's For You', was her fourth release, reaching No. 7 in the charts. John and Paul visited Cilla in the studio during the recording of the track, and Paul played piano on it.

Cilla covered the Righteous Brothers' hit 'You've Lost That Lovin' Feeling' and looked like beating them to the top of the charts. There was controversy at the time because many people believed that the Righteous Brothers' single was so good it should have been given a clear run. In fact, Andrew Loog Oldham, manager of the Rolling Stones, took out an advertisement in the *New Musical Express* imploring record buyers to pick the original version rather than Cilla's. Cilla had been No. 2 in the chart and the Righteous Brothers No. 3. The following week the Righteous Brothers leap-frogged over her to the No. 1 position.

By 1966, Cilla began to feel that Brian was neglecting her. For the first time he didn't attend the opening night of one of her shows. She found she could no longer contact him by phone and had to talk to secretaries or assistants. When appointments were made, he cancelled them or simply didn't turn up. She discussed the situation with her boyfriend, Bobby Willis, and they decided to seek representation elsewhere. Bobby phoned NEMS and left a message for Epstein that Cilla would soon be looking for a new manager.

Epstein had become dependent on drugs by this time, but the thought that Cilla might leave him proved so distressing that he arranged for Cilla and Bobby to meet him at his Chapel Street home for lunch.

When they were together he broke down and cried, telling her: 'There are only five people I love in the world. And that's the Beatles and you, Cilla. Please don't leave me, my Cilla, please.'

Touched by the depth of his emotion, Cilla agreed – and the next day Brian arranged for BBC TV to showcase her in her own series. This new direction was to turn Cilla into one of Britain's most popular mainstream entertainers, establishing her career for the next few decades and reaping her awards such as Best Female Entertainer of the Year for several years to come.

Epstein died in 1967, before the series he set up for Cilla was televised.

The first series of nine 50-minute shows, simply called 'Cilla', began in February 1968. Paul McCartney penned a number called 'Step Inside Love' as the show's signature tune, which became a Top 10 hit for her. This was the third song Paul had penned which Cilla had recorded and Paul made an acoustic version of the song as a demo for her.

Incidentally, George Harrison once wrote a song specifically for Cilla called 'I'll Still Love You'. Arrangements were made for her to record it during a hectic summer season at Blackpool and she travelled to London on a Sunday to do so, with George producing and Ringo playing drums. Unfortunately, Cilla had toothache and a swollen mouth at the time and the session didn't work.

The initial show was seen on Tuesday, 9 February and her special guest was Ringo Starr. The two of them appeared in a comedy sketch and sang a duet, 'Do You like Me Just A Little Bit?'. Paul's father, Jim McCartney, who used to play it when he had a jazz band, had suggested the number. Ringo also performed 'Act Naturally' and appeared in a comedy sketch in which he was a ventriloquist and Cilla was his dummy.

As he was the first Beatle to appear solo on another artist's show, his fellow Beatles sent along a number of telegrams to the BBC studios where he was recording the show: 'Come home, Jim. All is forgiven. Love. Your Buddies and Pals', 'We will be watching. Luv Herbert and Family' and 'Big Brothers are watching and wishing you well. Love from your Big Brothers'.

At the beginning of 1969, Cilla and Bobby were married and during the year, to celebrate her 25th birthday, she had plastic surgery on her nose. Cilla had fractured it when she was fourteen, but its shape hadn't concerned her until Bobby began urging her to have an operation to improve her profile on television.

For the next few years she continued to receive awards as Britain's top female singer by publications such as *New Musical Express* and *Disc,* but by the mid-1970s she'd become firmly established as an all-round entertainer, appearing in cabaret, pantomimes and summer seasons at holiday resorts. She also became a mum, giving birth to three boys, Ben, Robert and Jack, between 1974 and 1980.

By this time she was no longer achieving any success on record and her career as a singer gave way to her new status as a television personality. She and her family had settled down in a seventeen-acre estate in Buckinghamshire in a house formerly owned by Sir Malcolm Sargent.

Under a lucrative contract with London Weekend Television, which made her Britain's highest-paid female TV star, she started hosting the shows 'Blind Date' and 'Surprise, Surprise'.

Cilla was awarded an OBE in 1997 and in 1998 *Bobby's Girl,* a biography by Douglas Thompson, was published. Sadly, Bobby was diagnosed with cancer and died on Saturday, 23 October 1999.

Blackbird

A song written and recorded by Paul for *The Beatles* double album. Paul originally recorded the song solo in Studio Two at Abbey Road on Tuesday, 11 June 1968 while, at the same time, John was experimenting with sound effects for 'Revolution No 9' in Studio Three. Paul's voice was double-tracked in parts. The song was said to have been inspired by a newspaper report that Paul had read concerning race riots in America.

Some sounds of blackbirds singing were also added to the track, taken from a sound effect recording, 'Volume Seven: Birds of a Feather'.

The number was also included on the compilation *The Beatles Ballads.*

Paul performed the number on his 1975/76 tour with Wings and it is also featured on his *Wings Over America* album.

The number was included on the *Anthology 3* CD.

Black Dyke Mills Band, The

A famous British brass band. Paul selected them to record his composition 'Thingumybob', the theme tune of London Weekend Television's comedy series starring Stanley Holloway which was first networked in Britan on 2 August 1968.

On Sunday afternoon, 30 April of that year, Paul travelled to Bradford in Yorkshire to record the single, which he also arranged. The band, conducted by Geoffrey Brand, also produced an instrumental version of 'Yellow Submarine' for the flip, which Paul produced. The single was issued in Britain on Apple 4 on 6 September 1968, but failed to register in the charts. In America, 'Yellow Submarine' became the 'A' side when the disc was issued on Apple 1800 on 26 August 1968.

Although the band never recorded for the Apple label again, Paul was to feature them on a Wings album over a decade later, in 1979, when they performed on 'Winter Rose' and 'Love Awake' for his *Back To The Egg* album.

Blackjacks, The

When guitarist Ken Brown was sacked from the Quarry Men because Mona Best had paid him a share of the fee (despite the fact that he didn't perform because of a cold), he approached Mona's son, Pete, and suggested that they form a group, with Pete on drums. Pete Best had been considering becoming a drummer and took up the opportunity. With Pete on drums and Brown on rhythm guitar, the other members of the Blackjacks were Charles Newby on lead guitar and Bill Barlow on bass guitar. The band immediately began a residency at the Casbah Club playing a repertoire consisting mainly of numbers by Jerry Lee Lewis, Carl Perkins, Little Richard and Chuck Berry, rock 'n' roll classics such as 'Twenty Flight Rock', 'Whole Lotta Shakin' Goin' On', 'Sweet Little Sixteen', 'Rock And Roll Music', 'Honey Don't', 'Tutti Frutti', 'Long Tall Sally' and 'Memphis Tennessee'.

On 6 August 1960, the Silver Beetles found that their gig at the Grosvenor Ballroom had been cancelled and they drifted over to the Casbah Club to see if there was any work. They watched the Blackjacks and were particularly impressed by Pete's brand-new drum kit.

Paul McCartney phoned Best with the offer to join them as drummer and go with them to Hamburg. As the Blackjacks were virtually on the point of disbanding, with Brown soon to move down to London and Newby still a chemistry student, Pete, who had now abandoned the idea of going to Teacher's Training College, accepted the offer.

Coincidentally, John Lennon's first name for his skiffle group had been the Black Jacks.

Blacklers, Great Charlotte Street, Liverpool L1

Large department store in the city centre, situated opposite the former site of NEMS first record store, which had originally been managed by Brian Epstein.

When George Harrison left Liverpool Institute with no qualifications in 1959 and failed to obtain a job working for Liverpool Corporation, he went to the Youth Employment Centre in Dale Street and was told there was a position for a window dresser at Blacklers department store. When George went for the job it had already been taken, but he was told the maintenance department was looking for an apprentice electrician.

George was to comment, 'So I got a job cleaning all the lights with a paint brush, all those tubes to keep clean, and at Christmas I kept the Grotto clean.'

George began working at the store in 1960 and was paid £1.10s (£1.50) per week, but at the age of seventeen was able to tell his boss he was leaving – this was to go on tour in Scotland backing Johnny Gentle.

Mona Best bought her son Pete a drum kit at the store, which so impressed the Beatles when they saw him playing it that they invited him to join them.

The store was closed in the eighties and was converted into smaller commercial units.

Blair Hall, Walton Road, Walton, Liverpool WA4

One of the venues used as a jive hive by Walter Hill, who ran Peak Promotions, under which he organised weekly dances at four venues, the others being Holyoake Hall, the David Lewis Theatre and Columba Hall, Widnes.

The Beatles made their debut at the venue on Sunday, 5 February 1961. The Remo Four was also on the bill. Drummer Harry Prytherch comments:

It was the first time we ever saw the Beatles. Anybody who played at Blair Hall will know that it had a sloping stage. I'd played there quite a lot, but Pete Best hadn't.

He set up his drum kit – and Pete was very very heavy on his bass drum which, to me, was a lot of the Beatles' sound in those early days. The really heavy sound was coming from Pete's bass drum and it started sliding on the stage so I immediately ran round the back and got some string out of my case,

which I always carried round with me, specially for Blair Hall.
We tied it round Pete's bass drum and then we tied it round
his seat – and that stopped his bass drum from sliding on the
stage, no matter how hard he hit it.

The only other appearances by the Beatles at Blair Hall were for
a run of three consecutive Sundays on 16, 23 and 30 July 1961 and
on Saturday, 29 July 1961.

Blair, Lionel

British television personality, actor, choreographer, who met the
Beatles socially at various events such as the parties at Alma
Cogan's house or in the Ad Lib Club. He also appeared with them
on the Mike and Bernie Winters TV show 'Big Night Out'.

He says, 'One of the most exciting shows we did was with the
Beatles, and later, when the show moved to Blackpool and changed
its name to 'Blackpool Night Out', they came on again and did their
latest hit, which was "Help!" I invented a little kick movement
which the Beatles could do with me on the show, and the day after
the programme letters poured in asking how to do the kick.'

As a result, Brian Epstein asked him to develop the movement for
a tour he was promoting, which Epstein nicknamed the 'kick tour'.
The bill included the Everly Brothers, Cilla Black and Billy J.
Kramer. Blair compered the show and performed a dance number
involving the kick.

He also appeared with the Beatles at the London Palladium on
the *Night Of A Hundred Stars*.

Blair was also engaged to provide choreography for *A Hard
Day's Night*. He said, 'It was just like "Blackpool Night Out",
when I had first worked with the Beatles, so it went off very easily.
Dick [Lester] was one of those directors who thought I was a bit of
a joke because I played the fool a bit during breaks.' Blair was also
hired to choreograph the 'Hamlet' strip scene with Laurence
Harvey in the Peter Sellers/Ringo Starr film *The Magic Christian*.

Blake, Peter

Prominent contemporary British artist, born in Dartford, Kent, in
June 1932. He became one of the country's most popular painters
during the 1960s.

Blake was awarded the CBE and his retrospective exhibition at
the Tate Gallery in 1983 was the most successful show ever held at
the gallery for a living artist.

It was London gallery owner Robert Fraser who recommended
that Blake, one of his clients, design a new cover for the album

Sergeant Pepper's Lonely Hearts Club Band after he had dissuaded the Beatles from using a psychedelic design by the Fool.

The basic concept for the album had been evolved. Blake commented:

> They'd established that there would be another persona that they'd invented and I said well, perhaps we could pretend that you'd just done a concert and we were posing for a photograph. So what we evolved was that we'd build it in the studio. It wasn't a collage, which not many people realise. There have been a great many rip-offs of it and they've always cut up photography and stuck it down. Well, we built the whole thing life-size and made a platform for them to stand on – and the flowers were all delivered and built – and then they came in and posed and the photographs were taken.
>
> I said (to the Beatles), each of you make a list (of people they wanted to appear on the cover). John made a very comprehensive list. Paul did, too, and the lists were fascinating. George's list was all Indian gurus at that point and I think Ringo just sort of agreed with everything. I don't think he actually gave me a list. He said that what the others were doing was fine. I made a list too, and Robert Fraser did. On my list I'd put Leo Gorcey and Huntz Hall from the Bowery Boys and as it is, there's only Huntz Hall because Leo Gorcey must have been down on his luck because he wrote and said, 'Could you pay me a fee?' and EMI weren't prepared to do that, so he had to come out.

Among Blake's other choices were Johnny Weissmuller, Bobby Breen, Shirley Temple, W.C. Fields, Tony Curtis, Dion, sculptor H. C. Westerman – and Sonny Liston. The Sonny Liston waxwork was obtained by Blake when he went to Madame Tussauds to borrow figures for the tableau and discovered they were about to melt Liston down. So he bought it, included it in the tableau and still retains the waxwork at his home.

His then wife, American sculptor Jann Howarth, aided Blake on the project and they were paid only £200 between them.

Michael Cooper, who was a business partner of Robert Fraser's, was to take the photographs in his studio in Flood Street, Chelsea. Blake said: 'I worked in the studio for a fortnight constructing the set, fixing the top row to the back wall and putting the next about six inches in front and so on, so that we got a tiered effect.'

Blake was also to use the Beatles as an inspiration for some of his paintings. They include *The Beatles (1963–68),* a 48 × 36 in. acrylic on hardboard that was based on magazine photographs and had a space left on it for autographs. He also painted an oil-on-canvas *Beatles (1963–7)*, which is in the collection of Colin St John Wilson and was used as the cover of George Melly's Penguin paperback *Revolt into Style* in 1967.

Blake also created a collage in 1973 entitled *A Souvenir For John (Lennon)* which featured a drawing of a circus performer holding a barrel over his head while balancing another barrel with the words 'Mr Kite'. Underneath and in large letters was the message, 'For John'.

Blake was also to design the poster for *Live Aid* in 1985. In 1995 he was approached by Apple to discuss the design for the *Beatles Anthology* series. He was to say:

> After a few minutes I realised that they were asking me to pitch for the job. They were asking five other people as well as me, so not only was it a way for them to get some free ideas, it was also bloody insulting. I decided that I didn't want to do it, so I called back to tell them.
>
> I said, you either want me to do it, or you don't. And they said, well the person we really wanted was David Hockney! So I called their bluff and gave them David Hockney's home number and said go on, call him, and if he does want to do it, then great and if not, then come back to me. So they called David and he didn't want to do it as I suspected. I meanwhile had to put my offer in writing, and the big tactical error I made was mentioning that this would be a good opportunity to recompense me for paying so little for *Sgt Pepper*. I didn't hear anything after that. I'm not surprised, but I'm not going to start auditioning at my age.

In October 1998, Blake instigated proceedings against Apple, insisting that he should be paid lost royalties he felt were still owed to him for designing the *Sgt Pepper* sleeve – as he was only paid £200 for an image which has become one of the most copied images in the world. Apple was to comment, 'That's just the way the business works. His contract said he would get a one-off payment and that is what he accepted at the time.'

Blue Angel Club, 108 Seel Street, Liverpool L1

Nightclub opened by Allan Williams on 22 March 1961 on the premises of what had formerly been the Wyvern Social Club. The Silver Beetles had auditioned at the Wyvern on 10 May 1960 for impresario Larry Parnes. Williams had taken over the premises at the time and was planning his new club. On 12 August 1960, Pete Best auditioned for the Beatles at the club.

Williams called it the Blue Angel after the Marlene Dietrich film and had a large blow-up photograph of Dietrich in a scene from the film on the club wall.

On the club's opening night, cabaret artist Alma Warren appeared, backed by the Terry Francis Quartet. Allan intended the club to be a sophisticated night spot and, at first, didn't want members of the local groups to frequent the club. However, within a short time it became the main late-night watering hole for the Mersey Beat scene and presented the beat music in the basement. There was a bar in the basement and one on the ground floor and the first floor had a casino run by Williams' brother-in-law Barry Chang.

The Beatles frequented the club on a regular basis, as did Brian Epstein and most members of the Mersey Beat scene. One evening Bill Harry asked Epstein if he would listen to a girl singer and arranged for Cilla Black to get on stage and sing 'Boys' with the group who were performing that night. He then introduced Cilla to Epstein who arranged to meet her at his office the next day and then signed her up.

The Beatles never performed at the club, although the Rolling Stones did. When they were performing at Southport, Bill Harry called them at their hotel and they drove into Liverpool and did a free show at the Angel for the members of various Mersey groups.

Allan Williams used the lid of a grand piano as a 'wall of fame', with signatures from the famous. Celebrities from around the world visited the club including Bob Dylan, Allen Ginsberg and Judy Garland.

Blue Gardenia Club, The, Greek Street, London W1

A late-night club in London's Soho district which, in 1961, was being managed by Brian Casser, former leader of one of Liverpool's top bands, Cass & the Cassanovas.

When promoter Sam Leach had brought the Beatles down to perform at the Palais Ballroom, Aldershot on 9 December 1961, the gig hadn't lived up to expectations due to lack of advertising. After they'd finished performing and had had a number of drinks, Sam suggested they all drop in to the Blue Gardenia Club to see Cass.

They set out from Aldershot at 1.00 a.m. and when they reached the club, John, Paul and Pete got up on stage while George was having a chat with someone who'd recognised him.

Blue Jay Way

Song penned by George. He wrote it in August 1967 soon after arriving in America with Pattie. They'd rented a house on a street called Blue Jay Way. Derek and Joan Taylor, who were living in Los Angeles at the time, were due to pop around to see them. Derek had phoned to say that because of the fog they'd been delayed and were having difficulty locating the house. George was tired from jet lag but decided he wanted to remain awake and see Derek and Joan, so he sat at a small Hammond organ and began to compose a song about the fact that he was waiting for Derek – and called it 'Blue Jay Way'. He completed the number back home in Esher and the number was recorded in September 1967 and included on the *Magical Mystery Tour* soundtrack album and EPs.

Of interest is the fact that a number of technical effects were added when the song was recorded at Abbey Road in September 1967, including the use of the ADT (Artificial Double Tracking) machine devised by Ken Townsend.

Blue Moon Of Kentucky

Number penned by Bill Monroe and originally recorded by him in 1947. It was the version by Elvis Presley, recorded in 1954, which inspired the Quarry Men to use the number in their act, with Paul McCartney singing lead vocals.

Blue Suede Shoes

Classic rock 'n' roll number penned by Carl Perkins in 1955. Perkins had a million-seller with the song and was only prevented from reaching No. 1 in the charts by Elvis Presley's 'Heartbreak Hotel'. Elvis also recorded the number, although the version which inspired the Quarry Men was the original Perkins one. John Lennon was lead vocalist on their number, which remained in their repertoire when they became the Beatles, and they continued to perform it until late into 1961.

Bony Moronie

A hit for Larry Williams, who penned the number, in 1957. The Quarry Men immediately included it in their repertoire, with John Lennon on lead vocals. It was an indication of their musical direction, away from skiffle into rock 'n' roll, like so many other Liverpool groups, who also included the number in their act. The group continued to perform it when they became the Beatles, although it was dropped at the end of 1961.

Bonzo Dog Doo Dah Band, The

An eccentric outfit originally formed as the Bonzo Dog Dada Band in 1965. They comprised Vivian Stanshall (vocals/trumpet/devices), Rodney Slater (saxophone), Neil Innes (vocals/piano/guitar), Roger Ruskin Spear (saxophone/props/devices) and 'Legs' Larry Smith (drums).

Their initial singles, 'My Brother Makes The Noises For The Talkies' and 'Alley Oop', were released in 1966 and their debut album, *Gorilla*, was issued the following year.

The group was featured in *Magical Mystery Tour* performing 'Death Cab for Cutie' as an accompaniment to topless striptease artist Jan Carson. The sequence was filmed at Raymond's Revuebar in London on Monday, 18 September 1967. The Beatles inserted the word 'Censored' over Jan's breasts to prevent the scene being cut from the television transmission.

The Beatles also hired the Bonzos to perform at their special *Magical Mystery Tour* party, held at the Royal Lancaster Hotel, London, on 21 December 1967. During their show, Freddie Lennon and members of the Beach Boys got up to sing.

In 1968 the group were having problems recording a single called 'I'm The Urban Spaceman', penned by Neil Innes. They approached Paul McCartney to produce it for them and he agreed.

Ruskin Spear commented: 'We really needed someone we would all respect to produce us, and Paul was asked if he could come down and help us out.'

Paul turned up for the session at Chappell's Recording Studio in Bond Street. He showed the bass player Joel Druckman what to play. Spear noted that 'he wouldn't play the bass line on the record. In the end he did play some ukulele. He thrashed along with Neil Innes and Viv Stanshall, out in the corridor, and you can hear it plucking in the background.'

It was decided that Paul should be credited with a pseudonym, Apollo C. Vermouth. Roger said, 'Of course, it was cleverly leaked to the press that it was really Paul McCartney. He was only with us for a day but it is extraordinary what he achieved.'

The record was issued in Britain in October 1968 and reached No. 5 in the charts, but it didn't make any impact when it was released in the States in December. When the album *Urban Spaceman*, which contained the track, was issued in America in June 1969, Paul's name had replaced the Apollo C. Vermouth credit.

During 1968 the Bonzos supported Cream at the Saville Theatre, Brian Epstein's West End concert venue. They disbanded in 1970.

Songwriter Neil Innes was later involved with the Rutles and penned the songs for that Beatles lampoon. He was to become a popular guest at Beatles conventions.

George Harrison formed a friendship with 'Legs' Larry Smith, who became a regular visitor to Friar Park, and George was to write a song about him called 'Ladies And Gentlemen His Name Is Legs', which featured on the 1975 album *Extra Texture – Read All About It*.

Viv Stanshall recorded 'Sir Henry At Rawlinson's End', which was turned into a film starring Trevor Howard. He became a voice-over artist, but tragically died in March 1995 in a fire at his north London home. He was 53 years old.

Boone, Pat

Clean-cut American singing star who, between 1955 and 1962, had a staggering 27 major hits in the charts, including 'Ain't That A Shame', 'Long Tall Sally', 'Friendly Persuasion', 'April Love' and 'Speedy Gonzales'.

The Beatles included one of his numbers, 'Don't Forbid Me', in their repertoire and while the singer was touring in Britain he heard the Beatles' 'From Me To You' and decided to record it when he got back home to America – unfortunately, his record label, Dot Records, advised him against it.

The Beatles' sudden domination of the American charts in 1964 began to affect all sales by other acts and Boone commented, 'The Beatles were selling ALL the records, so the rest of us were twiddling our thumbs, saying, "What's going on here?"' An astute businessman, and noting the effect the Beatles were having on American youth, he obtained a merchandising licence to manufacture lithographs of oil paintings of the Beatles. He decided to promote them in a nationwide campaign by having each set numbered, allowing 30 numbers to be picked which would give 30 young Beatles fans tickets to attend the show at the Convention Centre, Las Vegas, on 20 August 1965.

The promotion was a big success and proved lucrative to Boone, who sold hundreds of thousands of the lithographs.

He turned up at the Las Vegas concert with his wife and daughters and was introduced to the Beatles backstage between shows. He showed them the lithographs and Paul noticed that one of the paintings, based on a photograph showing him holding a cigarette, no longer featured the cigarette. He pointed this out to Boone who mentioned that Leo Janssen, the artist, had anticipated that Boone wouldn't like to merchandise a product in which someone was smoking. Paul said, 'Well, Pat, you know, if we smoke, we smoke.'

Bootlegs

A 'bootleg' recording is one which has been issued without permission and which does not provide royalties to those to whom royalties should be paid. Despite the fact that legislation has been passed in both the United States and Great Britain effectively making 'bootlegs' illegal, the practice has survived. In the case of the Beatles there is more bootleg material than on any other act.

The material broadly derives from four main sources: their live appearances; club and concert shows; radio, film and TV performances, basically recorded from the radio or television; studio outtakes, recordings of material, some of it unreleased or not of a standard to be released, which have been illegally smuggled out of the recording studio. There are also various bootlegs of interviews.

There are so many hundreds of Beatles' bootlegs that to include a complete discography is outside the scope of this book. There are, in fact, several books and magazines which have specialized in documenting bootleg material, including *You Can't Do That! Beatles Bootlegs & Novelty Records, 1963–1980*, by Charles Reinhart, published by Pierian Press.

Among the sources from which radio bootlegs have been taken are: BBC radio shows such as 'Pop Go The Beatles', 'From Us To You', 'Saturday Club,' 'The Alan Freeman Show' and Radio Luxembourg transmissions.

Recordings from television shows have included 'People and Places', 'Top of the Pops', 'Around The Beatles', 'The Royal Variety Performance', 'Sunday Night At The London Palladium', 'The David Frost Show', 'Blackpool Night Out', 'Drop In', 'The Ed Sullivan Show', 'Shindig', 'Thank Your Lucky Stars' and 'Our World'. These also include individual appearances by Ringo Starr in 'Cilla' and John Lennon in 'Rock And Roll Circus'.

Bootlegs have been issued of numerous live show appearances including the Star Club, Hamburg shows; a Winter Gardens Theatre, Bournemouth concert; an Apollo, Ardwick concert; a Washington Coliseum concert; a Festival Hall, Melbourne concert; a Hollywood Bowl concert; an Empire Stadium, Vancouver concert; a Palais de Sports, Paris concert; a Shea Stadium concert, and a Nippon Budokan Hall, Japan concert.

Studio outtakes have included the Decca audition tapes; the Parlophone audition tapes; *Let It Be* outtakes and dozens of outtakes of particular numbers, such as 'Lucille', 'I Forgot To Remember to Forget', 'I'll Be On My Way', 'Sure To Fall', 'Crying, Waiting, Hoping', 'A Shot Of Rhythm And Blues', 'How Do You Do It', 'My Girl Is Red Hot', 'Dizzy Miss Lizzie', 'Keep Your Hands Off My Baby', 'Soldier Of Love', 'I Got A Woman', 'Little Child',

'Colliding Circles', 'What's The New Mary Jane', 'Annie', 'Not Unknown', 'India' and 'Stand By Me'.

There have also been bootlegs of soundtracks from *Yellow Submarine, Let It Be* and various promotional films, such as 'Strawberry Fields Forever' and 'Penny Lane'.

Another bootleg source has been that of the Beatles' interviews. Bootlegs in this vein have included material from *Ed Rudy's American Tour* album, Murry the K interviews, the *Hear The Beatles Tell All* album, an interview by disc jockey Tom Clay, a Kenny Everett interview and various interviews from Brian Matthew's thirteen-part radio series 'The Beatles Story'. There have even been such oddities as *I Apologise*, which was a bootleg recording of the press conference at the Astor Tower Hotel, Chicago, in which John Lennon apologised for his 'greater than Jesus' statement and a reading of excerpts from *A Cellarful Of Noise* by Brian Epstein.

The quality of the bootleg recording varies, as does the production. Some albums are cheaply produced, others are as lavish as the professional releases. There are bootleg albums, EPs and singles and the individual titles run into the hundreds. Here are some examples of the titles of bootleg Beatles albums: *Abbey Road Revisited, ABC Manchester 1964, Alive At Last In Atlanta, Alpha Omega, And The Beatles Were Born, Around The Beatles, The Beatles By Royal Command, Beatles Happy Birthday, Beatles In Italy, The Beatles Introduce New Songs, Beatles Live In Washington DC, Christmas Message From Liverpool, Elvis Meets . . . The Beatles, Five Nights In A Judo Arena, Indian Rope Trick, The Last Beatle Record* and *Twickenham Jams*.

One of the most famous bootlegs was the anthology *Alpha Omega*, a four-volume collection issued in America by Audio Tape Inc on ATRBH 3583. When this was originally issued early in 1973 it was actually advertised on radio and television. There was quite a demand for the unauthorised recordings which contained virtually every number the Beatles ever recorded. As a result of this particular bootleg set, EMI decided to issue two double albums of Beatles material almost immediately and *The Beatles 1962–1966* and *The Beatles 1967–1970* were issued in both Britain and America in April 1973.

Borashallen, Bockasjogatan, Boras, Sweden

Fourth stop on the Beatles' first-ever foreign tour. They appeared at the Borashallen on Monday, 28 October 1963 when they gave one performance at 7.30 p.m. The group were booked to give nine concerts at five venues for a total fee of £2,000 during their very short Swedish tour.

They received an enthusiastic reception from the Swedish audience.

Boston Gardens, Boston, Massachusetts

A sports arena which was the home of the Celtics and the Bruins. For the Beatles' appearance there on Saturday, 12 September 1964, the 13,909 tickets had sold out within a matter of hours.

There were intriguing little dramas taking place at most of the Beatles' American gigs and one of the stories here concerned a youth who escaped from reform school, held a male fan at knifepoint and stole his ticket. The police were able to apprehend the escapee because the fan remembered his seat number.

A black limousine with an escort of six motorcyles proved to be an effective decoy, while the Beatles sped away in a single car.

Boyd, Jennie

One of Pattie's two younger sisters. For a time Jennie was a model and then worked in the Apple Boutique. She joined the Beatles and party on their trip to Bangor to see the Maharishi and also went to Rishikesh with them.

In May 1968, Jennie also went on holiday to Greece with Cynthia Lennon, Donovan, Gypsy Dave and Alexis Mardas. Jennie and Alexis were with Cynthia when she arrived home and found John and Yoko together in Kenwood, in dressing gowns. Jennie and Alexis were shocked and embarrassed by the situation and Cynthia asked if she could stay with them for a few days. They agreed and she went to the small house they shared together – but as friends, not lovers.

Following the collapse of the Apple Boutique, Jennie and Pattie went into the antique business with a stall called Juniper in Chelsea Market, but they closed it at the beginning of 1969 because it entailed getting up early in the morning.

Jennie became the inspiration for Donovan's hit 'Jennifer Juniper'.

She married Mick Fleetwood, drummer with Fleetwood Mac, and went to live in America. They divorced, were reconciled, then split up again.

Jennie has a Ph.D. in philosophy and in 1992 interviewed 75 musicians, including George and Ringo, for her book *Musicians In Time*.

Boyd, Pattie

Born Patricia Anne Boyd on 17 March 1944, Pattie first arrived in London in 1962 with ambitions of becoming a model. She was brought to the attention of the British public when she appeared in a series of television commercials for Smith's Crisps. The commercials were produced by Dick Lester and when he was commissioned to direct the Beatles' debut movie *A Hard Day's Night,* he booked Pattie for the role of one of the schoolgirls who meet the Beatles on a train travelling from Liverpool to London.

She was present on the first day of filming and was to say, 'I met them and they said hello. I couldn't believe it. They were so like how I'd imagined them to be. They were just like pictures of themselves coming to life. George hardly said hello. But the others came and chatted with us.'

When filming began, Pattie said she could feel George looking at her and was embarrassed. She was also terrified of John and, when she came to ask for their autographs near the end of the first day's shooting, she was too scared to ask for John's. John was later to refer to her as Batty Pattie. When she asked George for his autograph she asked him if he could sign for her two sisters, Jennie and Paula, as well. He put two kisses under the autographs for the two sisters and seven kisses under the autograph for Pattie.

He came into the carriage where Pattie was sitting with another girl, Pru, and asked her to come out into the corridor on her own. He asked if she would go out with him that night and she said no. This was because she had a steady boyfriend she'd been going out with for two years. The following Tuesday, George asked her out again. This time she told her boyfriend it was all over and accepted George's invitation. He was enchanted by her and said she reminded him of his favourite film star, Brigitte Bardot. By the end of the week she'd introduced him to her mother and sisters.

The following week was Easter and Pattie and George joined John and Cynthia for a weekend in Ireland. The media besieged their hotel and Pattie and Cynthia had to dress up as maids and were smuggled out of the rear entrance in a laundry basket and driven to the airport in a laundry van.

By the end of the month, George took her to see a bungalow he was considering buying in Esher. The bungalow was called Kinfauns and within four weeks George had bought it for the two of them to live in together. He proposed to her there. Pattie was to say, 'We lived together for about a year before we got married. My mother knew, but she never mentioned it.'

Pattie became worried by the press interest, the crowds and the threatening letters. Also physical attacks by female fans, which were the lot of Beatles wives and girlfriends. Once, when she went to The Beatles Christmas Show in Hammersmith with Terry Doran, a group of girls started punching her. Then they took their shoes off and shouted, 'Let's get her.' They started kicking her and Pattie punched one in the face while Terry got one against the wall and held her tight. They were shouting and swearing, but Pattie managed to escape. However, she was to become a popular figure with teenagers and wrote a column on the British rock scene for America's 16 *Magazine* called 'Pattie's Letter From London'.

George actually had to ask Brian Epstein for permission to get married. He drove to Brian's house in Chapel Street, Belgravia, in December 1965 and left Pattie in the car outside while he went in to see his manager. He emerged ten minutes later to tell Pattie: 'It's all right. Brian has said we can get married in January. Off we go!' Pattie commented, 'God has spoken!'

When John Lennon was told, he said, 'January's a bit soon, she must be in the club.'

The couple were wed at Epsom Register Office, Surrey, on Friday, 21 January 1966, with Paul McCartney in attendance, and spent their honeymoon in Barbados. When George was busy touring it was Pattie who became interested in spiritual matters. Pattie revealed that her interest in religion had been sparked by the trip she and George made to India in September 1966, although the trip had been made simply for George to study Indian music.

Of the five weeks spent in India, she commented, 'We had really gone so George could study the sitar under Ravi Shankar. We met Ravi's guru, his spiritual guide. You can't be in India without being aware of everything. We went to a meeting at Benares, the Holy City on the Ganges. Millions of people had come for a big festival which went on for three days.'

Pattie was the first member of the Beatles' circle to join the Maharishi Mahesh Yogi's Spiritual Regeneration movement, attending a lecture in February 1967. She encouraged the others to attend his lecture at the Hilton Hotel, London, on Thursday, 24 August 1967. As a result of this meeting, they all began a ten-day course on Transcendental Meditation, held at University College, Bangor, in North Wales.

Her vivacity and beauty made headlines – she was an ideal Beatles bride in the eyes of the media, and proved to be the inspiration for several of George's songs, including 'Something', 'If I Needed Someone', 'For You Blue' and 'It's All Too Much'. After six years of marriage, however, the couple began to drift apart.

Since George had frowned on her having a modelling career, the 26-year-old Pattie felt isolated in the large Friar Park mansion. She wanted to raise a family but never seemed to get pregnant and both of them went for fertility tests. Pattie was willing to adopt a child, but George wasn't. Gradually, they began to engage in arguments.

Against George's wishes she decided to become a model again and agreed to appear in an Ozzie Clark fashion show. Towards the end of 1973 she had her first extramarital affair, with Ronnie Wood, who was then a member of the Faces.

While they were ensconced at Friar Park in Henley-on-Thames, Pattie was not unaware of the interest George's best friend Eric Clapton showed in her. In an effort to revive George's interest, or to make him jealous, she began to flirt with Eric and soon Eric realised he had fallen in love with her.

Eric wrote a song declaring his love, which he based on a 1,000-year-old Persian book by Nizami called *Layla and Majnun*. The song 'Layla' was included on an album Eric made under the pseudonym Derek & the Dominoes and George was invited to play on it. The number entered the British Top 10 in 1972 and again in 1982.

Eventually, Pattie left George, telling him she was taking a holiday. She settled for a while in Los Angeles with her sister Jennie, who was married to Mick Fleetwood. Clapton had gone to Miami to record his comeback album *461 Ocean Boulevard* and then set off on an American tour. Pattie joined him.

When George heard the news, he said, 'If she had to go off with someone, better Eric than some dope.'

George invited Eric and Pattie to Friar Park one evening. Another guest present was actor John Hurt. George had laid out two guitars and two small amplifiers, and when Eric turned up late with Pattie, George invited him to play – it was the equivalent of a duel, with the woman they loved there to watch. With six people present, the two guitarists played for two hours and spectators say that George had provided Eric with the inferior guitar and amplifier, but the opinion was that Eric won, even though he'd had too many brandies. Eric was to comment, 'I know exactly how to play in a situation like that. If someone makes the mistake of exaggerating, or being a bit too flamboyant, you win by being simple. Let them overdo it.'

Pattie was divorced from George in 1977 and married Eric on 27 March 1979 in Tucson, Arizona. On their return, a wedding reception was held in the back garden of Clapton's home, Hurtwood Edge, in the village of Ewhurst, Surrey, 25 miles from London. George and his second wife Olivia were among the 200 celebrity guests. Clapton had hired workmen to erect a platform for a jam session and at 9 p.m. Jim Capaldi sat down on drums. Paul McCartney started playing bass. As the jam went on it featured Ginger Baker on drums, Paul on bass, Denny Laine and eventually Clapton on guitars, George and Ray Cooper (of Elton John fame) on keyboards. Then Paul asked Lonnie Donegan up and Lonnie did a skiffle session. Next it was Paul on bass with Ringo on drums and George, Clapton and Denny on guitars. Then Mick Jagger jumped up and joined them singing the old Eddie Cochran song 'Something Else'.

Pattie and Eric were married for seven years, but they broke up in 1986. She later took up a profession as a photographer working from a studio in the Fulham area of London, where she also settled. In the early 1990s she invested in a modelling agency for older women called Déjà Vu, but it was a financial disappointment. She then went on to found a new charity with Barbara Bach called Sharp, which aimed to aid drug addicts and alcoholics.

Boyd, Paula

Pattie's youngest sister. When artist Rory McEven invited Pattie and George to a party in Chelsea, Pattie had gone into town to pick up a dress at Ozzie Clark's showroom. When she returned to her car she found someone had put a packet of cigarettes on her dashboard. Inside was a phone number, a man's name and the message 'Phone me'. There was also a tiny piece of hashish. When she returned home the police raided the house and the chip of hashish was found in the cigarette packet. Pattie suspected she had been set up. She phoned George, who took two hours to get home, and they were taken in for questioning. Their solicitor Martin Poulden got them out. They rushed back home and got ready for the party. When they arrived, Princess Margaret and Lord Snowdon were there. They went to the royal couple and explained that they'd been busted.

'Oh my, what a shame,' said the Princess.

'Can you help us?' asked George, 'Can you sort of use your influence to eliminate the bad news?'

The Princess was horrified at the suggestion. Just then, Paula joined the group, produced a joint from her purse and lit it. She noticed people glaring at her and thought they considered her rude for not passing the joint, so she extended it to Princess Margaret and said, 'Here, do you want this?'

The Princess and Lord Snowdon fled the party.

In 1969, when Eric Clapton had his passionate fixation on Pattie, he made approaches to Paula and they lived together at his mansion Hurtwood Edge for two months. Eric comments, 'I started living with Pattie's younger sister Paula because of their similarity in character and in looks. It was like a side route into Pattie, that was my way of thinking.'

He was also to say, 'I invited Pattie's sister Paula to come and hear me sing "Layla" for the first time. When she heard that vocal, she packed her bags and left my home in great distress. Because she realised it was about Pattie and that I'd been using her.'

Boys

A number penned by Luthor Dixon and Wes Farrell which was the flipside of the Shirelles' most popular single 'Will You Still Love Me Tomorrow', which was released in November 1960. Soon after, numerous Liverpool groups including the Beatles were performing the number, which provided a vocal vehicle for Ringo Starr when he was a member of Rory Storm & the Hurricanes. When Cilla Black used to sing occasionally with the Hurricanes, this was the number she wanted to perform, but she had to sing along with Ringo, both of them using the same mike. When the Beatles performed the song, it was drummer Pete Best who sang it.

When Ringo joined the Beatles, he also sang the number with them. Apart from the version on *The Beatles Live! At the Star Club In Hamburg, Germany: 1962* album, the group recorded the number on their *Please Please Me* album and on several BBC radio programmes, including 'Side By Side', 'Saturday Club', 'Pop Go The Beatles' and 'From Us To You'.

Ringo wrapped up the number during one take on the *Please Please Me* album, recorded on Monday, 11 February 1963.

'Boys' was included on the compilation *Rock 'n' Roll Music* and a live version is found on *The Beatles At the Hollywood Bowl* album. American albums featuring the number include *Introducing The Beatles, The Beatles Vs The Four Seasons, Songs, Pictures and Stories Of the Fabulous Beatles* and *The Early Beatles*.

A single of 'Boys' coupled with 'Kansas City/Hey! Hey! Hey!' was issued on Capitol Starline 60066 on 11 October 1965. The highest position it reached was No. 102 in the American charts.

The version, which the Beatles recorded for the radio show, 'Pop Goes The Beatles' was included on the *Live At the BBC* CD and another version was included on the *Anthology 1* CD.

Brambell, Wilfred

A British character actor noted for his portrayal of the grizzled rag-and-bone man, Steptoe, in the long-running BBC TV series 'Steptoe And Son'.

He co-starred with the Beatles in *A Hard Day's Night* as John McCartney, Paul's eccentric grandfather, who travels down to London with them and causes chaos wherever he goes.

At the time of filming he commented: 'I was worried about how someone like myself would fit in with these Beatles. I liked their music but I was no expert and I felt the whole thing could easily become a fiasco. Instead, they positively amazed me with their cool and professional approach.'

Wilfred travelled to Liverpool for the northern premiere of the film but refused to attend the opening as he claimed he had been slighted by officials at the civic reception.

He died of cancer on 18 January 1985 at the age of 72.

Bramwell, Tony

A childhood friend of George Harrison who became an office boy at NEMS in Liverpool after Brian Epstein had signed the Beatles.

George met him while he was working as a delivery boy and the two began to chat about skiffle and rock 'n' roll. George was suitably impressed when he heard that Tony had met Buddy Holly during his British tour. Tony recalls, 'I used to lend George all my Buddy Holly records so he could try to learn the various chords and riffs. We played them all so much that by the time we'd finished they were just about ready for the bin.'

From NEMS office boy he graduated to handling various assignments and soon became one of those close friends they always had around who was also capable of doing a good job of work. He travelled to America with them and wrote reports of their activities for various publications, including the *Beatles Monthly*.

Brian Epstein appointed him stage manager at the Saville Theatre and after Brian's death he joined Apple, involving himself in a number of tasks, including record production and the film company Subafilms.

He was also Apple's chief record-plugger and proved particularly adept at getting radio and TV spots for the Apple signings.

Tony was a dab hand with the camera and many of his photographs of Apple acts, such as Mary Hopkin, were syndicated throughout the world.

He remained in charge of Apple promotion until 1970 and then spent a year in Los Angeles running Apple Music.

Tony next worked for Harry Saltzmann's music-publishing company, then produced a Big Three album and became an independent promotions man, whose acts included Paul McCartney and the Moody Blues. By the end of the 1970s he was ensconced in an executive position at Polydor Records, retaining his independence.

The former NEMS office boy also became one of London's most eligible bachelors, dating an assortment of Miss Worlds and celebrities such as Christine Keeler, and for a number of years he lived with Swedish actress Julie Ege. He later married, began to represent

Phil Spector in Britain and moved to the south coast.

Commenting on his own career, he was to say, 'I started in 1963 as the Beatles' roadie and toured the world with most of the Mersey Beat bands through to 1965. Then I became head of NEMS Presentations and Subafilms, Brian Epstein's production and film companies. This involved producing and directing promotional films and stage shows with the Beatles, the Who, Jimi Hendrix, the Bee Gees and Cream.'

Bravo, Lizzie

A Brazilian girl, Lizzie was sixteen years old and a student living in Compayne Gardens, near to Abbey Road, when she waited outside the Abbey Road Studios on Sunday, 4 February 1968, hoping to catch a glimpse of the Beatles.

There were a number of other girls crowded outside the studio when Paul emerged looking for two fans to provide some falsetto harmonies on their current recording. He picked on Lizzie and another girl called Gayleen Pease and the two of them were asked inside to contribute some vocal harmonies to 'Across The Universe'. Lizzie and Gayleen were asked to sing the line 'Nothing's going to change my world' several times.

On the twentieth anniversary of the Beatles' recording career, a limited edition of 2,000 copies of a twelve-inch single was issued in Brazil with one side featuring Lizzie discussing her experiences in Portuguese. The 'B' side contained 'Love Me Do' and 'The Beatles Movie Medley'.

Bresner, Sergeant Buddy

The policeman assigned to guard the Beatles when they arrived in Miami Beach. He took over as their personal police bodyguard on Friday, 14 February 1964, and also acted as their adviser and friend. Buddy had been chosen for the job because he had previously looked after celebrities in the district, and he was given two dozen officers to command.

That evening the Beatles accepted the offer of having dinner at his home, where they met his wife Dottie and his children Barry, Andy and Jeri. Dezo Hoffman, who was also present, was struck by how Paul seemed so completely at home with the children. 'The unbelievable patience he had with those kids was incredible,' Dezo said. 'They didn't let him alone for a moment. He sat there reading to them, in a way that was obviously not an inconvenience to him at all – he was completely at home.'

Buddy then took them back to the Deauville Hotel which had a couple of nightclubs. They went in to see comedian Don Rickells, who gagged: 'Look at this, a police sergeant guarding four Zulus when all over the city there's fighting and burglary going on.' After the show John was tired and went to bed, but the others went to the second nightclub to see comedian Myron Cohen and singer/dancer Carol Lawrence. Comedian Cohen liked the Beatles and later commented, 'So long as they are still only TRYING to stamp out the Beatles in thirty years' time, who cares?

Part of Bresner's duties consisted of conducting bed checks every night to make sure there were no girls in their rooms – and no drugs. After they'd been to visit Cassius Clay (Muhammad Ali), Bresner took the lads to their very first drive-in movie, Elvis Presley's *Fun In Acapulco*.

The Beatles loved Miami so much they decided to stay on there for a few more days and Bresner arranged some other outings, including a visit to Star Island.

When he retired from the police force he became the owner of a construction business.

Brian Poole & The Tremeloes

A group from Dagenham, Essex, who auditioned for Decca Records at their West Hampstead Studios on 1 January 1962 on the same day as the Beatles had their recording audition. As it turned out, Decca's Dick Rowe agreed to take on one of the two groups recorded by Mike Smith that day, and it was eventually decided on the Tremeloes, presumably because they lived in closer proximity to London. In those days, prior to the motorway, it took several hours to travel from Liverpool to London.

Brian Poole & the Tremeloes had no record success until after the Beatles had become a major chart group. They then adopted the style that was known as **Mersey Beat**, initially covering 'Twist And Shout' four months after the Beatles had included the number on their debut album *Please Please Me*. They followed up with 'Do You Love Me', a number which had been released by another Mersey Beat band, Faron's Flamingos – although the Flamingos' version was relegated to the 'B' side on the decision of London executives.

'Twist And Shout' gave the Tremeloes a No. 4 position in the charts and 'Do You Love Me' reached No. 1. Initially, the north/south divide was evident when northern fans were annoyed to see a group from the south achieve success by what they regarded as 'pinching' the new sound from the north.

Brian Poole & the Tremeloes enjoyed some further hits until 1965: 'I Can Dance', 'Candy Man', 'Someone Someone', 'Twelve Steps To Love', 'Three Bells' and 'I Want Candy'. Brian Poole turned solo – but it was the Tremeloes who found success on their own, achieving a dozen further hits.

The original group comprised Brian Poole, vocals; Rick West, lead guitar; Alan Blakely, rhythm guitar; Alan Howard, bass guitar; and Dave Munden, drums. Blakely died of cancer in 1996.

Poole's two daughters Karen and Shellie found success in the 1990s as Alisha's Attic.

92 Broadway Avenue, Wallasey, Merseyside L45

The McCartney family lived in this house, situated across the Mersey from Liverpool, for almost two years in 1942 and 1943. Jim and Mary McCartney had moved into the small house with baby Paul, but decided to move back to Liverpool after Mike McCartney was born because the street was close to the docks and suffered some of the worst air raids.

Brodax, Al

Hungarian–American cartoon producer, whose cartoon productions had included *Popeye, Beetle Bailey* and *Krazy Kat*. He'd originally worked at the William Morris Agency handling the King Features account. King Features then approached him asking him to head a television and motion picture department for them.

In 1964 he negotiated with Brian Epstein, on behalf of his company, for a licence to produce a series of animated Beatles cartoons featuring Beatles songs. The 35-year-old New Yorker arranged a deal in which Epstein and the Beatles took fifty per cent of the fees. Brodax was both writer and producer of the series, which became the highest rating Saturday morning show of its time when it was originally screened in America in 1965.

During preliminary discussions for the series, Brodax also expressed his desire to make an animated feature film of the Beatles. Epstein told him that if the television cartoon series was a success, he would agree to him making a feature film.

The animated shorts, with each episode based on the title of a Beatles song, began airing by ABC in America in September 1965 and ran for two years.

Initially, Brodax experienced difficulty in contacting Epstein to finalise a deal for the feature. This was in 1965 when Brian was rarely in his office, due to his increasing addiction to drugs. Several meetings were cancelled and at one time, Brodax had to hang around for ten days for an appointment. But he persevered with the project, which was called *Yellow Submarine*. He'd even paid major writers such as Joseph Heller, author of the bestseller *Catch 22*, to prepare ideas for the feature, but Epstein seemed uninterested. It was Wendy Hanson who finally bullied Epstein into a meeting, and he nearly sacked her because of it.

Epstein liked the title and agreed to Brodax going ahead with the film, promising that the Beatles would provide four original songs for it.

Brodax did not enjoy his meetings with Epstein who, he claimed, treated him in a cavalier manner, but his persistence was rewarded with an animated film that became a classic of its kind. He allegedly didn't get on with the Beatles either and was said to have referred to Ringo as a 'clutz' and Paul as 'a wise-ass'.

He went on to write, direct and produce a number of TV shows in America, including 'Make A Wish' and in 2000 was planning a live action film called *Fish Story*.

Brodziak, Kenn

The Australian promoter who took the Beatles down under to tour in June 1964.

Brodziak, who had previously brought major names such as Marlene Dietrich and Sophie Tucker to tour Australia, arrived in London in July to book acts. At a meeting at the booking office of agent Cyril Berlin he was offered the choice of six groups and he liked the sound of the Beatles best and decided to book them. On 5 July 1963 he made a verbal contract to promote the Beatles in Australia at £1,000 per week.

The Beatles' career began to take off in a major way and the group could have demanded a considerably larger fee than the modest verbal deal. Brian Epstein sent a note to Berlin, 'You'll think me a very naughty boy, but I want £1,500 per week for Australia.'

Meanwhile, Brodziak was getting worried. He didn't have a contract and the fame of the Beatles was spreading to such an extent that there was great interest shown by rival promoters in bringing the group to Australia. In fact, Epstein was offered a considerably increased sum for an Australian tour via Tito Burns, but decided to honour his verbal agreement. He sent a telegram to Brodziak, 'I made an agreement and I will stick to it. The Beatles will come to Australia'.

The contracts were finally signed on 10 January 1964.

Brodziak tied in with Dick Lean, managing director of Stadiums Limited, who controlled a number of venues, for the fourteen playing dates, with Lean handling the security and supports while Brodziak was in charge of the staging. A Melbourne rock singer, Johnny Chester, was booked at £125 a week, together with a four-piece band called the Phantoms and New Zealand rock singer Johnny Devlin.

Bron, Eleanor

British actress who first rose to fame on the 'satire boom' in the early sixties, appearing at London's first satirical nightclub, the Establishment, and as a resident performer on the TV series 'Not So Much A Programme . . . More A Way Of Life'.

She made her film debut in *Help!* in 1965 and the *Sun* newspaper ran a story headed 'The Beatles' First Leading Lady' in which they wrote: 'Miss Bron, who has made a name for herself with pitiless send-ups of upper-class English women, will herself be an upper-class woman of a type: a mysterious Eastern princess who wants to be loved by the Beatles. She will thus become the Beatles' first leading lady (the woman interest in *A Hard Day's Night*, the Beatles' first film, was minimal). But the film people are not anxious to push this point too hard: it might upset some of the Beatles' girl fans.'

Eleanor portrayed a mysterious princess called Ahme, who comes to the boys' rescue on several occasions when they are pursued by Clang, leader of a religious cult, and his gang of murderous thugs.

During the filming in the Bahamas, the press kept trying to talk her into posing for photographs in a bikini, but she refused. She was surprised to see a *Daily Mail* photo-story headed 'Bron the Beatle Tamer', with a photograph of Paul McCartney on a bike talking to a dark-haired girl in a bikini with her back to the camera. It wasn't her!

While she was filming, Eleanor struck up a friendship with John Lennon and they used to spend time together drinking in the hotel bars, discussing politics and philosophy. When the Beatles were staying in Benedict Canyon in Beverly Hills prior to their Hollywood Bowl concert, Eleanor visited John there and spent a few hours with him. John was later to claim that she had been one of his conquests, but Eleanor denies they were ever lovers, pointing out that John was married to Cynthia and she had a boyfriend at the time.

Eleanor's recollections of filming with the Beatles are to be found in the *Pillow Book Of Eleanor Bron*, published by Jonathan Cape in 1985.

Brook Brothers, The

A British pop duo comprising brothers Geoffrey and Ricky Brook, from Winchester, Hampshire. They first began their musical career in a skiffle group in 1956. As a duo they made their recording debut in 1960, but it was when they joined Pye Records, with Tony Hatch as their producer, that they gained the tag 'the British Everly

Brothers' and enjoyed success with hits such as 'Warpaint' and 'Ain't Gonna Wash For A Week'.

They were added to the bill of the Beatles' fourth nationwide tour in November 1963. They also appeared in the film *It's Trad, Dad!*, directed by Richard Lester and starring Helen Shapiro, before they signed to Decca as the Brooks. The duo disbanded soon after.

Brookfield House

A fifteenth-century oak-beamed mansion in Elstead, near Guildford, Surrey. Peter Sellers bought the house and spent £50,000 on renovations. The house was set in several acres of ground and had its own lake, paddocks, walled gardens and barns. Sellers had a gymnasium, changing rooms, sauna and private cinema built into the barns.

When filming *The Magic Christian,* Ringo Starr discovered that Sellers was going to put the house on the market. He offered him £70,000 for it and Peter agreed. John Lennon also liked the house and offered him £150,000 for it, but Sellers decided to keep his word to Ringo. Ringo bought the house and lived there from mid-November 1968 until 5 December 1969. He later sold it to American singer Stephen Stills, who composed the song 'Johnny's Garden' there.

In 1998 the property was put up for sale for £1.7 million and the Society of Dead Comics had erected a plaque there in honour of Sellers.

Brooks, Elkie

One of Britain's major female vocalists.

Her real name was Elkie Bookbinder and she was a cabaret singer in Manchester before turning to rock music.

She appeared with the Beatles on 'Another Beatles' Christmas Show', at the Odeon, Hammersmith from 24 December 1964 to 16 January 1965. Elkie then changed her image from dance band singer to aggressive female rocker in the early seventies with Dada and Vinegar Joe. She was to enjoy success as a major concert performer and recording artist with over thirteen chart singles, including 'Pearl's A Singer', 'Lilac Wine', 'Fool If You Think It's Over' and 'No More The Fool'.

Her brother is Tony Mansfield, former drummer with Billy J. Kramer and the Dakotas.

Brown, Joe

Popular, blond-haired singer/guitarist who was first spotted by TV producer Jack Good performing at a dance in Southend.

Good featured him on his shows such as 'Oh Boy!' and Brown was soon to become a well-established show-biz star.

Born in Lincolnshire on 13 May 1941, his family moved to London's East End when he was two years old.

Brown's string of hits began with 'Darktown Strutter's Ball' in 1960 and he began appearing at live gigs backed by his band the Bruvvers.

In 1962 he was No. 3 in the charts with 'A Picture Of You', when Brian Epstein booked him on behalf of NEMS Enterprises for two consecutive gigs, with the Beatles in support, part of Epstein's plan to present the group on bills with established acts. 'A Picture Of You' was one of Epstein's favourite records at the time which is presumably why the Beatles included it in their repertoire, with George on vocals, even though it was untypical of their style.

Their first gig with Brown was at the Cambridge Hall in Southport on 26 July 1963, followed by a Tower Ballroom appearance the next evening. On the 27 July show, apart from Brown and the Beatles, the other acts were the Statesmen, the Big Three, Steve Day & the Drifters and the Four Jays.

In 1967 Brown recorded 'With A Little Help From My Friends', which became a minor hit for him, reaching the position of No. 32 in the British charts in June of that year.

Brown was to marry Liverpool singer Vicki Haseman, former student at the Junior Art School and a member of the female vocal groups the Vernons Girls and the Breakaways.

Their daughter Samantha Brown was later to become a hit recording artist in her own right in the eighties.

Sadly, Vicki died of cancer on 16 June 1991.

Brown, Ken

A Liverpool guitarist who played alongside a sixteen-year-old George Harrison in the Les Stewart Quartet in 1958, at a time when John Lennon's group the Quarry Men were dormant.

They were practising at a venue called Lowlands when George's girlfriend, Ruth Morrison, mentioned that a new coffee club was opening nearby and they might be seeking a resident group. Brown went along to see Mona Best and secured the band a residency, due to begin when the club opened on Saturday, 29 August 1959.

Early that Saturday, Brown went to Stewart's house and sat in the lounge with Stewart and George. There seemed to be a bad atmosphere in the room and Brown asked Stewart what was up. Stewart accused him of missing practice and continued to argue after Brown explained that he'd been helping out at the Casbah in order to secure a place for them to play. Stewart accused him of receiving money for helping out, which Brown denied.

Stewart told him, 'I'm not playing there.'

Brown asked George not to back out on him too, so George followed him out of the house, with Brown suggesting that they get a group together for that evening. George mentioned that he had two friends and would contact them.

Brown waited patiently at the Casbah for two hours, then George returned with John, Paul and Cynthia.

They decided to use the name of John's group, the Quarry Men, and began their residency that evening. Among the numbers played were 'Three Cool Cats' sung by John and 'Long Tall Sally', sung by Paul. Brown played Hofner guitar and the group used his ten-watt amplifier.

The new club was the subject of a story in the local newspaper, the *West Derby Reporter*. It noted how Kenneth Brown, David Hughes and Douglas Jenkins had helped to decorate the club and make it shipshape, adding: 'Kenneth Brown is also a member of a guitar group which entertains the club members on Saturday nights. The other members of the group, who call themselves the Quarry Men, travel from the south end of the city to play.'

In 1965, Brown told a reporter how his days with the group came to an end during a dispute which took place six weeks after the group had got together:

> One night, just as we were due to start a Saturday session, I felt a crippling pain in my leg. I could barely stand, but insisted on doing something, so Mrs Best asked me to take the money and the door and, for the first time, John, Paul and George played without me.
>
> Just as everyone was going home I was in the club when Paul came back down the steps. 'Hey, Ken, what's all this?' he said. 'What?' I asked him. 'Mrs Best says she's paying you, even though you didn't play with us tonight.' 'That's up to her,' I replied, as Paul bounded back up the stairs, still arguing with Mrs Best. They all came downstairs to me. 'We think your fifteen bob should be divided between us, as you didn't play tonight,' said Paul. So of course I didn't agree. 'All right, that's it then!' shouted McCartney, and they stormed off down the drive towards West Derby village, shouting that they would never play the Casbah again.

This left the club without a resident group, so Brown approached Pete Best and suggested they form a group on their own. The result was the Blackjacks, who began playing regularly at the club until Pete was approached by the Beatles to join them for their Hamburg

trip. The Blackjacks were on the verge of splitting up as Chas
Newby was soon to start college and Brown was about to marry his
girlfriend, Marcia, and move to London.

In December 1960, when Stuart Sutcliffe remained in Hamburg,
Best suggested that Brown rejoin them as bass guitarist for some of
their Liverpool gigs, even though he was then in London, but the
other members vetoed the suggestion.

The last time that Brown saw the group was on 16 March 1963,
when Neil Aspinall phoned him to say that they were in a jam as
they'd run out of money and were due to appear in Sheffield the
next night – could he lend them £20?

Brown was to relate: 'Eventually, I agreed and they all turned up
at our flat. Neil came to the door, then Marcia, and I went down to
the van to see the boys. I handed over the money, which they repaid
six weeks later.'

Over August Bank Holiday 1999, Brown joined Pete Best and
Chas. Newby at the Casbah to celebrate the club's fortieth anniversary.

Brown, Peter

One of Brian Epstein's close friends, Peter was born in Bebington in
the Wirral, across the river from Liverpool. He worked for a time in
Henderson's, one of Liverpool's large department stores, before
becoming the manager of the record department in another store,
Lewis's, which was quite close to the NEMS branch in Great
Charlotte Street.

When Epstein went on to run the new NEMS store in
Whitechapel he talked the 22-year-old Brown into taking his place
as manager of the Great Charlotte Street shop.

In 1965, when he'd settled in London, Brian asked Brown to
move to the capital as his personal assistant. Brown worked from
offices in Stafford Street and dealt with a variety of matters relating
to the Beatles, ranging from contractual dealings to arranging social
events.

Brown was invited to spend the weekend with Brian and
Geoffrey Ellis at Epstein's country house at Kingsley Hill over the
Bank Holiday weekend in August 1967. Epstein decided to leave
them and returned to London. Brown later received a call – Brian
had been found dead.

In the power vacuum left by the death of the Beatles' Manager,
several people tried to hustle their way into taking Brian's place.
Brown, similar to Brian in so many ways, looked after their affairs
for a while and became General Manager of Beatles & Co and then
became an executive at Apple Corps in Savile Row. In his book *The*

Longest Cocktail Party, author Richard DiLello describes Brown as 'The impeccable Signor Suave of the Apple diplomatic corps and personal assistant and social co-ordinator to the Beatles'.

It was Peter Brown who accompanied John and Yoko to Gibraltar and acted as best man at their wedding. John mentions Peter by name on his single 'The Ballad Of John And Yoko'.

When Allen Klein moved in he found it very easy to get rid of the majority of the Apple staff, some of whom had been associated with the Beatles since the early Liverpool days. However, he found it more difficult to sack Brown or Neil Aspinall. At Apple the directors resigned each year and then were automatically reappointed. Klein made sure that when Brown's resignation came in, his directorship was not renewed.

In 1970 Peter left Apple to join Robert Stigwood's organisation and then moved to America.

In the eyes of Beatle fans, his copy book was blotted when he began to write what was to become known as a 'kiss-and-tell' book. He'd been approached by writer Stephen Gaines and the two were to receive a substantial advance payment for a book on the Beatles. As an 'insider', Peter would have access to the surviving members of the band and their relatives and friends. He told them he was writing a book about the period of the sixties in general. When *The Love You Make: An Insider's Story Of The Beatles* was first published in January 1983 by McGraw-Hill, it infuriated Peter's former colleagues who had co-operated by discussing their memories, because the book did not portray the Beatles in a sympathetic light, was written like an exposé, suggested that Yoko Ono was responsible for the Beatles' break-up and intimated that she turned John into a heroin addict. It also revived some of the inaccurate stories that had appeared in previous books such as *Shout!* – in particular, the suggestion that Brian Epstein fell in love with John Lennon the moment he saw him, which became his main reason for signing up the Beatles. This unsubstantiated tale, which was originally told to Philip Norman by a gay friend of Epstein's in Liverpool, is false. Epstein was genuinely excited by what was happening on the Mersey scene and saw it as providing him with an exciting challenge to his creative talents.

Brown, Roberta 'Bobby'

A girl who lived in Buchanan Road, Wallasey, 'over the water' from Liverpool, who launched the Beatles' first official fan club in May 1962 (an unofficial club had been launched the year previously).

Bobby was a Cavern Club regular, began to advertise her club in

Mersey Beat, and was aided in her efforts by friends such as Frieda Kelly.

Bobby passed over the running of the club to Frieda when she became engaged to be married, early in 1963.

In December 1963 she wrote about the Beatles' fan club in a letter to *Mersey Beat*:

> The Fan Club has now been operating since April last, and the amount of members accumulated during this time, which has risen tremendously to one thousand, has made our efforts seem well worthwhile. Our members come from all over the country, from such places as Glasgow, Lancaster, Blackpool, Essex, Doncaster, Sussex, I.O.M., Northern Ireland – and even further afield from Hamburg, Belgium and Rhodesia. My daily post is fantastic, an average of thirty letters a day!
>
> Recently I visited the Star Club in Hamburg, with a number of fans, to see the Beatles. How pleased they were to see that they were appreciated there just as they had been by the numerous fans in this country. It is most rewarding to see after a hard struggle from the bottom that they have reached the top in their own special field of entertainment. It is the 'get up and go' quality which these boys possess that makes the Fan Club well worth running. Early next year we're going to organise a 'Fan club festival' in which the boys really 'meet' their fans.

Bobby also ran two special coach trips for fans, one to the Playhouse, Manchester in which the Beatles, Brian Epstein, Jim McCartney and Bill and Virginia Harry joined them on the trip. The other was to the Plaza, St Helens, to encourage ballroom manager Harry Bostock to provide them with more bookings at the venue.

Browne, Tara

A close friend of the individual members of the Beatles and John and Paul in particular. He visited Paul at the McCartney home Rembrandt in the Wirral and became a good friend of Mike McCartney, too. His other friends included Brian Jones of the Rolling Stones and Spencer Davis of the Spencer Davis Group and he visited the London 'in' clubs such as Sibylla's and the Bag O' Nails regularly.

Tara was married to Noreen, daughter of an Irish farmer, and they had two children, Dorian and Julian. However, he was estranged from his wife and dating a nineteen-year-old model Suki

Potier when he was involved in a fatal car crash. The 21-year-old Tara, a member of the Guinness family and heir to one million pounds, which he was to receive on his 25th birthday, died on 18 December 1966. He was driving his Lotus Elan sports car when he crashed into the back of a van in South Kensington. He was killed, but Suki escaped with bruises and shock, saying that Tara had swerved the car to protect her. Her father, Gilbert Potier said, 'I am certain Mr Browne saved my daughter. It was very courageous.'

When John Lennon read about the accident in the *Daily Mail* newspaper he included a reference to it in his song 'A Day In The Life', which was featured on the *Sgt Pepper's Lonely Hearts Club Band* album.

Another item from the *Daily Mail*, regarding holes in the road in Lancashire, was also included in the words of the song.

Bryce, Leslie

Photographer who became the official photographer for Sean O'Mahony's *The Beatles Book* (later to become the *Beatles Monthly*), which gained him an access to the Beatles which was denied other photographers. As a result he took many exclusive picture sessions and travelled around the world with the group, taking literally thousands of photographs.

Leslie had previously worked under renowned photographers such as Baron and Lord Snowdon and passed on many tips to the Beatles who were genuinely interested in photography, particularly Ringo.

Because he was present with the Beatles on numerous occasions, he was one of the many people who were given the tag 'the Fifth Beatle'.

Burns, Tito

A leading British impresario of the sixties. The former accordionist/bandleader had become a prominent manager and agent, representing acts such as Cliff Richard. He had the foresight to phone Brian Epstein in Liverpool following the release of 'Love Me Do' to enquire about the Beatles' availability for live shows.

Epstein wrote to him offering the Beatles to perform for £250 per week during January and February 1963, although Burns didn't take up the offer, merely filing the letter.

In the autumn of 1963 he phoned Epstein in Liverpool again on behalf of an Australian promoter, Harry Miller, whom he represented. Burns knew that Epstein had discussed an Australian tour with another promoter, but had only been offered £2,000.

Burns offered Epstein £7,000 if the Beatles would agree to tour

Australia for Miller. Although Epstein hadn't signed any contract with the other promoter, he felt that he'd given his word and therefore refused the offer from Burns.

However, the two became friends. Burns had begun building a powerful show-business company and represented a number of artists ranging from Liverpool's the Searchers to Dusty Springfield.

At one time the two discussed the possibility of uniting their respective organisations and becoming partners. However, Brian couldn't come to terms with the idea that Tito should be able to close any deals in which the Beatles were involved and the merger didn't take place.

Busch Stadium, Stadium Plaza, St Louis, Missouri

On Sunday, 31 August 1966 the Beatles had performed a noon concert in Cincinnati while the 8.30 p.m. open-air show in St Louis drew an audience of 23,143. Unfortunately, being an open-air venue it was vulnerable when the rain began to pour, and a tarpaulin cover was fitted over the stage area. Local promoters were Stix, Baer and Fuller and the show's compere was Nick Charles. Due to the bad weather the Beatles went on in the middle of the show, to be followed by the Cyrkle and the Ronettes, who saw a dwindling audience as everyone began to leave following the Beatles' performance.

Because of the 'Jesus controversy' a local pastor told his congregation that anyone attending the Beatles' concert would be excommunicated.

Byrds, The

An American band who, although they'd originally formed as a folk trio called the Jet Set, became heavily influenced by the Beatles in 1964 and changed their style.

They comprised Gene Clark (vocals/tambourine/rhythm guitar), Jim (Roger) McGuinn (vocals/lead guitar), David Crosby (vocals/rhythm guitar), Chris Hillman (bass) and Michael Clarke (drums).

McGuinn was to comment: 'We each heard them (the Beatles), saw them in *A Hard Day's Night,* and I personally went out and got a Rickenbacker 12-string guitar like George had and David got a Gretch and our drummer got Ludwig drums and we just patterned ourselves after the Beatles individually.'

They used the name the Beefeaters for their Elektra single 'Please Let Me Love You' in 1964, but by the end of the year had changed their name to the Byrds and signed with CBS, where they had a chart hit with their first release, 'Mr Tambourine Man'. George Harrison once called them 'The American Beatles'.

Derek Taylor became their publicist and travelled to England with the Byrds in 1965. He sent the Beatles copies of their debut album, also called *Mr Tambourine Man*.

The group met up with the Beatles socially on several occasions. Paul and Jane Asher joined three members of the group for a night out at the London nightspot the Scotch of St James. A few weeks later Paul and George attended the Byrds' recording session for the Bob Dylan song 'The Times They Are A Changing'.

Dave Crosby has been credited with bringing Ravi Shankar's music to the attention of George Harrison.

Gene Clarke died on 24 May 1991, the year in which the Byrds were inducted into the Rock 'n' Roll Hall of Fame.

Byrne, Gay

Irish TV presenter who worked for Granada Television in the early 1960s, hosting a programme called 'People and Places', which focused on people and events in the north-west of England.

Byrne had originally read out a news item regarding a clip of the Beatles filmed at the Cavern and became the first person to announce the Beatles on TV when they made their television debut and performed 'Love Me Do' for the show on 7 November 1962. The Beatles received a fee of £35. The programme was to change its name to 'Scene At 6.30' and Gay later returned to Ireland where he became the Republic's leading television personality, hosting the Dublin-based chat show 'The Late, Late Show'.

On 7 November 1963 the Beatles performed in Dublin. To celebrate the thirtieth anniversary of the event, Byrne hosted a two-hour Beatles TV special in Ireland on the same day in 1993.

Byrne had also hosted their 'Beat Show' radio programme, recorded at the Playhouse Theatre, Manchester, on 3 July 1963, in addition to recording an interview with the Beatles and Ken Dodd for Granada's 'Scene At 6.30' on 25 November 1963.

Cabana Motor Hotel, Dallas, Texas

The hotel where the Beatles stayed on Friday, 18 September 1964, prior to their appearance at the Dallas Memorial Coliseum. On their way to the hotel from the airport they passed the area where President John F. Kennedy had been shot and John Lennon asked, 'Is it safe?'

The group and their entourage filled the entire ninth floor of the hotel, which was under siege from hundreds of fans. Many were hiding in the building and armed police stalked the hotel searching them out. Mal Evans brought three members of the Dallas Beatles Fan Club to meet the group – Yolanda Hernandez, Marie Leggett and Stephanie Pinter who spent a few hours with the members of the group.

During the crush of fans outside the hotel, a plate glass window was smashed and three fans were hospitalised. Paul McCartney rang them up and talked to them at the nearby Methodist Hospital.

Cabaret Club, 28 Duke Street, Liverpool

One of the main Merseyside cabaret night spots in its time. A club totally unsuited to the proponents of the Mersey sound – the club catered for an older age group who preferred cabaret performers such as Lita Roza at the venue.

For some reason, Brian Epstein attempted to introduce the Beatles into the cabaret circuit and his influence resulted in a booking at the club on 25 July 1962. It was a total disaster.

Caird Hall, City Square, Dundee, Angus, Scotland

Venue where the Beatles appeared on the final date of a three-day
mini-tour of Scotland on Monday, 7 October 1963. They were to
return to the venue for the second and last time on Tuesday, 20
October 1964 during which they were interviewed in their dressing
room by June Shields for the Grampian TV show 'Grampian Week'.
The five-minute excerpt was screened on Friday, 23 October.

Calder, Tony

Calder worked in the Decca Press Office in the same room as Tony
Barrow, who wrote the sleeve notes for the Beatles' Decca albums.
He left Decca to set up his own PR firm in partnership with Andrew
Loog Oldham. When Brian Epstein offered the job of Beatles Press
Officer to Barrow, he turned it down and Epstein offered it to
Oldham, whom he met at 'Thank Your Lucky Stars'.

Epstein had asked Barrow's advice on promotion and when
Barrow pointed out that new records needed a press release,
Epstein commissioned him to provide one for the Beatles' 'Love Me
Do'. As he was still working for Decca, Barrow arranged for Calder
and Oldham to post out all the releases to the relevant newspapers.

Caldwell, Iris

Blonde sister of the late Liverpool Beat group leader Rory Storm.
Her first boyfriend was George Harrison in the days before he was
interested in music. Iris was only twelve at the time, George was
fourteen. Her mother Vi said, 'George used to come and watch TV
three times a week. He and Iris used to sit there holding hands. It
was the first time either of them had ever taken any interest in
someone of the opposite sex. At Iris' fourteenth birthday party, I
remember George turned up in a brand new Italian-style suit
covered with buttons. As in most teenage parties, they kept on
playing kissing games and somehow or other, George and Iris
always ended up together.'

When she was seventeen her boyfriend was Paul McCartney and
she claimed that 'Love Me Do' was a song Paul had written for her.

Her romance with Paul lasted for twelve months, and for at least
six months they were serious enough about each other to be what
Northerners would call 'going steady'. She commented, 'Epstein
was not very pleased that I was going out with Paul and I wasn't
allowed to go anywhere with the group in case any of their fans saw
me. But every night after they'd appeared at the Cavern, Paul would
come round to our house – and when they went away to Hamburg
he used to write me the most fantastic letters.'

The romance came to an end when Jane Asher entered the picture. Iris was to say, 'I'm quite sure there were many other girls around at that time . . . and then when he came back from London once and said that he had met Jane Asher I didn't want to go out with him anymore, though we remained good friends and kept a good relationship.'

Iris married singer Shane Fenton in 1964 and they went on the road as a double act. In the seventies Shane was to change his name to Alvin Stardust and had the chart success which had eluded him in the sixties. The couple had two children, but divorced several years later and Iris remarried in 1983.

Caleb

A long-haired Tarot card reader who was hired by the Beatles to work at Apple. No one seemed to know his surname, so he was always referred to, simply, as Caleb.

He was given the power to authorise or approve all Apple business dealings, which he would do using the Tarot cards, an ancient method of divination. At one time he replaced John Lydon as manager of the Apple boutique. Caleb was also an I Ching diviner and would regularly visit the various members of Apple staff and use three coins to advise on various decisions. He also used to compile daily in-house horoscopes.

Caleb eventually became bored with people asking him to predict the positions of records in the charts and left, later to end up in an asylum.

Cambridge Hall, Lord Street, Southport, Lancashire

Venue in the main thoroughfare of a smart seaside town, close to Liverpool.

On Thursday, 26 July 1962, NEMS Enterprises promoted a concert at the venue starring Joe Brown & the Bruvvers, who were No. 3 in the British charts at the time with 'A Picture of You'. It was one of two bookings by NEMS Enterprises of the blond-haired cockney guitarist who first rose to fame in Britain after his appearances on the TV programme 'Six Five Special'. He was a popular recording artist at the time and had an engaging personality. His chart hits included 'Dark Town Strutters Ball', 'Shine' and 'What A Crazy World We're Living In'. At the time of this engagement he was No. 3 in the charts with 'A Picture Of You', a number which the Beatles had recently featured in their act, with George Harrison on vocals.

The Beatles were second on the bill to Joe Brown on this occasion.

Canadian Broadcasting Company, The

On Saturday, 19 December 1969, the Canadian Broadcasting Company screened a 45-minute discussion programme between John Lennon and Marshall McLuhan from the University of Toronto. McLuhan was a noted intellectual, author of the best-seller *The Medium Is The Message* and head of the University's Department of Culture and Technology.

During the discussion, John mentioned that his initial interest in becoming a musician had been sparked off by hearing Elvis Presley. McLuhan pointed out that John's way of approaching music was by forming a band and that the English were more team-orientated than the Americans. McLuhan then went into a detailed theory of the growth and decline of pop festivals. The conversation touched on a few other topics and John mentioned that the Beatles had had to change because there was a danger in remaining the same, and that they had to avoid getting in a rut.

Candie Auditorium, The, Candie Gardens, St Peter Port, Guernsey, Channel Isles

The Beatles travelled the thirty-mile distance between Jersey and Guernsey in a twelve-seater plane for this concert promoted by Baron Pontin, the holiday camp millionaire, on Thursday, 8 August 1963. The group performed nine numbers at the sell-out show.

Candlestick Park, San Francisco, California

Venue which was the scene of the Beatles' final public concert on Monday, 29 August 1966.

Backstage visitors included Joan Baez and Mimi Farina.

A temporary stage had been erected in the middle of the Baseball Park, surrounded by a six-foot fence, and over 200 police were on patrol to supervise the 25,000-strong audience, with 20,000 seats unsold.

The show began at 8 o'clock and support acts included the Cyrkle, the Ronettes (without Ronnie Spector), Bobby Hebb and the Remains. The master of ceremonies was Gene Nelson, one of the leading DJs of KYA-AM, who remarked that the wind conditions would make the sound quality better across the Bay, commenting, 'With the breeze out here, you will see the Beatles, but they may hear them better in Alameda.'

Paul had asked PR man Tony Barrow to record the concert for him and Tony used a Philips cassette recorder with a Beyer microphone.

After the Ronettes had finished the set, the Beatles made their way to an elevated stage on the second base, which was protected by two fences, one a six-foot police barrier, the other a ten-foot cyclone fence.

The group, wearing dark green double-breasted Edwardian suits, began their performance at 9.27 p.m. with Chuck Berry's 'Rock And Roll Music' and went straight into 'She's A Woman'. Paul then said, 'Thank you very much everybody and hello, good evening. We'd like to carry on with a song, not surprisingly, written by George, and this was on our *Rubber Soul* LP and the song is called "If I Needed Someone".'

George took over lead vocals on the song and John then said, 'Thank you everybody. We'd like to carry on now, carry on together, one together and all for one, with another number which used to be a single record back in, er, er, a long time ago and this one's about the naughty lady called "Day Tripper".'

They then performed the number and went straight into 'Baby's In Black'. During the number a group of gatecrashers attempted to storm the field, but were intercepted by security men. George then announced, 'We'd like to carry on with something very old indeed and this one was recorded about 1959! It's called "I Feel Fine".'

George then said, 'Thank you. Like to carry on with a song from *Yesterday And Today*, and this one was a single as well, and it features Paul singing a very nice song called "Yesterday".'

Paul then said, 'It's a bit chilly,' referring to the fact that a cold wind was blowing in from the north California coast, and continued, 'We'd like to do the next number now which is a request for all the wonderful backroom boys on this tour. The song is called "I Want To Be Your Man". To sing it ... Ringo!'

Incidentally, Mort Feld, the soundman that night, was to comment, 'Ringo came out and on the first number he sat down and playfully swung the boom mike out and the counterweight came around. For the balance of the show he sang into the counterweight.'

After the number, the boys thanked Ringo and he thanked them. John shouted out, 'Lovely working with you, Ringo!' before continuing with the introduction, 'We'd like to do another song from our BBC album, and this one's called "He's A Real Nowhere Man, Sitting In His Nowhere Land", oh yes!'

When the song finished, Paul had noticed a fan running across the field towards the stage. 'We'd like to carry on, certainly, definitely, but shall we just watch this for a bit. Just watch,' he said. After the police had caught the girl fan, Paul said, 'The next song is called "Paperback Writer", one ... two ... three ... four!'

After the number he thanked the audience and commented, 'We'd like to say it's been wonderful being here in this wonderful sea air! Sorry about the weather, and we'd like to ask you to join in and clap, sing, talk, do anything. Anyway, the song is . . .' He was in the middle of saying 'Good night', then realised he shouldn't be tipping the audience that it was the last number. The group performed 'Long Tall Sally', then rushed into the Loomis armoured van, which had been waiting behind the stage with the engine running. They had finished their performance at 10.00 p.m.

If only the promoters Tom Donahue and Bobby Mitchell, who were disc jockeys at KYA-AM, had known that it was to be the Beatles' final concert, they would have ensured that the 20,000 empty seats were filled.

When the Beatles flew out of San Francisco following their final American concert, George Harrison remarked, 'Well, that's it. I'm not a Beatle any more.'

Tony Barrow auctioned off his tape at Sotheby's in London in 1988, and it was subsequently turned into a bootleg album. The official photographer for the show was Jim Marshall and his photographs were later to be featured in a special book of the concert by Eric Lefcowitz called *Tomorrow Never Knows: The Beatles' Last Concert.*

Cannibal & The Headhunters
An American band who appeared on the bill of the Beatles' US tour of 1965. At the time Cannibal & the Headhunters had a Top Ten hit in the charts with 'Land Of 1000 Dances'.

Can't Buy Me Love
Paul wrote 'Can't Buy Me Love' when the Beatles were in Paris in January 1964, staying at the George V hotel. They had a grand piano installed in the corner of the sitting room of their suite, near to the window, and composed several numbers there.

John gave him a hand, but it was mainly Paul's work, which is why he was upset when critics assumed that the title referred to prostitution. He commented: 'Personally, I think you can put any interpretation you want to anything, but when someone says "Can't Buy Me Love" is about a prostitute, I draw the line. That's going too far.'

As EMI urgently needed new Beatles material, George Martin recorded them in the Pathe Marconi Studios in Paris while he was over there to overdub some German vocals on to 'She Loves You' and 'I Want to Hold Your Hand'.

Martin advised them not to start with the verse line beginning

'I'll buy you a diamond ring my friend . . .' but to begin with the chorus. 'We've got to have an introduction, something that catches the ear immediately, a hook,' he told them.

Although the basic vocals were recorded on the Paris session, which took place on 29 January, Paul didn't put on the final vocal track until 25 February following the group's return from their debut tour of America.

Advance sales for the single reached one million in Britain and 2,100,000 in America, the highest advance sales for a single ever recorded at the time.

It was issued in Britain on 20 March 1964 on Parlophone R5114 and went straight to No. 1 in the charts, remaining in that position for four weeks. It was issued in the US on 16 March on Capitol 5150 and became the first record ever to go straight to No 1 simultaneously in both Britain and the United States.

When it reached No. 1 in the *Billboard* charts on 4 April 1964 the chart for that week was: 1. 'Can't Buy Me Love'. 2. 'Twist And Shout'. 3. 'She Loves You'. 4. 'I Want To Hold Your Hand'. 5. 'Please Please Me'.

It was the biggest domination of the Top Five ever – and the group also had a fantastic domination of the Hot 100 in general as, when 'Can't Buy Me Love' celebrated its second week at No. 1, the Beatles had no less than fourteen singles in the chart.

They were: 1. 'Can't Buy Me Love'. 2. 'Twist And Shout'. 4. 'She Loves You'. 7. 'I Want To Hold Your Hand'. 9 'Please Please Me'. 14. 'Do You Want To Know A Secret'. 38. 'I Saw Her Standing There'. 48. 'You Can't Do That'. 50. 'All My Loving'. 52. 'From Me To You'. 61. 'Thank You Girl'. 74. 'There's A Place'. 78. 'Roll Over Beethoven'. 81. 'Love Me Do'.

The single also created a record by giving the Beatles the most consecutive No. 1 singles in the *Billboard* chart. It immediately followed 'She Loves You' in the No. 1 spot, which had directly followed 'I Want To Hold Your Hand' at the top. The number was included on the *A Hard Day's Night* album, the 1965 compilation EP *The Beatles Million Sellers*, the 1966 album *A Collection Of Beatles Oldies (But Goldies)*, the 1973 compilation *The Beatles 1962–1966*, the 1979 *Hey Jude* album, the 1980 *Beatles Box* and various other compilations. The group also performed it on one 'Saturday Club' and two 'From Us To You' BBC radio programmes.

The 'B' side was 'You Can't Do That'.

Several weeks after the Beatles' single was released, jazz singer Ella Fitzgerald issued her version, which reached No. 30 in the British charts. Ella's was the most famous version, apart from the Beatles' own, but there have actually been more than seventy different versions of the song by artists such as Mary Wells, Brenda Lee, Gerry Mulligan and the Supremes.

The Beatles' recording of 'Can't Buy Me Love' was also included in their movie *A Hard Day's Night,* becoming the last number in the film, heard as the group rushed down the fire escape at the end of their show to horseplay in a field.

The version the Beatles performed on the radio show 'From Us To You' was included on *The Beatles Live At The BBC* CD. The version they recorded in Paris while they were appearing at the Olympia Theatre is included on the Beatles' *Anthology 1* CDs.

Capitol Cinema, Dock Street, Cardiff, Wales

The Beatles made their first appearance at this Welsh cinema on Monday, 27 May 1963 as part of their tour with Roy Orbison. They headlined their own show when they appeared at the venue for the second time on Saturday, 7 November 1964. Their third and final appearance at the Capitol was also the last date of their final British concert tour when they performed there on Sunday, 12 December 1965.

The venue has long since been demolished.

Capitol Records

An American label founded in Los Angeles in the forties by Glen Wallichs and lyric writer Johnny Mercer. The company is based at Capitol Tower on Hollywood and Vine, a 13-storey building shaped like a stack of records.

In the fifties EMI Records in Britain began to experience a number of problems. In 1952 the American Columbia label left EMI to place its roster of artists, who included Doris Day, Johnnie Ray, Frankie Laine and Guy Mitchell, with Phillips Records. Then EMI also lost their contract with RCA-Victor. As American products were vitally important for the British and European market, in 1955 Sir Joseph Lockwood, with great foresight, decided to buy an American label outright and purchased Capitol Records for nine million dollars.

Although they owned Capitol, they did not want to pressure the label into accepting British artists, but gave Capitol the right of first and second refusal on British recordings.

With the success in Britain of 'Please Please Me', EMI decided to offer the record to Capitol. 'They wouldn't take it at any price,' said Sir Joe.

As Beatlemania grew in Britain and Europe, and following the success of 'From Me To You', George Martin offered Capitol the British chart topper. They refused it. Capitol President Alan

Livingston was to send a memo, 'We don't think the Beatles will do anything in this market'. With their third massive No. 1 hit in the UK, 'She Loves You', George Martin tried again and in August 1963 told Capitol, 'For God's sake, do something about this. These boys are breaking it, and they're going to be fantastic throughout the world. So for heaven's sake, latch on to them.' For the third time Capitol said they considered that the Beatles had no prospects in America.

EMI were frustrated that their own American branch refused to handle their biggest British and European act, so they contacted another of their American subsidiaries, Transglobal. Transglobal usually made special deals with other American labels for EMI products which had been rejected by Capitol. Transglobal's Paul Marshall arranged for the small label Vee Jay Records to issue the singles 'Please Please Me' and 'From Me To You' and the album *Introducing The Beatles*. But they had no success and dropped their option. Marshall then placed 'She Loves You' with Swan Records. This was also unsuccessful.

Up to this time, EMI had exerted no major pressure from its chief executives, but Brian Epstein was becoming annoyed at the negative response from Capitol and told EMI to use their clout. He also phoned Alan Livingston personally and told him, 'Mr Livingston, we just don't understand it. The Beatles are doing very well in England, why don't you release them over there?' Livingston told him that he would listen to their records and call him back. By this time, word was beginning to filter through to America that the Beatles were becoming a phenomenon in Europe. EMI's Senior Executive L. G. Wood had called Capitol's Lloyd Dunn, who was Vice-President in charge of Merchandising and Sales, to use his muscle. EMI's Tony Palmer had also put pressure on Dave Dexter Jr, Capitol's A&R man, who said that he would agree to release the next Beatles record. Epstein had also got in touch with Brown Meggs, Director of Eastern Operations for Capitol. Livingston got back to Epstein and said he'd agree to release a single and an album by the group. Brian told him, 'I'm not going to give them to you unless you agree to spend $40,000 promoting this song.' He was referring to 'I Want To Hold Your Hand'. This was a vast amount of money for promotion as the largest amount the company had ever spent on the promotion of a record up to that time was $5,000. Livingston decided to take the gamble and it became the biggest single promotional campaign in the history of the record industry and included a crash publicity programme with posters and window stickers and the manufacture of five million 'The Beatles are coming' badges.

Although Capitol were literally forced to take what became the biggest-selling recording artists in history, they didn't seem to learn their lesson. Following the success of the Beatles in America, EMI's Columbia label then offered Capitol the Dave Clark Five. Capitol rejected them and they went on to have 24 American hits. Capitol also turned down the Animals, who were to have fourteen US hits; Herman's Hermits, who were to have eighteen; the Hollies, who were to have twelve; Manfred Mann, who were to have four; Gerry & the Pacemakers, who were to have seven; Lulu, who had four, including the chart topper 'To Sir With Love'; and the Yardbirds, who had six – among others.

On 11 November 1963, Brian Epstein met Brown Meggs in New York to discuss the release of 'I Want to Hold Your Hand', on 26 December 1963. The commitment from Capitol at the time still wasn't one hundred per cent and even the publishing rights to 'I Want To Hold Your Hand' had been given to MCA at a nominal fee and Capitol had to contact them for clearance on the publishing rights. Meggs and his colleagues had been uneasy about the record and, in particular, their promise that they would press 200,000 copies. As it happened, due to a growing demand, the orders outstripped that figure and during December three production plants – Capitol's, CBS's and RCA's – were all at work in an effort to press a million copies by the New Year.

The 14 December issue of *Cash Box* headlined their lead story: 'Capitol Gets The Beatles For US', and mentioned that Brown Meggs had announced that the first album *Meet The Beatles* would now be issued in January instead of February. In the 28 December issue of *Cash Box*, another Capitol story on the Beatles read: 'It was in one of Hamburg's rowdy and raucous strip joints, the Indra Club, that they were discovered by a young English talent agent and promoter, Brian Epstein.' A Capitol press release at the time called 'National Record News' had such innacurate information as: 'In those days they called themselves a variety of things – the Quarry Men, Moon Dogs or Moonshiners. It was early 1958 and they spent most of their time playing in the cellar of a friend's home in Liverpool for kicks.' The press release also referred to Paul as 'Paul McCatney'.

Capitol's first Beatles release, 'I Want To Hold Your Hand', became the company's fastest-selling record up to that time and their biggest seller, eventually achieving sales of over five million copies.

When George Martin accompanied the Beatles on their first trip to America, he was irked at how Capitol had implied that they had literally discovered the group. In his autobiography *All You Need Is Ears* he commented that when he arrived in America with the group, Capitol were embarrassed at his presence because they had been implying that the Beatles were theirs. He observed, 'At the Beatles' first press conference in New York, Alan Livingston ran the whole show. He kept me away from the press, which I must admit seemed a mite peculiar. To top it all, he introduced the Beatles as *the* Capitol recording artists – words which came ill from the lips of the man who had turned them down three times!'

It was ironic that the company which had been rejecting the Beatles for a year suddenly switched around to the extent that by April 1964 the Capitol Records' switchboard was answering calls with the message, 'Good morning: Capitol Records, home of the Beatles!'

Capitol distributed the Beatles' records in America between 1964 and 1968 and then handled the American distribution for Apple Records.

A few days after the release of 'I Want To Hold Your Hand', the album *Meet The Beatles* was issued on 20 January 1964. Within its first week it sold 750,000 copies and by December 1966 American sales had reached five million. Capitol was originally to issue different albums from the British releases.

Because American record companies paid higher royalties if more than ten tracks were featured on an album, many Beatles tracks were cut from the Capitol releases and put out as singles in the US. *Meet The Beatles* was a twelve-track album which differed from the British *With The Beatles*, because it had had five tracks removed and replaced with three others.

Capitol's second Beatles single 'Can't Buy Me Love' achieved the biggest advance order for any previous single – two million, eventually selling over three million copies in America. When it entered the American charts on 28 March 1964, 'She Loves You' was No. 1, 'I Want to Hold Your Hand' No. 2, 'Twist And Shout' No. 3, 'Please Please Me' No. 4 and 'I Saw Her Standing There' No. 27.

When Capitol issued *The Beatles Second Album* they used five tracks from the *With The Beatles* album, four tracks from American singles and two previously unreleased tracks from the British EP *Long Tall Sally*. It became Capitol's fastest-selling album up to that time.

Capitol next tried the EP format by issuing *Four By The Beatles* in May 1964, which included tracks from two Capitol albums, *Meet The Beatles* and *The Beatles Second Album*.

In the meantime, United Artists had originally signed the Beatles to a film contract in order to secure them for a soundtrack album which, when released, went to No. 1. Under the agreement with EMI/Capitol they could only feature eight of the songs from the film

A Hard Day's Night and the rest of the tracks they padded out with instrumental versions of Beatles tunes. Capitol also had the right to release five of the official soundtrack songs and used a number of them as singles and then used all five tracks on *Something New*, an album issued a month after United Artists' *A Hard Day's Night*.

Capitol Records continued to achieve incredible record success with the Beatles' products throughout the balance of the group's career.

Caravelles, The

A British singing duo featuring two former office girls, Lois Wilkinson and Andrea Wilson.

Their single, a reworking of Tennessee Ernie Ford's 'You Don't Have To Be A Baby To Cry', was a British chart entry, reaching the No. 6 position in August 1963, and was an even bigger hit in America, where it reached No. 3 in the charts.

The girls were booked to appear with the Beatles on their very first American concert at the Coliseum, Washington, DC, on Tuesday, 11 February 1964.

The Caravelles didn't have any further major hits and Wilkinson left to embark on a solo career under the name Lois Lane. Wilson continued using the Caravelles name for a number of years with various other female singers.

Carfax Assembly Rooms, Cornmarket Street, Oxford

The Beatles only appeared at this venue once, on Saturday, 16 February 1963. The engagement was the first booking they undertook for promoter John Smith.

Carlton Theatre, Arcade Halls, Sinclairtown, Kirkcaldy, Scotland

The Beatles performed two concerts at this venue. There was a capacity audience of 1,500 at each of the shows on Sunday, 6 October 1963. It was their only appearance in the town. The Beatles had actually been booked by the town's Raith Ballroom but, because Brian Epstein had decided that the Beatles would now only perform in theatres, the concert was moved to this theatre.

In the song 'Cry Baby Cry' there is mention of the 'Duchess of Kirkcaldy'.

Carnegie Hall, New York City

On Wednesday, 12 February 1964, the Beatles became the first rock 'n' roll act to perform in concert at the famous Carnegie Hall. The booking had originally been arranged by promoter Sid Bernstein the previous year, who was promoting the two concerts independently under his Theatre Three Productions Company. Norman Weiss of G.A.C. had concluded the deal on Bernstein's behalf during a visit to Paris in January 1964.

Bernstein had set the date for Abraham Lincoln's birthday and it fortunately tied in with the Beatles' huge American success immediately following their sensational 'Ed Sullivan Show' appearance and their single 'I Want To Hold Your Hand' topping the American charts.

As the 6,000 tickets had been sold out in advance, Bernstein requested extra seats on the stage itself. This was granted, although the management insisted that these seats be reserved for older customers only. Among the VIPs who shared the additional seats on stage were Lauren Bacall and Mrs Happy Rockefeller, although other celebrities were unable to be accommodated. Bernstein was to say, 'It's a status symbol for the kids to be here, just as it's a status symbol for the 300 adults here tonight. I had to turn down David Niven, William Zeckendorf and Shirley MacLaine for tickets, I just didn't have one left.'

The Beatles travelled by train for two hours from Washington and arrived at New York's Penn Station and took taxis to their hotel where they showered, changed and refreshed themselves before moving on to Carnegie Hall for the two 34-minute shows, which took place at 7.45 p.m. and 11.15 p.m. Among the other acts on the bill were a folk group called the Briarwoods. One of the Beatles' backstage visitors was British singer Shirley Bassey, who was appearing at Carnegie Hall the following week.

Each house had a 2,900 capacity and there were 362 policemen handling security around the hall.

Capitol Records had wanted to record the two shows but their attempts to do so had been blocked by the American Federation of Musicians.

Bernstein himself took to the stage to ask the audience to comport themselves in the presence of the foreign press. Also making on-stage announcements was disc jockey Murray the K who joked and told the audience not to leave their seats or throw things at the stage. 'We have people especially to deal with things like that – but I'm sure you won't let it happen,' he said.

For both shows, the Beatles grossed $9,335.78.

Carnival of Light

An avant-garde psychedelic event at the Roundhouse, London, which took place in January 1967. Paul McCartney had promised the organisers that he would prepare a sound effects tape for them and during some early *Sgt Pepper* sessions, on Thursday, 5 January 1967, the Beatles spent part of their evening session at Abbey Road's Studio Two recording a bizarre series of sounds, which resulted in a tape of electronic noises lasting thirteen minutes and 48 seconds. Paul then took the tape along to the Roundhouse organisers.

No announcement was made when the tape was played at the 'Carnival Of Light' and the audience were unaware that they were listening to a Beatles tape. The unusual Beatles recording remains in the Abbey Road vaults under the description 'Untitled'.

Carol

A song written and recorded by Chuck Berry in 1958. The Beatles introduced it to their repertoire in 1960, with John taking lead vocals. They performed the number on their 'Pop Go The Beatles' broadcast on 16 July 1963 but never recorded it for release on record. A version of the Chuck Berry number, which they performed live on radio, was included on the *Beatles Live At The BBC* CDs.

Casbah Club, The, 8 Haymans Green, West Derby, Liverpool

A club situated in the basement area of a fifteen-room Victorian house which the Best family moved into after the war. They comprised John and Mona Best and their sons Peter and Rory.

As there were so many friends calling in to see her sons and as they wanted a meeting place of their own, Mo Best suggested that they could redecorate the cellars and turn them into a club. There was plenty of room as the basement comprised seven adjoining rooms. The idea developed and she began to have in mind something like the nearby Lowlands club, with live groups at the weekend, with the club open during the week as a coffee bar where the youngsters could dance to a jukebox.

Work began on the decoration with Mo, Peter, Rory and a number of friends, including a girl called Ruth Morrison. When Mo said they'd have to find a group, Ruth suggested the Les Stewart Quartet who played at the Lowlands club. Ken Brown and George Harrison came round to see Mo, although it was Ken who seemed most enthusiastic about the project. Ken began to spend his spare time helping to convert the cellars into a club and spent weekends working there, with the result that group leader Stewart argued with him about the amount of time he spent helping out there. Brown left the Les Stewart Quartet and George joined him.

Bench seats and a counter were fitted in and Mrs Best painted a dragon on the ceiling. There was a table in the foyer where Mo would issue the tickets and there were tables and a fireplace, espresso coffee machines and in a small room a bar which sold coffee, sweets, soft drinks, hot dogs and crisps.

George Harrison turned up with John Lennon and his girlfriend Cynthia Powell and they helped with painting the walls shortly before the official opening. John used gloss paint on the walls instead of putting on an undercoat and the paint was not completely dry on the opening night. The conversion of the basement rooms into the club took two months. Mona's favourite film at the time was *Algiers*, which starred Charles Boyer. People mimicked his saying, 'Come with me to the Casbah', whenever the film was mentioned, although that line of dialogue was never in the actual movie. Mona settled on calling the club the Casbah.

When the club officially opened on Saturday, 29 August 1959, the resident band was the Quarry Men. The doors opened at 7.30 p.m. and each Saturday the Quarry Men appeared on stage at 8.00 p.m. Membership was two shillings and sixpence (12½p) per annum and entrance at the door cost one shilling (5p). During the first year the club enrolled more than 1,000 members.

The group had, in fact, not been active since January 1959 and George Harrison had joined the Les Stewart Quartet that month. They only got together again to take up the residency at the new club. When Les Stewart refused to take up the residency following his argument with Brown, Mrs Best had wondered how she would find a replacement. George said he had two friends and brought Paul and John down.

The four-man line-up of John Lennon, Paul McCartney, George Harrison and Ken Brown played without a drummer, using Brown's ten-watt amplifier, and they initially received £3 a night between them. This line-up played at the club each Saturday on 29 August, 5, 12, 19 and 26 September, 3 and 10 October. On 10 October, Brown arrived at the club, but he had a bad cold. Mrs Best told him he could help out and paid him a quarter of the group's fee, even though he didn't play. John, Paul and George were furious and stalked out of the club, giving up their residency. Brown encouraged Pete Best to form a group with him and, as the Blackjacks, they took over the residency and the club went from strength to strength, building up a loyal membership and booking various local bands such as Rory Storm & the Hurricanes.

John, Paul and George didn't return to the Casbah until 3 August 1960 when they dropped into the club after their booking at the Grosvenor Ballroom, Wallasey, had been cancelled. They were then called the Silver Beetles and had been booked for their Hamburg debut that month, although they still hadn't found a drummer. They noticed Pete playing with the Blackjacks and Paul McCartney phoned him to invite him to audition with them. He did – and he was invited to join the Beatles.

The first date they played on their return from Hamburg was the Casbah Club on 17 December, when Pete arranged for them to have a temporary bass player, Chas Newby, as Stuart Sutcliffe was still in Germany.

Pete and Mona Best now took charge of all the Beatles' bookings and, in addition to the Casbah gigs, formed Casbah Promotions to run dances at St John's Hall, Tuebrook, and Knotty Ash Village Hall, where they booked the Beatles regularly.

Their 1961 Casbah appearances took place on 8, 15, 22 and 29 January; 12, 19 and 26 February; 5 and 19 March; 6, 13 and 27 August; 10 and 24 September; 22 October; 19 and 24 November; 3 and 17 December. Dates in 1962 were on 7, 14, 21 and 28 January; 4, 11, 18 and 25 February; 4, 11, 18 and 25 March; 1 and 7 April; and 24 June. This date saw the Beatles' final appearance at the club which was closed down a few days later following a death in the Best family.

The Beatles gathered together on the Casbah premises on 10 December 1961 with Brian Epstein to discuss their management contract with him.

The Casbah Club played an important part in the career of the Beatles. If it had not opened, the Quarry Men would probably not have re-formed and there would never have been any Beatles. The club provided them with their first residency and a base with regular money when times were tight. In fact, the Bests prevented the Beatles from disbanding in their early days by providing a number of bookings, including their own promotions, which helped to keep them working full-time as a group. The Casbah also provided them with their first regular drummer, Pete Best, their first road manager, Frank Garner – and their regular road manager, Neil Aspinall. In some ways it could be called the first 'Home of the Beatles'.

Casey, Howie

A Liverpool musician who had learned to play sax while in the army. He formed Derry & the Seniors in November 1959. The line-up comprised Howie (saxophone), Derry Wilkie (vocals), Jeff Wallington (drums), Billy Hughes (rhythm/vocals), Brian Griffiths (lead) and Phil Whitehead (bass).

They appeared regularly around Merseyside at venues such as

Blair Hall, Wilson Hall and the Jacaranda. Because of the Jacaranda connection, clubowner Allan Williams booked them for the Liverpool Stadium Show with Gene Vincent on Tuesday, 3 May 1960.

Williams had staged the event with London impresario Larry Parnes and the bill featured a number of Liverpool groups. Parnes was impressed and asked Williams to arrange an audition as he was seeking bands to back his various artists, such as Billy Fury, Johnny Gentle and Duffy Power.

The Silver Beetles were also present at the audition, which took place on Tuesday, 10 May at the Wyvern Social Club in Seel Street. When Casey was later asked what he thought of them, he said: 'Quite frankly, I wasn't too impressed and I can't remember the group singing. I believe they played a lot of instrumentals and Shadows numbers.'

Following the audition, the Seniors were booked by Parnes to back one of his bands for a season at Blackpool, a deal arranged by Williams. As a result, they turned professional.

When the season was cancelled, a furious Casey arrived at the Wyvern (which Williams was transforming into his Blue Angel Club) with his band, ready to give Williams a severe beating. A frightened Williams promised he would take them to London and find work for them.

They drove down south and Williams took them to the 2 I's coffee bar in Old Compton Street, Soho. Fortuitously, the German clubowner Bruno Koschmider was present at the 2 I's, having arrived in London to seek some bands for his Kaiserkeller Club.

It was one of those million-to-one coincidences, because Williams had been in contact with Koschmider about booking groups for Hamburg, telling him that Liverpool had the best rock 'n' roll groups in the world. Koschmider had arrived in the country and, when inquiring about groups, had been directed to the 2 I's.

Williams arranged for the Seniors to go on stage and they were booked to appear at Koschmider's Kaiserkeller Club for a season from 31 July 1960. Howie was to describe it as 'seven hours a night, 16 quid a week, sleeping in cupboards, being crazy'.

Koschmider asked Williams to send along another Liverpool group. Allan first approached Rory Storm & the Hurricanes, but they were booked for a season at Butlins. He next asked Gerry & the Pacemakers, but Gerry said no. As a last resort he booked the Beatles, who had been playing in his Jacaranda cellar.

When Williams wrote to Casey, mentioning that the Beatles were to replace them, Howie wrote back, probably remembering the Wyvern Club audition, complaining that the scene in Hamburg was great and that he'd be ruining it for everyone 'by sending that bum group the Beatles'.

The Beatles duly arrived, to be met at the Kaiserkeller by Howie, who told them that they were booked at a smaller club called the Indra at the shoddy end of the Grosse Freiheit.

Howie observed: 'They had very, very pointed shoes in grey crocodile. They had mauve jackets with half-belting at the back. The length of their hair caused a great stir around the area – it was thick at the back, almost coming over their collars.'

Once the Beatles appeared in Germany, Howie was able to reappraise them and was suitably impressed. At one point the Beatles' bass guitarist, Stuart Sutcliffe, joined his band.

In 1963, Howie told *Mersey Beat*:

The girls used to rave over Pete Best – he was the star boy. He was a great fellow and the one I liked most. He was very quiet and didn't rave as much as the others, Pete really did fit in with the group then – but their style is more sophisticated now, as they have improved musically. He used to swap ideas with our drummer, Jeff Wallington.

Paul had terrific talent and used to play left-handed guitar. He didn't actually play it, he had the amp turned down low.

The manager of the Kaiserkeller decided to discontinue having a jukebox in the interval, and wanted to put a group on instead, so he split our group in two. He arranged for Stu to play with us. So the second unit of the Seniors was myself on sax, Stan Foster on piano, Stu on bass and a terrific German modern jazz drummer.

All we could do with Stu was to play 12-bar blues – he couldn't venture out of that – and I noticed more than ever how self-critical he was about his music all the time.

He used to sketch around the club, drawing patrons and members of the groups, such as Derry Wilkie. In fact, he left the group during the trip and remained in Germany to study at Hamburg Art College.

The Beatles did their nut because Stu was playing with us. A woman close to the Indra complained about the noise and the police closed the club. The Beatles then came to the Kaiserkeller and reunited with Stu.

The Seniors finished their residency on 1 October, when Rory Storm & the Hurricanes replaced them. They tried to find other work, ran out of money and had to be repatriated.

When they returned to Liverpool at the end of the year, their equipment was stored at the Top Ten Club in Soho Street, a new rock 'n' roll club based on the Hamburg-style clubs, to be opened by Allan Williams. Unfortunately, it was burned down, allegedly by operators of a protection racket. With all their equipment destroyed, the Seniors disbanded in December 1960.

They were reborn in January 1961 as Howie Casey & the Seniors. Apart from Howie and Derry, the line-up comprised Freddie Fowell, who was later to become Freddie Starr (vocals), Frank Wibberley (drums), Brian Griffiths (guitar) and Phil Whitehead (bass). They were signed with Fontana and became the first Liverpool group to make a record in their own right.

The record company placed them with a London agent. Howie commented: 'They had no idea how to cope with us. They were used to nice boys-next-door cabaret groups – but we were the ugliest bunch of rowdy drunken gits you ever saw! Eventually they got us a residency at a club in Ilford called Twist at the Top, and we really thought we'd cracked it. We got nice new shiny bronze suits! Opening night was great, but it went downhill fast and closed!'

This line-up suffered financial problems and disbanded in December 1961. In January 1962, Howie launched the group again, with Derry, Freddie, Frank and Brian plus Frank Bowen and Lou Walters on bass guitars.

They appeared at all the major Liverpool venues, but rarely played outside the north-west, despite having three singles and an album released.

Howie decided to disband the group in June 1962. Lou returned to Rory Storm & the Hurricanes, Frank Bowen joined Lee Curtis, Derry Wilkie fronted the Pressmen, Frank Wibberley teamed up with the Lee Eddie Five, Freddie was to form Freddie Starr & the Midnighters, Brian was to join the Big Three and Howie joined the Dominoes.

After a number of years in Germany with Kingsize Taylor & the Dominoes, Howie returned to Britain and became a successful session man in London.

Paul McCartney asked him to join Wings on their 1975 world tour and 1979 tour of Britain. He also played on a number of Wings recordings, including the albums *Band On the Run* and *Back To The Egg*.

In 1995 he recorded an album in Britain with Tony Sheridan and Roy Young.

Howie's first wife was Scottish singer Barry St John, who he originally met in Hamburg. He was later to marry Sheila McKinley who toured with the Beatles in Scotland in 1964, part of a supporting act the McKinley Sisters.

Casino Ballroom, Lord Street, Leigh, Lancashire.

The Beatles appeared at this venue only once, during a break in their tour with Helen Shapiro, on Monday, 25 February 1963. The Cavern disc jockey had been hired by Brian Epstein to produce the show, which was billed as a NEMS Enterprises' Showdance.

Cassanova Club, Fraser Street, Liverpool L3

One of several clubs which opened on the premises of Samson & Barlow's, a Liverpool catering firm, who had spacious rooms to let on their premises in the city centre.

Promoter Sam Leach opened his Cassanova Club here on 9 February 1961, and two days later, on 11 February, he booked the Beatles for the first time. A club of that name had originally been launched above the Temple restaurant in Dale Street by Cass & the Cassanovas and the Beatles played there on Sunday, 10 January 1960, in an afternoon interval break. Sam was to take over the venue and moved the club to Samson & Barlow's.

While it was called the Cassanova, the Beatles appeared there on 14, 16, 21 and 28 February and 7 and 12 March 1961. The Tuesday, 14 February appearance was a 'Valentine's Night Rock Ball' with tickets priced at 4/6d. The posters announced: 'Four Rockin' Bands starring the originators of "The Atom Beat", The Sensational Beatles; Rockin' the Sound Waves, The Cassanova Big Three; Rory Storm & The Hurricanes and Introducing Mark Peters & The Cyclones'. Mark Peters (real name Peter Fleming) was said to be Liverpool's first disc jockey when he became DJ at the Locarno Ballroom in 1959. The group appeared on a number of bills with the Beatles and Brian Epstein booked them several times. Mark later fronted Mark Peters and the Silhouettes and made some unsuccessful records. In the seventies he went to work in Sri Lanka.

The Cassanova was closed by the police soon after these appearances due to the noise of the groups. Leach reopened it as the Peppermint Lounge in March 1963, naming it after the famous club in New York. The Blott Brothers took over the venue and began to run it successfully. Until February 1963, following the demise of the Cassanova Club, the venue had been reopened as a nightclub, the New Compton.

The Blotts got the club on-stream and promoted bands there on Thursdays, Fridays, Saturdays, Sundays and Tuesdays. Capacity was 350 people and prices varied from four shillings on Tuesdays to eight shillings and sixpence on Saturdays. There were three groups each night, four on Saturdays and regulars included Earl Royce & the Olympics, the Blackwells, the Chessmen, the Karacters and the Kirkbys.

Casser, Brian

Also known as Casey Jones and Casey Valance. A Newcastle-born musician, who originally led one of the top Liverpool groups, Cass & the Cassanovas, from December 1959 to December 1960.

During their relatively short span, Cass & the Cassanovas were regarded by many locally as Liverpool's top band. The group made their debut at the Corinthian Club, Slater Street, in 1959.

Cass played lead/vocals, Adrian Barber was on guitar and Johnny Hutchinson on drums. Soon after their formation, Hutch brought Johnny Gustafson to see the group and suggested he join. Johnny didn't have a guitar but Adrian converted a Hoyer Acoustic and put bass strings on it.

Of the Liverpool acts appearing on the Gene Vincent concert at the Liverpool Stadium on Tuesday, 3 May 1960, Cass & the Cassanovas received top billing.

It was Cass who also suggested that Silver Beetles find themselves a drummer, suggesting Tommy Moore. Cass also suggested to John Lennon that the group call themselves Long John & the Silver Men.

Allan Williams allowed Cass to sleep overnight in the Jacaranda Club in Slater Street and Cass claimed that he'd been using the club phone in the early hours to make long-distance calls to a Hamburg promoter. He was trying to fix up a booking in Hamburg for the Cassanovas and had been speaking to a representative of Bruno Koschmider. Cass claimed that Koschmider's representative called him back at the Jacaranda one afternoon when he wasn't there and Williams talked to him and told him he could supply him with as many groups as he needed.

The other members of the group eventually ousted Cass from the band and they became the Big Three. Cass then moved on to London where he came to manage a Soho club in St Anne's Court, the Blue Gardenia. The Beatles dropped in to see him on 9 December 1961 following their abortive appearance in Aldershot.

It has also been said that it was Cass who arranged for Howie Casey & the Seniors to perform at the 2 I's coffee bar when Allan Williams drove them down to London, which led to their Hamburg booking.

Cass formed another band in late 1963, and when he had a debut record issued on EMI's Columbia label called 'One Way Ticket', he wrote to *Mersey Beat*.

His letter read: 'Since coming to London three years ago I have been doing a great deal of film work, but films were not really my ambition. When everything started to happen in Scouseland, I really felt left out. So I decided to return to the singing scene.'

The line-up of his band Casey Jones & the Engineers, between

August and October 1963, comprised Casey Jones (vocals), Eric Clapton (guitar), Tom McGuinness (guitar), Dave McCumisky (bass) and Ray Smith (drums). He later moved to Germany where he had several chart entries with his group, now named Casey Jones and the Governors. They also recorded two albums for the Gold 12 label, *Casey Jones & the Governors* and *Don't Ha Ha*.

Catcall

A number by Paul McCartney which was recorded by Chris Barber & his Jazz Band. Paul had originally written the instrumental in the late fifties when he was a member of the Quarry Men, under its original title 'Catswalk'.

Just as the sixties were dominated by the three Bs: Bardot, the Beatles and Bond, so the traditional jazz boom in Britain in the late fifties was dominated by the three Bs: Chris Barber, Acker Bilk and Kenny Ball.

Barber's Jazz Band appeared in Liverpool regularly in the mid-fifties featuring Lonnie Donegan, who later had success with 'Rock Island Line' and helped popularise the British skiffle boom.

When Barber recorded 'Catcall' on 20 July 1967, Paul and Jane Asher attended the session and at the end of the recording added their voices to the finale. The single was issued on 20 October 1967 on Marmalade 598-005, but it wasn't a hit. The track was later included on Barber's album 'Battersea Rain Dance'.

Cathy's Clown

A chart topper for the Everly Brothers, Don and Phil, early in 1960 which was included in the Beatles' repertoire for a short time during that year.

Cavendish Avenue, St John's Wood

Paul purchased a three-storey brick detached Georgian townhouse from physician Desmond O'Neill on 13 April 1965 for £40,000. He immediately hired H. F. Wilkins, a decorating firm based in Kilburn High Road, to refurbish the house. Paul also engaged John and Marina Adams and briefed them on the refurbishing, which was to cost £20,000. He moved in during March 1966. He had a housekeeper Mrs Kelly, who lived in with her husband, but he fired them when they sold a story to an Australian magazine. There was a music room in which he composed 'Penny Lane', 'Getting Better' and 'Hey Jude' where he also worked with John in composing numbers for the *Sgt Pepper* album. Among the art collection which Paul had in the house were some paintings by Magritte, a sculpture by Takis, a commissioned painting from Peter Blake based on

Edward Landseer's *Monarch of the Glen* and a chrome sculpture by Eduardo Paolozzi called *Solo*.

Paul moved out of Cavendish Avenue in 1970, although he still owns it and the house remains a listed building.

Cavern Club, The, 10 Mathew Street, Liverpool

The most famous club in the world during the early to mid-sixties when it was known as 'The Home of the Beatles'.

Originally the premises comprised a small group of cellars below seven-storey warehouses which, during the war, had been used as air-raid shelters. For a while wines and spirits were stored there and in 1958, Alan Sytner, son of a local doctor, noticed that the premises were empty. Sytner had been running jazz nights at the nearby Temple restaurant. He'd recently been to Paris and was impressed by a jazz cellar he'd visited called Le Caveau Francais Jazz Club. He immediately took over the lease of the basement and the club opened officially as the Cavern on 16 January 1957, with a local jazz band, the Merseysippi, topping the bill. Over 1,000 people queued to get in, but only 600 were allowed entrance.

The club was reached by walking down eighteen stone steps. At the bottom of the steps was a table where admission was paid. There were three long arches with a stage at the end of the centre aisle, where rows of wooden seats were placed. Patrons danced in the outer aisles. Only soft drinks were served and initially just traditional jazz was presented at weekends. Then skiffle was presented each Wednesday and modern jazz each Thursday. By 1959 Sytner had got married and moved to London, leaving the running of the club to his father.

Financially, the Cavern wasn't faring well and Sytner decided to sell. He found a buyer close to home – Ray McFall, the Sytner family's accountant, who had been financial adviser to the Temple Jazz Club and acted as cashier twice a week at the Cavern. Ray purchased the club on 1 October 1959 for £2,750. Music had always been a leading interest in his life and his tastes ranged from the classics to all forms of pop music.

Yet the Cavern had been run strictly on the lines of a jazz club – with no rock 'n' roll polluting the atmosphere. The only bands apart from jazz bands to be employed were skiffle groups. When the Quarry Men had appeared at the club on 7 August 1957 and played some Elvis Presley numbers, Sytner had sent them a note: 'Cut out the bloody rock!' When Rory Storm & the Hurricanes appeared and performed 'Whole Lotta Shakin'' they were fined for playing a rock 'n' roll number.

However, the times were changing and McFall began to change

the club's policy. In the early summer of 1960 a radical departure from previous jazz club policy appeared – rock 'n' roll. Ray decided to take a chance and pioneer lunchtime sesssions. From Tuesday to Friday they featured one day of jazz and three days of rock 'n' roll. Although the sessions were successful, Tuesday jazz performances lacked the audiences of the other days. In January 1961 the Tuesday jazz was replaced by rock and the Tuesday lunchtimes picked up. In March 1961 the lunchtime sessions were extended to Monday.

Experiments in evening sessions had begun on Wednesday, 25 May 1960, when the first rock 'n' roll evening was presented with the two top local bands Cass & the Cassanovas and Rory Storm & the Hurricanes.

Ray was to tell Tony Barrow in 'On The Scene At The Cavern': 'A dozen or more suburban halls on the outskirts of Liverpool had been flourishing as a result of the increasing demand for beat groups. I decided to make the Cavern into Liverpool's first city-centre rock 'n' roll club. At the time I couldn't have dreamed of the destiny which lay ahead for many of the groups I began to use on Wednesdays. To me the introduction of a new rock 'n' roll night merely meant the drawing in of a separate crowd which wouldn't have visited the Cavern before. I knew that some of the jazz followers would give the Wednesday groups a try but I was equally interested in attracting the rockers who had been filling the ballrooms and club halls outside town.'

In February 1961 Tuesday became the Bluegenes guest night, in which they presented some of the top rock 'n' roll groups in the area, and their first 'guest night' on Tuesday, 21 March 1961 featured Dale Roberts & the Jay Walkers, the Remo Four and the Beatles. The Beatles were making their evening debut at the club and exactly one month prior, on 21 February, they had made their first appearance at a lunchtime session. In April, modern jazz sessions, which had been tottering on the brink for some time, stopped.

The Beatles began a stream of appearances which included their 'Welcome Home' session on Friday, 14 July 1961, with Johnny Sandon and the Remo Four and the White Eagles Jazz Band. The Beatles began their own series of resident nights on Wednesday, 2 August 1961, and made a total of approximately 292 appearances until their last one on 3 August 1963 for which they received a fee of £300.

There were too many Cavern appearances by the Beatles to list individually, but among their 1961 gigs were those on Tuesday, 25 July, when they appeared on another Bluegenes guest night, along with Gerry & the Pacemakers and the Remo Four; Friday, 1

September, when they were the only rock group, playing during the interval of a traditional jazz bill; and Saturday, 23 December, when they performed with Gerry & the Pacemakers and Johnny Sandon and the Searchers on an all-night session featuring several jazz bands. Their 1962 engagements at the club included acting as a support, along with Gerry & the Pacemakers, to the Saints Jazz Band from Manchester; Wednesday, 28 February, when they appeared with Gerry & the Pacemakers and Johnny Sandon and the Searchers; Thursday, 5 April, when they had their own fan club night, with the Four Jays also performing; Saturday, 7 April, when they performed a two-hour show in between two sets by the Saints Jazz Band; Saturday, 9 June, when they had their 'Welcome Home' evening following their Hamburg season; Sunday, 1 July, which saw the first Cavern evening which had no jazz content at all and featured the Beatles, the Swinging Bluejeans, Gene Vincent and Sounds Incorporated; Wednesday, 1 August, with Gerry & the Pacemakers and the Merseybeats; Tuesday, 28 August, when they appeared on another Bluegenes guest night, along with Gerry Levene and the Avengers, the first group from Birmingham to appear at the Cavern; Sunday, 9 September, when they appeared with Billy J. Kramer and the Coasters and jazz singer Clinton Ford; Wednesday, 9 September, when Simone Jackson, a London singer, became 'the girl who sang with the Beatles', when the group backed her performance – also on the bill were Manchester's Freddie & the Dreamers; Friday, 12 October, when they appeared on a bill with their idol Little Richard; Wednesday, 5 December, when they shared the bill with Gerry & the Pacemakers; Sunday, 16 September, when they made their final appearance prior to their Hamburg season in December. Their 1963 shows at the Cavern included Sunday, 20 January, when they appeared with the Dennisons, the Swinging Bluejeans and the Merseybeats; Sunday, 3 February, was a 'rhythm and blues marathon' – appearing with the Beatles were Manchester's the Hollies, making their Cavern debut, and the Merseybeats, the Fourmost, the Swinging Bluejeans and Kingsize Taylor and the Dominoes; Friday, 12 April, a Good Friday session in which the Beatles topped the bill over seven other local groups, who included the Road Runners, Faron's Flamingos and the Dennisons; Saturday, 3 August, was a Bank Holiday special; the Beatles were supported by the Merseybeats, the Road Runners, Johnny Ringo and the Colts, the Escorts and the Sapphires.

Commenting on their 'Welcome Home' session on Saturday, 9 June 1962, which immediately followed their trip to Hamburg, Bob Wooler told Tony Barrow: 'You might have expected the Beatles to be tired after their strenuous Hamburg session. On the contrary they gave one of their finest-ever performances and seemed to draw extra inspiration from the feverish reaction they were getting from the one thousand fans who packed the place that evening. Although the national newspapers didn't invent the word "Beatlemania" until a year later, I would say that the Cavern reception given to John, Paul, George and Pete Best that Saturday was just as enthusiastic, just as genuine as the nationwide acclaim which was to follow. I would qualify this statement with one further observation. Cavern members didn't use the Beatles as an excuse for hooliganism. They cheered and screamed and showed their excitement in a dozen ways – but they were still an orderly audience with a respect for the club itself and its surroundings.'

As success began to spread across the Mersey scene, Ray undertook a policy of expansion and the Cavern soon became the most famous club in Britain. There was even a group called the Caverners (Kenny Smith (lead), Steve Roberts (bass), Mark Farrell (rhythm), Colin Roberts (drums)) and Beatles PR man Tony Barrow wrote a book *The Cavern*, which was published by Souvenir Press.

McFall organised a Cavern trip to Hamburg in which 36 members of the club flew to the German city for two days to visit the Star Club and see the Kubas (formerly the Koobas) and Ricky Gleason and the Top Spots from Liverpool and Tony Sheridan backed by the Bobby Patrick Big Six. Ray was to forge a friendship with his counterpart at the Star Club, Manfred Weissleder. He carried a letter from the Lord Mayor of Liverpool to the Burgomeister of Hamburg which read: 'I have heard with interest that during the last few years groups of young Liverpool rock 'n' roll musicians have visited Hamburg. I feel confident that these visits will result in the formation of friendships amongst members of the younger generation, a happy augury for the future.'

The Cavern now had a Junior Cavern Club, membership of which cost 6d (3p) and admission cost members 2s (10p) and visitors 2s 6d (12½p). The sessions took place between 1.00 p.m. and 4.00 p.m. each Saturday and featured two groups and Top Twenty discs, was strictly for thirteen to sixteen-year-olds and began on 1 February 1964. A sign was displayed which read: 'Adults are not admitted unless accompanied by children!'

The club became the subject of worldwide media attention, with TV cameramen from America, France, Sweden and Germany focusing their cameras on the heady atmosphere; radio teams included several radio stations from India, the Russian news agency Tass, the Canadian Broadcasting Company – and a whole host of magazine journalists from American publications such as *Time*, *Life* and *Newsweek*. Celebrities from around the world took to dropping into the club, including film stars such as Anna Neagle, musicians such as Chet Atkins, classical conductor Arthur Fiedler and dozens of others.

Ray continued his expansion plans and launched a management/agency called Cavern Artistes Ltd, representing a number of acts, including the Michael Allen Group, the Clayton Squares, the Excelles, the Hideaways, the Kubas, the Notions, Earl Preston's Realms and the St Louis Checks.

On 3 November 1963 he bought the premises next door to the Cavern, extended the width of the club and began building a recording studio, Cavern Sound, which opened on 15 October 1964 with £10,000 worth of equipment. The studio handled demonstration tapes, tape-to-disc transfers, master recordings, pressings, pressings for distribution to major labels and recordings for commercial radio. The first group to record there was the Clayton Squares and the studio was run by engineers Peter Hepworth and Nigel Greenburg. During alterations the old stage had to go and Ray had the idea of selling pieces of the original stage as 'Beatleboard' to Beatles fans who would like a souvenir of the stage on which the group had performed so many times. Beatleboard cost five shillings (25p) a piece, the proceeds being donated to Oxfam. There were so many requests from all over the world that it took four months to fulfil the orders.

On Saturday, 13 September 1964, there was a 'Caverncade', a parade through the streets of Liverpool by groups on decorated floats, the proceeds being donated to Oxfam.

There was even a weekly half-hour radio show which took place at the club. Called 'Sunday Night at the Cavern', it was broadcast on Radio Luxembourg each Sunday at 10.30 p.m. commencing on 15 March 1963. The show was hosted by Bob Wooler who played the latest chart records and introduced a group live from the Cavern stage each week.

Unfortunately, McFall had taken on too many enterprises and overextended his capital, with the result that, in February 1966, he had to declare himself bankrupt. The loyal troglodytes (one of the names by which the Cavern 'regulars' were known) wished to support McFall and keep the club open, but the bailiffs were called in. The irate Cavernites staged a sit-in. Frieda Kelly, the Beatles fan club secretary, took part in the siege by blockading the stairway of the Cavern with chairs. On stage, moral support came from the music of the Hideaways. Eventually, the police entered the club and removed its struggling inhabitants. The cave dwellers continued their protests and a petition was sent to Prime Minister Harold Wilson at Lime Street Station as he arrived in Liverpool on a visit.

Following the bankruptcy proceedings, the club was acquired by Joe Davey, who ran Joe's Café, and Alf Geoghegan. It was officially reopened on 23 January 1966 by Harold Wilson, while Ken Dodd and local MP Bessie Braddock were also present. The first group to take the stage after the reopening were the Hideaways, who had been the last group to play at the club (the group also appeared at the Cavern more times than any other band, a total of 412 appearances). The Beatles were unable to attend, but sent a telegram.

The Cavern changed hands again and was taken over by another local club-owner, Roy Adams. Although he ran the club successfully, Roy couldn't fight the local bureaucracy. The corporation decided they needed to fit an extraction duct for the underground railway in the premises and Adams was given notice to quit. The club was forced to close on 27 March 1973 and the bulldozers razed the site. The Cavern itself was buried in rubble and when the railway work had been completed, the site was turned into a car park.

Adams obtained the premises directly opposite and opened the New Cavern Club. Arthur Dooley created a Beatles sculpture for the outside wall. The premises were taken over by Roger Eagle who reopened the venue as Eric's in 1976 and a whole new generation of Mersey talent found an outlet – Elvis Costello, Frankie Goes To Hollywood, China Crisis, Orchestral Manoeuvres In The Dark, Echo and the Bunnymen, Teardop Explodes, A Flock of Seagulls, the Lotus Eaters, Wah! and many more.

Following John Lennon's murder, Liverpool architect David Backhouse approached Royal Life Insurance Limited to develop the site. They were orginally going to call it the Eleanor Centre, after 'Eleanor Rigby', but it was then dubbed Cavern Walks and £9 million was spent on the scheme. Backhouse designed the basic plans for the complex in only two days, producing an original design of a structure seven storeys high with an almost Victorian look to it. He also included provision for the restructuring of the original Cavern Club. The original bricks of the club were still buried below the car park in the packed earth and a number of the original bricks were used in the reconstruction. For some reason, the new Cavern was built parallel to Mathew Street, in contrast to the original, which had been built at a right angle to the street. As a result, instead of merely walking down eighteen steps into a club, a new entrance with a large spiral staircase had to be constructed.

The Cavern Walks complex was also to have a shopping centre, offices, an 'Abbey Road' pub, a restaurant, a Beatles museum, a central atrium where the shopping malls merged and an eye-catching statue of the Beatles.

Cynthia Lennon was asked to provide a design for the terracotta tiles that would face parts of the new building. On 25 April 1984 she unveiled a small commemorative plaque, placed on an outside wall, inscribed 'To John' and containing the lyrics to 'In My Life'.

In the centre of the atrium itself – which reaches up past the entire seven floors with a wall-climber lift, candy-pink lamp-posts, valuted ceilings and hanging gardens of foliage – is the controversial £40,000 statue by John Doubleday, who says, 'It is the largest figurative group in bronze commissioned in Britain for 25 years, in fact since Epstein's Bowater House Group. It has been a considerable professional challenge. Above all, I have tried to capture the raw energy of the Beatles as they were when they were playing at the Cavern.'

At the time the local council ordered the destruction of the original Cavern to make way for the air vent, Liverpool bureaucrats spurned any efforts to promote the image of the Beatles in Liverpool, turning down requests for a statue and to name Liverpool streets after the Beatles. However, after the death of John Lennon, all that changed. Eventually even a series of streets was named after the group and further accolades were given to the Cavern. In April 1984, EMI issued a special sixteen-track album *Tribute To The Cavern*, to be sold exclusively at the club. All the tracks were recorded during the 1963/4 period, although none of them was actually recorded at the club. Among the artists represented were the Beatles, Billy J. Kramer & the Dakotas, the Fourmost, Gerry & the Pacemakers, the Swinging Bluejeans and Cilla Black.

However, there had been albums recorded at the Cavern in the past. George Martin had originally considered recording the Beatles during a live session at the Cavern, but decided that there were too many technical difficulties. The Big Three were recorded live at the club and an EP *The Big Three Live At The Cavern* issued on Decca DFE 8552 in July 1964. The group also recorded a number called 'The Cavern Stomp'. In March 1964 Decca issued an album on Decca LK 4597 which was recorded live at the club and called *Live At The Cavern*. Four of the acts were from Liverpool – the Big Three, Beryl Marsden, the Dennisons and Lee Curtis, while other acts featured were Dave Berry & the Cruisers, Bern Elliott & the Fenmen, the Fortunes and Heinz & the Marauders.

Abbey Road Studios also produced a 45-minute film, *Cavern Beat*, which was screened at the newly opened venue twice a day during the summer of 1984. The film was narrated by Terry Sylvester, former member of the Escorts and the Hollies, and included film of the Cavern's history and the groups who appeared there, with a soundtrack which included various Mersey groups and the Beatles tracks 'Penny Lane', 'Strawberry Fields Forever', 'A Hard Day's Night', 'I Feel Fine', 'Twist and Shout', 'She Loves You', 'Please Please Me', 'Love Me Do' and 'Some Other Guy'.

During 1984 there was also a musical play *Cavern Of Dreams*, presented at the Liverpool Playhouse.

Caxton Hall, Caxton Street, London W1

Originally built in 1878, the building was at one time the home of Westminster Town Hall. The premises later became Britain's most celebrated Register Office because it was the place where many celebrities were married, including Elizabeth Taylor, Diana Dors, Peter Sellers and Roger Moore.

Mary (Maureen) Cox and Ringo were married at the hall on 11 February 1965. The Registrar who conducted the ceremony was Mr D. A. Boreham. George and John were present at the ceremony while Paul was on holiday in Hammamet, Tunisia, at the time. The best man was Brian Epstein.

The hall had a famous history and was the venue where the suffragettes planned their campaigns. Winston Churchill also made his wartime speech from the hall.

Pattie Harrison attended a lecture on Transcendental meditation at the Caxton Hall in February 1967, which led her to encourage George, together with the other members of the Beatles, to attend the Maharishi's lecture at the Hilton Hotel a few months later.

Civil marriages ceased to be carried out at the hall in 1977, and in 1991 the building was demolished to make way for a £28 million redevelopment programme.

Cayenne

An instrumental penned by Paul McCartney when he was a teenager, probably inspired by the Shadows. The number was included on the Beatles' *Anthology 1* CDs.

CBS Studio, 50 Broadway & West 53rd Street, New York City

The former Maxine Elliott Theatre which became the CBS Studio base for the 'Ed Sullivan Shows'.

It was quite a coup for Brian Epstein to have the Beatles booked for the show, particularly as bill toppers, for despite their fame in Europe, they were virtually unknown in America at the time of the booking.

Although Ed Sullivan believed the group were going to become major stars, he contested Epstein's insistence that they receive top billing as no British group had made it big in the States before. Brian Epstein got his way and the group were booked for three shows, although the $4,500 fee was very low – ten years previously Colonel Tom Parker had insisted on $50,000 for Elvis Presley to appear on three Sullivan shows (although some reports did say that the Beatles fee was $10,000 or $12,000). Another factor is that Sullivan Productions paid for the Beatles' air fares.

The theatre provided seating for an audience of 728 people and there was an unprecedented demand of over 60,000 ticket requests.

The Beatles had to become members of the AFRA trade union before they could begin rehearsing for the show. At the time, George Harrison was suffering from flu and remained behind at the Plaza Hotel while the group dropped into the studios on Saturday, 8 February 1964. Neil Aspinall stood in for George at the rehearsals and a concerned Ed Sullivan was assured that George would be present at the show itself. 'He'd better be or I'm putting on a wig myself,' Sullivan said.

On 9 February there was a dress rehearsal and the taping of another 'Ed Sullivan Show' to be broadcast on 23 February.

The show itself drew the biggest audience for an entertainment programme in the history of television. An estimated 73,000,000 viewers saw the performance and it was reported that the crime rate among teenagers throughout America dropped to virtually zero that night.

Conductor Leonard Bernstein had requested tickets for his two daughters and Wendy Hanson, Epstein's PA, arranged seats for them in the front row. She also escorted Bernstein to the Beatles' dressing room. After he'd left, John Lennon told her: 'Look, luv, could you keep Sidney Bernstein's family out of this room.'

Brian Epstein had approached Sullivan with the request, 'I would like to know the exact wording of your introduction.' Sullivan replied, 'I would like you to get lost.'

The show went on the air at 8.00 p.m. and Sullivan opened with the words: 'Now, yesterday and today, our theatre's been jammed with newspapermen and hundreds of photographers from all over the nation, and these veterans agree with me that the city never has witnessed the excitement stirred up by these youngsters from Liverpool, who call themselves the Beatles. Now, tonight, you'll twice be entertained by them – right now and in the second half of the show.' Sullivan also read out a congratulatory telegram from Elvis Presley (it had actually been sent by Colonel Parker) and the Beatles opened with Paul singing 'All My Loving'. This was followed by 'Till There Was You', also sung by Paul. During this number their christian names were flashed on the screen and when it was John's turn, there was also the comment, 'Sorry girls, he's married'. They ended the first part of their show with 'She Loves You'. Sullivan then announced that they would be back in the second half of the show and that the three numbers they'd played had been dedicated to Randy Parr (daughter of the TV host Jack Parr). When the Beatles returned they performed 'I Saw Her Standing There' and 'I Want To Hold Your Hand'. During the last number, one of the mikes went dead.

Other acts on the bill that evening included Frank Gorshin, the impressionist, comedian Charlie Brill, the Broadway cast of *Oliver*, with singer Georgia Brown, David Jones (who would later become a member of the Monkees) and Tessie O'Shea.

The show's producer was Bob Precht and the musical director was Ray Bloch.

The Neilson ratings indicated that it was Sullivan's highest rating show with 45.3 per cent of all TV sets in America tuned to the programme.

The performance was widely reported in the American press the next day and the *Herald Tribune* was to comment that the Beatles were: '75% publicity, 20% haircut and 5% lilting lament', while *Newsweek* reported: 'Visually they are a nightmare: tight, dandified Edwardian beatnik suits and great pudding bowls of hair. Musically they are a near disaster, guitars and drums slamming out a merciless beat that does away with secondary rhythms, harmony and melody.'

Evangelist Billy Graham had decided to watch television on the Sabbath to see what all the fuss was about, and later commented: 'They're a passing phase. All are symptoms of the uncertainty of the times and the confusion about us.'

Ed Sullivan died in 1974 and the studio is now known as the Ed Sullivan Theatre.

Centennial Hall, Adelaide, South Australia

Adelaide had not been included on the initial plans for the Beatles' tour of Australia and the citizens of that city launched a major campaign for Adelaide to be included on the itinerary. After promoter Kenn Brodziak received a petition with over 80,000 signatures he contacted London asking for an extension to the tour to include Adelaide and was granted it.

The only venue in Adelaide where the concert could be held was the Centennial Hall, which was run by the Royal Agricultural and Horticultural Society. Their usual booking fee for the hall was £65, but they demanded £440 per night for the Beatles' appearances. Brodziak telegrammed Adelaide disc jockey Bob Francis to tell him that the bookings would be cancelled due to the exorbitant demands.

To add the further dates to the tour, Brodziak was required to come up with a further £12,000, which was more than he was paying the Beatles for the rest of the tour – and it would cost him all his profits from the four shows. Fortunately some Adelaide businessmen, eager that the visit should take place, undertook to finance and promote it themselves.

The Adelaide concerts created a world record for queues for Beatles tickets and thousands of applicants began to take place in a massive queue and 250,000 people came to watch the phenomenon as fans queued for 60 to 70 hours for their tickets. Several people in the queue were hospitalised for exhaustion and all 12,000 tickets went within five hours.

When the Beatles arrived in the city there were 200,000 people lining the streets to watch the motorcade.

At that evening's show the Beatles performed the same set they had played in Denmark and Holland – and they would repeat it throughout the Australian tour. It was: 'I Saw Her Standing There', 'I Want To Hold Your Hand', 'You Can't Do That', 'All My Loving', 'She Loves You', 'Till There Was You', 'Roll Over Beethoven', 'Can't Buy Me Love', 'This Boy' and 'Long Tall Sally' or 'Twist And Shout'.

The group appeared for two nights at the Centennial Hall on 12 and 13 June 1964.

Chains

A song penned by the husband and wife songwriting team Gerry Goffin and Carole King. It was issued as a single by the Cookies in November 1962 and rapidly became a popular number with Liverpool bands. George Harrison took over on lead vocals for the Beatles version, which he recorded for the *Please Please Me* album. George also sang the number on the BBC radio shows 'Here We Go', 'Side By Side' and 'Pop Go The Beatles'.

The number was included on the British EP *The Beatles No. 1*, the compilation *The Beatles Collection* and the American albums *Introducing The Beatles*, *The Beatles vs The Four Seasons* and *The Early Beatles*.

Channel, Bruce

Singer from Dallas, Texas, who had a major hit in 1962 with 'Hey Baby'.

Five weeks after the record entered the British Top Ten, Brian Epstein booked him to top the bill of a NEMS Enterprises promotion at the Tower Ballroom, New Brighton, on Thursday, 21 June 1962. This was part of Epstein's policy to place the Beatles as second on the bill to an established artist and thus give them prestige. He promoted the event with large advertisements in *Mersey Beat*.

Channel was accompanied by his harmonica player Delbert McClinton, whose performance on the record added to its commercial appeal. John Lennon in particular, was struck by McClinton's harmonica sound, which became a big influence over the following two years and is particularly evident on the 'Love Me Do' recording.

Apart from McClinton, Channel was also backed by a group called the Barons, although they weren't the Liverpool group of that name.

The rest of the bill comprised Liverpool acts with the Beatles and Howie Casey & the Seniors advertised as recording artists. The show, which attracted an audience of 2,500, was compered by Bob Wooler and also featured the Big Three and the Four Jays.

Chants, The

A five-piece vocal harmony group who proved to be Liverpool's most popular black vocal act.

The Chants evolved in the Liverpool 8 district, the Toxteth area, which they felt was totally isolated from the rest of Merseyside, part of it being almost a Liverpool equivalent of Harlem, where the black community had their own cultural influences. The music the Chants listened to was reflected in their own cultural heritage as they were brought up on what was to become known as R&B, which was introduced to them by the black GIs who came to Liverpool 8 from American bases such as Burtonwood. This included doo-wop recordings by outfits such as the Del Vikings, along with the music of artists such as Johnny Otis, Little Richard and the Miracles – this was before these artists became mainstream and their music became the embryonic influence of the Shades, their original name.

Their first approach to the Beatles was reported in an item in *Mersey Beat* in 1963:

Last year, Joe Ankrah and his brother Eddie joined a vocal group called the Shades, whose only appearances were in Stanley House, Upper Parliament Street. Due to the fact that a rock 'n' roll group in London had the same name, the group decided to call themselves the Chants.

Joe went along to the Tower Ballroom during an appearance by the Beatles. He had a chat with Paul McCartney, who asked him to bring the group for an audition. The Beatles liked the group so much that they provided backing for them on a number of appearances.

In fact, when they turned up at the Cavern for an audition but didn't have a backing group, the Beatles offered to provide backing for them, but Brian Epstein objected. John Lennon overruled him and the Chants made their Cavern debut on Wednesday, 21 November 1962, with the Beatles providing their backing.

The group's leader, Joe Ankrah, wanted to form an American-style vocal group and the Chants were his third attempt. The other members were Edmund Ankrah, Nat Smeda, Alan Harding and Edmund Amoo.

Joe first met Paul McCartney at the Tower Ballroom, New Brighton, on 12 October 1962. He 'blagged' his way into Little Richard's dressing room after the concert and Paul spotted him leaving. Paul wanted to find out who he was and was fascinated when Joe told him about being in an accapella group. He then gave Joe a note, signed by himself, for the Chants to produce at the Cavern when the Beatles returned from Hamburg. They did this, turning up for one of the lunchtime sessions. They waited for the Beatles to come off stage and 'waylaid' them when they left the dressing room as the gig emptied. Paul introduced them to the rest of the group and then beckoned them on to the stage.

Eddie Amoo recalls:

> They went 'apeshit' when we started to sing. I can still see George and John racing up to the stage with their mouths stuffed with hot dogs or whatever. The invitation to make our Cavern debut was given as soon as we finished 'A Thousand Stars' for them. They insisted we perform that very night. Everything happened completely spontaneously from that point.
>
> The Beatles themselves offered to back us when we told them we'd never worked with a band before. We then rehearsed four songs with them and then we ran home to tell all and sundry that we had 'made it'!
>
> When Brian Epstein arrived at the Cavern that night he refused to allow the Beatles to back us, but they collectively persuaded him to change his mind – and when he heard us he invited us to appear on many subsequent appearances with them.

On that Cavern debut, the Chants, backed by the Beatles, performed 'Duke Of Earl', 'A Thousand Stars', '16 Candles' and 'Come Go With Me' before an enraptured audience, their set lasting approximately twenty minutes.

Local MP Bessie Braddock took an interest in the group as they were from her Liverpool district, the Exchange ward, and she arranged for them to be the only other Liverpool group present at the Beatles' civic reception at Liverpool Town Hall.

Despite his initial frustration at the Beatles agreeing to back the Chants against his wishes, Epstein took over the management of the group early in 1963, but only for a short time, and without any formal signing. The group found him ineffectual as a manager and he agreed to release them. They then signed with Manchester agent Ted Ross, who arranged a recording deal with Pye Records. However, they were later to consider they had committed 'professional suicide' by signing with Ross, although they were grateful for what he tried to do for them.

On the special all-Beatles edition of the TV show 'Juke Box Jury', the first record played to them was the Chants' 'I Could Write A Book', which they voted a hit – but it became a miss, despite their positive comments.

The Chants' debut disc, 'I Don't Care', flipside 'Come Go With Me', was released on 17 September 1963. Their second, 'I Could Write A Book', flipside 'A Thousand Stars', was released on 1 January 1964. Their third was 'She's Mine', flipside 'Then I'll Be Home', in June 1964, and their final release for Pye was 'Sweet Was The Wine', flipside 'One Star', on 11 September 1964.

Eddie Amoo wrote 'One Star', credited to Stanley Houseman, as a tribute to Stanley House, where they'd made their first appearance. Stanley House was a social meeting place in the Toxteth area where young met old and black met white to drink, dance and play football, table tennis, snooker and generally mix together.

The group never found record success, despite further releases with Fontana, Page One, Decca and RCA and strong singles such as 'Man Without A Face'.

After they broke up, Joey and Edmund Ankrah joined a group called Ashanti and enjoyed a degree of success on the television show 'New Faces'. Eddie Amoo joined a Liverpool soul group, The Real Thing, who finally found UK chart success in June 1976 with 'You To Me Are Everything', which also reached No. 5 on its re-release in April 1986.

The Real Thing were still active at the close of 1999, with Eddie commenting:

We have seen our flagship song recorded by Philip Bailey of Earth Wind & Fire and Courtney Pine, one of our leading sax players. 'Can You Feel The Force' was probably our biggest seller in terms of sales and is still being covered and sampled all over the world. We also have two songs in the all-time top 100 of the *Guinness Book of Records*.

I had 13 years of struggle and scraping with the Chants –
and plenty of fun also – and 23 years of being in a hit band, I
think the balance has been more than redressed.

24 Chapel Street, Belgravia, London SW1

Georgian brick house which Brian Epstein bought for £60,000 on
20 December 1964.

The five-storey building had a private garage, a small servant's
quarters, a formal dining room and roof garden. Brian's staff
included his chauffeur Brian Barratt, a Spanish couple – Antonio,
the butler and his wife Marie, the cook. As Brian had ceased working
at his Stafford Street office and now used Chapel Street as his base,
his secretary Joanne Newfield travelled there each day from Edgware.

Brian liked to hold dinner parties at the lavishly decorated house
and on 19 May 1967 held a special *Sgt Pepper* party for the press.
His PA Peter Brown described the elite get-together as being 'for the
ten most important representatives of the press to listen to the new
album and enjoy a "family" dinner with one or two of the Beatles
around the dining table'.

Press people included Don Short of the *Daily Mirror* and among
the photographers was Linda Eastman. Fare included fine wines,
caviar and poached salmon. Disc jockey guests included Alan
Freeman, Jimmy Savile and Kenny Everett, and Everett was to
observe that the Beatles were dressed in colourful clothes, with
John wearing red trousers and a green shirt decorated with a yellow
flower design.

The Chapel Street address was where Brian was found dead on
27 August 1967. He'd intended to spend the weekend at his
country house in Kingsley Hill in Sussex with Geoffrey Ellis and
Peter Brown as his guests. He'd arrived home to Chapel Street on
the Friday with promises that he'd return. Peter Brown phoned his
private number after midnight to see if he'd arrived safely and
Antonio answered it, explaining that he was unable to contact
Brian on the intercom.

Later, still unable to contact his employer, Antonio phoned
Kingsley Hill but Geoffrey and Peter were out lunching at a local
pub. He next called Joanne Newfield and Alistair Taylor who
arrived at Chapel Street. They managed to contact Peter Brown on
the phone, who suggested they get hold of his own GP, Dr John
Gallway, who lived nearby. When Dr Gallway arrived a decision
was taken to break down the doors of Brian's bedroom. Antonio
and Brian Barrett broke down the doors and Brian was found dead.

At the coroner's inquest the verdict was that he had died of an
overdose of Carbitol.

Chapman, Norman

A Liverpool youth, who became a member of the Silver Beetles for a short time during the summer of 1960.

When Tommy Moore left the group following a gig at the Jacaranda coffee bar on Monday 13 June of that year, the Beatles were desperate for a replacement. They were pondering over the problem one night while sitting in the coffee bar when they heard the sound of drumbeats from across the street. Almost directly opposite the Jacaranda in Slater Street was a picture-framing establishment. Norman Chapman worked there as a picture-framer and renovator, and played drums as a hobby, practising on a hire-purchase kit in the offices of the firm in the evenings.

They went into the street, trying to find where the sound was coming from. They knocked on the doors of the National Cash Register Office and Chapman popped his head out of an upstairs window of the building. They offered him the position of drummer with the band. Chapman, an imposing six-foot-two in height, accepted the job. However, he only managed to appear with them on three Saturday night gigs at the Grosvenor Ballroom, Birkenhead, on 18 and 25 June and 2 July, before he was called up for National Service and was conscripted for two years in Kenya and Kuwait. In later years he was to say that he did not regret being 'called up'.

Chapman became a teacher in the south of England and used to fascinate his students with tales of his brief spell with the Silver Beatles. He continued playing drums and was a member of a trio when he died in 1995 at the age of 58.

Charles, Tommy

Manager of WAQY, a C&W radio station in Birmingham, Alabama, who, on 31 July 1966, announced that the station wouldn't play any more Beatles records and requested that his listeners burn records and photographs of the group because of John Lennon's alleged statement that the Beatles were bigger than Jesus Christ. He presided over a publicised bonfire where Beatles records were burned.

Other stations followed suit. One of them, radio KLUE, which had organised a public bonfire of Beatles records on 13 August, had their transmission tower struck by a bolt of lightning the very next morning which knocked their news director unconscious and caused extensive damage to equipment!

Charts

'Love Me Do' was the Beatles' very first chart entry, although it was not a massive hit in its first year of release. It reached its highest position of No. 17 in one London music paper for one week only, was No. 27 for one week in another, but at least managed to make its presence felt in all four London musical weeklies, reaching No. 24 in *Disc* and No. 32 in *Record Mirror*, in addition to the *Melody Maker* and *New Musical Express* placings.

However, as was to be expected, it reached No. 1 soon after release in the North's only music paper: *Mersey Beat*. The full Top Twenty of the 18 October 1962 issue was as follows:

1. 'Love Me Do', the Beatles
2. 'Telstar', the Tornadoes
3. 'The Locomotion', Little Eva
4. 'It Might As Well Rain Until September', Carole King
5. 'Sheila', Tommy Roe
6 'Ramblin' Rose', Nat King Cole
7. 'She's Not You', Elvis Presley
8. 'Devil Woman', Marty Robbins
9. 'What Now My Love', Shirley Bassey
10. 'You Don't Know Me', Ray Charles
11. 'I Remember You', Frank Ifield
12. 'It'll Be Me', Cliff Richard
13. 'Let's Dance', Chris Montez
14. 'Reminiscing', Buddy Holly
15. 'Don't That Beat All', Adam Faith
16. 'Things', Bobby Darin
17. 'Venus In Blue Jeans', Mark Wynter
18. 'Speedy Gonzales', Pat Boone
19. 'Send Me The Pillow', Johnny Tillotson
20. 'It's Started All Over Again', Brenda Lee

The most prestigious British chart of the sixties was the *New Musical Express* chart. The *NME* was the music weekly with the largest circulation and had, in fact, been the publication which had run Britain's first-ever chart listing on 14 November 1952. The Beatles first entered the *New Musical Express* chart on Wednesday, 24 October 1962. To indicate the type of music popular at the time of the Beatles' record debut, the full Top Thirty of this date follows, with background details on the artists.

1. 'Telstar', The Tornadoes (Decca) – A group produced by the late Joe Meek, a major British record producer who committed suicide in 1967. This was the first million-seller by a British group in America. The most notable member of the Tornadoes was the blond-haired guitarist Heinz. He

enjoyed brief fame as a solo artist, but never maintained his success and took on numerous jobs over the years before settling into a bakery in Eastleigh, Hants.

2. 'The Locomotion', Little Eva (London) – A Goffin-King composition, recorded by the couple's babysitter, Eva Boyd. Eva had one or two minor hits before settling down as a housewife.

3. 'Sheila', Tommy Roe (HMV) – American singer, born in Atlanta, Georgia, whose 'Sheila' didn't hit the British charts on its original release in 1960. The Beatles included this number in their repertoire and were to tour with Roe and another American singer, Chris Montez, in 1963. Tommy also appeared on the Beatles' first-ever American concert at the Washington Coliseum on 11 February 1964.

4. 'Ramblin' Rose', Nat King Cole (Capitol) – A fine balladeer who, sadly, died of lung cancer in 1965 at the age of 45. Several years later, his daughter Natalie Cole pursued a career as a singer.

5. 'It Might As Well Rain Until September', Carole King (London) – One half of the tremendously successful songwriting team of Goffin and King. In the late sixties, Carole maintained her career as a singer with a succession of hit albums.

6. 'Venus In Blue Jeans', Mark Wynter (Pye) – Handsome solo singer who covered American hits. First discovered singing in Peckham in 1959. After his spell as a British hitmaker he moved to Australia. Over the years he has turned to the stage and on his return to England he performed in pantomime and Shakespeare.

7. 'Let's Dance', Chris Montez (London) – This number and 'The More I See You' were the biggest hits by this American singer who toured Britain with Tommy Roe, billed above the Beatles. Apart from a minor revival of interest in the seventies for his early records, nothing much has been heard of him since.

8. 'Lovesick Blues', Frank Ifield (Columbia) – Coventry-born Ifield moved with his parents to Australia at the age of nine. When he returned to Britain he had a string of hit records, including four chart toppers.

9. 'You Don't Know Me', Ray Charles (HMV) – American singer who first rose to fame in 1959 with 'What'd I Say'. Born in Georgia, Charles became blind at the age of six due to an illness. He performed a distinctive style of rhythm and blues and had many hits before concentrating on music publishing and record promotion.

10. 'What Now My Love', Shirley Bassey (Columbia) – Born in the Tiger Bay area of Swansea in 1937, Shirley went on to become one of Britain's major international stars and was later to find her biggest recording successes with James Bond numbers such as 'Goldfinger' and 'Diamonds Are Forever'. She also had hits with George Harrison's 'Something' and Paul McCartney's 'Fool On The Hill'.

11. 'Swiss Maid', Del Shannon (London) – The song was written by Roger Miller and gave Michigan-born singer Shannon an international hit. He later became fabulously wealthy dealing in real estate and bought a large ranch in California. Tragically, he died from a gunshot wound, presumably self-inflicted.

12. 'Sherry', the Four Seasons (Stateside) – A major American vocal group whose lead singer Frankie Vallie carved a successful solo career. Valli had a massive hit with the theme song from *Grease*. The Vee Jay label in the States issued an album *The Beatles vs The Four Seasons* in October 1964.

13. 'She's Not You', Elvis Presley (RCA) – One of popular music's legendary figures, who died in August 1977. The Beatles once had a private meeting with Elvis at his home in California. At one time Paul wrote a number specially for Elvis, but nothing came of it.

14. 'Devil Woman', Marty Robbins (CBS) – This was one of a series of international hits by a country singer who was a leading exponent of C&W music in Nashville.

15. 'It'll Be Me', Cliff Richard (Columbia) – Britain's most popular solo singer and the only recording artist to have No. 1 hits in five different decades. With his group the Shadows he was the major British sensation until the Beatles made their bow.

16. 'She Taught Me How To Yodel', Frank Ifield (Columbia) – Although he has settled in Hounslow, London, Ifield is particularly popular in Australasia and the Far East, where he still tours.

17. 'I Remember You', Frank Ifield (Columbia) – Three records in the Top Twenty for Frank – the sort of achievement which the Beatles were soon to enjoy around the world.

18. 'Lonely', Acker Bilk (Columbia) – A survivor of the Traditional Jazz boom which hit Britain in the late fifties and brought Acker his biggest hit 'Stranger On The Shore'. The clarinettist/bandleader still tours Europe regularly.

19. 'No One Can Make My Sunshine Smile', the Everly Brothers (Warner Bros) – Another classic act from the golden age of the fifties. The duo ceased performing together

in 1973 and there were rumours of a feud between the brothers, but Don and Phil were reunited in 1984 and came to Britain. Paul McCartney was at their Albert Hall concert and penned 'On The Wings Of A Nightingale' for them, which gave the Evs their first hit in the singles chart for over a decade.

20. 'Don't That Beat All', Adam Faith (Parlophone) – Major British solo singer of the early sixties who found success in another sphere as an actor. His most notable TV series was 'Budgie' and he took over the role vacated by Ringo Starr in *Stardust*. He entered the field of management with Leo Sayer and still makes occasional TV appearances.

21. 'It Started All Over Again', Brenda Lee (Brunswick) – At one time this tiny Georgia-born singer was the top female vocalist in the world. She left the recording scene in 1967 to settle down in her home in Nashville and in the seventies turned to country music. A compilation of her original hits entered the British charts in 1980.

22. 'Send Me The Pillow You Dream On', Johnny Tillotson (London) – A spell in the army doing compulsory service seemed to end the career of this singer, whose biggest hit was 'Poetry In Motion'. He attempted several comebacks but never equalled his early success.

23. 'The Pay Off', Kenny Ball (Pye) – Another survivor from the Traditional Jazz scene of the fifties who continues to pursue a career on the club and cabaret circuit, making frequent television appearances. A regular at the Cavern Club at the time the Beatles began appearing there.

24. 'If A Man Answers', Bobby Darin (Capitol) – Sadly, this brilliant singer died of a heart attack in December 1973. He had eighteen chart singles and once even rivalled the popularity of Frank Sinatra himself.

25. 'Bobby's Girl', Susan Maugham (Philips) – Pretty, dark-haired singer from County Durham who made several records. This single was her only Top 30 entry. She pursued a career in pantomime and cabaret and still makes occasional appearances on television.

26. 'Because Of Love', Billy Fury (Decca) – At one time the closest rival to Cliff Richard in the pre-Beatle years. This late, lamented singer had to curtail a promising career due to ill health following 26 British chart hits. Born in Liverpool, he once shared the same class at school as Ringo Starr and the Silver Beetles auditioned to be his backing group in 1960.

27. 'Love Me Do', the Beatles (Parlophone) – The first chart
    entry of the most sensational group in the history of popular
    music.
28. Reminiscing', Buddy Holly (Coral) – A seminal influence on
    the Beatles, who recorded some of his songs. The name
    'Beatles' was actually inspired by the name of Holly's
    backing group the Crickets. Paul McCartney was to become
    the publisher of Holly's songs. The singer died in an air
    crash in October 1959.
29. 'Roses Are Red', Ronnie Carroll (Philips) – One of several
    former danceband singers who had regular chart success in
    the fifties and early sixties. His last chart entry was 'Say
    Wonderful Things' in 1963.
30. 'The James Bond Theme', John Barry (Columbia) – Former
    leader of the John Barry Seven who became a major sound-
    track composer following his association with the James
    Bond movies. Paul McCartney penned the theme tune for
    'Live And Let Die'.

The first British charts were published on 14 November 1952 in the
New Musical Express. The initial chart listed 12 records and was
later enlarged to 20, then to 30. On 10 March 1960 the trade magazine *Record Retailer* inaugurated a Top 50 chart.

From 19 February 1969 the chart began to be compiled for *Record
Retailer* by the British Market Research Bureau. As the same chart
was also used by the BBC, this became recognised as the major chart
in Britain. *Record Retailer* later changed its name to *Music Week*
and in 1983 the compilation of the charts was undertaken by Gallup.

However, during the sixties, the most important chart was still
the one compiled by *New Musical Express*. The *NME* chart was
also broadcast weekly on Radio Luxembourg and printed in
national publications such as the *Daily Mail*. The *Record Retailer*
chart was not really recognised by any major media outlet in the
early sixties and it was not until later in the decade when it was
compiled by the British Market Research Bureau that the BBC
began to use it. The BBC had previously compiled its own chart
based on the combined statistics of the *New Musical Express*, *Disc*,
Melody Maker and *Record Mirror* and from this chart they chose
the artists for 'Top Of The Pops'.

The positions reached by the Beatles in the *Record
Retailer/Music Week* singles charts were:

'Love Me Do' reached No. 17.
'Please Please Me' reached No. 2.

'From Me To You' reached No. 1.
'She Loves You' reached No. 1.
'I Want To Hold Your Hand' reached No. 1.
'Can't Buy Me Love' reached No. 1.
'Ain't She Sweet' reached No. 29.
'A Hard Day's Night' reached No. 1.
'I Feel Fine' reached No. 1.
'Ticket To Ride' reached No. 1.
'Help!' reached No. 1.
'Day Tripper'/'We Can Work It Out' reached No. 1.
'Paperback Writer' reached No. 1.
'Yellow Submarine'/'Eleanor Rigby' reached No. 1.
'Penny Lane'/'Strawberry Fields Forever' reached No. 2.
'All You Need Is Love' reached No. 1.
'Hello Goodbye' reached No. 1.
'Magical Mystery Tour' reached No. 2.
'Lady Madonna' reached No. 1.
'Let It Be' reached No. 2.
'Yesterday' reached No. 8.

A number of Beatles singles were re-released in the seventies and
eighties and these were their positions in the *Music Week* chart:

'Hey Jude' reached No. 12.
'Paperback Writer' reached No. 23.
'Strawberry Fields Forever' reached No. 32.
'Get Back' reached No. 28.
'Help!' reached No. 37.
'Back In The USSR' reached No. 19
'Sgt Pepper's Lonely Hearts Club Band'/'With A Little Help
From My Friends' reached No. 63.
'Beatles Movie Medley' reached No. 10.
'Love Me Do' reached No. 4.
'Please Please Me' reached No. 29.
'From Me To You' reached No. 40.
'She Loves You' reached No. 45.
'I Want To Hold Your Hand' reached No. 62.
'Can't Buy Me Love' reached No. 53.
'A Hard Day's Night' reached No. 52.
'I Feel Fine' reached No. 65.
'Ticket To Ride' reached No. 70.
'Eleanor Rigby'/'Yellow Submarine' reached No. 63.
'Penny Lane'/'Strawberry Fields Forever' reached No. 65.
'All You Need Is Love' reached No. 47.

'Hello Goodbye' reached No. 63.
'Lady Madonna' reached No. 67.
'Hey Jude' reached No. 52.

The album positions were:

Please Please Me reached No. 1.
With The Beatles reached No. 1.
A Hard Day's Night reached No. 1.
Beatles For Sale reached No. 1.
Help! reached No. 1.
Rubber Soul reached No. 1.
Revolver reached No. 1.
A Collection Of Beatles Oldies reached No. 7.
Sgt Pepper's Lonely Hearts Club Band reached No.1
Magical Mystery Tour, an import album, reached No. 31.
The Beatles reached No. 1.
Yellow Submarine reached No. 4.
Abbey Road reached No. 1.
Let It Be reached No. 1.
A Hard Day's Night, a reissue, reached No. 39.
Help!, a reissue, reached No. 33.
The Beatles 1962–1966 reached No. 3.
The Beatles 1967–1970 reached No. 2.
Rock 'n' Roll Music reached No. 11.
The Beatles Tapes reached No. 45.
The Beatles At The Hollywood Bowl reached No. 1.
Love Songs reached No. 7.
Rarities reached No. 71.
Beatles Ballads reached No. 17.
20 Greatest Hits reached No. 10.

The *Melody Maker* has been Britain's longest-running British music weekly. Here are the *Melody Maker* chart positions of the Beatles EPs and singles until the band broke up:

'Love Me Do' entered the charts on 27 November 1962 at No. 48, eventually reaching No. 21 with a chart life of sixteen weeks.
'Please Please Me' entered the charts on 19 January 1963 at No. 47 and eventually reached No. 1 for two weeks with a chart life of eighteen weeks.
'From Me To You' entered the charts on 20 April 1963 at No. 19 and eventually reached No. 1 for six weeks with a chart life of twenty weeks.

'My Bonnie' entered the charts on 15 June 1963 at No. 30, dropped to No. 46 the next week then left the charts.

Twist and Shout (EP) entered the charts on 27 July 1963 and No. 14 and eventually reached No. 2 with a chart life of 31 weeks.

'She Loves You' entered the charts on 31 August 1963 at No. 12 and eventually reached No. 1 for five weeks, with a chart life of 31 weeks.

The Beatles Hits (EP) entered the charts on 28 September 1963 at No. 44, eventually reaching No. 14 with a chart life of twelve weeks.

'I Want To Hold Your Hand' entered the charts on 7 December 1963 at No. 1 where it remained for four weeks with a chart life of eighteen weeks.

All My Loving (EP) entered the charts on 8 February 1964 at No. 42, eventually reaching No. 12 with a chart life of twelve weeks.

'Can't Buy Me Love' entered the charts on 28 March 1964 at No. 1 where it remained for three weeks with a chart life of fourteen weeks.

'Ain't She Sweet' entered the charts on 13 June 1964 and No. 36, eventually reaching No. 24 with a chart life of six weeks.

Long Tall Sally (EP) entered the charts on 4 July 1964 at No. 20, eventually reaching No. 14 with a chart life of thirteen weeks.

'A Hard Day's Night' entered the charts on 18 July 1964 at No. 1 where it remained for four weeks with a chart life of fifteen weeks.

A Hard Day's Night (EP) entered the charts on 28 November 1964 at No. 48, reaching No. 34 with a chart life of four weeks.

'I Feel Fine' entered the charts on 5 December 1964 at No. 1 where it remained for six weeks with a chart life of thirteen weeks.

'Ticket To Ride' entered the charts on 17 April 1965 at No. 1 where it remained for five weeks with a chart life of twelve weeks.

'Help!' entered the charts on 31 July 1965 at No. 1 where it remained for four weeks with a chart life of thirteen weeks.

'We Can Work It Out'/'Day Tripper' entered the charts on 18 June 1966 at No. 1 where it remained for four weeks with a chart life of ten weeks.

'Yellow Submarine'/'Eleanor Rigby' entered the charts on 13 August 1966 at No. 4, eventually reaching No. 1 for three weeks with a chart life of twelve weeks.

'Penny Lane'/'Strawberry Fields Forever' entered the charts on 25 February 1967 at No. 3, eventually reaching No. 1 for three weeks with a chart life of ten weeks.

'All You Need Is Love' entered the charts on 15 July 1967 at No. 3, eventually reaching No. 1 for three weeks with a chart life of eleven weeks.

'Hello Goodbye' entered the charts on 2 December 1967 at No. 3, reaching No. 1 where it remained for four weeks with a chart life of ten weeks.

Magical Mystery Tour (two EPs) entered the charts on 16 December 1967 at No. 17, eventually reaching No. 1 for one week with a chart life of ten weeks.

'Lady Madonna' entered the charts on 23 March 1968 at No. 3, eventually reaching No. 2 for two weeks with a chart life of seven weeks.

'Hey Jude' entered the charts on 7 September 1968 at No. 1 where it remained for four weeks with a chart life of thirteen weeks.

'Get Back' entered the charts on 26 April 1969 at No. 2, eventually reaching No. 1 for five weeks with a chart life of thirteen weeks.

'The Ballad Of John And Yoko' entered the charts on 7 June 1969 at No. 15, eventually reaching No. 1 for three weeks with a chart life of ten weeks.

'Something' entered the charts on 9 November 1969 at No. 26, eventually reaching No. 4 with a chart life of ten weeks.

'Let It Be' entered the charts on 14 March 1970 at No. 15, eventually reaching No. 3 with a chart life of eight weeks.

The Beatles releases in America during 1963 failed to chart. The situation changed the following year and recording history was made on 31 March 1964 when the first five places in the American Top Hundred singles chart were:

1. 'Twist And Shout', the Beatles
2. 'Can't Buy Me Love', the Beatles
3. 'She Loves You', the Beatles
4. 'I Want To Hold Your Hand', the Beatles
5. 'Please Please Me', the Beatles

A similiar previously unprecedented chart blitz had also taken place in Australia when on 27 March 1964 the first six places in the Australian Top Twenty were:

1. 'I Saw Her Standing There', the Beatles
2. 'Love Me Do', the Beatles
3. 'Roll Over Beethoven', the Beatles
4. 'All My Loving', the Beatles
5. 'She Loves You', the Beatles
6. 'I Want To Hold Your Hand', the Beatles

The American trade publication *Billboard* runs a Hot 100 chart of the best-selling singles in America. The chart differs from the British chart, not only in the fact that it includes the hundred best-selling records of the week, but also because it includes chart placings for the flipside of discs, which is why the Beatles have 30 different titles among the singles chart entries for 1964 alone.

Here are the details of the Beatles' positions in the *Billboard* chart until they group's eventual break-up:

'I Want To Hold Your Hand' entered the charts on 18 January 1964 at No. 45 and was No. 1 for seven weeks with a chart life of fifteen weeks.

'She Loves You' entered the charts on 25 January 1964 at No. 69 and was No. 1 for two weeks, with a chart life of fifteen weeks.

'Please Please Me' entered the charts on 1 February 1964 at No. 68 and eventually reached No. 3 with a chart life of thirteen weeks.

'I Saw Her Standing There' entered the charts on 8 February 1964 at No. 68 and eventually reached No. 14 with a chart life of eleven weeks.

'My Bonnie' entered the charts on 15 February 1964 at No. 67 and eventually reached No. 26 with a chart life of six weeks.

'From Me To You' entered the charts on 7 March 1964 at No. 86 and eventually reached No. 41 with a chart life of six weeks.

'Twist And Shout' entered the charts on 14 March 1964 at No. 55 and eventually reached No. 2 with a chart life of eleven weeks.

'Roll Over Beethoven' entered the charts on 21 March 1964 at No. 79 and eventually reached No. 68 with a chart life of four weeks.

'All My Loving' entered the charts on 28 March 1964 at No. 71 and eventually reached No. 45 with a chart life of six weeks.

'Do You Want To Know A Secret?' entered the charts on 28 March 1964 at No. 78 and eventually reached No. 2 with a chart life of eleven weeks.

'Can't Buy Me Love' entered the charts on 28 March 1964 at

No. 22 and eventually reached No. 1 for five weeks with a chart life of ten weeks.

'You Can't Do That' entered the charts on 4 April 1964 at No. 65 and eventually reached No. 48 with a chart life of four weeks.

'Thank You Girl' entered the charts on 4 April 1964 at No. 79 and eventually reached No. 35 with a chart life of seven weeks.

'There's A Place' entered the charts on 11 April 1964 for one week only at No. 74.

'Love Me Do' entered the charts on 11 April 1964 at No. 81 and eventually reached No. 1 for one week with a chart life of fourteen weeks.

'Why?' entered the charts on 18 April 1964 at No. 88 for one week only.

'P.S. I Love You' entered the charts on 9 May 1964 at No. 64 and eventually reached No. 10 with a chart life of three weeks.

'Four By The Beatles' (EP) entered the charts on 13 June 1964 at No. 97 and eventually reached No. 92 with a chart life of three weeks.

'Sie Liebt Dich' entered the charts on 27 June 1964 for one week only at No. 97.

'A Hard Day's Night' entered the charts on 18 July 1964 at No. 21 and eventually reached No. 1 for two weeks with a chart life of thirteen weeks.

'Ain't She Sweet' entered the charts on 18 July 1964 at No. 90 and eventually reached No. 19 with a chart life of nine weeks.

'I Should Have Known Better' entered the charts on 25 July 1964 at No. 75 and eventually reached No. 53 with a chart life of four weeks.

'And I Love Her' entered the charts on 25 July 1964 at No. 80 and eventually reached No. 12 with a chart life of nine weeks.

'If I Fell' entered the charts on 1 August 1964 at No. 92 and eventually reached No. 53 with a chart life of nine weeks.

'I'll Cry Instead' entered the charts on 1 August 1964 at No. 62 and eventually reached No. 25 with a chart life of seven weeks.

'I'm Happy Just To Dance With You' entered the charts on 1 August 1964 for one week only at No. 95.

'Matchbox' entered the charts on 5 September 1964 at No. 81 and eventually reached No. 17 with a chart life of eight weeks.

'Slow Down' entered the charts on 5 September 1964 at No. 99 and eventually reached No. 25 with a chart life of seven weeks.

'I Feel Fine' entered the charts on 5 December 1964 at No. 22 and eventually reached No. 1 for three weeks with a chart life of eleven weeks.

'She's A Woman' entered the charts on 5 December 1964 at No. 46 eventually reaching No. 4 with a chart life of nine weeks.

'Eight Days A Week' entered the charts on 20 February 1965 at No. 53 and eventually reached No. 1 for two weeks with a chart life of ten weeks.

'I Don't Want To Spoil The Party' entered the charts on 20 February 1965 at No. 81 and eventually reached No. 39 with a chart life of six weeks.

Four By The Beatles (EP) entered the charts on 27 February 1965 at No. 81 and eventually reached No. 68 with a chart life of five weeks.

'Ticket To Ride' entered the charts on 24 April 1965 at No. 59 and eventually reached No. 1 for one week with a chart life of eleven weeks.

'Yes It Is' entered the charts on 1 May 1965 at No. 71 and eventually reached No. 46 with a chart life of four weeks.

'Help!' entered the charts on 7 August 1965 at No. 42 and eventually reached No. 1 for three weeks with a chart life of thirteen weeks.

'Yesterday' entered the charts on 25 September 1965 at No. 45 and eventually reached No. 1 for four weeks with a chart life of eleven weeks.

'Act Naturally' entered the charts on 25 September 1965 at No. 86 and eventually reached No. 47 with a chart life of seven weeks.

'We Can Work It Out' entered the charts on 18 December 1965 at No. 36 and eventually reached No. 1 for three weeks with a chart life of ten weeks.

'Day Tripper' entered the charts on 28 December 1965 at No. 56 and eventually reached No. 5 with a chart life of ten weeks.

'Nowhere Man' entered the charts on 5 March 1966 at No. 25 and eventually reached No. 3 with a chart life of nine weeks.

'What Goes On?' entered the charts on 12 March 1966 at No. 89, moved to No. 81 the following week, then dropped out.

'Paperback Writer' entered the charts on 11 June 1966 at No. 28 and eventually reached No. 1 for two weeks with a chart life of ten weeks.

'Rain' entered the charts on 11 June 1966 at No. 72 and eventually reached No. 23 with a chart life of seven weeks.

'Yellow Submarine' entered the charts on 20 August 1966 at No. 52 and eventually reached No. 2 with a chart life of nine weeks.

'Eleanor Rigby' entered the charts on 27 August 1966 at No. 65 and eventually reached No. 11 with a chart life of eight weeks.

'Penny Lane' entered the charts on 25 February 1967 at No. 85 and eventually reached No. 1 for one week with a chart life of ten weeks.

'Strawberry Fields Forever' entered the charts on 25 February 1967 at No. 83 and eventually reached No. 8 with a chart life of nine weeks.

'All You Need Is Love' entered the charts on 22 July 1967 at No. 71 and eventually reached No. 1 for one week with a chart life of eleven weeks.

'Baby You're A Rich Man' entered the charts on 29 July 1967 at No. 64 and eventually reached No. 34 with a chart life of five weeks.

'Hello Goodbye' entered the charts on 2 December 1967 at No. 45 and eventually reached No. 1 for three weeks with a chart life of eleven weeks.

'I Am The Walrus' entered the charts on 9 December 1967 at No. 64 and eventually reached No. 56 with a chart life of four weeks.

'Lady Madonna' entered the charts on 23 March 1968 at No. 23 and eventually reached No. 4 with a chart life of eleven weeks.

'The Inner Light' entered the charts on 30 March 1968 for one week only at No. 96.

'Hey Jude' entered the charts on 14 September 1968 at No. 10 and eventually reached No. 1 with a chart life of nineteen weeks.

'Revolution' entered the charts on 14 September 1968 at No. 38 and eventually reached No. 12 with a chart life of eleven weeks.

'Get Back' entered the charts on 10 May 1969 at No. 10 and eventually reached No. 1 for five weeks with a chart life of twelve weeks.

'Don't Let Me Down' entered the charts on 10 May 1969 at No. 40 and eventually reached No. 35 with a chart life of four weeks.

'The Ballad Of John and Yoko' entered the charts on 14 June 1969 at No. 71 and eventually reached No. 8 with a chart life of nine weeks.

'Come Together' entered the charts on 18 October 1969 at No. 23 and after six weeks, during which it reached No. 2, it was tied in with the 'Something' position for a further ten weeks, reaching No. 1 for one week.

'Something' entered the charts on 18 October 1969 at No. 20 and, after six weeks, during which it reached No. 3, it was tied in with the 'Come Together' position for a further ten weeks, reaching No. 1 for one week.

'Let It Be' entered the charts on 21 March 1970 at No. 6 and eventually reached No. 1 for two weeks with a chart life of fourteen weeks.

'For You Blue'/'The Long And Winding Road' entered the charts on 23 May 1970 at No. 35 and eventually reached No. 1 for two weeks with a chart life of ten weeks.

Here are the positions which the Beatles' albums reached in the *Billboard* charts:

Meet The Beatles reached No. 1.

Introducing The Beatles reached No. 2.

The Beatles With Tony Sheridan And Their Guests reached No. 68.

Jolly What! The Beatles And Frank Ifield On Stage reached No. 104.

The Beatles Second Album reached No. 1.

The American Tour With Ed Rudy reached No. 20.

A Hard Day's Night reached No. 1.

Something New reached No. 2.

The Beatles vs The Four Seasons reached No. 142.

Songs, Pictures And Stories Of the Fabulous Beatles reached No. 63.

The Beatles Story reached No. 7.

The Beatles '65 reached No. 1.

The Early Beatles reached No. 43.

Beatles VI reached No. 1.

Help! reached No. 1.

Rubber Soul reached No. 1.

Yesterday . . . And Today reached No. 1.

Revolver reached No. 1.

Sgt Pepper's Lonely Hearts Club Band reached No. 1.

Magical Mystery Tour reached No. 1.

Unfinished Music No. 1 – Two Virgins, John Lennon and Yoko Ono, reached No. 124.

The Beatles reached No. 1.

Wonderwall Music, George Harrison, reached No. 49.

Yellow Submarine reached No. 2.

Unfinished Music No. 2 – Life With The Lions, John Lennon and Yoko Ono, reached No. 174.

Electronic Sounds, George Harrison, reached No. 191.

Abbey Road reached No. 1.

Wedding Album, John Lennon and Yoko Ono, reached No. 178.

Live Peace In Toronto, Plastic Ono Band, reached No. 10.
Hey Jude reached No. 2.
In The Beginning reached No. 117.
Let It Be reached No. 1.
The Beatles 1962–1966 reached No. 3.
The Beatles 1967–1970 reached No. 1.
Rock 'n' Roll Music reached No. 2.
The Beatles At The Hollywood Bowl reached No. 2.
Live! At The Star Club In Hamburg, Germany: 1962 reached No. 111.
Love Songs reached No. 24.
Rarities reached No. 21.
Reel Music reached No. 19.

There were three main trade music publications in America during the sixties: *Billboard*, *Cash Box* and *Record World*. The chart positions of the Beatles in *Record World* were as follows:

'She Loves You' reached No. 1.
'Roll Over Beethoven' reached No. 35.
'I Want To Hold Your Hand' reached No. 1.
'My Bonnie' reached No. 31.
'Please Please Me' reached No. 5.
'All My Loving' reached No. 32.
'Twist and Shout' reached No. 1.
'Can't Buy Me Love' reached No. 1.
'Do You Want To Know A Secret' reached No. 3.
'Love Me Do' reached No. 1.
'Ain't She Sweet' reached No. 13.
'A Hard Day's Night' reached No. 1.
'I'll Cry Instead' reached No. 28.
'And I Love Her' reached No. 16.
'Matchbox' reached No. 22.
'I Feel Fine' reached No. 1.
'Eight Days A Week' reached No. 1.
'Ticket to Ride' reached No. 1.
'Help!' reached No. 1.
'Yesterday' reached No. 1.
'We Can Work It Out'/'Day Tripper' reached No. 1.
'Nowhere Man' reached No. 1.
'Paperback Writer' reached No. 1.
'Yellow Submarine'/'Eleanor Rigby' reached No. 1.
'Penny Lane'/'Strawberry Fields Forever' reached No. 1.
'All You Need Is Love' reached No. 1.

'Hello Goodbye' reached No. 1.
'Lady Madonna' reached No. 2.
'Hey Jude' reached No. 1.
'Get Back' reached No. 1.
'The Ballad Of John And Yoko' reached No. 7.
'Give Peace A Chance', Plastic Ono Band, reached No. 10.
'Something'/'Come Together' reached No. 1.
'Cold Turkey', Plastic Ono Band, reached No. 26.
'Instant Karma!', John Ono Lennon, reached No. 3.
'Let It Be' reached No. 1.
'The Long And Winding Road' reached No. 1.
'Got To Get You Into My Life' reached No. 9.
'Ob-La-Di, Ob-La-Da' reached No. 75.
'Sgt Pepper's Lonely Hearts Club Band'/'With A Little Help From My Friends' reached No. 103.
'The Beatles Movie Medley' reached No. 39.

Beatles album placings were:

Meet The Beatles reached No. 1.
Introducing The Beatles reached No. 1.
The Beatles Second Album reached No. 1.
The American Tour With Ed Ruby reached No. 32.
A Hard Day's Night reached No. 1.
Something New reached No. 2.
Songs, Pictures and Stories of the Fabulous Beatles reached No. 79.
The Beatles Story reached No. 13.
Beatles '65 reached No. 1.
The Early Beatles reached No. 29.
Beatles VI reached No. 1.
Help! reached No. 1.
Rubber Soul reached No. 1.
Yesterday . . . And Today reached No. 1.
Revolver reached No. 1.
Sgt Pepper's Lonely Hearts Club Band reached No. 1.
Magical Mystery Tour reached No. 1.
Unfinished Music No. 1 – Two Virgins, John Lennon and Yoko Ono, reached No. 56.
The Beatles reached No. 1.
Wonderwall Music, George Harrison, reached No. 33.
Yellow Submarine reached No. 2.
Unfinished Music No. 2 – Life With The Lions, John Lennon and Yoko Ono, reached No. 124.

Abbey Road reached No. 1.

Wedding Album, John Lennon and Yoko Ono, reached No. 108.

Live Peace In Toronto 1969, Plastic Ono Band, reached No. 18.

Hey Jude reached No. 1.

In The Beginning: The Beatles reached No. 139.

Let It Be reached No. 1.

The Beatles 1962–1966 reached No. 4.

The Beatles 1967–1970 reached No. 1.

Rock 'n' Roll Music reached No. 2.

The Beatles At The Hollywood Bowl reached No. 7.

The Beatles Live! At The Star Club In Hamburg, Germany: 1962 reached No. 165.

Love Songs reached No. 36.

Rarities reached No. 26.

Rock 'n' Roll Music – Volume One reached No. 134.

Rock 'n' Roll Music – Volume Two reached No. 137.

Reel Music entered the *Record World* chart at No. 90 on 10 April 1982 which saw the final issue of the publication.

The chart positions of the Beatles singles in *Cash Box* were as follows:

'She Loves You' reached No. 1.

'Roll Over Beethoven' reached No. 30.

'I Want To Hold Your Hand' reached No. 1.

'My Bonnie' reached No. 29.

'Please Please Me' reached No. 3.

'All My Loving' reached No. 31.

'Twist and Shout' reached No. 1.

'Can't Buy Me Love' reached No. 1.

'Do You Want To Know A Secret' reached No. 3.

'Love Me Do' reached No. 1.

Four By The Beatles EP reached No. 86.

'Ain't She Sweet' reached No. 14.

'A Hard Day's Night' reached No. 1.

'I'll Cry Instead' reached No. 22.

'And I Love Her' reached No. 14.

'Matchbox' reached No. 17.

'I Feel Fine' reached No. 1.

Four By The Beatles EP reached No. 68.

'Eight Days A Week' reached No. 1.

'Ticket To Ride' reached No. 1.

'Help!' reached No. 1.

'Yesterday' reached No. 1.

'Boys' reached No. 73.

'We Can Work It Out'/'Day Tripper' reached No. 1.

'Nowhere Man' reached No. 2.

'Paperback Writer' reached No. 1.

'Yellow Submarine'/'Eleanor Rigby' reached No. 1.

'Penny Lane'/'Strawberry Fields Forever' reached No. 1.

'All You Need Is Love' reached No. 1.

'Hello Goodbye' reached No. 1.

'Lady Madonna' reached No. 2.

'Hey Jude' reached No. 1.

'Get Back' reached No. 1.

'The Ballad Of John and Yoko' reached No. 10.

'Give Peace A Chance', Plastic Ono Band, reached No. 11.

'Something'/'Come Together' reached No. 1.

'Cold Turkey', Plastic Ono Band, reached No. 32.

'Instant Karma', John Ono Lennon, reached No. 3.

'Let It Be' reached No. 1.

'The Long And Winding Road' reached No. 1.

'Got To Get You Into My Life' reached No. 3.

'Ob-La-Di, Ob-La-Da' reached No. 47.

'Sgt Pepper's Lonely Hearts Club Band'/'With A Little Help From My Friends' reached No. 92.

'The Beatles Movie Medley' reached No. 14.

The positions of the Beatles albums in the *Cash Box* charts were:

Meet The Beatles reached No. 1.

Introducing The Beatles reached No. 2.

The Beatles With Tony Sheridan And Their Guests reached No. 43.

Jolly What! The Beatles And Frank Ifield On Stage reached No. 73.

The Beatles Second Album reached No. 1.

The American Tour With Ed Rudy reached No. 55.

A Hard Day's Night reached No. 1.

Something New reached No. 2.

Songs, Pictures and Stories of the Fabulous Beatles reached No. 100.

The Beatles Story reached No. 7.

Beatles '65 reached No. 1.

The Early Beatles reached No. 24.

Beatles VI reached No. 1.

Help! reached No. 1.
Rubber Soul reached No. 1.
Yesterday . . . And Today reached No. 1.
Revolver reached No. 1.
Sgt Pepper's Lonely Hearts Club Band reached No. 1.
Magical Mystery Tour reached No. 1.
Unfinished Music No. 1 – Two Virgins, John Lennon and Yoko Ono, reached No. 82.
The Beatles reached No. 1.
Wonderwall Music, George Harrison, reached No. 39.
Yellow Submarine reached No. 3.
Unfinished Music No. 2 – Life With The Lions, John Lennon and Yoko Ono, reached No. 118.
Abbey Road reached No. 1.
Live Peace in Toronto 1969, Plastic Ono Band, reached No. 18.
Hey Jude reached No. 2.
In The Beginning: The Beatles reached No. 94.
Let It Be reached No. 1.
The Beatles 1962–1966 reached No. 1.
The Beatles 1967–1970 reached No. 2.
Rock 'n' Roll Music reached No. 4.
The Beatles At The Hollywood Bowl reached No. 3.
Live! At The Star Club, In Hamburg, Germany: 1962 reached No. 183.
Love Songs reached No. 28.
Rarities reached No. 20.
Reel Music reached No. 18.

The Beatles were a musical phenomenon on a global scale and their records also dominated the charts in non-English-speaking countries. At one time it was believed that the Beatles would have to record in foreign languages in order to capitalise on the charts in some of the non-English-speaking countries and they actually recorded two of their numbers in German. However, despite the fact that *'Komm Gib Mir Diene Hand'/'Sie Liebt Dich'* topped the charts in West Germany, they never had to repeat the exercise as their records continued to be popular in the English language – the language of rock 'n' roll. Here are the West German singles chart positions as they appeared in the trade publication *Der Misikmarkt*:

'My Bonnie' reached No. 32.
'Twist And Shout' reached No. 10.
'She Loves You' reached No. 7.

"I Want To Hold Your Hand' reached No. 1.

'Misery' reached No. 37.

Komm Gib Mir Diene Hand'/'Sie Liebt Dich' reached No. 1.

'All My Loving' reached No. 32.

'Please Please Me' reached No. 20.

'Can't Buy Me Love' reached No. 24.

'Do You Want To Know A Secret' reached No. 34.

'Long Tall Sally' reached No. 7.

'Please Mr Postman' reached No. 47.

'A Hard Day's Night' reached No. 2.

'If I Fell' reached No. 25.

'I Should Have Known Better' reached No. 6.

'I Feel Fine' reached No. 3.

'Rock 'n' Roll Music' reached No. 2.

'Eight Days A Week'/'No Reply' reached No. 7.

'Ticket To Ride' reached No. 2.

'Kansas City' reached No. 18.

'Help!' reached No. 2.

'Yesterday' reached No. 6.

'We Can Work It Out' reached No. 2.

'Michelle' reached No. 6.

'Nowhere Man' reached No. 3.

'Paperback Writer' reached No. 1.

'Yellow Submarine' reached No. 1.

'Penny Lane' reached No. 1.

'All You Need Is Love' reached No. 1.

'Hello Goodbye' reached No. 1.

'Lady Madonna' reached No. 2.

'Hey Jude' reached No. 1.

'Ob-La-Di, Ob-La-Da' reached No. 1.

'Get Back' reached No. 1.

'Ballad Of John And Yoko' reached No. 1.

'Something'/'Come Together' reached No. 3.

'Let It Be' reached No. 2.

'Long And Winding Road' reached No. 26.

'Got To Get You Into My Life' reached No. 22.

Chart placings for the Beatles albums were:

Beatles For Sale reached No. 1.

Something New reached No. 38.

Yeah Yeah Yeah (A Hard Day's Night) reached No. 5.

With The Beatles reached No. 34.

Beatles '65 reached No. 9.

Beatles VI reached No. 15.
Help! reached No. 1.
Rubber Soul reached No. 1.
Beatles Greatest reached No. 38.
Yesterday . . . And Today reached No. 13.
Revolver reached No. 1.
Sgt Pepper's Lonely Hearts Club Band reached No. 1.
Magical Mystery Tour reached No. 8.
The Beatles reached No. 1.
Yellow Submarine reached No. 5
Abbey Road reached No. 1.
Let It Be reached No. 4.
The Beatles 1962–1966 reached No. 2.
The Beatles 1967–1970 reached No. 2.
Rock 'n' Roll Music reached No. 10.
Live! At The Star Club In Hamburg, Germany: 1962 reached No. 21.
The Beatles At The Hollywood Bowl reached No. 10.
20 Golden Hits reached No. 4.

Chelsea Town Hall, Kings Road, London SW3

The venue chosen for the press reception to promote 'Give Peace A Chance', the first single from the Plastic Ono Band. Apart from John and Yoko, there were no confirmed members of their new musical concept at the time, so the Plastic Ono Band was to be represented by clear plastic robotic pieces of sculpture with bits of recording equipment attached. The robots were on display on 3 July 1969, when the reception took place, but John and Yoko weren't. They'd been involved in a crash in Scotland on 1 July and had been detained in hospital. Ringo Starr and his wife Maureen deputised for them.

Chester, Johnny

A rock 'n' roll star from Melbourne who had been booked as support for numerous touring rock shows in Australia on the bill with the Everly Brothers, Roy Orbison, Connie Francis and Bobby Rydell. Chester had had nine chart hits and was compering his own TV show 'Teen Time' when he was offered a spot on the Beatles' Australian tour. He accepted a rather derisory fee of £125 a week, but was upset when told he couldn't use his own backing band the Chessmen, but had to be backed by the Phantoms, who had also been booked for the tour.

Following the Sydney appearances, writer Charles Higham wrote in the *Bulletin* newspaper: 'Excitement was followed by bathos as Johnny Chester, wearing boots the colour of cherries with pointed

toes, a pallid suit and a cerise tie, sang "Fever" in the dark with lumi-
nous blue cuffs and a face that, because of some trick of lighting,
now matched both boots and tie.'

Chester continued to find success as an entertainer in Australia
for many years to come, although he changed his act and developed
into a Country singer.

Chiffons, The

An American girl vocal group of the early sixties comprising
Patricia Bennett, Barbara Lee, Sylvia Peterson and Judy Craig. The
girls appeared with the Beatles on the bill of their very first major
concert appearance in the States, at the Washington Coliseum on
11 February 1964, less than a year after the girls' biggest hit, 'He's
So Fine', a number penned by their manager Ronnie Mack.

In 1971 when George Harrison's first solo single 'My Sweet
Lord' entered the charts, Bright Tunes, the American publisher of
'He's So Fine' instituted legal proceedings in March of that year
claiming that 'My Sweet Lord' was an unauthorised plagiarism of
the Chiffons' hit. The court case dragged on until 1976 when it was
finally resolved with George paying $587,000 to Bright Tunes – by
that time, the publishing company was under the ownership of
Allen Klein.

Child Of Nature

One of the many songs John Lennon wrote during his stay at
Rishikesh in India. He made a home demo disc of the number during
The Beatles white album sessions, but it was never recorded in a
studio. Later, he completely rewrote the number and retitled it
'Jealous Guy'.

Chipmunks, The

The brainchild of Ross Bagdasarian. Bagdasarian, professionally
known as David Seville, was experimenting with recording speeds
until he hit on a novelty sound which reminded him of chipmunks.
This led him, in 1958, to create the fictitious Chipmunks, who were
named Alvin, Theodore, Simon and Dave. Seville's productions of
Chipmunks records went on to sell over 30 million copies before his
death in 1972. The Chipmunks line-up comprised Theodore and Dave
on guitars, Simon on drums and Alvin on harmonica and drums!

One of his most interesting productions was the album *The
Chipmunks Sing The Beatles Hits*, which was issued in America on
24 August 1964 on Liberty LST 7388 and in Britain on 19 February
1965 on Liberty LBY 1218. The tracks were: 'All My Loving', 'Do
You Want To Know A Secret?', 'She Loves You', 'From Me To You',

'Love Me Do', 'Twist And Shout', 'A Hard Day's Night', 'P.S. I Love You', 'I Saw Her Standing There', 'Can't Buy Me Love', 'Please Please Me' and 'I Want To Hold Your Hand'.

Bagdasarian also created the Bedbugs, a novelty group based on the Beatles, who appeared in a segment of the American TV series 'F Troop'. The character Corporal Agarn decides to leave the army to manage the Bedbugs, four young musicians from Boston who wear collarless suits and sport long hair. Four of his army buddies don't want him to leave so they form another group, the Termites, wearing Beatle wigs. The show ends with the information that the Bedbugs left for Liverpool, England, became a big hit and even performed before the Queen.

Chiswick House

A country estate in Surrey whose grounds were used during the making of the promotional film of 'Paperback Writer'. The group had been filming at EMI's No. 1 studio the previous day and completed their movie among the lawns, statues and lush gardens of the estate.

The Beatles, Director Michael Lindsay-Hogg and the crew paused for a luncheon break at three in the afternoon when food was brought over from Twickenham Studios, about half an hour's journey away. They all dug in to chops and veg, with red wine and rice pudding to follow – with the exception of Paul, who settled for cold meat and salad.

The film had its premiere on BBC TV's 'Top Of The Pops'.

Cilla (TV Show)

Before he died, Brian Epstein negotiated with the BBC for Cilla Black to have her own peak time television show. This move was to provide her with a new career which continued when the recording side was on the wane.

The weekly 50-minute show made its debut on BBC 1 on 6 February 1968 and the series was to feature many top names, including Tom Jones, Donovan, Tony Bennett and Harry Secombe.

Paul McCartney specially wrote a theme song for the series called 'Step Inside Love', which provided Cilla with a Top Ten hit in Britain. Ringo Starr also agreed to be her guest on the first show, making him the first Beatle to appear solo on another artist's show.

Ringo said, 'Without John, Paul and George, I feel vulnerable – like a sultan with three hundred wives who, one day, goes out to buy an ice cream for himself.'

His fellow Beatles sent him a greetings telegram: 'From All Your Big Brothers'.

Ringo and Cilla performed a duet of an old 1920s number 'Do You Like Me Just A Little Bit', which had been suggested by Paul's father, Jim McCartney, who used to play the number when he had a jazz band. Ringo also appeared solo singing 'Act Naturally' and joined Cilla in a comedy sketch in which he was a ventriloquist and Cilla was his dummy.

Cincinnati Gardens, Cincinnati, Ohio
This appearance was almost cancelled when the Musicians Union demanded that local groups should appear. The branch office was deluged with phone calls and surrounded by angry fans, and they withdrew their request – after all, the other acts on the bill were American.

The Beatles arrived at the former boxing ring at 6.00 a.m. and backstage they talked to Elvis Presley on the telephone for the first time. They then held a press conference in a private room. They appeared on stage at 9.35 p.m. before an audience of 14,000 people.

Cinema Cyrano, Versailles, France
The venue where the Beatles made their first concert appearance in France on the evening of Wednesday, 15 January 1964. It was ten miles outside Paris and the show was, in effect, a dress rehearsal for their imminent three-week season at the Olympia Theatre, Paris, starring the same bill – Trini Lopez, Sylvie Vartan and the Beatles, with some variety acts.

The 2,000-seater cinema was sold out for the performance, which began at 9.00 p.m.

On their way to the theatre, the Beatles' Austin Princess had broken down and they completed their journey in a borrowed Cadillac, remaining in their dressing-room until it was time to go on stage. They were introduced shortly before midnight, then a juggling act came on stage. When they finally began their performance there was a mild reception. They didn't make any announcements in French as Trini Lopez had done earlier. A boy dressed up as French rock 'n' roll idol Johnny Hallyday came on to the stage and had to be carted off by Mal Evans. Eventually, when John broke into 'Twist And Shout', and Paul began to sing a Little Richard number, the audience came alive.

Among the celebrities in the audience were Francoise Hardy, Johnny Hallyday, Richard Anthony and Petula Clark.

When they returned to their hotel they received a call from New York informing them that 'I Want To Hold Your Hand' was No. 1 in the American charts.

Circus-Krone-Bau

Venue situated in Marsstrasse, Munich, Germany. The Beatles flew to Munich from London airport at 11.05 a.m. on Thursday, 23 June 1966 on BEA flight BE 502, a Comet aircraft, and on landing ninety minutes later were picked up in a white Mercedes and driven to the Bayerischer Hof Hotel. While there they were presented with a trophy by *Bravo* magazine, which had sponsored the three-venue West German tour, which had been called Bravo Blitztournee.

The following day, 24 June, they presented two shows at the Circus-Krone-Bau, which was basically a winter circus and during summer months was available for rock shows.

The first concert took place at 5.15 p.m. and the second at 9.00 p.m. Cliff Bennett & the Rebel Rousers opened the show, followed by German band the Rattles and then Peter & Gordon. When the Beatles took the stage they wore bottle green suits with green collars and performed 'Rock 'n' Roll Music', 'She's A Woman', 'If I Needed Someone', 'Day Tripper', 'Baby's In Black', 'I Feel Fine', 'Yesterday', 'I Wanna Be Your Man', 'Nowhere Man', 'Paperback Writer' and 'I'm Down'.

The second concert that evening was filmed by the German TV station ZDF (Zweites Deutsches Fernsehen) and transmitted as a 45-minute programme 'Die Beatles' on Tuesday, 5 July at 8.00 p.m.

Cirkus, Lorensbergsparken, Goteborg, Sweden

Third stop on the Beatles' brief tour of Sweden. The group's appearance at the Cirkus on Sunday, 27 October 1963 proved to be one of the busiest of their tour dates as they gave no less than three performances at the venue that day – at 3.00 p.m., 5.00 p.m. and 8.00 p.m.

City Barge, The, No 27 Strand-On-The-Green, London W4

A pleasant riverside pub in Chiswick, London, originally built in 1484. It featured in a scene in *Help!*.

The scene was filmed on 24 April 1965 and stuntmen deputised for the Beatles as the script required them to be hurled through the pub windows!

Interiors of the pub, including the scene where Ringo is trapped in the cellar with a tiger, were actually filmed inside a studio – the City Barge does not have a cellar.

City Hall, Northumberland Road, Newcastle-Upon-Tyne, Northumberland

The Beatles made their debut at this venue on Saturday, 23 March 1963. Their next appearance took place on Saturday 8 June 1963 as part of their tour with Roy Orbison. They headlined their own show when they next appeared at the hall on Saturday, 23 November 1963, and their final appearance took place on Saturday, 4 December 1965.

City Hall, Fisherton Street, Salisbury, Wiltshire

One of the promotions arranged by John Fallon for his Jaybee Clubs. The booking had been settled in April 1963 for a fee of £300. Brian Epstein offered the promoter £200 if he would cancel the gig, but was refused and the group appeared at the venue on 15 June. The hall was packed to capacity and the local newspaper was to report, 'It was the first appearance in Salisbury of a group who shot to fame last year and have been called the most exciting group since the Shadows – the Beatles.

'Queuing for tickets began as early as 3.00 p.m. In all there were about 1,500 teenagers – the largest number ever to attend a personal appearance locally.'

City Hall, Barker's Pool, Sheffield

The penultimate appearance of the Helen Shapiro Tour took place at this venue on Saturday, 2 March 1963. The billing in the local paper read:

ARTHUR HOWES presents
Britain's International Teenage star
HELEN SHAPIRO
Special Guest Star
DANNY WILLIAMS
KENNY LYNCH
THE BEATLES
THE KESTRELS
THE HONEYS
Compere:
DAVE ALLEN
THE RED PRICE BAND

There were two performances, the first at 6.10 p.m., the second at 8.40 p.m., and ticket prices were: Circle 8/6. 6/6. 5/6. Stalls 8/6. 7/-. 5/6. 4/-. Balcony 5/-. 3/6. Platform 3/6.

The group returned to the City Hall two weeks later on Saturday, 16 March as part of another Howes tour, billed locally as:

ARTHUR HOWES presents
(In Association with Evelyn Taylor)
America's exciting
CHRIS MONTEZ
America's fabulous
TOMMY ROE
THE BEATLES
THE VISCOUNTS
THE TERRY YOUNG SET
DEBBIE LEE
TONY MARSH

The ticket prices were the same as those of their previous City Hall appearance.

They next appeared at the City Hall as part of the Roy Orbison Tour on 25 May.

When they returned to the venue later that year, on Saturday, 2 November, they were bill-toppers in their own right.

The local paper, the *Star*, had organised a competition in which six of their readers would win a trip to the ABC Television Studios in Birmingham to meet the Beatles. Reviewing the concert in the *Star*, journalist Francis Mullins called it 'the night when Sheffield went Beatle-barmy' and described how 4,000 'frenzied scream-agers' yelled themselves hoarse during the two shows at the hall.

Three girls in the audience fainted. Seventeen-year-old Joyce Elgie, a secretary from Worksop in Notts was carried from the hall in tears and treated for hysteria by local St John Ambulance men – then allowed to return to the hall to watch the rest of the show.

Reviewing the City Hall concert for the local press was eighteen-year-old Anthea Linacre, a former head girl of Dore and Totley High School in Sheffield, who was training to be a journalist. In her lengthy review, she made some personal assessments of the individual performances:

The image of the Beatles was McCartney, who was delightful. It was he who won the hearts of the audience with his cheeky smile and boyish appeal.

Ringo Starr, the drummer, who, physically, has to take a back seat anyway, was truly the team's anchor. Pleasant and efficient with few frills, he was what we expected.

But George Harrison, the youngest Beatle, his head held low, hiding his lean good looks, was for the most part unanimated. True, he mustered the occasional smile and a shake of his silky brown hair to set his fans swooning.

John Lennon might have been a guard on Buckingham Palace duty for all the movement we received from him. Not an expression crossed his face except when a straw boater floated on to the stage and he had the inspiration to put it on for a moment.

The Beatles rushed off the stage at the end of the show and, escorted by the police and still in their stage clothes, they piled out of a side door, into a waiting car and were off to a hotel in Doncaster. Fans spilled out of the hall quickly, hoping to see their idols, and they refused to budge, even when a police message was put over the loudspeakers that the Beatles were already out of the city.

At midnight there were still over 250 fans milling outside the stage door, convinced that the group hadn't left the venue.

Their final appearance at the City Hall took place on 9 November 1964. Peter and Jeff Stringfellow dropped in to see Epstein at his London office to petition him to ensure that Sheffield was on the itinerary of their next concert tour. The brothers impressed Brian and he not only agreed to the gig, but offered the brothers the opportunity of compering the City Hall concerts that evening instead of the tour compere Bob Bain.

There was one unfortunate muddle that evening. The *Sheffield Star* had a pop music supplement called Top Stars Special and its editor Roy Shepherd had spent weeks arranging with Brian for the Beatles to meet up with Sheila Parkin, the Olympic long jumper, between shows. Sheila was to present the group with their Top Stars Popularity Poll Award. Derek Taylor had phoned Neil Aspinall at 7.30 to let him know about the arrangement, but Sheila was told she wouldn't be able to see them, that they were too tired to meet anyone. She left the hall disappointed and furious at the snub. Derek Taylor commented, 'I can't understand why it happened. The Beatles knew of the arrangements and had agreed to them. All I can say is that this has been a desperate year for them. The night before they came to Sheffield, they played in Liverpool and, after their shows, were surrounded by strange faces.'

When he heard what had happened, Brian personally invited her to meet them in London on an expenses-paid trip where she could make a proper presentation – and Sheila agreed.

The Beatles stayed overnight at the Park Hall Residential

Country Club in Spinhill, near Sheffield, having landed on the lawn in front of the building by helicopter. The club later became the Parkhall Hotel and Restaurant.

City Park Stadium, New Orleans, Louisiana

The Beatles appeared at this venue before an audience of 12,000 fans on Wednesday, 16 September 1964.

During their cavalcade from the airport, hundreds of fans lined the route and the group were taken to the Congress Inn, where they settled in Room 100, a three-room suite. Mayor Schiro had officially declared 16 September as 'Beatles Day' and he presented each of them with a key to the city and also a certificate of honorary citizenship. A local Councilman, Daniel Kelly, arrived at their rooms to present them with the proclamation regarding 'Beatles Day', but never got around to making the presentation.

For the first and only time on the tour, Brian Epstein allowed a newsreel cameraman to film the group's press interview. Among the questions and answers were:

Q: 'What do you think of topless bathing suits?'
George: 'We like them, we've been wearing them for years.'
Q: 'What do you expect to see when you visit Dallas?'
Paul: 'Oil wells.'
Q: You've experienced both – what's the difference between poverty and riches?'
John: 'Money'.
Q: 'Dave Brubeck told the *Dallas News* that America is reaping the harvest from the musical garbage it exported to England years ago. Comment?'
John: 'Quite true.'
Q: 'What is your chief gripe against the United States"?
Paul: 'The quality of your tea.'
Q: 'Will the draft break up your group?'
John: 'There is no draft in England anymore. We'll let you Yanks do the fighting.'
Q: 'Don't you think it's morally wrong to be influencing your fans with your atheist views?'
Paul: 'We're not atheists, we're agnostics. The story which said we're anti-Christ is not true. We simply don't know enough about it.'

After the press conference, much to their delight, the Beatles bumped into Fats Domino and had a long chat with him.

They began playing on stage at the stadium at 9.25 p.m. and

within fifteen minutes several hundred fans rushed on to the field. Police and mounted policemen charged the fans, some wielding nightsticks, although no sticks actually hit any of the teenagers. Ringo said of it later, 'It was like watching the police play stickball with the kids.'

Civic Arena, Auditorium Place, Pittsburgh, Pennsylvania

The Beatles appeared before an audience of 12,603 at the venue on Monday, 14 September 1964. There were 4,000 fans waiting for them at Greater Pittsburgh Airport and when they flew in their escort was far bigger than that given for a presidential visit. There were 120 policemen and deputies, twenty members of the Allied Detective Agency and fifteen members of the Allegheny County Mounted Police. There was a motorcade to the Civic Arena along streets lined with thousands of fans.

The group fielded questions at a press reception at 6.00 p.m. in the venue's conference room, dined and then performed.

They were due to be whisked away in a police car, but it was blocked by fans and they ran through an underground passage to a waiting limousine which sped them back to the airport.

Also on the bill was Clarence 'Frogman' Henry, a singer born in New Orleans in 1937, whose hits included 'Ain't Got No Home', 'But I Do', and 'You Always Hurt The One You Love'.

Incidentally, the promoter who booked the show was Pat DiCesare. He was a 24-year-old entrepreneur who borrowed $5,000 from his father, who mortgaged his home, to gamble on placing a deposit to book the group. His gamble paid off and the concert was a sell-out with attendance topping 12,000. Unfortunately, DiCesare didn't get to see the show – he was drafted!

Civic Hall, Whitby Road, Ellesmere Port, Wirral, Cheshire

Although part of Merseyside and situated only nineteen miles from Liverpool's city centre, this industrial town was to be graced with only one Beatles appearance. This took place at the Civic Hall on 14 January 1963. The group appeared before an audience of 700 people. The dance was organised by the Wolverham Welfare Association.

Clapton, Eric

One of the world's foremost rock guitarists, Eric was born in Ripley, Surrey, on 30 March 1945 and was raised by foster parents.

He took to the guitar at the age of seventeen and his first band was called the Roosters. In October 1963 he joined Casey Jones & the Engineers, but his stint with the band only lasted for seven gigs. The line-up comprised Casey Jones (Brian Casser), vocals; Eric Clapton, guitar; Tom McGuinness, guitar; Dave McCumisky, bass; and Ray Stock, drums. Casser had formerly been the leader of a popular Mersey Beat group Cass & the Cassanovas. Eric then joined the Yardbirds and they supported Billy J. Kramer on a 1964 tour before appearing on *The Beatles Christmas Show* at the Odeon, Hammersmith. It was during the Christmas show that Eric and George Harrison got to know each other and their long and enduring friendship began.

When Eric became a member of Cream, the group was booked to appear at Brian Epstein's Saville Theatre and was also, along with the Beatles, one of the stable of groups with NEMS Enterprises when Epstein brought Robert Stigwood and his discoveries into the company.

Eric's friendship with George Harrison had blossomed and he began to work with him quite closely. 'Badge' was a number he co-wrote with George from a Cream recording – and George played rhythm on the session and was credited as L'Angelo Misterioso. Eric joined George on the recording of Jackie Lomax's 'Sour Milk Sea' and also played on the soundtrack for Harrison's *Wonderwall* album. George also brought him in to perform on the Beatles number 'While My Guitar Gently Weeps'. This created a precedent – bringing in another rock musician into a Beatles session. The event occurred on Friday, 6 September 1968. Eric was giving George a lift into town from Surrey, where they both lived, and on the spur of the moment suggested he join him in the studio to play a solo overdub on the track 'While My Guitar Gently Weeps'. Eric protested – it was unheard of for anyone else to play on a Beatles track, but George told him, 'It's my song!'

Following the break-up of Cream, Eric became part of another supergroup, Blind Faith – but the band only had a short career. His first public appearance after Blind Faith was as a member of the Plastic Ono Band at the Toronto Rock 'n' Roll Revival Show in which he played with Lennon, Klaus Voormann, Alan White and Yoko Ono. Also on the bill were Bo Diddley, Jerry Lee Lewis, Chuck Berry and Little Richard. The group performed rock 'n' roll for half an hour and then Yoko joined them. Clapton said, 'A few people started to boo, but it turned into howling along with Yoko. Yoko has the same effect on people as a high-pitched whistle has on a dog. Her voice is spine-chilling. Very weird. John and I played some feed-back guitar while she was singing.'

Eric also played on 'Cold Turkey' and appeared at the Unicef Concert at the Lyceum, along with George, John and Yoko on 15 December 1969.

He joined George Harrison for recording sessions at Olympic Studios, along with Rich Grech, Denny Laine and Trevor Burton, but they proved abortive.

Eric became obsessed with George Harrison's wife Pattie and wrote a love song for her on his double album *Layla And Other Assorted Love Songs*. He said at the time, 'It was actually about an emotional experience, a woman that I felt deeply about and who turned me down, and I had to kind of pour it out in some way. It was the heaviest thing going at the time. I didn't consciously do it, though, it just happened that way. That was what I wanted to write about most of all.' Describing how the affair began, Eric Clapton said that George had, 'Once grabbed one of my chicks and so I thought I'd get even with him one day, on a petty level, and it grew from that, you know. She was trying to attract his attention, trying to make him jealous, so she used me, you see, and I fell madly in love with her.'

His emotional problems led to him becoming a heroin addict and when he travelled to New York to appear on the *Concert For Bangladesh*, which was taking place in August 1971, he was too sick to attend rehearsals at Nola Studios and Jesse Ed Davis was brought in to play second lead to George. On the night before the concert, Eric didn't attend the last run through – but he did manage to turn up for the actual concert.

When Eric performed some solos on George's numbers, his record company didn't like it, so Ringo suggested he use the pseudonym 'Eddie Clayton', which was no doubt due to the fact that Ringo was once a member of the Eddie Clayton Skiffle Group. Eric was to appear on a number of George's albums, including *All Things Must Pass* and *The Concert For Bangladesh*.

The two appeared on a European tour with Delaney and Bonnie and over the years teamed up on a number of occasions, including a concert at Guildford Civic Hall on 7 December 1978 and a *Prince's Trust Rock Gala* on 5 and 6 June 1987, along with Ringo. George also joined Eric on a twelve-show tour of Japan in December 1990.

Strangely enough, their friendship, although strained, didn't bust up when Eric wooed George's wife Pattie and eventually married her.

Clarabella

A number popularised by American group the Jodimars in 1956, although it wasn't a hit. The Beatles introduced it into their repertoire and performed it during 1960, 1961 and 1962 with Paul McCartney on lead vocals. A radio version of the number from the show 'Pop Go The Beatles' was included on *The Beatles Live At The BBC* CD.

Cleveland Stadium, Cleveland, Ohio

The Beatles appeared at this massive baseball stadium, home of the Cleveland Indians, on Sunday, 14 August 1966. The stadium had a capacity of 50,000, but as parts of the rear-of-stage areas had a poor view, the tickets were limited to 30,000. Due to the size of the stadium there was only one show that evening, but crowds of fans poured on to the actual field and the appearance by support acts the Cyrkle and the Ronettes were delayed for half an hour while police tried to control the crowd. When the Beatles did appear the show was held up as 2,500 fans invaded the field while the group were playing 'Day Tripper'.

Cliff Bennett & The Rebel Rousers

Originally formed in 1961, by Cliff Bennett from Slough, who got the group together primarily for German bookings. It was while they were in Germany that they made many friends among the Liverpool bands while appearing at the Star Club.

The group comprised Cliff Bennett (vocals), Dave Wendells (lead guitar), Maurice Groves (sax), Sid Phillips (sax), Roy Young (keyboards), Frank Allen (bass guitar) and Mike Burt (drums). When Frank Allen left the band in 1964 to join the Searchers, he was replaced by Bobby Thompson from Kingsize Taylor & the Dominoes. In one of his later bands, Cliff employed Howie Casey, Liverpool's famous sax player.

They were respected but remained unsuccessful until 1964 when they had a hit with 'One Way Love'. The Beatles had recommended the band to Brian Epstein who then signed them to NEMS Enterprises and Paul McCartney produced the group performing the *Revolver* album number 'Got To Get You Into My Life'. Issued on Parlophone 5489 on 5 August 1966 in Britain and on ABC 10842 in America on 29 August 1966. The record reached No. 6 in the British charts.

Cliff Bennett & The Rebel Rousers also joined the bill of the Beatles' tour of Germany and Japan in June 1966.

Paul next produced their *Got To Get You Into My Life* album, issued by Parlophone on PCS 7017 on 27 January 1967 in Britain. The group were never to achieve recording success again and disbanded in 1969.

Cliff went on to form a few more bands, including Toe Fat and Shanghai, before retiring from the music world for good.

Cliff Roberts & The Rockers

A Liverpool group who were one of the handful of bands chosen to audition for Larry Parnes and Billy Fury at the Wyvern Club on Tuesday, 10 May 1960. The Rockers appeared after Cass & the Cassanovas, Derry & the Seniors and Gerry & the Pacemakers, and immediately before the Silver Beetles.

Cliff and his group were on the Saturday, 14 May 1960 bill at Lathom Hall when the Silver Beats (this was the only time they used this name) auditioned that night for promoter Brian Kelly. The Rockers were also the house band at the Grosvenor Ballroom, Liscard, during several of the Beatles' appearances there in 1961. Among the other gigs they shared with the Beatles was 'The Beatles Farewell Show' at Aintree Institute on Saturday, 11 March 1961.

Clivedon, Buckinghamshire

The country house of Lord Astor, which doubled as Buckingham Palace during the filming of *Help!* in 1965. The scene in which the Beatles play cards was filmed in the luxurious Madam Pompadour room and Lord Astor himself treated the four to a cup of tea – poured from a grecian urn!

C'mon Everybody

The last of three Eddie Cochran hits in the American charts. 'C'mon Everybody' reached No. 35 in the US in 1959, although it reached No. 6 in Britain the same year.

The Quarry Men introduced the song into their repertoire that year and continued to perform the number when they became the Beatles.

Cochran, Eddie

Legendary American rock 'n' roll singer born in Oklahoma in 1938. Cochran appeared in a few movies, including *The Girl Can't Help It* and *Untamed Youth*, and had three chart hits in America with 'Sittin' In The Balcony', 'Summertime Blues' and 'C'mon Everybody', although he wrote and recorded several other numbers which became rock classics.

Cochran was due to appear on a major show at Liverpool Stadium on 3 May 1960 with Gene Vincent, but was killed in a road accident on 17 April 1960 in Wiltshire, England. In June, his 'Three Steps To Heaven' topped the British charts and became his biggest British hit, although it failed to make the charts in America.

The singer was one of the Beatles' early influences and they included four of his songs in their repertoire, 'Three Steps To Heaven', 'Twenty Flight Rock', 'I Remember' and 'C'mon Everybody'.

Cocker, Joe

A singer who was born in Sheffield on 20 May 1944. He began his career in 1961 with the Cavaliers, who changed their name to Vance Arnold & the Avengers. Joe was offered a one-record deal by Decca in 1964 and recorded a lavish version of 'Georgia On My Mind' with orchestral backing. At the Decca board meeting to select new releases, Dick Rowe turned the single down and Joe had to go into the studio and record another number quickly. He reluctantly recorded the Beatles' 'I'll Cry Instead'. Supporting him on the record was guitarist Big Bill Sullivan and vocal backing was from the Ivy League. The single failed to register and it was reported that Joe only received the equivalent of 50 pence in royalties.

His biggest hit was another Lennon and McCartney number, 'With A Little Help From My Friends'. Cocker decided to record it in 3/4 time and the single reached the top of the charts. He was also to perform it at the Woodstock Festival. A friend took the single to Apple and played it to the Beatles, who sent Joe a telegram: 'The Record's Absolutely Great. Love. John. Paul. George And Ringo.' They also took out some press advertisements in praise of the record.

Joe was invited up to Apple and initially met George, who sang 'Old Brown Shoe' and 'Something' for him. Joe later recorded 'Something'. Later that same afternoon, Paul arrived and played Joe a couple of songs on the piano. One of the numbers was 'Golden Slumbers' and Joe told Paul: 'I'd love to record that one.' Paul told him he couldn't have it, but offered him 'She Came In Through The Bathroom Window', which he did record. The number gave him a Top 30 entry in the US and he was to base himself in America from the 1970s.

Later in his career he was also to record 'You've Got To Hide Your Love Away'.

Cogan, Alma

Britain's top female singer of the fifties who had twenty records in the charts. She became such a close friend of Brian Epstein that there were even rumours that they would marry. Alma attended many parties with the Beatles and became a good friend of theirs. Immediately prior to their June 1964 tour they attended Alma's birthday party at her home at 4 Stafford Court, Kensington, where she lived with her mother, Faye. Other guests included Brian Epstein, Noel Coward, Sir Joseph Lockwood, George Martin, Chuck Berry and Carl Perkins.

Her last few records were covers of Lennon & McCartney songs.

On 11 November 1965 her version of 'Yesterday' (Columbia DB 7757) was released and later in the month, on 28 November, her double 'A' side 'Eight Days A Week'/'Help!' (Columbia DB 7786) was issued. John and Paul attended her recording session for 'Eight Days A Week' on 9 October 1965.

Tragically, she died of cancer at the age of 34 on 26 October 1966.

Twenty years later when EMI released the double album *Alma Cogan: A Celebration*, there was a gatefold sleeve picturing Alma with the Beatles and a brief sleeve note penned by Paul McCartney.

Coleman, Ray

He was a journalist with the *Manchester Evening News, Brighton Evening Argus* and *Leicester Evening Mail* before becoming a music journalist and joining *Melody Maker* in 1960. He later became editor of *Disc & Music Echo*. When John Lennon became disenchanted with the fortunes of Apple, he told Ray all about it for an interview which appeared in *Disc & Music Echo* on 18 January 1969. This was the interview in which John told him that Apple was losing money every week. John said, 'If it carries on like this, all of us will be broke in the next six months.' As a result of the article, Allen Klein made his move to take control of the Beatles. Paul McCartney was upset about the piece and, when Ray dropped into the Apple office, told him, 'This is only a small company and you're trying to wreck it. You know John shoots his mouth off and doesn't mean it.'

Ray became editor-in-chief of *Melody Maker* in 1970 and at the end of the decade left the publication to become a full-time biographer. In 1984 he wrote the two-volume work *John Winston Lennon* and *John Ono Lennon*, with the co-operation of Cynthia Lennon and Yoko Ono. The following year *Survivor*, his authorised biography of Eric Clapton, was published. He also penned the first major autobiography of the Beatles' manager, *Brian Epstein: the Man Who Made the Beatles,* in 1989, with the co-operation of Epstein's family. His last Beatles-related book was *Paul McCartney: Yesterday & Today*.

Ray died of cancer on Wednesday, 10 September 1996 at the age of 59. Paul McCartney was to comment, 'Ray was a lovely man and much admired by everyone in the business. He had a marvellous sense of humour and a good heart.'

Coleman, Sid

Coleman was manager of EMI's own publishing company Ardmore & Beechwood, when he played his part in the Beatles' story in 1962.

In April of that year, Brian Epstein was in London seeking a recording contract for the group. He'd been turned down by a number of labels, but was now armed with the tapes of their Decca audition. He went to EMI's HMV Shop in Oxford Street which offered the service of transferring tapes to disc. Epstein went into the store and made his way to the room where acetates were made. In his autobiography he mentions meeting Kenneth Boast, 'an exceedingly pleasant and interesting executive with the HMV Retail Store within the mighty EMI company'.

The man transferring the tapes to disc was engineer Ted Huntley who, noticing that a number of the songs were originals, commented: 'I don't think these are at all bad.' He told Boast, and Brian was asked if he'd be interested in meeting Coleman, who had an office on the top floor of the building. Brian, keen on any beneficial contacts, agreed and Boast phoned Coleman who asked Brian to come straight up.

He listened to the tapes and asked Brian if they had a recording contract. Together with his assistant Kim Bennett he believed that the group had something and offered to publish two of the songs, 'Love Of The Loved' and 'Hello Little Girl'. Brian demurred, saying he'd prefer to have a recording contract before agreeing to any publishing deal. Coleman considered the EMI A&R men – Norrie Paramor, Wally Ridley and Norman Newall – however, all had groups on their books, so he called George Martin's office. George's secretary Judy Lockhart-Smith answered and a meeting was arranged for the following day.

There are some conflicting reports regarding the actual details of the initial contact. Bennett is reported to have said that Martin took some persuading, that he wasn't keen initially on the meeting with Epstein. Martin, on the other hand, in his autobiography says his response, on receiving the call from Coleman, was: 'Certainly, I'm willing to listen to anything. Ask him to come and see me.'

Martin did take the Beatles and they transformed the fortunes of EMI. Unfortunately, Ardmore & Beechwood did such a poor job promoting 'Love Me Do' that Brian decided not to sign with the company.

In his autobiography *All You Need Is Ears* Martin points out that on the release of 'Love Me Do': 'Ardmore & Beechwood, the EMI publishers, whose Sid Coleman had first put Brian Epstein on to me, did virtually nothing about getting the record played.' Yet Ted King, an ex-Radio Luxembourg DJ working for BBC radio at the time on 'Twelve O'Clock Spin', was one of the first people to play 'Love Me Do' because he said he was pressured to do so by Kim Bennett of Ardmore & Beechwood.

Coliseum, Seattle, Washington

The Beatles' concert on Friday, 21 August 1964 drew 14,045 fans and there were 50 police, four deputies, a fire chief and fourteen firemen plus 100 Navy volunteers to control them.

There was a backstage press conference and as the Beatles were walking back to their dressing room a girl fell 25 feet down an air vent on to the concrete floor in front of Ringo. When she came to he asked, 'Are you sure you're all right, luv?' and she ran away into the crowd. Among the visitors to their dressing room was Charmaine Smith, the current Miss Teenage America, who later commented, 'They're really nice. As soon as the kids find something new, the Beatles will be on the way out.'

The group went on stage at 9.30 p.m. and finished at 10.00 p.m., but it took them over an hour to leave the stadium. Their Cadillac, sent ahead on a dummy run, was swamped by fans who squashed the trunk, caved in the roof and ripped off the door handles. The group finally made their escape in a darkened ambulance.

The venue was also the site of one of the final appearances they made in America at the end of their last tour, on Thursday, 25 August 1966. There were two performances with only 8,200 tickets sold for the matinee show, although the evening concert was sold out.

Rumours abounded that Paul and Jane Asher were meeting in Seattle and were getting married there following the evening show. When asked about it, Paul said, 'Tonight? Yeah. I'm not confirming it. It's a joke. How did it all start, does anybody know?' He was then asked if he knew Jane. He winked and said, 'Yeah. I've heard of her.' George commented, 'If she comes in tonight, we'll miss her. We're going out tonight.'

During their press conference, the Beatles were made honorary citizens of Washington State.

The gross income of the concerts was $118,071, the biggest single day's gross in entertainment history in Seattle.

Collection Of Beatles Oldies (But Goldies), A

EMI wanted to have a new Beatles album available for the Christmas market at the end of 1966, although *Revolver* had only been issued in August and was still gathering sales. The group's new album project *Sgt Pepper's Lonely Hearts Club Band* wouldn't be ready for some months, so the record company assembled this collection of tracks, compiling various previously released album and singles tracks. One of the tracks, 'Bad Boy', hadn't been available in Britain before, although it had been included on the American album release *Beatles VI*.

It was issued in Britain on Parlophone PCS 7016 on 9 December 1966 and reached No. 6 in the charts, becoming the first Beatles album not to hit the top spot.

The tracks were, Side One: 'She Loves You', 'From Me To You', 'We Can Work It Out', 'Help!', 'Michelle', 'Yesterday', 'I Feel Fine', 'Yellow Submarine'. Side Two: 'Can't Buy Me Love', 'Bad Boy', 'Day Tripper', 'A Hard Day's Night', 'Ticket To Ride', 'Paperback Writer', 'Eleanor Rigby', 'I Want To Hold Your Hand'.

The front cover was a painting designed by David Christian and the back cover featured a photograph of the Beatles by Bob Whitaker.

Collingham, Anne

Fictitious head of the Beatles Fan Club in Britain. When Tony Barrow was involved in the organisation of the Beatles Fan Club from offices in Monmouth Street in London he created the name Anne Collingham. The name was even used aside a regular column of fan club news in *Beatles Monthly* and a photograph of 'Anne Collingham' appeared in the publication. This was a picture of one of the several girls who worked full-time on the fan club from the Monmouth Street offices.

Collins, Joe

Born into a large London Jewish family in 1902, Collins' first job was as an office boy with Moss Empires. He later set up a business partnership with Lew Grade and for over fifty years was at the heart of British showbusiness. Two of his daughters found fame, Joan as an actress and Jackie as an author. He initially booked the Beatles in February 1963 for a summer ball for the *People* newspaper, but the newspaper later cancelled the engagement. He was then asked to help set up the first Beatles Christmas Show and booked them into the Astoria, Finsbury Park, for two weeks, engaging Peter Yolland as producer and Rolf Harris. He was to say, 'When I looked at the printed programme for that Christmas show, I noted the credit I had been given: "Brian Epstein wishes to acknowledge with gratitude the invaluable assistance of Joe Collins in the presentation." I was actually co-producer.' He met the Beatles for the first time on opening night. He continued his association with Brian Epstein who asked him to co-produce the next Beatles Christmas Show with him at the Odeon, Hammersmith. He also co-produced Gerry's Christmas Cracker for Brian, but it didn't prove as successful as the Beatles' shows.

Joe was backstage with the Beatles on a number of occasions and noticed how they sought a bit of peace and quiet in their dressing room and were often irritated by visitors.

He was with them at the Odeon, Hammersmith, when a Scandinavian representative of EMI came into the dressing room. He sat around for a while, watching them tune their guitars and he tried to make conversation.

'Tell me, what is the best thing about being a Beatle?' asked the rep. John Lennon looked at him and without registering any expression on his face said, 'Best thing about being a Beatle? Well, I guess it has to be that we meet EMI sales reps from all over the world.'

Colston Hall, Bristol, Avon

The Beatles made their debut at this venue on 15 March 1963 as part of the Tommy Roe/Chris Montez tour. Their second appearance took place during their autumn tour on 15 November 1963.

10 November 1964 saw the last gig of the Beatles' UK tour at the venue and the manager of the hall, Ken Cowley, was furious when an incident occurred as they finished 'If I Fell' and were about to begin their finale. Four local students had managed to gain access to the stage lighting gantries and they tipped bags of flour on to the Beatles' heads. However, the lads took it in good spirit, shook the flour from their guitars and carried on.

Come And Get It

A number which Paul McCartney composed for the Ringo Starr film *The Magic Christian*. Before the Beatles gathered for a recording session on Thursday, 24 July 1969, Paul went into Abbey Road's No. 2 studio and cut a demo disc of the number.

It had been decided that Apple band Badfinger would sing the song over the titles of the movie and Paul produced their version of the song at Abbey Road on 2 April 1969.

The single was issued in Britain on 5 December 1969 on Apple 20 and reached No. 4 in the British charts. It was issued in America on Apple 1815 on 12 January 1970. Paul's original demo, featuring himself on vocals, drums, bass and piano was included on the Beatles' *Anthology 3* CDs.

Come Together

The song had its origins when Timothy Leary was planning a life in politics, intending to stand for the Governorship of California, and his wife asked John Lennon if he could write a campaign song. John began writing the number, but Leary's visions of a political career crumbled when he was imprisoned for his advocacy of drugs.

When John was initially composing the tune he said he was writing obscurely round an old Chuck Berry tune called 'You Can't

Catch Me'. He added. 'I left the line in, "Here come old flat-top".
It is nothing like the Chuck Berry song, but they took me to court
because I admitted the influence once years ago.'

A settlement was made in which John agreed to include two
Chuck Berry songs on an album, which resulted in 'You Can't
Catch Me' and 'Sweet Little Sixteen' being featured on his 1975
album, *Rock 'n' Roll*.

The court action wasn't the only problem associated with the
song. John had mentioned the words 'Coca Cola' and the BBC
banned the number because it broke their code regarding advertising on TV.

'Come Together' was the last song recorded for the *Abbey Road*
album and was the first track on the LP. The number was also used
as the flipside of the single 'Something' and also included on the
compilation album *The Beatles 1967–1970*.

It was one of the numbers John performed at the *One To One*
concert in August 1972.

Aerosmith performed the song in the film *Sgt Pepper's Lonely
Hearts Club Band* in 1978 and their single of the song reached No.
20 in the American charts that year. Take One of the Beatles' original Abbey Road Studios recording was included on the Beatles'
Anthology 3 CDs.

Comic Books

Over the years the Beatles have been the subject of several comic
strips.

They appeared in the American Dell Comics' *Strange Tales*, No.
130, in March 1964. This issue featured a story entitled 'Human
Torch and the Thing Meet the Beatles'. Dell also published a special
Beatles comic in the autumn of 1964, named *The Beatles*. The
comic was one of their 'Dell Giant' series and was a strip outlining
the group's history to that date. There were also pin-up stories and
some text on the individual members.

In September 1964 DC Comics featured a story, 'Redheaded Beatle
of 1000 BC', in Issue 79 of their *Jimmy Olsen* comic. The group
were also included in *Batman* No. 222 and were featured on the
covers of a number of comics aimed at girls, including *Girls Romance*
No. 109, *Heart Throbs* No. 101, *My Little Margie* No. 54 and
Summer Love Nos. 46, 47 and 48. Issue 121 of *Mad*, published in
September 1968, sported a cover with Alfred E. Neuman as the
Maharishi Mahesh Yogi with caricatures of the Beatles.

In 1968 Gold Key Comics, published by the Western Publishing
Company in the US, issued *Yellow Submarine*, which was the story
of the film related in comic form.

The most interesting seventies comic book venture was the Marvel 'Super Special' edition of *The Beatle Story*, with visuals by George Perez and Klaus Jenson. Oddly, the illustrations seemed to evoke the atmosphere of the forties rather than the sixties – Brian Epstein is seen stalking off into a rainy night, dressed in trilby and raincoat, like some denizen of a film noir tale. Liverpool's tiny Casbah Club is depicted as a spacious nightclub, peopled by sophisticated couples sitting at tiny round tables. The Beatles themselves are shown using expensive equipment, whereas in those days they didn't even have mike stands.

The group are depicted as a bunch of Cockneys in the comic, continually calling each other 'Mate', and using words such as 'ruddy' and 'blooming'. At one point Paul says, 'This is ruddy insane, we're getting gongs!'; at another George says, 'Stress doesn't bother me like it did before, mates'; and Ringo comments, 'It'll tie in ruddy well with the TV taping, too.'

Published in 1978, *The Beatles Story* contains 39 pages of comic strip in colour, supplemented by several articles and photographs, including a pin-up poster, discography, filmography and group history.

The following year the Pendulum 'Illustrated Biography' series issued *Elvis Presley/The Beatles*, a comic book tracing the careers of both acts.

The most significant strip devoted to the Beatles appeared as a serial in the British teen paper *Look In* in 1981, under the name 'The Beatles Story'. The complete strip was published in April 1982 as a *TV Times/Look In Special*. The strip was padded out with thirteen photographs, three of which were in colour.

The strip's artist was Arthur Ranson and the text was written by Angus P. Allan. Ranson produced some exquisite black-and-white drawings, based on well-known Beatles photographs.

Unfortunately, the words that Allan put into the Beatles' mouths were not as accurately conceived as the illustrations, although their absurdity is, at times, extremely amusing.

Despite the passage of years which has elapsed since the Beatles disbanded, new books and magazines are published regularly – and the same applies to comic books. An eight-issue series called *The Beatles Experience* is a bi-monthly comic launched in March 1991 by Revolutionary Comics of San Diego, California. The text is by Todd Loven and the illustrations by Mike Sagara.

In November 1991, Personality Comics of New York issued a series of four comics entitled *Personality Comics Presents The Beatles*, each one devoted to an individual member of the group.

Concert For Bangladesh, The

George Harrison's most ambitious project, coming almost a year after the Beatles had disbanded, led to speculation that the *Concert for Bangladesh* in August 1971 would see the Beatles reunite on stage. It wasn't to be.

Ravi Shankar, distraught by the horrific events in his country, appealed to George for ideas on a way to help the refugee problem out there. The civil war in Pakistan, with the western sector fighting the eastern sector which had declared itself as the nation of Bangladesh, had resulted in the exodus of ten million refugees into India. A million people had died from disease and starvation and there were countless orphaned children.

Ravi had in mind a modest concert, hoping to raise an amount in the region of £25,000. George once again proved his entrepreneurial skills, aiming for a brilliantly ambitious concert that would provide a souvenir three-album set, a television special and a cinema film. The project was destined to earn almost $15 million for the troubled country of Bangladesh.

George immediately began contacting musician friends of his and spent the month of June and the early part of July 1971 phoning fellow musicians. On a visit to Disneyland with Peter Sellers and Ravi Shankar it was suggested that Peter Sellars be compere of the event. However, as he was involved in the post-production of *Being There*, George took on the task. Mick Jagger had just settled in France and was unable to obtain a visa in time.

George decided to hold the concert at a venue where he could obtain maximum promotional exposure and chose Madison Square Garden in New York City. He set the date for Sunday, 1 August 1971.

The Beatles had last made an appearance at Candlestick Park in San Francisco in 1966, and it was just possible that George might have pulled off the ultimate coup and gathered them together again for the gig. Ringo Starr, who was filming *Blindman* in Spain, was one of the first people George called, and he immediately agreed to appear. John Lennon also agreed to appear but, when he arrived, the ever present Yoko was at his shoulder. She became quite furious when George quietly explained that he would only be requiring John's presence on stage and not hers. Yoko created such a scene with John that there was a violent argument. John's glasses were broken, he furiously left her and travelled to the airport for the first plane to Europe – and ended up in Paris. Yoko had dreamed of appearing at the concert and wanted to make New York their new home. Within a few days they had both cooled down and were reunited at Tittenhurst Park, only to leave England and settle in America for good the next month.

Paul felt that the Beatles had only recently split up and considered that it would be pointless if one of the first moves was to get back together again. He said he'd only agree if the other three would drop the legal action against him instigated because of his wishes for a legal dissolution of the Beatles. This was unacceptable to them at the time.

There were to be two performances that August evening at the 20,000 seater arena and both shows completely sold out within six hours of the box office opening.

The Bangladesh Concert was Eric Clapton's only appearance for a long time. He'd ceased appearing the previous year and was not to perform again until 1973. The problem was his addiction to hard drugs. When he arrived in New York, he sent his girlfriend Alice Ormsby-Gore, daughter of the former British Ambassador, out on to the streets trying to score heroin for him. Eric was terribly ill the night before the concert and didn't attend the rehearsals at the West 57th Street studios. Jesse Ed Davis was ready to take over as Clapton's stand-in. Allen Klein arranged for Dr William Zahm to treat him and on the day he was able to appear on stage.

The concert opened when George introduced Ravi Shankar who began a stirring set of Indian music – Ravi on sitar, backed by Ali Akbar Khan on sarod and Alla Rakha on tabla and Kamala Chakravarty on tamboura. A bearded George then appeared on stage in a white suit and orange shirt and opened with 'Wah-Wah'. Ringo Starr was on drums, Eric Clapton on guitar, Leon Russell on piano, Billy Preston on keyboards, Jesse Ed Davis on electric guitar, Jim Horn leading a brass section, Jim Keltner on drums, Klaus Voormann on bass, Claudia Linnear leading a nine-piece gospel chorale and three members of Badfinger playing acoustic guitars. The ensemble performed 'My Sweet Lord', 'Awaiting On You All', 'Beware Of Darkness', 'That's The Way God Planned It' (a Billy Preston showpiece), 'It Don't Come Easy' (Ringo's showpiece), 'Jumpin Jack Flash'/'Young Blood' (Leon Russell's showpiece), 'While My Guitar Gently Weeps' (the genius of Eric Clapton), 'Something', 'Here Comes The Sun', the latter performed by George, who played six-string acoustic guitar, as did Peter Ham of Badfinger. George then introduced Bob Dylan, saying 'I'd like to bring on a friend of us all – Mister Bob Dylan.'

Dylan, now also sporting a beard, appeared dressed in jeans and a denim jacket and opened with 'A Hard Rain's Gonna Fall' and followed with 'Mr Tambourine Man', 'Blowin' In The Wind', 'It Takes A Lot To Laugh, It Takes A Train To Cry' and 'Just Like A Woman'. He was joined on the last number by

George on slide guitar, Ringo on tambourine and Russell on bass. George finished the set with a performance of the number 'Bangladesh'.

There was a party after the show and guests included the Who and Grand Funk Railroad.

CBS TV broadcast a version of the concert and a film was also made, directed by Saul Swimmer and distributed by 20th Century Fox. This was premiered the following year on 23 March 1972 in New York. George had worked with the director on the film, putting together the best excerpts from both shows, and Bob Dylan had also involved himself in the editing of the 4 hours of footage into 90 minutes of screen time. It was originally screened in thirteen major cities on 70mm film with six-track sound. There was also a version issued for general release in 35mm film with four-track sound. The movie was previewed at New York's DeMille Theatre and among the celebrity guests were John and Yoko, Jerry Rubin and Nino Tempo, although John left the cinema in the middle of Dylan's performance.

This, the first of the legendary rock-charity events, was soured by the intransigence of the income tax officials who insisted on their pound of flesh, despite the worthiness of the cause. Record companies had waived their royalties, but the British and American governments insisted on heavily taxing the event. George commented, 'The law and tax people do not help. They make it so that it is not worthwhile doing anything decent.' George lobbied in Britain and even had a two-hour meeting with Patrick Jenkins, a governmental financial undersecretary, which had been arranged for him by MP Jeffrey Archer. No matter how sincerely George presented the case of the suffering innocents of Bangladesh and how urgently they needed help, he was facing hard-nosed officialdom. Jenkins was unmoved, he refused to waive demands for tax. 'Perhaps you people would prefer it if I were to move out of England, like virtually every other major British pop star, and take my money with me?' said George. 'That, sir, would, of course, be entirely up to you,' said Jenkins. Naturally, sickened by this unyielding attitude, George personally paid a cheque for one million pounds to the tax authorities.

Difficulties arose with the triple album, with record dealers charging extra money for the package, and pocketing it. UNICEF was able to receive an early cheque for $243,418.50, the proceeds of the concert itself, but the rest of the urgently needed money took almost a decade to collect, with accusations being made against Allen Klein regarding the financial administration, which he took legal action against and then dropped.

Concert Hall, Argyle Street, Glasgow, Scotland

The Beatles appeared at this venue only once. Their performance on 5 October 1965 was the opening night of a three-day tour of Scotland, promoted by Albert Bonici.

Condon, Richard

American author of several best-sellers, including *The Manchurian Candidate*.

When a property for the Beatles' third film was being considered, United Artists' head of production Bud Ornstein suggested Condon's novel *A Talent For Loving*. Condon was an old friend of his and he loved the book and suggested to Brian Epstein and the Beatles that they buy the film rights, which they did. The novel was a Western, set in 1871 and concerned a dramatic horse race set over distances of hundreds of miles.

A meeting was arranged between Condon and John Lennon in which the author discussed his ideas on the treatment of the film with John.

On 10 February 1965 it was announced in the press as their third movie, which was to be financed by Brian Epstein's Pickfair Films, a company he formed with Bud Ornstein on 21 December 1964. On 16 June 1965 it was announced that the film was postponed due to weather conditions in Spain, where it was to be filmed, and on 13 December it was announced that the project had been abandoned because the Beatles couldn't fit it into their heavy schedule.

In fact, the real reason seems to be that the Beatles weren't satisfied with Condon's script.

They decided to tell the author personally and arranged for him to fly to London where they gave him their reasons for not continuing with the project.

When Ornstein moved to Paramount he talked the studio into producing it and the film was made in 1968 with Richard Widmark and Topol. The Beatles still owned the property and had a share in the profits.

Connolly, Ray

A Merseyside writer who was a student of social anthropology at the London School of Economics. He then became a journalist writing for the *Liverpool Daily Post* before graduating to Britain's largest evening newspaper, the *Evening Standard* in London. When he joined the paper in 1967 as a columnist specialising in the show-business field, he wrote about the Beatles on numerous occasions and interviewed them regularly.

Several of his Beatles interviews were collected in his book *Stardust Memories*, published in Britain by Pavilion in 1983. They included his first interview with Paul, which took place at the Cavendish Avenue house. Their conversation touched on a number of topics, ranging from the *Magical Mystery Tour* film to the group's forthcoming trip to India. An interview with Ringo was conducted in March 1968 and Connolly painted a happy picture of Ringo's home in Weybridge and his life with his wife Maureen and son Zak. His interview with Yoko Ono took place in October 1968 and began with a chat about the *Two Virgins* album and *Bottoms* film. The rest of the interview covered her childhood and years prior to meeting with John. Another interview with Paul took place in a Soho restaurant in April 1970 and was a detailed discussion of the Beatles' breakup. Later that year, Ray interviewed John at Tittenhurst Park. Yoko also joined in the conversation, which concentrated on John's solo career.

He became a confidant and learned many of their secrets, the biggest of which was the story of John's intention to leave the Beatles. Ray respected John's wishes that he keep the story on ice. Four months later, Paul was able to make his own announcement to the press and John regretted that he had asked Ray to withhold the story.

Ray also travelled to Toronto and stayed at Ronnie Hawkins' farm during John and Yoko's visit there. After John's period of being househusband, Ray was one of the journalists invited to New York to interview John about his future plans. His interview was set for 9 December 1980. On 8 December Yoko called him to inform him of the tragedy.

Connolly is one of a handful of major freelance columnists in Britain and his writings frequently appear in publications ranging from the *Sunday Times* to the *Standard*. His books/film scripts include *That'll Be The Day* and *Stardust*, the latter winning him the Writers' Guild of Great Britain Award for the best original screenplay.

Among his published works is a biography of John entitled *John Lennon: 1940–1980*, published by Fontana in 1981. Among his unpublished works is a brilliant film screenplay on the life of John Lennon called *Working Class Hero*.

Continuing Story Of Bungalow Bill, The

A song which John wrote when he was at the Maharishi's ashram in India. He commented that it 'was written about a guy in Maharishi's meditation camp who took a short break to go shoot a few poor tigers, and then came back to commune with God. There used to be a comic character called Jungle Jim, and I combined him with Buffalo Bill. It's a sort of teenage social comment song, and a bit of a joke.'

During the recording session on Tuesday, 8 October 1968 Yoko Ono spoke one line of the song and Maureen Starkey joined in on the chorus. Chris Thomas played mellotron on the track which was featured on *The Beatles* white album.

Convention Center, Philadelphia, Pennsylvania

Mersey Beat reader Sheila Dress of Pennsylvania wrote to the Liverpool-based newspaper about the Beatles' appearance here on 2 September 1964.

Their concert in Philadelphia on 2 September was exactly the same (as the Atlantic City one) except that it started at 8 o'clock. One act, the Righteous Brothers, was replaced by Clarence 'Frogman' Henry. Unfortunately, we didn't have such good seats in Philadelphia as Atlantic City, so we couldn't see as well. We could hear them all right though.

Philadelphia's Convention Hall is smaller than Atlantic City's, so there were only about 12,037 teenagers there. The kids were much noisier though and everyone had to stand on the back of their seats to see anything because the seats weren't elevated.

Rose DeWolf, reporter for the *Inquirer*, wrote of the Philadelphia Press Conference: 'The Beatles were asked, "What's the best city you've ever played in?" They answered, "Liverpool".'

Another newspaper reported a question and answer session with the group:

Q (to Paul McCartney): 'Do you find any difference in teenagers of different countries you visit?'
A: 'Only in their accents.'
Q: 'What do you think of serious music?'
A (Lennon): 'It's rock 'n' roll. Of course, all music is serious, it depends on who's listening to it.'
Q: 'What do you know of Elvis Presley?'
A (Ringo Starr): 'Some of his earlier stuff is good. Don't care for what he's been doing recently.'
Q: 'Where would you be with crew-cuts?'
A (Lennon): 'I don't think it would make any difference. Our sound was the original thing. The funny part came later.'

The police chief in Philadelphia spent two weeks preparing for the Beatles' appearance there and Ringo told him: 'You chaps gave us the safest and most protection we've had in any city.'

Convention Hall, Atlantic City, New Jersey

George Hamid, who owned the Steel Pier in Atlantic City, had booked the Beatles to appear at the Convention Hall three days after the Democratic Party National Convention had been held there, on 30 August 1964.

Despite the fact that the population of Atlantic City was only 60,000, the concert was completely sold out in advance, with over 19,000 fans crammed into the hall.

Police were stationed outside the hall at 5.00 p.m. as there were already almost 1,000 fans gathered. When the Beatles' party arrived almost an hour later, the crowds surged forward. A fan jumped in between a radio car and the Beatles' limousine and had her legs jammed between the vehicles.

The police helped the group to get into the stage door and a press conference took place, supervised by Derek Taylor. There were various questions, one of which asked, of all the cities they had been to, which one did they like most and Lennon answered, 'Liverpool'.

A 15 ft high platform had been specially erected in front of the stage and the group played on this, protected from the audience, who remained in their seats, by a line of eighteen policemen.

After the show, it seemed it would be impossible for them to leave the hall in the limousine. A marked laundry truck was requested and the Beatles climbed inside and made their escape.

Mersey Beat printed a report of the Beatles in Atlantic City and Philadelphia by reader Sheila Dress, who came from Philadelphia. She wrote: 'The Fab Four were in Atlantic City's Convention Hall on Sunday, 30 August, and their concert was scheduled to start at 8.30 p.m.

'My two sisters, a girlfriend and I went down to Atlantic City for the day (about 70 miles from Philadelphia) and walked on the Broadwalk (promenade). Atlantic City is the most popular seaside resort in New Jersey and is much like Blackpool.

'At 7.00 p.m. we went down to Convention Hall to get in and the waiting line was blocks long on either side of the hall. We didn't get in until 8.20. Fortunately, all tickets had been sold months before, so that problem was eliminated.

'Convention Hall is a huge place and 20,000 kids were on hand to see the Beatles. The master of ceremonies gave everyone a strict lecture about sitting down in their seats, but that wasn't observed too well. Four other acts: the Bill Black Combo, the Exciters, the

Righteous Brothers and Jackie De Shannon preceded the Beatles. Everything was pandemonium when they finally came on! We had seats in the eleventh row centre orchestra, so we could see and hear pretty well. My youngest sister and I took pictures, but none of them came out. To sum up their performance, they were absolutely FAB! They were only on for 30 minutes and sang 11 songs, but it was still great.'

Co-op Ballroom, Doncaster, Yorkshire

The Beatles appeared only once at this venue on the evening of 8 August 1962. They had been booked to appear at the Cavern that night but were allowed to cancel their appearance there for the Co-op Ballroom gig.

Co-operative Hall, Market Street, Darwen, Lancashire

The Beatles appeared at this venue on Friday, 25 January 1963. Tickets were 6/- and available from four local shops: Nightingale's Record Shop, Co-op Travel Agency, Walsh's Cycle Shop and Nelson's Grocer Shop.

Due to fog the Beatles were five minutes late going on stage, but gave a performance which the local paper reviewed under the headline: 'Teenagers Entertained By TV Stars'. It read:

'Fabulous!' That was the comment everyone made who heard the Beatles at the Co-operative hall on Friday night.

Delayed by fog, the group went on stage five minutes after arriving to give a rip-roaring 60 minute performance such as Darwen youths have never heard in the town before!

Right from the first minute of their appearance the audience showed their delight in more ways than one. A packed hall; a star group ably supported by local groups namely: the Mustangs, the Electones, the Mike Taylor Combo, combined to make a very successful night.

The Beatles were the main attraction at the dance held by the Baptist youth club. Mr T. Proudfoot, who organised the dance, said: 'This was the climax to three dances, which we held before, and it was well worth the work involved.'

Everyone who attended – and many more – are asking the question 'when are they coming again?' The answer: As soon as possible!!!

In fact, the Beatles were never to return to the venue.

Co-operative Hall, Long Street, Middleton, Lancashire

The Beatles only appeared once at this venue, on Thursday, 11 April 1963. Tickets were priced at 7/6d. The hall itself had originally opened on 4 November 1871 and was closed and demolished in August 1963, only four months after the Beatles appeared there.

The gig was promoted by Barry Chaytow, who remembered the Beatles arriving one hour before they were due on stage, accompanied by Clive Epstein. He also recalled John having trouble removing his knitted tie. Frustrated, he said that anyone who could get it off could keep it. Local photographer Jamie Lowe cut the tie off with scissors, but gave it back to John.

Also on the bill were the Country Gents and Shaun & Sum People.

The Beatles performed for one hour and played: 'Till There Was You', 'Love Me Do', 'From Me To You', 'Keep Your Hands Off My Baby', 'A Taste Of Honey', 'Long Tall Sally', 'Please Please Me', 'Baby It's You', 'Some Other Guy', 'To Know Her Is To Love Her', 'I Saw Her Standing There', 'Clarabella', 'Memphis Tennessee', 'Sure To Fall', 'Thank You Girl' and 'Twist And Shout'.

The local paper the *Middleton Guardian* reported:

> The group is a tightly knit one. Drummer 'Ringo' Starr joined the Beatles in August last year, but the others are original members. George Harrison (lead guitar) and Paul McCartney used to go to the same school, and John Lennon (lead guitar) is Paul's next door neighbour.
>
> Did they think that 'Love Me Do' would be the hit which it was? 'You just don't know when you record it,' said Paul McCartney. 'Sometimes you make a record, which you think is great and it flops. Other times you make something which you don't think will go anywhere and it's a hit.'

Cooper, Michael

The photographer who took the famous photograph of the *Sgt Pepper's Lonely Hearts Club Band* cover.

Michael was a prominent British photographer who worked closely with art gallery owner Robert Fraser and, as a result, photographed a number of the major painters of the time, including Duchamp, Magritte, Claus Oldenberg, Larry Rivers, Brigit Riley, Jim Dine and Rauchenberg. Fraser gave them all their first show in London and Michael was there to photograph them.

As a result of Fraser becoming an adviser for the *Pepper* sleeve, he hired Cooper to take the photographs and the special display was constructed in Cooper's studio in Chelsea. Cooper's four-year-old son Adam was present and years later he was to recall, 'There were lots of people milling around the studio at first, then when the shoot was about to commence, they cleared the studio.

'My grandparents were invited to the end-of-the-shoot party at my father's studio in Flood Street where the sessions took place. They were of that age group, middle-aged, middle-of-the-road, and I still don't think they've got over it to this day. They walked into this place and a whole cross-section of weird people were in there, from models from different agencies, to the Beatles, to Robert Fraser, Michael, Peter Blake and lots of people wearing colourful sixties gear. My grandparents walked into this scene and didn't know what was going on, but they were impressed by the whole set-up.'

Cooper also took many shots of the Rolling Stones and was responsible for the cover of *Her Satanic Majesties Request*. Michael devised the 3D effect, but Allen Klein decided that it was too expensive, so only a limited number of 3D copies were issued. Keith Richards remarked about how Cooper was proud of his record collection – with his own two covers at each end, one the *Sgt Pepper* cover, the other *Her Satanic Majesties Request*.

Michael Cooper took photographs of the Beatles during a concert peformance and also took hundreds of shots of John and Yoko at their exhibition at Robert Fraser's gallery. A colleague commented: 'For the John and Yoko exhibition they had people walking up and down Oxford Street with signs promoting it, but people didn't believe John and Yoko would be there. Hardly anyone turned up at first and they were just closing down when suddenly hundreds and hundreds of people started turning up and the gallery became packed.'

In 1972 Cooper became depressed and committed suicide. He left behind over 17,000 photographs. He'd always planned to have a book of his work published which he intended to call *Blinds and Shutters*. Fourteen years after his death, *Blinds and Shutters* was finally published in a lavish limited edition of 5,000 copies by Genesis Publications. It had been put together by Cooper's son Adam, together with a friend, Perry Richardson, and the help of Bill Wyman.

Corbett, Bill

A driver hired by John in 1964 to become the chauffeur of his recently acquired £5,000 Rolls Royce. Corbett had originally been an employee of a car hire firm that had assigned him to drive the Beatles around in an Aston Martin.

In August 1964 in an article in the *People* newspaper, Corbett said:

> When I took the job nine months ago I found I had to start learning an entirely new technique of driving. The art of moving off through a dense mob of half-crazed Beatles fans is something no driving school teaches.
>
> The biggest menace is not the fans thronging around the front of the car. A gentle nudge with the bumper, accompanied by a blast on the hooter, usually gets them out of the way. It is the girls clinging on to the door handles who worry me. If I drive away too slowly they will try to climb into the car or on the roof. If I put me foot down and speed away they will still cling on desperately and be dragged dangerously along the road.

Cordet, Louise

A teenage girl singer and Decca recording artist who was booked by Arthur Howes to appear on the Roy Orbison/Beatles British tour of May/June 1963.

Louise was promoting her new single 'Round And Around'. Her previous releases were 'I'm Just A Baby' and 'Who's Sorry Now?'. Her only chart hit was 'I'm Just a Baby', which had reached No. 13 in the British charts in May 1962.

In October 1963 the young French singer had her version of 'From Me To You' issued. A number which she sang in the French language.

Cornell, Lyn

Blonde-haired member of the Vernons Girls, the all-female singing group from Liverpool. She was a member of the vocal outfit when they recorded 'We Love The Beatles'. Later she joined a group called the Carefrees with Betty Prescott, another former Vernons girl.

The other members were Barbara Kay, Johnny Evans, John Stevens and Don Riddell. The group recorded 'We Love You Beatles', which was issued in the US on London International 10614 in 1964 and reached No. 39 in the *Billboard* charts, with a chart life of five weeks, making it the most successful Beatles novelty single ever recorded.

As a solo singer, Lyn was booked to appear on the special all-British edition of the US TV series 'Shindig' on which the Beatles appeared. Lyn had lived quite close to Paul McCartney in Liverpool and during rehearsals at the Granville Theatre, Fulham, she was able to talk over old times with Paul.

Lyn was also married to Andy White, drummer on the recording sessions for 'Love Me Do' and 'P.S. I Love You'.

Corn Exchange. St Paul's Square, Bedford, Bedfordshire

The Beatles appeared here only once, on the evening of Thursday, 13 December 1962. Joe Brown & the Bruvvers had originally been booked to appear but, as they were unable to fulfil the engagement, the promoters sought an alternative and managed to book the Beatles, only days before the group left for their final season at the Star Club, Hamburg. Admission was 3/- and the support act was folk duo Robin Hall and Jimmie MacGregor.

Corrine, Corrina

A traditional song which the Beatles added to their repertoire in 1960. Joe Turner had recorded a version of the number in 1956 but the Beatles were probably influenced by the Ray Peterson version which reached No. 9 in the American charts in 1960. The Beatles dropped it from their repertoire at the end of 1961.

Coventry Theatre, Hales Street, Coventry, West Midlands

The Beatles made only two appearances at this theatre, both in 1963. The first took place on 24 February 1963 as part of the Helen Shapiro tour. Their second appearance was part of their own autumn tour on 17 November.

Cowan, Norman

Doctor to Brian Epstein, George Martin and Gerry Marsden. Cowan was the man who broke down the door to Brian Epstein's room and discovered his body. He told the coroner that Brian had suffered from glandular fever in July 1966 and that he took Tryptizol, Librium and Carbrital. He took two tablets of Carbrital each night.

Coward, Noel

The late British playwright, composer and actor, who was knighted in 1970. The celebrated figure kept a diary and noted in his entry for Saturday, 6 June 1964 that he'd finished up at Alma Cogan's London flat at 12.20 a.m. where he met two Beatles. They were John Lennon and Paul McCartney.

The following year, on Wednesday, 23 June 1965, he noted, 'The Beatles have all four been awarded MBEs, which has caused a considerable outcry. Furious war heroes are sending back their bravely won medals by the bushel. It is, of course, a tactless and major blunder on the part of the Prime Minister, and also I don't think the Queen should have agreed. Some other decoration should have been selected to reward them for their talentless but considerable contributions to the Exchequer.'

In the biography *Noel Coward* by Philip Hoare, the author writes: 'Back at Les Avants, Noel heard news of the Beatles' MBEs. . . . A week or so later, he saw the noisy youths in concert in Rome. "The noise was deafening throughout," and he was unable to hear "a word they sang or a note they played, just one long, ear splitting din," with the fanatical audience "like a mass masturbation orgy".'

Coward went backstage to see the group, and was told by Brian Epstein to go to their hotel. There he was told they would not see him, 'because that ass David Lewin had quoted me saying unflattering things about them months ago'. Lewin had interviewed Coward shortly after he had met Lennon and McCartney at one of Alma Cogan's Kensington parties, and had recorded Coward as saying, 'The Beatles, those two I met seemed nice, pleasant young men, quite well behaved and with an amusing way of speaking. Of course they are totally devoid of talent. There is a great deal of noise. In my day the young were taught to be seen and not heard – which is no bad thing.' Coward insisted their publicist find one of the group, and she returned with Paul McCartney, to whom he explained 'gently but firmly that one did not pay much attention to the statements of newspaper reporters. The poor boy was quite amiable and I sent messages of congratulations to his colleagues, although the message I would have liked to send them was they were bad-mannered little shits.'

Despite the criticisms from Coward, Paul McCartney recorded 'A Room With A View' for the Noel Coward tribute album in 1998.

Cow Palace, San Francisco, California

Site of the first gig on their first American tour on 19 August 1964.

The entire stadium of 17,130 seats was sold out, bringing in receipts of $91,670 of which the Beatles' share was $47,600. The promoter was Paul Catalana.

The show began at 8.00 a.m. with the Bill Black Combo, followed by the Righteous Brothers, backed by the Exciters and then Jackie de Shannon.

Backstage, the boys were introduced to Joan Baez and Derek Taylor arranged a press conference at which there were a number of simplistic questions such as 'Do the Beatles have pillow fights?' Ringo was to make the plea, 'Please don't throw jelly beans – they're dangerous.'

A sheriff's deputy had spotted film star Shirley Temple in the audience and brought her backstage with her husband Charles Black and their eight-year-old daughter Lori. Brian Epstein had a ban on celebrity photos being taken at the time, but it was waived and the historic picture was taken by her husband.

The group took the stage at 9.20 a.m. Dressed in dark blue suits, they were on a stage surrounded by seats and were pelted by a hail of jelly beans, which mainly hit Ringo. Paul later commented, 'We'd step in them and they'd stick to our guitar leads and our shoes. The kids must've thought I was trying out new dance steps, but I was always just trying to get unstuck. And – we didn't even eat them!'

There was such a hail that the show was stopped twice while an announcer told the audience. 'You're hurting the Beatles!'

The group performed ten numbers in 30 minutes and then went backstage, planning to be driven to the airport and fly to Las Vegas. Their limousine driver didn't pull away quickly enough and the car was swamped by fans whose weight began to tell on the car roof. Security men pulled the Beatles out of the car and put them in an ambulance in which there were several drunken sailors who had been involved in a brawl at the show.

The Cow Palace opened their first American tour and it was also the venue where they finished their American tour in 1964 on 31 August. The group performed a matinee before 11,700 fans and an evening show before an audience of 17,000.

Crawdaddy Club, Station Hotel, Kew Road, Richmond, Surrey

One of Britain's first R&B clubs, launched in 1962 by the slightly eccentric, but immensely talented Giorgio Gomelski, on a loan of five pounds he'd received. It was known as the Crawdaddy Blues Club.

Giorgio was the son of a Russian father and French mother, had been born in the Caucasus and had travelled widely. Brian Jones approached him about booking the Rolling Stones and he agreed. The deal was that they would split the takings 50-50, after the band had been paid a minimum guarantee of fifteen pounds per gig.

For the first few gigs, Giorgio earned no money at all, but the audiences began to grow. Giorgio began to take over management responsibilities and Brian suggested he sign them to a contract, but Giorgio never got around to it.

When *Please Please Me* was at the peak of its success, Giorgio managed to talk the Beatles into coming to the club to see the Stones and they arrived on the evening of 21 April 1963. It was the start of a long-lasting relationship between the two bands.

As a result of the Beatles' visit, George Harrison was able to recommend the Stones to A&R man Dick Rowe, who signed them to Decca.

Crawford, Marie

Under her maiden name of Maguire, Marie is known to Beatles fans as the girl who helped teach Ringo Starr to read.

Marie, who was four years older than Ringo, then known as Ritchie Starkey, lived in the same street. In June 1943 her family moved into 10 Madryn Street, in the Dingle area of Liverpool. Ritchie and his mother, Elsie, lived next door at No. 9.

Marie would come and look after Ritchie when his mother went out to work. Since Ritchie had suffered academically due to the length of time he'd spent in hospital, Marie would spend one hour, twice a week, reading to him and going over spelling lists with him. Elsie paid her 6d an hour.

When Ritchie had to spend another lengthy period in hospital, Marie brought him a present – a drumming record, 'Bedtime for Drums' by Eric Delaney.

During the 1980s, Marie became an official Beatles guide in Liverpool.

Crittle, John

A clothes designer who came to London and was sponsored at the Royal College of Art by Lord Montague. Crittle next set up Dandy Fashions, one of the first fashion boutiques in the Kings Road, with his partner Tara Browne. During 1966 he was designing clothes for the Beatles, the Rolling Stones, the Who, Procol Harum, Elvis Presley and Jimi Hendrix and became known as 'the tailor to the stars'.

He claimed to earn £10,000 a week, which he blew on drugs and drink, drove an E type Jaguar and had an affair with Marianne Faithful.

Through his friend Pete Shotton, Crittle became close to the Beatles organisation and he was appointed to run Apple Tailoring. John Lennon was to say, 'We bought a few things from him and the next thing we knew, we owned the place.'

It became Apple's second boutique, was situated at 161 New Kings Road and the large sign on the shop façade above the windows read: Civil And Theatrical Apple Tailoring By John Crittle.

A launch party and a press reception were held to celebrate the opening of the boutique on 22 May 1968 with John and Yoko and George and Pattie Harrison in attendance. Crittle designed the costumes for the shop and staged a fashion show at the launch party.

It was a short-lived venture. A few months after the opening, the Beatles relinquished control of the shop and handed it back to Crittle on 31 July 1968.

Crittle met Andrea Williams in a nightclub and they married at Chelsea Register Office in 1967. Their daughter Marnie Mercedes Darcey Pemberton Crittle was born in April 1969.

After the Apple Tailoring venture, Crittle opened a restaurant called GHQ in Fulham, but fled to Australia when the taxman chased him for £3 million in back taxes.

He left his wife and daughter behind and has remained in Australia ever since, living on a cattle farm at Mullumbimby, New South Wales. His daughter, under the name Darcey Bussell, was to become the Royal Ballet's youngest-ever leading ballerina.

In 1998 the 55-year-old Crittle had only one lung and was suffering from acute emphysema. He was given just one year to live.

Crosley Field, Findlay Street at Western Avenue, Cincinnati, Ohio

The Beatles had been due to appear at this venue on Saturday, 20 August 1966. A canopy used to protect the electrical equipment from rain failed to do so and there was a possibility that members of the Beatles could be electrocuted. There were backstage arguments between Brian Epstein, the American agents and the local promoters Dino Santangelo and Steve Kirk due to the fact that 35,000 fans were already in the arena.

Minutes before they were due to go on stage the Beatles insisted that they had Brian Epstein's word that there was no danger from the wet equipment and, as he couldn't assure them, they refused to go on. The gig was rearranged to take place at noon the next day, Sunday, 21 August.

Thousands of fans were unable to attend the show the next day and, due to the fact that the show actually went ahead, they were not entitled to get refunds. There were about 10,000 attending the noon show. After the Beatles performed their lunchtime concert they had a 350-mile journey to St Louis for their performance at Busch Stadium that evening.

Crown & Mitre Hotel, Carlisle, Cumberland

The hotel where the Beatles stayed following their appearance at the ABC Cinema, Carlisle on 8 February 1963.

The group were appearing on the bill of the Helen Shapiro tour. After the show they were relaxing at the hotel when Helen mentioned that someone had invited them all to attend a Young Conservatives' dance being held in the hotel ballroom on behalf of the Carlisle Golf Club, but she'd turned the offer down. Helen was later to say that it was very cold, everyone was bored and the Beatles said they would drop into the dance. Helen quickly went to her room to make up and joined the Beatles and Kenny Lynch as they approached the private function. They passed the entrance desk into the dance area, but because the Beatles were wearing leather jackets they were asked to leave. They hadn't even entered the main ballroom, but they all left.

On 11 February, the event made front-page news in the *Daily Express*, which blew the incident out of all proportion, sympathised with Helen, but castigated the Beatles. Helen was later to mention it was not the organisers of the dance who objected to the Beatles' attire, but personnel from the hotel itself.

Cry Baby Cry

A track on *The Beatles* double album, composed by John while he was in India. It's partly based on the nursery rhythm 'Sing A Song Of Sixpence'. The number is about the King of Marigold and his family, the Duke and Duchess of Kirkcaldy and a midnight séance.

Commenting on the number, John Lennon told Beatles biographer Hunter Davies, 'I've got another one here, a few words, I think I got them from an advert – "Cry baby cry, make your mother buy". I've been playing it over on the piano.'

John also played piano and organ on the track while George Martin added harmonica. During one of the recording sessions, on Tuesday, 16 July 1968, engineer Geoff Emerick decided that he could no longer work with the Beatles due to what he perceived as a deteriorating atmosphere between them.

Strangely enough, when David Sheff was interviewing John in September 1980 he was asking John to comment on each of the songs he'd written. When he asked about 'Cry Baby Cry', John said 'Not me. A piece of rubbish.'

An early take of the number was included on the Beatles' *Anthology 3* CD.

Cry For A Shadow

The first Beatles composition to appear on record.

The song was mainly composed by George Harrison, with John Lennon's approval, and was really a parody of the Shadows'

'Frightened City', which George had done as a spoof to fool Rory Storm. The number had gone under the working title 'Beatle Bop'.

When Bert Kaempfert recorded the Beatles as a backing band for Tony Sheridan in May 1961, they asked if they could cut some tracks of their own. John sang on 'Ain't She Sweet'. Kaempfert had asked them if they had any original compositions of their own. John and Paul did play a couple of their own compositions for Kaempfert, but he was unimpressed with their songs, although he felt George's cod-Shadows style on 'Cry For A Shadow' was suitable and suggested that they record it.

'Cry For A Shadow' was included on Tony Sheridan's German album *My Bonnie* in June 1962 earning itself the honour of being the first original composition by a Beatle to find itself on record.

The news of the recording was announced on the front page of issue No. 2 of *Mersey Beat*. The number was included on the Beatles' *Anthology 1* CDs.

Crying, Waiting, Hoping
One of Buddy Holly's lesser-known compositions, which was originally included on the flipside of 'Peggy Sue Got Married' in 1959. The Beatles included it in their repertoire in 1960, with George Harrison on lead vocals. It was one of the numbers they recorded at their Decca audition. The group also performed the number on their radio show 'Pop Go The Beatles' on 6 August 1963. A live performance of the Beatles playing the Buddy Holly number on the radio was included on *The Beatles Live At The BBC* CDs.

Cumberland Gap
Traditional folk number, typical of the material utilised during the British skiffle boom of the fifties. It provided Lonnie Donegan with a No. 1 chart hit in 1957 and the Quarry Men, like thousands of skiffle groups around the country, included it in their repertoire, John Lennon took over on lead vocals during the Quarry Men performances, although they had dropped the number from their act by the end of 1959.

Curtis, King
American rock 'n' roll saxophonist, born Curtis Ousley in Fort Worth, Texas, on 7 February 1934. He made his professional debut at the Apollo Theatre, New York, and moved to the Big Apple at the age of 20.

Curtis became a leading session musician, dubbed 'king of the tenor saxophone', and also became a member of the Coasters, and his hits with them included 'Charlie Brown', 'Yackety-Yak' and 'Poison Ivy'.

His King Curtis Band appeared on the Beatles' American tour in 1965.

When 'Reminiscing', composed by Curtis, became a posthumous hit for Buddy Holly in 1962, the Beatles included it in their repertoire, with George Harrison on lead vocals. They performed it at the Star Club in Hamburg and it is included on the *Star Club* double album.

In 1971, John Lennon hired Curtis to play on his *Imagine* album sessions and Curtis appears on the tracks 'It's So Hard' and 'I Don't Want To Be A Soldier'.

Shortly after the *Imagine* sessions, on 13 August 1971, Curtis was stabbed to death outside his apartment in Harlem following a fight with a Puerto Rican youth, Juan Montanez, who stood trial for his murder.

Curtis was only 37 years old.

Cyrkle, The

An American group originally formed by students of Lafayette College, Pennsylvania, under the name the Rondells. They comprised Tom Dawes (vocals/guitar/banjo/sitar), Don Danneman (piano/guitar) and Marty Fried (drums). Fred Pickens joined them on organ.

The group was brought to Brian Epstein's attention in 1966 by Nat Weiss, his American attorney, who had spotted the band performing in Atlantic City.

Epstein suggested that Weiss go ahead and sign them, and they became the first act of a new management company, Nemperor Artists, which Brian formed with Weiss to handle American acts.

Weiss arranged for them to perform in New York's Greenwich Village during one of Epstein's trips. Brian then suggested that they change their name to the Circle and it was John Lennon who suggested that the spelling be altered to Cyrkle.

The group was signed to Columbia Records and Weiss sent Epstein several demo discs. Brian picked a number called 'Red Rubber Ball', penned by Paul Simon and Bruce Woodley of the Seekers, predicting it would sell a million copies. It did, reaching No. 2 in the American charts.

A few months later they had their second and final big hit, 'Turn Down Day', which reached No. 16 in the *Billboard* charts. The group was also booked to appear on the Beatles' final US tour in August 1966.

Dakotas, The

A Manchester band who backed the singer Pete MacLaine. They began playing regularly in Liverpool and during 1962 appeared at the Cavern on the same bill as the Beatles on a number of occasions: Wednesday, 25 July, Wednesday, 19 September and Friday, 30 November. On Friday, 10 August they appeared with the Beatles and Johnny Kidd & the Pirates (whose guitarist was Mick Green) on a 'Riverboat Shuffle' along the River Mersey on the *Royal Iris*. They also appeared with them at the Cavern on Wednesday, 30 January 1963.

As Pete MacLaine & the Dakotas, they also appeared on the Little Richard/Beatles concert at the Tower Ballroom, New Brighton, on Friday, 12 October 1962.

When Brian Epstein signed Billy Kramer, his backing band, the Coasters, refused to turn professional. Epstein asked a number of Liverpool bands, including the Remo Four, to provide backing for Billy, but they refused.

He then approached the Dakotas. Like the Mersey groups before them, they turned his offer down. He then promised that they would be able to record in their own right as the Dakotas and they agreed, shedding Pete MacLaine ¬ not as traumatic as Pete Best being shed by the Beatles, but another case of a musician being tossed out in the cold.

A news item in *Mersey Beat*, headed 'Manchester Furious About Dakotas Change-over' read: 'We are informed that terrific feeling has been aroused in Manchester concerning the parting of the ways between Pete MacLaine and the Dakotas. "Billy Kramer won't fit" say many of the Dakotas' Mancunian fans. Pete MacLaine and his new group the Clan received a harsh reception at the Oasis Club, Lloyd Street. Although the fans seem up in arms about the change-over, Brian Epstein informs us that, "All parties concerned parted amicably."'

Almost word for word what he said about the dumping of Pete Best.

The Dakotas comprised Mike Maxfield (lead guitar), Robin McDonald (rhythm), Ray Jones (bass) and Tony Mansfield – Elkie Brooks' brother (drums).

Despite immediately being sent to the Star Club, Hamburg, to develop an act together, the Dakotas and Kramer never really got on well and didn't build a rapport.

Their first single together, the Lennon and McCartney composition 'Do You Want To Know A Secret?', topped the British charts, and they followed up with a series of hits, 'Bad To Me', 'I'll Keep You Satisfied' and 'From A Window', all penned by Lennon and McCartney. Kramer then picked 'Little Children', which became their third chart-topper. Their final hit together was 'Trains And Boats And Planes', which reached No. 12.

The Dakotas did record three singles and an EP for Parlophone under their own name, and their first release, an instrumental, 'The Cruel Sea', reached No. 18 in the charts in July 1963. It was their only solo hit.

Ray Jones left the band in August 1964. Robin then took over on bass and Mick Green joined as rhythm guitarist.

Dallas Memorial Coliseum, Dallas, Texas, USA

The Beatles appeared at this venue on Friday, 18 September 1964, in a promotion by Super Shows Inc of Washington DC. Earlier that day there had been a telephone call reporting that a bomb had been planted in the area. The police carried out a thorough search and no bomb was found, although two fans were found hidden under the bandstand and a further four in a washroom. The Beatles arrived and before their 30 minute performance, participated in a press conference at 7.00 p.m. It was to be their last press conference in America that year.

There were 200 police present in the auditorium and another 200 on stand-by. The police chief, Jess Curry, arrived with his daughter and two grandchildren.

Dalrymple Hall, Seaforth Street, Fraserborough, Aberdeenshire, Scotland

The Silver Beetles made the third appearance of their seven-venue Beat Ballad Show Tour of Scotland backing Johnny Gentle at this venue on Monday, 23 May 1960. Fraserborough was a fishing town eighty miles east of Inverness, which had a population of 11,000 in 1960. The support acts were the girl/boy duo Lena and Stevie and Rikki Barnes And His All Stars.

Dance In The Street
Number recorded by Gene Vincent and his Blue Caps in 1958 which the Beatles introduced into their repertoire in 1960 and continued performing until late in 1962.

Darktown Skiffle Group
A Liverpool skiffle group which Ritchie Starkey joined in 1958 when his former group, the Eddie Clayton Skiffle Group, disbanded.

Darktown Strutters Ball
Traditional song which the Beatles introduced into their repertoire in 1960 and continued to perform until late in 1962. The Beatles probably included the number in their stage act following the version by Joe Brown & the Bruvvers which reached No. 6 in the British charts in March 1960.

Dave Clark Five
A group from Tottenham in London. When the Mersey sound began to dominate the British music scene, the status quo had been seriously breached. The agents, managers, recording studios and media were all in London. Until the emergence of the Beatles, London had a complete grip on the music scene.

There was a determined effort to bring control back into the hands of the top London entertainment agencies. The Dave Clarke Five and Brian Poole & the Tremeloes both recorded 'Do You Love Me'. Originally a vocal number by the Contours on Motown, it had been adapted into a beat version by a popular Liverpool band, Faron's Flamingos, who included it in their stage act. They recorded it for a small London label, Oriole, who inexplicably placed it on the 'B' side of the record. The Dave Clark Five and Brian Poole & the Tremeloes immediately came out with a version very close to the Flamingos' sound and both entered the charts with it.

There was media saturation on the Dave Clark Five. Their next record, 'Glad All Over', hit the No. 1 spot and the media had a field day: 'Tottenham Sound Has Crushed The Beatles' were the headlines in the *Daily Express*; cartoons in the *Evening Standard* dismissed the Beatles as old-fashioned. Despite the fact that the media went all out to promote the Dave Clark Five as the group to take over from the Beatles, it never happened.

The Dave Clark Five did become a major hit band, particularly in America where the publicity drive was completely opposite to that in Britain. Rather than being pushed as London's answer to Liverpool, the group were promoted as if they were a Mersey Beat band. Since 'Glad All Over' had replaced 'I Want To Hold Your Hand' at the top of the British charts, the Americans believed that the Dave Clark Five was the next big group from Liverpool. Epic Records exploited this belief by advertising them in *Billboard* as having 'the Mersey sound with the Liverpool beat'. In fact, the Motown Museum in Detroit still displays a framed photograph of the Dave Clark Five and the Supremes with the caption 'Liverpool meets Detroit'.

The group comprised Dave Clark (drums), Mike Smith (keyboards/vocals), Rick Huxley (bass), Denis Payton (tenor sax/guitar) and Len Davidson (guitar). During the next ten years they were to have 22 hit records in Britain and 24 in America. They'd originally formed as an instrumental group and had made their debut with 'Chaquita' on the Ember label. They moved to Pye records, but were also unsuccessful with their releases. In 1963 they signed with Columbia and their first release, 'Mulberry Bush', was also a miss. They also recorded Mitch Murray's 'I Like It', but never released it and it became a chart topper for Gerry & the Pacemakers. Then came 'Do You Love Me', and the group never looked back.

Drummer Dave Clark proved to have an astute business sense and did much to steer the group to success, while the main musical asset was vocalist Mike Smith, who wrote most of the group's material.

In 1965 they made the film *Catch Us If You Can*, which was directed by John Boorman.

The group finally disbanded in August 1970.

David & Jonathan

A vocal duo who enjoyed a six-week residency in the British charts with the Lennon & McCartney number 'Michelle'. Issued on Columbia DB 7800 on 13 January 1966 it entered the charts on 29 January and reached No. 11. They issued another Beatles cover, 'She's Leaving Home', in June 1967, but it didn't reach the charts. The two singers were actually a songwriting team, Roger Cook and Roger Greenaway, who later had a number of hits in their own right. Greenaway had originally been a member of the Kestrels, a vocal group who had toured twice with the Beatles in 1963.

David Lewis Theatre, The, Great George Place, Liverpool L1

An unusual architecturally interesting building complex which housed a large theatre and hotel. The main local promoter to use the venue was Wally Hill who presented regular rock 'n' roll shows at the theatre with groups such as Carl Vincent & the Counts and Karl Terry & the Cruisers.

The Beatles never actually appeared at the David Lewis Theatre. However, on 17 October 1961, a number of girls who attended the Cavern regularly had formed a Beatles fan club in September and had pooled their money to raise five pounds to hire a room at the David Lewis for their first (and only) fan club gathering. The Beatles agreed to come along.

They had no PA equipment with them and couldn't really perform properly, although Paul sang some ballads and Pete Best was coaxed to sing 'Matchbox', 'Peppermint Twist' and the Elvis Presley number 'A Rose Growing Wild In The Country'. Paul's father Jim McCartney was also in attendance.

The David Lewis was levelled by developers in the late eighties.

Davies, Hunter

The Beatles' official biographer.

Davies had been working on the *Sunday Times* since 1960 and was currently in charge of the Atticus column when he first interviewed Paul McCartney for an item published on 18 September 1966. Davies had penned a novel, *Here We Go Round The Mulberry Bush*, which was being filmed. The director, Clive Donner, suggested that Paul McCartney might be approached to provide the music, as he'd done for *The Family Way*. Davies met Paul again and he seemed interested initially. Then, finally, he said 'no'. It was during his discussions with Paul that Davies asked if he could write a book about the Beatles. Paul suggested that he contact Brian Epstein and helped him to draft a letter. Davies then met Epstein at his Chapel Street home in January 1967 and Brian said he would ask the individual members of the group. At the meeting the following week there was a positive response and Davies suggested that the Beatles receive one-third of the book deal.

For almost eighteen months, Davies travelled around with the Beatles, interviewed their parents, other relatives and friends and compiled over 150,000 words in note form. His completed manuscript contained enough to fill two volumes. However, the agreement he'd arranged with the Beatles meant that the book could be subject to cuts made by the Beatles themselves or relatives such as

John's Aunt Mimi – and that is what happened, resulting in a book which, due to the censoring, left certain aspects of their story out. Davies didn't like having to smooth the rough edges, but had no choice.

During the time he spent with the Beatles, at Abbey Road recording sessions and at their homes, he managed to retrieve a number of items, with their permission, which they'd thrown away – these were mainly scraps of paper on which they'd been composing songs. As a result, a few years later, when the Beatles became interested in their own history, Davies was able to give both Paul and George some of their original handwritten items. He was also able to save a number for posterity and loan them to the British Museum.

The book was first published on 14 September 1968 with a cover by Alan Aldridge and, since Brian Epstein had recently died, Hunter dedicated the book to him.

Hunter also wrote Brian's obituary for *The Times* and was commissioned to prewrite obituaries for each member of the group, John was the only member who asked him to show him his obituary.

Davies' authorised biography was reprinted in 1985 with a lengthy introduction, which is a fascinating account of the story behind the original edition.

Davis, Billie
British singer, born Carol Hedges in Woking, Surrey, in 1945. Robert Stigwood discovered her and she duetted with Mike Sarne on his hit record 'Will I What?' In 1963 she charted in her own right with 'Tell Him'.

It was while 'Tell Him' was entering the charts that Billie was booked to appear with the Beatles on their nationwide tour on Tuesday, 26 February at the Gaumont, Taunton, when the headliner, Helen Shapiro, was laid low with a heavy cold. Billie also appeared with them the following night at the Rialto, York.

Helen resumed her place on the tour the following evening.

Of her experience, Billie commented: 'I remember the Beatles sitting in the front row watching me rehearse. I was having terrible trouble with them as they'd been on the road a few weeks and I was having to lock my dressing room door.'

Davis, Rod
A member of the Quarry Men who first met John Lennon at St Peter's Sunday School in Woolton, when he was five years old. He was also in the same class as Pete Shotton, Nigel Whalley, Ivan

Vaughan and Geoff Rhind. He remembers going into Quarry Bank School one morning and Eric Griffiths asked him if he wanted to join a skiffle group. He asked who was in it and was told there was John Lennon, Pete Shotton on washboard and Bill Smith on bass. He didn't have a banjo prior to joining the group, but bought one for £5. Rod recalls their first rehearsal was in an air raid shelter in Pete Shotton's back garden and they also went to John's mother's place to practice. One of their first gigs was at Childwall Golf Club when they wore a stage uniform of white shirts and black jeans. Rod recalls they used the name Blackjacks, although Pete Shotton disagrees and doesn't remember the name Blackjacks being used. When he left the Quarry Men, Rod bought a guitar and in September 1957 joined a jazz group.

Dawsons Music Shop, Widnes, Lancashire
A record store in Widnes, the town fifteen miles from Liverpool. The Beatles made a rare personal appearance at the shop on 6 October 1962, the day after 'Love Me Do' was released. The group were well known in the area and the store advertised regularly in *Mersey Beat*. The Beatles autographed copies of their debut single for half an hour after their arrival at 4.00 p.m.

Day By Day
A regional television programme produced by Southern TV. The Beatles were due to appear on the show on Tuesday, 12 November 1963, but their spot was cancelled when Paul McCartney came down with gastric flu. They were due to appear at the Guildhall, Portsmouth, that evening, but the show was postponed until 3 December. However, 'Day By Day' reporter Jeremy James managed to interview the group in their Guildhall dressing room, which was then broadcast that evening.

A Day In The Life
A John/Paul collaboration, but one in which they each wrote separate parts, John penning the beginning and end of the number and Paul composing the middle section. Paul had already written some of the lyrics for another song, but decided to incorporate them into the number that John had been writing.

There is a long chord at the end of the song which lasts for 42 seconds and it has been suggested that it was only intended to be heard by Martha, Paul's dog!

John's section was inspired by two separate items: the death in a car crash of Guinness heir Tara Browne, a friend of the Beatles; and a story that he'd read in the *Daily Mail* concerning holes in the roads in Blackburn, a town in Lancashire. John had a copy of the *Daily Mail* newspaper resting on the piano when writing the song and noticed the short news item. It appeared on page 7 of the 17 January 1967 issue, the lead item in the 'Far And Near' column, and read: 'There are 4,000 holes in the road in Blackburn, Lancashire, or one twenty-sixth of a hole per person, according to a council survey. If Blackburn is typical, there are two million holes in Britain's roads and 300,000 in London.'

Paul's rather cheery section, according to Steven Norris, a former schoolmate at the Liverpool Institute who became Conservative MP for Oxford East, was based on a bus journey they used to take to school together. In a *Daily Mail* interview in 1985, Norris commented: 'Everyone says that "A Day In The Life" was about drugs, but Paul always claimed it was about catching the bus to school. I agree. It's exactly what we used to do. Went upstairs and had a smoke, somebody spoke and I went into a dream. That's just how I remember it. Getting sleepily out of bed, dragging a comb across your head, then going out and catching the bus, upstairs to the top deck like we all did, still not properly awake and having an untipped Woodbine.'

In fact, it was only ever John's part of the song that was said to be about drugs. The BBC banned it nonetheless. It has never been clear why they thought the holes in the road referred to holes caused by a drug addict's hypodermic needle. Paul commented: 'It was banned on the basis of the line about how many holes does it take to fill the Albert Hall. Somebody got the idea it was how many holes there are in their arm. I think they heard it was something to do with drugs and that was the only part they could find that sounded like drugs.' The reference to the English army winning the war was inspired by John's appearance in the film *How I Won The War*.

There was originally a 24-bar gap when John and Paul's contributions were put together in the studio. At one of the sessions, on Friday, 10 February 1967, Paul told George Martin that he considered the best way to fill the gap was with a build-up by a 90-piece orchestra. Martin took on the technical task of putting the complex number together and hired 40 musicians from the Royal Philharmonic and London Symphony Orchestras. They were Erich Gruenberg, Granville Jones, Bill Monro, Jurgen Hess, Hans Geiger, D. Bradley, Lionel Bentley, David McCallum, Donald Weekes, Henry Datyner, Sidney Sax and Ernest Scott on violins; John Underwood, Gwynne Edwards, Bernard Davis and John Meek on violas; Francisco Gabarro, Dennis Vigay, Alan Dalziel and Alex Nifosi on cellos; Cyril MacArthur and Gordon Pearce on double-bass; Roger Lord on oboe; Clifford Seville and David Sandeman on flutes; David Mason, Monty Montgomery and Harold Jackson on trumpets; Raymond Brown, Raymond Premru and T. Moore on trombones; Michael Barnes on tuba; Basil Tschaikov and Jack Brymer on clarinets; N. Fawcett and Alfred Waters on horns; and Tristan Fry on percussion.

The Beatles had originally planned to film the *Sgt Pepper* sessions as a television movie and Tony Bramwell from Apple Films was in charge of shooting the 'A Day In The Life' session, but the plan for the TV film was dropped when the BBC banned the song. The promotional film remained in the archives until it was screened as part of the *Beatles At Abbey Road* exhibition in 1983.

The Beatles had insisted that the orchestra members wear full evening dress and they gave them carnival novelties to wear – including red noses and funny hats, upside-down spectacles, false eyes and fake bald heads. The Beatles had also invited a host of friends to add to the party atmosphere, including Pattie Harrison, Marianne Faithfull, Mick Jagger, Donovan, Keith Richard, the Fool, Mike Nesmith of the Monkees and the staff of the Apple Boutique.

Apart from its appearance on the *Sgt Pepper* album, the number was also included on *The Beatles 1967–1970* compilation in 1973 and *The Beatles Box* in 1980. A version of the number was included on the Beatles' *Anthology* 2 CD.

Day Tripper

A John Lennon composition. John commented, 'That was a drug-type song in a way because she was a day tripper. I just liked the word tripper.' At another time he was to say, 'Day trippers are people who go on a day trip, right? Usually on a ferryboat or something. But it was kind of, you know – you're just a weekend hippie.' In fact, John wasn't quite satisfied with the number because he felt that he'd rushed the song while he was working to a deadline.

'Day Tripper' was issued as the first of four eventual Beatles double 'A' sides. The other track was 'We Can Work It Out'. In America it was issued on Capitol 5555 on 6 December 1965, although the Americans preferred to promote the 'We Can Work It Out' side, which reached No. 1 in all three charts. 'Day Tripper' reached No. 5 in *Billboard*, No. 10 in *Cash Box* and No. 15 in *Record World*.

In Britain the single was issued on Parlophone R5389 on 3 December 1965 and became the group's tenth consecutive No. 1 and their third Christmas No. 1. The Beatles performed the number during tours in 1965/66 and on their 'The Music Of Lennon & McCartney' TV show. It was also included on *A Collection of*

Beatles Oldies (But Goldies), the American album *Yesterday And Today*, *The Beatles 1962–1966* and *20 Greatest Hits*, and they lip-synched both 'Day Tripper' and 'We Can Work It Out' for 'Hullabaloo', the American TV show.

Otis Redding had a hit with the song in 1967 and reached No. 6 in the British charts with it. The number was included on the CD compilation *Past Masters Volume Two*.

DC Stadium, 2001 E Capitol Street, Washington, DC

The Beatles' final tour of America was fraught with tension due to the hostile atmosphere created by the reaction to the 'Beatles are bigger than Christ' interview. When the Beatles appeared on Monday, 15 August 1966, outside the stadium, dressed in full robes, stalked the Imperial Wizard of the Maryland Clan and five Klansmen from Prince George's County Ku Klux Klan.

The show, promoted by the Feld Brothers, began at 6.00 p.m. before an audience of 32,164 fans. Other acts on the bill were the Cyrkle, the Ronettes, the Remains and Bobby Hebb.

The Beatles performed eleven numbers. During the show, someone who still brooded over the 'Jesus' statement jumped on stage and attacked John. Ringo rushed from his drums and pulled the attacker off.

The venue is now called the RFK Stadium.

Dear Prudence

Prudence Farrow was actress Mia Farrow's younger sister who had a playful personality. The sisters became friendly with the Beatles who interested Prudence in the Maharishi Mahesh Yogi and she, in turn, interested her sister in the teachings of the guru, resulting in the two sisters travelling to Boston in January 1968 to hear the Maharishi speak to Harvard law students. The sisters decided to study under the Maharishi at Rishikesh.

While there, Prudence became intensely serious and spent so much time meditating in her cottage that she rarely came out. The Beatles were aware of this and John was asked to contact her and make sure she came out more often and mixed with people. He was to say, 'She'd been locked in for three weeks and was trying to reach God quicker than anyone else.'

The incident inspired John to write 'Dear Prudence'. The Beatles began recording the number at the 8-track Trident Recording Studio in London on Wednesday, 28 August 1968, and it was included as a track on *The Beatles* double album.

Deauville Hotel, Miami, Florida

The site of the Beatles' second live performance for the 'Ed Sullivan Show'. The Beatles arrived in Miami on National Airlines Flight 11, with a pilot who wore a Beatle wig. When the plane touched down at Miami International Airport at 4.00 p.m. there were over 7,000 fans waiting. The group's arrival caused a riot in which glass windows were smashed and chairs were torn to pieces, resulting in over $2,000 worth of damage.

They arrived at their hotel, which had been nicknamed 'Beatle Central'. The suite had three bedrooms and John and Cynthia had one room and Paul and Ringo another. George was disgruntled to find he had to share a room with disc jockey Murray the K.

Local police sergeant Buddy Bresner was in charge of their safety and supervised a Beatle Patrol of two dozen officers.

Murray the K took them to the Peppermint Lounge to see Hank Ballard and they also watched the Coasters perform in the Mau Mau Lounge of the hotel.

On Saturday, 15 February, they rehearsed before a live audience, dressed in their grey suits with velvet collars, and later, after a trip to the swimming pool, rehearsed without an audience and dressed in their swimming trunks in the Napoleon Room of the hotel.

George Martin arrived at the Deauville and was able to tell them that the recordings he'd made at the Carnegie Hall concert had come out fine – although the album was never to be released. Then, on Sunday, 16 February, the group performed their television show before a live audience of 3,200 people. Their numbers were 'She Loves You', 'This Boy', All My Loving', 'I Saw Her Standing There', 'From Me To You' and 'I Want To Hold Your Hand'.

The Beatles were to remain at the Deauville for a week during which they took in more shows, including the Don Rickles show at the hotel, saw Elvis Presley's *Fun In Acapulco* at a drive-in and visited Cassius Clay's (Muhammed Ali) training camp. A local millionaire, Bernie Castro, lent them his luxurious houseboat in his absence. It had a full staff, including butler and chef, and they were able to enjoy barbecued steaks on board. During their time off they were also able to write 'Can't Buy Me Love'.

The group finally flew out of Miami at 5.18 p.m. on 21 February 1964.

Decca Audition, Decca Studios, Hampstead Studio No. 3, 165 Broadhurst Gardens, London NW6

In December 1961, the American music trade publication *Cash Box* carried the following story: 'One of the most constructive moves to be made by Decca for many months is the formation of a new production team to handle the company's pop single output. Spearheaded by A&R manager, Dick Rowe, who will be directly responsible to the chairman, Sir Edward Lewis, the team is completed by Dick Rowe, Rowe's assistant and co-producer Mike Smith, Peter Attwood, recording engineer of three years standing and Tony Meehan, former drummer for the Shadows. Rowe, who will act in an advisory capacity. feels that this youthful team with their fingers on the teenage pulse, will be more than capable of producing the kind of sound that makes for chart success.'

Such a story would seem to bode well for the Beatles who, nine days after the story appeared, turned up on New Year's Day, 1962, for their Decca recording audition. From an initial approach by Brian Epstein to Tony Barrow, who then put in a word, followed by Epstein's meetings with Decca executives such as Dick Rowe and Beecher-Stevens, to a Liverpool meeting where Epstein wined and dined Mike Smith, the road led to the West Hampstead studios of Decca on an icy cold New Year's morning.

On New Year's Eve, Brian Epstein caught the train down to London and stayed overnight with his Aunt Frida in Hampstead. The Beatles were to travel down by van with Neil Aspinall. Neil, a pal of Pete Best, had become their road manager and one of their staunchest champions. He bought a van for £80 to drive them to their gigs, initially charging them a fee of around five shillings a trip. For the London trek he borrowed a larger van, loaded in the boys and their equipment and set out on a journey that took ten hours because of lack of visibility in the snowy weather. They were lost in Wolverhampton and arrived in London at 10 o'clock at night.

The Beatles and Neil were booked into the Royal Hotel in Russell Square, but soon after arriving they went into the streets of the West End where they witnessed various capers, including the revellers in Trafalgar Square and some pot smokers who wanted to use their van.

The group arrived at the recording studios for their 11 a.m. appointment and met Brian, who was furious that Mike Smith was late.

Smith then rejected their amplifiers and told them to plug their guitars into the studio speakers.

Brian and the Beatles had discussed their repertoire. John wanted to perform a strong rock 'n' roll set, like they played at the Cavern, but Brian wanted them to play safe, telling them not to play numbers such as 'One after 909' and concentrate on standards such as 'Till There Was You'. He also suggested that they play as few of their own original compositions as possible. John and Paul weren't happy about this, but decided to take Brian's advice.

When the red light in the studio went on they began to perform and they were obviously nervous. Paul's voice began to crack and George was having trouble playing the guitar.

At one point Epstein began to criticise John's voice. John went mad and shouted at him. Everything stopped, the red light went off and Epstein rushed out of the room and didn't return for half an hour.

The group performed fifteen songs, with Paul taking lead on 'Like Dreamers Do', 'Till There Was You', 'Sure To Fall', 'Love Of The Loved', 'September In The Rain', 'Besame Mucho', and 'Searchin''. John was lead vocalist on 'Money', 'To Know Him Is To Love Him', 'Memphis', and 'Hello Little Girl'. George sang 'The Sheik of Araby', 'Take Good Care Of My Baby', 'Three Cool Cats' and 'Crying, Waiting, Hoping'.

The session finished around 2.00 p.m. and they listened to the playback and all seemed pleased with the session.

Brian then took them all to a restaurant in Swiss Cottage to celebrate and the Beatles and Neil then drove back to Liverpool.

Tony Barrow contacted Mike Smith to ask him if he would be signing the group. Smith said he'd have to wait for Dick Rowe to return from America, but felt confident that the Beatles would get their contract.

As it turned out, Smith had recorded another band that afternoon, Brian Poole & the Tremeloes, and Decca decided to sign them up rather than the Beatles. The precise details regarding this decision have never been clearly laid out. It is suggested that Smith liked the Beatles and wanted to sign them, but was either vetoed or asked to choose one of the two groups. There was certainly a suggestion that the Tremeloes were on Decca's doorstep whereas the Beatles were located over 200 miles away and for the sake of communication, it would be easier to sign the Tremeloes.

Yet, if Rowe and Smith were on-the-ball as the *Cash Box* item suggested, why didn't they at least see the potential in the Beatles' repertoire? A third of the songs performed at that session were to become chart hits. Three of the Beatles numbers, 'Love Of The Loved', 'Hello Little Girl' and 'Like Dreamers Do', provided hits for Cilla Black, the Fourmost and the Applejacks and two other numbers they performed, Chuck Berry's 'Memphis' and Berry Gordy's 'Money', were to provide hits for Dave Berry and Bern Elliott & the Fenmen.

When the Decca rejection was finalised, Brian was given the Decca tapes to use in his attempts to secure the group a recording contract.

However, Decca retained the master tapes of the Beatles session in their vaults and in the late seventies and eighties, bootleg albums and singles of the session began to appear followed, later on, by releases of the packages by legitimate record companies, even though the actual legalities of the rights have never been put to the test in court. EMI did not claim any rights to products recorded before the group signed with the label, but Decca itself did not release any of the tracks on its own label and it is unclear who actually sold rights to various record labels.

Bootleg singles began to appear in America in 1977 on a label called Deccagone. They were 'Three Cool Cats' c/w 'Hello Little Girl' issued on Deccagone PRO 1100 in April 1977; 'The Sheik of Araby' c/w 'September In The Rain' issued on Deccagone PRO 1101 in August 1977; 'Memphis, Tennessee' c/w 'Love Of The Loved' issued on Deccagone PRO 1102 in November 1977; 'Searchin'' c/w 'Like Dreamers Do' issued on Deccagone PRO 1103 in November 1977; 'Sure To Fall' c/w 'Money' issued on Deccagone PRO 1104 in February 1978; 'Crying, Waiting, Hoping' c/w 'Till There Was You' issued on Deccagone PRO 1104 in October 1978 and 'To Know Him Is To Love Him' c/w 'Besame Mucho' on Deccagone PRO 1106 in February 1979. Following the release of the fourth single, an album *The Deccagone Sessions* was available to fans containing eight of the Decca tracks, plus some radio material. More singles followed and in December 1979 another album called *The Decca Tapes* was issued on Circuit Records LK 4438-I.

UDL (United Distributors Lyrics Ltd) began to package ten of the tracks in an album called *Dawn Of The Silver Beatles* (although the Beatles had dropped the name 'Silver' from their name before the Decca sessions), issued by PAC Records, a mail order firm in Phoenix, Arizona, on 16 April 1981 on PAC Records UDL 2333. Various other tracks were issued, coupled with material by other artists, and Backstage Records issued *Like Dreamers Do*, which was a three-album package containing Decca tracks, excerpts from press interviews and an interview with Pete Best, issued on Backstage Records BSR 1111 in May 1982. During the same year, a company called Audio Fidelity Enterprises issued twelve of the tracks on an album called *The Complete Silver Beatles*, on Audio Fidelity AFELP 1047 in September 1982 and on Audio Rarities AR 2452 in October 1982 and followed with two budget album releases, *The Silver Beatles Vol. 1* in October 1982 on Phoenix PHX 352 and *The Silver Beatles Vol. 2* in October 1982 on Phoenix PHXC 353. All of these albums were aimed specifically at the American market. In Britain, Breakaway Records issued *The Audition Tapes* (Breakaway BWY 72) in

December 1983. Tracks from the sessions have also been mixed with Star Club recordings for other album packages.

Decca Records

Along with EMI, Decca was one of the major record labels at the same time Brian Epstein was seeking a recording contract for the Beatles. Over the years Decca has, rather unfairly, been dismissed as the record label which turned down the Beatles.

It was, in fact, the first label to be enthusiastic enough about the group to grant them a recording audition. EMI, on the other hand, saw all of its pop labels dismiss the group out of hand without even considering an audition. It was only by a fluke that George Martin, on EMI's non-pop label Parlophone, eventually did sign the Beatles up.

At a time when the British charts had been dominated by American artists, cover versions of American hits, solo singers, jazz bands and former singers with dance bands, Decca had decided to actively seek new British talent in the pop field and had briefed Dick Rowe and his assistants Mike Smith and Tony Meehan to do just that. This would have seemed an auspicious moment to sign the Beatles.

Epstein had experienced great difficulty in his efforts to obtain a recording contract for the Beatles. He'd approached Les Cox of Pye Records, but was refused even an audition for the group. Philips Records was also uninterested, together with the minor label Oriole. Epstein had even considered approaching Woolworths' Embassy label, but this was a label which only covered current hits on budget releases and didn't actually sign up any artists.

On Epstein's urging, EMI's marketing manager Ron White had approached all three recording managers who looked after EMI's pop music labels: Norrie Paramor, Walter Ridley and Norman Newell all expressed their disinterest in the Beatles. The fourth EMI house A&R man George Martin was on holiday at the time, so White didn't approach him. However, he was able to contact Epstein to tell him that EMI was not interested as Martin's label Parlophone, wasn't really a pop label and Martin had been recording comedy artists such as Peter Sellers and the 'Beyond The Fringe' team. As it turned out, the Beatles were able to enter EMI through the back door, via the piece of luck which drew Brian Epstein to have acetates made at Oxford Street's HMV store.

Decca, on the other hand, sent Mike Smith up to Liverpool to see the group. He was enthusiastic and arranged an audition. The audition took place and a satisfied Smith would have signed them up, but was given the option of signing only one of the two groups he'd

recorded that day. The decision came down in favour of Brian Poole
& the Tremeloes because of their proximity to London. If the
Tremeloes had come from Sheffield, Decca would no doubt have
signed up the Beatles. But even leaving out the hypothetical situation, Decca was the only company which directly expressed enough
interest in the group to grant them a proper recording audition,
prior to the set of circumstances in which fate drew Epstein and
Martin together.

Decca was able to offset the stigma of 'turning down' the Beatles
when it signed up the Rolling Stones – ironically, on the recommendation of George Harrison. George just mentioned the group to
Dick Rowe when both of them had been participating in the judging
of a beat contest in Liverpool. It probably didn't enter George's head
to formally recommend them to his own record company. If he had,
EMI would surely have signed them up. Yet it was Decca who signed
them up and the Rolling Stones benefited. Due to the success of the
Beatles, the Stones were able to demand and get an equitable royalty
on their records, more than the Beatles received from EMI, a situation which was to rankle the members of the Beatles when they
realised that the Rolling Stones made far more money from selling
less records than they did.

Decca was also to sign up the Beatles' former drummer, Pete Best,
and Ringo Starr's former group, Rory Storm & the Hurricanes, but
didn't have success with either of them.

Epstein was also to deal with Decca and signed up the Big Three
to them. Decca issued a number of records by other Mersey Beat
acts, including Freddie Starr & the Midnighters, Lee Curtis and
Beryl Marsden, but didn't have much success with them. It's interesting to note that the only non-Epstein group from Liverpool to
reach No. 1 was the Searchers. The media were firmly locked in on
Epstein and his stable, who received the lion's share of the media
attention and promotion during the 1963–64 period.

Defeat of the Dog, The

One of a series of avant-garde films which Paul made in 1966.
Another was called *The Next Spring Then*. Paul screened the two
films for journalist Patrick Skene Catling and they were mentioned
in his article that appeared in *Punch* magazine on 23 November
1966. Catling commented: 'They were not like ordinary people's
home movies. There were over-exposures, double-exposures,
blinding orange lights, quick cuts from professional wrestling to a
crowded car park to a close-up of a television weather map. There
were long still shots of a grey cloudy sky and a wet, grey pavement,
jumping Chinese ivory carvings, and affectionate slow-motion

studies of his sheepdog Martha and his cat. The accompanying music, on a record player and faultlessly synchronised, was by the Modern Jazz Quartet and Bach.'

These are also the films Paul screened for director Michaelangelo Antonioni. They pre-date John's first forays into experimental films, which he didn't begin until 1968, establishing that Paul was the first member of the Beatles to experiment in avant-garde music and film.

Sadly, they are believed lost, being among the number of Paul's home movies that were stolen from his Cavendish Avenue house.

Delaney, Patrick

A former member of the Guards, Patrick, more familiarly known as 'Paddy', joined the Liverpool Parks Police and later became a doorman at the Locarno and Grafton ballrooms in West Derby Road, Liverpool. In 1959 he was asked if he would work on the Cavern door one night. Believing it to be a proper club, he turned up in a dinner-suit with matching tie and cummerbund. He then became the regular doorman at the Cavern until the venue closed, spending a total of seven years working for the club.

When Ray McFall originally engaged him he told Paddy that there were fights going on almost every night as a group of hooligans had virtually taken control of the club. Paddy agreed to take on the job for one pound per night if he could have some other men to help him. He soon cleaned up the place.

Paddy became a friend of the Beatles and often chatted with them at the door, following a few incidents in which he initially almost stopped them from entering because of their appearance. For a time he also worked for *Mersey Beat*, helping to deliver copies locally.

His memories of the years he served at the Cavern written in a manuscript 'The Best Of Cellars', remain unpublished.

Delfont, Bernard

In the sixties, together with his brothers Lew and Leslie Grade, Delfont was part of the triumvirate which virtually controlled British showbusiness. Among the ventures under Delfont's control was the annual Royal Variety Show. Delfont was to book the Beatles for the show on 4 November 1963, saying that his ten-year-old daughter had recommended the group. When he sent the list of artists, with the Beatles' name on it, to Buckingham Palace for approval, there was no objection.

Delfont also ran a large management and agency group and Brian Epstein had several meetings with him, some of them in the South of France, to discuss Delfont purchasing NEMS and the

Beatles. Eventually, Delfont offered Brian £150,000 in exchange for 50 per cent of Brian's companies. Epstein seriously considered the offer but when he mentioned it to the Beatles, John Lennon wouldn't hear of it and said that the group would break up if he tried to sell them. Epstein later leased the Saville Theatre from Delfont.

For his services to charity, the entertainments industry and the Royal Variety Show, Delfont was given a peerage and became Lord Delfont. He also became Chairman of a vast entertainment group called First Leisure.

He died in 1999.

De Montfort Hall, Granville Road, Leicester

The major concert venue in Leicester. The Beatles appeared there for the first time on the last date of their Tommy Roe/Chris Montez tour on 31 March 1963. Their second appearance took place there on 1 December 1963 during the group's autumn tour of the UK. Their third and final appearance at the De Montfort Hall was the second date of their winter tour of Britain on 10 October 1964.

Dennisons, The

Many people predicted major success for this highly popular Liverpool group who first formed in 1961 and began their career with a Saturday night residency at the BICC Club in Melling. They comprised Eddie Parry (vocals), Ray Scragge (rhythm), Clive Hornby (drums), Steve McLaren (lead) and Alan Willis (bass).

They appeared on Cavern bills with the Beatles during 1962: on Wednesday, 25 July, Saturday, 13 October and Sunday, 25 November. Their 1963 Cavern appearances with the Beatles took place on Sunday, 20 January and Friday, 12 March.

When record companies heard that they were drawing crowds in Liverpool like the Beatles used to, they rushed there and Decca managed to sign them.

The group made their recording debut in July 1963 with 'Come On Be My Girl', a number they'd written backstage at the Cavern. It reached No. 47 in the charts. They followed up with their version of Rufus Thomas' 'Walkin' The Dog' in February 1964. The 'B' side, 'You Don't Know What Love Is', was written specially for them by Ben E. King, with whom they were touring at the time. The record reached No. 36 in the charts and when it was played on 'Juke Box Jury', one of the panellists, *Carry On* star Sid James, commented: 'If I knew who that feller was, I'd buy him a drink.'

Their third and final single was 'Nobody Like My Babe', released in November 1964. Although it had a very commercial sound, it didn't enter the charts.

Vocalist Parry left in 1965 and the group disbanded two years later.

Clive Hornby became an actor and appeared in a production of *In His Own Write* at the Playhouse Theatre, Liverpool, in 1968. He found fame as Jack Sugden in the long-running British TV soap 'Emmerdale'.

Steve contracted multiple sclerosis and died in 1993 and Eddie succumbed to a heart attack in 1995.

Denver, Karl

A folk singer, born Angus McKenzie in Glasgow on 16 December 1934. A former merchant seaman, he entered show business at the age of 23, formed the Karl Denver Trio with Kevin Neill and Gary Cottrell and enjoyed eleven British chart hits between 1961 and 1964, including the Top 10 entries 'Marcheta', 'Mexicali Rose', 'Womoweh' and 'A Little Love, A Little Kiss'.

When the Beatles recorded for the BBC Light Programme's 'Side By Side' at the Piccadilly Studios in London on Monday, 1 April 1963, they duetted with the Karl Denver Trio on the number 'Side By Side', a song originally penned by Harry Woods in the 1920s.

Denver's group was the resident band on the half-hour show in which their performances would alternate with those of their guest group. They always opened the show singing 'Side By Side' with their guest of the week.

At this particular session, the Beatles recorded two editions of the show, transmitted on Monday, 22 April and Monday, 13 May. They were to appear as Denver's guests on one further programme in the series.

The trio also appeared with the Beatles on 'Shindig', the American ABC networked pop show, in an edition recorded at the Granville Studio, Fulham Broadway, London, on Friday and Saturday 2 and 3 October 1964.

Denver later settled in Manchester and in 1989 had further success when he recorded 'Wimoweh' with the Happy Mondays. He teamed up with the band again in 1990 to record 'Lazyitis'.

He died in 1998.

De Shannon, Jackie

American singer/songwriter, real name Sharon Myers, who was born in Hazel, Kentucky, on 21 August 1944.

She penned 'Dum Dum' and 'Heart In Hand' for Brenda Lee in collaboration with Sharon Sheeley, and 'When You Walk In The

Room', a number she co-wrote with Jack Nitzche, became a hit for the Searchers.

Her own singing career took second place to her songwriting success and she penned hits for numerous artists, including Marianne Faithfull, the Byrds and Helen Shapiro.

Jackie had a Top 10 hit with 'What The World Needs Now Is Love' in 1965. In 1969 she had her biggest hit with 'Put A Little Love In Your Heart', which reached No. 4 in the American charts.

Although her own version of 'When You Walk In The Room' wasn't a chart hit, it led to her being booked on the first Beatles tour of America in the autumn of 1964, for which she was paid $1,250 per week. Soon after, she released an album, *Breakin' It Up On The Beatles Tour*.

Her first performance with the Beatles was at the Cow Palace, San Francisco, and she was very nervous. Paul came over to her and said, 'I've heard some of your music, and it's really good and it's gonna be great so don't worry about it.'

Jackie performed an up-tempo repertoire on the tour, with numbers such as 'Shout' and closed the first half of the show.

Devil In Her Heart

Number, originally called '(There's A) Devil In His Heart' by female vocal group the Donays in 1962. Penned by Richard B. Drapkin, the record wasn't a major hit for the Donays, but the Beatles adapted the number and included it in their stage act with George Harrison on lead vocals. They recorded the number on Thursday, 18 July 1963, and it was included on their *With The Beatles* album. It was also included on their American release *The Beatles Second Album*. A version recorded on the *Pop Go The Beatles* radio show in 1963 was included on *The Beatles Live At The BBC* CDs.

Devlin, Johny

Singer who appeared with the Beatles on their tour of Australia and New Zealand. Devlin was a rock 'n' roller from New Zealand who had begun singing in 1958 and received the first domestic Gold Disc awarded in that country. He moved to Australia and settled in Sydney where he had seven hit records within a two-year period. Shortly before the Beatles tour he had a new chart hit, 'Stomp The Tumbarumba'.

As an A&R man for RCA Records, Devlin had been trying to get another singer a place on the bill, but it was decided that he'd be an ideal attraction himself, being popular in both Australia and New Zealand. He managed to gain immediate press publicity by insuring himself against injury on tour – for £25,000!

After instrumental group the Phantoms opened the show, Devlin was next on the bill, with backing from the Phantoms. His repertoire consisted of fifties rock 'n' roll numbers and he bought himself a black leather suit for the tour which led one critic to describe him as 'an overstuffed suitcase'. Another commented that: 'He looked and behaved like a skin diver with St Vitus's Dance.' Not all reviews were as ungallant. Charles Higham in the *Bulletin* newspaper wrote: 'Introduced by a flabby compere named Alan Field, Johnny Devlin looked fat, well past the dreaded bourne of 30, and far from the condition that once won him the title of Mr West Coast of New Zealand. Nevertheless he was, for my money, unquestionably the best performer of the evening. Clad in pitch-black leather from toe to tippet, he looked at first like an animated suitcase; then he unzipped, screamed, shook from head to toe and turned into a blackberry jelly with legs.'

Backstage at the Sydney Stadium, Devlin co-wrote a pop song with Paul McCartney called 'Won't You Be My Baby'. Paul insisted that Johnny take all the credit and it became his first single after the tour.

Devlin continued to perform successfully in Australia for many years after the amazing tour.

Dexter Jr, David

Dave Dexter was a Capitol Records A&R executive based in Hollywood. Each month he would receive a cardboard container with a selection of records issued by EMI in Britain. Dexter had once taken a chance by selecting a Cliff Richard record which, despite promotion, failed to make an impact on the American market and the general opinion was that British discs wouldn't be successful in the US. In 1962 one of the records included in the monthly box was 'Love Me Do'. Other Beatles singles were passed over to Dexter as they were released in the UK, but were turned down.

Dexter had formerly been a journalist on *Downbeat*, the jazz magazine, and a jazz producer.

EMI, embarrassed by their major act being constantly turned down by their American subsidiary, decided to pull some strings. L. G. Wood, an executive at the Manchester Square offices in London, contacted his Capitol counterpart Lloyd Dunn to plead the case for 'I Want To Hold Your Hand'. Dunn told Dexter to put it on their schedule. Dexter told him that he'd already decided to do so. He mentioned that while he'd been at the London offices of EMI during his annual visit there, the disc had been brought to his attention by Tony Palmer and he said that the first four bars of the record convinced him they had a hit.

Dexter was to process the Beatles' records for the American market and was also involved in compiling Beatles albums for Capitol, including the deluxe souvenir *Help!* album. He wrote a book, *Playback*, and Chapter 19 deals with his work for the Beatles.

He retired from Capitol Records in 1974 and died from a heart attack on 19 April 1991 in Sherman Oaks, California. He was 74 years old.

Dietrich, Marlene

The legendary Hollywood star who was born in Germany in 1904. Her many films included *The Blue Angel*, *Destry Rides Again*, *Stage Fright*, *No Highway*, *Rancho Notorious*, *Witness For The Prosecution* and *Judgement At Nuremberg*.

Dietrich embarked on a second career as an international cabaret star and on 4 November 1963 appeared on the Royal Variety Show with the Beatles. This took place at the Prince of Wales Theatre in London and was attended by the Queen Mother, Princess Margaret and Lord Snowden.

When asked how she felt about the group, she said 'The Beatles? I thought they were wonderful – who doesn't?'

In his book, *Dietrich: The Story Of A Star*, author Leslie Frewin pointed out that Dietrich was in great form when she rehearsed with the group and was philosophical in recognising that the majority of those who had paid £50,000 to the Variety Artists Benevolent Fund largely wanted to see the Beatles. She didn't mind and lined up with them at rehearsals and agreed to be photographed.

While admitting that the Beatles stole the show, Frewin pointed out the figures analysed from the television ratings when the show was screened on 10 November. It was discovered that when the Beatles were appearing 2,394,000 people in the London area were viewing, but when Dietrich appeared, the number shot up to 2,525,000, although it was pointed out that earlier viewers might have been watching an Ingrid Bergman film on the other channel while the Beatles were on, only to switch over when the film ended.

The Beatles chose Marlene as one of the 68 figures on the cover of their *Sgt Pepper's Lonely Hearts Club Band* album, where she is nicely positioned on the front right-hand side, close to the Beatles themselves.

There was another anecdote concerning the Royal Variety Show which put a different slant on the relationship between Marlene and the Beatles. In the book *My Fabulous Brothers* by Rita Grade Freeman it says there were difficulties between the Beatles and Marlene during rehearsals.

Comedian Dickie Henderson commented, 'That lady is without

doubt one of the all-time great superstars, but she's also one of the all-time great pains in the backside.'

Rita Freeman observed: 'She went on behaving petulantly and selfishly. Then when she had finished at long last, a group of photographers swept down to the front stalls. "Not now, darlings!" she said to them, "come back in an hour when I've got my make-up on." She then left the stage and four very unassuming young men began their rehearsal. They were playing guitars and singing, and all the cameras flashed them for the next 15 minutes. By the time Marlene returned, now resplendent in a sequined gown and wearing full make-up, there wasn't a photographer in sight – those four young men who had reaped all the publicity were the Beatles, invited to appear in their first Royal show!'

Marlene Dietrich died in Paris, May 1992.

Dig A Pony

Track recorded at Apple Studios on 22 January 1969 as part of the ill-fated 'Get Back' sessions. The John Lennon composition was first heard by the public when it was included among the songs the Beatles sang at their Apple rooftop session on 30 January 1969. The track was included on the *Let It Be* album and Billy Preston played electric piano.

Phil Spector had worked on the tapes, deleting an introduction in which John and Paul say, 'All I want is . . .' In fact, the number was originally going to be called 'All I Want Is You'.

John wasn't quite happy with the song and once described it as 'another piece of garbage'. An alternative version was included on the Beatles' *Anthology 3* CD.

Dig It

Number featured on the *Let It Be* album. The song credits read Lennon/McCartney/Harrison/Starr, but although all members contributed to the composition, it was mainly written by John, who sings lead vocals. Heard in the background is Paul's six-year-old stepdaughter Heather and the lyrics give namechecks to various people and institutions, including singers Doris Day and BB King, Manchester United soccer chief Matt Busby and the BBC and CIA.

The group recorded two versions of the number; the second, which was recorded on Sunday, 26 January, is the one used on the album, although in severely truncated form. One piece from the first version was tacked on to the end of the number, when John announces, 'That was "Can You Dig It" by Georgie Wood. Now we'd like to do "Hark The Angels Come".' Incidentally, 'Wee' Georgie Wood was a show business midget who appeared on variety bills, pantomimes and radio comedy shows.

DiLello, Richard

A New Yorker, born 28 September 1945, who became acquainted with Derek Taylor in San Francisco. He arrived in Britain in November 1967, then left for North Africa for four months before returning to London and asking Taylor for a job. Derek was able to provide him with a post as an assistant press officer to himself at Apple.

Richard became known as 'the House Hippie', and he took on the task of photographer and chronicler of the Apple days as he documented the day-to-day life in the Savile Row building.

He eventually rose to be Chief Press Officer, a post which lasted only a short time. Journalist Anne Nightingale ran a story describing a crumbling Apple empire, which provided Allen Klein with the ammunition he needed in order to sack him.

DiLello's amusing account of his Apple escapades was published in book form as *The Longest Cocktail Party* in 1973.

He is now a TV and movie scriptwriter in Los Angeles.

147 Dinas Lane, Huyton, Liverpool L36

Address of Paul McCartney's auntie Jin. On 18 June 1963 it was the site of Paul's eventful 21st birthday party.

It was decided to hold the party there because Jim McCartney felt that too many fans knew the Forthlin Road address and it would be impossible to hold the function there.

A marquee was erected in the back garden and the host of guests included Brian Epstein, Mike McCartney, John and Cynthia, Ringo and Maureen, George, the Fourmost, the Scaffold, the Shadows, Billy J. Kramer and disc jockey Bob Wooler.

John got drunk and took exception to a remark Wooler made to him relating to John's recent holiday in Spain with Brian Epstein, intimating that John was homosexual. John beat him so severely he had to be pulled off by Billy Kramer and members of the Fourmost. John then attacked a girl.

The next day when asked to apologise, John was unrepentent and said, 'He called me a queer.' An apology was sent on his behalf and a short item about the incident appeared on the back page of the *Daily Mirror*, written by Don Short.

Dingle Vale Secondary Modern, Dingle Vale, Liverpool L8

Ringo attended this school when he was eleven, but was not allowed to take the eleven-plus examination as his primary school teachers believed he wouldn't be able to pass it. He was the only

Beatle not to attend a grammar school. He attended Dingle Vale
between the ages of eleven and fifteen, but at the age of thirteen
suffered from pleurisy and spent his final two years in hospital. He
left the school with no qualifications. After leaving, he needed to go
back to the school 'to get the certificate to prove I'd left. You needed
that to get a job. They didn't even remember I'd been there.'

However, a school report by teacher S. Roberts judged him: 'A
quiet, thoughtful type, although working rather slowly. Academic
work will no doubt improve in time as he is trying to do his best.'

The school was later to become Shorefields Comprehensive
School.

Discs A-Go-Go

A television pop programme produced for the regional TV station
TWW, which covered 'Wales and the west'. The Beatles appeared in
the programme miming to 'Love Me Do', recorded at the
company's Bristol studio at TWW Television Centre, Bath Road,
Bristol, Somerset, on Monday, 3 December 1962. The show's theme
studio setting was described as 'the gayest coffee bar in town'.
Despite being recorded, no copy of the programme currently exists.
The series also screened the promotional film for *Help!* on Monday,
26 July 1965.

Dizzy Miss Lizzy

A song written and recorded by Larry Willliams in 1958. It was a
number very popular with Liverpool groups and the Beatles
included it in their repertoire in 1960 while Mersey Beat band the
Escorts issued it as a single in 1964.

John took over on solo vocal and the Beatles performed it on
their last BBC radio recording, 'Ticket To Ride', in June 1965. The
same year it was included on their *Help!* album and it later surfaced
on *The Beatles Collection, Rock And Roll Music* and the American
Beatles V album. One of the performances from the radio was
included on *The Beatles Live At The BBC* CDs.

Dodd, Ken

Popular Liverpool comedian who was also a successful recording
artist who had seventeen British chart hits between 1960 and 1975,
including 'Love Is Like A Violin', 'Happiness' and 'Tears'.

The Beatles appeared on a charity show at the Albany Theatre,
Maghull, with Dodd topping the bill on 15 October 1961, and
reports suggest he wasn't too enthusiastic about their appearance,
although it's true that they were out-of-place on a bill of variety
artists appearing before local councillors and civic dignitaries.

Fame began to come to both acts at around the same time and during an appearance on the Granada programme, 'Scene at 6.30', Ken Dodd joined the Beatles in a humorous dialogue, with Gay Byrne as the referee. They also appeared once on 'The Ken Dodd Show' a BBC radio programme, although Dodd's agent turned down the opportunity of booking the group twice as he didn't think they'd last.

When Dodd appeared in pantomime in 1964 he commented, 'When I found out I was doing pantomime in Liverpool, I knew I had to pick out at least one Beatle to do a little impersonation. I picked Ringo, got myself tight trousers and a wig and included it in the show. Fantastic reception! Fantastic! But then Liverpool lads have got to stick together, haven't they?'

Dodd, Les

A dance promoter from Wallasey, 'over the water' from Liverpool, who had been promoting dances at the Grosvenor Ballroom, Liscard, and the Institute, Neston, since 1936 via his company, Paramount Enterprises.

He ran '21 plus' nights weekly in two halls, strictly for adults, with advertisements which declared 'No Jiving! No Rock 'n' Roll! No Teenagers!'

But the impact of young music on Merseyside was so strong that Dodd reluctantly began booking local groups on Saturday night 'swing sessions' at the Grosvenor – and Thursday evening dances at the Institute.

Allan Williams had formed Jacaranda Enterprises, a part-time agency, to book a few groups locally and the first gig he arranged for the Silver Beetles was via Dodd. It took place at the Institute, sited in Hinderston Road, Neston, Wirral in Cheshire, on 2 June 1960. Dodd booked them for six Thursday night gigs at the venue. He also booked them for his Grosvenor Hall dances, beginning on Saturday, 4 June 1960.

Both venues became noted for violence and a sixteen-year-old boy was nearly beaten to death in front of the Beatles at the Institute during one of their sessions. They were also quite nervous when they turned up at the Grosvenor without Tommy Moore – who had quit as their drummer – only to find a tough local teddy boy called Ronnie joining them on stage to play drums and telling them he was going to join the group!

The local newspaper wrote about their June appearance at the Institute:

'The Big Beat' featured a double bill at Neston Institute on Thursday evening when the resident Silver Beetles from

Liverpool were supported by Keith Rowlands and the Deesiders from Heswall.

Well known locally for their performances at the Glee Club and the Jazz Club and Le Macabre, the Deesiders are Ronnie Aston on drums, guitarists Pete Bolt and John Sanders and the guitar-playing vocalist Keith Rowlands, who has been signed as a guest artiste with the Silver Beetles on Thursday nights.

Next month the Beetles are leaving Neston to go on tour with teenage idol Dickie Pride.'

From June to August 1960, all the Silver Beetles' bookings, with the exception of a single Jacaranda coffee bar appearance, were for Les Dodd at his two venues. This came to an end when Wallasey Corporation cancelled Dodd's season at the Grosvenor due to the violence. The Beatles had been due to play there on Saturday, 6 August, but Dodd had to cancel their appearance as the venue was now closed to rock 'n' roll.

Dodger Stadium, Elysian Park Avenue, Los Angeles, California

The penultimate American concert appearance. It was the biggest single show of the Beatles' final US tour, attended by 45,000 fans at the mammoth baseball stadium on Sunday, 28 August 1966. The radio station KRLA promoted it.

The Beatles had difficulty escaping from the arena after the show, but finally managed to get away in an armoured car.

The local newspaper reported:

As the quartet tried to leave by the main gates scores of delirious teenagers climbed over the limousine and it was forced to turn back.

The Beatles then fled to offices under the grandstand as crowds charged the 151 foot high entrance gates.

Time and again, police were forced to hit out with their clubs, to keep the fans off the gates.

Youths then charged the gates with wooden barricades which had been set up to keep the crowds back.

They hurled sticks and bottles at police until they were finally turned away with a shoulder-to-shoulder charge by officers who cleared a sort of no-man's-land between the crowds and the exit gates.

Meanwhile, the Beatles, virtually imprisoned beneath the grandstand by fans stampeding from one spot to another in the vast outdoor stadium, made good their escape by armoured car at the opposite end of the field.

Veteran film star Edward G. Robinson was sitting in the audience with cotton wool in his ears, but left the stadium a few minutes before the Beatles appeared on stage.

Doelen Hotel, Amsterdam, Holland
Hotel in Amsterdam where the Beatles stayed on the evening of 5 June 1964 during their brief visit to Holland on their world tour.

Donegan, Lonnie
Musician, once known as 'the king of skiffle', who was born Anthony Donegan on 29 April 1933 in Glasgow, the son of a violinist in the National Scottish Orchestra. When he completed his army service in 1949, he began playing in various jazz bands. His stage name allegedly came about in 1952, when he was appearing on the same bill as legendary blues guitarist Lonnie Johnson in London and the compere mistakenly announced him as 'Lonnie Donegan' – he decided to keep the name.

During the same year he joined Ken Colyer's Jazzmen on guitar and banjo, where he was reunited with a former army buddy, Chris Barber. During the band's show he was given his own spot, accompanied by Colyer on guitar, Barber on bass and Bill Colyer on washboard, performing the style of music generally known as 'skiffle'.

Donegan had a massive hit with 'Rock Island Line' in 1956 and during the next six years enjoyed a total of 32 chart hits. He sparked off a skiffle boom and during its height it was estimated that there were 5,000 skiffle groups in the country.

Among Donegan's appearances in 1956 was a concert at the Empire Theatre, Liverpool. Paul McCartney was in the audience and he became inspired. Also, during a school lunchtime he'd gone down to the theatre to glimpse his idol and noticed that Donegan was writing notes to the employers of factory girls, explaining why they were late – they'd spent time in their dinner hour waiting for him. Paul was very impressed by the gesture and felt that this was the way that stars should behave.

Donegan's Liverpool appearance sparked Paul's desire for a guitar and his father, Jim, bought him one for £15.

A fourteen-year-old George Harrison, who'd originally met Paul on the bus on the way to the school they both attended, went round to Paul's house to look at his teach-yourself-to-play book. George recalled: 'We learned a couple of chords from it and managed to play "Don't You Rock Me Daddy'O".'

The Donegan appearance also sparked off George's desire for a guitar and he bought a second-hand one from a boy in school for £3, which his mum had lent him.

George's brother Harry was to say: 'Lonnie Donegan was appearing at the Empire and of course George just had to go. In fact, he borrowed the money from our parents so that he could see every single show! Anyway, he found out where Lonnie was staying, which happened to be in a house in Speke, so George went round and hammered on the door until he came out and gave George his autograph. Of course, he immediately raced home to show everyone.'

In an interview with *Disc*, George Harrison was to comment: 'Lonnie and skiffle seemed made for me . . . it was easy music to play if you knew two or three chords, and you'd have a tea-chest as bass and washboard and you were on your way.'

They were similar to the comments he made to Hunter Davies in the official biography of the Beatles, when he said that Lonnie Donegan was the first person to make an impression on him musically: 'I'd been aware of pop singers before him, like Frankie Laine and Johnny Ray, but never really taken much interest in them. I don't think I thought I was old enough for them. But Lonnie Donegan and skiffle just seemed made for me.'

The king of skiffle was also a catalyst for the sixteen-year-old John Lennon. He'd listened to the music on Radio Luxembourg and thought that it wasn't difficult to play, so he asked his Aunt Mimi if she could get him a guitar. He also bought a 78rpm record of 'Rock Island Line', which he later sold to a schoolmate, Rod Davis. Rod was also inspired by Donegan and bought a banjo for £5 from an uncle and joined John Lennon's new skiffle group, the Quarry Men.

Included in the Quarry Men's repertoire were several skiffle numbers popularised by Donegan, including 'Rock Island Line', 'The Cumberland Gap', 'Midnight Special', 'Railroad Bill' and 'Worried Man Blues'.

Ringo Starr also entered the music world during the skiffle era and joined the Eddie Clayton Skiffle Group in 1957.

In the late 1970s, Paul suggested that Lonnie re-record some of his skiffle hits. The album *Puttin' On the Style,* produced by Adam Faith in Los Angeles, was released in January 1978. Among the musicians backing him were Ringo Starr, Elton John, Leo Sayer, Brian May of Queen and Lonnie's regular band. Ringo appeared on the tracks 'Have a Drink On Me' and 'Ham 'n' Eggs'.

Following a mild heart attack in 1986, Donegan went into semi-retirement, moving to the Costa del Sol, where he lives with his second wife, Sharon, and their three sons, Peter, David and Andrew.

Although the group were later to be influenced by a range of American rock 'n' roll stars such as Carl Perkins, Elvis Presley, Buddy Holly, Chuck Berry, Little Richard and Gene Vincent, it was really Donegan, a British musician, who set the ball rolling.

Donovan
Folk singer, born Donovan Phillip Leitch in Glasgow, Scotland, on 10 May 1946.

Bob Dylan first introduced him to the Beatles at the Savoy Hotel, London in May 1965. He became a friend of the group and wrote a song in tribute to them called 'For John And Paul'. The name of the song was changed to 'Sunshine Superman' when it was released and it reached No. 2 in the British charts in December 1966.

Donovan was also at Rishikesh with the Beatles during a six-week period in 1967 and he composed 'Hurdy Gurdy Man' before the four Beatles, Beach Boy Mike Love and actress Mia Farrow. George Harrison immediately added a new verse to the song. Unfortunately, Donovan's record company Pye talked him out of including George's verse on the finished track as they wished releases of singles to be kept to a length of under three minutes. The record reached No. 4 in the British charts.

Mickie Most produced the number and Jimmy Page, John Bonham and John Paul Jones backed Donovan on it. The George Harrison verse, the third in the song, was reinstated in 1990 on a CD *The Classics Live*. Donovan also included George's verse in his live performances in 1991.

While in India, Donovan taught John some guitar styles and John was to comment, 'Donovan is as important and influential as Bob Dylan and we are listening: the man's a poet.'

Paul and George attended Donovan's Royal Albert Hall appearance on Sunday, 15 January 1967, and all four Beatles went to see him on the opening night of his week-long engagement at the Saville Theatre on Monday, 24 April 1967.

George Harrison was to give him his first lesson in playing the sitar in January 1967.

During 1968 it was alleged that Paul McCartney made a guest appearance on Donovan's 'Atlantis' single playing tambourine and providing some backing vocals – but Donovan denies this. He does confirm that Paul dropped into the studio during the recording of 'Mellow Yellow' and at one point sang the words Mellow Yellow.

A fifteen-minute session between the two artists, also from 1968, has been captured on an American bootleg album *No. 3 Abbey*

Road, NW8. The interlude was taken from a studio warm-up between Donovan and Paul. In their book, *The End Of The Beatles,* authors Harry Castleman and Walter J. Podrazik mention that the two stars sat down together with acoustic guitars and exchanged songs-in-the-works, with Paul offering 'Blackbird' and 'Heather' and Donovan selecting numbers from what eventually became *HMS Donovan.*

Donovan married Linda Lawrence in 1970 and the couple had two children, Oriole and Astrella.

Don't Bother Me

The first George Harrison composition to appear on a Beatles album.

When *Mersey Beat* editor Bill Harry met George in Liverpool clubs such as the Blue Angel and the Cabin, he pointed out that the first mention of an original Beatles song in *Mersey Beat* was 'Cry For A Shadow', in issue two. This was mainly a George Harrison composition and Harry kept mentioning that George should get down to writing songs himself and not leave everything to John and Paul. It got so that every time George went to a club Harry would ask him if he was writing a song. When George was about to go out one night he felt he might bump into Harry, so he started writing a number which he called 'Don't Bother Me'. In his book *I. Me. Mine,* George says he completed it in a hotel in Bournemouth when on tour in 1963.

The Beatles bgan recording the number on Wednesday, 11 September 1963, and it was included on their *With The Beatles* album in November 1963 and on the American *Meet The Beatles* album in January 1964.

Don't Ever Change

A Gerry Goffin and Carole King number issued as a single by the Crickets in June 1962. The Beatles immediately added it to their repertoire, with George performing the number on stage, although when they included it on their 'Pop Go The Beatles' radio show on 27 August 1963, John and Paul shared the vocal honours. The group never performed the number for release on record. However, the Pop Go The Beatles performance was included as a track on *The Beatles Live At The BBC* CDs.

Don't Forbid Me

Pat Boone had a No. 1 hit in America with this song in 1956. The Beatles introduced it into their repertoire in 1960, but had dropped it by the beginning of 1962.

Don't Let Me Down

Another composition written by John, which he dedicated to Yoko. Recordings began during the *Get Back* sessions and the number was issued as the flipside of the 'Get Back' single in April 1969.

Billy Preston played electric piano on the track and it was one of the numbers performed on the Apple rooftop session and was included in the film *Let It Be*.

The track was included in the compilation albums *The Beatles 1967–1970* and *Hey Jude*. The number was included on the CD compilation *Past Masters Volume Two*.

Don't Let The Sun Catch You Cryin'

A number which had been recorded by Ray Charles in 1960. The Beatles included the song in their stage repertoire the same year but had dropped the number by the following year. Paul McCartney sang lead vocal. It is a completely different number than 'Don't Let The Sun Catch You Crying', which Liverpool group Gerry & the Pacemakers took to No. 6 in the British charts in 1964.

Don't Pass Me By

Ringo's first self-penned composition to appear on a Beatles album. Ringo had attempted to write numbers before, but his fellow Beatles had always commented that they sounded too much like other tunes. Ringo had been working on this number over a period of time and it became the second song to be recorded for *The Beatles* double album. When recording began, it was dubbed 'Ringo's Tune', then 'This Is Some Friendly' and finally, 'Don't Pass Me By'. Ringo's love of country music came to the fore in this tale of a girl who was late for a date because she was delayed in a minor crash.

Strangely enough, when he began writing the song in 1963 he revealed the fact to the *New Musical Express*, saying, 'Every time I play it to the lads they just laugh.' But he also mentioned in the interview then that the title was 'Don't Pass Me By'.

He wrote the lyrics, then played the number to the other members of the group during a BBC recording session at the Paris Theatre. He'd hoped it would be an album track which Paul could sing. He was told that the tune was just like a particular 'B' side on a Jerry Lee Lewis record.

In addition to playing drums, Ringo played piano and to add to the country feel, violinist Jack Fallon was brought in to provide a country fiddle sound.

Commenting on his songwriting efforts to *Music Echo*, he said, 'I usually get a first verse and then I find it impossible to get anywhere else with the song. I can't say, "Now I'm going to write." I just have to be around a guitar or piano and it just comes. Usually, what I do if I'm in the mood is to put the tape on if I've got a tune, and then I play the same tune like a hundred times with different words. Then I take the tape off and get it all typed out and then I pick the lines out that I'll put together.' A version of *Don't Pass Me By* was included on The Beatles' *Anthology 3* CDs.

Dooley, Arthur

One of the colourful characters who was part of the Mersey scene in the late 1950s and early 1960s. A tall, powerfully built working-class card-carrying member of the Communist Party, he became a noted sculptor and was the subject of a 'This Is Your Life' TV programme and a TV play by Alun Owen.

Arthur had been a friend of the Beatles during their early career when they used to frequent clubs such as the Jacaranda and the Blue Angel. Eventually he created a piece of sculpture dedicated to them which, in 1974, was fitted to a wall in Mathew Street, Liverpool, directly opposite the site of the Cavern Club.

Dick jockey Peter Prince launched an appeal to raise £500 to enable Arthur to work on his tribute. £1,300 was raised, the balance being donated to a Liverpool boys' club.

Arthur worked mainly in metal and the piece is typical of his style. It depicts a Madonna holding three babies – a fourth is separated from the group and is flying away. The three babies represent John, George and Ringo and the solo figure represents Paul. The initials MJPGR, with the M standing for Madonna, surround the piece. Directly above the sculpture, in a reproduction of a typical street sign, is the legend 'Beatles Street, Liverpool 2'.

Arthur died on Friday 7 January 1994, aged 64.

Doran, Terry

One of Brian Epstein's original circle of drinking companions and gay friends. They first met in a Liverpool pub in 1959.

Once the Beatles had achieved nationwide success, Brian decided to go into business with Terry, who was a car salesman. They formed a partnership and launched a company called Brydor Autos, based in Hounslow, Middlesex. Brian reasoned that since the Beatles and other members of the organisation were buying cars, it would be a sensible move to direct the business Terry's way.

Brian immediately purchased a silver Bentley convertible and a black Mini-Cooper. Among the other immediate customers were John Lennon who bought a green Ferrari and a Mini Minor, Ringo

Starr who bought two Minis, a Land Rover and a Facel Vega, and George Harrison who bought a Maserati and an E-type Jaguar.

Although Clive Epstein was in charge of the company's books, he had a difficult time balancing them because Brian kept taking cash out. If they were selling so many cars, Clive asked regularly, where was the money? In fact, Brian was using cash from Brydor Autos to fund his passion for gambling. Consequently, the company didn't last very long.

Terry, a charming and entertaining man, had by that time become a close friend of the individual members of the Beatles – with John and George in particular. When John tired of going out to clubs in favour of sitting at home watching television or listening to Dylan records – and George also tired of clubbing – Terry and Pete Shotton used to take Cynthia and Pattie out for nights out on the town, mainly dancing in clubs.

Terry also used to join John on his LSD trips and the two of them once began spray-painting the front of John's house with aerosol paint cans.

In the song 'She's Leaving Home', penned by both John and Paul, there is a line referring to 'a man from the motor trade'. It is commonly alleged that this refers to Terry, although Paul has denied this.

When John was writing 'A Day In The Life', he was stuck for an ending to the line, 'Now they know how many holes it takes to fill' and needed something to rhyme with 'small'. It was Terry who suggested 'the Albert Hall'.

When the Beatles set up their Apple Empire, Terry was appointed head of Apple Music in September 1967. The publishing company was situated in an office above the Apple Boutique in Paddington Street. Initially Mike Berry, who formerly worked for Sparta Music, aided him, Jack Oliver was his personal assistant and there were two secretaries, Dee Meehan and Carol Paddon. Terry was also appointed manager of the publishing company's first signing, Grapefruit. John Lennon thought of the name – which was the title of Yoko Ono's book.

In November 1968, Terry took the group away from Apple, commenting: 'I like the Beatles as friends, but not as bosses . . . there is too much driftwood at Apple.'

He then replaced Frankie Hart as George's personal assistant and worked for him for several years, at one time basing himself at the Dark Horse offices in Los Angeles. Terry then continued his duties as PA, working from Friar Park. At one time he managed the estate for George, but George next appointed his brother Harold as manager. When George's son Dhani was born, Terry was sacked as

PA amid rumours that George didn't want someone who was gay to be around his offspring.

Terry then returned to the motor trade.

Dorchester Hotel, Park Lane, London WI

One of London's most famous and prestigious hotels, originally built in 1930. The Beatles were invited to the twelfth Annual Variety Club of Great Britain Awards, which took place at the hotel on Thursday, 19 March 1964. The group received an award as Show Business Personalities of 1963, which was presented to them by Prime Minister Harold Wilson. Other award recipients at the lunchtime ceremony included Julie Christie and James Fox, jointly winning the Most Promising Newcomer of 1963 award; Jean Metcalfe as Radio Personality of 1963; Margaret Rutherford as Film Actress of 1963; Dirk Bogarde as Film Actor of 1963; Wilfred Brambell and Harry H. Corbett, joint winners of BBC TV Personality of 1963; Patrick Macnee and Honor Blackman as joint ITV Personality of 1963; Sir Michael Redgrave as Stage Actor of 1963; and Maggie Smith as Stage Actress of 1963. There was also a special award presented to Sean Connery.

On Thursday, 23 April 1964, the Foyle's Literary Luncheon was held at the hotel and John Lennon was guest of honour. The event paid tribute to his best-selling book *In His Own Write* and although John was expected to give a speech to the gathering of celebrity guests, all he could muster were the words, 'Thank you very much, and God bless you.'

Following the premiere of *A Hard Day's Night* at the London Pavilion on Monday, 6 July 1964, the Beatles were guests at a private party at the Dorchester. Brian Jones and Keith Richards of the Rolling Stones turned up, uninvited, but were warmly received by the Beatles, who greeted them with glasses of champagne. Princess Margaret and Lord Snowdon also attended the party.

The Dorchester was also the scene of the post-premiere party for *Help!* on Thursday, 29 July 1965.

John and Yoko met Allen Klein there on Tuesday, 28 January 1969, a meeting which resulted in John agreeing to him becoming his representative. On 1 December 1983, Paul, Ringo, George and Yoko met at the Dorchester Hotel to discuss the dissolution of Apple. After eleven hours of talk, Yoko told the press, 'We've just been having dinner and a chat with friends.'

Dorn, Beno

Master tailor, famous on Merseyside due to his flair for publicity and the inclusion of his photograph in the numerous ads he took in the local papers under the slogan 'The master tailor for impeccable handmade clothes'.

When Brian Epstein decided to smarten up the Beatles' image in 1962 he took the group 'over the water' to Dorn's shop at Grange Road West in Birkenhead. Brian and the Beatles finally decided on the sort of suits which should be worn and Dorn made them grey tweed suits with matching ties for £40 each (but later discounted to £30) which they wore for the first time on stage at the Heswall Jazz Club on 24 March 1962 when they played for the Barnston Women's Institute. They also wore the suits for their 'new image' photo session with Albert Marrion.

Douglas, Craig

British singer who enjoyed a string of chart hits from 1959 with 'A Teenager In Love' straight through to 1963 with 'Town Crier'. His eleven chart entries included the No. 1 hit 'Only Sixteen' plus 'The Heart Of A Teenage Girl' and 'When My Little Girl Is Smiling'. The former milk roundsman was born in Newport, Isle of Wight, in 1941 and made his film debut in *It's Trad, Dad.*

The wholesome singer appeared on the bill at the Empire Theatre, Liverpool on Sunday, 28 October 1962. Little Richard was the bill-topper and there were eight acts on the concert, presented by NEMS Enterprises.

Trailering the Empire show, *Mersey Beat* wrote: 'Recording, films and concerts are everyday parts of Craig Douglas' life, for this nineteen-year-old former tractor driver has several hits to his credit, and has the good looks which make him a natural choice for film parts – he has appeared in *Climb Up The Wall, The Painted Smile* and *It's Trad, Dad.*

Douglas closed the first half of the show and the Beatles became his backing group for this performance which was billed as 'Their first appearance at the Empire'. It was a prestigious event for the Beatles, part of Brian Epstein's plan to build them up by presenting them on major venues on bills with star names. They'd only previously appeared at the Empire in talent competitions as the Quarry Men.

Douglas-Home, Sir Alec

The British Prime Minister and leader of the Conservative Party when Beatlemania first blossomed. At a Conservative Party rally, Douglas-Home commented on the Beatles by describing them thus: 'The Beatles are now my secret weapon. If any country is in deficit with us, I only have to say the Beatles are coming.'

When the Beatles returned to England following their short

Swedish tour on 29 October 1963, Heathrow was so crowded with
fans that Sir Alec Douglas-Home, due to fly to Scotland, was held
up in his car by the crowds. The Queen Mother was also due to
arrive from Ireland and Ed Sullivan, puzzled by all the chaos, asked
whether the crowds were gathered to meet the Queen Mother – and
was told, for the first time, about the Beatles. The new Miss World
was also at the airport – and was totally ignored.

Dovedale Road Primary School, Dovedale Road, Liverpool 18

The primary school which John Lennon attended between 1945
and 1951. One of his fellow pupils was Jimmy Tarbuck, who was
to become one of Britain's leading comedians. George Harrison
also attended the school between 1948 and 1950. As George was
three years John's junior, it is doubtful whether the two ever met
during their period at the school.

Do You Want To Know A Secret?

Number penned by John which was originally given to George
Harrison to sing lead vocal on when the Beatles recorded it on 11
February 1963, during their marathon session for their *Please
Please Me* album. This version was also included on the group's
first EP *Twist And Shout*. It was also released in America on the Vee
Jay label as the flipside of 'Thank You Girl' in 1964 and reached
No. 2.

The Beatles performed the song on several of their BBC radio
shows, including 'Here We Go', 'On The Scene', 'Side By Side',
'Saturday Club', and two 'Pop Go The Beatles'.

The most successful version was by Billy J. Kramer & the
Dakotas, the Beatles' stablemates in Brian Epstein's NEMS
Enterprises. Kramer's version was issued in Britain on Parlophone
R 5023 in April 1963 and topped the British charts. Later that year,
in September it was issued in America on Liberty 55586.

John claimed his inspiration for the number came from a
memory of a Walt Disney film he'd seen as a child.

Dream Baby

Number composed by Cindy Walker recorded by several prominent
rock artists including Roy Orbison, Del Shannon and Bruce
Channel. The Roy Orbison single had only been issued in Britain
for a few weeks when the Beatles performed it on their first radio
show 'Teenager's Turn' on 8 March 1962. With Paul on lead vocal,
it became the first song recorded on the radio by the Beatles.

Drive My Car

Number penned by Paul, although John helped him to tighten up the lyrics and both feature on lead vocals. It was recorded on Wednesday, 13 October 1965, and became the opening track on the *Revolver* album.

It was also included on their *Nowhere Man* EP, *The Beatles 1962–1966* and *Rock 'n' Roll Music* compilations and the American album *Yesterday and Today*.

Drop In

Title of a Swedish television show on which the Beatles featured on Wednesday, 30 October 1963. They recorded the show before a live audience at a small theatre at Narrenteatern in the Stockholm amusement park, Grona Lund. Originally, the group were to perform just two numbers, 'She Loves You' and 'Twist and Shout', but the show's presenter, Klas Burling, persuaded them to add the additional numbers 'I Saw Her Standing There' and 'Long Tall Sally'.

The show was broadcast on Sunday, 3 November 1963 at 7 p.m.

Dr Robert

A song featured on the *Revolver* album, with John singing lead. It was also included on the American album *Yesterday ... And Today*.

The Beatles began recording the number on Sunday, 17 April 1966.

Dr Robert Freymann was said to be the inspiration for the song. John penned the number, with help from Paul in the middle section of the number.

Freymann was a sixty-year-old German doctor whose surgery was on East 78th Street in New York. He had been the doctor present at the death of legendary jazzman Charlie Parker and many New York musicians used his services. John was one of a number of celebrities who obtained amphetamines from him. Prescribing amphetamines was not illegal, although Freymann was to lose his licence for six months in 1968 and was eventually struck off by the New York Medical Society for malpractice. He died in 1987.

Other sources have cited Dr Charles Roberts, who reputedly had a practice on 49th Street, also in New York. However, writer Steve Turner says that Charles Roberts didn't exist but was an alias used by biographer Jean Stein in her book on Warhol protégée Edie Sedgwick, which hid the identity of another doctor who freely prescribed amphetamines. On the other hand, Joel Schumacher, in his biography *Edie: An American Biography,* wrote: 'There were other father figures in New York at that time – the acid doctors. A friend of mine – well, an ex-friend of mine – told me about this terrific doctor where you'd get these vitamin shots – Dr Charles Roberts ... I went one night, got this shot, and it was the most wonderful shot in the world.'

Commenting on the song, Paul McCartney said: 'Well, he's like a joke. There's some fellow in New York, and in the States we'd hear people say, "you can get everything off him; any pills you want." It was a big racket, but a joke too, about this fellow who cured everyone of everything with all these pills and tranquillizers, injections for this and that; he just kept New York high. That's what "Dr Robert" is all about, just a pill doctor who sees you all right.'

Dunbar, John

The man who introduced Paul McCartney to Robert Fraser. Born in Mexico of a Russian mother, Tatiana, and a Scottish father, Robert. John's father had met Tatiana when he was stationed in Russia during the war and the couple also had twin daughters, Jenny and Margaret. He began to study natural science at Churchill College, Cambridge, changing to a history of art course. He first met Marianne Faithfull at a Valentine's Ball at Cambridge and the two began their romance. Dunbar's sister Marianne was going out with Gordon Waller, one half of the duo Peter & Gordon, and introduced them to Peter Asher – and they then became part of the Paul McCartney circle. The couple were married on 6 May 1965 in Cambridge, with Peter Asher as Best Man. John was 22 and Marianne was 18, and their son Nicolas was born in November of that year.

They settled at 20 Lennox Gardens and Paul and Jane Asher were frequent visitors, meeting a variety of artistic people including poet Peter Brown.

Together with his former school chum Peter Asher and Barry Miles, he opened an avant-garde bookshop and gallery called Indica, in Mason's Yard, London, helped by a £3,000 donation from Paul McCartney.

Dunning, George

A Toronto-born animator who directed the Beatles' *Yellow Submarine* film. In the 1940s he had worked on avant-garde shorts, such as *Cadet Rouselle,* made in 1945. In the early 1950s he worked in America at UPA on 'The Gerald McBoing Boing Show' and was also to work on advertising commercials. He was associated with Al Brodax when he produced the Beatles' cartoon series for King Features. Dunning moved to London where he established TVC in 1956, a company making advertising commercials and films for educational, corporate and industrial purposes. In 1962 his short film *The Flying Man* won the Grand Prix at the Annecy International Animation Festival. Dunning had also worked on the Beatles' cartoon series for King Features and Al Brodax hired him to direct the Beatles' feature-length animated film, and it was Dunning who engaged innovative artist Heinz Edelmann.

Discussing *Yellow Submarine,* Dunning commented, 'The film, apart from story and plot, was designed as an "experience". Feature film audiences want this "sensation" or "experience". Since the film was made of drawings and paintings, we decided to bring in all the images familiar to the popular mind that we could.'

He died in 1979.

Durband, Alan 'Dusty'

Paul McCartney's favourite teacher at Liverpool Institute. He taught Paul for the three years leading up to Paul taking his O level GCEs.

Of the sixth-form teacher of English, Paul claimed he was the only teacher he liked. He mentioned that Durband told the boys about books such as *Lady Chatterley's Lover* and Chaucer's *The Miller's Tale*, pointing out that they weren't dirty books but examples of good literature.

Durband was nicknamed 'Dusty'.

When Paul's mother died and Paul turned up at school the next day, acting quite normally, Durband felt sympathy for his pupil and anticipated the torment he must have been going through. He then sent a note to the other teachers asking them to be tolerant of Paul if they noted any strangeness in his behaviour.

Durband commented, 'He'd had a bad break, his mother had died. He did go through a rough patch then. I think it shattered him a lot; maybe it made him turn to other things, like practising his guitar and getting away from the school environment, which was very academic.'

Dusty had a passion for literature and the theatre and once, when he was trying to raise money for a Liverpool theatre which was under threat from closure, Paul told him, 'If I'd got it, I'd give it to you, sir.'

Each year Durband was in charge of the school play and one year the production was George Bernard Shaw's *Saint Joan*. Paul was very keen on appearing in it and auditioned for the part of the Earl of Warwick. The part went to another student, Peter Sissons, who was later to become a television newscaster.

Durband commented, 'All he (Paul) got was a non-speaking role in the last act of the play, as a monk.'

Years later Dusty was told that Paul had been very upset that he didn't get the part. Durband said, 'He just didn't have the talent – he was very quiet in his speech. Peter Sissons, meanwhile, had a huge booming voice . . . but Paul was talking down in his throat, swallowing his words.'

When Paul announced that he was going to Hamburg with his group, Durband told him, 'Go to Teacher's Training College. We can't all be Tommy Steele, you know.'

Alan Durband was to become Head Teacher at Liverpool Institute and he died in September 1994 at the age of 67.

Dylan, Bob

One of the most influential singer/songwriters to emerge in the sixties, he was born Robert Allen Zimmerman on 24 May 1941 in Duluth, Minnesota. He first adopted the name Dylan in 1959. It was suggested that this was in tribute to the Welsh Poet Dylan Thomas – but this theory has been disputed.

The Beatles were first introduced to Dylan's music by American journalist Al Aronowitz who originally met the Beatles in 1963 while reporting for the *Saturday Evening Post*. While the group were appearing at the Olympia Theatre, Paris, in January 1964 they visited a radio station and picked up Dylan's two albums *Bob Dylan* and the *Freewheelin' Bob Dylan*, having only previously heard his hit single 'Blowin' In The Wind', and they played the albums continuously while in Paris.

When they arrived in New York the following month, Aronowitz introduced them to Dylan.

When the group returned to America later in 1964 to tour, they were staying at the Delmonico Hotel in New York when Dylan visited them again. He'd been driven from his home in Woodstock by his friend and roadie Victor Mamoudas in company with Aronowitz and they were taken straight to the Beatles' room. When they began to talk, Dylan suggested that they smoke marijuana. The Beatles had been introduced to pills in Hamburg and now took them on prescription, but they'd been wary of trying marijuana which they regarded as a 'drug'. When they told him they hadn't smoked it before, Dylan was amazed and pointed out that on their number 'I Want To Hold Your Hand', which he thought was a drug song, they'd sung the words 'I get high'. John explained that the words were actually 'I can't hide'. They bolted the doors, put towels around every cranny, pulled the blinds and drew the curtains while Dylan lit a joint and instructed them how to smoke it. Then he passed it on to John, who seemed scared and passed it straight to Ringo. Ringo finished the joint and Dylan rolled half a dozen more. Ringo was the first to start laughing and they all spent several hours together, chatting, giggling and laughing. Paul enjoyed the effects of the drug and said, 'I was thinking for the first time. Really thinking.' For the next few years they were able to compose songs under the influence of marijuana.

Over the years, Dylan and the Beatles were to meet on many occasions and become firm friends. Initially, John came under Dylan's influence and they met socially, but gradually the firmer ties were between Bob and George.

On 9 May 1965, all four members of the Beatles attended Dylan's concert at the Royal Albert Hall in London. This was the tour in which Dylan was receiving criticism from critics and fans alike because he had abandoned the acoustic guitar and 'gone electric'. During the concert, members of the audience began to boo and the Beatles shouted at the hecklers, 'Leave him alone – shut up!' George called the members of the audience who had walked out 'idiots' and commented, 'It was all still pure Dylan, and he has to find out his own directions. If he felt he wanted electrification, that's the way he had to do it.' He added, 'Who's laying down rules?' The Beatles' general comment on the show was, 'Great, just great.'

On 13 and 16 August 1965, Dylan visited them at the Warwick Hotel in New York and in May 1966 when he was in London, Paul and Neil Aspinall met him at Dolly's Club and went back to his room at the Mayfair to spend several hours chatting. In October 1968, George and Pattie spent two weeks at Dylan's home in Woodstock, New York. George and Ringo also visited Dylan in Nashville during the recording of 'Nashville Skyline'. George and Pattie, Ringo and Maureen, John and Yoko and Neil and Mal attended Dylan's concert at the Isle of Wight on 31 August 1969. After the concert he joined John, Yoko and George in a helicopter trip to Tittenhurst Park.

Early in 1970 George was again invited to Woodstock. This was over Thanksgiving and George was accompanied by Mal Evans. Dylan also presented George with a painting, which he displayed at home in his bungalow, Kinfauns. After the third day they got their guitars out. George said, 'Write me some words', and Bob said, 'Show me some chords, how do you get those tunes?' and the song 'I'd Have You Anytime' was born, with Dylan contributing the bridge. The number surfaced on a bootleg album in America called 20 x 4. During 1970 Dylan also showed John and Yoko around Greenwich Village.

When George was making 'All Things Must Pass', Dylan recommended Peter Drake to play the pedal steel parts and George had Drake flown in from Nashville to appear on the album. George also included the number he'd co-written with Dylan, 'I'd Have You Anytime', together with the Dylan composition, 'If Not For You'.

One of their most successful teamings was at George's *Concert For Bangladesh*, when Bob appeared for twenty minutes with a five-song set.

Bob Dylan also had a marked influence on John Lennon, particularly on the lyrics of John's own compositions. In 1964 John said 'I was not too keen on lyrics in those days. I didn't think they counted. Dylan used to come out with his latest acetate and say "Listen to the words, man", and I'd say, "I don't listen to words"' It soon became obvious that Dylan inspired John, who began to wear a Huck Finn cap like Dylan and to pen songs such as 'I'm A Loser' and 'You've Got To Hide Your Love Away'.

At one time while Dylan was at John's Weybridge home for dinner, they played records and talked. John said, 'We swapped addresses and said we'd exchange ideas for songs, but it never happened. He said he sent me things, but he got the address wrong and it never arrived.'

Dylan liked John's 'Norwegian Wood' and took the tune and rewrote his own lyrics to it, resulting in 'Fourth Time Around'. John used Dylan's 'Masters Of War' as an inspiration for his 'Working Class Hero' and when John produced an album for Nilsson he included a new arrangement of 'Subterranean Homesick Blues'. In his song, 'Yer Blues', John wrote: 'Feel suicidal, just like Dylan's Mr Jones,' which was referring to a character in a Dylan song called 'Ballad Of A Thin Man'. Dylan, under his real name of Zimmerman, is also mentioned in the lyrics to John's composition 'God'.

Bob Dylan is one of only two contemporary music figures featured on the cover of the *Sgt Pepper's Lonely Hearts Club Band* album and the Beatles performed five Dylan songs during their *Let It Be* sessions.

In the mid-eighties George was to form a recording group called the Traveling Wilburys with Bob Dylan, Roy Orbison, Tom Petty and Jeff Lynne.

Eamonn Andrews Show, The

The Beatles appeared on this television show, filmed live from Teddington Studios on 11 April 1965.

Andrews, a talk-show host, had worked for BBC Television for a number of years, but had decided to make a move to the commercial channel. His associate Tom Brennan thought it quite a coup to be able to secure the Beatles to appear on the new chat show, only a few weeks after its initial launch. Not only would the Beatles perform two of their latest hits live, but they would also be interviewed at length by Andrews. In fact, the entire show was devoted to the Beatles.

Both John and Paul were very amused to note that Andrews thought Ringo was George and vice versa and laughed when Andrews addressed Ringo as George.

On his forthcoming Easter Sunday show, Andrews had a family of boys from Merseyside as his guests and thought it would be a good idea to present them with an Easter egg with the Beatles' signatures in icing on it. When this suggestion was put to the Beatles management prior to the show, a message came back that they were not skilled in the art of writing in icing sugar and couldn't do it on the live show. Andrews told his producer, 'Sod them, we'll get somebody just to write their names on it with icing. Just John, Paul, Ringo and . . .' 'George' his producer reminded him. Andrews said that they could forge the Beatles' signatures because the Beatles wouldn't admit that they refused to do such a thing for a bunch of kids and the kids themselves wouldn't know the difference.

Andrews had the egg made with the forged signatures and presented the youngest of the Merseyside boys with it on his Easter programme – and was proved right, there were no complaints forthcoming from the Beatles' camp.

When Andrews was hosting a show called 'Today' for Thames Television, John and Yoko appeared on the programme on 1 April 1969 to discuss 'Bagism' and encouraged Andrews to climb into a large white bag with them.

Early Beatles, The

A Capitol album issued in America on ST 2309 on 22 March 1965. This was material obtained by Capitol after Vee Jay Records ceased trading and mainly comprised material which had originally appeared on the *Introducing The Beatles* album and had been re-packaged several times since by Vee Jay. Despite the familiarity of the material and the fact that it had been issued for the fifth time, the album sold over a million copies and reached No. 24 in *Cash Box*, No. 29 in *Record World* and No. 43 in *Billboard*.

There were differences between this release and the original *Introducing The Beatles* album as Capitol took out 'I Saw Her Standing There', 'Misery' and 'There's A Place' and added 'Love Me Do' and 'P.S. I Love You'.

The track listing was, Side One: 'Love Me Do', 'Twist And Shout', 'Anna (Go To Him)', 'Chains', 'Boys' and 'Ask Me Why'. Side Two: 'Please Please Me', 'P.S. I Love You', 'Baby It's You', 'A Taste Of Honey' and 'Do You Want To Know A Secret'.

Eastman, John

Linda McCartney's brother. He was a graduate of Stanford and NYU Law School and joined his father Lee's law firm in New York. When Paul McCartney asked Lee Eastman for advice on how to sort out the financial mess at Apple Corps, Eastman recommended John.

John Eastman flew to London and met the Beatles. John, George and Ringo were considering hiring Allen Klein, but decided that they could also hire Eastman, if only to placate Paul, and he was hired as General Counsel.

The first thing he suggested was that the Beatles buy NEMS. He started negotiations, but they fell through and the company was sold to Triumph Investments. Eastman blamed Klein and Klein blamed Eastman. The Beatles would have been satisfied retaining both men to look after their interests, but it was obvious that the two couldn't work together, so Eastman was in the McCartney corner and Klein with Lennon, Harrison and Starr. Paul's ties with

Eastman became stronger when he married Linda and John became his brother-in-law. Paul refused to sign with Klein and retained Eastman as his representative. It was Eastman who advised him that he had no choice but to file writs against John, George, Ringo and Apple in order to dissolve the Beatles partnership.

Eastman, Lee V

Linda McCartney's father, the son of Russian/Jewish immigrants to New York. At the age of sixteen he won a scholarship to Harvard University, from which he graduated. He changed his name from Epstein to Eastman. His wife Louise was killed in a plane crash in 1962.

As a lawyer, he was to represent many famous painters and the walls of his house were decorated with the works of clients such as Franz Kline, Willem de Kooning, Robert Rauschenberg and Richard Lindner. Together with his son, John, he was set to represent the Beatles in their financial affairs in 1969 until Allen Klein appeared on the scene with the same idea in mind. Klein won, although the Eastmans continued to represent Paul. Their firm, Eastman and Eastman, founded MPL Communications to handle Paul's business affairs and encouraged him to purchase song copyrights. Eastman and his son concentrated on entertainment and their clients included David Bowie, Billy Joel and Andrew Lloyd Webber. Eastman, a collector of modern art, also represented the estate of playwright Tennessee Williams.

Lee died in a New York hospital following a stroke on Tuesday, 30 July 1991. He was 81 years old and survived by his second wife Monique, two other daughters, two sisters, three stepsons and nine grandchildren.

Easy Beat

A Sunday morning BBC radio programme broadcast between 10.30–11.30 a.m. The show was presented by Brian Matthew and produced by Ron Belchier at the Playhouse Theatre in London.

The Beatles appeared on four 'Easy Beat' shows, all of which took place in 1963. The first was broadcast on 7 April and the group performed 'Please Please Me', 'Misery' and 'From Me To You'. On their second appearance on 23 June they performed 'Some Other Guy', 'A Taste Of Honey', 'Thank You Girl' and 'From Me To You'. Their third performance on 21 July featured 'I Saw Her Standing There', 'A Shot Of Rhythm And Blues', 'There's A Place' and 'Twist And Shout'. Their final appearance on 20 October saw them performing 'I Saw Her Standing There', 'Love Me Do', 'Please Please Me', 'From Me To You' and 'She Loves You'.

Eckhorn, Peter

At the age of 21, after returning home from sea, his father presented Peter Eckhorn with club premises at 136 Reeperbahn in Hamburg. The premises had been called the Hippodrome and formerly hosted a topless circus. Eckhorn decided to open a rock 'n' roll club which he called the Top Ten Club and launched it in late October 1960.

Observing the success Bruno Koschmider was having in his Grosse Freiheit clubs with British rock 'n' roll bands, Eckhorn astutely hired Horst Fascher, the Kaiserkeller's 'bouncer', who had developed a rapport with the bands. Through Fascher he was able to book Tony Sheridan & the Jets to open the Top Ten. As a follow-up band he wanted to book the Beatles. The Jets had completed their contract for Koschmider and were ready to go home, but Eckhorn managed to get some of them to stay and remain with Sheridan.

The Beatles made a few appearances at the club before Koschmider saw to it that they had to return to Liverpool. Members of the Jets remained for a further two months, but then left, although Sheridan had agreed to remain as the club's resident singer. Gerry & the Pacemakers was the next band to appear.

In the meantime, Eckhorn made arrangements for the Beatles to return and booked them for a short season from 27 March 1961. The group was so popular he renewed their contract twice and they appeared at the club until 2 July.

In 1962, Peter made a special visit to Liverpool to sign up the Beatles for another season at the club. This time he had to deal with their new manager, Brian Epstein. The money that Epstein demanded, 500 marks for each Beatle per week, was far higher than Eckhorn had intended to pay. He offered 450 marks each and Epstein said he'd let him know. Eckhorn was also unsuccessful in his bid to book Gerry & the Pacemakers again.

In the meantime a new club was being prepared in Hamburg – the Star Club. The owner, Manfred Weissleder, did exactly what Eckhorn had done to Koschmider – he poached Horst Fascher. Three weeks after Eckhorn's visit to Epstein, Fascher arrived in Liverpool to book the Beatles and agreed to Epstein's demand for 500 marks. This ended the group's association with the Top Ten Club.

Peter engaged Iain Hines, former member of the Jets, to become booking manager for the club, but its heyday had passed.

Peter Eckhorn died on 19 May 1978 from kidney insufficiency. He was 39 years old. His wife took over the running of the Top Ten until 1981 and then began renting the club out, with new promoters turning it into a discotheque.

Eddie Clayton Skiffle Group, The

Liverpool skiffle group formed in 1957, when Ritchie Starkey was working as an apprentice engineer at H. H. Hunt & Sons. At the time he had no thoughts of taking up the drums as a career. He recalled, 'I remember my mum saying a neighbour was in a band and why didn't I have a go. I thought it was a jazz group – I was mad on jazz. When it turned out to be a silver band, playing in the park and sticking to the marches and all that, I chucked it in. I lasted just one night.'

His stepfather had bought him a drum kit for £10 in London and brought it back by train.

He got together with his friend Eddie Miles, who also worked for the firm. With three other band members from Hunts, the line-up was Eddie Miles (using the stage name Eddie Clayton because he felt it sounded better than his own name), guitar/vocals; Ritchie Starkey, drums; Roy Trafford, tea-chest bass; John Dougherty, washboard; and Frank Walsh, guitar. They originally began playing during lunchbreaks in the works canteen. Ritchie's grandfather then lent him £50 to put down as a deposit for a brand new kit.

The group made their debut at the Peel Street Labour Club and became resident there, also initially appearing at Wilson Hall, Garston. They also appeared at the Cavern on Tuesday, 31 July and Wednesday, 4 December 1957. Their 1958 Cavern appearances were on Wednesday, 29 January, Friday, 7, Monday, 10, Sunday, 16 and Sunday, 23 February and Saturday, 8 and Friday, 28 March. They also appeared at various skiffle contests taking place at venues such as St Luke's Hall.

Their nearest approach to a group uniform consisted of shirts in the same colour as their bootlace ties. The group was also to enjoy a residency at the boys' club meetings at the Florence Institute in Dingle.

Ritchie's mother, Elsie, was to recall in *Mersey Beat:* 'Ritchie joined the Eddie Clayton Skiffle Group with Ed Miles, the boy who lived next door, Roy Trafford and Johnny Dougherty – they all worked together in the same place. Eddie used to take his guitar to work every day. He was a smashing fellow – if ever a lad should have got somewhere he should have. I believe he's with Hank Walters & his Dusty Road Ramblers.'

The group disbanded because Eddie was getting married. Ritchie then went on to join the Darktown Skiffle Group.

Interestingly enough, Eric Clapton used the alias Eddie Clayton when he guested on the *Ringo* album.

Edelmann, Heinz

Czech-born graphic artist who was artistic director of *Yellow Submarine*. He had already established himself as an internationally renowned artist with his work in typography, book design, illustrations, posters, comic strips and cartoon animation, when he was approached by Charlie Jenkins to work on *Yellow Submarine*. Initially, he was hired for a two-month period, but found himself working around the clock for eleven months. He slept for four hours every other day and the ordeal caused him major health problems. He suffered food poisoning, nearly lost his eyesight and took two years to recover his health after the project was finished.

Edelmann also designed all the characters, including the Blue Meanies. They were originally designed as Red Meanies, but an assistant misread Edelmann's instructions and coloured them blue.

He continued his career as a world-renowned graphic artist with acclaimed book designs, illustrations and posters. In addition, he became a teacher for thirty years until he retired as a Full Professor at the Stuttgart Academy of Fine Arts.

Edelweiss Hotel

Alpine hotel situated in Obertauern, Austria, where the Beatles stayed during the filming of *Help!* They occupied room numbers 501–507 during March 1965.

For the skiing scenes, four Austrian skiers were hired as doubles, each wearing identical clothes to their Beatle counterparts. Frank Bogensberger doubled for John, Herbert Lurzer for Paul, Gerhard Griens for George and Hans Pretscherer for Ringo.

The Beatles had been accompanied by Cynthia, Maureen and Pattie and one morning Maureen walked out of the Edelweiss, moved towards Ringo and gave him a kiss – then realised it was Ringo's double, Hans!

During their stay at the Edelweiss, the producers hired Gloria Makk, Miss Austria 1964, to act as their contact, translator and ski coach.

After the Beatles vacated the hotel on Monday, 22 March the rooms they stayed in were visited by numerous fans who took towels and sheets as souvenirs.

Edgwater Inn, Seattle, Washington

Hotel where the Beatles stayed on 21 August 1964 while appearing at the Seattle Center Coliseum.

The hotel manager, Don Wright, found his hands full with the consequences of Beatlemania. Fan mail and gifts of cakes and cookies were pouring into the hotel, security staff had to scour every nook and cranny – and four teenagers were found hiding in the toilets, three under a bed in one room and a further two under a bed in another, while 1,000 Beatles fans besieged the front of the hotel.

The Beatles had their own suite and were able to fish out of their windows which overlooked Elliott Bay.

When the Beatles left at lunchtime the next day, manager Wright heard that fans intended tearing up the Beatles' suite for souvenirs, so he sold the orange rug that had carpeted their room to MacDougall-Southwick, a company which intended to cut it up and sell the pieces as souvenirs. The Beatles had heard rumours that the hotel staff had planned to take their bedsheets and sell them, so they poured milk, orange juice and alcohol over them.

102 Edith Grove, London SW10

Street branching off the fashionable Kings Road in Chelsea where Mick Jagger, Brian Jones and Keith Richard shared two rooms on the middle floor of this address in 1962.

In the building they had a two-room flat and had to walk up several flights of stairs to the grimy toilet. Wallpaper was hanging from the walls and the place was in disarray. It was to their flat that the Stones invited the Beatles on 21 April 1963, after the Fab Four had travelled to see the Stones at the Crawdaddy Club at the invitation of Giorgio Gomelski.

After the gig, the Beatles and Stones retired to Edith Grove where they chatted throughout the night. They got on well and became very good friends, although there were obvious differences in musical tastes at the time with the Stones not showing interest in the Beatles' enthusiasm for Chuck Jackson and the Beatles remaining indifferent to Mick Jagger's collection of rare Jimmy Reed albums.

Eight Days A Week

A John Lennon composition. When John was asked to recall the number in 1980 he said that he'd written the song quite quickly as it was considered as a title track for the Beatles' next film, which turned out to be called *Help!*

The group began to develop the number when they started recording it on Tuesday, 6 October 1964, and it ended up featuring what is probably the first fade-in to a pop record – as opposed to a record fading out.

The track was considered as a single, but found its way on to the *Beatles For Sale* album and the *Beatles For Sale* EP.

It was issued as a single in America on Capitol 5371 on 15 February 1965 with 'I Don't Want To Spoil The Party' on the flip and reached the No. 1 position in the charts.

The track was also included on the American *Beatles VI* album. A version made up of parts from three of the takes of the number was included on The Beatles' *Anthology 1* CDs.

Eleanor Rigby

Together with 'Yellow Submarine', this number was issued in Britain as the second double-A sided single by the Beatles on Parlophone R5493 on 5 August 1966 and in America on Capitol 5715 on 8 August. It became a No. 1 hit and the number was also featured on the *Revolver* album, issued in Britain on the same day. A few months later, in December, it resurfaced on *A Collection Of Beatles Oldies (But Goldies)* and also appeared on several other albums, including *The Beatles 1962–1966* in 1973, *The Beatles Box* in 1980 and *20 Greatest Hits* in 1982. It was re-released amongst a batch of singles to celebrate the group's twentieth anniversary in 1982.

From what Paul had said about the song in the sixties, it was assumed that Eleanor Rigby was a figment of his imagination, yet in 1984 stories in the press suggested that Eleanor Rigby had been a real person. This was because a tombstone for an Eleanor Rigby had been discovered in the graveyard of St Peter's Church in Liverpool, the same church where John and Paul had first met. She had died on 10 October 1939. Could he have seen the gravestone as a young man and held the name in his subconscious? Or is it just coincidence?

When the *Sun* newspaper ran a story about the song in 1984, it published a photograph of former dancehall compere Tom McKenzie posing at the side of the gravestone and commented that Tom was also the Father McKenzie referred to. Yet in Paul's version of the origin of the number, Father McKenzie was also fictitious.

Here is what Paul has said at various times to the press: '[It] started off with sitting down at the piano and getting the first line of the melody and playing around with words. I think it was "Miss Daisy Hawkins" originally; then it was her picking up the rice in a church after a wedding. That's how nearly all our songs start, with the first line just suggesting itself from books or newspapers.

'At first I thought it was a young Miss Daisy Hawkins, a bit like "Annabel Lee", but not so sexy; but then I saw I'd said she was picking up the rice in church so she had to be a cleaner; she had missed the wedding and she was suddenly lonely. In fact she had missed it all – she was the spinster type.

'Jane [Asher] was in a play in Bristol then, and I was walking around the streets waiting for her to finish. I didn't really like "Daisy Hawkins" – I wanted a name that was more real. The thought just came: "Eleanor Rigby picks up the rice and lives in a dream" – so there she was.

'The next thing was Father McKenzie. It was going to be Father McCartney, but then I thought that was a bit of a hangup for my

Dad, being in this lonely song. So we looked through the phone book. That's the beauty of working at random – it does come up perfectly, much better than if you try to think it with your intellect.

'Anyway, there was Father McKenzie, and he was just as I had imagined him, lonely, darning his socks. We weren't sure if the song was going to go on. In the next verse we thought of a bin man, an old feller going through dustbins; but it got too involved – embarrassing. John and I wondered whether to have Eleanor Rigby and him having a thing going, but we couldn't really see how. When I played it to John, we decided to finish it.

'That was the point anyway. She didn't make it, she never made it with anyone, she didn't even look as if she was going to.'

The number was recorded in April 1966 and scored by George Martin who said he was inspired by the work of film composer Bernard Herrmann, particularly on his scoring of *Fahrenheit 451*. Paul sang lead with backing vocals from John and George. Apart from that, the Beatles weren't featured as the instrumental backing was provided by eight session men: Tony Gilbert, Sidney Sax, John Sharpe and Jurgen Hess on violins; Stephen Shingles and John Underwood on violas and Derek Simpson and Norman Jones on cellos.

The number has also become one of the most popular Beatles songs to be recorded by other acts with over 200 recorded versions, including those by Diana Ross & the Supremes, Paul Anka, Frankie Valli, the Four Tops, Johnny Mathis and Vanilla Fudge. The Ray Charles version reached No. 25 in the British charts in 1968 and Aretha Franklin's version reached No. 23 in the American charts. A backing track for the song was included on the Beatles' *Anthology 2* CDs.

Electronic Sounds

The second and final album to be released on Apple's specialist label Zapple Records. It was issued in America on Zapple ST 3358 on 26 May 1969 and reached No. 191 in the *Billboard* charts, although failing to find a place in either the *Cash Box* or *Record World* charts.

It was issued in Britain on Zapple 02 on 9 May 1969 and, like George's first solo album venture *Wonderwall*, failed to achieve a placing in the British charts.

The concept of Zapple was that it was to be an experimental label, which was certainly true in this case. George had recently acquired a Moog synthesizer (an instrument developed in America by Dr Robert Moog during 1963/4) and was experimenting with sounds on the new instrument when he decided to put them down on record – on what is probably the first album to consist entirely of synthesised sounds.

There were only two tracks on the LP. The first side was called 'Under The Mersey Wall', the second, 'No Time Or Space'.

George recorded 'No Time Or Space' in California in November 1968 and recorded 'Under The Mersey Wall' in the studio at his home in Esher in February 1969. 'Under The Mersey Wall' was probably a reference to the *Liverpool Echo* column of a similar name by journalist George Harrison.

George was to comment, 'All I did was get that very first Moog synthesizer with the big patch unit and keyboards you could never tune, and I put a microphone into a tape machine. Whatever came out when I fiddled with the knobs went on tape.'

When he'd been recording in California, George had hired an engineer for the session called Bernard Krause. Krause later told a magazine that he had created the music as a demonstration tape for the synthesizer and that George had taken his tapes. It seems unlikely, as Krause didn't press the matter.

George also designed the album sleeve, using two paintings by himself, and he also wrote the sleeve notes, using the pseudonym Arthur Wax, in which he commented, 'There are a lot of people around, making a lot of noise, here's some more.'

On its original release, Apple press officer Richard DiLello wrote of 'Under The Mersey Wall', 'In February 1969, in a mounting vortex of decibels, there came to pass a wrecked chord of environmental sound that went beyond the genre of hashish cocktail music. The bass line has been milked through the Moog machine and, lo and high, we behold electronic music ... music that becomes sounds that flood the mind, not to forget the soul, o solo mio.'

The comments on 'No Time Or Space' were equally flowery: 'In California, through the machine-gun of his mind, George thought aloud to himself and in his composure he has exposed the thought patterns beating on his brow, and diametrically opposed, he has exposed, through the medium of the Moog, a pottage of space music. And on and on we go ... George Harrison versus Godzilla and King Kong in space.'

When *Electronic Sounds* was issued on CD in 1996, George declined to write some new sleeve notes. He commented, 'It could be called avant garde, but a more apt description would be, (in the words of my old friend Alvin) "Avant garde clue!"'

His 'old friend Alvin' referred to Ten Years After guitarist Alvin Lee.

Elizabethan Ballroom, Co-operative House, Parliament Street, Nottingham

Brian Epstein approached Bill Harry for permission to use the *Mersey Beat* name in a showcase he'd wanted to promote on behalf of NEMS Enterprises which would be a package tour of Liverpool acts. Permission was given and Epstein called the series *Mersey Beat Showcase*.

The first of them took place at the Elizabethan Ballroom on 7 March 1963 and the Beatles were bill-toppers with support from Gerry & the Pacemakers, the Big Three and Billy J. Kramer & the Dakotas. Bob Wooler compered the shows. For this debut, NEMS Enterprises hired two coaches and in addition to the groups, eighty fans were able to join the bands on the journey for a modest 25 shillings (£1.25), which included entrance to the show.

There were a total of six *Mersey Beat Showcase* packages, all in 1963, and the others took place on 19, 24 and 25 April and 14 and 16 June. Further presentations planned for 17, 18, 19, 20 and 23 June were cancelled by Epstein.

Ellis, Geoffrey

One of Brian Epstein's closest friends. The two met as regulars at the Royal Court Theatre in Liverpool. Ellis who was four years older than Brian, had studied for the bar at Oxford University. When Ellis became an executive for the Royal Life Insurance Company he was posted to New York in June 1958, but he and Brian corresponded on a regular basis. Ellis was later to work for Walter Hofer, a lawyer acting on Brian's behalf in America.

Brian asked Ellis to join his organisation and he became a senior executive at NEMS in October 1964 and a director the following year. He ran the day-to-day office administration.

Brian invited Geoffrey and Peter Brown as his house guests to Kingsley Hill for the weekend on 25 August 1967. During the evening he left them to return to Chapel Street and was found dead on 27 August.

Ellis later worked for the Dick James Organisation and John Reid Enterprises.

Ellis, Royston

British 'Beat' poet who first met the Beatles in June 1960 when he was booked for a poetry recital at Liverpool University. John and Stuart invited him to stay for a week at the Gambier Terrace flat and they also booked him for a 'poetry to beat' session at the Jacaranda.

While he was at the Gambier Terrace flat he introduced the Beatles to their very first drug experience. He cracked open a Vick inhaler and showed them the strip of benzedrine inside. It was nick-named a 'spitball' and you chewed it. The amphetamine kept you awake all night in a state of excitement.

Ellis recalled that in conversations with Paul he told him of his ambitions to be a 'paperback writer' and said that he used the phrase so often in his conversations that perhaps Paul subcon-sciously recalled it when he came to write the song.

The Record Mirror reported in July of that year that Ellis was thinking of bringing a Liverpool group called the Beetles [sic] to London to back him on his poetry readings, but nothing came of it.

Ellis did, in fact, form a close association with Cliff Richard & the Shadows and penned the paperback books *Jiving To Gyp, Driftin' with Cliff Richard* and *The Big Beat Scene*. He also penned a biography of the Shadows.

He met the Beatles again in August 1963 when they appeared in the Channel Isles. John spent the night with Ellis and his girlfriend Stephanie at their flat in Guernsey.

Ellis travelled to the Canary Isles with Cliff & the Shadows during the filming of *Wonderful Life* and stayed there for a while. He left in 1966 to live in the Caribbean where he enjoyed success with a number of best-selling plantation novels under the pseu-donym of Richard Tressilian. He later settled in Sri Lanka with a new profession as a travel writer.

El Rio Club, El Rio Ballroom, Queen Victoria Street, Macclesfield, Cheshire

A booking originally arranged for 19 January 1963 on a provi-sional basis, the booking was then confirmed and took place on 23 January 1963, with Wayne Fontana & the Jets in support.

Local boy Fontana, real name Glyn Ellis, was to find record success within the year. When he went into a Manchester studio to record his first single for the Fontana label, his backing group failed to turn up. Some session musicians were in the studio and backed him on record; they were Eric Stewart on guitar, Bob Land on bass and Rick Rothwell on drums. As the Mindbenders they became Fontana's backing group. Together they had ten chart hits between 1963 and 1966, including 'Hello Josephine', 'Um Um Um Um Um Um' and 'Game Of Love'. In 1966 the Mindbenders split with Fontana and had four hits, beginning with 'A Groovy Kind Of Love'.

Stewart went on to become a member of the highly successful

group 10cc. and later recorded with Paul McCartney, beginning with the 'Tug Of War' album. He said, 'I meet Paul fairly often and we've known each other since way back when he was with the Beatles and I was with the Mindbenders. We used to play the Cavern together, we used to play the same kind of music, American R&B and we're both from the North, we have the same accent, the same sense of humour. After I had a car accident a while back, Paul phoned me up to see if I was all right. I said I was, but in fact I was still rather messed up and still had to use drugs and all that. But Paul asked me if I felt like playing on his new LP so I said "Great!"'

Stewart also played on Mike McGear's solo album *McGear*.

Embassy Theatre, The Broadway, Peterborough, Northamptonshire

The Beatles made their debut at this East Coast venue on 2 December 1962. Brian Epstein had managed to trace the telephone number of Arthur Howes, one of Britain's major tour promoters. Coincidentally, Howes lived in Peterborough. He related to Beatles biographer Hunter Davies the call received on Saturday afternoon: 'He [Brian] said he had a great group, was there anything I could fit them into? He told me their names, Beatles, and I laughed . . . but I've never turned down a group without first hearing them. I said there was a show at Peterborough they could join.'

The Beatles cancelled a booking they had at the Cavern that evening, but didn't fare too well at the gig and, indeed, didn't even receive applause, which isn't too hard to understand as Frank Ifield topped the bill with Julie Grant, Ted Taylor and Susan Cope as support acts. Howes was to comment: 'It was a Frank Ifield show so I suppose it wasn't so surprising, they loved him so much that the show was good enough to take ten minutes of a bad group.'

Ifield had enjoyed spectacular success that year, reaching No. 1 in the charts with 'I Remember You' and remaining in the Top Twenty from 14 July until 1 December. He followed up with another No. 1 hit in November, 'Wayward Wind', and had several further hits.

Journalist Lyndon Whittaker, writing in the local newspaper, reported: 'The "exciting" Beatles rock group quite frankly failed to excite me. The drummer apparently thought that his job was to lead, not to provide rhythm. He made far too much noise and in their final number, "Twist And Shout", it sounded as though everyone was trying to make more noise than the others. In a more mellow mood, their "A Taste Of Honey" was much better and "Love Me Do" was tolerable.'

The group hadn't been paid a fee for the gig, just their expenses from Liverpool, and Howes was prepared to take a further chance with them, booking them on his next nationwide tour promotion which was headlined by Helen Shapiro.

They were due to return to the Embassy again as part of a tour on which they were bottom of the bill and only received £80 a week. The date was set for 10 February 1963 but they had to travel to London for a recording session and were excused from the gig and replaced by Peter Jay & the Jaywalkers.

However, only a short time was to pass before they appeared at the Embassy again on their next tour, on a bill headlined by American singers Chris Montez and Tommy Roe. The Beatles made their second and final appearance at the theatre on 17 March 1963.

Emerick, Geoffrey

He was twenty years old when he worked on his first Beatles track, 'Tomorrow Never Knows'. Geoff first began working as a tape operator on Beatles sessions on Wednesday, 20 February 1963 for the recordings of 'Misery' and 'Baby It's You'. Later he became a recording engineer, replacing his former boss Norman Smith as engineer on the Beatles' recordings in April 1966. Emerick became George Martin's assistant and was involved in many further Beatles recordings, receiving a Grammy Award for his work on the *Sgt Pepper* album. He also won a Grammy for his work on Paul McCartney's *Band On The Run* album. He also worked on Paul's *Venus And Mars* and *London Town* albums. In addition, he also mixed the tapes for *The Beatles At the Hollywood Bowl* album and was presented with a Lifetime Achievement Award for his services to the music industry by BASCA (British Academy of Songwriters, Composers and Authors).

Paul was Best Man at Geoff's wedding in January 1989.

Together with George Martin, Emerick entered the EMI vaults to work on the mass of unreleased Beatles tapes to remaster and release them as three double CDs in the *Anthology* series.

EMI Records

Over the years there has been too much emphasis placed on the fact that Decca Records turned down the Beatles. Decca Records at least took the trouble to arrange a studio audition and seriously considered signing the group. EMI, on the other hand, originally turned the Beatles down without even granting them an audition, and it was only by an unusual set of circumstances that they entered EMI by 'the back door', and transformed the fortunes of the company.

EMI originated in 1931 as the Gramophone Company, but

changed its name to Electrical and Mechanical Industries. The company was involved in various activities, including the production of wooden cabinet TV sets, but when Sir Joseph Lockwood became Chairman in 1954 he ended the production of the cabinets and concentrated on the production of records. In 1955 he made the decision to buy an American record company, Capitol, for three million pounds.

EMI Records, who now described themselves as 'The greatest recording organisation in the world', were actually the very first company Brian Epstein approached. Being a major record retailer he was able to set up a meeting in London with EMI marketing manager Ron White, who agreed to approach the company's four house producers: Norrie Paramor, Walter Ridley, Norman Newell and George Martin. Martin was on holiday at the time, but the other three A&R men told White they weren't interested. These A&R men handled EMI's pop labels, but George Martin's Parlophone label was not strictly a pop label and therefore White wrote back to Epstein formally rejecting the Beatles on behalf of EMI.

Epstein went into the HMV shop to have acetates made and was sent to see publisher Sid Coleman, who then arranged a meeting with George Martin, which led to the Beatles' signing with the Parlophone label. Even that set of circumstances is not straightforward. Epstein's assistant Alistair Taylor confirms that Parlophone began to play around with Epstein to the extent that he became frustrated and threatened to withdraw his business if EMI didn't give the Beatles a recording contract. Taylor was to tell writer Ray Coleman, 'EMI took them on sufferance because Brian was one of their top customers. I saw Brian in tears, literally, because Martin promised to phone back, and day after day went by and George Martin was never available, always 'in a meeting'. I saw Brian thumping the desk and in tears because George Martin hadn't phoned back.' According to Taylor, when Epstein finally got hold of Martin he told him that NEMS as a shop would jettison EMI's HMV, Parlophone and Columbia labels. The result was an offer of a recording test.

Parlophone was not one of EMI's pop-orientated labels and in the six years leading up to the signing of the Beatles had only had one Top Ten hit, 'Stop You're Driving Me Crazy', by the Temperance Seven. George Martin had once auditioned Tommy Steele, but had turned him down – and Steele became Britain's leading rock 'n' roll star. George had been recording stage revues and comedy records with artists such as Peter Sellers, Peter Ustinov and Flanders and Swann.

Martin admits that EMI had nothing to lose financially by taking on an unknown group such as the Beatles. He said, 'To say I was taking a gamble would be stretching it, because the deal I offered them was pretty awful.'

The contract offered them one penny in royalties per single – with no advance payments – and on overseas sales they would only get half of that. A twelve-track album would be regarded as six cuts. There were three one-year options with an increase of a quarter of a penny (a farthing) at the end of the first year and an increase of a halfpenny at the end of the second year. There was a new agreement in January 1967 which gave the Beatles 10 per cent of an album's wholesale price. Epstein dealt with Len Wood, EMI's Managing Director, who was to say, 'When we exercised the first option, and the royalty rate went up as a result, I asked George Martin to bring the royalty rate for the following option forward so that the Beatles got more rewards now . . . but at the same time get for EMI an extra year or two's option.' Brian couldn't give him an option beyond September 1967 because his management contract with the Beatles ended on that date.

EMI did, however, lose the Beatles' publishing. EMI's Chairman Sir Joseph Lockwood was justifiably frustrated not to have the Beatles' lucrative songwriting activities under the wing of EMI's own publishing company Ardmore & Beechwood, who had published the first two songs without a contract.

When the Beatles' contract with EMI expired in 1966 there were six months of negotiations before a deal was signed on 27 January 1967. Under the deal the Beatles received 10 per cent of the retail price of their records, which was double the normal royalty and the highest royalty given to an artist at the time. The contract was to last for nine years, which gave EMI the benefit of the individual recordings of John, Paul, George and Ringo for six years after the split in 1970.

The small Parlophone label benefited not only from the incredible success of the Beatles records, but also from the string of other acts Epstein placed with the label – Cilla Black (No. 1 with 'Anyone Who Had a Heart' and 'You're My World'); Gerry & the Pacemakers (No. 1 with 'How Do You Do It', 'I Like It' and 'You'll Never Walk Alone') and Billy J. Kramer (No. 1 with 'Bad To Me' and 'Little Children').

The Beatles' success also transformed the company's American arm, Capitol Records.

During the years the association between the Beatles and EMI worked very well, most particularly when the Beatles themselves were in the driving seat. When their nine-year contract ended on 6

February 1976 and EMI then had the right to issue any back catalogue material, there were a few things the Beatles in their solo
years weren't happy with (although they didn't have much say in
the matter) – such as the choice of album covers and compilation
selections. They hated the cover of *Rock 'n' Roll Music* and the
company, unbelievably, turned down John Lennon's offer of
designing the cover himself. George Harrison was also upset at
their selection of tracks for *The Best Of George Harrison* compilation.

Empire Pool, Empire Way, Wembley, Middlesex
Site of the prestigious *New Musical Express* Poll Winners Annual
concerts in the mid-sixties.

The *New Musical Express* had the largest circulation of any
music paper in Britain and had a powerful influence on the music
business. The NME concerts comprised a bill of the main winners
of their Readers' Polls and were filmed by ABC Television for
screening on the commercial channel.

The Beatles made their debut on the show in front of an audience
of eight thousand fans on the afternoon of 21 April 1963. On that
occasion the bill toppers were Cliff Richard & the Shadows. The
Beatles performed 'Please Please Me', 'From Me To You', 'Twist
and Shout' and 'Long Tall Sally'. Paul introduced the last song with
the words, 'Here's a song immortalised by that great gospel singer,
Victor Sylvester!' The Beatles performed in the late second half of
the bill, immediately before Cliff Richard & the Shadows. Other
artists on the bill were Joe Brown & the Bruvvers, the Springfields,
Adam Faith, Mike Berry, the Brook Brothers, the Tornadoes, Kenny
Ball, Gerry & the Pacemakers, Jet Harris and Tony Meehan, Frank
Ifield, Mark Wynter and Joe Loss & His Orchestra.

Their second appearance took place on 26 April 1964 and this
time they topped the bill. They were introduced by Murray the K
and then performed 'She Loves You', 'You Can't Do That', 'Twist
And Shout' and 'Can't Buy Me Love'. The ABC TV show was
screened on 10 May as 'Big Beat '64' and repeated on 8 November.

The 11 April 1965 appearance found them performing 'I Feel
Fine', 'She's A Woman', 'Baby's In Black', 'Ticket To Ride' and
'Long Tall Sally'. The ABC TV concert film was screened on 18
April. Other artists on the bill included the Rolling Stones, Dusty
Springfield, the Moody Blues, Wayne Fontana and Tom Jones. The
Beatles were presented with their awards by American singer Tony
Bennett.

The Beatles' fourth and final Empire Pool appearance for the
New Musical Express 1965–66 Annual Poll Winners All-Star

Concert on 1 May 1966 was also the group's last live concert appearance in Britain. Due to contractual reasons, the Beatles' and the Rolling Stones' appearances on this particular concert were not filmed by ABC TV.

The four performed a fifteen-minute act comprising 'I Feel Fine', 'Nowhere Man', 'Day Tripper', 'If I Needed Someone' and 'I'm Down'. Paul McCartney commented: 'There's nothing like going on in front of a really big audience. It's like a little break coming after all those weeks locked away in the studios. We'd have gone on all night, honest!'

The huge bills on these concerts featured an average of fourteen live acts. Other artists appearing on the bill of their last concert were: the Spencer Davis Group, Dave Dee, Dozy, Beaky, Mick & Tich, the Fortunes, Herman's Hermits, Roy Orbison, the Overlanders, the Alan Price Set, Cliff Richard, the Rolling Stones, the Seekers, the Shadows, the Small Faces, Sounds Incorporated, Dusty Springfield, Crispian St Peters, the Walker Brothers, the Who and the Yardbirds.

Empire Stadium, Exhibition Park, Vancouver, Canada

The Beatles' appearance in British Columbia was part of a fourteen-day fair, the Pacific National Exhibition, during which they were to give one performance at the Empire Stadium on Saturday, 22 August 1964. It was their first show in Canada and was also broadcast live by the local radio station CKNW.

There was an audience of 20,261 inside the arena and thousands outside the stadium who couldn't get tickets. The 100 police found it difficult to control the crowds and crash barriers were buckled.

The Beatles appeared on stage at 9.23 p.m., and after their show were driven away in three limousines with a police motorcycle escort. One boy, in an attempt to stop the cars, threw his bicycle in front of the leading police motorcycle, but the escort just swerved to the side and carried on.

Commenting on the show, local music critic William Littler wrote: 'Seldom in Vancouver's entertainment have so many (20,261) paid so much ($5.25 top price) for so little (27 minutes), as did the audience which screamed at the Beatles in Empire Stadium on Saturday night. I have had to subject my eardrums to more than a little of the cacophony which currently dominates the hit parade, but the stuff shouted by these Liverpudlian tonsorial terrors left me particularly unimpressed.' Describing them, he wrote: 'Paul is cute and panders to his audience with assorted gestures. He and John shout with great energy in close harmony. George plays an especially vigorous guitar and is more restrained otherwise. Ringo just bobs and bashes away.'

Empire Theatre, Lime Street, Liverpool L1

Liverpool's main theatre for live entertainment, situated in the heart of the city centre. The Quarry Men made their debut at the Empire at 3.00 p.m. on 9 June 1957 when they auditioned for Carroll Levis' *Search For The Stars* talent show. This was a talent show which was presented at the main theatres throughout the country, highlighting local talent. There were numerous heats, and the winners appeared on a short spot on Levis' television show. This particular heat was won by the Sunnyside Skiffle Group.

The Quarry Men's next appearance at the theatre, when they used the name Johnny & the Moondogs, was also as part of the Carroll Levis auditions. Levis held these auditions over three Sunday afternoons on 11, 18 and 25 October 1959. The winners were the Connaughts, a showgroup whose main member, Nicky Cuff, had previously been in the Sunnyside Skiffle Group. The Moondogs had also gained sufficient points to win them an appearance in the finals in Manchester.

The Beatles' first Empire appearance as part of the official bill took place on Sunday, 28 October 1962, on a co-production by Epstein's NEMS Enterprises and Ray McFall of the Cavern Club. There were eight acts on the bill, which was topped by Little Richard and included Craig Douglas, Jet Harris, Kenny Lynch and Sounds Incorporated. There were two houses that evening and the Beatles were the third act on stage, following the Breakaways. They performed four numbers and remained on stage to provide backing for singer Craig Douglas.

On 24 March 1963 they returned to the Empire as part of the bill of the Chris Montez/Tommy Roe tour and were back on 26 May 1963 on their Roy Orbison tour.

On the afternoon of 7 December 1963 they appeared on a special all-Beatle 'Juke Box Jury', filmed from the stage of the theatre as part of their special northern fan club convention and the live show for their fans later in the afternoon was also filmed by the BBC and screened later the same evening as 'It's The Beatles'.

Their third Empire appearance in 1963 took place on 22 December when they previewed their first Christmas show.

It was almost a year later when they made their next appearance on 8 November 1964.

The Beatles' final concert at the Empire took place on 5 December 1964. It was also the last time they appeared in

Liverpool. The demand was such that there were over 40,000 applications for tickets.

Empire Theatre, High Street, Sunderland, Tyne & Wear

The Beatles made their debut at this venue during their Helen Shapiro tour on 9 February 1963. Their second and final appearance at the Empire took place on 30 November 1963.

End, The

The penultimate track on the *Abbey Road* album. Actually, considering that there was a gap of twenty seconds following this track and that the last track 'Her Majesty' was only 23 seconds long, in some ways it is considered to be the last song featured on the last recorded album by the Beatles, making its title 'The End' quite appropriate.

Work first began on the number, under its working title 'The Ending', at Abbey Road on Wednesday, 22 July 1969. Ringo performed a drum solo – his first recorded drum solo on a Beatles release – while there were guitar solos from John, Paul and George.

A 30-piece orchestra was overdubbed on to the track on Friday, 15 August 1969, comprising one bass trombone, one trombone, one string bass, three trumpets, four horns, four cellos, four violas and twelve violins. 'The End' is the final track on the *Anthology 3* CDs as it was the final track on their final album.

EP

The initials stand for Extended Player. This four-track disc with a picture sleeve, which played at 45 rpm, was a record format available in Britain throughout the 1960s. The cost was around 55d, which was an attractive price, being far cheaper than the cost of two singles. An EP record chart was introduced in 1960 in *Record Retailer*. By 1967 the sales of EPs had shrunk to such an extent that the chart was dispensed with. During the life of the chart, the Shadows emerged as the most successful artists, spending a total of 461 weeks in the listings. Cliff Richard, the Beatles and Elvis Presley followed them. The record which spent most consecutive weeks at the top of the chart, a total of 213, was the EP *Shadows To The Fore*.

Prior to the release of the Beatles' first EP, the most successful EP release in Britain had been Elvis Presley's *Follow That Dream*, which had reached No. 11 in the *New Musical Express* charts.

Generally, EPs contained both sides of two recent singles. Beatles'

EPs included titles such as *The Beatles Hits*, which was the normal EP-type compilation of two singles; extracts from albums, such as *Beatles For Sale No. 1* and *No. 2*; and a third type which featured four songs which you weren't able to buy on other British releases – such as the *Long Tall Sally* EP.

Twist And Shout, issued on 12 July 1963 on GEP 8882, comprised 'Twist And Shout', 'A Taste Of Honey', 'Do You Want To Know A Secret' and 'There's A Place'. It reached No. 4 in the *New Musical Express* chart.

Their next EP, *The Beatles Hits,* was issued on 6 September 1963 on GEP 8880 and comprised 'From Me To You', 'Thank You Girl', 'Please Please Me' and 'Love Me Do'. It reached No. 14 in the charts.

The Beatles (No. 1) was issued on 1 November 1963 on GEP 8883 and comprised 'I Saw Her Standing There', 'Misery', 'Anna (Go To Him)' and 'Chains'. It reached No. 24 in the charts.

All My Loving was issued on 7 February 1964 on GEP 8891 and comprised 'All My Loving', 'Ask Me Why', 'Money (That's What I Want)' and 'P.S. I Love You'. It reached No. 13 in the charts.

Long Tall Sally was issued on 19 June 1964 on GEP 8913 and comprised 'Long Tall Sally', 'I Call Your Name', 'Slow Down' and 'Matchbox'. This fifth EP release was the first to contain previously unreleased tracks and reached No. 11 in the charts. The chart positions quoted are those for the singles charts. There was also an EP chart and this record topped it.

Extracts From The Film 'A Hard Day's Night' was issued on 4 November 1964 on GEP 8920 and comprised 'I Should Have Known Better', 'If I Fell', 'Tell Me Why' and 'And I Love Her'.

Extracts From The Album 'A Hard Day's Night' was issued on 6 November 1964 on GEP 8924 and comprised 'Anytime At All', 'I'll Cry Instead', 'Things We Said Today' and 'When I Get Home'.

Beatles For Sale was issued on 6 April 1965 on GEP 8938 and comprised 'No Reply', 'I'm A Loser', 'Rock And Roll Music' and 'When I Get Home'.

Beatles For Sale No. 2 was issued on 4 June 1965 on GEP 8938 and comprised 'I'll Follow The Sun', 'Baby's In Black', 'Words Of Love' and 'I Don't Want To Spoil The Party'.

The Beatles Million Sellers was issued on 6 December 1963 on GEP 8946 and comprised 'She Loves You', 'I Want To Hold Your Hand', 'Can't Buy Me Love' and 'I Feel Fine'.

Yesterday was issued on 4 March 1966 on GEP 8948 and comprised 'Act Naturally', 'You Like Me too Much', 'Yesterday' and 'It's Only Love'. Interestingly, a different member of the group takes lead vocal on each track.

Nowhere Man was issued on 8 July 1966 on GEP 8952 and comprised 'Nowhere Man', 'Drive My Car', 'Michelle' and 'You Won't See Me'.

Their thirteenth and final EP was *Magical Mystery Tour,* issued on 8 December 1967 on SMMT ½ as a set of two EPs comprising the tracks 'Magical Mystery Tour', 'Your Mother Should Know', 'I Am The Walrus', 'The Fool On the Hill', 'Flying' and 'Blue Jay Way'. The package came with a 24-page booklet and a gatefold sleeve.

Over a decade later, in December 1981, Parlophone issued *The Beatles' EP Collection* on BEP 14 in a boxed set containing all the above EPs, plus an extra bonus EP called *She's a Woman,* which comprised the tracks 'She's a Woman', 'Baby You're a Rich Man', 'This Boy' and 'The Inner Light'.

One other EP was issued in Britain during the 1960s. This was *My Bonnie,* issued on Polydor NH 21-610 in July 1963 and containing the tracks 'My Bonnie', 'Why', 'Cry For a Shadow' and 'The Saints'. It made no impact on the charts.

Extended players weren't as common in America as they were in Britain.

On 23 March 1964, Vee Jay issued *Souvenir Of Their Visit To America (The Beatles)* on V JED 1-903 which contained four tracks from the *Introducing The Beatles* album: 'Misery', 'A Taste Of Honey', 'Ask Me Why' and 'Anna (Go To Him)'. The record failed to make a chart placing.

The first Capitol EP was *Four By The Beatles,* issued on 11 May 1964 on EAP 2121, and comprised two tracks each from the *Meet The Beatles* and *The Beatles Second Album* LPs. They were 'Roll Over Beethoven', 'All My Loving', 'This Boy' and 'Please Mr Postman'. The EP reached No. 92 in the *Billboard* charts and No. 86 in *Cash Box,* but didn't receive a placing in the *Record World* charts.

Capitol next issued *4 By The Beatles* on 1 February 1965 on R5365. This comprised tracks from the *Beatles '65* album: 'Honey Don't', 'I'm A Loser', 'Mr Moonlight' and 'Everybody's Trying To Be My Baby'. The EP reached No. 68 in both the *Cash Box* and *Billboard* charts. Capitol decided to abandon plans for any further Beatles releases in the EP format.

Epsom Registry Office, Epsom, Surrey

Site of the marriage between George Harrison and Pattie Boyd on 21 January 1966. The honour of Best Man went to both Paul McCartney and Brian Epstein. John and Ringo weren't in attendance as they were on holiday in Trinidad at the time, but both sent flowers, greetings and presents. Brian Epstein, Neil Aspinall and Mal Evans were in attendance, together with the parents of the bride and groom. The wedding plans had been kept secret and a short press conference was arranged after the event in which a member of the press asked, 'How on earth did you manage to keep it a secret?' George replied, 'Simple. We didn't tell anyone.'

There was a reception afterwards at George's bungalow Kinfauns and Mrs Harrison told a friend: 'I felt as if I had lost everything. Quite silly, really. As we were in the car with them returning from the ceremony, George took my hand and said, "It doesn't mean because I'm married I don't need you anymore, Mum. We need you more now." He's such a lovable son, and cares about how people feel.'

George and Pattie then went off on honeymoon to Barbados.

Epstein, Brian Samuel

The Beatles' first manager, born at a private nursing home at 4 Rodney Street, Liverpool, on 19 September 1934. His mother was Malka (known as 'Queenie'), daughter of a furniture manufacturer in Sheffield, and his father was Harry Epstein, whose family owned a furniture store in Liverpool.

The family moved to Prestatyn in north Wales for a short time in 1939 at the onset of World War II and then spent three years in Southport where the five-year-old boy attended Southport College. He was also educated at Croxton Preparatory School and at the age of ten he was expelled from Liverpool College for drawing obscene pictures. He then attended Wellesley School in Aigburth. His parents, however, feeling that there were elements of anti-Semitism in the local schools, sent him to a Jewish boarding school, Beaconsfield School in Frant, Sussex. He spent two years there, briefly attended Claysemore, near Taunton, and then Wrekin College. He left Wrekin in the summer of 1950 to begin work at a branch of the family business, I. Epstein & Sons in Walton Road, Liverpool.

Brian had ambitions of becoming a dress designer, but his father forbade it and insisted he work as a salesman in the store.

At the age of eighteen he was conscripted for National Service. His first choice was the Royal Air Force, but they rejected him. He began the two-year stint in the Royal Army Service Corps at Aldershot where he was discharged after ten months, ostensibly because he was deemed to be emotionally and mentally unfit, although it was said he had been found importuning in a public toilet while dressed in an officer's uniform. For a time he worked at Clarendon Furnishing in Hoylake, a branch of the family firm, where he proved to be successful.

Brian had other aspirations than to spend his life working in a family business and, due to his interest in the theatre and a friendship he had established with some actors and actresses appearing at the Playhouse Theatre, he decided he wanted to join RADA (Royal Academy of Dramatic Arts).

He then revealed to his family that he was homosexual, shocking his father and younger brother, Clive, but receiving sympathy from Queenie. He was then allowed to study at RADA, passing the audition on 18 September 1956, his 22nd birthday.

It was alleged that he was once again found importuning in a public toilet and he left the course to return to the family business in 1957.

Scandal followed when he attempted to pick up a man in a public toilet in Liverpool and became the victim of blackmail. The family informed the police and at the trial Brian was referred to as 'Mr X'. By that time Harry had opened a new NEMS store in Great Charlotte Street and he placed Brian in charge of the ground-floor record section while Clive ran the electrical and domestic goods department on the first floor. Singer Anne Shelton performed the opening ceremony. The branch proved so successful that Brian was placed in charge of an even larger branch of the store at 12–14 Whitechapel. His friend Peter Brown, from Lewis's record department, replaced him in the record section at Great Charlotte Street. Singer Anthony Newley was engaged to open the Whitechapel branch.

Early in July 1961 he was approached by Bill Harry to stock copies of the new publication, *Mersey Beat,* which contained news of the remarkable music scene in Liverpool, with the first issue featuring a biography of the Beatles written by John Lennon. Brian ordered a dozen copies, which sold out almost immediately. He ordered increasing numbers over the next few days before ordering 144 copies of the second issue.

This was published on 20 July 1961 and the cover announced 'Beatles Sign Recording Contract!' Below an Astrid Kirchherr photograph of the Beatles in Hamburg was the detailed story of their recording there.

With dozens of youngsters coming into his store asking for copies of *Mersey Beat*, and with the details of the unique music scene in the city in the first two issues, Epstein became intrigued. He invited Harry into his office to discuss the local scene and was quite fascinated – and also asked if he could become the paper's record reviewer.

In the third issue, dated 3 August 1961, his first column 'Stop the World – and listen to everything in it. Brian Epstein of Nems', was published.

With each delivery of *Mersey Beat*, Epstein would invite Harry for a chat and it was obvious that he was beginning to see the potential of this huge musical movement that was literally on his doorstep.

The fourth issue of *Mersey Beat* featured a full-page feature by Bob Wooler extolling the merits of the Beatles, expressing his conviction that they were the No. 1 band around.

When Epstein decided to become involved in the local scene, it was the group featured in every issue of *Mersey Beat* which interested him and he phoned Harry to arrange for him to visit the Cavern, where he could see the Beatles perform for the first time.

Brian, accompanied by his personal assistant, Alistair Taylor, dropped into the club at 12.30 p.m. on Thursday, 9 November 1961.

By then he was completely aware of the Beatles and they were aware of him. Brian had noticed the members of local groups who came into NEMS to listen to new releases in the record booths and often chatted to people like Gerry Marsden to ask them about their choice of repertoire. The Beatles also dropped into NEMS regularly and local promoter Sam Leach had arranged for Brian to sell tickets to his Tower Ballroom promotion Operation Big Beat. This took place on 10 November and Brian had been selling tickets for more than two weeks prior to the gig. The posters in NEMS prominently featured the Beatles as the bill-topping band.

Brian went into the Cavern bandroom to have a brief chat with the group and dropped in to see them a month later. He left a message with George Harrison suggesting that he would like to arrange a meeting with them at NEMS. John Lennon asked disc jockey Bob Wooler to join them, telling Epstein that Bob was his father. Paul was ten minutes late, which irked the punctilious record store manager. A second meeting at NEMS was held a few days later. Then, on Sunday, 10 December, he met up with the group in the afternoon at the Casbah Club.

This time his assistant Alistair Taylor was with him and it was agreed that Brian would become their manager. The first contract would be for a five-year period from 1 February 1962. Epstein's commission was to be 10 per cent of any income up to £1,500 per year and 15 per cent above that amount.

The formal signing took place at Pete Best's home on Thursday, 24 January 1962. All four Beatles and Alistair Taylor signed it, but Brian didn't. A second management contract for five years was drawn up on Monday, 1 October 1962. By 1963, Brian had increased his commission to 25 per cent. It was fortuitous that he hadn't signed the original contract, which would have limited him to 15 per cent for the first five years.

Brian might have given up control of the Beatles in the early stages of his management. According to reports, he was offering a slice of his management percentage to several different people – all of whom refused.

It was said that in 1963 he offered Joe Collins (father of Joan and Jackie) a share of the Beatles and in 1964 Epstein reputedly approached Lew Grade and told him he was ready to sell the Beatles. When John Lennon heard about it, he told Epstein: 'If you do sell, we'll never play again. We'll disband.'

Mike and Bernie Winters, in the biography *Up A Pagoda Tree,* revealed that they were appearing at the London Palladium when Jack Murray called to see them in their dressing room and showed Mike a magazine picture of the group. 'They're big up north,' he said. 'Their agent had a record shop and doesn't know what to do with them. I've got them for 16 to 20 weeks, and I can have a permanent share of their contract if I want to. Do you want to come in with me?'

Mike told him: 'I'm not gambling any more, Jack. Bernie and I are going to work on our act and try to make a go of it. Thanks all the same.'

While there may be some truth in the story from Mike and Bernie's point of view, it is not accurate to say that Jack Murray had the Beatles signed up for 16 to 20 weeks of that year, which he obviously didn't.

It has also been reported that Epstein offered impresario Larry Parnes a share in the Beatles, but was also rejected.

In the book *The Life and Times of Little Richard,* Richard claims that after the Beatles came off stage at the Liverpool Empire, where Richard had been topping the bill, Epstein approached him and said: 'Richard, I'll give you 50 per cent of the Beatles.' Richard commented: 'I couldn't accept 'cos I never thought they would make it.'

It was essential for Brian to secure the group a recording contract. Initially, he thought he would have a great deal of clout due to his position as a prominent north-western record dealer. The family now had nine record stores in Liverpool with a stock of half a million records. Brian had also organised the Liverpool branch of the Gramophone Retailers' Association. However, this seemed to cut no ice and he was turned down by all of the EMI pop labels (Parlophone wasn't approached regarding the Beatles at this time as George Martin was on holiday). Epstein received an official letter from Ron White of EMI Records on Monday, 18 December 1961 confirming that the company was not interested in signing the group. Pye and the various other labels also turned him down, and he began to despair.

Through Tony Barrow, he'd put a foot in the door at Decca and followed through, stressing his position as a record dealer. Decca arranged a recording audition for the group, but they were turned down.

Brian didn't actually like pop music at the time and really had no idea of the group's intrinsic value. He'd signed the Beatles quite simply because they had been established as the No. 1 group locally, as he'd read in the pages of *Mersey Beat*.

His initial attempts to alter the Beatles' image met with some resistance from John Lennon and Pete Best, who didn't like the idea of discarding their leathers in favour of mohair suits. The leather image seemed popular. Youngsters began wearing leather jackets and coats and even Epstein took to wearing leather, yet he insisted they wear mohair suits.

This cleaning up of the image – telling them not to smoke on stage, not to swear, not to clown around – actually wasn't part of a clever plan. Brian was simply following convention in smartening up an image to make it palatable to the moguls who controlled the entertainment industry and were a generation above the kids they manipulated. Most groups on television, like the Shadows, wore smart suits, so Epstein made the Beatles conform. Although it's hypothetical, it would have been interesting to see how the Beatles fared if they'd been allowed to continue with their leather image – it would certainly have excited the youngsters they appealed to. After all, in those days rock 'n' roll meant rebellion to the kids.

Epstein attempted to make suggestions about their music – such as the type of songs to perform at their Decca recording audition – which was taking his brief too far.

As their career progressed they made sure Brian never interfered with their music again. During one recording session, he had switched on the studio intercom and said: 'I don't think that sounded quite right, John.' Lennon turned to him and said: 'You stick to your percentages, Brian. We'll look after the music.'

With the rejection by Decca, Brian was determined to plough ahead, although there seemed nowhere else to go. He was becoming despondent, realising how important a record contract was to the band. On the advice of Paul Murphy, on 8 May 1962 he went to London's HMV store to have the Decca tapes transferred to acetates and was put in touch with Sid Coleman of EMI's publishing company Ardmore & Beechwood. Coleman fixed up a meeting between Epstein and George Martin of the Parlophone label.

Parlophone wasn't one of EMI's pop labels and had basically been a label for middle-of-the road singers such as Matt Monro, comedy discs such as Peter Sellers' and Sophia Loren's 'Goodness

Gracious Me' and the recordings of revues such as 'Beyond The Fringe' and 'Flanders And Swann'.

Even after the initial approach had been made, Epstein found that Parlophone treated him in a cavalier way and he was often driven to tears of frustration when George Martin didn't answer his calls. Eventually, he had to threaten to boycott EMI labels at his stores.

A recording audition was arranged and Brian was so convinced that they had passed it that he was to send telegrams to the Beatles and Bill Harry confirming that they had a recording contract with Parlophone. Paul sent him a return telegram: 'WATCH OUT ELVIS.' While John's cable read: 'HOW SOON SHALL WE BE MILLIONAIRES.'

The deal Brian signed on behalf of the Beatles was pathetic and George Martin was to describe it as 'pretty awful'. There were no advance payments and they would only receive one penny per single – and half of that on overseas sales. A twelve-track album would be regarded as only six cuts. There were three one-year options with an increase of a quarter of a penny at the end of the first year and an increase of a halfpenny at the end of the second year.

Although it's true that Epstein didn't have much of an option at the time, the Beatles were to earn such staggering sums for EMI that he should have been able to renegotiate with the company before he eventually did. This occurred shortly before his own contract with the Beatles ran out. After all, he was able to increase the percentage in his own contract with them from 15 to 25 per cent.

John and Paul in particular were simmering with anger for years at the pathetic royalties they received – particularly when they discovered that, after the Rolling Stones had been with Decca for three years, Allen Klein had appeared and renegotiated their contract, obtaining for them an advance of almost £3 million. The Stones were then earning far more from records than the Beatles, even though they were selling much fewer.

Although Brian cultivated the image that he was an astute businessman, his deals in his brief time as a manager didn't really bear it out. Apart from the far from lucrative record deal, he signed a publishing deal for the Beatles with publisher Dick James which resulted in the group losing control of their own songs for ever. It was rumoured at the time that James' small independent music publishing company was in financial trouble. Epstein had been rattled by being asked to wait in the reception area at one of the music publishing companies he'd intended to negotiate with. Due to the simple fact that James managed to get the Beatles on the TV show 'Thank Your Lucky Stars', Epstein decided to sign with him.

Arguably, the initial arrangement was fair in relation to music publishing deals at the time, but Epstein could have arranged his own publishing company and appointed James to administer it. In addition, he could have ensured that the later shares were fairer to John and Paul, whose songs were, after all, what made Northern Songs such a valuable company.

Northern Songs was formed in 1963 with James and his partner, Charles Silver, owning 50 per cent of the company. Against the wishes of John and Paul, it became a public company in 1965 with James and Silver owning 23 per cent while John and Paul had only 15 per cent each. In March 1969, James sold his shares to ATV without offering the Beatles a chance to buy them.

If Brian's recording and publishing deals left something to be desired, his negotiations regarding their film career were also suspect. United Artists, keen to release a Beatles soundtrack album, were willing to offer the Beatles 25 per cent. At the meeting to discuss the deal, Brian pre-empted their offer by telling them: 'I wouldn't consider anything under seven and a half per cent.' Fortunately, their lawyer David Jacobs was able to finalise a deal in which they eventually received 25 per cent – but he asked only for gross, not net. Also, producer Walter Shenson's lawyer negotiated a better deal for his client.

United Artists didn't really believe that the Beatles were a long-term prospect and Shenson's lawyers suggested that the rights to the Beatles' films be given to the producer after fifteen years. United Artists agreed. Epstein should have taken that route on behalf of the Beatles. As a result, the films are owned by Shenson and have proved very lucrative for him.

The worst deal of all related to Beatles merchandise. Prior to the group's first trip to America, Brian asked his solicitor, Jacobs, to find someone to handle the merchandising. Jacobs met a young man called Nicky Byrne at a cocktail party and proposed he take over the merchandising for the Beatles.

Jacobs asked him what percentage he would require and Byrne said 90 per cent. Jacobs immediately agreed and informed Epstein, who also agreed. Without any advance fee or discussion, he had given away 90 per cent of the Beatles' merchandising rights to an unproved person who had no previous experience of merchandising, leaving 10 per cent to be shared by the Beatles, Brian and NEMS Enterprises.

Byrne flew to New York and within a week Capitol Records had offered to buy him out for $500,000, with the money being paid into the Bahamas for him and also allowing him to retain a half interest in the company. He turned them down. The young man seemed to have more of an idea of the Beatles' value than Epstein himself.

When Epstein realised the full extent of his gaffe, he was horrified. By August 1964, Jacobs had renegotiated the deal, raising the Beatles' royalty to 46 per cent, but by that time Epstein had instructed NEMS Enterprises to begin negotiating with US firms directly. Court proceedings were instigated against him.

Due to the legal problem, a large number of major firms, including Woolworth, backed out of negotiations and it was said that approximately $100,000,000 worth of merchandising deals were lost. To make matters worse, Byrne won his case and NEMS Enterprises had to settle with him for a substantial cash payment.

The fact was, Brian had never been a successful businessman. His parents initially refused to support him in NEMS Enterprises unless his brother, Clive, became a partner to look after the business side of things. At the time they had no faith in Brian's ability.

He was to take on several other ventures, which lost a great deal of money. He employed the experienced agent Vic Lewis as managing director of NEMS Enterprises. Lewis arranged a British tour for the Four Tops, working out that it would be profitable if it attracted the fans, but would at least break even with the deal he negotiated. Behind his back, Brian flew to Detroit and amended the contract, giving concessions such as agreeing to pay the group's tax, their air fares and adding bonuses to the deal. NEMS Enterprises lost £10,000 on the tour. He also lost a greater amount when he flew in the Four Tops for a single appearance at his Saville Theatre.

Brian never understood the music young people loved. It basically didn't appeal to him. He liked classical music, jazz and middle-of-the-road. The Beatles, Gerry & the Pacemakers and Billy J. Kramer had been voted Nos 1, 2 and 3 in *Mersey Beat* polls when he signed them, and he also signed Cilla Black on the urging of *Mersey Beat*. Yet he was never to really understand the sort of music they'd been playing and turned the rock 'n' rollers into straight pop and middle-of-the-road performers. Gerry, who'd been rocking away in Liverpool and Hamburg, was placed in the pantomime *Babes in the Wood* in 1963 and in 1965 Brian booked three of his acts into pantomimes, Cilla in *Little Red Riding Hood,* Billy J. in *Mother Goose* and Gerry in *Cinderella*.

Despite his initial success, some of the other Mersey groups he signed left him because they realised he had no idea how to manage them and had no understanding of their music – they included the Big Three, the Chants and the Merseybeats. Apart from his early Liverpool signings, he seemed to have no success with his other acts, primarily because he had no real idea about rock 'n' roll and pop music. The Rustiks, the Silkie and Michael Haslam, for example, vanished without trace. He couldn't even launch his Liverpool signing Tommy Quickly to stardom, and when he signed up the talented Paddy, Klaus & Gibson he didn't know what to do with them and they eventually disbanded.

In spite of the fact that he couldn't tell a good band from a bad one, he sat on several talent competition panels, including 'Ready, Steady, Win!' and 'Beat Time for Oxfam'.

Brian also didn't like acknowledging credit and was a great self-publicist. In the opening of his autobiography, *A Cellarful Of Noise,* he created the apocryphal story that he'd never heard of the Beatles until a boy came into his store and asked for their record. He made himself available for as many television and radio shows and media interviews as possible. In a relatively short time he appeared on 'Juke Box Jury', 'Panorama', 'Desert Island Discs', 'The Eamonn Andrews Show', 'Late Night Line-up', 'The David Frost Programme', 'Tonight', 'Celebrity Game', 'For Art's Sake' and 'Let's Find Out'. He also compered the American TV show 'Hullabaloo'.

He was often moody and petulant with his staff, several of whom left him following disputes – Brian Somerville, Derek Taylor and Wendy Hanson along them.

In fact, there was a great deal of incredible luck during his management of the Beatles. The timing was right for a supergroup to appear because young people were demanding their own idols for perhaps the first time. He was unable initially to get them a recording contract, and it was only by pure accident that his path led to Parlophone. Luck again intervened when leading American TV host Ed Sullivan was at Heathrow Airport to see the Beatles arrive and booked them on his show.

Although Capitol Records in America had continued to refuse to release the Beatles' records, when they eventually planned to, disc jockeys in different parts of America began playing 'I Want To Hold Your Hand'. As a result, the release date was moved forward and it became a hit despite Capitol's initial lack of enthusiasm. The Beatles also arrived in America a few months after President Kennedy had been assassinated and were able to draw America out of its mourning and put a smile on its face. Apart from Brian's attempt at plasticising the Beatles' image with the original mohair suits, the visual look that mattered – their 'moptop' hairstyle and collarless suits – had their origins in Hamburg. It's hard to find any specific plan or deal or management structure devised by Epstein that led to the success of the Beatles.

Towards the end of his life there were suicide attempts. He had neglected his business because of his addiction to drugs and gambling and was virtually ready to hand his show business empire over to Robert Stigwood, who seemed to have more musical acumen than Brian with his signing of acts such as the Bee Gees and Cream.

Because he was letting his business affairs slip, Brian was neglecting his acts and Cilla, Billy J. and Gerry wanted to find new managers. It took all his powers of persuasion to get them to remain with him. His contract with the Beatles was nearing its end and he was worried that they wouldn't renew it. Without their knowledge, he made a deal with EMI to increase their percentage, but also contracting them to pay NEMS Enterprises royalties for Beatles records for years after his own contract had expired.

On Friday, 23 August 1967, Brian planned to spend time at his country home with his friends Geoffrey Ellis and Peter Brown. When he arrived he phoned his mother in Liverpool to tell her that after the weekend he was going to join the Beatles at their Transcendental Meditation studies in Bangor, north Wales, after which he would visit her in Liverpool. During the course of the evening he became restless, due to the fact that a number of other friends he'd invited for the weekend hadn't arrived, so he drove back to London.

On Saturday morning his mother rang Kingsley Hill and spoke to Peter Brown and Geoffrey Ellis, who told her Brian had returned to London. She then rang his Chapel Street home and his butler, Antonio, told her that Brian was still asleep, so she requested that he wasn't to be disturbed. On Sunday at noon, Antonio and his wife, Maria, attempted to contact Brian on the intercom. As there was no reply, they phoned Kingsley Hill, but Brown and Ellis were out, so Antonio got in touch with Brian's secretary, Joanne Newfield, who arrived with Alistair Taylor. They phoned Peter Brown, who'd returned to Kingsley Hill. He advised them to contact his own doctor, John Gallway, who lived nearby. When the doctor arrived he instructed that the doors to Brian's room be broken open. His body was found on the bed.

The coroner's verdict was that he had died by an accidental overdose of the drug carbitol.

Brian Epstein was 32 years old at the time of his death and, despite the coroner's verdict, writers have perpetuated the myth that he had committed suicide. Philip Norman's book *Shout!* hinted at a murder plot, as did Albert Goldman's *The Lives Of John Lennon,* both ridiculous suppositions.

Brian's body was buried at the Jewish Cemetery in Long Lane, Aintree, Liverpool, in Section A, Grave H12.

Epstein, Clive

Brian Epstein's brother, younger by 22 months. Clive's early years proved him a more successful and less troubled person than Brian. He excelled at Wrekin College and did well in the army, where he became a sergeant in the Royal Army Education Corps.

When the Epstein family opened their large NEMS store in Charlotte Street in Liverpool's city centre, Clive ran the electrical and domestic goods section while Brian handled the record department.

With Brian's discovery of the Beatles and the decision that he wished to manage them, the Epstein family agreed to the formation of NEMS Enterprises. The company was launched on 26 June 1962 with a share capital of £100. The brothers shared 50 per cent of the company equally and Clive was appointed Company Secretary.

On 27 April 1964 NEMS Enterprises increased its share capital to £10,000. Brian's share was increased to 5,000, Clive's to 4,000 and each member of the Beatles received 250 shares.

Clive was a scrupulously fair man, extremely popular with those he dealt with and, in some eyes, a more reliable person to deal with than Brian. Nevertheless, he always maintained a low profile. He didn't display the entrepreneurial skills of Brian, was slowly methodical in all of his dealings and was more at home working in Liverpool than in London. Paul once described him as a 'provincial furniture salesman'.

On Brian's death in August 1967, Clive was appointed Chairman of NEMS Enterprises. He realised that the Beatles and Robert Stigwood were not compatible and a deal was arranged which led to Stigwood leaving NEMS with his various acts such as the Bee Gees and Cream. A new company, NEMS Holdings, was formed with Clive as Chairman and Vic Lewis as Managing Director.

Although eternally suspicious of 'the men in suits', as Clive was a known and trusted friend, the Beatles appeared to accept him as Brian's successor until their NEMS contract expired.

It was Clive who first planted the seed which was to become Apple Corps. He realised that a vast proportion of their income, about two million pounds, would go to the taxman unless they diversified and he suggested that they should invest in retail outlets – shops. Paul was excited about the idea and initially visualised a department store in which everything would be white. Paul said, 'It would be great. We could have a department where they sell nothing but white clothes, another where you can buy white furniture – even a white grand piano – and still another where you can buy white pets.'

NEMS Holdings continued to act as agent for the Beatles, taking 25 per cent of their royalties, but was not really expanding or advising the group on their ventures such as *Magical Mystery Tour*. Clive didn't like the constant commuting to London from his Liverpool home.

He felt comfortable in Liverpool, had married Barbara Mattison and settled down. They had two children, a son Henry and a daughter Joanna. There were also the estate duties of half a million pounds hanging over the heads of the Epstein family following Brian's death.

When Clive was approached at the latter part of 1967 by a City merchant bank, Triumph Investment Trust, who wanted to buy NEMS, he gave it serious thought, but didn't immediately respond. He was approached again by Leonard Richenberg, representing Triumph, who made him a good offer, but he still demurred. Clive had felt that he was morally obliged to let the Beatles have first offer on buying NEMS and told Richenberg in January 1969 that he was going to sell NEMS to the Beatles' company Apple.

In the meantime, the Beatles' financial affairs were complicated. Paul had engaged Linda's brother John Eastman to look after the Beatles' affairs, while the other three Beatles had decided on Allen Klein. There were mix-ups between the two. Klein met with Clive and asked him to defer a decision about selling NEMS until he examined the accounts. In February, Clive received a letter from Eastman, part of which read: 'As you know Mr Allen Klein is doing an audit of the Beatles' affairs vis-à-vis NEMS and Nemperor Holdings Ltd. When this has been completed I suggest we meet to discuss the results of Mr Klein's audit as well as the propriety of the negotiations surrounding the nine-year agreement between EMI, the Beatles and NEMS.'

Clive was furious and sent back a note: 'Before any meeting takes place, please be good enough to let me know precisely what you mean by the phrase "the propriety of the negotiations surrounding the nine-year agreement between EMI, the Beatles and NEMS".'

Six weeks after he had told Triumph he would be selling NEMS to Apple, Clive closed the deal with Richenberg.

Eastman blamed Klein and said that while he had been negotiating to obtain NEMS from Clive, Klein had turned up and told the Beatles, 'Forget it, I'll get you NEMS for nothing because the Epsteins owe you money.' However, Clive maintained that it was Eastman who persuaded him against selling NEMS to the Beatles.

Clive remained on Merseyside where he built up a successful furniture business. He later decided to return to show business and in the late seventies teamed up with Joe Flannery to manage a Liverpool band Motion Pictures. He was also intending to go into partnership with Sid Bernstein.

Tragically, Clive died of a heart attack during a skiing holiday with his wife Barbara, on 2 February 1988. His funeral took place on 5 February at Greenbank Drive Synagogue in Liverpool.

Epstein, Harry

A Jewish furniture retailer from Liverpool. Harry's father Isaac was a penniless Polish immigrant who opened a furniture store, I. Epstein & Sons, in Walton Road, in 1901. Harry took over the running of the business. While on holiday in St Anne's-on-Sea he met Malka Hyman, daughter of a family who were also in the furniture business – they owned the Sheffield Cabinet Ltd. The couple were married in Sheffield in 1933 and immediately moved to 197 Queen's Drive in Liverpool.

Harry and Malka (who was known as 'Queenie') had two sons, Brian and Clive. When Harry expanded his business he brought his two sons in as Directors.

The family also decided to support Brian in his plans to manage the Beatles, but insisted that Clive should join him to advise on business matters.

In 1966 Harry had a heart attack and was admitted to Sefton General Hospital in Liverpool. In 1967 Harry and Queenie moved to Bournemouth where he was to convalesce and recuperate. Queenie found him dead in bed on the morning of 17 July. He was 63 years old.

His son Brian died several weeks later.

Epstein, Queenie

Although Jewish, Malka Hyman had been educated in a Catholic boarding school and had anglicised her first name which, roughly translated in Yiddish, means Queen.

Her family owned the Sheffield Cabinet Company and at the age of eighteen she met and married 28-year-old Harry Epstein. A five-bedroom house in Queen's Drive, Childwall, Liverpool, was given to the couple as her dowry.

Queenie had two sons, Brian and Clive. When Brian revealed that he was homosexual, Queenie was supportive and always poured her love on to her son.

Sadly, she was to see her husband and both sons pass away before her. She died at Lourdes Private Hospital, Mossley Hill, Liverpool, on 14 December 1996. She was 82 years old.

Ernst Merck Halle, Hamburg, Germany

The Beatles arrived at Central Station at 6.00 a.m. on Sunday, 26 June 1966 and were surprised to see an old friend waiting for them on the platform – Bettina Derlin, the buxom barmaid from the Star Club. They were then driven in a black Mercedes to the Schloss Hotel in Tremsbuttel, about thirty miles from Hamburg, where they slept until 1.30 p.m. and were driven to the Ernst Merck Halle for their two final concerts in West Germany.

Manager Brian Epstein had left the hall by a side entrance. On his return he found he had forgotten his stage pass and the security guards refused to allow him in. He eventually persuaded a policeman to go inside the hall to verify his identity and was allowed in shortly before the concert commenced.

A number of friends came to greet them backstage, including Bettina, Cattia, a former girlfriend of Paul's, Gibson Kemp, former drummer with bands such as Rory Storm & the Hurricanes, with his girlfriend Astrid Kirchherr, former fiancée of Stuart Sutcliffe, and Bert Kaempfert and his wife.

This was the Beatles' first visit to Hamburg since January 1963 and was to be their last ever concert in the city.

In the 5,600 capacity venue they performed eleven songs during a thirty-minute set.

Outside the hall, fans ran riot and 500 police were used to control them, with the aid of water cannons.

Escorts, The

A popular Liverpool band who never quite achieved their potential.

They comprised Terry Sylvester (guitar), John Kinrade (guitar), Mike Gregory (bass) and Pete Clarke (drums), although an earlier member, when they first formed in 1961, was John Foster. John was Ringo Starr's cousin and Ringo arranged for the group to have a residency at the Blue Angel Club.

The group appeared on the bill with the Beatles at several Cavern appearances including the Beatles' very last gig there on 3 August 1963. Tickets went on sale almost two weeks prior to the gig and were sold out in half an hour. The Beatles were paid £300 for the appearance and although Brian Epstein told Bob Wooler that the group would return, they never did.

Paul McCartney produced the Escorts single 'From Head To Toe' coupled with 'Night Time', issued on 18 November 1966 on Columbia DB 8061, but it fared no better than their previous releases.

Terry Sylvester was later to join the Hollies.

Eubanks, Bob

Boss and disc jockey at KRLA, the No. 1 station in Hollywood. He then became host of the TV show 'The Newlywed Game'. Bob also

owned a chain of clubs with the Cinnamon Cinder in North
Hollywood and others in Long Beach and Alhambra. He was trying
to book the Beatles for Los Angeles a month before their debut
appearance on the 'Ed Sullivan Show'. He originally offered them
$7,500, then $25,000 against 60 per cent of the gate to play the
Hollywood Bowl. He took a second mortgage on his house to
promote the concert and sold out the 18,000 seats at $3.50 a ticket.

The show took place on Sunday, 23 August 1964.

The Hollywood Bowl officials told Eubanks when he booked the
venue that it would be physically impossible to sell out the show at
the Bowl in one day. Three hours after the box office opened, every
ticket had been sold.

Eubanks approached Brian Epstein and tried to arrange a second
show at the Bowl, but Epstein refused.

Eubanks was later to offer Derek Taylor a job when he left
NEMS Enterprises. Taylor left England and settled in Hollywood as
a member of Eubanks' Prestige Promotions. One of the tasks he had
was to conduct interviews with the Beatles in the Bahamas during
the filming of *Help!* This proved an embarrassment both to Derek
and the Beatles, although the tapes were never aired.

Evans, Mal

The friend the Beatles called 'Big Mal'.

He was 26 years old and working as a telecommunications engineer at the Post Office building near to the Cavern when he decided
to drop into the club one lunchtime. He became fascinated by the
venue and began to attend regularly, becoming friendly with
George Harrison, whom he asked back to his house one day to
listen to his records. George suggested that he should ask for a job
at the Cavern door where his 6ft 2in size would make him an ideal
'bouncer'. George introduced him to Ray McFall, and Mal began to
work the Cavern door in his spare time, together with fellow
doormen Tony Buck, Sean Conneelly and Pat Delaney.

He'd been working there for three months when, in 1963, Brian
Epstein offered him the job as equipment road manager to the
Beatles. This job was nicknamed 'the humper' and was the lowest
in the pecking order of road managers, being the person who
humps the gear around, unloading it from vans and setting it up –
a position formerly occupied by Neil Aspinall, whose other duties
precluded him from continuing with the job.

At the time, Mal lived in Mossley Hill with his wife Lil and they'd
just had a baby son. She advised him against taking the job, but he
went ahead and joined the team as assistant to Neil. He travelled
the world with the group and wrote of his adventures with them in

Beatles Monthly. He also appeared briefly as a long-distance swimmer in *Help!* and followed up with appearances in *Magical Mystery Tour* and *Let It Be.* He also had a cameo role in the spaghetti western *Badman,* in which Ringo appeared as a villain.

Since he was always at the Beatles' side in the recording studios, he was often asked to participate. He played Hammond organ on 'You Won't See Me' on the *Rubber Soul* album; sang in the chorus of 'Yellow Submarine'; played bass harmonium on 'Being For The Benefit Of Mr Kite' and played one of the pianos on 'A Day In The Life' on the *Sgt Pepper* album; the tambourine on 'Dear Prudence' and trumpet on 'Helter Skelter' on *The Beatles* double album; the anvil on 'Maxwell's Silver Hammer' on the *Abbey Road* album; and backing vocals on 'You Know My Name (Look Up The Number)'.

Following three years of globe-trotting with the Beatles he was given a job as one of their personal assistants when they ceased touring. In 1968 he was appointed an executive at Apple and took an interest in the recording activities there, discovering a group called the Iveys. He produced their record, 'No Matter What'. They changed their name to Badfinger.

He also helped to co-produce a record by Jackie Lomax.

When Apple began to shed its staff in the wake of Allen Klein, Mal moved to America.

He'd become estranged from his wife and two children and found himself at a loose end, experiencing difficulty in coping with an uneventful existence after the intense excitement of the Beatles years.

He began to write a book of his experiences called *Living The Beatles Legend* with a collaborator, John Hoernle. Grosset and Dunlap were to publish the book and the deadline for delivering the manuscript to the publishers was Monday, 12 January 1976.

At the time he'd moved into a rented duplex at 8122 West 4th Street in Los Angeles with his new girlfriend Fran Hughes and her four-year-old daughter.

On the evening of Sunday, 4 January 1976 he'd been in a depressed state and had taken valium. Hughes was worried and called Hoernle, who came over and began to talk to Mal. The two of them went to an upstairs bedroom and continued talking. Mal seemed doped and groggy and picked up an unloaded 30–30 rifle. Hoernle tried to take it from him and there was a scuffle prompting Hughes to call the police, saying 'My old man has a gun and has taken valium and is totally screwed up.'

Four police officers arrived and two of them, David D. Krempa and Robert E. Brannon, went upstairs. Mal saw them and pointed the rifle at them. They told him to put it down, but he didn't and they fired six shots, four of them hitting him and killing him instantly. He was forty years old.

Mal had been an Honorary Sheriff of Los Angeles County.

He was cremated in Los Angeles on Wednesday, 7 January 1976 and his ashes placed in a pot and posted to England, but were lost in the post. Eventually they were recovered from the Lost Letter office.

Evans, Malcolm

Not to be confused with the Beatles' road manager of that name.

Evans, a former junior executive of Rediffusion Television, was 25 years old when he was invited by Nicky Byrne to become one of the shareholders of the Beatles' merchandising company Seltaeb for a fee of £1,000.

Byrne made Evans Vice-President of the company and three weeks before the Beatles toured Australia, Evans flew there to visit Stephen, Jacques and Stephen, a Sydney law firm, to brief them on protecting the merchandising rights.

Following Evans' visit, a large amount of Seltaeb-approved merchandise began to flood the Australian stores – stockings, calendars, bracelets, wallpaper, plastic wigs, dolls, trays and posters. However, a large amount of the goods weren't sold as the Australians weren't as enthusiastic about merchandising souvenirs as the American fans.

Everett, Kenny

A zany British disc jockey and television personality, born Maurice James Christopher Cole in Liverpool on Christmas Day 1944. He worked in an office and in a bakery, before beginning his show-biz career with Radio Luxembourg. He next joined the pirate ship Radio London. Kenny was the official pirate radio reporter invited to accompany the Beatles on their final tour in August 1966. He then joined BBC's Radio 1 on its launch in 1967.

On Saturday, 20 May 1967 the BBC show 'Where It's At' transmitted a pre-recorded feature by Everett on *Sgt Pepper's Lonely Hearts Club Band,* including interviews with John, Paul and Ringo. Another pre-recorded interview by Everett, in which he talked to Paul McCartney and discussed 'All You Need Is Love', was transmitted on 'Where It's At' on Saturday, 1 July 1967.

On the edition of 'Where It's At' on Saturday, 25 November 1967, an eighteen-minute interview with John Lennon by Everett and Chris Denning was broadcast.

Some of his interviews with the Beatles were issued as an Apple promotional single in Italy under the title 'Una Sensazionale Intervista dei Beatles'.

Everett edited the Beatles' fifth and final Christmas fan club record. He used his real name, Maurice Cole, on the 1969 edition.

On Saturday, 27 January 1968, Everett visited John at his home in Weybridge to record an interview for 'The Kenny Everett Show', which was broadcast on Radio 1 on 4 February.

Everett also visited the group while they were recording at Abbey Road on Thursday, 6 June 1968 and recorded an interview that was broadcast on 'The Kenny Everett Show' on Sunday, 9 June.

On Thursday, 14 August 1969, Everett again dropped by the Abbey Road Studios while the Beatles were mixing some tracks and recorded an interview with John Lennon which was broadcast in two parts on his 'Everett Is Here' radio series on Saturday, 20 and Saturday, 27 September.

It wasn't merely the fact that Kenny shared the same Liverpool roots as the Beatles that led to his becoming such a personal friend of the group. He also had a wacky sense of humour that appealed to them, particularly to Lennon. Kenny was also anarchic in his approach to his radio and television shows, another aspect of his talent that they liked.

His autobiography, *The Custard Stops At Hatfield,* published in October 1982, featured many anecdotes about his relationship with the Beatles.

Kenny died from an AIDS-related illness on Tuesday, 4 April 1995. He was 50 years old.

Everybody's Got Something To Hide Except Me And My Monkey

One of the longest titles of a Beatles track, this John Lennon number had no title when they began recording it in June/July 1968. A title 'Come On, Come On', the opening words to the song, was considered, but then John confirmed it was to be 'Everybody's Got Something To Hide Except Me And My Monkey' and commented, 'That was just sort of a nice line that I made into a song. It was about me and Yoko. Everybody seemed to be paranoid except for us two, who were in the glow of love.' It was included as a track on *The Beatles* double album.

Everybody's Trying To Be My Baby

A number written and recorded by Carl Perkins, which featured on his *Teen Beat* album, issued on 18 August 1958. The same album included his songs 'Matchbox' and 'Honey Don't', which were also recorded by the Beatles.

The Beatles began performing the song in 1961 with George on lead vocals. A live version is to be found on *The Beatles Live! At The Star Club In Hamburg, Germany 1962* album and the group recorded it for their November 1964 album *Beatles For Sale*. It's also to be found on The *Beatles Collection, Rock 'n' Roll Music* and their Capitol EP *4 By The Beatles*. The group performed the number twice on 'Saturday Club' and also sang it on three other BBC radio shows, 'Pop Go The Beatles', 'Top Gear' and 'Ticket To Ride'.

George Harrison was lead vocal on the track when the Beatles recorded it on 18 October 1964.

The 'Top Gear' version was used on *The Beatles Live At The BBC* CD and the version used on the *Anthology 2* CD was from their Shea Stadium appearance.

Every Little Thing

Track from the *Beatles For Sale* album. It's not clear as to who actually wrote it, although John credited it to Paul in a *Playboy* interview.

Recording began on Tuesday, 29 September 1964, and the number also appeared on the *Beatles For Sale* EP. It was included on the American album *Beatles VI* and the compilation *Love Songs*.

Exciters, The

A New York quartet who appeared with the Beatles on their first American tour. Led by Herb Rooney and his wife, Brenda Reid, the group had reached No. 4 in the US charts with their single 'Tell Him' in 1962.

Exis, The

The name the Beatles called the group of students who began to attend their gigs in Hamburg. They included Klaus Voormann, Astrid Kirchherr, Jurgen Vollmer, Detlev Birgfeld and Peter Markmann who were generally clad in black clothes, like the French Existentialists.

The Exis had their own nicknames for the Beatles. They called John 'the Sidie Man', George 'the Beautiful One' and Paul, 'the Baby'.

Extracts From The Album *A Hard Day's Night*

Issued two days following the release of the Beatles' sixth EP, with a slightly different cover by Bob Freeman, the sales didn't warrant a Top 30 chart entry.

The EP was issued on Parlophone GEP 8924 on 6 November 1964 and contained the tracks 'Any Time At All', 'I'll Cry Instead', 'Things We Said Today' and 'When I Get Home'.

Extracts From The Film *A Hard Day's Night*

The Beatles' sixth British EP. This was the first of the Beatles EPs not to enter the Top 30 – and no subsequent Beatles EP was to do so either. Their EP sales were never to equal those of the first five releases again, although the material was repackaged product which had already achieved fantastic sales when issued on albums and singles.

The cover featured the same Bob Freeman shot used on the album cover and the EP was issued on Parlophone GEP 8902 on 4 November 1964. The tracks were: 'I Should Have Known Better', 'If I Fell', 'Tell Me Why' and 'And I Love Her'.

Fab Four, The

One of the most frequently used of the nicknames given to the
Beatles, along with 'the Moptops'.

The phrase began to be used by disc jockeys and other members
of the media after the release of the *With The Beatles* album. In his
sleeve notes, when writing about George Harrison's 'Don't Bother
Me', Tony Barrow used the superlative 'The fabulous foursome',
which then led the media to dub them 'The Fab Four'.

Fairfield Hall, Park Lane, Croydon, Surrey

The Beatles appeared at this venue on Thursday, 25 April 1963
as part of the Mersey Beat Showcase with Gerry & the
Pacemakers, the Big Three and Billy J. Kramer. Originally, as the
Beatles and the other Liverpool bands weren't very well known
in the south of England at the time, promoter John Smith
booked them in January and he also booked singer John Leyton
to top the bill. On the night of the concert, Leyton was unable
to perform as he was ill.

The Beatles returned to the venue on Saturday, 7 September
1963.

Faithfull, Marianne

Singer, born in Hampstead, London, on 29 December 1946. She
was the daughter of Baroness Erisso von Sacher-Masoch and Dr
Glynn Faithfull, a psychologist.

The family originally lived in Ormskirk, on the outskirts of

Liverpool while Marianne's father worked on his doctorate at Liverpool University.

When Marianne was six years old her parents separated and she attended St Joseph's Convent School in Reading.

At the age of seventeen she met John Dunbar at a Valentine's Ball at Cambridge. The two began a relationship and John introduced her to Paul McCartney during visits to the Ashers' house in Wimpole Street. While John was abroad she attended a birthday party for actress Adrienne Posta. During the party she was spotted by Andrew Loog Oldham, manager of the Rolling Stones, who considered she had a 'virginal' appearance that would contrast with the Stones' image. He signed her up and she had immediate record success with her debut disc 'As Tears Go By', penned by Mick Jagger and Keith Richards. She was still attending convent school at the time of the record release.

She married Dunbar on 6 May 1965 at Cambridge, with Pete Asher as Best Man.

The couple moved into a flat at 29 Lennox Gardens, Knightsbridge, and one of the regular visitors was Paul McCartney. Paul told her he'd give her a song and actually wrote one for her called 'Etcetera', but decided it wasn't good enough to record. As a result, Marianne became Paul's personal choice to record 'Yesterday' and during an evening at a party he played her an acetate of his version. When she recorded 'Yesterday', he attended her recording session at Decca Studios on 11 October 1965 and the record was released on 22 October 1965. She was booked to appear on Granada's TV special 'The Music Of Lennon McCartney' singing 'Yesterday'. Paul McCartney began singing the number for 22 seconds and the camera then moved to Marianne, who completed the song. The eighteen-year-old singer was three months pregnant at the time, so the camera concentrated on a head and shoulders shot throughout.

However, it was singer Matt Monro who reached No. 8 in the British charts with the number while Marianne barely scraped in, her highest position being No. 36.

Her son Nicholas was born on 10 November 1965.

Marianne then left her husband to live with Mick Jagger and was later to tell the *New Musical Express*, 'My first move was to get a Rolling Stone as a boyfriend. I slept with three and decided the lead singer was the best bet.'

She and Mick were present at various Beatles functions, beginning with the 'Yellow Submarine' recording on Wednesday, 1 June 1966, when she joined several others in producing background noises to the track. They joined the Beatles on their trip to Bangor to see the Maharishi and were also among the group of celebrities at the Beatles' feet as they performed 'All You Need Is Love' on the 'Our World' programme.

In February 1965 her mother approached Brian Epstein and asked him to manage Marianne, but he told her he would not manage another female singer as long as he had Cilla Black.

Marianne was to become dependent on drugs, her relationship with Jagger floundered and she ended up a registered heroin addict, living in a squat.

She was to conquer her addiction and received critical acclaim for albums such as *Broken English,* released in 1979. Her autobiography *Faithfull* was published in 1994.

37 Falkner Street, Liverpool L8

A ground floor flat which Brian Epstein rented in 1961.

During John and Cynthia's wedding lunch at Reece's Restaurant when they were married on 23 August 1962, Epstein told the couple that they could have the use of the flat for as long as they wished and gave them the key.

That evening the Beatles were appearing in Chester and Cynthia began moving her things into the flat. Their 'honeymoon' proved to be a strange one as John went on to London from Chester and began appearing at gigs in various cities.

When John eventually did manage to turn up at the flat, Cynthia told him that, as she was pregnant, she'd been afraid she might miscarry. Aunt Mimi insisted that John and Cynthia come back to live with her as she was concerned about Cynthia being left alone in the flat so often in her delicate state.

It was while John and Cynthia were residents in the flat that John wrote 'Do You Want To Know A Secret?' Later, John was to comment, 'I was in the first apartment I'd ever had that wasn't shared by fourteen other students – girls and guys at art school. I'd just married Cyn and Brian Epstein gave us his secret little apartment that he had in Liverpool to keep his sexual liaisons separate from his home life. And he let Cyn and I have that apartment.'

Falling In Love Again

A song which Paul performed during the early career of the Beatles in Liverpool and Hamburg. The number was originally sung by Marlene Dietrich in the classic German silent film *The Blue Angel*.

Paul sang the number at the Star Club when Adrian Barber was recording and this version can be heard on the Star Club recordings, first issued in June 1977 as a two-album set by Lingasong.

Fallon, John

A Canadian-born musician, more commonly known as Jack. His early career, displaying his versatility on double-bass and violin, saw him performing with many major names, including Duke Ellington and Guy Lombardo. He also established himself in Britain as a session man.

In the early sixties he ran a prominent London booking agency, the Cana Variety Agency, in addition to organising promotions under the name Jaybee Clubs.

Fallon booked the Beatles into their first venue in the south following their signing with Epstein (their only other southern appearance had been for Sam Leach), at the Subscription Rooms, Stroud, on 31 March 1962. He also booked them into the Subscription Rooms on 1 September 1962; McIlroys Ballroom, Swindon, on 17 July 1962; the Town Hall, Lydney, on 31 August 1962; and the City Hall, Salisbury, on 15 June 1963.

Several years later, Fallon was approached by Abbey Road Studios in his capacity as session man and when he arrived at the studios on 12 July 1968 he found it was a Beatles recording session and he was to play country guitar on Ringo Starr's 'Don't Pass Me By'.

Family Way, The

A British film which presented Paul McCartney with his first opportunity to compose film music. In 1967 he was asked to provide the score for *The Family Way*, which starred Hayley Mills, Hywel Bennett and John Mills.

A former lorry driver from Liverpool, Bill Naughton, who had penned the highly successful *Alfie* in 1966, had written a play *All In Good Time*, on which the movie was based. On its release its theme of an unconsummated marriage earned it an 'X' certificate. Produced by the Boulting Brothers, it was set in Lancashire and concerned the newlywed Jenny (Hayley Mills) and Arthur (Hywel Bennett), who set off on their honeymoon only to discover that their travel agent has absconded with their money. The mental strain of living with Arthur's parents makes Arthur impotent. The film follows the further stresses this unfortunate problem brings, especially when parents and friends find out.

The Family Way was premiered at the Warner Theatre, London, on 18 December 1966, with Paul receiving his first screen credit as a solo composer. He produced 28 minutes of music for the film, arranged for him by George Martin. A soundtrack album (Decca SKL 4847) was released on 6 January 1967 and two singles, 'Love In The Open Air' coupled with 'Theme From The Family Way'

(United Artists UP 1165) and 'Love In The Open Air' coupled with 'Bahama Sound' (United Artists UA 50148), were released on 23 December 1966 and 24 April 1967 respectively.

Fans! Fans! Fans!

A British ATV documentary shown on 29 July 1964. The programme, on fan adulation and hysteria, was originally to have been called 'The Road To Beatlemania'.

Farrow, Mia

At the age of 22, actress Mia Farrow, who had appeared in a hit TV series 'Peyton Place', married Frank Sinatra and starred in *Rosemary's Baby*, set out on a spiritual odyssey, having studied alternative and Eastern philosophy which she regarded as 'a mathematical formula for mind expansion'.

It was her sister Prudence who introduced her to the teachings of the Maharishi Mahesh Yogi, on the recommendation of the Beatles, who had become friendly with the two sisters shortly before Mia made *Rosemary's Baby*.

In January 1968, Mia and Prudence flew to Boston to see the Maharishi and decided to travel to Rishikesh and study under him for three months. Mia had been meditating for two hours a day at the ashram for nearly a month when she heard that the Beatles were to arrive. Aware of the media circus which surrounded them, she considered that the tranquility she'd found would be compromised. 'I got into a panic,' she said. 'I had nightmares of armies of press invading.' As a result, after the Beatles had arrived, she decided to explore other parts of the country and set out on a three-week journey across India. She had decided that the Maharishi wasn't the teacher she was looking for and told the *Ladies Home Journal*: 'Everyone made the mistake of trying to make a Christ figure out of him. He's a man. No religious man should try and become another pope-like figure. His edifices are bound to crumble.' However, she did acknowledge some value in his teachings and was to say, 'The Maharishi did do one thing right. He put meditation in terms that the Western world could understand. That was important.'

It has been reported in a number of books that John and George decided to confront the Maharishi and leave Rishikesh because they'd been told he'd made sexual advances to Mia Farrow. This is not true. The girl in question was a young meditator from California.

Farrow, Prudence

One of actress Mia Farrow's younger sisters. It was Prudence who first introduced Mia to the teachings of the Maharishi Mahesh

Yogi. The two sisters had become close friends of the Beatles in London, particularly since both girls refused to be awed by them. It was the Beatles who first turned Prudence on to the Maharishi. The two sisters had been at Rishikesh for almost a month when they heard that the Beatles were coming to the ashram. While there Prudence remained by herself in her room meditating for a long time and wouldn't come out to communicate with anyone, so John was picked as the person to persuade her to come out of her solitude and experience the reality of life. The task inspired him to write the song 'Dear Prudence'.

Fascher, Horst

A former featherweight boxer, who represented both Hamburg and West Germany. Horst was born in Hamburg on 5 February 1936. He became a bouncer on the door of the Kaiserkeller Club when the Beatles made their first appearance there in 1960. He used tough methods to control any violence in or out of the club and employed some of his friends from the Hamburg Boxing Academy, who were soon known as 'Hoddel's Gang'. His efficiency at controlling trouble led to an invitation from Peter Eckhorn to move to the Top Ten Club before being head-hunted by the Star Club where he later began managing the venue on behalf of Manfred Weissleder.

Horst had a fearsome reputation because he had served a prison term for manslaughter following a street fight in which he'd accidentally killed a sailor.

He became a good friend of the Beatles, although observers say there was an initial tension. It was alleged that when George Harrison made a remark about him being a Nazi, Horst punched him. It is also alleged that when John Lennon made a similar remark, he took him into the gents' toilet and urinated over him. Horst particularly objected to such comments as his family had hidden a Jewish family from the Nazis during the Second World War.

When Adrian Barber recorded the Beatles during their December 1962 appearances at the Star Club, Horst could be heard singing on the track, 'Hallelujah, I Love Her So', although he is uncredited. His brother Fred also got up on stage to sing 'Be-Bop-A-Lulu', but is credited as Herr Obber – German for 'Mr Waiter' – as the sleeve note writers were unsure of who was on the tracks. This recording took place at a Star Club party when various people were invited on stage to do a turn.

Horst was to marry Ali, the daughter of Faron, leader of Faron's Flamingos, and the couple had a child, Rory. The marriage didn't last and, sadly, the baby died in an accident in Hamburg caused by a faulty cot.

Horst and his next partner had a baby girl who suffered from a rare heart problem. Paul McCartney generously came to his aid by hiring a team of specialists to fly over from New York and operate at Great Ormond Street Hospital, London. Paul also arranged for Horst and his partner to fly to London and stay while the operation took place. Unfortunately, the baby couldn't be saved and Horst was plunged into depression, having seen both his children die within a year of each other.

Since the 1960s, Horst has reopened a venue called the Star Club on several occasions in different parts of Hamburg and did so once again in 1994. When he opened a Star Club in the Grossnerumark district on 15 December 1978, headlined by Tony Sheridan, both Ringo Starr and George Harrison were present for the first night.

Fell, Ray

Apart from its group and football teams, Liverpool was also famous for its comedians – and the many successful funnymen from Liverpool included Ken Dodd, Tommy Handley, Arthur Askey, Ted Ray, Norman Vaughan and Jimmy Tarbuck.

Ray Fell was yet another Liverpool comedian and the Beatles booked him to co-compere their second *Christmas Show* at the Odeon, Hammersmith. Unfortunately, Ray was one of the local comedians who never made the big time.

Fenton, Shane

Born Bernard Jewry, he adopted the stage name Shane Fenton and led a group called the Fentones in the sixties, before changing his name to Alvin Stardust in the seventies and achieving fame with a series of chart hits.

He frequently appeared on Merseyside and was featured in *Mersey Beat*. Shane became friendly with the Beatles and when they were appearing at the Granada, Mansfield in early 1963, a town where Shane's parents lived, he recalls: 'There were hundreds of girls blocking all the streets nearby – but being in the business I knew that if you went through the shop of the local chippie, through his back room, and then up over the roof of the cinema dressing-room and down a fire escape, you could get into the cinema backstage. I'd already worked with them a few times, so I went over the roof and found them trapped in their dressing-room. They said they were starving, because they hadn't been able to leave the cinema since they arrived there during the afternoon, so I went back home . . . and told my mother all about it and she made them up a picnic basket full of food, with containers full of hot soup and piles of salmon sandwiches, which I took to them backstage, again going over the roof, and they were absolutely knocked out.'

He also appeared on a bill with them at the Albert Hall and on a promotion at the Empire Theatre, Liverpool. Backstage at the Empire, Brian Epstein offered Shane the number 'Do You Want To Know A Secret?' and said that he could record it if he would let Brian be his manager. Shane turned him down, saying he already had a manager.

Shane was to marry Iris Caldwell, sister of Rory Storm and former girlfriend of George Harrison and Paul McCartney. The two of them formed a double act and later opened a club on the outskirts of Liverpool. They had a couple of children, but were later divorced. Shane changed his name to Alvin Stardust and had thirteen British chart hits between 1973 and 1985, including 'My Coo-Ca-Choo' and 'Jealous Mind'. He married actress Liza Goddard, but that marriage also ended in divorce.

Festival Hall, Brisbane, Australia

The Beatles made the final appearance of their Australian tour at this theatre on 29 and 30 June 1964, when they performed at four concerts, two shows per evening, to capacity audiences of 5,500 at each show.

When they arrived in the capital of Queensland they were pelted at the airport with missiles from a faction who later admitted they were students making a protest. As a result of the missile hurling, the Beatles restricted their public appearances. When they did go on stage at the Festival Hall, the faction was present and hurled numerous missiles on stage, including sweets, coins, food and drink. Two youths ran forward and tossed a metal biscuit tin on to the stage. A message of apology was later given and a meeting arranged between representatives of the protesters and the Beatles. Three protesters apologised to the Beatles at their hotel and said that their actions had been 'a protest against materialism'.

Between shows on the first night at the Festival Hall, the Beatles were visited backstage by Sir Henry Abel Smith and his wife Lady May Smith, who said that the Beatles were 'quite decent chaps'.

Festival Hall, Melbourne, Australia

The Beatles appeared for a total of six concerts over three nights at this venue in the state of Victoria.

They appeared twice nightly on Monday, 15 June, Tuesday, 16 June, and Wednesday, 17 June 1964, and drew capacity crowds, attracting audiences of 45,000 to the six appearances.

Ringo re-joined the group after an illness for the first of the shows, which was also recorded by the Nine Television network and broadcast under the title 'The Beatles Sing For Shell'.

Field, Alan

A comedian from the north of England, whose main work took place in working men's clubs. He was hired to compere the Beatles' tour of Australia.

Unfortunately, his blunt, adult-orientated humour didn't go down well at the concerts, and his time on stage was cut back after every performance. One observer commented, 'He just died slowly every night.' Field appeared in every city on the tour with the exception of Adelaide, where Bob Francis took over the compering honours.

Field remained in Australia to become resident compere on a television show called 'The Go! Show!', and later returned to England and the northern clubs.

Fifth Beatle, The

'The Fifth Beatle' is a term which has been applied to several people, some close associates of the group, others with only a tenuous connection.

The first person looked upon as 'the fifth Beatle' was their original bass guitarist Stuart Sutcliffe who was, literally, 'the fifth Beatle' because he was the fifth member of the group. They became a quartet when he left.

Drummer Peter Best also has some claim to the title because there were four members of the group when he joined: John, Paul, George and Stuart, so he became the fifth member and remained with them during the formative days between August 1960 and August 1962.

Their original road manager Neil Aspinall has often been referred to as 'the fifth Beatle' and is possibly the most likely claimant to the title, having been associated with them longer than anyone else, someone whom they'd always trusted and relied upon, and who still administrates their Apple empire for them.

Manager Brian Epstein was also referred to as 'the fifth Beatle', but due to the age and class barriers between them, his title of Manager is more apt.

George Martin, their recording manager, was tagged 'the fifth Beatle' because of his contribution to their recorded sound. It was a symbiotic relationship because Martin's technical expertise and the Fab Four's musical innovations provided a revolution in the sound of popular music in the sixties.

Jimmy Nicol, who deputised for Ringo Starr, who was ill, on the

Beatles' European and Far Eastern tour in 1964, including some Australian dates, has also been referred to as 'the fifth Beatle'.

A self-styled 'fifth Beatle' was American disc jockey Murray The K, who bestowed the title on himself when he ingratiated himself with the Beatles on their arrival in New York in February 1964. Brian Epstein was furious and told him to stop doing so.

The most tenuous of all was American journalist Ed Rudy, who joined the entourage travelling with the Beatles on their American tour in 1964. He issued an album of his interviews with the group called *The Beatles American Tour With Ed Rudy*, in which the sleeve notes claimed: 'The Beatles call Ed Rudy "the fifth Beatle".'

The term was also applied to keyboards player Billy Preston who recorded with the Beatles on the 'Get Back' sessions. When the single was issued in April 1969, the record was credited to 'The Beatles with Billy Preston'.

Films

The Beatles only appeared in three feature films as a group. A three-picture deal had been arranged with United Artists and the first two, *A Hard Day's Night* (1963) and *Help!* (1965), were produced by Walter Shenson and directed by Richard Lester.

There was great difficulty in finding a third project which the Beatles would agree to film, 'Shades Of A Personality', in which each member would portray a facet of one man's multiple personality, was rejected, as was Joe Orton's controversial 'Up Against It'. The rights to film the Western 'A Talent For Loving' was acquired by the group, but they rejected it, also turning down a comedy version of 'The Three Musketeers' with their favourite film star Brigitte Bardot as Lady De Winter.

They agreed to the filming of the animated *Yellow Submarine*, believing this would fulfil the terms of their three-picture deal, but it didn't and they eventually decided to utilise their planned TV documentary on the making of an album, and turned it into the film *Let It Be*.

Before the group split up, individual members were involved in a number of film ventures. Ringo appeared in *Candy*, *The Magic Christian*, *Blindman* and *200 Motels*, and in his solo career has appeared in numerous movies and TV specials including *Born To Boogie* (which he directed), *That'll Be The Day*, *Son Of Dracula*, *Lisztomania*, *Sextette*, *The Caveman* and others.

Paul made two avant-garde films in 1966, *The Next Spring Then* and *The Defeat Of The Dog*, and composed the music for the 1967 film *The Family Way*, starring John and Hayley Mills. He was to score music for several other films, including the 1973 James Bond

movie *Live And Let Die*, which was awarded a Grammy and nominated for an Oscar. He has been involved in many film ventures in
his solo career, including the feature film based on his own script,
Give My Regards To Broad Street in 1984, which also featured
Ringo.

John appeared in Dick Lester's 1967 feature film *How I Won The
War* and began making avant-garde films with Yoko the same year.
Over the years they included: *Two Virgins*, *Rape*, *Honeymoon*, *Self
Portrait*, *Up Your Legs*, *Fly*, *Apotheosis*, *Erection*, *Ten For Two*,
The One To One Concert and *Imagine*.

George composed the music for the feature film *Wonderwall* in
1969, and composed the soundtrack for the 1971 documentary on
Ravi Shankar, *Raga*. His main involvement in film began after the
breakup of the Beatles when he founded Handmade Films.

Fitzgerald, Ella

The legendary jazz vocalist who was born in Newport News, Virginia,
on 25 April 1918. The seal of approval for the songwriting team of
Lennon/McCartney came in 1964 when Ella had a British chart hit
with 'Can't Buy Me Love' several weeks after the Beatles' own version
was released. Ella reached the position of No. 30 and her interpretation of the song was the most famous one, apart from the Beatles'
own. There have been about seventy different versions of the song by
artists such as Mary Wells, Brenda Lee, Gerry Mulligan and the
Supremes.

Some of the songs Ella wrote herself were awful. One was called
'Ringo Beat' and included lyrics such as 'Don't knock the rhythm of
the lads today, Remember they're playing the Ringo way.' At the
Nice Jazz Festival on 21 July 1971 she sang a bossa nova medley
which included The Beatles' 'Something', the Carpenters' 'Close to
You' and Del Shannon's 'Put A Little Love In Your Heart'.

Ella, who had ninety hit records during her long career, was 78
years old when she died in 1996.

Fixing A Hole

A track from the *Sgt Pepper* album on which Paul sings lead. There
has been some confusion regarding the harpsichord player. Neil
Aspinall claimed in *Beatles Monthly* that it was Paul, but others
claim it was George Martin. George Harrison provides a guitar
solo.

Commenting on the song, Paul has said, 'The song is just about the
hole in the road where the rain gets in; a good old analogy – the hole
in your make-up which lets the rain in and stops your mind from going
where it will. It's you interfering with things; as when someone walks

up to you and says, "I am the Son of God." And you say, "No, you're not; I'll crucify you," and you crucify him. Well, that's life, but it is not fixing a hole.'

There were the inevitable suggestions that fixing a hole referred to a drug 'fix'. Paul said, 'If you're a junky sitting in a room fixing a hole then that's what it will mean to you, but when I wrote it I meant if there's a crack or the room is uncolourful, then I'll paint it.'

When the Beatles began recording the number at Regent Sound Studios on Thursday, 9 February 1967, it was the first recording session they'd done for EMI in Britain ouside the familiar Abbey Road Studios as the Abbey Road facilities were fully booked that night.

Flannery, Agnes
When the Beatle City Museum opened in Liverpool in 1985 one exhibit was a photograph of Agnes Flannery, then 76, in her youth. It was accompanied by a notice that the photograph of her inspired the Beatle 'bob'.

Her son Joe claimed that when the Beatles visited him at his Aintree flat early in their career they noticed a picture of his mother when young. Apparently, John fell in love with it.

Joe says, 'John picked up the photo, admired the hairstyle and said to Paul McCartney, "That's the way I want our hair to look."'

'Compare the photo of my mother and John Lennon and the hairstyles are remarkably similar. I have spoken on a number of occasions with Astrid (Kirchherr) and she has told me that she never ever said that she created the hairstyle. In fact the group went to a barber's at Horne Brothers at the corner of Paradise Street and Lord Street.'

Agnes said: 'The picture that intrigued John was taken at a studio in Bold Street, Liverpool, when I was just sixteen, two years before I married. I'm delighted to hear that the photograph is going on exhibition in Beatle City Museum. I'm sure many folk will be thrilled to learn the true story of how the Beatles came by their distinctive hairstyle which, incidentally, I'd created for myself by washing and trimming my own hair in that particular way.'

Agnes died in her home in December 1998 at the age of 91.

The Floral Hall Ballroom, The Promenade, Morecambe, Lancashire.
The Beatles appeared twice at this ballroom, in a seaside resort in the north-west of England, quite close to Merseyside. Their first

appearance took place on Wednesday, 29 August 1962 and their last on Friday, 18 January 1963.

Floral Hall, The, The Promenade, Southport, Lancashire.

The Beatles played in the nearby seaside town of Southport on numerous occasions early in their career, and this venue was particularly impressive because it was a proper theatre, in contrast to the local jive hives they'd been appearing in.

They made their debut at the hall in a 'Rock 'n' Trad Spectacular' on Tuesday, 20 February 1962, on a bill with several Mersey groups, including Gerry & the Pacemakers and Rory Storm & the Hurricanes, together with the jazz outfit the Chris Hamilton Jazzmen. Later that year, on Tuesday, 20 November, they appeared at the theatre again, performing two shows in the course of the evening.

During 1963 they appeared at the venue twice, on Tuesday, 23 April and on Tuesday, 15 October.

Flying

An instrumental recording featured in *Magical Mystery Tour* and issued on the EP set and album of *Magical Mystery Tour*.

The Beatles considered they needed some instrumental background music to their film and began recording what was only their third instrumental number. The first was 'Cry For A Shadow', which they'd recorded for Polydor in Hamburg in 1961, and their second the unreleased '12 Bar Original', recorded in 1965.

When they first began recording the number at Abbey Road studios on 28 September 1967, it went under the title 'Aerial Tour Instrumental'. All four members of the group contributed to the composition, which was one of only three Beatles numbers credited to Harrison/Lennon/McCartney/Starkey, the others being 'Dig It' and 'Christmastime (Is Here Again)'.

John played organ and mellotron, George and Paul were on guitars and Ringo on drums and maracas. All four participated in a vocal chant.

The original recording was a lengthy nine minutes and thirty-one seconds long and it was edited down to a more reasonable length of two minutes and fourteen seconds.

Follow The Beatles

A 30-minute BBC television production. The documentary concerned the making of the Beatles' debut film *A Hard Day's*

Night and also included footage of the Beatles recording in the Abbey Road Studios.

'Follow The Beatles' was screened on 3 August 1964.

Fontaine, Dick

First television director to capture the Beatles on film. Fontaine worked for Granada Television, the station with the franchise to cover the north-west of England. Mona Best had originally written off to David Plowright of Granada, suggesting that the company use the Beatles on one of their programmes. A shoal of letters from Liverpool were organised to be sent to the station, resulting in Granda dispatching some scouts to watch the group perform at Southport's Cambridge Hall on 26 July and the Cavern on 1 August.

Filming was approved, and Fontaine moved in with his camera crew to film them performing at the Cavern during the lunchtime session on 22 August 1962. The idea was for them to film some live clips to be used on a programme called 'Know The North'. Fontaine filmed them performing 'Some Other Guy' and 'Kansas City/Hey, Hey, Hey', but the resulting film, due to the technical difficulties of filming inside the dank cellar, wasn't considered satisfactory and was scrapped.

Later, when the Beatles began to make their impact in Britain, Granada sought the original copy of the film, but only the clip of 'Some Other Guy' survived. They first broadcast it in 1963 and it has been aired several times since.

Fool On The Hill, The

Paul McCartney composition which he wrote for the *Magical Mystery Tour* movie. The sequence was filmed in France. Three flautists were engaged – Christopher and Richard Taylor and Jack Ellery – with George and John adding harmonicas and George Martin playing piano. Before it was included on the *Magical Mystery Tour* double EP and album, it was pruned by 90 seconds. The number was also included on the compilations *The Beatles 1967–1970* and *The Beatles Ballads*.

Sergio Mendes and Brazil 666 reached No. 6 in the American charts with their cover of the number in 1968 and Shirley Bassey had a minor hit with it in Britain in 1971. Two versions of the number were included on the Beatles' *Anthology 2* CDs.

Fool, The

Josje Leeger and Marijke Koger were both born in Amsterdam in 1943. The two eventually met and teamed up as a design group,

together with Marijke's boyfriend Simon Postuma, and for a while
they ran a boutique in Amsterdam called The Trend.

In 1966 they moved to London, and while there they met
Canadian-born Barry Finch (also born in 1943) and his partner
Simon Hayes, who ran a public relations company handling artists
for Robert Stigwood and the Saville Theatre for Brian Epstein. The
work of the Dutch designers, who decided to call themselves the
Fool, was shown to Epstein, who commissioned them to do some
design work for the Saville.

Commenting on the origin of their name, Simon said, 'It represents Truth, Spiritual Meaning and the circle which expresses the
Universal circumference in which gravitate all things.'

Barry Finch then joined the team and Simon Hayes was
appointed their business manager. The group specialised in
costumes, interior design and painting. They began to design
clothes for the Beatles and their wives and girlfriends, including the
outfits the group wore on their 'All You Need Is Love' segment of
the 'Our World' programme. They also painted the fireplace in
George's bungalow, George's guitar and Mini, and John's Rolls-
Royce, piano and caravan.

Another completed commission was a design for the centre-
spread of the *Sgt Pepper* sleeve, but it wasn't used.

The Fool interested the Beatles in funding them to design outfits
for the Apple Boutique in Baker Street and a great deal of controversy was aroused by a large mural, designed by the Fool and
executed by 40 art students, which covered the outer walls of the
boutique. Local traders demanded its removal and it eventually had
to be painted over with whitewash.

The shop opened on 7 December 1967, but lost so much money
that the Beatles decided to close it down and offer the remaining
stock free to all comers. By this time the Fool had made arrangements to move to America and were given a large amount of money
to record an album for Mercury Records. The album, entitled *The
Fool* and recorded by Graham Nash, was issued in 1968, but
proved unsuccessful.

The group began designing theatres in America and also opened
a design company in Los Angeles called The Chariot. Josje and
Barry were married in July 1969 and later returned to Holland.
They settled down in Amsterdam with their six children, Violet
Dawn, Titus Blue, Scarlet Arrow, Jade Moon, Daniel Haze and
Amber Blue, and continued to design costumes and sets for pop
artists in succeeding years. Josje died in July 1991. She was 47 years
old.

Simon and Marijke recorded some singles together, produced by

Graham Nash, which were released in 1972, under the name Seemon and Marijke. The couple finally split up in 1975 and Simon eventually returned to Holland in the mid-eighties.

For Arts Sake

Title of a magazine programme produced by Southern Television, one of Britain's regional TV stations. On Wednesday, 20 May 1964, Brian Epstein appeared on the show discussing his career.

For No One

A composition by Paul featured on the *Revolver* album. John Lennon was later to comment, 'That was one of my favourites of his.'

Paul wrote it in March 1966 in a chalet while he was on a skiing holiday in Switzerland with Jane Asher. His working title was 'Why Did It Die?' It has been suggested that perhaps his love affair with Jane was fading.

John and George didn't participate in the recording. After Paul and Ringo had recorded the number on Monday, 9 May 1966 with Paul on piano and overdubbing on clavichord, and Ringo playing drums and overdubbing cymbals and maraca, a French horn solo was added several days later on 19 May. George Martin contacted Alan Civil, principal horn player with the Royal Philharmonic Orchestra, and he was able to overdub the French horn obligato on to the song. Sadly, Civil died of a liver complaint on Sunday, 19 March 1989. He was sixty years old.

'For No One' was included on the compilations *Love Songs* and *The Beatles Ballads,* and Cilla Black also recorded it as a single, although it didn't bring her any chart success.

For You Blue

A country blues number penned by George Harrison and first recorded on 25 January 1969 at Apple Studios in Savile Row, under the working title 'George's Blues'. The working title was then changed to 'Because You're Sweet And Lovely', before it was eventually called 'For You Blue'.

John Lennon added a bottleneck guitar solo to the track, which George had described as a simple twelve-bar blues number.

George sang solo vocal on the number which was included on the *Let It Be* album in May 1970, and in the lyrics, George makes a passing reference to the bluesman Elmore James: 'Elmore James got nothing on this, baby.' The number was also featured on *The Best Of George Harrison* album.

'For You Blue' was issued in America as a double 'A' side with

'The Long And Winding Road', on Apple 2832, on 11 May 1970 where it reached No. 1 in the charts.

Both tracks had been subject to a production mix by Phil Spector, although, while Paul McCartney was upset at what Spector had done to 'The Long And Winding Road', George made no comment about Spector's work on his own track – but was obviously content and asked Spector to produce his solo album *All Things Must Pass*. A version appeared on the Beatles' *Anthology 3* CDs.

Ford, Emile

Singer, born Emile Sweetman in Nassau on 16 October 1937. Ford arrived in London at the age of seventeen and formed his group the Checkmates in 1959. He topped the charts that year with 'What Do You Want To Make Those Eyes At Me For?' and followed up with 'Slow Boat To China'. After several other hits, his final chart entry was 'I Wonder Who's Kissing Her Now' in 1962.

He met the Beatles on 24 November 1961. Ford dropped in at the Tower Ballroom, New Brighton, and took the stage to sing with Rory Storm & the Hurricanes, whose drummer at the time was Ringo Starr.

Mersey Beat arranged for him to be photographed by Dick Matthews backstage with the Beatles and published the picture on their front cover.

On 6 April 1962, Emile Ford and the Checkmates topped the bill at the Tower Ballroom, New Brighton, *A Night To Remember* concert with the Beatles (advertised as The Beetles on posters for the event). Also on the bill were Gerry & the Pacemakers, Howie Casey & the Seniors, Rory Storm & the Hurricanes, the Big Three and the Original Kingtwisters.

From 1962, Ford began producing records by other artists, moved to Sweden for ten years, then returned to Britain to set up a company, EFOS (Emile Ford Objective Sound Monitoring System). In 1993 he won the Black Music Industry Association's Award for Businessman of the Year.

Forest Hills Tennis Stadium, Queens, New York City

Arena in New York where the Beatles appeared on 28 and 29 August 1964, performing a one-hour show on each occasion to a 16,000 capacity audience. Tickets had been sold out months in advance, and the shows had been promoted by Sid Bernstein. Their concert was taped and broadcast by the radio station WBOX.

On Friday, 28 August, officials at the stadium at first refused to allow the Beatles to arrive by helicopter, but the New York Police Department insisted it was necessary and they got their way.

Backstage, Benny Goodman, the legendary jazzman, arrived with his two daughters, although the conversation proved to be strained, with Brian Epstein showing his annoyance at what he considered an intrusion.

When Norman Weiss realised the helicopter pilot had gone, he was annoyed. No one had told the pilot to wait, but Weiss refused to let the Beatles go on stage until the helicopter returned, and there was a delay. They eventually began their peformance at 9.50 p.m. During the show a young girl rushed down the aisle, scaled a 15-foot-high fence and rushed straight for the Beatles. She was within six feet of them when she was eventually downed by two security guards and, in the struggle, a production man, Harry Hennessey, got knocked clean off the stage. The action of the girl had taken the 200 policeman on duty and the squad of Burns Security Guards completely by surprise.

The following night, Saturday, 29 August, there were 150 policeman and 100 security guards, and almost 50 screaming youngsters were prevented from mobbing the stage. One girl got through and hugged George, before fainting. Another youth reached the stage, but was pulled off, knocking out a number of footlights. Over 50 girls fainted from hysteria.

The numbers peformed were: 'A Hard Day's Night', 'All My Loving', 'Boys', 'Can't Buy Me Love', 'If I Fell', 'I Want To Hold Your Hand', 'Long Tall Sally', 'Roll Over Beethoven', 'She Loves You', 'Things We Said Today', 'Twist And Shout' and 'You Can't Do That'.

20 Forthlin Road, Allerton, Liverpool L18

Paul, his parents and brother Mike moved into this house in 1955 when Paul was thirteen. It became the family home until 1964. The next occupier was Mrs Sheila Jones who moved in with her husband and three children and lived there for 34 years.

The house had a back garden, which overlooked a police-training field, and Jim McCartney planted a black mountain ash beneath Paul's bedroom window. It was a three-bedroom terraced council house.

It was at Forthlin Road that Mary McCartney discovered she had cancer, from which she died in 1956.

One of the McCartneys' neighbours was Tom Gaul, who'd moved next door into No. 18 two years previously with his two sons. He enjoyed a friendly relationship with Paul and when fans used to gather outside the front door of No. 20, he'd let Paul clamber over the backyard fence and rush out the front of his house into a waiting car.

He has said that Paul told him that the essence of some of the lyrics of 'Yesterday' concerned the death of Paul's mother.

Forthlin Road was where numerous Lennon and McCartney songs were composed. As Jim McCartney was out working at the Cotton Exchange during the day, John and Paul used to spend their time around Jim's piano in the small front parlour, filling exercise books full of lyrics to the songs they composed. They included 'The One After 909', 'I Saw her Standing There', 'Love Me Do' and 'When I'm Sixty Four'.

Paul's bedroom was the smallest room in the house, where his father rigged up extension cables and headphones from the radio in the parlour so they could listen to Elvis Presley and Little Richard on Radio Luxembourg.

The McCartneys eventually moved from the house in the spring of 1964, when Paul had bought a new home for his father – Rembrandt, 26 miles away in Heswall.

Sir John Birt, Director General of the BBC, was on a visit to Liverpool to show his children his birthplace and they all took the Magical Mystery Tour coach trip. That was when he noticed that the house was up for sale. He felt that the house had a certain historical significance and suggested to Martin Drury, director of the National Trust, that it should be restored to what it was when Paul lived there.

The National Trust purchased the property for £55,000 and spent three years restoring it at a cost of £47,000. It was officially opened to the public on 29 July 1998.

In the visitors' guide, Paul comments: 'My dear mother Mary had great aspirations for our family and was very proud when we moved to Forthlin Road. She and dad would have found it very hard to believe that the house is now National Trust property. You expect them to own places like Blenheim Palace, not a little terraced house like ours. But they would have been chuffed about it and so am I.'

He was to add, 'I was living at 20 Forthlin Road when I first met John Lennon and it was here that he and I rehearsed with the Beatles. John and I would sometimes sag off school to go back to my house to write many of our early songs. I was still living at the house when the Beatles found worldwide fame, so my memories of it are closely connected with those times.'

Forum, Montreal, Quebec, Canada

Ringo had received a death threat from a fanatic in Montreal who threatened to kill 'the English Jew'. When the Beatles arrived at

Dorval Airport at 2.20 p.m. on Tuesday, 8 September 1964, there were 5,000 fans at the airport awaiting them, but there was also a heavy police presence from the Royal Canadian Mounted Police and the Dorval Municipal Police Force. Detectives accompanied the group as they were driven straight to the Forum, where they were to appear on two shows before an audience of 21,000.

The death threat was taken seriously and when the Beatles took to the stage at 5.20 p.m. a detective crouched down behind Ringo's drums, and Ringo also crouched low while he played. He was to comment on the presence of the detective behind him: 'God knows what he was trying to do. I mean there's an assassin out there trying to get me and he's sitting next to me on stage as if someone in the back of a 12,000 seater is gonna go – Bang! – and he's gonna catch the bullet?' He also remarked, 'No one was seeing much of me that day. It was the worst gig of my life.'

Between shows they posed for photographs and had a press reception. When asked if any of them spoke French, Ringo replied 'Nein', and when asked who their leader was, Paul said 'It depends on who shouts the loudest.'

There were 75 Royal Mounted Police at the airport when they returned and Ringo's detective escort had remained by his side from the moment of their arrival, until they finally boarded their plane to Florida. Once inside the plane, Ringo commented, 'I am English. But I'm not Jewish.'

4 By The Beatles

The second EP to be issued by Capitol in the States. *4 By The Beatles* was released on 1 February 1965 on Capitol R 5365. The four tracks were taken from the American album *Beatles '65* and were: 'Honey Don't', 'I'm A Loser', 'Mr Moonlight' and 'Everybody's Trying To Be My Baby'.

This was Capitol's second attempt at utilising the EP (Extended Play) format with the Beatles, although it was not a popular format in America. Once again, it wasn't a totally successful venture, even though it reached No. 68 in the *Cash Box* and *Billboard* charts, and Capitol didn't repeat the experiment again.

Four By The Beatles

The EP (Extended Play) format was not an established format in America, but Capitol Records decided to try an experiment and issued an EP by the Beatles, probably inspired by the fact that Vee Jay Records had recently attempted such an experiment a few weeks earlier with *Souvenir Of Their Visit To America: The Beatles*.

They combined two of the most successful of the Canadian import singles on the EP, although the tracks were also available on albums – two on the *Meet The Beatles* album and two on *The Beatles Second Album*. *Four By The Beatles* was issued on Capitol EAP 2121 on 11 May 1964 with the tracks being: 'Roll Over Beethoven', 'All My Loving', 'This Boy' and 'Please Mr Postman'.

Compared to the sales of Beatles singles and albums, it wasn't a success, reaching only No. 92 in *Billboard* and No. 86 in *Cash Box*.

Capitol only tried the experiment one further time, the following year, with the similarly titled *4 By The Beatles* which was also deemed unsuccessful.

Fourmost, The

Brian (Owie) O'Hara and Joey Bowers originally teamed up as the Two Jays at the age of thirteen, performing for a season at the Isle of Man. They were joined by Billy Hatton and Brian Redman and in September 1959 called themselves the Four Jays. Owie played lead, Billy was on bass, Joey on guitar and Brian on drums. The three guitarists also vocalised.

The group had a rock/jazz/comedy act, but each member was pursuing a career and initially decided to remain semi-pro. Joey turned down an offer to join Jan Ralfini's Band at the Locarno, Billy turned down the opportunity of backing his friend Billy Fury, Owie refused the offer of joining a television group and Brian a position with the Nat Allen Band.

As the Four Jays, their Cavern appearances with the Beatles in 1961 took place on Wednesday, 26 July, Wednesday, 18 October, Wednesday, 15 November and Wednesday, 13 December. Appearances in 1962 were on Wednesday, 24 January, Thursday, 5 April, Saturday 9 June, Sunday, 15 July and Wednesday, 20 October. They also appeared as special guests on a Beatles Fan Club night on Thursday, 5 April 1962 and on a bill with the Beatles at the Tower Ballroom on Thursday, 21 June 1962.

By mid-1962 an argument resulted in Joey leaving the group and Mike Millward, former member of Bob Evans & the Five Shillings, replaced him. Redman left the group for three months to play in Hamburg on the assurance that his position with the group was safe, but on his return Owie told him they'd decided to keep his replacement, Dave Lovelady. Later that year the group changed its name to The Four Mosts, having learned that a southern group called the Four Jays was managed by London impresario Lou Prager. Under their new name they appeared with the Beatles in 1962 on Sunday, 21 October, Sunday, 25 November, Sunday, 9 December, Wednesday, 12 December and Sunday, 16 December.

Their 1963 Cavern appearances with the Beatles as the Fourmost (their name slightly altered once again) were on Wednesday, 23 January, Sunday, 3 February and Friday 12 April.

By the time Brian Epstein signed them on 30 June 1963, their line-up had changed to Mike Millward, Billy Hatton, Brian O'Hara and Dave Lovelady.

According to Dave, they were the second group that Brian approached and asked to turn professional. They turned him down, preferring to remain semi-professional. He made them a management offer three times and it was only after Gerry & the Pacemakers and Billy J. Kramer had their initial chart hits that they decided to sign with NEMS.

The quartet appeared on many other Merseyside gigs with the Beatles. As the Four Jays they were billed on the Operation Big Beat 3 at the Tower Ballroom, New Brighton, on Friday, 29 June 1962 and the Little Richard/Beatles Tower concert on Friday, 12 October 1962.

Following his usual practice, Epstein placed them with George Martin, but they found they had no original material strong enough for them to record. Owie asked John Lennon if he had a number he could give them and John told him he had one that he'd written while sitting on the toilet. When they appeared with the Beatles at the Queen's Theatre, Blackpool, on 4 August 1963, John told them that the number they could have was called 'Hello Little Girl', which he'd penned in his teens and had included in the group's repertoire since 1958. The Beatles had also recorded it at their Decca and Parlophone recording auditions.

John was to say: 'This was one of the first songs I ever finished. I was then about eighteen and we gave it to the Fourmost. I think it was the first song of my own that I ever attempted to do with the group.'

He also commented that it was loosely based on a couple of old standards which his mother used to sing to him when he was a small child and was an attempt to capture the mood of those songs written in the 1930s.

Billy Hatton told *Mersey Beat:* 'We arranged to go to John Lennon's house, and they gave us a copy of the words. We hadn't heard the number before, and George and John gave us a rough idea of it by taping the tune. We received the tape at 4 o'clock on Monday morning.

'As we had to record on the following Wednesday, we had two days in which to make an arrangement good enough to put on disc. As a matter of fact, when we were recording, we were just learning the song as we went along and were tremendously encouraged by A&R man George Martin.'

'Hello Little Girl' reached No. 9 in the British charts. Their next release was unusual in that it was a Lennon and McCartney number that the Beatles hadn't used on an album and was written specifically for the Fourmost. A romantic number called 'I'm In Love', it reached No. 17 in the British charts.

They appeared in The Beatles Christmas Show at the Finsbury Park Astoria in north London in December 1963, during which they performed 'Hello Little Girl'.

The group was arguably the very first beat group to perform impressions. Dave Lovelady was to comment: 'We did them long before the Barron Knights and the Rockin' Berries.'

The Finsbury Park audience were given an opportunity to see this side of the Fourmost as Brian O'Hara sang 'White Christmas', during which he did impressions of Elvis Presley, Gracie Fields, Adam Faith, Dean Martin – and the Beatles. They issued an EP called *The Fourmost Sound* and appeared in the film *Ferry 'Cross the Mersey,* with their NEMS stablemates Gerry & the Pacemakers and Cilla Black.

Their biggest hit, 'A Little Loving', which reached No. 6 in the charts, wasn't by Lennon and McCartney. The Fourmost had gone to Dick James to ask him if he had a number for them to record and he played them several tracks that didn't excite them. Then James remembered a song that had come in that morning's post. He played them the demo of 'A Little Loving', written by Juliet Mills's husband, Russell Alquist, and although Owie hated it, the others liked the number enough to vote it in as their next single.

They had three remaining hits in their career, 'How Can I Tell Her?', 'Baby I Need Your Lovin' and 'Girls Girls Girls', but they were never to have a hit in America.

From 13 May 1964 they were booked to appear for a four-month season at the London Palladium on a bill with Frankie Vaughan, Cilla Black and Tommy Cooper. It was so popular that the run was extended until December.

Sadly, just before the Palladium season began, Mike Millward became seriously ill with leukaemia and needed radium treatment. He had to enter Clattterbridge Hospital in the Wirral, where he died. A special show, *A Night for Mike,* was presented at Liverpool's Grafton Ballroom on Tuesday, 5 April 1966.

Mike's place was filled by a number of different Liverpool musicians over a period of time, including George Peckham, Ian Edwards and Frank Bowen. Eventually, Joey Bowers, an original founder member of the band, returned to the fold.

Paul McCartney discovered a song called 'Rosetta', which he felt would be suitable for the group, and offered to produce it for them, which he did.

Dave Lovelady commented: 'Paul liked the way we could mimic instruments with our voices, our "mouth music" if you like. Brian O'Hara was a trumpet and we were the trombones. We used it on "Rosetta" and the Beatles did the same thing on "Lady Madonna". There were proper instruments on our record as well. I was playing piano at the session, but Brian O'Hara told me to play it badly. I soon found out why: Paul said, "Look, I'll do the piano bit," and so he ended up playing on our record.'

The number was released by CBS on Friday, 21 February 1969, but failed to reach the charts.

The band continued appearing in cabaret during the 1970s, but split in 1978. Three of the members – Joey Bowers, Billy Hatton and Dave Lovelady – teamed up with Joey's wife to form a quartet called Clouds, which performed on a semi-pro basis in Liverpool clubs until 1993. Owie found three other musicians and continued performing for a time and then sold them the name the Fourmost for a reputed £1,000. He was said to have regretted it. The group then appearing as the Fourmost had no association with the original hitmakers and was locally referred to as the Fraudmost or the Four Almost.

Sadly, Owie hanged himself on 17 June 1999. The coroner reported that he had committed suicide due to depression over financial problems.

Four Nights In Moscow

Another Beatles mystery. The song was reputed to have been a number which John Lennon wrote for Ringo to record as a solo single. Various Beatles books have suggested that the Beatles recorded the number in June 1969, but didn't release it.

However, the Beatles didn't visit the recording studios that month. John and Yoko were in Canada and on their return took Julian and Kyoko on a motoring trip to Scotland. George and Pattie were on holiday in Sardinia, Paul and Linda in Corfu and Ringo and Maureen in the south of France.

Another story purports that 'Four Nights In Moscow' was the title of a track on a lost Beatles album. This resulted from a fake story in a British music weekly at the beginning of the seventies which reported that the group had recorded an album, the master tapes of which were stolen in the summer of 1969. The group were said to have paid a huge ransom for its return, but were cheated by the thieves and never retrieved it.

Perhaps this made-up tale inspired Paul in his screenplay for *Give My Regards To Broad Street*, which concerned the loss of the master tapes of an album he'd made.

Four Tops, The

A Motown group of four vocalists comprising Levi Stubbs, Abdul Fakir, Renaldo Benson and Lawrence Payton. Their hits included 'I Can't Help Myself', 'It's The Same Old Song' and 'Reach Out, I'll Be There'.

In October 1966, while in Detroit, Epstein negotiated with Motown to bring the Four Tops to the Saville Theatre. The quartet had already been set to tour Britain from January 1967 for NEMS in a deal negotiated by Vic Lewis. Vic, as managing director of NEMS, had worked out a contract which would make the tour profitable for NEMS if there were reasonable audiences on the ABC and Odeon cinemas circuits. He had also made sure that even if there was a poor response, the tour would break even. Epstein rearranged the contract in Detroit, magnanimously offering the group bonuses and first-class air fares. He also agreed to pay the group's taxes. As a result, NEMS lost £10,000 on the tour. One of the dates on the NEMS 1967 tour was an appearance at the Royal Albert Hall on 28 January, which Paul McCartney and George Harrison attended.

Brian also lost money when he brought the group to Britain to appear at the Saville Theatre on 13 November. The backdrop to their stage act had been designed by Paul McCartney, who couldn't attend because he was holidaying in Kenya at the time with Jane Asher. John Lennon and George Harrison attended. They were also guests at a special party Epstein threw for the Four Tops at his Chapel Street house. Also at the celebration were Mick Jagger, Keith Richards and Charlie Watts of the Rolling Stones, Georgie Fame, Donovan, Eric Burdon and Hilton Valentine of the Animals and Chris Curtis, drummer with the Searchers.

Fox And Hounds, The, Gosbrook Road, Caversham, Berkshire

A pub which had recently been taken over by Paul McCartney's cousin Elizabeth and her husband Mike Robbins. Paul and John took a break there during April 1960, during which they worked behind the bar for a week. They also made appearances singing and playing acoustic guitars while calling themselves the Nerk Twins on 23 April.

Francis, Bob

A disc jockey at the Adelaide radio station 5AD who orchestrated the 'Bring The Beatles To Adelaide' campaign. He was rewarded for his efforts by being present with the Beatles for almost all of the time they were in Adelaide, joining them on the balcony of the town hall for their first public appearance and conducting various interviews with them. He was also selected to compere their Adelaide shows.

He later became station manager at 5AD.

Fraser, Robert Hugh

One of the leading figures in the British art world of the 1960s, born in London in August 1937. He was to open his first art gallery, the Robert Fraser Gallery, at 69 Duke Street on Wednesday, 15 August 1962, where he exhibited painters such as Peter Blake, Claes Oldenberg, Bridget Riley and Lichenstein.

Fraser held regular dinner parties at his flat at 20 Mount Street, attended by celebrities such as Paul McCartney, Terry Southern, Keith Richard, Anita Pallenberg and Brian Jones.

In addition to promoting Pop Art and various new painters and sculptors at his prestigious gallery, he was a friend and adviser to both the Beatles and the Rolling Stones in the field of art.

Fraser dissuaded the Beatles from using a psychedelic design by the Fool for their *Sgt Pepper* album. Although the Fool design had been completed, Fraser advised the Beatles that it would date rapidly. He also joined Brian Epstein in a meeting with Sir Joseph Lockwood to champion the idea of the famous Pepper tableau. Fraser became an adviser and was eventually paid £1,500 by EMI. He recommended that artist Peter Blake was brought in to design the sleeve, and also hired his regular photographer Michael Cooper to take the pictures.

Along with Blake and the Beatles, Fraser also made a list of characters to be included on the actual sleeve and was present at the construction of the tableau and the shoot of the final photo session.

Apart from being a homosexual, Fraser was hooked on drugs. He'd been a heroin addict since 1965, had introduced Paul McCartney to cocaine and in the famous raid on Keith Richard's house in 1967 was busted, along with Mick Jagger and Keith Richard. Jagger and Richard were freed because they'd been in possession of soft drugs. Fraser had been caught with heroin and was sentenced to six months in Wormwood Scrubs.

On Monday, 1 July 1968, John Lennon held his first art exhibition 'You Are Here' at Fraser's gallery. The main focus of the exhibition was a huge circular white canvas with the words 'You Are Here'. There were lots of charity collection boxes on display and the students of Hornsey Art College sent along a rusty bike with the message: 'This exhibit was inadvertently left out.' John immediately placed it in the exhibition.

Fraser contracted AIDS and died of AIDS-related pneumonia and meningitis in January 1986.

A biography, *Groovy Bob: The Life And Times Of Robert Fraser*, by Harriet Vyner, was published in October 1999.

Freddie & The Dreamers

A Manchester group who appeared on *Another Beatles Christmas Show*, which played for three weeks, twice-nightly at the Odeon, Hammersmith, London, over Christmas 1964. Freddie & the Dreamers appeared on stage immediately after the Beatles had performed a sketch as four Arctic explorers coming across the Abominable Snowman (a costumed Jimmy Savile).

Freddie & the Dreamers were a popular group whose hit records spanned two years from 1963–1965 and were: 'If You Gotta Make A Fool Of Somebody', 'I'm Telling You Now', 'You Were Made For Me', 'Over You', 'I Love You Baby', 'Just For You', 'I Understand', 'A Little You' and 'Thou Shalt Not Steal'.

The group successfully promoted a comedy-rock act and comprised Freddie Garrity (vocals), Roy Crewsdon (rhythm guitar), Pete Birrell (bass guitar) and Bernie Dwyer (drums).

Free As A Bird

The first 'new' Beatles single since 1970.

George Harrison was the one who originally thought of the three surviving Beatles utilising a recording by John Lennon to reunite the Beatles on song. Yoko Ono provided the mono home demo that John had recorded in 1977 and Jeff Lynne was called in to record the number using 48 track technology.

Commenting on the finished song, Paul said: 'We took the attitude that John had gone on holiday saying "I finished all the tracks except this one, but I leave it to you guys to finish it off".'

The video of the number received its world television premiere on Sunday, 19 November 1995 when ABC TV screened the first instalment of the five-part six-hour TV documentary.

Freeman, Robert

A photographer who, between 1963–1965 acted in a semi-official capacity to the Beatles. In 1963 he requested a photo session with the Beatles and wrote a request to Brian Epstein, who asked him to submit samples of his work. Freeman sent a series of photographs he had taken of jazz musicians, which resulted in Epstein inviting him to take photographs of the Beatles in Bournemouth. During the photo assignment the group mentioned their forthcoming album and said they needed a cover. Freeman suggested it be in black and white and took photographs of them wearing black turtleneck sweaters, which resulted in the cover for *With The Beatles* (in America, *Meet The Beatles*), although EMI initially resisted the idea of a mono cover.

When John was looking for a London flat for himself, Cynthia and Julian, Freeman suggested the apartment below him in Emperor's Gate. When he accompanied the Beatles on a five-day trip to Sweden, he shared a room with John, and he also travelled to Paris with them in January 1964 and on their first trip to America. He was asked to design both John's books *In His Own Write* and *A Spaniard In The Works*, and also took colour and black and white shots when commissioned to provide the cover for the soundtrack to *A Hard Day's Night*. He also designed the film's opening titles. The other album covers he designed and photographed were *Beatles For Sale*, *Help!* and *Rubber Soul*.

Robert was commissioned to photograph the marriage of Ringo and Maureen, and another of his photographs provided the cover to the *Long Tall Sally* EP.

Between 1963 and 1965 he had taken hundreds of shots of the group in various settings, from outdoor locations in Austria and the Bahamas to backstage shots in dressing rooms and sessions at Abbey Road. His final important assignment with them came when he took the photographs for *Rubber Soul* in John's back garden at Weybridge.

Several collections of his Beatle photographs have been published in book form, including *Beatles Ltd*, George Newnes (1964); *Yesterday: Photographs Of The Beatles*, Weidenfeld & Nicolson (1983) and *The Beatles*, Octopus (1990). Paul McCartney wrote the introduction to *Yesterday*, in which he described Freeman's large, grainy prints as 'artistic without being pretentious' and commented, 'I have a feeling that Robert Freeman's photos were amongst the best ever taken of the Beatles.'

Friar Park, Paradise Road, Henley-on-Thames, Oxfordshire

Ornate Victorian mansion with 120 rooms, bought by George Harrison for $350,000, in February 1969. The building had originally been built for Sir Frank Crisp, a City of London solicitor, in 1889 and was erected on the site of a thirteenth century Friary.

The spired and turreted building, with a red brick and yellow low-stone exterior, had been owned by nuns of the Order of St John Bosco for over a decade and since they could no longer afford the upkeep, the building was about to be knocked down.

It was in quite a state of disrepair when George bought it and he and Pattie initially lived in the labourer's cottage on the grounds while the main building was restored.

He had a suite of two bedrooms, bathroom and dressing-room turned into a recording studio, and installed a cinema.

He paid tribute to the original owner with 'The Ballad Of Sir Francis Crisp' on his *All Things Must Pass* album.

George had his brother Harold take over the task of managing Friar Park from a gatehouse office. His brother Peter was engaged to oversee the team of full-time gardeners attending the large grounds, which were spread over forty acres, with gardens, fields, hedges and caves.

He then had a sign placed outside the gates, stating 'absolutely no admittance' in ten languages.

Friday Spectacular

A Radio Luxembourg show in which artists mimed to their records in front of an invited audience. The Beatles appeared on a series of 'Friday Spectacular' performances. They recorded a show at EMI House in London on 8 October 1962 which was transmitted on 12 October. The following month they appeared on the show on 16 November and it was transmitted on 23 November. For their show recorded on 21 January 1963, which was transmitted on 25 January, they actually performed live on the show for the first time, playing 'Please Please Me', 'Carol' and 'Lend Me Your Comb'. Their final appearance took place on 11 March 1963, for transmission on 15 March. The presenter was Muriel Young.

Friedrich Ebert Halle, Alter Postweg 30, Harburg, Hamburg

Venue where the Beatles recorded with Tony Sheridan for producer Bert Kaempfert on Thursday, 22 and Friday, 23 June 1961. The sound engineer for the session was Karl Hinze. Although Stuart Sutcliffe turned up for the sessions, he didn't play. Kaempfert had arranged for mobile recording equipment to be installed on the stage of the auditorium. When they began recording 'My Bonnie' there were coke bottles on the stage and George Harrison knocked one over. Bert told him, 'All coke bottles off the stage.'

John, Paul, George and Pete then recorded five numbers – 'My Bonnie Lies Over the Ocean', 'When The Saints Go Marching In', 'Why (Can't You Love Me Again)', 'Nobody's Child' and 'Take Out Some Insurance On Me Baby'. The group also recorded two tracks without Sheridan, 'Ain't She Sweet' and 'Cry For A Shadow'.

From A Window

Billy J. Kramer's fourth single with a Lennon & McCartney song-writing credit. The number had been penned by Paul McCartney, and John and Paul cut an acetate of the song for Kramer and George Martin to listen to. The Beatles never recorded the number themselves, and Kramer's vesion was issued in Britain on Parlophone R 5156 on 17 July 1964, and in America on Imperial 66061 on 12 August 1964. It reached No. 13 in the British charts and No. 23 in the American.

From Me To You

The Beatles' third single, which John and Paul wrote on 28 February 1963, while travelling by coach between York and Shrewsbury on a leg of their Helen Shapiro tour. Their inspiration had been the title of the letters column in the *New Musical Express*, which was called 'From You To Us'. John commented, 'We nearly didn't record it because we thought it was too bluesy at first, but when we'd finished it and George Martin had scored it with harmonica it was alright.'

The song became their most performed number on their series of BBC radio shows and they featured it fifteen times – three times on 'Easy Beat', once on 'Swinging Sound '63', three times on 'Side By Side', twice on 'Saturday Club', once on 'Steppin' Out', four times on 'Pop Go The Beatles' and once on 'Beat Show'. They also adopted the number for their 'From Us To You' radio series.

The single was issued on Parlophone R 5015 in Britain on 11 April 1963 and became a No. 1 hit, with 'Thank You Girl' on the flip. It was issued in America by Vee Jay Records on VJ 522 on 27 May 1963, but failed to make the charts. They reissued it in America on VJ 581 on 30 January 1964 coupled with 'Please Please Me'. The 'From Me To You' side reached No. 41 in the charts.

The number was included on their second British EP *The Beatles Hits*, the compilations *A Collection Of Beatles Oldies (But Goldies)*, *The Beatles Hits 1962–66* and *20 Greatest Hits*. It was in *The Beatles Box* set and Vee Jay included it on the album *Jolly What! The Beatles and Frank Ifield On Stage*. In Britain EMI issued a press release to go with the single, which read:

> Vocally and instrumentally this new deck matches the high spirits of PLEASE PLEASE ME with John, Paul and George chanting and harmonising expertly. BUT don't get the idea that this is a carbon copy of their last single – in fact it is the most unusual number THE BEATLES have recorded to date.

In defiance of the tiresome trend towards weepie lost-love wailers, FROM ME TO YOU is a rip-rockin' up tempo ballad which has a happy-go-lucky romantic story-line.

EAR-CATCHING HIGH SPOT: Those unexpected falsetto-voice high-kicks on the line 'If there's anything I can do'.

OFF-BEAT FINALE: Sudden switch of speed and rhythm for that end-of-the-track instrumental climax.

UNANIMOUS VERDICT: The sturdy beat plus the unique Beatle-blending of harmonica, guitars and voices plus the thoroughly infectious tune make FROM ME TO YOU another dead-cert Number One chart-smasher!

'From Me To You' was also reissued as a single yet again by Vee Jay, as the flipside of 'Please Please Me' on OL 151 Oldies 45, on 10 August 1964.

There have been numerous covers of the song and it became the very first Beatles number to be covered by an American artist, when Del Shannon issued it in the US and it provided a minor chart hit for him. Their publisher Dick James also recorded the number and there have been several foreign language versions, including *'Lo Tendras Amor'* in Spanish, *'Meidan Yhteinen'* in Finnish and *'Des Bises De Moi Pour Toi'* in French. A version of the number was included on the Beatles' *Anthology 1* CDs. The number was also included on the CD compilation *Past Masters Volume One*.

From Us To You

Four BBC radio programmes broadcast during holiday periods. The Beatles adapted their number 'From Me To You' to become the show's theme 'From Us To You'.

Produced by Bryan Marriott, the first show was transmitted on 26 December 1963. The two-hour show, which was presented by Rolf Harris, had guest appearances from Joe Brown and the Bruvvers, Susan Maughan and Kenny Lynch. The Beatles performed 'From Us To You', 'She Loves You', 'All My Loving', 'Roll Over Beethoven', 'Till There Was You', 'Boys', 'Money', 'I Saw Her Standing There', 'I Want To Hold Your Hand' and 'From Us To You'.

The second in the series, presented by Alan Freeman on 30 March 1964 (Easter Monday), featured the group performing 'From Us To You', 'You Can't Do That', 'Roll Over Beethoven', 'Till There Was You', 'I Wanna Be Your Man', 'Please Mr Postman', 'All My Loving', 'This Boy', 'Can't Buy Me Love' and 'From Us To You'. Their guests were the Swinging Bluejeans, Vince Hill and Acker Bilk and his Paramount Jazz Band.

Alan Freeman also presented the third show on 18 May 1964

(Whitsun Bank Holiday). The group performed 'From Us To You', 'I Saw Her Standing There', 'Kansas City/Hey! Hey! Hey!', 'I Forgot To Remember To Forget', 'You Can't Do That', 'Sure To Fall In Love (With You)', 'Can't Buy Me Love', 'Matchbox', 'Honey Don't' and 'From Us To You'.

Their final programme was presented by Don Wardell on 3 August 1964 (August Bank Holiday Monday) and the Beatles performed 'From Us To You', 'Long Tall Sally', 'If I Fell', 'I'm Happy Just To Dance With You', 'Things We Said Today', 'I Should Have Known Better', 'Boys', 'A Hard Day's Night' and 'From Us To You'.

From Us To You (Recording)
The Beatles had adapted the chorus of their number 'From Me To You' as the title of a series of four BBC radio programmes. The track was included as the first musical number on their *The Beatles Live At The BBC* CD, released in November 1994.

Frost, David
Television celebrity who first found fame on BBC TV's satirical series 'That Was The Week That Was'. He was to emerge as one of the most renowned television interviewers on both sides of the Atlantic, hosting shows for the BBC and ITV in Britain, as well as having his own series in America.

John and George appeared on his 'The Frost Programme' during a break in their Abbey Road session on 29 September 1967. It was broadcast the following day. The two chatted about the Maharishi and his Transcendental Meditation and how it had affected them personally. John mentioned that he had stopped using drugs long before he met the Maharishi. He said that he thought of God as a huge amount of energy, like electricity. The discussion went so well that Frost invited them both back to his show on 4 October – an offer which they took up.

Paul McCartney appeared with Frost later that year, on 27 December, to discuss the critical bashing received by the screening of *Magical Mystery Tour* on television.

On 4 September 1968 Frost visited the Beatles at Twickenham Studios where they were filming a promotional performance of 'Hey Jude', which he introduced and broadcast on 8 September on 'Frost On Sunday'. A clip of this was used on American TV stations and has cropped up in various film compilations. 'Frost On Sunday' was the new title of his show as it had changed channels and was then screened by London Weekend Television.

John and Yoko also appeared on his show to discuss conceptual art. Frost was quite sceptical and made some disparaging comments about John's badge, which displayed the words 'You Are Here'. John made his attitude to art quite clear: 'Our bodies are art, everything around us is art, the world is a gallery.' He commented that the public would enjoy creating art of its own. For the purposes of demonstration, Yoko had brought along a nail board and members of the audience were invited to knock a nail in. They all said how much they had enjoyed the experience.

By the late sixties, Frost had become a regular transatlantic traveller, flying back and forth across the Atlantic to host shows in New York and London. On his American show on 23 February 1969 his guest was Paul McCartney, who introduced his new Apple protégée, Mary Hopkin. On 29 March 1970 Ringo Starr performed 'Sentimental Journey', accompanied by the George Martin Orchestra. Ringo made a further appearance on Frost's show that year, with his co-star of the film *The Magic Christian*, Peter Sellers. Clips from the movie were shown and the two stars duetted on 'Octopus's Garden'.

George guested on 3 December 1971; John and Yoko also put in an appearance in the New York studios on 13 January 1972. George Harrison and guitarist David Bromberg appeared in December 1972 playing together on the numbers 'Suffer To Sing The Blues', 'The Hold Up', and 'Bangladesh' and George and Ravi Shankar played some Indian music together.

On 21 May 1975, David Frost hosted a special tribute to the Beatles in America. It was screened on ABC TV and entitled 'Salute To The Beatles'. He was to host a similar tribute in 1977.

Frost also had a radio programme on the BBC Light Programme, called 'David Frost At The Phonograph'. Paul McCartney recorded an interview with Frost on 1 August 1966 which was broadcast on the show on 6 August.

Frost On Sunday

David Frost's television show had changed channels to London Weekend Television and was now known as 'Frost On Sunday' when it was transmitted on Sunday, 8 September 1968 with the world premiere of the 'Hey Jude' video clip. At the time the Musicians Union had banned miming on all television shows.

However, Frost had visited the group at Twickenham Studios on Wednesday, 4 September when they were filming the promotional video, backed by a 36-piece orchestra. George Martin had composed a theme tune for the show and Frost taped the Beatles performing the theme. He said, 'Magnificent, magnificent. Beautiful, beautiful, beautiful. A perfect rendition!' Then announced, 'Ladies and

Gentlemen, there you see the greatest tea room orchestra in the world. It's my pleasure to introduce now, in their first live appearance for goodness knows how long in front of an audience – the Beatles.' It appeared as if they were performing live, but they weren't.

There was an audience of 300 with John on guitar, Paul on an upright piano, George on a six-string bass and Ringo back behind the drum kit for the first time since quitting the group on 23 August. While the crew was setting up, Paul kept the audience entertained with a selection of 'oldies' on his piano.

Michael Lindsay Hogg directed the promotional film.

A clip of the show was used on American TV stations and has cropped up in various film compilations.

Fury, Billy

A Liverpool singer, born Ronald Wycherley on 17 April 1941. His parents were Albert and Jean and he also had a brother, Albert, three years younger than himself, who became a pop singer, calling himself Jason Eddie.

Prior to the Beatles, he was Liverpool's most successful pop artist.

In a small Liverpool studio in 1958, Ronnie cut several songs and sent a demo tape and picture to Larry Parnes. He then went to a Parnes Extravaganza Show at the Essoldo, Birkenhead, for a successful audition. Parnes was to rename him Billy Fury.

He became Decca's biggest-selling artist of the time, with 26 hits between 1961 and 1966. During this period he spent 268 weeks in the charts. His hits included 'Halfway To Paradise', 'Jealousy', 'I'll Never Find Another You', 'Last Night Was Made For Love', 'Once Upon A Dream', 'Like I've Never Been Gone', 'Wondrous Place' and 'In Summer'.

Fury was reared in the same area of Liverpool as Ringo Starr, the Dingle, where he attended St Silas's Junior School and Dingle Vale Secondary School, along with Ringo and Fury's best friend, Billy Hatton, who was later to become a member of the Fourmost.

On 10 May 1960, Billy and his manager, Larry Parnes, attended an audition at the Wyvern Club in Seel Street, Liverpool. Parnes had been impressed by the Liverpool bands appearing in a Gene Vincent concert and had asked one of his assistants, Mark Foster, to contact Allan Williams to arrange an audition. He wrote: 'Duffy Power will be touring Scotland from June 2nd to 11th inclusive and Johnny Gentle will be touring Scotland from June 16th to 25th. For these two periods, as agreed, we are willing to pay your groups £120, plus the fares from Liverpool.'

The letter also added: 'We will make arrangements for Mr Parnes to come and audition your groups to select the most suitable. He will also bring Billy Fury as Billy will want one of these four groups for his own personal use. Incidentally, the idea of Billy wanting a group from his own home town will provide several interesting press stories and publicity tie-ins.'

There were actually five Mersey groups at the audition: Gerry & the Pacemakers, Cass & the Cassanovas, Cliff Roberts & the Rockers, Derry & the Seniors and the Silver Beatles.

During the afternoon, Stuart Sutcliffe drew Fury's portrait and John Lennon asked for and received his autograph. Although Fury didn't get his backing group, the Silver Beatles were chosen to tour Scotland with Johnny Gentle. Billy himself decided that he liked the Silver Beatles best, Parnes hadn't liked the appearance or age of Tommy Moore and hired Cass & the Cassanovas to back Billy on a tour.

All four Beatles went to the Empire Theatre, Liverpool, on Sunday, 21 October 1962, prior to their Cavern appearance that evening, to see Billy perform at a show there.

Fury made his film debut in 1962 in Michael Winner's *Play It Cool* and also starred in *I've Gotta Horse* in 1965.

The singer had been plagued by ill health since he was a child, when rheumatic fever had left him with a weak heart. Several tour appearances had to be cancelled due to his recurring heart problems and he was hospitalised on a number of occasions, which caused him to cease live performances in 1967 and spend most of his time on a farm, breeding horses.

He appeared with Ringo Starr in a cameo role as Storm Tempest in *That'll Be the Day* in 1973, performing 'Long Live Rock', a number written specially for him by Pete Townshend. As the character led a group performing in a holiday camp, it must have reminded Ringo of his days with Rory Storm at Butlins. During the filming there was a jam session with Ringo on lead guitar, David Essex on bass, Graham Bond on drums, Harry Nilsson on tambourine and Billy Fury on vocals.

Billy's heart finally gave out on Friday, 28 January 1983, at a time when he was in the process of recording a new album and had just had a new single enter the charts.

Futurist Theatre, Foreshore Road, South Bay, Scarborough, Yorkshire

The Beatles first appeared at this venue in the Yorkshire seaside resort during their autumn tour of the UK, on Wednesday, 11 December 1963. Their second and final appearance took place on Sunday, 9 August 1964.

3 Gambier Terrace, Liverpool L8

Less than 100 yards from the entrance to Liverpool College of Art, this Georgian terrace, directly opposite the Anglican Cathedral, was where art student Rod Murray managed to rent a first floor flat in 1960. He'd previously been dwelling in nearby Percy Street, where Stuart Sutcliffe had also been renting a flat.

The Gambier Terrace accommodation was more salubrious than Rod's previous place – and more expensive. He talked Stuart into sharing it with him and John Lennon became a third tenant, although he had some difficulty in persuading his Aunt Mimi to allow him to leave the comforts of her home in Menlove Avenue.

John liked the freedom of Gambier Terrace and his girlfriend Cynthia was able to stay overnight with him on several occasions, telling her mother she was spending the night at her friend Phyllis MacKenzie's house. Rod Murray's girlfriend Margaret Dizley also slept there on a number of nights.

The flat's proximity to the college, Liverpool Institute, Ye Cracke, the Philharmonic pub and the Liverpool 8 area in general, proved advantageous to the young students and the Silver Beatles were also able to rehearse there. One night, after meeting poet Royston Ellis and backing him on a poetry to rock session at the Jacaranda, they brought him back to the flat and he introduced them to some soft drugs such as benzedrine.

Bill Harry and his girlfriend Virginia were also regular visitors and one night, after they'd been so involved in discussions that they missed the late night bus, John took them in the bathroom and provided blankets and pillows, suggesting they sleep in the bath, which they did.

The flat was spacious, with high ceilings, although it was very sparsely furnished as the impecunious art students couldn't afford much in the way of furniture.

During 1960 the *Sunday People* newspaper was 'exposing' Beatniks – the British youngsters, inspired by America's Beat Generation, who had 'dropped out of society'. Journalists usually used Allan Williams's coffee bar as a meeting place and Allan had established friendly relations with the local press corps. When the reporters from the *Sunday People* asked him if he knew of a dirty flat where they could take photographs of Beatniks in filthy conditions, Allan said he'd fix something up for them.

He asked John, Stuart and Rod if the newspaper could take photographs in their flat and was able to talk the naïve youngsters into granting their permission. Of course, the flat was quite a nice-looking one, despite the lack of furniture, but it didn't take Williams long to set about making the place scruffy, placing empty beer bottles on the floor, rumpling up old newspapers and scattering them about, making the furniture askew and generally turning the flat into a messy place. The pictures were taken and were published in the *Sunday People* on 24 July, under the title 'The Beatnik Horror'.

Due to this staged event, Beatle chroniclers mistakenly write that the Gambier flat was a slum, which it wasn't. Another Gambier Terrace fable is that there was a coffin in it. The original rumours, which began after Stuart's death, implied that Stu had slept in a coffin. He didn't. He slept on a camp bed which his mother collected from the flat in 1961. Over twenty years later, writer Albert Goldman was suggesting that John Lennon slept in a coffin there, complete with silver lining – pure fantasy.

Once John and Stuart left for Hamburg, Rod was in a dilemma. He just couldn't afford to pay the rent himself. When they didn't return to the flat – with John going back to his Aunt Mimi's and Stuart remaining in Germany, Rod was in further trouble because of the back rent. He contacted Mrs Sutcliffe, who paid off Stuart's part of the debt and hired a mini-van to collect both Stuart's and John's possessions.

One or two items of John's were left in the flat, including some exercise books which Rod was able to auction off at Sotheby's in 1984 for £16,000.

Garland, Judy

Legendary singer and Hollywood star. When Judy was living in England, Brian Epstein was introduced to her by Lionel Bart while they were attending the Manchester premiere of the *Maggie May* musical. Judy was among the many guests at the special show party held at Liverpool's Blue Angel Club later that evening – although Allan Williams actually threw her out of the club!

The singer provided one of the highlights of 'The Night Of A Hundred Stars' at the London Palladium on 23 July 1964 when she sang the song most associated with her – 'Over The Rainbow'. The Beatles were also on the bill.

Judy was among the celebrity guests, along with the Beatles, who attended a party at Epstein's Knightsbridge home on 12 August 1964. Paul McCartney spent a great deal of time talking to her that evening and there were later rumours that he would be writing a song specially for her.

The Beatles' press agent Brian Somerville formerly handled Judy's publicity and Epstein's solicitor David Jacobs also represented her.

In October 1964 Brian Epstein and Lionel Bart announced that they would be promoting a Judy Garland concert, but it never took place.

The singer/actress died in 1969.

Garner, Frank

First road manager for the Beatles, although he only worked for them for a couple of months. Garner was a 'bouncer' at the Casbah Club when Mona Best asked him if he could act as a driver for the Beatles.

Frank's first assignment was their Litherland Town Hall gig on 20 December 1960. In addition to driving the group, he also humped their kit. For this he was paid the same amount as the members of the group – one pound. Their fee for that evening was six pounds and there were five members in the band. Stuart Sutcliffe was still in Germany at the time and Chas Newby deputised on bass guitar.

Garner continued to act as roadie for the next few months but began to find that he couldn't do two jobs at once, particularly at weekends, and by the autumn of 1961 Pete Best asked Neil Aspinall, who was lodging in his house, if he could take over the job from Frank, which he did.

Garry, Len

A member of John Lennon's group The Quarry Men at the age of fourteen, from June 1957 until the middle of 1958. He played tea-chest bass. Len left the skiffle group when he contracted tubercular meningitis and had to spend seven months in hospital. He became an architect and in 1965 married his girlfriend Susan. In 1971, together with their two sons Robert and Jonathan, they left Liverpool and settled in the south of England where their daughters Ruth and Jane were born. They emigrated to New Zealand in 1987, but returned to Liverpool in 1988. In 1992, Len teamed up with former Quarry Men John 'Duff' Lowe and Rod Davis to make some records and they were later joined by other original members, including Pete Shotton, Colin Hanton and Eric Griffiths to appear in concerts and at Beatles conventions around the world. In 1997, Len's autobiography *John, Paul & Me: Before The Beatles* was published.

Gator Bowl, East Adams Street, Jackson, Florida

At the time of the gig. Hurricane Dora had swept over Jacksonville causing terrible damage. President Johnson had arrived to inspect the damage and when the Beatles flew in on Friday, 11 September 1964, to appear at the Gator Bowl, their plane had to circle Imeson Airport until the President's plane had flown out. His police escort had remained to take the Beatles into town and they were driven to the George Washington Hotel in a cavalcade of police cars and motorbikes.

There was a press reception at the hotel with 150 attendees asking questions such as 'Does your hair require any special care?' and 'How do you all feel about you and the President coming to town on the same day?' to which John replied, 'Amazing.'

The Beatles had originally refused to appear at the venue until they were assured that the audience wouldn't be segregated. John was to say, 'We never play to segregated audiences and we're not going to start now. I'd sooner lose our appearance money.'

Winds of 40 mph were whipping through the stadium and, due to the devastation caused by Dora, 9,000 of the 32,000 ticket holders didn't make it to the concert.

The show started at 8.30 p.m. but, when the Beatles were due to appear, a camera team from LA had entrenched themselves backstage and refused to move. Derek Taylor faced the audience and told them: 'The Beatles are one hundred feet away. They came thousands of miles to be here and the only thing preventing their appearance are those nasty cine-cameramen.' He pointed to them and the boos began. 'Now if you want the Beatles to perform here tonight,' he said, 'tell the police to make the cameramen leave.'

The entire audience began chanting 'Out! Out! Out!' and police moved forward and hustled the eight-man team away.

The winds continued throughout the show unabated and Ringo's drums had been nailed down. At one time an attendant held Ringo down because he thought he'd be blown away!

Gaumont, Barker's Pool, Sheffield

Their one and only appearance at this cinema was one of the very last concert dates the group performed in Britain. 'The Beatles Show' was presented at the Gaumont on Wednesday, 8 December 1965 during their final British concert tour.

Manager Harry Murray decided on a simple trick to get the Beatles into the theatre. They'd phoned him five minutes before they were due to arrive and he told them to come straight to the front entrance. While police and security men were gathered at the stage door, the Beatles' car arrived at the front of the cinema and they walked straight in, in sight of the large queues, before anyone could realise what was happening.

Ringo commented: 'It was unusual for us. Normally we have to hide in vans or go in through back entrances. They did not realise outside what was going on.'

The group was provided with a TV set in their dressing room where they watched the programme 'No Hiding Place'.

During the show the usual missiles were hurled at the stage and a pear drop caught Paul in his left eye, causing him to blink throughout the rest of the performance. Ringo said, 'Another half inch and Paul would have been blinded for life.'

Compering the show was a local lad, Jerry Stevens of Seagrave Avenue, Gleadless. He said: 'It is a big experience working with the Beatles and I have learned a lot. I said before I met them I thought they were the greatest. Now I think they are even better than I thought they were.'

During the show, Jerry presented them with two Top Stars Special Awards. The first was for being voted the most popular group by the Sheffield readers of the paper, the second was for 'Help!', voted the most popular single of the year.

Following the show the Beatles stayed at a country club near Sheffield before moving on to their next venue in Birmingham.

Gaumont, Westover Road, Bournemouth, Hampshire

The Beatles appeared at this venue three times, making their debut there for a one-week season with two shows per night for six nights from 19–24 August 1963. They were driven to the gigs in a Ford Zephyr and their outfits comprised black velvet jackets with white shirts, together with string ties and grey-striped trousers, Support acts were Billy J. Kramer & the Dakotas and Tommy Quickly. During one of the performances a fan threw a five-inch metal safety pin at the stage which narrowly missed Paul's face.

The chief technician at the venue taped their live performances during the week on reel-to-reel tapes. Thirty-five years later, on 10 December 1998, he put a tape up for sale at Christie's auction house in London. Their spoken introductions can be heard with John cracking their joke about their favourite American group being Sophie Tucker and Paul saying that 'I Saw Her Standing There' had been 'recorded by that great coloured gospel singer, Victor Silvester'.

The songs on the tape included 'Roll Over Beethoven', 'Thank You Girl', 'Chains', 'From Me To You', 'A Taste Of Honey', 'I Saw Her Standing There', 'Baby It's You', 'Boys', 'She Loves You', 'Twist And Shout' and an instrumental verse of 'From Me To You'.

Their second appearance on 2 August 1964 had the Kinks, Mike Berry and Adrienne Posta in support and their final show at the Gaumont took place on 30 October 1964, with Mary Wells, Tommy Quickly, Sounds Incorporated, Michael Haslam, the Remo Four, the Rustiks and Bob Bain in support.

Gaumont, New Victoria Street, Bradford, Yorkshire

The venue for the Beatles' first ever Christmas stage show. The group previewed their Christmas show here for one evening on Saturday, 21 December 1963. Their guest artists were Billy J. Kramer & the Dakotas. It was the first of two northern previews for 'The Beatles Christmas Show', without the costumes, sets or comedy sketches which were to be featured in the London season at the Astoria, Finsbury Park.

The Beatles also made their major theatre tour debut here on Saturday, 2 February 1963 as part of the Helen Shapiro Tour. The group received £30 per show which, after Brian Epstein's 25 per cent commission had been deducted, left each member with £5.

There were two performances that night and Paul commented, 'We went on that opening night with Helen looking like a gang of Red Indians with war paint. But it was fun, and it was a challenge.' John was to say, 'It really was a relief to get out of Liverpool and try something new. Back home we'd worked night after night on the same cramped stage. Bradford wasn't very far away, but at least it was different as a field. We'd all started feeling tired, jaded, tied down, with the club scenes. Touring, with a different venue every night, was a real lift.' Their first performance that night was recorded by ABC TV and part of it was broadcast on 'Thank Your Lucky Stars'. The actual order of billing ran: Helen Shapiro, Danny Williams, Kenny Lynch, the Beatles, the Kestrels, the Red Price Orchestra, the Honeys and compere Dave Allen.

Local journalist Gordon Sampson was to write:

A great reception went to the colourfully dressed Beatles, who almost stole the show, for the audience repeatedly called for them while the other artists were performing! Undoubtedly their best number was an unusual vocal treatment of 'A Taste Of Honey', sung by left-handed bass guitarist Paul McCartney, with the others harmonising.

Their current hit, 'Please Please Me', with which they closed, was the most popular. They also sang their first success, 'Love Me Do', 'Beautiful Dreamer', 'Chains' and 'Keep Your Hands Off My Baby'.

Their longest British tour, their fourth, also commenced at this theatre on Friday, 9 October 1964. This time the Beatles were top of the bill and earning £850 per show, which comprised two performances per day at 6.15 and 8.40. Also on the bill were Mary Wells, Tommy Quickly and the Remo Four, Michael Haslam, the Rustiks, Sounds Incorporated and compere Bob Bain.

They performed 'Twist And Shout', 'Money', 'Can't Buy Me Love', 'Things We Said Today', 'I'm Happy Just To Dance With You', 'I Should Have Known Better', 'If I Fell', 'I Wanna Be Your Man', 'A Hard Day's Night' and 'Long Tall Sally', with Ringo gaining the biggest applause of the evening for his rendition of 'I Wanna Be Your Man'.

Actor Richard Harris and his wife dropped into the dressing room to see them although both John and George weren't in the mood for visitors. John wrapped himself in a green plastic mac and lay down behind a sofa while George pretended to be asleep.

Harris said, 'Hello, do you mind if we come in?'

Paul and Ringo said, 'Of course' and Harris said, 'We just popped round to say hello.'

'Hello,' said Paul.

Harris then said 'How's it going, then?' and Paul answered, 'Great!'

Looking at George pretending to be asleep in the chair, Harris said, 'What's the matter with George?'

Paul said, 'He's tired.'

Mrs Harris then asked, 'Where's John?'

Paul pointed to where John was wrapped in the plastic mac and said, 'He's there.'

'What's the matter with John?' asked Harris.

'He's tired too,' said Ringo.

Mrs Harris then said, 'We just wondered if you could give us an autograph for the children.'

'Yes, of course,' said Paul.

She handed over a piece of paper, saying, 'You must have signed thousands of these.'

'Yes,' said Ringo.

Then Harris said, 'I suppose you're so used to it you just sign anything that's put in front of you. How about a cheque then?'

Paul said, 'OK.'

The couple then said their goodbyes and thank yous and left.

Gaumont, Hallgate, Doncaster, Yorkshire

All three appearances by the Beatles at this cinema took place in 1963. Their debut occurred on Tuesday, 5 February as part of the Helen Shapiro Tour, followed by a visit the following month on Friday, 22 March as part of the Tommy Roe/Chris Montez package and, finally, as bill toppers in their own right on Tuesday, 10 December. Australian broadcaster Dibbs Mather interviewed them in their dressing room during their last visit to the venue for programmes distributed abroad – *Dateline London* and *Calling Australia*.

Gaumont, Piccadilly, Hanley, Stafforsdhire

Site of the Beatles' final date on the Helen Shapiro Tour on Sunday, 3 March 1963. The group had begun the tour in the opening spot and had gradually risen to the more prestigious position of being the last act in the first half – generally regarded as second on the bill. They returned for their second and last appearance at the cinema several weeks later on Sunday, 19 May on their tour with Roy Orbison.

Gaumont, St Helen's Street, Ipswich, Suffolk

The Beatles played here during their tour with Roy Orbison on Wednesday, 22 May 1963. Their second appearance there was on Saturday, 31 October 1964.

Gaumont State Cinema, 195–199 Kilburn High Road, London NW6

A picture palace originally built in 1937, when it became the largest cinema in Europe.

During the 1950s and 1960s the venue presented many famous live performances on stage, including Bill Haley, Ella Fitzgerald and Duke Ellington.

The Beatles made their debut appearance in a ballroom within the Gaumont State on 9 April 1963 and also performed on stage at the large cinema itself on 23 October 1964.

It finally closed its doors in 1980.

Gaumont, Commercial Road, Southampton, Hampshire

The Beatles first appeared at this cinema during their tour with Roy Orbison on Monday, 20 May 1963. They returned to the venue for the final date of their autumn tour on Friday, 13 December 1963 and their last appearance at the venue took place on Friday, 6 November 1964, during which Tony Bilbow interviewed them for the programme 'Day By Day'.

Gaumont, Corporation Street, Taunton, Somerset

The Beatles first appeared at this cinema during their tour with Helen Shapiro on Tuesday, 26 February 1963. However, this was the first of two dates on which Helen didn't appear due to her having contracted a cold. Her stand-in that night was Billie Davis, who had a chart hit called 'Tell Him'.

Their next and final appearance at the venue took place later the same year on Thursday, 5 September.

Gaumont, Snow Hill, Wolverhampton, West Midlands

When the Beatles first appeared at this venue on Thursday, 14 March 1963, as part of the Tommy Roe/Chris Montez Tour, John Lennon was ill and only Paul, George and Ringo appeared in the Beatles' spot. They next appeared on Tuesday, 19 November 1963, as headliners in their own right. During the evening Sean O'Mahony and Leslie Bryce of *Beatles Monthly* visited the boys backstage. Mahony had brought along ten hats of various styles from Dunn of Regent Street for the boys to pose in.

Also backstage were journalist Mike Hennessy and Tony Bramwell of NEMS. The group wore black mohair suits with velvet collars and during their set a fan threw a white bunny on stage which John kept, presumably for Julian.

Gaumont, Foregate Street, Worcester

The Beatles first appeared at this cinema on Tuesday, 28 May 1963 during their tour with Roy Orbison. They returned to the venue on Wednesday, 4 September 1963 as the first of a series of four bookings by promoter John Smith.

Gentle, Johnny

Singer, born John Askew near Scotland Road, Liverpool, on 8 December 1936. He became an apprentice and in 1957 made his own guitar. He teamed up with Bobby Crawford and the two began making appearances at local social clubs.

When his apprenticeship ended in 1958, Johnny became a ship's carpenter on a cruise liner. Following the initial voyage, he entered a talent competition at Butlin's under the name George Baker – but Jimmy Tarbuck won the contest. By that time he'd changed his name again to Rick Damone.

He moved to London and worked on a building site while writing to various record companies and agencies and received a response from leading impresario Larry Parnes. Initially, Parnes suggested he call himself Tim McGee, but Johnny didn't like the name so Parnes said: 'Your name is Johnny and you're a quiet guy – how about Johnny Gentle!' He also appointed him a tour manager – another Scouser called Hal Carter.

Johnny's debut record was the self-penned 'Wendy', but it wasn't successful. He followed with 'Milk', but it only managed to reach No. 28 in the charts. An EP, *The Gentle Touch*, followed.

In 1960, Parnes co-promoted an event with Liverpool coffee bar owner Allan Williams at Liverpool Stadium. Initially, it was to be topped by Eddie Cochran and Gene Vincent, but Cochran was killed in a road accident.

With Vincent now topping the bill, Williams also featured local bands Cass & the Cassanovas, Rory Storm & the Hurricanes and Gerry & the Pacemakers.

The event took place on 3 May and Parnes saw the potential of the Liverpool bands and thought it might be a good idea to use one of them as a backing band for Fury and others to back Duffy Power and Johnny Gentle on tour.

An audition was held at the Wyvern Club in Liverpool on 10 May, which resulted in the Silver Beetles being selected to back Johnny on his Scottish tour. Their fee was £120, which was to include their fares from Liverpool. At the time the group comprised John Lennon, Paul McCartney, George Harrison, Stuart Sutcliffe and Tommy Moore.

Gentle, then twenty years old, has been quoted as saying, 'When I first saw them I wondered what on earth Parnes had sent me.' But he was later to deny this, claiming that he immediately liked their youth and enthusiasm.

The tour began on 20 May 1960 at the Town Hall, Alloa, Clackmannanshire. Other gigs were on 21 May at the Northern Meeting Ballroom, Church Street, Inverness; on 23 May at the Dalrymple Hall, Fraserburgh, Aberdeenshire; on 25 May at St Thomas's Hall, Keith, Banffshire; on 26 May at the Town Hall, Forres, Morayshire; on 27 May at the Regal Ballroom, Leopold

Street, Nairn, Nairnshire, and on 28 May at the Rescue Hall, Peterhead, Aberdeenshire.

The group name was never actually used in the promotion of the tour, as the billing read 'Johnny Gentle and his group'. However, three members of the band decided to use stage names. Paul used the name Paul Ramon, George adopted the name Carl Harrison and Stuart called himself Stuart de Stael. It has been suggested that John called himself Johnny Silver, but he denied this.

Johnny first met the group half an hour before they were due to go on stage together and they had time for only twenty minutes of rehearsals before their performance. Duncan McKinnon wasn't impressed with the show but Johnny explained that they needed rehearsal time together and, after practising the next day, the stage show improved.

McKinnon had also complained about their stage gear, so Johnny gave George a black shirt to wear, as Paul and John were wearing black shirts. It was the nearest they got to a uniform appearance on stage.

Johnny had a room to himself and the Silver Beatles shared two rooms. Sometimes they were put in different hotels. Johnny recalled the best hotel they stayed in was in Inverness, overlooking the river. It was while they were at the hotel that he played a song he'd written called 'I've Just Fallen For Someone' to George and John. Gentle was having difficulty with the middle eight and John came up with something he'd written which fitted in. Johnny decided to use Lennon's middle eight in his song and he actually recorded the number for Parlophone the following year under the name Darren Young. The record sold about 3,000 copies.

Gentle was to say that, despite their rawness as a group, he was impressed with them and urged his manager to sign them up. However, Parnes specialised in representing solo singers and wasn't interested in the problems associated with managing bands.

Parnes commented: 'Johnny used to phone me virtually every night and say, "Come up to Scotland and see these boys. I've given them a spot in my act and they're doing better than I am." He was very honest. I always said that if I'd found the time to go up to Scotland he might have been the fifth Beatle. Who knows?'

Following the tour, Johnny appeared with them once more. He visited Merseyside and on 2 July dropped in to the Jacaranda Club with his father. He was told that the group was appearing that night at the Grosvenor Ballroom, Liscard, and went over to the gig and joined them on stage.

Gentle asked Parnes to book them again as his backing band, but they were appearing in Hamburg at the time.

His singing career was unsuccessful, despite changing his name to Darren Young. He also joined vocal outfit the Viscounts for a time.

He moved to Jersey for a while, but couldn't maintain a living as a singer and in the early 1970s began his own joinery business.

This has proved to be very successful. Johnny married, had two children – Gavin and Donna – and is now a granddad.

Happily ensconced in Kent, he had a brief return to the limelight when the *Beatles Anthology* was released and the press became interested in that first Scottish tour. He also participated in the BBC radio show 'The Beatles In Scotland' and Merseyside rock historian Ian Forsyth then persuaded him to put his story down on paper. The result was *Johnny Gentle & The Beatles, First Ever Tour,* published in 1998.

Gerry & The Pacemakers

Liverpool's nearest rivals to the Beatles.

Leader Gerry Marsden had joined his first skiffle group at the age of fourteen and named one of his skiffle bands the Mars Bars. In 1959 the group had become a rock 'n' roll band and Gerry was accompanied by his brother Freddie on drums, Les Chadwick on guitar and Les Maguire on piano.

Although the group were a rock 'n' roll band they didn't have the same hard edge as groups such as the Big Three, the Dominoes or the Beatles, but their music was infectious and they had a huge local following. Gerry had an astonishing repertoire of 250 songs and among the numbers performed regularly by the band were 'Jambalaya', 'Skinny Minnie', 'What'd I Say' and 'Will You Love Me Tomorrow?'

In his own personal Top Ten of local groups, published in the 5 October 1961 issue of *Mersey Beat, Cavern* disc jockey Bob Wooler placed Gerry and the Pacemakers directly behind the Beatles at No. 2.

Mindful of the publicity the local groups were receiving in *Mersey Beat,* Brian Epstein began talking to Marsden when the singer was in the NEMS, Whitechapel, shop, looking at records. Epstein, aware of the youngsters who frequented his shop, began to ask Gerry about his selection of records.

Gerry, who was born on 24 September 1942, was nineteen at the time and an apprentice working for British Rail. In January, Bob Wooler's personal preferences were reflected in the first official *Mersey Beat* Poll. The Beatles were at No. 1, Gerry & the Pacemakers at No. 2. As Epstein had already signed up the No. 1 group, it was only natural that he next sign up their closest rivals. Interestingly enough, the following year, soon after Billy J. Kramer was voted into the No. 3 position of the *Mersey Beat* Poll, Epstein signed him up. In fact, an analysis of the poll results will show that Epstein signed up the highest-placed acts in the poll who were not already committed to a manager, such as the Fourmost, the Remo Four and the Merseybeats (the latter didn't stay with him for long).

Gerry & the Pacemakers made their Cavern debut in October 1960 and appeared at most of the leading Mersey venues, often on the same bill as the Beatles – during their 19 October 1961 appearance at Litherland Town Hall the two groups joined as one and called themselves the Beatmakers! They also went to Germany where they had the opportunity of meeting some of their idols – Fats Domino, Jerry Lee Lewis and Gene Vincent.

Freddie Marsden was to tell broadcaster Spencer Leigh, 'The Beatles appealed to a different audience from us. They had more of a beatnik following. There was always friendly rivalry between us. Despite their rawness, Paul McCartney used to get a great reception for the sentimental songs like "Over The Rainbow" and we thought we'd have to get a song that would go over just as well. We tried "You'll Never Walk Alone" a few times and it went down excellently. We'd be playing rock 'n' roll and then all of a sudden we'd stop and do "You'll Never Walk Alone".'

Gerry was proud when, one day, after the number had been a No. 1 hit, he heard Liverpool supporters begin to sing the number at football matches. It soon became the main football anthem, not only in Liverpool, but throughout Britain. He was to re-record the number almost a quarter of a century later and see it reach No. 1 again – a record no other artist has achieved.

When George Martin visited Liverpool on 9 December 1962 to see the Beatles perform at the Cavern and assess the technical difficulties involved in recording them live at the club, Brian Epstein also took him across the River Mersey to see Gerry & the Pacemakers performing at the Majestic Ballroom, Birkenhead. Martin was impressed and signed them. He gave them the Mitch Murray number 'How Do You Do It?', which the Beatles had rejected, to record. They reached the No. 1 position with the single at the end of March 1963 and, because the *Record Retailer* chart was the official industry chart, Gerry & the Pacemakers reached the No. 1 spot before the Beatles. They also reached No. 1 with their next two releases, 'I Like It' and 'You'll Never Walk Alone'. It was a unique achievement – no other artist had ever scored a hat-trick of chart toppers with their first three recordings. It was a record which has never been topped, although it was equalled at the beginning of the eighties by another Liverpool band, Frankie Goes To Hollywood, who, ironically, had Gerry's 'Ferry 'Cross The Mersey' on the flipside of one of their chart toppers.

Just as they'd appeared on many local bills together, the Beatles and Gerry & the Pacemakers found themselves sharing bills on nationwide concert appearances, including the Brian Epstein series of 'Mersey Beat Showcase' gigs which featured the Beatles, Gerry & the Pacemakers, the Big Three and Billy J. Kramer & the Dakotas. The two groups also topped the bill on a special NEMS Enterprises promotion at the Tower Ballroom, New Brighton, on Friday, 14 June 1963. They also toured with the Beatles and Roy Orbison in May and June 1963.

Epstein attempted to pattern the career of Gerry & the Pacemakers on the model of the Beatles' success. They were placed with the same recording manager, George Martin, had publicity photographs by Dezo Hoffmann, suits by Dougie Millins, and Epstein even talked Sean O'Mahoney into publishing a Gerry & the Pacemakers monthly magazine similar to the *Beatles Monthly*. Just as the Beatles had a Christmas show, Epstein had a similar one for Gerry, 'Gerry's Christmas Cracker' – and following the success of *A Hard Day's Night*, he also arranged for Gerry & the Pacemakers to appear in a black and white feature film, *Ferry 'Cross The Mersey*, scripted by Tony Warren, who'd created the northern soap opera 'Coronation Street'. Epstein also tried the same tack in America, arranging for Gerry to appear on 'The Ed Sullivan Show' and on tour over there.

Despite such a push, the career at the top was relatively short-lived for Gerry & the Pacemakers. Trying to fit them into the same pattern as the Beatles didn't work. They were different groups; the Pacemakers needed specific attention paid to their own individuality and style as an act. Brian Epstein didn't really have that much time to spend on them as his attention was fully directed on the Beatles' career. The Pacemakers had enjoyed three No. 1 hits in 1963 and three further hits in 1964: 'I'm The One', which reached No. 2, 'Don't Let The Sun Catch You Crying', which reached No. 6, and 'Ferry 'Cross The Mersey', which reached No. 8. They had their last hit, 'I'll Be There', in 1965, which reached No. 15. They disbanded soon afterwards and Gerry starred for some time in the West End musical *Charlie Girl*, before becoming a host on children's television programmes.

In the seventies he re-formed Gerry & the Pacemakers with different personnel and has been touring on and off ever since. In 1985 he issued his own tribute to the Beatles, an album *Lennon/McCartney Songbook* (K-Tel ONE 1274) with his personal rendition of Lennon & McCartney classics. Paul McCartney provided the sleeve notes, in which he commented, 'In Liverpool his group was probably the biggest competition to the Beatles and I remember all too well sweating the outcome of our local newspaper popularity poll, hoping that we could scrape together the necessary points to beat their band. That's how close it was!'

Get Back

The single that was credited to 'The Beatles with Billy Preston', making Preston the only musician to officially share label billing with the Beatles at their request.

The Beatles had first met Preston in Hamburg and when George Harrison went to the Royal Festival Hall to attend a Ray Charles concert, he saw Billy perform on stage. George renewed the acquaintanceship and took Billy along to the Apple Studios where the group were recording. They then invited him to spend the next two weeks recording and filming with them on their 'Get Back' project, with Preston playing electric organ. Billy was later to say, 'I didn't even know until the record was out that they had put my name on it. It was something that I could have never asked for or no manager could negotiate, just something they felt for me.' Billy was also presented with a Gold Disc for his contribution to the single.

The number was a Paul McCartney composition, but it had seen many changes and the song had been rehearsed at the Twickenham sessions, although in a different form. Paul had originally written it as a satire on the British immigration laws, with such controversial lines as 'Don't dig no Pakistanis taking all the people's jobs'. Although Paul was making a political comment, aimed at attitudes towards immigration from people such as Enoch Powell, the MP, and also mentioning political figures such as Harold Wilson and Edward Heath, he was not being 'racist' as the *New Musical Express* accused him of being several years later when they heard some of the various recordings of the song. Different versions of the number in its early stages have been called by several names, including 'Commonwealth', 'Commonwealth Song', 'White Power' or 'No Pakistanis', and have cropped up on numerous bootleg albums.

Recordings of the new version began on Thursday, 23 June 1969, at the Apple Studios in Savile Row, with Preston. Apart from producer George Martin, Glyn Johns acted as engineer and Alan Parsons became tape operator on a Beatles disc for the first time. Recordings continued on other days at Apple and the number was also included in the group's live performance on the roof of the Apple building.

The single was issued in Britain on 11 April 1969 on Apple R 5777 with 'Don't Let Me Down' as the flip. A slightly earlier release date had been planned, but the Beatles halted the release and re-mixed the track.

In America it was issued on 5 May 1969 on Apple 2490 and entered the charts at No. 10, equalling their feat with 'Hey Jude'. An advertisement in *Billboard* stated, 'It's the first Beatles record which is as live as can be, in this electronic age.'

Over 4½ million copies were sold worldwide and the single was No. 1 in Australia, New Zealand, Canada, Germany, France, Spain, Norway, Denmark, Holland, Belgium, Malaysia and Singapore.

Rod Stewart recorded a version of the number for the *All This And World War II* film soundtrack which, when issued as a single, reached No. 10 in the American charts.

The song was included on *The Beatles 1967–1970* compilation, EMI's *A Monument To British Rock, Volume 1, Rock 'n' Roll Music* and *20 Greatest Hits*.

When 'Get Back' was originally recorded it was produced by George Martin and his version can be found on the single and on compilations such as *The Beatles 1967–1970* and *Rock 'n' Roll Music*. When the 'Get Back' project tapes were handed to Phil Spector to re-dub and edit, his version became the one that was featured on the *Let It Be* album. A version was included on the Beatles' *Anthology 3* CDs and the number was also featured on the CD compilation *Past Masters Volume Two*.

Getting Better

A track on the *Sgt Pepper* album which was penned by Paul with some aid from John on the lyrics of the middle eight. Most of John and Paul's collaborations had been written in their early days in Liverpool and by the mid-sixties and their 'studio years' they mainly wrote individually, and this is one of the few occasions during those times when they did some work on a song together. Beatles biographer Hunter Davies was present in the studio when John began to help Paul with one of the verses in the song.

The number had its origin when Paul had driven to Primrose Hill, near St John's Wood, in the spring of 1967 to take his dog Martha for a walk. It was a sunny day and Paul recalled a phrase often used by Jimmy Nicol, the drummer who deputised for Ringo during part of the Beatles' world tour in 1964. Jimmy's phrase was a piece of positive homespun philosophy: 'It's getting better.' Paul mentioned to John at their next meeting that 'It's Getting Better' sounded like a good title for a song.

Additional instruments on the track included George Harrison playing a large four-string Indian instrument called a tamboura and George Martin playing piano.

Gibb, Russ
A disc jockey on the Detroit radio station WKNR-FM in 1969. Gibb, also known as 'Uncle Russ' was a popular figure in Detroit at the time and also co-owned the Grande Ballroom, one of the city's main concert venues. A caller to his show suggested various oddities on Beatles releases, intimating at secret messages. Gibb then opened his phone lines the next day to add to the story. Fred LaBour, a student reviewing the *Abbey Road* album for the *Michigan Daily*, also heard the caller and began to use the clues and develop others to spark off what became, with the encouragement of Gibb, the 'Paul Is Dead' affair.

Ginsberg, Allen
An American Beat Generation poet and Gay Rights activist. He travelled to England in 1965 and began to involve himself in poetic activities in London, aided by Barry Miles, who was later to write a Ginsberg biography. On 10 May, Ginsberg attended the Bob Dylan concert at the Royal Albert Hall and was invited to the after-show party at the Savoy Hotel, held in the suite of Dylan's manager Albert Grossman. In Dylan's suite the Beatles were there with their wives and girlfriends and Neil Aspinall and Mal Evans. Ginsberg was asked to join them.

The poet was particularly impressed with the Beatles and spent a week up in Liverpool. Of his experiences there, he was to say, 'Liverpool is at the present time the centre of the consciousness of the human universe.'

John and Cynthia and George and Pattie were invited to Ginsberg's birthday party in London. When they turned up they were startled to find a naked Ginsberg, with a pair of jockey shorts on his head and a 'Do Not Disturb' sign on his penis. They soon left, with Lennon commenting, 'You don't do that in front of the birds.'

In 1996 Paul recorded 'The Ballad of the Skeletons' with Ginsberg. Ginsberg had recorded the basic track of his poem in New York with guitarists Mark Ribot, David Mansfield and Lenny Kaye. He then sent the tape to Paul in England and Paul added organ, drums and maracas. When Ginsberg recited the poem at the Royal Albert Hall on 16 October of that year, Paul joined him on stage for its performance.

Ginsberg died of liver cancer on Friday, 4 April 1997. He was seventy years old.

Girl
A John Lennon Composition featured on the *Rubber Soul* album. John commented, 'This was about a dream girl. When Paul and I

wrote lyrics in the old days we used to laugh about it like the Tin
Pan Alley people would. And it was only later on that we tried to
match the lyrics to the tune. I like this one. It was one of my best.'
He was also to add later on that he eventually found the 'dream
girl' – Yoko!

The track, which John had to write under a tight deadline for the
album, was recorded in one day, 11 November 1965, and John said
that he had Paul and George sing the word 'Tit' over and over on
the backing vocals.

The number was also included on the *Beatles 1962–1966* and
Love Songs compilations. Two groups, St Louis Union and Truth,
had Top 20 hits in the British charts with the number.

Give Peace A Chance

A number which John wrote as the first single for the Plastic Ono
Band. Although Yoko Ono gave him a little help on the number, the
song was credited to Lennon & McCartney due to a verbal agreement the two had to credit all their songs to the joint name.

When John was growing more politically aware, he'd always felt
the desire to write a political anthem, like 'We Shall Overcome' had
been used in the Civil Rights marches in America. 'Give Peace A
Chance' became the anthem of the anti-Vietnam marches in America.

The song was recorded on portable equipment in Room 1742 of
the Queen Elizabeth Hotel, Montreal, on 26 May 1969, during
John and Yoko's eight-day bed-in there. They had a large number of
friends visiting them during the stay and a number of them took
part in the recording, singing the chorus, including poet Allen
Ginsberg, youth-culture spokesman Timothy Leary and his wife
Rosemary, comedian Tommy Smothers, Derek Taylor, the
Canadian chapter of the Radha Krishna Temple, disc jockey
Murray The K, comedian Dick Gregory, singer Petula Clark and a
priest and a rabbi.

The song, credited to the Plastic Ono Band, was issued in Britain
on Apple 13 on 4 July 1969 where it reached No. 2 in the charts. It
was issued in America on Apple 1809 on 7 July 1969 and reached
No. 14 in the charts.

The number on the flipside was 'Remember Love'.

'Give Peace A Chance' was included on John's *Live Peace In
Toronto* and *Shaved Fish* albums and he performed it at the
Toronto Rock 'n' Roll Revival Concert, at a peace demonstration in
New York in May 1972 and at the 'One To One' concert in 1972.

Its use as a peace anthem has been powerful, although there may
have been more controversy attached had it not been for some self-
censoring on John's part. He was to comment, 'The real word I used

on the record was "masturbation", but I'd just got into trouble for "The Ballad Of John And Yoko" and I didn't want any more fuss, so I put "mastication" in the written lyrics. It was a cop-out, but the message about peace was more important to me than having a little laugh about a word.'

Glad All Over

Not to be confused with the hit by the Dave Clark Five. This number was composed by Bennett/Tepper/Schroeder and recorded by Carl Perkins in 1957. The Beatles added it to their repertoire, with George taking over lead vocals, and they performed it on two of their BBC radio shows, 'Saturday Club' and 'Pop Gear'. The Beatles never issued it as a record, although their Mersey Beat mates the Searchers recorded it in 1964. One of the Beatles radio performances was included on *The Beatles Live At The BBC* CDs.

Glass Onion

A composition by John which was included on *The Beatles* double album. The song contained references to five other Beatles compositions: 'Strawberry Fields Forever', 'I Am The Walrus', 'Lady Madonna', 'Fool On The Hill' and 'Fixing A Hole'.

Paul McCartney was to comment, 'John wrote the tune "Glass Onion", I mean he wrote it mainly, but I helped him on it, and when we were writing it we were thinking specifically of this whole idea of all these kind people who write in and say "Who was the walrus, John? Were you the walrus?" or "Is Paul the walrus?" So John, I mean, he happened to have a line go "Oh yeah, the walrus was Paul" and we had a great giggle to say "Yeah, let's do that", let's put this line in 'cause everybody's gonna read into it and go crackers 'cause they all thought that John was the walrus – "I am the walrus" you know, and it goes kind of insane after a while. So eventually he said, "Let's do this joke tune 'Glass Onion' where all kinds of answers to the universe are," but we thought it was a joke. Now someone the other night told me he'd met this feller who chartered a yacht and was going out into the middle of the ocean 'cause he knew the spot where to go through the glass onion. Now this feller hasn't been seen since!'

John was to say, 'I was just having a laugh because there'd been so much gobbledegook about "Pepper", play it backwards and you stand on your head and all that. Even now, I just saw Mel Torme on TV the other day saying that "Lucy" was written to promote drugs and so was "A Little Help From My Friends" and none of them were at all – "A Little Help From My Friends" only says get high in it, it's really about a little help from my friends, it's a sincere message.'

In 1980, John was to add a further comment about 'Glass Onion': 'That was me just doing a throwaway. I threw the line in – "the walrus was Paul" – just to confuse everybody a bit more. It could've been "the Fox Terrier was Paul". It's just a piece of poetry!' A version of the number was included on the Beatles' *Anthology 3* CDs.

Glenpark Club, Lord Street, Southport, Lancashire

The Beatles appeared at this venue in November 1961.

Globe Cinema, High Street, Stockton-on-Tees, Durham

The Beatles made their first appearance at this venue on Friday, 22 November 1963 during their autumn tour, the day of President John F. Kennedy's assassination. They returned to the cinema for the last time on Thursday, 15 October 1964 and were interviewed in their hotel room during the day regarding the current general election for the TV programme 'North-East Newsview', which was transmitted the following day.

Golden Slumbers/Carry That Weight

'Golden Slumbers' was originally an English hymn, based on a 400-year-old poem by Thomas Dekker. Paul's stepsister Ruth approached him one day when he was composing on the piano and showed him the sheet music of 'Golden Slumbers', asking if he could read music. He admitted he couldn't, but was intrigued by the number and composed his own lyrics to one of the verses. He then contributed some further additions and the finished song appeared on the *Abbey Road* album with another of Paul's songs, 'Carry That Weight'. They were both recorded as one number on Wednesday, 2 July 1969.

'Golden Slumbers/Carry That Weight' was recorded by Apple band Trash and reached No. 27 in the *New Musical Express* charts in Britain. Another version by Orange Bicycle was a flop.

Goldmann, Peter

A Swedish director whom the Beatles employed when they decided to make videos of 'Strawberry Fields Forever' and 'Penny Lane'. They'd decided to make special filmed inserts for programmes such as 'Top Of The Pops'. John mentioned that they found great difficulty appearing on television programmes to promote their singles and a simpler solution would be to make a promotional film which could be used at home and abroad.

It was really the beginning of the pop promo as we know it,

although Goldmann had come to the Beatles' attention because of some acclaimed promotional films he had made for the Troggs and Donovan.

The Beatles weren't actually shown performing the two numbers in the film because of a Musicians' Union ruling in Britain which had recently been introduced which prevented groups from miming to their records.

Filming took place in February 1967 and as they were involved in recording an album, they couldn't make it up to Liverpool, so a team went up to the Mersey port to produce some background scenes to be spliced into the film. The 'Penny Lane' film, with its intercut shots of Liverpool, had John wandering around some London streets, then featured the Beatles riding horses in Stratford, London, a sequence filmed on a Sunday morning. They rode into the countryside, which was actually Knole Park Estate, near Sevenoaks in Kent. Ringo's drums were set up near a large banqueting table, bedecked with a candelabra, and the four sipped champagne from teacups, before John overturned the table and the group began to play their instruments.

The 'Strawberry Fields' promo had a strange, surrealistic air as Goldmann had devised the image of a huge tree strung with wires like a giant piano, with the wires leading to a keyboard on the ground.

Goldmann was to say, 'I found that Ringo was very well informed on camera and photographic techniques, and Paul was a most entertaining conversationalist. But the group had all informed me that I was the director and so I must direct. I was amazed to find, that there was a ban in Britain which prevented the Beatles from miming to their disc – I cannot think that this serves any useful purpose.'

The two films were first screened on 'Top Of The Pops' in Britain, but only in mono. The colour films made their debut in America on the 'Ed Sullivan Show'.

Gone, Gone, Gone

A number written and recorded by Carl Perkins in 1959. The Beatles performed the song in their stage act for a short period of time in 1960. Perkins was a major inspiration to the Beatles and during their career they performed no less than ten of his numbers on stage.

Good, Jack

A London-born impresario who originally devised one of Britain's first TV rock shows, 'The 6.5 Special'. His other shows included 'Oh Boy!', 'Boy Meets Girl' and 'Wham!' before he moved to

America in 1962. He returned to England specially to produce the 1964 special 'Around the Beatles' and a British edition of his American show 'Shindig', in which the Beatles starred.

Goodbye

A song which Paul McCartney wrote specially for his protégée, Mary Hopkin. He made a demo disc of the number, but it was never considered as a composition for the Beatles.

Paul also produced Mary recording the number and it was issued in Britain on Apple 10 on 28 March 1969 and in America on Apple 1806 on 7 April 1969. The number was Mary's second single and the follow-up to her international No. 1 record 'Those Were The Days', which had sold over five million copies. 'Goodbye' reached No. 2 in the British charts.

Good Day Sunshine

Composition by Paul McCartney. When recording began on Wednesday, 8 June 1966, the song's title was then 'A Good Day's Sunshine'.

The song was included as a track on the *Revolver* album and it was a number Paul was particularly proud of and he was to feature it in his film *Give My Regards To Broad Street*.

Good Morning, Good Morning

A John Lennon composition featured on the *Sgt Pepper's Lonely Hearts Club Band* album.

John felt that there should be some brass on the number and the three saxophonists from Sounds Incorporated – Barrie Cameron, David Glyde and Alan Holmes – performed on the track, together with two trombonists and a French horn player. At a later session, John felt that the sounds of animals should be included. A bizarre set of effects was used which began with a cock crowing and ended with a hen clucking. All other animal noises were introduced in between, including sounds of lions, horses, sheep, elephants, dogs, cats and a cow. The sounds were taken from sound-effect tapes, 'Volume 35: Animals and Bees' and 'Volume 57: Fox-hunt'.

John had originally been inspired to write the number after listening to a television advertisement and commented, 'I often sit at the piano working on songs with the television on low in the background. If I'm a bit low and not getting much done then the words of the telly come through. That's when I heard "Good morning, good morning". It was a cornflake advertisement.' Take No. 8 from the original studio recording sessions was included on the Beatles' *Anthology 2* CDs.

Goodnight

A children's lullaby which John had originally written for his five-year-old son, Julian. It was used as a vehicle for Ringo and featured as the final track on *The Beatles* double album.

At the initial recording session Ringo made some brief spoken invitations to children to settle into bed while he sang them the song. This was dropped from the final version of the number. Initially it was also considered to record the song in a simple way with John backing Ringo's vocal on acoustic guitar. George Martin eventually opted for a much more lavish production and conducted an orchestra of 26 musicians and also added a choir of eight voices. The members of the Mike Sammes Singers who provided the vocals were Ingrid Thomas, Pat Whitmore, Val Stockwell, Irene King, Ross Gilmour, Mike Redway, Ken Barrie and Fred Lucas. An alternative take of the number was used on the Beatles' *Anthology 3* CDs.

Got To Get You Into My Life

A song penned by Paul and featured on the *Revolver* album, issued on 3 August 1966. It's another number in which the influence of Motown is evident, and Paul was to comment that he wrote the song after being introduced to marijuana – and was to refer to the number as 'an ode to pot'. Paul sang a double-tracked solo vocal, with brass backing from Ian Hamer, Les Condon and Eddie Thornton on trumpet and Alan Branscombe and Peter Coe on tenor saxophones. John played rhythm, George lead, Ringo drums and tambourine and George Martin organ.

Paul had originally booked two members of Georgie Fame & the Blue Flames, Eddie Thornton on trumpet and Glenn Hughes on baritone sax. On the morning of the recording, Hughes fell sick and he was to die soon afterwards in a house fire. Another member of the Blue Flames, Peter Coe, replaced him. When his name was mentioned in the press as having recorded with the Beatles, Thornton was booked for sessions with several acts, including the Rolling Stones, the Jimi Hendrix Experience, the Small Faces and Sandie Shaw.

On the same day that *Revolver* was released, Cliff Bennett & the Rebel Rousers issued 'Got To Get You Into My Life' as a single. Paul produced their version, which reached No. 6 in the British charts.

American band Earth, Wind & Fire recorded a version for the Robert Stigwood film, *Sgt Pepper's Lonely Hearts Club Band,* and this reached No. 4 in the US charts in August 1978, although it only reached No. 30 in Britain.

The Beatles' version was included on the compilations *The Beatles 1962–1966* and *Rock 'n' Roll Music*.

There was also an American single issued. This followed a revival of interest in *The Beatles* white album following an American television dramatisation of the Charles Manson trial called 'Helter Skelter'. Capitol decided to rush-release a single of 'Helter Skelter', but at the last minute realised that the public might consider it in bad taste and then placed it on the flipside of 'Got To Get You Into My Life'. It was issued on Capitol 4274 on 31 May 1976 and rose to No. 3 in the charts.

The number remained one of Paul's favourite songs and he included it in his repertoire during the Wings British Tour of 1979.

A version of the Beatles' recording was included on the *Anthology 2* CD.

Grade, Sir Lew

At the time of the emergence of Beatlemania in England, three brothers – Lew and Leslie Grade and Bernard Delfont, were the most prominent showbusiness impresarios in the country, with interest in television, theatres, agencies and management companies.

Lew was born Louis Winogradsky at Tokmak in the Ukraine on 25 December 1906, the eldest of three brothers. His family emigrated to Britain when he was five. He won the world Charleston championships at the Royal Albert Hall when he was nineteen and entered a career as a dancer. In the early 1930s he teamed up with Joe Collins to form an agency, Collins & Grade. He was in at the ground floor of commercial television, involved in the formation of ATV and later became managing director, then chairman.

In 1964 it was rumoured that Brian Epstein had approached Lew Grade and said he was ready to sell the Beatles. When he heard about it, John Lennon told him, 'If you do sell, we'll never play again. We'll disband.'

In November 1964, Brian Epstein had meetings with Lew Grade and a few days later made an announcement that he would never sell the Beatles.

Grade was to acquire control of the Beatles' songwriting company, against their wishes. He was then head of ATV, who successfully took control of Northern Songs in March 1969 despite a fierce battle by the Beatles to prevent him gaining a foothold in their publishing company. Grade had already lost a similar battle in which he tried to take over Chappell's Music, but this time he was able to arrange a deal with Dick James, who sold his shares to Grade without informing the Beatles.

When Grade had been an agent, James had been one of his clients.

The shares ATV bought from James enabled them to gain a stranglehold on Northern Songs and then obtain a controlling interest.

When Paul came to compose material for his first solo single, 'Another Day', the songwriting credits were attributed to Mr and Mrs McCartney, which caused a slight panic at ATV Music. Paul commented: 'Lew Grade suddenly saw his songwriting concession, which he'd just paid a lot of money for, virtually to get hold of John and I, he suddenly saw that I was claiming that I was writing half my stuff with Linda.'

ATV Music instigated legal action and the case actually went to court. Paul won the case but, to settle the matter with Lew Grade, he agreed to appear on a TV special, 'James Paul McCartney', for ATV. It was described as 'a personal project of Sir Lew Grade, realised through the genius of Paul McCartney and the expertise of producer Gary Smith and director Dwight Hewison'.

The TV show was filmed in various places: on location in Scotland; in the Chelsea Reach pub in New Brighton where Gerry Marsden, former leader of Gerry & the Pacemakers, joined Paul and locals in a rousing singalong; and at ATV's Boreham Wood studios in front of a live audience with Paul and Wings performing 'Big Red Barn', 'The Mess', 'Maybe I'm Amazed' and 'Long Tall Sally'.

Paul also performed a medley of 'Bluebird', 'Michelle', 'Heart of the Country', 'Mary Had a Little Lamb' and 'Yesterday'. Finally, Paul ended the show singing 'Yesterday' to his own acoustic guitar accompaniment.

The show's major number was a Busby Berkeley-style spectacular to the tune of 'Gotta Sing, Gotta Dance', a number Paul had written for Twiggy. This featured a long-haired Paul, with moustache, in a white tail-suit, dancing with a host of showgirls whose costumes and make-up were half-male, half-female.

There were also scenes of Linda taking photographs of Paul and a clip from the James Bond movie *Live and Let Die*. Other numbers in the show were 'Little Woman Love', 'Uncle Albert', 'Another Day', 'Oh Woman Oh Why' and 'Hi Hi Hi'.

The programme was first screened in America on 16 April 1973 and in Britain on 7 June of the same year. Paul was to comment: 'You could say it's fulfilling an old ambition. Right at the start I fancied myself in a musical comedy. But that was before the Beatles. Don't get me wrong. I'm no Astaire or Gene Kelly and this doesn't mean the start of something big. I don't want to be an all-rounder. I'm sticking to what I am.'

Sir Lew also managed to arrange John Lennon's appearance on the television tribute 'Salute To Sir Lew Grade', which was screened on 13 June 1975. However, John produced a sardonic stunt by having the members of Etc, his backing group, wear masks with the large image of a face on the back of their heads.

This gave them the visual effect of having two faces and many people said that this was John's way of calling Sir Lew 'two-faced'. John and his band performed three numbers on the show, 'Slippin' And Slidin'', 'Stand By Me' and 'Imagine'.

Sir Lew died in London on 13 December 1998.

Grafton Ballroom, West Derby Road, Liverpool L6

One of Liverpool's two major ballrooms, along with the Locarno, both situated next to each other in West Derby Road. Both venues were part of the Mecca ballroom chain and the Quarry Men appeared at the Grafton when skiffle contests were held at the venue.

The Beatles first appeared here as a band on 3 August 1962. A local promoter, Albert Kinder, who had previously specialised in jazz concerts, booked a bill of local rock 'n' roll groups, featuring the Beatles, Gerry & the Pacemakers and the Big Three.

Among the group's repertoire at the time were numbers such as 'Darktown Strutters Ball', 'Ain't She Sweet', 'Falling In Love Again', 'Some Other Guy', 'Hey Baby', 'Lay Down Your Arms', 'Don't Ever Change', 'A Picture Of You', 'Besame Mucho', 'I Remember You', 'Shimmy Shimmy', 'A Shot Of Rhythm & Blues', 'Sharing You', 'Mr Moonlight', 'Red Hot', 'Please Mr Postman' and their own 'Love Me Do' and 'P.S. I Love You'.

Their next appearance took place on 10 January 1963 when they topped a bill of five local groups. Their penultimate visit was at a special concert in aid of the National Society For the Prevention of Cruelty to Children on 12 June 1963 and they requested that Bill Harry introduce them on stage. Their final appearance at the venue took place on 2 August 1963.

Granada Cinema, St Peters Street, Bedford

The group made their debut at this venue on Wednesday, 6 February 1963 during their tour with Helen Shapiro. They only made one further appearance at the Granada, which took place the following month on Tuesday, 12 March as part of the Tommy Roe/Chris Montez Tour. John had become the victim of a heavy cold and had to remain in bed. The three remaining Beatles went ahead with the show, although some of John's numbers had to be adapted for Paul or George to take over on lead vocals.

This was the group's first appearance at a Granada cinema and during their career they were to appear at a total of seven different Granada venues.

Granada Cinema, 281 Barking Road, East Ham, London E6

The Beatles appeared here for the first time on Saturday, 9 March 1963. It was the opening date of their second tour, coming five days after the end of their tour with Helen Shapiro. The American singers Tommy Roe and Chris Montez headlined the tour.

The Beatles' repertoire on this tour was: 'Love Me Do', 'Misery', 'A Taste Of Honey', 'Do You Want To Know A Secret?', 'Please Please Me' and 'I Saw Her Standing There'.

Traffic chaos resulted when 6,000 fans gathered outside the cinema on Saturday, 9 November 1963, when the Fab Four were due to appear as part of the autumn tour.

At 3.50 p.m. the Beatles' car sped to the stage door and they began rehearsing and ate cheese sandwiches from the nearby Granada Café. The local newspaper reported: 'Souvenir-hunters mobbed 34-year-old John Perdoni when he left with the dirty cutlery and he had to be rescued by the police. He escaped more lightly when he took them their supper of steak and chips (for Ringo Starr and George Harrison) and egg salad (for Paul McCartney and John Lennon) later in the evening. Nobody noticed as he slipped in the front entrance.'

During the afternoon they were visited by four local office girls who had baked them a cake. They also had several other visitors to their dressing room, including George Martin who was able to tell them that 'I Want To Hold Your Hand' had pre-sales of a million copies – an unprecedented achievement in Britain. John Lennon commented, 'That's great, but how do we top that?' Other guests included Alun Owen in the first of several meetings he had with the boys to discuss the script for *A Hard Day's Night*, Alistair Taylor and the group's press man Tony Barrow.

Their last number came to an end at 11.08 p.m. and they made a dash for it down the stairs to the stage door, into their waiting limousine and sped away.

Paul dropped into the cinema on Saturday, 27 November 1965 to watch the Scaffold make their first appearance on a nationwide tour with the Manfred Mann/Yardbirds package. Paul's brother Mike was a member of the Scaffold.

During the 1970s the cinema was transformed into a bingo hall and social club.

Granada Cinema, West Gate, Mansfield, Nottingham

The Beatles only appeared twice at this venue, both times in 1963. They made their debut at the venue as part of the Helen Shapiro Tour on Saturday, 23 February and returned the next month as part of the Tommy Roe/Chris Montez Tour on Tuesday, 26 March.

Granada Cinema, Castle Gates, Shrewsbury, Shropshire

The Beatles only appeared once at this venue. It took place during their tour with Helen Shapiro on 28 February 1963. This was also the day in which John and Paul composed 'From Me To You' on their way to the gig.

Granada Cinema, Mitcham Road, Tooting, London SW17

The Beatles only appeared once at this London venue, performing two shows on the evening of Saturday, 1 June 1963. Prior to their appearance they had spent eight hours in the studio recording programmes for their radio series 'Pop Go The Beatles'.

Granada Cinema, 186 Hoe Street, Walthamstow, London WE17

Another London venue in the Granada chain where the Beatles first appeared on Friday, 24 May 1963 during their tour with Roy Orbison. They returned the following year on Sunday, 24 October 1964.

On Monday, 28 March 1966, George and Ringo dropped by the cinema to see a Roy Orbison concert performance.

The venue was transformed into a bingo hall and social club in the 1970s.

Granada Cinema, 186 Powis Street, Woolwich, London SE18

The Beatles only made one appearance at this venue, which took place on Monday, 3 June 1963. They were appearing on a bill with Roy Orbison. The cinema became a bingo hall and casino in the 1970s.

Grandstand

A BBC television sports programme. When the Beatles returned from America on the morning of 22 February 1964, they held a press conference in the Kingsford-Smith Suite at Heathrow Airport, which was filmed by BBC TV and included as an excerpt in the 'Grandstand' programme that afternoon.

Grapefruit

John Lennon thought up the name for this group, possibly because *Grapefruit* was the name of a book by Yoko Ono or perhaps because of the fruit association of the Apple organisation.

As Apple Records had not been formed when the Beatles took an interest in the group, they were signed by Apple Publishing and publishing head Terry Doran became their manager.

They comprised George Alexander (bass guitar), John Perry (lead guitar), Pete Swettenham (rhythm guitar), and Geoff Swettenham (drums). Most members of the band had been in the line-up of Tony Rivers & the Castaways, who had been signed to NEMS Enterprises.

They had a minor hit with their first release 'Dear Delilah' on RCA 1656, which reached No. 21 in the British charts in February 1968. On 17 January 1968, the day before the single was released, John, Paul and Ringo attended an RCA reception for the band. Paul McCartney directed a promotional film for Grapefruit's 'Elevator' single, filmed at the Albert Memorial on 26 May 1968. In August of that year they reached No. 25 in the British charts with 'C'mon Marianne', issued on RCA 1716.

Doran was eventually to obtain the group's release from Apple as he said the company wasn't doing enough for the band. They had no further chart success.

Graves, Elsie

Richard 'Ringo' Starkey's late mother. She was one of fourteen children and her maiden name was Gleave. She married Richard Starkey in 1936. Both of them worked in a bakery at the time and after they were married they moved to No. 9 Madryn Street, Dingle, where their son Richard was born on 7 July 1940.

By the time Ringo was three his father had left the family home, although he continued to send a sum of money each week. But it wasn't enough and Elsie had to move to a smaller house in nearby Admiral Grove and take on a job as barmaid, engaging relatives or friends to look after her son who always referred to his mum as Elsie.

Elsie married Harry Graves in 1953 and when Ringo became famous he bought his mother and stepfather a new house in a fashionable area of Liverpool.

Graves, Harry

This Romford-born painter and decorator entered the lives of Ringo and his mother Elsie when Ringo was eleven. Harry moved to

Liverpool to work for Liverpool Corporation. He was introduced to Elsie Starkey by mutual friends, the Maguires. He began dating Elsie and Ringo took to him straight away. The boy was quite pleased when, on 17 April 1953, Harry married his mother and referred to him as his new 'step-ladder'.

The relationship between the boy and his stepfather was very strong and it was Harry who bought Ringo his first drum kit during a visit to Romford. It cost slightly under £10 and Harry lugged it to Liverpool by train. He also persuaded the engineering firm Henry Hunt & Sons to engage Ritchie as a trainee joiner.

When Ritchie, now known as Ringo Starr, wanted to continue playing with groups in Liverpool, Elsie and Harry attempted to persuade him to remain at Hunts, without success.

Once Ringo had become wealthy, he bought Elsie and Harry a bungalow in the Gateacre Park area of Liverpool.

Harry died of pneumonia on Saturday, 27 August 1994 at the age of 87. Ringo and Barbara attended his funeral service at Huyton Cemetery on 1 September.

Green Street, Mayfair, London W1

The Beatles shared an apartment here in an area quite close to Marble Arch, from October 1963 until March 1964, but had to move as they were unable to renew the lease. They'd heard that a flat was available when Brian Epstein moved into Whaddon House in Knightsbridge and Ringo, George and Paul rented the floor below.

Gretty, Jim

The former rotund chief salesman at Frank Hessy's music store, originally based in Whitechapel and then in Stanley Street, Liverpool. He sold guitars and other instruments to most of the Mersey Beatsters in the late 1950s and early 1960s. He obtained the initial job as demonstrator at Hessy's after he suggested to owner Frank Hessy that a good way of selling guitars would be for him to give free lessons to anyone who bought a guitar. So Hessy rented another shop and each Monday Jim would spend an hour and a half teaching a group of thirty to forty youngsters.

It was Jim who sold a guitar to Mimi Smith when she dropped in one day in 1957 with her nephew John Lennon. Jim also acted as a variety agent and was later to book the Beatles on some dates locally, although they weren't on the rock 'n' roll bills the band were used to. They included the variety show at the Albany, Maghull, and the Pavilion Theatre appearance with the Royal Waterford Showband.

Jim was also a performer and was quite well known as a country music singer/guitarist. He offered advice to all the groups and once built a 'wall of fame', a panorama of photographs of all the local bands, which stretched along Hessy's main showroom wall.

He died in 1992 at the age of 78.

Griffiths, Eric

Eric was a neighbour of John Lennon in the Woolton area and was invited to become the original lead guitarist with the Quarry Men. One of the main reasons why he was asked to join the skiffle group was because he had a new guitar and was friendly with a boy called Colin Hanton, who had a new set of drums and could also be enticed to join them.

Once Paul McCartney joined the group, he wanted to take over Eric's position as lead guitarist himself. He tried it once at the Broadway Conservative Club, but it didn't work. By that time the group felt there was a surfeit of guitarists in the group and they wanted George Harrison to become lead guitarist as he was a better player than Eric. They offered Eric the job as bass guitarist, but he couldn't afford to buy the required amplifier, so the group decided he had to go.

Manager Nigel Whalley was told to approach Hanton and tell him of their plans. Eric wasn't invited to Paul's house for their next rehearsal and, when he phoned them during the practice sessions, he was told they didn't want him in the group any more.

Eric was a member of the Quarry Men from March 1957 until mid-1958. At the time he left he was working as an apprentice engineer, but he gave it up to join the Merchant Navy. He got married at the age of 24 and eventually joined Her Majesty's Prison Service, settling in Scotland with his wife and three children in 1972. He became Head of Planning and Production for the Prison Service and later left it to open a dry cleaning chain in Edinburgh, where he now lives.

He was asked to team up with other former Quarry Men members for the 40th anniversary of the opening of the Cavern in 1997 and occasionally appears with the reformed group.

Grosvenor Ballroom, Grosvenor Road, Liscard, Wallasey, Cheshire

Venue run by promoter Les Dodd. When Allan Williams decided to act as an agent for some local bands, Les Dodd was the man he initially arranged some dates for the Silver Beetles with, firstly at the Institute, Wirral, and then at the Grosvenor on Saturday, 4 June

1960. Williams said that their pay was £10, of which he received £1. A further £1 was paid to the bouncer and the balance to the five members of the group: John, Paul, George, Stu Sutcliffe and drummer Tommy Moore.

The group were calling themselves the Silver Beetles at the time and two days later they appeared on a special Monday session to celebrate the Whitsun Bank Holiday on a bill with Gerry & the Pacemakers. The gig ran from 8.00 p.m. to midnight and admission was 3/- (15p).

Their next appearance on 11 June is described in detail in Allan Williams' book *The Man Who Gave The Beatles Away*. Tommy Moore had decided not to play with the group anymore due to his full-time job at the Garston Bottle Works and the protestations of his common law wife. The group arrived at the Grosvenor without a drummer, although their equipment, with Moore's drumkit, had been set up for them. John asked if anyone from the audience would like to join them on drums and a local thug called Ronnie, leader of a gang, volunteered. Unfortunately, he enjoyed the episode so much he wanted to become their permanent drummer. They were afraid of turning him down in case his gang beat them up, so they phoned Allan Williams, who arrived at the ballroom and sorted the situation out.

Tommy Moore was to make one last appearance with them at the Grosvenor.

Their 18 June appearance was on the occasion of Paul McCartney's 18th birthday and they returned to the venue on 25 June.

They appeared there several times in July. On their 2 July gig they were joined on stage by Johnny Gentle, whom they'd recently backed on a tour of Scotland. Other dates included 9, 16, 23 and 30 July.

They were next due to appear on 6 August, but the gig was cancelled. The Grosvenor had a bad reputation because of the rowdiness caused by some of the hooligans who attended the dances. The ballroom was owned by the local council and when residents of Grosvenor Street presented a petition to the council complaining about the noise caused by the dances, they banned further rock sessions from the hall.

The ban was only temporary. The Beatles next appeared at the Grosvenor on 24 February 1961 and their 10 March gig there was the last booking arranged for them by Allan Williams.

Their final appearance there was on Friday, 15 September 1961. The evening session lasted from 7.15 p.m.–11.00 p.m. and the support band was Cliff Roberts & the Rockers, the resident band at the ballroom.

Grosvenor House Hotel, 88–89 Park Lane, London W1

The Beatles appeared on an evening cabaret show in the ballroom of this prestigious hotel in aid of a charity for spastics on Monday, 2 December 1963. They were to perform before an audience in evening dress and were uncomfortable appearing on a cabaret-style bill before such an audience – and were never to appear at a similar engagement again. They performed 'I Saw Her Standing There', 'From Me To You', 'This Boy', 'I Want To Hold Your Hand', 'Till There Was You', 'She Loves You' and 'Twist And Shout'.

Grosvenor Rooms, Prince of Wales Road, Norwich

The Beatles only appeared at this venue once, on Friday, 17 May 1963, the day prior to the opening of their tour with Roy Orbison.

Gruenberg, Erich

Leader of the orchestra of 41 male musicians on the 'Day In The Life' track on the *Sgt Pepper* album. Gruenberg, who had attended the Guildhall School of Music at the same time as George Martin, was one of Europe's foremost violinists and was previously leader of the London Symphony Orchestra and the Royal Philharmonic.

Recording manager George Martin realised that when they recorded the track Gruenberg had a giant monkey's paw on his bow hand and was wearing coloured-paper spectacles, novelties which the Beatles had been handing out to the musicians. They'd done this because the session was being filmed for a proposed TV documentary, which was never completed.

He was to comment: 'The Beatles were very charming and musical, expressing their personalities like all truly successful people by being quite themselves. They had a good spirit and in the studio there was a sense of occasion and momentum . . . They sent me a copy of the record which I still have.'

He also led the musicians on 'She's Leaving Home' and was leader of eight violinists who performed on 'Within You, Without You'.

Grugenhalle, Essen, Nordrhein-Westfalen, Germany

The Beatles left their hotel in Munich to travel in a motorcade in the early morning of 25 June 1966 to the railway station where they boarded the special train which had been used by Queen Elizabeth the previous year on her royal trip to Germany. The group and their party, which included Brian Epstein, Neil Aspinall, Tony Barrow,

Mal Evans and Alf Bicknell, had a suite of rooms aboard the train comprising a large dining-room, lounge and four bedrooms and bathrooms.

The train arrived in Essen at 4.30 p.m. and among the crowd on the platform were three men dressed as barbers, wearing bald-topped wigs and carrying giant combs. The group were driven to the Grugenhalle in a white Mercedes, with a motorcade. They performed two shows and arrived back at the railway station at 12.30 a.m.

Guildhall, The Square, Portsmouth, Hampshire

The Beatles made their debut at this theatre on Saturday, 30 March 1963 as part of the Tommy Roe/Chris Montez Tour. During their autumn tour later that year they were due to appear at the venue on Tuesday, 12 November. They arrived at the venue, but Paul was suffering from an attack of gastric flu and the performance had to be postponed. The Beatles spent the evening at The Royal Beach Hotel in Southsea where a doctor visited Paul, and the group resumed their tour the following day. The Guildhall appearance was re-scheduled for Tuesday, 3 December 1963.

Guitar Boogie

Composition by Arthur Smith, recorded by Arthur Smith & his Crackerjacks in 1946. The Quarry Men used the instrumental in their repertoire between 1957 and 1959.

Haig Dance Club, Haig Avenue, Moreton, Wirral, Lancashire

Venue 'over the water' from Liverpool, on the Wirral peninsula, where the Quarry Men appeared for a single performance one Friday night in November 1957.

Hair Style

The hair style developed by the Beatles didn't raise any eyebrows on Merseyside, where it wasn't actually radically different from the hair style of the other local groups. It barely raised attention in the British media once Beatlemania began to sweep the country (although in their first national newspaper story in London's *Evening Standard*, Maureen Cleave mentioned their 'weird' hair: 'French styling, with the fringe brushed forwards') but it caused a sensation in America when the Beatles arrived there in 1964. The affectionate term 'Moptops' was created and almost every comedian in the country cracked gags about the hair style. Hundreds of thousands of Beatles wigs were manufactured and it eventually led to the American youth growing their hair longer than had been previously acceptable for the young male.

The hair style caused amusement in various countries and in Sweden it was referred to as the 'Hamlet' cut while in Germany it was described as a 'mushroom'.

It is generally acknowledged that the style was first developed in 1961 by Stuart Sutcliffe's girlfriend Astrid Kirchherr. Mrs Millie

Sutcliffe commented: 'As for the haircut, it started when Stuart's hair was falling down and sticking out. One night Astrid had been moaning about his hair and then took him into the bathroom and cut it.'

Hunter Davies, in his authorised biography of the Beatles, corroborates this version: 'It was at this time [1960–1961] that Astrid got round to telling Stu that she didn't like his greasy, Teddy boy hair style. She said he would suit the sort of style that Klaus [Voormann] and Jurgen [Vollmer] had. After a lot of persuading, Stu let her do a special style for him. She brushed it all down, snipped bits off and tidied it up.

'Stu turned up at the Top Ten that evening with his hair in the new style, and the others collapsed on the floor with hysterics. Halfway through he gave up and combed his hair high. But thanks to Astrid, he tried it again the next night. He was ridiculed again, but the night after, George turned up with the same style. Then Paul had a go, though for a long time he was always changing it back to the old style as John hadn't yet made up his mind. Pete Best ignored the whole craze. But the Beatle hair style had been born.' Pete didn't adopt the style simply because he didn't think it suited him, but would have adopted it if asked. Years later he was to wonder if this was one of the reasons why he was sacked.

Philip Norman, in his book *Shout!*, had this to say: 'She [Astrid] did away with his Teddy boy hair style, cutting it short like hers, then shaping it to lie across the forehead in what was called the French cut, although high-class German boys had worn a similar style since the days of Bismarck.'

Ray Coleman, in his book *John Winston Lennon*, covers the incident in detail: 'Tired of the fast-scissored, traditional formula of Hamburg hairdressers and looking for something that would emulate her own sense of the eccentric, Astrid had cut Klaus's hair for years. She never combed his hair backwards, always out from the side, and it was always longer than the accepted length ... Stuart, the first to have his hair cut and styled by Astrid, faced John's scorn when, one night, he arrived at the club for work with what later became known as the Beatle haircut ... Paul, always more conscious than the others about his appearance, was the next to ask Astrid to style his hair ... John was the last Beatle to succumb to the Beatle cut. Only Pete Best declined, retaining his quiff and Teddy boy aura that attracted the girls.'

Jurgen Vollmer, one of the students in Hamburg who befriended the Beatles, puts forward his own claim in his book *Rock 'n' Roll Times*: 'When I moved to Paris in late 1961, John and Paul visited me and decided to have their hair like mine. A lot of French youth wore it that way. I gave both of them their first "Beatles" haircut in my hotel room on the Left Bank.'

As a joke, George Harrison once told a reporter that it was the result of the way their hair fell after being in the local swimming baths. The story was taken as fact!

The Beatles never wore wigs, but Beatle wigs were manufactured in vast quantities in America – although they looked more like the hair style of Mo Howard of the Three Stooges than the Beatles style, and when the group first arrived in America photographers and journalists kept tugging their hair, asking them if they were wearing wigs.

The wigmania took off when the Beatles made their February 1964 visit to America. The media seemed obsessed with the hair style. New York radio station WMCA ran a competition for listeners to paint or draw someone in a Beatlewig – either celebrity pictures clipped from newspapers or photos of friends. The most popular subjects were: Nikita Krushchev, Mayor Wagner, Alfred E. Newman (of *Mad* magazine), Brigitte Bardot and the Jolly Green Giant.

Capitol Records instructed all their sales staff to wear Beatle wigs during the working day until further notice and issued a memo: 'Get these Beatle wigs around properly, and you'll find yourself helping to start the Beatle Hair-Do craze that should be sweeping the country soon.'

When the group held their first American press conference, they were asked questions such as 'Will you be getting a haircut?' and 'What's the greatest threat to your career – dandruff or nuclear warfare?' Such questions continued throughout the press conferences that year during their autumn tour: 'What excuse do you have for your collar-length hair?' 'What do you do with your long hair in the shower?' 'Do you have any plans for a haircut?' 'Does your hair require any special care?' and so on. When Paul was asked 'Do you ever go unnoticed?' he replied, 'When we take off our wigs.'

When they arrived in America in February, the *New York Herald Tribune* reported: 'The Beatles' hairstyle is a mop effect that covers the forehead, some of the ears and most of the back of the neck.'

An example of the way in which the Beatles altered the style and fashions of the sixties is provided by the fact that the male youth of America began to grow their hair long, in contrast to the almost military short back and sides of previous years.

Hallelujah, I Love Her So

Number composed by Ray Charles and recorded by him in 1956. It was also recorded by Eddie Cochran in 1960 and he promoted it when he was in Britain in March of that year, shortly before his death. Ray Charles was popular among Liverpool bands and several of them included the number in their repertoire. The Beatles included it in their stage act, with Paul McCartney on lead vocals. However, when the number was recorded at the Star Club in December 1962, a friend of the Beatles, Horst Fascher, sang the lead vocal with them and it is this version which is to be found on the album *The Beatles Live! At The Star Club In Hamburg, Germany: 1962*. A version appeared on the Beatles' *Anthology 1* CDs.

Hambleton Hall, St David Road, Page Moss, Huyton, Liverpool 14

Situated in the suburbs of Liverpool, this large hall was booked by freelance promoters to present local bands.

Wednesdays, Saturdays and, occasionally, Sundays were the main evenings on which dances took place. Bob Wooler ran a few free-lance promotions of his own at the venue and remembers the time the Beatles told the audience to go out and buy their German single 'My Bonnie'.

Paul McCartney remembers it as a rough place. He commented, 'They used fire extinguishers on each other one night there. When we played "Hully Gully". That used to be one of the tunes which ended in fighting.'

Wally Hill and Vic Anton were two promoters who booked groups regularly at the venue and they booked the Beatles through the 1961 period. Billed as 'The Sensational Beatles', they made their debut at the hall on 25 January 1961 on a bill with Derry & the Seniors and Faron & the Tempest Tornadoes. Their subsequent appearances that year took place on 1, 8, 15 and 22 February; 8 and 20 March; 3 and 17 September; 15 and 29 October; 12 and 26 November; and 10 December. Their last appearance at the venue took place on 13 January 1962. Hambleton Hall later became a Probation Office.

Hamburg, Germany

Interestingly enough, Hamburg, the largest city in West Germany, is on the same latitude as Liverpool – 53 degrees north. Like Liverpool it is a major seaport, and lies on the River Elbe.

Unlike Liverpool, Hamburg had no thriving music scene in 1960 when the Beatles first appeared there. The St Pauli district, a large red-light area of the city, was an area of sex and violence, with clubs catering for the sexual needs of visitors – strip joints, female mud wrestling, nude circuses and so on.

Through a set of circumstances Bruno Koschmider, who owned

two strip clubs, the Kaiserkeller and the Indra, began booking groups into his clubs in 1960. The first group he booked following a visit to London was called the Jets, the other was Liverpool's Derry & the Seniors. Liverpool club owner Allan Williams arranged with Koschmider for the Beatles to appear at one of the Hamburg venues from August 1960. Believing they were appearing at the Kaiserkeller, they were disappointed to end up in a much smaller club called the Indra. They were the only rock 'n' roll group to perform at the former strip club, which was closed by the police at the beginning of October that year. The Beatles then appeared at the Kaiserkeller from 4 October until 30 November, second on the bill to another Liverpool band, Rory Storm & the Hurricanes, whose drummer was Ringo Starr. On 15 October, John, Paul and George, with Ringo on drums, made a recording of the number 'Summertime' at the small Akustik Studios, near to Hamburg's main rail station.

Hamburg had no real competition to offer the Beatles as, unlike Liverpool, there were few rock 'n' roll musicians. The Jets, with their lead vocalist/guitarist Tony Sheridan, were the only non-Liverpool band they encountered and they were, to some extent, influenced by Sheridan. He was nicknamed 'the Teacher' by the Liverpool bands, who were impressed by his stage style.

The most important consequence of their appearances in Hamburg was that it completely transformed the group's stage show. Koschmider, with his constant appeals for them to 'make a show', and the extremely long hours of playing they were contracted to, led the Beatles to develop an act.

There were other bonuses resulting from their Hamburg visits. Their visual look changed. Their 'teddy boy' image was to be replaced with the 'rocker' image when they bought leather jackets and trousers in the Reeberbahn and their 'teddy boy' hair styles were to be replaced by what was to become their trademark hair style. A group of Hamburg students, including Astrid Kirchherr, Klaus Voormann and Jurgen Vollmer, became firm fans of the group and bass guitarist Stuart Sutcliffe decided to remain in Hamburg, study art and marry Astrid. His days in the group were already numbered, though, as Paul McCartney wanted to take over his spot as bass guitarist.

The second Hamburg rock 'n' roll club, the Top Ten, opened in October 1960 and the Jets were the first band to be booked there. The owner, Peter Eckhorn, booked the Beatles to replace them immediately following their Kaiserkeller season. Koschmider discovered this and was furious. His contract stated that the Beatles could not appear at another venue within 40 miles of his clubs and he even made threats of physical violence to them. They didn't take much notice of this because Horst Fascher, the former 'minder' at the Kaiserkeller, had now moved to the Top Ten and they were under his protection.

Koschmider was revenged. The under-aged George Harrison was deported and Pete Best and Paul McCartney were also sent back to Liverpool for allegedly trying to 'burn down' Koschmider's cinema, the Bambi Kino.

It was an indication of the fact that the Beatles were still relatively unknown in their own home of Liverpool when they were billed as 'direct from Hamburg' on a Litherland Town Hall appearance on 27 December 1960 – many of the girls in the audience thought they were a German group and were impressed at their grasp of the English language! This particular gig proved to be a sensation, established them locally and was an indication of just how well the long hours of playing in the German city had improved their act.

Their second trip to Hamburg commenced with appearances at the Top Ten Club from 27 March 1961. Koschmider's brief flirtation with rock 'n' roll had ended. The Indra had reverted to a strip club when the Beatles had left the previous October and the Kaiserkeller was also to revert back to a strip club called the Colibri.

The appearances at the Top Ten were much more fun than the Kaiserkeller. The money and accommodation were better, for a start, and Peter Eckhorn was much more sympathetic to the needs of the musicians than Koschmider. The group performed from 7.00 p.m. until 2.00 a.m. with a fifteen-minute break each hour. George Harrison commented, 'We performed like a gang of lunatics. It was all right once we got the hang of it all and it was great fun. The boss would send up cups of coffee on stage and we'd take turns to take a nap.' There was a curfew in the St Pauli district and after 10.00 p.m. no one under the age of eighteen was allowed in the area. Paul McCartney was to say, 'We'd try out my sort of numbers from the Top Twenty. In a way it was marvellous – simply because we could experiment. Tired? We were dead whacked but we got great kicks out of watching the audiences, seeing the way they reacted to different gear.'

Their Top Ten contract was extended twice and they performed there for 98 nights. During this time they built up a great following in Hamburg and also made their first recordings for an established recording company when they backed Tony Sheridan during some recording sessions with A&R man Bert Kaempfert in May 1961. They only received a session fee rather than royalties and the recordings have been released and re-released on a regular basis ever since. It was during this trip to Hamburg that Stuart officially left the group and his position was taken over by Paul.

Their third visit to Hamburg found them appearing at a third venue, the Star Club. By this time the group were under the management of Brian Epstein and despite Peter Eckhorn's attempts to book them for the Top Ten Club, the proprietor of the Star Club, Manfred Weissleder, was the one to agree to pay Epstein's demand for an increased fee. Weissleder's right hand man was once again Horst Fascher, who had been the Beatles' friend when he worked for Koschmider, then Eckhorn and then Weissleder. The Star Club was the best of the Hamburg venues, specially catering for the audiences who wanted the best in rock 'n' roll. Weissleder was prepared to pay what was needed to attract the best names and apart from booking all the major Liverpool bands, he also engaged the leading American names – Little Richard, the Everly Brothers, Gene Vincent. For a brief time, the Star Club was the greatest rock 'n' roll venue in the world. The Beatles' first appearance there lasted for seven weeks from 13 April to 31 May 1962. During their appearances there they shared the bill with Little Richard and Gene Vincent.

The Beatles appeared for their second visit to the Star Club later the same year, from 1 to 14 November 1962. It was a brief appearance as the band were now becoming a major name in Britain and they were to perform their third and final visit at the Star Club between 18 and 31 December 1962. It was during this visit that Adrian Barber recorded them on tape, resulting in albums of material of their performances at the Star Club being released for decades later – although Barber never received either acknowledgement or remuneration for his efforts.

Their club days in Hamburg were over, although the Hamburg scene was of less importance than their grounding in Liverpool. The Hamburg scene was not unique – merely three main clubs (ignoring the Indra), over a short period of time. The long hours in the clubs made the group a fòrce to be reckoned with, it was their 'baptism of fire'. But it would have meant nothing if there hadn't been that vital scene in Liverpool with hundreds of groups performing in hundreds of venues from the mid-fifties.

The handful of Hamburg clubs glittered brightly for a few years in the sixties, providing work for dozens of British groups, mainly from Liverpool, but also including groups from various parts of Britain including Cliff Bennett & the Rebel Rousers, Alex Harvey, Dave Dee, the Fortunes, Bern Elliot and the Fenmen and others.

The only other appearance the Beatles were to make in Hamburg was at the Ernst Merck Halle on 26 June 1966 during a brief tour of West Germany, Japan and the Philippines. That evening, many old friends dropped by to see them.

Yet another dimension to the Hamburg experience was that the young men from a relatively inhibited environment were plunged

478   HAMILTON, DAVID

into a situation in which there were no restrictions regarding drugs and sex. During their period in Hamburg the members of the group (with the exception of Pete Best) took pills such as Preludin and Captogen and indulged in sex almost nightly with a variety of females ranging from girl fans to prostitutes.

They also witnessed violence of a kind which was even more outlandish than in the violent city of Liverpool – muggings, gas guns, clients in the audience being beaten with clubs, and so on. This obviously had some effect on the band mentally.

A detailed account of their days in Hamburg is to be found in Pete Best's autobiography *Beatle!*.

Hamilton, David

A well-established British disc jockey/compere who, because of his diminutive size, was nicknamed 'Diddy' by Ken Dodd.

In 1963, Hamilton worked for ABC TV in Manchester, whose area covered part of the north of England and the Midlands. The company was based in Didsbury, Manchester, and Hamilton was a continuity announcer when he was given the job of interviewing the Beatles for a special edition of 'ABC At Large'. At the Didsbury Studios on Saturday, 2 March, during his late night talk show, he interviewed Brian Epstein, the Beatles and Gerry and the Pacemakers. Also included in the programme was a conversation he had with Bob Wooler which had been filmed during a visit to the Cavern.

In his book, *The Music Game,* Hamilton wrote: 'Brian was charming and articulate, but Messrs Lennon, McCartney, Harrison and Starr were a different story. They acted as though they were above it all. Other groups were pleased to be on TV to advertise their wares, the Beatles' attitude was clearly that they didn't need it. Lennon, in particular, was prickly and difficult with a sarcastic wit. Between them, they made me understand the problems of one man trying to interview four when they are not keen to co-operate.'

Kennedy Street Enterprises paid Hamilton 10 guineas (£10.50) to compere a Beatles show at Urmston on Monday, 5 August 1963.

In the 1980s, Hamilton began regular broadcasting with Capital Radio, London's major radio station, and he included a special 'Beatle Break' in his show several times a week.

Hamilton, Richard

An artist, who had studied at the Royal Academy and Slade School, who was credited with the invention of 'Pop Art'. Robert Fraser introduced him to the Beatles. Following the success of the *Sgt Pepper* sleeve designed by Peter Blake, Paul McCartney figured they could seek their next sleeve design concept from another established artist.

They had already engaged several artists to come up with ideas for an album that they were originally going to call *A Doll's House*. They then found that a British band called Family had used a similar title for their latest album, *Music In A Doll's House*.

One designer suggested a transparent cover that revealed a colour photograph each time the record was taken out of the sleeve.

Fraser showed the Beatles a sample of Hamilton's work – a collage he'd made of newspaper clippings concerning the Rolling Stones' drug trial.

Paul immediately suggested to Hamilton, who was 45 years old at the time, that he should do something similar as the cover of their new album. Instead, Hamilton suggested that they opt for stark simplicity by having a plain white cover. He also suggested that each copy of the album be numbered to produce the effect of a limited edition and that they should include a collage of the Beatles, which would be autobiographical.

Hamilton also asked if they had released an album simply called *The Beatles*. They hadn't, so it was decided to use the name as the double album title.

All his suggestions were taken up and the plain white sleeve had the name *The Beatles* embossed on it and an individual serial number, which is why it became known as the white album.

Inside the sleeve was the poster collage and four colour photographs of the individual Beatles, taken by John Kelly. The collage was as Hamilton had suggested. He'd asked Paul to collect a sample of Beatles pictures and Neil Aspinall and Mal Evans assembled a selection of old photographs which Jeremy Banks co-ordinated into the overall design.

Paul took all the photographs up to the Highgate house where Hamilton lived with his girlfriend Christine and they worked for a few days in his studio, placing the photos in a line on a ten-foot long table until the final design of the collage was realised.

One of the photographs was a tiny shot of Paul in the nude, although he is discreetly posed behind a white column. This caused an outcry in the British press with headlines such as 'Paul goes nude.' Derek Taylor was furious and commented, 'All this work, all these tracks, all this talent – and all their dirty little minds focus on is one tiny picture.' Strangely, the press ignored a far larger picture in the collage of John in the nude.

Hamp, Johnny

At the time the Beatles released their first British single, 'Love Me Do', Johnny Hamp was a producer at Granada Television, a station which was transmitted over a large area of Lancashire. He first booked the Beatles on his 'People And Places' programme on 17 December 1962 and used the group regularly.

A few years later he was to comment: 'I first saw the Beatles in a club in Hamburg. They were very scruffy characters but they had a beat in their music which I liked.'

Coincidentally, it was on 17 December (1965 this time) that Johnny produced his most ambitious Beatles enterprise, a major TV special called 'The Music Of Lennon & McCartney'.

In 1982, when he was Granada's Head of Light Entertainment, he intended to produce a show to tie in with the 20th anniversary of the 'Love Me Do' release. He found such a wealth of interesting material in the archives that the programme wasn't finished until 1983 and, under the title 'The Early Beatles', was first broadcast on 1 January 1984.

Hanover Grand Banqueting Suite, Mayfair, London W1

Venue booked by the Beatles for a special Christmas party for forty of their fan club secretaries from all parts of Britain. The event took place on Sunday, 17 December 1967, and was attended by John and George who had just returned from Paris where they had been visiting the Maharishi. Ringo was on his way back from Rome where he'd been filming *Candy* and Paul was in Scotland. The fan club secretaries, apart from enjoying the company of John and George and special guests such as Spencer Davis, were treated to a preview screening of *Magical Mystery Tour* prior to its debut on BBC Television. As an added bonus they were also shown the film *The Beatles At Shea Stadium*.

Hanson, Wendy

Personal assistant to Brian Epstein. Wendy was born in Huddersfield and was a cousin of financier Lord Hanson.

She was efficient, discreet, could type 90 words a minute and wrote 140 words a minute in shorthand. Her qualifications took her to New York at the age of eighteen where she worked as secretary to conductor Leopold Stokowski for two and a half years. She also acted as temporary secretary to President Kennedy.

It was while he was in America in 1964 that Epstein asked Capitol Records to provide him with an English secretary during his thirteen-day stay. Wendy was working for Gian-Carlo Menotti at the time, but agreed to take up the temporary post and joined Brian at the Plaza Hotel. She was approximately the same age as

Brian and he was impressed with her authority and efficiency, with the result that when he needed a personal assistant the following year, he offered her the position.

Epstein often chastised members of his staff, depending on his mood. Some were able to take the insults, others weren't and, over a period of years, a number of his staff left following disagreements with him.

Brian had berated his personal assistant Derek Taylor in front of a number of friends over a trivial incident regarding a ride in a limousine. Taylor, feeling that this was one humiliating scene too many, resigned. This gave Epstein the opportunity to hire Hanson and he contacted her and offered her £2,000 a year to work for him. She accepted and returned from America to work in the Argyle Street offices of NEMS on 12 October 1964. On that same day Epstein had written a letter to Taylor which read, in part: 'I write now to advise you of the appointment of Miss Wendy Hanson as my personal assistant. Miss Hanson assumes her responsibilities in this capacity from today, Monday October 12th ... at this stage I must advise you that I will appreciate your understanding it is necessary that you relinquish your duties as personal assistant, and at the same time I will be most grateful if you can give to Miss Hanson your co-operation and help, in order that she may smoothly settle in to this position.'

The reason why Wendy decided to join Epstein at this time was because of an ill-fated affair she'd had. A change of scene was needed.

However, just like Derek Taylor, Brian Somerville and so many other associates of Brian's, she found that his tantrums led him to insult his aides over often trivial items and she quit her post as personal assistant several times. On each occasion he refused to accept her letters of resignation, would take her out to dinner and then talk her out of it.

It was Wendy who suggested he move into his own office at Hille House in Stafford Street and, while there, she also became personal assistant to the Beatles.

However, Brian's whims, moods and tantrums proved too much even for her to cope with. One evening he phoned her at 10.00 p.m. to say that he'd lost the address of a recording studio he was due to be at. Then he began shouting at her over the phone. She told him she wasn't his nanny and refused to put up with his attitude any longer. She sent in her letter of resignation the next day and went to work for film producer David Puttnam. This was in December 1966. She'd worked for Brian for three years. The Beatles sent her a farewell gift and Brian wrote her a letter and requested that they keep in touch. A few months later he phoned her and asked if she could get permission to use images of certain famous people on the cover of the *Sgt Pepper* album. She did.

In 1991 she was injured falling down the stairs at her home in Cortona, Italy, and failed to regain consciousness. She died on 27 January. She was 56 years old.

Hanton, Colin

An apprentice upholsterer in 1958 when he was asked to join the Quarry Men. The group only wanted him as a member because he'd bought a new drum kit for £38 on hire purchase from Hessy's. His father was manager of a co-operative shop and the group often practised at his house on Saturday afternoons.

Colin liked to drink Black Velvet (a mixture of Guinness and mild bitter) and although he was two years older than the other members of the group he was so small that he looked younger than he was and always carried his birth certificate around to enable him to drink in pubs.

Early in 1959 the group were booked by George Harrison's father to appear at the Picton Lane Busmen's Social Club Saturday night dance in Wavertree. Mr Harrison, who was master of ceremonies for the evening, had told them that the manager of a local cinema would be dropping in to watch them play with a view to giving them a series of bookings in the intervals between films.

During the interval the boys went to the bar and had too many pints to drink, with the result that they gave a disastrous performance and heard no more from the cinema manager. On the way home, the upset Hanton had a furious argument with the others and decided he'd never play with them again. He got off the bus with his drums before he'd even reached his own stop and the other members of the Quarry Men never saw him again.

Happiness Is A Warm Gun

John Lennon composition which was Paul McCartney's favourite number on *The Beatles* double album.

George Martin showed John the cover of an American gun magazine which had the caption 'Happiness is a warm gun in your hand'. John thought it was an outrageous title. 'A warm gun means that you've just shot something,' he said.

Originally, the song was put together from three unfinished songs John had worked on. Although the themes of the songs were completely different, he managed to weld them together into this number.

When discussing the song he said, 'I think it's a beautiful song. I like all the different things that are happening in it. Like "God", I had put together some three sections of different songs, it was meant to be – it seemed to run through all the different kinds of rock music.'

The song was banned by the BBC because they thought there was sexual symbolism in the number. Members of the media speculated that the 'H' in happiness stood for heroin.

John said, 'It wasn't about "H" at all.'

A version of the number was included on the Beatles' *Anthology 3* CDs.

Hard Day's Night, A (Album)

The soundtrack album for the Beatles' debut film *A Hard Day's Night* was issued in Britain on Parlophone PCS 3058 on 10 August 1964 and reached No. 1 in the charts.

The album contained thirteen new Lennon & McCartney numbers and was the only album to feature Lennon & McCartney songs exclusively. Several numbers which appeared on the actual film soundtrack weren't included on the album, including 'I Wanna Be Your Man', 'All My Loving', 'She Loves You' and George Harrison's 'Don't Bother Me'.

The album also contained some numbers which weren't featured in the film.

The track listing on the British release was, Side One: 'A Hard Day's Night', 'I Should Have Known Better', 'If I Fell', 'I'm Happy Just To Dance With You', 'And I Love Her', 'Tell Me Why' and 'Can't Buy Me Love'. Side Two: 'Any Time At All', 'I'll Cry Instead', 'Things We Said Today', 'When I Get Home', 'You Can't Do That' and 'I'll Be Back'.

In America the album was issued by United Artists on UAS 6366 on 26 June 1964. This version included only numbers which were featured in the actual film, together with a number of instrumental tracks by the George Martin Orchestra.

The track listing was, Side One: 'A Hard Day's Night', 'Tell Me Why', 'I'll Cry Instead', 'I Should Have Known Better' (George Martin Orchestra), 'I'm Happy Just To Dance With You' and 'And I Love Her' (George Martin Orchestra). Side Two: 'I Should Have Known Better', 'If I Fell', 'And I Love Her', 'Ringo's Theme' (George Martin Orchestra), 'Can't Buy Me Love', 'A Hard Day's Night' (George Martin Orchestra).

Capitol Records were to use three tracks from the British *A Hard Day's Night* soundtrack on their *Something New* album: 'Things We Said Today', 'Any Time At All' and 'When I Get Home'.

Hard Day's Night, A (Film)

In 1963 Capitol Records in America were still refusing to issue Beatles products. Noel Rodgers, the British representative for

United Artists Records, was witnessing Beatlemania first-hand in London and was convinced that it would inevitably reach the States. He approached Bud Ornstein, the British production head of United Artists' film division, with the suggestion that they offer the Beatles a three-picture deal in order to obtain three Beatles soundtracks. They were both primarily interested in obtaining the Beatles on record for UA and didn't initially realise how big the films would be.

Because of this they opted for a cheap budget and approached Walter Shenson who'd been making low-budget films in Britain, asking him to produce. Shenson chose **Dick Lester** as his director.

When the meeting to discuss the deal was arranged with Brian Epstein, Ornstein and Shenson had agreed that they would be prepared to give the Beatles 25 per cent of the net profits. They were surprised when Epstein said, immediately, 'I wouldn't consider anything under 7.5 per cent.' Fortunately, when the final contracts came to be signed, the Beatles' lawyer David Jacobs had renegotiated the deal for 25 per cent, although it would have been more lucrative to have asked for a percentage of the gross as opposed to net, due to the reputation the film world had for creative accounting.

In an *Evening Standard* interview, Shenson commented: 'Now I've got the Beatles, do I need stars? Are they necessary, even playing bit parts? My guess is, no. It would be all wrong to have say Kenny More or Dirk Bogarde appearing with the boys, though maybe not Margaret Rutherford. I have a hunch the fans would love her. But say, just say, it was Hayley Mills, will they feel resentment of her?'

A teenage daughter of a friend then said to him, 'Oh Mr Shenson, I'm just praying there'll be no love interest in your Beatles film!' He took the girl's advice and decided not to include any romances for the Beatles. He also eschewed big name stars, giving the largest non-Beatles role to Wilfred Brambell, known for his leading role in the BBC TV sit-com 'Steptoe And Son'. Others in the cast included Liverpudlian actor Norman Rossington as Norm, the group's road manager (a role said to be based on Neil Aspinall, who was to marry Bud Ornstein's daughter several years later).

Rossington was to tell *Beatles Monthly*: 'I've never before met a bunch of characters who are so obviously interested in everything going on around them. Always a smile for the lowlier characters on the film set. Always a quick gag if there was any hold-up.'

Another Liverpool-born actor was Deryck Guyler, who portrayed a police sergeant. Actor John Junkin portrayed the group's second road manager, Shake, and Kenneth Haigh, who played the part of Simon, an advertising executive, didn't want his name in the film's credits. Shenson explained, 'He's a Shakespearean actor and, like a lot of established people back then, he didn't want to be associated with the Beatles. He got a lot of money for one day's work and we agreed not to use his name. But today he lists *A Hard Day's Night* in his credits wherever he goes.'

Victor Spinetti was cast as a manic television director and he was to appear in further Beatles projects. Anna Quayle appeared as Millie and a touch of glamour was added with the casting of ex-Miss World, Rosemarie Frankland, as a showgirl. Margaret Rutherford, who'd appeared in both of Shenson's 'Mouse' movies, didn't appear in *A Hard Day's Night*, but visited the set and told Shenson: 'I'm so glad you're making a film about the Beatles. They're my favourite group.' George Harrison was to return the compliment when he told a 'Ready, Steady, Go!' audience that Margaret Rutherford was his favourite actress.

George, in fact, benefited in many ways from this first film. He'd always felt slightly awed by the talent of John and Paul and, added to the fact that he was the youngest member of the group, had tended to stay in the background at interviews; yet he proved to be a natural actor. Shenson said: 'George came along well with his acting, so I asked the writer for another short scene for him because I liked his "shirt scene". He [the writer] came up with the "shaving scene". The art director put a bath tub in, so I said to the director, 'Why don't we put John in the bath?" ' He didn't have any dialogue, but the scene became John's instead of George's.

George also met his future wife on the set. There were four schoolgirls featured in an early scene: Pattie Boyd, Tina Williams, Pru Bury and Susan Whitman. Pattie was a model who had appeared in a series of Smiths Crisps TV ads directed by Dick Lester, who had hired her for the Beatles' movie. George seemed enchanted by her from the moment he met her and a real-life romance began which more than made up for the one aspect the movie noticeably lacked.

The film was budgeted at £200,000, the production company was Proscenium Films and Shenson's production assistant was Dennis O'Dell. It was decided to film in black and white and Robert Freeman, the group's photographer friend, was hired to create the title sequence, while George Martin was appointed musical director. He provided instrumental versions of 'This Boy', 'I Should Have Known Better', 'And I Love Her' and 'A Hard Day's Night'. The director of photography was Gilbert Taylor and the scriptwriter was Alun Owen.

Walter Shenson was to comment: 'I don't want to take anything from Dick [Lester] who did a terrific job, but I don't think enough credit has been given to Alun's script. Everyone assumed we just got the Beatles together and winged it. Actually, the film was very tightly scripted and not improvised at all. So much of the idiom that became famous – like George's use of the word "grotty" for grotesque – were Alun's inventions.'

The other major contributor to the film's success was, of course, director Richard Lester, who had previously worked with Shenson on the pop film *It's Trad, Dad*, starring Helen Shapiro, whom the Beatles had backed on their first major British tour.

The official announcement about the making of the film was given in December 1963. Shooting began on 2 March 1964 and lasted for two months. Twickenham Studios, Middlesex, was the setting for the interior scenes and location shooting took place at several sites in the London area. The Beatles are shown at Marylebone Station at the beginning of the film where they are pursued by hordes of fans, causing them to make an ingenious escape by dodging through the doors of taxis. St Margaret's Field in Gatwick was used for the scene in which they engage in a bit of horseplay during a break in rehearsals for their TV show. It was also where the final scene – in which the boys are picked up by a helicopter – was filmed.

The Scala Theatre in Charlotte Street, London, was the setting for their performance before an audience on the television show. (In fact the group actually performed to rows of empty seats. The audience was admitted after the group had left the theatre and did all their screaming to a film of the Beatles' performance.)

The street scenes and police station sequences were filmed in Clarendon Road in Notting Hill Gate. The train sequences were filmed over six days, mainly on the route between London and Minehead; during this period the cast and crew travelled approximately 2,500 miles by train. The scenes of Ringo by himself were filmed in Kew and the pub scene was shot in an actual pub near Twickenham Studios, where most of the movie was filmed.

The guards-van scene in which the Beatles perform 'I Should Have Known Better' in front of four schoolgirls, was filmed in the studios, among crates of live chickens. It had been suggested at one time that the chickens should be let loose during the sequence, but it was felt that they might end up stealing the scene!

Among the many suggestions for a title were: *What Little Old Man?*, this is one of the first sentences uttered in the film; *Beatlemania*, a term which, by then, was gaining widespread usage; *On The Move*; *It's A Daft, Daft, Daft, Daft, Daft World*; *Travelling On*; *Moving On* and *Let's Go*. Reports at the time all claimed that the title *A Hard Day's Night* had come from Ringo. *Beatles Monthly*, for instance, wrote: 'Ringo hit on *A Hard Day's Night*. Earlier, he'd been asked if he'd had a haircut and said, "No, it's the same difference." He often comes out with strangely worded quotes. And after a long day's work, as the hands on the clock reached into the early hours, he said casually, "Boy, this has been a hard day's night".'

Walter Shenson also credited Ringo as the person who thought up the title. However, in John Lennon's first book *In His Own Write*, published on 23 March 1964, there is a story called 'Sad Michael' in which John wrote: 'He'd had a hard day's night that day, for Michael was a Cocky Watchtower.'

Although Alun Owen had tried to ensure that all four received an equal share of the action, it was Ringo's role which seemed to catch the critics' attention. George also had an interesting scene in an advertising agency. A sequence featuring Paul was cut from the finished film. He had appeared with Isla Blair who was dressed as a Shakespearean actress, but it ended up on the cutting room floor because it was felt that Paul had been too self-conscious.

The scene occurred following George's adventure in the advertising agency and his confrontation with the teenage model Susan Campey. Paul has set out in search of Ringo who has managed to get himself lost. Paul wanders around the Notting Hill area, coming across an old church hall that sports a sign 'TV Rehearsal Room'. A group of figures dressed in costume emerge and pass him. He enters and notices a girl moving about the huge room. She is dressed in theatrical costume and is quoting Shakespeare. After some moments, the girl notices Paul and pauses in her speech. He asks her to continue but she tells him to go away as he's spoiled her solitary rehearsal. He remains and begins to chat with her, although she tells him he'll be thrown out when the others return. She guesses he's from Liverpool and they then discuss acting, although Paul admits he's only done Shakespeare in a school play.

She tells him she likes acting for herself and he considers such an attitude to be selfish, telling her that actors and actresses should act for an audience. He tells her that he'd approach her part acting in the manner of a Liverpool scrubber. He points out that this is a clearer way of explaining the character of the role she has been rehearsing. Paul has to utter such lines as: 'I know your sort – two Cokes and a packet of cheese and onion crisps and suddenly it's love and we're stopping in an empty street doorway. Gerrout of it! Ah, you're lonely all right, you're smashin', but come round here and tell all that to me Mum – you won't, will you? You're just after me body and you can't have it, so there!' Paul remembers his

mission to find Ringo and says his farewells. As he leaves he hears
the actress return to the rather artificial voice she'd been using when
he first heard on her rehearsal. Then she pauses and begins again,
using a much more naturalistic mode of speech, just as Paul had
suggested.

The basic story of the film, as outlined in a synopsis by United
Artists at the time of the release, is as follows:

'Once upon a time there were four happy Liverpool lads called Paul,
John, George and Ringo and they played their music all over the
country. Now, when they'd finished playing in one place they'd run to
the nearest railway station and go on to a new place to play some more
of their music, usually pursued by hundreds of young ladies.

'On the day of our story, John, George and Ringo get to the
station and fight their way into the railway compartment where
they meet up with Paul, who has a little old man with him, a very
dear little old man. Anyway, who is he? The little old man is
"mixing" John McCartney, Paul's grandfather (Wilfred Brambell).
Grandfather is dedicated to the principle of divide and conquer. The
mere sight of a nice friendly group of clean-cut lads like the Beatles
brings him out in a rash of counterplots.

'Norm (Norman Rossington), the boys' road manager, who is
conducting a war of nerves with John, the group's happy anarchist,
collects Grandfather and together with Shake (John Junkin), the
general dogsbody, he retreats to the restaurant car for coffee,
leaving the boys to settle in for their journey to London and a live
television show. However, a well-established first-class ticket holder
(Richard Vernon) drives the boys out of their carriage by being
pompously officious, so they go and join Norm, Shake and
Grandfather in the restaurant car.

'By this time Grandfather has managed to get Norm and Shake at
each other's throats and Paul warns the others that this could be
only the beginning. Sure enough, Grandfather has started a
campaign of dissension that leads to frightening schoolgirls, a
proposal of marriage to a chance acquaintance and general chaos
culminating with Grandfather being locked in the luggage van
where he and the boys complete their journey making music.

'When the boys arrive in London, they go to their hotel where
Norm leaves them to sort out their fan mail. However, Grandfather
has noticed that a certain amount of good-humoured banter is
directed at Ringo. Here, thinks Grandfather, is the weak link in the
chain. Instead of staying in the hotel the four boys sneak out to
enjoy themselves at a twist club and Grandfather, trading his
clothes for a waiter's suit, heads straight for a gambling club,
passing himself off as Lord John McCartney.

'Again the boys have to rescue him, much to the old man's indignation.

'The following day sees the boys plunged into the bustle of the television world. Press conferences, rehearsals, make-up, running from place to place, being shepherded by the harassed Norm and got at by the television show's neurotic director (Victor Spinetti), and always in the background is Grandfather, interfering, disrupting and needling Ringo.

'Only for a moment are the boys free. They can enjoy themselves playing in a large, open field, but even that doesn't last. John, however, does make the most of every second; he is always for the here and now. Paul tries keeping things on an even keel and George has a blind doggedness that sees him through. But the strain begins to tell on Ringo.

'Grandfather, of course, plays on this, pointing out the barrenness of Ringo's life and finally goading him into walking out into the world, outside of the group.

'The other three boys go out searching for Ringo, leaving Norm to fume and the director to worry himself to near collapse at the possibility of no show.

'Meanwhile, Ringo has found the world outside not too friendly, and through a series of encounters and misunderstandings, gets himself arrested. He is taken to the station, where he meets up with Grandfather who has been taken into protective custody. Grandfather storms at the Police Sergeant (Deryck Guyler) and manages to escape, leaving Ringo behind in the police station.

'He gets back to the television theatre and tells the boys, who, pursued again, but this time by the police, go and rescue Ringo.

'Finally they are able to do their show in front of a live audience.

'The show does well but as soon as it is finished, again it is the mad dash on to the next plane for the next show. The past thirty-six hours have been a hard day's night. The next thirty-six hours will be the same.'

The Beatles' music obviously played a major part in the film and it was introduced in a refreshingly natural way, unlike the forced musical breaks in so many rock 'n' roll films. The movie featured 'A Hard Day's Night', 'I Should Have Known Better', 'If I Fell', 'I'm Happy Just To Dance With You', 'And I Love Her', 'Tell Me Why', 'Can't Buy Me Love', 'Any Time At All', 'I'll Cry Instead', 'Things We Said Today', 'When I Get Home', 'You Can't Do That' and 'I'll Be Back'.

The film was given a Royal World Premiere at the London Pavilion before HRH Princess Margaret and the Earl of Snowdon to aid the Dockland Settlements and the Variety Club Heart Fund on Monday, 6 July 1964, at 8.30 p.m.

Piccadilly Circus had to be closed to traffic as there were literally thousands of fans crowding the area. After the show the group went on to supper at the Dorchester Hotel. The northern premiere took place in Liverpool on 10 July at the Odeon Cinema, following a civic reception at the Town Hall. The film then went on general release in Britain on 2 August. It was premiered in America at the Beacon Theatre in New York on 12 August and opened in 500 cinemas throughout the country the next day.

Both British and American critics were, in the main, captivated by the film.

Leonard Mosley of the *Daily Express* wrote: 'It's a mad, mad, mad, mad film, man. Nothing like it since the Goons on radio and the Marx Brothers in the thirties', a feeling which was echoed by Cecil Wilson of the *Daily Mail*, who commented: 'As crazily inconsequential, as endearingly insolent, as infectiously pleased with themselves – as funny as the Marx Brothers.'

The Times was to observe: 'Mr Richard Lester has had a real go, and a lot of his bright ideas come off very well; the way, for instance, that several of the numbers are treated as contrapuntal soundtrack accompaniments to screen action of quite another sort; the outbursts of Goonish visual humour; the freshly observed London locations and the vivid glimpses of backstage (or in this case behind-the-screen) show business life.'

A most quotable comment came from Andrew Sarris of the American magazine *Village Voice* who described the film as 'the "Citizen Kane" of jukebox movies'.

A Hard Day's Night proved to be an international success, bringing in almost $14 million on its initial release. There were various foreign language versions; in Italy it was known as *Tutti Per Uno*, in Germany as *Yeah Yeah Yeah die Beatles*, in France as *Quatre Garcons dans le Vent* and in Holland as *Yeah Yeah Yeah, Daar de Beatles*.

The film began to receive television screenings from July 1968. Walter Shenson thought that it had not been fully exploited despite the fact that an unprecedented number of prints had been released so that it could be issued in 500 US theatres simultaneously. He felt that Proscenium Films had underrated the movie, and failed to consider the possibility that it might have a long life span as far as commercial cinema release was concerned.

He commented: 'I'm angry with United Artists. I don't think they ever had the respect for the Beatles' films that they deserve. They considered them exploitation films and let them go for stupid hundred dollar bookings and TV. They should have held them back.'

Fifteen years after the release of *A Hard Day's Night*, Shenson regained control of the film. He prepared it for re-release in the US with a Dolby stereo soundtrack in 1981 and licensed its release as a video cassette in America and Britain in 1984. MPI issued a video documentary about the film on Tuesday March 28, 1995 called *You Can't Do That: The Making Of A Hard Day's Night*. Phil Collins hosted the documentary. It also included a performance of 'You Can't Do That', from a concert sequence at the Scala Theatre, which had been cut from the film, but had been screened in America on the 'Ed Sullivan Show' on Sunday, 24 May 1964.

Miramax obtained rights to re-issue the movie to theatres in a year 2000 release.

Hard Day's Night, A (Single)

Once the title for their debut film had been confirmed, John and Paul were asked to come up with a song to match it. It was the first time they'd been specifically commissioned to write a song and John was the first to produce the completed number. This was perhaps appropriate as, although all reports credited Ringo with coming up with the phrase, it had actually appeared in one of John's written sketches prior to this time.

Recording of the single began on Thursday, 16 April 1964, and George Martin added piano to the track.

The single was issued in Britain on Parlophone R 5160 on 10 July 1964 and became the Beatles' third single to reach No. 1 one week after release. It was issued in America on Capitol 5222 on 13 July 1964 and also reached No. 1 in the charts. The million-seller also brought the group a Grammy Award as 'Best Vocal Group Performance of 1964'.

The flipside was 'I Should Have Known Better'.

It was included as part of their repertoire on their American tour in 1964, their Finsbury Park Astoria Christmas shows and on their European and American tours in 1965.

Apart from being the first track on the *A Hard Day's Night* album, the number was also used extensively on compilation albums, including *A Collection Of Beatles Oldies (But Goldies), The Beatles 1962–1966, The Beatles At The Hollywood Bowl, Reel Music* and *20 Greatest Hits*. It was also one of the numbers on the medley single *The Beatles Movie Medley* in 1982.

Peter Sellers recorded a version which reached No. 15 in the British charts in 1965 and the Ramsey Lewis Trio recorded an instrumental version which reached No. 29 in the *Billboard* charts in 1966. Take One of their original Abbey Road studio recording was included on the Beatles' *Anthology 1* CD.

Harris, Rolf

Australian singer/comedian/cartoonist who had his first British chart hit in 1960 with 'Tie Me Kangaroo Down Sport'. Harris moved to Britain and in 1963 was asked by the BBC to interview the Beatles. Aware of their reputation for 'taking the mickey' out of interviewers, he broke the ice by asking, 'Ringo, what do you think of spaghetti?'

He was booked on the bill of their 1963 Christmas Show at the Finsbury Park Astoria and drew a cartoon souvenir of the show which was sent to UK members of the Beatles Fan Club.

An incident during the run of the show occurred when John and Paul used an off-stage mike to cut in on Rolf's act. He rushed backstage and lambasted them on their unprofessional conduct. He was to observe, 'I got more respect from that point but less friendship.'

Harrison, Dhani

George and Olivia Harrison's only child. George named him Dhani because of 'dha' and 'ni', notes of the Indian music scale. Although it is also the Sanskrit word for 'wealthy'.

Dhani was born on 1 August 1978 at Princess Christian Nursing Home in Windsor, some four weeks before his parents were married. He was reared at George and Olivia's 33-acre Gothic mansion, Friar Park, where he lived a somewhat cosseted life, being chauffeured around in a gold Mercedes or the Porsches of George's various friends.

Initially educated in the Montessori method at the Dolphin School, near Twyford, he was then enrolled at the fee-paying Shiplake College. From an early age he has been schooled in a spiritual way of life and meditates regularly. George and Olivia commented: 'We can instil the right values in our son. It is his nightmare that he should grow up spoiled.'

George invited him on stage to play guitar at the Royal Albert Hall during an appearance to promote the Maharishi Mahesh Yogi's political party in 1992, although Dhani says he does not want to become a musician. He also denies press reports that his ambition is to become a botanist. Following his first term at Shiplake in 1995, he decided to study design technology.

Harrison, George

George Harrison was born on 25 February 1943 at 12 Arnold Grove, in the Wavertree area of Liverpool, to Louise and Harold Harrison. The new baby had two brothers, Peter and Harry, and a sister, Louise.

When George was five his family moved to Upton Green, Speke, and he attended Dovedale Primary School with his brother Peter. In September 1954 he became a pupil at the Liverpool Institute. His interest in music was aroused with the skiffle boom and he initially bought a guitar from a schoolmate, but it was damaged and difficult to play. His mother helped him to obtain a proper guitar and he formed a group called the Rebels with his brother Peter and best friend Arthur Kelly, although the skiffle group only appeared for a single gig at the local British Legion club.

When George left the Institute he was sent by the Youth Employment Centre to Blackler's store to apply for the job as a window-dresser. That job had been taken, but he found employment at the department store as a trainee electrician. In the meantime, his interest in music continued, although he had failed an audition to join Alan Caldwell's Texans (who were to become Rory Storm & the Hurricanes). He did manage to find a place with the Les Stewart Quartet, who had a residency at Lowlands club in West Derby. George had also developed a friendship with another Institute boy whom he met while travelling to school on the No. 86 bus – Paul McCartney, and he attended a few of the gigs performed by the Quarry Men, the group Paul was a member of.

During the early part of 1959, the Quarry Men had virtually ceased to exist. When Ken Brown, a fellow member of the Les Stewart Quartet, had an argument with Stewart, George walked out with him and suggested he contact John and Paul to join them in a residency at the Casbah Club. The Quarry Men then re-formed on 29 August with John, Paul, George and Ken. A different argument ended with Brown leaving the group in October.

In 1960 the group had become the Beatles and, with new drummer Pete Best, set off for Germany in August. They appeared at the Indra Club, then at the Kaiserkeller. When an opportunity came to appear at the rival Top Ten Club, Kaiserkeller owner Bruno Koschmider revealed that George was under-age and would have to return home. George told Beatles biographer Hunter Davies, 'At all clubs they used to read out a notice every night saying that all people under eighteen had to leave. Someone eventually realised I was only seventeen, without a work permit or a resident permit. So I had to leave. I had to go home on my own. I felt terrible.'

When the newspaper *Mersey Beat* reported on the Beatles' recording activities in Hamburg, it mentioned that George had written the only Beatles original composition recorded – 'Cry For A Shadow'. George had also co-written with Paul a number called 'In Spite Of All The Danger', which was the first original song the group recorded when they made a demonstration record in

Kensington, Liverpool, in 1958. Over the next few years of the Beatles' success, the main focus of attention was John and Paul, in particular because of their songwriting. George felt frustrated because he believed his work wasn't being taken seriously by the others. He eventually began writing seriously with 'Don't Bother Me' and began to emerge as a talented songwriter in his own right, although he still had to fight to have his numbers accepted on the group's albums. His compositions included: 'I Need You' and 'You Like Me Too Much' on the *Help!* album; 'Think For Yourself' and 'If I Needed Someone' on the *Rubber Soul* album; 'Taxman', 'Love You Too' and 'I Want To Tell You' on the *Revolver* album; 'Within You, Without You' on the *Sgt Pepper* album and 'Blue Jay Way' on the *Magical Mystery Tour* EP set. 'The Inner Light' became George's first song to be included on a single when it was issued as the flipside of 'Lady Madonna'. His compositions on *The Beatles* double album were 'While My Guitar Gently Weeps', 'Piggies', 'Long Long Long' and 'Savoy Truffle'. Other compositions by George included: 'Only A Northern Song' on the *Yellow Submarine* album; 'Old Brown Shoe', which became the flipside of the 'Ballad Of John And Yoko' single; and 'Something' and 'Here Comes The Sun' on *Abbey Road*. It was Allen Klein who finally made the decision to place a George Harrison song as the 'A' side of a Beatles single and this happened with 'Something'. On the Beatles' final album, *Let It Be*, George had two numbers, 'I. Me. Mine' and 'For You Blue'.

George did not have as large a profile in the Beatles' set-up as John or Paul, but he did attract the fans. Even in the Hamburg days the Exis referred to him as 'the Beautiful One'. During the filming of *A Hard Day's Night* he met and fell in love with teenage model Pattie Boyd and the two were married on 21 January 1966. The following two years proved to be a very important period for George. Apart from his marriage, he developed a close friendship with guitarist Eric Clapton and he met two men who were to alter the direction of his life. The first was Indian musician Ravi Shankar, whom George was introduced to in June at a party at the home of Peter Sellers, the other was the Maharishi Mahesh Yogi. These two 'Men from the East' were to have a profound effect on both George's musical and spiritual life, even though his association with the Maharishi was brief. From Shankar he developed a love of Indian music, learned to play the sitar, and opened up his songwriting to new influences. Transcendental meditation was also to prove beneficial to him and he received inspiration from Indian philosophy and travelled to Bombay in January 1968 to record tracks for the album *Wonderwall* with Indian musicians.

With his new interests, George also began to develop confidence in his own abilities and was no longer prepared to take a back seat in the Beatles' activities. Following a dispute with Paul he walked off the set of the *Let It Be* film in January 1969. He returned, but he was determined never again to appear on stage with the Beatles, despite Paul's attempts to have the group appear in public again. Paul's urgings did, however, result in their last public appearance on the roof of the Apple building in Savile Row. During the year George and Pattie had been busted for drugs at their home and he vowed never to keep any drugs at his home again. He also became interested in the Hare Krsna movement and recorded the Radha Krsna Temple performing 'The Hare Krsna Mantra'. He also met his Divine Grace A. C. Bhakivedanta Swami Prabhupada.

The Beatles were, by now, effectively finished as a group and George produced a series of solo albums and singles.

In April 1984, George announced that he had cut his last record, stating that he'd decided to retire from the music business to concentrate on film production. Fortunately, he changed his mind concerning recording, but he did channel most of his efforts into film-making when he founded HandMade Films in partnership with Denis O'Brien in 1978.

George triumphed in August 1971 when he presented *The Concert For Bangladesh* at Madison Square Garden, in which he was surrounded by a host of stars, including Ringo Starr, Bob Dylan, Eric Clapton, Billy Preston, Badfinger and Ravi Shankar.

In 1974 he went on the road again and performed 50 concerts in North America. His marriage with Pattie was breaking down and she became involved in a love affair with George's best friend, Eric Clapton. The couple were divorced on 9 June 1977. By that time George was in love with Olivia Arias and the couple were living together at George's palatial mansion, Friar Park in Henley. Olivia gave birth to their son Dhani on 1 August 1978 and the two were married the following month, on 2 September. In 1979 George had his autobiography *I. Me. Mine* published in a special limited edition.

During the eighties George began to make a number of appearances on stage and television, including a special TV tribute to the career of Carl Perkins. George was also to become part of a unique band called the Traveling Wilburys, which also included Roy Orbison, Bob Dylan, Tom Petty and Jeff Lynne, and they were instantly successful with their debut album *The Traveling Wilburys* in 1988.

The world was shocked on 31 December 1999 when an intruder attacked George in his Friar Park home, stabbing him in the chest.

Olivia saved his life, hitting the attacker on the head with a table lamp. Fortunately, George soon recovered from the injury.

Harrison, Harold Hargreaves

George's father, who was born in Liverpool on 28 May 1909, the son of Henry Harrison and Jane Thomson. His father was killed in the First World War and his mother had to raise several children by herself. Harold left school at the age of fourteen to become a delivery boy and at the age of seventeen went to sea. He joined the White Star Line, serving on cruise ships, eventually becoming a first class steward.

In 1929, during one of his trips home, he met his future wife, Louise, while she was working in a Liverpool greengrocer's, asked for her address and began writing regularly to her. They were married on 20 May 1930.

Long sea voyages were not conducive to married life and he left the sea in 1936, spending fifteen months on the dole before finding a job as a bus conductor. By the beginning of the Second World War he had been promoted to driver.

Harold and Louise lived in Liverpool's Wavertree area, where their four children, Louise, Harry, Peter and George, were born. On the birth of George, Harold was to describe him as 'A tiny, squalling, miniature replica of myself.'

Harold's social life revolved around the Liverpool Corporation Centre for Conductors and Drivers at Finch Lane. He became a leading union official and also the Saturday evening master of cere-monies at the Speke Depot Social Club, of which he was chairman. He and Louise also ran a ballroom dancing class at the club for over ten years.

On 1 January 1959, Harold booked his son's group, the Quarry Men, to appear at a special social club Christmas Party at Wilson Hall, Garston.

When the Beatles became internationally famous, Harold and Louise were particularly close to fans, inviting them into their home and answering fan mail by the sackload.

In 1965, George asked Harold how much he earned as a bus driver. Harold told him his pay was still £10 a week, so George offered to pay him £30 a week if he'd retire early. He then bought his mum and dad a £10,000 bungalow in three acres of land in the village of Appleton, near Warrington in Cheshire.

Harold continued to visit George at Friar Park and occasionally travelled with him on tours – for example, the Dark Horse Tour.

After a lifetime of heavy smoking, he died of emphysema in May 1978. George was to claim that on the eve of his father's death he had a dream in which Harold bade him farewell.

Harrison, Harry

One of George Harrison's elder brothers, known as Harry Junior. When Harry was called up for National Service, his girlfriend Irene McCann used to keep George company, taking him to shows, including the Lonnie Donegan shows at the Empire Theatre. She said that George was like a little brother and referred to him as 'our kid'. She married Harry after he'd completed his National Service and the Quarry Men played at their wedding reception on 20 December 1959.

Harry was a mechanic, but later in life he went to work for George at Friar Park as his estate manager.

Harrison, Louise (Mother)

George's mother was born Louise French. She first met Harry Harrison on a street corner in Liverpool in 1929 and the couple were married on 20 May 1930, at Brownlow Hill register office. Louise worked at a local greengrocer's shop and gave up her job when her first child Louise was born in 1931, to be followed by Harold in 1943, Peter in 1940 and George in 1944. Her husband became a bus conductor and for ten years the two of them ran ball-room dancing lessons at the conductors' club.

Louise was supportive of George's interest in music and bought him an acoustic guitar for £3 when he was thirteen. When he joined the Quarry Men she let them rehearse in her drawing room, and she visited the Cavern to give support to the Beatles.

When the Beatles began to receive such a huge volume of fan mail she would go to the Beatles Fan Club office in Liverpool city centre and take home the letters to George, reading all of them, up to 2,000 a month between 1963 and 1966, and answering as many of them as she could, personally.

In 1965 George bought his parents a new house in Appleton, near Warrington. Tragically, Louise was only to spend five years there. She became terribly ill and suffered for twelve months before dying of a brain tumour on 7 July 1970.

A group of Beatle fans formed the Louise F. Harrison Memorial Cancer Fund.

Harrison, Louise (Sister)

George's elder sister, now known as Louise Kane. Harold and Louise's first child, she was named after her mother when she was born in 1931. She studied at a training college in Liverpool before marrying an American, Gordon Caldwell, and the couple moved to America in April 1954. Louise and Gordon had two children and in

the spring of 1963 moved to Benton, Illinois, 200 miles from St
Louis, a small town with a population of 8,000. They lived for five
years at 113 McCann Street, a two-storey house with a porch and
bay window.

On Monday, 16 September 1963 her brothers George and Peter
flew in via New York and St Louis to stay with Louise and her
family in Benton. It was the day 'She Loves You' was issued in the
States.

Commenting on the holiday, George said: 'I've wanted to go
there [America] for years, but I could never afford it before. Also,
this may be my last chance for a while, 'cause it may be ages before
the Beatles can get two weeks free again.'

During their vacation they went camping in Shawnee National
Forest.

Louise had played the *Please Please Me* album to the Four Vests,
a local group, and two of the members, Gaby McCartney and
Kenny Welch, showed George around the town. He was invited to
sit in with the group when they played at the VFW dance hall in
Eldorado, a nearby town. Welch lent him his Rickenbacker guitar
on which George played some Hank Williams numbers. Kenny
remarked: 'He'd never seen one before and he liked it really well.
He wanted to buy it.' Kenny wouldn't sell the guitar to him so
George bought one in another nearby town, Mount Vernon.

Commenting on George's visit, Louise said: 'That was the only
experience any one of the Beatles ever had of living in this country
as a normal human being. Nobody had ever heard of him.'

In February 1964, when the Beatles arrived for their triumphant
visit to America, George fell ill and a doctor was called to his room
at the Plaza Hotel. Louise moved into the adjacent room and
nursed him.

Louise began to prepare Beatles reports for eighteen radio
stations across America and in 1965 an album *All About The
Beatles,* on Recar Records (2012), was issued. It was a compilation
of her interviews with five American radio stations: WMEX
Boston, WNDR Norfolk, WHK Cleveland, WKNR Detroit and
KIMN Denver.

It was Louise who phoned George to inform him that John had
been murdered.

Louise was divorced in 1982 and later settled in Saratoga,
Florida. In 1992 she returned to the public eye when she began
appearing at Beatles conventions, promoting a non-profit making
environmental organisation, We Care Global Family Inc.

In 1999 the original house in Benton, Illinois, was prevented from
demolition and turned into 'A Hard Day's Nite Bed and Breakfast'.

Harrison, Olivia

Born Olivia Trinidad Arias in Mexico in 1948, she was educated in America and graduated at Hawthorne High School, California. She remained in Los Angeles and went to work in the merchandising office at A&M Records. She was then moved to Dark Horse Records as a secretary – George's Dark Horse was a small subsidiary label of A&M.

Olivia was 27 in 1974 when George first met her in the company offices. They talked together on the phone on numerous occasions and when George was returning to the States to work he asked a friend to check her out.

Their relationship deepened and they became virtually inseparable. When George fell ill following a number of problems relating to his marriage breakdown and a slump in his recording career, he suffered from serum hepatitis, but didn't respond to treatment. Olivia recommended that he visit Dr Zion Yua, a noted Chinese acupuncturist, who cured him.

George and Olivia then spent the winter in Britain, preferring a traditional cold Christmas to the heat of Los Angeles. George also took her to visit Liverpool.

The pair lived together in Los Angeles, initially at George's $700,000 Beverly Hills mansion, which had a guest house, tennis court, swimming pool and all the trimmings. They found that it was too big for their needs and sold it for a smaller home with a greater sense of privacy.

When they stayed with Ringo and Nancy Andrews for a time in Hollywood Hills, an observer commented:

> There was a serene and calming presence that George and Olivia gave off. George had fresh flowers placed in the home and there was incense burning, pictures of holy men, the smell of curried rice dishes – long grain rice – wafting in from the kitchen. They're both health-food eaters.
>
> You know something is going on when they're around but it isn't something George shoves down your throat. They are both very thoughtful, and he has a great sense of humour. She is a lovely woman, far from the Hollywood-model type, far too spiritual. The harmony between them is clear and apparent to anyone around them.

It became obvious that Olivia was not particularly impressed by the lavish lifestyle of Los Angeles and the two of them moved to the tranquillity of the English countryside, to George's mansion, Friar Park, in Henley-on-Thames.

The couple were unable to marry until George's divorce from Pattie was finalised. This took place on Thursday, 9 June 1977 and they then planned their wedding for May 1978, but postponed it due to the death of George's father. Their son Dhani was born on Tuesday, 1 August 1978. George and Olivia were eventually married by special licence at Henley Register Office some four weeks later, on Saturday, 2 September, in a secret ceremony at which the only guests were Olivia's parents, who had flown in from California. The couple then went on honeymoon to Tunisia.

Harrison, Peter

One of George's elder brothers, who became a panel beater and welder before George asked him to move south with his family and oversee the gardeners at Friar Park.

Peter joined George in his short-lived band the Rebels, but Peter was basically uninterested in the guitar. He accompanied George on his first visit to America in September 1963.

Harry Lime Theme, The

Instrumental number popularised in the 1949 film *The Third Man*. It was composed by Anton Karas who performed the number on a zither. Paul McCartney mentioned that the Silver Beatles played 'The Harry Lime Theme' when they backed Janice the Stripper at the New Cabaret Artistes Club.

Harvey, Alex

Scottish musician, born 5 February 1945, who, when he formed a skiffle group, was dubbed 'the Tommy Steele of Scotland'. He appeared with the Beatles at the Town Hall, Alloa, Scotland, on 20 May 1960, the first date of their Scottish tour as backing band to Johnny Gentle. He formed the Alex Harvey Big Soul Band in 1959 and they appeared regularly in Hamburg. He died of a heart attack in Belgium on 4 February 1982. He was 46 years old.

Haslam, Michael

A singer from Lancashire, who was 24 years old when he was signed to Brian Epstein in 1964.

Godfrey Winn, a leading show business writer for women's magazines, saw Haslam performing in a Bolton pub. A short time later he was dining with Brian Epstein and Cilla Black and raved over his discovery. Brian then set off for Bolton with Winn and arrived to witness a Sunday evening show by Haslam at the White Hart pub. Epstein was impressed and after the show told Haslam he would like to manage him and would put him on the next Beatles tour.

Epstein also arranged a Parlophone recording contract for the singer, who was to be recorded by George Martin. Haslam appeared on the Beatles' sell-out tour in October 1964 and also appeared on their Christmas show at the Odeon, Hammersmith in December of the same year. Despite the massive exposure, he had no record success. His first release was 'Gotta Get Hold Of Myself'. His second was the prophetic-sounding 'There Goes The Forgotten Man'. When his contract lapsed after two years. Epstein didn't bother renewing it.

Haslam's sister Annie later became a star in her own right in the seventies as lead singer with Renaissance.

Hawke, Jim

Former British soldier who remained in Germany after World War II. He married a German girl, Lilo, and at the beginning of 1960, together with their daughter Monica, they took over the running of the British Sailors' Society in Hamburg, known as the 'Mission'.

When the Beatles arrived in Hamburg, Iain Hines and Tony Sheridan of the Jets introduced them to the delights of the Mission, which were English breakfasts with lots of milk and cornflakes, and very cheap meals – steak, egg and chips.

Hawke made British musicians very welcome at the Mission and the Beatles would often arrive there at 11.00 a.m. and stay until 3.00 p.m. or 4.00 p.m. One of the rooms had a piano in it and John and Paul used it to compose songs on.

On one occasion John and Paul called on Tony and Iain to join them on their walk to the Mission, but the two members of the Jets refused to join them as they were embarrassed because the two were wearing German army forage caps and Tony and Iain told them they'd be 'lynched' walking around dressed like they were – particularly as the caps had a white swastika painted on them. John and Paul left and Tony and Iain trailed them ten minutes later. A man spat at them and a number of Germans began to follow them, so Tony and Iain broke into a run and fled to the Mission. They asked Jim Hawke why they had been picked on. He explained that they were wearing T-shirts – which they'd been given by some American sailors – with the initials D.D.R. on them. This meant D-Type Destroyer. However, in German eyes the initials meant Deutsche Democratic Republic – East Germany, which resulted in their hostile reception on the streets.

Jim Hawke became a kind friend to the Beatles and, aware of their financial hardships, ensured that they enjoyed hearty meals at a fraction of the price they'd have paid elsewhere in St Pauli.

Haworth, Jann

An American sculptress who was married to British artist Peter Blake. Gallery-owner Robert Fraser, who acted as their representative, commissioned both of them to devise an album sleeve for *Sgt Pepper's Lonely Hearts Club Band* and paid them £200.

Haworth had exhibited at the 'Young Contemporaries' show at the ICA in 1963 and one of her exhibits from that show, a doll of Shirley Temple, was placed on the sleeve wearing a 'Welcome Rolling Stones' shirt.

Paul McCartney invited Jann and her husband to his home to hear tracks from the album as an inspiration. Once, when Jann was travelling in a car with Paul in Hammersmith, she pointed out a municipal flower clock and suggested that, rather than lettering, a grouping of flowers spelling 'Beatles' should be used.

In photographer Michael Cooper's studio, Jann helped to build the background to the tableau and, together with her husband, pasted the life-size photographic blow-ups to hardboard. She also tinted all of the original black and white photographs.

Together with Blake, she also designed the special colour card contained inside the sleeve which featured a set of army stripes, badges and a moustache which could be used as cut-outs. In addition, the card contained a painting of Sergeant Pepper and a Beatles photograph.

Haworth and Blake separated in 1979.

Hear The Beatles Tell All

An album originally issued in the United States in September 1964 on Vee Jay PROP 202. The record contained interviews with all four members of the group, conducted by Dave Hull, plus a John Lennon interview conducted by Jim Steck. The album was issued in Great Britain in March 1981 on Charly Records CRV 202.

Hebb, Bobby

Nashville singer who appeared on the Beatles' 1966 North American tour. Born 26 July 1941, Hebb had appeared at the Grand Ole Opry at the age of twelve. He later moved to New York and in memory of his brother Hal (a member of the doo-wop group the Marigolds), who died the day after President Kennedy was assassinated, he wrote 'Sunny', which reached No 2 in the US charts in August 1966. Hebb also entered the UK Top 20 with the number – as did Georgie Fame with a cover version. It was his biggest hit and later efforts such as 'Sunny 76' and 'My Pretty Sunshine' failed to make an impact.

On the Beatles tour, the Remains backed Hebb.

Hello Goodbye

Paul McCartney composition issued as a single with John's 'I Am The Walrus' as the flip. Released in Britain on Parlophone R 5655 on 24 November 1967, it was No. 1 for seven weeks. It was issued in America on Capitol 2056 on 27 November 1967 and also topped the charts.

John Lennon wasn't pleased that the number was chosen as the 'A' side of their single, with 'I Am The Walrus' as the 'B' side. He considered 'Walrus' a much better number and cynically referred to 'Hello Goodbye' as 'typical Paul'.

The song was included on the American album of *Magical Mystery Tour* in 1967, the 1973 double album *The Beatles 1967–1970* and the EMI album version of *Magical Mystery Tour*, issued in November 1976. It was also selected for their second twenty-track compilation *20 Greatest Hits* in 1982.

The promotional film of the number couldn't be screened in Britain due to a new musicians' union ruling which banned miming to records – on the supposition that it kept live musicians out of work! Its planned screening on BBC 2's 'Late Night Line-Up' on 23 November was scrapped and the film was replaced on 'Top Of The Pops' with a film clip from *A Hard Day's Night*.

When the song was recorded in October 1967 it had the working title 'Hello Hello', and was recorded during the *Magical Mystery Tour* sessions. Paul was lead vocalist, with backing from John and George, and Paul also played piano, bongos and conga drums on the session while John played organ and lead guitar, George played lead and tambourine and Ringo played drums and maracas. Two viola players were brought in to play on the session – Leo Birnbaum and Ken Essex.

There was a reprise ending which the group referred to as 'the Maori finale' and when the group were making their promotional film of the number at the Saville Theatre, they featured a number of girl dancers wearing grass skirts. Take 16 from the original recording sessions was included on the Beatles' *Anthology 2* CDs.

Hello Little Girl

A number penned by John in his teens and included in the group's repertoire in 1958. John was to comment, 'This was one of the first songs I ever finished. I was then about 18 and we gave it to the Fourmost. I think it was the first song of my own that I ever attempted to do with the group.' John was also to say that he'd loosely based the song on a couple of old standards which his mother used to sing to him when he was a small child, and the song was an attempt to capture the mood of those songs written in the 1930s. The Beatles performed the number on their Decca and Parlophone recording auditions in 1962. The number was included on the Beatles' *Anthology 1* CDs.

Help! (American Album)

The American album of *Help!* was issued by Capitol on SMAS 2386 on 13 August 1965. It was the first album in history to have an advance order of over one million copies.

Unlike the version of the album which was issued in Britain and the rest of the world, the Capitol album only contained the seven Beatles songs from the movie. Capitol replaced the new Beatles tracks with seven soundtrack instrumentals from the film by the George Martin Orchestra.

Capitol advertised the package as a 'Special Movie Souvenir Package' but the Beatles were annoyed at the release containing only half of the Beatles numbers from the British version of the *Help!* album.

The track listing was, Side One: 'James Bond Theme', 'Help!', 'The Night Before', 'From Me To You Fantasy', 'You've Got To Hide Your Love Away', 'I Need You', 'In The Tyrol'. Side Two: 'The Bitter End/You Can't Do That', 'You're Going To Lose That Girl', 'The Chase', 'Another Girl', 'Another Hard Day's Night', 'Ticket To Ride'.

Help! (British Album)

The soundtrack of the Beatles' second film, issued on PCS 3071 on 6 August 1965. The songs from the film were featured on Side One of the album which reached No. 1 in the British charts.

The tracks were, Side One: 'Help', 'The Night Before', 'You've Got To Hide Your Love Away', 'I Need You', 'Another Girl', 'You're Going To Lose That Girl', 'Ticket To Ride'. Side Two: 'Act Naturally', 'It's Only Love', 'You Like Me Too Much', 'Tell Me What You See', 'I've Just Seen A Face', 'Yesterday', 'Dizzy Miss Lizzy'.

Help! (Film)

Work on the second Beatles movie *Help!* began on 24 February 1965, with an eleven-week shooting schedule and double the funds of their first film.

Initially, Dick Lester and Joe McGrath had written an original treatment. According to McGrath, it had been based on an old film idea. A doctor tells Ringo that he is terminally ill. Depressed, Ringo pays £500 to a contract killer, who is a master of disguise. As he doesn't want to face death directly, Ringo has asked the killer to murder him when he least expects it. The next day the doctor informs him that there has been a mistake, the X-rays he'd consulted had belonged to someone else, and therefore Ringo isn't terminally ill. Not able to contact the contract killer, he panics and tells the other Beatles to track down the killer before he can carry out his assignment.

Lester's recollection of that initial treatment is slightly different. He has Ringo complaining that he can't cope with his stress-filled life any longer. Sitting in a bar he moans: 'I can't go on anymore.' The person sitting next to him says: 'If you haven't got the courage to put an end to it yourself, I'll do it for a price. I'm a professional assassin.' Ringo gives him a cheque. The next day he wakes up and realises what he's done and panics.

This treatment was dropped when Lester discovered that a film with a virtually identical plot was already being filmed in Hong Kong. It was *Les Tribulations d'un Chinoise en Chine*, with Jean Paul Belmondo.

Lester then contacted Marc Behm, an American writer living in Paris (who'd penned the Audrey Hepburn movie *Charade*), to come up with a synopsis vaguely based on the idea that Ringo was being attacked by various people and didn't know why. Once the synopsis had been written, Lester then contacted Charles Wood, who had penned the screenplay for Lester's previous film, *The Knack*.

He felt that Behm's story had no 'Englishness' to it and wanted Wood to rewrite it to suit the Beatles and bring in a degree of 'Englishness'. This resulted in appearances of or references to various British icons ranging from James Bond to the Queen, with scenes in Scotland Yard, Buckingham Palace and with the British Army on Salisbury Plain.

Wood completed the revised script in ten days, commenting, 'It was just an assignment. I don't think I did a particularly good job.' Bud Ornstein wasn't too enthusiastic about it either, but he needed to get another Beatles movie off the ground.

The Behm/Wood screenplay didn't manage to capture the Beatles' humour in the same way as Alun Owen had in *A Hard Days Night*, although there are touches of Scouse wit. While watching the belly dancer Durra perform in a restaurant, the boys quip, 'Doesn't the blood rush to your stomach?' At another point in the movie, John picks up a season ticket out of his soup and says, 'I'd like a bit of seasoning.' When a Scotland Yard superintendent sarcastically remarks 'So you're the famous Beatles. How long do you think you'll last?' John replies: 'And the Great Train Robbery – how do you think that's going?'

It was decided that the filming should begin in Nassau in the Bahamas and the cast and crew of seventy flew out on 22 February in a chartered Boeing 707. The temperature in the Bahamas was 90 degrees, but the Beatles couldn't afford to get a tan as they would next be filming a sequence in Austria that would be appearing prior to those shot in the Caribbean. Cast and crew left for Austria and the ski resort of Obertauern on 13 March. Producer Walter Shenson was to comment: '(*Help!*) is essentially a holiday picture. It was filmed in two totally contrasting holiday resorts. We travelled from calypso to yodel with a lot of yeah, yeah thrown in.'

A special wardrobe was made for the Beatles' Austrian scenes. All four wore black skin-tight trousers and ankle-length ski boots in black sealskin. John sported a black cape lined with white satin while Ringo wore a tight-fitting black sweater with white rings around the sleeves. George also wore a black sweater but with a white stripe down each sleeve while Paul had on a loosely cut ski jacket in lustrous sealskin.

Filming was completed on 13 May, the rest of the film's scenes being shot in London, Salisbury Plain (with permission from the War Office) and Twickenham Studios. While *A Hard Day's Night* had cost only $500,000 to make, *Help!* (filmed in Eastmancolor) cost $1.5 million.

This Walter Shenson–Subafilms production was once again distributed by United Artists and directed by Dick Lester.

The film begins with the tribute: 'Respectfully dedicated to the memory of Elias Howe who in 1846 invented the sewing machine.' Title cards are used at various points in the film bearing such inscriptions as 'Intermission' and 'End of intermission': the scene in which Paul is miniaturised and dodges around the floor of his flat is heralded by a card reading 'The adventures of Paul on the Floor'.

By the time the cameras had started rolling, an official name still hadn't been confirmed. It was initially known as *Beatles Two,* and for a time called *Eight Arms To Hold You.*

John and Paul began composing numbers for the film even before they saw the script. A total of fourteen numbers were originally produced. They gave nine to Dick Lester who selected seven for the soundtrack. The original fourteen songs were 'I Need You', 'Another Girl', 'Ticket To Ride', 'Yes It Is', 'The Night Before', 'You Like Me Too Much', 'Tell Me What You See', 'You've Got To Hide Your Love Away', 'If You've Got Trouble', 'You're Going To Lose That Girl', 'That Means A Lot', 'Help!' 'I'm Down' and 'Wait'.

'Yes It Is', 'You Like Me Too Much', 'Tell Me What You See', 'If You've Got Trouble', 'That Means A Lot', 'I'm Down' and 'Wait' were dropped from the actual soundtrack.

Other members of the cast were Leo McKern as Clang, Eleanor Bron as Ahme, John Bluthal as Bhuta, Warren Mitchell as Abdul, Peter Copely as a jeweller and Dandy Nichols as a neighbour. Bruce Lacey plays Lawn Mower (he mows a lawn – situated in a drawing room – with two pairs of false teeth) and Mal Evans pops up from time to time as a Channel swimmer who has lost his way.

The official synopsis outlined the story as follows:

In the Eastern Temple of the Goddess Kaili, a human sacrifice is about to be made. But the executioner, the High Priest Clang, is stopped by the beautiful Ahme, priestess of the cult who has discovered that the victim is not wearing the sacrificial ring essential for the ritual.

On the other side of the world the Beatles are performing. Ringo sits on the stage playing the drums and amongst his many rings is – the ring – a present from an unknown fan of another continent.

In the days that follow a series of mysterious events make no sense to the Beatles. At home, on the street, a strange force seems to be directed at Ringo. A gang of thugs descend upon the boys and attempt to amputate Ringo's entire hand – and the Beatles realise that it is Ringo's new ring they must have.

After several more attempts, Clang and his gang nearly succeed in stealing Ringo's whole person, but just in time he is saved by Ahme.

A few days later, while the boys are waiting for a meal in an Indian restaurant, the dreaded Clang and his henchman Bhuta appear disguised as waiters. They tell Ringo that since they cannot remove the ring from his finger he is to be sacrificed to the goddess. The boys flee to the nearest jewellers and ask the man to cut off the offending ring. But the metal breaks the files and the cutting wheel.

The boys call next at a science laboratory run by Professor Foot and his assistant Algernon who put Ringo through every machine they have – to no avail; the ring resists all the assaults known to science. Foot decides that the ring has properties, which could give the owner the power to rule the world, and he confides to Algernon that he must get the ring. So the Beatles have two more enemies who will stop at nothing to retrieve the ring. Ahme once again comes to the rescue and they all flee from the laboratory – to the Alps!

In no time the Beatles' winter sport activities are interrupted by the arrival of Foot and Algernon intent on mayhem to be joined almost at once by Clang and gang. After a frantic

chase through snow and ice up mountains and down ski lifts
the boys scramble to the nearest railway station and gasp to
the ticket man, 'London!'

Back home they confide their troubles to a Superintendent
of Scotland Yard and tell him they must have protection in
order to record in peace.

The next day the boys record two songs on Salisbury Plain,
under the protection of the British Army, but Clang and his
murderous thugs arrive and put the Beatles to flight. Ahme, in
a tank, rescues them in the nick of time.

Back in London the murder attempts increase and the Beatles
decide to leave the country until the heat is off. Heavily
disguised they fly off to the Bahamas. But, alas, the world is
too small a place for the Beatles, Clang and his gang and the
two power-drunk scientists. Soon, the whole fray is resumed.
But Ringo learns the formula, which releases him from the ring.
The ring slips off and he hands it to Clang who hastily hands
it on to Foot who tries to pass it on to Algernon and so on
down the line.

Ahme and the Beatles at last find peace and the dreaded
Kaili will have no more victims.

The film contains numerous clever touches and colourful scenes
– the four terraced houses that are really a single luxurious flat; the
emergence of animated snowmen on the slopes of the ski resort; the
Fab Four's appearance and members of a brass band in uniform
(very Sgt Pepperish); and the giant idol rising from the sea.

One of the best sequences was filmed in the cellar of a London
pub and featured Ringo and a lion. In the film, the animal, called
Sheba, has been brought up on classical music at the Berlin Zoo. To
calm the beast, the Beatles have to sing 'Ode to Joy' from
Beethoven's Ninth. While the scene was being filmed, the film's
insurance brokers insisted that the lion keeper stand close by armed
with a safari gun.

The world premier of *Help!* took place at the London Pavilion on
29 July. Crowds began to gather at 8.00 a.m. and by evening there
were 10,000 people massed in Piccadilly. The statue of Eros was
boarded up for its protection and 250 policemen were needed to
handle the crowds. The area was so packed that John's Rolls-Royce
was held up for twenty minutes.

Princess Margaret and Lord Snowdon attended the event. The
Princess, when talking to Ringo about *A Hard Day's Night*, said,
'You were a trifle pessimistic about that one. I enjoyed it very much
and I have been looking forward to this one. I've come with an

open mind.' The premiere was sponsored by the Variety Club of Great Britain in aid of the Docklands settlement and the Variety Club's Heart Fund. £6,000 was raised for these two charities.

The film opened at 250 leading cinemas throughout the United States on 11 August and was the official British entry at the International Film Festival in Rio de Janeiro from 15–26 September, where it won first prize.

The critics weren't as universally enthusiastic about *Help!* as they had been about *A Hard Day's Night*. *The Spectator* noticed the slight stylistic influence of the Bond films (there were even a few bars of music on the soundtrack parodying the Bond music) and headed its review 'Beatles on the Bond Trail'. The reviewer commented: 'Ringo, the oddity and outsider, in so far as any one of them can be called that, is, as he was before, both hero and victim, certainly the most individual character.

'*Help!* is almost consistently funny, sometimes almost confusingly fast, and above all a contrast to its predecessor. Its social satire is directed inwards as much as out . . . the Beatles put latchkeys into four identical front doors which, with carefully primitive exteriors, all open into a single opulent interior, a schoolboy millionaire's dream of gadgets and instant marvels – sunken beds, rising wurlitzers, orangeade-making machines and pigeon-holed sandwiches.'

Writing in the *Daily Express*, Clive Barnes commented: 'These boys are the closest thing to the Marx Brothers since the Marx Brothers.'

Kenneth Tynan, in his *Observer* review, wrote: 'The Beatles themselves are not natural actors, nor are they exuberant extroverts. Their mode is dry and laconic, as befits the flat and sceptical Liverpool accent. Realising this, Lester leaves it to his cameraman [David Watkin] to create the exuberance, confining the Beatles to dead-pan comments and never asking them to react to events with anything approaching emotion. He capitalises on their wary, guarded detachment. "There's something been in this soup," says John, having calmly removed from the plate a season ticket and a pair of spectacles. "Not a bit like Cagney" is George's response when a CID Superintendent favours the group with a patronising impersonation of Ringo.'

America's *Time* magazine commented: '*Help!*, in short, is a Beatle production rather than a Beatle movie. It must have cost, as the British say, a packet. It will certainly make, as the Americans say, a bundle.'

The film did go on to make a bundle and United Artists were obviously eager, along with Shenson and Lester, to make a third film with the group, but it never materialised. The Beatles were offered several scripts and ideas, but were unhappy with all of them. Perhaps *Help!* had been a disappointment to them.

Certainly, John never had anything positive to say about the film: '*Help!* was a drag, because we didn't know what was happening. In fact, Lester was a bit ahead of his time with the Batman thing, but we were on pot by then and all the best stuff is on the cutting-room floor, with us breaking up and falling about all over the place.' Some years later he was blunt and dismissive about the film, describing it as 'Crap!'

Walter Shenson summarised his own and the Beatles' feelings as follows: 'The Beatles finally decided to discharge the third film in their contract by filming the *Let It Be* recording session. They financed it with UA [United Artists] and gave me a small piece of the profit.

'I think if we'd had a sensational script of a great idea, we might have made a third film. But it just wasn't in the cards.'

Help! (Single)

Number written by John Lennon for the film *Help!* He was to describe it as one of his first 'message' songs, which was his own personal cry for help, and it became one of his particular favourites.

In 1970, John was to tell Jann Wenner in a *Rolling Stone* interview, 'The only true songs I ever wrote were "Help!" and "Strawberry Fields Forever". They were the ones I wrote from experience, not projecting myself into a situation and writing a nice story about it, which I always found phoney. On "Help!", the lyric is as good now as it was then. It was just me singing *help*, and I meant it.'

He told David Sheff during a *Playboy* magazine interview, 'It was my fat Elvis period. You see the movie; He-I-is very fat, very insecure, and he's completely lost himself. And I'm saying about when I was so much younger and all the rest, looking back at how easy it was.'

The song was issued in Britain on Parlophone R 5305 on 23 July 1965 and topped the charts for four weeks. It was issued in America on Capitol 5476 on 19 July 1965 where it also reached the No. 1 position. 'I'm Down' was the flip.

The number was also featured on the soundtrack album *Help!* and on several compilations, including *A Collection of Beatles Oldies (But Goldies)*, *The Beatles 1962–1966*, *Reel Music*, *20 Greatest Hits* and the American *The Beatles Rarities*.

'Help!' was recorded on Tuesday, 13 April 1965. The Beatles' second film had used a working title and as soon as the name *Help!* was decided on, both John and Paul were asked to come up with a title song. As with *A Hard Day's Night*, John was the first to produce a number. The track, taken from a live performance, was included on the Beatles' *Anthology 2* CDs.

Helter Skelter

While in Scotland Paul read an interview with Pete Townshend in *Melody Maker* claiming that 'I Can See For Miles' which the Who had just recorded was 'the loudest, most raucous rock 'n' roll, the dirtiest thing they'd ever done'. When Paul read this he was inspired and wanted to top this claim, immediately writing 'Helter Skelter'.

They first began recording the number at Abbey Road on Thursday, 18 July 1968, recording three versions, including one which turned out to be a 27-minute jam, and those versions were scrapped.

It was decided to record the number from scratch on Monday, 9 October 1968, and as George Martin was on holiday, Chris Thomas produced the track.

Various instruments were used on the backing and Mal Evans attempted to play a trumpet. The session was a long one and at the end of the recording, Ringo cried out, 'I've got blisters on my fingers!'

The song was featured on *The Beatles* double album, issued in November 1968.

A helter skelter is a spiral slide found at British fairgrounds, although an American hippie, Charles Manson, leader of a cult in Los Angeles, claimed there were hidden meanings in the song. On hearing the Beatles album, Manson was convinced that the group was imparting a secret message heralding an Armageddon. He believed that 'when the Helter Skelter came, the Black Panthers, led by "Rocky Raccoon", would rise and execute the "Piggies".'

He sent members of his sect out to commit murder, and among the victims was Sharon Tate, wife of film director Roman Polanski.

It was John Lennon who was asked to testify at Manson's trial, but he refused. He was asked to comment on Manson's state of mind and said: 'Well, he's barmy. He's like any other Beatles kind of fan who reads mysticism into it. I mean, we used to have a laugh putting this, or the other in, in a light-hearted way. Some intellectual would read us, some symbolic youth generation wants it, but we also took seriously some part of the role ... but, I don't know, what's "Helter Skelter" got to do with knifing somebody? I never listened to the words properly, it was just a noise.'

Manson was caught, put on trial in 1969 and jailed. A bestselling book called *Helter Skelter* by Vincent Bugliosi and Curt Gentry, the prosecuting attorneys at the trial, was filmed as a television dramatisation called 'Helter Skelter', featuring some of the white album tracks. This resulted in Capitol rush-releasing 'Helter Skelter' as a single on Capitol 4274 on 31 May 1976. However, although they'd sent a special single of 'Helter Skelter' to disc jockeys for promotion, when they released the single they placed it on the flipside of 'Got To Get You Into My Life', in case anyone accused them of exploiting the Manson case. The single reached No. 3 in the American charts.

When Bono of U2 covered the song, he introduced it with the words, 'This is a song Charles Manson stole from the Beatles, and we're stealing it back!'

'Helter Skelter' was also included in the 1976 compilation *Rock 'n' Roll Music* and the American 1980 compilation *The Beatles Rarities*. A four and a half minute version was issued on the *Anthology 3* CD.

Her Majesty

At 23 seconds in length, the shortest Beatles track on record.

As Paul lived in St John's Wood, quite close to Abbey Road Studios, he often arrived far earlier than his fellow Beatles and sometimes began recording. This was one of his efforts which he recorded before the others arrived on Wednesday, 2 July 1965.

When the tracks for *Abbey Road* were being remixed on Wednesday, 30 July, second engineer John Kurlander played it to Paul who told him to throw it away. After Paul had left, Kurlander picked the small piece of tape off the floor and stuck it on the end of the edit tape. Eventually, Paul heard it again and decided it could be used on the album.

The number was the closing track on the *Abbey Road* album. Paul had composed the number in tribute to Queen Elizabeth II and copies of the LP were sent to Buckingham Palace.

Paul played acoustic guitar and sang solo on the number.

Here Comes The Sun

A George Harrison composition which he wrote one day in Eric Clapton's garden. He'd become bored with the business problems of Apple and decided to take the day off, rather like 'sagging off school', and went to see Eric Clapton. It was while he was walking in the garden with one of Eric's acoustic guitars that he composed the number, which was featured as one of the tracks on the *Abbey Road* album.

It was recorded on Ringo's 29th birthday, 7 July 1969, and there were only three Beatles present at the session as John was indisposed with an injury.

George was gaining more confidence in himself as a musician and songwriter, after years under the Lennon and McCartney shadow, and was taking more control of how his own songs were recorded. In this instance he supervised most of the overdubbing sessions.

Some years later, in 1976, Steve Harley & Cockney Rebel had a hit with the number when they issued it as a single in Britain, where it reached No. 10 in the charts.

'Here Comes The Sun' is included in the compilations *The Beatles Ballads, The Beatles 1967–1970, The Best Of George Harrison* and on *The Concert For Bangladesh* LP. In addition to performing it on *The Concert For Bangladesh*, George also played the number on 'Saturday Night Live', with Paul Simon in November 1976.

Here, There And Everywhere

One of Paul McCartney's compositions that he regards as one of his favourite numbers. In 1980, John Lennon also said, 'That's one of my favourite songs of the Beatles.'

Paul recalls that when the Beatles were in Obertauern, Austria, filming *Help!,* he shared a room with John. After a day's filming he played a cassette of numbers for the *Revolver* album and when he played 'Here, There And Everywhere', says: 'I remember John saying "you know, I probably like that better than any of my songs on the tape".'

The number was written while Paul was sitting beside John's swimming pool at his Weybridge home. It was recorded over three days in June 1966 for the *Revolver* album and it was suggested that Paul had been inspired to write it after listening to the Beach Boys' album *Pet Sounds* and, in particular, 'God Only Knows'.

When asked about the Lennon and McCartney songs and this title in particular, Paul commented: 'This one was pretty much mine, written sitting by John's pool. Often I would wait half an hour while he would do something – like get up. So I was sitting there tottling around in E on the guitar.'

In addition to *Revolver,* the number surfaced on compilation albums such as *Love Songs* and *Beatles Ballads.* Paul was also to feature the number in his film *Give My Regards To Broad Street.*

In 1970, country music singer Emmylou Harris reached No. 30 in the British charts with her single of the song.

An alternative version of 'Here, There And Everywhere', Take 7 from June 1966, was included on the Beatles' *Anthology 2* CD.

Here We Go

A BBC radio show produced in Manchester by Peter Pilbeam and presented by Ray Peters. The Beatles made four appearances on the

programme, recorded at the Playhouse Theatre, Manchester. The
first was recorded on 11 June and transmitted on 15 June 1962
when they performed 'Ask Me Why', 'Besame Mucho' and 'A
Picture Of You'.

The Beatles travelled to the gig by coach, which collected its
passengers outside Liverpool College of Art. Apart from the Beatles
there were members of their local fan club, Bill and Virginia Harry
of *Mersey Beat* and Pete Mackey, a member of the Art College
Students' Union. Pete had boarded the coach under false pretences,
in the guise of a fan. His brief had been to recover the Students'
Union amplifier which had been lent to the Beatles some years previously. When he did confront John Lennon and asked for its return,
John told him quite bluntly that he'd sold it in Hamburg and if he
had any problems he'd better discuss it with their manager, Brian
Epstein. After the gig, there was hysteria outside the Playhouse and
while John, Paul and George managed to board the coach, Pete Best
wasn't so lucky and was trapped by hordes of Manchester girls. He
found the ordeal terrifying as the girls tried to pull out tufts of his
hair and almost ripped his mohair suit to pieces. He finally escaped,
but Jim McCartney, Paul's father, who had also joined the coach
trip, was annoyed at him and said, 'Why did you have to attract all
the attention? Why didn't you call the other lads back?' Pete tried
to explain that he'd been trapped and it hadn't been his fault, but
Jim told him, 'I think that was very selfish of you.'

The Beatles' second appearance on the programme was recorded
on 25 October and transmitted on 26 October and was the show in
which Ringo Starr made his radio debut and they performed 'Love
Me Do', 'A Taste Of Honey' and 'P.S. I Love You'. They also
performed 'Sheila', the current chart hit by Tommy Roe, but their
version wasn't transmitted. On 25 January 1963, a show recorded
on 16 January, they performed 'Chains', 'Please Please Me' and
'Ask Me Why' although their performance of 'Three Cool Cats'
wasn't transmitted.

On their final appearance on 12 March 1963, recorded on 6
March, they performed 'Misery', 'Do You Want To Know A
Secret?' and 'Please Please Me'. Their version of 'I Saw Her
Standing There' was not transmitted.

Hessy, Frank

Frank Hesselberg opened his musical instrument store, Frank
Hessy, in Whitechapel, Liverpool, in 1934 and it became the city's
most famous music store. In the mid-1950s, with the burgeoning
music scene, local youngsters flooded the shop, wanting musical
instruments on hire purchase.

Mimi Smith bought her nephew John Lennon his first guitar at Hessy's for £15 – and later threatened to throw it into the dustbin, after telling him: 'The guitar's all right as a hobby, but you'll never make a living out of it.' Years later he had the phrase engraved on a silver plaque which he sent to her.

Stuart Sutcliffe also purchased his first bass guitar, a Hohner President, from Hessy's. Although the story goes that he bought it with the £65 he received for selling a painting to John Moores, he actually took out a hire-purchase agreement and did not buy it outright, as is popularly supposed.

Hessy funded a music magazine, *Frank Comments,* mainly written and illustrated by Bill Harry.

His chief salesman was Jim Gretty, a local entertainer who encouraged the groups and occasionally booked them on his own promotions.

Although there were other musical instrument stores in Liverpool such as Crane's, Rushworth & Dreaper's and Cramer & Lea, Hessy's had a particular affinity with the local groups.

The shop was featured in the film *Ferry 'Cross the Mersey,* and had its own 'Wall of Fame', a panoramic display of photographs of dozens of local groups.

Frank Hesselberg retired to Tel Aviv, where he died in 1983 at the age of 74. His store continued to supply instruments to local groups, but eventually closed down after 61 years in July 1995, when a fashion chain bought the premises.

Heswall Jazz Club, Barnston Women's Institute, Barnston Road, Heswall, Cheshire

The Beatles made their debut at this venue on the Wirral on Saturday, 24 March 1962. They topped the bill above the local jazz band, the Pasadena Jazzmen. Entrance was by ticket only at seven shillings and sixpence (37½p) and the venue was open from 7.30 p.m. until 11.15 p.m. The Beatles were billed as 'Mersey Beat Poll Winners! Polydor Recording Artists! Prior to European Tour!' The European tour referred to their April visit to the Star Club in Hamburg.

It was a smart, new-look Beatles who appeared that night wearing their Beno Dorn suits for the first time.

Their next appearance at the venue took place on 30 June, headlining above the Big Three, when they were now advertised as Parlophone Recording Artistes and the last of their three appearances, all of them in 1962, took place on Tuesday, 25 September.

Hey, Bulldog

Recorded on Sunday, 11 February 1968, it was one of the last songs the Beatles recorded before they left for India.

They hadn't originally intended to record that day as they were in the studio to film a promo for 'Lady Madonna', but decided that since they were in the studio they might as well record a song. John has commented, 'Paul said we should do a real song in the studio, to save wasting time. Could I whip one off? I had a few words at home so I brought them in.'

It has also been said that there was originally no reference to 'Bulldog', but as they started recording, Paul started barking to make John laugh and they decided to call the number 'Hey, Bulldog'.

John had brought Yoko into the studio for the first time and she said, 'I went to see the Beatles' sessions and in the beginning I thought, "Oh well". So I said to John, "Why don't you do something more complex?"' He noted, 'I was doing "Bulldog", it was embarrassing.'

The song was included in the *Yellow Submarine* film, but producer Al Brodax didn't like it and cut it from the American prints.

The number was included on the *Yellow Submarine* soundtrack album and the *Rock 'n' Roll Music* compilation.

Hey Good Lookin'

A number penned by country music's legendary Hank Williams and recorded by him in 1951.

The Beatles were probably influenced by the later version by their hero Carl Perkins. The Beatles performed the number in their stage act in 1960 and 1961, with John Lennon on lead vocals.

Hey Jude

This was the Beatles' longest single at seven minutes fifteen seconds and their first to be issued on the Apple label. It was released in Britain and America on 26 August 1968, in the UK on Apple R522 and in the US on Apple 2276, with 'Revolution' on the flip.

It went to No. 1 on both sides of the Atlantic and in at least ten other countries around the world. In the UK it received the Ivor Novello Award for the highest number of record sales in Britain during 1968 and in America it had the longest spell of any Beatles single at No. 1 – a total of nine weeks. At over seven minutes it was the longest single to reach No. 1 up to that time. The single was re-released in 1982 as part of the batch of Beatles records celebrating their twentieth anniversary. It was also featured on *The Beatles*

1967–1970 compilation and a *Hey Jude* album was issued in the
States in 1970 and in Britain in 1979. The song has also been
included on *The Beatles Ballads* compilation and *The Beatles Box*
set in 1980.

During one of the recording sessions for the track, on Tuesday, 30
July, a film team from the National Music Council of Great Britain
shot colour footage for their documentary *Music!* The 45-minute
film, directed by Michael Tuchner and produced by James Archibald,
was a documentary covering music in general, from classical to pop,
and was shown as a second feature to *The Producers* at the Prince
Charles Theatre, London, and then went on general release in Britain
on 12 July 1971. The 'Hey Jude' sequence lasted for five minutes.

During a session on Tuesday, 1 August, which took place at
Trident Studios, the orchestral accompaniment, using 36 instruments, was added.

Discussing the origin of the song, Paul says: 'It was going to be
"Hey Jules" but it changed. I happened to be driving out to see
Cynthia Lennon. I think it was just after John and she had broken
up, and I was quite matey with Julian. He's a nice kid, Julian. And
I was going out in me car just vaguely singing this song. I started to
sing "Hey Jules, don't make it bad", and then I changed it to "Hey
Jude", you know, the way you do. It was just a name. It was just
like "Hey Luke" or "Hey Max" or "Hey Abe" but "Hey Jude" was
better.

'To one feller "Hey Jude" meant Jew, "Juden Raus – Jews Get
Out". At the time we had the Apple shop, I went in one night and
put whitewash on all the windows and rubbed out "Hey Jude" as a
big ad. I thought it was a great thing, nothing happening in the shop,
let's use the window as a big advertising thing for the record. So I
did this "Hey Jude" right across the window and some feller from
a little Jewish delicatessen rang up the office the next day. He said
"If my sons vere vif me, I'd send von of them around to kill you.
You are doing this terrible thing wif the Jewish name. What you
want? Juden Raus, you trying to start the whole Nazi thing again?" '

Although Paul said that Julian Lennon was his inspiration, other
people have thought it was inspired by them. Journalist Judith
Simons of the *Daily Express* thought it referred to her. John Lennon
believed that Paul had produced a subliminal message to him in
which he blessed John's new relationship with Yoko. In September
1968, John told *Rolling Stone* magazine, 'Well when Paul first sang
"Hey Jude" to me – or played me the little tape he'd made of it – I
took it very personally. Ah, it's me! I said. It's me. He says, "No, it's
me".' 'Hey Jude' is regarded as one of their major classics and has
been recorded by hundreds of different artists, covering a wide

musical spectrum, including Chet Atkins, Count Basie, Petula Clark, Bing Crosby, the Everly Brothers, Ella Fitzgerald, Stan Kenton, Joe Loss and His Orchestra, Wilson Pickett, Elvis Presley and Dionne Warwick.

The only version to reach the chart apart from the Beatles one was Pickett's.

'Hey Jude' received the American award for being 'The Most Performed Song' in 1968, 1969 and 1970. A shorter version than the original single was included on the Beatles' *Anthology 3* CDs. The number was also included on the CD compilation *Past Masters Volume Two*.

Hey Jude (The Beatles Again)

Capitol Records had been receiving orders for the proposed *Get Back* album when instructions came from Apple that the album would not be issued and all promo copies were to be recalled. Since they had received so many orders for a Beatles album, Capitol decided to produce their first collection of tracks not previously found on Beatles albums in the US. Initially the collection was called *The Beatles Again* and was given the catalogue number SO-385. Then it was decided to call the album *Hey Jude* and the photograph from the reverse of the album was placed on the cover and it was issued on Apple SW 385 on 23 February 1970. The album was a massive seller and reached No. 1 in *Record World* and No. 2 in *Cash Box* and *Billboard*.

The tracks were, Side One: 'Can't Buy Me Love', 'I Should Have Known Better', 'Paperback Writer', 'Rain', 'Lady Madonna', 'Revolution'. Side Two: 'Hey Jude', 'Old Brown Shoe', 'Don't Let Me Down' and 'The Ballad Of John And Yoko'.

Hey, Man

Title of a proposed stage musical based around the daily life in the Apple building. The idea had first been mooted by Mike Connor, head of the Apple office in Los Angeles.

It was agreed that George Harrison would write the music and Derek Taylor would provide the lyrics. Both George and John Lennon encouraged Derek in the project and there was talk of the musical opening at New York's Shubert Theatre.

Taylor told the music paper *Disc*: 'For everyone life is a mixture of fact and fiction – often this office is like *Alice In Wonderland* – and since Apple is constantly surrounded and involved in music, it seemed a natural subject to base a musical around.'

However, Derek found that he was unable to produce lyrics and the project was dropped.

Highlight

A BBC Overseas Service radio programme. Paul McCartney was interviewed for the show on 14 July 1964 and the interview was transmitted on 18 July. It was also transmitted on the BBC Home Service on 11 September under the title 'A Beatle's Eye View'.

High Park Farm, Nr Machrihanish, Argyllshire, Scotland

At the height of their romance, Jane Asher recommended to Paul that he invest in a farm which they could use as a retreat and in June 1966 they went to view High Park Farm in Scotland.

Farmer's wife Janet Brown commented, 'Our farm had been up for sale for a while now but what a surprise my husband and I had when we saw the famous pair – Paul told me that it had always been his ambition to own a farm in Scotland.' Paul purchased the farm and Jane helped him furnish it. The farm comprised 183 acres near Machrihanish, the nearest town being Campbeltown.

The affair with Jane over, Paul continued to enjoy relaxing at the faraway retreat, which was greeted with equal enthusiasm by Linda when the couple were married.

The area was too bleak and hilly for cows, so Paul bought sheep, almost 200 of them. However, he couldn't bear the thought of killing them and rarely sent any to market, allowing them to breed. For some time Paul sheared the sheep himself with some hand shears, sending the wool to the Wool Marketing Board. The couple also grew lots of vegetables on the farm and stabled horses with names such as Drake's Drum, Honor and Cinnamon, along with ponies such as Coconut, Cookie and Sugarfoot.

Paul took to farm life and Linda once bought him a tractor as a Christmas present.

Hilton Hotel, Park Lane, London W1

In February 1967 Pattie Harrison had attended regular meetings of the Spiritual Regeneration Movement and had been given her own 'mantra', a secret word to chant. George was also beginning to show an interest in spiritual matters at the time. A girl friend told Pattie about Transcendental Meditation and she attended a lecture at Caxton Hall. The Maharishi wasn't at that particular meeting, but Pattie joined.

In August, George and Pattie noticed advertisements in the newspapers announcing that the Maharishi Mahesh Yogi would be at the Hilton Hotel giving a lecture on TM. George suggested that they attend and also contacted the other members of the Beatles.

On Thursday evening, 24 August 1967, George, Pattie, Paul, Jane Asher and John and Cynthia attended the lecture which was held in the ballroom of the Hilton and cost 35p entrance at the door. (Ringo was with Maureen at Queen Charlotte's Hospital as she'd given birth to Jason five days previously.) Following the lecture, the Beatles asked for and received a private audience with the Maharishi, during which he suggested that they all attend a gathering he'd arranged at the University College of Bangor during the coming weekend.

Hippodrome Theatre, Hurst Street, Birmingham

The Beatles first appeared at the Hippodrome as part of the Tommy Roe/Chris Montez tour on 10 March 1963. After the show John came down with a heavy cold and had to miss the next three gigs, which went ahead with three Beatles only.

When the Beatles next appeared at the theatre on 9 November 1963 their popularity in Britain had increased to such an extent that plans had to be made to escort them in and out of the Hippodrome through the massive throng of fans.

'Operation Beatles' was the plan and the group were first taken to the local Digbeth Police Station where they drank hot cups of tea and signed autographs while a special van was prepared. They were driven to the theatre and the van drew up quickly outside the stage door. All four members of the Beatles were wearing police helmets and they jumped out of the van and briefly posed for photographers, standing among a group of policemen, before being smuggled into the theatre. John Lennon later quipped, 'Me in a copper's hat. No one will ever believe this.'

Hippodrome Theatre, Middle Street, Brighton, Sussex

The Beatles appeared three times at this southern seaside resort venue.

They made their debut there on Sunday, 2 June 1963 during their tour with Roy Orbison.

Their second appearance took place on Sunday, 12 July on the first of five Sunday concerts at seaside resorts. Jimmy Nicol & the Shubdubs were also on the bill, but the drummer who had once substituted for Ringo never met the group that night. Liverpool's the Fourmost were also appearing and George Harrison was involved in a minor road accident in his new E-Type Jaguar on his way to the show.

Their third and final appearance at the theatre took place on Sunday, 25 October 1964.

Hippodrome Theatre, Hyde Road, Ardwick Green, Manchester

The theatre where Johnny & the Moondogs travelled to appear in the finals of the 'Star Search' talent contest, organised by Carroll Levis and offering the winners a brief spot on his television show.

The date was 15 November 1959 and this was the first time the group had ever travelled outside Merseyside for a performance and they didn't even have enough money to enable them to stay overnight in Manchester, resulting in them leaving the theatre before the end of the show in order to catch the last train back to Liverpool.

Hippy Hippy Shake, The

Number composed and recorded by Chan Romero in 1959 which became very popular with Mersey Beat groups. The Swinging Bluejeans took their version to No. 2 in the British charts and No. 24 in the American.

Paul took lead vocals on the Beatles' version of the number which is captured on *The Beatles Live! At the Star Club In Hamburg: 1962* album. The group also recorded it on two BBC 'Saturday Club' and three 'Pop Go The Beatles' radio shows. The 'Pop Go The Beatles' radio performance was included on *The Beatles Live At The BBC* CDs.

Hofer, Walter

The Attorney who represented Brian Epstein and NEMS in America.

It was Dick James who recommended Hofer to Epstein and when Brian visited New York, Hofer invited him to his offices in West 57th Street and also held a cocktail party in his honour. Brian hired Hofer, although he considered his fees to be extravagant.

It was Hofer's office which received notices that Brian was obliged to make an appearance in a New York court in the Seltaeb case.

In American civil cases the contesting parties have the right to examine each other, with sworn testimony before a trial. Hofer mentioned the notices to Epstein, but didn't stress their urgency. As a result, since Brian hadn't responded to the legal notices to appear, the Supreme Court granted a judgment against Epstein, the Beatles and NEMS for default. It cost Brian a great deal of money to sort the problem out.

Hofer died in November 1984.

Hoffmann, Dezo

A photographer who was born in a small Hungarian village shortly after World War I. He studied journalism in Prague and then became a clapper boy for legendary film cameraman Otto Heller. During his military service he was sent to Abyssinia as a newsreel cameraman to cover Mussolini's invasion. He then returned to Prague only to be sent to film the Olympic Popular, the Social Democrat-organised series of games prior to the 1936 Olympics. It was here that he was caught up in the opening events of the Spanish Civil War. He was actually hanged in the street, cut down in the nick of time, and decided to stay on with the 800 volunteers who were determined to fight fascism and who were the first stirrings of the International Brigade. He was actively involved in the fighting in and around Madrid and it was at this time that he met Hemingway and Capra. He was badly wounded and, following Franco's victory, was interned in a prison camp until the outbreak of World War II. He joined the Czech army, escaped to Gibraltar, then to England where he organised the Czech Brigade of volunteers and soldiers.

He then became involved with the Ministry of Information as a newsreel cameraman, took a crash course in English and went around the theatres of war in Burma, India, Tobruk and El Alamein. During the allied landings he was wounded twice and eventually discharged from the army in 1945. He then moved to Leicester where he married. The couple had two children before Dezo decided to move to London where he established himself as a show business photographer, photographing stars such as Marilyn Monroe, Charlie Chaplin, Marlene Dietrich, Frank Sinatra and Louis Armstrong.

In 1955 he joined *Record Mirror*, the weekly show business newspaper. In 1962 he received a letter from a reader in Liverpool who waxed enthusiastically about a group called the Beatles. Dezo became interested in this relatively unknown band and began taking photographs – which was to result in him taking more photographs of the Beatles than any other photographer.

He photographed their first Abbey Road Studios audition with George Martin in June 1962, and travelled to Liverpool to take numerous exclusive shots in April 1962, including pictures of them in their homes, at the Cavern, in Sefton Park and at their hairdressers. Until he had a dispute with John Lennon on the set of *A Hard Day's Night* over a photograph that had been printed in *Tit Bits* magazine, he was present covering almost every major event in their career. Following the argument he continued taking shots of the Beatles, but not so frequently.

His collections of Beatles photographs are the most complete visual/photographic documentation of their career during 1963–64 in existence. The thousands of shots include them performing at Stowe

School, the Liverpool Empire, the Albert Hall, at the BBC radio recordings, television shows, during their trips to Paris and America, appearances at Twickenham Studios, during the Christmas Show at the Hammersmith Odeon and their Royal Variety performance.

In addition to his photographs appearing in publications throughout the world, there have also been a number of books of his work printed. They include: *The Beatles* (Shinko Music, 1975), *With The Beatles* (Omnibus Press, 1982), *The Beatles Conquer America* (Omnibus Press, 1984) and *John Lennon* (Columbus Books, 1985).

In the early 1970s, Dezo and John met up at the Plaza Hotel in New York and settled their differences.

He died on Wednesday, 26 March 1986 following a heart attack that left him in a coma. Apple Corps was to buy the rights to his Beatles photographic collection.

Hoffmann, Rosa

Born on 21 April 1900, she was the toilettenfrau of the Indra Club when the Beatles first appeared there in June 1960.

The Beatles had spent almost all of their money on their trip from Liverpool and were very hungry when they settled in on their first night in Hamburg. Rosa gave them a few German marks and sent them to the nearby Harold's Café for potato fritters, cornflakes and chicken soup.

She used to provide them with soap and towels, washed their shirts and socks and gave them chocolate bars. She even allowed Paul to live in her bungalow in dockland and said: 'I remember when young Paul used to practice guitar on the roof of my little place. We used to get crowds of burly old Hamburg dockers, just listening. They shouted out things in German, but Paul couldn't understand them. In Hamburg, even when people didn't understand what the Beatles were singing, they took to the group – especially to Paul when he did his Little Richard act, they really took to him.'

The Beatles called her 'Mutti', because she acted like a mother to them.

When the Beatles moved to the Kaiserkeller and Top Ten Clubs, she moved with them and when the Beatles appeared at the Star Club they found that Rosa had become the toilettenfrau there, too.

The St Pauli district in those days was not as seedy as has been made out and was visited by lots of respectable couples in much the same way as visitors flock to Soho in London. The area changed into a more sinister place many years later, with the introduction of hard drugs. Still, amphetamines such as preludin and captogen were available over the pharmacist's counter, and the groups used to take 'uppers' regularly, to keep them going through their long sessions and the unsociable hours. When Henri Henriod heard that the police were about to raid the club for drugs, he was baffled – no drugs were allowed to be sold at the club. He was then told that Rosa, who had a big sweet jar full of 'prellies' in the toilet, was supplying the Beatles (with the exception of Pete Best) and other musicians with tablets.

Henri called her to the office and sacked her – until the doorman, Ali, intervened and told him that Rosa didn't get any money for the pills. The financial rewards from the selling of the pills went to an English road manager who, as a result of the incident, was dubbed 'Terry the Pill'.

Rosa died on Tuesday, 15 March 1988 in Peter Eckhorn's house, then owned by his widow, Christa.

Holder, Owen

Scriptwriter whose most successful script was for the film, *A Funny Thing Happened On The Way To The Forum*.

In 1966 he proposed a script for the Beatles' third film, which he called 'Shades Of A Personality'. Reporting on the story, the *New Musical Express* commented that it would: 'focus on one member of the group (yet to be chosen) who will supposedly have a split personality with four different sides to his character. Besides his real self he will imagine himself in turn as three other people. The three other Beatles.'

The film was to be shot in Malaga, Spain, in September 1967 with Michelangelo Antonioni directing. The *NME* was later to announce: 'John Lennon will play the part of the man himself, while the three other Beatles will portray each of the faces of his split personality – "the dreamer", the "human being" and the man as perceived by the outside world.'

Producer Walter Shenson regarded Holder's script as being dull and he passed it over to playwright Joe Orton to see if he could brighten it up. Orton commented: 'Basically it [the idea] is that there aren't four young men. Just four aspects of one man. Sounds dreary, but as I thought about it I realised what wonderful opportunities it would give.'

Orton developed the idea and came out eventually with a script which was totally different from the original, which he called 'Up Against It'.

Hold Me Tight

A number penned by Paul in Forthlin Road and said to be influenced by the music of American girl group the Shirelles. The Beatles first began playing the number in 1961 and it was part of their Cavern Club repertoire. They recorded it for their *Please Please Me* album on Monday, 11 February 1963, but it was left off the album and that particular tape was lost. The group re-recorded the number on Thursday, 12 September 1963, and it was included on the *With The Beatles* album and the American release *Meet The Beatles*.

'Hold Me Tight' was the rare instance of a number being rejected for one Beatles album, but eventually placed on another.

Hollies, The

Northern group, once referred to as 'Manchester's Beatles', who appeared on the same bill as the Beatles at the Cavern on Sunday, 3 February 1963.

Allan Clarke and Graham Nash had been singing together for a number of years as a vocal duo using various names, including the Guytones, the Two Teens and Rikky & Dane. In 1959, as Rikki & Dane, they appeared on a 'Carroll Levis Discovery Show' with Johnny & the Moondogs, who comprised John Lennon, Paul McCartney and George Harrison, who performed 'Think It Over'. They were to see the Beatles for the first time at the Oasis Club, Manchester.

The Hollies themselves were formed in 1962, with Eric Haydock on bass, Don Rathbone on drums and Tony Hicks on guitar. Like several other Manchester bands, they began travelling to Liverpool to appear at the Cavern and appeared on several bills with the Beatles.

When they earned the tag 'Manchester's Beatles', they told *Mersey Beat*: 'Our sound is completely different and the comparison has probably been made because we wear leather pants. The reason why we wear leather is because it's more serviceable and you can do anything with leather and it still stays the same. If you analyse the Beatles' sound you will find it's entirely different from ours – and we hope people will stop associating our name with theirs.'

It was while they were playing at the Cavern that they were discovered by Ron Richards, who signed them to the Beatles' record label, Parlophone. They had hits with their first two singles 'Just Like Me' and 'Searchin''. Shane Fenton at one time managed them and when Rathbone became their road manager Bobby Elliott, a member of Fenton's band, replaced him on drums.

When their cover of George Harrison's 'If I Need Someone' entered the charts in December 1965, Harrison made some uncomplimentary remarks about it: 'They've spoilt it. The Hollies are all right musically, but the way they do their records they sound like session men who've just got together in a studio without ever seeing each other before.'

This caused a great deal of controversy and Graham Nash replied: 'Not only do those comments disappoint and hurt us, but we are sick of everything the Beatles say or do being taken as law. The thing that hurt us most was George Harrison's knock at us as musicians. And I would like to ask: If we have made such a disgusting mess of his brainchild song, will he give all the royalties from our record to charity?'

George's comments seemed to have affected the record sales and the disc only reached No. 20 in the charts, their previous release 'Look Through Any Window' having reached No. 4 and their next single 'I Can't Let Go' reaching No. 2.

There seemed to be no hard feelings later on as Graham was invited as one of the guests at the recording of 'All You Need Is Love'.

The Hollies were one of the most successful groups to emerge from the beat boom and had a total of 31 hit singles and several hit albums between the ears 1963–88, more hits than any other British band, including the Beatles. They included 'Stay', 'Just One Look', 'Yes I Will', 'I'm Alive', 'I Can't Let Go' and 'He Ain't Heavy, He's My Brother'.

Graham was to leave the band and settle in America where he became part of the successful Crosby, Stills & Nash group. Liverpudlian Terry Sylvester, former member of the Escorts and the Swinging Bluejeans replaced him in the Hollies. Graham joined them for a reunion album *What Goes Around* in 1983 and teamed up with them again in 1995 to record 'Peggy Sue Got Married'. With Allan Clarke the head, the group were still embarking on concert tours in 1999.

The group continued to have hits during the 1970s and embarked on an anniversary tour of Britain in 1986 – and later returned to the charts with a re-release of one of their hits of 1969, 'He Ain't Heavy, He's My Brother'.

Holly, Buddy

One of rock 'n' roll's greatest legends, who died in an air crash, along with Ritchie Valens and the Big Bopper, on 3 February 1959.

He was a seminal influence on the Beatles and the group played several of his numbers on their early gigs and recorded his 'Words Of Love' and 'Crying, Waiting, Hoping'. When they appeared on the Carroll Levis talent show in Liverpool during their early career they performed two of Holly's numbers, 'Think It Over' and 'It's So Easy'.

Although George Harrison was quoted as saying that the name Beatles was inspired by the motorcycle gang 'The Beetles' led by Lee Marvin in *The Wild One*, it is generally acknowledged that the group chose the title when seeking a similar name to that of Holly's backing group, the Crickets. Stuart Sutcliffe is said to have thought of the name Beetles and John Lennon replaced one of the 'e's' with an 'a'.

(Incidentally, *The Wild One* was banned in Britain for more than a decade after it was made, therefore the Beatles could not have seen it before choosing a name.)

Holly's manager, Norman Petty, was to present Paul McCartney with the cufflinks Holly was wearing at the time of his death.

Paul McCartney was the major Holly fan and his MPL Communications managed to purchase the Buddy Holly music catalogue of approximately 38 Holly compositions. From 1976 Paul began to run an annual 'Buddy Holly Week' on the anniversary of the singer's birth. Holly's widow, Maria Elana, commented: 'Paul told me that Buddy had more influence on his early songwriting than any other singer. Paul was very gracious and I appreciated what he had to say.'

John Lennon was to pay his own tribute to Holly on his 1975 album *Rock 'n' Roll*, which featured the track 'Peggy Sue'. When discussing his initial interest in music, John commented: 'I started off with a banjo at fifteen which my mother taught me to play. My first guitar cost ten pounds. It was one of those advertised in the paper you sent away for. Julia got it for me. I remember it had a label on the inside which said, "Guaranteed Not to Split". My mother used to say she could play any stringed instrument there was, and she really did teach me quite a lot. The first tune I ever learned to play was "That'll Be The Day" by Buddy Holly.'

Hollywood Bowl, The, Los Angeles, California

On Sunday, 23 August 1964, the Beatles became the first rock 'n' roll act to perform at the prestigious, open-air venue in the Hollywood hills which had previously been the setting for symphony concerts. All 18,700 seats were sold and thousands of fans roamed outside the Bowl in the hills, with further fans climbing on to trees.

Backstage the group were visited by Lauren Bacall and they went on stage at 9.30 p.m. for a 35-minute show, with John Lennon setting the scene by announcing, 'Welcome to you in the trees.'

There was an element of drama that night with the fervour of so many fans who couldn't get into the Bowl – and one fan gave birth to a son in the car park.

Capitol Records recorded the show and the group rushed off stage at 10.05 p.m. and were spirited away in a limousine to a rented mansion where a private party had been arranged. Among the guests were Joan Baez and film starlet Peggy Lipton.

The Beatles returned to the Hollywood Bowl for two further concerts the following year, on 29 and 30 August. Their second concert was also recorded by Capitol Records. The album of the Hollywood Bowl concerts was not released until almost thirteen years later.

Holyoake Hall, Smithdown Road, Liverpool L15

A building originally erected on behalf of the Co-operative Society at the beginning of the century and situated only a few hundred yards away from Penny Lane. The entire first floor was used as a ballroom from the thirties. The Quarry Men made a few appearances here during 1957 and 1958 when the venue booked skiffle groups. The Beatles only appeared at the venue twice when promoter Wally Hill booked them on 15 July and 22 July 1961.

Many of the top Liverpool bands appeared regularly at the venue in the early sixties, where they reported that the large hall was ideal for dances, but the 'bouncers' proved to be over-zealous and groups were often arguing with them over their rough treatment of fans.

Honey Don't

A Carl Perkins composition which was the flipside of his million-seller 'Blue Suede Shoes' in 1956. The Beatles included the number in their repertoire in 1962 with John on lead vocals. From August 1963 it provided a vocal spot for Ringo and he continued to perform it until late in 1964.

It was Ringo who sang the number when the Beatles recorded it on Monday, 26 October 1964, for the *Beatles For Sale* album. It was also included on the American *4 By The Beatles* EP and *Beatles '65* album. The version from the *Pop Go The Beatles* radio show was included on *The Beatles Live At the BBC* CDs.

Honeymoon Song, The

A number composed by Greek musician Theodorakis and featured in the 1959 film *Honeymoon*.

There were several versions of the tune, the most notable being an instrumental by Manuel and the Music of the Mountains. There was also a French-language version by Petula Clark.

The Beatles began performing the song on stage in 1961 with Paul on lead vocals. They recorded it on the BBC radio show 'Pop Go The Beatles' on 6 August 1963 and when Apple Records was launched several years later, Paul produced a version by Mary Hopkin. The radio show performance of the number was included in *The Beatles Live At The BBC* CDs.

Honey Pie

Number penned by Paul which was included on *The Beatles* double album. Paul played piano and sang solo while John played electric guitar and George Harrison played bass. It was recorded at Trident Studios, London, on 1 October 1968 and a few days later George Martin recorded several musicians for a brass backing sound which he had scored. They were Dennis Walton, Ronald Chamberlain, Jim Chester, Rex Morris and Harry Klein on saxophones and Raymond Newman and David Smith on clarinets.

Commenting on the number in a Radio Luxembourg interview, Paul said, 'My Dad's always played fruity old songs like this, and I like them. I would have liked to have been a 1920s writer because I like that top hat and tails thing.' A version of the number appeared on the Beatles' *Anthology 3* CDs.

Hopkin, Mary

A young, blonde-haired folk singer, born in Pontardawe, near Swansea in South Wales on 3 May 1950, who came to the attention of Paul McCartney via Twiggy, the popular model. Twiggy and her manager Justin De Villeneuve had been invited to dinner at Paul's Liverpool home. Twiggy mentioned that she'd seen a talented girl singer on 'Opportunity Knocks' and predicted that she would win and appear on the show the following week. Paul watched the programme the next week and the seventeen-year-old Mary Hopkin did win.

Paul had Derek Taylor trace her number and call her. He then spoke to her, recalling the moment in a *Melody Maker* feature: 'This beautiful little Welsh voice came on the phone and I said: "This is Apple Records here; would you be interested in coming down here to record for us?" She said: "Well, er, would you like to speak to my mother?" and then her mother came on the line and we had a chat and two further telephone conversations and later that week Mary and her mum came to London.'

Paul decided to produce her first single himself. He chose the song 'Those Were The Days', a number he had first heard several years previously in London's Blue Angel Club. Gene and Francesca Rankin had performed the number. Paul had liked the song so much he'd at one time suggested that the Moody Blues record it, and had played it to Donovan during their time at Rishikesh. It became the second Apple release, following 'Hey Jude', and sold

five million copies worldwide after being released in Britain on 30
August 1968 on Apple 2 and in America on 26 August on Apple
1801. It followed 'Hey Jude' into the No. 1 spot in the British
charts and reached No. 2 in America, being kept off the top slot by
'Hey Jude'.

Mary also sang the number in Italian, French, Spanish and
German. The hits on the continent led to Paul recording her singing
two more numbers in Italian, 'Quelli Erano Giorni' and 'Lontano
Dagli Occhi', and another song in French, 'Prince en Avignon'.

Paul then decided to produce an album in which he selected most
of the tracks, numbers such as 'Inchworm', 'There's No Business
Like Show Business', 'Love Is The Sweetest Thing', 'Someone To
Watch Over Me' and 'Lullaby Of The Leaves', mainly songs from
musicals. Mary, on the other hand, was a folk singer. Her favourites
were three folk songs penned by Donovan. He'd written two of
them specially for her – 'Lord Of The Reedy River' and 'Voyage of
the Moon', while the third, 'Pebble and the Man', he'd previously
recorded himself. Harry Nilsson also composed a number for the
album at Paul's request, 'The Puppy Song'. Paul also designed the
cover of the album, which was released in Britain on 21 February
1969 on Apple Sapcor 5 and in America on 3 March. The album
was called *Postcard* and was promoted at a special press reception
at London's Post Office Tower on 13 February 1969. Paul turned
up with Linda, Donovan performed and Jimi Hendrix was among
the guests. Both Paul and Donovan played acoustic guitars on the
three tracks.

Paul also appeared in 'A Day In The Life Of Mary Hopkin', a
special insert in 'Magpie', the ITV children's programme, which
was filmed at the Apple office.

Mary's second Apple single 'Goodbye' was also specially written
and produced by Paul and reached No. 5 in Britain and No. 13 in
America.

Paul also produced her version of 'Que Sera Sera', issued in
France on 19 September 1969 on Apple 16 and in America on 15
June 1970 on Apple 1823.

However, he ceased being involved in her recordings because she
was more enthusiastic about singing folk material, which Paul
wasn't really interested in.

Although record producer Tony Visconti was later to say '. . . the
next record was "Goodbye" which was somewhat prophetic, and
Paul's rather cruel way of saying goodbye, because Mary read it in
the papers that Paul wasn't going to produce her anymore. He
never told her personally, but he was just that sort of way in those
days – the Beatles were very sheltered people, and they left all their

dirty work to the people around them, but since then Paul and Mary have become friends again, so everything's OK.'

Dissatisfied with the managers offered her by Apple, Mary chose her sister Carol to be her manager. Within a year her relations with Apple became strained and her Apple material was produced initially by Mickie Most, then by Tony Visconti. Visconti produced her album *Earth Song/Ocean Song* and the two were married in 1971. The couple had a daughter, Jessica, and Mary became more interested in rearing her daughter than performing and left Apple in 1972 and had no further hits. They were later divorced and Visconti went on to marry May Pang, John Lennon's former live-in lover.

She was later to make the occasional recording, appearing on David Bowie's 'Low' in 1977 and recording an album in the Welsh language, *The Welsh World Of Mary Hopkin*, in 1979.

Cynthia Lennon was to record 'Those Were The Days' in 1995.

Hot Chocolate

A popular British band who had a string of chart hits spreading over two decades and who became the only group to have had a hit in the British charts in every year of the seventies.

When singer Errol Brown teamed up with Tony Wilson, the two of them decided they'd like to make their debut recording 'Give Peace A Chance'. Since they wanted to make some alterations to the lyrics they had to seek the permission of the songwriters and sent a tape to Apple.

John Lennon arranged to see them and suggested that Apple could release the disc. As they had no group name at the time, one of Apple's press officers, Mavis Smith, suggested they call themselves the Hot Chocolate Band. John Lennon recommended the name, although they cut it to Hot Chocolate after they made their recording debut with 'Give Peace A Chance', coupled with 'Living Without Tomorrow'. The single was issued in Britain on Apple 18 on 10 October 1969 and in America on Apple 1812 on 17 October, although it failed to make the charts.

Following that release they joined Mickie Most's Rak Records and have had a large number of hits, including 'Brother Louie', 'Emma', 'You Sexy Thing', 'Every One's A Winner' and 'No Doubt About It'.

Hound Dog

An Elvis Presley chart topper of 1956. A Jerry Leiber/Mike Stoller song which the Quarry Men included in their repertoire in 1957 with John Lennon on vocals. It was also included in the Beatles' repertoire until 1961.

How Do You Do It?

A number which songwriter Mitch Murray had originally written for
singer Adam Faith. Faith didn't record the song and Murray took it
along to George Martin's assistant, Ron Richards. Richards liked the
number and called Dick James, who snapped up the publishing rights.
Richards retained the acetate for a while but was unsure whom to
place the song with. When George Martin was looking for material
for the Beatles, Richards played him the acetate and Martin decided
the Beatles should record the number and sent a copy up to Liverpool.

Martin was pleased with the number and claimed that it would
turn the Beatles into a household name. He was therefore quite
upset when John and Paul showed no interest in the song and said
that they'd prefer to record their own material. Martin ticked them
off and told them, 'When you can write material as good as this,
then I'll record it. But right now we're going to record this.'

The session took place on Tuesday, 4 September 1962, and the
Beatles didn't exactly put their heart into the recording. On the
same day they recorded 'Love Me Do'. Martin wasn't pleased with
the sound of that day's recording session and a new one was
arranged for Tuesday, 11 September, although they didn't record
'How Do You Do It' this time.

Following 'Love Me Do', the Beatles played Martin their version
of 'Please Please Me', which had been rearranged on Martin's
advice, and it was decided to issue the number as their next single,
with Martin acknowledging that, as far as the Beatles were
concerned, it was a better choice for them.

His faith in 'How Do You Do It' was vindicated when he
recorded Epstein's second Liverpool band, Gerry & the
Pacemakers. Their version of 'How Do You Do It' was issued on
Columbia DB 4987 on 14 March 1963 and was to reach the No. 1
position where it remained for four weeks.

Arguably, 'How Do You Do It' gave Gerry & the Pacemakers the
honour of being the first Mersey Beat group to top the British charts.
'Please Please Me' had seen the Beatles reach No. 1 in the *New
Musical Express*, *Melody Maker* and *Disc* charts but they only
reached No. 2 in the *Record Retailer/Record Mirror* charts. As the
Record Retailer chart was to include Top 50 placings and because
it was later changed to *Music Week* and carried the official chart
compiled by the British Market Research Bureau, researchers generally use the Record Retailer chart placings in their statistics. To be
quite fair, the most important British chart in 1963 was the *New
Musical Express* chart, which was also printed in some national
newspapers – and the chart placings in the BBC TV show 'Top Of
The Pops' were assembled from the placings in *New Musical*

Express, Melody Maker and *Disc* – and 'Please Please Me' had topped all those charts. Finally, what had been intended as the Beatles first Parlophone release eventually found its way on to the Beatles' *Anthology 1* CDs.

Howes, Arthur
One of the major British promoters of the sixties who was the main tour operator for the Beatles between the years 1964 and 1966.

Howes was the biggest presenter of 'pop package shows', in which a handful of recording artists, with a current or recent hit in the charts, would appear on a countrywide tour, generally on the ABC, Gaumont or Odeon Cinema circuits.

In November 1962 Brian Epstein tracked down Howes' phone number and called him at his home in Peterborough one Saturday afternoon. Howes agreed to try out the Beatles to see how they would go down on a theatre tour and put them on a bill topped by Frank Ifield at the Embassy Cinema, Peterborough on 2 December. They cancelled a Cavern booking and set off for the Northamptonshire venue, but their appearance didn't receive a good response from the audience. To his credit, Howes saw potential in the band and agreed to book them as a support on the bill on his forthcoming Helen Shapiro tour for £80 per week. They received the same amount for the second tour he billed them on, with Tommy Roe and Chris Montez. Howes featured them on a third tour that year, but this time as bill toppers on an autumn tour which commenced on 1 November.

Apart from the Roy Orbison tour and some short minitours, all the Beatles' succeeding British tours were organised by Arthur Howes.

Howes became a group manager when he took over the management of Rory Storm & the Hurricanes, as a favour to Brian Epstein. Howes died in London on 12 February 1987 at the age of 63.

Hullabaloo
An American coast-to-coast television series, produced by Jack Good, in which Brian Epstein had a five-minute spot as host and interviewer. During the Epstein segments of the shows, recorded at Shepperton Studios, Brian introduced and interviewed Gerry & the Pacemakers, Marianne Faithfull, Freddie & the Dreamers and Andrew Oldham.

Hully Gully
A number recorded by the Olympics in 1959. The Beatles included it in their repertoire in 1960. The group never recorded the number

and although there is a version of 'Hully Gully' on one of the later releases of the Star Club albums, the track is not by the Beatles.

Hulme Hall

Merseyside venue situated in Bolton Road, Port Sunlight, Cheshire. It was a small hall with a capacity of 450, across the River Mersey from Liverpool in a pleasant town that Viscount Leverhulme had built for his employees in 1888.

The Beatles appeared at the venue four times in 1962. They were booked on their debut appearance there on 7 July for a local golf club dance. Their second appearance on 18 August saw Ringo make his first public appearance with the group, following two hours of rehearsal. They were engaged for a dance promoted by the Horticultural Society.

R. E. Smith, director of the Horticultural Society, had booked the group on the urging of his son Geoff. Mr Smith contacted Brian Epstein and there was an agreement for the Beatles to play for a minimum of sixty minutes and a maximum of eighty minutes for a fee of £30.

The posters announced: 'Port Sunlight Society, Seventeenth Annual Horticultural Show, Hulme Hall, Port Sunlight, Saturday 18 August 1962. A dance will be held on the evening of the show in the above hall from 7.45pm to 11.30pm starring the North's No 1 rock combo, the Fabulous Beatles, now recording for Parlophone, supported by the 4 Jays. Tickets 6/- each.'

Smith also booked them to appear on 6 October. Their final appearance at the hall took place on 27 October at a dance organised by the Recreational Organisation. It was prior to their performance that Monty Lister interviewed them for his radio shows broadcast at the Cleaver and Clatterbridge Hospitals. This was the first radio interview the Beatles had and Lister was accompanied by two friends, Malcolm Threadgill and Peter Smethurst, who also took part in the interview, which was broadcast to the Wirral hospitals the next day.

Huntley, Ted

A link in the chain of events leading to the Beatles' recording contract in 1962.

Ted was working at the HMV shop in Oxford Street, London, in charge of cutting discs for customers. When Brian Epstein came into the shop to have acetates made of some Beatles numbers, Ted, a former engineer at EMI studios, was impressed by the group's sound: something which several A&R men with different record companies had not been. After a chat with Brian he discovered that the group did not have a publishing contract so he phoned Sid Coleman of EMI's publishing company, Ardmore and Beechwood, who were in the same building, and recommended that he meet Brian. Sid was also impressed with the material and called George Martin's office to arrange a meeting between Epstein and the Parlophone A&R man.

Huntley later left EMI to run a hotel in Jersey in the Channel Isles.

Chris Hutchins

A British journalist and former reporter for the *New Musical Express*. At the time of the Beatles' rise to prominence in Britain, the *NME* was the most influential music publication in the country.

Hutchins first met the Beatles in Hamburg in November 1962, when he visited the Star Club to interview Little Richard.

Once the Beatles had made their impact in Britain, Hutchins, whom they called Chrisp Hutchy or Chrispy Hutch, covered their activities on a regular basis, travelling to America with them in February 1964 and staying at the Plaza in New York.

Following their appearance at the Albert Hall on Thursday, 18 April 1963, Shane Fenton drove Paul, John, George and Jane Asher to Chris Hutchins' Chelsea flat, and that's where Paul's romance with Jane began.

His biggest contribution to the Beatles' story took place when he arranged their famous meeting with Elvis Presley during their American tour of 1965.

Chris was later to become a gossip columnist for several British tabloids, including the *Sunday Mirror, Daily Express* and *Today.*

His reminiscences of his days with the Beatles are to be found in *Elvis Meets The Beatles,* a book he wrote in collaboration with Peter Thompson in 1994.

Hutchinson, Johnny

Regarded as one of Liverpool's top drummers in the Mersey Beat era, the Maltese-born Johnny was a member of Cass & the Cassanovas, who became the Big Three when Brian Casser left the group. Johnny sat in with the Silver Beetles at their Larry Parnes audition when their drummer Tommy Moore turned up late.

Johnny made his debut on drums at the age of 18 at the Corinthian Club with Cass & the Cassanovas and also did the occasional gig with a modern jazz band. When the group became the Big Three, Johnny turned down a two-year contract with Johnny Kidd & the Pirates to remain with them.

According to Cilla Black, when Pete Best was sacked from the

Beatles, Hutchinson was first choice as his replacement. Then the Beatles had second thoughts because of his belligerency and felt they needed a drummer with a more subordinate personality and chose Ringo. In the few dates between Best's departure and Ringo's joining, Hutchinson played drums with the band. It has also been suggested that Epstein, aware that Hutchinson was regarded as Liverpool's top drummer, offered him the Beatles seat, but he turned it down.

Epstein was to sign up his group, the Big Three, and they had some minor hits with 'Some Other Guy' and 'By The Way', but they disagreed with Brian's style of management and convinced him that he should release them from their contract. There were various line-up changes, with Hutchinson being the only consistent member, but the group disbanded in the mid-sixties.

Huyton Parish Church Cemetery, Stanley Road, Huyton, Liverpool L36

Final resting place of the Beatles' original bass guitarist Stuart Sutcliffe whose grave is No. 552 in the 1939 section of the cemetery.

Stuart had died of a cerebral haemorrhage on 10 April 1962 and his body was flown back to Liverpool to be buried the same week as the Beatles went to Hamburg.

I Am The Walrus

A bizarre yet fascinating surrealistic composition from John Lennon, featured in the *Magical Mystery Tour* film. The 'I Am The Walrus' sequence was shot in West Malling, Kent, in September 1967.

Recording began on Tuesday, 5 September 1967, four days after the death of Brian Epstein. On Wednesday, 27 September, there were various overdubs, on to the track using sixteen musicians and sixteen singers. The musicians were Sidney Sax, Jack Rothstein, Ralph Elman, Andrew McGee, Jack Greene, Louis Stevens, John Jezzard and Jack Richards. On cellos were Lionel Ross, Eldon Fox, Bram Martin and Terry Weil. Gordon Lewin played clarinet and Neil Sanders, Tony Tunstall and Morris Miller were on horns. The voices were provided by the Mike Sammes Singers: Peggie Allen, Wendy Horan, Pat Whitmore, Jill Utting, June Day, Sylvia King, Irene King, G. Mallen, Fred Lucas, Mike Redway, John O'Neill, F. Dachtler, Allan Grant, D. Griffiths, J. Smith and J. Fraser. On Friday, 29 September 1967, a radio was tuned in to the BBC's Third Programme and some lines from a production of *The Tragedy of King Lear* were included on the track.

The number was included on the *Magical Mystery Tour* double EP release in Britain, the American album of *Magical Mystery Tour* and a later British album release of *Magical Mystery Tour*. It was also issued as the flipside of 'Hello Goodbye' in both Britain and America and was featured on the compilations *The Beatles 1967–1970*, *Reel Music* and the American *The Beatles Rarities*.

John was said to have been inspired to compose some of the

verses after hearing the sound of a police siren in the distance while sitting at his home in Weybridge.

The song was banned by the BBC because John mentions 'knickers' in the lyrics, which caused him to comment: 'It always seems to happen now that people misinterpret what we write or say. We're happy with the words and I don't see how they can offend anyone.' A version was included on the Beatles' *Anthology 2* CDs.

I Call Your Name

A song written by John, who commented, 'I like this one. I wrote it very early on when I was in Liverpool, and added the middle eight when we came down to London.'

They gave the number to Billy J. Kramer who included it as the flipside of another Lennon & McCartney song, 'Bad To Me', on his second single. It was issued in Britain on Parlophone R5049 on 26 July 1963 where it reached No. 1, losing its place a few weeks later to the Beatles' 'She Loves You'. In America it was issued on Liberty 55626 on 23 September 1964 and rose to No. 9.

When the Beatles came under pressure to produce a number of songs for a new album, they dug out the number and recorded it themselves on 1 March 1964. As it turned out, it wasn't required for an album, but they included it on their EP *Long Tall Sally*, which was released in June 1964. The Beatles also performed the number on the radio show 'Saturday Club' on 4 April 1964.

The Beatles version was included on their compilations, *Rock 'n' Roll Music* and *Rarities* and in America on *The Beatles Second Album*. It was also used on the *Beatles Box* and *The Beatles Collection* sets. The number was included on the CD compilation *Past Masters Volume One*.

I Don't Want To See You Again

The third Paul McCartney composition to be recorded by Peter & Gordon. The Beatles never recorded the number, although a demo disc may have been prepared for the duo's recording manager Norman Newall.

This was the least successful of the Lennon & McCartney numbers to be given to Peter & Gordon and didn't provide them with a British chart hit, although it reached No. 16 in America. It was issued in Britain on Columbia DB 7356 on 11 September 1964 and in America on Capitol 5272 on 21 September 1964.

I Don't Want To Spoil The Party

A John Lennon composition featured on the *Beatles For Sale* album which caused John to comment: 'That was a very personal one of mine. In the early days I wrote less material than Paul because he was more competent on guitar than I. He taught me quite a lot of guitar really.'

Recording began on Tuesday, 29 September 1964, and in addition to appearing on *Beatles For Sale*, the track was included on the *Beatles For Sale* (No. 2) EP. In America it surfaced as the flipside of the single 'Eight Days A Week', issued on 15 February 1965, and on Capitol's *Beatles VI* album.

I Feel Fine

A number which John penned during a recording session. The group performed the song on their radio shows 'Top Gear' and 'Saturday Club' and it was issued as a single with 'She's A Woman' on the flip. It was issued in Britain on Parlophone R5200 on 27 November 1964 and hit the No. 1 spot, where it remained for six weeks. It was issued in America on Capitol 5327 on 23 November 1964 and also reached No. 1, selling a million copies within the first week.

The Beatles used amplifier feedback on the number for the first time and it was a song they performed live on a number of occasions, including their 1964 Christmas shows and on tours in 1964 and 1965.

John often experimented with tape recorders at his small studio in Kenwood and may have developed the idea of the song's opening with a single note of feedback there. Discussing the song with David Sheff in a *Playboy* interview, John told him, 'That's me, including the guitar lick with the first feedback ever recorded. I defy anyone to find an earlier record – unless it is some old blues number from the twenties – with feedback on it.'

'I Feel Fine' was the Beatles' sixth No. 1 hit in both Britain and America and the American radio plays began before the official promotion was planned when KRLA in Los Angeles began airing a copy it had obtained on 6 November, playing the song every hour. The station's programme director Reb Foster commented on his scoop to *Billboard* magazine, saying, 'We've received calls from Florida, New York, St Louis, Denver and Cleveland stations, offering us money and queries about where we picked up the single.'

The number was included on the compilations *A Collection Of Beatles Oldies (But Goldies)*, *The Beatles 1962–1966* and *20 Greatest Hits*. It was also found on the American album *Beatles '65* and the *Beatles Box* set.

The *Top Gear* radio performance was included on *The Beatles Live At The BBC* CDs. A version from their performance on the TV show *Blackpool Night Out* was included on the Beatles' *Anthology 2* CDs. The number was also included on the CD compilation *Past Masters Volume One*.

Ifield, Frank

Singer born in Coventry in 1937 who went to live in Australia from 1946 to 1959. When the Beatles first entered the charts with 'Love Me Do', Ifield's 'Wayward Wind' was in the Top Five. The singer had fifteen records in the British charts between 1960 and 1966, including 'I Remember You', 'Lovesick Blues' and 'Confessin''.

When promoter Arthur Howes agreed to give the Beatles a try-out, he placed them on a bill with Ifield at the Embassy Cinema, Peterborough, on 2 December 1962.

The reception to the Beatles was poor, obviously due to the type of audience attracted to top-of-the-bill singer Ifield. The report in the local newspaper read: 'It is easy to see why Frank Ifield has been so popular in this country. No pseudo American accent; no sulky Presley look. Frank Ifield is himself and he flashed many a happy smile as he breezed through a confident performance at the Embassy on Sunday.

'As expected his well-known songs "I Remember You", "Lovesick Blues" and "She Taught Me How To Yodel" were sung, in addition to "Lonesome Me" and "Lucky Devil".

'Ifield came well up to expectations, but the supporting artists failed to please, just as a year ago Billy Fury, Eden Kane, Karl Denver, the Allisons and Chas McDevitt all appeared on the same show. Since then there has been a gradual decline in the standard of supporting artists.

' "The exciting Beatles" rock group quite frankly failed to excite me. The drummer apparently thought that his job was to lead, not to provide rhythm. He made far too much noise and in their final number "Twist and Shout" it sounded as though everyone was trying to make more noise than the others. In a more mellow mood, their "A Taste Of Honey" was much better and "Love Me Do" was tolerable.'

In 1964, Vee Jay Records in America issued the album *Jolly What! The Beatles And Frank Ifield On Stage* on 26 February. The album was only a minor hit and the title was misleading as all tracks by both artists were studio recordings and were not taken from the one and only night they appeared on the same stage.

I Forgot To Remember To Forget

A Stanley Kesler/Charlie Feathers composition which Elvis Presley recorded in 1956. The Beatles introduced the number into their repertoire in 1962, with George on lead vocals. They performed the song on their BBC radio show 'From Us To You' on 18 May 1964. The performance with George on lead vocals from the second *From Us To You* radio show was included on *The Beatles Live At The BBC* CDs.

If I Fell
Number composed by John Lennon and included on the *A Hard Day's Night* album. It was also one of the tracks on the *Extracts From The Film 'A Hard Day's Night'* EP. The song was included on the *Love Songs* compilation and in America it was issued as the flip-side of the single 'And I Love Her', which was issued in July 1964.

The Beatles included the number in the repertoire of their summer tour of America in 1964.

If I Needed Someone
In his book *I. Me. Mine* George describes this song by saying that it is like a million other songs written around the D chord: 'If you move your finger about you get various little melodies.'

George performed the number on stage during the Beatles' British tour of 1965 and their world tour in 1966. Recording of the number began in October 1965 and the song was included on the *Rubber Soul* album. It was also featured on the American release, *Yesterday ... And Today* and on *The Best Of George Harrison* album.

The Hollies recorded the number, but George criticised their version so much that it probably influenced the record-buying public's attitude and the single didn't sell as well as other Hollies records. The group hit back at George for his criticism.

If You Gotta Make A Fool Of Somebody
The one and only American hit by James Ray, who took it to No. 22 in the US charts in December 1961. The Beatles included it in their stage repertoire shortly afterwards with Paul McCartney on lead vocals. The group included it in their stage act and it was a popular number at the Cavern.

Manchester group Freddie & the Dreamers recorded the number and it became their first chart hit in May 1963 and reached No. 3 in the British charts.

If You've Got Trouble
A track which John and Paul composed specially for Ringo to record for the *Help!* album. A fast rock number, it was recorded on Thursday, 18 February 1965, and Ringo's voice was double-tracked.

Ringo had been featured singing at least one song on each Beatle album and, as he didn't write songs himself at the time, he generally covered numbers by other artists. John and Paul thought they'd provide the vehicle for him this time, but the number was not deemed satisfactory; it was left off the album. The number was eventually included on the Beatles' *Anthology 2* CDs.

I Got A Woman

A 1955 Ray Charles composition previously recorded by a large number of artists, including Elvis Presley and Bill Haley. The Beatles introduced it into their act in 1961, with John on lead vocal. They performed the number on their BBC radio appearances on 'Pop Go The Beatles' and 'Saturday Club'. The 1963 'Saturday Club' version of 'I Got A Woman' was included on the November 1994 CD *The Beatles Live At The BBC*.

I Got To Find My Baby

A Chuck Berry composition which he recorded in 1960. The Beatles introduced it into their repertoire in 1961 with John taking lead vocals. The group performed the number on 'Pop Go The Beatles' and 'Saturday Club'. The version from *Pop Go The Beatles* was included on *The Beatles Live At The BBC* CDs.

I Just Don't Understand

A chart hit for Ann-Margret in 1961 who took the song to No. 17 in the American charts. The Beatles began performing the number, with John Lennon on lead vocals, during 1961 and 1962.

Ann-Margret, truncated from her full name of Ann-Margret Olson, was once known as 'the female Presley' and had the potential to become a major female rock star. She appeared with Elvis in *Viva Las Vegas* and the two were romantically linked. Her name was also linked romantically with that of Ringo Starr and Ringo had to deny a romantic relationship several times during the conferences on the Beatles' first American tour. Their radio performance of the number on *Pop Go The Beatles* was included on *The Beatles Live At The BBC* CDs, another example of a Beatles performance which had never been previously issued or an official release.

I'll Be Back

An early John Lennon composition. John said that he'd originally begun to write it while playing a Del Shannon number on his guitar. He just reworked the chords of the Shannon number and came up with a completely different song – 'I'll Be Back'.

It was one of the tracks used on the *A Hard Day's Night* album –

an LP almost dominated by Lennon compositions. 'I'll Be Back' was also included on the American album *Beatles '65* and the compilation album *Love Songs*.

I'll Be On My Way

A number penned by Paul McCartney which was used as the flip-side of Billy J. Kramer's debut single 'Do You Want To Know A Secret?' Issued in April 1963.

The Beatles didn't record the number in a recording studio, but did tape a version of the song on Thursday, 4 April 1963 that was broadcast on the BBC radio show 'Side By Side' on Monday, 24 June 1963. It was this version which found its way on to the November 1994 *The Beatles Live At the BBC* CD.

I'll Cry Instead

A John Lennon composition. John was to comment: 'We were going to do this in *A Hard Day's Night* but the director Dick Lester didn't like it, so we put it on the flipside of the album. I like it.'

When recording was first begun on Monday, 1 June 1964, it was taped in two parts. As Dick Lester wasn't impressed by the number it was left off the film soundtrack and a short version was included on the British album *A Hard Day's Night*. The same version appeared on the British EP *Extracts From The Album 'A Hard Day's Night'*.

In America, Capitol wanted to issue it as a single and, due to the fact that it had been recorded in separate parts, they were able to extend its length and also repeated one of the verses in the editing, making the song longer. This is the version that was included on the American *A Hard Day's Night* album although the shorter version, from the British LP, was the one used on the American *Something New* album.

'I'll Cry Instead' was issued as a single in the States on Capitol 5234 on 20 July 1964, with 'I'm Happy Just To Dance With You' on the flip. It reached No. 25 in the charts.

In 1981, when Walter Shenson re-released the film *A Hard Day's Night,* the song was finally heard in the film – it was included at the beginning of the movie, over a montage of still photographs.

I'll Follow The Sun

One of the many numbers that Paul wrote in the very early days of his songwriting career, although exactly where and when is unclear. Some sources claim that he wrote the number at his Forthlin Road home in Liverpool. Paul was sixteen at the time and recovering from the 'flu. He was standing in the parlour with his guitar, looking out of the window through the lace curtains, when he began to write the song.

The number wasn't recorded until Sunday, 18 October 1964 and was included on their *Beatles For Sale* album. The number was also included on the *Beatles For Sale* (No 2) EP, the *Love Songs* compilation and the American *Beatles '65* album.

Paul recalls that they didn't record the song until their fifth album because he felt it initially didn't fit in with the hard R&B/rock 'n' roll and black leather image of their early career. However, Pete Best recalls him playing the number on piano in Hamburg in 1960 in between sets at the Kaiserkeller Club.

Explaining why it wasn't included on earlier Beatles releases, Paul commented, 'It wouldn't have been considered good enough. I wouldn't have put it up.'

When discussing *Beatles For Sale* in *Mersey Beat*, Paul commented: 'There are still one or two of our very early numbers which are worth recording. Every now and then we remember one of the good ones we wrote in the early days and one of them, "I'll Follow The Sun", is on the LP.'

Their performance from their second appearance on the 'Top Gear' radio show was included on *The Beatles Live At The BBC* CD.

I'll Get You

A John Lennon composition which, when the Beatles began recording it on Monday, 1 July 1963, had the working title 'Get You In The End'.

It originally surfaced as the flipside of 'She Loves You'. In America, the single was issued on the Swan label in September 1963. In May 1964 Swan released '*Sie Liebt Dich*' as a single, with 'I'll Get You' on the flip.

In the meantime, when Capitol acquired the track they included it on their release *The Beatles Second Album* in April 1964. A version of the song was also included with the *Rarities* album in the British *The Beatles Collection* set. The number was included on the CD compilation *Past Masters Volume One*.

I'll Keep You Satisfied

Another Paul McCartney number for Billy J. Kramer, featured as the 'A' side of his third single. It was issued in Britain on Parlophone R 5073 on 1 November 1963 and reached No. 4 in the charts. It was issued in America on Liberty 55643 on 11 November 1963 and reached No. 30.

The Beatles never recorded this number and didn't even tape it during their numerous BBC radio sessions, although it is likely they made a demo tape of the number for George Martin and Billy J. Kramer to listen to prior to the recording.

I Lost My Little Girl

Reputedly the first song that Paul McCartney ever wrote. He immediately introduced it into the Quarry Men's repertoire when he joined the group, but the band dropped the number when they became the Beatles.

When Paul was unsuccessful in his attempt to become lead guitarist with the new group in the New Clubmoor Hall, Liverpool, on 18 October 1959 he is said to have attempted to recover his pride by playing John this number after the show. John was suitably impressed.

I'm A Loser

Number penned by John which the group performed on their 'Top Gear', 'Saturday Club' and 'Ticket To Ride' radio appearances. They also featured it on their 1964 Christmas show, during their European tour in 1965 and on their January 1965 'Shindig' TV show appearance.

It was included on the *Beatles For Sale* album and within a short time Marianne Faithfull had included the song on her debut album.

'I'm A Loser' is also to be found on the American album *Beatles '65* and the EPs *Beatles For Sale* and *4 By The Beatles*.

John was said to be influenced by Bob Dylan when he wrote the semi-autobiographical number, which was originally considered for release as the Beatles' last single of 1964, along with 'No Reply' and 'Eight Days A Week'. Eventually, 'I Feel Fine' was chosen. A 'Top Gear' radio performance was included on *The Beatles Live At The BBC* CDs.

I'm Down

A Paul McCartney composition which the Beatles recorded on Monday, 14 June 1965. The track appeared as the flipside of the 'Help!' single and was also included on the compilation album *Rock 'n' Roll Music* and the British version of *Rarities*.

The group performed the number on stage during their world tours in 1965 and 1966 and also on their 'The Ed Sullivan Show' appearance in September 1965. The number was included on the CD compilation *Past Masters Volume One*.

I'm Gonna Sit Right Down And Cry (Over You)

Originally written by Joe Thomas and Howard Biggs in the early 1950s and recorded by Biggs. Elvis Presley recorded the number in

1956, but his single wasn't a hit. The Beatles added it to their repertoire in 1960 with Elvis enthusiast John Lennon on lead vocals. Their version of the song from the 'Pop Go The Beatles' broadcast was included on *The Beatles Live At the BBC* CD in November 1994.

I'm Happy Just To Dance With You

John wrote this number specially for George to sing in *A Hard Day's Night*, in the days before George found the confidence to be a songwriter in his own right, although John was also to say, 'I would never have sung it myself.' Apart from being featured on the *A Hard Day's Night* soundtrack, it was issued as the flipside of the single 'I'll Cry Instead', which was released in America in July 1964. Due to the fact that 'B' sides received placings in the US charts, 'I'm Happy Just To Dance With You' reached No. 95. In the same month it was included on Capitol's American album *Something New*. In 1982 the song was used as the flipside of 'The Beatles Movie Medley' single.

The number was recorded on Sunday, 1 March 1964 – the first time the Beatles had been into a studio to record on a Sunday.

I'm In Love

Brian Epstein was conscious of the potential of using Lennon & McCartney numbers for his other acts and was to ask John and Paul for numbers for Cilla Black, Billy J. Kramer, the Fourmost and Tommy Quickly to record.

He was careful not to ask them for their best numbers and usually requested early songs that they'd written and didn't intend to record for themselves. One of these was a pre-Beatles composition by John Lennon called 'I'm In Love' which Brian obtained for the Fourmost as their follow-up to John's other early number, 'Hello Little Girl', which gave the group a Top Ten hit.

'I'm In Love' was issued on Parlophone R 5078 in Britain on 15 November 1963 where it reached No. 12 in the charts. It didn't fare so well in America, not charting at all when it was issued on Atco 6285 on 10 February 1964.

I'm In Love Again

A single by Fats Domino. It was the first rock 'n' roll record that George Harrison remembers hearing, although it was never included in the Beatles' repertoire.

I'm Looking Through You

One of the many songs inspired by Jane Asher – but not in such a loving frame of mind as most of the others. Paul was angry with her

because she had gone to Bristol to appear in a play. He was to
comment, 'My whole existence for so long centred around a bachelor life: I don't treat women as most people do. My life generally
has always been very lazy and not normal. I knew I was selfish. It
caused a few rows. Jane went off to Bristol to act. I said, "OK then,
leave, I'll find someone else." It was shattering to be without her.
That was when I wrote "I'm Looking Through You" – for Jane.'

The number first surfaced on the 1965 *Rubber Soul* album and
has also been featured in the 1978 *The Beatles Collection* set. A
version of the number appeared on the Beatles' *Anthology 2* CD.

I'm Only Sleeping

A lazy atmosphere, a laid-back feeling prevails in the lyrics of
John's song requesting he be left alone to sleep and dream. Some
lengthy recording sessions took place to get this track down for the
Revolver album, including the use of a 'backward guitar sound'.
The number was also used on the American album *Yesterday . . .
And Today*. The number was included on the Beatles' *Anthology 2*
CDs.

I'm So Tired

Composition which John wrote during his stay at Rishikesh and
which he later regarded as one of his favourite songs.

The introspective lyrics denote weariness, a desire for peace of
mind after three weeks of virtual sleeplessness. There is also the
mention of his addiction to cigarettes and a curse on Sir Walter
Raleigh who is referred to as 'a stupid get'.

The number was included on *The Beatles* double album. A mix
of three of the studio recording takes, was included on the Beatles'
Anthology 3 CDs.

I'm Talking About You

A Chuck Berry composition which he released as a single in June
1962. The Beatles introduced it into their repertoire the same year,
with John on lead vocals. The group performed it during their last
season at Hamburg's Star Club and it's one of four Chuck Berry
numbers contained on *The Beatles Live! At The Star Club In
Hamburg, Germany: 1962* album. It became a popular number
with British R&B bands and the Beatles performed the song on the
BBC radio show 'Saturday Club' on 16 March 1963.

I. Me. Mine

A George Harrison composition that was said to have been based
on the music of a song George saw performed by an American

marching band on TV. When discussing the songs in his book *I. Me. Mine*. George wrote: 'Allen Klein thought it was an Italian song – you know, "Cara Mia Mine" – but it's about the ego: the eternal problem.'

When the song was recorded on Saturday, 3 January 1970 there were only three Beatles present in Studio Two at Abbey Road because John was on holiday in Denmark. George was able to give a short, amusing speech to the folks gathered in the studio: 'You all will have read that Dave Dee is no longer with us. But Micky and Tich and I would just like to carry on the good work that's always been done in number two.'

A version of the song had originally been attempted at Twickenham Film Studios, but only 94 seconds of it had been recorded. As the excerpt was to be used in the *Let It Be* film it was decided to record the number for the soundtrack album with just George, Paul and Ringo.

This version lasted for 1 min. 34 secs., which is the length Glyn Johns let it remain when he mixed the tapes – only including a brief piece of dialogue at the beginning in which George says, 'Are you ready, Ringo?' and Ringo answers, 'Ready, George!'

The Johns version was not used as Allen Klein gave the tapes to Phil Spector to whip into shape. Spector overdubbed a brass and strings section and made an extended re-mix of the number, lengthening it to 2 min. 25 secs. for the album. In the *Let It Be* film, John and Yoko are seen waltzing to the number.

A version of the number was included on The Beatles' *Anthology 3* CD.

Imperial Ballroom, Carr Road, Nelson, Lancashire

A large ballroom situated in a town near to Merseyside. The Beatles first appeared here on Saturday, 11 May 1963 before a capacity crowd of 2,000 and returned to a further capacity house on Wednesday, 31 July 1963.

Indiana State Fair Coliseum And Grandstand, Indianapolis, Indiana

The Beatles performed two shows on Thursday, 3 September 1964, as part of the Indiana State Fair. The site was at the home of the famous Indianapolis 500 Racetrack. The first show took place at 5.00 p.m. in the Indiana State Fair Coliseum and the second at 9.30 p.m. at the Grandstand. There were approximately 30,000 people at the two shows.

In between the shows the Beatles took part in a press conference at the Radio Building. A phone call had reported that there was a bomb in the building, but a bomb squad discovered it was a hoax. Present at the conference was the obligatory beauty queen – Miss Indiana State Fair.

Indica Gallery, Masons Yard, London W1

Gallery and specialist bookshop opened by Peter Asher, Barry Miles and John Dunbar in the sixties. Peter Asher was Jane's brother and Paul McCartney had designed the shop's wrapping paper, which he donated to them as a gift.

Barry Miles was a contributor to the fashionable 'underground' paper *International Times* and John Dunbar, a Cambridge graduate, was married to singer Marianne Faithfull.

It was Dunbar who invited John Lennon to 'Unfinished Paintings & Objects by Yoko Ono', an exhibition at the gallery, which ran from 9–12 November 1966.

Dunbar had told John, 'Some amazing things will be happening. Yoko sometimes puts people into bags to create a living, breathing work of art!' John thought the idea of the Japanese girl sticking people into bags was sexy and decided to attend the preview.

He was immediately struck by an apple on display. 'There was an apple on display there for two hundred quid. I thought that was fantastic.' He noticed a black canvas attached to the ceiling. A tiny magnifying glass was dangling from its side by a chain and a step ladder was conveniently placed. He climbed up the ladder leading to the canvas, picked up the magnifying glass and peering through its lens read the tiny word 'Yes'.

'It was positive. I was relieved,' he said.

John Dunbar was eager to introduce John to Yoko and when he did, Yoko handed him a card on which the word 'Breathe' was printed. He panted on it.

John then noticed an exhibit called 'Hammer A Nail In' and asked if he could 'Bash a nail in'. Yoko, who claims she had not been particularly aware of the Beatles, that the only one she knew by name at the time was Ringo, was reluctant to allow John's request because the official opening didn't take place until the following day. Dunbar was anxious that John's wish be granted as he'd intended approaching him at some future date to sponsor exhibitions. 'He's a millionaire. He's one of the Beatles,' he impressed upon Yoko. So she said, 'OK. You can hammer a nail in if you pay me five shillings.' He paused, then offered to pay her an imaginary five shillings in exchange for knocking in an imaginary nail with an imaginary hammer.

'And that's when we really met,' said John. 'That's when we locked eyes and she got it and I got it.'

Indra Club, 34 Grosse Freiheit, Hamburg, Germany

The club where the Beatles played their first 200 hours of music in Hamburg and underwent their 'baptism of fire', transforming themselves from an average group into something special, due to the long hours, the frenetic show caused by pills, booze and the insistent demands to 'make a show'.

Crammed into Allan Williams' mini-van in company with his wife Beryl, his brother-in-law Barry Chang, his friend Lord Woodbine and the German waiter Georg Sterner, the five Beatles finally arrived at the Kaiserkeller Club in the Reeperbahn where they believed they would be playing. The group who were currently performing were Derry & the Seniors and as the Beatles entered the club during one of the group's breaks, leader Howie Casey told them that they wouldn't be playing there, but at a little strip club down the road. This was confirmed by the pugnacious little promoter Bruno Koschmider who took them down the Grosse Freiheit where, at the seedy end of the street, they found a tiny club with its neon sign shaped like an elephant.

Koschmider had decided to turn his small strip club into a rock 'n' roll venue. The Beatles were appalled at the narrow room with its low stage, jukebox, heavy curtains and thick carpet (which were to muffle the sound), as Koschmider hadn't bothered to alter it from its strip club decor. The acoustics were pathetic. The group were appalled still further when they were shown their awful lodgings in the adjacent Bambi Kino.

After their 36-hour journey the group went on stage at the club that very night, 17 August 1960, and played for four-and-a-half hours to an uninterested audience of half a dozen people.

Their contract called for them to perform four-and-a-half hours each evening during the week and six hours each Saturday and Sunday evening. For this they were paid DM30 (ten pounds) a week, which Bruno paid them each Thursday. Their contract also stipulated that they couldn't play any other venue within a radius of 40 kilometres without Koschmider's permission.

Initially disgruntled, they slowly began to change their act, urged on by Koschmider's pleas to 'make a show'. They began to take Preludin pills supplied by the toilet-frau Rosa (Pete Best didn't indulge), which made them dehydrated, causing them to swill back copious quantities of beer, usually sent up on stage for them by members of the audience. Their on-stage antics included mock fights amongst themselves, horse-play, John imitating a spastic and doing the goose-step, much to the frustration of Koschmider, who had formerly been in a Panzer division. In fact, John and Paul provided most of the on-stage action and John increased his verbal attacks on the audience, calling them 'krauts', 'nazis' and 'German spassies' (Spastics). Strangely enough, members of the audience found this funny and more beer was ordered for the group on stage.

Although there was a little old lady living in a flat above the club, she was nearly deaf and Pete Best maintains she never complained about the noise they were creating. However, other nearby residents complained to the police – and although the area provided every variation of sex, a cornucopia of drugs and drinks around the clock, noise wasn't tolerated. The police kept warning Koschmider about the noise and they finally took action. The Beatles arrived at the Indra one night to find that the police had closed it down, 48 nights after it had been turned into a showplace for the group. During that time the Beatles had transformed their act, had increased the takings at the Indra and had begun to build a local following. Koschmider moved them to the Kaiserkeller for the duration of their contract.

I Need You

One of the two George Harrison compositions featured on the *Help!* album. During recording, George introduced a wah-wah pedal for the first time on a Beatles session.

The number was also included on the *Love Songs* compilation.

In My Life

A reflective, autobiographical composition by John which was featured on the *Rubber Soul* album and the compilations *The Beatles 1962–1966* and *Love Songs*.

John originally commented, 'I wrote that in Kenwood. I used to write upstairs where I had about ten Brunell tape recorders all linked up . . . I'd mastered them over the period of a year or two – I could never make a rock and roll record but I could make some far out stuff on it. I wrote it upstairs, that was one where I wrote the lyrics first and then sang it. That was usually the case with things like "In My Life" and "Universe" and some of the ones that stand out a bit.'

Interestingly enough, the concept of the song originally began as the story of a bus journey from John's home in Menlove Avenue to Liverpool city centre, mentioning every place on the way which John could remember. It included mentions of Penny Lane, Strawberry Fields and the Tram Sheds depot. 'In My Life' was written well before either 'Penny Lane' or 'Strawberry Fields' were composed by Paul and John respectively. John found that his original concept for the song turned out to be boring, so he rested, and then the lyrics of the song began to flow. He was to add, 'Now Paul helped write the middle eight melody. The whole lyrics were already written before Paul had even heard it. In the song, his contribution melodically was the harmony and the middle eight itself.'

The song was one of George Harrison's favourites and he rearranged the music and lyrics when he performed the number himself during his Dark Horse tour in 1974.

Inner Light, The

The first of George Harrison's compositions to find its way on to a Beatles single. It was the flipside of the March 1968 release 'Lady Madonna'.

George had appeared on a 'David Frost Show' with John Lennon, discussing meditation, and, as a result, received a letter from Juan Mascaro, a Sanskrit teacher at Cambridge University, who wrote to say how much he had enjoyed 'Within You, Without You'. Mascaro also enclosed a book called *Lamps Of Fire* in which there was a translation of a poem from the Tao Te Ching called 'The Inner Light'. George put the poem to music and wrote it specially for Mascaro.

George recorded the instrumental part of the number at the EMI Studios in Bombay, India, on 12 January 1968, using Indian musicians. He completed the vocals on 6 February at Abbey Road's Studio One, with John and Paul adding their vocal harmonies the following day.

The track was also included on the *Rarities* compilation and the 1981 release *The Beatles EP Collection*.

Paul, perhaps not comprehending the importance of Indian music in George's mind, or the validity of its influence in the composition of his songs, commented, 'George wrote this. Forget the Indian music and listen to the melody. Don't you think it's a beautiful melody? It's really lovely.' The number was included on the CD compilation *Past Masters Volume Two*.

In Spite Of All The Danger

A number which the Quarry Men recorded in 1958 at Percy Phillips' Studio in Kensington, Liverpool. They could only afford one copy at 17/6d and each member of the band borrowed it. The last member to have it was John Lowe, who left the group at the end of 1958 because he couldn't take a piano to gigs. He had it in a drawer for many years and, when he eventually discovered it again, he wanted to put it up for auction. Paul McCartney bought it from him for an undisclosed sum. He then had both sides of the acetate placed on to master tapes at Abbey Road Studios. The new master tapes were then taken to the Orlake pressing plant in Dagenham, Essex and around two dozen copies on 10 in 78 rpm shellac were made, together with a similar number of vinyl 7 in 45 rpm singles.

The recording was included on the Beatles' *Anthology 1* CD.

Institute, The, Hinderton Road, Neston, Wirral, Cheshire

Promoter Les Dodd had been running ballroom dancing events at this venue since the thirties, but had decided to present some jive dances.

Allan Williams secured the Silver Beatles a short residency at the hall and they made their debut there on Thursday, 2 June 1960. All their appearances took place during that year on consecutive Thursdays – on 9, 16, 23 and 30 June and 7 July.

On their 16 June appearance the support band was Keith Rowlands & the Deesiders.

International Amphitheatre, 42nd and Halsted Streets, Chicago, Illinois

The Beatles first appeared here during their debut American tour on 5th September 1964. Their limousines drove them from the Stockyards Inn where they had conducted a press conference and then drove them to the amphitheatre where the entire 15,000 tickets had sold out in a matter of hours. There were 4,000 frantic fans outside the stadium who hadn't been able to obtain tickets and several of them were threatening to commit suicide.

The Beatles ran on to the stage via a stairway draped in gold cloth at 9.20 p.m. and their performance went underway with Paul yelling, 'Why don't you join in? Clap your hands, stomp your feet, maybe even shout!' During the performance someone threw a raw steak at Ringo and Paul was hit in the face by a flashbulb.

To protect the Beatles, their fans and the amphitheatre, there were 320 policemen, firemen and private guards in attendance. The policemen were issued with cotton to stuff in their ears.

Immediately after the show had finished the group were herded off in limousines to the airport.

The Beatles began their final tour of America at this venue on Friday, 12 August 1966. They'd arrived the day previously and held a press reception at the Astor Towers Hotel due to the controversy caused by John Lennon's comments comparing the popularity of the Beatles to that of Christ. There were two concerts at the amphitheatre, one starting at 3 p.m., the other at 7 p.m. They were virtual sell-outs, with 13,000 fans attending each of the shows and gross takings of $136,000. The Beatles performed 'Rock 'n' Roll Music', 'She's A Woman', 'If I Needed Someone', 'Day Tripper', 'Baby's In Black', 'I Feel Fine', 'Yesterday', 'I Wanna Be Your Man', 'Nowhere Man', 'Paperback Writer' and 'Long Tall Sally'. While they were performing, 200 Andry Frain ushers, 100 firemen and 84 Burns detectives formed a solid line in front of the stage.

Support acts on this tour were the Remains, who backed Bobby Hebb, and the Ronettes (sans Ronnie Spector) and the Cyrkle.

Introducing The Beatles
The first Beatles album to be released in America, issued on 22 July 1963, on VJLP 1062. It didn't make the charts. It was reissued with the same catalogue number on 27 January 1964 and reached No. 2 in the *Billboard* and *Cash* Box charts, and No. 1 in the *Record World* chart.

The tracks were, Side One: 'I Saw Her Standing There', 'Misery', 'Anna (Go To Him)', 'Chains', 'Boys', 'Ask Me Why'. Side Two: 'Do You Want To Know A Secret', 'A Taste Of Honey', 'There's A Place', 'Twist And Shout'.

Invicta Ballroom, High Street, Chatham, Kent
The Beatles only made one appearance at this ballroom, on Saturday, 12 January 1963.

I Remember
A number recorded by Eddie Cochran in 1959. The Beatles performed it during 1960 and 1961.

I Remember You
A No. 1 hit for singer Frank Ifield in Britain in 1962 which the Beatles immediately included in their repertoire.

The group performed it during their Star Club set and it is included on *The Beatles Live! At The Star Club In Hamburg, Germany: 1962* album.

Iron Door Club, The, 13 Temple Street, Liverpool L2
A cellar club quite close to the Cavern, which began as a jazz club, called the Liverpool Jazz Society. The Beatles made their debut there on a special session promoted by Sam Leach.

The event took place on 11 March 1961. Sam had decided to

feature twelve top local groups, who would replace each other on the hour, on a massive twelve-hour music marathon commencing at 8.00 p.m. on Saturday and finishing at 8.00 a.m. on Sunday.

The bill comprised the Beatles, Kingsize Taylor & the Dominoes, Rory Storm & the Hurricanes, Gerry & the Pacemakers, the Big Three, the Searchers, the Four Jays (later to become the Fourmost), the Remo Four, Howie Casey & the Seniors, Ian & the Zodiacs, Faron & the Flamingoes and Karl Terry & the Cruisers.

There was so much condensation dripping down the walls that the Beatles had to stand on their amplifier covers to avoid being electrocuted because they had American equipment which was wired differently. Paul said, 'The heat was "shocking!" '

Although the club only held 1,000 people, over 2,000 eventually saw the show. Queues continued until after midnight when the younger members of the audience left to catch their last bus home. Admission price was 6/6d (32½p) for members and 7/6d (37½p) for non-members.

The Beatles returned to the club for an appearance a few days later on 13 March and also on Wednesday, 15 March, on a five-hour afternoon session with Rory Storm & the Hurricanes and Gerry & the Pacemakers. Their final appearance at the venue that month was on 17 March.

When they next played the venue on 1 March 1962 it had undergone a name change to the Storyville Jazz Club. They also appeared there on 8 March.

They made their final appearance at the club on 15 March on a bill advertised as the 'Beatles' Farewell Party'.

I Saw Her Standing There

Penned by Paul in the living room of Forthlin Road under the working title 'Seventeen'. John Lennon amended it slightly, altering the line 'never been a beauty queen' to 'you know what I mean.'

It became the opening track on their debut album *Please Please Me*. When it became a hit, Paul discussed the genesis of the song in an interview for the magazine *Beat Instrumental*.

On the subject of learning to play an instrument, Paul advised that rather than use a tutor, aspiring musicians should learn to play by stealing bits and pieces from other guitarists they could listen to. He commented: 'Here's one example of a bit I pinched from someone: I used the bass riff from "Talkin' About You" by Chuck Berry in "I Saw Her Standing There". I played exactly the same notes as he did and it fitted our number perfectly. Even now, when I tell people about it, I find few of them believe me; therefore, I maintain that a bass riff hasn't got to be original.'

It next surfaced on *The Beatles (No. 1)* EP. In America it was included on the *Introducing The Beatles* and *Meet The Beatles* albums. The number was also included on the *Rock 'n' Roll Music* album.

The group had performed it as part of their repertoire during their Star Club season in Hamburg and this raw version is to be found on *The Beatles Live at the Star Club In Hamburg, Germany: 1962* albums.

Within weeks of *Please Please Me* being released, Duffy Power issued a single of the number on the Beatles' own Parlophone label in May 1963, backed by the Graham Bond Quartet. Ron Richards produced it. He told Power, whose real name is Ray Howard, 'The Beatles think you're the best R&B singer in the country.' It failed to make an impact on the charts.

A version by John Lennon and Elton John is to be found on the flipside of Elton's 1975 single 'Philadelphia Freedom'. John had appeared on stage with Elton at Madison Square Garden in 1974 and this number was recorded at the concert. John had announced it as '. . . a song written by an old fiancé of mine called Paul.' The John Lennon performance was also included on an EP issued by DJM Records in 1981, which reached No. 24 in the New Musical Express chart in Britain.

The Beatles also recorded it before a live audience on the 'Easy Beat' BBC programme in 1963. This version was included on *The Beatles Live At The BBC* CD in November 1994. The version on the *Anthology 1* CD was from a Swedish radio recording and Take 9 from the Beatles' original studio session was also included on the *Anthology 1* CD.

I Should Have Known Better

One of the several John Lennon compositions for *A Hard Day's Night*. John plays harmonica on the track and George played his twelve-string Rickenbacker guitar for the first time on record. A group called the Naturals covered the number and reached No. 26 in the British charts with it.

Apart from the album *A Hard Day's Night*, the number was used on the EP *Extracts From The Film 'A Hard Day's Night'* and was the flipside of the 'Yesterday' single, issued in Britain in March 1976. It was featured on the compilation albums *Hey Jude* in 1979 and *Reel Music* in 1982 and was one of the numbers included on 'The Beatles Movie Medley' single in 1982.

At the initial recording session on Tuesday, 25 February 1964, John kept laughing over his harmonica playing, causing the others to laugh, too. They re-recorded the number the following day.

It's All Too Much

A George Harrison composition which was called 'Too Much' when the Beatles first began recording it on Thursday, 25 May 1967, at De Lane Lea recording studios in Kingsway, London. George took lead vocals with John and Paul adding backing vocals and handclaps. At the session George sang a few bars from 'Sorrow', a hit single by the Merseys. When recording resumed on 2 June the title had been changed to 'It's All Too Much' and four trumpets and a bass clarinet were overdubbed on to the track.

At that time the number was more than eight minutes in length, but it was later edited down.

The song had been written for the *Yellow Submarine* movie and is one of the numbers featured on the film soundtrack. A shorter version, with one of the verses taken out, is to be found on the *Yellow Submarine* album, issued in January 1969, almost two years after George wrote it.

It's For You

The majority of Lennon & McCartney songs given to other artists to record during the sixties were composed by Paul. This number, which he gave to Cilla Black for her fourth British chart hit, reached the No. 8 position. It didn't fare too well in the States where Cilla only enjoyed one Top Forty chart placing in her entire career, although it did enter the lower regions of the charts.

Cilla recorded the number on 2 July 1964 and John and Paul attended the session, with Paul playing piano on the track.

The number was issued in Britain on Parlophone R 5162 on 31 July 1964 and in America on Capitol 5258 on 17 August 1964, with 'He Won't Ask Me' on the flip.

It's Only Love

Composition by John, recorded on the afternoon of Tuesday, 15 June 1965, and featuring John on acoustic guitar and George on his tone pedal guitar. The number had the working title 'That's A Nice Hat'.

The number was included on the British *Help!* album and the *Yesterday* EP. It was also one of the two songs from *Help!* to be excluded from Capitol's American version of the *Help!* album and was featured on the American *Rubber Soul* album. The song was also included on the *Love Songs* compilation.

Bryan Ferry performed the number on his hit British EP *Extended Play* in 1976 and, following John's death, it became a minor hit for Gary 'US' Bonds in 1981 – ironically, because John had said that he disliked it and described it as a 'lousy' song with 'abysmal lyrics'. Take Two of the studio recording found its way on to the Beatles' *Anthology 2* CDs.

It's So Easy
Number composed by Buddy Holly and Norman Petty. Holly was one of the major influences of the Quarry Men and they included this number, recorded by Buddy Holly & the Crickets, in their repertoire in 1958.

It's The Beatles
A 30-minute BBC 1 TV show filmed at the Empire Theatre, Liverpool, on 7 December 1963 and screened the same evening.

The Beatles had returned to their home town to appear at a special Northern Area Fan Club convention before 2,500 members of their fan club. In addition to the actual concert, they also filmed a 'Juke Box Jury' show from the Empire stage that afternoon, and after their fan club performance they rushed to the Odeon Cinema, only fifty yards away, for yet another show.

After the 'Juke Box Jury' sets had been cleared away and the BBC television cameramen and lighting crew had organised their equipment, the afternoon filming of the special show began, their first performance in Liverpool for four months.

Ringo's drumbeat introduced 'From Me To You' and with the counting of 'one, two, three, four' they went straight into 'I Saw Her Standing There'. After 'thank yous' from Paul they went into 'All My Loving', a ballad from their latest album, and then George introduced and took lead vocals on 'Roll Over Beethoven'. John said, 'Thank you folks, the next number is a sort of special number which we only do every night', explaining that Ringo was going to do his new number, but hadn't learnt it, so they went into 'Boys'. John then introduced 'Till There Was You', with the words, 'The next song is definitely off the new LP but a lot of you'll probably remember this at the Cavern as well, er, it's a song from the musical *The Muscle Man* sung by Peggy Lee.' They followed the number, which was from *The Music Man* and had given Peggy Lee a hit single, with 'She Loves You'. After further 'thank yous' it was the turn of George to sing the B-side of their latest single, 'This Boy'. 'I Want To Hold Your Hand' followed. Paul encouraged the audience participation while John said 'Shut up' and then launched into 'Money' and 'Twist And Shout'. They then ended with 'From Me To You'.

The concert was screened later the same day from 8.10 to 8.40 p.m.

It's The Beatles (Radio Luxembourg)
A weekly fifteen-minute series on Radio Luxembourg which was first broadcast on 23 December 1963. The second episode was aired on 30 December 1963.

It Won't Be Long
Number penned by John which was included on the *With The Beatles* album, issued in November 1963 and which also appeared on the American *Meet The Beatles* album in January 1964.

It was recorded on Tuesday, 30 July 1963, and became the opening track on the album.

I've Got A Feeling
A number composed by both John and Paul in which each sings his own verses. There was a version recorded in the studio and they also performed the number on their Apple rooftop session. When Phil Spector was given the tapes of the 'Get Back' sessions, he mixed two versions of this track, the studio track and the live track, and decided to use the live rooftop track for the release on the *Let It Be* album. The number opened Disc Two on the Beatles' *Anthology 3* CDs.

I've Just Seen A Face
A folk-rock song which Paul composed for the *Help!* movie and on which he sings solo on the soundtrack recording. It was the first number he recorded on Monday, 14 June 1965, the same day he recorded 'I'm Down' and 'Yesterday'. The number was included on the *Help!* soundtrack album and also on the American version of the *Rubber Soul* album and the compilations *The Beatles Box* and *The Beatles Collection*.

When Paul was composing it the song became one of his Auntie Gin's favourites, so the working title of the song was 'Auntie Gin's Theme'. The George Martin Orchestra recorded an instrumental version of 'I've Just Seen A Face' under the title 'Auntie Gin's Theme'.

Paul performed it on the Wings world tour of 1975/6 and it became one of the tracks on the *Wings Over America* album.

Ivor Novello Awards, The
Prestigious annual awards presented by the Songwriters' Guild of Great Britain and named in honour of the late, famous British composer Ivor Novello.

The Beatles received five awards on 25 October 1964. They were:

1. The most outstanding contribution to British music in 1963. 2. The most broadcast song, 'She Loves You'. 3. The top-selling record, 'She Loves You'. 4. The second top-selling record, 'I Want To Hold Your Hand'. 5. The second most outstanding song of the year, 'All My Loving'.

On 25 March 1967 they received two awards for the year 1966. They were: 1. The most performed work, 'Michelle'. 2. The top-selling single, 'Yellow Submarine'.

In March 1968 they received three awards: 1. Best British song, musically and lyrically, 'She's Leaving Home'. 2. Best instrumental theme of the year, 'Love In The Open Air' (Paul's theme for the film *The Family Way*). 3. Second best-selling record of the year, 'Hello Goodbye'.

On 19 May 1969 they received an award for 1968: 1. The top-selling single in Britain, 'Hey Jude'.

On 10 May 1972 they were presented with two awards: 1. Best-selling British single, 'Get Back'. 2. Most requested song on the radio, 'Ob-La-Di, Ob-La-Da'.

They also received awards for 'Help!' and 'Yesterday'.

I Wanna Be Your Man

A number penned by Paul McCartney and John Lennon.

On 10 September 1963 John and Paul had been present at a Variety Club lunch at the Savoy Hotel where they had received an award as Top Vocal Group of the Year.

They were in a taxi and went into the West End and in Jermyn Street bumped into Andrew Loog Oldham, co-manager of the Rolling Stones. He told them that he was on his way to visit the group at their rehearsals, but they were having difficulty finding material for their second single.

John and Paul said they had an unrecorded song which might be something suitable and went along with him to Ken Colyer's Studio 51 club in Soho.

While there they borrowed the Stones' instruments to play them part of a number they had been composing called 'I Wanna Be Your Man'. Bill Wyman was to recall his amazement that Paul played his bass guitar backwards. They had only played the first verse and chorus as the number was incomplete and the two asked if they could be excused for a few minutes and went into another room. After about ten minutes they returned and said that they had just finished the middle eight and last verse and played it to them.

The Stones recorded it at Kingsway Studios with their other co-manager Eric Easton producing. It was issued in Britain on 1

November 1963 and brought them their first Top Twenty hit. They also released it in America on 17 February 1964.

On Wednesday, 11 September 1963, the very next day after they'd given the number to the Rolling Stones, the Beatles recorded the song themselves at Abbey Road Studios as a vehicle for Ringo Starr. It was included on the *With The Beatles* album. It was also later included on the compilation album *Rock 'n' Roll Music*. A version was included on *The Beatles Live At The BBC* CDs and their track from the *Around The Beatles* TV show was included on the Beatles' *Anthology 1* CDs.

A group called the Rezillos had a minor hit with the song in the British charts in September 1979.

I Want To Hold Your Hand

Possibly the most significant Beatles single of them all: the one that made the breakthrough in America and changed the direction of the charts irrevocably, eventually selling over fifteen million copies throughout the world, making it the biggest selling British single of all time.

John and Paul originally composed the song in the Harley Street house of Jane Asher's parents and when they recorded it on Thursday, 17 October 1963, it was the first time they'd had the benefit of EMI's new four-track machine.

Brian Epstein left for New York on 5 November 1963 with a copy of the disc and played it to Brown Meggs, Director of Eastern Operations for Capitol Records. The company had already turned down four of the Beatles' British chart records, but Meggs thought 'I Want To Hold Your Hand' would be suitable for the American market and a release date of 13 January 1964 was set with a pressing of 200,000 copies. Washington disc jockey Carroll James began to play a copy which his British air stewardess girlfriend had obtained for him and other radio stations took it up, resulting in Capitol advancing the release date to 27 December and increasing the pressing to one million copies.

The Beatles were at the George V Hotel in Paris when they were given the news that 'I Want To Hold Your Hand' was No. 1 in the American charts.

When they arrived for their triumphant first visit to America, part of the media loved them, another part treated them as a joke. Commenting on 'I Want To Hold Your Hand', William Williams of Radio WNEW in New York said, 'They want to hold your hand – a lot of people would like to hold their noses!'

More than fifteen years later a British vocal duo of David Van

Day and Thereze Bazar, known as Dollar, recorded the number and reached No. 11 in the British charts with it in January 1980.

A track from their appearance on the *Morecambe & Wise Show* was included on the Beatles' *Anthology 1* CDs. The number was also included on the CD compilation *Past Masters Volume One*.

I Want To Tell You

One of the three George Harrison compositions to find its way on to the *Revolver* album.

At the time, apparently, George had some difficulty in deciding on a title for his song. At the session on Thursday, 2 June 1966, George Martin asked George what the title of the number was. George had already come up with a song without a title which they were currently calling 'Granny Smith' (it became 'Love You To') and John Lennon, commenting to George that he never seemed to have a title for his songs, told him to call it: 'Granny Smith Part Friggin' Two!'

Engineer Geoff Emerick suggested that they call it 'Laxton's Superb', which was the name of another British apple, but by the next day the name had been changed to 'I Don't Know', before it eventually received its official name 'I Want To Tell You' on 6 June.

Emerick was later to comment that there seemed to be pressure to complete George's songs in as short a time as possible, while compositions by John and Paul took as long as was deemed necessary.

I Want You (She's So Heavy)

A John Lennon song, with Yoko as his inspiration. Rehearsals for the song began at Apple Recording Studios in January 1969 during the 'Get Back' session when it was called simply 'I Want You'. The next session was at Trident Studios in February when, on one of the takes, Paul McCartney sang lead vocal. Further recordings and overdubs took place at Abbey Road Studios in April and August of that year.

The track was included on the *Abbey Road* album and at seven minutes and 44 seconds in length, it was the longest number issued by the Beatles next to 'Revolution 9', which mainly consisted of tape loops put together by John.

I Will

A love song which Paul dedicated to Linda. George wasn't present when the number was recorded in September 1968. It was included on *The Beatles* double album and later featured on the *Love Songs* compilation album. Take One of one of Paul's favourite melodies was included on the Beatles' *Anthology 3* CDs.

A version was included on the Beatles' *Anthology 1* CDs.

I Wish I Could Shimmy Like My Sister Kate

A number recorded by the Olympics in 1961, although it wasn't a chart hit. The Beatles must have appreciated this R&B group from Los Angeles, who only had two US chart hits – 'Western Movies' and 'The Bounce', as they included three of the group's numbers in their stage act: 'I Wish I Could Shimmy Like My Sister Kate', 'Hully Gully' and 'Baby . . . (Please Don't Go)'.

'I Wish I Could Shimmy Like My Sister Kate' was included in the Beatles' repertoire in 1961 and was popular at the Cavern. They continued performing it until late in 1962 with John Lennon on lead vocals.

Jacaranda Club, The, 23 Slater Street, Liverpool L1

The coffee bar which Allan Williams opened in September 1958. At the time, coffee bars were very fashionable and this particular area of Liverpool was honeycombed with them. Quite close to the 'Jac' was a coffee bar called the Studio, frequented by the models and students from Liverpool College of Art; local painter Yankiel Feather ran the Basement, directly to the rear of Mount Pleasant Register Office where John and Cynthia were married; 50 yards from the Jac, in Duke Street, were the Zodiac and Boomerang coffee bars; in Mount Pleasant was Streates, where poetry readings were held – and there were many more.

Allan saw an advertisement in the *Liverpool Echo* which read 'suitable premises for a club' and went to Slater Street. The premises to let were formerly occupied by Owens Watch Repair Shop and the lease was owned by a man in the sweetshop next door who demanded an extra £150 for 'goodwill and fittings'. Allan raised the money and managed to engage a group of West Indians to play in a steel band by offering them ten shillings (fifty pence) each.

Shortly before opening the club, Allan had been trying to think up a suitable name. He eventually decided he'd call it the Samurai, because he'd recently seen the film *The Seven Samurai*, when a friend, Bill Coward, who'd just read a book called *The Jacaranda Tree*, suggested Jacaranda.

The clientele was mixed – solicitors, doctors, art students, musicians – and two of the girls who served there as waitresses, Mary

Larkin and Terry Shorrock, found themselves on the cover of the first issue of *Mersey Beat* after their photograph had been taken with rock 'n' roll star Gene Vincent.

The ground floor had a large glass window looking out on to Slater Street and there were small padded benches and coffee tables, a tiny kitchen, an outside loo for the Gents and steps leading to the tiny basement where the steel band played and steps leading upstairs to the Ladies loo.

Among the art students who went there were John Lennon, Stuart Sutcliffe, Rod Murray and Bill Harry and among the musicians George, Paul and Pete of the Beatles, Gerry Marsden, Cass & the Cassanovas and Rory Storm.

At one time Allan asked Stuart to paint some murals in the club, which he did, with the help of Rod Murray, although in later years Allan was to claim that John Lennon painted them with Stuart.

All appearances made by the Silver Beetles took place between May and August 1960, about a dozen appearances in all. Allan booked them mainly on Monday evenings when the Royal Caribbean Steel Band had a night off. They were crammed into a corner of the stone-floored basement and as there wasn't any room for equipment, their girlfriends had to sit opposite them on chairs holding broom handles to which the microphones were attached. Their first appearance at the Jac took place on 30 May and on 13 June Tommy Moore appeared with them for the last time. When the Silver Beetles asked Pete Best to join them, they held his audition at the Wyvern.

In later years the club was turned into a late night drinking club called the Maxie San Suzie then, following the death of John Lennon and the subsequent upsurge of interest in the Beatles, it reverted back to its original name, with a flamboyant giant placard above the club premises which featured a painting of the group in their 'Sgt Pepper' personae and the words 'The place the fab four first played'.

Jack Paar Show, The

'The Jack Paar Show' broadcast a short clip of the Beatles performing 'She Loves You' on the evening of Friday, 3 January 1964. The highly rated NBC show screened the excerpt less than two weeks before 'I Want To Hold Your Hand' entered the American charts. The excerpt was likely to have been a clip filmed by Pathe News at the Manchester concert on 20 November 1963. There was also a fragment of a performance of 'From Me To You'.

Jack Paar may take the credit for being the first person to introduce the Beatles on a major American television entertainments show, but he marred the historic occasion by making snide remarks about their haircuts and the fans they attracted, with comments such as 'I understand scientists are working on a cure for this'.

News of the Beatles' impact in Europe had been filtering into the States and at the Beatles concert at the Winter Gardens, Bournemouth, on 16 November 1963 no less than three US camera teams were filming the group, including CBS and ABC. As a result, a clip from that show was screened on 7 December 1963 on 'The CBS Evening News with Walter Cronkite' which showed the screaming fans at the concert and clips of the NEMS staff tackling the huge Beatles mail sacks.

However, it is generally acknowledged that Paar was the first person to actually introduce them via a film on a major entertainment show.

When the Beatles appeared on the 'Ed Sullivan Show' on 9 February 1964 their first three numbers were dedicated to Paar's daughter, Randy.

Jackson, Simone

The Beatles provided backing for Simone Jackson at the Cavern on Wednesday, 12 September 1962.

The sixteen-year-old London singer was making a special appearance at the club and compere Bob Wooler was later to comment: 'She was one of the very few favoured people to be backed by the Beatles. In their earlier Hamburg days they had accompanied singer Tony Sheridan and they were sufficiently impressed by a Liverpool group of coloured singers called the Chants to play for them too. I can recall only two other occasions when the Beatles backed other people. Once was when they did their very first theatre date at a Liverpool Empire Sunday concert and accompanied Craig Douglas at the end of the first half. The other was when, as a novelty item, they backed Ray McFall himself at the Cavern for two numbers – Presley's "Can't Help Falling In Love" and Vic Damone's "Tender Is The Night". But Simone Jackson was something rather special. She had a superb voice with great soul and feeling in her delivery. The Beatles thought a lot of her and so did the capacity crowd at the Cavern.'

Simone was represented by the Tito Burns agency and had only been singing professionally for five weeks.

Note: the Beatles did back other people, including Davy Jones.

Jacobs, David

A prominent show business lawyer whose clients included Diana Dors, Judy Garland and Laurence Harvey. He was an imposing figure, 6 ft 2 ins tall. What made him more striking was the fact that he was a homosexual who often wore stage make-up on his face. He used to hold lavish parties at his home at 2 Princes Crescent, Hove, where Ringo and Maureen were to spend their honeymoon.

Jacobs was responsible for the abortive merchandising deal with Nicky Byrne, which caused Brian Epstein so much frustration and lost the Beatles an estimated $100,000,000. Sixteen months after Brian's death, on 15 December 1968, Jacobs was found hanging in the garage of his Hove home. He'd suffered a nervous breakdown and hadn't been to his Pall Mall offices for a month.

Although the inquest rendered a verdict of suicide, there were many rumours surrounding the death of the 56-year-old lawyer, who had asked for police protection shortly before his death. John Merry, a private detective who had worked for Jacobs on numerous occasions, commented, 'I last heard from David two days before his death. He telephoned my secretary and told her it was urgent that I contact him. When I rang back he burst out, "It's no good John. I'm in terrible trouble. They're all after me." I asked who "they" were and he gave me six names – famous people in show business. I told him not to worry.'

Jacobs, David (DJ)
A British television personality who was the host of the popular BBC TV series 'Juke Box Jury' throughout the sixties.

He travelled to Liverpool with the Beatles for their civic reception and the northern premiere of *A Hard Day's Night* and presented an all-Beatles edition of 'Juke Box Jury' from the stage of the Empire Theatre, Liverpool. Jacobs claimed that this edition of the programme gave them their biggest-ever audience. He said that around 23 million viewers watched it.

Brian Epstein, Jane Asher and the individual members of the Beatles also appeared on various editions of his show.

'Juke Box Jury' was revived by BBC 2 in the late eighties with Jools Holland as the host.

Jailhouse Rock
Another Jerry Leiber/Mike Stoller composition which Elvis Presley took to the top of the American charts in 1957. It was included in the Quarry Men's repertoire sung by John Lennon. He continued performing it until late in 1960.

James, Carroll
The disc jockey credited with being the first person to play a Beatles record on the American airwaves.

James was a jock at WWDC-AM, the Washington DC radio station, when he received a letter from a listener, fifteen- year-old Marsha Albert Thompson requesting that he play 'I Want To Hold Your Hand' by the Beatles. As the single hadn't been released in the States, he asked his girlfriend, a stewardess with BOAC (British Overseas Airways), to bring a copy of the record back from England. When he aired the single on 17 December 1963 he invited Marsha into the studio to introduce it. He said, 'We played the record and I said to the radio audience, "We'd like to know what you think about the record. Don't call. Please write."' Despite that particular request, listeners began phoning straight away and the switchboard became jammed. James played the single again, an hour later.

James gave Marsha his copy of the actual record he'd played, although she was to lose it in the passage of time.

Capitol Records had intended to issue 'I Want To Hold Your Hand' in America in late January 1964 as a build-up to the Ed Sullivan appearance, but the response in Washington was confusing them. It had proved to be so popular that it was being played every day, once an hour. Initially, Capitol considered taking an injunction against the station for playing it when it hadn't been officially released, but decided to bring forward the release date and issued it on 27 December 1963. James had been playing it for ten days, calling it 'a WWDC exclusive'.

In an effort to take advantage of James' promotion, Capitol wanted to immediately ship hundreds of copies to Washington. They had to obtain publishing clearance first and contacted Walter Hofer, Brian Epstein's legal representative in New York. He told them that because of the lack of response by Capitol to Beatles products, the publishing rights to the number had been sold to MCA Records for a nominal sum, simply to give them a foothold in America. In the meantime, one of James' friends had taped the number and sent it to a disc jockey in Chicago, who also began having an immediate response – and he sent a tape along to a disc jockey in St Louis. With all this going on, Capitol seemed to have little choice but to bring the release date forward.

When the Beatles appeared in their first American concert at the Washington Coliseum on 11 February 1964, James was able to introduce the group on stage. During the same day he recorded a ten-minute interview with the Beatles, using as his theme the various questions which listeners had sent to him. For example, what would Paul have been when he grew up if he hadn't joined the Beatles? Paul said he might have become a teacher, but felt it was a good thing he had become a Beatle because 'I think I would have been a bad teacher'. James asked John whether he liked tea or coffee. John told him he preferred tea. 'How about tea bags?' asked James. 'I don't like them,' John answered, 'they get stuck in me teeth.'

The most perplexing part of the interview came from the conversation with George. When James asked him about what he would have become without the Beatles, George said, 'I wanna be a baggy sweeger.' James asked, 'A baggy sweeger?' 'Oh yeah,' said George, 'you know, in every town there's 25 baggy sweegers and every morning they get up and go to the airport and baggy sweeger all around.'

In 1984, twenty years after the event, James issued an album *The Carroll James Interview with the Beatles – February 11, 1964* on Carroll James CJEP-3301.

James died from cancer at the age of sixty on Monday, 24 March 1997.

James, Dick

The Beatles' music publisher, born Richard Leon Vapnick in London's East End in 1920. He left school when he was fourteen and became a professional singer at the age of seventeen in 1937 when he joined Al Berlin and his Band, who were resident at the Cricklewood Palais. Among the names he used were Isaac Vapnick and Lee Sheridan. During the war he joined the Medical Corps and continued to play in a band and in 1942 he made his first record with Primo Scala's Accordion Band. In 1945 he changed his name to Dick James. He appeared with various bands, including those run by Henry Hall, Stanley Black and Cyril Stapleton, but in the early fifties he lost his hair and became a song-plugger. He also began to record in the mid-fifties and his recording manager was George Martin, who produced James singing 'Tenderly' and 'Robin Hood'. Other chart hits for James were 'The Ballad Of Davy Crockett' and 'Garden Of Eden'. His biggest hit with Martin was 'Robin Hood', issued on the Parlophone label in 1955. The number became the theme tune for the TV series starring Richard Green and reached No. 9 in the charts. He ceased singing professionally in 1959 and worked as an assistant to Sidney Bron, the music publisher, until he formed his own music publishing company in September 1961. Incidentally, Bron was the brother of actress Eleanor Bron.

Mitch Murray had brought along one of his songs to Ron Richards at EMI. Richards liked the acetate of 'How Do You Do It?' and phoned Dick James, who acquired the publishing rights to it. The song had been composed by Murray and Peter Callender and James approached Martin with the number and told him that it would be just right for a vocal group. Martin said that it might do for this new band from Liverpool. James laughed and said, 'Liverpool? A group from Liverpool – you gotta be kidding?' (That's the way James himself recalled it, although chroniclers have also written that he'd said, 'Liverpool? So what's from Liverpool?')

The Beatles did not like the song, but Martin insisted that they record it and they did, on Tuesday, 4 September 1962, along with 'Love Me Do'. Martin was considering 'How Do You Do It?' as the Beatles' follow-up single, but John and Paul stressed that they wanted to record one of their own compositions and Martin agreed that a re-recorded version of 'Please Please Me' would be right for their second release. He was to comment, 'I still think the boys were too self-opinionated when they had that dispute, but they were right in the end.'

'Love Me Do' had been published by Ardmore and Beechwood, EMI's publishing arm, but Brian Epstein was dissatisfied with the promotion of the record and complained to George Martin that Ardmore and Beechwood hadn't pushed it. 'When the next one comes off I don't want to give the publishing to them.' Brian wanted to approach an American company, Hill and Range, and sign up with them because, 'They do all the Elvis Presley stuff.' He saw someone from Hill and Range, but Martin told him, 'They don't need you, they've already got Elvis. You need someone who's hungry.' He then suggested his former singer James, who he knew was having a struggle with his new company but who he considered was honest and would be dedicated.

Martin phoned James to tell him that they weren't issuing 'How Do You Do It?' as the Beatles' next single, but arranged a meeting between James and Epstein to discuss the plugging of 'Please Please Me'.

Brian Epstein had meetings arranged with various publishing representatives, including Alan Holmes of Robbins Music, David Platz of Essex Music and Dick James. On the day he was due to meet James for an 11.00 a.m. appointment, he had a prior meeting at 10.00 a.m. at Francis, Day and Hunter, another EMI subsidiary. The punctilious Epstein sat in the reception office at Francis, Day and Hunter's for 25 minutes. The man he was meeting hadn't turned up and it was suggested that he play the acetate to the office boy. Epstein stalked out and immediately went to the nearby James office at 132 Charing Cross Road, arriving half an hour early. James asked Brian if he could publish 'Please Please Me'. Brian asked him what he could do for the Beatles. James then picked up the phone and called Philip Jones, producer of the new television show 'Thank Your Lucky Stars'. He told Jones about the record and asked him to listen. He put it on the record player and Jones listened over the phone and agreed to book them for the following show. James turned to Epstein and said, 'Now, can I publish the song?'

The 44-year-old James had asked his sixteen-year-old son, Stephen, the night before the meeting what he thought of the Beatles. Stephen told him the Beatles were great, which gave James the confidence to tell Epstein that 'Please Please Me' would be a No. 1 record. Impressed, Epstein told him that if he could make the record No. 1 he would have a long-term contract for Lennon & McCartney.

A deal was struck. James suggested that they form a company called Northern Songs, which would be administered by Dick James Music. James would have a half stake in the company and Brian and the Beatles the other half. The actual split would be 55 per cent for Dick James with John, Paul and Brian sharing the remaining 45 per cent.

Northern Songs was formed in January 1963 and during the next four years, John and Paul added more than 100 songs to the company's original catalogue of 59 songs, despite the fact that their contract demanded only a minimum of six songs per year. John and Paul were to have a company called Lenmac Enterprises which owned the rights on the first 59 songs, but this was acquired by Northern Songs before its flotation.

It was in 1965 that James persuaded Epstein that Northern Songs should go public on the Stock Exchange. John and Paul were reluctant to take that path, but they had no choice. Since the original formation the shares had altered slightly. James now owned 37.5 per cent, John and Paul owned 15 per cent each, Epstein owned 5 per cent, NEMS owned 7.5 per cent and Ringo and George each had 0.8 per cent. At the time of the company's flotation, with five million shares, John and Paul's percentage was worth £267,000 to each of them, George and Ringo had had their shares upped to 1.6 per cent which was worth £27,000 to each of them. Charles Silver, who was the accountant for Northern Songs, was made Chairman and together with the company's Managing Director, Dick James, he shared 37 per cent.

John and Paul had taken a lot of persuading to agree to the flotation. Their misgivings were correct, from their point of view. Paul had said that they never owned their songs – and this proved to be true. Since their original deal with James, they were minor shareholders of their own compositions. They were never able to gain control of their songs, which were very personal to them, and over the years they were sold to various companies, and the Beatles were never able to gain possession of their work.

In December 1964, Dick James became a singer again and recorded a medley of Beatles hits, backed by a chorus of 100 voices. It was a party record for Christmas, called *Sing A Song Of Beatles* and released on 7 December on Parlophone R 5212. The number comprised a medley of 'From Me To You', 'I Want To Hold Your Hand', 'She Loves You', 'All My Loving', 'I Should Have Known Better' and 'Can't Buy Me Love'. Paul McCartney commented, 'Very good indeed – a lot of fun.'

The attitude of John and Paul to James appeared calm on the surface, but they regarded him as one of 'the men in suits', their term for the men who take control of the work of creative people and turn it into profit for themselves. They also resented the way he insisted on referring to them as 'the boys', a term they found patronising.

Once, while they were editing *Magical Mystery Tour* in Old Compton Street, James dropped in and told them that Barbra Streisand wanted to record some of their songs for her new album. This was nothing new, Lennon & McCartney songs were being recorded by major artists all the time. James remained in the studio and when Paul asked him why he was still there, he said, 'Well, if you and John just write a few songs for her ...' There was an atmospheric silence for a moment or two, then John told him to 'Fuck off!'

When Allen Klein moved into Apple, attempts were made to buy Northern Songs for the Beatles. James had already been approached by Sir Lew Grade in 1968, but told him that he didn't want to sell. Grade suggested that he should come back to him any time he wanted to make a deal. Then, in March 1969, James went to Grade and, together with Charles Silver, sold his Northern Songs shares to Associated Television Corporation. This was without the Beatles' knowledge. The first John heard about it was when he read it in the newspapers on 28 March. Paul was on honeymoon with Linda at the time.

According to John Eastman, James had decided to sell because he was afraid that Allen Klein would get control of Northern Songs and Klein had even threatened him with litigation. On top of that, the Beatles had refused to extend their contracts and the relationship between James and the Beatles was strained.

In mid-March the negotiations had begun with Silver, James and Jack Gill, the ATV Finance director. Then James told Grade that the deal was off, that there were too many complications surrounding it. A meeting was arranged between lawyers and representatives from the banks and James and Silver. Grade arrived at the meeting before the lawyers and put forward a proposition. Within five minutes they'd done a deal.

The Beatles attempted to buy Northern Songs but failed and it passed into the hands of Sir Lew Grade in 1969.

Dick James had become a multi-millionaire. From a small company which was teetering at the time he met Epstein, James was able to become fabulously rich on the songs penned by Lennon and McCartney. They felt he'd betrayed them by not allowing them a chance to buy control of the company from him which would have enabled them to buy their own songs.

James continued to thrive, becoming publisher to stars such as Elton John.

He died on 1 February 1986, aged 65.

James, Ian

A classmate of Paul McCartney's at the Liverpool Institute. The two friends virtually taught each other to play guitar, passing tips, playing together.

They also used to wander round the visiting fun-fairs, trying to pick girls up. They began to look and dress alike, sharing the same hairstyle, the DA, and both wore white sports jackets and drainpipe trousers. Paul said they wore the jackets because of the song 'A White Sports Coat' and described his jacket as having 'speckles in it and a flap on the pockets'.

It was Ian who taught Paul the chords he played to John at their first meeting.

Janice The Stripper

Fulsome-figured striptease dancer from Manchester hired to appear at Allan Williams' New Cabaret Artists Club, which was managed on his behalf by Lord Woodbine.

Janice, surname unknown, refused to perform unless she had a backing band and Williams offered the Silver Beatles ten shillings each to back her. So, for one week early in June 1960 the four boys backed Janice's performance twice nightly at the seedy little shebeen.

She gave them printed sheet music of Beethoven and Khachaturian, which they couldn't read and they ended up playing their own versions of such standards as 'The Harry Lime Theme', 'September Song', 'Moonglow', 'Begin The Beguine' and 'It's a Long Way to Tipperary'.

Paul McCartney wrote about the experience in a letter to Bill Harry:

John, George, Stu and I used to play at a Strip Club in Upper Parliament Street, backing Janice the Stripper. At the time we wore little lilac jackets ... or purple jackets, or something. Well, we played behind Janice and naturally we looked at her, everybody looked at her, just sort of normal. At the end of the act she would turn round and ... well, we were all young lads, we'd never seen anything like it before, and we all blushed ... four blushing red-faced lads.

Janice brought sheets of music for us to play all her arrangements. She gave us a bit of Beethoven and the Spanish Fire Dance. So in the end we said 'We can't read music, sorry, but instead of the Spanish Fire Dance we can play 'The Harry Lime Cha Cha', which we've arranged ourselves, and instead of Beethoven you can have 'Moonglow' or 'September Song', take your pick ... and instead of the 'Sabre Dance' we'll give you 'Ramrod'. So that's what she got. She seemed quite satisfied anyway.

The Strip Club wasn't an important chapter in our lives, but it was an interesting one.

Jelly Babies

Small soft sweets, made by the confectionery firm Bassetts. They were in the shape of little babies and came in many colours. During their tour with Roy Orbison, fans began throwing jelly babies on stage because they'd heard that George liked them. This soon became a standard procedure at concerts and increased to an extent where it became dangerous with literally thousands of the sweets being hurled at the group during their shows.

The situation was far worse in America because they did not have the very soft jelly babies, but a hard-coated jelly bean.

George was to comment: 'They hurt. Some newspaper had dug out the old joke which we'd forgotten about, when John once said I'd eaten all his jelly babies. Everywhere we went I got them thrown at me. They don't have soft jelly babies in America but hard jelly beans like bullets.'

After their first American concert at the Washington Coliseum, Ringo commented, 'Some of them even threw jelly beans in bags and they hurt like hailstones.'

Jessie's Dream

Actress Jessie Robins was featured as Ringo's Aunt Jessie in the *Magical Mystery Tour* film. Jessie, who is rather stout, has a nightmare in which she dreams of a waiter (played by John Lennon), who shovels lashings of spaghetti on to her dining-table by the spadeful. For this sequence, the Beatles worked out a piece of incidental music which they called 'Jessie's Dream'.

They recorded the incidental music privately, not in a recording studio, and it was credited to McCartney/Starkey/Harrison/Lennon.

Jets, The

The first British rock band to perform in Hamburg. Some of the members were present in the 2 I's coffee bar in London when Bruno Koschmider arrived looking for bands for the Kaiserkeller. Pianist Iain Hines said he had a group and made up a name, the Jets, gathering individual musicians within 24 hours. However, Iain failed to show up at Liverpool Street Station when the group departed on 4 June 1960. The Jets began rehearsing on the boat over to the Continent. They comprised Tony Sheridan on lead guitar and vocals, Pete Wharton on bass guitar, Colin Milander on vocals and rhythm guitar, Rick Richards (also known as Rick Hardy) on vocals and rhythm guitar, and Del Ward on piano and vocals.

They hadn't managed to find a drummer to join them. They arrived at the Kaiserkeller at 2 a.m. on 5 June and found the club had a Trixon drum kit. The various members tried to play on it and it was decided that Del Ward, who'd hardly touched a set of drums before, should become their drummer.

After they'd played at the Kaiserkeller for a few weeks, Hines turned up wanting to be included in the line-up. Koschmider said he was quite happy with the band as it was, and if Iain wanted to join them, he wasn't prepared to pay them any more money. The members wouldn't agree to Iain joining them as it would have resulted in them taking a 17½ per cent cut in their pay, so Iain then went back to London.

They signed a new contract with the Kaiserkeller on 30 June, but were then approached by Peter Eckhorn who offered them five marks extra a night to play at his Bavarian bar in the Reeperbahn. There must have been some pressure applied to Koschmider because he agreed to free them from their contract.

They played their final date at the Kaiserkeller on Wednesday, 6 July and opened at the new club on Saturday, 9 July.

As the club, which was in a building formerly called Der Hippodrom, had no proper name, they suggested it be called the Top Ten Club, after a venue they'd played in Berwick Street, London.

They initially played one hour, followed by a half-hour break, and in the evenings they played from 7 p.m. to 3 a.m. Business had boomed to such an extent that Eckhorn decided to present non-stop music.

During their season there, the Beatles occasionally joined them on stage for a jam and were due to take over the residency at the club when the Jets' season came to an end.

One night, when the Beatles played on stage at the Top Ten with Sheridan, Colin and Iain got up on stage with them and the set included a seventy-minute version of Ray Charles' 'What'd I Say?'.

Horst Fascher had been appointed manager of the Top Ten and, on 6 August, Richards joined Fascher on a trip to London to find new musicians. The idea was to form two bands for the Top Ten. Iain Hines was recruited, along with Chas Beaumont, former lead guitarist with the Worried Men.

It was planned that Sheridan would lead a trio, with himself backed by Pete Wharton on bass and Ingo Jones on drums. Jones was a former member of German band Fats and his Cats. The second band would comprise Richards, Hines, Beaumont and Del Ward. Unfortunately, on the journey back the car crashed on the autobahn and Richards was hospitalised. In the meantime, Jones had been sacked and replaced by a black GI, Tony Kavanagh. Colin Milander had fallen in love with a girl called Antje and decided to leave the group and take a job in a brewery.

Despite the long-term contract they'd signed, Eckhorn told the Jets in October that he wanted new bands and got rid of them, replacing them with Gerry & the Pacemakers. Wharton, Kavanagh, Beaumont and Richards began playing in the Bambina Bar in the Hamburg suburb of Pferdemarkt, while Sheridan began playing in a club in the Reeperbahn called Studio X.

Colin left the brewery, returned to England with Iain and joined the Echoes, backing various artists including Gene Vincent, Dickie Pride, Vince Eager and Ricky Valance. Later, Iain was to return to Hamburg and become booking manager at the Top Ten. Richards began a new career in cabaret in Germany before returning to Britain. Ward joined an Indonesian cabaret group the Tilman Brothers and Wharton returned to England to run the family business.

Johanneshows Isstadion, Stockholm, Sweden

This massive ice-hockey stadium saw the appearance of the Beatles on their second and last visit to Sweden when, on 28 and 29 July 1964, they performed a total of four concerts, two per night.

During their first concert, John and Paul received mild electric shocks from an unearthed microphone.

Also on the bill were the Kays, the Moonlighters, the Streaplers, Jimmy Justice, the Mascots and the Shanes.

The capacity of the arena was 8,500 although their audiences varied from 6,500 to 3,000.

John F. Kennedy Airport, New York City

Scenes of adulation greeted the Beatles when they flew in to John F. Kennedy Airport on Pan Am Flight 101 at 1.35 p.m. on 7 February 1964.

The group had flown out of Heathrow Airport, ensconced in the first-class section of the plane. Among the other first-class passengers were Cynthia Lennon, Brian Epstein, Phil Spector and George Harrison of the *Liverpool Echo*. Also on the plane were photographer Dezo Hoffmann and Cavern Club boss Ray McFall, who alighted wearing a fur hat he'd bought in Hamburg. Other seats in the plane were occupied by pressmen and businessmen who were trying to obtain Beatles merchandising rights. The businessmen kept sending notes to Epstein, who ignored them. Neil Aspinall and Mal Evans spent a great deal of time forging the Beatles' signatures on photographs.

There were 5,000 fans gathered at the airport, mainly on the balcony above the customs hall, waving banners with messages such as 'Welcome to Beatlesville USA' and singing 'We love you Beatles, Oh yes we do'.

As the passengers alighted, each was given a Beatle kit with the compliments of Capitol Records. This comprised a 'signed' photograph, an 'I like the Beatles' badge and a Beatles wig.

There was a 100-man police cordon holding back the crowds and escorting the Beatles to the customs hall and one policeman said, 'I think the world has gone mad', while another commented, 'Boy, can they use a haircut!'

All their luggage was thoroughly examined in the customs hall, while airport officials said that they had experienced nothing like it since General MacArthur had returned from Korea.

Brian Sommerville, the group's press agent, had arrived a few days earlier to co-ordinate the press and there were 200 press representatives waiting for them on the first floor of the main terminal.

The 200 journalists and photographers were almost impossible to control and they ignored Sommerville's request for order – until John Lennon shouted at them to 'Shut up!' This was greeted with applause, followed by a quiet spell during which Sommerville was able to introduce each member of the group and the question and answer session began.

Q: 'Are you in favour of lunacy?'
Paul: 'Yeah. It's healthy.'
Q: 'Will you be getting a haircut?'
All: 'No!'
George: 'We had one yesterday.'

Q: 'Will you sing something?'

John: 'No, we need money first.'

Q: 'Which one of you is really bald?'

Paul: 'I'm bald.'

John: 'We're all bald.'

Q: 'Is there any truth to the rumour that you're really just four Elvis Presleys?'

Ringo: 'No, nah, we're not.' (His voice mimicking Elvis.)

Q: 'What is the secret of your success?'

Ringo: 'We have a press agent.'

Q: 'What do you think of the campaign in Detroit to "Stamp out the Beatles"?'

John: 'We have a campaign to stamp out Detroit.'

Q: 'Are you part of a social rebellion against the older generation?'

Paul: 'No, it's a dirty lie.'

All: 'Yeah, a dirty lie.'

Q: 'Ringo, why do you wear two rings on each hand?'

Ringo: 'Because I can't fit them through my nose.'

Q: 'Do you think it's wrong to set such a bad example to teenagers, smoking the way you do?'

Ringo: 'It's better than being alcoholics.'

Q: 'What do you think of the criticism that you are not very good?'

George: 'We're not.'

Q: 'What do you believe is the reason you are the most popular singing group today?'

John: 'We've no idea. If we did we'd get four long-haired boys, put them together, and become their managers.'

Q: 'What do you miss most now that your fame prohibits your freedom?'

Ringo: 'Going to the movies.'

George: 'Having nothing to do.'

John: 'School, because you don't have much to do there.'

Paul: 'Going on buses.'

Q: 'What do you do when you're cooped up in a hotel room between shows?'

George: 'We ice-skate.'

Q: 'How did you find America?'

Ringo: 'We went to Greenland and made a left turn.'

Q: 'Would you like to walk down the street without being recognised?'

John: 'We used to do that with no money in our pockets. There's no point in it.'

Q: 'How do you keep your psychic balance?'

Ringo: 'The important thing is not to get potty. There's four of us, so whenever one of us gets a little potty, the other three bring him back to earth.'

Q: 'Does all the adulation from teenage girls affect you?'

John: 'When I feel my head start to swell, I look at Ringo and know perfectly well we're not supermen.'

Q: 'How do you feel about the invasion of your privacy all the time?'

Ringo: 'The only time it bothers us is when they get us to the floor and really mangle us.'

Q: 'Do you speak French?'

Paul: '*Non*.'

Q: 'Do you have any special advice for teenagers?'

John: 'Don't get pimples.'

Q: 'What would you do if the fans got past the police lines?'

George: 'We'd die laughing.'

Q: 'What will you do when the bubble bursts?'

George: 'Take up ice-hockey.'

Paul: 'Play baseball.'

Q: 'Has success spoiled the Beatles?'

John: 'Well, you don't see us running out and buying bowler hats, do you? I think we've pretty well succeeded in remaining ourselves.'

Paul: 'The great thing about it is that you don't have big worries anymore when you've got where we have, only little ones – like whether the plane is going to crash.'

Q: 'What is the biggest threat to your careers, the atom bomb or dandruff?'

Ringo: 'The atom bomb. We've already got dandruff.'

After the press reception the Beatles made their way to the Plaza Hotel.

John F. Kennedy Stadium, Broad Street and Patterson Avenue, Philadelphia, Pennsylvania

There was only one performance, at 8 p.m. on Tuesday, 16 August 1966, sponsored by George A. Habib. The local disc jockey who hosted the show was Ed Hurst. The Beatles arrived in a florist's truck and George was to quip: 'We came disguised as a bouquet . . . or a wreath, depending on your viewpoint.'

It was a hot and humid evening, which saw constant streaks of lightning flashes throughout the show. The crowd thundered with screams and shrieks when the announcement blared 'Ladies and Gentlemen

... The Beatles!' When they reached the stage the announcer said, 'Please do not stand on your seats or enter the playing field ... Relax and enjoy yourselves ... and now ... the Beatles!' The four were dressed in green double-breasted suits with mustard yellow open-collared shirts and began with Paul saying, 'Hello, Philly.' They opened with 'Rock 'n' Roll Music', followed by 'She's A Woman', 'If I Needed Someone', 'Day Tripper', 'Baby's in Black', 'I Feel Fine', 'Yesterday', 'I Wanna Be Your Man', 'Nowhere Man' and 'Paperback Writer'. Paul then took the mike and said, 'Well, this will be our last tune. Sorry, but we don't want to be hit by lightning, you know. We hope you enjoyed the show, and we'll see you again, maybe next year. This last song is one that we've been doing forever, it seems. It's a Little Richard song called "Long Tall Sally".'

Although the stadium had a seating capacity of 60,000, there were only 20,000 in the audience that day.

Johnny & The Hurricanes

Tenor saxophonist Johnny Paris was born in Walbridge, Ohio, in 1940 and founded this instrumental group in 1957. Their hits between 1959 and 1961 included 'Red River Rock', 'Reveille Rock', 'Beatnik Fly', 'Down Yonder', 'Rocking Goose', 'Ja-Da' and 'Old Smokey/High Voltage'.

The group topped the bill at Hamburg's Star Club when the Beatles made their debut there in 1962.

Johnny & The Moondogs

A stopgap name adopted by the Quarry Men when they entered the Carroll Levis talent competitions in 1959. They thought it would be a more suitable name as most successful groups at the time had the name of a lead singer in the title. John, Paul and George used the name when they performed at a couple of heats at the Empire Theatre, Liverpool in October 1959 and at the Hippodrome Theatre, Manchester in November.

George commented: 'For this we dreamed up a new name, Johnny & the Moondogs. There were just the three of us and I remember we were on a Buddy Holly & the Crickets kick at the time. So, of course, we sang "Think It Over" and "It's So Easy".'

Carroll Levis asked the boys what the name Moondog meant. They'd made it up, but told him that it referred to a Red Indian who banged tin cans!

The Liverpool heats were won by another band, but Johnny & the Moondogs had received enough applause to be booked into the special heat at Manchester's Hippodrome Theatre on 15 November. The winner of the Manchester show would be given the opportunity of appearing for two minutes on Levis' ATV television show 'Discoveries'.

It was the boys' first performance outside of Liverpool but they had to leave before the end of the show in order to catch the last train home. As all the acts appeared singly in a finale to receive audience applause, which determined the winner, Johnny & the Moondogs never had the opportunity of appearing on 'Discoveries'.

The name Johnny & the Moondogs was used from October 1959 until January 1960.

Johnny B. Goode

A classic rock 'n' roll recording by Chuck Berry, originally released in 1958, which became a standard item in the repertoire of most rock groups, including the Beatles, who began performing the number in the late fifties, before they had even decided on the name the Beatles. John was lead vocalist on the number, which the group performed on their BBC radio appearance on 'Saturday Club' on 15 February 1964. A Saturday Club recording was included on *The Beatles Live At The BBC* CDs.

Johns, Glyn

A leading British record producer/engineer who had worked with a number of top bands such as the Rolling Stones and the Who when he received a phone call from Paul McCartney in December 1968, inviting him to work with the Beatles as balance engineer on a current project. Paul explained that they were producing their own television show and intended making a documentary and an album from it. The project, then called 'Get Back', eventually turned into *Let It Be*.

The tapes which Glyn recorded, together with George Martin, were later given to Phil Spector to mix. Glyn was to comment: 'I cannot bring myself to listen to the Phil Spector version of the album – I heard a few bars of it once, and was totally disgusted, and think it's an absolute load of garbage.'

Glyn's first association with the Beatles occurred when he acted as second engineer on Jack Good's television special 'Around the Beatles' at IBC Studios on 19 April 1964.

As a vocalist, Glyn recorded 'I'll Follow The Sun' from the *Beatles For Sale* album. His single was issued on Pye 7N 15818 on 2 April 1965.

Paul later called Glyn, this time to work on the *Red Rose Speedway* sessions, but it was said that he felt Paul's work on the album was too slow and he walked out on the session.

John used to humorously refer to him as Glynis (an injoke referring to Glynis Johns, the British actress of fifties' films).

Jolly What!

Jolly What! England's Greatest Recording Stars The Beatles & Frank Ifield On Stage was an unusual album which has become a collector's item.

Issued by Vee-Jay Records in America on Vee-Jay 1085 on 26 February 1964, it reached No. 104 in the *Billboard* charts and No. 73 in *Cash Box*. The reason for its poor showing was that most American Beatles fans already had the few Beatles tracks on the album.

The Vee-Jay label had been given the opportunity of picking up some Beatles tracks for release in America in 1963 after Capitol Records had turned the group down. Once the build-up began in 1964, Vee-Jay decided to take advantage of the material. They'd released an album *Introducing The Beatles* (the tracks from the British debut album *Please Please Me*) in July 1963 with no success. They re-released the album in January 1964 and it reached No. 2 in *Cash Box* and *Billboard* and No. 1 in the *Record World* charts. As the company was unable to obtain any more Beatle cuts due to the fact that Capitol had now realised the group's potential, Vee-Jay placed four of the tracks from *Introducing The Beatles* – 'Please Please Me', 'From Me To You', 'Ask Me Why' and 'Thank You Girl' – on to this album, which also contained eight Frank Ifield cuts – 'Any Time', 'Lovesick Blues', 'I'm Smiling Now', 'Nobody's Darling', 'I Remember You', 'The Wayward Wind', 'Unchained Melody' and 'I Listen To My Heart'.

The cover blurb implied that the album had been recorded live, which was untrue. All the tracks were studio cuts. By sheer coincidence, the Beatles and Frank Ifield had once actually appeared on the same show in Peterborough.

The original album sleeve was a rather bland affair sporting a drawing of an Edwardian-type figure with a long moustache and spectacles, obviously illustrating the 'Jolly What!' phrase. The album was re-pressed with a different cover featuring a painting of the four in their collarless jackets.

The sleeve notes read:

The tremendous surging influence that has of recent months been felt by the European Recording artists has never been equalled as on this album. Without any question The Beatles and Frank Ifield are the most popular recording stars in Europe. The Beatles are considered a phenomenon on the

American scene in that this is the first time that a European based recording act has so captivated the American public from both TV and recording standpoint.

It is with a great deal of pride and pleasure that this copulation [sic] has been presented.

Jones, Brian

Blond, charismatic founder-member of the Rolling Stones, born in Cheltenham on 28 February 1942.

Giorgio Gomelsky, who acted as manager of the group for a time, invited the Beatles to see the Stones at the Crawdaddy Club, Richmond. They became friends and Brian, in particular, found the Beatles' music exciting and wanted the Stones to adopt Beatles-style harmonies.

In the early days of the group, Brian had been looked upon as their leader. However, the power in the band began to revolve increasingly around Mick Jagger and Keith Richards, primarily because they wrote the group's material. Although Brian had innovative ideas and was one of the first British musicians to be influenced by ethnic music, his role in the group continued to be eroded. This caused him to turn increasingly to drink. He was in love with Anita Pallenberg, but when she slept with both Keith Richards and Mick Jagger, he became depressed still further, took solace in drugs and was constantly depressed. John Lennon was to comment, 'From being brilliant he became the kind of person you dread ringing you up. He was in a lot of pain but I was going through so much myself that it seemed there was nothing I could do to help.'

Brian left the Stones in 1969, announcing on 9 June: 'The music of Mick Jagger and Keith Richards has, to my mind, progressed on a tangent as far as my own tastes are concerned.'

In May 1967 he had played saxophone with the Beatles on their track 'You Know My Name (Look Up The Number)', which wasn't released until March 1970 when it was used as the flipside of 'Let it Be'.

Brian had expressed his desire to join the Beatles and thought he might end up as the fifth member of the band.

He was found drowned in the swimming pool of his Sussex house on 3 July 1969. He was 27 years old.

Jones, Davy

Black American singer who had appeared on several major US TV shows, including the Ed Sullivan, Walter Winchell, Arthur Godfrey and Alan Freed Shows, before moving to Britain in 1960 and signing with Pye Records.

In 1961, at the age of 22, he made several appearances in and around Liverpool, getting to know the local groups and promoters before moving on to the Continent. He'd first appeared in Liverpool on Tuesday, 3 May 1960 at Liverpool Stadium on the Allan Williams promotion headlined by Gene Vincent, which featured Liverpool bands such as Cass & the Cassanovas, Rory Storm & the Hurricanes and Gerry & the Pacemakers. Williams hadn't booked the Beatles as they were still relatively unknown locally.

Jones made his debut with the Beatles on Friday, 24 November 1961 when he dropped by the Tower Ballroom, New Brighton, where the group was appearing on the second 'Operation Big Beat' promotion. Two black singers turned up unannounced at the venue that evening – one was Emile Ford, who took to the stage and performed with Rory Storm & the Hurricanes, the other was Jones, who went on stage during the Beatles' performance and sang two numbers with them.

His first official booking with them was a Cavern lunchtime session on Friday, 8 December 1961. Ray McFall booked the singer and, as Jones didn't have a backing band, arranged for the Beatles to do the honours. During the evening he headlined 'The Davy Jones Show' at the Tower Ballroom, which also featured the Beatles, Rory Storm & the Hurricanes, Dale Roberts & the Jaywalkers, Kingsize Taylor & the Dominoes, Derry & the Seniors and Steve Day & the Drifters. Once again, the Beatles provided backing for Jones, who had been advertised as 'Saturday Spectacular television star and Reprise recording artist'.

He was photographed on both occasions for *Mersey Beat*.

Jones was later to renew his acquaintance with Liverpool bands when he began appearances at the Star Club in Hamburg.

Jones, Peter

A prominent British music journalist who wrote the first-ever paperback book on the Beatles' story, entitled *The True Story of the Beatles*, under the name Billy Shepherd, a pseudonym he was to use for his features on the Beatles in the *Beatles Book* magazine.

During his term as editor of *Record Mirror* he became the first journalist on a national music paper to interview the Beatles, in August 1962. An account of the interview is given in the November 1978 issue of the *Beatles Book*. Peter, whose small office at *Record Mirror* was based at 116 Shaftesbury Avenue, received a call from photographer Dezo Hoffmann, whose studio was only a few streets away. He'd just finished a photo session with the Beatles and said, 'I have four boys from Liverpool I would love you to meet.' He brought them around to meet Peter, accompanied by Brian Epstein. There were only three chairs in the office. Epstein told him that the group were probably the most popular vocal and instrumental band in the North of England. Peter was to interview the group on numerous occasions.

He was later to become European representative of *Billboard* magazine.

Jones, Philip
Producer of the popular 'Thank Your Lucky Stars' television pop show of the sixties.

When Brian Epstein was meeting Dick James in his Charing Cross Road office in January 1963 to discuss the possibility of James promoting 'Please Please Me', James immediately contacted Jones by phone in Epstein's presence. He asked Jones if he'd book the Beatles for the programme and Jones, although a friend of James, pointed out that he had to listen to artists' records before he decided on booking them. Undismayed, James immediately put 'Please Please Me' on the record player and Jones listened to the song on the phone. He then booked them for the next available show.

The group travelled to Birmingham on 13 January 1963 to record the show, which was transmitted on 19 January. As the show was networked, 'Thank Your Lucky Stars' became their first national TV appearance and Jones was to book them for numerous further appearances.

Joseph Williams Primary School, Naylorsfield Road, Belle Vale, Liverpool L25
The school where both Paul and Mike McCartney were moved when Stockton Wood Road became overcrowded. It was a half-hour bus ride from the McCartney home in Speke, but the two boys used to enjoy the journeys on the double-decker buses. It was the first school built in Liverpool after the war and it was situated in a conservation area.

Their headmaster John Gore, whom they called 'Pop', used to take them for nature walks, and they enjoyed their trips into the neighbouring countryside. However, for a period at the school, Paul was very unhappy because he'd put on weight and some of the pupils called him 'fatty'.

Paul was an apt pupil and came top in most subjects regularly. He did not have any difficulty in passing his 11-Plus examination and gaining entrance to the Liverpool Institute.

Juke Box Jury

A popular BBC 1 television show hosted by David Jacobs which made its debut on 1 June 1959, heralded by the theme 'Hit And Miss' by the John Barry Seven. The show was swiftly moved from a Monday evening to Saturday, where it remained for eight years, then was moved to Wednesday nights on 27 September 1967, at the same time moving from a studio in Manchester to one in London. A panel of celebrities would vote on the current week's record releases and vote them either a hit or a miss. Pop stars, actors and actresses and TV personalities in general composed most of the panels and they included a range of celebrities from Jane Asher to Brian Epstein.

John made his only solo appearance on the panel on Saturday, 22 June 1963, for the programme which was transmitted on Saturday, 29 June. His fellow judges were actress Caroline Maudling, actor Bruce Prochnik and TV personality Katie Boyle. Records reviewed were: 'Southend', Cleo Laine; 'So Much In Love', the Tymes; 'Devil In Disguise', Elvis Presley; 'The Click Song', Miriam Makeba; 'On Top Of Spaghetti', Tom Glaser; 'Flamenco', Russ Conway; 'First Quarrel', Paul and Paula; and 'Don't Ever Let Me Down', Julie Grant. The only record voted a hit was 'Devil In Disguise'. However, John caused upset to Elvis fans who wrote in several letters of complaint after he was critical of the new Presley single and referred to the King as 'today's Crosby', suggesting that he return to using rock 'n' roll material.

George made his only solo appearance when he guested 'live' on Saturday, 25 July 1964. George's fellow celebrities were actress Alexandra Bastedo, comedian Reg Varney and singer Carole Ann Ford. The records played were: 'I Should Have Known Better', the Naturals; 'What Am I To You', Kenny Lynch; 'Soulful Dress', Sugar Pie De Santo; 'How Can I Tell Her', the Fourmost; 'Heart', David Nelson; 'Spanish Harlem', Sounds Incorporated; 'All Grown Up', the Crystals; 'She's Not There', the Zombies; and 'Ain't Love Grand, Ain't Love Proud', Tony Clarke.

Ringo also recorded a 'Juke Box Jury' that day, which was transmitted the following week on Saturday, 1 August. Jacobs introduced him by saying, 'A gentleman known in the trade as Ringo Starr.' Ringo was initially nervous and commented, 'I'm not worried about what records they'll play. I'm OK judging records – just as long as I don't get too carried away and get too outspoken.'

His fellow judges were Katie Boyle, comedian Ray Martine and actress Judy Cornwall. The records reviewed were: 'Thinking Of You Baby', the Dave Clark Five; 'A Summer Song', Chad Stuart and Jeremy Clyde; 'Don't It Make You Feel Good', the Overlanders; 'It's For You', Cilla Black; 'Move It Baby', Simon Scott; 'I Wouldn't

Trade You For The World', the Bachelors; and 'Not for Me', Sammy Davis Jr.

Brian Epstein was to make two appearances on the show, the first on Saturday, 26 October 1963 and the second on Saturday, 29 February 1964. The waxwork models of the Beatles from Madame Tussauds were displayed on the programme on Saturday, 30 May 1964.

The outstanding highlight took place on Saturday, 7 December 1963 when a special all-Beatles edition of the show was filmed from the stage of the Empire Theatre, Liverpool. It was broadcast the same day in the early evening to a television audience of 23 million viewers.

The records reviewed by John, Paul, George and Ringo were: 'I Could Write A Book', the Chants; 'Kiss Me Quick', Elvis Presley; 'Hippy Hippy Shake', the Swinging Bluejeans; 'Did You Have A Happy Birthday?' Paul Anka; 'The Nitty Gritty', Shirley Ellis; 'I Can't Stop Talking About You', Steve Lawrence and Edie Gorme; 'Do You Really Love Me?' Billy Fury; 'There, I've Said It Again', Bobby Vinton; 'Love Hit Me', The Orchids; and 'I Think Of You', the Merseybeats.

The Beatles voted the Chants, Elvis Presley, the Swinging Bluejeans, Billy Fury, Bobby Vinton and the Merseybeats as hits. The records which actually charted were by Elvis, the Swinging Bluejeans, Billy Fury, Bobby Vinton and the Merseybeats. Four of the records, 'I Could Write A Book', 'Hippy Hippy Shake', 'Do You Really Love Me?' and 'I Think Of You' were by Liverpool artists.

When reviewing 'Hippy Hippy Shake', John Lennon said, 'I prefer Bill Harry's version.' This was an in-joke by John referring to the fact that *Mersey Beat* had been encouraging a Liverpool group to record the number. As a result, record stores throughout the land were inundated by requests from Beatles fans asking for Bill Harry's version of 'Hippy Hippy Shake', a record which didn't exist.

The BBC was keen to present another all-Beatles panel on the programme and approached Brian Epstein in July 1964, but he turned the proposal down.

There were a total of 433 'Juke Box Jury' shows, the final one being screened on 27 December 1967.

There were short-lived attempts to revive it, with Noel Edmunds hosting it in 1979. A further attempt was made to revive it in 1989 with Jools Holland in the chair, but the series lasted less than a year.

Julia

John's song, named in honour of his mother. Yoko was said to have given him some small help with the lyric and she is herself mentioned in the song – as 'Ocean Child'.

This was the only completely solo John Lennon number recorded while he was a member of the Beatles. When he recorded the number at Abbey Road on Sunday, 13 October 1968, neither Paul, George or Ringo were in the studio and John sang the song himself, playing acoustic guitar.

'Julia' was included on *The Beatles* double album. Capitol also issued it as the flipside of the single 'Ob-La-Di, Ob-La-Da' in America on Capitol 4347 on 8 November 1976. Take two of the original studio recording of the number was included on the Beatles' *Anthology 3* CDs.

Junk

A song Paul wrote in India which had the original working title of 'Jubilee'. He'd originally recorded it for the *Abbey Road* album, but it wasn't used and he included it on his 1970 Apple album, *McCartney*. The number finally appeared on an official Beatles release when it was included on the Beatles' *Anthology 3* CDs.

Junkin, John

A British comedian/actor who portrayed a road manager called Shake, loosely based on Mal Evans, in the film *A Hard Day's Night*.

Junkin had heard that the Beatles were only hiring Liverpool actors for the road manager roles, which seemed to be confirmed when Norman Rossington was employed to portray Norm. So Junkin affected a Liverpool accent and pretended to be a 'scouser'. Once the filming was underway he couldn't keep up the pretence, but the boys appreciated his nerve and were amused by it.

Kaempfert, Berthold

A major German bandleader/composer, born in Hamburg, who was an A&R man at Polydor in 1961 when Alfred Schacht of Aberbach Music approached him about recording an artist he'd seen in the Top Ten Club. Schacht had visited the club, was impressed by Tony Sheridan and suggested that Kaempfert should record him. The 37-year-old recording manager/talent scout visited the Top Ten, agreed with his friend's assessment and signed Sheridan to a recording session. On Tony's recommendation, he hired the Beatles to back him on the sessions.

The Beatles began a three-day recording stint, backing Tony Sheridan at the Harburg Friedrich Ebert Halle, which was in an infants' school, on 22 June 1961.

Kaempfert chose two numbers, 'My Bonnie Lies Over The Ocean' and 'When The Saints Go Marching In', and Sheridan also sang 'Why (Can't You Love Me Again)'. Kaempfert had also decided to name the group the Beat Brothers on the record release. The Beatles, who were paid a flat fee of 300 marks (around £26) for the session and did not receive any royalties, asked Kaempfert if they could record some other numbers. He asked them what original material they had, but they couldn't come up with anything original, apart from the George Harrison instrumental 'Cry For A Shadow'. Kaempfert advised them to start writing their own material if they intended to make a name for themselves. He also recorded them performing 'Ain't She Sweet'.

'Cry For A Shadow' was actually an instrumental George had

composed (with a little help from John) on their previous Hamburg trip when Rory Storm asked him if he knew the Shadows' 'Frightened City'. It was a parody of the Shadows style which George had considered calling 'Beatle Bop'. On the third day in the studio they only managed to cut one number with Sheridan, 'If You Love Me, Baby'.

On 1 May 1961 the Beatles signed a recording contract with Bert Kaempfert Produktions for one year, but renewable for periods of one year, in which they agreed to record four songs per year.

When Brian Epstein took over the Beatles and was negotiating a British contract for them, he wrote to Kaempfert on 20 February 1962 asking him to release them. Kaempfert wrote, 'I do not want to spoil the chance of the group to get recording contracts elsewhere, but I do think that we should have the chance to make recordings with the group for the Polydor label whilst they are in Hamburg.'

A few years later, Kaempfert told the British musical weekly, *Melody Maker*: 'One day Brian Epstein wrote to me asking under what conditions I'd release the Beatles. I said there's no conditions, you can take them. Polydor didn't want them, they were only interested in Sheridan.'

When the Beatles performed at the Ernst Merck Halle, Hamburg, on 26 June 1966, Bert was among the backstage visitors. As soon as they saw him, the Beatles began singing 'Strangers In The Night'.

Kaempfert became a major recording artist and composer in his own right and his first million seller was 'Wonderland By Night', which topped the American charts. In 1961 the Bert Kaempfert Orchestra was voted 'Number One Band of the Future' in a *Cash Box* poll. In 1965 Bert composed the music for the film *A Man Could Get Killed* and one of the numbers he composed was 'Strangers In The Night', which was to provide Frank Sinatra with his first No. 1 hit for several years. Other major hits by Kaempfert included 'Bye Bye Blues', 'A Swinging Safari', 'Spanish Eyes' and '*Danke Schön*'.

Kaempfert, who was married with two daughters, began his first British tour in 1980. In June of that year he died of a heart attack shortly after arriving in Spain.

Kaiserkeller, 38 Grosse Freiheit, St Pauli, Hamburg, Germany

A large club in the notorious red-light district of Hamburg which was run by Bruno Koschmider. The events which led up to the Beatles appearing at the Kaiserkeller (King's Cellar) had their origins in the Jacaranda Club, Liverpool.

The main attraction at the Jacaranda was the Royal Caribbean Steel Band. Allegedly, one day Allan Williams arrived at the club to discover that the band had not turned up and they later contacted him to say that they were playing at a club in Hamburg and suggested that he come over and book some groups into the German city.

Williams decided to act on the tip and recorded a number of local acts on a tape recorder in the cellar of the Jac. They were the Silver Beatles, Cass & the Cassanovas, Gerry & the Pacemakers, folk group the Spinners and a jazz band, Noel Walker's Stompers. He then set off on a weekend trip to Germany, via Amsterdam, accompanied by his friend Lord Woodbine.

Arriving in Hamburg they couldn't locate the club where the steel band were playing and when Lord Woodbine went off with a stripper, Williams decided to explore the red-light district. Someone mentioned the Kaiserkeller club to him and he took a cab there and was quite impressed by the size of the venue. He observed that the decor was in a nautical style with glass floats on the walls, fishing nets, a bar shaped like a ship and various brass portholes on the walls.

The German band on the stage were making music which was having no impact on the audience, who ignored it and continued drinking and talking. When the band took a break and the jukebox began to blast out rock 'n' roll records by Elvis Presley and others, he noticed a complete change of atmosphere, with members of the audience crowding on to the dance floor.

He stopped a waiter and requested to see the manager and was eventually taken to Koschmider's office. Koschmider couldn't speak English and their discussion was held through an interpreter. Williams impressed on Koschmider that he needed rock 'n' roll groups at the club, that the best rock 'n' roll groups came from Liverpool and that he was agent for a number of them. Williams then told him about the tapes and they were put on a tape recorder, but all that came out was a racket – the tapes had become demagnetized during the trek from Liverpool to Hamburg. Koschmider suggested that he send him some more tapes.

There is a slight variation to the story. Brian Casser, of Cass & the Cassanovas, maintained that Williams allowed him to sleep overnight at the Jacaranda. Cass had heard from contacts that a German clubowner called Koschmider was looking for bands to book. Eager to find work for his own band, Casser discovered Koschmider's number and phoned him, using the Jacaranda telephone after the club had closed for the night. He says he convinced Koschmider that he should book Liverpool groups. Casser then alleges that Koschmider rang the Jac during the day when he wasn't around and Allan Williams took the call and decided to act as agent instead. The explanation couldn't be as straightforward as this, because Koschmider didn't speak English, therefore any call would have had to be made by someone who could translate for him.

Following Williams' trip to Hamburg, he had problems with a group called Derry & the Seniors. As a result of Williams arranging for them to tour with one of Larry Parnes' acts, they'd turned professional, only to discover that the tour had been cancelled. Howie Casey arrived at Williams' Blue Angel Club, determined to take it out of his hide and Williams escaped a physical beating by offering to take the group down to the 2 I's in London and get them work.

By an amazing coincidence, when they arrived at the 2 I's, Bruno Koschmider was there. Intrigued by the idea of booking British rock 'n' roll clubs into the Kaiserkeller, and not knowing the difference between London and Liverpool, he'd arrived in England and had been directed to the 2 I's. As a result he'd booked a group called the Jets. Williams arranged for the Seniors to go on stage and Koschmider agreed to book them at a fee of 30 Deutschmarks per man per day. The group began playing at the Kaiserkeller on 31 July 1961.

Koschmider contacted Williams for more bands and the Beatles eventually wended their way to Germany, only to be booked into the Indra Club, a seedier venue at the wrong end of the Grosse Freiheit.

The Seniors ended their season at the Kaiserkeller and on 1 October, Rory Storm & the Hurricanes took over. On 4 October they were joined by the Beatles and the two groups took split shifts at the venue. The Beatles appeared from 4 October–30 November, a total of 58 nights.

Both groups got up to high jinks at the club, with Lennon taunting the customers with shouts of '*Sieg heil! Sieg heil!*'. One night he walked on stage clad only in a pair of swimming trunks and turned his back on the audience, pulling down his trunks to show his bare bottom. The Hurricanes and the Beatles also had a bet as to who could break the stage, which was a flimsy affair supported by crates. Nightly they'd become more energetic, jumping up and down in an effort to crack the stage. Eventually it happened when the Hurricanes were playing and a furious Koschmider fined the group 65 Deutschmarks. It was while they were playing at the club that they were discovered by a German student Klaus Voormann, who brought along his friends such as Astrid Kirchherr and Jurgen Vollmer, all of whom would play their part in the Beatles' story. Also among the regulars were prostitutes from the Herbertstrasse who continually ordered waiters to send drinks to the group on stage.

As their season neared its end, they were determined to remain in Hamburg and move on to another club, the Top Ten Club in the Reeperbahn, where Tony Sheridan was appearing. When Koschmider heard about their plans he was furious and told them that their contract forbade them to play in any venue within a 40-mile radius of his clubs without his permission. A number of incidents then occurred, which soon put paid to the Beatles' plans for appearing at the Top Ten.

A letter from Koschmider was handed to George Harrison, which read:

> I the undersigned, hereby give notice to Mr GEORGE HARRISON and to BEATLES' BAND to leave on 30 November 1960.
> The notice is given to the above by order of the Public Authorities who have discovered that Mr GEORGE HARRISON is only 17 (seventeen) years of age.

George was deported, but the others elected to stay. Then Koschmider reported to the police that Pete Best and Paul McCartney had tried to set fire to his Bambi Kino and they were both arrested and deported.

The Kaiserkeller wasn't able to compete with the groups playing at the Top Ten Club and by the time the Star Club opened on the premises opposite to the Kaiserkeller, Koschmider had reverted the club back to a cabaret/strip joint and given it a new name, the Colibri.

Kansas City/Hey! Hey! Hey!

Two separate compositions combined, which, when the Beatles recorded them as one, resulted in royalties for both Leiber and Stoller and Little Richard. Jerry Leiber and Mike Stoller had originally written 'Kansas City', although it was called 'K.C. Loving' when the first version by Little Willie Littlefield was released in 1952. Richard, under his real name, Richard Penniman, composed 'Hey! Hey! Hey!'. He, in fact, recorded the two numbers separately in 1959, then recorded them as a medley later the same year and this is the version that the Beatles adopted in 1961, with Paul on lead vocals.

They performed it on stage during their last Star Club season and it appears on *The Beatles Live! At The Star Club In Hamburg, Germany: 1962* album. The group also performed it on BBC recordings for 'Pop Go The Beatles', 'From Us To You', and 'Saturday Club'. The number was also featured on their 1964 album *Beatles For Sale* and is to be found on the collections *The Beatles Box* and *The Beatles Collection*, their compilation *Rock 'n' Roll Music* and the American album *Beatles VI*.

Kass, Ron
When he was appointed divisional head of Apple Records, Kass was 33 years old and married to film star Joan Collins. He had headed the International Division of Liberty Records and the Beatles were looking for an experienced professional to head their record company.

Kass travelled regularly arranging the various deals for the label, launching it in 67 countries, and also set up an Apple office in California.

His own office was situated on the ground floor at Savile Row, with white walls, an expensive sound system, and two desks with Danish chrome and wood chairs. He shared his office with his secretary Carol Chapman.

However, by August 1968 he had gone, one of the victims of the wholesale sacking at Apple by Allen Klein, to be replaced by Jack Oliver, who had no experience of running a record company. Kass's office was then taken over by John and Yoko.

Kass became chairman of Warner Bros Records in London in 1974. When his wife went to America to star in 'Dynasty', Ron had to make a decision about whether to move to the States permanently. However, the marriage broke down and the couple divorced.

Ron died of cancer in Los Angeles on Saturday, 17 October 1986 at the age of 51.

Kaufman, Murray
A New York disc jockey, known as Murray the K. He received a copy of 'She Loves You' in October 1963 from a promotion man called Bud Helliwell. He recalled that he included it in a record contest in which he played five records and asked listeners to vote on them. 'She Loves You' came third to 'Coney Island Baby' by the Excellents and a Four Seasons single. Murray continued playing the Beatles single for two and a half weeks. Nothing seemed to happen, so he dropped it and went off to Miami in mid-January for his vacation. Suddenly, while listening to the radio there, it seemed as if every other record being played was the Beatles' 'I Want To Hold Your Hand'. Then he received a phone call from his programme director Joel Chaseman at 1010 WINS, telling him to return to the station as the Beatles were coming. 'Get yourself an exterminator,'

Kaufman told him, but his director was firm, Murray's job was on the line, so he cut short his holiday to attend the Beatles' airport press conference.

Before the Beatles arrived he announced on his station the airline, flight number and approximate time that the Beatles would be arriving.

He contacted the Beatles by phone at the Plaza Hotel, where they were staying, and conducted a radio interview with them over the phone. This tickled their interest and they didn't object when he turned up at the hotel. They were apparently aware of him from the sleeve notes he'd made on various record albums, and he told them: 'You're what's happenin', baby.'

Murray was to become the omnipresent disc jockey during that first trip.

Soon he was literally running their social life, taking them to New York nightclubs to meet starlets such as Tuesday Weld and Stella Stevens, and visiting the Playboy Club – all the time recording interviews.

When the group booked into the Deauville Hotel in Miami, to record another 'Ed Sullivan Show', Murray flew to Florida and shared a room with George Harrison, much to George's frustration. He continued taking them to nightclubs, such as the Peppermint Lounge in Miami, where they watched a show by country singer Hank Ballard.

When Murray was with the Beatles in Washington DC, a reporter asked: 'What the fuck is Murray The K doing here?' George replied, 'Murray's the fifth Beatle.' Kaufman then had the audacity to continually refer to himself as 'the fifth Beatle', a liberty which infuriated Brian Epstein so much that he threatened legal action.

Kaufman was even hired to compere their two concerts at Carnegie Hall, during which he announced: 'This is your fifth Beatle talking, I'm what's happening, and for one or two of you who want to leave your seats or throw things, we have people to take care of you.'

Despite Brian's fury at his calling himself the fifth Beatle, he was aware of the massive radio publicity Kaufman gave the group, and when the 'Around The Beatles' show was being planned by Rediffusion Television in London, he suggested that Murray the K be compere of the show. John Lennon, who considered Kaufman a phoney, talked Epstein out of it.

Over the years, Murray kept in touch, visiting them in London, where he attended their appearance at the *NME* Award Winner's Concert at Wembley Stadium and interviewed them during the filming of *A Hard Day's Night*.

He also travelled to the Queen Elizabeth Hotel, Montreal, some years later when John and Yoko had a bed-in, and was one of the celebrities present (including Petula Clark and Timothy Leary) who provided the background clapping on the 'Give Peace A Chance' recording.

His interviews from New York, Miami, London and Washington were contained on an EP, *The Beatles And Murray the K As It Happened*. The interviews he conducted in 1965 are to be found on bootleg albums such as *Soldier Of Love* and *Murray the K Fan Club*.

His autobiography *Murray the K Tells It Like It Is, Baby,* was published in America in 1966 with an introduction penned by George Harrison. He also appeared as himself in the film *I Wanna Hold Your Hand* in 1978, which concerned the adventures of a bunch of youngsters attempting to see the Beatles on their first American visit.

Kaufman was technical adviser to the 'Beatlemania' stage show and participated in a major Beatles festival held at Knotts Berry Farm in 1980. Tragically, he died in Los Angeles of cancer on 21 February 1982.

Kaye, Peter

A name which began appearing under Beatles photographs in 1961 with the appearance of the *Mersey Beat* newspaper. Peter Kaye was not a person, it was the name of a studio launched in the late fifties by photographer Bill Connell, who set up a photographic studio/shop in Park Lane in Liverpool's Dingle area, a few blocks from where Ringo Starr lived. He hired Les Chadwick, a former pupil at the Junior School of Art, as his assistant.

When Bill Harry launched *Mersey Beat* he sought out Les as one of his main photographers and a deal was made: in exchange for advertisements and by recommending to local groups that they should use his services, 'Peter Kaye' would take photographs commissioned by *Mersey Beat*. This resulted in the studio, mainly Les Chadwick, but occasionally Bill Connell, taking literally hundreds of shots of the Beatles and local groups on behalf of the publication.

In 1987 a book of the studio's work was published called *Beatles In Liverpool*. Sadly, it was the year in which Bill Connell died.

K.B. Hallen, Peter Bangsvej, Frederiksberg, Copenhagen, Denmark

The Beatles made only a single appearance in Denmark throughout their career. This took place at the K.B. Hallen on Thursday, 4 June

1964 on the opening date of their 27-day world tour. Ringo was ill in hospital at the time and drummer Jimmy Nicol deputised.

The group performed two shows at the K.B. Hallen, the first at 6.00 p.m., the second at 9.30 p.m. At each of the performances there was a capacity audience of 4,400.

Their repertoire was: 'I Want To Hold your Hand', 'I Saw Her Standing There', 'You Can't Do That', 'All My Loving', 'She Loves You', 'Till There Was You', 'Roll Over Beethoven', 'Can't Buy Me Love', 'This Boy' and 'Long Tall Sally'.

Keep Your Hands Off My Baby

A Gerry Goffin/Carole King composition, recorded by Little Eva in 1962 and included in the Beatles' repertoire in 1963, with John taking lead vocals. The group performed the song on their 'Saturday Club' appearance for BBC radio on 26 January 1963. The January 1963 *Saturday Club* performance was included on *The Beatles Live At The BBC* CDs.

Kelly, Arthur

Childhood and school friend of George Harrison. Arthur, George and Peter Harrison played guitars in the Rebels, a skiffle group supplemented by two other friends on washboard and tea-chest bass, who made a single appearance at the British Legion Club in Speke. When the fourteen-year-old George began dating Iris Caldwell, Arthur made it a foursome when he started dating Iris's best friend. Mrs Vi Caldwell used to call the two boys Arthur and Martha.

When George made the transference from the Les Stewart Quartet to the Quarry Men, the skiffle group had been without a bass player since the departure of Len Garry. John Lennon suggested that George become their bass player, but he didn't like the idea and told Arthur that he could become bass player with the Quarry Men if he could find the necessary £60 to buy a bass guitar. Arthur couldn't – and possibly missed out on becoming a member of the Beatles.

Arthur did become famous in his own right, as an actor, mainly in stage and television productions with Liverpool subjects. He portrayed Bert in the West End stage production of 'John, Paul, George, Ringo ... And Bert' and George came to see him in the play. Arthur was to appear in various productions, including the highly acclaimed television series 'The Boys From The Black Stuff'.

Kelly, Brian

One of the handful of Liverpool promoters who helped to build up the network of local venues which provided Mersey groups with the opportunity to develop their music in front of live audiences on a regular basis.

Kelly promoted 'Beekay' dances, the first of which took place at the Savoy Hall, Bath Street, Waterloo, on 11 May 1959. He then built up a number of other regular promotions at Lathom Hall, Seaforth; Alexandra Hall, Crosby; Aintree Institute, Litherland Town Hall; and a venue in Skelmersdale.

Like several other promoters, Kelly would have bands appearing at 'auditions'. In other words, if he hadn't seen a band perform before, he would let them play at his venue for no fee as an 'audition'.

He first booked the Silver Beats for an audition at Lathom Hall on Saturday, 14 May 1960 on a bill that included Kingsize Taylor & the Dominoes, Cliff Roberts & the Rockers and the Deltones.

They passed the audition!

Kelly next booked them to appear the following week, on Saturday, 21 May. However, they never turned up because they had set off on their brief Scottish tour with Johnny Gentle.

One of their most important early bookings took place at Litherland Town Hall on Tuesday, 27 December 1960. It was their debut appearance at the venue. Kelly hadn't booked the Beatles since their failure to turn up at his Lathom Hall promotion, but Bob Wooler had talked him into booking them at a fee of £6.

As it was a late booking, their names didn't appear in the local newspaper advertisements, which had already been placed, announcing the groups: Kingsize Taylor & the Dominoes, the Searchers, the Del Renas and the Deltones. Entrance to the show was 3s (15p) and Kelly managed to place their name on a number of hand painted posters: 'Direct from Hamburg, the Beatles!'

Their line-up that night was John, Paul, George, Pete and Chas Newby. They had just returned from Hamburg, where they had literally transformed their music and appearance, and gave a dynamic performance. Members of the audience, due to the posters, initially believed they were a German group, because they were virtually unknown locally.

Present at that particular gig were Pete Best's brother Rory and the Bests' lodger, accountancy student Neil Aspinall.

Over two decades later, John Kennedy of Kingsize Taylor & the Dominoes, who opened the show, told Radio Merseyside reporter Spencer Leigh: 'We used to open and close the show there. We'd do our spot and then go to the White House for a few pints. We never got to the pub that night. We'd just reached the door when they started off. And that was it. We stayed there all night and watched them. They were brilliant. There was something raw and animal about them.'

Discussing his involvement in the Beatles' career in an article published in *Mersey Beat*, Kelly revealed:

> I was organising a dance at Litherland Town Hall to be held on Boxing Day, 1960, but I was short of a group. On Christmas Day I received a phone call from Bob Wooler who said, 'I've found a group for you at the Jacaranda and they're free. They want eight pounds. Will they do?'
>
> 'Not at that price they won't,' I said. 'A group just won't increase my attendance enough to warrant that' . . . we finally agreed to pay them six pounds.
>
> On their first appearance I was completely knocked out by them. They had a pounding, pulsating beat which I knew would be big box office. When they finished playing, I posted some bouncers on the door of their dressing room to prevent other promoters who were in the hall entering. I went inside and booked them solidly for months ahead.
>
> I had a huge poster made with 'The Beatles' written in large fluorescent lettering. The poster caused a certain amount of curiosity and I remember the first reaction to their name. 'Beatles – you've spelt it wrong, mister.' 'Beatles – where've you dragged them from?' 'Beatles – who are they?'
>
> The group went from strength to strength at Litherland and built up a fantastic following. Even then, the songwriting talents of Lennon and McCartney were evident. On stage they'd say, 'Here's a song we've just written – if you don't like it you needn't clap.'
>
> The group went away to Germany. When they returned we did reasonable business with them, but they had lost Stuart and seemed downhearted and had temporarily lost their lustre.
>
> They were the first really noisy group to appear on Merseyside – and amplifiers were insufficient to cope with their sound. I worked on the amplification for them – and received a great deal of business for Alpha Sound. Groups on Merseyside seemed to play wilder and louder and more of them approached me to help with their amplification.

Brian booked them for Lathom Hall during a two-month period in 1961 on Friday, 20, Saturday, 21, Saturday, 28 and Monday, 30 January and Saturday, 4, Monday, 6, Friday, 10, Saturday, 11 and Saturday, 25 February. The last date was George Harrison's eighteenth birthday.

Their Litherland Town Hall appearances during 1961 were on

Thursday, 5 and Thursday, 26 January; Thursday, 2, Tuesday, 14, Thursday, 16 Tuesday, 21 and Tuesday, 28 February; Thursday, 2 March; Monday, 17, Monday, 24 and Monday, 31 July; Monday, 7 August; Thursday, 7, Thursday, 14, Thursday, 28 September; Thursday, 19 and Tuesday, 31 October. Their last appearance at Litherland Town Hall took place on Thursday, 9 November.

Kelly also booked the Beatles for a total of 31 appearances at Aintree Institute. They made their debut there on Saturday, 7 January 1961 and also appeared on Saturday, 7, Friday, 13, Saturday, 14, Wednesday, 18, Saturday, 21, Friday, 27 and Saturday, 28 January; Wednesday, 8, Friday, 10, Wednesday, 15 Saturday, 18 Wednesday, 22 and Saturday, 25 February; Wednesday, 1, Saturday, 4, Wednesday, 8 Saturday, 11 March; Friday, 21 and Friday, 28 July; Friday, 4 Saturday, 12, Friday, 18, Saturday, 19 and Saturday, 26 August; Saturday, 2, Saturday, 9 Saturday, 16 and Saturday, 23 September; Saturday, 28 October; and Saturday 11 November. Their last appearance at the venue took place on Saturday, 27 January 1962.

Their fee for the Aintree Institute was now £15 and by that time Brian Epstein was now their manager. Kelly paid them for the gig in coins. A furious Brian Epstein was to recall the incident in his biography and said they were paid '. . . in sixpences and florins and even halfpennies and I kicked up an awful fuss, not because £15 isn't £15 in any currency, but because I thought it was disrespectful of the Beatles.' As a result, Epstein ensured that they never appeared at the venue again.

Brian Kelly died in 1993.

Kelly, Frieda

The longest-lasting fan club secretary to the Beatles. The first official Beatles Fan Club was originally formed in May 1962 and run by Bobbie Brown. Frieda, who worked for Princes food firm, met Bobbie at the Cavern and began to help her with the club work. Due to the association, Frieda was employed as a shorthand typist in the NEMS Enterprises management office, operating from Whitechapel, at six pounds ten shillings a week. When Bobby became engaged in 1963, Frieda took over the running of the club, initially having to ask the Beatles to have a whip-round to pay for the postage. Brian Epstein then agreed to pay the fan club's running costs and Frieda shared a small office with Brian's secretary, Beryl Adams.

Frieda had been born in Ireland on 14 July 1945 and arrived in Liverpool when she was thirteen. She worked in an office in the city centre and attended the Cavern regularly. Once officially in charge of the fan club she was pleased to find, on her first day at the job, that there were two fan letters, but as time passed she was receiving up to 400 letters a day.

When NEMS Enterprises moved down to London, Frieda's father refused to let her go, so she remained in Liverpool and moved into new offices in Hackins Hay which she shared with *Mersey Beat*. Soon the club boasted more than 16,000 members to whom she would send a membership card, a photograph, a quarterly newsletter and, eventually, a Christmas record. She was the only full-time member and was helped by some part-time workers. As the club grew and the HQ was moved to London, Frieda continued to handle the Northern Area of the club and in October 1966 became joint national secretary.

Frieda was one of those stout 'Cavernites' who went down fighting when the Cavern was due to be demolished, and on 28 February 1966 was involved in the sit-in at the Cavern, entertained by the Hideaways group, who kept on playing when the barricades were torn down by the police.

When she moved to North John Street and Castle Street, when Apple took over the funding of the club, she had two full-time helpers, Elsa Breden and Edith Yates. She also had part-time helpers Sandra Malloy and Margie Travers, who were paid a wage. Casual workers included John McCartney (Paul's cousin), Ringo Starr's cousin Pat and schoolgirls Lynn Edwards, Lillian Boyle and Linda Shepherd. Officially, it was a 10 a.m. – 5.30 p.m. job, but Frieda willingly worked regularly until late at night.

Late in 1967 she became the official secretary and took over the full running of the club. The London office was closed. Frieda was also working for both NEMS and Apple.

On 4 April 1968, Frieda married Brian Norris, former member of the Realms and the Cryin' Shames.

When she was expecting her second child, Rachel, in March 1972 (her son Timothy was born in 1968) she decided she no longer wanted to run the club, particularly as the Beatles had disbanded. She put it to Apple who agreed that the club would close when the membership fee was up in March. The Beatles said they would not have another official fan club without Frieda as she ran it from 1962 until 1975 (it took three years to run everything down).

In the 1990s she began working full-time for solicitors in the Wirral.

Kelly, John

A photographer whose pictures were used in the *Magical Mystery Tour* booklet, enclosed with the *Magical Mystery Tour* record package. Kelly also took a series of colour portraits of the Beatles, four of which were used as inserts in *The Beatles* white album. Paul employed Kelly as the official photographer of his wedding to Linda in 1969.

Ken Dodd Show, The

Liverpudlian comedian Ken Dodd had his own radio series on BBC's Light Programme, produced by Bill Worsley. This was broadcast on Sundays from 2.30–3.00 p.m.

The show was recorded in front of a live audience and the Beatles recorded their single appearance on the programme on 9 October 1963 at the Playhouse Theatre, London, for a transmission on 3 November, which was repeated on 6 November. The group performed a single number, 'She Loves You', but didn't participate in any comedy sketches with Dodd.

Dodd's agent had told him that he could have the Beatles for two appearances on his programme. 'I'm not sure, what do you think?' asked Dodd. 'I think we should just have them for one show because they're going to be one of these groups that fade overnight,' said the agent – so only one appearance was booked.

Kensington Recording Studio, 53 Kensington, Liverpool L7

A small studio in Liverpool situated in the back room of a house belonging to Percy Phillips. Phillips owned the studio and there was also an outside sign which sported his name.

It was Paul McCartney's idea that the Quarry Men should record here in the summer of 1958, at a time when they hadn't been appearing at gigs locally. When Paul had seen the sign with Phillips' name on it he had mistakenly thought that it had something to do with the Philips record label. He found that they could record a double-sided single for less than one pound and the group booked a session.

Despite the fact that John and Paul had already begun to write songs together and had filled an exercise book with their lyrics, they didn't record a Lennon & McCartney song, but settled on Buddy Holly's 'That'll Be The Day' and another song. John commented: 'I didn't want to push my songs on the group, but Paul had written one with George Harrison called 'In Spite Of All The Danger', and we did that one for the other side.'

John sang lead vocal on 'That'll Be The Day' and Paul did the honours on 'In Spite Of All The Danger'.

Performing at the session were John, Paul, George, Colin Hanton and John Lowe. The cost of the recording was 17s.6d. and each of the boys contributed 3s.6d. They couldn't afford to buy a copy each and John Lowe was to retain the acetate. John later went back to the studio to buy a copy, but Phillips never kept master tapes. 'It was too late,' said John, 'our stuff had been wiped off by another recording session by some Country and Western singer.'

Paul eventually bought the record back from Lowe in July 1981.

Kenwood. Cavendish Road, St George's Hill, Weybridge, Surrey

It was the Beatles' financial adviser Walter Strach who advised the four members that they should invest some of their untaxed income in property – in other words, they should all buy a house. He lived in a property called Elmsleigh in Weybridge, twenty miles south-west of London, and suggested that the area was a convenient place for them to settle. John and Ringo both bought properties in the area, sometimes described as 'the stockbroker belt' or 'Britain's Beverly Hills', although Paul, who opted to stay in London and bought a house in Cavendish Avenue, St John's Wood, commented: 'Bankers and stockbrokers live there. They can add figures and Weybridge is what they live in and they think it's the end.'

John paid £40,000 for the 27-room Kenwood in July 1964. The house had been built in 1913 for Norman Johnson, an adviser to the last Liberal Prime Minister, Lloyd George. The mock Tudor house was on the side of St George's Hill and John spent a further £30,000 on renovations. He was later to park a painted caravan on one of the lawns. While Cynthia was away on a short holiday in May 1968, John and Yoko recorded 'Two Virgins' together in the music room John had installed. They then made love. Cynthia arrived the next morning to find the two of them together. It was home to John, Cynthia and Julian until 10 December 1968 when it was put up for sale, weeks after John and Cynthia's divorce.

When it was resold in 1994, the asking price was £950,000. John left Weybridge in 1969 for the Georgian mansion in Ascot, Tittenhurst Park.

Kesey, Ken

An American author and hero of the counter-culture in the 1960s. The Oregon-born Kesey became a guinea pig for controlled experiments into lysergic acid diethylamide in 1959 while still a student at Stanford University. In 1966 he bought an old 1939 yellow International Harvester schoolbus, fitted it out with a sound system to play rock music, aerosolled the bus with day-glo mandellas and set out on a celebrated 'acid trek' with a group of friends called the Merry Pranksters. They were all high on the hallucinogenic drug LSD. The main destinations of the Pranksters' bus were rock concerts – one of them being a Beatles show. Their exploits became the subject of Tom Wolfe's book *The Electric Kool-Aid Acid Test*.

The psychedelic bus trip also triggered Paul McCartney into developing the idea of *Magical Mystery Tour*.

Kesey's novels included *One Flew Over The Cuckoo's Nest* and *Sometimes A Great Notion*, both of which were turned into feature films.

Peter Asher and Derek Taylor were considering Kesey as the first artist in a proposed spoken word series of albums from Apple. At the Beatles' request he arrived in London, along with San Francisco chapter members of Hells Angels as part of a posse named the California Pleasure Crew.

Paul McCartney had tentatively called the spoken word series *Paperback Writings* and John Lennon handed Kesey a tape recorder and typewriter and he was provided with a small rear office in the Savile Row building.

Following a visit to Amsterdam, he returned to Apple to find they'd changed the locks and sacked the staff. His tapes and notes were either stolen or thrown away.

'They wouldn't even let me in through the door, so I figured it was time to go home,' he said.

Kestrels, The

A West Country vocal group, whose members included Tony Burrows and Roger Greenaway.

The Kestrels first toured with the Beatles on the cinema tour headlined by Helen Shapiro which commenced on 22 February 1963. They also accompanied the Beatles on a six-week tour of England and Ireland later that year, commencing on 1 November.

The Kestrels issued a single of Lennon & McCartney's, 'There's A Place', and also recorded 'Please Please Me' as a track on their album, released on Pye's Piccadilly label.

Burrows was to join several other groups, including the Ivy League, the Flowerpot Men and Edison Lighthouse, while Roger Greenaway teamed up with Roger Cook to form David and Jonathan, who had a chart hit with 'Michelle', and he later achieved success as a songwriter.

Kinfauns

A luxury bungalow situated in Claremont Drive, the Fair-Mile Estate, near Esher, Surrey. It is set back from the road and hidden by trees and bushes in a wooded estate owned by the National Trust. Soon after meeting Pattie Boyd, George took her with him to view the property as a place where they could live together.

He purchased Kinfauns in June 1964 but, despite its isolation, he found he had to remove the sign 'Kinfauns' because fans still managed to find it. At one time they actually gained entrance to the bungalow, stole George's pyjamas and left a nasty note for Pattie. On another occasion, George found two girls hiding under his bed – they'd crawled through a window Pattie had left open for their pet cat. After that George had electronically-operated gates fitted.

The bungalow comprised two long wings separated by a rectangular courtyard in which there was a heated swimming pool. The curved floor-to-ceiling windows of the living room looked out on to a landscaped yard, and the bungalow was surrounded on three sides by a twelve-foot high brick wall and on the fourth by a hedge of fir trees. Near the changing rooms at the pool was a reproduction of one of John's drawings in marble mosaic. George had his own music room containing his guitars, Indian instruments and jukeboxes. He'd wanted a mini-recording studio with the music rooms, so a wall between two small rooms was knocked down to accommodate it. However, he was to find that it was still not big enough to house the musical equipment he was adding to his collection. George and Pattie had also bought an antique bed, which couldn't fit in their bedroom, so they put it into storage. As they'd outgrown the bungalow, they left Kinfauns in 1969 and moved into Friar Park in 1970.

King's Hall, Showgrounds, Balmoral, Belfast, Northern Ireland

There was controversy surrounding this appearance because the boys had received an invitation to appear at the Royal Command Performance two weeks before the gig. John Lennon commented, 'There was never any intention to snub the Queen' and Paul McCartney said, 'We couldn't let the Belfast fans down.'

The show took place on 2 November 1964 and with an audience of 17,400 it was the largest audience the Beatles had ever appeared before in the United Kingdom.

There were hundreds of fans crowding Aldergrove Airport and the Beatles arrived an hour late, due to fog at Heathrow. Four fans managed to slip through the security net and as Ringo became the first Beatle to step on the tarmac, they hurried forward and all managed to obtain autographs. The group were taken straight from the airport to the King's Hall and sat around in a tiny back room for over three hours. They huddled in their black top coats around an electric fire and John Lennon was heard to comment, 'They told us that we were getting food about two hours ago but it hasn't come yet – we are all starving.'

The Belfast promoter who set the appearance up was Trevor Kane, although the official notice was: 'Brian Epstein and Arthur Howes in conjunction with George Connell and Trevor Kane presents . . .' Tickets could be reserved at 20/-, 15/- and 10/- and unreserved seats in the balcony were 7/6d.

Ian Starrett reviewed the event for *Mersey Beat*:

For the second time since they hit the top, Liverpool's fabulous Beatles flew into Northern Ireland recently for two fantastic performances in the King's Hall.

Because of fog their aircraft was an hour later than was scheduled. When the Merseyside Four eventually did fly into Aldergrove Airport a tight security net fell around the group and they were immediately whisked off to Belfast.

The strangest party of fans in the King's Hall was composed of soldiers of the 1st Battalion the King's Regiment – the Beatles' home town regiment. The group had hoped to visit the soldiers in Berlin earlier this year so instead they sent them 300 free tickets for the Belfast show. The regiment is now stationed at Ballykinlar, which is just outside Belfast.

Pandemonium reigned inside the hall. The yells were deafening when John, Ringo, George and Paul took the stage, dressed in immaculate black suits. Frantic teenage girls stripped off their clothes, others fainted and had to be carried from the hall. It was fantastic, incredible and completely disproved the critics who predicted that the Beatles were finished.

The fanatical 17,500 fans composed the biggest night's crowd known in Britain for any pop show – yet another record added to the boys' long list of achievements.

No matter where they roam, the Beatle lads are always thinking about the Mersey scene. On arrival in Belfast they immediately sent a telegram ('Hope it's a right Royal rave') to their old colleague Cilla Black who appeared that night on the Royal Command Show.

Typical of the fans in the hall that night were two 14-year-old youngsters Margaret Whiteside and Florence Magill from Lurgan.

They travelled to the airport to greet the Beatles on their arrival and then went to the King's Hall. Before the show dark-haired Margaret proudly showed me the autograph she had obtained at the airport.

It was Paul McCartney's. When Paul appeared on stage she went frantic with joy. When the show was over she broke down and wept.

As I left the hall she tried to say goodbye, but the words didn't come. She slumped over her seat with tears running down her face. Only one of 17,500 victims of Beatlemania.

King's Hall, Northgate, Blackburn, Lancashire

The town of 4,000 potholes! The Beatles made a single appearance at this venue on 9 June 1963, which was also the last night of their tour with Roy Orbison.

King's Hall, Stoke-on-Trent

The Beatles appeared on two bookings on the evening of 26 January 1963. The first was at the El Rio Club in Macclesfield and the second at this venue in Stoke-on-Trent, 21 miles away. The group returned to the venue on a bill with fellow Liverpool groups on a *Mersey Beat Showcase* promotion on 19 April 1963.

Kingsway Club, The Promenade, Southport, Lancashire

A club situated in the seaside town of Southport, close to Liverpool. Brian Epstein had obtained a series of bookings at the club for the Beatles shortly after he'd become their manager. They made their debut there on Monday, 22 January 1962. Admission was 2/6d before 8 o'clock and 3/- afterwards. Epstein, in his plans to promote the Beatles, had publicity photographs run off and one was given to each of the attendees at the gig. The club's compere Ron Appleby was to observe that the girls tore around the photograph until they had a picture of Pete Best, which they then stuck to their jumpers – an action which caused Brian some frustration. However, it's interesting to note that Epstein was now personally writing their advertisements and the copy he penned for this particular gig read: 'THE BEATLES. Come and meet "PETE, PAUL, JOHN and GEORGE" The Group Everyone has been asking for – Now they're here, at the KINGSWAY NEXT MONDAY – ONLY 2/6. Come and hear them play their latest record. It's sensational.' Why did Epstein himself place Pete Best's name first when advertising the group?

The gig was the first of a series he'd obtained for them at the club and the other dates were Monday, 29 January, Monday, 5 February, Monday, 26 February, Monday, 5 March and Monday, 23 July.

On their second appearance there on 29 January, Pete Best was ill and Ringo Starr, then with Rory Storm & the Hurricanes, took his place.

Kirchherr, Astrid

A pale-skinned, blonde girl of an ethereal beauty who became engaged to Stuart Sutcliffe.

Astrid was born in Hamburg in 1938 into a middle-class family in the respectable Altona suburb of Hamburg. Her father was an executive for the Ford Motor company.

From an early age she showed a flair for art and design and was enrolled at the Meister Schule to study dress design. It was here that she met a student from Berlin called Klaus Voormann who became her boyfriend. Rheinhardt Wolf, who ran a photographic course at the school, felt that Astrid had potential as a photographer and she changed her course from dress design to photography. When she completed her course, Wolf hired her as his assistant.

It was in October 1960 that Astrid and Klaus had a row which resulted in Klaus wandering around the St Pauli district and being lured into the Kaiserkeller by the sound of Rory Storm & the Hurricanes. That night he saw the Beatles and was so impressed he began telling Astrid and his friends. On his third visit to the club, Klaus was joined by Astrid and Jurgen Vollmer. She was reluctant to make the trip and was initially frightened when she arrived at the club, but the sight of the Beatles fascinated her and she noticed Stuart Sutcliffe immediately and was later to say, 'I fell in love with Stuart that very first night.'

With her ghostly pale skin and dark clothes, Astrid looked uniquely appealing to the Beatles and Stuart was immediately smitten. Her friends, who were nicknamed 'Exis', after existentialists, began to gather every night at tables near the stage to watch the Beatles.

After a week she gathered up the nerve to ask them if she could take photographs of them and the group agreed. Her first location shooting with them took place at a fairground in the local park, Der Dom. After the session she invited the group to tea at her home in Altona and all but Pete Best took up the offer, Pete only refusing because he had to buy some drumsticks to replace the ones he'd broken.

Astrid's mother was charmed by the group and also took a particular liking to Stuart.

Over the next few weeks Astrid began to take other photographs of the group and some of her later shots – portraits in which one half of the face was in shadow, was to pre-date the famous Bob

Freeman *Around The Beatles* cover. Her mum was concerned about the terrible accommodation the group had at the Bambi Kino and invited Stuart to stay in the attic room of their house. Almost two months after they first met, in late November 1960, Stuart and Astrid became engaged and exchanged rings, in the German fashion.

When Bruno Koschmider caused the police to deport George, Astrid and Stuart drove him to the station. Paul and Pete were next bundled off unceremoniously to Liverpool by the police following the Bambi incident and then John left. He was later followed by Stuart who, because he had tonsilitis, was to take a more comfortable route home – by airplane, funded by Astrid. It was Astrid who helped to organise their next trip to Hamburg, in March 1961, when they appeared at the Top Ten Club.

Astrid was more mature than her young lover from Liverpool and began to influence him in many ways, particularly regarding his looks and dress. She initially changed his hair style, shaping it across his forehead in a style which was then currently popular in France. This was to become the basis for the famous Beatle 'moptop'. At first, the rest of the group ridiculed Stuart's new style. Then George agreed to try it and Astrid shaped his hair. Paul tried next and finally John agreed to have Astrid style his hair. Pete was the only Beatle who wasn't asked to try out the new style.

She next made a leather jerkin and trousers for Stuart, which resulted in the other members of the group buying some leather outfits from a Hamburg store. When Astrid made Stuart a black corduroy jacket without lapels, in a style then being popularised by Pierre Cardin in Paris, the other members initially ridiculed him – but the collarless style was later to feature in the Beatles' image.

The relationship between Stuart and Paul had been deteriorating, mainly because Paul wanted to take over on bass. One night he made a remark about Astrid and the two began to fight, with the stronger Paul beating up his smaller colleague. By that time Stuart had realised that art meant more to him than music and as he had been unable to return to Liverpool College of Art, he was encouraged by two friends, who were students at Hamburg State Art College, to apply there. He obtained a grant and left the group to study under Eduardo Paolozzi.

When the Beatles returned to Liverpool in July 1961 Stuart remained in Hamburg with Astrid and they planned to get married as soon as he finished his course.

A few months later, Stuart fell down the narrow steps leading from his attic studio and banged his head severely. Soon after, he began to experience terrible headaches and blackouts, although the

only one who associated the fall with the headaches at the time was
Stuart's mother in Liverpool.

The pain became so violent that Stuart remained in his attic,
looked after by Astrid and her mother. A specialist was called in
and X-rays were taken, but nothing showed up on them. Three
doctors were consulted and all were equally puzzled. Stuart had to
take special massages under water, which didn't seem to help, and
one day, on returning from a massage, he told Astrid's mother he'd
seen a white coffin and asked her if she'd buy it for him.

On 10 April 1961, Astrid was at work in the photographic studio
when she received a call from her mother. Stuart was so bad that
she was calling the hospital. Astrid rushed home and joined Stuart
in the ambulance – but he died in her arms at 4.30 p.m. on the way
to hospital.

The distraught Astrid met the Beatles at Hamburg airport to tell
them the tragic news.

Astrid was later to marry Gibson Kemp, former drummer who
had replaced Ringo Starr in Rory Storm & the Hurricanes. They
were later to divorce.

Klaatu

In 1973 rumours began to abound that the Beatles had reformed to
record under the assumed name of Klaatu. An album by Klaatu was
issued on 3 August 1976 by Capitol, the Beatles' American label.
Entitled *Klaatu*, it contained the tracks: 'Calling Occupants of
Interplanetary Craft', 'California Jam', 'Anus of Uranus', 'Sub Rosa
Subway', 'True Life Hero', 'Doctor Marvello', 'Sir Bodsworth
Rugglesby III' and 'Little Mevtrino'.

Klaatu remained relatively unknown until disc jockey Charlie
Parker of WDRC in Providence, Rhode Island, played one of the
album tracks on his show. Hundreds of listeners phoned in to ask if
Klaatu were actually the Beatles. Then an article by Steve Smith
appeared in a newspaper in Providence, Rhode Island, claiming
that Klaatu were the Beatles. In what became known as 'the Klaatu
Konspiracy', numerous 'facts' were trotted out, in a similar way to
the 'Paul is dead' affair, and over 150 alleged clues linking Klaatu to
the Beatles were revealed, such as: 'At the University of Miami,
voice prints of Klaatu and a recent McCartney album were made –
and found to be the same … In Australia a disc jockey said that
Klaatu was a missing Beatles album called "Sun" … One of the
tracks from the album, "Sub Rosa Subway", was played backwards
at different speeds, using a vera-speed low-frequency oscillator, and
the vocals were sharpened with a set of filters. This message was
found: "It's us, it's the Beeeeeeatles!"'

Various newspapers and disc jockeys took up the story and within an eight-week period over 300,000 copies of *Klaatu* were sold.

When questions were asked as to the group's identity – as no mention of group members was made on the album sleeve – Capitol Records commented that they had never actually seen the group. Frank Davies, the group's manager, had brought them the tape of the band – and had not told them anything about Klaatu. When he was asked directly if Klaatu were the Beatles, Davies refused to either confirm or deny.

Despite the fact that the group members were later identified as John Woloschuk (also known as L. M. Carpenter and Chip Dale), Terry Draper, David Long and Dino Tome, the fascination in the 'Klaatu are really the Beatles' craze persisted. In Australia, Beatles fan John Squires issued a 34-page booklet entitled *Under an Assumed Name: The Beatles Secret Re-Union*, gathering hundreds of tenuous associations in order to prove his theory, including the fact that Ringo Starr appears as the character Klaatu from *The Day The Earth Stood Still* on the cover of his *Goodnight Vienna* album.

The group released five albums before they eventually disbanded. Several years later, David Long became head programmer in a computer room at George Martin's AIR Studios. Draper became a roofing contractor and Woloschuk an accountant in the Toronto music industry. The group's fifth and last album *Magentalane*, was only issued in Canada in October 1981. The group toured to promote it, then disbanded in August 1982. *Magentalane* was finally released in the US on 19 September 1995 and was the only album with a sleeve featuring photographs of the band and the names of the musicians.

Klein, Allen
American manager and music publisher, born in Newark, New Jersey, on 13 December 1931.

When he entered the music business, after studying accountancy, he formed some music publishing companies and became manager of Bobby Darin, the Shirelles, Sam Cooke and Bobby Vinton.

Klein's great strength was in discovering overlooked fees and royalties and obtaining monies for the artists from record companies. This much-publicised activity led to his being given the nickname the 'Robin Hood of Pop'.

He was a tough negotiator and together with his wife, Betty, set up his ABKCO Industries (short for Allen and Betty Klein).

When the 'British Invasion' of America occurred he was able to negotiate deals for several UK bands, including the Rolling Stones, the Dave Clark Five, Donovan, Herman's Hermits and the Animals. For the Rolling Stones he arranged a deal in which they received a $1,250,000 advance against 25 per cent of the wholesale – 75 cents per album. The Beatles were only receiving 15 per cent in Britain and 17.5 per cent in America.

Ironically, in the light of subsequent events, it was Paul McCartney who first suggested that Klein should act on behalf of the Beatles.

When Klein read the issue of *Disc & Music Echo* in which John Lennon had revealed to editor Ray Coleman, 'If Apple goes on losing money, all of us will be broke in six months,' he saw his opportunity. He contacted Lennon and met up with him and Yoko Ono at the Dorchester Hotel in London on Tuesday, 28 January 1969.

Lennon was impressed and sent a message to Sir Joseph Lockwood at EMI, which read: 'Dear Sir Joe – from now on Allen Klein handles all my stuff.'

Klein also met up with George and Ringo and they agreed to arrange a meeting for him with all four Beatles. Paul walked out of the meeting.

By that time Paul had decided he wanted John Eastman to represent him and a compromise was agreed for a while – that Eastman and Klein should both work as the Beatles' advisers.

There was a great deal of conflict, during which the Beatles lost their opportunity of buying NEMS Enterprises, and also Northern Songs.

Klein was one of the factors in the break-up of the group, although he had boosted their income by re-negotiating their contracts with EMI and Capitol and by sacking almost all of the staff at Apple.

In fact, within eighteen months Klein had earned the Beatles more money than Epstein had earned for them in his entire years of management.

However, Paul was disenchanted and on Thursday, 31 December 1970 he instigated a High Court action to place the group's affairs in the hands of the receiver, a move he was advised to take as the only way of ridding himself of Klein.

Although the Beatles' finances weren't as bad as they'd been pictured (they had £6,549,668 in the bank), it was revealed that their affairs were in a mess, that they didn't have enough money to pay their taxes and that there were hardly any accountants left at Apple to tackle their accounts.

In his 1971 *Playboy* interview Klein commented: 'The music business is about 99 per cent no-talent losers who can't stand a winner in their midst. I'm a winner and if they want to sour grape my success by calling me names, let them. I don't give a shit.'

Paul was successful in his action, although it took six years for Apple to be finally rid of Klein, who agreed to a pay-off of $4 million. The other three had eventually come to the same conclusion about Klein as Paul.

On Friday, 29 January 1971 he was convicted of ten counts of 'unlawfully failing to make and file return of Federal income taxes and FICA taxes withheld from employees' wages.' The conviction was upheld on appeal.

In May 1979, Klein was jailed for two months for tax evasion – this related to income he'd taken from illegal sales of George Harrison's charity album *The Concert For Bangladesh*.

In 1987 the surviving Beatles and the estate of John Lennon took out a £2,000,000 lawsuit against their former manager over a set of photographs used on the seventeen-year-old album *Let It Be*. Their US lawyers claimed that Klein had wrongfully withheld the negatives of the session.

In 1996, Klein was still living in New York, although it was reported that he was suffering from ill-health.

Knight, Terry

American musician who, with his group the Pack, had a minor hit in 1966 with 'I (Who Have Nothing)'. He was acting as Master of Ceremonies on an American promotional tour for Twiggy in 1967 when she decided to fly him to Britain to see Paul McCartney, who was looking for artists for Apple. Paul forgot all about the meeting and was in Scotland with Linda while Terry was waiting to see him in London. He eventually flew back to America without seeing Paul.

His group the Pack had broken up, then reformed as Grand Funk Railroad and he became their manager.

In 1969, under his own name, he recorded a single dealing with the 'Paul is dead' rumour called 'Saint Paul', issued on Capitol 2506.

Knotty Ash Village Hall, Junction of Eaton Road and East Prescot Road, Knotty Ash, Liverpool L12

Mona Best, already booking the Beatles regularly into the Casbah Club, began a series of promotions over a six-month period at this local venue. The group made their debut there on 15 September 1961 and further bookings included 22 September, 20 October, 27 October, 10 November and 17 November.

The following year, on Saturday 17 March 1962, local promoter Sam Leach booked the Beatles and Rory Storm & the Hurricanes on a 'St Patrick's Night Gala'.

His main reason for the promotion was to raise some ready cash to pay for his engagement to Joan McEvoy, to be celebrated in style at her mother Dolly's house, nearby in Huyton. After the show, the Beatles and the Hurricanes attended the party which lasted until the following afternoon.

Komm, Gib Mir Deine Hand

A German language version of 'I Want To Hold Your Hand'. The Beatles recorded the number at EMI's Pathe Marconi Studios in Paris on Wednesday, 29 January 1964, at the request of Odeon, the west German outlet for EMI Records. George Martin travelled to Paris to record the group, accompanied by engineer Norman Smith.

During the session they also recorded a German version of 'She Loves You', for the flipside of the single, which reached the Top Ten on its release in Germany. The Beatles never repeated the exercise.

The track was included on the *Rarities* album and the American album *Something New*. The recording was included on the CD compilation *Past Masters Volume One*.

Kosh, John

The designer of the book included with the *Let It Be* album. It was a lavish production, prepared by Kosh, written by Jonathan Cott and David Dalton, with photographs by Ethan Russell and Mal Evans. Kosh designed the entire package for the *Let It Be* album, including the cover design with the black background.

Kosh was later to design the covers for the Ringo Starr albums *Beaucoups Of Blues*, *Rotogravure* and *Bad Boy*.

Koschmider, Bruno

Small, pugnacious former circus clown, fire eater and acrobat who was the first club owner to book British rock 'n' roll groups into Hamburg.

He ran strip clubs in the Grosse Freiheit in the notorious St Pauli district, the large Kaiserkeller (King's Cellar) and the smaller Indra Club.

Stories regarding how he first booked the British bands into his clubs vary. Iain Hines says that Bruno came over to London looking for groups and was advised to seek them in the 2 I's. Hines found out what he was there for and immediately formed a group on the spot called the Jets. Koschmider booked them and they became the first band to play at the Kaiserkeller. Allan Williams says that he travelled to Hamburg to find his Royal Caribbean Steel Band. He stumbled into the Kaiserkeller and asked to see the owner, was introduced to Koschmider and convinced him he should book British rock 'n' roll groups. By a series of coincidences, he happened to be at the 2 I's club in London with the Liverpool band Derry Wilkie & the Seniors where he bumped into Koschmider again. As a result, the Seniors became the first Mersey group to be booked into Hamburg. Williams then booked the Beatles and travelled over with them, although Koschmider made them play at the smaller Indra Club. When the Indra was closed by order of the police, he had the Beatles fulfil their contract at the Kaiserkeller as second on the bill to another Mersey band, Rory Storm & the Hurricanes. For some reason, while he paid the Beatles a low fee and they had to rough it up in inadequate sleeping quarters at the Bambi Kino, he paid the Hurricanes more money and they were able to board at the Seamen's Mission.

Koschmider was strict in his dealings with the groups and laid down the law. His method of controlling them was by confrontation – unlike Peter Eckhorn and Manfred Weissleder, who offered incentives. Koschmider forbade them to appear anywhere else within a 40-mile radius of his club, fined groups if they infringed his stringent rules, and therefore never built up any loyalty between himself and the bands, which resulted in him having to revert his venues back to strip clubs while the Top Ten and the Star Club enjoyed success with the bands.

When he discovered the Beatles were going to play at the Top Ten, he allegedly arranged for George Harrison to be deported. Arguably, he was already aware of Harrison's age, but was able to have the 'protection' of booking him into his club with impunity. He withdrew that 'protection' and sent George the following letter dated 1 November 1960:

> I the undersigned, hereby give notice to Mr GEORGE HARRISON and to BEATLES' BAND to leave on November 30th 1960.
> The notice is given to the above by order of the Public Authorities who have discovered that Mr GEORGE HARRISON is only 17 (seventeen) years of age.
>
> BRUNO KOSCHMIDER

Koschmider was a tough individual who dealt with customers in his club roughly. He made threats to the Beatles regarding their physical well-being, but didn't carry them out because the group were under the protection of Horst Fascher, who had moved to the Top Ten Club.

His revenge came when Pete Best and Paul McCartney returned to the Bambi Kino to collect their belongings and singed some walls when they set light to some contraceptives they pinned to the wall to provide themselves with some light. Koschmider informed the police that they had attempted arson and they were deported.

Kramer, Billy J.

Liverpool singer, real name William Ashton, who was originally a member of Billy Forde & the Phantoms. When his guitar was stolen he became lead singer and the group changed their name to Billy Kramer & the Coasters.

He saw many early Beatles gigs and recalls, 'The first time I heard of them was when they played at the Litherland Town Hall. I remember Cliff Roberts & the Rockers were on at the time, but the only group who knocked me out were Kingsize Taylor & the Dominoes. I was a group freak. Bob Wooler announced that the next week they would be presenting a group just back from Hamburg – the Beatles. I stopped in my tracks. I thought, I must go and see them.

'The Beatles had Stu playing bass on that occasion, McCartney had a black and green Rosetti guitar, Lennon had a Rickenbacker and George had a Gretsch.

'When the Coasters had been given an audition by Brian Kelly at the Aintree Institute, the venue opposite the Coronation pub in Linacre Lane, we had to travel to the gig by 61 bus, me, the boys and all our gear. That was when I had my first meeting with Lennon. He was just lounging about in the dressing room and I asked him about his Rickenbacker guitar and he let me have a go of it. I'd seen the Fender guitar and the Gibson and the Gretsch, but I hadn't seen a Rickenbacker. The fact that he had one must have put him on the market. Paul was there with his Rosetti, unplugged and with strings missing.

'I also remember them on the Bluegenes night at the Cavern. They'd come back from Hamburg and Stu had left. I was freaked out by the whole band when I saw them at the Cavern. McCartney, Lennon, Harrison and Pete Best. McCartney was playing bass and they were into leather. It was a lot slicker, the space between numbers had tightened up a lot and the vocal backings and everything, the whole thing flowed better. They had a restricted repertoire but I realised that Lennon and McCartney had a character.'

Billy Kramer & the Coasters were voted No. 3 in the *Mersey Beat* Poll, following the Beatles and Gerry & the Pacemakers. Despite this, Billy was about to leave the group and take up a full-time post with British Rail at Rugby. He'd been down to Rugby to discuss his new job and his parents had agreed that he should take it up. His manager at that time was Ted Knibbs and he phoned Billy to arrange a meeting in Liverpool city centre. 'I had no idea what Ted had in mind,' says Billy. 'I was about to tell him I was packing it all in. He took me up to NEMS, introduced me to Brian Epstein and Brian said he wanted to manage me. I was so knocked out, I completely lost my appetite for remaining with British Rail. Shortly afterwards I was called in to a meeting with Brian at his office and John Lennon was there. Brian said to me, "John's come up with an idea. He thinks your name would sound much better if we added the initial 'J' to it. How does Billy J. Kramer sound?" I said, "That's OK by me, but what do I say to the press if they ask me what the 'J' stands for?" John said, "You can tell them it stands for Julian." To tell you the truth, I didn't like the name Julian and refused to use it. I didn't know at the time that John had a son and had named him Julian in memory of his mother.'

The Coasters refused to turn professional and Brian Epstein sought a new group to back him. He asked the Remo Four during a Cavern appearance. Their lead singer at the time was Johnny Sandon and they told Brian that they'd like him to manage them, but wouldn't back Billy as they were happy with Sandon. Epstein next approached Manchester's the Dakotas who initially turned him down. When he offered them the chance to record as the Dakotas in their own right, they took up the offer, shedding their lead singer Pete Maclaine. Epstein immediately sent Billy and the group to Hamburg for a Star Club season for them to work on their act. Group and singer never really got on well together.

The Dakotas comprised Mike Maxfield (lead guitar), Robin McDonald (rhythm guitar), Ray Jones (bass guitar) and Tony Mansfield (drums).

The group was featured on a number of Beatles gigs and their debut record was the Lennon & McCartney composition 'Do You Want To Know A Secret?' which George Harrison had sung on the *Please Please Me* album. It was issued on R 5023 by Parlophone in Britain on 26 April 1963 and reached No. 2 in the charts. It was issued on 55586 by Liberty in America on 10 June. The 'B' side of the record was 'I'll Be On My Way', which Paul McCartney had written specially for Billy.

Billy hadn't been Epstein's first choice to record 'Do You Want To Know A Secret?'. He'd originally offered it to Shane Fenton if the singer would be prepared to let Epstein manage him. Fenton told him he already had a manager and Epstein gave the number to Billy, who wasn't particularly keen on it.

His second single was 'Bad To Me', a number which John had

written for him in Spain. It was issued on R 5049 by Parlophone on 26 July 1963 and topped the British charts. It was issued on 55626 by Liberty in America on 23 September, where it reached No. 9 in the charts. The flipside was 'I Call Your Name.'

The third Lennon & McCartney number Billy recorded was 'I'll Keep You Satisfied', which was issued on R 5073 by Parlophone on 1 November 1963 and on 55643 by Liberty in America. It reached No. 4 in Britain and No. 30 in the US.

His fourth and last Lennon & McCartney single was penned by Paul. 'From A Window' was issued on R 5156 Parlophone on 17 July 1964 and on 66061 by Imperial in America on 12 August. It reached No. 10 in the British charts and No. 23 in the US.

Billy's other hits included 'Little Children' and 'Trains And Boats And Planes'.

He asked Paul McCartney if he could provide him with another song and Paul offered him 'Yesterday'. Billy turned it down.

One Lennon & McCartney number which Billy recorded has never been released. It's called 'One And One Is Two'. It was mainly written by Paul. John and Paul worked together on the number in their suite at the George V Hotel in Paris after a show at the Olympia Theatre. They had to send a tape off the next day to Dick James for Billy J. Kramer to record. Paul sat at the piano while John sat at a table playing guitar. They had a microphone leading from the tape recorder strapped to a floor lamp. As they were singing 'One and one is two . . .' George popped his head round the door and suggested, 'Can't you take one of the "one and one is two's" out?' At another time he interjected, 'Can't you do something with "do" or "Jew"?' John said, 'I'm a lonely Jew. How's that?'

The song was duly sent to James and recorded by Billy, but John wasn't happy with the number and is said to have advised Billy, 'Release that and your career is over.' So it was never released, although a version by the Strangers with Mike Shannon was issued in 1964 and flopped.

Ray Jones, former member of the Dakotas, died in January 2000.

Krause, Bernie

A classically trained American musician. Also a former folk singer, Krause became an expert on synthesizer music and recorded a number of synthesizer albums as one half of the duo Beaver & Krause. He was also to work on the soundtrack of films such as *Apocalypse Now*, *The Graduate*, *Performance* and *The Illustrated Man*. When George Harrison was recording the *No Time Or Space* half of his *Electronic Sounds* album in California, he met Krause during a recording session for Jackie Lomax. He then invited Krause to collaborate with him on the synthesizer recording. Krause was originally to have his name appear on the cover of the album, but when it was released he discovered his name had been taken off the outer sleeve and there was just a small credit on the inner sleeve.

He was later to claim that he had actually created most of the work on *No Time Or Space* and that George had simply taken his tapes.

Kubas, The

A Mersey group who formed in April 1963. At one time they were managed by Brian Epstein and were in the film *Ferry 'Cross The Mersey*, although their sequence ended up on the cutting-room floor.

There were several variations in personnel, but their basic line-up was Keith Ellis (bass), Stu Leithwood (rhythm), Tony O'Reilly (drums) and Roy Morris (lead).

They signed a contract with Columbia and their first release was 'Magic Potion' in January 1965. By the time of their second release, 'Take Me for A Little While', in November 1965, which was issued on Pye Records, they'd altered the spelling of their name to the Koobas. The following month they appeared on the Beatles' final tour of Britain from 3 to 13 December.

Late in 1965, Tony Stratton-Smith became enthusiastic about the group and signed them up. Unfortunately, despite major promotion, they never made the big time. Following the release of their album *The Koobas* in 1968 and an appearance as support band to a Jimi Hendrix Experience tour of Switzerland the same year, they disbanded.

Kungliga Tennishallen, Lidingovagen, Stockholm, Sweden

The second date of the Beatles' short tour of Sweden. They performed two shows at the hall at 5.00 p.m. and 8.00 p.m. on Saturday, 26 October 1963.

Due to the enthusiastic crowds, a cordon of forty policemen, armed with truncheons, surrounded the stage. The force of the fans, however, overpowered them at first and George Harrison was knocked over. The police then restored order.

Interestingly enough, the bill topper at this event was not the Beatles but Joey Dee & the Starliters.

Labour Club, Peel Street, Liverpool L7

Situated in the Dingle area, quite close to where Ringo spent his childhood. The Labour Club was one of the many scores of small working men's drinking clubs which booked local entertainers. It was the venue of the first gig by the Eddie Clayton Skiffle Group which included Ringo on drums, Roy Trafford on tea-chest bass, Eddie Miles on guitar and three other musicians. The full line-up comprised three guitars, drums, washboard and bass. Ringo was to comment in the *Beatles Book*, their monthly magazine, some years later: 'The organiser got a bit drunk and seemed to forget all about paying us. Whatever happened, we didn't get a penny.' The organiser threatened a law suit. However, Ringo stuck to his story and said he'd be prepared to go to court and swear to it. The club manager withdrew the action.

There was no such person as Eddie Clayton – although Eric Clapton was to use the name as a pseudonym on an album many years later.

Labour Club, Devonshire Road, High Park, Southport, Lancashire

There were almost 350 clubs in the Merseyside Clubs Association. These clubs were for various union and political organisations and provided entertainment, generally with cabaret-style singers, comedians, speciality acts and Country music. Occasionally, such clubs featured local rock 'n' roll bands. The Beatles appeared at a handful of such clubs at the onset of their career and the group made one appearance at this venue early in 1961.

LaBour, Fred

A student and aspiring journalist in 1969 when he helped to spark off the 'Paul Is Dead' rumours. LaBour was asked to review the new *Abbey Road* album for the University of Michigan newspaper *The Michigan Daily*. On the eve of writing his piece he was listening to Detroit disc jockey Russ Gibbs' radio show and was intrigued by a caller who related some strange things he'd noticed on previous Beatles releases.

LaBour commented, 'This guy was saying that if you played part of "Revolution No 9" backward, they were saying "Turn me on, dead man," and that in "I Am The Walrus" or was it "Strawberry Fields Forever?" you could hear "I buried Paul", and that it all meant that Paul was dead. I was astonished at the craziness of this, so the next day I led off the review with those and a bunch of other observations I made up. It was a satire on seeing things that aren't there, but people took it seriously.'

Other Detroit papers picked up his report and then it spread to Chicago and New York. Newspapers and radio stations were eager to interview him and he told them, 'Sure it's all true, I made it up myself', but they took no notice of his disclaimer and more and more 'death' clues began to pile up by an assortment of people.

Lots of the original LaBour 'clues' were easily disproved such as the statement he made regarding John's words 'Here's another clue for you all, the walrus is Paul' on 'Glass Onion'. LaBour said that walrus was Greek for 'corpse'. This could easily be checked out and proven to be wrong.

LaBour decided to cease accepting interviews because things were getting out of hand. He said, 'People were calling me up crying. You've got to be careful what you write because people are liable to believe you.'

He later became a songwriter in Nashville and joined a band called Riders in the Sky, using the name Too Slim.

Lady Madonna

In addition to writing the song, Paul also designed the press advertisements to promote it.

The single was issued in Britain on Parlophone R 5675 on 15 March 1968 and was the last Beatles single on that label. It was also the last American single to use the Capitol label.

The flipside was George Harrison's 'The Inner Light', his first song on a Beatles single.

The number topped the charts in Britain while in America it reached No. 2 in *Cash Box* and *Record World* and No. 4 in *Billboard*.

There is a brass section of four saxophones, with jazzman Ronnie Scott leading Harry Klein, Bill Povey and Bill Jackson.

The track was included on a number of compilations, including *The Beatles 1967–1970*, *Hey Jude* and *The Beatles Box*. A live version of the number is also included on *Wings Over The World*.

At the time of the original release, Paul mentioned that the arrangement of the number was based on an old song called 'Bad Penny Blues'. Coincidentally, that number had been a minor hit for Humphrey Lyttelton in 1956 on a single produced by George Martin. A version was included on the Beatles' *Anthology 2* CDs. The number was also included on the CD compilation *Past Masters Volume Two*.

Lady Mitchell Hall, Cambridge

The event which took place at this venue on 2 March 1969 marked the first time that a member of the Beatles made a solo appearance without his fellow members of the group. John and Yoko appeared as part of an avant-garde jazz concert with saxophonist John Stevens. Yoko provided the high-pitched vocals and John performed on guitar. Their entire set was recorded and later issued as Side One of the *Unfinished Music No. 2: Life With The Lions* album.

La Scala Ballroom, Runcorn, Cheshire

A regular venue for Mersey bands, situated only fourteen miles from Liverpool. The Beatles didn't make their debut there until 16 October 1962 and their only other appearance at the ballroom was on Tuesday, 11 December. The latter gig was a NEMS Enterprises promotion organised by Bob Wooler and also featuring Johnny Sandon and the Remo Four and the Merseybeats.

Las Vegas Convention Centre, Las Vegas, Nevada

Venue where they appeared on 20 August 1964, the second date of their first American tour. The Beatles flew into Las Vegas twelve hours ahead of schedule, arriving at 1.45 a.m., and were driven to the Sahara Hotel where they stayed overnight, almost under siege. A police escort took them to the Las Vegas Convention Centre at 3 p.m. There were two shows at the venue that day, a matinee at 4.00 p.m. and an evening show at 8.00 p.m., both of which were advance sell-outs, with a total audience of around 16,000.

The ban against having celebrities backstage, which Brian

Epstein had introduced, had been broken the day previously when Shirley Temple visited them. When Liberace came backstage saying, 'I want to meet these young artists who are doing such amazing things', Derek Taylor realised it was a ban that it wouldn't be diplomatic to enforce and Liberace met the lads – as did Pat Boone.

There were the inevitable hails of jellybeans and during the evening show there was a bomb threat during the second performance – but it was bogus.

Lathom Hall, Lathom Avenue, Seaforth, Liverpool L21

The venue was originally built in 1884 as a cinema. It became one of several venues, including Litherland Town Hall and Aintree Institute, promoted by Brian Kelly.

It was standard practice in Liverpool to offer groups 'auditions', which would actually take place at a live show. In other words, the promoter would regularly have groups playing for free with the enticement that he might book them.

Under the name the Silver Beats, the group auditioned for Kelly at Lathom Hall during the interval on Saturday, 14 May 1960 on a bill which included established Liverpool bands Kingsize Taylor & the Dominoes, Cliff Roberts & the Rockers and the Deltones. As a result of their brief performance, Kelly booked them for the following week, on Saturday, 21 May. He advertised the event, which was the first time the group had officially appeared in an advertisement. Despite the fact that they'd only auditioned, the advertisement billed: 'Silver Beats, Dominoes, Deltones.'

In spite of the top billing, they didn't turn up for the gig. Instead, they left on a tour of Scotland backing Johnny Gentle without informing Kelly who, as a result, didn't book them again for several months until Bob Wooler talked him into it.

Drummer Cliff Roberts recalled the Silver Beats' appearance that first night on 14 May and said they were a scruffy bunch whose drummer hadn't even brought his kit and asked if he could borrow Cliff's. Roberts had a brand new Olympic kit that he hadn't even used on stage himself, so he naturally refused. However, he agreed to play with the Silver Beats and they performed six numbers together, 'four rock 'n' roll standards that all of the groups played, and two originals that they had to teach me.' He says that the group then disappeared and he didn't see them until eight months later when they appeared on the bill at the Alexandra Hall, Crosby on Thursday, 19 January 1961, where, says Roberts, 'They wore black leather, had brand new instruments and played brilliantly.'

All their subsequent appearances at Lathom Hall took place during the first two months of 1961, by which time Kelly was paying them an average of eight pounds and tenpence a performance. Their appearances at the venue took place on 20, 21, 28 and 30 January and 4, 6, 10, 11 and 25 February. Their last performance on Saturday, 25 February took place on George Harrison's eighteenth birthday.

It was at Lathom Hall on 14 May 1960 that an incident occurred with troublemakers. In 1966, Neil Aspinall was to recall that the group was often a target for gangs who would shout insults at them because they were either looking for a fight or were annoyed that their girls fancied the foursome. For the sake of peace, the group ignored the taunts.

'But it wasn't easy,' said Neil. 'At Lathom Hall . . . two troublemakers followed Stu Sutcliffe into the dressing-room muttering things like "Get your hair cut, girl!" John and Pete saw this and went after them. A fight broke out and John broke his little finger . . . It set crooked and never straightened.'

Pete Best was also to recall the Lathom Hall incident. He said:

When we'd done our session and came off, we changed, which didn't take an awful lot of time because we basically played in the clothes which we stood up in. Stu went out, followed by John and myself.

These lads started a fight with Stu after picking on him. We got to know about it because some people ran back to the side of the stage where we had come from and said, 'Stu's getting the living daylights knocked out of him.'

So John and I dashed out. We threw a couple of punches, sorted things out and pulled Stu back in again. Then we turned to the lads and said, 'What the hell's going on? What the hell are you picking on him for? He hasn't done anything. We're only here to do a job, we're playing; so go away and behave yourselves.' And it was left at that.

The fact that John and I had pitched in and got involved made these lads feel a certain amount of respect for us . . . as a result of the fight John broke a little finger. He still managed to play for a couple of gigs after that. He hadn't complained . . . the next time we saw him he had a splint on it.

When people talk of Stu being beaten up, I think it stems from this incident. But I don't remember Stu getting to the stage where he had his head kicked in, as some legends say, alleging that this caused his fatal brain haemorrhage.

For as long as I was with the band I can only remember two

incidents when fists were thrown and Stu was involved. The Lathom Hall incident aside, the other occasion was at the Top Ten Club, and that was between Paul and Stu. Paul took the mick out of Astrid and Stu lost his temper and took a swing at him.

Stuart was never injured during the Lathom Hall gig, but this is where another apocryphal Beatles story had its origins. In *The Man Who Gave the Beatles Away*, by Allan Williams and Bill Marshall, journalist Marshall admitted that he just took the bones of Williams' memories and elaborated on them, exaggerating the violence, swearing and sex.

In the book he writes: 'It was on such a night that Stuart Sutcliffe received the injuries, which I believe hastened his death a couple of years later. Stuart was attacked outside Litherland Town Hall, where the Beatles played regularly, and was kicked in the head by a local thug. From then on he complained to me often of severe headaches.' This is hindsight presuming too much. According to Stuart's mother, who Stuart revealed everything to, his headaches only began following a fall in Hamburg.

Despite the fact that the Williams story was false, it was taken up and elaborated on by writers such as Philip Norman and began to take on a life of its own. In Chet Flippo's book *McCartney: The Biography*, he writes: 'In the middle of a jive night at Lathom Hall in Seaforth . . . that was the night that Stu was attacked and kicked in the head by teds who didn't like the Silver Beats' looks.'

Yet Pete Best, though confirming that John suffered a broken finger, clearly states that Stuart was never kicked in the head and was relatively unharmed.

Even more bizarre is Albert Goldman's accusation in *The Lives of John Lennon* that John was responsible for Stuart's death: 'He had gotten into a quarrel with Stu at Hamburg . . . suddenly John was seized by one of his fits of uncontrollable rage. He lashed out with hands and feet . . . when he came to his senses he looked down and saw Stu lying on the pavement.'

Goldman said that, as a result, John felt completely responsible for Stu's death. This is complete fiction, but of such stuff, myths are made.

Lawdy Miss Clawdy

Composition written and recorded by Lloyd Price in 1952. As there were no record charts in existence at the time, there was no way to gauge record hits. When the charts came into being, Price had ten hit records. The Quarry Men included this number in their repertoire which was gradually moving away from skiffle music and veering towards rock 'n' roll.

Leach, Sam

A Liverpool promoter, who first began booking groups into the Mossway Jive Club at Mossway Hall in 1958 and later went on to run various clubs such as the Cassanova Rock 'n' Swing Club where he booked the Beatles for the first time in February 1961.

Promoting under 'The Leach Organisation', Sam began to launch bigger promotions on Merseyside than the other local impresarios and used the Beatles regularly. Another of his major gigs was the Rock Around The Clock twelve-hour session at the Iron Door Club (also called the Liverpool Jazz Society) in March 1961.

Another highlight took place on 10 November that year when Sam launched the first of his *Operation Big Beat* promotions at the Tower Ballroom, New Brighton, a venue which had a 5,000 capacity. He had the Beatles appearing on further *Operation Big Beat* shows at the Tower on 24 November and 8 December 1961. Hundreds of tickets for Sam's first *Operation Big Beat* show were on sale at Brian Epstein's branch of NEMS in Whitechapel, and the Beatles' name was very prominent in the tickets, posters and leaflets for the gig and it would have been almost impossible for Epstein not to have been aware of the event – if the stories of how interested he was in every detail are to be believed. Sam, himself, had desires of managing the Beatles and he also had ambitions of launching a record label, Troubadour Records, with the Beatles and Gerry & the Pacemakers as his initial releases. First in the studio were to be the Beatles recording 'Twist And Shout' and 'Stand By Me', but Sam couldn't raise the necessary capital to carry it off. In an effort to promote the group in the South, he booked the Palais Ballroom in Aldershot for four consecutive Saturday nights, with the Beatles appearing on the first of the shows on 9 December 1961.

Once Brian Epstein had become the Beatles' manager, he also began local promotions at venues such as the Tower Ballroom. Admittedly, he did approach Leach to run the gigs in partnership with himself, but Sam was unhappy about the proposed division of profits and declined. Basically, Brian wanted his brother Clive involved and suggested a three-way split which Sam, having established the Tower as a venue for beat music, didn't regard as a fair deal.

Sam held several parties, to which the Beatles were invited. They included his Iron Door celebration on 11 November to toast the success of *Operation Big Beat*. After one of his shows at Knotty Ash Village Hall, they attended his engagement party.

When the Beatles made such an impact in America, Sam published a magazine called *Beatles on Broadway* which proved very lucrative for him.

Leander, Mike
A producer and arranger who arranged 'She's Leaving Home' for Paul. George Martin had to record Cilla Black at the time and Paul was anxious to have the number arranged, so he engaged the freelance Leander. This was to upset Martin, who was to comment, 'I couldn't understand why he was so impatient all of a sudden. It obviously hadn't occurred to him that I would be upset.' Leander was paid £18 for the rights to his arrangement. Within seven months he was called on to arrange the instrumental 'Shirley's Wild Accordion' for *Magical Mystery Tour*.

Leave My Kitten Alone
A number composed by John/Turner/McDougal which Little Willie John recorded in 1959. The Beatles included it in their repertoire in 1961, the same year that Johnny Preston's version was issued.

The group recorded it at Abbey Road, with John on lead vocals, on Friday, 14 August 1964, during their *Beatles For Sale* album sessions. It was intended for the album, but the group wasn't satisfied with how it was turning out and abandoned it after five takes. It was eventually released over thirty years later on the *Anthology 2* CD.

Lend Me Your Comb
Composition by Kay Twomey, Fred Wise and Ben Weisman, recorded by Carl Perkins in 1957 and included in the Beatles' repertoire in 1961 when John and Paul shared vocal honours.

It was part of the group's repertoire during their final Star Club season and is found on *The Beatles Live! At The Star Club In Hamburg, Germany: 1962* album. The group also recorded it for their BBC radio show 'Pop Go The Beatles' on 16 July 1963. Although this is a version recorded live on the 'Pop Go The Beatles' radio series, it was not included on *The Beatles Live At The BBC* CDs but is found on the Beatles' *Anthology 1* CDs.

Lennon, Alfred
John's father, born in Liverpool on 14 December 1912. When his father Jack died of a liver disease in 1921, Alfred was nine years of age and was placed in the Bluecoat School, which took in orphans.

Alfred remained at the school until he was fifteen years old and then left to take up his first job as an office clerk. It was during this period, in 1927, that he met Julia Stanley, a fourteen-year-old girl, in Sefton Park. He chatted her up and asked her to sit with him, and she told him she would on condition he got rid of his silly bowler hat. He immediately threw it into the lake. The couple then began to date and continued doing so over a period of ten years, in between Alfred's voyages abroad as a merchant seaman.

In 1930, at the age of sixteen, Alfred was drawn to the sea and signed up as a ship's waiter. In between voyages he stayed at the Stanley house in Newcastle Road, Wavertree, and taught Julia how to play the banjo.

It was Julia who finally suggested that they should get married and they did, at Mount Pleasant Registry Office on 3 December 1938. No member of their family was present and after the ceremony the couple went to the Trocadero Cinema where they spent their 'honeymoon'. Later that evening Julia went back home to Wavertree and Freddie went to his digs; he left the next day on a three-month trip to the West Indies. He was also away at sea in October 1940 when John was born.

While at sea, Fred had arranged to pay sums of money to the company he worked for, which Julia could collect from the branch in Liverpool. He was now a head waiter and as it was wartime and he was in New York City, he was asked to report to a ship sailing to Britain. However, he was to be an assistant steward on the voyage and not head waiter and he bemoaned the fact to the Captain, who suggested that he get drunk and miss the boat, which he did. He was then interned on Ellis' Island until another ship, this time sailing for North Africa, was available. When they reached North Africa he said that one of the cooks asked him to bring a bottle of vodka from his cabin and while Fred was drinking from it a party of police arrived to investigate some thefts and arrested him for stealing the vodka. He was jailed for three months and his money was stopped. Unable to provide Julia with any cash, he wrote her letters and suggested she enjoy herself by going out with other men. He later regretted the suggestion because she took him up on it – and he lost her.

In 1945 she gave birth to another child and had the baby adopted by a Norwegian couple. She also began living with John Dykins and placed her son John with her sister, Mimi, in Menlove Avenue.

Docking in Southampton in the summer of 1946, Fred phoned Aunt Mimi and asked if he could take John to Blackpool. Mimi felt she couldn't refuse this request from the boy's father and Fred picked up the five-year-old and took him to stay in a friend's flat in Blackpool.

During the few weeks they were in the northern seaside resort, Fred told John of his desire to take him to New Zealand. The idea appealed to Fred because his friend was emigrating there and, at the time, Fred was earning money on the side through black market deals.

Julia arrived at the flat demanding that John be returned to her. Fred asked the boy whether he wanted to go to New Zealand with him or return to Liverpool with his mother, and John opted for Fred's proposal. However, when Julia left the house he changed his mind and ran after her. Fred did not see his son again for twenty years. When Julia returned to Liverpool she placed the boy into Mimi's care once again.

In 1964, Fred had finally abandoned life on the ocean wave and was working as a porter in the Greyhound Hotel, Hampton, near London, for ten pounds a week. The *Daily Express* newspaper traced him and wanted to set up a meeting between him and his now famous son.

Fred went along to the set of *A Hard Day's Night* and entered the dressing-room. John wouldn't talk to him but asked him to leave his address. John sent a letter to the Greyhound with a note to: 'Dear Alf, Fred, Dad, Pater, Father, Whatever', with £30 enclosed.

John began to send Fred a regular twelve pounds a week and the ex-seaman moved into a flat in Kew, basking in the limelight as a minor celebrity, having his life story printed in the weekly magazines and gracing the London nightspots. He even found himself with a manager, Tony Cartwright, who co-wrote a song with him called 'That's My Life', which was issued as a single in December 1965 by Pye Records on their Piccadilly label. The company issued a press handout which read:

Fifty-three-year-old Freddie Lennon, father of John, has made his first record. It is entitled 'That's My Life (My Love And My Home)'.

Mr Lennon has been an entertainer in an amateur capacity for most of his life. He comes from a musical family, for his father was one of the original Kentucky Minstrels, and taught him to sing when he was young.

Most of Freddie's childhood was spent in an orphanage, for he was born into a large family and in those difficult times parents could not afford to feed so many children. At the orphanage, Freddie always took a major part in concerts, played his harmonica to the other children and generally showed an inclination towards the stage. He once sang at a theatre but the orphanage authorities were dismayed at the thought of one of their boys going on to the stage, so Freddie's early dreams were quickly dampened.

After leaving the orphanage at the age of 15, Freddie worked in an office, but the call of the sea was strong, and he joined his first ship as bell boy at the age of 16. He stayed at sea for 25 years and travelled the world.

Freddie was always connected with entertainment on board ship, and has acted as compere, produced numerous concerts, sang in New York clubs and even conducted an orchestra in Lisbon. He has many interesting stories to relate about his adventures at sea.

At the age of 25 Freddie married, and his son John was born three years later. He was the only child.

When he left sea 12 years ago, Freddie took a job as a waiter, and later worked in holiday camps at northern resorts. He came to live in London seven years ago. Over the years, Freddie was always interested in songwriting, but he never took it seriously. Six months ago he met Tony Cartwright, who is now his manager. Together they wrote 'That's My Life (My Love And My Home)' – a story about Freddie's life. The song was taken to a music publisher, accepted and recorded.

By the close of 1967 Alfred and his son were reconciled and Fred often dropped around to John's house in Kenwood. At the time a romantic relationship began between Fred and a nineteen-year-old student called Pauline Jones. At 56, Fred was almost three times her age.

Fred proposed and Pauline's parents were furious and had her made a ward of court, but the two eloped to Scotland where they were married. They then went to live in Brighton with John paying the rent for their flat. When their first son David was born they took him to see John at Tittenhurst Park. John was in a foul mood and tossed them out, seemingly upset at the thought of seeing his half-brother, which may have set off painful memories.

Years later, when Fred was dying, John spoke to him by phone from America on several occasions, although Fred could hardly speak a word in return. When Fred died John offered to pay for his funeral, but Pauline rejected the offer.

Lennon, Cynthia

Born Cynthia Powell in Blackpool on 10 September 1939. Her mother and two brothers, Tony and Charles, had been evacuated to the northern seaside town during World War II. The family then returned to Hoylake where Cynthia spent her childhood.

She sat an entrance examination which provided her with a place at the Junior Art School in Gambier Terrace and at the age of eighteen began her studies at Liverpool College of Art in September 1957.

Her close friend at the college was Phyllis Mackenzie and the two, like all beginners at the college, took part in the two-year Intermediate Course which provided them with the basic groundwork in the techniques of art. One of the various subjects which were part of the Intermediate Course was Lettering and joining Cynthia and Phyllis in the Lettering class were two other students, John Lennon and Jonathan Hague. As Hoylake on the Wirral was regarded as a 'posh' place, John began to make snide remarks to Cynthia.

Despite his apparent roughness, compared to the boyfriends she'd had, Cynthia found herself attracted to him and at one of the school parties he began dancing with her and asked her out. Embarrassed, she told him she was engaged to a chap in Hoylake. 'I didn't ask you to marry me, did I?' he snapped back. Yet Cynthia and Phyllis were invited to join John and his friends at Ye Cracke pub after the party and the two began to date regularly.

Completely besotted by John, Cynthia began to change her appearance to please him and allowed her blonde hair to grow long and began to wear tight black sweaters, very short, tight skirts, high-heeled shoes and black stockings and suspenders. This sort of blatant attire caused her some embarrassment at the times when she waited to meet up with John outside Lewis's store in Liverpool. The clothes belied the timid girl she really was. John liked Brigitte Bardot and therefore Cynthia tried to style herself on the looks of the French actress.

Cynthia began to travel with the Beatles to their local gigs, although she often had to stay in the background because of the possible hostile reaction she'd receive from the group's fans. She also became friendly with Paul McCartney's girlfriend Dot Rhone. When the Beatles appeared at the Top Ten Club in Hamburg from 27 March–2 July 1961, Cynthia and Dot were invited over to stay with them for a couple of weeks.

When Cynthia returned to Hoylake her mother revealed that Cynthia's cousin and his wife, who were emigrating to Canada, had invited her to travel with them and act as nanny to their children. She wanted to take up their offer, but was worried about Cynthia. Cynthia told her she would rent a room from John's Aunt Mimi. She tried to act like a daughter rather than a lodger, but found that the relationship with Mimi was strained and decided to move out. She eventually moved into a small flat and managed to persuade Dot Rhone to rent out the room next to her.

In 1963 a doctor confirmed that Cynthia was pregnant and when she told John, he said that they would have to get married. John's Aunt Mimi wasn't too pleased to hear the news and didn't attend the wedding. The ceremony itself was to be a hush-hush affair due to the increasing popularity of the Beatles nationwide and Brian Epstein suggested a special licence. On 23 August 1963 the couple were married at the Registry Office in Mount Pleasant, with her brother Tony and his wife, Paul McCartney, George Harrison and Brian Epstein in attendance. Brian was also to let the newly married couple have access to his private flat in Faulkner Street. On the wedding night, John left for a gig at the Riverpark Ballroom, Chester and was to spend most of the time over the next few months performing. The pregnant girl found herself very lonely during this period as John was on the road and hardly ever at the flat. A concerned Aunt Mimi requested that Cynthia move in with her.

On Monday, 8 April 1963 at 7.45 a.m., Cynthia gave birth to a baby boy, John Charles Julian Lennon, at Sefton General Hospital.

When Julian was six months old, Cynthia's mother returned from Canada and found a flat in Trinity Road, Hoylake, where Cynthia and Julian could join her. When John managed to take a break from touring, the couple were able to take a belated honeymoon in Paris, spending a week at the George V Hotel.

On Cynthia's return to Hoylake she was tracked down by the press who had heard rumours of the marriage and the story eventually broke in the newspapers. Now that the marriage was out in the open, John arranged for Cynthia and Julian to move down to London with him and a photographer friend, Bob Freeman, arranged for them to move into a flat in Emperor's Gate, Knightsbridge. The accommodation was not really suitable, as there were too many steps for Cynthia to negotiate with a child in a pram, and the address was known to Beatle fans who would gather outside.

However, on the Beatles' return from America, John bought a large house, 'Kenwood', in Weybridge, Surrey, and the family were able to move into their six-bedroomed home at the end of July 1964.

Cynthia travelled to America with the Beatles and the fans were not hostile to her – as they would later be to Linda McCartney and Yoko Ono. However, Cynthia never seemed to lose her timidity and was often unable to get back into hotels where she was staying with John and the Beatles. When they were staying at the Deauville Hotel in Miami, Cynthia was attempting to return to the hotel when a security guard refused to let her pass. She identified herself but he didn't believe her. It took a group of fans, who realised who she was, to talk in strong terms to the guard to allow him to let her back into the hotel.

She was able to settle down in Kenwood, more content in the role of a housewife than a celebrity, although enthusiasts even launched a Cynthia Lennon Fan Club. There were holidays and she enjoyed the socialising with other Beatles wives and girlfriends – Pattie, Jane and Maureen.

Inevitably perhaps, the idyll came to an end. Cynthia seemed to believe it was as a result of drugs and in her autobiography, *A Twist Of Lennon*, commented: 'As far as I was concerned the rot began to set in the moment cannabis and LSD seeped its unhealthy way into our lives.' She hated drugs herself and when someone slipped LSD into a drink of hers one day, she thought she was going insane.

Cynthia was also aware that when the Beatles were on tour, attractive model girls were among the many females who threw themselves at the group, and their constant tours abroad worried her. She began to lose confidence in her looks and in 1967 decided to have plastic surgery on her nose. When she was at the London Clinic, following the operation, John sent her a bouquet of red roses and a card which read: 'To Cyn, a nose by any other name. Love from John and Julian'.

However, Cynthia began to feel estranged from John and the Beatles' circle because she shunned drugs, and she could see that the others were obviously influenced by the effects of LSD in the way a colourful world of psychedelia seemed to open up with the lyrics of the *Sgt Pepper* album, and John having his Rolls-Royce painted in psychedelic colours. She felt outside of things and decided that she'd have to get back on John's wavelength to save the marriage. John had been asking her to take LSD for some time and she agreed, while John helped her through the trip. She regarded it as hell on earth and hated every moment. John kept telling her that he loved her and would never leave her, but when she looked at him the hallucinations made her see an animal-type person with razor sharp teeth, laughing at her. She realised that she would never be happy taking drugs.

By the time Cynthia joined the group at Rishikesh to study Transcendental Meditation, Yoko Ono had entered the picture, Brian Epstein had died and the Beatles had decided to launch Apple Corps. She enjoyed Rishikesh and believed that Transcendental Meditation had done John a lot of good, but she was sad that John and George severed their relationship with the guru so drastically.

The first time Cynthia had met Yoko was at a meditation session in London. She then began to notice the letters Yoko sent to John at Kenwood asking for his help in promoting her book *Grapefruit*.

Dot, the Lennons' housekeeper, had also told Cynthia that Yoko had been turning up at the house regularly trying to see if John was at home.

When things began to get on top of Cynthia, John suggested she go on a holiday for two weeks during a time when he would be recording. Donovan and Gypsy Dave were travelling to Greece with Jennie Boyd and Alexis Mardas and John suggested she join them. When Cynthia arrived back at Kenwood, accompanied by Jennie and Alexis, she found John and Yoko in the house together. Confused, she asked John if he'd come out to dinner. He refused. She'd noticed a pair of Japanese slippers placed outside the guest bedroom door and asked Alexis and Jennie if she could stay with them for a few days and left.

The opinion of people who knew both John and Cynthia at the time was that Cynthia should have stood her ground and demanded Yoko be thrown out of the house. If she had responded strongly as an outraged wife, then there was a strong possibility that John might have remained with Cynthia, perhaps taking Yoko on as a mistress. The fact that Cynthia capitulated proved to be her downfall.

That evening Cynthia and Alexis sat up drinking wine together and she awoke the next morning to find herself in bed with him. She felt disgusted with herself. She returned to Kenwood to find that Yoko had gone, and there was a reconciliation. John told Cynthia he was bored with Yoko. However, John left for New York a few days later, refusing to take Cynthia with him. Cynthia didn't want to remain at Kenwood by herself, so she took a brief holiday in Italy with Julian and her mother. One day Alexis Mardas arrived to tell her that John was divorcing her and that he would testify to adultery on John's behalf. Cynthia became terribly depressed and ill, having to remain in bed for several days. When she returned to London there was a divorce petition citing her adultery with Alexis Mardas.

However, it was decided that it would be better for all concerned if it was John who admitted to his adultery with Yoko, which is what happened when Cynthia was granted a decree nisi on 8 November 1969.

The following year, on 31 July, Cynthia married Roberto Bassanini at Kensington Register Office. Roberto had been the son of the hotel owners at the resort where Cynthia had been on holiday the previous year. At the ceremony, Julian was a page boy and Twiggy and Justin de Villeneuve were present. However, the marriage wasn't to last and after her divorce from Bassanini she married businessman John Twist and the couple moved to Ireland for a short time with Julian, then settled down in Ruthin, North Wales. Her autobiography *A Twist Of Lennon* was published in paperback in April 1978. When her marriage to Twist ended in divorce and after John's death, Cynthia reverted to the name Cynthia Lennon. Despite all that had happened, Cynthia remained in love with John.

Julian left home to seek a career in showbusiness and Cynthia attempted to make a living as an artist – the settlement John had made her following their divorce hadn't been large in comparison to his earnings. There were several exhibitions of her paintings and she was also involved in a number of design commissions. For a time she was involved in the West End restaurant Lennon's, but settled in the Isle of Man, and in 1991 finally put all her personal memorabilia relating to John up for auction.

With her long term partner Jim Christie she opened a restaurant, Bunter's in the Isle of Man, but it was later to close. Her life story was serialised in *Hello!* magazine, starting in April 1994. During the 1990s she began appearing regularly at Beatles conventions around the world and in January 1995 made her recording debut with *Those Were The Days*. In 1996 she and Jim relocated to Dorset and they later moved on to France. Her relationship with Christie ended in 1998 and during June and July 1999 she had an exhibition of her art works at the KDK Gallery in London, along with her former art school friend Phyllis McKenzie, calling the exhibition Lennon & McKenzie. In August she placed some of her works on permanent exhibition at the Beatles Experience in Liverpool.

Lennon, John

John Winston Lennon was born at 6.30 p.m. on 9 October 1940 at Oxford Street Maternity Hospital, Liverpool, to Julia and Alfred Lennon. The seaport of Liverpool had been subject to recent heavy raids by the Luftwaffe, but at the time of John's birth, there was a lull in the bombing.

Fred Lennon was away at sea and rarely saw his son. His mother Julia liked to enjoy herself and didn't seem to relish the responsibility of rearing a child at that time with the result that the young boy was left in the care of his Aunt Mary 'Mimi' Smith and Uncle George in the pleasant Woolton area of Liverpool.

John seemed fated to be reared by his aunt when Julia decided to live with another man, John Dykins, and eventually bore him two daughters. She'd previously given birth to another daughter by a soldier of brief acquaintance but was forced by her father to put the baby up for adoption.

In 1946 Fred returned to Liverpool and took his son on a short
holiday to the nearby seaside resort of Blackpool where he made
plans to emigrate to New Zealand with John. Julia turned up and
took her son back to Liverpool, returning him to Mimi's care.

John went to Dovedale Primary School where he began to betray
the streak of rebelliousness which was to remain with him for the
rest of his life. He also began to take an interest in drawing.

Tragedy struck in 1955 when his kindly Uncle George died,
leaving the troubled young boy to internalise another grief. Despite
the love his authoritarian aunt gave him, the fact that he was not
reared by his own mother and father was a factor in his outlook on
life.

John began attending Quarry Bank Grammar School in
September 1952 and struck up a friendship with another young
'tearaway', Peter Shotton. The two friends became inseparable and
were always getting into trouble at school for crazy pranks and
insolence to teachers. Their academic work suffered. It was during
this period that John began to display his creative abilities as a
writer and artist with a series of exercise books containing his
drawings and humorous stories, which he dubbed 'The Daily
Howl'. As a youngster he loved books and would prefer them as
presents. His favourites included the Lewis Carroll *Alice* books and
Richmal Crompton's *Just William* novels – these stories of a scamp
of a schoolboy probably influenced his behaviour and he possibly
identified with the character.

When the skiffle boom spread throughout Britain, John was one
of the many boys who decided to form a group of his own and in
May 1955 he gathered his school friends into a band he called the
Quarry Men.

There were various changes in personnel, but the most important
event occurred at Woolton Parish Church Fete on 6 July 1957 when
he met schoolboy Paul McCartney who was soon to become a
member of the group.

John's own preference for rock 'n' roll and his love of Elvis
Presley soon began to have its effect on the Quarry Men as they
shed the traditional folksy numbers and developed into a rock 'n'
roll group. Although John was the leader of the group, his musical
relationship with McCartney grew to the extent that they became a
songwriting team and developed a vocal-harmony style. There were
many suggestions and pressures for them to adopt the current style
of having a leader's name at the front of the group. Suggestions
included Long John and the Silver Men. At one time they used the
name Johnny & the Moondogs for a series of talent contests, but
generally resisted efforts to make them into a group with a front

line singer. This pressure continued until they signed with Parlophone. George Martin initially thought of changing their style and having Paul McCartney as the leader, but then changed his mind.

In September 1957, John enrolled at Liverpool Art College. He met Cynthia Powell, who was to become his first wife, Stuart Sutcliffe, who became his best friend and the Fifth Beatle, and Bill Harry who published his first works and promoted the Beatles' career locally.

In 1960 the Beatles travelled to Hamburg and many stories filtered back to Liverpool of John's escapades there. In July 1961 his first published work appeared in *Mersey Beat* and he contributed a column called 'Beatcomber'. Later the same year the group met Brian Epstein who became their manager and the following year they signed with Parlophone. In the meantime, John married Cynthia on 23 August 1962 and she gave birth to their son Julian on 8 April 1963. Within a few weeks John went on a brief holiday to Spain with Brian Epstein, and when local disc jockey Bob Wooler made a snide remark about the trip, John beat him up.

The Beatles were enjoying international success when John's first book *In His Own Write* was published on 23 March 1964 and became a best-seller. In January 1965 he appeared on the TV programme 'Not Only . . . But Also', reading his poetry, and on 24 June of that year his second book *A Spaniard In the Works* was published. During the same year his father Fred re-entered his life and the Beatles received their MBEs. In 1966 there was a degree of anti-Beatle fervour in America following comments John had made in an interview with Maureen Cleave, in which he said that the Beatles were more popular than Jesus, and he reluctantly made a public apology. At the end of the year the Beatles had decided to cease touring and in November John met the Japanese artist Yoko Ono at the Indica Gallery in London.

The Beatles had begun to experiment with various drugs, including LSD, and in August 1967 met the Maharishi Mahesh Yogi. During the same month their manager Brian Epstein was found dead from an accidental drug overdose. John's ties with Yoko grew stronger and he sponsored an exhibition of her work called *Yoko And Me* at the Lisson Arts Gallery in October. Later that month *How I Won The War*, in which he played his first solo feature film role, was premiered.

Following the Beatles' stay at the Maharishi's ashram in India, John and Cynthia split up and he began to live with Yoko. A play *In His Own Write*, based on John's books, was staged at the National Theatre in June and John's first art exhibition, *You Are*

Here, opened at the Robert Fraser Gallery. John and Yoko were raided by the police while staying at Ringo's flat in Montague Square and John was fined for possession of cannabis. John and Yoko's album *Unfinished Music No. 1: Two Virgins* was issued in November and created international controversy due to the cover, which showed the pair in a full frontal nude pose. John also appeared on the unshown *Rolling Stones Rock 'n' Roll Circus*.

In 1969, John was disillusioned with the Beatles' Apple empire and revealed as much to journalist Ray Coleman. As a result Allen Klein appeared on the scene and, with John's support, was able to take control of Apple. In the meantime Yoko's divorce from Anthony Cox came through in February and John and Yoko were married in Gibraltar on 20 March.

John and Yoko began making a series of avant garde films together, which included: *Apotheosis, Clock, Erection, Fly, Freedom Films, Imagine, Self Portrait, Smile* and *Up Your Legs Forever*. In May 1969 they bought an imposing mansion in Ascot called Tittenhurst Park and issued their second album *Unfinished Music No. 2: Life With The Lions*. During the year they also travelled to Toronto where they met Canadian Prime Minister Pierre Trudeau and they recorded the peace anthem 'Give Peace A Chance'. 1969 was also the year in which John introduced the Plastic Ono Band on record. In November the couple issued their *Wedding Album* and John returned his MBE to the Queen.

An exhibition of John's erotic lithographs opened at the London Arts Gallery on 15 January 1970 which was raided by the police. During the year there were further Plastic Ono Band releases, John and Yoko travelled to Los Angeles to undergo Primal Therapy under Dr Arthur Janov and Cynthia Lennon remarried. In January 1971 *Rolling Stone* magazine published the first part of a lengthy interview with John in which he vented his spleen. By March a receiver had been appointed to wind up the Beatles partnership and John and Yoko flew to New York. They came to Britain for a short time before returning to America in September, with John never to set foot in Britain again. During 1972 John fought to obtain a Green Card and was involved in a number of political protests, and his album *Some Time In New York City* included a number of songs based on the political causes he supported. During 1973 Ringo Starr bought Tittenhurst Park and John left Yoko to fly to Los Angeles with their secretary May Pang, with whom he was having an affair. What John called his 'long weekend' eventually ended and he returned to live with Yoko in New York in January 1975. Their son Sean was born in September of that year.

In 1976 John received his Green Card and at the end of the year decided to go into semi-retirement and rear Sean personally. He was to describe himself as a 'house husband' during this period. In late August 1980 he began recording his first album in six years and agreed to a number of interviews prior to him becoming active in the music scene once again. On 8 December he was shot dead outside the Dakota Building. In early 2000 it was alleged that both the FBI and MI5 had files on Lennon, including evidence supposedly showing that Lennon donated funds to the IRA. At the time of writing, the FBI files may be made public following a lengthy US court battle, although the final outcome remains unclear.

Lennon, Julia (nee Stanley)

John's mother, a slim, auburn-haired woman of a decidedly unconventional nature. Julia was one of the five daughters of George and Annie Stanley and was born on 12 March 1914. Julia first met Freddie Lennon in Sefton Park when she was only fourteen. Despite the disapproval of her father, Julia, known in the family as Juliet, married Freddie at Mount Pleasant Registry Office on 3 December 1938, several years after they had first met. As a joke, she put down her profession as 'Cinema usherette' on the wedding certificate, because she loved going to the pictures so much. In fact, after the wedding, Freddie and Julia spent the evening at the Trocadero, her favourite cinema. Then she went back to her parents' home, he went back to his lodgings and the next day Freddie sailed to the West Indies as steward on a ship.

Their only child together was John Winston Lennon, born in October 1940. Julia became pregnant again in 1944 by a young Welsh soldier 'Taffy' Williams, but refused to divorce Freddie and marry him. In fact, she was totally uninterested in the soldier and when he proposed she told him to 'get lost!'

Her father was furious and gave her an ultimatum: she had to have the baby adopted or leave the house. At first it was suggested that her childless sister Mimi could rear the child, but Mimi did not want to have anything to do with an illegitimate child. The baby, Victoria Elizabeth, who had been born on 19 June 1945, was adopted.

Freddie spent almost the entire period of the war years at sea and Julia, who worked for a time as a waitress at a cafe in Penny Lane, moved in with one of her customers, John Dykins. Mimi disapproved of the situation and insisted that Julia give John to her to rear. Eventually, Julia agreed to do so. When Freddie returned from sea at the war's end he insisted on taking John on a holiday to Blackpool. There he made plans to move to New Zealand with

John. Then Julia turned up and demanded that he return her son to her. John at first said he wanted to remain with his father, but then ran after his mother when she began to leave. When Julia arrived back in Liverpool she returned John to Mimi's keeping.

Julia settled down with Dykins, although they were never married as Julia was never divorced from Freddie. She gave birth to two daughters; Julia, born 5 March 1947, and Jacqui, born 26 October 1949.

Over the years, John was able to visit his mother frequently and she obviously had a profound effect on him. She was very pretty, had an off-beat sense of humour, was musical and totally unconventional. For instance, she used to do the housework wearing a pair of old woollen knickers on her head. Sometimes she'd wear a pair of spectacles without lenses and when talking to someone would suddenly put her fingers through the empty lens to scratch her eye.

Her new home was in Blomfield Road, close to where John lived with his Aunt Mimi. Soon he'd bring along his friends to meet her and they were all charmed, particularly Pete Shotton, who was delighted by her wacky humour.

She was also to influence John in his interest in music. Her grandfather, William Stanley, a part-time musician, had taught her to play banjo when she was a child. She used to sing to John and taught him how to play 'That'll Be The Day' on the banjo. John said, 'My mother could play any stringed instrument there was,' and Paul McCartney was to comment, 'Julia was lively and heaps of fun and way ahead of her time. Not too many blokes had mothers as progressive as she was.'

On 15 July 1958 she was killed. She'd left her house at 7.00 p.m. to see Mimi. After her visit, Mimi told her, 'I won't walk you tonight, Julia. I'll see you tomorrow.' Nigel Whally, who was managing John's group at the time, had dropped by to see if John was in and witnessed the accident. Julia stepped off the pavement to cross to the central reservation on the dual carriageway when she was hit by a car which sent her spinning. She died instantly. Her body was taken to Sefton General Hospital. The off-duty policeman who had driven the vehicle was taken to court, but was acquitted.

The tragedy was to affect John deeply, particularly as he had a tendency to let things boil up inside him and not show his emotions outwardly. His feelings were a mixed bag of guilt, resentment of her for leaving him, frustration at not having a normal family life and emotions which were finally to resolve themselves when he underwent 'Primal' therapy many years later. John named his young son

Julian after his mother and wrote a number of songs dedicated to her: 'My Mummy's Dead', 'Mother' and 'Julia'.

Lennon, Julian

John's first son and the first child born to any member of the Beatles. The group were currently promoting their new single 'Please Please Me' and John's marriage to Cynthia had been kept secret from the world in general.

Accompanied only by her friend Phyllis Mackenzie, Cynthia was rushed to Sefton General Hospital in Smithdown Road, Liverpool, and gave birth to Julian at 7.45 p.m. on Monday, 8 April 1963. There was some difficulty at the actual birth as the umbilical cord was wrapped around the child's neck, but he proved to be a healthy baby. Cynthia then requested a private room and John visited her there a week later.

When Cynthia left hospital with Julian she returned to Menlove Avenue where she had been staying with John's Aunt Mimi. When Cynthia's mother returned from Canada six months later, they decided to return to Trinity Road, Hoylake, their previous home.

In November Julian was christened at Trinity Road parish church, although John was unable to attend. His full name is John Charles Julian Lennon. The first name was chosen in honour of John, the second in memory of Cynthia's father and the third in memory of John's mother.

News of the marriage and the birth of Julian eventually found its way into the press. The three were able to unite as a family at last and move into a flat in Emperor's Gate, Kensington, London. This proved inconvenient and they later moved to St George's Hill Estate in Weybridge, Surrey, where Julian attended the local prep school.

When Julian was four years old he brought home a picture of a school friend which he'd drawn and called it 'Lucy In The Sky With Diamonds'. This inspired John to write a song of the same name.

At one time there was a kidnapping threat and Julian was guarded day and night, both at home and at school.

When Yoko Ono entered the picture, John and Cynthia's marriage was doomed. Alexis Mardas conveyed a message to Cynthia that John was going to divorce her and take Julian away from her. Paul McCartney was particularly upset by the split and felt sorry for Julian, an emotion which led him to composing 'Hey Jude'.

After the divorce, John had access to Julian who joined his father and Yoko on numerous occasions, visiting the filming of the Rolling Stones' *Rock And Roll Circus* and joining them on a trip to Scotland with Yoko's daughter Kyoko in June 1967.

Later that same year another of his drawings was immortalised, this time as the sleeve of *Christmas Time Is Here Again*, the Beatles' Christmas record, issued in December.

In 1970 Cynthia married hotelier Roberto Bassanini, but the marriage was a brief one and they parted shortly afterwards. The divorce came through in 1973 and she married businessman John Twist in 1976. They settled in Ruthin, North Wales, where Julian attended the local school and Cynthia teamed up with Angie McCartney, ex-wife of Mike McGear, to open a venture called Oliver's Bistro.

During the remainder of the seventies, Julian led a more-or-less normal life, out of the limelight, attending the local school and making friends in Ruthin. Julian's life was shattered when John Twist had to tell him that his father had been murdered, and he lay on the floor in a state of shock for hours.

Yoko wanted him to come straight to New York, but said that she didn't want Cynthia to come with him, so he was accompanied by one of his Ruthin friends, Justin.

Julian's life changed completely following the tragedy. Cynthia and John Twist became estranged, and she reverted to the name Cynthia Lennon and began to tour America with her paintings, also leaving North Wales for a new home in Wiltshire.

When he returned from America, Julian decided that the time had come for him to leave home and he moved to Chiswick in London. He became a favourite topic of the gossip columns, attracting escorts like moths to a flame. He'd had girlfriends in Ruthin such as Sally Hudson and a girl called Amanda, but the models who now pursued him in London were totally different.

He'd been befriended by an old Etonian Kim Kindersley who took him round all the fashionable clubs, from Tramps to Stringfellows. At Tramps he was approached by Stephanie La Motta, who became one of the series of girls he hit the headlines with.

He was given a nineteenth birthday party at Stringfellows, which received considerable press coverage, with models such as Sian Adley-Jones stripping to the waist for the photographers. For the next few years, models found that a date with Julian ensured them press coverage. Some examples include Kate Latto, featured in a *Daily Mirror* newspaper story in January 1982 under the heading 'Julian's Blonde'. Two months later the *Sunday Mirror* newspaper was featuring 'The New Girl For "So Shy" Julian' in a story which began: 'This beautiful blonde is the new girl in Julian Lennon's life. Model Jordana ... has been wined and dined ... by [Julian] since they met at a London nightclub.' The stories continued and a topless Debbie Boyland was featured in the *Sunday People* news-paper in April 1983 under the heading 'Love And Sun For Lennon' in a story beginning: 'Delicious Debbie Boyland and her lover Julian Lennon . . . are Barbados bound.' His club exploits caused controversy, such as the occasion when he was photographed with a blonde holding a gun to his head at L'Escargot club.

In the years immediately following John's death, Julian seemed only newsworthy for his partiality for blondes. His musical career seemed to be almost non-existent, despite the fact that he'd been signed up by Tariq Siddiqi.

When he was eighteen, Cynthia had said he could play the guitar better than his father. At one time he had a band called the Lennon Drops and in April 1982 the London *Evening Standard* in a story enti-tled 'Julian's Chilling Debut', wrote that Julian was about to 'astonish the world with the release of a chillingly brilliant debut record'. The number was 'I Don't Wanna Feel It Any More', which John himself had actually recorded during the *Double Fantasy* sessions but had never released.

In March 1983, reports appeared in the British press that Julian had joined Quasar, a group led by Paul Inder, son of Lemmy of Motorhead. Paul was also managed by Siddiqi. In May 1983 there was some controversy because Siddiqi organised the group's appearance on the roof of the old Apple building in Savile Row. Even Paul Inder's mother couldn't stomach this blatant use of Julian and said, 'The whole idea of using the memory of the Beatles and using John Lennon's son in this way is sick.'

In the years following John's death, there was always controversy regarding Julian's inheritance. Some papers described him as 'The heir to John's vast fortune – estimated to be more than £50 million'. However, Julian began to bemoan the fact that he was broke and began offering to tell his story to newspapers – for a price.

A series did appear in the *News Of the World* newspaper in January 1982 in which Julian talked to Polly Hepburn. The head-line ran 'All You Need Is Love. The Beatles Said It, But I Wish Dad Had Shown Me Some'.

Julian claimed that John had offered him marijuana when he was only twelve years old, described his visits to John in America and said other boys often threatened to beat him up because he was the son of a Beatle, and other rather innocuous stories. Yoko granted him an allowance of 100 dollars a week, a sum which was criticised when the news leaked out. Julian said: 'Yoko decided to give me a hundred dollars a week some time ago, but it is not mine by right. The papers say I'm heir to a fortune worth millions, but Yoko has total control of everything. I will get half the trust fund cash, about two hundred thousand dollars, when I am 25. The other half goes to Sean.'

Yoko replied to the criticism by saying, 'Poor Julian is probably very confused. It all has to do with Cynthia. She is not getting any money from John's estate, rightly, and she is very hurt by this. It's hard for Julian to please his mother without saying bad things about me. John never gave him any allowance. Julian was complaining that he didn't have enough money to be able to buy beer so I said "How much will cover that?" How much do most kids his age get? Should he grow up differently from other kids?'

Julian eventually succeeded as a musician in his own right, with tours and chart records. He moved to Los Angeles and settled in America.

Lennon, Sean

The only offspring of John and Yoko was born on John's 35th birthday, 9 October 1975, at New York Hospital. Yoko had had three miscarriages before the birth of their son, which was obviously one of the high points in their lives. John was to say, 'I feel higher than the Empire State Building.' At one time he considered calling his newborn son George Washington United States Of America Citizen Lennon.

The couple had almost given up hope of having a child together, but decided to try again on the advice of an acupuncturist. John said, 'We went through all hell trying to have a baby, through many miscarriages and other problems. He is what they call a love child in truth. Doctors told us we could never have a child. We almost gave up. We were told something was wrong with my sperm, that I abused myself so much in my youth that there was no chance. Yoko was 43, and so they said no way. But this Chinese acupuncturist in San Francisco said, "You behave yourself. No drugs, eat well, no drink. You have a child in eighteen months." We had Sean and sent the acupuncturist a Polaroid of him before he died, God rest his soul.'

Having experienced a childhood without any direct parental care, and harbouring a guilt for letting his career take precedence over seeing his first son Julian grow up, John decided that he would spend virtually his entire waking life in the company of Sean. He did this for a period of time which lasted five years.

In the Dakota apartments, John became a house husband, caring for Sean, feeding him, teaching him, and doting on him while Yoko went out to work, controlling the couple's many business interests. For the first year of Sean's life, John took Polaroid shots of his son every single day. When Sean began to draw, John had all the sketches framed. He was finding a satisfaction in life he had never experienced before.

John's life revolved around Sean's meals. He would rise at six in the morning to plan breakfast. The two would have this at around seven-thirty, when they would both 'communicate'.

Then at ten o'clock when Sean was involved in other things, John would be planning the next meal.

He didn't mind the role-reversal of having Yoko take care of business while he looked after the home. He'd finally ridden himself of that chauvinism so associated with males from the north of England.

It was during his holiday in Bermuda with Sean that John finally decided to resume a musical career. However, fate tragically brought this to a chilling end.

Sean is left with memories, the treasure of five years of close intimacy, rare between father and son. Nothing will compensate him for his loss. Life must have seemed puzzling for such a child, growing up in a world in which he was forever surrounded by bodyguards.

Lennon & McCartney Songbook, The

An hour-long BBC radio show, transmitted on the *Light Programme* on Bank Holiday Monday, 29 August 1966. The theme was cover versions of Lennon & McCartney songs and both John and Paul were interviewed for the programme at Paul's Cavendish Avenue house on 6 August.

Only one Beatles number was played on the show, 'Good Day Sunshine' from their *Revolver* album, issued earlier that month. All other music on the programme was by various artists who covered Lennon & McCartney songs, including Ella Fitzgerald, the Mamas and Papas, Pat Boone, Peter Sellers and Nancy Sinatra.

Leonard, Barry

Leonard worked as Brian Epstein's personal assistant in London for a short time. He quit when he said that the strain of managing the Beatles was too great. He then gave a story to the *Daily Express* newspaper in which he said that Paul McCartney intended leaving the Beatles and was attempting to lose his Liverpool accent.

Les Ambassadeurs, Hamilton Place, London W1

Fashionable club where the Beatles held a private party in June 1965 to celebrate the MBE awards they'd received. The club was also the setting for a special Magic Christian party hosted by Ringo and Peter Sellers.

On 24 October 1979, it was booked by *The Guinness Book Of Records* for a special party in honour of Paul McCartney.

Leslo

Name of the Greek island which the Beatles purchased in 1967, intending it to be an idyllic retreat where they would create their own community.

When the Beatles were in the recording studio one night, John suggested that they should find themselves a Greek island on which they could build houses, a studio and a school. He suggested that Julian could be taught there and they could invite Bob Dylan's children to be educated on the island. Alexis Mardas, who was present in the studio with them, immediately said that he knew an island off the Greek mainland which could be bought quite cheaply. The following day Peter Brown sent Alexis and Alistair Taylor off to Greece to make the arrangements for the purchase. They located a tiny cluster of islands in the Aegean; the large main island of 100 acres contained four beaches and there were five smaller islands with sixteen acres of olive trees. The Beatles would be able to buy them all for £90,000.

When the group heard about it they all wanted to leave for Leslo at once. At the time Alexis didn't tell them about the political situation in Greece, which was under the control of a military junta that had banned both long hair and rock music.

Alexis, who was the son of a Greek military officer in the junta, contacted a Greek official and impressed on him the tremendous publicity value the Beatles would be for Greece. As a result, they struck a deal. As VIPs the Beatles and their party would not be searched at the airport. They would also pose for publicity photographs with the Minister of Tourism. The Beatles were unaware that such a move would mean that they were literally endorsing the junta.

Alexis warned John that he should not criticise the junta in the press. Despite the warning, John arrived dressed in army uniform and began saluting every soldier in sight. The Beatles were driven around for fourteen hours, having photographs taken all the time which were then sent all around the world by wire service.

When the Beatles saw the islands they loved them and immediately agreed to purchase them. They instructed their accountants, Bryce Hanmer, who then had to apply to the British government, due to the fact that they wished to buy foreign property. Because of the economic situation, the movement of capital outside the UK was severely restricted. Bryce Hanmer had to make the arrangements directly with James Callaghan, the Chancellor of the Exchequer. He wrote to them, allowing them the transfer of

£95,000 outside the country, adding, 'But not a penny more – I wonder how you're going to furnish it?'

Bryce Hanmer were not happy about the deal. They advised the Beatles that they would have to pay the British government a premium of 25 per cent per pound on the £95,000, and that as the group only had funds of £137,000, it could prove disastrous for them.

The Beatles shunned the advice, deciding they were going to establish a community on Leslo with their families and John commented, 'It will be amazing. We'll be able to just lie naked in the sunshine together. There will be no hassles with the police because there won't be any police. The kids won't bother us because there won't be any kids. We can set a studio up and just make our albums, swim about in the Aegean and get stoned.'

They bought the islands, but the intricate financial hassles became too complicated for them and they lost interest. They sold the islands back to the Greek government, making a profit of £11,400.

Les Stewart Quartet, The

During 1959, when the Quarry Men had all but disbanded, George Harrison joined the Les Stewart Quartet, who had a residency at Lowlands Club in West Derby. He joined the group in January and remained with them until August of that year. Their line up comprised: Les Stewart (guitar/vocals), Geoff Skinner, Ken Brown (guitar/vocals) and George Harrison (guitar/vocals). When Ken Brown, who was also in the group, fixed up a residency at the new Casbah Club, Les Stewart refused to let the group appear, accusing Brown of missing rehearsals to help out in decorating the new club. George and Brown left the band to team up with John and Paul to re-form the Quarry Men and take up the Casbah residency.

Lester, Richard

He was born in Jenkinstown, Philadelphia, in 1932. During his last year at the University of Pennsylvania he managed and performed with the Vocal Group who made regular appearances on local television stations in America. He became a stagehand at the TV station WCAU-TV and eventually a director, but left after two years, becoming a roving reporter.

As a musician, Lester then toured the world playing guitar and piano in various bars and clubs throughout continental Europe and North Africa. He then moved to Britain in 1955 where he wrote a musical for television, *Curtains for Harry*. He also starred in a short-lived television series, 'The Dick Lester Show', co-starring with Alun Owen. He became associated with Peter Sellers and

Spike Milligan, co-writing and directing some of their TV series such as 'A Show Called Fred' and 'Son Of Fred'. In 1959 he made his first film *The Running, Jumping and Standing Still Film,* with Peter Sellers and Spike Milligan. He made his first pop film *It's Trad, Dad,* in 1962, which starred Helen Shapiro, and directed a number of television commercials, including one for Smith's Crisps, which featured Pattie Boyd.

He had directed *Mouse On The Moon* for producer Walter Shenson which resulted in him being commissioned to direct the Beatles' first film. In it he helped to fashion a style using hand-held cameras. Discussing *A Hard Day's Night,* he said, 'I made it for a tiny salary. No share in the profits.' However, Walter Shenson decided to give him one half of one per cent.

Lester worked with Shenson on the Beatles' next film *Help!* although he didn't want Alun Owen to write the script for the movie. He was lined up to direct the Beatles' third film for Shenson, but it didn't happen. At one time he planned to feature them in a comedy remake of *The Three Musketeers,* but they turned the project down. He was later to make three feature films based on the Musketeer idea.

It was Lester who hired John Lennon for his solo film debut in 1966 in *How I Won The War.*

Twenty-five years after his first association with the Beatles, Lester approached Paul McCartney to say he'd like to direct a film of his 1989/90 world tour. The result was the 1991 release *Get Back: The Movie.* Lester became involved in the tour from its inception and made the eleven-minute film which began each concert, played on a giant split screen behind the stage and cataloguing, with documentary archive and McCartney's home movie footage, Paul's rock 'n' roll career from the 1960s onwards.

Lester was to say, 'Paul's audience brings a lot of romantic and nostalgic baggage with it and with the use of twenty-five years of music, including classic Beatles songs and the extraordinary newsreel footage that we were able to obtain, we tried to recreate that feeling of romantic nostalgia that hopefully makes the film work well on an emotional, as well as a musical level.'

Among Lester's other films are *The Knack ... And How To Get It, A Funny Thing Happened On The Way To The Forum, Petulia, The Bed Sitting Room, Robin And Marian, Superman II* and *Superman III.*

Let It Be (Album)

The Beatles' thirteenth album was also their last. *Let It Be* was issued in Britain on PX1 on 8 May 1970 as part of a special boxed package which also included the glossy book *The Beatles Get Back*. An album without the book was issued on PCS 7096 on 6 November 1970. When it was issued in America on AR 34001 on 18 May 1970, it had the highest advance sales on record for that time – a total of 3,700,000.

Let It Be was salvaged from an original project which was to be called 'Get Back'. An album of that name was to have been issued in August 1969, but the Beatles cancelled it. It was decided to tie in a book, film and album under the title of *Let It Be*, but the project had dragged on for a long time. The Beatles had asked Glyn Jones to edit their hours of tapes from the sessions and he did compile a 44-minute master tape, but Allen Klein decided to bring in Phil Spector. Spector's tone seemed to please John and George, but not Paul.

John Kosh designed the cover, which had a photograph of each member of the band on a black background.

The album tracks were, Side 1: 'Two Of Us', 'Across The Universe', 'I. Me. Mine', 'Dig It', 'Let It Be', 'Maggie May'. Side 2: 'I've Got A Feeling', 'One After 909', 'The Long And Winding Road', 'For You Blue' and 'Get Back'.

Let It Be (Film)

The film originally started life as a proposed television documentary on the making of an album. Paul had suggested the project, John was also keen on the idea, while Ringo was content to go along with what the others wanted, although George was reluctant right from the start. The television special was conceived to promote their new album, which was to be called *Get Back*, and would be screened at the end of the month in which the album was released. It was then decided that another half-hour documentary would be made showing how the television special had been made.

Initial plans were for the Beatles to perform three shows at the Roundhouse in January 1969 and have them edited into a one-hour TV special which would be broadcast around the world.

The Beatles were by now having great difficulty maintaining a relationship as a team and the problem of their contract with United Artists for a third feature film remained. The group had mistakenly believed that *Yellow Submarine* had completed their three-film contract with United Artist, but it hadn't and it was decided to give United Artists the footage the group had been filming at their recording sessions at Twickenham and Apple Studios.

The Beatles had hated recording at the bleak Twickenham Studios, particularly as they weren't able to film in the evenings as they'd planned, but were told they had to record from early in the morning if they were to use the studio's facilities. John Lennon was to remark, 'You couldn't make music at eight o'clock in the morning or ten or whatever it was, in a strange place with people filming you and coloured lights.' Filming began at Twickenham Studios on 2 January 1969 under the project title of 'Get Back' and lasted until 17 January. The group then left Twickenham and resumed filming at Apple Studios for the remainder of the month, culminating with the famous rooftop session on 30 January.

By the time they had completed filming in January 1969, they had almost 30 hours of music and 96 hours of film in the can, and the movie took a full year to edit. Plans to edit it down into two one-hour television documentaries to be screened on consecutive nights were dropped.

When they were discussing ideas for the documentary, director Michael Lindsay-Hogg suggested that they go and film a sequence in a Roman amphitheatre he'd seen in Tunisia. George protested, pointing out the impracticality of it, due to the difficulties they would have in transporting all the personnel and equipment to Africa, not forgetting the cost. Other locations were put forward including an ocean liner, a Liverpool Cathedral and the Houses of Parliament. John succinctly commented, 'I'm warming up to the idea of an Asylum.' The location eventually became the rooftop of Apple's Savile Row building.

George's unhappiness and frustration was all too obvious and at one point, on 10 January, he walked out of the sessions, keeping away for a few days because he felt that Paul had been treating him as an inferior. Paul had, in fact, even been talking down to John, saying, 'Now look, son', but was far more patronising in his attitude to George and at one point told him, 'I always seem to be annoying you.' When Paul began to make suggestions on how he should play, George said, 'All right, I'll play whatever you want me to play. Or I won't play at all if you don't want me to play.'

Another reason why George walked out concerned the fact that he did not want to make any further concert appearances with the Beatles, and was upset by talk of going to Africa or finding alternative venues. He was later to accept the idea of the Apple rooftop performance.

When George eventually returned he brought in Billy Preston to join them on the sessions on 22 January, hoping the presence of another musician would reduce the tension in the air.

United Artists' description of the film in their publicity releases read, 'The picture gives an intimate view of the Beatles as musical creators and performers and shows them rehearsing, reading, philosophising and relaxing. *Let It Be* is presented by Apple, an ABKCO-managed company and was produced by Neil Aspinall and directed by Michael Lindsay-Hogg.' Actually, Dennis O'Dell was also producer of the film.

The colour movie was 81 minutes in length, was given a 'U' certificate and won an Oscar in the 1970 Academy Awards for 'Best Original Song Score: Music & Lyrics by the Beatles'.

Lindsay-Hogg's style of direction was criticised and, in the case of a review by Michael Goodwin in *Rolling Stone* magazine, was literally savaged. Paul also seemed to have his own ideas on how *Let It Be* should have been filmed and was to remark, 'Get bright lights so you see everything, instead of moody lighting, that kind of thing. With everything here, it hardly needs scenery. Really, it should be about him and his drum kit, it really looks great, beautiful sitting there. Then John and his guitar and his amp, sitting there, actually showing it at that minute. The scenery would just be the other things around, like the scaffolding and other cameras.'

Lindsay-Hogg was able to present his own point of view in a *Rolling Stone* interview and regarding the rooftop session, mentioned that they'd had an idea of introducing an actor in a policeman's uniform who would come to interrupt the session and be quite rude to them. He said, 'But when we shot it honestly, and the real Bobbies arrived, it was so charming we didn't do that. They called in the Black Marias and all that, but they were quite nice. We thought it would be good to show how nice some policemen can be.'

Critic Michael Goodwin once again found it hard to credit that actors weren't used as policemen and commented: 'In the last part of the film, a sequence where the Beatles play on the rooftop of the Apple building, there are these cops who come up to investigate the noise. We first see them outside, in the street, as they walk up to the front door of the building. They open the door (this is shot from outside), and as they do so there is a cut to a reverse angle, in which we see them complete the action (opening the door) from the inside. Now this is a perfectly reasonable editing sequence for a film shot in a studio, with actors, but I find it a little hard to believe that such a perfect matching shot could have been made in a documentary situation. So the next logical question is: Were those cops or actors?'

There are 22 numbers featured in the film, most of them performed during the studio recording. The group are seen playing, talking, eating, relaxing; the various people who appear in the film include Billy Preston, Derek Taylor, Yoko Ono, Mal Evans, Michael Lindsay-Hogg, Heather McCartney and George Martin. The

Twickenham Studios setting is featured for approximately an hour's screen time and the film's most exciting moment is when the Beatles emerge on to the Apple roof, overlooking Burlington Gardens. There are edited sequences of the 40 minutes they spent there, including the entry of the police and comments from people below. One man, incapable of appreciating that fun in life needn't be restricted to outside business hours, comments: 'This kind of music is very good in its place, but it's a bit of an imposition when it disrupts all the business in the area.' The critics were generally unenthusiastic about the movie (although nowhere near as ferocious as the TV pundits who had savaged *Magical Mystery Tour*).

Nina Hibbin of the *Morning Star* wrote: 'For those who expected it to throw some light on the development of the Beatles phenomenon, it is disappointingly barren ... Paul McCartney, now very much the guiding spirit of the team, comes over as a thoroughgoing professional who, one can imagine, may switch off his Beatleself out of studio hours and change into a quite different person at home. George Harrison, with his strong-boned face and shut-in expression, looks as if he could fit into any tough and isolated position – as a shepherd in Bulgaria or the manager of a suburban sub-post office. John Lennon and Ringo Starr appear to be the true individualists, as far as the film allows us to glimpse their individuality, with Beatle eccentricities running through their veins.'

In the *Sunday Telegraph*, Tom Hutchinson wrote: 'It is only incidentally that one glimpses anything about their real characters – the way in which music now seems to be the only unifying force to hold them together: the way Paul McCartney chatters incessantly even when, it seems, none of the others is listening.'

Alexander Walker, in his *Evening Standard* column, wrote: 'Yoko passes by like Lady Macbeth sleepwalking. An aimless camera catches the others in inarticulate chitchat; like most of us who consciously fool about for home movies they are dull and unfunny.

'A flicker of interest is provided by the folk standing out in the street when their comments – generally flattering – are caught in TV-style spot interviews.

'I'm told the film was made to complete the three-picture deal with United Artists made some years ago. If so, this explains why it looks like a chore. Let it pass.'

Dick Richards of the *Daily Mirror* wrote: 'Domestic touches are added by Paul McCartney's little stepdaughter frisking around the studio and by Yoko, who sits broodingly at her husband's elbow throughout, looking like an inscrutable miniature Mother Earth.

'This seems to inhibit John Lennon more than somewhat, especially when he and Yoko perform an ungainly waltz which will win them no Astaire-Rogers medals, and it is McCartney who comes over as the dominant figure and the musical boss.'

Despite the film's various shortcomings, there was no denying the excellence of the movie's soundtrack. Fans were treated to a host of numbers, which included: 'Don't Let Me Down', 'For You Blue', 'Maxwell's Silver Hammer', 'Besame Mucho', 'Two Of Us', 'Octopus's Garden', 'I've Got A Feeling', 'You've Really Got A Hold On Me', 'Oh Darling', 'The Long And Winding Road', 'One After 909', 'Shake Rattle And Roll', 'Jazz Piano Song', 'Kansas City', 'Across The Universe', 'Lawdy Miss Clawdy', 'Dig A Pony', 'Dig It', 'Suzy Parker', 'Let It Be', 'I. Me. Mine' and 'Get Back'.

Let It Be was premiered at the London Pavilion on 20 May 1970. A number of celebrities attended the occasion, such as Jane Asher and Cynthia Lennon, though none of the Beatles turned up for the film's launch, which perhaps gave some indication of their opinion of it. George, at least, had a good excuse – he was recording his *All Things Must Pass* album that evening with Phil Spector.

John was to comment: 'It was hell making the film. When it came out a lot of people complained about Yoko looking miserable in it. But even the biggest Beatle fan couldn't have sat through those six weeks of misery. It was the most miserable session on earth.'

Lewis, Brian

A business consultant and legal adviser from Wallasey who, in 1968, at the age of 44, joined the Beatles' Apple Corps in Savile Row. He worked in the Accounts department on the third floor. Other members of the full-time staff who handled Beatles accounts included Brian Cappociama, Ronald Tolson and Allan Lewis.

After Allen Klein took over the Beatles' affairs, Lewis resigned.

Lewis, Jerry Lee

Major American rock star who was an early influence on the Quarry Men, who performed a number of his songs in their repertoire, including 'Whole Lotta Shakin' Goin' On', 'High School Confidential', 'Mean Woman Blues' and 'Fools Like Me'.

The blond-haired Louisiana-born singer/keyboards player first emerged internationally with two hits in 1957, 'Whole Lotta Shakin' Goin' On' and 'Great Balls Of Fire', followed by 'Breathless' and 'High School Confidential' in 1958.

Lewis's popularity had declined following a controversial tour in 1958 when it was revealed that his new bride, Myra, whom he brought to England with him, was only thirteen years old – and his cousin! Jerry Lee was 22 at the time.

As one of the original rock 'n' roll idols, Lewis was very popular on Merseyside and on Thursday, 17 May 1962, Bob Wooler presented him at the Tower Ballroom, New Brighton, where he topped the bill with ten local bands in support: the Big Three; the Pressmen; the Undertakers; the Strangers; Vince Earl & the Zeros; Billy Kramer with the Coasters; Lee Castle & the Barons; Kingsize Taylor & the Dominoes; Steve Day & the Drifters; and Rip Van Winkle & the Rip It Ups.

Lewis returned to England in 1963 when he'd been booked for a tour of Europe which included appearances at the Star Club, Hamburg and the Olympia, Paris. He was also to appear for a week in Scotland. Promoter Don Arden contacted Brian Epstein to suggest that the Beatles appear on the tour, but Brian said that apart from the fact that they were already booked for a tour supporting Roy Orbison at the same time, their days as a supporting band were over and they would be headlining their own tours in the future.

Almost a year later, when the Beatles were beginning to receive publicity in America, Jerry Lee was asked to comment on the group. Among the things he said were: 'These Beatles lack just one thing. Talent. I hate to say this, but I ain't afraid to say it. They're a great bunch of boys but they're just doing what Elvis started back in '56 ... they've done well in the States because there've been no big rock 'n' roll groups in America for five years ... the Beatles are limited.'

But the Beatles were responsible for a revival of interest in rock 'n' roll and, because they mentioned their influences in interviews, lots of the rock 'n' roll stars such has Jerry Lee found that they were back in favour with the public again, which was probably why Jerry Lee changed his tune. In the June 1964 issue of *Beatles Monthly*, there was a full-page feature on Lewis entitled 'Thank You Beatles' in which he praised them for reviving his career.

He said: 'I'd heard of the Beatles way back before they hit the big time – heard about them from friends who'd played in Germany. Reports were great and I felt real flattered when they mentioned me to those friends, or even told reporters about how they'd liked my original work.' He also added: 'I kinda feel an affinity with the boys. It's all too easy to drop your own principles if it means you're gonna earn more loot. But the fact that they kept on and on now means that there's a whole lotta interest in Beat music, played by white performers – and it stretches right around the world.'

Jerry Lee Lewis was invited to appear on the 'Around The Beatles' TV special, but had to turn it down because of prior commitments.

In 1988 a feature film biopic was made called *Great Balls Of Fire*, with actor Dennis Quaid portraying Lewis.

Lewis's, Ranelagh Street, Liverpool L1

Huge department store, situated in the centre of Liverpool. The corner entrance doors opposite the Adelphi Hotel were a favourite rendezvous for couples. This is where John would often arrange to meet Cynthia during the early days of their romance.

Rearing high above the doors was a controversial statue of a well-endowed naked man, by the eminent sculptor Jacob Epstein. Adding to Cynthia's embarrassment at having to stand beneath such a sculpture was the fact that, to please John, she used to dress quite sexily, often wearing short, tight skirts, fishnet stockings and high-heeled shoes. The Beatles also performed at a special event on the top floor of the store on 28 November 1962. The occasion was a staff dance for the 527 Club called 'Young Idea Dance'.

Peter Brown, who was later to become Brian Epstein's assistant, was also manager of Lewis's record department.

Lewis, Vic

Former jazz musician and bandleader who became a major agent. Lewis was born in Brent, London, on 19 July 1919. After many years running his own band he formed a show business agency. With the success of the Beatles in Britain, Lewis contacted Norman Weiss of America's GAC and suggested he see the Beatles with a view to booking them in America. As GAC represented Trini Lopez, who was on the bill with the Beatles at the Olympia, Paris, Weiss saw them ahead of any other American agent and was able to make a deal.

Lewis didn't receive any commission from the contact, but he was repaid in kind in 1965 when Weiss suggested to Brian Epstein that he buy Lewis's agency and appoint him to the board of NEMS Enterprises. Epstein bought the Vic Lewis Organisation and made Lewis a director of his management/agency/show business company.

After Brian Epstein's death, Clive and Queenie Epstein asked Lewis to become Managing Director of NEMS. He was also approached by Robert Stigwood who wanted to place him in charge of the Stigwood Agency. Lewis decided to stay with NEMS, although he later declared that it was a mistake on his part. On 23 October 1969 he issued an orchestral album of covers of Beatles songs called *Beatles My Way* on the NEMS record label. NEMS was sold to Triumph Investments and Lewis remained. He also stayed for a while when the company was bought by an organisation called Worldwide, but eventually quit in 1977.

In 1987 his biography *Music & Maiden Overs* (Chatto and Windus) was published, which Lewis had written in collaboration with former Beatles Press Officer Tony Barrow.

Leyton Baths, 819–847 High Road, Leyton, London E10

An indoor swimming pool in London, originally designed by the Leyton Borough engineer and surveyor A. P. Howell and opened in 1934. It had been converted to a dance hall and featured top groups live each Friday evening. The Beatles appeared here on Friday, 5 April 1963 after a presentation ceremony at EMI Records where they had been presented with their first-ever silver disc for the 'Please Please Me' single. They had also given a short performance for EMI executives.

At Leyton Baths they were on a bill with Peter Jay & the Jaywalkers and performed their forthcoming single 'From Me To You' and most of the songs contained on their *Please Please Me* album, to a capacity audience. They wore maroon mohair suits with velvet collars.

Disc jockey Norman Scott was working at the venue that night and offered to buy them some drinks backstage after the show. He asked if he could take a photograph of the band and began to count from one to three. John shouted out 'Three!' so loudly that he startled the other Beatles, and Paul, who'd been holding a tube of toothpaste, squeezed it so hard that a length of paste squirted down his trouser leg!

Peter Jay & the Jaywalkers were to join the Beatles tour later that year, from 1 November to 13 December – and it was rumoured that a tape recording was made of the two bands having a jam session together. The group made several singles but didn't achieve major success.

Like Dreamers Do

A Paul McCartney composition which the Beatles included amongst the thirteen numbers at their Decca recording audition. The song was later recorded by the Applejacks who reached No. 7 in the British charts with the number.

It was one of Paul's early compositions and was included in the repertoire of the Quarry Men and was part of the Beatles' stage act until late in 1962.

Lindsay-Hogg, Michael

Michael Lindsay-Hogg was director of the celebrated weekly television show 'Ready, Steady, Go!', on which the Beatles appeared several times.

His closer association with the Beatles began when he was engaged to direct some of their promotional films, beginning with *Paperback Writer* and *Rain,* filmed at EMI's Abbey Road Studios and on location at Chiswick House on Thursday and Friday, 19 and 20 May 1966. Lindsay-Hogg was also to direct Wings' *London Town* promo in 1978. He also directed *The Rolling Stones Rock 'n' Roll Circus* in 1968, which featured John and Yoko, and which was eventually released on video thirty years later.

Lindsay-Hogg was hired to direct the promos for *Hey Jude* and *Revolution* at Twickenham Studios on Wednesday, 4 September 1968.

The Beatles then hired him as director of their *Get Back* project, a proposed television special on the making of their new album, meant to be called *Get Back*. He began filming the project on Thursday, 2 January 1969 at Twickenham Studios and the documentary eventually evolved into the film *Let It Be*.

A review by Michael Goodwin in *Rolling Stone* magazine savagely criticised his direction of the film. It said that with a good director the audience can sit back and relax, knowing that everything was under control. However, 'Here, you are constantly busy doing work that Lindsay-Hogg should have done, but didn't; cutting the bad stuff, rearranging the good stuff, placing the camera properly – really basic directorial responsibilities.'

Lindsay-Hogg was given an opportunity to speak in his own defence in a *Rolling Stone* interview in which he commented: 'It's lucky there is a movie. There was a big push all the time to get them going. Even though half of them were always behind it, the trouble was it was never the same half.

'It was a terribly painful, frustrating experience. It's not that I don't like them – I do. It's just that when we were trying to make the film, every day there was a different one to hate.'

Lindsay-Hogg was later to direct the acclaimed television series 'Brideshead Revisited'.

In October 1999 he directed *Two Of Us*, a TV movie featuring Aidan Quinn as Paul McCartney and Jared Harris as John Lennon in a film about a fictional meeting between the two of them in New York in 1976.

Lister, Monty

Wirral disc jockey who broadcast two regular shows, 'Music With Monty' and 'Sunday Spin', for the patients of Cleaver and Clatterbridge hospitals on the Wirral, over the River Mersey from Liverpool.

Monty attended the Beatles' gig at Hulme Hall, Port Sunlight, on 27 October 1962 and was able to record an interview with the

Beatles. He'd brought along two friends, Malcolm Threadgill and Peter Smethurst, to help him out on the questioning, and the interview was broadcast to the two hospitals the following day.

During the seven-minute interview the Beatles mentioned their trips to Hamburg, their Polydor recording with Tony Sheridan, 'Love Me Do' and their forthcoming single. Ringo commented on being the newcomer and Paul said, 'John Lennon is the leader of the group.'

The interview, the Beatles' first-ever actual radio interview, was included as a free disc in Mark Lewisohn's book *The Beatles Live!* in 1986.

Litherland Town Hall, Hatton Hill Road, Litherland, Liverpool L21

This was one of the venues used by local promoter Brian Kelly, who booked the Beatles for their debut appearance there on Tuesday, 27 December 1960. All their other appearances took place in 1961: 5 and 26 January; 2, 14, 16, 21 and 28 February; 2 March; 24 and 31 July; 7 August; 7, 14, 21 and 28 September; 19 and 31 October; and 9 November.

Bob Wooler was the man who talked Kelly into booking the group, at a fee of six pounds. As it was a late booking, their names didn't appear in the local newspaper advertisements, which had already been placed, announcing the Searchers, the Del Renas and the Deltones. Entrance to the gig was three shillings (fifteen pence). Kelly managed to place their name on some posters with the tag: 'Direct from Hamburg, the Beatles!' As they weren't all that well known in Liverpool at the time, this led to a number of members of the audience believing that they were a German group. Their lineup that night was John, Paul, George, Pete and Chas Newby.

The Beatles had already contacted Newby in October with the offer to join them in the place of Stuart Sutcliffe, but he'd turned them down. He agreed to appear with them for a few dates in Liverpool, beginning with their first gig at the Casbah Club.

The Searchers were to become a major recording group and John McNally was to comment: 'That was the first time I heard a drummer playing fours on a bass drum. It was a wall of sound and these were the days before you had your big PAs. They did rock 'n' roll stuff just like the Americans, but with more rawness to it and in a Liverpool accent. There was no way we could follow them with our tinny sound.'

Pete Best's brother Rory was also in the audience, along with accountancy student Neil Aspinall, a lodger at the Bests.

This was one of the most important events in the Beatles' early career as it was the gig that transformed their fortunes locally. They had been virtually unknown in Liverpool prior to their trip to Hamburg, but were such a dynamic outfit on their return that they stunned everyone with their performance. Faron, leader of local group Faron's Flamingos, was transfixed and remembers every incident of that night, down to the fact that George Harrison was wearing cowboy boots with a star on them. Also in the audience were Rory Storm, Johnny Guitar and Ringo Starr of the Hurricanes, who had returned from Hamburg the day previously.

Brian Kelly, impressed by the immense excitement the Beatles had generated, immediately booked them for a string of dates at all his main venues, and Bob Wooler was later to devote an entire page of *Mersey Beat* to them, extolling their performance that night.

In the article, the only Beatle he mentioned by name was Pete Best: 'Musically authoritative and physically magnetic, example the mean, moody, magnificence of drummer Pete Best – a sort of teenage Jeff Chandler.' This was because, strangely enough, Best had become the most popular Beatle with Liverpool audiences. So much so, in fact, that for their Valentine's night appearance at Litherland on Tuesday, 14 February 1961, Wooler talked the other members into the unusual step of placing Pete Best and his drums to the forefront of the band. This stratagem didn't work as the fans immediately surged forth and dragged Pete from the stage!

For the Monday, 7 August gig, the Litherland Town Hall classified advertisement in the *Liverpool Echo* carried the message: 'Hear Pete Best Sing Tonight.' Pete Best had been talked into performing the song 'Pinwheel Twist', while Paul took over on drums.

The Monday, 21 September appearance saw them share a bill with Gerry & the Pacemakers and Rory Storm & the Hurricanes.

On Thursday, 19 October, the Beatles and Gerry & the Pacemakers combined to make a single appearance as the Beatmakers. Gerry Marsden wore George Harrison's leather outfit and George, who played lead, wore a hood. Paul played bass and wore a nightie and Freddie Marsden and Pete Best played one drum each. It was so much fun that Karl Terry, leader of Karl Terry & the Cruisers, who were also on the bill that night, joined them on stage to sing. The numbers performed by the Beatmakers that evening were: 'Whole Lotta Shakin'', 'What'd I Say', 'Red Sails' and 'Hit The Road, Jack'.

Interestingly enough, their final appearance at the venue was on Thursday, 9 November – earlier that day Brian Epstein had visited a Cavern lunchtime session to see the Beatles for the first time.

Little Child

Recorded over two sessions in September 1963 for the *With The Beatles* album, this track, composed by John Lennon, with a little help from Paul, was one of the songs on which John played harmonica. It was also included on the American *Meet The Beatles* album.

Little Queenie

A Chuck Berry composition which Berry recorded in 1959. The Beatles included it in their repertoire in 1960, with Paul on lead vocals. They performed the number at Hamburg's Star Club and it is to be found on the various pressings of the Star Club recordings.

Little Richard

One of the classic rock 'n' roll stars, born Richard Penniman in Macon, Georgia, in 1932.

Paul McCartney was a Richard fan and performed hits in the Quarry Men days. In fact, Paul was the Beatles Little Richard specialist and the numbers he performed which had been recorded by the star included 'Long Tall Sally', 'Lucille', 'Ooh! My Soul', 'Tutti Frutti', 'Good Golly, Miss Molly' and 'Kansas City/Hey Hey Hey'.

The Beatles finally met their idol when they appeared with him at the Star Club for a brief season in April/May 1962, during which they became friends, with Richard giving Paul tips on how to perform his numbers and George making the acquaintance of Richard's keyboards player, Billy Preston.

Brian Epstein booked Little Richard for a NEMS Enterprises presentation, *Little Richard At The Tower*. This was for a spectacular show at the Tower Ballroom, New Brighton, on 12 October 1962. It was a five-and-a-half-hour show, with entrance costing only ten shillings and sixpence (52.5p) with a support bill comprising the Beatles, Billy Kramer with the Coasters, the Dakotas with Pete MacLaine, the Four Jays, Lee Curtis & the All Stars, the Merseybeats, Rory Storm & the Hurricanes and the Undertakers. Little Richard also appeared at the Cavern that day when the Beatles appeared at a lunchtime session. Backstage at the Tower, Bill Harry had commissioned photographer Les Chadwick to cover the event on behalf of *Mersey Beat* and arranged a photograph of Richard and the Beatles together.

In an interview for *Mersey Beat* at the time, Little Richard said, 'Man, those Beatles are fabulous. If I hadn't seen them I'd never have dreamed they were white. They have a real authentic Negro sound.'

Epstein also booked Little Richard to top the bill at Liverpool's Empire Theatre later that month on 28 October. He tried to include Sam Cooke on the programme, but the singer was unavailable, so Craig Douglas was second on the bill and during his spot he was backed by the Beatles. Jet Harris, Kenny Lynch and Sounds Incorporated were also on the bill and the Beatles had their own spot.

In the book *The Life And Times Of Little Richard* (Charles Wood, Harmony Books, 1984), Richard claims that after the Beatles came off stage at the Empire, Brian Epstein approached him and said, 'Richard, I'll give you fifty per cent of the Beatles.' Richard commented, 'I couldn't accept 'cos I never thought they would make it.'

Richard also said that he developed a close relationship with Paul, 'but me and John couldn't make it. John had a nasty personality.' With Paul the obvious Richard enthusiast, the two were bound to get on together and Richard said, 'Paul is like my blood brother. I believe if I was hungry, Paul would feed me. We're that tight. Paul is a humanitarian.'

When Apple Records was launched and George Harrison began producing other acts, he said, 'Little Richard, that's who I'd love to record. He's a fantastic character with a fantastic voice – and whether he's singing rock or gospel, he's still great.'

Little Theatre, The, Houghton Street, Southport, Lancashire

The Beatles made a special appearance at this small theatre on the morning of 27 August 1963. They gave a private live performance before an invited audience which was filmed for the BBC documentary 'The Mersey Sound'.

Live At The BBC

Between 1962 and 1965 the Beatles recorded 58 radio shows for the BBC. A selection of the 300 tracks recorded almost thirty years earlier became the first new Beatles LP for seventeen years when it was issued as a double CD in Britain on Apple 7243 8 31796 2 6 on Wednesday, 30 November 1994. It was issued in the US on Capitol C2-31796 on Tuesday, 6 December 1994. The cover featured a Dezo Hoffmann photograph, taken on 4 April 1963, of the Beatles walking by the BBC's Paris Theatre in Lower Regent Street, London. The package also contained a 48-page booklet with notes by Derek Taylor and Kevin Howlett. A US advance double cassette was issued on Capitol C4-31796 on 14 November 1994.

The CD entered the *Billboard* chart in America at No. 3
The press release noted:

The album, compiled by George Martin with the co-operation
and agreement of Apple and the BBC, brings together for the
first time as an authorised release, 56 songs recorded by the
Beatles for broadcast by the BBC in the early sixties. Of the 56
songs, 41 were either written, performed and/or produced by
American rock 'n' roll icons including Chuck Berry, Carl
Perkins, Little Richard, Elvis Presley, Smokey Robinson,
Buddy Holly, Ray Charles, and many others.
    In fact, 30 of the songs were never studio recorded by the
Beatles and the vast majority were their favourite rock 'n' roll
classics which had been in the Beatles' stage repertoire from
their earliest days in both Liverpool and Hamburg.
    In addition to the music, the album includes dialogue
between the Beatles and BBC disc jockeys Brian Matthew and
Alan Freeman and the packaging contains extensive information about the recordings, a background on the Beatles and
the BBC and many rare photographs taken during the various
sessions.

The first CD contained: 'From Us To You', 'I Got A Woman',
'Too Much Monkey Business', 'Keep Your Hands Off My Baby',
'I'll Be On My Way', 'Young Blood', 'A Shot Of Rhythm & Blues',
'Sure To Fall (In Love With You)', 'Some Other Guy', 'Thank You
Girl', 'Baby It's You', 'That's All Right (Mama)', 'Carol', 'Soldier
Of Love', 'Clarabella', 'I'm Gonna Sit Right Down And Cry (Over
You)', 'Crying, Waiting, Hoping', 'You Really Got A Hold On Me',
'To Know Her Is To Love Her', 'A Taste Of Honey', 'Long Tall
Sally', 'I Saw Her Standing There', 'The Honeymoon Song',
'Johnny B Goode', 'Memphis, Tennessee', 'Lucille', 'Can't Buy Me
Love' and 'Till There Was You'.
    CD 2 contained: 'A Hard Day's Night', 'I Wanna Be Your Man',
'Roll Over Beethoven', 'All My Loving', 'Things We Said Today',
'She's A Woman', 'Sweet Little Sixteen', 'Lonesome Tears In My
Eyes', 'Nothin' Shakin' (But The Leaves On The Trees)', 'The
Hippy Hippy Shake', 'Glad All Over', 'I Just Don't Understand', 'So
How Come (No One Loves Me)', 'I Feel Fine', 'I'm A Loser',
'Everybody's Trying To Be My Baby', 'Rock And Roll Music',
'Ticket To Ride', 'Dizzy Miss Lizzy', 'Kansas City/Hey Hey Hey',
'Matchbox', 'I Forgot To Remember To Forget', 'I Got To Find My
Baby', 'Ooh! My Soul', 'Don't Ever Change', 'Slow Down', 'Honey
Don't' and 'Love Me Do'.

It leapt straight to No. 1 in *Music Week* chart on 10 December 1994.

Liverpool

The city was founded by King John in 1207 when he discovered that the Mersey estuary was a suitable base for him to send his armies across to Ireland. A castle was built and a town began to grow around it. In the seventeenth century a Liver Bird was chosen to adorn the seal of the town.

Liverpool began its rise as one of the most important seaports in the world in 1760 when 69 Liverpool ships established a trade triangle trip to Africa. The slave trade ceased in 1807, but the city remained a major port, although its influence began to wane with the building of the Manchester Ship Canal. This venture instigated by businessmen resulted in Manchester becoming the business centre of the North of England and Liverpool's influence slowly vanished.

Its prominence as a seaport had resulted in a cosmopolitan population, a large percentage of which came from Ireland, resulting in the city often being referred to as 'the capital of Ireland'. There were also a large number of Welsh immigrants and in addition, Liverpool accommodated one of the largest Chinese communities in Europe, over 8,000 gathering in the Chinatown area near the city centre. Ironically, the great houses built in what is now the Liverpool 8 area on the profits of the slave trade became the homes of the black community in a Liverpool harlem.

Stuck on the north-west coast of England, Liverpool was isolated from the main events. Manchester became the northern home of the media, housing the television and radio stations and the northern offices of the national press. News from the north generally emanated from Manchester and little was heard of the events on Merseyside.

Liverpudlians were called 'Scousers' (a name derived from a stew for seamen called lob scouse), had adenoidal accents, a self-deprecating wit and were noted for their comedians and football teams. If asked why so many comedians came from Liverpool, a scouser would reply, 'Because you have to be a comedian to live here', referring to the poverty, slums and general lack of work in the area. Liverpool comedians included Arthur Askey, Tommy Handley, Ted Ray, Norman Vaughan and Ken Dodd. Other entertainers who had risen to national prominence via the local clubland scene included Frankie Vaughan, Lita Roza, Michael Holliday and Billy Fury.

The music scene which grew and developed on Merseyside in the fifties was unique, although the skiffle boom which spawned it wasn't. In fact, the skiffle boom was a national phenomenon in Britain in 1956 following the success of Lonnie Donegan with 'Rock Island Line'. Skiffle groups sprang up throughout the country, but died away a few years later when the bubble burst. In Liverpool, however, the skiffle groups turned to rock 'n' roll and a number of circumstances resulted in an amazing scene in which music began to dominate the city, with literally hundreds of groups performing in clubs, cellars, private houses, ice rinks, synagogues, youth clubs, church halls, swimming baths, town halls, seaside piers, coffee bars, ballrooms, ferry boats, cinemas, social clubs, colleges, department stores and pubs. Among the skiffle groups who became rock 'n' roll bands were the James Boys (formed in 1956, later to develop into Kingsize Taylor & the Dominoes), the Ralph Ellis Skiffle Group (formed in 1957 and later to develop into the Swinging Bluejeans), the Raving Texans (formed in January 1957 and later to develop into Rory Storm & the Hurricanes), the Eddie Clayton Skiffle Group (formed in early 1957 with Richard Starkey on drums) and the Quarry Men, who were to become the Beatles. At the same time, there were groups who had been inspired directly by rock 'n' roll, such as the Bobby Bell Rockers, who formed in October 1956, probably Liverpool's first real rock 'n' roll band.

A number of independent promoters began running weekly dances at local venues which featured several groups per night. This resulted in a large range of venues across the Merseyside area which provided hundreds of local groups with regular work. The promoters included Brian Kelly, Charlie McBain, Les Dodd, Albert Kinder, Dave Forshaw, Mona Best, Doug Martin, Sam Leach, Wally Hill and Vic Anton. The venues were often called 'jive hives' and the music and promotions were referred to as either 'twist' or 'jive', and it is at such dances, in the local church and town halls, that the Liverpool music scene was nurtured and grew. In addition, there were regular venues such as the Mardi Gras (run by Jim Ireland) and various ballrooms including the Locarno, Grafton, Plaza and La Scala.

When the *Mersey Beat* newspaper was launched in July 1961, everyone was amazed to discover that there was so much activity on Merseyside. The coverage of the music scene had been virtually non-existent and the new publication revealed just how extensive the local scene was. An entertainments guide (later lampooned by John Lennon) provided details of jazz clubs, coffee clubs, cabaret shows and jive halls. Among the jive halls listed were: Alexandra Hall; Aintree Institute; Blair Hall; Bootle Town Hall; Civic Hall, Ellesmere Port; David Lewis Theatre; Empress Club; the Grosvenor; Hambleton Hall; La Mystere, Maghull; Litherland Town Hall; La

Scala, Runcorn; Lathom Hall; Mossway Hall; Merrifield Old Swan; Orrell Park Ballroom; Quaintways, Chester; St John's Hall, Tuebrook; St Luke's Hall, Crosby; Town Hall, Skelmersdale; Wavertree Town Hall and Wilson Hall, Garston. There were many more. The name Mersey Beat had been devised by Bill Harry to describe an area rather than the beat of the music and the area covered included the whole of Merseyside, with Liverpool, Widnes, Warrington, St Helens, Skelmersdale, Crosby, Formby, Southport, the Wirral, Birkenhead, New Brighton, Chester and Ellesmere Port. Within the Merseyside conurbation at that time resided what was probably the greatest concentration of rock 'n' roll groups in the world, considerably more than 350 of them within that compact area. Bob Wooler and Bill Harry published a list of almost 300 groups in the 19 October 1961 issue of *Mersey Beat* and the humour and variety of the names was intriguing. They included Ahab & his Lot, Al Quentin & the Rock Pounders, Bennie & the Jumpin' Beans, Bruce & the Spiders, Dave & the Devil Horde, Eddie & the Phantoms, Foo Foo's Flashy Falcons, Hank's Hoppers, Johnny Apollo & the Spartans, Gerry Bach & the Beethovens, Vince Earl & the Zeros, Eddie Falcon & the Vampires, the G Men, the FBI, Ogi & the Flintstones, Pete Picasso & the Rock Sculptors, Johnny President & the Senators, Rikki & the Red Streaks, Rip Van Winkle & the Rip It Ups, Ray Satan & the Devils and Wump & his Werbles.

When the Beatles began to achieve success and the British media focused its attention on the Liverpool groups, they described the sound as 'Mersey Beat', taking the name from the newspaper and referring to a particular style, which also became known as the 'Liverpool Sound'. It referred to the Liverpool groups who were suddenly appearing in the charts – the Beatles, the Searchers, Gerry & the Pacemakers and the Swinging Bluejeans, who all had the four-man line-up of lead, rhythm and bass guitars, plus drums. However, the versatility and variety of the Mersey bands was far more extensive. There were line-ups featuring brass instruments, there were septets, quintets, trios and duos. There were also a large number of female artists who included all-girl rock bands such as the Liver Birds, the Blue Notes, the Demoiselles, the Fast Cats, the Rontons, the Three Bells, the Kandies and vocal groups such as the Vernons Girls, Collage, the Charmers and the Mystics. There were also many groups with female singers – Jenny & the Tall Boys, Three Hits & a Miss, Irene & the Santa Fe's, the Galaxies with Doreen, Joan and the Demons, Carol & the Corvettes, Vikki Lane & the Moonlighters and Tiffany's Dimensions. There were also a number of female solo vocalists – Beryl Marsden, Cilla Black, Barbara Harrison, Irene Carroll, Lorraine White, Rita Hughes, Rita

Rodgers, Barbara Grounds, Karina, Barbara Dee, Christine Ching, Vickie Cheetham and Jacki Martin.

In the Liverpool 8 district there were a number of black vocal harmony groups, influenced by Tamla Motown and including the Chants, the Sobells, the Challengers and the Poppies. There was also a thriving folk music scene in Liverpool, due to its heritage as a seaport, and folk music was performed mainly in pubs. The most popular Liverpool folk artists were the Spinners, originally the Gin Mill Skiffle Group, and they were to become Britain's most popular folk group over a period of more than 25 years until they disbanded in the late eighties.

Growing alongside the rock 'n' roll scene, which was to become known as the Beat scene, was a healthy Country Music scene. There were over 40 Country bands playing at their own clubs such as the Black Cat Club and Wells Fargo and at many local clubs and factories. They even formed a Country Music Association and held a Grand Ole Opry annually at the Philharmonic Hall. They included the Hillsiders, Hank Walters & his Dusty Road Ramblers, the Boot Hill Billys, Phil Brady & his Ranchers, the Blue Mountain Boys, the Missouri Drifters, the Nashpool Four, the Country Four, Johnny Gold & the Country Cousins, the Miller Boys and the Foggy Mountain Ramblers.

A number of Country groups and rock bands also appeared on another thriving local entertainments scene – Clubland. There were over 330 clubs affiliated to the Merseyside Clubs Association. These social clubs were run by unions, local stores and factories. An example would be the Speke Bus Depot Social Club where George Harrison's father Harry was chairman. It was because of these clubs that Liverpool was able to develop so many comedians, and ones who grew popular during the Beatles' rise to fame in the early sixties included Ken Dodd, Jimmy Tarbuck, Johnny Hackett and Ray Fell.

Also active in Liverpool was a thriving poetry scene with Streates coffee bar in Mount Pleasant as the main venue for regular appearances by the local poets. Bill Harry also organised the North's very first Poetry-To-Jazz concert at the Crane Theatre. The Mersey poets who achieved national fame included Roger McGough, Brian Patten and Adrian Henri. At the same time, a number of writers were developing locally, including playwrights Willy Russell and Alan Bleasdale and horror specialists Clive Barker and Ramsey Campbell.

Such was the highly exciting and creative scene in which the Beatles developed. Competition between bands was strong, but amicable. Many Beatles scribes who were unaware of what really happened on the Mersey scene, have written that as soon as the

Beatles achieved fame, everyone in Liverpool took up a guitar; the opposite was true, the scene was incredibly active long before the Beatles ever made a record.

The dimension of the Hamburg scene was added to the equation, with Liverpool groups gaining experience playing long hours at a stretch. However, with so many venues on Merseyside, groups such as the Beatles would be working three or four nights a week, often appearing at two and sometimes three different venues in a night – and also appearing at lunchtime sessions at places such as the Cavern. There was also a further area dominated by Liverpool bands, as from May 1962 – American bases in France, where the groups also played for long hours and developed their musical skills further.

By 1961 with so many venues, larger local promotions, the establishment of the *Mersey Beat* paper, the popularity of the Cavern (which had now turned exclusively to beat groups) and the interest taken in the Beatles by Brian Epstein, the Liverpool scene was ready to explode nationally.

Another apocryphal story is that groups derived their repertoires from American records brought back by seamen. Beatles scribes who talk of 'Cunard Yanks' are perpetuating a falsity. When *Mersey Beat* featured a story 'Why Liverpool?' in which various members of the local scene gave their versions of why the scene happened locally, a member of a country music band mentioned that his repertoire was made up of songs brought back from America by seamen. While this may have been the case with a handful of country bands, it was not the case with the beat groups – as Paul McCartney has confirmed. The records by Little Richard, Buddy Holly, Carl Perkins, Elvis Presley, Chuck Berry, Gene Vincent, Jerry Lee Lewis and Eddie Cochran, which made up the backbone of local repertoires, were easily available. So were the Tamla Motown records at the onset of the sixties. Groups were able to listen to Radio Luxembourg and bands would raid the record bins at local stores to find lesser known rock records which they could include in their act – numbers by the Coasters and Ray Charles, songs such as 'The Hippy Hippy Shake' and 'Some Other Guy'. A study of the Beatles' repertoire prior to 1961 would find that the numbers by other artists which they performed were readily available on record in Britain – and not a single one obtained from a 'Cunard Yank'. Most Liverpool bands will confirm that the 'Cunard Yank' aspect is nonsense.

The Beatles' sense of humour which so endeared the media at press conferences was typical of the scouse wit; a prime example occurred when the Beatles held their first recordings with George Martin and he asked them if there was anything they didn't like.

'Well, I don't like your tie for a start,' said George Harrison. Alun Owen was able to capture this local humour effectively in the script of *A Hard Day's Night*. The Beatles also popularised a number of Liverpudlian phrases such as 'Fab', 'Wack' and 'Gear'.

Following the initial success of the Beatles, other Liverpool acts who reached the charts during the sixties included Gerry & the Pacemakers, Billy J. Kramer, Cilla Black, the Big Three, the Cryin' Shames, the Dennisons, the Escorts, the Fourmost, David Garrick, the Long & the Short, the Merseybeats, the Mojos, Tommy Quickly, the Scaffold, the Searchers, the Swinging Bluejeans, the Undertakers and Whistling Jack Smith.

The success of the Beatles also resulted in the huge beat boom in Britain and the British invasion of America. The British scene, controlled from London, later returned to its policy of running everything from London, which meant that bands had to travel to the capital as A&R men ceased talent-spotting in the provinces. The moguls also considered that Liverpool had been over-exposed and weren't really interested in discovering further new bands from the 'Pool. However, Liverpool continued to be a breeding ground for talent, always able to produce hit bands if the A&R people took the trouble to seek them out.

In 1976 there was talk of another Mersey Beat boom when Liverpool Express, the Real Thing, Our Kid and Supercharge entered the Top Twenty – then the Sex Pistols hit the scene and the entire media became dominated by the Punk Rock explosion. Liverpool continued to produce talent with groups such as Orchestral Manoeuvres in the Dark, Echo and the Bunnymen, Teardrop Explodes and Wah! and, amazingly, in the British charts of 28 January 1984 there were more Mersey acts in the Top Twenty than at any time since the original Mersey wave in 1963. The positions were:

1. 'Relax', Frankie Goes To Hollywood
2. 'Pipes Of Peace', Paul McCartney
3. 'That's Living Alright', Joe Fagin
6. 'Nobody Told Me', John Lennon
9. 'Wishful Thinking', China Crisis
17. 'The Killing Moon', Echo and the Bunnymen
19. 'Love Is A Wonderful Colour', Icicle Works

Liverpool College Of Art, Hope Street, Liverpool L1

At the age of seventeen, John Lennon visited the college principal Mr Stevenson in June 1957 for an interview. William Pobjoy, headmaster of Quarry Bank School, had set up the interview. John was accepted and began his first term at the college in September of that year.

The college itself was part of the same building as the Liverpool Institute where, coincidentally, John's fellow Quarry Men members Paul McCartney and George Harrison were pupils. They were able to get together for rehearsals at lunchtime in the college's 'life rooms' on the top floor of the building.

John soon made friends with a couple of boys in his class, Geoff Mohammed and Tony Carrick. He also went out with a couple of girls, including Thelma Pickles and Helen Anderson.

As with all new students, he was entered for the Intermediate Course. One of the classes was to study 'Lettering' and he shared the lessons with Jonathan Hague, Cynthia Powell and Phyllis Mackenzie.

He also got to know Bill Harry, a student who had started an art college jazz magazine and was in charge of the college film society. Harry also encouraged the talents of other students. While at college he was selling his cartoons, using the pseudonym 'Kim' to professional publications such as *Time and Tide* magazine and the *Liverpool Echo*. He helped other students such as Mike Isaacson and Tony Ross to sell their cartoons to professional publications, too. Harry also co-edited Liverpool University's annual *Pantosphinx* magazine and contributed covers and poetry to the university monthly magazine *Sphinx*, in addition to helping to produce a music magazine for the local music store, Frank Hessy's. He became a close friend of Stuart Sutcliffe and, together with another student, Rod Murray, they became friends with John and used to meet frequently in the evening in local pubs and flats.

Both Bill and Stuart were members of the Students' Union Committee who ran the art college Saturday night dances and they booked John's group as a support at virtually all of the dances. Bill and Stuart proposed that the union buy PA equipment which the group could use.

John and Cynthia became lovers and eventually married. Stuart became a Beatle and Bill launched the *Mersey Beat* newspaper.

During his time at the college, John gained a reputation for causing trouble, although one of the tutors, Arthur Ballard, attempted to gain him a place in the new Graphic Design Department, without success.

John never returned to the college after the Silver Beatles toured Scotland with Johnny Gentle.

During the eighties the art college premises were changed to the Liverpool Polytechnic, Faculty of Art and Design.

Liverpool Echo, The

Merseyside's largest evening newspaper. Despite its dominance as the major Liverpool paper, the *Echo* didn't begin any extensive coverage of the Beatles until 1963.

Readers could only discover what was happening on the local rock 'n' roll scene in its pages by turning to the classified advertisements column, where local promoters advertised their gigs. These entries were placed under the heading 'Jazz', and despite pressure from the advertisers to have the heading changed to something more appropriate, the *Echo* refused to change it. Among their main rock 'n' roll advertisers were Ray McFall of the Cavern and Sam Leach, although Bob Wooler composed most of the advertisements for the local promoters in his own inimitable style. A typical example of one of Bob's classified advertisements would be:

Bob Wooler's Married!!
Yes cats Mr 'Big Beat' Bob
Wooler has been married to
the best rock sessions in
Liverpool. See him only on
Monday at
HAMBLETON HALL
Page Moss – Huyton
3 HOURS NON STOP ROCK
BEATLES
and the Ravin' Ravens
On Friday and Saturday at
AINTREE INSTITUTE
And every lunch time session
EXCLUSIVELY
AT THE CAVERN
Take Mr Big Beat's advice and go
to only the best in ROCK!

The record review column in the *Echo* was credited to 'Disker', although it was written, at the time, by Liverpudlian Tony Barrow who was then working in the press office at Decca Records in London. Brian Epstein wrote to 'Disker' to request mention of the Beatles in his column and received a letter from Barrow explaining that he could only publicise groups who actually had a recording contract. Barrow was to help Epstein obtain a Decca recording audition, was then able to mention the group in his column and later became the Beatles' Press Officer.

Brian also attempted to gain publicity for the Beatles in the *Echo* by writing to George Harrison, who penned the popular column 'Over The Mersey Wall'. The veteran Harrison, a former Fleet Street journalist, was not interested in writing about an unknown local group and rejected Epstein's plea. However, once the Beatles began to find success in the charts, Harrison became their main *Echo* contact and even travelled with the Beatles on the 1964 American tour.

The *Echo's* coverage then became extensive and they published several pop 'specials', including *Around The World With The Beatles*, which was a souvenir magazine they produced at Christmas 1964. Priced at two shillings (ten pence), the 32-page publication included four colour photographs, stories of the group's trips abroad and a large selection of early black and white photographs. On the death of John Lennon, they were to produce *Lennon*, a 50-page book reproducing *Liverpool Echo* articles on the Beatles and John Lennon from 1963 onwards.

Liverpool Institute, The, Mount Street, Liverpool L1

A high school for boys which was founded in 1825 as a Mechanics Institute, and was officially opened as a school on 15 September 1837. Charles Dickens lectured there in 1844 and famous pupils have included Sir Charles Lamb, Lord Mersey, Sir Henry Enfield and Sir Macalister of Tarbert.

In 1890 one half of the school became an Art College and brick walls were built to separate the two buildings internally. The Institute was changed from a fee-paying school to a grammar school in 1944, making it the oldest grammar school in Liverpool.

The school motto is *Non Nobis Solum Sed Toti Mundo Nati*, which means 'Not for ourselves alone but for the good of all the world'.

Paul McCartney entered the school when he passed his 11-plus examination. In the summer of 1957 he took two 'O' level exams and passed in Spanish, but failed in Latin. He took six further subjects in order to move up into the Sixth Form in 1958. He passed five and seemed to have a penchant for languages – apart from Spanish, he also has an 'O' level in German and French.

The boys nicknamed the school 'the Inny' and their headmaster, J. R. Edwards, 'the Baz'.

George Harrison was a year below Paul at the school. Other students included Paul's brother Mike; Neil Aspinall, who became the Beatles' road manager; Len Garry, a member of John Lennon's skiffle group the Quarry Men; Ivan Vaughan, who introduced Paul to John; Peter Sissons, who became a prominent TV celebrity in Britain; Les Chadwick, who was a member of Gerry & the Pacemakers; Colin Manley and Don Andrew, both members of the Remo Four; Bill Kenwright, who became an actor and later a leading West End theatre impresario; and Stu James who became a member of the Mojos.

'Dusty' Durband was Paul's Sixth Form teacher of English and Paul claimed he was the only teacher he liked and mentioned that Dusty told the boys about books such as *Lady Chatterley's Lover* and Chaucer's *The Miller's Tale*, pointing out that they weren't dirty books but examples of good literature.

One of Paul's classmates was Kenny Alpin, and Paul once used him as a scapegoat. He'd drawn a rather vulgar sketch of a naked woman for the amusement of his classmates, and had put it in his shirt pocket and forgotten about it. His mother discovered it there before washing the shirt and the embarrassed Paul told her that Kenny Alpin was the artistic culprit. His conscience got the better of him and two days later he confessed.

Paul and Mike used to catch the No. 86 bus to school and it was during these bus journeys that Paul first got to know George.

It had been anticipated that Paul would enter Teacher's Training College after leaving the Institute, but he took time off to tour Scotland with the Silver Beatles and then went off to Hamburg. He'd had a message from Mr Edwards asking him to visit the Head's office but he wrote back from Hamburg declaring that he'd resigned from the school: 'I said, "Dear Sir, I've got a great job in Germany and I'm earning fifteen pounds."'

Paul retained a fondness for the school and on Friday, 23 November 1979, arranged for Wings to give a special concert for the staff and students of the Liverpool Institute. The concert took place at the Royal Court Theatre, Liverpool, and Paul was to comment, 'It's my way of saying "Thank you" for some very happy years. Everyone seems to knock their schooldays but for me they have fond memories.'

Through Paul's vision, the Institute has now been revised as LIPA (Liverpool Institute of Performing Arts), a major stage school.

Liverpool Stadium, Liverpool

A large venue, close to Liverpool city centre and the Exchange Station, generally the centre for wrestling and boxing bouts. Although the Beatles never appeared at the venue, it does have some link with the Beatles story as it stimulated Allan Williams' interest in promoting local groups and led to Larry Parnes taking an interest in auditioning Liverpool bands.

Williams had decided to promote a rock 'n' roll extravaganza at the venue and contacted impresario Larry Parnes to book the package tour starring Eddie Cochran and Gene Vincent. The joint Parnes–Williams promotion featured the American stars and some support acts and Williams also added some Liverpool acts to the bill. It was to take place on Tuesday, 3 May 1960. Then tragedy struck when Cochran and Vincent were involved in a car accident, which was fatal for Cochran. Parnes informed Williams that although Vincent had been injured, he would still honour the booking, although his own suggestion was that it be cancelled. Williams wanted to go ahead and the promotion proved to be a success.

The three-hour show started at 8.00 p.m. and starred Gene Vincent, followed by Davy Jones, the black American singer who would later be backed by the Beatles in 1961, Italian rock group Nero & his Gladiators and Lance Fortune, Dean Webb, the Viscounts, Julian X, Colin Green & the Beat Boys and Peter Wynne. Liverpool acts Cass & the Cassanovas, Rory Storm & the Hurricanes, Gerry & the Pacemakers, Mal Perry, Bob Evans & his Five Shillings and the Connaughts were added attractions.

Stuart Sutcliffe, John Lennon, Paul McCartney and George Harrison were in the audience, having recently changed their name from the Quarry Men to the Beetles.

Parnes was impressed with the Liverpool acts and asked Allan Williams to arrange auditions for him to select local bands to back his artists on tour. This time Williams included the Silver Beetles on the list, at the request of Stuart Sutcliffe.

Liverpool Town Hall, Water Street, Liverpool L2

Setting for the amazing civic reception of Friday, 10 July 1964.

When news of the Beatles' attendance at the Odeon, Liverpool, for the premiere of *A Hard Day's Night* was announced, Alderman John McMillan put forward the idea of a civic welcome and the wheels were set in motion.

Following their world tour, the Beatles flew into Speke Airport on a red and white Britannia belonging to British Eagle Airways. They touched down at 5.25 p.m. to be greeted by a reception balcony crammed with 1,500 fans, the maximum allowed. Emerging from the aircraft, they were presented with bouquets of flowers by the air hostesses and were led to a special room where they held a brief press conference.

The Beatles then rode in a limousine, preceded by the Chief Constable's car and two motorcycle outriders. Three other official cars followed, together with two other motorcycle policemen on a route which took them along Speke Road, Woolton Road, Mather Avenue, Allerton Road, Smithdown Road, Croxteth Road, Princess Street, Catherine Street, Hardman Street, Leece Street, Bold Street, Church Street, Lord Street and Castle Street.

A number of people had been present in their party, including the disc jockey David Jacobs, who had been their host on the various BBC TV 'Juke Box Jury' programmes they had appeared on. Wilfred Brambell, the actor who starred as Paul's grandfather in *A Hard Day's Night*, had also arrived for the premiere and the group's movements were also covered by a travelling press corps which included George Harrison of the *Liverpool Echo*.

Describing the scene, David Jacobs commented: 'We travelled from Liverpool Airport with a plane of one of the smaller airline companies and I sat in the back, and it was extraordinary to see how very nervous the boys were. They were absolutely petrified that they would not be bothered with in Liverpool. Liverpool, after all, they said was their home and had a lot of stars and they thought that nobody would turn out to meet them.

'When we got near the airport they were eagerly looking out of their windows and we eventually saw the airport at a distance, and it looked like an enormous black mass of insects. The place was covered absolutely from side to side with thousands of people except the runway was kept clear. And we eventually got off the plane and within seconds the boys were surrounded by shouting fans. In this crowd I was getting lost and then a very sweet thing happened. George Harrison noticed it and suddenly stopped and came to collect me so that I could be with them. And then we went out for that nine-mile drive from the airport to the centre of town where we were due to come out on the balcony with the Lord Mayor and the boys were to receive the 'Freedom of the City'.

'I was in the car behind them and the nine-mile drive took a very long time. We drove very slowly and every inch of the way on both sides was crowded with people and the strange thing was – in sitting at the back of the car behind them I saw the faces of the people after they had seen the Beatles and the look on their faces was almost as if Jesus Christ had just gone past.'

They were due to arrive at the Town Hall at 6.30 p.m. and leave for the Odeon Cinema at 8.30 p.m., but the crowds of almost 200,000 people lining the route were given a treat as the Fab Four took their journey slowly in order to wave at their fans.

They actually arrived at the Town Hall at 6.55 p.m. to be greeted in the doorway by the late Bessie Braddock, a famous Liverpool MP of ample proportions, who also visited the band on one of their Liverpool Empire Theatre gigs. She had arranged for the Chants to attend the reception as they were one of the bands in her own Exchange Ward and had once been backed by the Beatles on an early Cavern appearance. The Beatles were then taken to a private room to enjoy a cup of tea and a chat with the Lord Mayor, Alderman Louis Caplan, who was to say, 'Liverpool is really proud of the Beatles. They are great ambassadors for the city and the inspiration they have given to youth clubs in Liverpool and throughout Britain was magnificent.'

The group were then taken out on to the Town Hall balcony to greet the thousands of fans outside, packing Castle Street, Water Street and Dale Street. They made two appearances on the balcony and then changed into dinner jackets and appeared on the Minstrel Gallery in the Town Hall ballroom, where they each said a personal 'Hello'. Paul then addressed the guests, saying, 'This has been our best ever welcome and we would like to thank you all very much.'

There were exactly 714 guests, including Lord and Lady Derby, the Bishop of Liverpool and numerous City councillors and officials. There were only a handful of representatives from the local music scene who had been invited, apart from the Chants. They were Ray McFall, owner of the Cavern, Bob Wooler, the Cavern compere, and Bill Harry, founder of *Mersey Beat*.

The Beatles were taken into a parlour where the Lady Mayoress showed them a large cake on which a map of the world in icing portrayed the message 'The City of Liverpool Honours the Beatles'. The cake was later presented to a local children's hospital.

The group then left the Town Hall and travelled up Dale Street and into William Brown Street where they entered London Road and reached the Odeon cinema where they attended the northern premiere of their debut film.

Livingston, Alan

When George Martin first approached him to issue the Beatles records in the States, Alan Livingston was currently President of Capitol Records.

Capitol was actually owned by EMI and Martin naturally turned to them first, sending a copy of 'Please Please Me' to the company.

Livingston jotted down a memo: 'We don't think the Beatles will do anything in this market', and Martin began looking for another outlet and eventually had the single issued on Vee Jay.

He then offered Capitol 'From Me To You' and the company turned it down again. The single was issued on Vee Jay. When Martin tried a third time with 'She Loves You', Livingston told him that in Capitol's opinion the Beatles had no prospects in America and the single was issued on a New York label, Swan.

Livingston, who was married to film actress Nancy Olsen, eventually had to bow to the inevitable when Brown Meggs, Director of Eastern Operations for Capitol, was visited by Brian Epstein in New York who played him a demo of 'I Want To Hold Your Hand'. Meggs agreed to release it and a date was set for 13 January 1964.

Capitol reputedly spent 50 thousand dollars on an initial promotion when the Beatles first flew into New York in February 1964.

When the Beatles were touring California, Livingston held a party for them at his Hollywood home on 24 August 1964.

Guests included Edward G. Robinson, Jack Palance, Gary Lewis, Tony Bennett, Gene Barry, Jane Fonda, Richard Chamberlain, Rock Hudson, Groucho Marx, Dean Martin, Hayley and Juliet Mills, James Stewart, Lloyd Bridges and famed gossip columnist Hedda Hopper. Brian Epstein and Derek Taylor were at first prevented from entering the grounds by security officers because they weren't carrying their invitation cards, but a gatecrasher called Hal York managed to get them in!

The following year, on 29 August, Livingston presented the Beatles with a Gold record for the *Help*! album at an afternoon press conference.

Locarno Ballroom, West Derby Road, Liverpool L6

For many years the premier Mecca Ballroom in Liverpool. The venue mainly featured dance bands and rarely booked any of the Mersey Beat groups, preferring their own resident beat group the Delemeres who comprised Mac McGibbon (bass), Dave Shipley (lead), Gordon Railton (rhythm) and Mike Wakefield (drums).

However, for a short time from 1963 they began to book some of the better known Liverpool names and presented the Beatles on a special Valentine's Night promotion on 14 February 1963. It was the only time the group appeared at the venue, although the Quarry Men had entered some talent contests there in the late fifties.

The Locarno regularly ran contests ranging from singing to beauty contests and during the skiffle boom, the Quarry Men entered a few of the talent contest heats at the ballroom.

In the seventies the ballroom was turned into a bingo hall and for a number of years, former Cavern DJ Bob Wooler acted as a bingo caller there.

Lockwood, Sir Joseph

In their dealings at the top level of EMI Records, the Beatles were in contact with Sir Joseph Lockwood, who was Chairman of EMI from 1954 until 1974.

Sir Joseph had been an asset to the company, overseeing the purchase of the small American record label Capitol Records, which was later to become such a major giant. He also appointed a young George Martin as head of the Parlophone label.

The man the Beatles called 'Sir Joe' was always available to advise and help them in personal and financial matters. He was the one who vetoed Gandhi as a figure for the *Sgt Pepper* album cover lest it offend record buyers in India. When John and Yoko were photographed in the nude for the *Two Virgins* cover, they showed Sir Joe the photograph. He refused to allow EMI to distribute the record. John asked him if he were shocked. He told him that he wasn't, that they should have had better bodies on the cover. 'They're not very attractive,' he said, referring to the figures of John and Yoko, 'Paul McCartney would look better than you.' He agreed to press the record if Apple took over the distribution.

When John and Yoko were involved in a drug bust, Paul contacted Sir Joe who immediately rang Paddington Green police station to contact John and advise him how to conduct himself.

Sir Joseph died on 6 March 1991 at the age of 86.

Lomax, Jackie

The Undertakers were one of the most stylish Mersey Beat bands, whose image matched their name. They wore undertakers' dress – black top hats and mourning coats – and their amplifiers were shaped like coffins. They were voted twelfth most popular group in the Mersey Beat poll in 1961 (the year the group were formed) and had risen to the fifth position the following year.

Members were Jackie Lomax (a former wages clerk at the Mersey Docks and Harbour Board), Geoff Nugent, Chris Houston, Bugs Pemberton and Brian Jones. They played all the main Liverpool venues and appeared at the Top Ten and Star Clubs in Hamburg.

The group signed with Pye Records and recorded 'Mashed Potatoes', which they wanted as their debut single. Pye decided otherwise and relegated it to the 'B' side of 'Everybody Loves A Lover'.

For their second single they wanted to issue 'Money' but Pye ignored them once again and placed it on the 'B' side of 'What About Us'. Bern Elliott & the Fenmen then recorded 'Money' and had a chart hit with the number. Pye relented and allowed the Undertakers to pick their next 'A' side, which was 'Just A Little Bit', which became their first and only chart hit. Pye claimed that they didn't sell records because of their name and talked them into changing it to the 'Takers. Geoff Nugent believes that the name change contributed to their downfall. As the 'Takers they recorded

'If You Don't Come Back', but at the moment the record began to sell, the record company ceased plugging it.

Some members of the group travelled to America and Jackie and Bugs teamed up with two American musicians to form the Lomax Alliance.

Jackie met Cilla Black at a party in 1966 and she told him, 'Brian Epstein's looking for you.' He contacted Brian who told him he was looking for a solo singer. Jackie asked him to listen to his band and Epstein signed up the Lomax Alliance and booked them on his showplace, the Saville Theatre in London. They also recorded an album with John Simon, but like the Undertakers tracks 'Hold On, I'm A-Comin', 'My Babe', 'Watch Your Step' and 'What's So Good About Goodbye', it remains unreleased.

After Epstein's death the Lomax Alliance disbanded and Jackie was signed to Apple. He had a voice with a remarkable range and George Harrison wanted to produce him. His debut single was one of Apple's first four releases on 26 August 1968 in America, on Apple 1802, and on 6 September in the UK on Apple 3. 'Sour Milk Sea' was also written by George and the flipside, 'The Eagle Laughs At You', was written by Jackie. Paul McCartney joined in on bass, Nicky Hopkins on piano, Eric Clapton on lead guitar, Ringo on drums and George and Jackie on rhythm guitars. The 'supergroup' angle of the record wasn't promoted and the single wasn't a hit.

Lomax's debut album *Is This What You Want?* was released in Britain on 21 March 1969 on Apple SAPCOR 6 and in America on 19 May on Apple ST 3354. Eric Clapton and Ringo played on the track 'You've Got Me Thinking', and George produced the album. George was interested in producing another record with Jackie, but Lomax wanted to record himself on a new song which he'd just finished called 'New Day'. This was issued in Britain on 9 May 1969 on Apple 11, with 'I Fall Inside Your Eyes' on the flip.

Paul McCartney had also been interested in Jackie and the night before he married Linda, Paul recorded Jackie singing 'Thumbin' A Ride' at a session in which George and Billy Preston also played. This appeared on the flipside of 'New Day' when it was issued in America on 2 June 1969 on Apple 1807. 'Thumbin' A Ride' was also featured as the flipside of Jackie's next British release, 'How The Web Was Woven', which George produced. It was issued on 9 March 1970 on Apple 1819.

His final Apple single was a re-release. 'Sour Milk Sea', coupled with 'I Fall Inside Your Eyes', was issued on 21 June 1971 in America on Apple 1834.

Like all of Jackie's previous releases, it failed to make the charts. This fact completely baffled the Beatles because Jackie had one of those rare and distinctive voices which have the potential of turning its owner into a superstar. The records were highly rated ones, and yet the public didn't go for them.

Another track George produced with Jackie, 'Going Back to Liverpool', remains unreleased.

When Allen Klein entered the picture, Jackie was lost in the office intrigues. Three of his appointments with Klein were cancelled and he eventually went to Warner, where he released two albums, then signed up with Capitol and for a while appeared with a group called Badger.

When Jackie's wife was involved in a serious road accident which almost crippled her, he gave up his musical career for a time to devote himself to looking after her.

He now lives in Los Angeles and appears on the occasional gig, as well as producing some new up-and-coming bands.

London Palladium, 8 Argyll Street, London W1

Site of the live ATV variety shows 'Sunday Night At The London Palladium'.

The group's debut there on Sunday, 13 October 1963, saw the birth of 'Beatlemania'. They were the bill toppers and performed five numbers to a television audience of fifteen million viewers: 'I Want To Hold Your Hand', 'This Boy', 'All My Loving', 'Money' and 'Twist And Shout'. Comedian Bruce Forsyth compered a section of the show called 'Beat The Clock' and other acts included singer Brook Benton, Des O'Connor and Jack Parnell & His Orchestra.

The show started at 8.25 p.m. There were such huge crowds of fans gathered that the Fleet Street newspapers had a field day taking shots of what appeared in the headlines the following day as 'Beatlemania!'. There was such a horde outside the Marlborough Street stage door exit that it was decided that the Beatles should slip out the front entrance of the theatre in Argyll Street and into a waiting chauffeur-driven Austin Princess. A police chief thought the car would be conspicuous parked directly outside the front entrance, so he had it moved 40 yards further up Argyll Street. Press Officer Tony Barrow tipped off some pressmen about their escape route and when they dashed out they couldn't find their car and were then pursued by fans. The shots made impressive spreads in the major nationals the next day.

Their next appearance at the theatre was also for a spot on Val Parnell's 'Sunday Night At the London Palladium' on 12 January 1964 topping a bill which included Alma Cogan and Dave Allen.

Their third appearance at the Palladium took place on Thursday, 23 July 1964, at a midnight performance of 'Night Of One

Hundred Stars', a charity revue in aid of the Combined Theatrical Charities Appeals Council. During the first half of the show the group performed a sketch called 'I'm Flying' and in the second half they performed a musical set. Among the many other artists on the bill were Zsa Zsa Gabor, Jane Asher, Laurence Olivier, Harry Secombe, Frankie Vaughan, Max Bygraves, Frankie Howerd, Richard Attenborough, Millicent Martin, Dora Bryan, Miriam Karlin, Wendy Craig, Angela Douglas, Adrienne Corri, Peggy Cummings, Eunice Gayson, Marti Stevens, Elizabeth Welch, Eve Arden, Hayley Mills, Sylvia Sims, Chita Rivera, Susan Hampshire, Rita Moreno, Ronnie Corbett, Wilfred Brambell, Judy Garland, Shirley Bassey, Marlene Dietrich and Buddy Greco.

Backstage, Laurence Olivier, who was compere of the show, personally requested that he be introduced to the Beatles.

London Pavilion, 3 Piccadilly Circus, London W1

Site of the British premieres of the Beatles films, a building which initially opened as a music hall in 1885 and became a cinema in 1934. The first Beatles event at the cinema was the premiere of *A Hard Day's Night* which took place on Monday, 6 July 1964, at 8.30 p.m. in the presence of Her Royal Highness The Princess Margaret and Lord Snowdon. The charity event was in aid of the Docklands Settlement and Variety Club Heart Fund. A crowd of 12,000 people gathered in Piccadilly Circus and they cheered and sang 'Happy Birthday, Ringo!' as it was Ringo's 24th birthday the following day. Ringo was pleased with the audience reaction to the film and said, 'They even standingly ovated.'

After the premiere, the group went off to the Dorchester Hotel for a special party, during which Paul gave his father a painting of Drake's Drum as a present for his 62nd birthday. Jim McCartney said, 'Very nice, son, thank you.' Then Paul surprised him by saying, 'It's not just a painting Dad, I've bought you the bloody horse and it's running at Chester next Saturday and Ripon next month.' Paul had spent £1,000 buying the gelding. Two surprise guests who turned up were Brian Jones and Keith Richard of the Rolling Stones. Later they joined the Beatles at the Ad Lib Club.

At the premiere of *Help!* which took place on Thursday, 29 July 1965 there were an estimated 10,000 people gathered in Piccadilly Circus. Once again, Princess Margaret and Lord Snowdon were in attendance. John arrived in his Rolls-Royce with Cynthia, Paul was accompanied by Jane Asher, and Ringo by Maureen. Other guests included producer Walter Shenson with his wife Gerry and publisher Dick James with his son Steven. After the film there was a party in the Orchid Room of the Dorchester Hotel.

The premiere of *How I Won the War*, in which John had a cameo role, took place at the Pavilion on Wednesday, 18 October 1967. John and Cynthia, Ringo and Maureen, Paul and Jane, and George and Pattie were in attendance and guests included Jimi Hendrix, Anita Harris, Cilla Black, Mama Cass Elliott, David Hemmings and Gayle Hunnicutt. After the film the Beatles attended a private party at Cilla Black's flat, located at Flat 20, 9b Portland Place.

The *Yellow Submarine* premiere took place on Wednesday, 17 July 1968, and once again huge crowds poured into Piccadilly Circus. Paul was in attendance as were John and Yoko, Ringo and Maureen, and George and Pattie. Guests included the Bee Gees, Ginger Baker, Twiggy and Grapefruit. After the show there was a party at the Yellow Submarine discotheque at the Royal Lancaster Hotel in Bayswater Road.

The final Beatles movie premiere took place at the London Pavilion on 20 May 1970 for *Let It Be*. Not a single member of the Beatles turned up, although two former lovers did, Cynthia Lennon and Jane Asher.

Other Beatles-related visits included one on Wednesday, 2 June 1965 when George Harrison and Brian Epstein attended the premiere of Richard Lester's *The Knack* while Paul and Linda attended the premiere of *Midnight Cowboy* on Thursday, 25 September 1969.

The London Pavilion closed its doors for the last time several years later and was redeveloped. It is now an entertainment complex, which includes Rock Circus, a museum of rock music that contains fibreglass animatronix figures of the Beatles among its exhibits.

Lonesome Tears In My Eyes

A number recorded by the Johnny Burnette Trio in 1956 on an album issued by Coral (CRL 57080) in the States. It was composed by Johnny Burnette, Dorsey Burnette, Paul Burlison and Al Mortiner. Johnny and his brother Dorsey were originally members of the Rock 'n' Roll Trio, a Rockabilly band. Johnny drowned in 1964 and Dorsey died in 1979. Johnny's son Rocky became an artist in his own right and had a big hit with 'Tired Of Toein' the Line'.

The Beatles introduced this Burnette number into their repertoire, with John Lennon on lead vocals, and performed it in their stage act during 1961 and 1962. A version appeared on *The Beatles Live At The BBC* CDs.

Long And Winding Road, The, (Single)

A composition by Paul McCartney which the Beatles originally began recording at Apple on Friday, 31 January 1969, for the 'Get

Back' sessions. The Beatles were becoming dissatisfied with the 'Get Back' project and Glyn Johns was handed the tapes to edit into album form. Johns' work was rejected and the following year Allen Klein brought in Phil Spector.

The number was said to be been inspired by the long road leading to Paul's Scottish farm. Paul also admitted that he had Ray Charles in mind when composing it. He explained that it didn't sound like Charles, but he had Charles on his mind when writing the number and wondered how Charles would have tackled it.

In April 1970, Spector altered 'The Long And Winding Road' substantially, introducing his own trademark, the 'Spector wall of sound', by utilising no less than fifty musicians on the track. They included Ringo on drums, two guitarists, three trombonists, three trumpeters, a harp, four cellos, four violas, eighteen violins and fourteen vocalists.

Paul was understandably furious at what Spector had done to his number and made his opinions vocal. His attitude about the post-production work on the *Let It Be* album differed from that of John and George. Paul felt that Spector had destroyed the documentary feel that had been the aim of the album. He was so incensed with the alterations that Spector had made to his song that he wrote a letter to Allen Klein angrily demanding that he have the changes removed. Klein ignored him. Paul was later to comment how he didn't like the violins and the female voices on the track and how nobody minded but him.

When Paul filed a writ in the High Court calling for the dissolution of the Beatles, he was to quote three reasons why he decided to leave the group, one of which was that Klein had authorised the alteration of 'The Long And Winding Road' without informing him.

Two versions of the number exist from the original recordings – one produced by George Martin, the other by Spector. Paul also performed it on tour with Wings, and this version is to be found on the *Wings Over America* album.

The track was featured on the Let It Be album and has also been included on several compilations: *The Beatles 1967–1970, Love Songs, The Beatles Ballads, Reel Music* and *20 Greatest Hits*.

The number was released in America as a single on Apple 2832 on 11 May 1970, coupled with 'For You Blue'. The two soundtrack numbers from *Let It Be*, selected by Allen Klein as a double A-side release, topped the charts in *Billboard, Cashbox* and *Record World*.

This was to be the final Beatles single issued in America, apart from reissued material, which began to be released from 1976.

During a seven-year period the Beatles had achieved twenty No. 1 singles in *Billboard*, 22 in *Cashbox* and 23 in *Record World*.

The version of 'The Long And Winding Road' which appeared on the *Anthology 3* CD was the original version recorded at Apple Studios on 26 January 1969 by George Martin with engineer Glyn Johns, which only features the Beatles and Billy Preston.

Long John Baldry

Influential British blues singer. A tall, blond figure, over six feet tall, Baldry first began singing in Soho pubs and coffee bars in the mid-fifties and later joined Blues Incorporated. While appearing at the Cavern in Liverpool, he became friends with Paul McCartney.

He was selected to be one of the guest artists on the Beatles' Rediffusion television special 'Around The Beatles'.

Long Long Long

A George Harrison composition which was included on *The Beatles* double album. John Lennon wasn't present at any of the recordings for this number. The love song isn't inspired by Pattie, as previous love songs were – George revealed that the 'you' mentioned in the number refers to 'God'.

Paul played Hammond organ on the song, which resulted in an interesting accident. There was a bottle of Blue Nun wine on the Leslie speaker and when Paul hit a particular note on the organ, the speaker vibrated and the sound of the bottle rattling can be heard at the end of the recording.

When recording began, the song had the working title 'It's Been A Long Long Long Time'.

Long Tall Sally

The first number Paul ever sang on stage. While holidaying at Butlin's camp in Wales, Paul and his younger brother Mike were asked up on stage by Mike Robbins, their cousin-in-law, who was a Redcoat (official camp steward). The duo sang the Everly Brothers' hit 'Bye Bye Love' and then Paul went solo, singing Little Richard's hit 'Long Tall Sally'.

This was also a number Paul performed in history teacher Cliff Edge's classroom at the Liverpool Institute, along with George Harrison and Don Andrews, and it became part of the early Beatles repertoire.

It became the title of the Beatles' fifth EP release in June 1964, which remained at No. 1 in the EP charts for seven weeks and reached No. 11 in the singles chart. It was included on the American release *The Beatles Second Album* in 1964, their *Rock 'n' Roll Music* compilation in 1976, *The Beatles Collection* in 1978 and *The Beatles Box* in 1980.

A live version of the number was featured on the *Live At Hollywood Bowl* album in May 1977 and it was also one of the tracks recorded at the Star Club in 1962, of which there have been various releases.

The number had been written by Little Richard under his real name Richard Penniman and Enotris Johnson and they'd originally called it 'The Thing', then 'Bald-Headed Sally' and finally 'Long Tall Sally'. The Little Richard version reached No. 3 in the British charts in 1956.

It was included in the repertoire in 1957 and became a highlight of the Beatles' early stage act. They performed it at the Star Club, Hamburg, and a version is to be found on *The Beatles Live! At The Star Club in Hamburg, Germany: 1962* album. The group also performed it on several of their BBC radio shows, including two 'Saturday Club' broadcasts, 'Side By Side', 'Pop Go The Beatles', 'Top Gear' and 'From Us to You'.

Long Tall Sally (EP)

The fifth Beatles British EP release. *Long Tall Sally* also became the first Beatles EP to contain previously unreleased tracks.

It was issued on Parlophone GEP 8913 on 19 June 1964 and reached No. 11 in the charts. It was very unusual for an EP to reach the singles charts, but the Beatles had managed it with every release. They had also popularised the EP, which resulted in a special EP chart and *Long Tall Sally* reached the No. 1 position in the EP charts and remained there for seven weeks.

The front cover photograph was taken by Robert Freeman and this time the sleeve notes were provided by Derek Taylor. The tracks were: 'Long Tall Sally', 'I Call Your Name', 'Slow Down' and 'Matchbox'. The track appeared on *Past Masters Volume One* and a radio recording was used on *The Beatles Live At The BBC* CDs while a further version was included on the Beatles' *Anthology 1* CDs.

Lopez, Trini

Artist who shared the triple-headlining bill at the Paris Olympia from 16 January–4 February 1964. The 25-year-old singer from Dallas, Texas, had just had a million-selling hit with 'If I Had A Hammer'.

His manager Norman Weiss of the powerful American agency GAC came to Paris to see him and while he was there confirmed the New York Carnegie Hall date for the Beatles on behalf of Sid

Bernstein. He was also able to arrange for GAC to represent the Beatles in America.

Lopez was to have a handful of hits in the sixties: 'Kansas City', 'I'm Comin' Home Cindy' and 'Gonna Get Along Without Ya Now'.

Lord Of The Rings, The

A fantasy trilogy written by an Oxford professor, J. R. R. Tolkien. It was first published in three volumes (The Fellowship Of The Ring, The Two Towers and The Return Of The King) in the mid-1950s and became a major cult in 1968 when the books appeared in a single volume as Lord Of The Rings.

Allegedly it was Apple Films chief Dennis O'Dell who, in 1968, first came up with the idea of the Beatles starring in the epic fantasy. He set out to secure the rights and find a top director. He approached David Lean who was fascinated with the idea, but wasn't available at the time.

O'Dell then approached Stanley Kubrick. Some years later, O'Dell was to tell film journalist Bob Neaverson, 'I sent the books round to be read by him. He read them, and his daughter berated him for not having read them.'

O'Dell travelled to Rishikesh and interested the Beatles in the project. After reading the books, Kubrick met up with John and Paul over lunch at MGM Studios, but turned the project down as he regarded it as unfilmable.

It was also claimed that the Beatles were now quite keen on adapting the epic as their third film and managed to interest the Italian director Michaelangelo Antonioni in the movie.

There are conflicting views about the entire background to the suggestion of filming Lord Of The Rings and Paul McCartney was to comment: 'John wanted us to buy the film rights to Lord Of The Rings. It was very much his idea. We talked about it for quite a while, but then I started to smell a bit of a carve-up because immediately John wanted to be Bilbo – wanted the lead and started to be a bit kinda "ooh, dear wait a minute." But things start to become difficult when somebody has taken the lead without consulting the others and then second lead goes and so you suddenly end up with Zeppo!'

Bilbo Baggins was actually the hero of The Hobbit, the prequel to The Lord Of The Rings. The Hobbit hero of the trilogy was his nephew Frodo.

Paul may have been mistaken about the casting, because it was announced that John had intended to portray the obsessive creature Gollum, George was to be the wizard Gandalf, Paul was to take the role of Frodo, the Hobbit, and Ringo was to portray Bilbo's friend

Gamgee. The four also asked Twiggy to appear in the movie with them.

Although some rumours purported that the author didn't like the idea of his book being turned into a vehicle for the Beatles, this is unlikely. Pete Shotton, in his autobiography *In My Life*, says that when a Beatles representative approached Tolkien's agent, he discovered that the film rights had been snapped up only a few days previously. Paul was to say, 'I'm not sure what the problem was, but I think that the Tolkein estate who control *Lord Of The Rings* wouldn't sell us the movie rights or maybe they'd already sold them to someone else.'

Another puzzling aspect is that O'Dell revealed that United Artists already owned the film rights to the books and were quite prepared for the script to be made into the third Beatles film – as long as the services of a name director should be secured.

As this didn't happen, attempts to transfer the film rights to Apple were unsuccessful. If this was really the case, wasn't Antonioni a major director? What happened to his reported interest in the project? Wasn't Dick Lester, who had made the previous two Beatles films, considered? As the Beatles were as big as ever and as they had made a fortune for United Artists with their films, how was it that the group were never informed that the company who they were contracted to already owned the rights to a film they wanted to make?

To add to the confusion, Tony Bramwell, who also worked for Apple Films in 1968, has said, 'We had lots of good ideas, including getting the rights to *Lord Of The Rings*. That was going to be directed by Patrick McGoohan with special effects by Ray Harryhausen. The Beatles were going to be the Hobbits.'

Director Ralph Bakshi eventually made a version of *Lord Of The Rings* in 1978, although he only filmed part of the trilogy, intending to complete the tale in a second film, which he never made.

Love In The Open Air

When this instrumental was issued with the composer credit given solely to Paul McCartney, it was the first piece of music to be released using the name of only one member of the Lennon & McCartney songwriting team.

Paul had composed the theme tune and incidental music for the 1967 film *The Family Way* and passed the music over to George Martin for him to fine-tune, compose and record. The George Martin Orchestra then recorded the film's soundtrack album, issued by Decca, and also released 'Love In The Open Air' coupled with 'Bahama Sound' as a single on United Artists UA 50148 on 24 April 1967.

Lovely Rita

A song by Paul which featured on the *Sgt Pepper* album.

Commenting on his inspiration for the song, Paul has said, 'I was bopping about on a piano in Liverpool when someone told me that in America they called parking meter women Meter Maids. I thought it was great and it got to be "Rita, Meter Maid" and then "Lovely Rita, Meter Maid" and I was thinking it should be a hate song, but then I thought it would be better to love her and if she was freaky too, like a military man, with a bag on her shoulders. A foot stomper, but nice.'

In Paul's song, the narrator sees Rita filling in parking tickets and notices that she has an almost military look with her cap and bag. He invites her out to tea, then takes her out to dinner – although Rita ends up paying the bill. He then takes her home, but doesn't quite make it with her as his two sisters are sharing the sofa.

Visually, artists interpret Rita as a very sexy woman. In the David Bailey colour photograph in *The Beatles Illustrated Lyrics*, she is a sluttish figure, smoking a cigarette, her cap askew, face heavily made up and her left hand pulling aside her jacket to reveal an ample cleavage. The Robert Rankin illustration in *Behind The Beatles Songs* depicts her clothed only in a hat and black stockings.

Real life Meter Maid Meta Davis claimed to have been Paul's inspiration. She retired after nineteen years as a Traffic Warden on Wednesday, 4 September 1985, when the media gave her story major coverage. She appeared on both BBC and ITV news that evening, pictured walking across the Abbey Road zebra crossing and discussing how she gave Paul his ticket (although she called him Paul 'McCarthy' in the interviews).

In 1967 Mrs Davis, who lives in St John's Wood, was giving Paul's car a ticket in Garden Road, when he turned up. She commented: 'He saw that my name was Meta and he laughed and said, "That would make a nice jingle, I could use that." We chatted for a few minutes and then he drove off. I didn't think any more of it, but later the song came out and although I knew the record was about me I never bought a copy.'

Paul didn't recognise her when, a few years later, she met him in the reception room of the local vet where she'd taken her cat. Paul was there with his dog and Meta says, 'We chatted about animals and he didn't recognise me out of uniform and I didn't tell him who I was.'

When the record was originally released in Australia it included Meta's name in the lyrics, but this was changed to Rita in other versions.

The number has also been recorded by several other artists, including Fats Domino and Roy Wood.

Love Me Do

A number Paul wrote one day when he was playing truant from school. John wrote the middle eight.

It became the Beatles' first single and was amongst the songs they recorded at their Parlophone recording audition on Wednesday, 6 June 1962, when Pete Best was a member of the group. Both George Martin and Ron Richards supervised the production of the session. When the group returned to Abbey Road Studios to record the number on Tuesday, 4 September 1962, Ron Richards rehearsed the group in Studio Three between 2.30 p.m. and 5.30 p.m. They then began recording with George Martin at 7.00 p.m. in Studio Three, initially recording 'How Do You Do It?' Next came 'Love Me Do', which took fifteen takes.

On their 6 June visit George Martin had commented that he wasn't happy with the drum sound. In fact, that was because he was used to a different style of drumming in the recording studios where producers had used show drummers rather than ones from rock 'n' roll bands. When the Beatles turned up with Ringo, Martin was unhappy with his drumming, too.

As he wasn't satisfied with the session, it was rearranged for the following Tuesday, 11 September. The Beatles told Martin that they thought Ringo was the best drummer in Liverpool, but Martin told them he'd be happier using Andy White as session drummer.

Ringo wasn't very happy when he arrived for his second recording session to find another drummer in place. He felt he would be kicked out of the group, just like Pete Best. The use of a session drummer, as it turned out, wasn't a reflection on either Pete Best or Ringo Starr – it was a common practice at the time. White was a show drummer who had appeared on many sessions and it was Ron Richards who had actually booked him, because he was used to working with him. Richards handled the recording session on 11 September in George Martin's absence. The first number recorded was 'P.S. I Love You' and an unhappy Ringo sat next to Ron Richards in the control box until the producer asked him to play maracas on the track. When they came to record 'Love Me Do', Richards asked Ringo to play tambourine.

Taking photographs at the session was Dezo Hoffmann and George tried to avoid the camera because he still had a black eye which a Pete Best fan had given him at the Cavern.

The record began with a distinctive harmonica solo by John. Discussing the harmonica, John had said, 'I can't remember why I took it up in the first place – I must have picked one up very cheap. I know we used to take in students and one of them had a mouth organ and said he'd buy me one if I could learn a tune by the next morning – so I learned about two. I was somewhere between eight and twelve at the time – in short pants anyway. Another time I was travelling to Edinburgh on me own to see me auntie and I played the mouth organ all the way up on the bus. The driver liked it and told me to meet him at a place in Edinburgh the next morning and he'd give me a good mouth organ. So I went, and he gave me a fantastic one – it really got me going.'

John had been particularly impressed by the distinctive harmonica opening by Delbert McClinton on the Bruce Channel hit 'Hey! Baby'. When the Beatles appeared on a bill with Channel at the Tower Ballroom, New Brighton, on Thursday, 21 June 1962, Lennon drifted over to McClinton and told him how much he liked the harmonica on the song and asked him how to play the intro. The two of them spent fifteen minutes together. John had actually performed 'Love Me Do' only two weeks previously at their Parlophone audition, but he was able to utilise the McClinton lesson when they recorded the number the following September.

'Love Me Do' coupled with 'P.S. I Love You' was issued on Parlophone R 4949 on 5 October 1962. The record had a red label which collectors can identify as the single with Ringo on drums – after all the problems about having a session drummer, the first single issued featured Ringo after all. However, in April 1963, further pressings of the single on a black label featured the version with Andy White on drums.

The single reached its highest position of No. 17 in one London music paper for one week only, was No. 27 for one week in another, but at least managed to make its presence felt in all four London musical weeklies, reaching No. 24 in *Disc* and No. 32 in *Record Mirror*, in addition to the *Melody Maker* and *New Musical Express* placings. It went straight to No. 1 in the *Mersey Beat* chart.

The version with Ringo playing drums was included in *The Beatles Box* set and on the American *Rarities* album.

The version with Andy White on drums appeared on the *Please Please Me* album, *The Beatles' Hits* EP, *The Beatles 1962–1966* compilation, the American *Introducing the Beatles* album, the Tollie single, the Oldies single, the Capitol Starline single and *The Beatles Collection* set.

The 'Love Me Do' single had originally been available in America as a Capitol of Canada import, but was issued on Vee Jay's Tollie label on Tollie 9008 on 27 April 1968 and reached No. 1 in the American charts, selling over a million copies. Vee Jay reissued it again on their 'Oldies 45' series on OL 151 Oldies 45 on 10 August 1964. It also failed to chart when Capitol released it on their Starline series on Capitol Starline 6063 on 11 October 1965.

To celebrate the twentieth anniversary of the Beatles' recording career in 1982, *20 Greatest Hits* was released and the compilation once again featured the Andy White version. It was discovered that the use of the White version over the past twenty years had been because the Ringo Starr master had disappeared. The original masters were discovered at the time of the anniversary and both versions were issued on the twelve-inch single on Parlophone 12R 4949 on 1 November 1982. This followed the re-release of the single in a picture sleeve on Parlophone R 4949 on 4 October 1982 and the release of a picture disc on RP 4949 on the same date. On the 30th anniversary of its original release, EMI celebrated the event by re-releasing the single on Compact Disc limited edition digipack CD, tape and 7″ single in October 1992. It was included as the last track on *The Beatles Live At The BBC* CDs in 1994 in a version from the radio show 'Pop Go The Beatles' and on *Past Masters Volume One*. The version featuring Pete Best was included on the *Anthology 1* CD.

Love Me Tender

An Elvis Presley number penned by Ken Darby and originally based on an 1861 ballad called 'Aura Lee', written by W. W. Fosdick and George R. Poulton. The number became the title song of Elvis Presley's debut film. The Beatles included it in their repertoire as a showcase for Stuart Sutcliffe and it is one of the few songs that their former bass guitarist sang while he was a member of the band.

Love, Mike

Vocalist with the Beach Boys. Mike became interested in Transcendental Meditation and was a student at Rishikesh when the Beatles went to study at the ashram. It was said that during the stay, Mike helped Paul to write 'Back In The USSR'. While they were there the Beatles taped a song live as a birthday present for Mike which they called 'Spiritual Regeneration', although it has also been called 'Transcendental Meditation'.

Love Of The Loved

One of the earliest of the Paul McCartney compositions and one which the Quarry Men included in their repertoire. It was also one of the handful of original songs they performed at their Decca Records audition.

Although written by Paul, John Lennon once considered offering the song to Liverpool singer Beryl Marsden, but Brian Epstein insisted on giving it to his latest signing Cilla Black as her debut record. Paul was also present at Cilla's recording session. The single

was released on Parlophone R 5065 on 27 September 1963 but it
wasn't a big hit for her and only reached the position of No. 30 in
the British charts for a single week. Paul was later to write some
other numbers specially for Cilla.

Love Songs
A 25-track double-album, issued after the Beatles' EMI contract
had ended, leaving the company with the rights to repackage any
back-catalogue material.

Love Songs was issued in both Britain and America in 1977. The
British release was issued on Parlophone 721 on 19 November and
the American double album on Capitol SKBL 11711 on 21
October. It reached No. 12 in the British charts and No. 24 in
America.

The Capitol package included a 28-page booklet featuring the
lyrics of the songs.

Both British and American albums contained the same cover
photograph, which was a shot by Richard Avedon which had originally been featured, in a slightly different form, on the cover of
Look magazine in 1967.

The tracks were – Record One/Side One: 'Yesterday', 'I'll Follow
The Sun', 'I Need You', 'Girl', 'In My Life', 'Words Of Love', 'Here
There and Everywhere'. Record One/Side Two: 'Something', 'And I
Love Her', 'If I Fell', 'I'll Be Back', 'Tell Me What You See', 'Yes It
Is'. Record Two/Side One: 'Michelle', 'It's Only Love', 'You're Going
To Lose That Girl', 'Every Little Thing', 'For No One', 'She's Leaving
Home'. Record Two/Side Two: 'The Long and Winding Road', 'This
Boy', 'Norwegian Wood (This Bird Has Flown)', 'You've Got To
Hide Your Love Away', 'I Will' and 'P.S. I Love You'.

Love You To
Although George Harrison used a sitar for the first time on record
on 'Norwegian Wood', he says that playing the instrument on that
particular track came about by accident. The first number which he
specifically wrote with the sitar in mind was 'Love You To'. This
was also the first of George's Indian-influenced numbers to be
recorded and, apart from playing the sitar himself, he hired Indian
musician Anil Bhaqwat to play tabla.

The working title of the song was 'Granny Smith', named after
the apple, as George seemed to complete his numbers before
deciding on a title at this time.

'Love You To' was featured on the *Revolver* album, although for
some reason the American release carried the misspelling 'Love You
Too', a mistake which completely altered the meaning of the title.

George was evidently fighting for his share of songs on Beatles albums and wrote three of the tracks featured on *Revolver.*

The number was recorded at Abbey Road on 11 April 1966 with overdubs added on 13 April. No other members of the Beatles were on the session and apart from Bhagwat, other unnamed Indian musicians performed – they were players from the North London Asian Music Circle.

'Love You To' was a love song to George's wife Pattie.

Lowe, John Charles

John Lowe, nicknamed 'Duff', shared the same class as Paul McCartney at Liverpool Institute. In January 1958, he joined the Quarry Men as pianist, appearing at a number of gigs with them, but leaving the band in January 1959.

During the summer of 1958, he recorded 'That'll Be the Day/In Spite Of All The Danger' with them at a small studio in Liverpool. Lowe maintained the only existing copy of the acetate and 23 years after it was recorded (in July 1981), he sold the disc to Paul McCartney.

He then moved to Ashton, near Bristol, where he works in the investment business. In the 1990s, he teamed up with Mike Wilsh, former member of the Four Pennies, to form the Pennies and a number of their gigs took place at the new Cavern in Liverpool during the annual Mersey Beat conventions. There he met up with other ex-members of the Quarry Men and they decided to record together and team up for occasional performances.

Lowlands Club, Hayman's Green, West Derby, Liverpool L12

One of the numerous small clubs in Liverpool which provided an outlet for local groups to play. The Quarry Men appeared at a Saturday night audition at Lowlands during the middle of 1958, but were unsuccessful in obtaining any bookings there.

The club was situated on the opposite side of the street, 50 yards down from the Bests' home, which was to become the Casbah Club in August 1959.

When the Quarry Men ceased appearing locally at the end of 1958, George Harrison joined the Les Stewart Quartet who appeared several times at Lowlands from January 1959.

Lucille

A Little Richard number by Penniman/Collins, first released in 1957. It was immediately adopted as part of the repertoire of the

Quarry Men after Paul had joined, with Paul taking over lead vocals, as he did with all Little Richard songs.

The Beatles featured the number on their BBC recordings for 'Pop Go The Beatles' and 'Saturday Club'.

Paul also recorded it for the Concert for Kampuchea on 29 December 1979 and this version is to be found on the 1981 double album *Concerts For Kampuchea*. A Saturday Club performance was included on *The Beatles Live At The BBC* CDs.

Lucy In The Sky With Diamonds

The inspiration for the song came when the four-year-old Julian Lennon returned from nursery school with a painting. When John asked him what the subject was, Julian told him, 'It's Lucy in the sky with diamonds.'

Purely because the initials of the song coincide with those of the drug LSD, which John had admitted taking, several radio stations banned the record, convinced it was a song advocating the taking of drugs.

The Beatles began rehearsing the song at Abbey Road on Tuesday, 28 February 1967, and the group began recording it the following day. In John's surrealistic lyrics can be detected the influence of his early love of Lewis Carroll's *Alice in Wonderland* books.

Paul McCartney was to comment: 'We did the whole thing like an *Alice in Wonderland* idea, being in a boat on the river, slowly drifting downstream and those great cellophane flowers towering over your head. Every so often it broke off and you saw "Lucy in the Sky with Diamonds" all over the sky. This Lucy was God, the big figure, the white rabbit. You can just write a song with imagination on words and that's what we like.'

John was never really satisfied with the Beatles' version of the number, voicing his opinion that they didn't really play well on it. He preferred the version by Elton John. When Elton recorded the number, John agreed to play guitar and sing backing vocals and the record was advertised as 'Featuring Dr Winston O'Boogie and his Reggae Guitars'. John also performed the number on stage with Elton John at Madison Square Garden in New York.

The number was featured on the album *Sgt Pepper's Lonely Hearts Club Band* and was included on the compilation *The Beatles 1967–1970*. A version was included on the Beatles' *Anthology 2* CDs.

Lush, Richard

Lush was an apprentice at Abbey Road Studios and had previously worked on recordings with Cliff Richard and the Shadows. He joined the recording team with George Martin and Geoff Emerick after engineer Phil McDonald became a cutting engineer in February,

1967, and was eighteen years old at the time he first made his debut as the Beatles' tape operator on Wednesday, 13 April of that year. Lush worked on numerous Beatles recordings, including the album *Sergeant Pepper's Lonely Hearts Club Band*. His final work on Beatles productions in the studios took place on Wednesday, 1 April 1970 when Phil Spector was in charge working on tracks for the *Let It Be* album. Richard had worked at Abbey Road from 1965 until 1973 when he then went to work at an EMI facility in Australia.

Lynch, Kenny

Popular British entertainer, born in London's East End, who had eight entries in the British charts between 1960 and 1983. His most successful singles were 'Up On The Roof', which reached No. 10 in 1962, and 'You Can Never Stop Me Loving You', which reached the same position the following year.

Kenny first met the Beatles on 28 October 1962 when he appeared on a bill at the Liverpool Empire, promoted by Brian Epstein. The Beatles asked him if he'd like them to provide backing for him, but he told them he'd already hired a backing band.

Their association continued when they both appeared on the Helen Shapiro tour, promoted by Arthur Howes, in 1963. John and Paul had written a number called 'Misery' for Helen, but apparently her record producer Norrie Paramor didn't like it. Kenny says that he was sitting next to John on the tour coach when Helen came to talk to them. John asked what Paramor thought about the song. When Kenny heard that she wasn't going to record the number he immediately seized on the opportunity. He said, 'I was leaning on the seat and I said to John, "Can you let me hear it?" and he played it to me on his guitar. I was going to record the number "You Could Never Stop Me Loving You" at the time, but I gave it to Johnny Tillotson and recorded "Misery" instead. Tillotson had a hit with his. I didn't. But I was the first person to record a Beatles number.'

'Misery' was released in Britain on 22 March 1963 on HMV Pop 1136. Kenny first played the single to John and Paul in Dick James' office and John Lennon admitted liking Kenny's rendition of the number but couldn't stand the guitar work. 'He gave me a bollocking because he didn't like the Bert Weedon guitar on it,' Kenny said, referring to the veteran British guitar player.

Incidentally, when Kenny was on tour with the Beatles, promoter Arthur Howes asked him to introduce the group on stage each night. He also appeared with the Beatles on 31 May 1964 on 'Pops Alive' at the Prince of Wales Theatre, London.

In 1973, Kenny was one of several personalities Paul McCartney picked to appear on the cover of his *Band On The Run* album. Kenny-commented: 'I travelled all the way down from Scotland to appear on the cover of the album and when I arrived at the session I said to Paul, "You owe me one." He said, "Right, I owe you one, Kenny", so I'm hoping he'll come on the cover of one of my albums.'

Lyndon, John

A former theatrical director who was hired by Brian Epstein to be Production Director for NEMS Enterprises. Lyndon introduced some innovations into the package show when he produced *Star Scene '65*, which starred several NEMS acts. He also staged the Sunday concerts at the Saville Theatre and was in charge of all NEMS theatre and cabaret presentations.

When the Apple Retail division was undergoing difficulties, the Beatles asked him to replace Pete Shotton and administer the Apple shops.

Lyntone Records

The record company which produced all the Beatles Christmas Records. The idea for the special Christmas messages to fans originally came from press officer Tony Barrow. He co-ordinated the project and the first Christmas disc was issued on 6 December 1963. For this release 30,000 copies were pressed in the basic format of a 33 rpm seven-inch flexidisc. Barrow took the 24 minutes of tape which the Beatles had recorded to Lyntone and, together with the company's director Paul Lynton, snipped the tape with scissors until they'd edited it down to a five-minute recording. They didn't keep a master copy and the rest of the recording ended up in the waste bin.

The records issued by Lyntone were:
'The Beatles Christmas Record', LYN 492, 6 December 1963.
'Another Beatles Christmas Record', LYN 757, 18 December 1964.
'The Beatles Third Christmas Record', LYN 948, 17 December 1965.
'The Beatles Fourth Christmas Record – Pantomime: Everywhere It's Christmas', LYN 1145, 16 December 1966.
'The Beatles Fifth Christmas Record – Christmas Time (Is Here Again)', LYN 1360, 15 December 1967.
'The Beatles Sixth Christmas Record – Christmas 1968', LYN 1743/4, 20 December 1968.
'The Beatles Seventh Christmas Record – Happy Christmas 1969', LYN 1970/1, 19 December 1969.
'From Then To You – The Beatles Christmas Record 1970', Apple LYN 2154, 18 December 1970.

Macbeth, David

British singer whose single chart hit was 'Mr Blue', which reached No. 18 in 1959. The former Newcastle footballer appeared in Liverpool several times during 1962 to promote his new release 'Roses Are Red', including the lunchtime pop sessions at the Crane Theatre and cabaret shows at the Cabaret Club and Speke Airport Cabaret Club.

He appeared on the Beatles/Roy Orbison tour, which commenced in May 1963.

Macdonna Hall, Corner of Salisbury Avenue and Banks Road, West Kirby, Wirral, Cheshire

Also known in Beatles annuls as Thistle Café, because when the Beatles appeared here for the first and only time on Thursday, 1 February 1962 the venue, a dance studio, was situated directly above the Thistle Café.

It was the group's first booking under Brian Epstein's aegis and Brian advertised the event as the 'Grand opening of the Beatle club'. Why he described it in this way is not known, because they never appeared at the venue again. It was an unlikely place for a gig and situated ten miles outside of Liverpool.

Epstein was able to secure eighteen pounds for the performance, a substantial sum for a small local venue at the time, and entrance cost four shillings and sixpence (22½p).

The support group was Steve Day & the Drifters.

Liverpool promoter Sam Leach claimed that on this evening John Lennon was ill and he was able to secure Rory Storm as a replacement for the gig. This seems unlikely as Rory couldn't even play a guitar – both George Harrison and Neil Aspinall denied such an occurrence, while many of Leach's claims can be taken with a pinch of salt.

The Thistle Café later became a restaurant called What's Cookin?

Macmillan, Iain

The photographer who took the famous cover shot for the *Abbey Road* album. Macmillan was only given a brief time to take the shots outside the Abbey Road Studios in St John's Wood at 10.00 a.m. on 8 August 1969. A policeman was able to hold up the traffic for a few minutes while Macmillan balanced on a stepladder and took six shots of the Beatles traversing the zebra crossing. Paul McCartney then picked the shot to be used from the six transparencies which Macmillan gave him. Paul had originally made a rough sketch of the basic idea for the photograph and Macmillan planned it out in more detail.

9 Madryn Street, Liverpool L8

Birthplace of Richard Starkey. The house was a small Victorian terraced one in Liverpool's Dingle area and Ringo's parents paid ten shillings (50p) per week in rent, which was to rise to fourteen shillings and tenpence (74p) per week.

The baby was born one week late, at midnight on 7 July 1940, one month before the Luftwaffe began bombing the city. Baby Richard weighed 10 lbs and was delivered by forceps.

His mother Elsie was 26 at the time and his father Richard was 28.

The bombing began when Elsie was still in bed recovering from the birth of her son, whom the couple had nicknamed Richie.

When Elsie and her husband split up in 1943, Elsie took her son to live in the nearby street, Admiral Grove, swapping the house with a friend as she didn't want to bump into her husband, who had moved to No. 59 Madryn Street.

Maggie May

A traditional sea shanty based on a Liverpool prostitute called Maggie May. Liverpool's Lime Street had the reputation of being one of the most notorious streets in the world during the days of the sailing ships because it was full of pubs and prostitutes. Maggie May became a Liverpool legend and there was even a musical,

Maggie May, penned by Alun Owen in the mid-sixties, and a Liverpool club of that name, run by Allan Williams.

The Quarry Men introduced 'Maggie May' into their earliest repertoire as the old sea shanty had recently been re-popularised during the skiffle boom by the Vipers Skiffle Group.

The Beatles recorded the number in January 1969 and the track was included on their *Let It Be* album. As the traditional song was out of copyright, the credits read: 'Trad. arr. Lennon/McCartney /Harrison/Starkey'.

Magic Christian, The

Ringo Starr co-starred with Peter Sellers in this 1969 movie, adapted from Terry Southern's novel of the same name. The 95-minute British film was directed by Joseph McGrath and produced by Dennis O'Dell, head of Apple Films. The movie's score was composed by Ken Thorne, while the theme song, 'Come and Get It', was written by Paul McCartney and performed by the Apple band Badfinger. Peter Sellers appeared as Sir Guy Grand, Ringo played Youngman Grand and guest stars in the movie were Richard Attenborough, Leonard Frey, Laurence Harvey, Christopher Lee, Spike Milligan, Roman Polanski and Raquel Welch.

Margaret Tarrant, in *Films And Filming*, wrote: 'The surreal world of the Goons and the picaresque fantasy world of the Beatles are combined in an essentially genial indictment of British capitalist society.' While another reviewer wrote: 'Ringo Starr continues to exploit the melancholy wanderer's role he made his own in *A Hard Day's Night*.'

Ringo's part had been specially written for the film (the character he played wasn't in the original book), and his role was mainly that of an observer, watching the various stunts which Sellers sets up.

Ringo appears as Youngman Grand, the adopted son of the world's richest man, Sir Guy Grand. Sir Guy resolves to show Youngman the extent to which people are obsessed by money and the ends they will go to obtain it. He seeks to prove that 'everyone has his price'. The lure of money encourages a traffic warden (Spike Milligan) to eat his own ticket and causes a snobby art gallery official (John Cleese) to sell him a Rembrandt. Before the man's horrified eyes, Sir Guy cuts out the nose in the painting, stating that he only collects Rembrandt's noses. He bribes the Oxford boat crew to lose the annual boat race against Cambridge and entices two beefy boxers to embrace each other in the ring during a bout. Money also persuades a famous Shakespearean actor (Laurence Harvey) to do a striptease in the middle of his soliloquy in *Hamlet*.

Sir Guy then takes Youngman on a cruise on the liner *Magic*

Christian, where his education into man's greed continues. At one point he is shown over the engine room of the boat by a whip-wielding Raquel Welch, to discover that it is in fact a galley with topless females at the oars.

The grand finale of the film occurs back on dry land in London where a giant vat has been filled with the most unspeakable detritus, including vomit, human excreta and pig's blood. Sprinkling it with money, Sir Guy stands back and watches as respectable, but desperately avaricious businessmen brawl amid the unsightly mess.

When filming was completed there was a special party held at Les Ambassadeurs Club in London. Among those in attendance were Ringo and Maureen and Paul and Linda. Ringo and Maureen and John and Yoko attended the Royal world premiere at the Odeon, Kensington, London, on 11 December 1969. The queues were taken aback by the sight of John and Yoko walking by them holding a banner proclaiming 'Britain Murdered Hanratty'.

Magical Mystery Tour (Album)

The album of *Magical Mystery Tour* was issued in America by Capitol Records on SMAL 2835 on 27 November 1967 and had the biggest initial sale of any Capitol album to that time, notching up sales amounting to eight million dollars within three weeks and eventually selling over three million copies.

The No. 1 album was packaged with a booklet of photographs from the film and contained three tracks which had been released as singles in 1967.

The American track listing was – Side One: 'Magical Mystery Tour', 'The Fool On The Hill', 'Flying', 'Blue Jay Way', 'Your Mother Should Know' and 'I Am The Walrus'. Side Two: 'Hello Goodbye', 'Strawberry Fields Forever', 'Penny Lane', 'Baby You're A Rich Man' and 'All You Need Is Love'.

Magical Mystery Tour (EP)

The soundtrack of *Magical Mystery Tour* was issued in Britain as a special double EP on Parlophone SMMT 1/2 on 8 December 1967. The package contained the two EPs and a special 24-page illustrated booklet of the film which had been edited by Tony Barrow, with a little help from Neil Aspinall and Mal Evans. It was lavishly illustrated with photographs by John Kelly and drawings by Bob Gibson. The tracks were – Record One: 'Magical Mystery Tour', 'Your Mother Should Know', 'I Am The Walrus'. Record Two: 'The Fool On The Hill', 'Flying', 'Blue Jay Way'. It was issued in America as an album, with the addition of three tracks previously issued as singles.

Magical Mystery Tour (Film)

The Beatles' television film was conceived before Brian Epstein's death, discussed with him and became the group's first solo venture after Brian died.

The concept was Paul McCartney's and he had planned the venture on a flight back to England from America where he'd been visiting Jane Asher during her theatre tour. While there he'd been reading about the adventures of Ken Kesey (author of *One Flew Over the Cuckoo's Nest*) and his Merry Pranksters who had been travelling cross-country by bus.

Paul's idea was for the Beatles to produce their own television spectacular, writing and producing it themselves, using the knowledge they had gleaned from Dick Lester and Walter Shenson while making their first two feature films. The Beatles reckoned that if *Magical Mystery Tour* proved a success on television, they would go on to produce their third feature film themselves.

Press officer Tony Barrow has said that Paul was originally hoping that *Magical Mystery Tour* would be suitable for cinema release and was disappointed to be told that this was out of the question.

The 55-minute special, edited down from ten hours of filming, featured six numbers: 'Magical Mystery Tour', 'Your Mother Should Know', 'I Am The Walrus', 'Fool On The Hill', 'Flying' and 'Blue Jay Way'. Two other songs they wrote for the projects were never issued – 'Jessie's Dream' and 'Shirley's Wild Accordion'.

The idea was a surrealistic mystery trip on a gaily-painted yellow and blue coach. The coach left London on Monday, 11 September 1967 and filming of the actual trip was completed on Friday, 15 September. Paul McCartney met up with the various Mystery Tour passengers at Allsop Place, near the London Planetarium, which the group had often established as a meeting place prior to some of their British tours. Painting still hadn't been completed on the bus and it arrived two hours later than its appointed 10.45 a.m. departure time. Once they set off they headed for Virginia Water, Surrey, to pick up John, Ringo and George as it was close to Weybridge where two of them lived. They then set off for the West Country and Hampshire, Devon, Cornwall and Somerset.

In all there were 43 passengers. Apart from the Beatles and film crew (Ringo was billed as Director of Photography), they included four fan club secretaries: Frieda Kelly, Barbara King, Sylvia Nightingale and Jeni Crowley. There were Neil Aspinall and Mal Evans, plus a small party of dwarfs. One of the dwarfs was Rayston Smith, who died in mysterious circumstances in 1989. His biography, *Little Legs*, revealed that he was a hit man who had killed several people and had served seven years in jail for manslaughter.

Neil was now the headman at Apple and was later to comment, 'We went out to make a film and nobody had the vaguest idea of what it was all about. What we should have been filming, if anything, was all the confusion, because that was the *real* mystery tour.'

Also on board were Luke Kelly, the coach driver Alf Manders, Bill Wall, Linda Lawson, Pamela and Nicola Hale, Elizabeth and Arthur Kelly, Liz Harvey and Michael Gladden. There were also a number of actors and actresses for whom basic parts had been outlined on which they could improvise. They included Scottish actor/poet/comedian Ivor Cutler, who portrayed Buster Bloodvessel, a passenger who travelled on all the mystery tours and who developed a passion for Ringo's Aunt Jessie, played by Jessie Robins. Paul had first spotted Cutler on the television show 'Late Night Line Up' and remembered him when casting for the special. One sunny morning, while John and George filmed a sequence at the Atlantic Hotel, Paul and Ringo set off for Tregurrian Beach where they filmed a romantic interlude between Cutler and Robins. The BBC cut this scene when the special was televised, although they reinstated it when they re-screened *Magical Mystery Tour* in 1979.

'Rubber Man' Nat Jackley was filmed by John and George at the Atlantic Hotel swimming pool for a comedy dream sequence in which he was joined by several girls in bikinis. This scene was also consigned to the cutting room floor. However, it was included in the cartoon storybook of *Magical Mystery Tour* that accompanied the film's soundtrack EP/album, as this was completed before the film was finally edited. Jackley was a British music hall comedian whose gimmick was his ability to twist his neck as if it were rubber. Jackley died at the age of 79 in September 1988.

There was also Little George Claydon, a tiny actor who played the Amateur Photographer; Maggie Wright as Maggie the Lovely Starlet, Paul's mini-skirted girlfriend; Shirley Evans, a professional accordionist; Derek Royce as Jolly Jimmy Johnson, the Tour Courier; and Mandy Weet as the Tour Hostess.

There were various other friends such as Paul's hairdresser, Leslie Cavendish, Paul's brother Mike McGear and the Apple electronics wizard Alexis Mardas.

Travelling through Devon and Cornwall, they picked up a few extra passengers, such as Spencer Davis (leader of the Spencer Davis Group) with his wife Pauline and their children. The family had been on holiday near Newquay. There was a clip of Winwood's group Traffic performing 'Here We Go Round The Mulberry Bush', but this ended up on the cutting room floor.

Most of the interior scenes had to be filmed at West Malling RAF Station near Maidstone, Kent, as Apple Films were unable to book Shepperton Studios in time. One of the scenes shot on Monday, 18 September was a sequence filmed in Paul Raymond's Revue Bar in Soho. It featured the Bonzo Dog Doo Dah Band performing 'Death Cab for Cutie', while popular stripper Jan Carson performed her act. Despite the fact that her bare breasts had a 'censored' strip covering them, the entire sequence was excised in Japan.

The sequence featuring Paul singing 'Fool On The Hill' was filmed in Nice, France, on Monday, 30 and Tuesday, 31 October. When Paul flew to France for the filming he forgot both his passport and his wallet – he was so used to someone else looking after those details! The French authorities wouldn't allow Paul any credit and filming was delayed while he arranged for money to be sent over from England.

The basic story concerns a coach trip that Ringo and his Aunt Jessie have decided to take. They visit a tour office and are talked into going on the Mystery Tour by a young man (John Lennon) wearing a thick moustache. Meanwhile: 'Away in the sky, beyond the clouds, live four or five magicians. By casting wonderful spells they turn the Most Ordinary Coach Trip into a Magical Mystery Tour.' The magicians, of course, are played by the four Beatles and Mal Evans, dressed in long wizards' robes and pointed hats. We meet them several times during the course of the journey. The coach has started off to the tune of 'Magical Mystery Tour' and the second number we are treated to is 'Fool On The Hill'. At one point, Paul has a chat with five-year-old Nicola Hale, a touching scene that wasn't planned or rehearsed.

Many of the episodic scenes during the trip are surrealistic, the most visually intriguing being the one set in front of the high, concrete walls of the deserted West Malling Aerodrome (the walls were finally demolished in 1991). There, 'I Am The Walrus' was filmed, with the Beatles in their animal masks and with egg-headed spectators and swaying policemen on top of the wall. The Marathon Race was held on the same set, with Ringo driving the coach followed by a line of egg-heads, four midget wrestlers, racing motorcyclists, a rugby team, a dozen children, five clergymen and a host of passengers scrambling across the airfield.

For 'Blue Jay Way', the slightly mystical George Harrison song, a host of people find their way inside a tiny tent to watch George perform the number seated amid swirling smoke clouds. In another scene, Paul plays Major McCartney, with Victor Spinetti as the Recruiting Sergeant. Victor couldn't take up the invitation of accompanying the Beatles on the trip, but took time off from the film he was making to act out this scene, which is a variation of his *Oh, What A Lovely War* role.

One of the strongest sequences is Aunt Jessie's Nightmare, in which the overweight Jessie dreams of lashings of spaghetti while a greasy-haired waiter (John Lennon) heaps pasta on to her table by the spadeful.

In the climactic scene, to the tune of 'Your Mother Should Know', the Beatles descend a grandiose staircase, dressed in white evening wear, to join a spectacular gathering of dancing couples and saluting girl cadets. Two hundred people were involved in this final scene, including 24 young girl cadets from the Women's Air Force who were locally based and 160 members of Peggy Spencer's formation dance groups.

The Beatles spent six weeks editing the film in a small office in Old Compton Street, Soho, London, engaging a professional film editor, Roy Benson, to help them. The 55-minute film was colourful, funny, mystical and musical. Unfortunately, it received almost universal condemnation from the critics after its initial screening in black and white on BBC 2 on Boxing Day, 1967, when a reported viewing audience of around 13 million people watched it, instead of the anticipated 20 million. TAM (Television Audience Measurement) estimated the viewing figures of other shows that evening as 'The Square Peg', a Norman Wisdom film – 17 million; 'Top of the Pops' – 15 million; 'David Frost Over Christmas' – 14 million; and the film *Brigadoon* – 13.5 million. In the Christmas ratings, *Magical Mystery Tour* was placed at No. 25. However, it must be recognised that BBC 2 was, and remains, a minority channel whose programmes don't generally approach the figures of ITV and BBC 1.

Negotiations had been taking place with CBS, NBC and ABC in America to buy the film for Stateside screening for $1 million (it cost $100,000 to make) but, following the harsh criticism in the British press, the US TV networks lost interest.

The American *Time* magazine was to report: 'Paul directed, Ringo mugged, John did imitations, George danced a bit and, when the show hit the BBC last week, the audience gagged.'

The show was repeated on BBC 2 on 5 January 1968 in full colour. In the meantime, Paul had appeared on TV and radio shows in an attempt to reply to the hostile reaction from the critics.

He was to ask: 'Was the film really so bad compared to the rest of Christmas TV?' He added: 'You could hardly call the Queen's speech a gasser! Our problem is that we are prisoners of our own fame. We could put on a moptop show, but we really don't like that sort of entertainment any more. Sure, we could have sung carols and done a first class Christmassy show starring the Beatles with lots of phoney tinsel like everybody else. It would have been the easiest thing in the world, but we wanted to do something different, we thought we would do a fantasy film without a real plot. We thought the title was explanation enough. There was no plot and it was formless – deliberately so and those people expecting a plot were probably disappointed.'

In 1968, *Magical Mystery Tour* was screened by Dutch Television on 10 February and it was sold to Japanese Television in April. In May it was shown at special screenings at selected cinemas in America, mainly in Los Angeles and San Francisco. A few months later it was premiered at the Savoy Theatre, Boston, where it received positive reviews.

In the years since it was first screened, *Magical Mystery Tour* has been reappraised. Many have now agreed that the virulent criticism at the time of its initial screening was unjust and perhaps biased, affording critics their first opportunity of knocking the Beatles, who had been riding high for so many years.

Magical Mystery Tour (Single)

The title song Paul wrote for his 'Magical Mystery Tour' concept. He also wanted to convey the sensation of excitement and jollity amid the car and coach noises as the trip got underway and another sound effects album from the Abbey Road archives was used, *Volume 36: Traffic Noise Stereo*, when the recording began on Tuesday, 25 April 1967. Later, four trumpeters were hired to overdub a brass section: Roy Copestake, Elgar Howarth David Mason and John Wilbraham.

The song was featured on the British double EP set of *Magical Mystery Tour*, the American album of the same name and also a British album of that title issued in 1976. The track was also featured on the *Reel Music* compilation.

Magnus, David

Born in 1944, photographer Magnus originally became Dezo Hoffmann's studio assistant, before turning freelance. He first photographed the Beatles at their Stowe School concert in April 1963, and from then until 1967 he photographed them on numerous occasions both on tour and in the studio. His photographs from the 'Our World' television session included the last photographs ever taken of Brian Epstein and the Beatles together, an image in which they were blowing trumpets together.

Maharishi Mahesh Yogi, The

For a brief time he was the Beatles' spiritual adviser.

Born Mahesh Prasad Varma in 1918, he graduated from the

University of Allahabad with a physics degree and then spent thirteen years studying Sanskrit and the scriptures under Guru Dev. He adopted the name Maharishi, which means 'the great soul', and devised a way of making an ancient form of meditation more palatable and marketable for the West in the shape of Transcendental Meditation. In 1959 he arrived in London to establish the International Meditation Society. By 1967 the movement boasted 10,000 British members and was also known as the Spiritual Regeneration Movement. This was the year in which Pattie Harrison first came across the movement when she attended a lecture on Spiritual Regeneration in February 1967 at Caxton Hall.

Pattie had plenty of time on her hands while George was involved in Beatle activities and she became intrigued with the mysticism of India as presented by the Maharishi. His methods of meditation had been developed in India thousands of years previously. What he did was repackage the goods, stamp them with a brand name, Transcendental Meditation, and sell them for consumption in the West. The Maharishi believed that by popularising TM he could help bring peace to the world due to the fact that the meditation technique inhibits violence and calms the spirit.

Pattie interested George and the other members of the Beatles in the movement and when notices began to appear on the advertisement hoardings of London Underground mentioning a personal appearance by the Maharishi at the Park Lane Hilton, all four Beatles decided to attend. The event took place on Thursday, 24 August 1967 and entrance was seven shillings and sixpence (37½p) per head. His talk impressed the Beatles who requested a private audience with him following the lecture. When they spoke to him he invited them to join him at a ten-day course on TM at the University College, Bangor, which was to begin that weekend. They all agreed to go and they even asked Brian Epstein. Brian told them that he had made other plans for that weekend, but that he'd try to join them in Bangor at a later date. It was during the course that they learned of their manager's death.

They turned to the Maharishi as their guru and agreed to spend three months at his ashram in Rishikesh in India. Ringo and Maureen stood it for ten days before returning to England, Paul and Jane Asher left after ten weeks – and the loyal John and George then had a bust-up with the spiritual leader.

This began when John invited Alexis 'Magic Alex' Mardas to the ashram. Alex had a knowledge of spirituality and mysticism and firmly believed that the Beatles were under the spell of a clever man who was attempting to manipulate them. Alex could not accept a spiritual leader who, in his opinion, was so obsessed with material things. The Maharishi had come to be known as the 'Giggling Guru', because of his habit of giggling. He seemed to act as if he didn't understand business affairs, and always had an accountant present at his meetings. When travelling he stayed at the best hotels and his quarters in Rishikesh were luxurious by Indian standards. Although he said, 'I deal in wisdom, not money' money was still a consideration, as Neil Aspinall and Peter Brown discovered when they tried to negotiate for a film to be made of the Maharishi and the Beatles at Rishikesh; the Maharishi haggled for a larger percentage of the film's potential proceeds.

The Maharishi was aware of Alex's suspicions and attempted to coerce him by offering him the commission of building a radio station at Rishikesh. Alex was more interested in proving to the Beatles that the holy man was using them. His opportunity came when a young nurse from California alleged that the Maharishi had made sexual advances to her.

As a result, both John and George confronted the Maharishi and left the ashram.

John, in particular, was furious at his idol. TM had benefited him greatly. It had broken his drug addiction and opened his creative juices – resulting in a large number of songs being written in Rishikesh. The angry John wrote a number called 'Maharishi', in which he intended to expose the holy man, but was persuaded into changing the title to 'Sexy Sadie' so as to avoid any possible legal suits.

The Beatles had obviously had too high aspirations regarding the abilities of the Maharishi. Neil Aspinall commented: 'John thought there was some sort of secret the Maharishi had to give you, and then you could just go home.' Paul said, 'We made a mistake. We thought there was more to him than there was. He's human. We thought at first that he wasn't.'

Despite the fact that the Beatles' association with him had been brief, the Maharishi's cause had blossomed with the international publicity. The money poured in as the converts grew and the Maharishi immediately began to buy property. In England alone he bought Mentmore Towers in Buckinghamshire, Roydon Hall in Maidstone, Swythamley Park in the Peak District and a Georgian rectory in Suffolk. He set up his headquarters in Switzerland and at one time he was reported to have an income of six million pounds per month, with two million followers worldwide, 90,000 of them in Britain.

Mahon, Gene

Dublin-born graphic designer who was working for an advertising agency in London when he became involved in the design of the sleeve for the *Sgt Pepper's Lonely Hearts Club Band* album. He was art director of the back sleeve which featured the photograph of the Beatles with Paul turning his back to the camera, over which were printed the lyrics to the songs. While working on the assignment, Gene first came into contact with Neil Aspinall and in February 1968 it was Neil who phoned him and invited him over to the Apple offices in Wigmore Street to discuss a commission. Neil told him that he needed a photograph of an Apple to be used as an image for the Apple label. Gene said the inspiration came to him in a flash. He suggested that on the 'A' side they feature a complete apple with no writing on it whatsoever and on the 'B' side the picture of an apple sliced in half with the label copy on it. He suggested that to avoid confusion they should have 'This Side' written on the left-hand side of the sliced apple, with the song title, artist's name, running time, publishing credits and so on while on the other side would be the words 'Other Side' with the title and the copy for the 'A' side.

Unfortunately, this idea couldn't be used because of the legal requirements which obliged a record company to place details of the contents on both sides of a disc.

Gene had photographer Paul Castell take a number of photographs of apples, both red and green, sliced and unsliced, against a variety of coloured backgrounds. The different two-and-a-quarter-inch transparencies were shown to the four Beatles, Neil and Ron Kass at various stages of development.

The design finally chosen was that of a green Granny Smith apple on a black background. Some final touches were added by Alan Aldridge on the actual lettering on the design.

From the initial commission to the final approval of the design, the project had taken six months to complete.

Mahon was also commissioned to work on other Apple record design projects.

Mailman Bring Me No More Blues

A number the Beatles recorded during the 'Get Back' sessions on Wednesday, 29 January 1969, although it wasn't released. The number was composed by writers Roberts/Katz/Clayton and originally featured as the 'B' side of Buddy Holly's 1957 release 'Words Of Love'. The Beatles introduced it into their repertoire in 1961.

A version was also included on the Beatles' *Anthology 3* CDs.

Majestic Ballroom, Conway Street, Birkenhead L41

When the Majestic Ballroom opened in 1962 it was a 'luxury venue' compared to some of the cellar clubs and local halls the

Mersey groups had been appearing in. It was one of 28 ballrooms around Britain run by the Top Rank organisation.

When the Beatles made their debut there on Thursday, 28 June 1962, it was their first ever appearance at a Top Rank venue. The Majestic rapidly became one of the top Merseyside venues, open throughout the week and presenting several groups each evening – for instance, the Saturday, 15 December 1962, bill comprised the Beatles, the Fourmost and Jenny & the Tall Boys.

The venue was managed by Bill Marsden and his office became a meeting place for various members of the Mersey scene who would gather in Bill's office for a drink to chat about the business. Regulars at these meetings were Brian Epstein, Bob Wooler, Bill and Virginia Harry, Joe Flannery and Ted Knibbs. During one of the evenings Flannery tried a joke by putting in a call to the office and claiming it was Colonel Tom Parker trying to contact Brian Epstein.

The Beatles' complete appearances for 1962 were: 28 June, 5 July, 12 July, 28 July, 17 August, 24 August, 8 September, 28 September, 15 October, 22 November, 29 November, 15 December. The 1963 appearances were: 17 January, 31 January, 21 February and 10 April.

On their 17 August 1962 appearance their drummer was Johnny Hutchinson. Following their 15 December 1962 show there was a special *Mersey Beat* Awards party at which the Beatles were presented with their first-ever award by Bill Harry: the *Mersey Beat* Shield for being voted No. 1 group in *Mersey Beat*.

For their 17 January 1963 appearance all tickets had been sold out in advance and 500 angry fans queuing outside were unable to see the show as the hall only had a 900 capacity. As a result, for the next Beatles appearance, there was an innovation: two separate performances. Although it was common to have two performances at a theatre concert, it had never been done before in a ballroom.

The new shows took place at 8.00 p.m. and 11.00 p.m. to capacity audiences. The two performances on the 21 February 1963 show took place at 7.30 p.m. and 11.50 p.m.

In 1964 a new manager, John Glass, took over the running of the ballroom and he received a telegram from the Beatles for the second anniversary which congratulated the Majestic on 'its bi-centenary or something'.

Majestic Ballroom, High Street, Crewe, Cheshire

The Beatles appeared at this Top Rank ballroom on two consecutive Monday nights in 1962, on 13 and 20 August.

A story in *Mersey Beat* newspaper headed 'All Change At Crewe' (referring to the fact that the Cheshire town contains one of Britain's main railway junctions) read: 'The Merseyside rock and roll scene has spread its wings to Crewe, due to the co-operation of two Top Rank managers, namely Bill Marsden of the Majestic Ballroom, Birkenhead, and Ron Ratty, his counterpart at the Majestic, Crewe.

'Bill, who has become well acquainted with Merseyside's top attractions, now books these groups for Crewe. The Beatles, Lee Curtis with the All Stars, Billy Kramer with the Coasters, the Big Three and Group One have all appeared at this exciting venue recently, and have been well received and enthusiastically welcomed by Crewe teenagers.'

For its rock 'n' roll nights, the ballroom used the slogan: 'The biggest rock since Blackpool rock!'

Majestic Ballroom, Witham, Hull, Humberside

The Majestics were a group of ballrooms in various British cities, owned by Top Rank. After the Beatles had proved successful at the Majestic Ballroom, Birkenhead, this led to other bookings on the circuit. They appeared here on Saturday, 20 October 1962. At 128 miles from Liverpool, it was the furthest distance from their hometown that they'd played. George wanted to drive the group van but crashed it in Goole, knocking down a factory fence. As a result he received a summons and a one-year driving ban.

They performed at the ballroom for the second and last time on Wednesday, 13 February 1963.

Majestic Ballroom, Seven Sisters Road, London N7

One of the largest venues in the Top Rank Majestic Ballroom chain. The Beatles appeared at the ballroom once, on Wednesday, 24 April 1963, headlining a Mersey Beat Showcase with Gerry & the Pacemakers, the Big Three and Billy J. Kramer. The occasion drew an audience of 2,000.

Majestic Ballroom, Mill Street, Luton, Bedfordshire

Another in the Top Rank chain of ballrooms. The Beatles appeared at this venue only once, on Wednesday, 17 April 1963.

Majestic Ballroom, Westgate Road, Newcastle-upon-Tyne, Tyne & Wear

The Beatles first appeared at this Top Rank Ballroom on 28 January 1963. Their second and final appearance at the venue on 26 June

1963 was their last-ever appearance at a Top Rank Ballroom. After they'd finished the gig, back at their hotel, John composed 'She Loves You'.

Majestic Theatre, Christchurch, New Zealand

The Beatles appeared at this theatre on the South Island on the final date of their brief tour of New Zealand, on 27 June 1964.

There were various incidents when the Beatles landed at Christchurch – at one point a thirteen-year-old girl threw herself on the Beatles' car and bounced into the road. Fortunately, she wasn't hurt and they took her into their hotel to have a cup of tea with them. When they went on to the balcony of their hotel to wave at the crowds they had to retreat when rotten eggs were hurled at them.

Maltz, Stephen

An accountant from the firm of Bryce Hanmer whom the company placed as Staff Accountant at Apple. Maltz was appointed a member of the Board of Directors at Apple, but became increasingly disenchanted at what he considered the mismanagement and profligacy of the company. Finally, in November 1968 he tendered his resignation after warning the Beatles that their finances were in disarray and that they would encounter major problems unless something was done. He sent each member of the Beatles a letter: 'After six years' work, for the most part of which you have given pleasure to countless millions throughout every country where records are played, what have you got to show for it? ... Your personal finances are a mess. Apple is a mess.'

The Beatles decided that they needed someone to manage their affairs properly and approached Lord Beeching, who had recently pruned British Rail to reduce its huge losses. He suggested they stick to making records, which they knew something about. The group approached other leading businessmen, including Lord Poole, chairman of Lazard's Bank. He offered to take the task on for nothing, but they never bothered to call him back or take advantage of the offer – an apathetic attitude which was possibly a reflection of what was wrong with Apple. Other businessmen such as Lord Goodman and Cecil King were considered and even Ronan O'Rahilly, the man who had launched the first British pirate radio station Radio Caroline – although talks broke down after Caleb, the Apple astrologer, told the Beatles that O'Rahilly didn't have the right 'vibes'.

Paul eventually decided on Lee Eastman and the other members of the Beatles turned to Allen Klein.

Manley Hall, Manley Hill Road, Sutton Coldfield, West Midlands

The Beatles only appeared once at this venue, on Friday, 1 February 1963. The same evening they also appeared at the Assembly Rooms, Tamworth, which was only eight miles away.

Manila, The Philippines

Capital of the Philippines. The Beatles were due to perform their concerts at the Rizal Memorial Football Stadium, promoted by Cavalcade International, in July 1966.

When the Beatles arrived in the Philippines they found themselves attending a press conference three hours later at the Philippine Navy Headquarters. The site had been chosen by the promoter because it was near to a harbour where he had hired a luxury yacht for the Beatles to live on during their stay. However, Brian Epstein didn't like the yacht and insisted that they be moved into the Manila Hotel.

The promoter, Ramon Ramos, provided an itinerary in which it was mentioned that prior to their arrival at the stadium at 4.00 p.m. they were to: 'Proceed to the Palace at 3.00 p.m. to call on the First Lady and from the Palace proceed to the stadium.' However, the itinerary stressed that the visit was dependent on 'approval of the Beatles and party'. Since the Beatles wanted to be at the stadium two hours before the show began, this wasn't practical, although the importance of the visit to the Palace wasn't stressed. Ramos, caught between the wishes of the Marcoses and those of the Beatles, decided to do nothing about it, neither telling the Palace that the Beatles couldn't make the appointment nor informing the Beatles that he hadn't let the Palace know they couldn't attend. A further complication was that although Ramos had mentioned a 3.00 p.m. meeting in the itinerary, the Palace had arranged the event for 11.00 a.m.

On 3 July, the *Manila Sunday Times* reported, 'President Marcos, the First Lady, and the three young Beatles fans in the family, have been invited as guests of honour at the concerts. The Beatles plan to personally follow up the invitation during a courtesy call on Mrs Imelda Marcos at Malacanana Palace tomorrow morning at 11 o'clock.'

At 11.00 a.m. the next morning representatives from the Palace arrived at the hotel to collect the Beatles. They were still asleep and Epstein refused to have them woken up. That afternoon they went to the stadium and performed a half-hour show before 30,000 people. At 6.30 p.m. they were back at their hotel. At 6.45 p.m.

there was a television announcement that the Beatles had snubbed Mrs Imelda Marcos and Ferdinand Marcos, plus 200 children who had gathered for the meeting. 'The children began to arrive at ten,' said the commentator. 'They waited until after two. At first we were told that a mob at the yacht basin was delaying the scheduled arrival of the Beatles, but then we learned that the group was not even aboard. At noon the First Lady decided properly and wisely not to wait any longer. 'The children have all the time in the world, but we are busy people,' she said. Lunch had been planned for the President's family and the Beatles, but the place cards were removed when the group failed to show.'

Beatles PR man Tony Barrow watched the announcement with horror and then called the news director of the TV station, Channel Five, and said there had been a mistake and asked them to arrange for Brian Epstein to explain the situation on the channel. A statement was drafted, which read: 'It goes without saying that we did not receive any sort of invitation. No enquiry was received by me or my staff travelling with the Beatles as to whether we could approve any afternoon visit to the Palace before the first concert. The first we knew of the two hundred waiting children was on television tonight.'

The statement was read out on television, but there was deliberate interference in the transmission and the sound quality was so bad that it was almost unintelligible. Immediately the statement was finished, the static mysteriously disappeared. Tony Barrow was to comment, 'His [Brian's] voice was not dubbed out but intentionally scrambled.'

The Beatles' second show had taken place that evening, 4 July, at 8.30 p.m. before 50,000 fans. Other acts on the bill were the Reycard Duet, the Wing Duet, the Lemons Three, Eddie Rayes & the Downbeats, Dale Adriatico and Pilita Corrales with music by Carding Cruz and his Orchestra.

Promoter Ramos refused to pay the Beatles their share of the gate receipts at the time and when newspaper reports claimed that the Beatles would be held and refused permission to leave until a tax bill had been settled, the Beatles' representatives pointed this out and also explained that their contract with the promoter clearly stated that Ramos, not the Beatles, would be responsible for any tax payments. However, Misael Vera, a commissioner with the tax office, insisted that tax must be paid by the Beatles. Brian Epstein eventually decided that it would be simpler to just pay the money and arranged that the Beatles' fee, minus the tax, be sent directly to him in London by the promoter.

A hate campaign against the Beatles was growing and there were telephone death threats to the Manila Hotel and the British Embassy. All the security guards protecting the Beatles were removed and the group and their party were intimidated and jostled as they made their way to Manila International Airport. However, the reports in the *Manila Times* were exaggerated, particularly a paragraph which read: 'Drummer Ringo Starr was floored by an uppercut. As he crawled away the mob kicked him. George Harrison and John Lennon received kicks and blows as they ran to the customs zone. Paul McCartney was relatively unhurt as he sprinted ahead. Manager Brian Epstein received the brunt of the mob's ire. He was kicked and thrown to the floor. As a result he suffered a sprained ankle and had to be helped to the customs area.' The Beatles, although harassed, were protected by their entourage and weren't physically assaulted. Brian Epstein was punched in the face and kicked. Mal Evans was kicked several times and knocked to the floor and Alf Bicknell, the group's chauffeur, received injuries which resulted in a damaged spine and fractured rib.

They had to suffer a barrage of heckling and booing, with cries of '*Beatles Alis Diyan!*' (Beatles Go Home!). Guillermo Jurado, the airport manager, ordered all the escalators to be shut down, forcing the Beatles to carry their luggage up several flights of stairs with a baying mob of 200 Filipinos at their heels.

The party eventually boarded a KLM flight to New Delhi, but shortly before take-off Tony Barrow and Mal Evans were asked to return to the terminal where they were told that there had been no record of their arrival two days previously and therefore they were illegal immigrants and wouldn't be able to leave. It was a bureaucratic mess deliberately concocted to intimidate the Beatles still further. Eventually, after almost 50 minutes, they were finally allowed to return to the plane and depart.

Brian Epstein was violently sick and was attended by a doctor for the following four days, once they had arrived in Delhi, and the Beatles were so angry at what they regarded as a bad cock-up that they discussed the subject of touring in general and the fact that they were expected to embark on another world tour the following year, and came to the decision that they would stop touring completely after the next American tour.

Mann, William

As music critic of *The Times* newspaper in London, on 27 December 1963 Mann wrote an in-depth article analysing the Beatles' music entitled 'What Songs The Beatles Sang', which was a prestigious feature which did much to enhance the Beatles' reputation as serious musicians. In describing their song 'Not A Second

Time' from the *With The Beatles* album, he wrote: 'But harmonic
interest is typical of their quicker songs too, and one gets the
impression that they think simultaneously of harmony and melody,
so firmly are the major tonic sevenths and ninths built into their
tunes, and the flat submediant key switches, so natural in the
Aeolian cadence at the end of "Not A Second Time" (the chord
progression which ends Mahler's "Song Of The Earth").'

He also wrote a major analysis of *Sgt Pepper's Lonely Hearts
Club Band* in an article entitled 'The Beatles Revive Hope Of
Progress In Pop Music', published in *The Times* on 29 May 1967.

He died at the age of 65 on 5 September 1989.

Manson, Charles

Born on 12 November 1943. Manson became the leader of a bizarre
cult he formed on release from prison that he named 'the Family'.
The members believed him to be some sort of satanic Messiah. Like
a Svengali, he seemed to hold his 'family' in a mesmeric power.

From the time of the release of *Sergeant Pepper's Lonely Hearts
Club Band* in 1967, Charles Manson believed the Beatles were
attempting to convey messages directly to him. He was convinced
that there were biblical predictions that applied to the Beatles,
particularly in the 'Book of Revelations'. He told one of his girlfriends that in verse 15: 'the four angels were loosened'.

To him, the four angels were the Beatles. He pointed out that
verse 3 stated: 'And there came out of the smoke locusts upon the
earth; and unto them was given power as the scorpions of the earth
have power.' As locusts and beetles are the same word in Hebrew,
he believed this confirmed the prediction. Another verse stated:
'Their faces were as the faces of men. And they had hair as the hair
of women.' References to 'breastplates of fire' and 'out of their
mouths issued fire and smoke and brimstone' Manson interpreted
as pointing to the electric guitars and voices.

As he gathered his notorious 'Family' and moved to Death Valley,
he began to believe he was a new Messiah. When he returned to the
group shortly after Christmas 1968 with *The Beatles* 'white' album,
it sent him into paroxysms of delight because he believed it had
been written with him in mind.

In January 1969 the group moved from Death Valley to a house
in Gresham Street in the San Fernando Valley. Manson was fever-
ishly studying the album, interpreting the 'messages'.

'Blackbird', for instance, meant that the black people, specifically
the radical group the Black Panthers, intended to destroy the white
race. He believed that 'Piggies' was a derogatory name the blacks
had devised for their white enemies, whom they would give 'a damn

good wacking'. In 'Happiness Is A Warm Gun' he believed the black race were being told how to exact their vengeance on the whites – 'bang, bang, shoot, shoot'.

Unaware that 'Helter Skelter' was the name of a British fairground ride, he believed it was the code word for an uprising in which the blacks would destroy the whites. He regarded 'Sexy Sadie' as refer- ring to one of his female acolytes whom he'd renamed Sadie Mae Gutz. 'Rocky Racoon', was to him a reference to black people: 'coons'. 'Revolution No. 1' and 'Revolution No. 9' also referred to the coming holocaust – 'Revelations' predicts a coming Armageddon.

In the 'Book of Revelation' of John 9, Manson equated it with 'Revolution No. 9'. St John says: 'So the four angels were set to kill a third of mankind. They had been held ready for this moment, for this very year and month, day and hour'.

Manson's acolytes set out on his orders and committed a series of horrific murders at three separate places, the first involving five killings, including that of Sharon Tate, the pregnant wife of film producer Roman Polanski. The second killings were a married couple, the LaBiancas.

The words smeared in blood at the murder scenes were from the Beatles' songs and the message 'death to pigs' was daubed on a wall near the dead Rosemary and Leno LaBianca. Leno had a fork piercing his stomach. In fact the LaBiancas had been stabbed with knives and forks, which are mentioned in the last line of George Harrison's 'Piggies' and were killed 'in the dead of night'.

Other words smeared in blood at the crime scenes came from 'Helter Skelter' and 'Revolution No. 9'.

Los Angeles District Attorney Vincent Bugliosi, who prosecuted, had a book of the trial published in 1971 called *Helter Skelter*.

Manson, together with three of his female followers who had committed the murders, were sentenced to death, although this was commuted to life imprisonment.

At the conclusion of his trial, Manson made a rambling state- ment: 'Like, Helter Skelter is a nightclub. Helter Skelter means confusion. Literally. It doesn't mean any war with anyone. It doesn't mean that those people are going to kill other people. It only means what it means. Helter Skelter is confusion. Confusion is coming down fast. If you don't see the confusion coming down fast, you can call it what you wish. It's not my conspiracy. It is not my music. I hear what it relates. It says "Rise!" It says "Kill!" Why blame it on me? I didn't write the music. I am not the person who projected it into your social consciousness.'

On the subject of Manson believing that the Beatles were sending special messages to him via the double album, John Lennon commented: 'Well, he's barmy. He's like any other Beatles fan who reads mysticism into it. I don't know what "Helter Skelter" had to do with knifing somebody.'

Maple Leaf Gardens, Carlton Street, Toronto, Quebec, Canada

The Beatles first appeared at this venue on Monday, 7 September 1964. There were over 10,000 fans awaiting their arrival at Toronto International and the group was whisked away to the King Edward Hotel, also besieged by fans. In fact, when the group arrived in their three-room suite they discovered a fourteen-year-old girl hiding in the linen closet.

The Beatles appeared on two shows in the arena that night, drawing a total of 35,522 people, breaking the attendance record, held since 1946 for a Toronto–Montreal hockey match.

Disc jockey/compere Jungle Jay Nelson introduced the first act, the Bill Black Combo, who were followed by the Exciters and Clarence 'Frogman' Henry. The Bill Black Combo returned to play one song, then were joined by Jackie de Shannon, who sang five numbers. The Beatles appeared on stage at 5.30 p.m.

Between shows there was a press conference and the Beatles were introduced to the Mayor, Michele Finney – who was also Miss Canada and the president of the Beatles Fan Club of Canada. Officials from the Canadian branch of Capitol Records presented them with a gold disc.

The Beatles left the arena after their second show at 10.30 p.m.

The event had gone smoothly, much to the relief of the Montreal police who, earlier that day, had received a death threat against Ringo,

They returned to Maple Leaf Gardens the following year for two performances on 17 August 1965. The arena's full capacity was for 18,000 people and for the first time it was completely full at both houses.

When the Beatles returned the following year on Wednesday, 17 August 1966, they once again performed two shows. There was an audience of 15,000 at the afternoon show and 17,000 at the evening show. During the show George was hit in the face by a flying object. There were 400 policemen on duty and 122 St John Ambulance personnel who treated 117 cases inside the building and 50 outside.

Mardas, John Alexis

When John Alexis Mardas first entered Britain on a student visa he was 21 years old, the son of a Greek military officer, said to be a member of the secret police for the junta who had recently come into power in Greece. He initially found work as a telephone repairman in Olympic Television before approaching John Dunbar of the Indica Gallery. He created some kinetic light sculptures and suggested that Dunbar become his agent. As a result the Rolling Stones bought a psychedelic light box he made and included it in their act. Brian Jones then introduced him to John Lennon, who dubbed him 'Magic Alex'.

The Beatles, and Lennon in particular, were completely fascinated by his electronic gadgetry, including the four tiny brooches he gave to each Beatle which bleeped and flashed at random. He was to come up with a number of electronic gizmos and suggestions of what he could create, given the money, which included a paint which glowed when connected to an electric current. He told them, 'One day it will replace conventional electric light as we know it.' He also constructed a tiny radio receiver which picked up and broadcast records being played on a special record player in another room; made a novel electric apple which trembled with light and music; and claimed he was working on a telephone which would automatically dial a number when you told it who you wanted to call.

Some of his other ideas seemed fantastical – an invisible curtain of ultrasonic vibrations which would screen the Beatles from their fans and an artificial sun which would illuminate the night sky by laser beams.

Alexis had been in Britain for some time and when the Beatles created a new branch of Apple for him – Apple Electronics – they also had to sort out the legalities which would allow him to remain in Britain. He'd only had a limited student visa and claimed that his passport had been stolen from his luggage. His visa had long since expired, so John asked Peter Brown to arrange Alexis' legal immigration to Britain through a solicitor.

Lennon was very gullible as far as Alexis was concerned, although he enjoyed the company of the young man who was now dubbed in the press as 'the Merlin of the Beatles Camelot'. When the Beatles were at Rishikesh, John missed him and summoned him over. Alexis had some experience of the search for spirituality and was appalled by what he found at the Maharishi's camp: 'An ashram with four-poster beds? Masseurs, and servants bringing water, houses with facilities, an accountant – I never saw a holy man with a bookkeeper!' In fact, Alex was completely disgusted with the situation and became alarmed when he heard that the Maharishi expected the Beatles to donate 10–15 per cent of their annual income to a Swiss account in the Maharishi's name. Alex

confronted the guru and told him that he was exploiting the
Beatles. He claimed that the Maharishi then tried to bribe him by
offering to pay him to build a radio station in the ashram grounds.
Although wine was forbidden, Alexis began to bring wine in for the
women of the ashram and began to win their confidence. A blonde
nurse from California told him that the Maharishi invited her to
private dinners in his quarters where they had chicken for dinner
and he made sexual advances to her.

Armed with this information, he sat arguing with John and
George, attempting to convince them of what he'd discovered.
Initially, George didn't believe Alexis and John was in doubt. Alexis
gathered further proof, which resulted in John and George's
confrontation with the Maharishi.

Alexis helped them in their bid to find a Greek island retreat and
he travelled with various members of the Beatles. He shared a mews
flat in central London with Pattie Boyd's sister Jennie, although their
relationship was said to be platonic. He joined George, Pattie, Jennie
and Neil Aspinall on their trip to the West Coast of the US in 1967.

He also holidayed in Greece with Cynthia, Jennie, Donovan and
his friend Gypsy Dave. On their return to England, Cynthia, Alexis
and Jennie arrived at Kenwood where they discovered John and
Yoko together. They all left and Cynthia was invited to stay at the
mews flat in Victoria. That evening she sat up drinking wine
through most of the night with Alexis and they crawled into bed
together. Cynthia was later to say that he practised black magic and
hypnotised her into doing it.

While John and Cynthia were estranged, Cynthia and her mother
Lil went on holiday to Italy. Alexis was sent over by John to give her
an ultimatum. Alexis told her that John would be accusing her of
adultery and that he had agreed to be the co-respondent and testify
on John's behalf. As a result she would lose Julian. The ploy didn't
work.

On Thursday, 11 July 1968, Alexis was married to Eufrosyne
Doxiades at the Greek Orthodox Church in Moscow Road,
London. The Beatles attended the ceremony.

In January 1969 the Beatles became unhappy with the lack of
atmosphere at Twickenham Studios and decided to record at Apple
in Savile Row. Alexis had promised them a 78-track recording
studio and had been working on it for months. When they arrived,
they found a disastrous situation. Most of the material was not
invented by Alexis, but was made by German manufacturers – and
was still in the packing cases. Far from there being 78 tracks available, there were none and no recording machines had been
installed. In addition, the heating and ventilation units of the

building were installed in a corner of the studio creating a continuous noise, wheezing and humming all the time. Alexis had even forgotten to install an intercom system between the studio and the control booth. The group had to appeal to George Martin who immediately sent down a number of engineers, together with a mobile recording unit.

Despite the fact that Alexis had not come up with any of the amazing inventions he'd promised them, but had merely provided some electronic toys, he remained in their favour. However, when Allen Klein arrived on the scene Alexis was soon to fade out of the picture.

Marietta Hotel, Obertauern, Austria

Site of the Beatles' only live performance in Austria, which took place on Thursday, 18 March 1965.

The occasion was the birthday of Dick Lester's assistant, Mr Read, and the film crew threw a party for them both at the hotel. The festivities lasted through the night, during which the Beatles performed for two hours with a repertoire comprising their hit songs and some standards such as 'Summertime'.

One old lady initially complained of the noise, but was invited to join the party – and did so!

Marine Hall Ballroom, The Esplanade, Fleetwood, Lancashire

Another venue where the Beatles only ever appeared once. It was a Lancashire fishing port and the gig took place on Saturday, 25 August 1962.

Marmalade

A Scottish band who covered the 'Ob-La-Di, Ob-La-Da' track from *The Beatles* double album. Their version of the song was issued on 4 December 1968 on CBS 3891. It entered the charts on 21 December and reached the No. 1 position. They spent two weeks at the top and a total of thirteen weeks in the charts. The group's line-up at the time was, Dean Ford (vocals), Junior Campbell (lead guitar), Pat Fairlie (rhythm guitar) and Raymond Duffy (drums).

A group called the Bedrocks also covered the number, but only reached No. 17 in the charts with it.

Marrion, Albert

Photographer engaged by Brian Epstein to take the first official photographs of the Beatles.

Marrion and his partner Herbert Hughes had established their photographic business which specialised in portrait and wedding photographs. Marrion had been the official Liverpool photographer covering the Blitz for the city and, with his partner, had a studio at 19 Smithdown Place, on the corner of Penny Lane, and another across the Mersey in Wallasey.

Marrion had taken photographs of Clive Epstein's wedding and Brian approached him to set up a photographic session with the Beatles. Marrion asked his partner to take the photographs, but Hughes refused. Marrion then handled the session himself at the studio at 268 Wallasey Village, Wallasey, on Sunday, 17 December 1961. Most of the thirty photographs taken that day weren't suitable because John Lennon kept horsing around and sticking his tongue out. Sixteen shots were selected and the main photo provided the front cover shot for Issue 13 of *Mersey Beat* which proclaimed 'Beatles Top Poll!'

Marsden, Beryl

A Liverpool singer, real name Beryl Hogg, who initially began performing with local groups at the age of fourteen. Beryl was generally regarded as the best female vocalist on the Mersey Beat scene and at one time John Lennon recommended that she be given the Lennon & McCartney number 'Love Of The Loved' to record, but was vetoed by Brian Epstein, who gave it to Cilla Black.

Beryl was initially managed by Joe Flannery, Epstein's friend/rival, and she appeared on several pop TV shows such as 'Thank Your Lucky Stars' promoting her early record releases such as 'I Know (You Don't Love Me No More)', her debut disc, released when she was sixteen, and 'When The Love Light Shines'. At the age of seventeen she was appearing on stage at the Star Club in Hamburg.

She was booked to appear with the Beatles on their last concert tour of Britain from 3–12 December 1964. Perhaps for the sake of nostalgia, the Beatles also had other Liverpool acts on the tour such as the Koobas and Steve Aldo.

Beryl moved to London and became a member of Shotgun Express with Rod Stewart and Peter Bardens, and later made some solo records while being managed by Tony Stratton-Smith. She returned to Liverpool, married and became a housewife. She then returned to her career as a vocalist in Liverpool in the seventies in a group she formed with Paddy Chambers called Sinbad, and finally settled in London where she became a Buddhist.

Marsh, Tony

The compere selected to present both the Chris Montez/Tommy Roe and the Roy Orbison tours in 1963 in which the Beatles were also on the bill. Tony was a popular comedian and compere and was booked to introduce many of the touring pop music shows before he was banned over a controversial incident.

During the Orbison tour on 23 May at the Odeon, Nottingham, the Beatles crawled into the orchestra pit and began making rude signs to Marsh as he was on stage, trying to upset his act. They were aware that Marsh was a practical joker. During that tour he told Roy Orbison that, as an American, he would need a passport to enter Scotland – and a worried Orbison believed him!

It was while he was compering a Rolling Stones tour that he got drunk and stood at the side of the stage and dropped his pants to distract Brian Jones. A woman who had brought her daughter to the show noticed this and complained to the management. As a result Marsh was taken to court and banned from all major touring circuits.

Martha My Dear

Track penned by Paul which was included on *The Beatles* white album. The number was recorded at Trident Studios and it seems that the double-tracked McCartney is the only Beatle to appear on the recording. George Martin arranged the backing by fourteen musicians: Bernard Miller, Dennis McConnell, Lou Sofier, Les Maddox on violins; Leo Birnbaum, Henry Myerscough on violas; Reginald Kilbey, Frederick Alexander on cellos; Leon Calvert, Stanley Reynolds, Ronnie Hughes on trumpets; Tony Tunstall on French horn; Ted Barker on trombone; and Alf Reece on tuba.

The title was inspired by Paul's Old English sheepdog, Martha, although the actual song is not about her.

Martha was born in 1966 and died of old age in the summer of 1982.

Martin, George

The Beatles' recording manager, often dubbed 'the fifth Beatle'. He was born in London in 1926. George joined the Fleet Air Arm when he was 17, and at the age of 21 was to enter the Guildhall School of Music for a three-year course, during which time Jane Asher's mother, Margaret, tutored him on oboe.

It was during his course at the Guildhall that he married his girl-friend Sheena, a former Wren. The couple were to have two children, Bundy and Gregory.

After working for a spell in the BBC Music Library, he was offered a job in 1950 working as an assistant to Oscar Preuss, head of the Parlophone label, which was part of EMI Records. EMI had several pop labels, such as Columbia and HMV, but

Parlophone specialised in classical, jazz, comedy and middle-of-the-road music.

Oscar's secretary was Judy Lockhart-Smith, who became George's secretary when Preuss retired in 1955.

When he was appointed head of Parlophone, Martin continued other duties, acting as A&R man and also producing recording sessions. He attended a revue in Notting Hill, performed by the duo Michael Flanders and Donald Swann, called 'At The Drop Of A Hat'. He recorded an album of it, together with other Flanders and Swann productions, and also recorded another revue *Beyond The Fringe*. The artists Martin recorded were off-beat and unlike the artists on the pop labels of EMI such as Columbia and HMV. He had success with Peter Sellers with *The Best Of Sellers* and also the singles 'Goodness Gracious Me' and 'Bangers And Mash' with Sellers and Sophia Loren. He recorded classical, jazz and comedy records and among the artists he recorded were Peter Ustinov, Bernard Cribbins, Sophia Loren, Johnny Dankworth, Cleo Laine, the Temperance Seven, Stan Getz, the Goons, Sir Malcolm Sargent, Sir Adrian Boult, Jimmy Shand, Shirley Bassey and Matt Monro.

The classically-trained A&R man was more at home with artists of this nature. In 1957 he was taken to the 2 I's coffee bar in Soho to see Tommy Steele, but decided to turn him down. Decca Records signed him the next day and Steele became Britain's first major rock 'n' roll star.

It was purely by chance that he became involved with the Beatles. Despite all the flak Decca were to receive in hindsight because they didn't sign up the group, they were the only company to travel to Liverpool to see them perform and to give the band a recording audition. The three pop labels of EMI, in addition to Pye, Philips and the other major and minor record companies, had turned the Beatles down flat without even allowing them the opportunity of such an audition.

Sid Coleman called Martin's office, but George was out. He chatted to Judy Lockhart-Smith, George's secretary, and arranged for Brian Epstein to meet Martin. Even then, the situation was not straightforward. Epstein, continually frustrated by his failure to obtain a recording contract for the group, began to apply what pressure he could.

Alistair Taylor, Brian's assistant at that time, confirms that Parlophone began to play around with Epstein to the extent that he became frustrated and threatened to withdraw his NEMS record store business if EMI didn't give the Beatles a recording contract.

Taylor was to tell writer Ray Coleman: 'EMI took them on sufferance because Brian was one of their top customers. I saw Brian in tears, literally, because Martin promised to phone back, and day after day went by and George Martin was never available, always "in a meeting". I saw Brian thumping the desk and in tears because George Martin hadn't phoned back'.

According to Taylor, when Epstein finally got hold of Martin he told him that NEMS as a shop would jettison EMI's HMV, Parlophone and Columbia labels.

Martin admitted that EMI had nothing to lose financially by taking on an unknown group such as the Beatles. He said: 'To say I was taking a gamble would be stretching it, because the deal I offered them was pretty awful.'

He then arranged an audition for Wednesday, 6 June 1962. It was Ron Richards, Martin's assistant, who actually took on the role of recording manager at the session. He was the one who usually dealt with the pop-style records and produced the discs for acts such as Paul Raven (later to become Gary Glitter), Shane Fenton & the Fentones, Jerry Lordan and Judd Proctor.

After he'd recorded four numbers with them, Richards was intrigued by their original material and, having listened to 'Love Me Do', sent for George Martin, who was in the canteen. Martin then took over the rest of the session.

It was while listening to the playback that Martin told them: 'You must listen to it, and if there's anything you don't like, tell me, and we'll try and do something about it.' George Harrison replied: 'Well, for a start, I don't like your tie.'

Over the succeeding weeks, Martin had to decide whether to sign the group. Initially, he'd begun thinking in terms of altering the structure to that of the more conventional line-up of the time – a lead singer with a backing group in the style of bands such as Cliff Richard & the Shadows. He was attempting to figure out who should be the frontman – John or Paul, a case of Paul McCartney & the Beatles or John Lennon & the Beatles. Finally, he decided to leave them as they were, and at the time seemed to have no quibble about Pete Best – although in hindsight, in his books, he has slightly altered the opinions he held at the time.

Having found he had nothing to lose by signing the Beatles, Martin presented them with a contract that paid a paltry royalty. Although their records were to make immense fortunes for EMI in subsequent years, the Beatles didn't receive a better slice until Allen Klein intervened.

When the Beatles returned to Abbey Road Studios on Tuesday, 4 September, they'd ousted Pete Best and replaced him with Ringo Starr. Ron Richards began rehearsing them in the afternoon and decided on two songs for the evening recording session: 'How Do You Do It?' and 'Love Me Do'. George Martin produced the session and insisted they record a Mitch Murray song, which Richards had obtained from Dick James. The Beatles were reluctant to do so and produced a lacklustre version.

Engineer Norman Smith was to comment: 'I've a feeling that Paul wasn't too happy with Ringo's drumming, and felt that it could be better. He didn't make a good job of it.'

This seemed to be confirmed by Richards, who was sole producer of the Tuesday, 11 September session and had booked a session man, Andy White, to play instead. This wasn't such an unusual move. As Richards was to remark: 'I used him [White] a lot at the time – he was very good.'

Martin was also unhappy with Ringo's drumming. He had commented that he was dissatisfied with the Beatles' drum sound when he'd originally heard them. This was mainly because Martin and other A&R men were used to a different style of drumming in the recording studio, where they used show drummers rather that ones from rock 'n' roll bands. It wasn't unusual for A&R men to employ a session drummer and this shouldn't have reflected badly on the ability of either Best or Starr.

Richards was used to working with White and preferred him at the session, and a worried Ringo thought, 'They're doing a Pete Best on me' when he noticed White in the drum seat. When the first number 'P.S. I Love You' was recorded, an unhappy Ringo sat next to Richards in the control box until the producer asked him to play maracas on the track. When they came to record 'Love Me Do', Richards asked Ringo to play tambourine. Fortunately for Ringo, Richards allowed him to play drums on one of the cuts of 'Love Me Do', and the versions by both White and Ringo were released.

If the version with Ringo had not been released they would never have got away with the suggestion that it was Pete Best who was 'not a good enough drummer'.

When 'Love Me Do' was issued, both Martin and Epstein were disappointed at Ardmore & Beechwood's promotion of the record and Epstein decided to sign with another publishing company. It was Martin who steered him into the arms of Dick James and a contract that was to lose Lennon and McCartney the rights of their songs forever.

For their second single, Martin wanted them to release the Mitch Murray composition 'How Do You Do It?'. He told them it would turn them into a household name and was upset when they said they didn't like the number and would rather record one of their own songs. Martin ticked them off and told them: 'When you can write material as good as this, then I'll record it. But right now we're going to record this.'

When they performed their new interpretation of 'Please Please Me', following advice he had given them about improving the song, he acknowledged that their own composition was better than 'How Do You Do It?' and 'Please Please Me' provided them with their first chart-topper.

Epstein then presented Martin with a string of acts: Gerry & the Pacemakers, Billy J. Kramer, Cilla Black and the Fourmost, almost guaranteeing him amazing success as an A&R man. The year 1963 brought him unprecedented acclaim, making him the first A&R man ever to achieve the top three places in the record charts with 'I Like It' by Gerry & the Pacemakers at No. 1, 'Do You Want To Know A Secret?' by Billy J. Kramer at No. 2 and 'From Me To You' by the Beatles at No. 3, with Martin's Mersey productions being placed at No. 1 for 37 weeks of the year.

This was largely due to the popularity of the artists and the songs themselves, not to any specific input that George contributed. Almost any A&R man would have had the same success given the artists and the material.

Yet he was not entirely supportive of all the new acts he was presented with. Billy J. Kramer still resents to this day the disparaging remarks made about him by Martin in his autobiography *All You Need Is Ears*. Also, when Brian Epstein brought him the song 'Anyone Who Had A Heart' for Cilla Black to record, Martin wanted Shirley Bassey to perform it as he didn't think Cilla was capable, even though it was to give her a No. 1 hit.

His knowledge of the Mersey acts, if his autobiography is anything to go by, is quite rusty. To take one example, he stated that Brian brought him a singer 'named Priscilla White. All her friends called her Cilla and Brian, for some reason best known to himself, didn't like the idea of Cilla White, so he'd gone to the other end of the spectrum and called her Cilla Black.' She had first been dubbed Cilla Black in a 6 July 1961 issue of *Mersey Beat* and had used the name ever since – a considerable time before Brian ever met her and over two years before she met Martin.

Having achieved such unprecedented success for EMI, George was taken aback when the company didn't even give him a Christmas bonus. When he asked why, he was told that his salary of £3,000 per annum was quite adequate and he was therefore not entitled to a bonus. Discovering that his productions had made a profit of £2,200,000 for EMI during 1963, he suggested that he should receive some form of commission or bonus. Being refused either, he left the company. The Beatles, who had been signed to the company by Martin with such a disgracefully low royalty arrangements, couldn't do the same.

So, fourteen years after joining EMI, Martin left to form Associated Independent Recordings (AIR), taking a number of EMI's leading A&M men with him, including Ron Richards, John Burgess and Peter Sullivan. In addition, a large number of the acts agreed to continue having their records produced by the new company. They included the Beatles, Gerry & the Pacemakers, the Fourmost, Billy J. Kramer, Cilla Black, P. J. Proby, the Hollies, Peter and Gordon, Adam Faith and Manfred Mann.

This resulted in a staggering loss of revenue for a company that didn't have the foresight or generosity to pay a modest bonus to the person who had completely transformed their fortunes.

Although the artists still had their product released by EMI, the independent producers now received a percentage commission on the recordings.

The success he'd achieved through the luck of having such a stable of acts placed in his hands established his reputation as the most successful A&R man in the world and the offers poured in for him to orchestrate music for movies. He even began recording in his own right with the George Martin Orchestra.

He released singles based on Lennon and McCartney numbers and an album, *A Hard Day's Night: Off The Beatle Track*. He composed a number of instrumental versions of their numbers for the soundtrack album of *A Hard Day's Night*. Other ventures included his album *George Martin Scores Instrumental Versions of the Hits*. Virtually all of his individual projects over those years were with Beatles or Beatles-related material.

Martin admitted that any A&R man could have achieved the same success with the Beatles during the first few years of their recording career. However, his real participation and input came in what were regarded as 'the studio years', when they ceased touring, and particularly in the production of *Sergeant Pepper's Lonely Hearts Club Band*.

This process evolved gradually. In the first stage of their recording career, which Martin called the first era of recording, John and Paul would play their numbers on acoustic guitars and George would make his suggestions. This was called a 'head arrangement', and it was to change at the next stage of their career, which occurred with 'Yesterday'. This number was the first Beatles track to use orchestration and was the first record on which George scored music for them, in addition to being the first time that instruments other than those used by the Beatles were included. With 'Yesterday', George began to exert a greater influence on their music, and as their records grew more sophisticated his input became more important.

By this time George had divorced Sheena and he married his

secretary, Judy, in August 1967. Brian Epstein hosted a dinner party
for the couple in his Charles Street house, with the Beatles and their
wives and girlfriends. George and Judy were to have two children,
Lucy and Giles.

The close relationship in the studio foundered when the studio
takes for the 'Get Back' project were handed to Phil Spector for him
to fashion into *Let It Be*. Ominously, this was the Beatles' thirteenth
album.

George became the subject of a BBC TV documentary, 'A Little
Help From My Friends', filmed at London's Talk Of The Town club
on 14 December 1969 and transmitted on 24 December.

Although he was to run a successful studio at AIR, Martin could
never escape his association with the Beatles, and in the succeeding
years people would be hard pushed to name his other record
successes or any major artists he created.

In November 1976, Robert Stigwood approached him to
compose the musical score for the movie *Sergeant Pepper's Lonely
Hearts Club Band*. The film proved a box-office disaster.

Bhaskar Menon, president of Capitol Records, contacted him in
1977 to listen to tapes from their vaults of recordings of the Beatles'
Hollywood Bowl concerts in 1964 and 1965, which Martin had
supervised. With the aid of Geoff Emerick, he worked on the tapes
at AIR Studios, enhancing them for commercial release by transferring the three-track recording to multi-track tape and remixing and
filtering until they had cleaned up the sound. The album *The
Beatles At The Hollywood Bowl* was issued in May 1977.

All You Need Is Ears, his autobiography, written with Jeremy
Hornsby, was published in 1979. In 1993 he became involved in the
production of a documentary on the making of *Sergeant Pepper* for
London Weekend Television's 'South Bank Show' and his book
Summer Of Love: The Making Of Sgt Pepper was published the
same year.

Martin then became involved in his biggest Beatles venture since
the 1960s: the three sets of double-CDs which were to comprise the
Anthology releases, with 150 tracks which Martin selected from the
Abbey Road vaults. With the help of Geoff Emerick and the latest
state-of-the-art technology, he enhanced the numbers for the series,
with *Anthology 1* being issued in November 1995.

The Beatles also recorded a new single 'Free As A Bird', with
'Real Love' on the flipside, which was released at the same time as
the double-CD. This release saw Paul, George and Ringo perform
together using demo tapes John had recorded in New York in the
1970s. However, the Beatles selected Jeff Lynne rather than Martin
to produce their new recordings.

When *New York Times* critic Allan Kozinn asked Paul McCartney why they chose Lynne rather than Martin, Paul commented: 'George is a very noble guy, and he's old now, and he will tell you that his hearing's not as good as it used to be. So when it came to who to work with, George Harrison brought up the fact that George Martin's hearing wasn't as good as it was. So George Martin was OK on all the old stuff. But perhaps for new stuff it required someone whose hearing was 100 per cent.'

In January 1996, at the age of seventy, George decided to retire after producing a tribute album featuring Beatles songs performed by a variety of celebrities. He announced his retirement, saying 'I am an old man and I don't want to do any more music.' He also cited increased deafness.

His Beatles tribute album was released on 15 March 1998 on Echo Records. He produced it with his son Giles. The tracks were: 'Come Together', Robin Williams and Bobby McFerrin; 'A Hard Day's Night', Goldie Hawn; 'A Day In The Life', Jeff Beck; 'Here, There And Everywhere', Celine Dion; 'Because', Vanessa-Mae; 'I Am The Walrus', Jim Carrey; 'Here Comes The Sun', John Williams; 'Being For The Benefit Of Mr Kite', Billy Connolly; 'The Pepperland Suite', George Martin; 'Golden Slumbers/Carry That Weight/The End', Phil Collins; 'Friends and Lovers', George Martin; 'In My Life', Sean Connery; 'Ticket to Ride', the Petropolis Choir and 'Blackbird' by Bonnie Pink.

In February 1999 he began a multi-media eight-city lecture tour of America called 'The Making of Sgt. Pepper', which opened on 18 February in Massachusetts and ended in Las Vegas. A month later he was inducted into the Rock and Roll Hall of Fame during a ceremony at the Waldorf Astoria, New York.

His retirement had a fitting end when he was knighted by the Queen and became Sir George Martin.

Marylebone Registry Office, Marylebone Road, London NW1

Paul and Linda were married at Marylebone Registry Office on 12 March 1969, the day after the Apple Press Office had issued a statement that they wouldn't be getting married.

Linda had obtained the licence and Paul, who had forgotten to buy a ring, had to persuade a jeweller to open his shop and he bought one for twelve pounds.

Shortly after 9.30 a.m. Paul arrived in a black Daimler. Linda's daughter Heather acted as a flower girl, Mal Evans was in attendance and the only other Beatles associate present was Peter Brown.

John and Yoko said they couldn't attend because they were working on their *Life With The Lions* album. George said he'd be too busy working at Savile Row and Ringo and Maureen said they were involved with domestic matters at home.

The press turned its attention to some weeping Apple Scruffs and distraught fans, such as Jill Pritchard, a hairdresser who'd heard the news on the radio and had rushed up to London, to stand outside the Registry office in the drizzling rain and weep.

Best Man was Paul's brother, Mike McCartney, who was late. The ceremony had been due to take place at 9.45 a.m. but the train bringing Mike from Liverpool had been delayed. Fortunately, there were no other marriages scheduled for that day and the Registrar was prepared to wait.

Coming out of the Registry Office there was a scuffle with the mass of press and weeping fans. One of the Apple Scruffs had been baby sitting and had brought her charge, whom she nicknamed Bam Bam, with her. In the crush the baby cried out and Paul said, 'Is he all right, Margo?' As the Daimler drove away the press corps swooped on Margo asking, 'Whose kid is it anyway?' and photographs of her with the 'mysterious child' appeared in the newspapers the next day, along with shots of the tearstruck Jill Pritchard.

There was a blessing ceremony at St John's Wood Church, a Roman Catholic church, after which the wedding party drove to Cavendish Avenue for a champagne toast. Angry McCartney fans forcibly pushed aside the gates and began to cram burning newspaper in the letterbox. The police had to be called. The party then made their way to the Ritz Hotel for the reception.

Marylebone Registry Office was also the setting for the marriage between Ringo and Barbara Bach on 27 April 1981. Wedding guests included George and Olivia Harrison and Paul and Linda McCartney. Sixty guests and relatives then celebrated at the London club, Rags. Barbara wore a cream satin suit, made by the Emanuels, who had designed the famous wedding dress for Diana, Princess of Wales.

Massey & Coggins

A Liverpool firm of electrical engineers.

Following the Beatles' first trip to Hamburg in 1960, Paul, who had left school against the advice of his father, abandoning his idea of becoming a teacher, felt guilty about not getting a regular job and approached the Labour Exchange. Initially he worked temporarily for a parcels delivery service, being laid off after the Christmas rush. He was then sent to Massey & Coggins where he received a wage of seven pounds per week.

He admits he was not very good at the job which consisted of him winding electrical coils all day long. Whereas fellow labourers would complete between eight and 14 coils per working week, Paul confessed he was lucky if he managed one and a half.

One of his workmates called him 'Mantovani' because of his long hair, and his boredom with the job was such that after two months he didn't bother turning up one morning.

Matchbox

Traditional blues number originally recorded in 1927 by artists such as Leadbelly and Blind Lemon Jefferson. Carl Perkins wrote his own version of the number and recorded it for Sun Records in 1957. It became part of the Beatles' repertoire in 1961 when it provided a vocal vehicle for drummer Pete Best. After Best left, the number was sung by Ringo, who performed it on the group's BBC radio shows 'Pop Go The Beatles' and 'From Us To You'.

Ringo's version of the song was recorded for their fifth EP *Long Tall Sally* and it appeared on the collections *The Beatles Box* and *The Beatles Collection*, the compilations *Rarities* and *Rock 'n' Roll Music* and the Capitol album *Something New*.

It was also released as a single in the States by Capitol with 'Slow Down' on the flip on 24 August 1964 and reached No. 17 in the charts.

A version sung by John is to be found on *The Beatles Live! At The Star Club In Hamburg, Germany: 1962* album. A version was included on *Past Masters Volume One* and a radio performance was included on *The Beatles Live At The BBC* CDs.

Mathew Street, Liverpool L2

A narrow, cobbled street in Liverpool's city centre which originally comprised a series of warehouses. The basement of No. 10, a fruit warehouse, was where the famous Cavern Club opened on 16 January 1957. When it changed from a jazz club to one which promoted the local rock 'n' roll bands, it became, for a time, the most famous club in the world.

Also in Mathew Street, on the opposite side, is the Grapes, a public house where the Beatles and many of the Liverpool bands used to drink. As the Cavern only sold soft drinks, the group members used to slip out the side entrance of the band room, which led to a narrow alley which was almost opposite the Grapes. As the band room at the Cavern was so tiny, and since there was no other room in the club where the members of groups could socialise between performances, they used the Grapes as their meeting place to talk to their managers and friends. When Pete Best was sacked from the Beatles on 16 August 1962, he was joined by Neil Aspinall when he went to the Grapes to ponder the unexpected dismissal.

When the warehouse buildings were razed to make way for an air vent for the underground railway system in 1973, the actual bull-dozing of the warehouse left the cellar club below filled with rubble.

In 1974 local sculptor Arthur Dooley had his piece of Beatles sculpture placed on the wall opposite the former Cavern site and shortly after John Lennon's death, a local architect, David Backhouse, walked down Mathew Street, was shocked at the mess, and decided to design a building on the site as a tribute, something with character and style – a fitting monument to the street's achievements during the sixties.

A main attraction of the new structure would be a resurrected Cavern Club, and when it came to rebuilding it was discovered that the original Cavern bricks were still mainly intact. So a number were sold off in aid of charity and the remainder used to build several yards of wall in the new club.

Following John Lennon's death, the 'John Lennon Worldwide Memorial Club' opened at 23 Mathew Street, opposite Cavern Walks on the premises formerly known as the Left Bank Bistro.

Two brothers, Ian and Muir Wallace, opened the Beatles Shop at 31 Mathew Street to coincide with the opening of Cavern Walks. Ian commented: 'To get it right we felt we had to have more Beatles gear than anyone else in the world. We wanted people to walk down the stairs and be confronted by such a sight they'd say, "Wow, where did all this come from?" '

The shop also has a Beatles statue at the front of the building, which was unveiled at a low-key ceremony on Tuesday, 2 April 1984. It was the work of Liverpool artist David Hughes, RA, who actually trained at the same art college as John Lennon before gaining entry to the Royal Academy.

Matrix Hall, Fletchamstead Highway, Coventry, Warwickshire

The Beatles only made one appearance at this venue, on Saturday, 17 November 1962. It was their first British appearance following their return from their second season at Hamburg's Star Club and their first appearance in the Midlands. Also on the bill were the Mark Allen Group and Lee Teri.

Matthew, Brian

Born 17 September 1928, he originally trained as an actor at RADA.

As a BBC radio host he worked with the Beatles more than any other radio personality in Britain. He presented 'Saturday Club', a prestigious radio show which was originally launched in 1958 as a showcase for up-and-coming talent.

Brian interviewed George and John at NEMS office in Argyle Street on Tuesday, 30 November 1965 for the 'Pop Profile' series.

He also recorded the Beatles on their first 'Saturday Club' on Tuesday, 22 January 1963.

Matthew was also the host on the radio series 'Easy Beat' and the Beatles recorded on the show for the first time at the Playhouse Theatre, London, on Wednesday, 3 April 1963.

Brian telephoned them for a 'Saturday Club' interview at the Plaza Hotel, New York, on Friday, 7 February 1964. He also interviewed them by telephone. The Beatles also chatted with him on Tuesday, 31 March for 'Saturday Club' for a programme broadcast on Saturday, 22 February 1964 on their return from America. He also hosted 'Top Gear', for which the Beatles recorded on Tuesday, 14 July 1964. Brian also appeared in a sketch with them for the TV show 'Thank Your Lucky Stars', recorded on Saturday, 14 November 1964.

During the filming of *Help!* he interviewed them by phone for 'Saturday Club' on Sunday, 14 March. He was also the host on their 'Thank Your Lucky Stars' show recorded on Sunday, 28 March and broadcast Saturday, 3 April. Matthew also joined them on their autumn 1965 tour of America.

Material from his interviews were gathered for a 45-minute documentary 'The Beatles Abroad' which was broadcast on Monday, 30 August 1965. They recorded with him for another 'Saturday Club' on Monday, 29 November 1965. He next interviewed them at the Playhouse Theatre, London, on Monday, 2 May for the 400th edition of 'Saturday Club'. He then recorded them at EMI Studios on Monday, 20 March 1967 for an overseas edition of 'Top Of The Pops' and for the radio show 'The Ivor Novello Awards' for 1966.

Matthew told Kevin Howlett in *The Beatles At the Beeb* book that although he worked with the Beatles so often, he wasn't very close to them on a personal level. He was to add: 'I suppose it's fair to say that I was close to Brian Epstein – I did count him as a personal friend.'

In fact, both Brians went into business together when they launched a theatrical project in Farnborough, Kent. The two theatre lovers intended to create a new theatre, the Pilgrim Theatre, at a cost of £38,000, which would present a festival of new and classical productions that could later be transferred to the West End. The theatre would also stage musicals, jazz concerts and films. A host of stars agreed to donate their services in a series of concerts to raise funds for the venture. They included Billy J. Kramer, the Searchers, Cilla Black, Gerry & the Pacemakers, Dusty Springfield and Kenny Ball & his Jazzmen. The project was abandoned in July 1965 when the Estates Committee of Bromley Borough Council turned down planning permission.

In 1972, Matthew compiled a thirteen-part radio series 'The Beatles Story' for the BBC.

Brian is also featured on *The Beatles Live At The BBC* CD. On the first disc he appears on the track 'Riding On A Bus', which are excerpts of a recording he made with the Beatles in November 1964. On the track 'Dear Wack!' Brian gets John to read out a listener's request. On Disc Two he appears on the opening track 'Crinsk Dee Night' in which they joke about their film career. He next appears on 'Have A Banana!' and 'Just A Rumour'.

Maxwell's Silver Hammer

A Paul McCartney composition, featured on the *Abbey Road* album. Paul was to comment: 'This epitomises the downfalls in life. Just when everything is going smoothly "bang bang", down comes Maxwell's silver hammer and ruins everything.'

Paul had written the number in 1968 and it was almost selected to be recorded for *The Beatles* double album. The group next rehearsed the number when they were at Twickenham Film Studios in January 1969 and a clip of them rehearsing the song is included in the *Let It Be* film.

Actual recording of the number began at Abbey Road on Wednesday, 9 July 1969. Backing vocals were provided by Paul, George and Ringo and an anvil was hired from a theatrical agency for Ringo to strike.

John Lennon didn't take much active participation in this recording as he made it plain that he didn't like the number and felt that Paul was pushing for it to be issued as a single.

In fact there were no less than four cover versions rush-released at the time of the *Abbey Road* album by Brownhill's Stamp Duty, Format, The Good Ship Lollipop and George Howe. None of them registered in the charts. A version was included on the Beatles' *Anthology 3* CDs.

Maysles, Albert and David

Two American filmmaking brothers who were noted for their early rock documentaries and, in particular, the 1964 documentary 'Yeah Yeah Yeah – The Beatles In New York', which they made for Granada Television.

David died on 3 January 1987. He was 54 years old.

MBE

The initials stand for Member (of the Order of the) British Empire and refer to a prestigious award presented in the Honours List in Britain annually. The MBE is actually the lowest grade of civil award and was instituted in 1917 by King George V.

The pop weekly *Melody Maker* had suggested in a March headline that the government: 'Honour the Beatles!' Harold Wilson, then Prime Minister of a Labour government, decided to put forward the names of the individual Beatles for MBE awards, while 75 youngsters from Pennsylvania had already written to the Queen suggesting that the Beatles be given a knighthood.

The announcement that the group would be awarded the MBE was issued in 11 June 1965, and the Beatles held a press conference the following day at Twickenham Film Studios to discuss it. George was to comment: 'I didn't think you got that sort of thing, just for playing rock 'n' roll music.'

The following day the first of many awards by disgruntled previous recipients was returned to the Palace. Over the next few days the irate former recipients making their protest included Hector Dupuis, a former Canadian MP; anti-aircraft expert James Berg; ex-Naval officer David Evans-Rees; another Canadian, Stanley Ellis; a Cyril Hearn; retired squadron leader Douglas Moffit – and a Colonel Frederick Wragg returned no less than twelve medals. Dupuis commented: 'The British House of royalty had put me on the same level as a bunch of vulgar numbskulls.' Ex-RAF squadron leader Paul Pearson returned his award with the comment, 'Because it had become debased.' Author Richard Pape, on returning his MBE, wrote: 'If the Beatles and the like continue to debase the Royal honours list, then Britain must fall deeper into international ridicule and contempt.'

Bernard Levin wrote in the *Daily Mail*: 'What humiliates us all about Mr Wilson's action is precisely that it has set the State's most formal stamp of approval on the mindless and ephemeral rubbish which the Beatles music is.'

On the other hand, hundreds wrote to Harold Wilson and the Queen expressing their approval. Lt General Sir William Oliver, retiring British High Commissioner to Australia, commented: 'I think the Beatles deserve their MBE.' Lord Netherthorpe echoed the sentiments, saying, 'They thoroughly deserve the award.'

The investiture took place in the Great Throne Room at Buckingham Palace at 11.10 a.m. on the morning of Tuesday, 26 October 1965 and there were a total of 182 people receiving medals from the Queen. Outside the Palace there was a crowd of 4,000 youngsters chanting, 'Long live the Queen, long live the Beatles!'

When the group arrived, John was accompanied by Cynthia and his Aunt Mimi; Paul by his father and Jane Asher; George by his mother, father and Pattie Boyd; and Ringo by his mother and step-father. Brian Epstein was also in attendance.

Epstein had been suffering depression because he was not mentioned in the Honours List and felt he wasn't put forward for an MBE because he was a homosexual and Jewish. It was apparent to many people that the fact that he wasn't given an honour was a snub. When he was dining at the Mirabelle with his friend Geoffrey Ellis, a noted actor sitting at the next table said, 'Look at that little boy over there – he couldn't get an MBE.'

However, the press was to print the quote that the MBE stood for 'Mister Brian Epstein', although different publications attributed the comment to Paul McCartney, George Harrison – and even Princess Margaret.

When the Queen presented the group with their silver medals, she said to Paul, 'How long have you been together now?' He replied, 'Oh, for many years.' Ringo said, 'Forty years.' The Queen then turned to Ringo and said, 'Are you the one who started it?' He replied, 'No, I was the last to join. I'm the little fellow.' The Queen turned to John and said, 'Have you been working hard lately?' and he replied, 'No, we've been on holiday.'

McBean, Angus

Veteran British photographer, born in Newbridge, Monmouthshire, in 1904. His work was highly regarded and Lord Snowdon acted as his assistant at one point. His work for the British film industry and theatre was well known and he began to gain commissions from record companies to photograph artists for album covers.

Following his work with acts such as John Leyton, Johnny Kidd and Marty Wilde, McBean was commissioned to produce a cover pic for the Beatles' debut album. Paul McCartney had already worked on sketches for the cover of an album tentatively called 'Off The Beatles Track', but the title *Please Please Me* was agreed on and McBean took a photograph of the four looking down from a position on the staircase at EMI House, in London's Manchester Square. He was then commissioned to provide covers for beat groups such as Freddie & the Dreamers and Billy J. Kramer & the Dakotas.

In 1969, for the cover of the 'Get Back' session, the photograph was originally to be taken by Dezo Hoffmann on the steps of Abbey Road Studios. John Lennon suggested that they return to the site of their first album sleeve, with a new McBean shot on the stairwell. It wasn't used on the 'Get Back' session, which became the *Let It Be* album, but the recreated scene was used on the 1970 retrospective album *The Beatles 1962–1966*.

McBean retired due to ill health and four-and-a-half tons of his glass negatives were purchased by Harvard University. In 1981 Quartet Books in Britain published a collection of his work entitled *Angus McBean*, which contained reproductions of the Beatles' covers.

He died in Ipswich General Hospital on 9 June 1990. He was 86 years old.

McCartney, Florence

Paul's paternal grandmother who was born in the Everton district of Liverpool at 131 Breck Road on 2 June 1874. On 17 May 1896, 21-year-old Florence, nee Clegg, married Joseph McCartney at Christ Church in Kensington, Liverpool. She was known as Florrie and had seven children, two of whom died in early childhood. She died on VE day in 1944.

McCartney, Heather

Linda's first daughter from her marriage to Melvin See. Heather was born on 31 December 1963.

During Paul's early visits to Linda in America, Heather, who seems to have brought out his paternal instincts, evidently charmed him and he acted as a baby-sitter to her in New York when she was five. Other famous baby-sitters included Al Kooper, Stephen Stills and Mike Bloomfield.

In 1969, when he married Linda, he formally adopted Heather. Heather came to live in Cavendish Avenue and enrolled at Robinsfield, a private school in St John's Wood. However, she never felt she fitted in and had difficulty forming friendships with other children.

When Wings began touring, Paul asked her whether she'd like to stay at home or join them on the road – she plumped for the travelling life. However, when she was thirteen Paul allegedly became concerned about the crowd she was mixing with in London to the extent that he decided to move the family, lock, stock and barrel, out to Sussex.

She took various jobs, including washing up in pubs, serving in a bar in a nightclub and working in a wildlife park. Then, in her late teens, Heather took an interest in photography. She got a job as a darkroom technician and, in 1981, becoming Ilford's Young Printer of the Year. The prize was for printing up a photograph she called *Waterfalls*, which was a snap she had taken of Carol and Steve Gadd in Montserrat, when Steve was a session drummer on Paul's *Tug Of War* recordings.

Her success encouraged her to attend art college and she became interested in pottery and design.

During her early twenties she says she had a personal identity crisis and was admitted to a Sussex clinic suffering from depression. She underwent therapy.

A few years later she travelled to Mexico and spent several months living with the natives of the Huichol and Tarahumara tribes, studying their lore. She felt liberated by the experience and returned to Britain with fresh inspiration. As a result of her new designs, Wedgwood hailed her as one of Britain's most exciting new talents.

Heather has settled in a small cottage a few miles from the McCartney farm near Rye, East Sussex.

She has always enjoyed the love of her parents and has also been financially secure, yet Heather has also remained vulnerable, with a feeling of insecurity and a lack of confidence.

In January 1999, Paul attended Heather's first collection of textiles, ceramics and other homeware at a trade exhibition in Atlanta, Georgia. Heather was now aged 36 and Paul commented, 'She has always been very talented in that way, even when she was very little. She started off as a potter, and now she has entered the interior design world.'

McCartney, James (Father)

Paul's father, generally known as Jim. He was born at 8 Fishguard Road, Everton, Liverpool, on 7 July 1902, the son of Joe and Florence McCartney.

He had two brothers and three sisters. A bad fall at the age of ten resulted in a broken eardrum, but this didn't prevent him from learning to play the piano by ear. He started work at the age of fourteen as a sample boy at A. Hanney & Co, the cotton brokers of Chapel Street, Liverpool, where he received six shillings a week.

At the age of seventeen he began playing ragtime music and his first public appearance with a band was at St Catherine's Hall, Vine Street. Even in those days gimmicks were considered useful in the promotion of bands, so they called themselves the Masked Melody Makers and wore black masks. But when they began to sweat, the dye from the masks ran down their faces, which put paid to that. Dressed in dinner jackets, they became known as Jim Mac's Band and performed locally for about five years, one of their notable appearances being at a local cinema where the film *The Queen Of Sheba* was playing. Their brief was to provide musical background for the silent movie. It was during this period that Jim penned an instrumental number called 'Eloise'.

At the age of 28 he was promoted to the post of salesman and his earnings rocketed to £250 per year. On 15 April 1941, at the age of 39, he married Mary Mohin at St Swithin's Roman Catholic church in the Gillmoss area of West Derby in Liverpool and they moved into furnished rooms in Anfield. The couple were to have two children, Paul and Michael.

The cotton exchange was closed during the war years and Jim went to work at Napiers, an engineering firm which produced engines for the Sabre plane. During the evenings he was on call as a voluntary fire-fighter. At the end of the war he found work as an inspector for Liverpool Corporation's Cleansing Department and later returned to his job at the cotton exchange.

His younger son Michael was to comment: 'We both owe him a lot. He's a very good man, and he's a very stubborn man ... it would have been easy for him to have gone off with other birds when Mum died, or to have gone out getting drunk every night. But he didn't. He stayed home and looked after us.'

In 1964 Paul asked his father to retire. He was then earning ten pounds a week. Paul also suggested that he move into a nice house 'over the water' and bought Rembrandt, a detached house in Baskervyle Road, Heswall, Cheshire, for £8,750.

On Jim's 62nd birthday, the same year, Paul presented him with a horse called Drake's Drum. Two years later he proudly led the steed into the winner's enclosure at Aintree after it had won the race immediately preceding the Grand National.

Paul was also to delight his father when he put the words to 'Eloise' and recorded the number in Nashville under the title 'Walking In The Park With Eloise'.

Jim was remarried on 24 November 1964 to a widow, Angela Williams. Over the next ten years Jim became crippled by arthritis and had to move to a nearby bungalow. As a result, Paul bought Rembrandt back from him. He died on 18 March 1976. Paul was performing on a European tour with Wings at the time. Jim's second wife Angela told Mike McCartney that just before he died, Jim had said, 'I'll be with Mary soon.' He was cremated at Landican Cemetery, near Heswall, on 22 March.

McCartney, James Louis

The only son of Paul and Linda McCartney, named after the respective fathers of Paul and Linda. James was born at the Avenue Clinic in St John's Wood, London, on 12 September 1977.

Rather publicity-shy, little has been revealed about him apart from a few of the accidents he has been involved in. In September 1989 he had a brush with death while surfing in high seas and apparently vanished for forty minutes. Then on 3 May 1995 he was driving a Land Rover which overturned, trapping him beneath it. He was airlifted to hospital, but the only injury he sustained was a broken ankle.

He began working for his father's music publishing company and had aspirations of becoming a drummer.

McCartney, Joe

Paul's paternal grandfather, who died before Paul was born.

Joe was born in Everton on 23 November 1866 and lived in the area all his life. He married Florence Clegg when he was 29 and worked throughout his life as a tobacco cutter at Cope's, a local tobacco firm. A keen amateur musician, his instrument was the big brass double-bass which he played in the line-up of two brass bands, one run by Cope's, the other by the local branch of the Territorial Army.

McCartney, Linda

Linda was born Linda Louise Eastman on 24 September 1942. Her father, Lee V. Eastman, was an affluent lawyer who had changed his name from Epstein and collected expensive works of art. Her father's speciality was copyright law in the showbusiness field and he once agreed to undertake legal work for songwriter Jack Lawrence in exchange for a song dedicated to his six-year old daughter. Lawrence penned 'Linda' late in 1947, and in 1963 it was recorded by Jan and Dean.

Linda's mother, Louise Eastman, was the daughter of a rich Cleveland family, the Linders, who owned major department stores. The family home was Scarsdake, Westchester County, in upstate New York. They also owned a house in East Hampton and a luxurious flat in Park Avenue.

Linda also had two younger sisters, Laura and Louise, and an elder brother, John.

During her formative years, Linda was used to mixing with celebrity guests who were invited to dinner parties at the house, such as William Boyd (the screen's Hopalong Cassidy), songwriter Hoagy Carmichael and jazz legend Tommy Dorsey.

Linda has said, 'All my teen years were spent with an ear to the radio.' She played truant from school to travel to shows at the Paramount Theatre in Brooklyn: 'They'd have twenty acts on, twenty-four hours a day. Alan Freed was the MC, but sometimes they'd get Fabian or Bobby Darin to MC. I remember seeing Chuck Berry sing "School Days" for the first time.'

She was educated at Scarsdale High School, followed by the

exclusive Sarah Lawrence School in Bronxville, near Scarsdale (where Yoko Ono had previously been a student).

In 1962, Linda's world fell to pieces when her mother died in a plane crash. Linda had gone to Princeton University to study history and art. Her mother's death affected her so much that she rushed into marriage with a fellow student, Melvin See. Linda recalled, 'My mother died in a plane crash and I got married. It was a mistake.' The two continued their studies at the University of Colorado.

She realised things wouldn't work out: 'When he [Melvin] graduated he wanted to go to Africa. I said, "Look, if I don't get on with you here I'm not going to Africa with you. I won't get on with you there."'

They'd moved to Tucson, Arizona, and Linda had become pregnant. She gave birth to her first daughter Heather on 31 December 1963. See, who was a geophysicist, still hoped that Linda would follow him to Africa but she wrote him a letter telling him she was getting a divorce.

The marriage had only lasted a year but, while she lived in Arizona, Linda had studied art history at the University of Arizona and had attended a short course on photography given by Hazel Archer at Tucson Art Centre. It was then that she first began taking photographs. She was to say, 'Arizona opened up my eyes to the wonder of light and colour.'

Linda's break into the professional world of photography had begun when she and Heather moved to New York. Linda was holding down a job as receptionist for *Town & Country* magazine when an invitation to cover a reception for the Rolling Stones on a boat on the Hudson came in – she snapped it up, and found she was the only photographer on board! The photographs established her reputation, she secured an unpaid, but prestigious position as the house photographer at the Fillmore East, a popular rock venue which featured major British and American acts, and began to receive commissions to photograph leading bands such as the Beach Boys.

She photographed the Beatles in 1965 in Austria during the filming of *Help!*, but says that she first met them officially at the Shea Stadium in 1966. She was to recall, 'It was John who interested me at the start. He was my Beatle hero. But when I met him the fascination faded fast and I found it was Paul I liked.'

In 1967 she came to London to photograph British acts such as the Animals and Traffic for a book she was working on with author J. Marks called *Rock And Other Four Letter Words*. On 15 May, Chas Chandler, ex-bass player of the Animals, took her to the Bag

O'Nails Club in Kingley Street and introduced her to Paul. They had their first real conversation that night and Paul asked her to join him at another club called the Speakeasy. A few days later, on 19 May, she was one of the select band of fifteen photographers from around the world who attended the private Sgt Pepper launch party at Brian Epstein's Chapel Street house. She managed to receive an invitation through Epstein's aide Peter Brown whom she'd provided with some photographs of the Rolling Stones.

In May 1969, Paul arrived in New York to promote Apple and gave a number of press conferences. At one of them, Linda slipped him her telephone number and he got in touch and spent a few days with her, meeting at Nat Weiss' flat. Heather charmed Paul to the extent that he baby-sat while Linda went out to take photographs at a rock gig.

He returned to London, then visited Los Angeles a month later and called up Linda with an invitation to join him. They spent a week together in a bungalow on the grounds of the Beverly Hills Hotel on Sunset Boulevard before Paul left once again. Linda returned to New York. In November she received an invitation from Paul to join him in London, just five months after he had split with Jane Asher.

'I came over,' she said, 'and we lived together for a while, neither of us talked about marriage, we just loved each other and lived together. We liked each other a lot, so being conventional people, one day I thought: OK let's get married, we love each other, let's make it definite.'

And the occasion did seem to be hastily arranged. Linda, four months pregnant with Mary, went to Marylebone Register Office on 11 March 1969 to book it for the next day at 9.45 a.m. Paul was in the studio recording Jackie Lomax singing 'Thumbin' A Ride' and, engrossed as he was in his work, forgot to buy a wedding ring. As he had an early start the next day, he had to persuade a local jeweller to open his shop after closing time. He bought a plain gold ring for twelve pounds.

On the morning of 12 March, determined fans, photographers and journalists, undaunted by the rain, gathered at Paul's Cavendish Avenue house from 6.00 a.m. onwards, hoping to catch a glimpse of the couple. Mike McCartney was best man, but his train from Liverpool was delayed and he arrived an hour late. He rushed into the Registry Office saying, 'Forgive me, it wasn't my fault. Have you been done?' Fortunately there had been no other weddings booked for that morning and Paul was able to answer: 'No, we've been waiting for you.' Linda's daughter Heather was bridesmaid and Peter Brown and Mal Evans were witnesses while

Linda wore a daffodil yellow coat over a fawn dress. None of the Beatles turned up as Paul had already started litigation to dissolve the group. Registrar Mr E. R. Sanders conducted the ceremony, and the marriage was blessed afterwards at the Anglican Church in St John's Wood by the Rev Noel Perry-Gore.

On the couple's return to Cavendish Avenue, the press was invited in and given champagne while Paul and Linda answered their questions. A rumour had spread that Linda was a rich heiress of the Kodak-Eastman family, but she quickly scotched it, saying she had nothing to do with them. Paul quipped, 'What? I've been done. Where's the money?' Once the press had been satisfied, Paul and Linda went on to the wedding reception proper at the Ritz Hotel, Piccadilly. Later that evening, Paul returned to the studios to complete the production of the Jackie Lomax single.

Unfortunately, around this time, Beatles fans that hung around Paul's house became quite nasty with Linda. While they had accepted Jane Asher as a suitable girlfriend and potential wife for Paul, they resented Linda and she received a degree of abuse from them.

One of the first songs which Paul wrote after the marriage was 'The Lovely Linda'. She also inspired 'Maybe I'm Amazed' and both songs were included on his solo debut album *McCartney*. Paul officially adopted Heather as his daughter and the couple had three more children, Mary, Stella and James Louis.

When Paul formed Wings he wanted Linda to tour with him. There were initially some cruel jibes about her being in the band and she suggested dropping out, but Paul insisted and taught her to play keyboards. She continued to pursue her career as a photographer with some success, and also recorded in her own right, initially using the pseudonym Suzi & the Red Stripes for her record 'Seaside Woman'. She was also involved in two animated films, The *Oriental Nightfish* and *Seaside Woman*.

Linda was to stretch herself still further. Concerned with the well-being of animals, she became a vegetarian and was to say, 'I don't eat anything with a face.' She aided various organisations including Greenpeace, Friends of the Earth, the Council for the Protection of Rural England, Lynx and the People for the Ethical Treatment of Animals. Her book, *Linda McCartney's Home Cooking*, published in 1989, became the biggest selling vegetarian cookbook of all time in Britain. In 1991 she launched her own line of ready-made vegetarian dishes in the UK and was to repeat the success in the US in 1994. Her second vegetarian book *Linda's Kitchen* was published in 1995. As a result of her efforts, she was presented with a Lifetime Achievement Award by PETA in December 1991.

Apart from her first book with J. Marks, her own published books of photographs included *Linda's Pictures, Sun Prints, Linda McCartney's Sixties, Portrait of an Era, Roadworks* and *Wide Open*. Her photographs were exhibited in over fifty galleries around the world, including the Victoria and Albert Museum in London.

Linda developed a growing authority as a musician in the various world tours undertaken with Paul. She appeared in a cameo role in the popular TV series 'Bread', set in Liverpool and scripted by Linda's friend Carla Lane

Paul and Linda have remained close throughout their marriage and have never been apart for longer than the nine days Paul spent in jail in Japan.

Sadly, Linda was first diagnosed with breast cancer in December 1995. She was to fight a two-and-a-half year battle with the cancer, but it spread rapidly to her liver.

Due to her illness, Linda was unable to attend Paul's knighthood ceremony at Buckingham Palace in March 1997, but rallied enough to be present at the Albert Hall premiere of *Standing Stone* in October, and she also attended Stella's Paris debut of her designs for Chloe the following day. It seemed as if there would be a remission when she was also able to attend the *Standing Stone* premiere at Carnegie Hall in November. Her last public appearance was at Stella's Paris show in March 1998.

She died in Arizona at McCartney's family ranch on April 17 1998.

Paul was to say: 'I lost my girlfriend, lover, wife and the mother of my children.' It was the same cancer which killed his mother when he was fourteen.

Paul made a statement following Linda's death:

This is a total heartbreak for my family and I. Linda was, and still is, the love of my life, and the past two years we spent battling her disease have been a nightmare. She never complained and always hoped to be able to conquer it. It was not to be.

Our beautiful children – Heather, Mary, Stella and James – have been an incredible strength during this time, and she lives on in all of them.

The courage she showed to fight for her causes of vegetarianism and animal welfare was unbelievable. How many women can you think of who would single-handedly take on opponents like the Meat and Livestock Commission, risk being laughed at, and yet succeed?

People who didn't know her well, because she was a very

private person, only ever saw the tip of the iceberg. She was the kindest women I have ever met, the most innocent.

All animals to her were like Disney characters and worthy of love and respect. She was the toughest woman who didn't give a damn what other people thought. She found it hard to be impressed by the fact that she was Lady McCartney.

When asked whether people called her Lady McCartney, she said, 'Somebody once did – I think.' I am privileged to have been her lover for 30 years, and in all that time, except for one enforced absence, we never spent a single night apart. When people asked why, we would say – 'What for?'

As a photographer, there are few to rival her. Her photographs show an intense honesty, a rare eye for beauty.

As a mother she was the best. We always said that all we wanted for the kids was that they would grow up to have good hearts, and they have.

Our family is so close that her passing has left a huge hole in our lives. We will never get over it, but I think we will come to accept it.

The tribute she would have liked best would be for people to go vegetarian, which, with the vast variety of foods available these days, is much easier than many people think.

She got into the food business for one reason only, to save animals from the cruel treatment our society and traditions force upon them.

Anyone less likely to be a business woman I can't think of, yet she worked tirelessly for the rights of animals, and became a food tycoon. When told a rival firm had copied one of her products, all she would say was, 'Great, now I can retire.' She wasn't in it for the money.

In the end she went quickly with very little discomfort, and surrounded by her loved ones.

Finally I said to her, 'You're up on your beautiful Appaloosa stallion; it's a fine spring day, we're riding through the woods. The bluebells are all out, and the sky is clear blue.'

I had barely got to the end of the sentence when she closed her eyes, and gently slipped away. She was unique and the world is a better place for having known her. Her message of love will live on in our hearts forever.

I love you Linda.

On 27 October 1998 an album of her music *Wide Prairie* was issued. Another posthumous release was her third vegetarian cooking book *Linda McCartney On Tour*.

McCartney, Mary (Daughter)

Paul and Linda McCartney's first child. She was born at the Marie Louise Clinic in London. Paul and Linda specially chose the clinic because Paul's mum was called Mary and Linda's mum was Louise. Mary was born at 1.30 a.m. on Thursday, 29 August 1969, although an earlier announcement had said she was due in December. She weighed 6lbs 8ozs and arrived slightly less than six months after the couple had wed. Two months after the birth, Paul and Linda took their new baby to Scotland with them. It was during this period that the 'Paul Is Dead' rumours first sprang up in America. In November they took Mary to America to show her to Linda's family.

For her 25th birthday, Paul and Linda organised a party for 1,000 people, allegedly costing £90,000. The glamorous brunette seemed the most confident of the McCartney offspring and began appearing in public in 1994 at opening nights. For the premiere of *Sirens* she wore a micro-mini and thigh length leather boots. When the photographers gathered, she said: 'Why are they taking my picture? I'm a nobody.'

She began to work in music publishing at her parents' company.

Mary married film director Alistair Donald in Rye, Sussex, on 26 September 1998, in a rose-coloured dress trimmed in antique lace, designed by her sister Stella. She gave birth to a 7lb baby boy Arthur Alistair Donald on 3 April 1999, making Paul the second Beatles grandfather.

McCartney, Mary (Mother)

Paul's mother was born Mary Patricia Mohin on 29 September 1909 at No. 2 Third Avenue, Fazakerley, Liverpool. Her mother, Mary Theresa Dahner, was a Liverpudlian and her father, Owen Mohin, an Irishman. The couple had four children – Wilf, Mary, Agnes and Bill. Sadly, Agnes died at the age of two, and was followed by her mother who died giving birth to a fifth child, who also died, in 1919, when Mary was only ten.

Her father came from Co. Monaghan and had immigrated to Glasgow in 1892 and then to Liverpool in 1905. After his wife's death he returned to Ireland with his family, but failed in his attempts at farming. He then returned to Liverpool where he set himself up as a coal merchant. He became so successful that he owned five delivery carts and at one point owned four racehorses. However, he was addicted to gambling and lost everything. On a trip to Ireland to buy horses in 1921, he met Rose, who became his second wife. When he returned to Liverpool, Rose and Mary didn't get on. Mary moved out of the house to live with her mother's relatives and became a trainee nurse at Alder Hey Hospital at the age of fourteen. She'd been christened a Catholic.

She later moved to Walton Hospital, where she was promoted to nursing sister at the age of 24. She married Jim McCartney in 1941 when she was 31 and the couple moved to Anfield.

When Paul was born at Walton Hospital, Mary gave up her position there to look after him. Her second son Michael was born eighteen months later. She became a health visitor for a while and then a midwife, which meant that she was on call virtually 24 hours a day. The family was given accommodation on the various council estates where she was on call to residents.

In 1947 they moved to St Thomas White Gardens in Everton, and when Paul was four years old moved to 72 Western Avenue, Speke, followed by 12 Ardwick Road, Speke, and in 1955 they moved for the last time to 20 Forthlin Road, Allerton.

Mary was concerned about both her sons making a success in life and was supportive in their schoolwork. She also smoothed out Paul's scouse accent, instilling in him the need to speak in as nice a way as possible, and had dreams of his becoming a doctor.

At the age of 45 she began to suffer from pains in her chest, but dismissed them as being part of the menopause. However, they persisted and were so intense at times that she took Bisodal. When she eventually saw a specialist, he diagnosed breast cancer. She underwent an operation, but it was too late – the cancer had spread. The operation exacerbated the condition and she died at the Northern Hospital on 31 October 1956, with rosary beads tied around he wrists. She'd said, 'I would have liked to have seen the boys growing up.'

The fourteen-year-old Paul, on hearing the news of his mother's death, said: 'What are we going to do without her money?' This initial reaction covered up his real grief, which set in later; his brother Mike believed the tragedy caused Paul to lose himself in music, which became an obsession.

Mary was buried at Yew Street Cemetery, Finch Lane, Huyton, on 3 November 1956. Both sons were to pay tribute to their mother, Mike by placing her photograph on the cover of his first solo album and Paul by immortalising her in 'Lady Madonna'.

Paul's first daughter Mary is also named after his mother.

McCartney, Mike (McGear)

Paul's younger brother Peter Michael McCartney was born on 7 January 1944 at Walton Hospital, Liverpool, and his first home was in Roach Avenue. He was baptised a Catholic, as was Paul, and he joined his brother at their first school, Stockton Wood Road Infants' School. When they moved to Ardwick Avenue in Speke, they shared the same bedroom and began to attend Joseph Williams Primary School in Gateacre.

Mike attended the Liverpool Institute, but his ambition was to enter Liverpool College of Art. Unfortunately, new rules made it mandatory for entrants to have five GCE (General Certificate of Education) passes and Mike was turned down. He was accepted for Birkenhead's Laird School of Art, but was unable to obtain a grant from Liverpool Corporation, so at the age of seventeen, he began his first job at Jackson's the Tailors in Ranelagh Street. The following year he began an apprenticeship at Andrew Bernard, a ladies' hairdresser in the same street.

In 1962 he was asked if he'd take part in a sketch at the Merseyside Arts Festival with a Post Office engineer, John Gorman, and a young teacher, Roger McGough. Mike agreed, but wanted to use a pseudonym. He suggested the name Michael Blank, and he was so credited in the programme. The three decided to stick together as a satirical trio, performing songs and sketches, and called themselves the Scaffold. In 1963 they were asked to appear regularly on Granada Television's weekly magazine programme 'Gazette', so they all gave up their jobs to become professional members of Scaffold. Mike changed his name to Mike McGear as the Beatles were now achieving such incredible success that he didn't want to appear as if he were exploiting his family name. In any event, he was used to pseudonyms as his first published photographs had appeared in *Mersey Beat* under the name Francis Michael.

The Scaffold were to prove a tremendous success. In 1968 they were appearing regularly on a BBC satirical show and were also doing live gigs at prestigious venues such as the London Palladium. During the seventies the Scaffold line-up was regularly supplemented by Neil Innes and Viv Stanshall of the Bonzo Dog Doo Dah Band and Andy Roberts of the Liverpool Scene, using the collective name Grimms. The Scaffold performed their final live gig on the *All Fools Show*, a charity affair at the Royal Albert Hall on 1 April 1977. There was a further reunion, on Granada Television in 1979 when they teamed up on the programme 'What's On' to celebrate the 10th anniversary of their No. 1 hit 'Lily The Pink'.

Mike had married Angela Fishwick in 1968 in a country church ceremony in Caerog, North Wales, with Paul as Best Man, accompanied by Jane Asher. The marriage produced three daughters, but began to break down in the late seventies and the couple were divorced in 1979.

After the demise of Scaffold and the collapse of his first marriage, Mike began to write children's books. He then married Rowena Home, a 21-year-old dress designer at St Barnabas Church in Penny Lane, Liverpool, on 29 May 1982. Over 600 fans gathered outside the church in the morning and waited for Mike to arrive at 2.30 p.m. and Rowena about ten minutes later. Paul was dressed in casual style with grey jacket, blue trousers and white sneakers, and there were five bridesmaids: Mike's three daughters (Benna, thirteen, Theran, eleven, and Abbi, eight) and Rowena's two sisters. The Reverend Harrington, who conducted the ceremony, recalled when Paul was a choirboy at the church and commented: 'He used to sit up there in the choirbox, making some kind of noise.' After the ceremony the wedding party left the church and headed for Hoylake for the reception. Later Mike and Rowena flew to Malta for their honeymoon.

The Scaffold enjoyed a successful recording career and their first single was produced by George Martin. It was '2 Days Monday', issued on Parlophone R5443 on 6 May 1966. John Burgess was the producer of their second single 'Goodbat Nightman', issued on 2 December of the same year on Parlophone R5548. They had a big chart hit with 'Thank U Very Much', produced by Tony Palmer and issued on Parlophone R5643 on 4 November 1967. Paul had bought Mike a Nikon camera and when Mike phoned him to thank him for the gift he chanted 'Thank you very much' on the phone. After the call the chant stayed in his head and he put it down on tape, then wrote 'Thank U Very Much'. Paul attended the recording session at Abbey Road, but told Mike the song was too oblique. When Mike pointed out that the entire song was oblique, Paul said, 'Have it your own way if you know so much.' The song became a spectacular hit and Paul phoned Mike and said, 'You were right . . . I was wrong.'

This was followed by 'Do You Remember', produced by Norrie Paramor and issued on Parlophone R5679 on 15 March 1968. Their next single '1–2–3' came out on 14 June 1968 on Parlophone R5703. Their biggest success, reaching the No. 1 spot in the British charts and proving to be the hit of the Christmas season, was 'Lily The Pink', issued on 18 October 1968 on Parlophone R5734. Other singles included 'Charity Bubbles', 'Gin Gan Goolie', 'All The Way Up', 'Busdreams', 'Liverpool Lou', 'Mummy Won't Be Home For Christmas', 'Leaving of Liverpool', 'Wouldn't It Be Funny If You Didn't Have A Nose?' and 'How Do You Do?'.

Paul's first involvement with his younger brother's recording career happened in 1968 when he produced the album *McGough & McGear*, released on Parlophone PCS 7047 on 17 May. He didn't produce the Scaffold's first album *The Scaffold*, but did produce their hit single 'Liverpool Lou', as well as Mike's solo album *McGear*, for which he wrote 'What Do We Really Know?' and 'Leave It' and co-wrote with Mike: 'Norton', 'Have You Got Problems?', 'Rainbow Lady', 'Simply Love You' and 'Givin' Grease A Ride'. He also co-wrote 'The Casket' and 'The Man Who Found God On The Moon', this time with Roger McGough.

At Island Records Mike recorded and released the single 'Woman' and an album of the same name in 1972. In 1973 Island issued the group Grimms' eponymous album, followed by a Scaffold album *Fresh Liver* and another Grimms LP *Rockin' Duck*. Mike then signed to Warners who issued *McGear* and *Sold Out* and a number of his singles.

Mike's popularity engendered an American Mike McCartney Fan Club and a fanzine called *Gear Box*. In the eighties he issued the series *Mike Mac's Black & Whites*, a collection of his photographs, which were also presented in a handsome range of postcards and posters. He began to tour American universities lecturing on his career, Liverpool and the Beatles and also completed a video about Liverpool, in addition to furthering his career as a photographer and recording various Liverpool bands – a busy, creative life for a man with such a large family (he and Rowena had three boys, in addition to the three daughters from his previous marriage, who were reared with Mike), who has also penned his autobiography, *Thank U Very Much: Mike McCartney's Family Album*, which was called *The Macs* in America.

McCartney, Paul

Paul was born at Walton Road Hospital in Rice Lane, Liverpool, on 18 June 1942, the first son of Mary and James McCartney. His brother Michael was born eighteen months later.

Mary McCartney was a midwife and the family moved to various addresses in Liverpool before settling at 20 Forthlin Road in 1955, where Mary died the following year of cancer of the breast.

When Paul passed his 11-Plus examination in 1957 he entered the Liverpool Institute, a popular high school near the city centre. While travelling to school on the bus he met with a younger student, George Harrison. Another Institute boy was Ivan Vaughan who invited Paul to a fete at St Peter's Church in Woolton where he introduced him to John Lennon, who was playing in a skiffle group he'd formed called the Quarry Men.

Paul had been interested in music due to the influence of his father, who had once led his own jazz band locally. Paul was able to play some songs to John and write down the lyrics which led to John inviting Paul to join the group.

The Quarry Men underwent changes and when the residency at the Casbah Club began they comprised John, Paul, George and Ken Brown. By that time they had introduced more rock 'n' roll numbers to their repertoire and Paul had been encouraging the group to perform their own original material. He began writing songs with John at Forthlin Road.

Although John was leader of the group, Paul was the one who seemed to have the greatest appetite for success and worked hard to achieve it. He developed a healthy respect for the media and became an ideal spokesman. He was also full of ideas which he was to continue to introduce to the group throughout the sixties, whether it was through his designs for album sleeves or scripts for a TV special such as *Magical Mystery Tour*. He was also the member who was most keen on public performances.

The left-handed Paul became the group's bass guitarist when Stuart Sutcliffe left the band in 1961. The majority of songs John and Paul wrote together were composed early on in their career, but once they became established, the two songwriters generally wrote their numbers individually, although they agreed to credit all songs as 'Lennon & McCartney' numbers. Paul, who had introduced numbers such as 'Till There Was You', 'Besame Mucho', and 'Falling In Love Again' to the early repertoire, veered toward romantic numbers and songs which indicated the influence of Hollywood musicals. Songs such as 'Yesterday', 'Michelle', 'When I'm Sixty-Four' and 'Lovely Rita' are typical of McCartney compositions, while Lennon opted for more biting compositions, harder, more experimental and rockier numbers than Paul. Paul's interest in the traditional musical was evident in the hour-long TV special 'James Paul McCartney', in 1973 when Paul performed numbers such as 'Gotta Sing, Gotta Dance'.

When the Beatles moved to London, Paul preferred to remain in the city centre, while his fellow Beatles opted for houses in the outer suburbs. Paul always seemed the 'culture vulture' of the quartet, attending the theatre and acquiring paintings by artists such as Magritte. His long-time girlfriend, Jane Asher, aided him in cultivating his artistic tastes. To the media they seemed the perfect couple, but their five-year romance came to an end because Paul continued to have affairs. Oddly enough, it was Paul rather than John who first began to experiment with avant-garde film-making.

After Brian Epstein was found dead in August 1967, Paul was determined to prevent the group from losing interest in their career and encouraged them to film *Magical Mystery Tour*; he even directed their promotional film for 'Hello Goodbye' that year.

Jane Asher suggested that he buy a farm in Scotland which could act as a retreat and he purchased property near Campbeltown. He'd also purchased a house in St John's Wood, quite close to Abbey Road Studios.

Paul was the first Beatle to become involved in a major solo venture when he composed the music for the feature film *The Family Way* in 1967. His interest in movies continued and he composed the title song for the James Bond film *Live And Let Die* in 1973. The following year he composed the theme for the TV series 'The Zoo Gang' and in 1983 composed the theme music for the Michael Caine film *The Honorary Consul*, while his biggest screen venture was the feature film *Give My Regards To Broad Street* in 1984.

In 1968 he began his affair with Linda Eastman and the couple were married in March 1969. Paul adopted Linda's daughter Heather and the couple had three children of their own, Mary, Stella and James.

During the filming and recording of the *Let It Be* project, tempers became frayed and George walked out of the project after an argument with Paul. He returned, but the Beatles were no longer the close team they used to be. A major split had developed between Paul and his three partners over the decision they made to appoint Allen Klein as manager, against Paul's wishes. Paul recorded a solo album *McCartney*, and had to argue with the other members and Allen Klein regarding its release date. It was finally issued in Britain on Apple PCS 7102 on 17 April 1970 and in America on Apple STAO 3363 on 20 April 1970. He was to form his own group called Wings, which had several changes of personnel, but whose line-up included his wife Linda on keyboards. Over the next 30 years he produced an amazing canon of works, releasing more albums and singles than any of the other ex-Beatles.

In 1979 Paul was awarded a rhodium-plated disc for his achievements which, by that time, had already brought him 43 songs which were million sellers and 60 Gold Discs. He had sold more records throughout the world than any other artist. Since then, Paul's achievements have continued and he became the only former Beatle to be knighted when the Queen dubbed him Sir Paul McCartney.

McCartney, Ruth

As Ruth Williams, she became a member of the McCartney clan at the age of five when, on 24 November 1964, her 34-year-old widowed mother Angela married 62-year-old Jim McCartney.

Ruth became Paul's stepsister, was given the McCartney surname and went to live in Rembrandt, the McCartneys' home in Hoylake on the Wirral. She recalls that Paul used to refer to her as 'Scabby' because she grazed her knees so often. After she'd broken her leg Paul bought her a pet dog which she called Hamish.

Jane Asher was a frequent companion of Paul's in the first three years of Ruth's life at Rembrandt and the young actress taught her to ride a bicycle. At school locally, Ruth came in for a fair amount of bullying from other children, jealous of her meeting the various famous guests who visited Rembrandt, such as Rod Stewart.

At the age of nine she was learning to play the piano and one day was attempting to play 'Golden Slumbers', a traditional hymn. She wasn't very successful, so Paul helped her out – and as a result he penned his own 'Golden Slumbers', which was included on the *Abbey Road* album. Ruth also recalls that Paul made up a song about her on the spur of the moment at a birthday party. As a young girl she observed the breakdown of Paul's romance with Jane Asher and the flowering of his relationship with Linda. Ruth, her mother and Jim were guests of Paul and Linda at the Campbeltown farm, where the conditions were very spartan, according to Ruth.

At fifteen, Ruth took an interest in choreography but claims that she didn't get much encouragement from Paul. Ruth spent twelve years in the McCartney family, but following Jim McCartney's death circumstances changed.

For a time Ruth led a dance trio called Talent, but didn't achieve much success. In 1981 she moved to King's Lynn where she shared a flat with her mother and worked as a salesgirl at the local Debenham's store. But the McCartney name still brought her to the attention of the press. She returned to her love of dancing and in March 1982 entered a 'Claim To Fame' dance competition at the Embassy Club in Mayfair, London, in which she won a heat. Julian Lennon had a sponsorship link with the competition and as a result their names were romantically linked by the press. Eventually Ruth went to live in Los Angeles to pursue a career in show business.

McCartney, Stella Nina

Linda McCartney's third child and the second child of both Linda and Paul. Stella was born in King's College Hospital in London on 3 September 1971. It was a difficult birth and, as the child was delivered by Caesarian section, Paul was banned from the operating theatre. He said: 'I sat next door in my green apron praying like mad. The name "wings" just came into my mind.' As a result he called his new band Wings. He'd initially considered Turpentine, then the Dazzlers, but the story went that he silently prayed that his child would be delivered 'on the wings of an angel.'

Stella grew up to be a strawberry blonde, tanned with freckles. Commenting on her early life, she said: 'We were very ordinary. When we were young, I shared a bedroom with my two sisters and brother, just like any other family. I went to the local comprehensive. There was never anything grand.' At the age of fifteen she took on work experience at Christian Lacroix in Paris and decided to become a fashion designer, enrolling at St Martins in London. She was in the class of '95 at Central St Martins and created a sensation at the graduate show by having her clothes modelled by Naomi Campbell, Kate Moss and Yasmin Le Bon. At the age of 26 she was appointed chief designer at Chloe, the luxury French ready-to-wear house.

McClinton, Delbert

An American musician, born in Lubbock, Texas, who specialised in harmonica. While with a band in Fort Worth, he was hired to work on the Bruce Channel recording session for 'Hey Baby' and provided the haunting harmonica solo which helped to make it a hit.

When Channel toured Britain he brought McClinton with him and the two appeared with the Beatles at the Tower Ballroom, New Brighton, on Thursday, 21 June 1962.

During the evening, John Lennon chatted with McClinton, who showed him how to play the harmonica passage. When the Beatles came to record 'Love Me Do', Lennon used the style McClinton had taught him.

McClinton was one of the country music artists who contributed to the 1995 Liberty Records release *Come Together: America Salutes The Beatles,* a tribute to the group by the stars of country music. McClinton recorded the track 'Come Together'. During the press call for the release, Matt Hurwitz interviewed him. His recollections of the Beatles indicate how perceptions and memories can differ, whether through point of view or passage of time.

He said: 'The Beatles were the opening act on about four of the shows we did . . . we were in New Brighton the first night we played with them, at a place called the Castle. It was an old castle, if I remember right, because when you looked out of the dressing-room window it was a sheer drop to the ocean.'

In fact, the Beatles appeared at only one gig with Channel and McClinton – at the Tower Ballroom, New Brighton. It wasn't a castle and didn't look down on the ocean: just the river Mersey!

The Barons backed Channel and McClinton, and the rest of the bill comprised the Beatles, the Big Three, the Four Jays and the Statesmen.

McFall, Ray

When Alan Sytner decided to sell the Cavern Club in Liverpool, he received an offer from Ray McFall, who worked on the accounts

for the Cavern and another nearby jazz venue. Ray took over the
operation from Sytner on 1 October 1959.

Ray was born in the Garston area of Liverpool on 14 November
1926 and during the war worked down the mines as a 'Bevan Boy'.
He married and moved to London in 1952, but decided to return to
Liverpool as an accountant two years later.

He began to work on accounts for the Sytner family and Alan
asked him to handle the accounts of the Cavern Club. He also
worked as a cashier on Sundays at the Temple Jazz Club and
fulfilled the same function at the Cavern on Thursdays and
Saturdays.

Once he'd taken control of the Cavern, Ray's new policies
became an important factor in the development of the Liverpool
sound. The Cavern had been primarily a jazz club and the local
rock groups mainly played on the 'jive hive' circuit. After taking
over the running of the club, McFall made a radical departure – he
introduced rock 'n' roll. He also pioneered lunchtime sessions.

By the end of February 1961 he'd stopped the modern jazz nights
as the musicians had failed to receive the support they'd deserved.
The club was now almost exclusively presenting rock 'n' roll, with
the Swinging Bluejeans running their customary guest night, during
which the Beatles made their evening debut on 21 March 1961.
This began a stream of appearances by the Beatles which included
their 'Welcome Home' session on Friday, 14 July 1961, with
Johnny Sandon and the Remo Four and the White Eagles Jazz
Band.

The Beatles also began their own series of resident nights on
Wednesday, 2 August 1961, and made a total of 274 appearances,
their final one taking place on 3 August 1963.

As success began to spread across the Mersey scene, Ray undertook a policy of expansion and the Cavern soon became the most
famous club in Britain.

McFall also launched a Junior Cavern Club, membership of
which cost sixpence (2.5p) with admission at two shillings (10p) for
members and two shillings and sixpence (12.5p) for visitors.

The sessions took place between 1.00 p.m. and 4.00 p.m. each
Saturday and featured two groups and Top Twenty discs, was
strictly for thirteen–sixteen-year-olds and began on 1 February
1964, with a guest appearance by Billy J. Kramer who was
promoting his latest single, 'Little Children'.

Ray continued his expansion plans and launched a manage-
ment/agency called Cavern Artists Ltd, and in November 1963 he
bought the premises next door to the Cavern, extended the width of
the club and began building a recording studio, Cavern Sound,

which opened on 15 October 1964. During alterations the old stage had to go and Ray had the idea of selling pieces of the original stage as 'Beatleboard' to Beatle fans who would like a souvenir of the stage on which the group had performed so many times. Beatleboard cost five shillings (25p) a piece, the proceeds being donated to Oxfam. There were so many requests from all over the world that it took four months to fulfil the orders.

On Saturday, 12 September 1964, there was a 'Caverncade' – a parade through the streets of Liverpool by groups on decorated floats the proceeds again were donated to Oxfam.

There was even a regular half-hour weekly radio show which took place at the club. Called 'Sunday Night At The Cavern', it was broadcast on Radio Luxembourg each Sunday at 10.30 p.m. commencing 15 March 1963. The show was hosted by Bob Wooler who played the latest chart records and introduced a group live from the Cavern stage each week.

Unfortunately, Ray had taken on too many enterprises and stretched his capital too far, with the result that he had to declare himself bankrupt, and the Cavern was sold.

While the Cavern had become famous, Ray had become a minor celebrity and began to travel widely. He joined the Beatles on their first trip to America, but while he was away, things began to deteriorate at the club, particularly in relation to the cash which was collected at the door each session, much of which became unaccounted for. Unfortunately, Ray couldn't salvage the situation and the club was never the same after he left, and it was eventually torn down to make way for an air vent for an underground railway in 1973. A decade later, a new Cavern was rebuilt on the site of the old.

Ray moved down to London and resumed his career as an accountant.

McGrath, Joe

A film and television producer. He first met the Beatles on Wednesday, 15 April 1964, when he was producing the show 'A Degree of Frost', which they appeared on that day. He also produced 'Not Only But Also . . .' on which John was featured in November 1964. On Tuesday, 23 November 1965 he was hired to direct the group on the first of ten promotional videos over an extended period of time that day. There were three versions of 'We Can Work It Out' and 'Day Tripper', two versions of 'I Feel Fine' and one version each of 'Help!' and 'Ticket To Ride'. In 1969, McGrath was also to direct the Peter Sellers/Ringo Starr film *The Magic Christian*.

McKenzie, Tom

A compere who believed he was the inspiration behind Father McKenzie in 'Eleanor Rigby'.

Tom, who first began compering in 1936, was born in Toxteth, Liverpool, and went to the same school as Ringo's stepfather. He compered the Beatles in shows for promoter Lewis Buckley on several occasions from early 1962 and was compere and master of ceremonies at the Memorial Hall, Northwich, for five years after it opened in 1961. The Beatles appeared at the venue on six occasions.

Tom recalled that the Beatles were booked on 6 July 1963 to crown the Northwich Carnival Queen and then played at a dance at the Memorial Hall. He said it was extremely hot and the Beatles were picked up from Ringo's aunt's home at Leftwich in a Parks' Steelworks van. The procession took so long to get round its route that the four were shut up inside the van, being driven round and round the town from half-past one to four in the afternoon. The crowning was a hurried affair because of fan fervour in the crowd and Paul put the crown on upside-down! Hundreds queued outside the Memorial Hall while the Beatles played inside, in spite of the torrential rain that followed the sunshine.

At one of the gigs, George had been left behind in the dressing room toilets and had to be smuggled out to the others, at Tom's suggestion, wearing a coach driver's hat and coat.

Tom fervently believed that he inspired Father McKenzie and commented: 'I think that when they wrote the song they had never forgotten me. They used to say that I treated them like a father and they were very amused when I told them of my days in the anti-aircraft artillery at Coventry, when I darned my socks at night to keep awake.'

Sadly, he died at the onset of the 1990s.

McKinnon, Duncan

An elderly pig farmer from Montrose who promoted the short Beat Ballad Show tour with Larry Parnes' intermediary for the Johnny Gentle tour of Scotland in May 1960, during which the Liverpool singer was backed by the Silver Beetles.

McKinnon, who'd received the nickname 'Drunken Duncan', didn't like the appearance of the Silver Beetles and, following their performance at Alloa, called Larry Parnes to complain. He wanted to send them home on the first train. He told Gentle he could find four buskers who played better. However, Gentle promised to make them smarten up their appearance and talked McKinnon into letting them continue.

Mean Mr Mustard

A number penned by John during his sojourn at Rishikesh in India. The number was included on Side Two of the *Abbey Road* album, which had some medley tracks.

'Mean Mr Mustard', about a peculiar chap who went around with a ten-shilling note stuck up his nose, was recorded as one song, not segued, with 'Sun King', although both tracks when originally recorded in July 1969 were recorded under the working title 'Here Comes The Sun King'. A version of the number was included on the Beatles' *Anthology 3* CDs.

Mean Woman Blues

Composition by Claude DeMetrius which was featured by Elvis Presley in his movie *Loving You*, in 1957, and also recorded by Jerry Lee Lewis. Roy Orbison had a hit with the number in 1963.

The Quarry Men introduced the song into their early repertoire and, being popularised by Presley, it was probably sung by John Lennon.

Meehan, Tony

Meehan was drummer with the Shadows, Cliff Richard's backing group and the most successful British pop group prior to the Beatles. He left the Shadows in September 1961 to join Decca Records as a record producer, his final single with the Shadows being the hit 'Wonderful Land'. Guitarist Jet Harris also left the band shortly after 'Wonderful Land' entered the charts.

Under Dick Rowe, the Decca A&R department was intending to search for new talent for pop singles. After the Beatles had auditioned for Decca, the group were rejected. Brian Epstein tried to convince Decca that they should sign the group, but Dick Rowe merely suggested that he hire Tony Meehan to produce a session for him. Epstein felt insulted at being asked to pay £100 in advance for the hire of the studio and Meeham's time to record the Beatles, but he went along to the West Hampstead studio where he had to wait for half an hour before Meehan saw him. Epstein reported in his autobiography that Meehan seemed uninterested in the group, insisted that he and Rowe were busy men and that Brian should phone Meehan's secretary to make an appointment for the Beatles to make the record. Feeling insulted, Epstein wrote a letter to Rowe saying that he would not be taking up the offer of Meehan making a record with the Beatles.

Meehan's version of the story is different. He said he talked briefly to Brian for five minutes, but their discussion had been friendly. Interestingly, Meehan teamed up with his former Shadow member Jet Harris to make records for Decca in 1963 and they had three chart records, including the chart topper 'Diamonds'.

Also of note is the fact that after leaving the Shadows, Harris made a couple of solo singles. One of them was 'Besame Mucho', one of the tracks the Beatles had recorded for Decca.

Meet The Beatles

Finally, twelve months after EMI had been asking Capitol to issue Beatles products, the American label decided to issue their first Beatles album.

They took the British release *With The Beatles* and altered it slightly, changing the name to *Meet The Beatles*. They used the same, famous half-light portrait shots of Robert Freeman's, although the actual cover design was slightly changed.

For the American release – as Capitol generally included less tracks on their albums than EMI – only nine of the original fourteen tracks from *With The Beatles* were used, together with 'I Saw Her Standing There', 'I Want To Hold Your Hand' and 'This Boy'.

The American LP was issued on Capitol 2047 on 20 January 1964, reached No. 1 in the charts and eventually sold over five million copies.

The full track listing is – Side One: 'I Want To Hold Your Hand', 'I Saw Her Standing There', 'This Boy', 'It Won't Be Long', 'All I've Got To Do', 'All My Loving'. Side Two: 'Don't Bother Me', 'Little Child', 'Till There Was You', 'Hold Me Tight', 'I Wanna Be Your Man', 'Not A Second Time'.

Memorial Coliseum, Dallas, Texas

The Beatles appeared at this arena on Friday, 18 September 1964. The show had been promoted by Super Shows Inc and the entire 10,000 tickets had sold out within a day.

The group arrived in Dallas and drove to the Cabana Motor Hotel. There was a telephone call reporting that a bomb had been planted in the auditorium. The opening was delayed while police searched the arena – no bomb was found, but fans were discovered hiding in washrooms and under the stage. There were 200 police in the auditorium and a further 200 were on stand-by. The Police Chief, Jesse Curry, brought along his daughter and two grandchildren. There was a press conference in the stadium at 7.00 p.m., the last one of the tour.

After the show, the Beatles were taken to the airport and flown to a ranch for a few days' holiday, while most members of their entourage remained at the hotel.

Memorial Coliseum, Portland, Oregon

During their 1965 tour of America, the Beatles performed two shows at this arena before a total audience of 20,000 on Sunday, 22 August 1965.

Newspapers reported the drama as one of the engines on the plane which flew them into Portland caught fire and emitted smoke.

Among the Beatles' visitors backstage that evening were Carl Wilson and Mike Love of the Beach Boys.

Memorial Hall, Chester Way, Northwich, Cheshire

Venue only 25 miles from Liverpool. The Beatles made their debut at the hall, also known as the Victory, on 23 June 1962. Other appearances took place on 15 September 1962, 1 December 1962, 27 April 1963, 6 July 1963 and 14 September 1963. Prior to their July 1963 appearance, the Beatles visited the Northwich Carnival where Paul McCartney crowned the Carnival Queen.

Memphis, Tennessee

Chuck Berry composition which he recorded in 1959, although he didn't enter the British charts with the number until October 1963.

The Beatles included the number in their repertoire in 1961, when it was sung by John.

They featured the song on several of their BBC radio recordings, including two 'Saturday Club' shows, two 'Pop Go The Beatles' shows and 'Teenager's Turn'.

The song also surfaced on *The Beatles Live! At The Star Club In Hamburg, Germany: 1962* album. A version from the Beatles' live performance on radio was used on *The Beatles Live At The BBC* CDs.

Mendips, 251 Menlove Avenue, Liverpool L25

The semi-detached home where John Lennon was reared by his Aunt Mimi and Uncle George from the age of five. The house was named after the Somerset hills. John spent more of his life at this home than any other, almost 20 years, until he eventually moved down to London. From his bedroom above the front door, he learned to play his acoustic guitar, and he continued to practise in the small front porch.

Mendips is a pleasant home, with a large garden in an extremely nice area of Liverpool, so different from many people's idea of the slum which writers often believed the 'working class hero' came from.

Mersey Beat

The title of the newspaper that gave the Liverpool sound its name.

Bill Harry was a student at Liverpool College of Art and had worked on a music magazine for the local music store, Frank Hessy's. He was at one time considering launching a jazz magazine called *Storyville/52nd Street* but, due to his friendship with John Lennon and Stuart Sutcliffe, decided to produce a newspaper promoting the local rock 'n' roll scene, which had been totally ignored by all the media. He'd even written to the national press asking them to cover what he considered as 'like New Orleans at the turn of the century, but with rock 'n' roll instead of jazz'.

A friend, Dick Mathews, who used to frequent the Jacaranda coffee club, knew that Bill was seeking finance to start the publication and introduced him to Jim Anderson, who provided the £50 needed to launch the magazine.

A small office was rented on the top floor of David Land, the wine merchant at 51 Renshaw Street and, as Bill was still studying at the Art College, the only full-time member of staff was his girl-friend Virginia.

At that time the local groups were referred to as rock 'n' roll groups and most of the venues were called 'jive hives'. The term 'beat' was seldom used. It was while Harry was sitting in the office late one night that he conceived the name. He was visualising the area he would cover and defined it in his mind as reaching 'across the water' to the Wirral, extending out to the seaside resort of Southport and to nearby towns such as Widnes and Warrington. He pictured it as a policeman's beat across Merseyside and came up with the name *Mersey Beat*.

The first issue was published on 5 July 1961. 5,000 copies were distributed through three wholesalers, Blackburn's, Conlan's and W. H. Smith, to 28 separate newsagents, to venues such as the Cavern and Mardi Gras, and to all the record and musical instruments stores in the city centre, including Cranes, Rushworths, Cramer & Lea and NEMS.

A particular interest was shown by Brian Epstein, manager of NEMS in Whitechapel, who initially ordered twelve copies. He then phoned for more when they immediately sold out. He ordered twelve dozen copies of Issue No. 2 (an incredible amount of copies for a single store in those days) and wanted to know all about the phenomenon that seemed to be happening on his own doorstep – the local music scene he read about in the paper.

The entire edition sold out and orders continued to increase over succeeding issues. The Beatles were strongly featured from the very first issue and they used to drop into the *Mersey Beat* office to help

Virginia out, answering the phone and typing – with John contributing a column.

When Harry had been planning the publication in 1960, he asked John to come up with a biography of the Beatles and, on their return from Hamburg, John gave him a piece which Harry called 'Being A Short Diversion On The Dubious Origin Of Beatles. Translated From The John Lennon'. John was so delighted with his piece being published in its entirety that he brought a huge bundle of stories, poems and drawings, some of which were then published under the name 'Beatcomber'. Harry conceived the pseudonym with deference to the humorous 'Beachcomber' column in the *Daily Express* newspaper. John Lennon also used to pay to take out classified advertisements.

The entire front page of Issue No. 2, published on 20 July 1961, was devoted to the Polydor recordings with 'Beatles Sign Recording Contract!' as the headline. It was illustrated with an Astrid Kirchherr photograph of the group in Hamburg.

The story read:

Bert Kaempfert, who may be remembered for his golden record 'Wonderland By Night' which reached the top of the American hit parade, contracted the Beatles for Polydor, Germany's top recording company. Under the contract they will make four records per year for the company.

At a recording session, the Beatles provided vocals and backing for three numbers for Tony Sheridan. Tony, a first class songwriter penned 'Why', a number familiar to readers through Gerry Marsden's excellent rendering. Apart from waxing 'Why', the Beatles recorded 'My Bonnie Lies Over The Ocean' opening in waltz-time, then breaking into a rock beat. Finally, the group provided good bass and drum backing to Sheridan for 'The Saints go Marching In', a very popular number in Germany.

The Beatles recorded two further numbers for Kaempfert on their own. One side, an instrumental written by George Harrison, has not yet been named – probable titles include 'Cry For A Shadow' and 'Beatle Bop'. The other side, 'Ain't She Sweet', featured a vocal by John Lennon. The boys weren't quite satisfied with these two numbers, so they sold the rights to Polydor. Thus, in fact, under the contract the Beatles still have four more records to make this year.

Bass guitarist Stuart Sutcliffe has remained in Hamburg and will shortly be marrying a German girl. At present he is studying at Hamburg Art College and has an English tutor.

The group have no plans for taking on another guitarist, but have decided to remain a quartet.

With this issue, in July 1961, all the Beatles' fans on Merseyside became aware of their Hamburg recordings. All the 5,000 copies of *Mersey Beat* in the Cavern and other venues, including the 12 dozen in NEMS store itself, provided the information which confirmed the local group as recording artists. Brian Epstein, who devoured the contents from cover to cover, invited Bill Harry to his office and wanted to know all about the local scene and the local groups. He was completely amazed that such a thriving music scene was literally on his doorstep. He also requested that he become record reviewer and his column 'Stop The World – And Listen To Everything In It', which was captioned 'Brian Epstein of Nems', began in Issue No. 3. He also took out advertising, which appeared on the same pages as Beatles features.

The Beatles were strongly featured in every issue and Harry also published letters, which Paul McCartney sent him, together with photographs by Mike McCartney.

When the Beatles brought Harry photographs by Astrid Kirchherr and Jurgen Vollmer for him to publish, *Mersey Beat* began to take on a look totally unlike that of the traditional music press, which was based in London. The photographic content, with the addition of photographs taken by Dick Mathews, Peter Kaye (Les Chadwick), Graham Spencer and other local photographers, was innovative for its time. The standard music papers usually printed publicity photographs taken in studios, *Mersey Beat* encouraged its photographers to take shots of the groups performing live on stage and in outside locations.

Bob Wooler wrote a major feature on the Beatles in which he described them as a 'phenomenon' in the 31 August 1961 issue – an article which impressed Epstein even further with a group he had already begun to make enquiries about. Wooler also placed them No. 1 in his own personal Top Ten in the 5 October 1961 issue and they topped the *Mersey Beat* poll, announced in issue No. 13 on 4 January 1962.

Paul McCartney wondered whether the Beatles had altered the results of the poll because they filled out a number of coupons for themselves. But most of the groups were doing this – and Rory Storm & the Hurricanes actually received the most votes, but over forty of them were disqualified.

Bill Harry and Virginia did the final count, eliminating the most obvious 'phoneys', and decided that the Beatles were definitely the winners and, after all, they'd been promoted so heavily in almost ever issue that it was virtually a foregone conclusion.

Local disc jockey Bob Wooler came into the *Mersey Beat* office and told Harry that his massive coverage of the Beatles was causing resentment among the other groups who were now calling the paper the *Mersey Beatle*. Harry later introduced a special section into the paper called 'Mersey Beatle'.

Once *Mersey Beat* had been published, the transformation in the local scene was enormous. What had been 'underground' became 'overground' and people began to realise just how vast the local music scene was. Events received more promotion and advertising, and the events became bigger.

The paper was now the offical HQ of the local scene, which now began to call itself the Mersey Beat scene – and the groups now began calling themselves beat groups instead of rock 'n' roll groups. The managers and group members visited the *Mersey Beat* offices daily and the paper's circulation was increasing to such an extent that larger offices had to be found, so the entire first floor of 51 Renshaw Street was taken over by the paper.

Once the Beatles and other Liverpool groups began to make their impact, first in Britain and then throughout the world, recording managers, television reporters and journalists of every persuasion descended on Liverpool and headed straight for the *Mersey Beat* office. There Bill and Virginia provided them with whatever help, information or contacts they needed, ranging from aiding Al Aronovitz of the *Saturday Evening Post* to Nancy Spain of the *News of the World*, helping to set up the recording sessions for the *This Is Mersey Beat* albums recorded by John Schroeder for Oriole, and organising scores of members of groups to assemble outside St George's Hall for a photograph for *Stern* magazine.

Working with Charlie Squires and Dan Farson on their production of the TV documentary 'Beat City' and aiding literally dozens of media people to meet and contact the groups, taking them round to all the venues ranging from the Cavern to the Blue Angel, was a welcome service they also provided for acts ranging from the Rolling Stones to Bob Dylan.

The publication continued to expand and introduced many innovations which were later adopted by the traditional music press – including the first gig guide, the first British Top 100 chart, the first weekly listing of all the record releases and so on. The newspaper had also expanded its coverage to take in the entire country, beginning with a section on the Manchester scene and one on the Birmingham scene, with coverage of groups from Sheffield, Newcastle, Glasgow and other provincial cities. By 1963, *Mersey Beat* had become the most imitated publication in the British Isles with no less than eighteen other publications based directly on it –

including *Midland Beat* in Birmingham, *Western Scene* in Bristol, *Scottish Beat* covering the Scottish scene, and so on.

Inevitably, London once again took complete control of the music scene and Mersey groups became *persona non grata*.

Bill and Virginia moved to London where Bill became news editor and feature writer for *Record Mirror*. He was also columnist for *Record Retailer*, feature writer for *Music Now*, pop columnist for *Weekend* magazine and columnist for *Valentine* and *Marilyn* magazines.

He then became personal press agent to the Kinks and the Hollies and over succeeding years became PR to over forty major acts, including Pink Floyd, Jethro Tull, Ten Years After, Procol Harum, David Bowie, Led Zeppelin, the Beach Boys, Free, Cockney Rebel, Supertramp, Hot Chocolate, Suzi Quatro and Kim Wilde. In the 1980s he returned to publishing, launching the album magazine *Tracks* and also *Idols: 20th Century Legends*. He has also authored eighteen books about the Beatles, including *Beatlemania: A History Of The Beatles On Film; Paperback Writers: A History Of The Beatles in Print; The Book Of Beatles Lists; Sgt Pepper's Lonely Hearts Club Band; The Ultimate Encyclopedia of the Beatles; The Encyclopedia of Beatles People;* and *The John Lennon Encyclopedia*.

Merseybeats, The

A Liverpool band who were called the Mavericks. Due to the success of the *Mersey Beat* newspaper, they approached Bill Harry, who had the name Mersey Beat copyrighted, to ask his permission to use the name the Mersey Beats. He agreed and, under that name, they began to find success. At the time they comprised Tony Crane (lead/vocals), Billy Kinsley (bass/vocals), Aaron Williams (rhythm) and John Banks (drums).

The group began a Monday night residency at St John's Hall, Bootle, and one of their special guests was the Beatles.

After Brian Epstein had been forced to sack Pete Best on the instructions of the other members of the Beatles, he continued to feel guilty about the deed and requested another meeting with Pete. He told him, 'I have an idea that might work. I'm thinking of signing the Mersey Beats and I'd like you to join them.' Pete felt that after being in Liverpool's top group it would be a retrograde step to join a new, young group who had not achieved any success and turned the offer down. Epstein decided not to sign them.

The group slightly altered their name from the Mersey Beats to the Merseybeats and became quite successful, with chart hits such as 'It's Love That Really Counts', 'I Think Of You', 'Don't Turn

Around', 'Wishin' And Hopin'', 'Last Night', 'I Love You, Yes I Do' and 'I Stand Accused'.

The group appeared second on the bill to the Beatles at the Beatles' final appearance at the Cavern Club on 3 August 1963.

Billy Kinsley left the group, to be replaced by Johnny Gustafson, formerly of the Big Three. Gustafson approached Epstein to be their manager, but Epstein declined.

The group disbanded early in 1966 soon after Billy Kinsley rejoined. Billy and Tony teamed up as the duo the Merseys and had a hit with 'Sorrow' and were finally signed up by Epstein to NEMS Enterprises. George Harrison took a line from 'Sorrow', relating to a girl with 'long blonde hair and eyes of blue', and included it on his *Yellow Submarine* composition 'It's All Too Much', in tribute to his wife Pattie.

The Merseys split up and Tony Crane reformed the Merseybeats with different musicians and is still actively leading the group today.

Billy Kinsley returned to Liverpool and, ironically, became involved in a group with Pete Best and the two have since worked together on various recordings. Kinsley has now rejoined the Merseybeats.

Mersey Beat Showcase

In 1963 the stranglehold London had on the British pop world was finally smashed with the flood of hit groups emerging from Merseyside. The national tours that year, on which the Beatles appeared, contained bills with various chart acts from around the country. Epstein decided to take advantage of the growing interest in the Liverpool sound by promoting a package of his own acts. He approached Bill Harry, who held the copyright to the name 'Mersey Beat', for permission to call his package *Mersey Beat Showcase*. Harry agreed, and Brian launched the first of the *Mersey Beat Showcases* at the Elizabethan Ballroom, Nottingham, on 7 March 1963. Groups on the bill were the Beatles, Gerry & the Pacemakers, the Big Three and Billy J. Kramer & the Dakotas – with Cavern disc jockey Bob Wooler as compere.

During the next six months Brian promoted a further six *Mersey Beat Showcase* presentations which included the King's Hall, Stoke-on-Trent on 19 April; the Majestic Ballroom, Finsbury Park on 24 April; the Fairfield Hall, Croydon on 25 April; the Tower Ballroom, New Brighton on 14 June and the Odeon, Romford on 16 June. On the final *Mersey Beat Showcase* in Romford, three of the acts, the Beatles, Gerry & the Pacemakers and Billy J. Kramer & the Dakotas, occupied the top three positions in the British charts.

Merseyside Civil Service Club, Lower Castle Street, Liverpool L2

The Beatles were booked for a series of four appearances at this small club near to Liverpool's Pier Head. All four gigs took place in November 1961. Their debut there took place on 7 November, followed by performances on 14, 21 and 28 November.

Mersey-Motown Sound, The

One of the major musical influences on the Liverpool groups in the early sixties was the Tamla Motown record label, created in Detroit by Berry Gordy Junior in 1959. Berry had originally derived the name Tamla from a Debbie Reynolds film *Tammy* and Motown was an abbreviation of the nickname of Detroit: Motor City. Berry actually used the name Tamla as a label in America in 1959 and Motown in 1961. The name Tamla Motown was used on the European releases.

In Britain in 1962, Tamla Motown was distributed by a small record label, Oriole, and the largest market for the records by the Detroit groups was on Merseyside.

At that time, the local music paper *Mersey Beat* began to feature Tamla Motown in each issue, profiling the artists and reviewing the latest releases. Oriole Records began to take half-page advertisements advertising Tamla Motown due to the interest aroused in the label in Liverpool.

When he received the latest Motown singles, *Mersey Beat* editor Bill Harry would take them down to the Cavern. When he took 'Fingertips' by Little Stevie Wonder, Ringo was there and requested it. Harry gave it to him. When Ringo later said it was his favourite, Harry told John Schroeder of Oriole who arranged for a complete Tamla Motown collection to be sent to Ringo.

The Tamla Motown numbers were included in the repertoire of the Liverpool bands. They adapted the songs to fit in with the developing Liverpool sound, the basic three guitars/drums/harmony line-up which produced a hybrid sound, known locally as 'the Mersey-Motown sound'.

This particular sound found its way on record when a number of Mersey acts recorded their own versions of Motown numbers: Faron's Flamingoes with 'Do You Love Me' and 'Shake Sherry', Ian & the Zodiacs with 'Beechwood 45789', Beryl Marsden with 'When The Love Light Shines' and so on.

Differing from the Mersey-Motown sound was the straight Motown-sounding presentation of numbers by the local black vocal groups such as the Chants, who performed numbers made popular by acts such as the Miracles and the Marvellettes.

In 1963 the Motown distribution in Britain went to EMI's Stateside label and the Motown artists soon began to have their first British hits, particularly since the Beatles had begun to mention the Motown artists in interviews.

1963 was also the year when the Beatles made their own Mersey-Motown recordings, with no less than three Motown numbers on their *With the Beatles* album: 'Please Mr Postman', 'You Really Got A Hold On Me' and 'Money (That's What I Want)'.

The Beatles also requested that Mary Wells be included on their autumn tour of Britain in 1964. Mary was later to pay her own tribute to the Beatles with an album of Lennon & McCartney songs.

Brian Epstein also became a fan of Motown artists and brought the Four Tops over to Britain to tour.

Paul McCartney was later to forge a close association with Motown artists, recording 'Ebony and Ivory' with Stevie Wonder and 'This Girl Is Mine', 'Say Say Say' and 'The Man' with Michael Jackson.

Ironically, the only reference to the Mersey-Motown Sound in the Motown Museum in Detroit is an inaccurate one. There is a picture of the Dave Clark Five with the Supremes which is captioned 'Liverpool Meets Detroit'.

Mersey Sound, The

The first major television documentary to concern itself with the Beatles and the Mersey sound. The programme, produced by Don Howarth, was first broadcast on BBC 1 on 9 October 1963 and was repeated on 13 November.

Howarth spent several weeks in Liverpool prior to the recording and filmed activities inside the *Mersey Beat* office: a conversation with a musician commenting on groups on the dole, a local promoter discussing protection rackets, scenes at the Iron Door Club with the Undertakers and Group One performing, and the Beatles commenting on their early careers, discussing fan letters, their home lives and their ambitions. There were scenes at NEMS record store, Rushworths music shop and outside Ringo's house in Admiral Grove. The group were televised performing on stage during their appearance at the Odeon, Southport and among the numbers they sang were 'Love Me Do', 'Twist & Shout' and 'She Loves You'.

Don Howarth told *Mersey Beat*: 'I visited Liverpool several months ago to see if the city was a good subject for a programme. I saw Bill Harry, Brian Epstein and several of the leading lights in the Beat scene, and visited several clubs including the Cavern and the

Iron Door. Within two days I knew that there was such atmosphere and excitement on the Mersey Beat scene that I just had to use it in a programme. When I brought the production unit down in August I decided to let the people on Merseyside make their own comments on the scene and allowed the people who were interviewed to talk freely. In that way a truer picture of the scene could be formed.'

This is the documentary in which Ringo, dressed smartly in a suit, walks past a bank of hairdriers at a hairdresser's declaring that his ambition is to make enough money to open his own salon.

Mersey View, Overton Hills, Frodsham, Warrington, Cheshire

A venue only twenty miles from Liverpool where Mersey Beat groups played on a regular basis.

The Beatles only appeared at the venue once, on Saturday 20 April 1963. Entertainment is still provided at the venue, which is now known as the Mersey View Country Club.

Metropolitan Stadium, Cedar Avenue, Bloomington, Minneapolis, Minnesota

The Beatles appeared at this large venue on Saturday, 21 August 1965, with ticket prices at $2.50, $3.50, $4.50 and $5.50. Only 25,000 seats in the 45,000-seater stadium were occupied. The concert began at 7.30 p.m. and there were a couple of local bands on the bill. The Beatles performed eleven numbers that night: 'She's A Woman', 'I Feel Fine', 'Baby's In Black', 'A Hard Day's Night', 'Help!', 'Ticket to Ride', 'Everybody's Tryin' To Be My Baby', 'I Wanna Be Your Man', 'Can't Buy Me Love', 'Slow Down' and 'I'm Down'. The Beatles landed at Minneapolis-St Paul International Airport at 4.15 p.m. to be greeted by 3,000 waiting fans. They climbed into a black Cadillac limousine and headed for the Met 'at speeds close to 65 miles an hour'. *The Minneapolis Tribune* also reported: 'While they were getting into the limousine, George Harrison waved to the crowd and smiled, but with his other hand he locked the car's door.

'A couple of rather heavy women who haven't been teenagers for a number of years, crashed through the police line. They touched Paul McCartney before they were pushed back by a number of policemen and Ray Colthan, the local backer of the Beatles show.'

Michelle

Song penned by Paul which first appeared on the *Rubber Soul* album issued on 3 December 1965. Within a month of the album's release there were over twenty cover versions of the number. In Britain both the Overlanders and David & Jonathan found themselves with a major hit, the former reaching the No. 1 spot. There were a staggering number of versions recorded by almost 700 artists throughout the world, including Booker T and the MG's, the Four Tops, Jan & Dean, Jack Jones, Johnny Mathis, Diana Ross & the Supremes, George Shearing, Sarah Vaughan and Andy Williams.

The Beatles' version was included on their EP *Nowhere Man*, issued in July 1966, and on several album compilations, including *A Collection of Beatles Oldies (But Goldies)* in 1966, *The Beatles 1966–1970* in 1973, *Love Songs* in 1977 and *The Beatles Ballads* and *The Beatles Box* in 1980.

Anthony Howard, who once worked for the Beatles organisation, claimed that the song had been inspired by his daughter Michelle. He said, 'Michelle was a great friend of the Beatles and they loved her. They wrote a song called "Michelle" which was done for her.' In January 1981 Michelle Howard hit the headlines in the British press with stories such as 'Drugs Battle of Beatles Michelle', when, aged 23, she was charged with shoplifting and possession of drugs.

Despite the claim, when Paul was appearing on the London Weekend Television chat show 'Aspel And Company' in 1984, he discussed the inspiration behind his songs and said, 'I just kind of make it up. "Michelle" – I've never met her. I make it up, that's how I write.'

Soon after writing the song, Paul said, 'I just fancied writing some French words and I have a friend (Ivan Vaughan) whose wife taught French and we were sitting around and I just asked her, you know, what we could figure that was French. We got words that go together well. It was mainly because I always used to think the song always sounded like a French thing, and I can't speak French really, so we sorted out some actual words.'

Mid-South Coliseum, South Fairgrounds, Early Maxwell Boulevard, Memphis, Tennessee

Site of the Beatles' first date in the American South on Friday, 19 August 1966, following the controversial statement by John about the Beatles being bigger than Christ. The anti-Beatles protestors were strong in the Southern states and, prior to their appearance at the Mid-South Coliseum, an anonymous phone call threatened that one or all of the Beatles would be shot on stage during one of the two concert appearances there. Protestors were also gathered at the roadsides with banners proclaiming 'Beatles Go Home'.

Six members of the Ku Klux Klan picketed the venue, which had a capacity of 13,300 and which drew 7,589 to the afternoon show at 4 p.m. and 12,539 to the evening performance at 8 p.m. During the third number in the evening performance a cherry bomb exploded and the Beatles thought it was a shot. Publicist Tony Barrow commented: 'Each Beatle just glanced at the others to see if one of them would drop. It says something for them that they didn't miss a note.' The bomb was thrown from a balcony and slightly injured four spectators. The culprits were a fifteen-year-old boy and a fifteen-year-old girl, who had a sack with 25 cherry bombs and the girl had a purse with 25 firecrackers.

Mike Cotton Sound, The

When beat music became a force in 1963, Mike Cotton, who'd formerly led a jazz band, steered his band into playing R&B. The Mike Cotton Sound, as they were now known, were booked to appear on *Another Beatles Show* at the Odeon, Hammersmith, London, in December 1964/January 1965.

They comprised Mike Cotton (trumpet), Johnny Crocker (trombone), Stu Morrison (banjo), Dave Rowberry (keyboards), Derek Tearle (bass guitar) and Jim Garforth (drums). Rowberry later became a member of the Animals.

Millings, Dougie

Well-known show business tailor. From the late fifties he had built up a business specialising in clothing stars of the entertainment world and by the time Brian Epstein visited him in 1963 he had 80 show business clients, including Cliff Richard & the Shadows, Tommy Steele, Billy Fury and Marty Wilde. Brian dropped into Millings' shop at 63 Old Compton Street in Soho, London W1, with Gerry Marsden and discussed with Dougie the possibility of him becoming the tailor for his various acts.

Dougie and his son Gordon provided the Beatles with their stagewear for several years, during which they produced 500 garments for the group, including the famous collarless jacket. This was based on sketches of a steward's jacket after discussions with Brian and the Beatles.

Dougie charged £31 per suit at the time and established a rapport with the group, who called him 'Dad'. In fact, they got on with him so well that they insisted he be given a cameo role in *A Hard Day's Night*. The part of 'A Tailor' was introduced, although most of it ended on the cutting room floor. In the film Dougie had to wear a frown of frustration due to his unsuccessful attempts to measure the group, because they were never able to stand still.

Dougie also made the suits for the original Madame Tussauds waxwork figures of the Beatles.

He'd moved to Great Pulteney Street by the time the Beatles were set to make their first tour of America and the wardrobe which he and Gordon made from lightweight wool and mohair were in dark grey and dark blue, with velvet collars. Half a dozen of each suit were made for each member of the group.

Milwaukee Arena, Milwaukee, Wisconsin

The Beatles made a single appearance at this venue on 4 September 1964.

When they flew into General Mitchell Field, there were over 1,000 fans at the airport, together with 65 policemen, 32 deputies and four airport police. Sheriff Michael Wolke had fire trucks ready to turn their hoses on the fans if they should break down the fence in the area they'd been herded into.

The Beatles' plane was then instructed to land on the opposite side of the field and the group left for their hotel without any of their fans seeing them.

A five-car motorcade took them to the Coach House Motor Inn where there was a press conference which John didn't attend as he had a sore throat. Most of the questions queried why the Beatles had avoided their fans at the airport – and they explained that it hadn't been their decision.

They took the stage at the Milwaukee Arena at 9.08 p.m., dressed in blue mohair suits. After the show they were driven back to their hotel and after dinner were each given antibiotic shots by the hotel doctor as all four were now suffering from colds.

Minoff, Lee

One of the screenwriters of the animated film *Yellow Submarine*. Producer Al Brodax, who was also a writer, felt that the Beatles considered him too old, so he decided to bring in a younger man and hired Minoff. Apparently John Lennon looked at Minoff's first draft and said, 'This is the bloody Flintstones.' Several other writers were brought in and numerous revisions made. Minoff was credited with the original story and the final screenwriter credits were attributed to Minoff, Al Brodax, Jack Mendelsohn and Erich Segal, although other writers such as Roger McGough were unaccredited. Minoff later became a psychoanalyst, based in New York.

Misery

A song John and Paul collaborated on which they completed on their tour coach during their Helen Shapiro tour.

They'd written the song for Helen Shapiro, but her recording manager turned it down. Kenny Lynch, who was also touring with them, showed interest in the number and asked if he could record it. His version was issued by HMV on 22 March 1963, but it didn't have any effect on the charts.

The Beatles recorded it themselves during their marathon *Please Please Me* album session, with John and Paul sharing vocals.

Apart from on the *Please Please Me* album, the song appeared on the EP *The Beatles No. 1*.

Its most frequent use was in America. Vee Jay included it on their *Introducing The Beatles, The Beatles vs The Four Seasons* and *Songs, Pictures and Stories Of The Fabulous Beatles* albums and on the EP *Souvenir Of Their Visit To America*. Capitol also issued it as the flipside of 'Roll Over Beethoven' on 11 October 1965 when it was released as part of the Capitol Starline series on Starline 6065. It was also used on the American release *The Beatles Rarities*.

Mod Odyssey. A

A seven-minute film, made by Tarot Associates Inc and produced by United Artists, which was used to promote the animated *Yellow Submarine* movie. It explained the title by stating: 'The most lasting work of Dante, Swift and Wells have been based on odyssey situations. In selecting *Yellow Submarine* for the Beatles' first full-length animated film, the producers were standing on firm literary ground.' The short was included on the 1999 DVD release of the *Yellow Submarine* songtrack.

Modern Jazz Quartet, The

The Modern Jazz Quartet had been established for almost fifteen years when they signed a short-term deal with Apple Records in 1968.

The group comprised John Lewis (piano), Milt Jackson (vibes), Percy Heath (bass) and Connie Kay (drums).

The Beatles had long been admirers of the MJQ and when the quartet appeared at the Liverpool Philharmonic Hall in April 1964, John Lewis told *Mersey Beat*: 'The Beatles are on record as saying they like our kind of music and I think you can say we appreciate their music, too. From the size and reaction of our audiences I'd say there is room enough for both styles in this city, though.'

They left Atlantic Records to sign with Apple, being the only established act to sign with the label.

The group recorded two albums for Apple, *Under The Jasmine Tree*, issued in Britain on 6 December 1968 and in America on 17 February 1969, and *Space*, issued in Britain on 24 October 1969, and in America on 10 November 1969.

Mods And Rockers

A ballet set to the Beatles' music which opened at the Prince Charles Theatre in London on 18 December 1963. The modern ballet ran until 11 January 1964.

Money (That's What I Want)

Song penned by Berry Gordy and Janie Bradford, which provided Barrett Strong with a hit in 1960. Gordy was to find great success building the Motown empire and this number is an example of the Motown influence on Liverpool groups which was called the 'Mersey-Motown Sound'.

The Beatles performed it at their Decca audition and this version has found its way on to various bootlegs and Decca audition outtake releases. The group also recorded it for their *With The Beatles* album, issued in November 1963. The Beatles performed the number on their 'Sunday Night At The London Palladium' appearance in October 1963. It was included on their EP, *All My Loving*, the American *Beatles Second Album* and *Rock 'n' Roll Music*.

John sings lead vocal on the track and he also performed it at the Toronto Rock 'n' Roll Revival Concert in 1969 and this version appears on his *Live Peace In Toronto* album.

A group from the south of England, Bern Elliott & the Fenmen, had a Top Twenty entry with the number shortly after the *With The Beatles* release, although they said that they first heard the Searchers performing it at the Star Club, Hamburg, and rushed straight back to England to record it. A version was included on the Beatles' *Anthology 1* CDs.

Monkees, The

The Monkees were a pop group created specially for television by two American producers, Bob Rafelson and Bert Schneider. They formed the Raybeat Company to produce a pilot sit-com for Screen Gems, based on *A Hard Day's Night*.

Acknowledging the work of director Richard Lester on the Beatles' debut film, Schneider commented: 'The Beatles made it all happen, that's the reality. Richard Lester is where the credit begins for the Monkees and for Bob and me.'

They initially considered using an existing group, the Lovin' Spoonful, but decided to use actors and organised a casting call by advertising in the newspaper daily *Variety*: 'MADNESS!! Auditions – folk and rock 'n' roll musicians/singers. Running parts for four insane kids, ages 17 to 21, with the courage to work.'

Some 437 hopefuls were interviewed, including Steve Stills, Paul

Williams, Danny Hutton (who became leader of Three Dog Night) and Charles Manson, who was to become involved in the Sharon Tate murder.

David Thomas Jones (vocals/guitar), more familiarly known as Davy Jones, had already been selected. Born in Manchester on 30 December 1946, he'd appeared as the Artful Dodger in *Oliver!* on Broadway, the stage version of *Pickwick* and in the TV series 'Ben Casey'.

In fact, it was as a member of the *Oliver!* cast that he appeared on the same 'Ed Sullivan Show' as the Beatles making their American debut in February 1964.

Robert Michael Nesmith (vocals/guitar) was born in Dallas, Texas, on 30 December 1942 and later moved to Los Angeles, where he appeared in several bands.

Peter Halsten Thorkelson (vocals/keyboards/bass guitar), more familiarly known as Peter Tork, was born in Washington DC on 13 February 1942, and George Michael Dolenz (vocals/drums), known as Mickey, was born in Los Angeles on 8 March 1945. Under the name Mickey Braddock he'd appeared as Corky in the series 'Circus Boy', had made appearances on shows such as 'Peyton Place' and had formed several bands.

The first name considered for the group was the Turtles, then the Inevitables and finally the Monkees.

NBC launched the series on 5 September 1966, the same day they launched another new series 'Star Trek'. A month before the debut of the show, a Monkees single, 'Last Train To Clarksville', was released and it was to top the charts. Publisher Don Kirshner had been asked to find songs for their first recordings and he engaged Tommy Boyce and Bobby Hart to write them. Hart said that the idea for the debut single 'Last Train To Clarksville' came after he'd heard 'Paperback Writer'. He mistakenly thought the Beatles were singing about a 'last train', and developed the idea.

Although the group had been formed especially for the series, it was decided to include music in all the shows and Don Kirschner gathered songs from a variety of songwriters, including Neil Diamond, Leiber and Stoller, Neil Sedaka, Carole King, Gerry Goffin and Barry Mann, and produced backing music to which the Monkees had only to add their voices.

Interestingly, on the programme's theme song the group sang 'no no no', a counterpoint to the Beatles' 'yeah yeah yeah.'

By 1967 the Monkees were at odds with Kirschner and wanted to produce their own material and perform the music themselves, which they were then allowed to do.

There were 58 episodes of the TV series, which lasted until 25

March 1968. The main audience for the group was a very young one and their appeal was described as 'Monkeemania'.

Brian Epstein's NEMS Enterprises was the company which first presented the group in Britain, booking them into the Empire Pool, Wembley, from 30 June to 3 July 1967. NEMS also held a party in their honour at the Speakeasy Club in London, which was attended by the Beatles, Lulu, the Bee Gees and numerous other celebrities.

In 1968 the group starred in a feature film *Head,* written by Bob Rafelson and Jack Nicholson, which also featured Annette Funicello, Victor Mature, Carol Dada, Teri Garr, Sonny Liston and Frank Zappa, with choreography by Toni Basil. Tork was unhappy with what he considered was manipulation of the group and left following the release of *Head.* The others continued as a trio for a short time and recorded a TV special, '33½ Revolutions per Monkee', on 14 April 1969. This was conceived and produced by Jack Good and also featured the Brian Auger Trinity, Julie Driscoll, Fats Domino and Jerry Lee Lewis.

In addition to the TV series, the Monkees had nine albums and fourteen singles released between August 1966 and May 1970. In their song 'Randy Scouse Git', they refer to the Beatles as 'the four kings of EMI'.

Incidentally Tommy Boyce, who had originally auditioned unsuccessfully to become a Monkee co-wrote 'The Monkees Theme' and 'Last Train To Clarksville' with Bobby Hart. Boyce and Hart teamed up with Mickie Dolenz and Davy Jones to perform as the Monkees in the 1970s but, early in 1997, Boyce committed suicide in Nashville by shooting himself.

34 Montague Square, Marylebone, London W1

After the flat in Whaddon Street, which George and Ringo shared, was burgled in April 1964, the two moved to separate premises.

Ringo moved to a single-bedroom, ground-floor flat in a long Victorian block near the new Swiss Embassy. By Christmas of that year, Maureen Cox had moved in with him.

After the couple were married and had moved into Sunny Heights, Ringo maintained the Montague Square flat and among the guests who stayed there were author William Burroughs and guitarist Jimi Hendrix.

John and Yoko were living at the flat on 18 October 1968 when six policemen, one policewoman and a sniffer dog raided the premises. They were led by Sergeant Norman Pilcher. John had been warned in advance of the raid and the flat had been thoroughly cleaned. The police found 1½oz of cannabis resin, which the couple seemed unaware was there, and they were taken to Paddington

Green where they were also charged with obstructing the police in the execution of a search warrant.

John was still adamant that the cannabis was not his, but because Yoko was pregnant and in order to have the charges against her dropped, he pleaded guilty to the charge on 28 November. He was fined £159 with twenty guineas costs, although he was found not guilty of obstructing the police.

On 19 February 1969 Ringo was served with a writ from the landlords Bryman Estates for 'misuse of property'. The landlords said they had no grouse against the Starkeys, just some of their guests, and they took civil proceedings against Ringo to bar Lennon 'and other undesirables' from the premises. Ringo was so upset he sold the leasehold to the premises on 28 February 1969.

Montez, Chris

American singer, born Christopher Montanez on 17 January 1943 in Los Angeles. 'Let's Dance' in 1962 was his first and only million-seller.

Although it was Montez' only British hit at the time, promoter Arthur Howes booked the singer to co-headline a tour with another American artist, Tommy Roe. When told that the second act on the bill was the Beatles, Montez commented: 'Who are these guys the Beatles? I try to keep up to date with the British scene, but I don't know their work.'

Despite the fact that the Beatles were now more famous in Britain than either of the two Americans, no British artist had previously topped the bill above an American act.

It was the Beatles' second package tour, which got under way five days after their first and commenced on Saturday 9 March 1963 at the Granada, East Ham.

'Let's Dance' was Montez' only claim to fame, but he did well with the number, taking it into the charts on three occasions, in 1962, 1972 and 1979.

Moody Blues, The

A group from Birmingham who formed in 1964 and comprised Denny Laine (guitar/vocals), Mike Pinder (keyboards), Ray Thomas (horns/vocals), Clint Warwick (bass) and Graeme Edge (drums). Brian Epstein interviewed them for the 'Hullaballoo' television show in 1965 and in September of that year he signed them to a management and agency contract. During 1965 they had a major hit with 'Go Now', a million-seller which reached No. 1 in Britain and the Top Ten in America. In December 1965 they joined the Beatles on their British tour.

Because of Epstein's initial enthusiasm, the group had believed that Brian would be managing them himself, but he appointed Alistair Taylor. By October 1966 they had become so discouraged that Laine and Warwick left, to be replaced by Justin Hayward and John Lodge, although their career seemed on the wane.

They were later to achieve success with best-selling albums such as *Days Of Future Passed*, *In Search Of The Lost Chord* and *On The Threshold Of A Dream*.

When Paul McCartney formed Wings, he brought Denny Laine into the group and the two of them co-wrote the massive hit 'Mull Of Kintyre'.

Moon, Keith

Before he died of a drug overdose in 1978 following one of Paul McCartney's annual Buddy Holly promotions, Moon was known as 'Moon The Loon', one of the zaniest personalities of the British rock scene.

The drummer with the Who formed a close relationship with Ringo Starr and they often went clubbing in each other's company and appeared in a number of films together, including *200 Motels*, *That'll Be The Day*, *The Kids Are Alright*, *Born To Boogie* and *Sextette*. On Ringo's 35th birthday, Moon and Ringo caused so much damage during a party that their Playboy membership cards were revoked.

Moon also acted as an 'uncle' to Zak Starkey and was the favourite drummer of Ringo's son.

Keith, who was one of the personalities sitting at the Beatles' feet during the 'All You Need Is Love' performance on the 'Our World' TV spectacular, made a solo recording of 'When I'm Sixty-Four'. Ringo played on his album *Two Sides Of The Moon* and when he became one of John Lennon's companions during his 'long weekend' in Los Angeles, Keith played on Harry Nilsson's *Pussycats* album, which John co-produced in 1974. Moon also appeared with John on his appearance at the Lyceum Ballroom *Peace for Christmas* concert on 15 December 1969.

In 1975 he accepted the special 'Hall of Fame' Grammy Award on behalf of the Beatles.

Moore, Tommy

A Liverpool drummer, he played with the Silver Beatles in 1960. The group had been performing without a drummer as the Quarry Men, but began changing their name and felt they needed someone in the drum seat. After Brian Casser had said that the name the Beatals was no good, they changed it to the Silver Beetles (also

Silver Beatles) and, on Casser's recommendation, they invited
Tommy Moore to join them.

At the time, Tommy was a fork-lift truck operator at the Window
Lane branch of the Garston Bottle Works. He was 26 years old, in
contrast to Lennon, who was 19. Apparently, during the short time
he was with them there was continual tension between him and
John, who was reputed to have needled him mercilessly.

Initially, he rehearsed with them at Gambier Terrace.

When they were due to audition for Larry Parnes at the Wyvern
Club, playing four numbers in a ten-minute set, Moore was late and
didn't turn up until halfway through their set. They began playing
with Johnny Hutchinson of the Big Three taking Moore's place –
and photographs of the audition, taken by Chenison Roland, show
Hutch in the drum seat.

As a result of the audition, the group was booked for a short tour
of Scotland, backing Johnny Gentle, although they weren't selected
as Billy Fury's backing group. Parnes said that this was because of
Moore, whom he felt was far older than the other members, and
also because he didn't dress in the same manner. Parnes didn't like
the fact that Moore had turned up late, either.

Despite the pressure from his girlfriend not to join them, Moore
took time off from his job to tour Scotland with them, which took
place between 20 and 28 May. On 23 May, when their regular
driver, Gerry Scott, needed to rest, Gentle took over as driver, but
crashed the van into the back of a two-door Austin saloon at the
crossroads outside Banff. An elderly gentleman and his wife, who'd
been shopping in Aberdeen, drove it. The only injuries suffered
were by Moore, who was catapulted forward with such force that
his face struck the equipment in the van. He was concussed and had
a front tooth knocked out. He was taken to the local cottage
hospital and had stitches in his upper lip. The promoter insisted on
them having a drummer so they forced the injured Moore, still
groggy from pain killing drugs, to play with them that night at
Fraserburgh.

At the end of the tour, Moore found he had only profited by £2.

Tommy decided to leave the group following their appearance at
the Institute, Neston, on 9 June and he didn't turn up at the
Jacaranda on 11 June to set off with them for their Grosvenor Hall
booking. Allan Williams and the Beatles went to Moore's house in
Fern Grove, Toxteth, to get him, but received a torrent of abuse
from his girlfriend, who leaned out of an upstairs window and
shouted: 'You can go and piss off! He's not playing with you any
more; he's got a job at Garston Bottle Works on the night shift.'

They all rushed to the works and found him driving his fork-lift, but he refused to go to the gig with them. So they arrived at the Grosvenor with Tommy's kit, but no drummer. When John mentioned this over the mike, a teddy boy called Ronnie got up on stage and joined them, thumping away at the drums and damaging Moore's kit.

Tommy actually made one further appearance with the band – at the Jacaranda on 13 June. He was to die of a stroke in 1981, soon after joining a local jazz band.

24 Moorfields, Liverpool L2

Site of the NEMS Enterprises office which Brian Epstein relocated to this address from Whitechapel on 6 August 1963. Brian and three of his staff moved into the premises, above the Wizard's Den magic shop. Inside the building, directly opposite the NEMS office, was the studio of photographer Harry Watmough, one of the regular *Mersey Beat* photographers, who had been commissioned to take some early studio shots of the Beatles wearing suits, when Pete Best was still a member.

Morecambe & Wise Show, The

Eric Morecambe and Ernie Wise were for many years regarded as Britain's top comedy duo and during the sixties and seventies their 'The Morecambe & Wise Show' was one of the highlights on British television.

The Beatles spent a day with the two comics recording at the ATV Studios, Boreham Wood, on 2 December 1963 for the networked ATV show which was not transmitted until 18 April 1964 and was repeated on 24 July. The Beatles performed three songs and appeared in a sketch with Eric and Ernie.

Morgue Skiffle Club, The, 'Balgownie', 25 Oakhill Park, Broadgreen, Liverpool L13

A skiffle club set in the cellar of a Victorian house and, during its brief existence, run by Alan Caldwell, leader of Al Caldwell's Texans. Caldwell was to change his name to Rory Storm and front the Hurricanes, whose drummer was Ringo Starr.

The Quarry Men were among the groups who appeared on the Morgue's opening night on 13 March 1959. The semi-occupied house was a former home for retired nurses. The club had walls painted black with white fluorescent skeletons dancing across them. The Morgue could accommodate an audience of 100 in cramped conditions, was open twice a week, on Tuesdays and Thursdays, but the Quarry Men only appeared a few times because the club was closed by the police on 22 April, presumably because it had no proper facilities.

Allegedly, at the 13 March gig, Paul McCartney was championing the cause of his young friend George Harrison, who played 'Raunchy' for them on his new Futurama guitar. John Lennon was impressed by the guitar, but not by George – although, as a result, George was allowed to sit in when regular lead guitarist Eric Griffiths didn't turn up and he soon became a full-time member.

Mosspits Lane Infants' School, Mosspits Lane, Wavertree, Liverpool L15

The first school which John Lennon attended. His Aunt Mimi enrolled him there on 12 November 1945, although the Admission Book shows his address as 9 Newcastle Road. For some reason, not explained, Mimi withdrew John from the school six months later and he moved to Dovedale Primary School on 6 May 1946.

Mossway Hall, Mossway, Croxteth, Liverpool L11

Small venue where the Beatles made a single appearance on 17 March 1961. It was their only booking for Ivamar Promotions, one of the handful of active local promoters. They were Jeff McIver and Doug Martin who promoted jive dances weekly at St Luke's Hall, Crosby, the Ivamar Club, Skelmersdale, and Mossway Hall.

Mother Nature's Son

One of the songs Paul composed during his sojourn in India. Paul recorded it on Wednesday, 9 August 1968. The recording sessions had finished at 10.00 p.m. and the other members of the Beatles had gone home. Paul remained behind and recorded an acoustic version of the song. A brass overdub was added later.

Paul is the only member of the Beatles on the track which was included on *The Beatles* double album, issued in November 1968. A version was included on the Beatles' *Anthology 3* CDs.

Mount Pleasant Registry Office, 64 Mount Pleasant, Liverpool L3

On 3 December 1938 Freddie Lennon married Julia Stanley in this registry office. They retired to a nearby public house with one of Freddie's brothers and a friend of Julia's and spent the evening at the Trocadero cinema before Julia returned to the Stanley home in Wavertree and Freddie spent the night in lodgings.

On 23 August 1963, John, Freddie and Julia's son, was married in the same room of the same registry office. His bride was a pregnant

Cynthia Powell and also present were Brian Epstein, Paul McCartney, George Harrison and Cynthia's brother Tony and his wife Margery. Ringo Starr, the new member of the Beatles, hadn't been invited. Paul signed the certificate as witness to the civil ceremony, which had been so disrupted by nearby construction work that Cynthia could hardly hear the words of the ceremony.

The party then retired to Reece's restaurant for their wedding breakfast.

Move Over, Dad

A Westward Television show on which the Beatles appeared during a tour in which they were appearing at the ABC Cinema, Plymouth. The show, aimed at teenagers in the south-west of England, was billed as 'a gay new show with the accent on the beat of the youth.' Stuart Hutchinson interviewed the group and the interview was screened on the next edition of the show at 5.15 p.m. on Saturday, 16 November.

Moynihan, Vyvienne

A prominent British figure in the arts and media whose career began immediately after the Second World War, when she joined the Q Theatre as assistant stage manager. She was soon to progress to stage director and company manager before moving to the West End.

She joined Associated Rediffusion, the original London television weekend contractor, in the mid-1950s, initially as casting director, then as manager of drama and eventually as manager of light entertainment. It was in this capacity that Brian Epstein initially contacted her in the autumn of 1962.

Moynihan, then 38 years old, listened to what Epstein had to say about the Beatles and suggested that she have someone see the group before she considered booking them. Epstein insisted that he come down to London to discuss the matter with her personally, which he did, and as a result Moynihan booked the Beatles for Rediffusion's 'Tuesday Rendezvous'.

Epstein also dealt with Vyvienne when he began negotiations for the 'Around The Beatles' television special, and she was also involved in the production of Cilla Black's TV series.

Brian then offered her a position in his own organisation, in charge of all work associated with theatres. He set her up in her own office in London's Cork Street where, as director of productions, she was involved in presentations featuring the Beatles and other artists and was also involved with the Saville Theatre.

Following Epstein's death, she moved to the Soviet Union for two years to produce documentaries, then returned to London where she joined the Central Office of Information. She moved to the advertising agency McCann Erickson, then formed her own consultancy business in 1984, which she ran successfully until retiring due to illness in 1993.

She died at the age of 74 on 19 August 1994.

MPTE Social Club, Finch Lane, Liverpool L14

One of the various Merseyside social clubs for members of the Liverpool bus services. George Harrison's father Harold was one of the social secretaries for the local union and organised various events at the different busmen's clubs.

Naturally, he took the opportunity of booking the group his son George was a member of – the Quarry Men.

On the skiffle group's appearance at the venue early in 1959, Mr Harrison told the boys that the manager of a local cinema was looking for a band to play in the intervals and would be watching their performance that evening. The Quarry Men had two spots and John and Paul got drunk during their break and the gig was a disaster, particularly with the two of them making fun of George, knowing that his father and mother were in the audience. Because of their unprofessionalism, drummer Colin Hanton left the band that night.

They never heard from the manager of the Pavilion, who booked the Darktown Skiffle Group instead – whose drummer was Ringo Starr.

Harold Harrison also booked the Quarry Men at social club gigs in Wavertree, Garston and Prescot.

The building housing the Social Club was later demolished.

Mr Moonlight

A number penned by Roy Lee Jackson and recorded by Dr Feelgood & the Interns in 1962. Dr Feelgood didn't have a hit with the number, but it became part of the repertoire of the Beatles and several other Mersey bands that year.

John Lennon was lead vocalist on the number and it was included in their Star Club performance and is found on the various Star Club recordings. The group also recorded the song for their *Beatles For Sale* album and it was included on their American EP *4 By The Beatles*. A version was included on the Beatles' *Anthology 1* CDs.

Municipal Stadium, West 3rd Street, Cleveland, Ohio

Due to the large size of this baseball pitch, home ground of the Cleveland Indians, there was only one show, the first in an outside arena, during their final American tour on Sunday, 14 August 1966. The ground had a capacity for 50,000, but only 30,000 tickets were on sale as most of the rear-seating area would have provided such a poor view of the concert. The stage was situated on second base, 125 feet away from the nearest person in the audience.

Extra security was taken for the Beatles and two black limousines, with their doors open and engines running, were positioned behind the stage throughout the Beatles' performance in the event that a quick escape might be necessary.

When the Beatles went on stage, they sang 'Rock 'n' Roll Music', followed by 'She's A Woman' and 'If I Needed Someone'. During the performance of 'Day Tripper', a mob of 3,000 began to rush to the stage and the police had to fall back, forming a cordon while the Beatles were whisked off stage into a trailer. The group were told, literally, to 'Run for your lives' and retreated to a caravan behind the stage. Fans were climbing on the roof, beating the windows and rocking the caravan. The event had been promoted by local radio station WIXY whose disc jockey Al Gates tried to soothe the crowd. After half an hour, with threats that the Beatles would not appear again if the audience didn't return to their seats, the group was able to take the stage and finish their act. They performed 'I Feel Fine', 'Yesterday', 'I Wanna Be Your Man', 'Nowhere Man', 'Paperback Writer' and 'Long Tall Sally'.

Municipal Stadium, Kansas City, Missouri

Thursday, 17 September 1964 was originally scheduled as a rest day during the Beatles' hectic American tour.

Charles O. Finley, owner of the baseball team the Kansas City Athletics, noticed that the Beatles weren't making an appearance in Kansas City during the tour and made a vow that he would bring them in. He went to see the group at the Cow Palace, San Francisco, and then visited Brian Epstein. While the Beatles were playing cards in their dressing-room, he offered Epstein $50,000 for them to appear at the Stadium. He didn't receive a reply, so he doubled the offer – and was told that several other promoters had offered to pay $100,000, so he then raised the sum to $150,000.

This was a world record price at the time and, realising the publicity and prestige value of such a price, Brian accepted.

The local police chief, on hearing that the deal had been done, commented, 'Personally, I would rather see an invasion from Mars than have to handle a Beatle concert.' But he assigned 350 police to the stadium, more than 40 per cent of the entire Kansas City Police Force.

It was pouring with rain when the Beatles flew into Kansas City, arriving at 2 a.m. They were taken by limousine to the Muehlebach Towers and booked into an eighteenth-floor terrace penthouse costing $100 a day. Earl Reynolds, vice-president of the hotel, had taken no chances and had the lobby stripped bare in case of trouble from souvenir-hunting fans.

At the stadium, the Bill Black Combo were followed by Jackie de Shannon and after the interval the Beatles came on and began a medley of 'Kansas City/Hey! Hey! Hey!', which they had put into their repertoire specially for the event.

Hundreds of fans rushed forward and broke through the barriers and the show had to be stopped. Derek Taylor went on stage and told the audience to settle down. If they didn't, he pointed out, the police would have to cancel the rest of the performance. Although the stadium had 41,000 seats, there were only 20,208 spectators – yet this was a record crowd for a concert.

Finley lost between $50,000 to $100,000 on the deal but gained a vast amount of publicity. There was only $100,000 taken but, despite the loss, Finley's manager Pat Friday presented the local children's Mercy Hospital with a cheque for $50,000.

On the reverse side of the ticket, Finley had a photograph of himself in a Beatle wig, pointing to a picture of Ringo. Underneath were the words: 'Yeah! Yeah! Yeah! Today's Beatles Fans Are Tomorrow's Baseball Fans. Charles O. Finley, President.'

The group performed twelve songs during a 31-minute set, and a report in the *Kansas City Times* the next day had a detailed review of the show, part of which read:

> But the event left some of the Beatle followers emotionally torn. As the crowds left the park, fully 10 minutes after all the shouting, there were groups of exhausted girls still seated in the playing field area and the stands:
> They were crying.
> Why?
> 'Because they [the B's] had just left and didn't say anything,' a girl explained, rubbing her eyes. 'Now they are gone forever.'
> 'Ah, they'll be back again,' a policeman said.
> 'What do you care?' the girl wept. 'You were down in front there and you didn't care and I was way back here and I couldn't even get close to them.'
> 'Now wait a minute, honey,' he said, 'It's not my fault.'
> Then he walked away.

Two enterprising local businessmen paid $1,000 to the hotel for the group's bed linen, comprising sixteen sheets and eight pillowcases. They then had them cut into 160,000 one-inch squares, advertised them for sale at $1 each and within a week had sold them all, making a profit of $159,000.

Following the concert the Beatles stayed at the Muehlebach Towers Hotel, which was demolished in 1996.

Muni, Scott

One of the top three New York disc jockeys who covered the arrival of the Beatles at J. F. Kennedy Airport on 7 February 1964. Scott worked for WABC and that day they changed the station's name to W-A-Beatles-C. Scott began interviewing the Beatles on that first day and continued covering their activities right up until their break-up.

In 1965 he was interviewing Ringo in a New York hotel suite when Ringo fainted. Scott found that he was worried about a family heirloom, a St Christopher medal which had been given to him by an aunt and which he'd lost. Scott then broadcast a message over the radio, promising that whoever returned it would get a hug and a kiss from Ringo and tickets to the Shea Stadium concert. It was quickly returned.

Scott left the station to open a club in New York, presenting bands such as the Rascals, but returned to radio in 1966 when he joined WOR-FM, changing to WNEW-FM the following year.

When John moved to New York, Scott interviewed him several times and when a new radio series called 'Ticket To Ride' was launched in February 1985, Scott became its host. The show interviewed artists whose careers have been inspired by the Beatles, in addition to the many people who were closely associated with the group.

Murphy, Paul

A Liverpool singer who made his stage debut at the age of thirteen in a school pantomime version of *Cinderella,* then became a member of various skiffle groups before appearing with the Rhythm Quintet. In 1957, together with Johnny 'Guitar' Byrne, he recorded 'Butterfly' and 'She's Got It' at Percy Phillips' studio in Kensington, Liverpool, the first local rock act to use the studio. The Quarry Men were to follow their example. At the beginning of 1959 he was vocalist/guitarist with Rory Storm's group the Raving Texans. He became a solo singer, using the stage name Paul Rogers, which had been given to him by Jim Gretty.

While appearing at Liverpool's Latin Quarter, comedians Mike and Bernie Winters spotted him. They recommended him to Walter Ridley of HMV. He appeared briefly with Johnny Kidd & the Pirates and sang with a big band, then made various solo appearances at the Zodiac Club in Duke Street.

HMV released his version of 'Four and Twenty Thousand Kisses' in 1961, a song which had been a hit at the San Remo Festival.

When Brian Epstein was in London with the Decca audition tapes, he bumped into Paul, who told him that no recording manager would listen to the tapes in the style they were, that he had to have acetates made. It was Paul who took him to the HMV Shop in Oxford Street to have the acetates cut, which then eventually led to the Beatles signing with Parlophone.

Paul moved to Germany and in 1963 became A&R man for Polydor in Hamburg. He signed up Tony Sheridan and commented: 'I want to show everyone in England "the Teacher", I also intend to send him to Liverpool and launch him from there.'

Paul also recorded a humorous disc about the Mersey Beat scene with Alex Harvey and produced an album with Kingsize Taylor & the Dominoes. He moved to various companies in Germany before returning to England in the 1970s to run Buk Records and achieve his ambition of launching Sheridan in Liverpool with a concert at the Philharmonic Hall.

When he was heading Buk Records he heard of the Adrian Barber tape of the Beatles at the Star Club which was in the hands of Kingsize Taylor and Allan Williams. He persuaded them to let him put the tapes through his company Lingasong, and released them as a double album. He later sold the distribution rights to Double H Licensing Corporation in America.

In 1998 he attempted to release a CD package of the Star Club recording with mail order TV advertising in Britain, but Apple successfully prevented him.

Murray, Mitch

A British songwriter who penned the pop song 'How Do You Do It', which he gave to Dick James to publish. James presented it to George Martin who believed it would provide a hit for the Beatles. The Beatles didn't like the number, but Martin insisted that they record it – and they were later to admit that they didn't put their heart and soul into the performance. Martin challenged them to come up with a better song and they produced 'Please Please Me'.

Acknowledging they were right, Martin issued the Lennon & McCartney number, although he was still convinced of the commercial potential of 'How Do You Do It' and recorded it with Gerry & the Pacemakers, who topped the charts with the song.

Brian Epstein also sought a Mitch Murray number for the Big

Three and he came up with 'By The Way'. This was totally unsuitable for one of Liverpool's top rock bands, but it provided them with a modest hit.

Murray teamed up with Peter Callender and continued to pen a string of pop hits including 'Bonnie And Clyde' and 'The Night Chicago Died', which resulted in his songs topping the 100 million sales mark.

He went into tax exile to Holland for a while and then moved to the Isle of Man, which also provided him with a tax haven. From that base he began to concentrate on composing radio jingles.

Museum Hall, Henderson Street, Bridge of Allan, Stirlingshire, Scotland

Penultimate show on the Beatles' five-day tour of Scotland, which took place on Saturday, 5 January 1963, when the British Isles was experiencing its worst spate of bad weather for decades.

Music Hall, The Square, Shrewsbury, Shropshire

Lewis Buckley was a promoter who booked the Beatles on numerous occasions, including the Friday, 14 December 1962 gig at this venue. Buckley also booked them for their second and last appearance at the hall on Friday, 26 April 1963.

Music International

A BBC 2 television show on which John Lennon was interviewed on 2 August 1965.

Music Of Lennon & McCartney, The

The title of a music spectacular conceived by Johnny Hamp of Granada Television, the producer and station which had given the group their first TV airing. Hamp had been made Head of Light Entertainment for Granada and after deciding he wished to pay tribute to the songwriting talents of John and Paul he had discussions with them which resulted in 'The Music Of Lennon & McCartney', the biggest spectacular yet produced by Granada Television. The programme was produced by Johnny Hamp and directed by Phil Casson.

The 50-minute programme was filmed over a two-day period in one of Granada's largest studios, Studio 6, on specially constructed sets. The completed show was fully networked at 9.40 p.m. on Friday, 17 December 1965.

The Beatles had wanted Ella Fitzgerald to sing 'Can't Buy Me Love', but she wasn't available. French singer Richard Anthony had been due to appear but was involved in a road accident shortly before the recordings and was replaced by Dick Rivers.

George Martin led a 25-piece orchestra in a rendition of 'I Feel Fine' and Paul introduced the American composer/pianist Henry Mancini with the words, 'Now we introduce our favourite composer, Henry Mancini, who is known to all his friends as Hank. Welcome to the Beatles' show, Henry.' Mancini played 'If I Fell' and Peter And Gordon performed their major hit 'World Without Love', with a dozen attractive female models decorating the background.

Esther Phillips flew in from America especially to perform 'And I Love Him' and Lulu, who had been driven up from London by Peter Noone of Herman's Hermits, belted out 'I Saw Him Standing There'. The Beatles closed the first half of the show with a rendition of 'Day Tripper'.

Six members of the Liverpool Philharmonic Orchestra appeared under the name Fritz Speigel's Barock And Roll Ensemble to perform 'She Loves You' in the style of Mozart. Peter Sellers, with a long wig and Shakespearean costume in the style of Richard III, rendered a theatrical interpretation of 'A Hard Day's Night'. Billy J. Kramer & the Dakotas performed their two hits 'Bad To Me' and 'Do You Want To Know A Secret'.

Cilla Black performed 'It's For You' and was followed by Paul McCartney who began singing 'Yesterday', and Marianne Faithfull appeared and completed the song. Organist Alan Haven performed another interpretation of 'A Hard Day's Night', with backing from drummer Tony Crombie, then the Beatles performed 'We Can Work It Out'. For the number, John Lennon played harmonium – it was the instrument used in 'Coronation Street' which was familiar to viewers of the soap opera as the harmonium in the corner of Ena Sharples' (Violet Carson) room. Incidentally, among the spectators who were witnessing the production were members of the 'Coronation Street' cast and disc jockey Jimmy Savile. Also appearing on the special was the Spanish dance star Antonio Vargas.

My Bonnie

The number was composed by Charles T. Pratt, who credited the song to J. T. Woods and H. J. Fuller, and it first appeared in a songbook called *Student Songs Of 1881*.

Ray Charles recorded a rock version of the number in 1958, which probably led Bert Kaempfert and Tony Sheridan to include it among the songs recorded at the Harburg Friedrich Ebert Halle on Thursday, 22 June and Friday, 23 June 1961, with the Beatles providing backing for Sheridan. One version included a slow German introduction, another a slow English introduction. This version credited Tony Sheridan as composer of the traditional arrangement.

The record was issued in Germany in June 1961 where, according to Kaempfert, it sold 100,000 copies. It entered the Top 40 and remained there for twelve weeks, although the highest position it attained was No 32. The single was credited to Tony Sheridan and the Beat Brothers, allegedly because Kaempfert decided that the Beatles' name sounded too like a German word for penis – peedles!

The number was eventually included on the Beatles' *Anthology 1* CD.

Nassau, The Bahamas

A group of 700 islands and islets which was first visited by Christopher Columbus in 1492. The capital of the Bahama Islands is Nassau, a city with a population of 3,000, resting on the 21-mile long New Providence Island.

The Beatles flew out to Nassau on 22 February 1965 to film scenes from their second movie *Help!*

The islands had been chosen as a location for the film for several reasons. One of them was financial. The Beatles' financial adviser Dr Walter Strach had set up temporary residence in Nassau in 1965. Walter Shenson and the Beatles were then able to set a Bahamian company Cavalcade Productions, which could receive proceeds in British sterling but would also be able to avoid some of the excessive British taxation of the time. However, when Harold Wilson devalued the pound in 1967, it was to cost the Beatles' Bahamian accounts approximately $200,000.

When they arrived, the group stayed in a house in the grounds of the Balmoral Club, close to Cable Beach.

The filming in Nassau took two weeks, from 24 February to 9 March, and the group flew out of the islands the day after filming there was completed.

George and Patti flew to Nassau for a ten-day holiday on 9 December 1964 prior to 'The Beatles Christmas Show'.

NEMS Enterprises

The company formed to direct the Beatles' careers.

Brian Epstein's family ran a furniture store in Walton Road, Liverpool, I. Epstein & Sons. The annexe to the furniture store sold pianos and sheet music and was called North End Music Stores (because it was in the North End of Liverpool). Eventually, just the initials N.E.M.S. were used. When the family decided to expand their business and launch a large store in the centre of Liverpool, they opened a branch of NEMS in Charlotte Street, run by Brian and his brother Clive. The family then opened a large record store at 12–14 Whitechapel and Brian was put in charge while his friend Peter Brown ran the record section at Charlotte Street.

When Brian wanted to become involved in the Mersey scene, initially signing the Beatles, his family agreed to support him, but his father Harry insisted that he should take advantage of his brother Clive's business acumen and Clive was appointed Company Secretary. NEMS Enterprises Limited was registered on 26 June 1962 with its £100 shares divided equally between Brian and Clive, and over the next five years Brian was to register no less than 65 other different companies. NEMS Enterprises Limited was formed as a theatrical, concert and variety agency and as new acts were signed, such as Gerry & the Pacemakers and Billy J. Kramer, the company moved to new offices at 24 Moorfields on 6 August 1963. By that time the company had expanded to a staff of three. The share capital was increased to £10,000 on 27 April 1964 with Brian receiving 5,000 shares, Clive 4,000 and each of the Beatles 250. Eventually, by December 1965 the shares had been changed still further and Brian owned 7,000, Clive 2,000, and the individual Beatles 250 each.

A concert promotions division, NEMS Presentations, was formed on 12 July 1963.

On 9 March 1964 the organisation moved to Sutherland House, Argyll Street, London, and the staff rose to fifteen. Geoffrey Ellis was appointed Executive Manager, Bernard Lee, who had formerly been with the Grade Organisation, headed the NEMS Booking Agency, Peter Brown became Brian's Personal Assistant, Tony Barrow the NEMS Press Officer, Alistair Taylor became Office Manager and various other members of the NEMS Liverpool staff moved to London. By 1966 there were 80 members of staff in five different London offices.

Brian had the opportunity to merge with various other powerful music business figures over the next few years, including Bernard Delfont and Tito Burns, but, to the frustration of his associates, he decided to merge with the Robert Stigwood Organisation and the merger took place on 13 January 1967. Epstein remained as Chairman and Robert Stigwood became joint Managing Director with Vic Lewis. Stigwood also had the option of buying 51 per cent of NEMS for £500,000 should Brian have wished to opt out of the business. When Brian died, Stigwood could have taken advantage of the option, but the Beatles told him that they would refuse to be associated with him and he never took the option up.

During the battle for Northern Songs and the entry of Allen Klein and the Eastmans into the picture, Clive Epstein had decided to let the Beatles buy NEMS. Due to a note which he received from Eastman suggesting that the NEMS contract with the Beatles had been improper, Clive sold his shares to Triumph Investments, who were able to take control of the company.

Newby, Charles

Rhythm guitarist with Pete Best's first band the Blackjacks. The group began a residency at the Casbah Club in late 1959 and also played at local weddings and social events in the West Derby Village area of Liverpool. The other members were Ken Brown and Billy Barlow.

In August 1960, Chas, as he was more familiarly known, was about to go to college and Brown was soon to leave for London when the Beatles asked Pete Best to be their drummer.

On their return to Liverpool from Hamburg in December 1960, the group was without Stuart Sutcliffe who had elected to remain in Hamburg with Astrid Kirchherr.

The Beatles needed a bass player to sit in with them for some of their local gigs and Best suggested Brown, who was currently living in London. John and Paul didn't like the idea as they had originally sacked him from the Quarry Men and reasoned that there would still be some bad blood between them. Paul McCartney felt that this might be his opportunity to become the group's bass guitarist, but Pete suggested Chas, who was currently on Christmas holiday from college, where he was a chemistry student.

When approached, Newby agreed to join the Beatles for a short time, borrowed a leather jacket and bass guitar, and made his debut with the band at the Casbah Club on 17 December 1960.

Newby was to make four appearances as a Beatle. The other dates were at the Grosvenor Ballroom, Birkenhead, on 24 December, Litherland Town Hall on 27 December and, finally, a return to the Casbah Club on 31 December.

It's interesting to note that the 'word' about the Beatles began to spread around the Liverpool scene following their Litherland appearance, while Newby played with the band.

John Lennon then approached him with the offer of joining them permanently on their next Hamburg season, but Newby turned him down, preferring to continue his college studies.

Years later he was to meet up again with Pete Best, who was researching his book *Beatle!* Chas was then working in industrial management in Birmingham and had fond memories of his brief time with the Beatles, observing how exciting it had been. Recalling those few gigs, he told Pete: 'I remember them vividly. It used to make my feet ache with all the stamping we had to put into the act, but I loved every minute.'

He also said that he had no regrets about turning down the offer to join the Beatles as a permanent member.

New Cabaret Artistes Club, 174a Upper Parliament Street, Liverpool L8

The cellar of this Victorian house was used as a strip club by Allan Williams and Lord Woodbine for a short time in 1960. Strip clubs were illegal in Liverpool at the time by order of the local Watch Committee.

When Williams had booked a large-breasted model called Janice, she insisted on having live musicians provide backing for her. The only group Williams could find at the time who weren't working during the day were the Silver Beatles and Williams offered them ten shillings each for two twenty-minute spots a night.

9 Newcastle Road, Wavertree, Liverpool L15

The Stanley home, where John Lennon's grandparents George and Annie brought up their five daughters. Julia lived here during the years of her courtship with Freddie Lennon and on their wedding night, Julia returned to Newcastle Road while Freddie went into lodgings and then off to sea.

John was reared at this address during the first five years of his life. It was suggested that as Julia liked going out and having a good time at night, the baby John was left alone in the dark on so many occasions that it traumatised him and left him in fear of the dark for the rest of his life.

John's Aunt Mimi, with no children of her own, wanted to rear John and eventually had her wish granted and took John away in 1945 to her home in Menlove Avenue.

New Clubmoor Hall, back of Broadway, Norris Green, Liverpool L11

A Conservative Club where Paul McCartney made his debut with the Quarry Men on Friday, 18 October 1957. The group had been booked by local promoter Charlie McBain, and entrance for members cost three shillings. There was an audience of approximately 100 people that night.

Paul had tried to convince the group that they should have some sort of stage uniform and he suggested white coats. They couldn't really afford to buy any at the time so their manager Nigel Whalley was able to borrow a couple of white jackets from the golf club where he worked. For the gig the group wore matching outfits with long-sleeved cowboy shirts, black string ties and black trousers. John and Paul wore the white sports coats.

The line-up that night comprised Colin Hanton on drums, Len Garry on tea chest bass, Eric Griffiths on guitar and John and Paul. John, Paul, Len and Nigel caught the 81 bus from Woolton and Eric and Colin met them at the venue.

They were due on stage at 9 p.m. and began with Paul singing 'Long Tall Sally'. On this occasion, Paul played lead guitar for the first and only time – and it was a disaster.

Paul played the old Arthur Smith hit 'Guitar Boogie', but ruined the guitar solo because he was playing his guitar upside down and backwards, as he still didn't know how to restring a guitar for a left-handed person.

After the show, aware that his debut as a lead guitarist hadn't gone down too well, Paul tried to impress John by playing him an original number he'd written called 'I've Lost My Little Girl'. John responded by trying out a few tunes he'd written and sought Paul's opinion – the Lennon and McCartney songwriting team was soon to develop.

The group returned to the venue on 23 November 1957, and performed their third and last gig at the club on 10 January 1959. By that time the line-up comprised John, Paul, George Harrison, Colin Hanton and John Lowe.

New Colony Club, 80 Berkley Street, Liverpool L8

A run-down house in the black quarter of the Liverpool 8 district provided the premises for a cellar shebeen, run by Lord Woodbine, which he called the New Colony Club. The Beatles appeared here for a couple of informal afternoon sessions in 1960 to help out their friend 'Woodie'.

Newfield, Joanne

Brian Epstein's personal secretary. She originally joined NEMS Enterprises as secretary to Wendy Hanson at the company's Stafford Street offices. She was 21 years old and the niece of dance band leader Joe Loss. Wendy had needed the services of an extra secretary at Hille House because in addition to her working as

Brian's PA, she was also virtually PA for the Beatles. She was not pleased when Brian decided to make Joanne his own personal secretary at his Chapel Street base. Joanne was paid £15 per week and her working hours were from 10.00 a.m.–6.00 p.m., although she was to work late on many occasions due to Epstein's disinclination to rise before noon on various days as a result of his increasing reliance on drugs. She was devoted to him despite the occasional displays of bad temper and rudeness.

When Hanson left NEMS in 1966, Joanne inherited her job. As Brian began to work increasingly from his home she'd moved office into a small room at the top of the house at 24 Chapel Street. On Friday, 1 September 1967, when the servants couldn't wake Brian up in his bedroom, she phoned Alistair Taylor and it was soon confirmed that Brian had died.

Joanne then fulfilled the same functions for Peter Brown at Apple. In 1968 she was to marry Colin Peterson, former drummer with the Bee Gees, and moved to live in New South Wales, Australia, where Colin became a recording manager.

Newley, Anthony

A major British actor/singing star. Brian Epstein chose him to open the Whitechapel branch of NEMS in 1959. George Harrison also met Newley during a visit to his sister Louise in St Louis and commented: 'America was really great. I met Tony Newley over there. He'd never heard of any of our numbers so I played him some of our records. When I left he said he wanted to record "I Saw Her Standing There".' Newley was as good as his word and the single was released in October 1963, making him the second artist to cover a Beatles number in America.

He died of cancer in April 1999.

New London Synagogue, Abbey Road, St John's Wood, London NW8

Close to Abbey Road Studios, the synagogue where the Memorial Service for Brian Epstein was held at 6.00 p.m. on 17 October 1967. A large crowd gathered and among the close friends attending and paying their respects were all four Beatles, George Martin, Dick James, Cilla Black, Billy J. Kramer, the Fourmost, Lulu, Lionel Bart and Bernard Delfont. The Beatles had originally meant to attend wearing their psychedelic clothes, but realised this might upset Brian's mother Queenie and they wore suits.

The service was conducted by Rabbi Dr Louis Jacobs B.A., assisted by Cantor George Rothschild. The choir was under the direction of Martin Lawrence and the order of service was: (1) Psalm 121 (2) Prayer (3) Psalm 23 (4) Scriptural Readings (5) Psalm 16 (6) Address (7) Memorial Prayer (8) Anthem (9) Alenu and (10) Adon Olam.

Rabbi Jacobs was to say, 'He encouraged young people to sing of love and peace rather than war and hatred.'

New Musical Express

As *Mersey Beat* had built the Beatles' reputation in the North from 1961, the *New Musical Express* began heavily promoting the group from 1963. It was the British music weekly with the largest circulation and one of its writers, Alan Smith, had been contributing to *Mersey Beat* under the name George Jones. Another *Mersey Beat* writer, Roy Carr, went on to become one of the main *NME* journalists. The *NME's* star writer was Chris Hutchins who, at one time, was about to take up Brian Epstein's offer of joining Bill Harry on *Mersey Beat* when the *NME* came up with a counter-offer.

It was Hutchins who was the main Beatles contact for *New Musical Express*, just as he was the paper's main contact for Elvis Presley and it was Hutchins, who travelled to America with the Beatles, who originally arranged their meeting with Elvis.

The *New Musical Express* featured a series of concerts in the sixties featuring artists who topped their annual popularity polls. The concerts, known as 'The Poll Winners' Concerts', were all held in Wembley and the Beatles appeared on the following dates: Empire Pool, Wembley, 21 April 1963; Wembley Stadium, 26 April 1964; Wembley Stadium, 11 April 1965; and Wembley Stadium, 1 May 1966. Their 1965 concert was screened on ABC TV and networked throughout the UK on 18 April of that year and their 1966 appearance was their last concert show in Britain.

From 1963–1976, places in the *NME* poll won by the Beatles both as a group and individually were:

SINGLE OF THE YEAR
1963 'She Loves You', the Beatles
1966 'Eleanor Rigby', the Beatles
1968 'Hey Jude', the Beatles
1970 'My Sweet Lord', George Harrison

ALBUM OF THE YEAR
1970 *Let It Be*, the Beatles

Bass Guitarist Of The Year
1972 Paul McCartney
1973 Paul McCartney
1974 Paul McCartney
1976 Paul McCartney

Vocal Personality Of The Year
1965 John Lennon

World Vocal Group	UK Vocal Group
1963 the Beatles	1963 the Beatles
1964 the Beatles	1964 the Beatles
1965 the Beatles	1965 the Beatles
1966 the Beatles	1966 the Beatles
1967 the Beatles	1967 the Beatles
1968 the Beatles	1968 the Beatles
1969 the Beatles	1969 the Beatles
	1970 the Beatles

New Orleans
First hit for Gary 'US' Bonds, which reached No. 6 in the American charts in 1960. Bonds, real name Gary Anderson, followed up with a No. 1 hit 'Quarter To Three' and had a further seven chart entries.

The number was penned by F. Guida and J. Royster and the Beatles included it in their stage repertoire during 1961.

Newsfront
An American television programme, produced by WNET-TV. John Lennon and Paul McCartney appeared on the show on 15 May 1968, promoting their launch of Apple Records; they also discussed politics on the New York TV show. The programme was repeated the following week on 22 May.

Incidentally, on 15 May they also appeared on the networked 'Tonight' show.

New Springfield Ballroom, Janvrin Road, St Saviour, Jersey, Channel Isles
Ballroom in the town of St Helier on the island of Jersey, the largest of the Channel Isles. Although closer to France than to Britain, the Channel Isles (which comprises four large islands: Jersey, Guernsey, Alderney and Sark, together with a number of smaller isles) is a British dependency and has been since 1066. Jersey itself is a sunny holiday resort, much favoured by the British and French and both

languages are in evidence in shop names, street signs and official notices.

The Beatles appeared at the Springfield Ballroom, before crowds of holidaymakers, as part of a five-day package promoted by John Smith, for which they were paid £1,000. They appeared at the Springfield on 6, 7, 9 and 10 August 1963.

Nicol, Jimmy

A British drummer, born on 3 August 1939, who had started his career as a drum repairer for Boosey & Hawkes. He'd begun playing drums with the Spotniks prior to forming his own group, the Shubdubs, who had signed with Pye Records.

During the morning of Wednesday, 3 June 1964, Ringo collapsed during a photo session the Beatles were having for the *Saturday Evening Post*, in Barnes. He was then taken to University College Hospital where it was diagnosed that he had tonsillitis and pharyngitis, with a temperature of 102 degrees. It was on the eve of the first leg of the Beatles' world tour that Brian Epstein felt they should go ahead with the tour using a substitute drummer. This was despite protests from George Harrison, who said: 'If Ringo's not going then neither am I, you can find two replacements.'

It was George Martin who suggested Nicol as the drummer had recently played on session for Martin with Georgie Fame & the Blue Flames and Tommy Quickly. Nicol had also performed on a Beatles soundalike album, *Beatlemania,* on the Top Six label and knew most of the Beatles' numbers.

Martin rang Nicol and arranged for him to audition and rehearse with the Beatles at Abbey Road at three that afternoon. At the rehearsal the four of them performed six numbers: 'I Want To Hold Your Hand', 'She Loves You', 'I Saw Her Standing There', 'This Boy', 'Can't Buy Me Love' and 'Long Tall Sally'. Journalist Dick Hughes, an Australian, was present at the rehearsals and says that Paul told him: 'This fellow is fine, but we just can't afford to be without Ringo at a real recording session, because the kids would always know that a record was one without him.'

Jimmy commented: 'I was having a bit of a lie down after lunch when the phone rang. It was EMI asking if I could come down to the studio to rehearse with the Beatles. Two hours after I got there I was told to pack my bags for Denmark.'

Immediately following the rehearsals, Jimmy was called into Brian Epstein's office, offered the job and given details of his remuneration in front of John, Paul and George. Epstein was to say: 'The difficulty was finding someone who looked like a Beatle and not an outcast.'

He rehearsed with them again the following day prior to their appearance at Copenhagen on 4 June 1964. Making his stage debut with them at the Tivoli Gardens that evening, he wore Ringo's stage suit, although the trousers were too short for him. The band performed ten numbers, cutting down from the eleven originally planned by leaving out Ringo's spot with 'I Wanna Be Your Man'.

After the show, George commented: 'Playing without Ringo is like driving a car on three wheels but Jimmy has grasped our rhythm very quickly.'

Jimmy also appeared in Hong Kong and on the first four shows in Australia.

Ringo was discharged from hospital on Thursday, 11 June. He teamed up with his fellow Beatles in Melbourne, Australia, and there was a single photo session in which all five were pictured together.

Jimmy left for Essendon Airport at 8.00 a.m. After packing his bags he was to comment: 'The boys were very kind but I felt like an intruder. They accepted me but you just can't get into a group like that – they have their own atmosphere, their own sense of humour. It's a little clique and outsiders just can't break it.'

He never said goodbye to the Beatles. 'They were still asleep,' he said. 'I didn't think I should disturb them.'

Brian Epstein and tour manager Lloyd Ravenscroft accompanied him to the airport. Brian presented him with a cheque for £500 and a gold Eternamatic wrist watch inscribed: 'From the Beatles and Brian Epstein to Jimmy – with appreciation and gratitude.'

Jimmy had thought that his brief spell with the Beatles would boost his career and had said, during the Australian trip, 'When I get home I won't have to run a group on fifteen or twenty pounds a night anymore.'

Unfortunately, he didn't have much success on his return. His group issued 'Husky' c/w 'Don't Come Back', which failed to make the charts. They were also booked to replace the Dave Clark Five, ironically because Dave Clark was ill, in a short season in Blackpool. While he was there Jimmy received a bundle of 5,000 letters from fans in Australia, sent on by a local DJ. Jimmy sent his thanks with the message that he'd go and live in Australia. On 12 July 1964 at the Hippodrome, Brighton, he appeared on a bill with the Beatles and the Fourmost, although they were said not to have met that night.

On 29 April 1965, Jimmy was declared bankrupt in a London court with debts of £4,066 and only £50 to his name. He said,

'Standing in for Ringo was the worst thing that ever happened to me. Up until then I was feeling quite happy turning over £30 to £40 a week. I didn't realise that it would change my whole life. I had half-a-million pounds worth of publicity and immediately I was offered three weeks at Blackpool standing in for Dave Clark at £350 a week. Everyone in the business said I couldn't miss. I was the hottest name there was. But after the headlines died, I began dying too. No one wanted to know me any more, I borrowed from everyone and anyone.'

When his group disbanded, Jimmy joined the house band on the television programme 'Come Dancing'. He later joined a Scandinavian instrumental act the Spotniks and while touring Mexico he met and married a Mexican Indian girl, Josephina.

The couple returned to Britain in 1987, penniless. Initially they lived with Jimmy's mother Edith in her tiny flat. By 1996 they had a small flat of their own in south London, with Jimmy trying to eke out a living through carpentry work.

Ironically, Howard, Jimmy's son from his first marriage, became a sound engineer and won a BAFTA award for his work on the television series 'The Beatles Anthology'.

Night Before, The
A number penned by Paul which was included on the *Help!* album and later surfaced on *Rock 'n' Roll Music*.

Night Of A Hundred Stars, The
A midnight charity revue presented by the Actors' Charitable Trust, which took place at the London Palladium on Thursday, 23 July 1964. It was hosted by Sir Laurence Olivier and was described as an event featuring 'stars of stage, screen and disc'.

The Beatles made an appearance along with a host of stars.

John Lennon contributed a sketch for the cover of the souvenir programme, and the Beatles appeared in a sketch, 'a flying ballet', during which they sang the Peter Pan song 'I'm Flying'.

The event raised £11,000 for the Combined Theatrical Charities Appeal Council.

Nilsson, Harry
An American singer/songwriter, born Harry Edward Nilsson III in Brooklyn, New York, on 15 June 1941. He moved to the West Coast in 1952.

In August 1967, Nilsson released an album *Pandemonium Shadow Show* on RCS 3874. It contained the track of his single 'You Can't Do That' (RCA 9298), whose lyrics included titles and lyrics from the Beatles songs 'I'm Down', 'Drive My Car', 'You're Gonna Lose That Girl', 'Good Day Sunshine', 'A Hard Day's Night', 'Rain', 'I Want To Hold Your Hand', 'Day Tripper', 'Paperback Writer', 'Do You Want To Know A Secret?', 'Yesterday' and 'Strawberry Fields Forever'.

The tribute came to the attention of Derek Taylor, who was also living on the West Coast at the time. He sent a copy of the album to Brian Epstein, calling Nilsson the best contemporary solo artist in the world, and added, 'He is the something the Beatles are.'

Harry's interpretation of their songs impressed John and Paul who, in an interview, said that he was their favourite singer.

His recording of 'Everybody's Talking' was chosen as the theme song for the film *Midnight Cowboy* and earned Harry his first Grammy award.

He became a close friend of the individual Beatles and topped the British charts with 'Without You', a number written by Pete Ham and Tom Evans, members of the Apple Records group Badfinger.

George and Ringo performed on his album *Son Of Schmilsson* and Derek Taylor produced *A Touch of Schmilsson In the Night*. John Lennon produced his *Pussy Cats* album and he appeared with Ringo Starr in two films, *Son of Dracula* and *Harry and Ringo's Night Out,* both produced in 1974.

Ringo was best man at the wedding of Harry and Una and became godfather to their children.

After John's murder, Nilsson toured America on a campaign for tighter handgun control.

In 1993 he suffered a heart attack from which he never fully recovered and died in Los Angeles on 15 January 1994 at the age of 52. Ringo played on his posthumously released 1995 album *The Harry Nilsson Anthology.*

Nippon Budokan Hall, Daikan-cho, Chiyoda-ku, Tokyo, Japan

Promoter Tatsuji Nagashima had booked the Beatles to appear on five shows at this impressive octagon-shaped hall, which could accommodate an audience of 11,000. However, because it had been regarded by many Japanese as a sacred place because of the traditional and honourable martial arts exhibitions which were the main feature of the hall, a number of death threats were made against the Beatles by right wing political groups. As a result the police presence was considerable, with a total of 35,000 security men involved during the visit and 3,000 policemen mixing with the audience at each of the concerts.

The Beatles flew out from London to Tokyo but, because of the danger from a typhoon called KIT, they had to stop off at Anchorage, Alaska for several hours. They eventually arrived at Tokyo International Airport at 3.40 a.m. on 29 June 1966. 3,000 police had guarded the airport for hours before the Beatles' arrival and 1,500 fans had turned up to greet the group. There were 15,000 uniformed policemen lining the route, drawn from all parts of Tokyo, and there were groups with banners stating 'Beatles Go Home'.

They were booked into the Presidential Suite of the Tokyo Hilton Hotel where a further 2,000 security guards were in place. Security was so tight that they weren't allowed outside the hotel and had to contend with a stream of screened visitors. During their stay an English-speaking guide, Mike Nakamura, accompanied them.

They performed a single concert on Thursday, 30 June, which was filmed in colour by the Japanese television channel NTV and screened on 1 July under the title 'The Beatles Recital, From Nippon Budokan, Tokyo'. Because of threats from an extremist student faction who were also incensed at the idea of a rock 'n' roll concert at the sacred hall, 250 armed police and plain-clothes detectives surrounded the stage at each performance and more than 2,000 police were present surrounding the building.

The Japanese Times reported that the show had been seen by 10,000 fans, was 'a howling, screaming success' and 'the kiddies screamed and waved their hankies, many with tears streaming down their faces'. The paper referred to the Beatles as 'bushy-haired heroes'. The performance lasted for thirty minutes and the newspaper reported: 'The only time in the whole half-hour the crowd quietened down enough to hear was when Paul sang "Yesterday".' On Friday, 1 and Saturday, 2 July they performed two concerts each day at the hall where the dressing-rooms had been specially decorated for their visit and stocked with food and drink. Many people, including Tetsusaburo Shimoya, the fifty-year-old President of their Japanese fan club, visited them. He presented each of them with a transistor radio.

Nobody I Know
The second number which Paul McCartney gave to Peter & Gordon to record, providing them with their second million-seller. The number was issued in Britain on Columbia DB 7292 on 29 May 1964 and reached No. 9 in the charts. It was issued in America on Capitol 5211 on 15 June 1964, but didn't chart.

Nobody's Child
This was one of the eight numbers recorded in Hamburg in May 1961 during the Polydor session in which the Beatles backed singer Tony

Sheridan. The Beatles merely provided instrumental backing to Sheridan's interpretation of the number, which has since been released on various singles and albums.

Noebel, Reverend David A

The Dean of the Christian Crusade Anti-Communist Youth University. He became an implacable critic of the Beatles and wrote numerous tracts about them in 1965, 1969, 1980 and 1982. In 1965, Noebel even embarked on a speaking tour to convince Americans that the Beatles were a dangerous arm of the Communist plot, saying they were part of a 'Communist master music plan to make our children mentally sick'. That year he wrote an article 'Beware The Red Beatles', in which he declared: 'In the excitatory state that the Beatles place these young stars into, these young people will do anything they are told to do.' In his book *Communism, Hypnotism And The Beatles*, he wrote: 'Pavlov experimented with animals in other areas as well, for example, in an area known as artificial neurosis. Here the scientist took healthy animals and using two conditioned reflexes, the excitatory reflex and the inhibitory reflex, caused these healthy animals to break down mentally with cases of artificial neurosis. As we shall see, this is exactly what the Beatles, in particular, and rock and roll in general, are doing to our teenagers.'

Non Stop Pop

A BBC radio programme. The Beatles were interviewed for the show by Phil Tate on 30 July 1963 and the programme was transmitted on 30 August 1963.

No One's Gonna Change Our World

A charity album, originally compiled following a suggestion by comedian Spike Milligan, on behalf of the World Wildlife Fund. A number of major British artists contributed to the project, including the Beatles, who donated their recording of 'Across The Universe', from which the phrase 'No One's Gonna Change Our World' was taken. George Martin co-ordinated the production of the project and the album was issued in Britain on SRS 50143 on 12 December 1969.

No Other Baby

The Vipers Skiffle Group were one of the handful of skiffle bands to make an impact on the British charts during skiffle's brief reign. Their hits were 'Don't You Rock Me Daddy-O', 'Cumberland Gap' and 'Streamline Train'.

One of the numbers they popularised and recorded in 1958 was 'No Other Baby', which the Quarry Men introduced into their repertoire, with John Lennon on lead vocals.

No Reply

A composition by John Lennon which was considered for release as a single, until it was decided to issue 'I Feel Fine'. The track then appeared on the *Beatles For Sale* album. It is also found on the *Beatles For Sale* EP and the American *Beatles '65* album.

The track was recorded on 30 September 1964 and George Martin played piano on the session.

Northern Meeting Hall, Church Street, Inverness, Inverness-shire, Scotland

Site of the second gig of the Silver Beetles' short tour of Scotland backing Johnny Gentle. On Saturday, 21 May 1960, they appeared at this venue, which was divided into two halls, with the main hall on the ground floor where Lindsay Ross and his band performed. The Silver Beetles appeared in an upstairs hall on a bill with Ronnie Watt and the Chekkers Rock Dance Band.

Norwegian Wood

Composition by John about a brief affair, possibly a one-night-stand. He wanted to describe his feelings regarding the affair without his wife Cynthia knowing. He commented, 'I was trying to write about an affair, so it was very gobbledegook. I was sort of writing from my experiences, girls' flats, things like that.

'I wrote it at Kenwood. George had just got the sitar and I said, "Could you play this piece?" We went through many different sort of versions of the song, it was never right and I was getting very angry about it, it wasn't coming out like I said. They said, "Well, just do it how you want to do it." And I said, "Well, I just want to do it like this." They let me go and I did the guitar very loudly into the mike and sang it at the same time and then George had the sitar and I asked him could he play the piece that I'd written, you know, dee diddly dee diddly dee, that bit, and he was not sure whether he could play it yet because he hadn't done much on the sitar but he was willing to have a go, as is his wont, and he learned the bit and dubbed it on after. I think we did it in sections.'

In fact, recording began on Tuesday, 12 October, when the song was called 'This Bird Has Flown', but John was dissatisfied with the result and they began re-recording it on Thursday, 21 October.

It was the first time a sitar had been used on a pop single. Ringo also played tambourine, maraca and finger cymbals.

John then decided to include the words 'This Bird Has Flown' as a sub-title.

The track was featured on the *Rubber Soul* album and was included on the compilations *The Beatles 1962–1966*, *Love Songs* and *The Beatles Ballads*. Take One of the studio recordings was included on the Beatles' *Anthology 2* CDs.

Not A Second Time

A John Lennon composition recorded on Wednesday, 11 September 1963, for the *With The Beatles* album. George Martin played piano at the session.

The number was one of the Beatles songs mentioned by *The Times* music critic William Mann in his feature 'What Songs The Beatles Sang', '. . . but harmonic interest is typical of their quicker songs too, one gets the impression that they think simultaneously of harmony and melody, so firmly are the major tonic sevenths and ninths built into their tunes, and the flat submediant key switches, so natural is the Aeolian cadence at the end of "Not A Second Time" (the chord progression which ends Mahler's "Song Of The Earth").'

Commenting on the article, John said, 'Really it was just chords like any other chords. That was the first time anyone had written anything like that about us.'

Not Guilty

A George Harrison composition, written in 1968, which the Beatles began recording for *The Beatles* double album. They recorded an incredible 101 takes of the number, more takes than they ever did on any other number, yet it still didn't find its way on to the album as originally planned.

George finally issued the song on his *George Harrison* album in 1979. A version was included on the Beatles' *Anthology 3* CDs.

Nothin' Shakin' But The Leaves On The Trees

A number penned by Cirino Colacrai, Eddie Fontaine, Dianne Lampert and Jack Cleveland which was recorded by Eddie Fontaine in 1958. The Beatles introduced it into their repertoire in 1960 with George Harrison on lead vocal. It was one of the numbers the group performed when they appeared at the Star Club and was one of the tracks recorded by Adrian Barber which has appeared on the various releases of the Star Club tapes. A version was included on the Beatles' *Anthology 3* CDs.

Not Only . . . But Also

BBC 2 comedy series featuring Peter Cook and Dudley Moore.

John Lennon was a friend of Cook's and they'd dined together a few times. On 9 January 1965, John appeared on the first edition of their new show reading excerpts from his book *In His Own Write*, alongside Dudley Moore and Norman Rossington. He also appeared in what was described as a 'surrealist sketch'.

His next appearance on the show took place on 26 December 1966 when he appeared in a sketch as a lavatory attendant. Dressed in a commissionaire's uniform and wearing 'granny' glasses, John was filmed outside a gentlemen's convenience in Broadwick Street, Soho, London W1. The word 'Gentlemen' remained above the loo, but a sign reading 'Members Only' was placed beneath it. The sketch, in which John appeared with Pete and Dud, concerned a 'Gentlemen's Club'.

Nowhere Man (EP)

The Beatles' twelfth British EP. All four tracks were taken from their album *Rubber Soul*, which had been released the previous year.

The EP was issued on Parlophone GEP 8952 on 8 July 1966 and contained the tracks: 'Nowhere Man', 'Drive My Car', 'Michelle' and 'You Won't See Me'.

Nowhere Man (Single)

A number John penned at Kenwood. He was to say, 'I was just sitting, trying to think of a song, and I thought of myself sitting there, doing nothing and getting nowhere. Once I'd thought of that, it was easy. It all came out. No, I remember now, I'd actually stopped trying to think of something. Nothing would come. I was cheesed off and went for a lie down, having given up. Then I thought of myself as "Nowhere Man" – sitting in his nowhere land.'

Recording began on Thursday, 21 October 1965, and the number was included on the *Rubber Soul* album and was also the title of the group's twelfth British EP. It was issued as a single in America on Capitol 5587 on 21 February 1966 with 'What Goes On' as the flip and reached No. 3 in the American charts. It was also featured on the American album *Yesterday . . . And Today* and the compilations *The Beatles 1962–1966* and *The Beatles Ballads*.

The Nowhere Man was brought to life in the film *Yellow Submarine* in the person of Hilary Boob, PhD.

A British vocal/instrumental group recorded 'Nowhere Man' and issued it as a single, which reached No. 47 in the British charts in March 1966.

Nurk Twins, The

When the pre-teen Paul and Mike McCartney participated in the family entertainment, performing before their relatives, they invented the name the Nurk Twins.

During the Easter holidays in April 1960, John and Paul hitch-hiked down South and stopped off at the Fox And Hounds, Gosbrook Road, Caversham, Berkshire, where the new tenants were Mike and Elizabeth Robbins. 'Beth' was Paul's cousin and she and her husband had been Redcoats at Butlin's. The McCartneys had spent a holiday at their camp in 1957 and Mike had encouraged the fifteen-year-old Paul and his thirteen-year-old brother Mike to take the stage together in a talent contest.

When John and Paul turned up at the Fox and Hounds, Mike suggested that they give a show at the pub and he gave them the name The Nerk Twins (remembering the childhood Nurk Twins?). The boys had been helping behind the bar and Mike thought they'd like the idea of entertaining in the tap room, where they performed sitting on stools playing acoustic guitars on the evening of 23 April and during lunchtime on 24 April.

Nya Aulan, Sundsta Laroverk, Karlstad, Sweden

Venue where the Beatles opened their Swedish tour on 25 October 1963. It was an unusual site for the group to be performing in as it was the hall of a secondary school. The Beatles performed twice that evening, at 7.00 p.m. and 9.00 p.m., to an audience of Swedish youngsters. Also on the bill were a group called the Phantoms.

The Beatles performed 'Long Tall Sally', 'Please Please Me', 'I Saw Her Standing There', 'From Me To You', 'A Taste Of Honey', 'Chains', 'Boys', 'She Loves You' and 'Twist And Shout'.

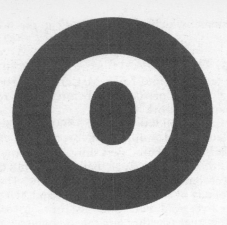

Oasis Club, 45/47 Lloyd Street, Manchester

Touted as 'Manchester's Cavern', a cellar-club in the nearby city to Liverpool. The Beatles made their Manchester debut there on 2 February 1962 advertised as 'Polydor's Great Recording Stars', on a bill with the Allan Dent Jazz Band. The club was owned by Manchester promoters Kennedy Street Enterprises and managed by Tony Stuart, who also ran his own jazz band.

The Beatles also appeared at the venue on 29 September and 8 December 1962 and made their final appearance at the club on 22 February 1963.

Ob-La-Di, Ob-La-Da

The Beatles began recording this number, penned by Paul, on 3 July 1968 and continued for several days. There were a number of changes over the various takes and at one time a number of session men were used, but that recording was rejected.

The number was completed on Tuesday, 19 July, with Paul on lead and John and George joining in on the chorus.

The lighthearted song had been inspired by reggae music and the number was originally intended to be a Beatles single, but John and George rejected it.

The song was recorded by both Marmalade and the Bedrocks in Britain and Marmalade topped the charts while the Bedrocks reached No. 17 with their version.

'Ob-La-Di, Ob-La-Da' was featured on *The Beatles* double album and also the compilation *The Beatles 1967–1970*.

Ironically, it was issued as a Beatles single in America years later on 8 November 1976 on Capitol 4347.

Alistair Taylor recalls an anecdote concerning the number. Paul received a phone call on behalf of a reggae musician called Scott who was in Brixton prison for failing to keep up with his wife's maintenance payments. Apparently, Scott ran a band called Ob-la-di, Ob-la-da and suggested that Paul may have got the title after seeing the name on the band's posters in South London. If Paul could deliver him £111 18s to have him released from Brixton, he'd drop all claims to the title.

Paul couldn't remember whether he'd ever seen a poster with that name on it, but he felt sorry for the guy and instructed Alistair to take the money to Brixton prison and arrange for Scott's release, which he did.

A version of the number was included on the Beatles' *Anthology 3* CDs.

Octopus's Garden

The second number penned by Ringo to appear as a Beatles track. It's a children's song with a similar ambience to 'Yellow Submarine'.

During the recording of *The Beatles* double album, Paul made a comment to Ringo that he'd fluffed while playing a tom-tom. Ringo walked out of the sessions threatening to quit. He spent the next fortnight on a yacht in the Mediterranean owned by Peter Sellers. While on the yacht the ship's chef regaled him with stories of the creatures who lived on the bed of the sea, which inspired Ringo to write the song.

He returned to Abbey Road to find 'Welcome home' banners on his drum kit.

A scene in the *Let It Be* film reveals George going through the number on a piano, working out the arrangement with Ringo and making various helpful suggestions. George Martin joins them and then John also enters the scene and begins to play drums with them.

The Beatles recorded the song on Saturday, 28 April 1969. George Martin was away at the time so the production was handled by Chris Thomas and the Beatles. On Thursday, 17 July, various sound effects were added to create an 'under sea' atmosphere. At Ringo's suggestion a mike was placed over him when he took a straw and began blowing bubbles in a glass of water to simulate the sound of being under water.

The number was included on the *Abbey Road* album, it is seen in the *Let It Be* film, and was included on *The Beatles 1967–1970* compilation and Ringo featured it in his 1978 TV special 'Ringo'.

Take Two from the official recordings was included on the Beatles' *Anthology 3* CDs.

Odd Spot Club, The, 89 Bold Street, Liverpool L1

When the Odd Spot opened in Liverpool city centre on 9 December 1961 the plan was to provide entertainment to a more affluent clientele than that which graced clubs such as the Cavern. The owners of the Odd Spot hoped to attract the middle-class patrons from the smarter areas of the city such as Childwall, Woolton and Aigburth.

The ground floor of the club was a restaurant area and live music was performed in the narrow basement. The Beatles made their debut here on 29 March 1962 and their second and last appearance occurred a few months later on 11 August.

For their 29 March appearance, Brian Epstein asked Alan Swerdlow, a former Liverpool Art College student, to take photographs of the Beatles' performance. The group were wearing their new suits, which they'd worn for the first time a few days previously at their Heswall Jazz Club gig. Swerdlow snapped a range of well-composed shots, although the only member of the Beatles he concentrated on taking solo shots of was Pete Best and one of the Best shots was used on the cover of *Mersey Beat* to announce their Parlophone recording deal.

John Dykins, who had lived with Julia Lennon before her death, worked in the Odd Spot restaurant for a time.

O'Dell, Dennis

Irish-born film producer whose association with the Beatles first began when he was Associate Producer of their debut film *A Hard Day's Night*. O'Dell also worked on *The Family Way*, for which Paul McCartney wrote the score, and *The Magic Christian*, which starred Ringo and Peter Sellers. When Apple Films was originally formed in February 1968 he was appointed a director, together with all four Beatles and Neil Aspinall. He was also a director of Apple Publicity.

O'Dell became involved in the production of *Magical Mystery Tour, Let It Be*, and *The Concert For Bangladesh*. The Beatles mention him by name in their song 'You Know My Name (Look Up The Number)'.

He was later to enter into partnership with George Harrison in the movie company Handmade Films.

Odeon, New Street, Birmingham

The Beatles appeared at this venue twice, on Sunday, 11 October 1964 and on Thursday, 9 December 1965.

Odeon, Winchcombe Street, Cheltenham, Gloucestershire

Venue where the Beatles opened their autumn tour of Britain in 1963. They appeared at the Odeon on Friday, 1 November with the Brook Brothers, with the Rhythm & Blues Quartet, the Vernons Girls, Peter Jay & the Jaywalkers and the Kestrels in support. Introducing the show was Canadian compere Frank Berry.

The Beatles performed 'I Saw Her Standing There', 'From Me To You', 'All My Loving', 'You Really Got A Hold On Me', 'Roll Over Beethoven', 'Boys', 'Till There Was You', 'She Loves You', 'Money' and 'Twist And Shout'.

Odeon, Renfield Street, Glasgow, Scotland

The Beatles first appeared at this venue on Friday, 7 June 1963. Their next appearance took place on Thursday, 30 April 1964. Following this concert, the Beatles all went on a month's holiday to exotic climes. Their third appearance at the cinema took place on Wednesday, 21 October 1964 and their last concert there was the opening date of their final UK tour on Friday, 3 December 1965.

Their repertoire on their last British tour was: 'I Feel Fine', 'She's A Woman', 'If I Needed Someone', 'Act Naturally', 'Nowhere Man', 'Baby's In Black', 'Help!', 'We Can Work It Out', 'Yesterday', 'Day Tripper' and 'I'm Down'.

Odeon, Epsom Road, Guildford, Surrey

The majority of appearances the Beatles made on the British cinema/theatre circuit were arranged by promoter Arthur Howes. However, there were a series of gigs at such venues arranged by other promoters.

Their appearance here on Friday, 21 June 1963, was presented by John Smith. Vic Sutcliffe was once again the compere, but after the Beatles were billed as headliners, the rest of the acts were listed under the slogan: 'The Jimmy Crawford Package Show' which comprised Lance Fortune, Jimmy Crawford, the Hayseeds, the Vampires, Rocking Henri, the Messengers and the Vikings with Michael London.

Odeon, Queen Caroline Street, Hammersmith, London W6

Setting for the second of the Beatles' seasonal theatre specials, called 'Another Beatles Christmas Show'. Once again devised and produced by Peter Yolland it opened on 24 December 1964 and presented two shows a night for twenty nights, with the exception of 24 and 29 December when there was only a single show. Proceeds for the 29 December appearance were in aid of the Brady Clubs and Settlement Charity.

The show opened with compere Jimmy Savile announcing the Mike Cotton Sound, who performed 'Yeh Yeh', a recent hit for Georgie Fame. They were then fronted by Brian Epstein's new discovery, singer Michael Haslam, who performed 'Scarlet Ribbons'. The next act to appear was the Yardbirds.

The co-compere Ray Fell, a Liverpool comic, appeared and told of four Arctic explorers in search of the Abominable Snowman. The Beatles, dressed in costumes suited to Arctic weather, then appeared in a humorous sketch. They were followed by Freddie & The Dreamers who performed 'Rip It Up', 'Bachelor Boy' and 'Cut Across Shorty'.

The second half of the show was opened by Elkie Brooks, Sounds Incorporated and Ray Fell. Then Jimmy Savile reappeared to introduce the Beatles, who were dressed in midnight blue mohair shirts. They performed 'Twist and Shout', 'I'm A Loser', 'Baby's In Black', 'Everybody's Trying to Be My Baby', 'Can't Buy Me Love', 'Honey Don't' (a vocal for Ringo), 'I Feel Fine', 'She's A Woman', 'A Hard Day's Night', 'Rock 'n' Roll Music' and 'Long Tall Sally'.

They next appeared at the venue on 10 December 1964 during their final British tour. The numbers they performed were 'I Feel Fine', 'She's A Woman', 'If I Needed Someone', 'Act Naturally', 'Nowhere Man', 'Baby's In Black', 'Help!', 'We Can Work It Out', 'Yesterday', 'Day Tripper' and 'I'm Down'.

While at the Odeon the boys were visited by Canadian DJ Dave Boxer of C.F.C.F. Radio who'd flown specially from Montreal with a petition from thousands of fans requesting that they visit the city on their next tour.

Odeon, The Headrow, Leeds, Yorkshire

The Beatles appeared at this venue twice in 1963. Initially on 5 June on their second tour, with Roy Orbison and Gerry & The Pacemakers, and on 3 November as bill toppers with Peter Jay & the Jaywalkers and the Brook Brothers in support. Part of this last performance was recorded, and part of the recording was used by the Performing Rights Society in a court case.

The group returned to the Odeon on 22 October 1964 heading a bill which also included Mary Wells, Tommy Quickly, the Remo Four, Michael Haslam, the Rustiks and Bob Bain.

Odeon, Loampit Vale, Lewisham, London SE13

The Beatles made their debut at this London venue on Friday, 29 March 1963 as part of the Tommy Roe/Chris Montez Tour. Their second and final appearance at the cinema took place on Sunday, 8 December 1963.

Odeon, London Road, Liverpool L3

The Beatles only made a single appearance at this major cinema venue in their home town of Liverpool. The occasion was on one of their busiest days since their touring career began. It took place on 7 December 1963. Earlier in the day the group appeared at the Empire Theatre, only 50 yards away, where they performed before members of their fan club and filmed two BBC shows, 'Juke Box Jury' and 'It's The Beatles'. They then rushed down a heavily policed side street to the Odeon for their concert, which had been specially added to their tour.

The Odeon was also the venue for the northern premiere of their film *A Hard Day's Night* on Friday, 10 July 1964. It was the day of their famous Civic Reception and after the group had left Liverpool Town Hall their car, which had a police motor cycle escort, was halted four times due to the massive crowds in the city centre. The group eventually managed to slip into the cinema by a side door in a side street.

The proceedings were opened by the Liverpool City Police Band who played 'Z Cars', the theme tune for a TV drama series about Merseyside police, followed by a Beatles medley. When the curtain opened, disc jockey David Jacobs introduced several personalities from the film, including Norman Rossington and Lionel Blair. There were also a number of star names in the audience, including Alma Cogan and Tommy Steele. When the Beatles returned there was an immense reception.

George walked forward and said 'Hello' to his parents and relatives and John wondered where all his relatives had got to. 'What happened to them at the Town Hall, I didn't get a chance to see them?' he said. Paul thanked everyone for the marvellous reception and Ringo mentioned that people had said they were finished with as far as the Liverpool people were concerned – 'But we proved them wrong, didn't we kids,' he said.

The film was then screened, applauded after each song.

In 1984, the Odeon was the site for the northern premieres of Paul's feature film *Give My Regards To Broad Street* on 28 November. That day Paul was presented with the Freedom of the City at a special ceremony.

Odeon, Llandudno, Caernarvonshire, Wales

The group was booked to appear for a week, heading a bill which also featured Billy J. Kramer and Tommy Quickly.

The short six-day season commenced on Monday, 12 August 1963 and finished on Saturday, 17 August.

Odeon, Dunstable Road, Luton, Bedfordshire

The Beatles only appeared at this venue once, on Friday, 6 September 1963.

Odeon, Oxford Street, Manchester

The Beatles only appeared at this venue once, on 30 May 1963. The appearance was during their tour with Roy Orbison and Gerry & the Pacemakers and their repertoire comprised: 'Some Other Guy', 'Do You Want To Know A Secret?', 'Love Me Do', 'From Me To You', 'Please Please Me', 'I Saw Her Standing There' and 'Twist And Shout'.

Interestingly enough, it was the show at which Derek Taylor first reviewed a Beatles performance. Derek was to loom large in their lives, becoming personal assistant to Brian Epstein, Beatles press officer and, later, press officer for their Apple empire.

At the time of the Odeon concert he was a columnist with the Northern edition of the *Daily Express*, penning his own 'Taylor On Saturday' column, but also interviewing show business personalities.

There were no press tickets available for this particular show, but Derek phoned the cinema manager, Mr Bint, and bought two front stall tickets for the first house at one pound each. Accompanied by his wife Joan he watched the show, then retired to a nearby public house where he met the *Daily Express* photographer Bill Gregory who had been unable to get shots of the Beatles, but had taken photographs of Gerry & the Pacemakers.

Derek's review appeared in 'The Critics' section of the Northern edition of the *Daily Express* the next morning. He described the concert '. . . as beneficial and invigorating as a week on a beach at the pierhead overlooking the Mersey'. He also wrote: 'I suppose there is not-yet-a-first-class musician among them. Last night's audience of screamers gave the ear little chance of picking up two consecutive notes.' Of their performance, he commented: Their stage manner has little polish but limitless energy, and they have in abundance the fundamental rough good humour of their native city', and he signed off with the words: 'It was marvellous, meaningless, impertinent, exhilarating stuff.'

Odeon, Angel Row, Nottingham

The Beatles debuted at this cinema on Thursday, 23 May 1963 as part of the Roy Orbison Tour. They were headliners when they next appeared on Thursday, 12 December 1963 and their final appearance took place on Thursday, 5 November 1964.

Odeon, South Street, Romford, Essex

The Beatles only ever made one appearance at this Essex cinema on Sunday, 16 June 1963. It was one of a handful of gigs promoted by John Smith, although billed as part of the 'Mersey Beat Showcase' series of concerts. Supporting the Beatles were Gerry & the Pacemakers, Billy J. Kramer & the Dakotas and the Vikings with Michael London.

The occasion was quite unique considering that the three Mersey bands that week occupied the top three positions in the British charts. The Beatles with 'From Me To You', Gerry with 'I Like It' and Billy J. Kramer with 'Do You Want to Know A Secret'.

The compare was Vic Sutcliffe.

The programme blurb on the Vikings read: 'The average age of the group is 21, lead guitar being the baby at 20. The group as such have been together for about a year and are well known for their efficient support to several prominent recording stars. "The Vikings Show Combo", who feature clavioline, already have their latest attack on the charts "in the can", titled "Valhalla" which is shortly to be released; they are appearing in Jersey in early August.'

The piece on Michael London read, 'Michael is a coloured, very good looking boy, he is 23 years of age, and has many records to his credit, including "Stranger On The Shore". He was born in Trinidad where he is at the top of the Hit Parade.'

The programme was a well-designed souvenir and included several photographs of the Beatles, together with articles on each of the acts appearing and a back page blurb proclaiming: 'Goodnight folks! Hope you enjoyed the show. Thanks for coming.'

When the Beatles arrived for their two shows there were over 2,000 teenagers outside the cinema and hundreds of girls surrounded their car, trying to wrench open the doors. The car's radio aerial was ripped from its fixing and the doors and bonnet were badly dented.

Several girls climbed on the roof and the driver reversed the car through the crowd and sought refuge in Romford police station. The Beatles were then taken to the rear entrance of the Odeon in a van.

Six girls were selected to go backstage and meet the group and included the local Carnival Queen, eighteen-year-old Maureen Cox. The local paper, the *Romford Recorder*, reported, 'During the two performances, girls pelted the stage with cards and gifts for Beatle Paul MacKenzie [sic] who was 21 last week.'

After the show, while Gerry & the Pacemakers and Billy J. Kramer struggled into the van at the stage door, the Beatles ran to the front of the cinema and into a waiting taxi. The crowd surged forth, traffic jammed and a policeman was hit on the head and struck in the eye by pennies.

The Beatles finally got away by taxi and switched to their own cars at the nearby Parkside Hotel.

Although Epstein had originally planned five more 'Mersey Beat Showcase' productions for the rest of June he cancelled them.

Odeon, High Street, Southend-on-Sea, Essex

The Beatles made their debut at this 2,100-seater venue on 31 May 1963 during their tour with Roy Orbison.

Their second and final appearance there took place on Monday, 9 December 1963. Five hundred fans had queued all night before the box office opened (some had camped outside in sleeping bags for as long as 36 hours) and the tickets were all sold out within a single day. The show was simply called *The Beatles Show* and the group arrived at the Odeon at 2.30 p.m. Since they were unable to leave the theatre during the day, Neil Aspinall organised food deliveries, mainly chicken for John, Paul and George while Ringo opted for fish and chips. There was also a selection of Chinese foods.

The first half of the show comprised sets from Peter Jay & the Jaywalkers and the Brook Brothers. When the Beatles appeared they performed a one-hour show, playing sixteen numbers, including 'Love Me Do', 'Roll Over Beethoven', 'Please Please Me', 'From Me To You' and 'She Loves You'. After 'I Want To Hold Your Hand' they left the stage, then returned for an encore during which they played a blistering version of 'Twist And Shout'.

Odeon, Lord Street, Southport, Lancashire

A venue in the main street of the nearby holiday resort to Liverpool. The Beatles first appeared at the Odeon on 1 March 1963 as part of the Helen Shapiro Tour. They next appeared for a week-long series of twice-nightly performances for five nights from Monday, 26–Friday, 30 August 1963. Their repertoire during the week comprised 'Roll Over Beethoven', 'Thank You Girl', 'Chains', 'A Taste Of Honey', 'She Loves You', 'Baby It's You', 'From Me To You', 'Boys', 'I Saw Her Standing There' and 'Twist And Shout'. Their performance of 'She Loves You' and 'Twist And Shout' was filmed for the BBC TV documentary 'The Mersey Sound'. Also on the bill were Gerry & the Pacemakers, the Fourmost, Billy Baxter, Tommy Quickly, Tommy Walls and Beryl, Gary And Lee and The Sons Of The Piltdown Men.

Odeon, The Centre, Weston-super-Mare, Somerset

The Beatles appeared at this seaside resort venue once, for a run of six nights from Monday, 22–Saturday, 27 July 1963. Generally, seaside resorts could present weekly bills rather than the usual one-nighters for package tours because of the large influx of holiday-makers who, being on holiday, sought entertainment every night, resulting in a higher proportion of people attending theatrical shows than in the provincial cities.

During their appearance at the Odeon, photographer Dezo Hoffmann arranged an afternoon session with the group on the beach at Weston-super-Mare. He brought along colourfully striped Victorian swimming costumes and straw boaters for the Beatles to wear. The session was originally undertaken as an assignment for the Souvenir Press book *Meet The Beatles* which was to retail for two shillings and sixpence.

Dezo commented: 'This session was for the American market, which as yet I hadn't been able to penetrate because the Americans didn't want to know about English pop groups. I knew I needed something strong, and since they were on a seaside tour, I had the idea of hiring bathing huts and old-fashioned costumes. They loved dressing up in silly costumes. John kept his on back at the hotel long after the session was over.'

Dezo had also brought along his cine-camera and fifteen minutes of film was taken of the Beatles larking about on the beach, playing leap-frog, go-karting on a track in the sand hills and taking donkey rides. The footage was in black and white and without sound. Many years later, on Friday, 3 December 1982, on Channel 4's pop show 'The Tube', ten minutes of Dezo's home movie was screened for the first time.

O'Donnell, Lucy

A girl who was in the same class as Julian Lennon at Heath House infants' school in Weybridge in 1967 and indirectly proved to be the inspiration for the creation of John Lennon's classic *Sgt Pepper* track 'Lucy In The Sky With Diamonds'.

Julian drew a picture of Lucy, whom he used to invite to his birthday parties, and showed it to his parents. John asked him what the painting was supposed to represent and Julian answered, 'It's Lucy In The Sky With Diamonds'. John was struck by the title and wrote the song, but for many years people wouldn't believe the story as they were convinced it was a song about drugs because the initials of the song, L.S.D., were the same initials as those of the hallucinogenic drug which John had admitted taking.

Lucy was the daughter of a journalist and later became a nursery nurse.

Oh Darling

Track from the *Abbey Road* album, penned by Paul. The Beatles originally began the recording of this track at the Apple Studios in Savile Row on 27 January 1969. Then Paul recorded the vocals by himself at Abbey Road's No. 3 studio over 17, 18, 22 and 23 July. He commented: 'When we were recording this track I came into the studios early every day for a week to sing it by myself because at first my voice was too clear. I wanted it to sound as though I'd been performing it on stage all week.'

Robin Gibb of the Bee Gees sang the song in the film version of *Sgt Pepper's Lonely Hearts Club Band* and his single of the number reached No. 24 in the American charts in 1978. A version of the number was included on the Beatles' *Anthology 3* CDs.

Old Brown Shoe

A George Harrison composition which he originally recorded by himself at Abbey Road on Tuesday, 25 February. It was George's 26th birthday and he treated himself to a session in the studios. Aided by engineer Ken Scott, George made demos of three of his numbers, including 'Old Brown Shoe'.

The number was recorded by the Beatles on Wednesday, 16 April, and Friday, 18 April 1969, and it was issued as the flipside of 'The Ballad Of John And Yoko'. It was also included on the compilation albums *The Beatles 1967–1970* and *Hey Jude*. A version was included on the Beatles' *Anthology 3* CDs and the number was also featured on the CD compilation *Past Masters Volume Two*.

Oldham, Andrew Loog

The illegitimate war child of a wealthy English woman and a Dutch-American bomber pilot who was killed before his birth, Andrew Loog Oldham adopted both his parents' names. In 1962, at the age of seventeen, he was working as a runner for Mary Quant. By the end of the year he was acting as a press agent for Mark Wynter and had formed a partnership in a PR firm with Tony Calder, setting up offices in Maddox Street.

Epstein had hired Tony Barrow to write a press release for 'Love Me Do', but, as Barrow was still working for Decca, he didn't have the facilities to post the releases to the relevant disc jockeys and publications, or set up the interviews. As Calder was a former colleague at Decca he contacted him and ended up taking Oldham to lunch at the Aeolian Hall. A deal was struck and Oldham and

Calder were involved in the promotion of the Beatles' debut record 'Love Me Do'.

Brian Epstein first met Oldham during the Beatles' recording for 'Thank Your Lucky Stars' on 13 January 1963. Oldham was present with Wynter and he began to advise Brian on how he should present the Beatles' image to the press. Brian was impressed and offered Oldham the job as full-time Beatles press officer, but he turned it down.

In April 1963, on a tip from journalist Peter Jones of *Record Mirror*, Oldham went to see a new band called the Rollin' Stones. He then contacted agent Eric Easton, who agreed to co-manage the group with him and provide the financial back-up to launch them. Oldham added a 'g' to Rollin'.

In the 1970s, in an interview in the *New Musical Express,* he recalled attending an early Beatles concert: 'I sat there with a lump in my throat. In one night you knew they were going to be very big. It was just an instinctive thing. From that night on, it registered subconsciously that when they made it, another section of the public was going to want the opposite.'

As a result he created an aggressive 'bad boy' image for the Rolling Stones – something which peeved John Lennon, who always claimed that the Stones had stolen the Beatles' original image.

Oldham also came up with the line: 'Would you let your daughter marry a Rolling Stone?'

In London early in the afternoon of 10 September 1963, when John Lennon and Paul McCartney were returning from a Variety Club luncheon at the Savoy Hotel to their flat in Green Street, they spotted Oldham and invited him into their cab. He then talked them into attending a Stones rehearsal at Studio 51 in Great Newport Street, where the two Beatles finished a number 'I Wanna Be Your Man', which gave the Stones a No. 2 hit and launched them into the major league.

Oldham and Epstein always remained on friendly terms and the two of them agreed that they would ensure that the release dates of the Beatles' and Rolling Stones' records didn't conflict.

Oldham was also one of the guests interviewed by Epstein for the 'Hullabaloo' show, an American NBC television series which Epstein recorded in London on 19 December 1964.

Oldham formed a company, Forward Look, with Lionel Bart to produce records and new talent, and their first release was 'As Tears Go By' by Marianne Faithfull. In 1967, Allen Klein supplanted Oldham as the Stones' manager. Oldham then went on to form Immediate Records with Tony Calder.

He's been a resident of Bogota, Colombia, since 1982, from where he manages top Argentinian band Ratones Paranoiacos (the Paranoid Mice), and in 1995 teamed up with Tony Calder and journalist Colin Irwin to write the book *Abba – The Name of the Game*.

Oliver, Jack

A young Londoner who joined Apple as assistant to Terry Doran of Apple Music. When the company moved to Savile Row, he was one of seven people who shared space in the Press Office. A few months later he moved to the Record Department on the first floor. When Allen Klein entered the picture and it was obvious that he was manoeuvring to oust Ron Kass, Oliver said he'd leave if Kass was sacked. When Kass did get the sack, to the surprise of almost everyone, Oliver was made head of Apple Records in his place, jumping from relative obscurity to the head of the Beatles' record label within twelve months.

Olympia Stadium, Grand River Avenue and McGraw Avenue, Detroit, Michigan

The Beatles first appeared at this venue, an indoor arena, on Sunday, 6 September 1964. There was the usual press conference, once again attended by various beauty queens, including Miss Michigan 1960, Miss Armed Forces and Miss Vermont. There were two shows at the venue that evening and a number of fans had been thrown out for hurling jellybeans at the group. At the press conference earlier, one question put to Paul was, 'Do you think girls should be thrown out of the show for throwing jelly beans?' Paul replied, 'No. It has become a bit of a trademark with our shows, but we'd prefer they throw nothing at all.'

The next time the group appeared at the stadium was on Saturday, 13 August 1966, on their final tour, during which they were escorted to the stadium by six motorcycle cops. 14,000 fans watched the 2 p.m. concert and 16,800 attended the 7 p.m. performance.

Olympia Theatre, Boulevard des Capucines, Paris, France

The Beatles were booked to appear at Paris' famous Olympia Theatre for three weeks from Thursday, 16 January 1964 until Tuesday, 4 February. Some reports claimed that they were only being paid £50 per performance. There were ten acts on the bill and it was never quite clear who was the actual bill-topper: the Beatles, Trini Lopez or Sylvie Vartan.

The group appeared at the Olympia for twenty days, with two, sometimes three, performances a day. Their repertoire for the theatre was: 'From Me To You', 'Roll Over Beethoven', 'She Loves You', 'This Boy', 'I Want to Hold Your Hand', 'Boys', 'Twist And Shout' and 'Long Tall Sally'.

France was a completely different market from Britain, particularly as far as musical tastes were concerned. In addition, they didn't release singles, but only issued albums and EPs – until 1967. Therefore, the Beatles had only had EPs issued by Odeon Records in France.

During the afternoon of Thursday, 16 January the Beatles performed before an audience of students. The evening performance seemed to draw from French society and the audience was dressed in tuxedos and evening gowns. Celebrities attending included Johnny Hallyday, Francoise Hardy, Petula Clark and Richard Anthony. It was one of their toughest audiences and the Beatles didn't seem to appeal to the French as much as they did to audiences in the rest of the world. During the show their amplification broke down on three different occasions and George voiced his opinion on stage that photographers had sabotaged the equipment.

Trini Lopez, who closed the first half of the show, had charmed the audience by speaking to them in French. The Beatles couldn't speak the language and made little attempt to do so. However, at one point John said 'Je me lève á sept heures' which caused one woman in the front row to cry out, 'How barbaric!' When the Beatles left the theatre there were two dozen police at the stage door, helping to hold back the mass of photographers.

After their cool reception the group returned to the George V Hotel. Years later, George Harrison was to comment: 'The audience at the Olympia was nothing like any audience we'd had before. They were much older people wearing tuxedos, as though they'd come to see a film premiere or watch a ballet. We were disappointed that there weren't any of the nice French girls we'd heard so much about. They were all kept at home in those days, because of the strict Catholicism in France.'

The French critics were harsh in their reviews and Victor Mulchrome, writing in the *Daily Mail*, commented: 'Beatlemania is still, like Britain's entry into the Common Market, a problem the French prefer to put off for a while.' The French newspaper *France Soir* referred to the Beatles as 'delinquents' and 'has-beens'.

On Sunday, 19 January, ORTF Radio recorded their show and on Wednesday, 22 January an ORTF TV camera crew filmed their performance.

Olympic Sound Studios, 117 Church Road, Barnes, London SW13

The studio manager at the time was Keith Grant and he actively sought to have the Beatles record at the independent studio where the Rolling Stones were now recording regularly. The Beatles booked Studio One at Olympic and recorded 'Baby You're A Rich Man' there on Thursday, 11 May 1967. It was the first Beatles number to be fully recorded and mixed outside of EMI's Abbey Road Studios.

The Beatles also recorded an early version of 'All You Need Is Love' at Olympic on Wednesday, 14 June 1967.

When the Beatles handed Glyn Johns the tapes of their 'Get Back' sessions and asked him to put the album together, he booked his favourite recording studios – Olympic Sound. Glyn began work on the album at Olympic on 10, 11 and 13 March and on 7 April 1969. He returned to Olympic with Steve Vaughan as his assistant on 5, 6, 7, 9 and 10 May when he completed his engineering of the tapes.

O'Mahony, Sean

The publisher of the Beatles Book Monthly. Sean worked on a magazine called *Pop Weekly* at the beginning of the sixties, but was a songwriter at heart, although his work had been rejected by A&R men such as George Martin and Dick James. He first contacted Brian Epstein to request an advertisement for 'Love Me Do' for *Pop Weekly*. He later left the magazine to launch his own *Beat Monthly* and contacted Epstein to arrange a feature on the Beatles. In January 1963 Sean read that 500 fans had been turned away from a Beatles show. Intrigued, he phoned Epstein and arranged to meet him at the Westbury Hotel, London, where he proposed a magazine devoted entirely to the Beatles. Brian said he'd discuss it with 'the boys'. The Beatles wanted to meet Sean to discuss his ideas and he met up with them when they were broadcasting a BBC radio show 'Pop Go The Beatles' on 1 June 1963. Later, Brian phoned him to tell him the deal was on. Epstein requested 50 per cent of the profits for the Beatles and it was eventually agreed that they would receive 33⅓ per cent.

80,000 copies of the first issue were printed and, at its height, the *Beatles Monthly* sold 350,000 copies per issue. The magazine continued for 77 issues over a six-and-a-half-year period and with issue 77, dated December 1969, Sean decided to cease publication. In a lengthy editorial entitled 'The End Of An Era', he put forward several reasons for his decision: the difficulty in obtaining photographs and gaining access to the Beatles; the fact that they were all approaching their thirties; their reluctance to maintain their group association; and preference for being interviewed or photographed individually.

The magazine's official photographer was Leslie Bryce who was afforded an access to the group denied other photographers with the result that he took literally thousands of photographs of them. There were cartoons and sketches contributed by artist Bob Gibson and a small core of regular feature writers.

The magazine was edited by 'Johnny Dean', a pseudonym that O'Mahony used. The Beatles' press officer Tony Barrow was also a regular contributor, although he used the alias Frederick James, and Peter Jones, then editor of *Record Mirror*, contributed items under the name Billy Shepherd. From the Beatles' own camp there were regular reports and occasional columns from Neil Aspinall and Mal Evans and photographs from Tony Bramwell.

During the next six years, O'Mahony received a considerable volume of mail from Beatle fans seeking back issues; he noted that copies of *Beatles Monthly* were selling at outrageous prices to collectors, and decided to reprint the entire run of issues. The publication was relaunched in May 1975 under the title the *Beatles Appreciation Society Magazine Book*. George Harrison objected to this and unsuccessfully attempted to prevent publication. The entire rerun of issues continued until September 1982. By that time, interest in the Beatles was still growing and O'Mahony decided to begin a new series of magazines using entirely new material. He had presented 1,000 photographs in the original 77-issue run, but still had over 4,000 photographs in his files. His new series, entitled the *Beatles Monthly Book*, was launched in October 1982.

Beatles Monthly used various editors during the reruns and new issues, including Lorna Read and Peter Doggett. Many of its regular writers such as Tony Barrow, Mark Lewisohn and Bill Harry continued to contribute to the new series.

O'Mahony was able to build a list of thriving magazines in his Beat Publications company, which included *Record Collector* and *Book Collector*.

One After 909, The

One of the very earliest of John Lennon's compositions, which he first performed with the Quarry Men in the late fifties. It was also included as part of the Beatles' stage repertoire until late in 1962.

Incredibly, it was not released as a Beatles number until 1970 when it was included as a track on the *Let It Be* album. The song had first been recorded on Tuesday, 5 March 1963, but was finally included on an album after the Beatles performed the number on the rooftop session on the Apple building.

The number 9 figured quite prominently in John's life and he used it more than once in his songs.

One And One Is Two

A song originally penned by Paul and John when they were staying at the George V Hotel in Paris in January 1964. It was written under pressure as they had to get a tape to London quickly as the number was due to be recorded by Billy J. Kramer. John Lennon wasn't too pleased with the number and commented: 'Billy J's career is finished when he gets this song.' Kramer didn't like it and insisted he record an American number he'd discovered himself called 'Little Children'. 'Little Children' gave Billy J. another No. 1 hit in Britain and his first Top Ten in the US. A British group, the Strangers with Mike Shannon, recorded 'One And One Is Two' and the single was issued by Philips on BF 1355 on 8 May 1964, but it failed to chart.

Only A Northern Song

A George Harrison composition, used in *Yellow Submarine*. Brian Epstein had promised the producers of the film four new titles. Some of them were tracks left over from the *Sgt Pepper* sessions, such as Paul McCartney's 'All Together Now' and George Harrison's 'It's All Too Much' (which was cut for the *Yellow Submarine* soundtrack because of its length). There was John's 'Hey Bulldog' which producer Al Brodax didn't like and left out of the American prints of the film. The final number was 'Only A Northern Song'.

This number was also originally planned for the *Sgt Pepper* album when recording first began on Monday, 13 February 1967. As usual, George hadn't come up with a title, so it was tentatively called 'Not Known'. When it was decided to leave the number off the *Sgt Pepper* album, George replaced it with 'Within You, Without You'.

The group continued recording the number, now known as 'Only A Northern Song', on Thursday, 20 April 1967, and it was eventually issued on the *Yellow Submarine* album on Friday, 17 January 1969. Another inaccurate story became part of Beatle lore. It was said the Beatles were at Abbey Road Studios one night and *Yellow Submarine* producer Al Brodax said they were still short of one number for the soundtrack. George asked everyone to wait and went into a room for an hour, returning with the number saying, 'Here, Al, it's only a northern song.' Embellishments on the story even have the London Symphony Orchestra waiting while George wrote the number.

Commenting on the song, George said, 'It was a joke relating to Liverpool, the Holy City in the North. The copyright belonged to Northern Songs Limited, which I didn't own, so "It doesn't really matter what chords I play, what words I say, or time of day it is, as it's only a northern song".' It was more of a comment about the Beatles song publishing company Northern Songs, which was mainly controlled by Dick James, whose percentage was more than those of John and Paul put together – George only received a nominal amount from the company, while at one time he was regarded as just a contract songwriter.

A version was included on the Beatles' *Anthology 2* CDs.

Ono, Yoko

Yoko, whose name means 'Ocean Child', was born in Tokyo, Japan, at 8.30 p.m. on 18 February 1933. Her parents were Eisuke Ono and his wife Isako, both of whose families were prominent in the Japanese banking world. Yoko's brother Keisuke was born in December 1936 and her sister Setsuko in December 1941.

When Yoko was two and a half years old she was taken to America where her father had been placed in a prominent position in a bank. Isoko returned to her home country with her children when Japan invaded China, fearing the backlash of anti-Japanese feeling in America. She returned to San Francisco with her children for a short time and Yoko attended school there. The family then had to return to Tokyo in 1943 due to the impending war.

As her family were rich and influential, Yoko didn't suffer the hardships of many of the Japanese people during the war; she continued with her education, becoming fluent in English. After the war the family returned to America, settling in the high-class Scarsdale area outside New York where Yoko attended the Sarah Lawrence School in 1953.

The 19-year-old girl didn't like the school and left in her third year to live in Manhattan with a young Japanese composer and musician, Toshi Ichiyanagi, whom she married against the wishes of her parents. They lived for a few years in Greenwich Village, but Yoko was reportedly unfaithful and they were divorced after six years, although Yoko gave signs of the strength of character and leadership evident in her later life. She encouraged Toshi in his musical career and talked him into returning to Japan where he received a degree of acclaim. The couple were divorced in 1963.

Yoko continued living in Chambers Street in New York, becoming part of an artistic sect called Fluxus, composed of painters, musicians and writers. She began to hold concerts and art exhibitions of her own, gaining a reputation as a creative conceptual artist. She married a film producer, Tony Cox, and the two had a daughter whom they named Kyoko.

In September 1966 the family moved to London to further Yoko's career, after accepting an invitation to attend a symposium called 'The Destruction of Art'. Even at this time it was very much a case of Yoko being the strong partner, advancing her career while her husband looked after the child.

Yoko began to involve herself in 'happenings' in London and gained attention when she appealed for volunteers to help her wrap up one of the stone lions in Trafalgar Square. She called this 'happening', 'Trafalgar Square Wrapping Event'. She also gained notoriety in the media for her film *Bottoms*, which featured the bare backsides of a number of 'Swinging London' personalities; and a 'happening' called 'Snip Piece' in which members of the audience cut off all her clothes with a pair of scissors. She had also, by this time, had a small book of conceptual ideas called *Grapefruit* published in a limited edition in Japan and America.

It was during the preview of her exhibition at the Indica Gallery on 9 November 1966 that the famous meeting with John Lennon took place. Yoko claimed she was relatively unaware of the phenomenon which the Beatles had become and said she was initially unimpressed when the gallery's co-owner John Dunbar urged her to speak to the 'millionaire'. The much reported incident of hammering in the imaginary nail took place and each realised that they had found a kindred spirit. In September 1967 John was to sponsor her *Half-Wind Show*, which was subtitled *Yoko Plus Me*.

Yoko began to pursue John with tenacity, writing him endless notes, following him around, and he began to take great interest in her conceptual ideas, keeping a copy of her book *Grapefruit* by his bedside, which he would regularly refer to.

It was in May 1968 when Tony Cox and Kyoko were in France and Cynthia was on holiday that Yoko arrived on John's doorstep at Kenwood in Weybridge. He suggested that they go upstairs to his studio and make some experimental tapes – the ones which were to eventually be issued as *Two Virgins*. Yoko reported, 'It was midnight when we started and it was dawn when we finished and then we made love.'

John's wife Cynthia arrived home, in company with Alexis Mardas and Jennie Boyd, to find Yoko ensconced in her home wearing a dressing-gown. It was obvious what had occurred. Cynthia left.

There was a brief attempt at a reconciliation, but it didn't work out and Cynthia was later to begin divorce proceedings.

Yoko began involving John in her conceptual creations, beginning with her acorn sculpture event at Coventry Cathedral in June 1968. The two made their involvement even more public when they attended the play *In His Own Write* on 18 June 1968. The couple were to move into Ringo's Montague Square flat together.

The British press took an immediate dislike to Yoko, and thus began the snide and hurtful comments which were to continue over the succeeding months and years and which were counted among the reasons which clinched the couple's decision to live in New York.

In July 1968, John held an exhibition called *You Are Here – To Yoko From John, With Love*. Yoko was pregnant at the time and when she was admitted to Queen Charlotte's Hospital later that month, John took to sleeping on the floor next to her bed. Unfortunately, she had a miscarriage – and was to have two more before she bore John a child. Before the year's end the couple had issued their *Two Virgins* album, telerecorded the Rolling Stones' *Rock & Roll Circus* and appeared at the Royal Albert Hall in the *Alchemical Wedding*. The two were to continue to work jointly in the creative and business fields, making records and films together, forming companies such as Bag One and Lenono, with Yoko appearing on the flipside of John's singles, on his albums and also recording five albums in her own right.

In 1969 John and Yoko continued to dominate the headlines, appearing on stage during a jazz concert in Cambridge and getting married in Gibraltar on 20 March – which they celebrated by holding their 'Bed-In For Peace' in Amsterdam. By May of that year John had officially changed his name to John Ono Lennon and the couple had moved into a large estate in Ascot called Tittenhurst Park. Following a trip to Montreal, the couple took John's son Julian and Kyoko on a visit to Scotland during which their car crashed. There were no serious injuries, although Yoko was later to attend Beatles sessions at Abbey Road resting in a double bed.

The vitriolic attacks in the media caused John a great deal of personal pain. He had made his choice, he loved Yoko and the two were inseparable. An attack on her was an attack on him. Why should outside people try to impose their preferences on him? He was aware that the other members of the Beatles did not like Yoko and this was more likely to have resulted in a breakdown between John and the other members of the group than Yoko's influence on John. He also resented the fact that certain people in Apple, whose security rested on the money he was putting into the company, also had an attitude towards her and talked about her behind her back.

It's also likely at the time that the British media couldn't come to terms with Yoko's independence, her determination to present her own ideas and to share them with John. Had a male been as 'pushy', no notice would have been taken. Yoko was perhaps ahead of her time in seeking equal rights with her man – and John was able to grasp this fact through reading books such as *The First Sex*. Although it may have seemed that, at times, Yoko was stifling John with her ideas – always at recording sessions, always wanting to take part in his stage appearances, wanting to write songs with him – at the same time she was stimulating him. John appreciated having his artistic horizons widened by someone else – just as had happened during his friendship with Stuart Sutcliffe.

But he could never understand why friends and foes alike all seemed to resent the woman he loved, and it was a constant source of frustration for him.

The Wedding Album, Live Peace In Toronto and 'The War Is Over' campaign occupied the remaining months of 1969, and in 1970, the year which the two christened 'Year One', they gained further notoriety when John's lithographs, some of them showing him in intimate sexual embrace with Yoko, were seized by the police. They also underwent Primal Therapy in America.

In 1971 Yoko and John appeared with Frank Zappa at the Fillmore East in New York, and began their efforts to obtain custody of Kyoko. It was during their search for Yoko's daughter that they decided to remain in America, settling in New York and beginning a battle for John to obtain his Green Card.

John was later to feel ashamed at the way they pursued Kyoko and her father. When Cox and Yoko had been divorced, Kyoko had remained with her father, but Yoko always had access to the child. It was then suggested that Yoko had a sudden desire to take custody of Kyoko following her miscarriage of John's child. Over the next few years, a battle for custody began initially when John and Yoko attempted to take Kyoko away from Majorca where she had been attending a nursery. They were prevented from spiriting her away from the island by the Spanish authorities. John and Yoko were accused of kidnapping and had to appear in court. The court officials took Kyoko aside and asked her if she would prefer to go with her father or her mother (shades of a five-year-old John's tug of war in Blackpool). She opted for her father. A legal battle began in earnest, with John calling in Allen Klein to help them, and the Lennons spent six months in courts in Texas, New York and the Virgin Isles. Despite the Lennons' wealth, Cox managed to flee with Kyoko to an unknown destination in America. John and Yoko had to admit defeat and were unable to trace them.

John and Yoko settled in the Dakota Building in New York, and over the next few years were involved in the making of various avant-garde films.

The major event in their lives was the birth of Sean Ono Lennon on 9 October 1975. Sean had been born following their reunion after eighteen months during which John had left Yoko to live with their secretary, May Pang, who had been hired when John had turned 33 years of age and was perhaps experiencing a restlessness or 'seven year itch'. It was said that Yoko had encouraged the relationship. John suddenly fled to Los Angeles with May and for the period described as his 'Long Weekend', she became his mistress. She continued to act as his secretary and helped to organise some of his West Coast recording projects. When John returned to Yoko, May resettled in New York where she became a professional manager of United Artists Music and she was later to marry a record producer Tony Visconti and write a book called *Loving John – The Untold Story*.

John decided to spend the next five years looking after Sean while Yoko attended to the couple's business affairs. While John reared Sean in their apartment in the Dakota Building, Yoko worked in the Lennon office on the ground floor of the building, turning their money into a vast fortune, reported to be in excess of a hundred million dollars – a figure which was to continue to increase over the years. She proved an astute businesswoman whose ventures included buying farms, real estate and breeding cattle.

This was a time when her own recording activities, in addition to those of John, were put on hold. Apart from her various recordings with John, she had become a recording artist in her own right, with her first solo album *Yoko Ono/Plastic Ono Band* issued in December 1970. This was followed the next year by her single 'Mrs Lennon', then another album in December, *Fly*. Her other recordings included the 1972 single 'Mind Train', the 1973 album *Approximately Infinite Universe*, followed the same year by two singles 'Death of Samantha' and 'Run Run Run' and another album *Feeling The Space*. She had no further releases for the rest of the decade.

In 1980, after the horror of John's murder, Yoko remained at the Dakota, having to employ bodyguards to look after Sean on a round-the-clock basis. She administered the huge funds which were donated on John's behalf to the Spirit Foundation, sending the money to various charities. She also began work on securing a memorial to John in Central Park, called 'Strawberry Fields'.

Yoko has done much to continue to perpetuate John's memory, participating in both television and feature films, recordings and radio shows and publishing posthumous books. In relation to the Beatles story she is still treated in a hostile way by writers who are probably prejudiced. Taking a different point of view, they could just as well concentrate on her considerable artistic ventures over the years, her courage and her incredible business acumen which has made her one of the richest women in America – and someone who has achieved success in what has undoubtedly been a man's world.

On The Scene

A BBC radio programme broadcast each Thursday from 5.00 p.m–5.30 p.m. Produced by Brian Willey, 'On The Scene' featured the Beatles performing 'Misery', 'Do You Want To Know A Secret?' and 'Please Please Me' on 28 March 1963. They'd recorded the programme on 21 March at the BBC studio in the Piccadilly Theatre, Denman Street. It was their only appearance on the show.

Ooh! My Soul

A number written and recorded by Little Richard. The Beatles included it in their repertoire in 1961 with Paul on lead vocals and featured the number on their 'Pop Go The Beatles' show on 27 August 1963. Their performance on 'Pop Go The Beatles' was included on *The Beatles Live At The BBC* CDs.

Open House

A BBC Radio 2 programme. Ringo appeared on the show on 31 March 1971 when he was interviewed by disc jockey Pete Murray.

Opera House, Church Street, Blackpool, Lancashire

A theatre in the main northern seaside resort. The Beatles only appeared twice at the Opera House, both occasions separated by only a few weeks. They made their debut at the theatre on 28 July 1964, immediately prior to their short tour of Sweden, and it was the site of their last British gig on 16 August 1964, prior to their American tour.

Orbison, Roy

Singer Roy Orbison was among several American artists who had been an early influence on the Beatles. In fact, the very first song the Beatles broadcast on BBC radio was 'Dream Baby', sung by Paul, which was broadcast on 'Teenager's Turn' on 8 March 1962, a month after the Orbison release.

John also claimed that it was Orbison's style which inspired him to write 'Please Please Me'.

Kennedy Street Enterprises booked Orbison to tour Britain from 18 May to 9 June 1963. They also booked the Beatles and Gerry & the Pacemakers as support acts. It was the Beatles' third tour within a relatively short time and they'd begun to build up such a large following that it was felt they warranted topping a concert bill in their own right.

Roy had enjoyed nine chart hits and was currently enjoying success with 'In Dreams'. He was to comment: 'When I arrived in London to tour England in 1963 I wore dark glasses because I'd lost my clear glasses.' Those dark glasses were soon to become something of a trademark.

Roy added: 'I arrived at a little theatre which had Beatles placards everywhere. There was very little of me. I'd had three years of hit records in Britain. I said, "What is a Beatle anyway?" and John Lennon tapped me on the shoulder and said, "I'm one." When he'd gone I asked them to take the placards down. I was earning three times their money. Then they approached me and said, "You're making the money, let us close the show."

'After their fourteenth or fifteenth encore, Paul and John grabbed me by the arm and said, "Yankee go home." They asked me how they could make it in the States and I told them: "Dress like you're doing, keep the hair, say you're British and get on a show like the Ed Sullivan Show." '

It was during this particular tour that the audience began pelting the Beatles with jelly babies for the first time as a result of a remark George had made in an interview.

The original billing for the tour had placed Roy's name above the Beatles, even though they actually closed the show. After one week, the billing was reversed. However, Roy continued to prove a major attraction. Reporting in a local paper on the tour's appearance at the Rialto Theatre, York, on 29 May, Stacey Brewer wrote: 'Roy Orbison got the biggest "hand" I've ever heard at the Rialto ... Don McCallion, manager of the Mecca-Casino, must have felt glad he had Roy booked for a return date in York – on September 18 ... Roy opened with "Only The Lonely" and, followed with a selection including "Cryin', Fallin' ", and, of course, his current chart entry, "In Dreams".'

Ringo Starr was to tell Beatles biographer Hunter Davies: 'It was terrible following him. He'd slay them and they'd scream for more. In Glasgow we were all backstage, listening to the tremendous applause he was getting. He was just standing there singing, not moving or anything. As it got near our turn, we would hide behind the curtain whispering to each other, "Guess who's next folks, it's your favourite rave." '

Roy became a good friend of the Beatles, although they were worried in June 1964 that they'd catch chicken pox from Roy's six-year-old son Roy Dewayne after Roy had brought the youngster to visit them – but they were given a clean bill of health by their doctor.

Roy underwent open heart surgery in 1979 but his career seemed to be given a new lease of life when he was invited by George to become part of the Traveling Wilburys and recorded a hit album with them. Two other Wilburys, Jeff Lynne and Tom Petty, produced a solo album by Roy, with George as guest – unfortunately, it was his last recording. Roy died of a heart attack in Nashville on 6 December 1988 at the age of 52.

Ormsby-Gore, Sir David

During the Beatles' first trip to Washington, Brian Epstein had arranged for them to attend an event at the British Embassy following their Washington Coliseum appearance.

Sir David Ormsby-Gore was the British ambassador at the time and the event was a formal staff dance to raise money for the National Association for the Prevention of Cruelty to Children. Ormsby-Gore had requested that the Beatles present the raffle prizes at the gala.

News of their appearance had circulated by word of mouth and a cordon of police had to circle the embassy. The Beatles, together with Brian, had a private meeting with Sir David and Lady Ormsby-Gore. Lady Ormsby-Gore then escorted them into the embassy rotunda, announcing: 'Attention! Beatles are now approaching the area.'

No one in their party was prepared for the behaviour from guests and staff, many of whom had had more than their fair share of punch that evening.

They were jostled and pushed around. There were condescending remarks such as 'those darling little baby boys' and one woman put her arm around Paul and asked: 'Which one are you?' 'Roger,' he told her. 'Roger what?' she asked. 'Roger McClusky the Fifth,' he said.

John Lennon was furious at the treatment and wanted to leave. When an embassy official told him, 'Come on, now, go do your stuff', he said, 'I'm getting out of here', but Ringo took hold of his arm and suggested that they get it over with.

When reports of the rude behaviour filtered out, the British press was incensed and Conservative MP Joan Quennell asked the Foreign Secretary, R. A. Butler, to look into the affair.

However, the real diplomat turned out to be Brian Epstein who, not wishing to make a fuss of the situation, sent a thank-you note to Lady Ormsby-Gore.

When his brother was killed in a car crash, Ormsby-Gore then inherited the title Lord Harlech. After his wife was killed in a car crash in 1967, there was talk that he would marry his close friend Jackie Kennedy. Instead, he married a New York journalist, Pamela Colin, who was eighteen years his junior.

In 1974, Lord Harlech's son Julian shot himself while suffering from depression. His daughter Alice fell in love with Eric Clapton and the two began to live together.

Lord Harlech was killed in a car crash in 1985. Death duties of more then £1 million caused severe financial hardships for the family. Eric Clapton left Alice and she was to become a drug addict and was found dead in a squalid bedsit in a rundown area of Bournemouth in April 1995. A needle was stuck in her arm. She was 43 years old.

Ornstein, George 'Bud'

The American head of United Artists in London in the early 1960s.

His wife Gwen was the niece of Mary Pickford, one of the co-founders of United Artists. One of his employees, Noel Rogers pointed out the appeal of the Beatles in Britain and Europe. Ornstein then discovered that the Beatles' contract with Capitol excluded film soundtracks and he calculated that if he could sign the group to a three-picture deal, this would enable United Artists to release three lucrative soundtrack albums. He hired producer Walter Shenson and they arranged a meeting with Epstein, intending to offer the Beatles 25 per cent of the film deal. Epstein pre-empted them by saying, 'I wouldn't consider anything under seven and a half per cent.' Fortunately, lawyer David Jacobs was able to finalise a deal in which the Beatles did receive 25 per cent, although it would have been more sensible for him to have asked for it to be gross rather than net.

On 18 December 1964, Ornstein quit United Artists to form Pickfair Films with Brian Epstein. They intended to produce Beatles films, beginning with a A Talent for Loving, but nothing came of it.

Ornstein's daughter Susan was to marry Neil Aspinall.

Orton, Joe

Controversial playwright, born John Kinsley 'Joe' Orton in Leicester. He was murdered at the age of 34 on 9 August 1967 by his lover Kenneth Halliwell at their bedsit in Noel Road, Islington. Halliwell then committed suicide.

Orton had written successful plays such as *Loot* and *Entertaining Mr Sloane.* Paul McCartney had been one of the 'angels' who backed the original stage production of *Loot,* donating £1,000.

In January 1966, producer Walter Shenson contacted Orton's agent Peggy Ramsay to say he had a script by Owen Holder called *Shades Of A Personality,* which he regarded as dull. He wondered if Orton could work on putting some life into it, in the hope that he could enliven it. However, Orton's ideas grew to such an extent that he ended up with a completely different concept and penned a screenplay called *Up Against It.*

He submitted a draft of his script to Brian Epstein and was invited to have dinner with Paul and Brian.

Of his meeting with Paul, Orton wrote: 'He was just as the photographs, only he'd grown a moustache. His hair was shorter, too. He was playing the latest Beatles record, "Penny Lane". I liked it very much. Then he played the other side – Strawberry something. I didn't like this as much.'

Brian Epstein gave him the go-ahead to continue, although his finished version of the screenplay didn't gain the approval of the Beatles.

Orton sent his script to Shenson and a month later it was returned. Orton was to comment: "No explanation why. No criticism of the script. And apparently, Brian Epstein had no comment to make, either. Fuck them.'

He rewrote the script and in April 1966 producer Oscar Lewenstein bought the rights to *Up Against It* for £10,000 plus 10 per cent of future production profits. Lewenstein had also approached Dick Lester to direct. Lester commented: 'We had a deal to prepare a version of that screenplay, but altered it so that instead of the Beatles, it would be Rolling Stone Mick Jagger and actor Ian McKellen plus two girls. In essence, the plan was now to turn it into a musical film.'

Orton was about to discuss the filming of it with Lewenstein and Lester when Halliwell battered him to death in his flat, before committing suicide himself.

Their bodies were found by Derek Taylor, a chauffeur sent to collect Orton for a meeting to discuss the screenplay at Twickenham Studios with Lewenstein and Lester.

The music chosen to be played at Orton's funeral was his favourite tune, the Beatles' 'A Day In The Life'.

A film company immediately bought Orton's screenplay, but all attempts at making it into a movie failed. After his death, several other writers attempted to work on it, but it remains unfilmed.

The script was published in book form in 1979 and it is fairly obvious why the Beatles turned it down. It is an anarchic comedy with sex, murder and politics in which the main characters end up killing a female British Prime Minister. Another minus was the fact that the part for Paul McCartney was so small in contrast to that of the other three.

The script was finally broadcast as a radio play on Radio 3 on 21 September 1997. A BBC spokesperson commented: 'The music and mood of sex, sin and revolution of the summer of 1967 is brought to life.' The play was adapted for radio by John Fletcher, who commented: 'As this is a Joe Orton play, I tried to be offensive to absolutely everyone, but if I left anyone out, I apologise.'

The cast included Leo McKern, who appeared with the Beatles in *Help!*, Sylvia Sims and Prunella Scales. Damon Albarn of Blur played George Harrison, Douglas Hodge portrayed John Lennon and Joe Fiennes played Ringo Starr.

Orton was portrayed by Gary Oldman in the film *Prick Up Your Ears*.

Osterreichischer Hof Hotel, Salzburg, Austria

Hotel at which the Beatles held their first Austrian press conference on 13 March 1965 during the filming of *Help!*

The group had landed at the Salzburg-Maxglahn Airport at 2.18 p.m. to be greeted by a large number of fans, with a small number wearing armbands stating 'Beatles Go Home'. They posed for a group of pressmen and then drove off to the Osterreichischer Hof Hotel, followed by the press corps, for the conference.

They then drove off to Obertauern, where they were filming, stopping on the way to eat lunch at a restaurant in the village of Werfen.

Our World

A spectacular television production that was transmitted live throughout the world by satellite on 25 June 1967 and lasted for six hours.

This unique event was the first time a worldwide satellite broadcast had been attempted and twenty-six different nations participated in the link-up which was to have the largest television audience ever, up to that time: 400,000,000 people.

The British contribution was a performance by the Beatles from the No. 1 studio at EMI's Abbey Road. After the group had accepted the invitation to appear, John and Paul wrote the song 'All You Need Is Love' specially for the occasion and it was screened 'live' in a party atmosphere, complete with streamers, balloons and placards proclaiming 'All You Need Is Love' in several languages.

The Beatles were backed by a thirteen-piece orchestra conducted by Mike Vickers which included Sidney Sax, Patrick Halling, Eric Bowie, Jack Holmes (violins); Rex Morris, Don Honeywell (tenor sax); Evan Watkins, Harry Spain, (trombones); Jack Emblow (accordion); and Stanley Woods, David Mason (trumpets).

The orchestra was dressed formally in evening suits while the Beatles and friends wore colourful flower-power gear. Among the friends sitting on the studio floor surrounding the group were Paul's brother Mike, Jane Asher, Pattie Harrison, Mick Jagger and Marianne Faithful, Eric Clapton, Keith Moon, Keith Richard, Graham Nash and his wife Rose and Gary Leeds of the Walker Brothers.

The group had recorded a backing track earlier, but they actually sang and played live when the show was broadcast and their song included excerpts from familiar tunes such as 'La Marseillaise', 'Greensleeves', 'In The Mood', and 'She Loves You'.

Overlanders, The
A British folk trio comprising Paul Arnold, Laurie Mason and Peter Bartholomew. Within a month of the release of the *Rubber Soul* album, the 'Michelle' track had been covered by twenty artists around the world. The most successful British cover was by the Overlanders who topped the charts with it for one week after it had been issued on Pye 7N 17034 on 13 January 1966. It entered the charts on 22 January and remained there for ten weeks. It was their only hit. The trio also featured the number on an album and an EP.

Owen, Alun Davies
Playwright, actor and director, born on 24 November 1925 in, according to some sources, Menai Bridge, North Wales, and according to others Liverpool. He certainly always regarded himself as a Liverpool Welshman and was to comment: 'Liverpool and Wales, they're the two things I really know, and yet I'm not completely at home in either place.'

Alun, son of Welsh-speaking parents whose father was a merchant seaman, was initially educated at Cardigan County High School prior to the family's move to Liverpool.

He married Mary O'Keefe at the age of sixteen in 1942, and the couple were to have two sons. His first stage play, *Progress to the Park,* was broadcast on the radio in 1958, and his first broadcast television play was *No Trams to Lime Street* in 1959. Other plays included *Ruffians* and *The Strain.*

Composer Lionel Bart contacted him to write a musical based on the Liverpool folksong 'Maggie May'. Alun told him: 'You've got to learn a whole new language. The Liverpool dialect, the real, pure Scouse is part-Irish, part-Welsh, part-catarrh.' He suggested Bart move to Liverpool to soak up the atmosphere.

It was during this time that Alun was approached to write the screenplay for *A Hard Day's Night,* apparently at the suggestion of Paul McCartney.

Brian Epstein wrote to Owen and then met him after the performance of one of his plays in Liverpool, telling him: 'Whatever you think, you must meet the boys. They're keen to see you – they admire your work.'

Owen met George Harrison in Liverpool's Blue Angel Club, but first got together with all four of them in October 1963 during the weekend following their 'Sunday Night at the London Palladium' appearance. He said: 'Getting to know them was remarkably easy. They are immediate people and I knew from that that it wouldn't be a colour film. The boys are essentially black and white people.' He travelled with them to Dublin and Belfast in November. He also joined them in Paris in January 1964, along with the film's producer, Walter Shenson.

He actually began writing the script in November 1963 and was virtually given a free hand. The only thing he was specifically asked to do was include a scene that would give them an opportunity to sparkle like they did at the press conference in New York in February 1964, so he introduced a press conference scene in a theatre lounge.

Alun was to say: 'I write by the minute not the page. I had a couple of false starts trying to write a fantasy film, but quickly realised that nothing could compare with their own fantastic lives. They are always on the move, usually from one box to another, hotels, cars, dressing rooms, but they know what they want. Where they are going.'

He also commented: 'In the film we see the boys in a world which has no future and no past and I've tried to incorporate into the script some of the fantastic and curious things which happen to the boys, the world they carry in them, by just being themselves. What I am doing is taking what I see in them and putting it down on paper. In fact, they emerge as four very different people.

'I want to give them things they want to do. They have a terrific joy in being alive and there is a great sense of fantasy in their humour. There is a conflict in the script and there is conflict in the way the boys send each other up. I'm sure the film will do very well in America. Americans will find the Liverpool accent easier to understand than, say, a Cockney one. Liverpool people hit their words when they talk. It's part of their aggressiveness.'

He was also to point out that because the dialogue was in short sentences and naturalistic, many people thought it was ad-libbed. It wasn't – he pointed out that the only member of the Beatles to ad-lib in the film was John Lennon.

Alun tried to ensure that all four received an equal share of the action, although it was Ringo's role that attracted the attention of the critics. Owen wrote individual scenes for each member, but the scene featuring Paul ended up on the cutting-room floor. Allegedly, Paul didn't carry it off and the scene proved too embarrassing to include in the finished print.

Alun was paid £1,200 for his screenplay. He was also nominated for an Oscar for his script and, since the critical reaction had been so enthusiastic, he believed that he'd have the opportunity of penning their second film. Unfortunately, this wasn't the case. Epstein told him that Richard Lester had already employed another scriptwriter for their next project, which may have been why Owen, perhaps ungenerously, commented: 'I don't get on very well with John, Ringo is fine, but not the greatest intellectual in the world. We had trouble with one scene with Paul . . . mind you, I like George very much.'

When Epstein heard that, he told Owen: 'What would you say if I told you that the one person who doesn't want you to work on this film is George Harrison?' Furious, Alun's wife Mary called him a liar.

Owen went on to complete *Maggie May*, which he set in contemporary times, featuring Mersey Beat music, and he booked a Liverpool group called the Nocturnes to appear in it.

The stars of the musical were Kenneth Haigh and Rachel Roberts. Interestingly enough, Haigh had appeared as an advertising executive in *A Hard Day's Night*. It was rumoured that he wanted his name kept from the credits, but as the reputation of the film grew he cited it as giving him one of his best cameo roles.

Sadly, Alun died on Tuesday, 6 December 1994 at the age of 69, following a short illness.

Oxford Street Maternity Hospital, Oxford Street, Liverpool L7

In the street continuing off Mount Pleasant, a few hundred yards from where both Julia Lennon and John Lennon were married.

It is close to the city centre and at 6.30 p.m on the evening of 9 October 1940, Julia Lennon gave birth to a son: Hunter Davies in *The Beatles* wrote: 'He was born during a heavy air raid' and Philip

Norman in *Shout!* confirmed, 'John . . . was . . . born . . . during one of the fiercest night raids by Hitler's Luftwaffe on Liverpool.'

This particular story is to be found in most books documenting John's birth. They are all untrue. Archivist Helen Simpson consulted the local papers for that entire week and found that there was a lull in the bombing on the night of John's birth. Other researchers have since found that the Luftwaffe gave Liverpool a miss on the night of John's birth.

Perhaps the only writer to include this fact in his book was David Stuart Ryan, author of *John Lennon's Secret*, who wrote, 'There were not – as he liked to imply – any bombs falling.'

Within twenty minutes of the baby's birth, his Aunt Mimi Smith was at her sister's bedside. It was she who gave him the Christian name John and she also picked the middle name Winston, no doubt due to the feelings of patriotism rife at the time.

A notice of the birth appeared in the *Liverpool Echo* on Saturday, 12 October.

LENNON – October 9, in hospital to JULIA (nee Stanley), wife of ALFRED LENNON, Merchant Navy (at sea), a son – 9 Newcastle Road.

Paddy, Klaus & Gibson

An interesting trio because it brought together two prominent members of Liverpool bands and one of the Beatles' friends from Hamburg.

Paddy, Klaus & Gibson formed in 1965 and comprised Paddy Chambers (lead guitar), Klaus Voormann (bass guitar) and Gibson Kemp (drums).

Paddy had been a member of several Mersey Beat bands including Faron's Flamingos and the Big Three.

Klaus had originally been inspired by former Beatles bassist Stuart Sutcliffe to take up the bass guitar.

Gibson Kemp was sixteen in 1962 when he replaced Ringo Starr in Rory Storm & the Hurricanes, inheriting Ringo's pink suit. He left the Hurricanes to join Kingsize Taylor & the Dominoes in Germany, where he married Klaus' former girlfriend Astrid Kirchherr, the late Stuart Sutcliffe's fiancée.

The trio actually formed in Hamburg, moved to Liverpool and then settled in London, where they were initially managed by Don Paul, a former member of the vocal group the Viscounts. Paul approached Tony Stratton-Smith and agreed to give him 10 per cent of his 25 per cent management commission in exchange for £250, which he urgently needed to buy equipment for the group.

'Stratters' agreed and set to work on the first of the several groups he was to manage, immediately securing them a residency at London's Pickwick Club, a haunt of celebrities, including Paul McCartney and Jane Asher.

Stratton-Smith began to work hard to gain recognition for the band, entertaining disc jockeys and journalists at the club while the group were performing.

It was probably a pity that John Lennon became so enthusiastic about the band that he encouraged Brian Epstein to take an interest. Once Epstein declared that he wished to take over as manager, Stratton-Smith and Paul reluctantly allowed the transfer, accepting a settlement of £3,000, although 'Stratters' felt they were making the wrong move, commenting: 'I had regrets because I think they should have made it. They weren't a Top 20 band but they had a marvellous live feel. I think the way I was handling them, building them through the clubs and delaying a record debut was, with hindsight, the best way. With NEMS, record after record came out and they were put on tours and I don't think they really had time to develop.'

Epstein signed Paddy, Klaus & Gibson on Sunday, 6 June 1965, securing them a contract with Pye Records, and the group were to release a total of three singles, beginning with 'I Wanna Know', flipside 'I Tried' on Friday, 9 July.

As with a number of acts signed by Brian following his initial Liverpool successes, they vanished without a trace.

There were plans at one time, suggested by Pete Townshend, to amalgamate the trio with the Who. However, when internal disputes within the Who were settled, the scheme was dropped and Paddy, Klaus & Gibson disbanded on Monday, 13 June 1966.

In interviews with music biographer Ray Coleman, Paddy was to comment that although he paid them £50 a week, Epstein got them very little work and 'to be honest the management side of things he completely cocked up.' He also told Coleman: 'I basically don't think he gave the band anything in management. I don't think he had a clue. But it was obvious after a while that he was getting emotionally very hung up on me and I tried my best to cope with it. I actually ended up in bed with him one day but after about five minutes I said, "Brian, I just can't handle this" and I got up and walked out.'

Paddy returned to Liverpool, where he joined the Escorts for a while and later teamed up with another former Stratton-Smith artist, Beryl Marsden, in a soul band called Sinbad. He then began managing clubs and was about to team up with former Faron's Flamingos team-mate Nicky Crouch when he became very ill and was hospitalised.

Gibson became a prominent record executive for Polygram and is now semi-retired in a village outside London.

Klaus continued his association with the Beatles, was a member of the Hollies, Manfred Mann and the Plastic Ono Band, and eventually returned to Hamburg. He was also invited to design the artwork for the *Anthology* series by the Beatles.

Palace Theatre Club, Turncoat Lane, Offerton, Stockport, Greater Manchester

A totally untypical Beatles booking. On 13 June 1963 they were booked to appear at this cabaret venue and at another cabaret club ten miles distant. Although there was a flourishing variety club scene in the North of England, Mersey Beat groups rarely played at such venues where the adult audiences went to drink and watch speciality acts, comedians, strippers and solo singers. It is ironic that the seventies saw the cabaret clubs becoming the main places of work for the surviving groups of the sixties beat scene.

Palais Ballroom, Queens Road, Aldershot, Hampshire

The scene of the Beatles' first performance in the South of England on Saturday, 9 December 1961. Enterprising Liverpool promoter Sam Leach, who had high hopes of recording and managing the Beatles, decided that he would try to arouse interest in the group from prominent London impresarios: he'd book the Beatles to appear in London and invite several major agents, such as Tito Burns, to see them. Unfortunately, he booked them into a venue in the out-of-the-way town of Aldershot, 37 miles from London. Naturally, no agents turned up.

Sam had contacted Bob Potter, who ran the hall, and booked the venue for five consecutive Saturdays, beginning on 9 December 1961. He had leaflets printed announcing a 'Battle of the Bands'. It was to be 'Liverpool vs London' with the Beatles representing Liverpool and Ivor Jay & the Jaywalkers appearing for the South.

The party set off at 5.00 a.m. on Saturday morning, Sam accompanied by photographer friend Dick Matthews and the Beatles travelling with their equipment in a van driven by one of Sam's bouncers, Terry McCann. There was no motorway at the time and the drive took nine hours. When they arrived Leach told the group that he'd promoted the gig in a big way and bought a copy of the *Aldershot News*, expecting to see a large advertisement publicising the event. There was nothing. Angrily he went to the newspaper office and discovered that the £100 advertisement didn't appear because he'd sent a cheque and only cash bookings were accepted from first-time advertisers. It was also explained that he hadn't left an address, so the paper couldn't contact him about the rule.

With no promotion, things looked grim. They were even grimmer when only four people turned up and Sam had to go round local pubs and coffee bars pleading with youngsters to come along. Eventually, eighteen people witnessed the Beatles performing their London(!) debut and, due to the fact that the record player didn't work, they had to play an extended set. As some consolation, Sam bought four crates of brown ale and they sat drinking and played a football match on the dance floor with some bingo balls. The noise they were making had led to a neighbour phoning the police to complain and when they emerged from the hall at 1.00 a.m. there were three police cars and four police vans. They were told to leave Aldershot and not return.

Leach suggested that they drive into London and they arrived at the Blue Gardenia Club in Greek Street, Soho, which was run by Brian Casser, former leader of one of Liverpool's top groups, Cass & the Cassanovas. The group took to the stage for a jam session and eventually set off back to Liverpool at 5.00 a.m. on Sunday morning. Sam managed to place an advertisement in the *Aldershot News* for the following week and a total of 210 youngsters paid the 5/- (25p) entrance fee to see Rory Storm & the Hurricanes. Despite this promising response, Sam cancelled the three remaining dates.

Palais Des Fetes, Nice, France

The Beatles made a final French appearance at this venue in the south of France during their fortnight tour of Europe in 1965. Slotted in between an Italian and Spanish concert on 30 June.

Palais d'Hiver de Lyon, Rue Louis Guerin, Villeurbanne, Lyons, France

The Beatles' second appearance in France during their two-week European tour in 1965. They performed two concerts at the venue on Tuesday, 22 June, at 8.00 a.m. and 10.00 p.m. with an audience of 3,500 at each show.

Palais Des Sports, Place de la Porte de Versailles, Paris, France

The Beatles opened their short European tour at this venue on Sunday, 20 June 1965. They appeared on two shows at the arena, the first at 3.00 p.m. and the second at 9.00 p.m. The second show was broadcast by both French television and radio and the two houses were full to the 6,000 capacity – something which hadn't happened for several years.

Their repertoire comprised: 'Twist and Shout', 'She's A Woman',

'I'm A Loser', 'Can't Buy Me Love', 'Baby's In Black', 'I Wanna Be Your Man', 'A Hard Day's Night', 'Everybody's Trying To Be My Baby', 'Rock And Roll Music', 'I Feel Fine', 'Ticket To Ride' and 'Long Tall Sally'.

The group received a tremendous reception after their final number, 'Long Tall Sally'. Ringo had a solo spot with 'I Wanna Be Your Man' and George had sung lead on 'Everybody's Trying To Be My Baby'. There was enthusiastic applause for Paul when he tried to introduce several songs in French.

The Yardbirds were also on the bill.

After the show, Francoise Hardy visited the group at the George Cinq Hotel and later they visited Castell's nightclub.

Palazzo Dello Sport, Piazza Kennedy, Genoa, Italy

The Beatles performed two concerts at this arena on 25 June 1965 as part of their European tour. There were only three Italian venues visited throughout the entire career of the Beatles and not one sold out.

The Palazzo Dello Sport could accommodate an audience of 25,000, but only 5,000 turned up to see the first show that afternoon, with a larger audience for the evening performance. Audiences generally during the European tour were disappointing after the fever pitch receptions which the Beatles had received around the world in 1963 and 1964.

Panorama

A BBC television current affairs programme. On Easter Monday, 30 March 1964, the entire programme was given over to the success story of Brian Epstein and the Beatles. Hosted by Richard Dimbleby, the special included an interview with Epstein, a short, filmed appearance by the Beatles shot during a break in the filming of *A Hard Day's Night*, and appearances by Gerry & the Pacemakers, Tommy Quickly, Cilla Black and Sounds Incorporated.

Paolozzi, Eduardo

An internationally-renowned Scots-born sculptor, the son of Italian immigrants. He was educated at art schools in Edinburgh and London. He took Stuart Sutcliffe under his wing when Stu wished to remain in Hamburg and continue with his art studies. Paolozzi recognised Stuart's potential, believed in his talent and not only arranged for him to become one of his students at Hamburg's State High School in June 1961, but also approached the Hamburg authorities to arrange for Stuart to receive a grant.

Discussing Stuart Sutcliffe, he said: 'He was always slightly ahead of the rest of the class. But when he finished some work he would walk away from it. He destroyed almost everything he painted or drew. Stuart was very intelligent, open to everything – not just to painting and pop but to every medium and experience possible. Had he lived he could easily have become *the* Beatle.'

Paul McCartney bought one of Paolozzi's works, entitled *Solo*, and used another on the cover of his album *Red Rose Speedway*. Paolozzi also designed the mosaics that decorate London's Tottenham Court Road underground station.

Paperback Writer

Paul wrote this song, although John helped with one or two words in the lyrics. Some sources claim it was written in connection with John's two books, hence the mention of nonsense writer Edward Lear in the fourth line.

A young man working for the *Daily Mail* wants to become a paperback writer. It is also suggested that Paul even worked out the man's name, a character called Ian Iachimore, which he devised because it sounded like his own name after it had been played backwards on a tape loop.

The number was used quite successfully as the theme tune of a television book series in Britain called 'Read All About It'.

The single was issued in Britain on R5452 on 10 June 1966 and reached No. 1 in the charts – although it didn't go straight to the No. 1 position on release as several of their other singles had. The flipside was 'Rain'. It also reached No. 1 in the States when it was issued on Capitol 5651 in May 1966.

The number was featured on several compilations, including *A Collection Of Beatles Oldies (But Goldies)*, *The Beatles 1967–1970*, the 1979 *Hey Jude* album and *The Beatles Box*. The number was included on the compilation *Past Masters Volume Two*.

Parade Of The Pops

A BBC Light Programme show on which the Beatles made their first live radio performance on 20 February 1963. The show was presented by Denny Piercy and produced by John Kingdon and broadcast each Wednesday between 12.30 p.m.–1.30 p.m. The group performed 'Love Me Do' and 'Please Please Me' at the Playhouse Theatre, London.

Paramounts, The

A group from Southend comprising Gary Brooker (keyboards/vocals), Robin Trower (guitar), Chris Copping (bass) and Barrie

Wilson (drums). They signed to the Parlophone label and the
Rolling Stones described them as 'The best R&B band in Britain'.
They had limited success and only one minor hit, 'Poison Ivy' in
1964. In 1965 they were signed up by Brian Epstein's NEMS organ-
isation and, as a result, were booked to appear on the Beatles' last
British tour in December of that year.

In 1967 Brooker formed Procol Harum and over a period of time
brought all the original members of the Paramounts into the band.

Paramount Theatre, New York City

Venue of the final appearance on the Beatles' first American tour.
The Beatles and several other artists appeared at this special benefit
in aid of the Retarded Infants Service and Cerebral Palsy of New
York.

Entitled *An Evening With The Beatles*, the charity show was
held on Sunday, 20 September 1964, before an audience of 3,682
people who had paid from five to 100 dollars a ticket. This
resulted in an audience which was a strange mix of teenage Beatle
fans and bejewelled New York elite, and when the fans began
screaming for their heroes, one onlooker commented, 'The kids
were making these people with diamonds very nervous.' Other
acts on the bill were Steve Lawrence and Edie Gormé, Leslie
Uggams, the Tokens, Bobby Goldsboro, the Shangri-Las, the
Brothers Four, Jackie De Shannon and Nancy Ames. The Beatles
were due to go on at 10.45 p.m., but because the fans were
screaming for the group continuously, the time allotted to each of
the other acts was cut drastically and the Beatles went on stage
three-quarters of an hour ahead of schedule to play ten songs in a
25-minute set.

Outside the crowds built up until there was a swell of 10,000
people, with 240 policemen trying to control them. Backstage, the
Beatles had a number of visitors, including Ed Sullivan and Bob
Dylan. By 10.45 p.m. they were in a limousine heading for the
Idlewild Motel.

The occasion raised almost £25,000 for the charity and the
Beatles were presented with an illuminated scroll which read: 'To
John, Paul, George and Ringo who, as the Beatles, have brought an
excitement to the entertainment capitals of the world and who, as
individuals, have given of their time and talent to bring hope and
help to the handicapped children of America.' John said, 'We do
these shows whenever we can simply because we want to. We don't
feel that it's any big deal on our part. We don't like talking about
them because when you can give something, even if it is only time,
then you should do it.'

Paris, France

French capital, which John Lennon and Paul McCartney were to visit in 1961. In September of that year, two weeks before his 21st birthday, John's Aunt Elizabeth, who lived in Sutherland, Scotland, sent John £40 as a coming-of-age present. Together with Paul he planned to visit Paris and after the Beatles had completed a gig at Knotty Ash Village Hall on 29 September 1961, the group took a break while John and Paul left for their fifteen-day trip abroad. Some reports have suggested that the two of them left without informing George and Pete, who were disgusted by the action, which almost caused the group to break up and resulted in Ray McFall and Bob Wooler lecturing John and Paul about acting irresponsibly. This isn't actually so, John and Paul had planned the trip and no bookings were made for the period they were away.

Stuart Sutcliffe had informed John by post that Jurgen Vollmer, their friend from Hamburg, had moved to Paris, and he provided them with his address. During the trip they visited Jurgen who was to write about the visit and said that they wanted to have their hair cut in the same style as his. So he gave both of them their first 'Beatles' haircut in his hotel room on the Left Bank. They then went to the Flea Market and bought some mod-style clothes. Jurgen wore a corduroy jacket and a sweater with cut-off sleeves, which was collarless – and John wanted to dress like this. Jurgen wrote: 'At that time, the rage in Paris was bell bottoms. The Beatles always wore very tightly cuffed, or "pegged" pants with pointed shoes or very pointed boots. They were "Teddy Boys" in the English fashion and dressed in black leather and black jeans ... John and Paul wanted to dress more in the Paris fashion, but they were afraid to look queer in their home town of Liverpool.'

While in Paris, Paul sent a lengthy letter to Bill Harry in Liverpool in which he wrote, 'It was 10 o'clock, it was, when we were entering the Olympia in Paris to see the "Johnny Hallyday Rock Show". The cheapest seats in "les theatre" (French) were seven and sixpence, so we followed the woman with the torch (English).

'When Johnny Hallyday came, everybody went wild – and loud was the cheering and many the dancing in the aisles, too. But the man said "sit down", so we had to.

'The excitement rose, the audience rose to dance, like the many boys and girls dancing along the back rows. Also old men, which is stranger still, isn't it.

'Meanwhile, later the same week, we go to "Les Rock Festival" held in a club in Montmartre, with Danny et les Pirates and many more groups for your evening's entertainment. Topping the bill was Vince (Ron, my boy, Ron) Taylor, star of English screen and Two I's.

'The atmosphere is like many a night club, but the teenagers stand round the dancing floor which you use as a stage. They jump on a woman with gold trousers and a hand microphone and then hit a man when he says "go away". A group follows, and so do others, playing "Apache" worse than many other bands. When the singer joins the band, the leather jacket fiends who are the audience, join in dancing and banging tables with chairs.

'The singers have to go one better than the audience, so they lie on the floor, or jump on a passing drummer, or kiss a guitar, and then hit the man playing it. The crowd enjoy this and many stand on chairs to see the fun, and soon the audience are all singing and shouting like one man, but he didn't mind.

'Vince (Ron, Ron) Taylor finally appeared and joined the fun, and in the end he has so much fun that he had to rest. But in spite of this it had been a wonderful show, lovely show . . . lovely'.

John and Paul stayed in Montmartre for a week and planned to travel on to Spain, but their money ran out. On their return to Liverpool they stopped off in London where they bought some Chelsea boots, which were later to become fashionable as 'Beatle boots'.

On 16 September 1963, John decided to take Cynthia on a belated honeymoon to Paris. The couple stayed at the luxurious George V Hotel and began to take in all the sights – the Eiffel Tower, the Arc de Triomphe, Montmartre – and John bought a movie camera. On their return to the hotel they found a note from Astrid Kirchherr which revealed that she was in Paris for a few days with a girlfriend. There was a phone number with the note and John and Cynthia contacted her and arranged to meet. The four of them had a night on the town, drinking rough red wine until dawn. They were so blotto they decided to go to Astrid's lodgings for coffee. After the coffee they drank another bottle of wine. John and Cynthia found they were in no state to return to the hotel and despite there being only a single bed, all four of them got into it and fell into a deep sleep. Brian Epstein had also arrived in Paris and John and Cynthia met up with him and all three returned to England together on 2 October.

The French market was a difficult one to break for an English-speaking act, but the Beatles were booked to appear at the Olympia in Paris for three weeks. John, Paul and George flew out on 14 January 1964 but Ringo remained in Liverpool and threatened not to go: He caught a plane and flew from Liverpool via London Airport the next day and the group appeared at the Cinema Cyrano in Versailles that night, opening at the Olympia on 16 January. The group had a suite at the George V Hotel and on their opening night received a telegram informing them that 'I Want To Hold Your Hand' had reached No. 1 in the *Cash Box* charts in America. They then had a celebration dinner, hosted by Brian Epstein and George Martin.

They were appearing at the Olympia for £50 a day and the male dominated audiences weren't as fervent as the group were used to. The group finished their short season at the Olympia on 4 February and flew back to London the following day. They next returned to Paris in June 1965 when they received a triumphant reception at the Palais De Sport.

Parkinson, Norman

Norman Parkinson, real name Ronald Parkinson Smith, was one of the major British photographers, particularly famous for his exotic fashion photographs featured in magazines such as *Vogue*.

He took photographs of the Beatles at Abbey Road in September 1963. A selection of them were published by Hutchinson in *The Beatles Book* in 1964.

His photographs of the Beatles were also featured in a special exhibition of Parkinson's work at the National Portrait Gallery in London.

He died in Singapore on 14 February 1991, aged 76.

Parnes, Larry

One of the most successful British pop impresarios of the late fifties and early sixties. Parnes, known as 'Mr Parnes Shillings And Pence', because of his reputed tightfistedness in paying his artists, first discovered Tommy Steele in 1956. He then began to build up a stable of pop singers, known for the stage names he devised for them – Billy Fury, Vince Eager, Marty Wilde, Duffy Power, Johnny Gentle, Dickie Pride and Lance Fortune.

Epstein first met Parnes backstage at the Liverpool Empire. Marty Wilde and Billy Fury were topping the bill and he was introduced to Parnes as a local record store manger. He told Parnes he was interested in the pop business and they had drinks together and Parnes introduced him to Marty and Billy in their dressing rooms.

Allan Williams approached Parnes about co-promoting a bill in Liverpool starring Eddie Cochran and Gene Vincent. He also arranged for groups to audition for Parnes, who was seeking a backing group for Fury. At the Wyvern Club, Parnes and Fury watched several Liverpool groups, including the Silver Beetles. Reports stated that, because Parnes wanted them to play a number without Stuart Sutcliffe, he was put off by Stu's lack of skill. Parnes denied this some years later, saying he thought the group were great, but had been put off by the middle-aged drummer (Tommy Moore), who joined them half-way through the session.

Parnes booked the Silver Beetles to appear on Johnny Gentle's short tour of Scotland.

When Epstein signed up the Beatles, he phoned Parnes and asked him if he'd book the group for Sunday gigs at Great Yarmouth. Parnes remembered the band and offered £25. Epstein wanted £50. He then visited Parnes' Marble Arch office and said that if Parnes would book the group for thirteen dates he would come down to £45 and give him first option on a five-year contract to promote all of Brian's artists worldwide. Parnes upped his offer to £35. Brian phoned his office again, asking for £40 and Parnes offered £37 10s. Brian put the phone down on him.

In November 1962 Parnes wrote to Epstein offering the Beatles a tour. Brian asked for £230 a week. Parnes offered £140. Brian wrote back requesting £200 for a seven-day week. Parnes then suggested that if the follow-up to 'Love Me Do' entered the Top Ten he would pay £230 a week; if it entered the Top Three he would pay £300 a week.

The two never came to a deal, although they maintained good relations and Brian often approached him for advice and it was Parnes who recommended Nat Weiss as a New York attorney and Dougie Millings as a tailor for Brian's bands. It has also been suggested that Epstein offered Parnes a share in the Beatles, but was turned down.

In 1967 Brian Epstein became ill through drug abuse and entered a private clinic in Putney. Parnes went to visit him and Brian told him of his worries – that the Beatles' contract would be ending in four months' time and he was concerned that they wouldn't re-sign with him. Parnes commented, 'Brian was very ill. He told me that the contract was coming to an end and he understood the boys were going to leave him because another man was taking over. My answer to Brian was "I could never see the boys leaving you. Ever. I think you're depressed over nothing."'

In 1982, when Paul was appearing on the radio show 'Desert Island Discs', he jokingly said that the Beatles hadn't been paid for their early Parnes tour. Parnes sued him and Paul made a public apology on the radio two years later. Parnes died on 30 July 1989 aged 59.

Parsons, Alan

A tape engineer at Abbey Road Studios who was contacted by George Martin to bring Abbey Road equipment down to the Apple

Studios in Savile Row when Martin discovered that the equipment
Alexis Mardas had built for Apple was useless. The date was
Thursday, 23 January 1969. Parsons then remained as a second
engineer on the Beatles' *Get Back* sessions until October 1969, and
the album was eventually issued as *Let It Be*. Parsons later created
a successful outfit called the Alan Parsons Project and was to
manage Abbey Road Studios for a time.

Past Masters Volume One
Part of a two-volume issue by EMI Records to utilise further Beatles
material that could be used for digital transfer to CD. The two-part
package included all their B sides and EP material which had never
been issued on an official Beatles album – together with their two
German language tracks and an alternative take of 'Across The
Universe'.

Both volumes were released simultaneously on a worldwide basis
on Tuesday, 8 March 1988.

Volume one was issued on Parlophone CDP7 90043-2. The tracks
were: 'Love Me Do', 'From Me To You', 'Thank You Girl', 'She Loves
You', 'I'll Get You', 'I Want To Hold Your Hand', 'This Boy', 'Komm,
Gib Mir Deine Hand', 'Sie Liebt Dich', 'Long Tall Sally', 'I Call Your
Name', 'Slow Down', 'Matchbox', 'I Feel Fine', 'She's A Woman', 'Bad
Boy', 'Yes It Is' and 'I'm Down'.

Past Masters Volume Two
Issued on Parlophone CD P7 90044-2 on Tuesday, 8 March 1988.
The tracks were: 'Day Tripper', 'We Can Work It Out', 'Paperback
Writer', 'Rain', 'Lady Madonna', 'The Inner Light', 'Hey Jude',
'Revolution', 'Get Back', 'Don't Let Me Down', 'The Ballad Of
John & Yoko', 'Old Brown Shoe', 'Across The Universe', 'Let It Be'
and 'You Know My Name (Look Up The Number)'.

Paul's Christmas Album
One of the rarest of the Beatle recordings. An album which Paul
McCartney made. There were only four copies pressed and in
December 1965 Paul gave a copy to each member of the Beatles.

Pavilion, North Parade, Bridge Road, Bath, Somerset
Venue where the Beatles appeared only once, on Monday, 10 June
1963, on the evening directly following the end of their Roy
Orbison Tour.

Pavilion Gardens Ballroom, St John's Road, Buxton, Derbyshire

The Beatles performed at this venue on Saturday, 6 April 1963. Their support act was a group called the Trixons. Police struggled on the stage with fans as they attempted to prevent the youngsters from reaching the Beatles during their performance.

Their second and final appearance at the ballroom took place on 19 October 1963.

Pavilion Theatre, Lodge Lane, Liverpool L8

A former Music Hall which, in the fifties, was mainly the setting for weekly 'nude' revues such as *Bareway To The Stars*, which featured tableaux of nude girls who weren't allowed to move on stage by order of the Lord Chamberlain. As long as they were 'frozen', they could pose in the nude. In contrast, Chris Barber & his Band always drew capacity houses at the Pavilion and his show included a special solo spot for Lonnie Donegan. The Pavilion, when Lonnie Donegan had his own show there, at the time of his major hit 'Rock Island Line', was attended by members of several local skiffle bands, including Paul McCartney, and that particular Donegan concert was said to have inspired a lot of local musicians to keep on playing after the skiffle boom had died.

The Beatles appeared at the Pavilion on Monday, 2 April 1962, for one night only (they'd previously appeared as the Quarry Men in a skiffle contest at the theatre in the late fifties). The concert was promoted by Jim Gretty and the headliners were the Royal Showband from Waterford in Southern Ireland, winners of the Carl Allen Award as 'the Outstanding Showband of the year' and advertised as 'Ireland's Pride'. The Beatles, on the other hand, were described as 'Merseyside's joy'.

The Pavilion was later turned into a snooker club.

Peggy Sue

Buddy Holly's first major hit record, which took him to No. 3 in the American charts and No. 6 in the British charts in 1957. The number became a rock classic and was included in the Quarry Men's repertoire, with John Lennon on lead vocals.

Pennebaker, D. A.

An American movie director who specialised in making rock films. John Lennon appeared fleetingly in Pennebaker's film of Bob Dylan's 1966 British tour, *Eat The Document*, and John, Yoko and the Plastic Ono Band appeared in his film of the 1969 Peace Festival

Sweet Toronto. Pennebaker was one of the personalities who allowed his legs to be filmed in John and Yoko's *Up Your Legs Forever.*

Penner, Peter
A photographer friend of Astrid Kirchherr. When the Beatles were first in Hamburg in 1960, they got to know Astrid and her friends, who used to visit them at the Kaiserkeller club.

At this time the Beatles wore typical 'Tony Curtis' style haircuts, which were popular in Liverpool then. They noticed that Peter Penner, who was one of the group of Astrid's friends who watched the Beatles' shows, had a special type of hairstyle. They discovered that Astrid had styled his hair for him. Later, she styled Stuart Sutcliffe's hair in the same way and the famous Beatle cut was born. A few years later, the Germans began to describe the Beatles' hair as 'Pilzenkopt' – mushroom shaped!

Penny Lane
A song penned by Paul in the autumn of 1966. The Beatles had decided to make a concept album inspired by their childhood in Liverpool. Digging into their memories, Paul produced 'Penny Lane' and John composed 'Strawberry Fields Forever'. When the time came for the song to be recorded, Paul had the number completely finished and had drafted out a rough arrangement for the brass section.

Paul was to comment: 'Penny Lane is a bus roundabout in Liverpool, and there is a barber's shop showing photographs of every head he's had the pleasure to know – no, that's not true they're just photos of hairstyles, but all the people who come and go/stop and say hello. There's a bank on the corner so we made up the bit about the banker in his motor car. It's part fact part nostalgia for a place, which is a great place, blue suburban skies as we remember it, and it's still there.

'And we put in a joke or two: "Four of fish and finger pie." The women would never dare say that, except to themselves. Most people wouldn't hear it, but "finger pie" is just a nice little joke about the Liverpool lads who like a bit of smut.'

Incidentally, the barber's shop was called Bioletti's.

The track was recorded in January 1967 and among the musicians who were to perform on overdubs were flautists Ray Swinfield, P. Goody, Manny Winters and Dennis Walton; trumpeters Leon Calvert, Freddy Clayton, Bert Courtley and Duncan Campbell; oboists Dick Morgan and Mike Winfield; and bassist Frank Clarke. Clarke was later to say, 'I've spent a lifetime playing with top orchestras yet I'm most famous for playing on "Penny Lane".'

Paul was still not satisfied with the track, and he was sitting at home watching the BBC2 TV show 'Masterworks' with David Mason performing Bach's Brandenberg Concerto No. 2 in F Major. He arranged for Mason to be hired to play trumpet on the 'Penny Lane' track and was satisfied with the finished result.

The number is one of the most uplifting and cheery of the Beatles songs and caused problems in Liverpool with fans stealing the actual Penny Lane street signs. It was an act later to be repeated at Abbey Road. It resulted in Liverpool Corporation ceasing to make street signs for Penny Lane, settling for painting the street name on buildings instead.

'Penny Lane' was issued as a double 'A' side with 'Strawberry Fields Forever' on Parlophone R5570 on Friday, 17 February 1967 when it became the first Beatles single since 'Love Me Do' not to hit the No. 1 spot. It was held at No. 2 by the Engelbert Humperdinck hit 'Release Me'. The British release received its world premiere broadcast on the pirate radio station Radio London, and Parlophone issued the first 250,000 in special bags with a full colour sleeve. It was issued in America on Capitol 5810 on Monday, 13 February 1967 with advance orders of over a million copies. This was a record in itself for Capitol with the highest quantity of a single ever pressed and shipped out in a three-day period. The number topped the charts in the US.

Another version of the number was included on the *Anthology 2* CD.

People And Places

A Granada television, early evening magazine programme, screened only in the north-west of England, which saw the Beatles' television debut on 17 October 1962 when the group performed 'Love Me Do' and 'Ooh! My Soul', for a fee of £35.

The Beatles travelled to the Manchester studio and were introduced by the show's host Gay Byrne. They were later to comment: 'Gay Byrne was the bloke who introduced us . . . made us feel at home and showed us round and generally took some of the fright out of the whole business.' Byrne was later to return to his native Ireland where he became a major TV celebrity.

The programme was screened live at 6.35 p.m. and ran for half an hour. It was to be produced by Johnny Hamp who filmed several Beatles shows over the years, including the special 'The Music Of Lennon & McCartney' in 1965 and the documentary 'The Early Beatles' in 1982.

Their planned appearance for 2 November was scrapped and they next performed on the programme on 17 December 1962, promoting 'Love Me Do' again. 'People And Places' changed its name to 'Scene At 6.30' during 1963.

Peppermint Lounge, The, Miami, Florida

A club where disc jockey Murray the K took the Beatles on Thursday, 13 February 1964. Country singer Hank Ballard was on stage that evening and the Beatles remained at the club for a couple of hours.

Peppermint Lounge, The, New York City

The famous American nightclub of the sixties, home of a noted band, Joey Dee & the Starliters. During their first trip to America in 1964 three members of the Beatles visited the Peppermint Lounge on 9 February. George Harrison had decided to return to the Plaza Hotel for a sleep after Murray the K had taken the group to visit the Playboy Club. John, Paul and Ringo accompanied the New York disc jockey to the lounge. Others in the party included John's wife Cynthia and press agent Brian Sommerville. The group declined to participate in the club's 'Twist Revue', but Ringo took to the dance floor to 'do the Twist' with Peppermint Lounge Captain Marlene Klaire, who was to comment later: 'It was that exhausting that it felt like a Beatle was on me, and I had to shake it off.'

During the evening a group called the Seven Fabulous Epics – featuring the Four Younger Brothers, alias the American Beatles – played Beatle numbers, while wearing Beatle wigs!

Incidentally, their old friend Adrian Barber, former member of the Big Three who had become stage manager at the Star Club, Hamburg, so impressed Joey Dee with the sound system that he had built at the Star Club that the singer invited Adrian to New York to build a sound system for the Peppermint Lounge.

7 Percy Street, Liverpool L8

The house at No. 7 was divided into flats. Art students Stuart Sutcliffe and Rod Murray rented rooms here.

Stuart's flat was on the ground floor rear, its solitary window overlooking a grimy backyard, surrounded by brick walls. Sparsely furnished, with a few high-back wooden chairs and a camp bed. Stuart was able to work in the flat during the long summer holidays as his mother agreed to support him financially. He also received tuition in the flat from art college lecturer Arthur Ballard.

Stuart carried on his work of painting and sketching at a prolific rate. He completed a portrait of Bill Harry, together with over two dozen sketches on pink foolscap paper, during a single afternoon. The painting was executed in a Van Gogh style, which Stuart had become quite adept at. It was in this single room that Bill and Stuart made plans to produce a book about Liverpool, projecting a positive image in visual and written terms. The book was never started as Stuart became involved with the Beatles as their bass guitarist.

When Stuart was about to be evicted from the Percy Street flat, he discussed the possibility of moving into Gambier Terrace where Rod Murray had recently found a flat, and John Lennon joined them.

Perkins, Carl

One of the original American rock 'n' roll legends, Carl was born on 9 April 1932 in Lake City, Tennessee. He signed with the legendary Sun Records, wrote and recorded the classic rocker 'Blue Suede Shoes' and a number of other rock 'n' roll standards.

A serious accident in 1956, in which his brother and manager were killed, left him hospitalised for a year. His career suffered a number of setbacks and he compounded his problems by drinking too much.

He rose from the doldrums when Chuck Berry invited him to tour with him in Britain in 1964, and during the trip he met the Beatles for the first time. His career, personal life and finances were boosted when the Beatles recorded three of his numbers: 'Matchbox', 'Honey Don't' and 'Everybody's Trying To Be My Baby'. With the royalties he was able to buy his parents a farm.

The 1964 tour was the first time either Carl or Chuck Berry had been to England and Carl said that he was in total shock because the tour was sold out every night and: 'The kids were bopping in the aisles.' On the last night of the tour the promoter invited him to a party. Carl told him that he was tired and had a 9.00 a.m. flight to catch the next day. However, the promoter insisted he go to the party – and when he arrived he discovered that it was a party thrown by the Beatles in his honour.

He told broadcaster Scott Muni: 'We wound up – John, Paul, George and Ringo – sitting on a couch and me sitting on a floor with a guitar.' The Beatles asked him what he was doing the next night and, although he was due to fly out in the morning, he told them he had no plans, so they invited him to their recording session at Abbey Road. When he arrived at the studio, no one had told him that the Beatles were going to record some of his songs. He said, 'George Martin said, "Are we ready to go?" and Ringo cut out on "Honey Don't". It was a magic time . . . I was in the studio when they cut "Honey Don't", "Matchbox" and "Everybody's Trying To

Be My Baby". And they did a version of "Blue Suede Shoes" which was never released."

Perkins actually visited Abbey Road on the afternoon of Monday, 1 June 1964 when they recorded 'Matchbox'.

The Beatles had also recorded a number of Perkins songs on their various BBC radio appearances: 'Everybody's Trying To Be My Baby', 'Matchbox', 'Sure To Fall', 'Lend Me Your Comb' and 'Honey Don't'. George Harrison had also used the stage name Carl Harrison in his tribute to Perkins when the Silver Beetles had toured Scotland with Johnny Gentle.

Over the years, Carl kept in touch with Paul, visiting him whenever he was in England. In 1981, Paul invited Carl to Montserrat to be one of the guests on the *Tug Of War* album. Carl was so delighted with the invitation that the night before he left for the island he sat down and composed a number, 'My Old Friend', in tribute to Paul. Paul composed the number 'Get It' for the two of them to record, and during the sessions they had a jam in which they played a number of Perkins classics, including 'Honey Don't', 'Boppin' The Blues' and 'Lend Me Your Comb'. Paul recorded all the jam sessions, in addition to studio conversations for his personal collection.

Carl played the number 'My Old Friend' on the day he was to leave Montserrat. Paul was so moved that he asked Carl if he had to leave that day and persuaded him to stay and record the number. Carl was to say that the song meant more to him than any other number he'd written, including 'Blue Suede Shoes'. On the track, Paul added backing vocals and played organ, rhythm guitar, drums and bass, but didn't use it on *Tug Of War*.

'Get It' was featured on the album and was also issued as the flipside of the 'Tug Of War' single.

Paul also produced Ringo performing Carl's number 'Sure To Fall' on the *Stop And Smell The Roses* album.

In October 1984, to celebrate the 30th anniversary of 'Blue Suede Shoes', Carl recorded a television special at Limehouse Studios in London called 'A Rockabilly Session – Carl Perkins And Friends'. Among the artists performing with him were George Harrison, Ringo Starr, Eric Clapton, Dave Edmunds, Rosanna Cash, Earl Slick, Slim Jim Phantom, Lee Rocker, Greg Perkins, John Davis, Mickey Gee, David Charles and Geraint Watkins.

Perkins is definitely one of the Beatles' major influences as can be seen from the fact that during their career they performed no less than ten of his compositions in their stage act. They were: 'Blue Suede Shoes', 'Lend Me Your Comb', 'Sure To Fall', 'Tennessee, Your True Love', 'Glad All Over', 'Everybody's Trying To Be My Baby', 'Matchbox', 'Honey Don't' and 'Gone, Gone, Gone'.

Carl underwent surgery for a blockage in his cartoid artery in June 1997. He suffered a stroke on 20 November and 2 December of that year. A third stroke left him partly paralysed on his left side, he was in a coma until the beginning of 1998 and died three weeks later on 19 January 1998 at Jackson Madison County General in Jackson, Tennessee. He was 65 years old.

His funeral took place on Friday, 23 January at Lambuth University, Jackson. Among the attendees were George and Olivia Harrison, Garth Brooks, Wynonna Judd, Ricky Skaggs, Billy Ray Cyrus, Jerry Lee Lewis and Johnny Rivers. Messages arrived from Paul McCartney, Elton John, Bob Dylan and Eric Clapton, and Ringo Starr sent flowers. Ringo sent a video message and George performed 'Your True Love'.

Carl's last album, released in 1966, had been *Go Cat Go*. It featured John Lennon with a live recording of 'Blue Suede Shoes' from the Toronto Rock 'n' Roll Festival; Paul McCartney performing 'My Old Friend'; Ringo Starr and his All Starr Band with 'Matchbox' and George Harrison performing 'Distance Makes No Difference', which he recorded at Friar Park.

Peter & Gordon

Rumour has it that when Paul McCartney told the other members of the Beatles that he'd just written a song that began 'Please lock me away ...' they laughed. It is known that John Lennon was certainly amused by it and it was a number which the Beatles never recorded themselves.

However, it was to launch the career of a young duo called Peter and Gordon.

The two of them met at Westminster Boys' School, had mutual interests (both were sons of doctors) and decided to team up as a folk duo Gordon & Peter, performing at the various school events and in some Soho folk clubs. They swopped the name around purely because it sounded better. They were spotted playing at the Pickwick Club by EMI A&R man Norman Newall in January 1964. By that time the Beat scene had thoroughly transformed the music industry to the extent that A&R men were continuously on the look-out for new talent (recording managers were called A&R men in those days – the initials stood for 'artists and repertoire').

Gordon Trueman Riviere Waller had been born in Braemer, Scotland, on 4 June 1945 and Peter Asher in London on 22 June 1944. One of Peter's sisters was Jane, an actress, and as her current boyfriend was Paul McCartney, Peter decided to talk him into giving them a song to record. They'd sent 63 demo tapes to record companies before their signing to Columbia and had been scheduled to record a song called 'If I Were You', but Peter realised that a number written by a member of the Beatles would virtually assure them of a hit.

Paul decided to complete an unfinished song, 'World Without Love', and the duo saw their debut record released in Britain on 28 February 1964 on Columbia DB 7225 and in America on 27 April 1964 on Capitol 5175. The Beatles never recorded the number and it wasn't part of their repertoire. Within two weeks it had topped the British charts. It eventually sold over 550,000 copies in Britain and became a million-seller worldwide.

Paul gave them a second composition 'Nobody I Know', which was another million-seller. The number was issued in Britain on Columbia DB 7292 on 29 May 1964 and reached No. 9 in the charts. It was issued in America on Capitol 5211 on 15 June 1964, but didn't chart. Peter & Gordon flew to the States to appear at the New York World Fair and on the 'Ed Sullivan Show' and became a major teen attraction.

'I Go To Pieces', a number given to them by Del Shannon, didn't make much impact in the UK, although it reached No. 9 in the United States. They then had a smash hit with Buddy Holly's 'True Love Ways', followed by 'To Know You Is to Love You' and 'Baby I'm Yours'.

The third Paul McCartney composition to be recorded by Peter & Gordon was 'I Don't Want To See You Again'. The Beatles never recorded the number, although a demo disc may have been prepared for the duo's recording manager Norman Newall.

This was the least successful of the Lennon and McCartney numbers to be given to Peter & Gordon and didn't provide them with a British hit, although it reached No. 16 in America. It was issued in Britain on Columbia DB 7356 on 11 September 1964 and in America on Capitol 5272 on 21 September 1964.

Paul then tried a little experiment. He'd wondered how well a composition of his would fare if it didn't receive the advantages of the Lennon and McCartney credit, so he penned a new song for Peter & Gordon, but insisted that the composer's credit should read Bernard Webb. The song was called 'Woman' and reached No. 28 in the British charts, faring better in America at No. 14.

Paul admitted that he'd written it but had wanted to see if he could enter the charts without using the magical Lennon & McCartney name. Webb was said to be an aspiring songwriter and a student in Paris. Paul also used the pseudonym A. Smith for the American release.

This was the fourth and last song which Paul gave to Peter & Gordon, and the flipside was 'Wrong From The Start'. It was issued in America in January 1966 and in Britain the following month. The song was also the first track on the duo's album of the same name, issued in March of that year.

They had one further British hit, 'Lady Godiva', and two other singles, 'Sunday For Tea' and 'The Jokers', which didn't reach the British charts but received low placings in the American Top 100.

Late in 1967, Peter suggested to Gordon that they should split due to the changing music scene. Gordon had several solo releases, without much success, while Peter joined the Beatles' new Apple company as head of A&R. One of his first moves was to sign up American singer James Taylor. Asher later settled in the States as Taylor's manager and also managed Linda Rondstadt.

Waller never found success in the recording field again and in 1973 appeared in the stage musical *Joseph and His Amazing Technicolour Dreamcoat* at the Edinburgh Festival, in London and in Australia. He later worked as a salesman selling photocopiers before settling down in Northamptonshire and becoming a partner in a company making radio commercials.

He surfaced in the 1990s to appear at a number of Beatles conventions.

Peter Jay & The Jaywalkers

A band from East Anglia who comprised Peter Jay (drums), Pete Miller (lead guitar), Tony Webster (rhythm guitar), Mac McIntyre (tenor sax/flute), Lloyd Baker (piano/baritone sax), Geoff Moss (acoustic bass) and Johnny Larke (bass guitar).

The group toured with the Beatles from 1 November until 13 December 1963. During their tour they had several jam sessions with the Beatles and the Brook Brothers, some of which were taped.

Peter Jay & the Jaywalkers disbanded in 1966.

Phantoms, The

A four-piece instrumental group from Melbourne who were booked as one of the support acts on the Beatles' Australian tour in June 1964. The band had previously had two instrumental records in the Melbourne charts (there wasn't a national Australian chart at the time) and were booked for the series of Beatles concerts Down Under.

For their appearances the group wore electric blue suits and were first on stage. They remained on stage to back singer Johnny Chester and then singer Johnny Devlin.

After they completed the tour the group changed from their Shadows-style and recorded a Beatle-ish number 'I Want You' and by the following year had transformed themselves into a beat group with the new name, MPD Ltd, and became quite successful in Australia.

Philharmonic Hall, The, Hope Street, Liverpool L1

Large concert hall which was primarily used for classical and jazz concerts. During the Mersey Beat days the local country music bands also ran an annual 'Grand Ole Opry' there.

On 10 May 1963 a special beat group contest was taking place at the venue with George Harrison and Dick Rowe among the judges.

The Decca A&R man sat next to George and while they were chatting, George said, 'We've seen a great band down in London called the Rolling Stones who are almost as good as our Roadrunners.' (He was referring to a popular Liverpool R&B group called the Roadrunners.)

Dick Rowe immediately left the hall, caught a train to London and went to see the Stones that evening, signing the group up for Decca and thus making up for the fact that he'd originally turned down the Beatles.

The contest in Liverpool was won by the Escorts – and they weren't signed up by Decca either, but eventually recorded for EMI's Columbia label.

Phillips, Esther

Singer, born Esther Mae Jones in Houston, Texas, on 23 December 1935. At the age of thirteen she began singing with the Johnny Otis Revue under the name Little Esther. She dropped the 'Little' in 1962 and had a number of hits, including 'Release Me' and 'What A Diff'rence A Day Makes'. She recorded the Lennon and McCartney composition 'And I Love Him', issued by Atlantic Records on 22 May 1965. Paul McCartney was so pleased with her rendition of the song at the time that he said it was the best cover version of any Beatles number. When John and Paul were involved in the making of Johnny Hamp's 'The Music Of Lennon & McCartney' for Granada Television, they sent a cable to Esther, who was performing in cabaret in Bermuda, inviting her to appear on their show to sing 'And I Love Him'. She completed her engagement in the West Indies and flew to Manchester to appear in the television special.

She was thrilled that they'd contacted her and said: 'I wanted so much to meet the Beatles in the States but every time I hit town on my own tour, they'd either just been or were coming the next week. I never met four young men before who are all in the genius class.'

Esther died of liver and kidney failure on 7 August 1984.

Phillips, Percy

The man who made the Quarry Men's first record. At the age of 59, Phillips converted the ground floor of his terraced house at 58 Kensington, Liverpool, into a recording studio. He spent £400 on equipment that comprised a tape recorder, MSS disc cutter, amplifier, four-channel mixer and microphones. The front room served as a waiting room for prospective clients and the large back room housed the studio, which was relatively primitive, compared to the professional studios of the time. It featured two large twin-track tape recorders, one microphone, which hung from the ceiling, a stand-up piano and a disc cutter, which produced a metal core 78rpm shellac disc.

The first group he recorded was local country and western outfit Hank Walters & the Dusty Road Ramblers.

John Lennon, Paul McCartney, George Harrison, Colin Hanton and Charles 'Duff' Lowe recorded two numbers there in the summer of 1958: 'That'll Be the Day' and 'In Spite Of All The Danger'.

Phillips was to comment: 'They came here to record a demo disc and as usual I recorded everything on tape in case there were any problems. But I used to wipe the tapes off. It was 17/6d to make both sides of the demo disc. They only had fifteen shillings, so I hung on to the disc until they came back with the rest.'

Phillips died in March 1984.

Photographs

Due to their phenomenal domination of the sixties, the Beatles became the world's most photographed subject during the decade and there were literally tens of thousands of photographs taken of the group. However, if a photographic history of the Beatles were to be outlined, certain photographers would stand out.

Within three months of the formation of the Quarry Men, a friend, Charlie Roberts, took the famous pictures of them performing on the back of a lorry at the Rosebury Street party on 22 June 1957.

The next important image was a box brownie photograph by schoolboy Geoff Rhind, who was a pupil at Quarry Bank School and took the historic shot of the Quarry Men playing at the Woolton Parish Church Fete on 6 July 1957. Leslie Kearney took the shot of the Quarry Men appearing at New Clubmoor Hall on 23 November 1957 and David Hughes photographed the Quarry Men at the Casbah Club in September 1959. Ken Beaton took a photograph of the Silver Beetles performing with Johnny Gentle at the Town Hall, Alloa, Scotland, on Friday, 20 May 1960, although the most important set of pictures of this period were taken ten days earlier at the Wyvern Club, Seel Street, Liverpool, by Chenison Roland whose set of shots include the Silver Beetles performing with both Johnny Hutchinson and Tommy Moore, with reaction shots of Larry Parnes and Billy Fury. Another unique shot was taken at Arnhem Cemetery on the Beatles' first trip to Germany where Stuart, Paul, George and Pete together with Allan and Beryl Williams and Lord Woodbine, are posing before a memorial which states 'Their name liveth for evermore'.

Hamburg, of course, is when the first really sensational photographs of the Beatles were taken by Astrid Kirchherr and Jurgen Vollmer. Astrid had studied photography at the Meister Schule and had been taken on as assistant to her former photographic tutor. Once she had become a friend of the Beatles, she arranged her first photographic session with them, initially meeting them in the Reeperbahn and then taking them to Der Dom, the city park, where she took a series of shots. Over the next few weeks she took them to other locations, including the docks and the railway yards. Jurgen also took photographs of the group, his main action pictures taken at a single session when the group were on stage at the Top Ten Club. He also took photographs of George by the Hamburg lake and of Astrid and Stuart together.

The large, grainy prints were atmospheric and not unlike the shots Bob Freeman was eventually to take for the *With The Beatles* album cover.

Following their Hamburg trip, the Beatles brought the Kirchherr and Vollmer photographs to Bill Harry at *Mersey Beat* with a request to print them. The first used was the photograph which Astrid took of them posing at Der Dom, the Hamburg fair, which was used on the cover of Issue No. 2. The photograph dominated the front page, alerted Liverpool to the fact that the Beatles had made a record in Germany and intrigued Brian Epstein. When the Beatles began to enjoy major success in Britain in 1963, some Fleet Street journalists came to the *Mersey Beat* office asking if they could borrow some early photographs of the Beatles for publicity purposes. *Mersey Beat* lent the prints at no charge, hoping that they could provide further promotion for the band, unaware of such things as photo agencies and their practices. As a result, and without permission, Astrid's photograph of the Beatles at Der Dom not only began to appear in publications throughout the world, but copyright was claimed by a London newspaper – even though the print betrayed a slight tear across the photograph, as in the original *Mersey Beat* print.

With the publication of *Mersey Beat* in 1961, the most complete documentation of Beatle photographs began to be assembled. The first major *Mersey Beat* photographer was Dick Matthews. Dick was a close friend of promoter Sam Leach and had once co-promoted dances with him at Mossway Jive Club in 1958. It was Dick who interested his friend Jim Anderson into lending Bill Harry £50 to launch *Mersey Beat*. Dick took some marvellous photographs for posterity, which were featured in the early issues, of the Beatles in their black leather image playing on stage at the Cavern and the Tower Ballroom. The atmosphere of the times is superbly captured in Dick's shots, especially the action ones on stage when it is obvious that the Beatles are enjoying themselves. He also took many informal shots of the Beatles with friends and at parties.

Another historic session took place on 17 December 1961 at Albert Mariott's studio in Wallasey. Thirty shots were taken and one of the photographs of the Beatles in black leather from this session was used on the cover of Issue 13, the January 1962 issue which announced 'Beatles Top Poll'. This has become one of the classic music paper covers of all.

Since *Mersey Beat* had changed their printers and were now handled by Swale's of Widnes who reproduced photographs from plastic blocks, the paper could now use more photographs. Les Chadwick, a former Junior Art School chum of Bill Harry, was working as a photographer for Peter Kaye Photography in Park Lane. This was a studio owned by Bill Connell. A deal was arranged in which Bill Harry commissioned Peter Kaye Photography to take pictures specifically for *Mersey Beat* in exchange for classified and display advertisements, and the rights to sell photographs to readers, with *Mersey Beat* recommending groups to commission the studio to take their publicity shots. This same deal was hammered out with other local photographers such as Graham Spencer and Harry Watmough resulting in a stream of studio, location and stage shots of the Beatles.

The photographs in music papers at this time were basically static studio shots, formally posed. *Mersey Beat* changed all that with the artistic quality of the Kirchherr/Vollmer pictures, the exciting action of the Matthews pics and the location work of the Peter Kaye Studio. Les Chadwick and Bill Connell decided to try something different and get away from the studio setting, taking photographs of the Beatles and other bands on locations such as building sites and ferry boats. London photographers and publications were later to follow suit.

The majority of Beatles photographs commissioned by *Mersey Beat* from Peter Kaye Photography were taken by Les Chadwick, although a few assignments were undertaken by Bill Connell. When Brian Epstein took over the management of the Beatles he initially had photographs taken by his family photographer Albert Marrion, and then commissioned a number of the *Mersey Beat* photographers to take publicity shots – including Peter Kaye and Harry Watmough.

Graham Spencer, who died in 1983, was a tall, pleasant, photographer with a quite distinctive personality and he documented the Beatles and Mersey Beat groups in a collection of hundreds of photographs in colour and black and white for the pages of *Mersey Beat*.

Harry Watmough was a photographer who specialised in cabaret artists' photographs and mainly took shots for the 'Clubland' section of *Mersey Beat*, although Brian Epstein, trying out each of the *Mersey Beat* photographers for publicity pic sessions, hired Watmough to take studio shots of them with their new mohair suits, looking very sartorial. This was in stark contrast to their previous wild, black leather image and while Pete Best was still a member of the band.

Due primarily to the Hamburg sessions of Kirchherr/ Vollmer and *Mersey Beat* in Liverpool, the Beatles were in the unique position of having a wide range of photographic images available before they'd even secured a recording contract in Britain. A situation which few other groups, if any, could boast of.

Mersey Beat also provided Mike McCartney with his publishing debut by printing his photographs of Paul and the Beatles, using the pseudonym Francis Michael. A selection of Mike's work documenting the early Beatles has been collected in poster/postcard collections, exhibitions and the book *Mike Mac's White And Blacks* (Aurum Press, 1986).

Another important set of early photographs was taken at the Odd Spot Club in Bold Street, Liverpool, on 22 March 1962 by Alan Swerdlow, a friend of Epstein's, who was a former student at Liverpool College of Art. Swerdlow was on the panel of the Students' Union Committee, along with Stuart Sutcliffe and Bill Harry, when they requested Union funds for the Beatles' PA equipment.

The next major photographic figure in the Beatles' life was Dezo Hoffmann, who had been acting as staff photographer to the London-based music paper *Record Mirror* since 1955. In response to readers' enquiries, Dezo went to Liverpool in 1962 to take some photographs of the band. He took photographs of their Abbey Road auditions on 6 June 1962 and for the next three years had numerous studio sessions and travelled with the group regularly, taking thousands of shots of the band, many of which have become famous Beatle images. In April 1963 he visited them in Liverpool, taking shots of them in Sefton Park (one used on the cover of the EP *Twist and Shout*), at the Cavern and having their hair cut at Horne Brothers. His work has been collected together to form several books, including *With The Beatles* (Omnibus Press, 1982) and *The Beatles Conquer America* (Virgin Books, 1984). It was mainly Dezo's work which was featured in the initial promotion of the Beatles in America early in 1964.

Veteran photographer Angus McBean took the famous shot of the group on the EMI stairwell for their *Please Please Me* album and the next photographer associated with their album covers was Robert Freeman, who began taking shots of the group in 1963 and travelled with them as a photographer and friend, eventually handling design and photography for five of their album covers. His cover of the *With The Beatles* album, with its black and white portraits in half light, remains one of the famous early images and Freeman has had several collections of his Beatle photographs published, beginning with *Beatles Ltd* (George Newnes) in 1964.

Norman Parkinson, a leading fashion photographer, next took shots of the group at Abbey Road Studios and a collection of the photographs was published as *The Beatles* (Hutchinson) in 1964.

Once they had become established as international stars, hundreds of different photographers took thousands of shots of the group – at concerts, in hotels, at leisure, with girlfriends, on holiday – and photographers such as Dezo Hoffmann and Robert Freeman were still taking shots of the group on a regular basis. There were also photographers specially commissioned to take official shots of the group and also to document specific events in their personal life such as the wedding of Ringo and Maureen Starkey.

There were also the publicity photographs taken to promote their various film projects.

For a time, Epstein employed Robert Whitaker as official photographer and among the many unique images which Bob captured were those taken for the notorious 'butcher' cover, featuring the Beatles in butchers' smocks holding pieces of raw meat and parts of the bodies of dolls. Whitaker was to produce a book of his Beatle pics in 1991.

One of the major images of the mid-sixties were the shots of the Beatles in their colourful military costumes used in the *Sgt Pepper* sessions, taken by photographer Michael Cooper, who documented the entire *Sgt Pepper* sleeve sessions in his Flood Street studio. Many of the images were published in his posthumous book *Blinds and Shutters*.

John Kelly was the photographer who provided the set of colour portraits enclosed with *The Beatles* double album package and Iain Macmillan took the famous *Abbey Road* shots, the most famous being the front cover photograph on the *Abbey Road* album, depicting the group walking across the zebra crossing. The photographs for their final album *Let It Be* were taken by Ethan Russell, who also provided the shots for the special *Get Back* book which was included in the package when the *Let It Be* album was originally issued.

During their career, other notable photographs of the Beatles include those taken by American photographer Richard Avedon and, in particular, his psychedelic portraits; the John and Yoko nude shots and the final live performance on the roof of the Apple building.

Picture Of You, A

This Beveridge/Oakman composition was a British hit for Joe Brown & the Bruvvers in 1962. An odd choice for the Beatles' repertoire, although it was one of Brian Epstein's favourite records at the time. George sang the number and the group performed it on their BBC radio show 'Here We Go' on 15 June 1962.

Pigalle, Piccadilly, London W1

An unusual venue for a Beatles show. The Pigalle was a sophisticated nightclub in the heart of London's West End. The Beatles appeared here on the evening of Sunday, 21 April 1963 following their appearance earlier that day at the *New Musical Express* poll winners' concert at Wembley.

The reason why Brian Epstein booked the group into this luxuriously decorated club with a wealthy middle-aged clientele was because he was seeking a West End showcase for the group, a place where he could invite the leading London booking agents and television producers to view the band.

The Beatles were advertised as 'The Most Sensational Group In England' and the show lasted from 8.00 p.m. to 11.30 p.m., admittance was 12/6d and the other act on the bill was Dave Anthony and the Druids.

To an audience of businessmen and their companions, the Beatles probably only had curiosity appeal. John Lennon noted the reaction and, with a degree of sarcasm, told them 'You can scream if you like, you know.'

The club was to undergo several transformations and name changes as times and tastes altered and in the 1980s became the fashionable discotheque, Xenon's.

Piggies

A George Harrison composition. When George was writing the number he needed a line to rhyme with 'backing' and 'lacking' and his mother came up with, 'What they need is a damn good whacking!'

He'd originally begun writing the number in 1966 but didn't finish it until 1968 when it was included on *The Beatles* double album.

Recording began on Thursday, 19 September 1968, and Chris Thomas was producer of the session and also played harpsichord on the track.

This was one of the numbers which Charles Manson believed was a special hidden message from the Beatles in which they called for a revolution. A version was included on the Beatles' *Anthology 3* CDs.

Pilbeam, Peter

The first BBC producer to book the Beatles for a radio show.

In 1962 he was holding auditions with new bands for the 'Teenager's Turn' programme, based in Manchester, and was impressed by the Beatles. In his audition report he wrote: 'An unusual group, not as "rocky" as most, more country and western with a tendency to play music.'

Commenting on their first radio appearance to Kevin Howlett in *The Beatles At The Beeb* book, Peter said: 'We used to get some terrific audiences down at the Playhouse for the teenage shows that we did, and we'd have the Northern Dance Orchestra on stage trying to look like teenagers with their chunky jumpers on, which we kitted them out with. We used to have a group in each programme, a guest singer and a presenter and it was the usual style of show that we did in those days for half an hour. The Beatles came on and did a very good show. I was very impressed with them and I booked them straight away for another date after that first show.'

'Teenager's Turn', on which the Beatles made their radio debut, was broadcast on 8 March 1962. The programme underwent a name change to 'Here We Go', still produced by Pilbeam, who booked the Beatles for four appearances on the show, broadcast on 15 June and 25 October 1962 and 25 January and 12 March 1963.

Pilchard

The title of a play which John and Paul tried to write in their early days together. Paul later described it as: '. . . a sort of precursor of *The Life of Brian*, about a working-class weirdo who was always upstairs playing. It was a down-market Second Coming. But we had to give it up because we couldn't actually work out how it went on, how you actually filled up all the pages.'

Pinwheel Twist

A number which Paul McCartney wrote for Pete Best to perform on stage. Best told broadcaster Spencer Leigh: 'Paul wrote the song and asked me to do it. He coupled it with Joey Dee's hit "The Peppermint Twist". I used to get up and do the twist on stage and Paul played my drums. It was a little novelty act and it went down well with the fans.'

When the Beatles performed the number, Paul took over on drums, George played Paul's left-handed bass right-handed and Pete sang.

Pittsburgh Civic Arena, Pittsburgh, Pennsylvania

This venue on Monday, 14 September 1964, drew a maximum capacity of 12,603. There was a huge police presence at the arena and a Beatles press conference was held at 6.00 p.m. in Conference Room A. After their show there, the Beatles had intended to leave the arena by police car, but the access was blocked by fans and they were smuggled out of another exit and left in a limousine heading straight for the airport.

Plastic Ono Band, The

In 1969 when John Lennon was more interested in cementing a creative partnership with Yoko than recording with the Beatles and soon after changing his name to John Ono Lennon, he created the name Plastic Ono Band. The first record under this name, 'Give Peace A Chance', was issued on 4 July 1969 (7 July in the US). John and Yoko had recorded the number at the Hotel La Reine Elizabeth in Montreal, Canada, with a various assortment of friends, including Tommy Smothers, Petula Clark, Rosemary and Timothy Leary, Rabbi Geinsberg, Allen Ginsberg and members of the Canadian Chapter of the Radha Krsna Temple.

The Plastic Ono Band was due to be promoted at a 'Give Peace A Chance' press reception at the Chelsea Town Hall on 3 July 1969. As John and Yoko had been involved in a car accident, Ringo and Maureen deputised for them – and as the Plastic Ono Band didn't exist as a group, some plastic robots were used as substitutes.

The second Plastic Ono Band single was 'Cold Turkey', issued on 24 October 1969 (20 October in the US). This time John and Yoko were accompanied by Eric Clapton on lead guitar, Klaus Voormann on bass and Ringo Starr on drums.

The Plastic Ono Band were not only a recording band, John

formed a group of musicians using that name to accompany him to Canada for the *Toronto Rock 'n' Roll Revival Concert*. They were Eric Clapton on lead guitar, Alan White on drums and Klaus Voormann on bass guitar. Their performance was recorded and it was issued as an album on 12 December 1969 as *The Plastic Ono Band – Live Peace In Toronto 1969*. John also formed a Plastic Ono Supergroup who made a single appearance at the Lyceum Ballroom in London on 15 December 1969. Among the group of musicians John arranged to play with him was George Harrison.

The next single was 'Instant Karma', credited to Lennon/Ono with the Plastic Ono Band. This was issued on 6 February 1970 (20 February in the US). The other musicians were George Harrison on guitar and grand piano, Klaus Voormann on bass guitar and electric piano, Alan White on drums and grand piano and Billy Preston on organ. The next album was recorded after John and Yoko had experienced Primal Therapy and was simply called *John Lennon/Plastic Ono Band*. It was issued on 11 December 1970 and the musicians, apart from John and Yoko, were Ringo Starr on drums, Klaus Voormann on bass guitar and Billy Preston on piano.

A single, 'Mother', credited to John Lennon/Plastic Ono Band, was issued in America, but not in Britain, on 28 December 1970.

The following single, issued on 12 March 1971 (22 March in the US), was called 'Power To The People', credited to John Lennon and the Plastic Ono Band, while the flipside 'Open Your Box' was credited to Yoko Ono and the Plastic Ono Band. The musicians supplementing John and Yoko were Klaus Voormann on bass guitar and Jim Gordon on drums.

Imagine was the next album, issued on 8 October 1971 (9 September in the US) and credited to John Lennon and the Plastic Ono Band, with the Flux Fiddlers. There were various musicians on individual tracks and included Klaus Voormann on bass guitar and piano, Alan White on drums, Nicky Hopkins on piano, Steve Brendel on upright bass, George Harrison on dobro, Ted Turner on acoustic guitar, Rod Linton on acoustic guitar, John Tout on acoustic guitar, Jim Gordon on drums, John Barham on harmonium, King Curtis on saxophone, Joey Molland and Tom Evans of Badfinger on acoustic guitars and Andy Cresswell-Davis on acoustic guitar.

The next release was *Some Time In New York City*, a double-album set issued on 15 September 1972 (12 June in the US). The first album was credited to John and Yoko/Plastic Ono Band with Elephants Memory plus Invisible Strings, the second to the Plastic Ono Supergroup and the Plastic Ono Mothers (because part of it was recorded at a concert with the Mothers of Invention).

A single followed, 'Happy Xmas (War Is Over)', credited to John and Yoko/Plastic Ono Band with the Harlem Community Choir, issued on 24 November 1972 (1 December in the US). No more releases used the name Plastic Ono Band although the *Mind Games* album was credited to John Lennon with the Plastic U.F. Ono Band, the single 'Whatever Gets You Thru The Night' to John Lennon with the Plastic Ono Nuclear Band and the *Walls And Bridges* album to John Lennon with the Plastic Ono Nuclear Band.

Playhouse Theatre, The, St John's Road, Manchester

Used by the BBC to record radio shows before live audiences in the sixties.

The Beatles appeared on their first radio session here on 7 March 1962. The show was called 'Teenager's Turn' and it was broadcast on the BBC's Light Programme between 5.00 p.m. and 5.30 p.m. the next day.

The group performed 'Dream Baby', 'Memphis Tennessee' and 'Please Mr Postman' before a live audience. Resident musicians on the programme were the NDO (Northern Dance Orchestra). The group recorded another number at the session, 'Hello Little Girl', but it was not broadcast. The show was produced by Peter Pilbeam.

The group were to return to the Playhouse for four sessions of a programme called 'Here We Go', also produced by Pilbeam. Their first 'Here We Go' show was recorded on 10 June 1962 and transmitted on 15 June. The group were heard performing 'Ask Me Why', 'Besame Mucho' and 'A Picture Of You' and among the vocal supporters in the audience were members of their Liverpool fan club who had travelled to Manchester by coach. The Beatles next appeared on 'Here We Go' on 26 October, having recorded the show the day previously, affording Ringo his first BBC Radio session. They performed 'Love Me Do', 'A Taste Of Honey' and 'P.S. I Love You'. Another number, 'Sheila', was not broadcast. On 16 January 1963 they performed at the Playhouse once again with 'Chains', 'Please Please Me' and 'Ask Me Why', all transmitted several days later on 25 January. Another number recorded for 'Here We Go' but not transmitted was 'Three Cool Cats'.

They returned to the venue on 6 March 1963 to record 'Misery', 'Do You Want To Know A Secret?', 'Please Please Me' and 'I Saw Her Standing There', but the latter wasn't broadcast when 'Here We Go' was transmitted on 12 March.

Plaza Ballroom, Halesowen Road, Old Hill, Dudley, Staffordshire

A Midlands booking which the Beatles undertook on 11 January 1963, during a severe winter in which there were fierce blizzards. That evening they had been engaged for a double-booking, but due to the nature of the weather they were unable to travel on to the Ritz Ballroom in Birmingham and the engagement there had to be rearranged.

They appeared at the Plaza for the second and last time on 5 July 1963. Also on the bill were a Birmingham band, Denny & the Diplomats, led by Denny Laine.

Plaza Ballroom, Queen Street, St Helens, Lancashire

The ballroom opened in 1956 and began to feature local groups in 1958 when the enterprising manager, Harry Bostock, held a rock 'n' roll group contest. It was also part of the company Whetstone Entertainments, which also promoted dances at the Orrell Park Ballroom in Liverpool and the Riverpark Ballroom in Chester.

In 1959 the Plaza switched to a policy of exclusively featuring groups and was open four nights a week: Friday, Saturday, Sunday and Monday. There were usually three groups per night and admission charges varied from 2s.6d. to 3s.6d.

Most of the top Mersey groups appeared there, including the Beatles, Gerry & the Pacemakers, the Fourmost, the Swinging Bluejeans, the Merseybeats and the Searchers.

The Beatles made their debut there on 25 June 1962 in a booking arranged by Brian Epstein for which they received £25. The Monday evening event was compered by Bob Wooler, entrance was two shillings and sixpence and the support band was the Big Three. The event lasted from 7.30 p.m.–11.00 p.m. and it was the Beatles' first appearance in St Helens and the first of a series of Monday night bookings. Promotional leaflets read: 'Harry Bostock presents his *Big Beat Bargain Night* starring the North's No. 1 Rock combo THE BEATLES, Just back from their Sensational German Tour. Now Recording Exclusively for Parlophone. They're terrific . . . you must see them! FIRST EVER APPEARANCE IN ST HELENS.'

The group also appeared there on 2 July, 9 July and 16 July.

Their last appearance at the venue took place on 4 March 1963 and it was the first booking for which they received a three-figure sum – £100.

Ballroom manager Harry Bostock was a Mancunian who had previously led bands in Birmingham, Manchester, Folkestone and

Liverpool. He could also play eight instruments, including piano, trumpet, saxophone, drums, violin and clarinet.

Plaza De Toros De Madrid, Madrid, Spain

The Beatles' first appearance in Spain, which took place in the main bullring at Madrid on 2 July 1965 when the group appeared in a single concert at 8.30 p.m. Among the other acts on the bill were Freddie Davis, the Martin Brothers, Michel, the Modern 4, the Rustiks and the Trinidad Steel Band.

Plaza De Toros Monumental, Avenue de les Corts, Catalanes, Barcelona, Spain

The final concert of the Beatles' fourteen-date European tour and their second and last appearance in Spain. The group appeared here on Saturday, 3 July 1965 and, like their previous Spanish appearance, it took place in a bullring.

Plaza Hotel, West 58th Street, New York City

Famous conservative American hotel where the Beatles stayed when they first arrived in New York. After the group had held their press conference at Kennedy Airport on Friday, 7 February 1964, they were driven straight to the Plaza in air-conditioned Cadillac limousines.

As they arrived they discovered the hotel was surrounded by crowds of fans, held in check by 100 New York City cops with a squad of mounted police.

The management issued a statement that they wouldn't have accepted the bookings if they'd known who the Beatles were. They had assumed they were English businessmen. There has been some doubt cast upon this story as the hotel certainly knew who the Beatles were – and the hotel staff queued up for autographs.

The group were taken to the ten-room Presidential Suites (Suites 1209 to 1216) on the twelfth floor, which overlooked 58th Street. One of the corridors was sealed off by guards from the Burns Detective Agency and there were two guards on duty around the clock. The suites contained expensive modern furniture in creams, browns and turquoise. Fan mail was brought to them there, and there was also camera and radio equipment stored there by the various media who came for interviews. While the Beatles were sitting around they took a call from Brian Matthew in London for an interview on 'Saturday Club'.

The next day, a Saturday, found George in bed with a throat problem. His sister Louise had arrived at the hotel and moved in to nurse him. The hotel doctor, Dr Gordon, told George, 'I'll have to get you fit, otherwise my young relatives will blunt all my needles.' He did, however, insist on a signed photo before starting treatment.

The rest of the group attended another press reception in the Plaza's Baroque Room during which one female reporter noticed Ringo smoking and told him that it set a bad example for teenagers. Ringo said, 'Who's a teenager? I'm 23', and an angry John Lennon rounded on her, 'We're not here to set examples for teenagers.'

New York disc jockey Murray the K breezed into their suite with the Ronettes, still recording his show. 'We're what's happening, Babe. We're Murray the K and the Beatles, Babe on W-I-N-S'. The Beatles admired his nerve and he became one of their regular escorts over the following few days, taking them to various nightclubs and restaurants and introducing them to starlets such as Stella Stevens, Tuesday Weld and Jill Haworth.

A report in the *New York Herald Tribune* read: 'The Beatles are all short, slight kids from Liverpool who wear four-button coats, stovepipe pants, ankle-high black boots with cuban heels and droll looks on their faces. The Plaza, one of the most sedate hotels in New York was petrified. The reservations were accepted months ago before the Plaza knew it was for a rock and roll group.'

Please Mr Postman

A number composed by Brian Holland, Robert Bateman and Berry Gordy which was recorded by the Marvelettes as their debut single and brought them a million-selling No. 1 entry in the States in December 1961. The Beatles included it in their repertoire in 1962 with John on lead vocal. They performed the number on their BBC radio shows 'Teenager's Turn', 'Pop Go The Beatles' and 'From Us To You'. They recorded it for their *With The Beatles* album. The track is also to be found on the American *Beatles Second Album* and *4 By the Beatles* EP and the collections *The Beatles Box* and *The Beatles Collection*.

Please Please Me (Album)

The Beatles' debut album, recorded in one marathon session on Monday, 11 February 1963. Recording manager George Martin was amazed at the staying power of the group as they continued recording far longer than originally planned, including the time allotted for their lunch break. By the evening, when they did take a break in the canteen, he was able to tell them that they just needed one more number to complete the album – and they immediately decided on 'Twist And Shout'.

The group recorded eight of their own compositions and six

other numbers which were then part of their stage repertoire. Paul had originally wanted to record 'Besame Mucho', but it was decided to include 'A Taste Of Honey', from the British stage play, instead.

'Please Please Me' was issued on Parlophone PCS 3042 on 22 March 1963 and reached No. 1 in the British charts, eventually selling over half a million copies.

The all-day session cost approximately £400 and was produced with George Martin, engineer Norman Smith and second engineer Richard Langham.

The tracks were – Side One: 'I Saw Her Standing There', 'Misery', 'Anna (Go To Him)', 'Chains', 'Boys', 'Ask Me Why', 'Please Please Me'. Side Two: 'Love Me Do', 'P.S. I Love You', 'Baby It's You', 'Do You Want To Know A Secret?', 'A Taste Of Honey', 'There's A Place', 'Twist And Shout'.

The American equivalent had a name change to *Introducing The Beatles* when it was issued by Vee Jay in July 1963.

Please Please Me (Single)

The Beatles' second single, issued on Parlophone R 4983 on 11 January 1963. The group had originally hoped to use the number as the 'B' side of 'Love Me Do', but George Martin was unhappy about the arrangement and suggested they put it aside. Martin had wanted them to issue Mitch Murray's 'How Do You Do It?' as a single, but acknowledged that the rearranged 'Please Please Me' was the right one. As soon as they'd completed recording on Monday, 26 November, Martin said to them, 'You've just made your first No. 1.' He was right, it went to No. 1 in most charts. The new arrangement owed something to Martin, as Paul commented: 'George Martin's contribution was a big one, actually. The first time he really ever showed that he could see beyond what we were offering him was "Please Please Me". It was originally conceived as a Roy Orbison-type thing, you know. George Martin said, "Well, we'll put the tempo up." He lifted the tempo and we all thought that was much better and that was a big hit.'

The number was penned by John who claimed that he'd thought of the idea when he remembered a Bing Crosby song which included the line, 'Please lend a little ear to my pleas'. The flipside of the single, which was originally issued on the red Parlophone label, was 'Ask Me Why'. Later the single was issued on the black label. It was included on their album *Please Please Me*, their EP *The Beatles Hits* and the compilation *The Beatles 1962–1966*. It was re-released in Britain in 1983 in different forms, one of them being a limited-edition picture disc.

In America it first surfaced as a Vee Jay single on VJ 498 with 'Ask Me Why' on the flip on 25 February 1963. It made no impact. It was re-released by Vee Jay on VJ 581 on 30 January 1964 with 'From Me To You' on the flip and reached No. 3 in the charts. Before Vee Jay closed as a company they reissued it as a single on OL 150 Oldies 45 on 10 August 1964, although it didn't chart and in October it was included on two Vee Jay albums, *The Beatles vs The Four Seasons* and *Songs, Pictures and Stories Of The Fabulous Beatles*. Capitol included it on their album *The Early Beatles* in March 1965.

Its release in Britain was greeted by enthusiastic reviews in the British press and it was also praised by radio disc jockeys. Brian Matthew said that the Beatles were 'Musically and visually the most accomplished group to emerge since the Shadows'.

'Please Please Me' provided a chart hit for David Cassidy in 1974. A version was included on the Beatles' *Anthology 1* CDs.

Polythene Pam

One of the songs which John had penned in India. The track was featured on the *Abbey Road* album, although at one time it had been considered for *The Beatles* white album. John commented: 'I wrote this one in India and when I recorded it I used a thick Liverpool accent because it was supposed to be about a mythical Liverpool scrubber dressed up in her jackboots and kilt.' John later revealed that it concerned a true incident when a friend of his unsuccessfully tried to involve him in an orgy. On the album the song ran straight into Paul's composition 'She Came In Through The Bathroom Window' and they were both recorded as one song at Abbey Road sessions on Friday, 25 July, and Monday, 28 July 1969. Extras included John on maracas, Paul on cow bells and piano and George on tambourine. A version was included on the *Anthology 3* CDs.

Pop Gear

A 68-minute film, directed by Frederick Goode. Produced by Associated British-Pathe, the movie went on general release throughout Britain on 18 April 1965.

Jimmy Savile hosted a string of groups in a format similar to the TV show 'Top Of The Pops'. The Beatles were shown singing 'She Loves You' and 'Twist And Shout', although both performances had been edited from the Pathe News feature recorded at the Apollo, Ardwick, Manchester, on 20 November 1963.

Other acts of interest in the movie included Billy J. Kramer & the Dakotas performing 'Little Children', Peter & Gordon with 'World

Without Love', the Fourmost with 'A Little Loving' and Tommy Quickly performing 'Humpty Dumpty'.

Pop Go The Beatles

A 1963 series of radio shows, hosted by the Beatles. The show's presenter was Terry Henebery and when discussions were taking place to decide what it should be called, Francis Line, a production secretary, suggested the title to Henebery. The Beatles began each show singing the title song 'Pop Go The Beatles', which was a variation of the traditional tune 'Pop Goes The Weasel'.

The first four shows were produced by Lee Peters and in each programme the Beatles featured a guest artist.

On the show's debut on 4 June 1963 which they had recorded on 24 May at the BBC's Studio 2 in Aeolian Hall in New Bond Street, London, the Beatles performed 'From Me To You', 'Everybody's Trying To Be My Baby', 'Do You Want To Know A Secret?', 'You Really Got A Hold On Me', 'Misery' and 'The Hippy Hippy Shake'. Their special guests were the Lorne Gibson Trio.

On the 11 June show, recorded at the BBC's Paris Studios on 1 June, they performed 'Too Much Monkey Business', 'I Got To Find My Baby', 'Young Blood', 'Baby It's You', 'Till There Was You' and 'Love Me Do'. Their guests were the Countrymen.

Their third show, transmitted on 18 June, Paul McCartney's 21st birthday, had also been recorded on 1 June, and the group performed 'A Shot Of Rhythm And Blues', 'Memphis Tennessee', 'A Taste Of Honey', 'Sure To Fall In Love (With You)', 'Money' and 'From Me To You'. Their guests were Carter Lewis and the Southerners, a group formed by John Carter and Ken Lewis. They had a minor hit in 1963 with 'Your Momma's Out Of Town', but by 1964 had changed their name to the Ivy League. Among the various members who passed through the Southerners' line-up were Jimmy Page (later to become leader of Led Zeppelin) and Viv Prince (later to become a member of the Pretty Things).

On the 25 June transmission, recorded at the BBC's No. 5 studio in Delaware Road, Maida Vale, on 17 June, they performed 'I Saw Her Standing There', 'Anna (Go To Him)', 'Boys', 'Chains', 'P.S. I Love You' and 'Twist And Shout'. A recording of 'A Taste Of Honey' was not transmitted. Their guests were the Bachelors, a popular Irish vocal trio who were to notch up thirteen chart hits between 1963 and 1967, including their No. 1 record 'Diane'. They comprised John Stokes, Con Cluskey and Dec Cluskey.

This was Peters' last stint as producer of the show, which had a break of three weeks to gauge the audience reaction, which proved positive. As a result, the programme returned on 16 July with a new producer Rodney Burke. The show was recorded on 2 July at Maida Vale and the Beatles performed 'That's All Right, Mama', 'There's A Place', 'Carol', 'Soldier Of Love', 'Lend Me Your Comb' and 'Clarabella'. Their guests were Duffy Power and the Graham Bond Quartet, who were to record the *Please Please Me* album track 'I Saw Her Standing There' as a single, released by Parlophone on 26 April 1963. Although they had the foresight to become one of the first artists to record Lennon & McCartney material, it wasn't a hit for them.

Three other numbers were recorded by the Beatles, but not transmitted – 'Three Cool Cats', 'Sweet Little Sixteen' and 'Ask Me Why'.

Their show on 23 July was recorded at the Aeolian Hall on 10 July and presented their performances of 'Sweet Little Sixteen', 'A Taste Of Honey', 'Nothin' Shakin' (But The Leaves On The Trees)', 'Love Me Do', 'Lonesome Tears In My Eyes' and 'So How Come (No One Loves Me)'. Their guests were Carter Lewis and the Southerners.

Their 30 July show had also been recorded on 10 July and the Beatles performed 'Memphis Tennessee', 'Do You Want To Know A Secret?', 'Till There Was You', 'Matchbox', 'Please Mr Postman' and 'The Hippy Hippy Shake'. Their guests were the Searchers.

The show on 6 August had been recorded at the Paris Studio on 16 July and featured the Beatles performing 'I'm Gonna Sit Right Down And Cry (Over You)', 'Crying, Waiting, Hoping', 'Kansas City/Hey! Hey! Hey!', 'To Know Her Is To Love Her', 'The Honeymoon Song' and 'Twist And Shout'. Their guests were the Swinging Bluejeans.

The 13 August programme had been recorded on 16 July when, in fact, three complete shows had been put in the can at the same time. On this programme the group played 'Long Tall Sally', 'Please Please Me', 'She Loves You', 'You Really Got A Hold On Me', 'I'll Get You' and 'I Got A Woman'. Their guests were the Hollies.

The show on 20 August had the Beatles performing 'She Loves You', 'Words Of Love', 'Glad All Over', 'I Just Don't Understand', 'Devil In Her Heart' and 'Slow Down'. Their guests were Russ Sainty and the Nu-Notes.

On 1 August the next two shows were recorded at the Playhouse Theatre, Manchester due to the group's commitments in the North. On the 27 August show the group performed 'Oh! My Soul', 'Don't Ever Change', 'Twist And Shout', 'She Loves You', 'Anna (Go To Him)' and 'A Shot Of Rhythm And Blues'. Their guests were the Cyril Davies Rhythm And Blues All Stars with Long John Baldry. Davies was an innovative harmonica player who'd originally performed with Alexis Korner between 1957 and 1962. He formed the All Stars at the close of 1962 and Baldry joined him in January 1963. Tragically, Davies died in January 1964 and the band broke up.

The Beatles' 3 September show saw them performing 'From Me To You', 'I'll Get You', 'Money', 'There's A Place', 'Honey Don't' and 'Roll Over Beethoven'. They also recorded 'Lucille', 'Baby It's You' and 'She Loves You', but these tracks weren't transmitted. Their guests were Brian Poole & the Tremeloes.

10 September heralded their thirteenth show and was recorded at the Aeolian Hall on 3 September, when in a lengthy session lasting almost nine hours, they recorded the next three shows. The group performed 'Too Much Monkey Business', 'Till There Was You', 'Love Me Do', 'I'll Get You', 'A Taste Of Honey' and 'The Hippy Hippy Shake'. Their guests were Johnny Kidd & the Pirates.

Their penultimate show on 17 September had them performing 'Chains', 'You Really Got A Hold On Me', 'Misery', 'Lucille', 'From Me To You' and 'Boys'. A version of 'A Taste Of Honey' was not transmitted. Their guests were the Marauders, a group from Stoke-on-Trent who had a minor hit with 'That's What I Want' in 1963.

For their final show on 24 September the Beatles selected 'She Loves You', 'Ask Me Why', 'Devil In Her Heart', 'I Saw Her Standing There', 'Sure To Fall (In Love With You)' and 'Twist And Shout'. Their guests were Tony Rivers & the Castaways, a talented group from Dagenham, noted for their vocal harmony, who were to cover the Beach Boys' 'God Only Knows' in 1966. At one time Geoff and Pete Swettenham and John Perry, who went on to form Grapefruit, were members.

Pop Inn

A BBC Light Programme chat show. On Tuesday, 9 April 1963 the Beatles arrived at the Paris Studio in London to rehearse for their live broadcast, which took place between 1.00 and 1.45 p.m. Their new single 'From Me To You' was played. Other guests on the programme that day were Liverpool comedian Arthur Askey, pianist Winifred Atwell and disc jockey David Jacobs.

Pops And Lenny

The Beatles made their second national BBC Television appearance on this children's show on Thursday, 16 May 1963. Lenny was a puppet featured by ventriloquist Terry Hall, whose catchphrase was 'Don't embawass me!' The Beatles performed 'From Me To You' and 'Please Please Me' and joined the finale with Patsy Ann

Noble, the Raindrops, the Ben Hayes Octet, and Terry and Lenny to sing 'After You've Gone'. The puppet was later featured on a show aiding children with reading difficulties, 'Reading with Lenny the Lion', until Terry decided to retire following the death of his wife in 1980 and settled in Coventry.

Pop's Happening

A programme produced by the pirate station Radio Caroline. Paul McCartney pre-recorded an interview for the show, which was broadcast on Sunday, 26 December 1965.

Pop '63

A Swedish radio show. The Beatles recorded for the show during their short Swedish tour on 24 October 1963. The group recorded the programme at the Karlaplansstudio in Stockholm. Among the numbers the group performed were: 'From Me To You', 'Roll Over Beethoven', 'Money', 'You Really Got A Hold On Me', 'She Loves You', 'Twist And Shout' and 'I Saw Her Standing There'. There have been bootleg releases of this transmission, although they have been mistakenly attributed to another Swedish radio show recorded a few days later, called 'Drop In'.

Precht, Bob

Producer of 'The Ed Sullivan Show'. Precht, who was also Sullivan's son-in-law, met Brian Epstein at his New York hotel to discuss booking the Beatles on the show. Sullivan had wanted to book the band after seeing Beatlemania in force at Heathrow Airport. Precht wasn't really aware of their appeal and had no idea how they'd suit American audiences and offered them a single appearance on the show. Brian insisted they be bill-toppers and after the discussion, a deal was struck in which the Beatles would headline two shows on consecutive Sundays, 9 and 16 February 1964. For each show they would receive $3,500, with Sullivan paying their air fares.

Presley, Elvis

The Beatles are the most famous group in popular music history and Elvis Presley is the most famous solo singer.

Born Elvis Aaron Presley on 8 January 1935 in East Tupelo, Mississippi, Elvis was to begin his phenomenal music career in 1954, just two years before John Lennon founded the Quarry Men.

In the British charts Elvis was to share the same number of No. 1 hits as the Beatles and remains the artist who has spent more weeks in the No. 1 position in the charts than anyone else. He's also spent more weeks in the charts than any other artist, had the largest number of hits and more Top Ten entries than any other artist. His chart success in America was also incredible, beginning with his No. 1 hit 'Heartbreak Hotel' in 1956 and stretching until 1981, a few years after his death at the age of 42 on 16 August 1977.

Elvis was a major influence on the Beatles and on John Lennon in particular. John once said, 'Nothing really affected me until I heard Elvis. If there hadn't been Elvis, there would not have been the Beatles.'

When the Quarry Men formed they began to introduce Elvis numbers into their repertoire, performed by either John or Paul, which included 'All Shook Up', 'Blue Moon Of Kentucky', 'Hound Dog', 'Jailhouse Rock', 'Mean Woman Blues', 'I Forgot To Remember To Forget', 'I'm Gonna Sit Right Down And Cry Over You', 'It's Now Or Never', 'That's All Right (Mama)' and 'Love Me Tender' (a showcase for Stuart Sutcliffe).

George Harrison was to comment, 'I remember at school there was all that thing about Elvis. When a record came along like "Heartbreak Hotel" it was so amazing. We know Elvis is great. He stopped being a rocker and they made him go into the army, and by the time he came out he was a clean, healthy American, doing clean, healthy songs and films. But basically he's got such a great bluesy voice.'

Paul McCartney was to say, 'Every time I felt low, I just put on an Elvis record and I'd feel great, beautiful.'

When Brian Epstein began touting the Beatles to the British record companies, he told them that the Beatles would become bigger than Elvis and when the Beatles eventually flew to America to appear on 'The Ed Sullivan Show', there was a congratulatory telegram from Elvis, which was read out on the air – although it was Colonel Tom Parker who had actually sent it.

During the group's first concert tour of America, when Brian Epstein arrived at the Hilton Hotel, San Francisco, he received a telegram from Parker offering to help as a friend and asking Brian to phone him up. Once the two were in touch with each other they became firm friends.

Journalist Chris Hutchins of the New Musical Express was travelling with the Beatles on their American tour in 1964 and on 30 August, when they were in Atlantic City, he passed on Elvis's private number, which Colonel Parker had given him, to Paul McCartney, who phoned Elvis in Memphis. He apologised for the fact that the Beatles hadn't been able to take advantage of an invitation to visit Elvis at Graceland because of security reasons and said, 'How do you do. I want to tell you that we all think it's a drag that we weren't able to get together with you.' Elvis told Paul that he'd just got an electric bass guitar which he was learning to play. Paul asked if Elvis would be coming to Britain. 'Soon, I hope,' Elvis said, then asked if the Beatles would be making a film in Hollywood. Paul said that they'd continue to make their films in England.

Elvis said, 'Tell the other Beatles that I think they're doing a great job' and the two of them then discussed records. Elvis remarked that he liked the cover of the *With The Beatles* album, with their faces in half light, and said it reminded him of the faces in the British movie *Children Of The Damned*. The conversation ended with them agreeing that they'd try to get together as soon as possible.

That event happened on a sunny evening in California, on Friday, 27 August 1965.

Chris Hutchins was once again the mediator and the Beatles arrived at Elvis's home on 565 Perugia Way, Bel Air, at 10.00 p.m. from nearby 2850 Benedict Canyon, where they were staying. Elvis met them at the door and he was dressed in a red shirt and grey trousers. After greeting them, he took them into the living-room where there were members of his 'Memphis Mafia'. The Beatles were accompanied by Brian Epstein, Neil Aspinall, Mal Evans and Tony Barrow.

The main room was large and circular and Priscilla Presley was also there. Initially there was a degree of nervousness and, to break the ice, Elvis said, 'Look, guys, if you're just going to sit and stare at me, then I'm going to bed.' Everyone laughed. George squatted on the floor, Ringo began to look through Elvis's record collection and Brian and the Colonel began to chat.

Elvis suggested that they sing and play together and three guitars were brought over, including an electric bass, and plugged into amplifiers. John played rhythm and Elvis was on bass. 'Now here's how I play bass,' he told Paul, 'Not too good, but I'm practising!' Paul played piano and George played third guitar. Elvis turned to Ringo and said, 'Too bad we left the drums in Memphis.'

Paul said, 'Elvis, lad, you're coming along quite well there on the old bass. Keep up the rehearsals and me and Mr Epstein will make you a star.'

While they were playing 'You're My World', John said, 'This beats talking, doesn't it?'

The jam session lasted for an hour, during which Elvis drank 7-Up and the Beatles drank scotch and coke. Elvis didn't smoke.

John knew that Elvis liked Peter Sellers, so he imitated his voice, saying, 'Zis is ze way it should be; ze small homey gathering wiz a few friends and a leetle music.'

Paul was later to say that their jam session was captured on Elvis's tape machine, but George denied that there was ever a recording.

In the meantime Parker had escorted Epstein into the games room and unveiled a roulette table which had been disguised as a coffee table. The two gamblers began to play. Epstein asked the Colonel if Elvis would be touring in the future and Parker told him, 'We'd love to hit the road, but we have to think of giving the maximum enjoyment to the maximum fans and the best way to do this is by making films, which can be seen by millions.'

Elvis and the Beatles began to discuss various topics, including songwriting, films, tours and records.

John said, 'When the fans went for you, you were up there all alone. With us, it's four against everybody and we can draw support from each other.'

When they were discussing life on the road, Elvis said, 'I remember once in Vancouver. We'd only done a number or two when some of the fans rushed the stage. It was lucky the guys and I got off in time. They tipped the whole damn rostrum over.'

He also told them, 'I once took off from Atlanta, Georgia, in a small two-engined plane and one of the engines failed. Boy, was I scared! I really thought that my number was up. We had to take everything out of our pockets that was sharp and rest our heads on pillows between our knees. When we finally got down safely the pilot was soaking in sweat, although there was snow on the ground outside.'

George then told him how the Beatles had been flying out from Liverpool when a window on the plane suddenly swung open.

Another topic was cars, with Elvis and John talking about their recently acquired Rolls-Royce Phantom Vs.

The meeting lasted for three hours and the Beatles left at 2.00 a.m. As they departed, John said, 'Tanks for de music, Elvis. Long live ze King.' Parker had given each of them a boxful of Elvis records. Epstein promised to send Parker a Shetland pony and Parker said he'd give Brian a cocktail cabinet. The Beatles invited Elvis to join them the following evening at Benedict Canyon, but he didn't make it – although some members of his entourage did.

Commenting on the meeting, Ringo said, 'Fantastic, He was just like one of us, none of the old Hollywood show-off thing.'

The Beatles as a group never met Elvis again. On the death of Epstein, Elvis sent a message to the Beatles expressing: 'Deepest condolences on the loss of a good friend to you and all of us'. George managed to visit Elvis backstage at Madison Square Garden in June 1972 and Ringo visited Elvis backstage at one of his Las Vegas shows.

Elvis was to record several Beatles compositions, including 'Hey Jude', 'Yesterday' and 'Something'.

Preston, Billy

Born in Houston, Texas, on 9 September 1946, Billy Preston began to carve a reputation for himself as a support musician in America. The Gospel Rock keyboards player first met the Beatles in Hamburg's Star Club in 1962 when he was a member of Little Richard's backing band. He was fifteen at the time and was befriended by George Harrison. He was also to back Sam Cooke and later became resident keyboards player on the 'Shindig' TV show.

It was while he was touring Britain with Ray Charles that he met up with George again, who introduced him to the other members of the Beatles and they bought his contract from Vee Jay Records and signed him to Apple Records.

He also became the first musician to be credited on a Beatles record when he performed on the 'Get Back' single, which was released with the credit 'The Beatles with Billy Preston'. At one time, because he was doing so much recording work alongside the Beatles, he was dubbed 'The Fifth Beatle'. It was said that the introduction of Preston at the sessions helped to soothe the tension between members of the group that had slowly been building up. Other Beatles tracks he performed on were: 'Let It Be', 'I.Me.Mine', 'I've Got A Feelin'', 'Dig A Pony' and 'One After 909'.

During his three years with Apple, Billy made two albums, *That's The Way God Planned It* and *Encouraging Words,* both co-produced by George. George also performed on Preston's later albums *I Wrote A Simple Song* and *It's My Pleasure*. During the sessions, George invited a number of friends to come to the studio, including Klaus Voormann, Keith Richard, Ginger Baker and Eric Clapton. Madeline Bell and Doris Troy also provided vocal backing on some tracks on Billy's first Apple album.

Among his Apple releases was a version of 'My Sweet Lord', the George Harrison number that he co-produced with George. It was issued in Britain on 4 September 1970 on Apple 29 and in the States on 3 December on Apple 1826.

The relationship with George continued and Preston performed on *The Concert For Bangladesh* and also on George's 1974 Dark Horse tour, in addition to the albums *All Things Must Pass, Extra Texture, Dark Horse* and *33⅓*. He also appeared on John's *Sometime In New York City* album and on Ringo's *Ringo* and *Goodnight Vienna*.

He played piano on the 'God' track on the *John Lennon/*

Plastic Ono Band album. Preston was also to feature in Robert Stigwood's 1978 film, *Sgt Pepper's Lonely Hearts Club Band*.

Preston was later to record for A&M Records and won a Best Pop Instrumental Grammy in 1976 for 'Outta Space'. He topped the American charts with 'Will It Go Round In Circles' in 1973 and 'Nothing From Nothing' in 1974. In 1975 he wrote 'You're So Beautiful' for Joe Cocker and his duet with Syreeta Wright in 1980, 'With You I'm Born Again', was an American Top 5 entry.

In 1991 he was accused of assaulting a teenage boy and the following year accused of sexually assaulting a handyman who refused to have sex with him. The sex charges were dropped when he agreed to plead guilty to cocaine and assault charges and he received a suspended sentence, although he had to spend nine months at a drug rehabilitation centre.

At the beginning of 1999 he was in jail for violating probation on a cocaine conviction when he was also charged and pleaded guilty to an insurance fraud.

Prince Of Wales Theatre, Coventry Street, London W1

Site of the 1963 'Royal Variety Performance' in aid of the Entertainment Artistes' Benevolent Fund. The first royal show was held in 1912 and attended by King George V who said that he would attend such a variety show once a year provided the profits went to the fund. Bernard Delfont became involved in 1958.

The 1963 show took place on 4 November and was attended by Her Majesty Queen Elizabeth The Queen Mother, Princess Margaret and Lord Snowdon.

With the appearance of Britain's pop phenomenon, huge crowds of teenagers were anticipated and 500 policemen were in attendance to control the crowds.

The Beatles were seventh on a nineteen-act bill which comprised: the Billy Petch Dancers, the Clark Brothers, Max Bygraves, Luis Alberto Del Parana and Los Paraguayos, Susan Maughan, the Beatles, Dickie Henderson, Francis Brunn, Buddy Greco, Nadia Nerina and members of the cast from *Sleeping Beauty*, Joe Loss & His Orchestra with Rose Brennan, Ross McManus and Larry Gretton, 'Steptoe & Son' – Wilfred Brambell and Harry H. Corbett, Pinky & Perky and Company – Jan and Vlasta Dalibor, Eric Sykes and Hattie Jacques, Michael Flanders and Donald Swann, Marlene Dietrich with Burt Bacharach at the piano, Tommy Steele and members of the *Half a Sixpence* company, Harry Secombe and the *Pickwick* company.

The Beatles were to perform four numbers: 'She Loves You', 'Till There Was You', 'From Me To You' and 'Twist And Shout'.

Backstage, John Lennon was apprehensive about the reaction they'd receive from the audience and said that if they were undemonstrative, 'I'll just tell them to rattle their fuckin' jewellery.'

They needn't have worried, the audience was fully behind them from the moment they walked on and Paul asked, 'How are yer – all right?' Between numbers he cracked a joke about Sophie Tucker being their favourite group and when John announced their final number, 'Twist And Shout', he said, 'Will people in the cheaper seats clap your hands? All the rest of you, if you'll just rattle your jewellery.'

This appearance was a major turning point in their career. The front-page headlines in the newspapers the next morning were ecstatic, with headlines such as 'Beatles Rock Royals'. But the most significant headline was the one splashed across the cover of the *Daily Mirror*, the biggest national of them all, with 6,000,000 readers – 'Beatlemania!' In a lengthy report it said: 'How refreshing to see these rumbustious young Beatles take a middle-aged Royal Variety performance by the scruff of their necks and have them Beatling like teenagers.'

'Beatlemania' had arrived! and was confirmed when the show was televised to the nation on the ATV network on 10 November 1963.

The group returned to the theatre on 31 May 1964. The occasion was a series of seven Sunday night pop concerts promoted by Brian Epstein which he called 'Pops Alive!' The Beatles were the fifth in the series and there were six support acts: Kenny Lynch, Cliff Bennett & the Rebel Rousers, the Vernons Girls, the Lorne Gibson Trio, the Chants and the Harlems.

The Beatles performed 'Can't Buy Me Love', 'All My Loving', 'This Boy', 'Roll Over Beethoven', 'Till There Was You', 'Twist And Shout' and 'Long Tall Sally'.

Princess Margaret

Her Royal Highness Princess Margaret was the royal who was very supportive of the Beatles. She was to say, 'I adored them because they were poets as well as musicians.' In addition to being among royals at the Prince of Wales Theatre for the Royal Variety Performance on 4 November 1963, together with her then husband Lord Snowdon, she also attended the London premieres of *A Hard Day's Night* and *Help!* At the premiere of *A Hard Day's Night* she asked Paul what he thought of their screen debut. He said, 'I don't think we are very good, Ma'am, but we had a very good producer and director.' She told him, 'You have nothing to worry about. It was fine.'

Princess Theatre, Kowloon, Hong Kong

The Beatles performed two shows at this theatre on 9 June 1964, as part of their world tour. Ringo Starr was ill at the time and drummer Jimmy Nicol was deputising.

The group and their party flew into Kai Tak Airport, Hong Kong, where over 1,000 fans had gathered. They were taken to the President Hotel, Kowloon, where they were booked into the fifteenth floor. Paul McCartney and Neil Aspinall immediately put in an order for suits to be made for them within 24 hours – something which Hong Kong had been noted for.

The group were asked to judge a Miss Hong Kong Pageant at the hotel, but were too tired to attend. There was some agitation as it was expected that the Beatles would be there. In order to smooth matters over, John Lennon turned up and the audience were happy.

When they heard that the promoters of the concerts at the 1,700-seater Princess Theatre had put a price of 75 Hong Kong dollars per seat on the tickets, they were highly critical of the huge charge, which amounted to the average weekly wage in the colony at the time.

There were 200 policemen outside the theatre to control the crowds, although the actual shows weren't fully booked due to the extravagant ticket prices.

The local newspaper *Sing Pao* didn't think too highly of the Beatles' performance and printed a review which commented: 'The incessant shrieking of fans was mental torture to those in the audience who came to appreciate music.' However, the other newspapers seemed more appreciative and the *Tin Tin Yat Po* said that 'Youth and its rhapsody had shaken Hong Kong'.

The *Hong Kong Standard* devoted the entire front page to the event, headlining: 'The Big Battle Of The Beatles'. The report contrasted the two shows at the theatre, the first before a mainly teenage audience who kept up such a wall of noise that the group couldn't be heard, and the more adult audience for the second concert who were actually able to hear the group perform.

The *Standard* reported: 'At the 7.30 show the predominantly teenage audience shrieked, screamed, applauded, stomped, cheered all through the 25 minutes of the Beatles' appearance.

'Despite the perfect sound system in the theatre – turned on full – the Beatles were singing a losing battle against the enthusiasm of the kids.

'At that show not a single number could be heard through. The Beatles were game though, and didn't appear to be disturbed by the din. They kept the show going and did their very best to out-shout the audience. But it was bigger than they.

'As the curtains drew closed on the last number, there was a dash by a vanguard of teenagers direct at the stage. But a flank of policemen blocked the way of the invading kids.'

The Beatles had originally planned to return to their hotel between shows to change and have a short rest, but they were advised by the police to remain in their dressing-room because of security problems.

The group performed ten numbers in each of their 25-minute appearances.

Princess Theatre, Torbay Road, Torquay, Devon

The Beatles only appeared once at this venue in the extreme south of England on Sunday, 18 August 1963, making two performances during the evening. Earlier that day they had recorded an appearance on 'Thank Your Lucky Stars' miming to 'She Loves You' and 'I'll Get You'.

Proby, P. J.

A Texas-born singer whose real name was James Marcus Smith. Producer Jack Good brought him over to Britain to appear on the 'Around The Beatles' television show and his subsequent success was meteoric. He began to tour and had a major hit with 'Hold Me'. He also recorded the Lennon & McCartney number 'That Means A Lot' which was released in America on 5 July 1965 on Liberty 55806 with 'Let The Water Run Down' as the flip. The single was issued in Britain on 17 September on Liberty 10215 with 'My Prayer' as the flip. Proby's downfall was caused by the almost hysterical reaction in the media to the fact that his trousers split on stage.

Promotional Films

Promotional films, or 'promos', are now a staple ingredient of most record releases and are also known as 'pop videos'.

Such marketing tools weren't readily available in the early sixties and when clips were generally used on television shows they were basically clips from pop movies or from live concert footage.

The Beatles hired Michael Lindsay-Hogg in 1966 to film promotional movies of their numbers 'Paperback Writer' and 'Rain' for use on programmes such as 'Top Of The Pops'. The filming sessions took place at Abbey Road recording studios on 19 May 1966 and a colour clip was filmed specially for use on 'The Ed Sullivan Show' which was transmitted on 5 June. This also included a brief introduction, with Ringo apologising for them not being there in person. They also filmed black and white clips for British television programmes. There were two films made of 'Paperback Writer' at Abbey Road, but the second version of 'Rain' was filmed at Chiswick House, West London, the following day. 'Top Of The Pops' featured both films on 2 June 1966.

In 1967 the Beatles engaged Peter Goldmann to direct the promotional films for 'Strawberry Fields Forever' and 'Penny Lane'. 'Strawberry Fields' was filmed at Sevenoaks, Kent, on Monday, 30 January, when night-time sequences were shot. The following day they returned to Sevenoaks to complete the daytime sequences. There were two different locations for 'Penny Lane'. A unit filmed location shots in Liverpool of Penny Lane, the bus shelter and the barber's shop. The Beatles were filmed riding horses in Stratford, East London, on 5 February and some of the additional scenes were shot in Angel Lane in Stratford. They returned to Sevenoaks on 7 February and filmed the sequences at the dinner table and with the large tree. The tree remained standing throughout the seventies and displayed a plaque relating to its use in the film. The tree has since been cut down. The clips were aired in America on ABC TV's 'Hollywood Palace' on 25 February, on 'American Bandstand' on 11 March, on Dick Clark's 'Where The Action Is' on 14 March and an edited version of 'Strawberry Fields Forever' was used on 'The Best On Record' Grammy Awards special on 24 March.

Later in 1967 the Beatles had planned to make a film surrounding the production of their *Sgt Pepper* album. This didn't come about, although the 'A Day In The Life' sequence was filmed in which there was a party atmosphere with a number of celebrated friends and an orchestra whose members wore funny noses and carnival masks. The film was banned by the BBC and never used as a promotional film, although it was shown in the special *The Beatles At Abbey Road* exhibition in 1983.

The other promotional film of 1967 proved controversial. Paul directed the promo for 'Hello Goodbye' with the Beatles performing the number on stage at the Saville Theatre, London. There were three clips made on 10 November, one in which they are dressed in Sgt Pepper uniforms, the other in casual clothes and the third which was made up of out-takes of the other two. Neil Aspinall flew to New York with copies for a number of American shows, including the 'Ed Sullivan Show', but the clip didn't fare well in Britain. The Musicians' Union still had their ban which prevented musicians miming to their records. As a result, the BBC decided not to use the clip on 'Top Of The Pops' on 21 November as planned. They attempted to make another clip themselves by filming the Beatles editing *Magical Mystery Tour*, but this didn't work out. The BBC also dropped plans to screen one of the Saville Theatre clips of 'Hello Goodbye' in colour on 'Late Night Line-Up' on 23 November.

The next Beatles promos were actually taken from David Frost's London Weekend Television programme 'Frost on Sunday', broadcast on 8 September 1968. They were promotional films for 'Hey Jude' and 'Revolution' and were filmed on 4 September at Twickenham Film Studios. David Frost was present at the filming as he appeared in an introduction to 'Hey Jude' for use on his programme. At the same time, a video was made of the performances for use on 'The Smothers Brothers Comedy Hour' in America. The 'Hey Jude' segment was transmitted on the 'Smothers Brothers' show on 6 October and the 'Revolution' clip on 13 October.

1969 was the final year in which the Beatles made promotional films, two for 'The Ballad Of John And Yoko' and one for 'Something'. In March 1970 when the 'Let It Be' single was issued, a promo was compiled from out-takes of the Twickenham Film Studios sessions.

There are, of course, many clips of the Beatles performing various songs, including 'Help', 'I Feel Fine', 'Day Tripper', 'We Can Work It Out' and 'Ticket To Ride', but these have come from clips of television appearances and weren't specially made as promotional films.

Pseudonyms

The first time the Beatles used pseudonyms was in 1960 when, known as the Silver Beetles, they embarked on a short tour of Scotland. Paul called himself Paul Ramon, because he felt the name sounded exotic and romantic; George called himself Carl Harrison in deference to Carl Perkins and Stuart Sutcliffe adopted the name Stu De Stijl, after the painter. Many years later some books reported that John called himself Johnny Silver, but he denied this, stating that he kept his own name for the tour, a fact which is backed by a press clipping of the time.

Incidentally, Paul was to use the name Paul Ramon again many years later. On 3 February 1969 he dropped in to see the Steve Miller Band who were recording 'My Dark Hour' in a London studio – and he contributed to the track under the name Paul Ramon.

The Beatles rarely found the use of pseudonyms necessary during the sixties, although there were one or two examples, such as the time Paul called himself Bernard Webb when he penned a number for Peter & Gordon, but the aliases appeared later in their careers when they were recording or guesting on other artists' records and when John began travelling.

John, in particular, loved pseudonyms, which is not surprising from the author of *In His Own Write*, which indicates a love of ridiculous names. Here are some of the pseudonyms used by the members of the Beatles.

JOHN LENNON Mel Torment, used when he recorded the number 'Scared'; John O'Cean, used when he appeared on Yoko Ono's *Feeling The Space* album – the moniker is obviously inspired by the Japanese meaning of Yoko's name 'Ocean Child'; Dr Winston O'Boogie, used on the *Mind Games* album – Winston was his real middle name and he used it on several pseudonyms; Mr Winston O'Reggae, used on his number 'Steel And Glass'; Dr Winston & Booker Table & The Maitre D's, used on his 'Beef Jerky' single, was obviously a pun inspired by Booker T & The MG's; Reverend Thumbs Ghurkin, used on his 'Old Dirt Road' song; Reverend Fred Ghurkin, one of the pseudonyms on the *Walls & Bridges* album, was also used when John travelled with Yoko and they booked into some hotels as the Reverend Fred and Ada Ghurkin; John Green, one of the pseudonyms John used when travelling.

PAUL MCCARTNEY Bernard Webb was the name he used when he penned the number 'Woman' for Peter & Gordon, as he was interested in seeing how well a number of his would be received without using the magic McCartney name – for the same number he also used the alias A. Smith. Apollo C. Vermouth was used when producing 'I'm An Urban Spaceman' for the Bonzo Dog Doo Dah Band. Apollo is obviously linked with Spaceman because of the American Apollo missions.

RINGO STARR Ringo, like Paul, was a person who used pseudonyms sparingly. The few he did use were not so far removed from his own name. R. S. were the initials he used for his appearance on David Hentschel's *Startling Music* album; Ritchie, used for his contribution to Stephen Stills' *Stills* album; Richie, the first name by which he is known to friends, this time without the 't', used on *The London Howling Wolf Sessions* album; Richie Snare, another thinly disguised alias, using his first name allied to 'snare', referring to drums, was used on the *Son Of Schmilsson* album; English Ritchie, another alias used on the *Stills* album; Ognir Rats, simply the name Ringo Starr (one 'r' missing) spelled in reverse, used in his 1978 TV show 'Ringo', which adapted the Mark Twain classic *The Prince and the Pauper* to a contemporary setting in which there are two identical men, one called Ringo Starr, the other Ognir Rats, who swop places.

GEORGE HARRISON Next to John, George seemed to enjoy hiding under an alias, although his pseudonyms were nowhere near as colourful as John's. Son Of Harry, used for his musical contribution to Dave Mason's album *It's Like You Never Left*; P. Roducer, used on the album *Splinter*, the group he produced; Hari Georgeson, used for his guest appearance on Billy Preston's *It's My Pleasure* album; The George O'Hara-Smith Singers, used when his voice was overdubbed to produce the effect of several voices on his *All Things Must Pass* album; Jai Raj Harisein, was another of the pseudonyms on the *Splinter* album – a name with a touch of Eastern promise; George Harrysong was the alias he used for his appearance on the *Son Of Schmilsson* album and was similar to that of his early music publishing company, Harrisongs Ltd; George O'Hara-Smith, the Irish-sounding hyphenated name, appears once again – on Ashton, Gardner & Dyke's *I'm Your Spiritual Breadman* album (the group had evolved from Liverpool band the Remo Four and George had promised to return the compliment when the Remo Four recorded for him on the *Wonderwall* soundtrack); George O'Hara was a name he used thrice, as an alias on two of Garry Wright's albums, *Footprint* and *That Was Only Yesterday*, and also on the Nicky Hopkins LP *The Tin Man Was A Dreamer*; L'Angelo Mysterioso, used on Cream's 'Badge' single. This was a song he co-wrote with Eric Clapton. He also used the name on Jack Bruce's album *Songs For A Tailor*.

P.S. I Love You

A number mainly written by Paul, with some help from John. The group originally recorded it as one of the tracks on their Parlophone recording audition on Wednesday, 6 June 1962, when Pete Best was a member of the band.

The Beatles next recorded it on Tuesday, 11 September, when Ringo was a member of the group. Ron Richards produced this session and he wasn't happy with the drumming on the original 'Love Me Do', so he hired drummer Andy White for the session. Ringo was in attendance but didn't play drums that evening. He sat quietly in the control box next to Richards and Richards asked him to play maracas on the 'P.S. I Love You' track.

The number was issued as the flipside of their British debut single 'Love Me Do' and was also included on the *Please Please Me* album and the *All My Loving* EP. Some years later it was selected for the *Love Songs* compilation On the twentieth anniversary of its release Parlophone issued it as a picture disc and a month later it was also issued on a twelve-inch disc.

In America Vee Jay included it on the *Introducing The Beatles* album. It was also issued on a single by Tolie and was re-released on Vee Jay's 'Oldies' series later in 1964 and on Capitol's 'Starline' series in 1965 – in all cases as the flipside of 'Love Me Do'. When the rights to the Vee Jay tracks were obtained by Capitol, they included 'P.S. I Love You' on their *The Early Beatles* album.

Public Auditorium

A 12,000-seater venue situated on East Sixth Street in Cleveland, Ohio. The Beatles flew into Hopkins Airport and were driven to the Sheraton Hotel. Although they were to be given the Presidential Suite, the Police Chief Richard R. Wagner felt that too many people would know they were there. He requested they be moved to another suite. Five hundred police had been called to duty, with leaves cancelled and officers and men placed on twelve-hour shifts at a cost of $15,000 in police overtime.

The Beatles' concert took place on Tuesday, 15 September 1964 and was promoted by the local radio station WHK. Tickets weren't on sale generally. There had been so many ticket requests that the station decided to computerise them and the machine then picked out the lucky 12,000 who had sent in postcards and would be permitted to buy tickets, which cost an average of $3.50.

Two press receptions had to be organised because of the insistence of the rival radio station KYW that they be given access to the Beatles.

Acts on the bill included Jackie De Shannon and the Bill Black Combo. As the show opened a police officer announced over the microphone: 'I'm not running this show, but I am responsible for your safety. If you get out of hand at any point, the show will be stopped immediately. You can make as much noise as you want as long as you behave.'

Following De Shannon's act, which she closed with the song 'I've Got The Whole World In My Hands', the DJs from WHK came on stage carrying boxes, to present the Beatles with gum chains which fans had sent to the station as presents for the group.

Ten minutes into the Beatles' performance, hordes of fans rushed the stage towards the barricades, with over forty policemen straining to hold them back. Some of the girls were trampled near to the barricades.

Deputy Carl C. Bare grabbed the microphone from John and shouted 'The show is over!' They obviously didn't quite understand him and continued playing 'All My Loving' until Bare pushed George away from his mike. The curtain dropped and the Beatles were led offstage with Ringo complaining, 'The police are stupid.'

This was the first time a Beatles show had ever been stopped in

America. The group began to change in their dressing room, but Derek Taylor asked them if he could talk the crowd into behaving. They agreed and he went to the police and made the same request. Then he went on stage and said: 'This is the first time the Beatles have ever encountered a situation like this. The Beatles are standing just a hundred feet away and they want to play for you, but you must not stand up.' Initially, he was booed. He continued: 'If you will not sit down, the police will be back. Do you want the Beatles?' The crowd roared 'Yes!' Then Derek said: 'Then sit down and I will bring you the Beatles. But if one more incident like this occurs, the show will be over. We can't risk any more injuries or the Beatles won't do the show.'

Then Police Sergeant Edwin Nahgorski announced: 'You can be as loud as you want, but you must remain in your seats. Do not stand up or the show will be over.'

Music critic Robert Finn, reporting in the *Cleveland Plain Dealer*, wrote: 'In twenty-plus years of concert-going, this music critic has often been moved, amused, charmed, and exalted by what he heard. But this is the first time he was terrified.'

Public Ear, The

A BBC radio series on the Light Programme. The Beatles made the first of three appearances on the show on Thursday, 3 October 1963 when they recorded an interview with Michael Colley at the NEMS offices in Argyle Street. This show was broadcast on Sunday, 3 November at 3.00 p.m. Their second interview was taped on Sunday, 5 January 1964 and broadcast on Sunday, 12 January. They recorded their final interview for the show in between filming *A Hard Day's Night* at Twickenham Film Studios on Wednesday, 18 March 1964. John read an excerpt from *In His Own Write,* George and Paul discussed *A Hard Day's Night* and were joined in the conversation by Ringo. The show was transmitted on Sunday, 22nd March at 3.00 p.m. and simultaneously by BFBS (British Forces Broadcasting Service) in West Germany.

Public Hall, Lune Street, Preston, Lancashire

The Beatles made their debut here on the evening of Friday, 26 October 1962. It was their first appearance in Preston, a town only thirty miles from Liverpool. The event was presented by the Preston Grasshoppers Rugby FC and top of the bill were Mike Berry & the Outlaws. Third on the bill was a big band, the Syd Munson Orchestra, and tickets cost 6/- . The group appeared at the venue for the second and last time on Friday, 13 September 1963.

Quarry Bank High School, Harthill Road, Liverpool L18

A Grammar School, founded in 1922. Its first headmaster was named George Harrison. Old boys from the school have included Labour Government Ministers William Rodgers and Peter Shore.

The school uniform was a black blazer with a red and gold stag's head badge which sported the motto *Ex Hoc Metallo Virtuten* which, translated, means 'From This Rough Metal We Forge Virtue'.

John Lennon became a pupil at the school in September 1952 and the twelve-year-old boy would cycle there each morning from his Menlove Avenue home one mile away, on his green Raleigh Lenton bicycle.

The school headmaster was E. R. Taylor, who found he had a couple of troublemakers on his hands in the form of Lennon and his mate Pete Shotton. The two were very disruptive, were always causing trouble at the school, were often disciplined by caning and were continually punished with detention. Academically, they were uninterested in studying and were both placed at the bottom of the 'C' stream where they remained for most of their school life. When John took his GCE 'O'-level examinations, he failed in every subject.

In 1956 a new headmaster arrived at the school, the 35-year-old William Ernest Pobjoy. He was less of a disciplinarian than his predecessor and John was pleased and surprised when Pobjoy not only allowed the Quarry Men to play at the school (they performed at a Sixth Form dance in July 1957), but encouraged him in his interest in skiffle music. Pobjoy also spotted John's potential as an artist, contacted his Aunt Mimi and arranged for him to attend Liverpool College of Art when he left Quarry Bank School at the end of July 1957.

Quarry Men, The

The skiffle group formed by John Lennon in the autumn of 1956, soon after his Aunt Mimi had bought him a guitar for £17 at Frank Hessy's store. His friend and classmate Pete Shotton was engaged to play washboard and another Quarry Bank School classmate, Bill Smith, was brought in on tea chest bass. Smith was only with the group for a matter of weeks and the honours on tea chest bass until the middle of 1958 were shared between Ivan Vaughan, and Len Garry. Nigel Whalley also played tea chest bass, but was mainly looked upon as the Quarry Men manager.

It was alleged that for one week John called the group the Black Jacks and then decided on the Quarry Men because of a line from the school song, which read 'Quarry Men, old before our birth'. The other members were Rod Davis on banjo, Eric Griffiths on guitar and Colin Hanton on drums. Their initial repertoire comprised mainly popular skiffle hits of the time such as 'Lost John', 'Railroad Bill', 'Cumberland Gap', 'Freight Train', 'Midnight Special', 'No Other Baby', 'Rock Island Line', 'Worried Man Blues' and the Liverpool sea shanty 'Maggie May'.

The group appeared at various parties and entered several of the numerous skiffle group contests locally, and a few months after their formation they took part in an afternoon audition at the Empire Theatre for the Carroll Levis Discovery competition, on Sunday, 9 June, without success. Historically interesting 1957 gigs by the group included their appearance at the party in Rosebery Street on Saturday, 22 June; their appearance at the Woolton Village Fete on Saturday, 6 July, where John and Paul met for the first time; their Cavern debut on Wednesday, 7 August, sans Paul McCartney, where they were chided for performing rock 'n' roll numbers such as 'Hound Dog' and 'Blue Suede Shoes'; and their gig at the New Clubmoor Hall on Friday, 18 October where Paul unsuccessfully attempted to take over on lead guitar.

As was apparent from their Cavern engagement, John was increasingly interested in performing rock 'n' roll and moving away from skiffle music

On their Cavern debut they appeared on a bill with Ron McKay's Skiffle Group, the Deltones Skiffle Group and the Darktown Skiffle Group. The Quarry Men played 'Come Go With Me'. Then they performed 'Hound Dog' and 'Blue Suede Shoes'. Cavern boss Alan

Sytner sent them the note 'Cut out the bloody rock.' Paul wasn't with them. On 24 January, Paul made his Cavern debut with them when they appeared on a bill with the Merseysippi Jazz Band.

Queen Charlotte's Maternity Hospital, Goldhawk Road, London W6

Maureen Starkey was admitted to the hospital for the birth of her first child. Zak was born on 13 September 1965. Two years later Maureen moved into the hospital again, to Ward D in the west wing on the fourth floor. Her second son Jason was born at 3.35 p.m. on Saturday, 19 August 1967, and weighed 8lbs 5½ozs. As Ringo had chosen the name Zak, Maureen was in line for the choice of a new name and suggested Jason.

Maureen returned to the hospital for a third time for the birth of her daughter Lee on 17 November 1970.

Yoko Ono was admitted to the hospital in November 1968. John insisted on being near her and slept in her room throughout the time she was there. Unfortunately, she suffered a miscarriage on 21 November. The picture of John and Yoko together in the hospital was displayed on the cover of their album *Unfinished Music No. 2: Life With The Lions*.

197 Queen's Drive, Childwall, Liverpool L18

A 5-bedroom house which was the family home of the Epstein family for thirty years. Brian Epstein lived here with his mother and father and brother Clive. They had a home-help and a live-in nanny. Soon after Brian signed the Beatles, John became a regular visitor. The two of them would discuss plans in the morning room. A cocktail party in Paul McCartney's honour was held at the house on 18 June 1963 to celebrate Paul's 21st birthday. When the Epsteins moved in the late sixties it became the home of the Dean of Liverpool.

Queens Hall, Sovereign Street, Leeds, Yorkshire

Despite heavy rain, an audience of 3,200 filled this large hall to capacity on Friday, 28 June 1963 when the Beatles appeared on the same bill as Acker Bilk and his Paramount Jazz Band. The Beatles performed two spots during the evening, the first lasting for twenty minutes.

Queens Hall, The, Victoria Road, Widnes, Cheshire

Brian Epstein, to enhance the local popularity of his bands, began to promote them on some of the larger venues in the Merseyside area. NEMS Enterprises ran a string of promotions at the Queens Hall in Widnes, twelve miles outside Liverpool.

The Beatles made their debut at the venue in a series of three Monday night gigs in 1962. On 3 and 10 September they were supported by Rory Storm & the Hurricanes, the group whose drummer they'd taken the previous month. They completed their trilogy of bookings on 16 September.

On 22 October 1962 they were back at the Queens Hall, this time with Lee Curtis & the All Stars on the bill. The All Stars had their new drummer Pete Best with them, but the Beatles never spoke to him.

Their final appearance at the venue, also promoted by NEMS Enterprises, was for two sell-out concerts on the evening of 18 February 1963.

Queens Hotel, The Promenade, Southport, Lancashire

A jazz club was situated on the ground floor of this hotel in the seaside resort close to Liverpool. It was called Club Django (after jazz guitarist Django Reinhardt) and mainly featured jazz bands. However, due to the increasing success of the Beatles locally, the organisers decided to book the Beatles and the group appeared at the club on 6 December 1962.

Queens Theatre, Bank Hey Street, Blackpool, Lancashire

The Beatles only appeared at this venue twice – with only a few weeks between each of the bookings. They made their debut there on Sunday, 21 July 1963 and their final appearance took place on Sunday, 4 August 1963. On their second visit there were so many fans outside the theatre that the group had to gain access by climbing over the roof of the building and crawling through a trapdoor.

Quickly, Tommy

Merseyside singer who appeared with his group on a bill with the Beatles at the Majestic Ballroom, Birkenhead, on Thursday, 31 January 1963, advertised as Johnny Quickly & the Challengers. Brian Epstein noticed him when he opened the show at a NEMS Enterprises Beatles promotion at the Queens Hall, Widnes. The seventeen-year-old telephone fitter didn't get to sign with Epstein until the following year when Brian changed his name to Tommy Quickly, taking him on as a solo artist and dispensing with his backing band, the Challengers.

Epstein then embarked on a massive promotional campaign to establish his new signing. As George Martin had enough acts to handle at that time, Brian contacted Ray Horricks of Pye, via Dick James, and Tommy was signed to the label. Brian then gave him a new backing band, the Remo Four, and a Lennon and McCartney number 'No Reply' to record. Slightly drunk, he found it almost impossible to record and after seventeen takes it was abandoned. This frustrated the Remo Four, who believed that a proper interpretation of the number would have brought them a hit. Tommy then made his record debut with another Lennon and McCartney number, 'Tip Of My Tongue', which was arguably not as strong as 'No Reply'. Epstein spent $30,000 on a promotional tour of America. Tommy was included on three Beatles tours, a Beatles Christmas show, plus a Gerry & the Pacemakers show, a Gerry & the Pacemakers tour and a Billy J. Kramer tour. On the 1963 Beatles Christmas show he performed 'Winter Wonderland' and 'Kiss Me Now'. Yet despite the major exposure, all five singles by Quickly failed to register and the singer left NEMS in February 1966.

His lack of success was puzzling, as he was an appealing young vocalist with a cheery personality, not unlike Peter Noone of Herman's Hermits. Perhaps it had something to do with his record product.

Radha Krsna Temple

The Radha Krsna Temple was founded in London in 1966 by his Divine Grace A. C Bhakjtivedanta Swami Prabhupada. The Swami had originally travelled from India to New York in September 1965 to bring the mahamantra to the West; he was 70 years old at the time. The mantra was a repetition of Krsna's name, chanted as a form of meditation. George Harrison was to say, 'Silent meditation is rather dependent on concentration, but when you chant, it's more of a direct connection with God.'

The Swami, with shaven head and distinctive robes, arrived in Britain with a small following, members of whom visited Apple and met up with George Harrison, who arranged for them to meet the Beatles at Kinfauns. They all had a vegetarian meal and after chanting began to talk, with John and George asking most of the questions. George then arranged for Apple to lease a building for them in Bury Place, Holborn. However, there were complaints from local residents about the renovation work, which was then suspended while an independent inquiry took place. In the meantime, John Lennon invited them to move into a conservatory at Tittenhurst Park on a temporary basis.

In September 1969 his Divine Grace, author of over 80 books on Vedic philosophy, moved into the annexe at Tittenhurst Park with his followers, where he was to hold a meeting with George and John. As problems with Bury Place continued, George helped to finance a 17-acre property, Pickett's Manor in Hertfordshire, which was renamed Bhakjtivedanta Manor in 1972.

George was impressed by the Swami who, with his self-inflicted poverty, presented a contrast to the Maharishi's commercial and material lifestyle. He advocated training in self-purification in which his followers did not eat meat, have illicit sex, gamble, take intoxicants such as drugs, alcohol, coffee or cigarettes. Unfortunately for George, he found he couldn't become a fully fledged devotee because he liked the occasional drink and smoke.

George decided to record the devotional chant and early sessions took place at George's bungalow with George on guitar and Billy Preston playing a synthesizer. Then a recording session took place at Trident Studios in London. This was more of a studio rehearsal and the final recording was made at EMI's Abbey Road Studios. There were a group of devotees chanting the mantra, Paul and Linda McCartney were operating the control console and George played organ. George was to comment, 'While the words don't alter, the tune it is sung to doesn't matter. You could sing it to "Coming Round The Mountain" if you wanted. All I've done on this is shorten it.'

The single 'Hare Krsna Mantra' by Hare Krsna Temple was issued in America on 22 August 1969 on Apple 1810 and in Britain on 29 August on Apple 25. The record entered the British Top 20, reaching the position of No. 17. This was followed by 'Govinda', which was issued in Britain on 6 March 1970 on Apple 25 and in America on 24 March on Apple 1821. The record reached No. 23 in the British charts. This was followed by an album, also produced by George, called *The Radha Krsna Temple*, which was issued in America on 21 May 1971 on Apple SKAO 3376 and in Britain on 28 May on Apple SAPCOR 18.

The first single actually enjoyed international success, particularly in the European charts, and reached No. 1 in Germany and Czechoslovakia. It also reached the Top Ten in Japan.

Swami Prabhupada died on 17 November 1977 at the age of 81. Before he died he took a gold ring from his finger, passed it to a disciple and told him, 'Please give this to George Harrison. He was a good friend to us all. He loves Krsna sincerely and I love him. He was my archangel!'

Radio Luxembourg

A commercial radio station which transmits its programmes to the UK from the Duchy of Luxembourg on the Continent. As the only alternative to BBC radio in the late fifties and early sixties, it promoted pop music and one of its most popular programmes was the weekly Top Twenty chart programme which played the twenty leading records in each week's *New Musical Express* chart listings.

The station's signal was stronger in the north of England and it was more popular there than in the south. It was the station which the Beatles used to listen to when they first became interested in music and it played a wider variety of records to appeal to young people than the BBC and also gave more opportunities to new artists. Rory Storm became the first of the Mersey Beat artists to appear on the radio when he managed to get a booking for his group the Raving Texans on Luxembourg's 'Amateur Skiffle Club' programme on 30 April 1958 with the group performing 'Midnight Special'.

Radio Luxembourg also transmitted sponsored programmes. The one sponsored by EMI Records was called 'The Friday Spectacular' and the Beatles recorded three shows in the series, transmitted from EMI House in London. When they appeared on 'Friday Spectacular', hosted by Muriel Young on 16 November 1962, they mimed on stage before an audience at EMI House to 'Love Me Do'.

Radio Luxembourg also began broadcasting a Beatles special called 'This Is Their Life' on 10 May 1964 and transmitted a second programme in the series on 17 May 1964.

From January 1965 Radio Luxembourg began running a fifteen-minute radio series devoted to Beatles records each Sunday evening at 8.45 p.m., introduced by Chris Denning.

In 1981 Radio Luxembourg ran a poll in which listeners voted for their all-time favourite Beatles number. They were:

1.   'Hey Jude'
2.   'She Loves You'
3.   'Yesterday'
4.   'Help!'
5.   'A Hard Day's Night'
6.   'Let It Be'
7.   'Can't Buy Me Love'
8.   'I Want To Hold Your Hand'
9.   'All My Loving'
10. 'Ticket To Ride'
11. 'Love Me Do'
12. 'Eleanor Rigby'
13. 'All You Need Is Love'
14. 'I Feel Fine'
15. 'Penny Lane'
16. 'Twist And Shout'
17. 'A Day In The Life'
18. 'Get Back'
19. 'Please Please Me'
20. 'Strawberry Fields Forever'

Raga

A film, originally to be called 'Messenger Out Of The East', which was a documentary co-produced by George Harrison and Ravi Shankar and released by Apple in 1971. The 96-minute documentary was based on Shankar.

George and Ravi held a press conference in Los Angeles to announce that the film would focus on Shankar's life and philosophy, taking in a general look at Indian religions and traditions. George made a brief appearance in the film taking a sitar lesson from Ravi. George also introduced Yehudi Menuhin, saying, 'Old friend Yehudi Menuhin, one of the great violinists, joins Shankar for an informal session while youthful George Harrison comes to the master to learn.' The film was produced and directed by Howard Worth, with a screenplay by Nancy Bacal.

George also produced the film's soundtrack album, *Raga*, which was issued on Apple SWAO 3384 on 7 December 1971. The tracks were: 'Dawn To Dusk', 'Vedic Hymns', 'Baba Teaching', 'Birth To Death', 'Vinus House', 'Gurur Bramha', 'United Nations', 'Raga Parameshwari', 'Rangeswhart', 'Banares Ghat', 'Bombay School', 'Kinnara School', 'Frenzy and Distortion', and 'Raga Desh'.

Railroad Bill

Traditional American railroad song popularised in Britain in 1957 by Lonnie Donegan & his Skiffle Group and included in the repertoire of virtually every skiffle group in the country, including the Quarry Men, who performed it in 1957 with John Lennon on lead vocals.

Rain

John Lennon composition which was used as the flipside of the 'Paperback Writer' single in June 1966. There is a degree of experimentation on this record in which both the music and the vocals have been slowed down technically in the recording studio. There is one sentence when John sings, 'Rain, when the rain comes they run and hide their heads', at the end of the record which is heard in reverse. John claimed that he inadvertently played the tapes backwards when he was at home and liked the effect so much he wanted it recreated on the record. George Martin contradicts the claim and says that it was his idea. He decided to take the line of vocal by John off the four-track and put it on another spool and experiment with playing it backwards.

The number is also found on the *Hey Jude* album and the *British Rarities* compilation. The number was included on the CD compilation *Past Masters Volume Two*.

Ramon, Paul

Pseudonym Paul used when the Silver Beetles toured Scotland as backing band to Johnny Gentle. Paul couldn't remember why he chose that particular surname, but he thought it was rather glamorous. So much so, that he was to use it again, many years later, when he recorded a track with the Steve Miller Band, 'My Dark Hour' in 1969. The American punk rock band the Ramones are reputed to have taken their name from this alias of Paul's.

Ramrod

Instrumental hit for Duane Eddy in 1958. George Harrison began to perform this number with the Quarry Men when the band included it in their repertoire.

Rarities (American Album)

An American album issued on Capitol SHAL 12060 on 24 March 1980. This is a different compilation from the British album *Rarities* which had originally been issued as part of *The Beatles Collection* in 1971 and as a separate album the following year.

Capitol had already stated that the American album *Rarities* would not be available in their limited-edition release of *The Beatles Collection*, but announced that they would be releasing *Rarities* as part of their Budget Line series. There was some initial confusion over this, unrelated to the fact that it was a different album from the British one of the same name.

In 1979 it was rumoured that Capitol had decided to issue an album of rare Beatles tracks, which they called *Collectors' Items*. The LP was given the catalogue number SPRO 9462 and the track listing was, Side One: 'Love Me Do' (the recording featuring Ringo on drums), 'From Me To You', 'Thank You Girl', 'All My Loving' (with the hi-hat introduction), 'This Boy' (which hadn't previously been released in stereo in the US), *'Sie Liebt Dich'*, 'I Feel Fine', 'She's A Woman' (which had never been released in stereo in the US), 'Help!', 'I'm Down'. Side Two: 'Penny Lane' (the promotional copy version), 'Baby You're A Rich Man' (not previously available in stereo in the States), 'I Am The Walrus', 'The Inner Light', 'Across The Universe', 'You Know My Name (Look Up The Number)'.

The rumour then claimed that a decision was made to scrap *Collectors' Items*, with Capitol ordering that all copies were to be destroyed. The story further claimed that Capitol employees smuggled copies out of the pressing plant which then became, literally, 'collectors' items'.

This story is untrue. *Collectors' Items* was a bootleg release and the bootleggers concocted this story themselves. They carefully produced a professional-style album cover, duplicating the Capitol logo and even adding the message 'For Promotional Use Only'.

The *Rarities* issued by Capitol in March 1980 is the only genuine one. Capitol had decided to compile a different selection of rare tracks for its own version of *Rarities*, aimed specifically at the American market, as the original American releases had differed from the British ones. Randall Davis compiled the tracks and also contributed the detailed sleeve notes, aided by research from Ron Furmanek and Walter Podrazik. The album reached No. 21 in the *Billboard* charts. The tracks were, Side One: 'Love Me Do', 'Misery', 'There's A Place', '*Sie Liebt Dich*', 'And I Love Her', 'Help!', 'I'm Only Sleeping', 'I Am The Walrus'. Side Two: 'Penny Lane', 'Helter Skelter', 'Don't Pass Me By', 'The Inner Light', 'Across The Universe', 'You Know My Name (Look Up The Number)'. The album ended with a two-second burst of sound from the inner groove of the British *Sgt Pepper* album, which hadn't been included on the American release. It was called 'Sgt Pepper Inner Groove'.

Rarities (British Album)

Originally, this album was a special bonus LP included in EMI's *The Beatles Collection* boxed set of the Beatles' original twelve studio albums issued with the catalogue number BC 13 on 2 December 1978. The extra album, *Rarities*, had the catalogue number PSLP 261.

EMI had announced that this special gift album would only be obtainable with *The Beatles Collection* and would not be released as an album in its own right. Various record retailers actually took the album from the set and sold it separately at the inflated price of eight pounds, which resulted in EMI making the decision to release the album as a separate entity, which they did in October 1979 on PCM 1001. The sleeve design remained the same, except for the addition of a review of the album by Hugh Fielder of the weekly music paper *Sounds*.

The album had been compiled by EMI's Mike Heatley, who worked for the company's International Division. Initially, the tracks were to be a collection of EP tracks and the flipsides of singles which hadn't been available on previous Beatles albums issued in Britain. This wasn't actually the case as eight of the seventeen tracks had been available on albums issued in Britain.

The album's original sleeve notes had claimed that nine of the seventeen tracks were in stereo, but this wasn't the case – only four of them were in stereo, this error was pointed out on the notes to the 1979 release which stated that twelve of the seventeen tracks were in mono. Heatley admitted that this had been due to a mistake on EMI's part as they'd intended to include stereo versions of 'Rain', 'Long Tall Sally', 'I Call Your Name', 'Slow Down', 'Matchbox' and 'I'm Down', but due to an error, the mono versions were used.

The album tracks were, Side One: 'Across The Universe' (this had previously been issued on the charity album *No One's Gonna Change Our World*), 'Yes It Is' (originally the flipside of 'Ticket To Ride'), 'This Boy' (the flipside of 'I Want To Hold Your Hand'), 'The Inner Light' (first time on an album for the flipside of 'Lady Madonna', although only in a mono version), 'I'll Get You' (the flipside of 'She Loves You'), 'Thank You Girl' (first time on an album for the flipside of 'From Me To You', although only a mono version), '*Komm, Gib Mir Deine Hand*' (first British release of the German version of 'I Want To Hold Your Hand'), 'You Know My Name (Look Up The Number)' (first album release for the flipside of the 'Let It Be' single), '*Sie Liebt Dich*' (first British release for the German version of 'She Loves You'). Side Two: 'Rain' (mono version of the flipside of 'Paperback Writer'), 'She's A Woman' (originally issued as a double-'A' side with 'I Feel Fine'), 'Matchbox' (mono version of the track from the *Long Tall Sally* EP), 'I Call Your Name' (another track from the *Long Tall Sally* EP), 'Bad Boy', 'Slow Down' (another track from the *Long Tall Sally* EP), 'I'm Down' (the flipside of 'Help!'), 'Long Tall Sally'.

Raunchy

The number which helped George Harrison to become a member of the Quarry Men. Paul McCartney was to comment, 'He could really play guitar, particularly this piece called "Raunchy", which we all used to love. You see, if anyone could do something like that it was generally enough to get them in the group. Of course, I knew George long before any of the others as they were all from Woolton and we hung out with the Allerton set. I can tell you we both learned guitar from the same book, and that despite his tender years, we were chums.'

'Raunchy' had been a massive instrumental hit in America in 1957 and Bill Justis and his Orchestra took the number to No. 2 in the charts. Justis had formerly been musical director of Sun Records in the fifties and died in 1982. Eric Freeman also had a hit with the number the same year and reached No. 4 in the American charts, and the third version of the song to chart that year was by Billy Vaughan & his Orchestra, who took the number to No. 10.

George began performing the instrumental with the Quarry Men and continued to play it with the Beatles until 1960.

Ready, Steady, Go!

Influential weekly music show from Rediffusion Television which was networked on ITV between 1963 and 1968. Cathy McGowan, Keith Fordyce and Michael Aldred were hosts of the show which was produced by Michael Lindsay-Hogg and screened early on Friday evenings. It was Britain's first live TV pop show.

The group made their debut ten weeks after the programme was launched, filming from Studio 9 in Kingsway, London, on 4 October 1963. The show was repeated on 8 November.

The group appeared on 20 March 1964, once again from the Kingsway studio and during the show they were presented with an award from *Billboard* magazine. Keith Fordyce announced: '. . . You've got a special award coming to you and *Billboard* magazine in America specially asked it be presented to you on this show and this is in recognition of the fact that two or three weeks ago you had in the American charts numbers one, two and three in their hit parade, all Beatles records, and that's an outstanding achievement and you've got the award of a type that's never been given before, for that. I might add I phoned the States just half an hour ago and they told me this week that it's one, two, three and four of your records and once more you've got another six in the Top Hundred, making ten altogether, so all I suggest is don't keep on with this or there'll be a second War of Independence.'

John and George were interviewed by Cathy McGowan from the programme's new Wembley studios on 16 April 1965 for a special edition called 'Ready Steady Goes Live!'

On 23 November 1964 they recorded 'I Feel Fine' and 'She's A Woman' for transmission on 27 November.

The programme ceased, despite its huge popularity, simply because Rediffusion lost its TV franchise and was obliged to amalgamate with ABC. Michael Lindsay-Hogg was later asked to direct some Beatles projects. The most famous personality created by the programme was Cathy McGowan, known as 'the Queen of the Mods', a pretty girl with long dark hair and a notable fringe which fell down on to her eyes. She married actor Hywel Bennett, although they were later divorced. For many years she shunned publicity, running her own successful clothing business although, in the late eighties, she returned to the media as a radio reporter.

Real Love

A number which John originally penned at the Dakota in 1977 under the title 'Real Life'. He incorporated some strands of the number in the songs 'I'm Stepping Out' and 'Watching The Wheels' and after changing the title to 'Real Love' he cut seven demos of the number in 1979. Yoko included it as the opening track on the soundtrack album of the 1988 film *Imagine*.

When the three surviving Beatles decided to issue some new singles to tie in with their *Anthology* releases, it was decided to use some tapes which John had made, to which they could add their own voices and instruments. The first release was 'Free As A Bird', the second, 'Real Love'.

It was released on Monday, 4 March 1996 and Paul was to comment: 'It was good fun doing it. Unlike "Free As A Bird", it had all the words and music and we were more like "sidemen" to John, which was joyful, and I think we did a good job.'

The official press release stated: 'The surviving Beatles decided to use as little state of the art equipment as possible to give a timeless Beatles feel to the single. To enhance the effect, Paul McCartney used a stand-up double bass originally owned by Elvis Presley's bassist, the late Bill Black. Both Paul and George used six-string acoustic guitars to augment the electric instruments and Ringo used his Ludwig drum kit. The result is a bona fide Beatles single with ageless appeal!'

Incredibly enough, BBC's Radio 1 banned the single from their playlist, making the statement: 'We have played "Real Love" a few times, but no, it's not on the playlist.'

This led to headlines in the national press: 'Beatles Banned by Beeb.' Paul wrote an article about the Radio 1 ban in the *Daily Mirror* newspaper on Saturday, 9 March 1996, in which he stated: 'Is Radio 1 as important as it was? As Ringo said to me about all this, "who needs Radio 1 when you've got all the Independent stations!"'

Some 91 per cent of the *Daily Mirror* readers voted in favour of having the new single on the radio.

The record reached No. 4 in the *Music Week* chart in Britain, but dropped out of the Top 10 after two weeks.

It was included on the *Anthology 2* CD as the opening track.

Rebels, The

A five-piece skiffle band formed by George Harrison which comprised George, his brother Peter and his best friend Arthur Kelly on guitars and two other friends on mouth organ and tea-chest bass. The bass had 'Rebels' painted in red across its front.

Their first and only gig was an audition at the nearby British Legion Club in Dam Wood Road, Speke. The group had been rehearsing at Arthur's house in Wavertree and in one of the bedrooms at the Harrisons' house. When the offer of the audition came up they trooped across to the Legion Hall. Horror of horrors, they discovered that the band who'd been officially booked that night had failed to turn up and they immediately had to set up on stage and play a lengthy set. They enjoyed it tremendously, were given ten shillings for their trouble, but were never to play together again.

George was to comment: 'I remember the Rebels had a tea-chest with a lot of gnomes around it. One of my brothers had a five-shilling guitar, which had the back off. Apart from that it was all fine. Just my brother, some mates and me.'

Red Hot

A number recorded by Ronnie Hawkins in 1959. Hawkins had a backing group called the Hawks who left him and changed their name to the Band. John and Yoko were to stay at Hawkins' farm in Canada during a visit to that country.

The Beatles included this number in their repertoire in 1961 with John Lennon on lead vocals.

Red Rocks Amphitheatre, Denver, Colorado

The Beatles performed here on Wednesday, 26 August 1964. The concert arena was twenty miles outside of Denver and there was no public transport, which was said to have accounted for the fact that only 5,000 of the 7,000 seats were taken. The concert was also considered to be expensive, with tickets costing $6.60 each.

The group were late on their arrival at the airport and stayed at the Brown Palace Hotel until the show. The Beatles performed for half an hour of the two-hour show, playing numbers such as 'If I Fell', 'Can't Buy Me Love' and 'A Hard Day's Night'. There were 250 policemen and reservists placed on concert detail and the altitude was such that the Beatles kept running out of breath during their performance, which began at 9.30 p.m., and had to regularly use some canisters of oxygen which had been provided on stage for them. As at other gigs, they were pelted with jelly beans.

Other artists on the bill were the Righteous Brothers, the Bill Black Combo, Jackie De Shannon and the Exciters.

Red Sails In The Sunset

The Beatles included this number in their repertoire in 1960. The number was originally penned by Jimmy Kennedy and Will Grosz and was first recorded by Joe Turner in 1959, although he didn't have a hit with it. The Beatles probably decided to perform the number after hearing Emile Ford & the Checkmates version in

1960. The song later became a minor hit in Britain for Fats Domino in 1963.

As part of their repertoire, the Beatles played it at the Star Club and it is one of the tracks on the various releases of the Star Club recordings.

Reel Music

A compilation from Capitol Records, co-ordinated by Randall Davis, who also penned the sleeve notes with Steve Meyer. The album contained tracks from the Beatles five films and came with a twelve-page booklet featuring an article and photographs from the films. The artwork on the sleeve was by David McMacken.

Reel Music was issued in the States on Capitol SV-12199 on 22 March 1982 and in Britain on PCS 7218 on 29 March 1982. In America the album reached No. 19 in the charts, although it did not chart in Britain.

The tracks on the album were, Side One: 'A Hard Day's Night', 'I Should Have Known Better', 'Can't Buy Me Love', 'And I Love Her', 'Help!', 'You've Got To Hide Your Love Away', 'Ticket To Ride', 'Magical Mystery Tour'. Side Two: 'I Am The Walrus', 'Yellow Submarine', 'All You Need Is Love', 'Let It Be', 'Get Back', 'The Long And Winding Road'.

Regal Ballroom, Leopold Street, Nairn, Nairnshire, Scotland

Venue of the penultimate gig of the Silver Beatles' brief tour of Scotland as a backing band to singer Johnny Gentle on Friday, 27 May 1960.

Regal Cinema, St Andrews Street, Cambridge

The Beatles made their first appearance at this venue on Tuesday, 9 March 1963 during their tour with Tommy Roe/Chris Montez. They returned to the cinema for the second and last time on Tuesday, 26 November 1963 during their own headlining autumn tour of the UK.

Regal Cinema, St Aldgate Street, Gloucester

The Beatles only appeared at this venue once, on 18 March 1963 during their Tommy Roe/Chris Montez tour.

Regal Cinema, Kirkgate, Wakefield, Yorkshire

The Beatles made a single appearance at this cinema during their tour with Helen Shapiro, on 7 February 1963.

Regent Dansette, High Street, Rhyl, Flintshire, Wales

A ballroom situated above a branch of Burton's, the tailors, where the Beatles appeared on Saturday, 14 July 1962. It marked the group's very first gig in Wales. In common with most advertising of the time, the music was categorised 'Jive-Twist-Rock!', the reference to 'Beat music' and 'Beat groups' came after the establishment of the *Mersey Beat* newspaper. Entrance was five shillings (25p) and the dance took place from 8.00 p.m. to 11.30 p.m. and the Beatles were supported by another Mersey band, the Strangers.

Remains, The

A group from Boston who appeared on the bill of the Beatles' last American tour in 1966.

The Remains were formed by vocalist/guitarist Barry Tashian after he'd been on a visit to England in 1964 and fallen in love with the sounds of the British beat groups. The other members were Bill Briggs on keyboards, Vern Miller on bass guitar and Chip Damiani on drums. The group moved to New York where their new manager John Kurland arranged for them to appear on the bill of the Beatles tour. However, they had to get a new drummer as Chip quit the band prior to the tour saying he didn't want to leave Boston. They engaged seventeen-year-old N. D. Smart, performing with him for the first time at the opening date in Chicago.

Discussing the tour in *Record Collector* magazine in 1992, Tashian recalled 'I was awe-struck. I was 19, and suddenly – the Beatles!' When asked if anyone actually listened to the group on tour, he replied: 'Some listened. We got some notices that were pretty good. Being the kids we were, ambitious and enthusiastic, our philosophy was to steal the show. But how could we steal the show from the Beatles? We tried, though!'

The group opened each concert playing twenty minutes of their own music before backing two other acts, Bobby Hebb and the Ronettes. The numbers in their own repertoire were 'Hang On Sloopy', 'Why Do I Cry', 'Doo Wah Diddy Diddy', 'Thank You', 'Don't Look Back' and 'I'm A Man'.

The Remains, who made a total of four singles and an album, disbanded soon after the tour, although they reformed for a short time for some live gigs in the 1970s.

Tashian's father had suggested he keep a diary of the tour and he was to use the journal as the basis of his book *Ticket To Ride*, published in 1997.

Rembrandt, Baskervyle Road, Heswall, Cheshire

Name of the house which Paul McCartney bought for his father in July 1964 for £8,750. Situated fifteen miles from Liverpool and overlooking the River Dee estuary, the five-bedroomed detached house even had its own wine cellar. A further £8,000 was spent on central heating, furnishing and decorations.

The removal of furniture from Forthlin Road took place at midnight to escape the fans gathered outside the house during the day. Mike McCartney was still living at home at the time and joined his father at Rembrandt. He was very impressed with the contrast between Forthlin Road and the new residence with its five bedrooms, wall-to-wall carpeting and three indoor bathrooms, although it seemed to be too much of a change for Jim McCartney who had lived his life on a relatively low income. Mike was to observe that the sudden contrast proved too much for him: 'Dad, a man of action who'd been striving for something "better" all his life, had suddenly been given it . . . on a plate.'

Jim was later to suffer from severe arthritis and found that he couldn't cope with Rembrandt, so Paul bought the house back off him and Jim moved into a small bungalow nearby.

Reminiscing

The Beatles introduced this King Curtis composition into their repertoire late in 1962, probably after hearing Buddy Holly's version. Holly had a posthumous hit with the number, reaching the British Top Twenty in October 1962 and also climbing to No. 2 in the US charts.

It was one of the numbers the group performed at the Star Club over the Christmas season that year and it is included on the various recordings from Adrian Barber's Star Club tapes.

George Harrison is lead vocalist on the song.

Remo Four, The

A Mersey group who first formed as a vocal outfit, the Remo Quartet, in 1958 and played at social clubs and weddings. They changed to rock 'n' roll music at the beginning of 1960 and were nicknamed 'Liverpool's Fendermen' because they were the first group on Merseyside to have a complete line-up of Fender guitars.

As the Remo Quartet they appeared on a number of Cavern bills with the Beatles, including the Beatles' first evening appearance on Tuesday, 21 March 1961. Other 1961 appearances included Wednesday, 19 July and Tuesday, 25 July.

When they appeared with the Beatles, on Saturday, 5 August,

they'd changed their name to the Remo Four, and under their new name appeared with them on Wednesday, 8 November, Tuesday, 14 November, Tuesday, 21 November, Wednesday, 29 November, Wednesday, 6 December and Saturday, 23 December, all in 1961. Their 1962 Cavern appearances with the Beatles included Wednesday, 17 January and Wednesday, 31 January.

Paul McCartney used to say that on his night off he'd visit the Cavern specially to see the Remo Four.

They appeared with the Beatles on various other gigs, including the 'Rock Around the Clock' all night session at the Iron Door Club on 11 March 1961 and as Johnny Sandon & the Remo Four at the Scala, Runcorn, on Tuesday, 11 December 1962.

The group comprised Keith Stokes (rhythm/vocals), Colin Manley, who was rated as Liverpool's top rock 'n' roll guitarist and was the first to play a Fender (lead), Don Andrews (bass) and Harry Prytherch (drums).

In December 1962 they became Johnny Sandon & the Remo Four in order to embark on a tour of US bases in France, when Roy Dyke replaced Prytherch and Johnny Sandon joined them. They made several further appearances on Beatles Cavern bills under the name Johnny Sandon & the Remo Four.

The group performed some original numbers, including an instrumental 'The Rat Race' and a number sung by Sandon, 'Spanish Main'. Their single 'Yes', flipside 'Magic Potion', was issued by Pye Records on 27 August 1963, but Johnny left on 18 December, after two years, to go solo.

The Remo Four turned down the offer of becoming Billy J. Kramer's backing band, but seemed fated to be cast in the role as a backing group and accepted the offer of backing Tommy Quickly.

The group thought that they were on the brink of success when they teamed up with Quickly, managed by Brian Epstein. They were included on the Beatles Christmas Show at the Finsbury Park Astoria and also joined the Beatles on their autumn tour of Britain in 1964.

The Remo were excited when the Beatles provided them with 'No Reply' to record and felt that it would be the single to take them and Tommy to the top of the charts. The Remo Four recorded the backing track, then double-tracked the guitars and added extra percussion, with Paul McCartney joining them on tambourine and John Lennon clinking Coke bottles in the background. Unfortunately, Quickly was slightly drunk and very nervous at the session and the single was never released.

The group then began to back a variety of singers, including Georgie Fame, Billy Fury and Billy J. Kramer. By this time, Tony Ashton had joined the group.

The personnel of the band comprised Manley, Ashton, Dyke and Phil Rogers in 1968, when George Harrison used them on the recording of the *Wonderwall* album.

Bass guitarist Kim Gardner teamed up with Roy Dyke and Ashton in the trio Ashton, Gardner & Dyke, and they were later to have a chart hit in 1971 with 'Resurrection Shuffle'. George Harrison was to play guitar on the 'I'm Your Spiritual Breadman' track on their album, *The Worst Of Ashton, Gardner & Dyke*.

When the group broke up, Colin began to back singers such as Clodagh Rodgers and Freddie Starr, before becoming a member of the Swinging Bluejeans. He died of cancer in April 1999. Johnny Sandon hanged himself at Christmas 1997.

81a Renshaw Street, Liverpool L1

Address of the *Mersey Beat* office.

When Virginia Sowry moved in as the only full-time member of staff at the beginning of 1961, the office was originally situated on the top floor of the building in one small back room. Due to the rapid growth of the publication there was an internal move to take over the entire first floor, comprising two large rooms, the following year. The offices were directly above David Land's, the wine merchants, and next door to the Renshaw Arms public house.

The offices became the meeting place for almost everyone on the Mersey Beat scene, ranging from the Beatles, Brian Epstein, Bob Wooler and including groups, managers, agents and promoters.

During the first few months the office was opened, the Beatles used to be regular visitors, as they hung around local coffee bars. They dropped in and would often help Virginia out by answering the phone. When they received some copies of their first single they brought a copy round to the *Mersey Beat* office to give to Virginia and personally signed it for her.

Virginia married *Mersey Beat* founder Bill Harry.

The local 'dole' office was also in Renshaw Street and when Ringo Starr went to collect his dole, he used to drop into *Mersey Beat*.

Rescue Hall, Peterhead, Aberdeenshire, Scotland

The final date of the Silver Beetles' short Scottish tour, on which they backed singer Johnny Gentle, took place at this venue on 28 May 1960.

The group arrived back in Liverpool the next day, while Gentle remained in Scotland. They were under the impression that they'd be returning to Scotland to back another Parnes signer, Dickie Pride, in July, on the same circuit, but it never transpired.

Revolution

John Lennon wrote 'Revolution' while he was in India. He had been feeling that it was time to start speaking up about the Vietnam War and decided he wanted to say what he thought about revolution. It became a complex composition for him and there were several versions of the number.

About 'Revolution' itself, he says, 'There were two versions of that song but the underground Left only picked up the one that said "Count me out". The original version which ends up on the LP said "Count me in" too; I put in both because I wasn't sure. There was a third version that was just abstract, musique concrete, kinds of loops and that, people screaming. I thought I was painting in sound a picture of revolution – but I made a mistake. You know. The mistake was that it was anti-revolution.' John pointed out that on the single version he'd said, 'When you talk about destruction you can count me out.'

On Thursday, 30 May 1968, the Beatles began recording the first version of 'Revolution', called 'Revolution 1'. They were to do a second version which was called 'Revolution 9' and in all, there were four different versions of the number.

The fourth version of 'Revolution' was issued as the flipside of the Beatles' 'Hey Jude' single in August 1968 and a slower version was issued on *The Beatles* White album – with John saying, 'Count me in', rather than, 'Count me out'.

There were many recording sessions for the versions of 'Revolution', including Friday, 31 May; Tuesday, 4 June; Monday, 10 June; Tuesday, 11 June; Thursday, 20 June; Friday, 21 June; Tuesday, 25 June; and Wednesday, 10 July 1968. During the session on 4 June, John sang the number lying flat on the ground with the microphone suspended above him on a boom. On the 21 June session he had some other musicians added to the track – trumpeters Derek Watkins and Freddy Clayton and trombonists Don Lang, Rex Morris, Bill Povey and J. Power.

During one of the afternoon sessions, visitors to the studio while they were recording a version of 'Revolution' included Lulu, Davy Jones of the Monkees and Twiggy.

The number was over ten minutes in length, but was edited down to three minutes and twenty-two seconds for the single and four minutes and thirteen seconds for the album.

The track was also featured on the compilation albums *The Beatles 1967–1970*, *Rock 'n' Roll Music* and *Hey Jude*. The Beatles were also seen performing the number on the TV shows 'Frost On Sunday' and 'The Smothers Brothers Comedy Hour'. The number was included on the CD compilation *Past Masters Volume Two*.

Revolution 9

Originally a piece of avant-garde music created by John and Yoko which the other three members of the Beatles didn't wish to be included on *The Beatles* double album. Eventually it was, together with 'Revolution', which is a different number.

John was to comment, 'All the thing was made with loops. I had about 30 loops going, fed them on to one basic track. I was getting classical tapes, going upstairs and chopping them up, making it backwards and things like that, to get the sound effects.'

This was a Beatles track with no singing. There are muffled sounds of conversation, Paul is heard playing piano, a voice keeps repeating, 'Number 9, Number 9', and a range of other unusual sounds are heard. John said, 'One thing was an engineer's testing tape and it would come up with a voice saying. "This is EMI Test Series Number Nine." I just cut up whatever he said and I'd number nine it. Nine turned out to be my birthday and my lucky number and everything. I didn't realise it; it was just so funny the voice saying "Number nine", it was like a joke, bringing number nine into it all the time, that's all it was.'

When 'Revolution 9' appeared on *The Beatles* album, its length of eight minutes and fifteen seconds made it the longest track of any Beatles recording.

Revolver

The Beatles' studio recordings were becoming more complex. Within a matter of weeks after the release of *Revolver,* the Beatles' touring days were over and their 'studio years' began – the type of music they were now experimenting with in the recording studio would have been difficult to present in their live stage performances.

The group originally intended to call the album *Abracadabra,* but discovered there had already been an album released using that title. They had then considered *Magic Circles, Freewheelin' Beatles, Bubble And Squeak, The Beatles On Safari* and *Four Sides To The Circle*. Ringo had even come up with the name *After Geography,* a twist on the word 'Aftermath'. Their use of the word *Revolver* referred to the motion of a record turntable – and not to a handgun.

The tradition of other artists covering numbers from Beatles albums to coincide with their release had already been established, but the 'cover' versions tied to this album were far more in number than usual. Singles quickly issued covering eight of the tracks were by artists such as Cilla Black and Cliff Bennett & the Rebel Rousers. Wayne Gibson, Marc Reid and Brian Withers covered 'For No One', the Tremeloes, Eyes and Glen Dale covered 'Good Day Sunshine'. The Fourmost and Episode Six covered 'Here, There And Everywhere' and Loose Ends covered 'Taxman'. Cliff Bennett & the Rebel Rousers were the winners, reaching No. 6 in the charts with 'Got To Get You Into My Life'.

Robert Freeman, who'd designed all their previous album sleeves, with the exception of *Please Please Me* cover, had come up with a circular photo-montage design, but this was rejected. The Beatles then turned to an old friend from their Hamburg days, Klaus Voormann, to design the album cover. When he'd originally contacted the Beatles at the Kaiserkeller Club, as a way of introduction he'd brought some designs of his, mentioning that he'd like to design record sleeves. This time he got his chance – and he was to receive a Grammy award for his design, which comprised a collage of his drawings of the individual Beatles.

George Harrison had begun to emerge as a songwriter in his own right and was represented on the album by three compositions.

Revolver entered the British charts at No 1 when it was issued on Parlophone PCS 7009 on 5 August 1966. The tracks were, Side One: 'Taxman', 'Eleanor Rigby', 'I'm Only Sleeping', 'Love You To', 'Here, There And Everywhere', 'Yellow Submarine', 'She Said, She Said'. Side Two: 'Good Day Sunshine', 'And Your Bird Can Sing', 'For No One', 'Dr Robert', 'I Want To Tell You', 'Got To Get You Into My Life', 'Tomorrow Never Knows'.

The Capitol *Revolver* album was issued on ST 2576 on 8 August 1966. The American album releases differed from the British ones, due to the American system of including fewer tracks on the LPs and also of including previously unreleased singles on albums. While the British album featured fourteen tracks, the American version only had eleven. 'I'm Only Sleeping', 'And Your Bird Can Sing' and 'Dr Robert' were left off the US release, although *Revolver* became the final American album to contain different tracks from the original British release.

Rhind, Geoff

Liverpool youth who took the photograph of the Quarry Men performing at the Woolton Village Fete on Saturday, 6 July 1957. He recalled that the music was 'extremely loud'. Geoff took the famous picture with his new black plastic Kodak Comer camera.

Rhone, Dorothy

Paul McCartney's first serious girlfriend, the inspiration behind 'Love Me Do' and 'P.S. I Love You'.

Dorothy, known as Dot, attended Liverpool Institute High

School for Girls and lived near the Childwall area with her parents
and siblings Billy, Anne and Barbara. Their mother Jessie and the
children lived in terror of their father, who was a drunkard.

It was while Dot was at the Casbah, Hayman's Green, that she
first saw the Quarry Men, and both John Lennon and Paul
McCartney attempted to chat her up. John nicknamed her Bubbles,
but since he already had a girlfriend, Cynthia, Dot started going out
with Paul.

Paul had many girlfriends in Liverpool, was particularly partial
to blondes and had lost his virginity to a baby-sitter two years
previously, but Dot became his first steady girlfriend and they dated
for three years.

After leaving school, Dot had jobs as a chemist's assistant and a
bank clerk.

Mike McCartney in his book *Thank U Very Much* recalls that
Dot was Paul's first real sweetheart. He has a photograph of Paul
holding her in his arms in the background of the Forthlin Road
house and she's pictured again, with her arms around Paul's neck,
in a photograph taken at Rory Storm's house.

Paul became her first lover at Christmas 1959, while Paul's father
Jim and brother Mike were absent from their house.

Once the Beatles began to do the rounds in Liverpool and
Hamburg she became a friend of another regular Beatle girlfriend,
Cynthia Powell.

Of their first meeting, Cynthia comments: 'Dot was lovely, seventeen years old, slim, short blonde hair (not out of a bottle), and the
most attractive pixie face you have ever seen. Dot was such a gentle
soul, she spoke almost in a whisper, blushed frequently and idolised
Paul.'

When the Beatles set off for their Top Ten Club season in
Hamburg in April 1961, they invited Cynthia and Dot to follow
them over. Cynthia took time off from Liverpool Art College as it
was the Easter holiday, but Dot had some difficulty in getting her
parents' permission for her first trip outside Britain.

The couple set off from Liverpool's Lime Street Station, travelling
by boat train via the Hook of Holland. When they arrived at
Hamburg station, a scruffy-looking reception committee of John
and Paul met them, exhausted by the long hours of playing and the
Hamburg night life.

Cynthia was to stay with Astrid Kirchherr at her home in Eims
Butteler Strasse, and Dot joined Paul on a barge on the river where
Paul had been staying with Tony Sheridan. The 'houseboat' was
owned by Rosa, the lavatory attendant at the Top Ten Club, who
had become an almost maternal figure to the boys, having previously

worked in Bruno Koschmider's clubs where she had dispensed supplies of Preludin to the band.

While they were in Germany, Paul bought Dot a gold engagement ring.

It was while she was working as a bank clerk that the sixteen-year-old girl found out she was pregnant. She revealed the fact to her parents and Paul told his father, Jim. In those days, rather than seek an abortion, the right thing to do was to get married and Jim McCartney began to make arrangements for a registry office wedding. Three months into the pregnancy, Dot had a miscarriage and the wedding never took place.

Several months after the German trip, Cynthia was living in a tiny room in a Liverpool house. When the room next to hers became vacant she persuaded Dot, who had now become her close friend, to move into it. It was in this boarding house that Cynthia discovered she was pregnant.

One evening Dot had just washed her hair and had put it in rollers. She was dressed in an old sweater and a pair of her mother's bloomers when Paul arrived. He took her into her room and told her that their affair was over. Dot was heartbroken. She packed her bags and went back to her parents' home.

Within a year of the break-up, Dot emigrated to Canada and the following year she married a German businessman, Werner Becker. The couple have three daughters, the first of which Dot called Astrid. In October 1997, as a 54-year-old grandmother, Dot revealed the details of her romance with Paul in a two-part series in the *Daily Mail* newspaper.

Rialto Ballroom, Upper Parliament Street, Liverpool L8

Part of a leisure complex that also included a cinema. The Quarry Men made a couple of appearances there in 1957. The Beatles made their debut at the venue, a Top Rank Ballroom, on 6 September 1962 on a gig promoted by Sam Leach. Also on the bill were Rory Storm & the Hurricanes, the Big Three and the Mersey Beats.

The Beatles' second and final appearance took place a few days later on Thursday, 11 October 1962 at an event promoted by Liverpool University Students' Union called 'Rock 'n' Twist Carnival'. Earlier that day the group celebrated the news that 'Love Me Do' had entered the *Record Retailer* Top 50 chart at No. 49.

The event, also advertised as a 'Rock & Twist Spectacular', featured Billy Kramer with the Coasters, the Undertakers and the Mersey Beats. It was part of a week of events, organised by the

cinema/ballroom managers Brian Collins and Vince Sumner to celebrate the Rialto's 35th anniversary. The event ran from eight until
midnight and price of admission was 5/-. Among the other events
that week was a special display of drawings by Bill Harry in the
foyer, together with photographs of Mersey Beat bands. There was
a Saturday morning party for kids and a Wednesday anniversary
dance with a Miss Top Rank election in the Regency Suite, plus an
Irish dance with a top Irish band. Friday night was Ladies' Gift
Night.

The Rialto was utterly gutted in the Toxteth riots of 1981.

Rialto Theatre, Fishergate, York, Yorkshire

Each of the four appearances the Beatles made at this venue took
place in 1963. Their first appearance occurred on Wednesday, 27
February, when they were on the bill of the Helen Shapiro Tour.
However, due to illness, Shapiro didn't appear. It was while they
were travelling by coach to the next gig that John and Paul were
reading the *New Musical Express* and were inspired to write 'From
Me To You'.

Their next appearance at the theatre found them on the bill of the
Tommy Roe/Chris Montez tour on Wednesday, 13 March. This
time it was John Lennon's turn to succumb to a severe cold and he
was not able to appear that night.

Their Wednesday, 29 May appearance was on the bill of the Roy
Orbison Tour, but when they returned on Wednesday, 27
November they were bill toppers in their own right and the final gig
was part of the Beatles' autumn tour.

Richards, Ron

A recording manager who became George Martin's assistant in
1962. Richards usually recorded the rock 'n' pop acts, while Martin
concentrated on the comedy, classical and variety artists. When the
Beatles turned up for their recording audition on Wednesday, 6 June
1962, it was Richards who initially recorded the session, while
George Martin left the studio to go to the canteen. Richards recorded
the Beatles performing 'Besame Mucho', 'P.S.I Love You', 'Ask Me
Why' and 'Love Me Do'. There was some excitement about the
number 'Love Me Do' and Martin was called up from the canteen.

For the session later that year, on Tuesday, 4 September, Richards
rehearsed the Beatles in the afternoon and Martin recorded two
numbers with them that evening. Norman Smith, present at the
session, remarked: 'I've a feeling that Paul wasn't too happy with
Ringo's drumming, and felt it could be better.' Apparently, this was
also the feeling of Richards and Martin.

The next session, on Tuesday, 11 September, was produced solely by Richards, who said: 'We weren't happy with the drum sound on the original "Love Me Do" so I booked Andy White for the remake. I used him a lot at that time – he was very good.'

The sequence of events seems to disprove the allegations about Pete Best and his drumming. White was booked because of disenchantment with Starr, not Best.

While the session took place, Ringo was initially asked to join Richards in the control box, then Richards, possibly taking pity on him asked him to play maracas on 'P.S.I Love You'. He then asked him to play tambourine on 'Love Me Do'.

The succeeding sessions were taken over by Martin who became the Beatles' recording manager rather than Richards who, as already mentioned, handled Parlophone's pop and rock acts. Richards was also credited on the Beatles' initial recording sheets as 'Artists' Manager', meaning he was their A&R man. It is possible that it all happened by chance. Richards was, indeed, credited as their artists manager and was the person actually recording them. During their 6 June session, balance engineer Norman Smith felt there was potential on the Beatles' own number 'Love Me Do' and asked the tape operator Chris Neal to fetch Martin from the canteen. Martin listened and then took over. The incident arguably lost Richards the opportunity of remaining recording manager for the act that was to become the world's leading group.

Righteous Brothers, The
One of the acts selected to support the Beatles on their first tour of America on 25 concerts in August and September 1964.

Vocalists Bill Medley and Bobby Hatfield weren't actually brothers and they'd just had a modest hit in America with 'Little Latin Lupe Lu'. They were among the list of potential acts who were available for the tour which GAC drew up for Brian Epstein's approval.

They received $750 a week during the tour. The following year they had their biggest hit, which became a pop classic, 'You've Lost That Loving Feeling', written by Phil Spector, Cynthia Weill and Barry Mann.

Cilla Black covered the song when it was issued in Britain, but the Righteous Brothers' version reached the No. 1 spot and Cilla's was right below at No. 2. The Righteous Brothers version entered the British charts again in 1969 and 1977.

Ringo's Theme
One of the four George Martin Orchestra instrumental themes which were included on Capitol's American release of the *A Hard*

Day's Night soundtrack album. The theme was used to provide atmosphere in Ringo's solo scenes where he was wandering along a canal bank and was actually just an instrumental version of 'This Boy'.

Rink Ballroom, Park Lane, Sunderland, Tyne & Wear

Another of the British venues where the Beatles only made a single appearance. This took place on Tuesday, 14 May 1963.

Ritz Ballroom, York Road, King's Heath, Birmingham

The Beatles made their debut here on Friday, 15 February 1963 as they were unable to reach the ballroom on the date originally booked, Friday, 11 January, due to blizzards. The rescheduled gig benefited the ballroom as the Beatles' latest single 'Please Please Me' was then near the top of the charts.

Ritz Ballroom, The Promenade, Rhyl, Wales

The Beatles appeared for two consecutive nights at this venue. Both houses at the ballroom in the Welsh seaside resort completely sold out. The dates were Friday, 19 and Saturday, 20 July 1963.

Ritz Cinema, Fisherwick Place, Belfast, Northern Ireland

The Beatles appeared here on Friday, 8 November 1963. The original plan was to have Peter Jay & the Jaywalkers arrive at the front of the house while the Beatles sneaked around the back wearing flat caps. The Commissioner of the Royal Ulster Constabulary vetoed this, saying 'The Beatles must be seen otherwise there will be riots.' The group had to enter the venue after 300 policemen forced a passage through the crowds of screaming fans.

Ritz Cinema, Gordon Street, Luton, Bedfordshire

The Beatles only appeared at this venue once, on their winter tour of the UK on Wednesday, 4 November 1964.

Riverpark Ballroom, Off Love Street, Chester.

Brian Epstein had secured four Thursday night bookings for the Beatles at the venue, but had a problem. He'd reluctantly been forced, on the urging of the other members of the group, to sack Pete Best. Ringo Starr, who was currently in Skegness with Rory Storm and the Hurricanes, agreed to replace him. Although Pete had said he'd appear with the group on their last few gigs before Ringo took over, he then quite naturally decided against it and drummer Johnny Hutchinson agreed to sit in with the group for this appearance on 16 August 1962.

On the second of their appearances, on 23 August 1962, it was John Lennon's wedding night. The Remo Four were on stage before the Beatles and John Lennon was furious that they had introduced some numbers that the Beatles also used in their repertoire. He got on to the stage and asked them if they were going to do any more numbers that the Beatles also played. They told him to get off the stage.

Their other two bookings at the venue took place on 30 August and 13 September 1962. The gig on Thursday, 30 August also featured Gerry & the Pacemakers and the compere was Bob Wooler. Tickets cost 3/-

Roadrunners, The

A Liverpool R&B group who formed in mid-1962. They initially played Chuck Berry numbers.

The Roadrunners soon became acknowledged as Liverpool's leading R&B band, following the usual path of top local groups by appearing at the major venues such as the Cavern and performing at the Star Club, Hamburg.

When George Harrison was telling Dick Rowe about the Rolling Stones in a conversation which directly led to Decca signing the group, he said: 'We've seen a great band down in London called the Rolling Stones who are almost as good as our own Roadrunners.'

Incidentally, Mackey had become president of the Students' Union at the Liverpool College of Art and was assigned to recover the Art College PA system lent to the Beatles, which was needed for the college dances. He travelled to Manchester on the fan club coach and approached John Lennon, who said: 'We've hocked it in Hamburg. If you need to know anything about it, just contact our manager.'

The group recorded a charity record, issued locally on 'Panto Day'. The *Pantomania* EP, featuring 'Cry Cry Cry', 'Fun At Twenty-One', 'If You Want to Know the Time' and 'The Leaving of Liverpool', was recorded at Cavern Sound and the proceeds went to Liverpool charities.

The Roadrunners appeared on three Cavern bills with the Beatles during 1963, on Sunday, 3 February, Friday, 12 March and on the Beatles' final Cavern appearance, on Sunday, 3 August.

Robbins, Mike

A former Butlin's redcoat who married Paul and Mike's cousin Betty. In 1957 the McCartney family visited Butlin's Holiday Camp in Filey. Mike and Betty were redcoats (official camp stewards). As Mike knew that the two boys used to sing the Everly Brothers' 'Bye Bye Love' to the family at home (calling themselves the Nurk Twins), he entered them for a National Talent Contest, organised by the Sunday newspaper the *People*, which was holding heats at the various Butlin's camps. He introduced them as the McCartney Brothers. They sang 'Bye Bye Love', then Paul sang a solo version of 'Long Tall Sally'. They weren't eligible for any prizes as they were under-age, but the thirteen-year-old Mike McCartney was too nervous to give a confident performance and was literally shaking.

Mike and Betty gave up their jobs as redcoats to run a pub, the Fox & Hounds in Berkshire. In April 1960 Paul and John visited the pub and performed on a Saturday night using the name the Nurk Twins.

The couple's children entered showbusiness and even had their own television series at one time. Their daughter Kate Robbins also became a recording artist in her own right and has occasionally guested as a backing vocalist on some of Paul's records. Paul took a hand early in her career and produced her recording 'Tomorrow', the song from the musical 'Annie', which was part of his own MPL publishing catalogue. The single was released in Britain on Anchor ANC 1054 on 30 June 1978, but didn't make the charts. Her biggest hit was 'More Than In Love', a song featured on the television soap opera 'Crossroads', which brought her to the No. 2 position in the British charts when the single was issued on BCA in May 1981.

Robinson, Smokey

Singer/songwriter, born in Detroit, Michigan, on 19 February 1940. He founded the Miracles in 1955. While in London he spent an evening in the company of John and Paul at the White Elephant Club on 29 November 1964. At the time the Miracles had already recorded 'You Really Got A Hold On Me', one of Smokey's songs which had been inspired by Sam Cooke's 'Bring It On Home To Me'. The Beatles had recorded the number on their *With The Beatles* album. Robinson was to comment: 'When they recorded it, it was one of the most flattering things that ever happened to me. I listened to it over and over again, not to criticise it but to enjoy it.' He also said, 'They were not only respectful of us, they were down right worshipful. Whenever reports asked them about their influences, they'd go into euphoria about Motown. I dig them, not only for their songwriting talent, but their honesty.'

Another track on their *With The Beatles* album was penned by John in 1961. It was called 'All I've Got To Do' and John said it was his attempt to do a Smokey Robinson. In 1980, when recording 'Woman', Yoko said that John sounded like a Beatle, but he told her, 'Actually, I'm supposed to be Smokey Robinson at the moment, my dear, because the Beatles were always supposing that they were Smokey Robinson.'

George Harrison dedicated Ooh Baby '(You Know That I Love You)' on his *Extra Texture* album to Smokey Robinson. He also wrote about him in his song 'Pure Smokey' on the *33⅓* album.

Rock And Roll Music

A Chuck Berry rock standard which he took to No. 8 in the American charts in 1957. The Beatles included it in their repertoire in 1960 and it became one of the few non-Lennon & McCartney compositions to remain in their repertoire for several years – they were still playing it in 1966 when their touring days came to an end.

John sang lead vocals on both the stage and recorded versions. It was recorded by them on Sunday, 18 October 1964, for their *Beatles For Sale* album and also included on their *Beatles For Sale* EP. It was featured on their *Rock 'n' Roll Music* compilation and the American album *Beatles' '65*. A version from their live performance on 'Saturday Club' was used on the *Beatles Live At The BBC* CDs.

Rock 'n' Roll Music (Double Album)

When the nine-year recording contract which the Beatles had signed in 1967 expired on 6 February 1976, EMI Records had the rights to release any Beatles material from the back catalogue and *Rock 'n' Roll Music* became the first of several special compilations from EMI.

On being told about the album, John Lennon wrote to EMI offering to design the sleeve. Inexplicably, he was turned down, much to his annoyance when he saw the final album sleeve, illustrated by Ignacio Gomez, which he didn't like. John Lennon wasn't the only one who didn't like the *Rock 'n' Roll* package as it was widely criticised as being cheap-looking. Ringo Starr also criticised the cover as being unsuitable.

The 28-track double album was issued in Britain on PCSP 719 on 10 June 1976 and reached No. 10 in the New Musical Express chart.

George Martin, at the request of Bhaskar Menon, President of Capitol Records, re-dubbed the tapes to enhance their quality – although he was never paid for his efforts, even though Capitol reportedly spent more money promoting this album than on any of their other Beatles releases. The only track not produced by George Martin was 'Get Back', which had been produced by Phil Spector.

The American release was issued on Capitol SKBO 11537 on 7 June 1976 and reached No. 2 in *Billboard*, No. 4 in *Cash Box* and No. 2 in *Record World*, prevented from reaching No. 1 by *Wings At the Speed Of Sound*.

The album tracks were, Side One: 'Twist And Shout', 'I Saw Her Standing There', 'You Can't Do That', 'I Wanna Be Your Man', 'I Call Your Name', 'Boys', 'Long Tall Sally'. Side Two: 'Rock And Roll Music', 'Slow Down', 'Kansas City/Hey Hey Hey', 'Money (That's What I Want)', 'Bad Boy', 'Matchbox', 'Roll Over Beethoven'. Side Three: 'Dizzy Miss Lizzy', 'Any Time At All', 'Drive My Car', 'Everybody's Trying To Be My Baby', 'The Night Before', 'I'm Down', 'Revolution'. Side Four: 'Back In The USSR', 'Helter Skelter', 'Taxman', 'Got To Get You Into My Life', 'Hey Bulldog', 'Birthday', 'Get Back'.

Rock 'n' Roll Music Volume 2

The compilation *Rock 'n' Roll Music* was originally issued as a double album in Britain on 10 June 1976. The album was split into two separate LPs and reissued on 27 October 1980 when it became the first Beatles album to be repackaged on a budget label. It was issued on Music For Pleasure, EMI's budget label. *Rock 'n' Roll Music* was issued on MFP 50506 and *Rock 'n' Roll Music Volume 2* on MFP 50507.

The tracks on *Rock 'n' Roll Music Volume 2* comprised what were originally Sides Three and Four on the original double album. They were, Side One: 'Dizzy Miss Lizzy', 'Any Time At All', 'Drive My Car', 'Everybody's Trying To Be My Baby', 'The Night Before', 'I'm Down', 'Revolution'. Side Two: 'Back In The USSR', 'Helter Skelter', 'Taxman', 'Got To Get You Into My Life', 'Hey Bulldog', 'Birthday', 'Get Back'. It was issued in America in October 1980 by Capitol Records on SN 16021, together with the Volume 1 package on Capitol SN 16020.

Capitol had deleted the original double album and issued Beatles albums for the first time on its budget line shortly after the death of John Lennon. They sold well enough to warrant a minor chart placing with Volume 1 reaching No. 134 in the *Record World* Chart and Volume 2 reaching No. 137 in the *Record World* chart.

Rocky Raccoon

A number penned by Paul when he was composing a Rishikesh. He had some help from both John Lennon and Donovan as he began writing it when the three of them were on the roof of one of the chalets at the ashram. He originally called it 'Rocky Sassoon'.

Recording began at Abbey Road on Thursday, 15 August 1968,

and among the additional instruments played were Paul on acoustic guitar and John on bass, with George Martin on honky-tonk piano. The number was included on *The Beatles* double album. A version was included on the Beatles' *Anthology 3* CDs.

4 Rodney Street, Liverpool L1

Site of a private nursing home where Brian Samuel Epstein was born on 19 September 1934. Rodney Street is Liverpool's equivalent of Harley Street and Brian was the first son of Harry and Queenie Epstein. Appropriately, he was born on Yom Kippur, the Jewish Day of Atonement.

Roe, Tommy

An American singer, born Thomas David Roe in Atlanta, Georgia, on 9 May 1942.

He formed his own group, the Satins, at the age of sixteen and enjoyed his first hit with 'Sheila' in 1962. The million-seller topped the charts in America and reached No. 3 in Britain. The Beatles liked the number so much they included it in their own repertoire, with George Harrison as lead vocalist.

Despite spending two years in the Army, Roe had a total of eleven chart singles in America between 1962 and 1971, including another chart-topper 'Dizzy'. He also had six chart hits in Britain, where he was very popular.

From 9 March 1963, Roe began a month-long tour of Britain, co-headlining with fellow American Chris Montez, and the Beatles were the main support band.

Roe also appeared on the bill of the Beatles' first American concert at the Coliseum, Washington DC, on 11 February 1964.

Rolling Stones, The

The group who were regarded as second only to the Beatles in popularity.

Georgio Gomelski, who was unofficially managing the Rolling Stones and presenting them at the Crawdaddy Club in Richmond, went along to the recording of 'Thank Your Lucky Stars' at Twickenham, where the Beatles were performing 'From Me To You' on 14 April 1963 and invited them down to the Crawdaddy Club, which was only three miles away, to see the Stones. Later that night, dressed in leather overcoats, they arrived at the gig. George Harrison was to comment, 'It was a real rave. The audience shouted and screamed and danced on tables. They were doing a dance that no one had seen up till then, but we all know as the Shake. The beat the Stones laid down was so solid it shook off the walls and seemed to move inside your head. A great sound.' The Stones invited the Beatles back to their flat in Edith Grove, Chelsea, and they all went and spent a few hours chatting about music. The Beatles invited the Stones to come along to their Albert Hall show the following Thursday, 18 April, and Brian, Keith and Mick turned up.

The line-up of the Rolling Stones was Mick Jagger (vocals), Brian Jones (guitar, vocals), Keith Richards (guitar, vocals), Bill Wyman (bass) and Charlie Watts (drums).

When George Harrison was judging a beat group contest in Liverpool, he told fellow panellist Dick Rowe about the Rolling Stones and Rowe immediately set off for London and signed the group to Decca Records. By that time the Stones were being co-managed by Andrew Loog Oldham and Eric Easton, and Oldham, who had turned down Epstein's offer of becoming press officer to the Beatles, had worked out an image for his group. The Beatles' tough image had been completely sanitised by Brian Epstein who had made them throw away their black leathers and dress smartly in mohair suits. This pleased Paul but enraged John Lennon. They were instructed not to swear or smoke on stage and the new image was obviously working, with the Beatles' clean-cut image appealing to all ages. Oldham wanted something in complete contrast to the 'lovable moptops', a rough, rebellious image, something to shock the establishment. He succeeded and one critic later commented: 'The Beatles became the kids who charmed a nation. The Stones were the louts who kicked it in the bollocks.' An American critic observed: 'If the Beatles are a wholesome lot, the Rolling Stones look like Neanderthal Teddy Bears.' John Lennon always considered that the Stones had stolen the original Beatles image. While the Stones were good little boys attending middle-class schools in the home counties, the black-leather Beatles were whoring in Hamburg, drinking and pill-taking and pounding out raw and savage R&B and rock 'n' roll music.

On 10 September 1963, John and Paul bumped into Andrew Oldham in Jermyn Street and he took them to the Stones' rehearsal at Studio 51, where they completed a song called 'I Wanna Be Your Man', which gave the Stones their first Top Ten hit. A few days later, on 15 September, the Rolling Stones opened *The Great Pop Prom* at the Royal Albert Hall, where the Beatles were bill toppers. The next month the Stones travelled from Manchester to Liverpool to pop into the Cavern Club to see the Big Three record. They were delighted to be mobbed by Liverpool girls asking for their autographs.

There was friendship on a personal level between the two bands and they were often meeting socially at clubs such as the Ad Lib and Scotch of St James, laughing at the fact that the press painted them as bitter rivals.

Brian Epstein and Andrew Oldham had come to an agreement that there would be no clash on release dates between the two groups. Oldham was later replaced as Stones' manager by Allen Klein and it was the Stones who recommended to the Beatles that they take him on board to run their Apple empire.

Following the success of the *Beatles Monthly*, publisher Sean O'Mahony also launched a *Rolling Stones Monthly*, but it only lasted for 30 issues.

On 26 April 1964, both groups appeared on the New Musical Express poll winners concert at the Empire Pool, Wembley. On 8 July 1964, Keith Richards, Brian Jones and Bill Wyman turned up at the *A Hard Day's Night* party at the Dorchester Hotel. On 18 May 1967, while the Stones were recording at Olympic Sound Studios in Barnes, John and Paul turned up and added backing vocals to 'We Love You'. Mick Jagger was to send them a bunch of flowers by way of a thank you. The next month Paul McCartney invited Brian Jones to a Beatles session at Abbey Road. Paul commented, 'To our surprise he brought along a sax. I remember him turning up in this big Afghan coat at Abbey Road and he opened up a sax case and we said, "We've got a little track here", so he played sax on it. It was a crazy record, a sort of "B"-side, "You Know My Name (Look Up The Number)" '. On 7 July 1967 Brian, Mick Jagger and Marianne Faithfull were among the guests at the live television transmission of 'All You Need Is Love' on the 'Our World' television broadcast.

On 5 August 1967 Mick produced Marianne singing 'When I'm Sixty-Four' and later the same month, on 26 August, the two of them joined the Beatles at the Maharishi Mahesh Yogi seminar in Bangor, Wales.

On 15 October 1967 the *People* newspaper ran a story that the Beatles and Stones were going into business together. The story read, 'They are looking for new studios in London, probably to record unknown pop groups. And they may make films together. There is no question of the two pop groups merging.'

On 17 October Les Perrin, the Stones' publicist, issued a press release, 'Mr Jagger states that preparatory conversations of a purely exploratory nature were held between him and Mr Paul McCartney. These conversations have not been resolved and any assumption to the contrary should be considered premature.' The Beatles office had issued a statement, 'We look upon any merger as a fusion of nine people's business talents in a new and exciting project. Nothing has changed since Brian Epstein's death, but the prospect of some professional tie-in between the Beatles and the Stones is very intriguing. What the boys are contemplating is a separate business project for opening up a joint talent centre that will build up on other people's talents, produce and distribute their records.'

On 20 January 1968 Brian Jones was once again in the recording studios with Paul McCartney, this time playing sax on a track for the album *McGear*, by Paul's brother Mike.

On 12 December 1968 *The Rolling Stones' Rock 'n' Roll Circus* was shot at Intertel Studios in Wembley. Among the guests were black fashion model Donyale Luna, the Who, Eric Clapton, John Lennon, Yoko Ono, Mitch Mitchell, Marianne Faithfull and Jethro Tull.

During the career of both groups there were many occasions when they acknowledged each other. The Beatles had 'Welcome Rolling Stones' on the cover of their *Sgt Pepper* album and the Stones had a picture of the Beatles on their *Satanic Majesties Request* album. George Harrison also had Keith Richard play guitar on his production of 'That's The Way God Planned It'.

Roll Over Beethoven

A number written and recorded by Chuck Berry in 1956, which provided him with his second American chart hit, although it only reached the position of No. 29 in June 1956. It was included in the Beatles' repertoire in the very early stages of their career, before they'd settled on their name. George was lead vocalist on their version of the number which they performed on three 'Saturday Club' shows, two 'From Us To You' shows and on their 'Pop Go The Beatles' and 'Steppin' Out' radio programmes. A live version of the number was recorded while they were at the Star Club and is included on *The Beatles Live! At the Star Club In Hamburg, Germany: 1962* album. The group recorded it for their *With The Beatles* album and the track is also to be found on *Rock 'n' Roll Music, The Beatles Second Album, The Beatles Box* and *The Beatles Collection*. Another live version was recorded at the Hollywood Bowl and issued on *The Beatles At The Hollywood Bowl* album. The number was also the opening track on their *Four By The Beatles* EP, issued by Capitol in May 1964.

A rock classic, the number was part of the standard repertoire of most Mersey groups, although it had never been a chart hit in Britain. 'Roll Over Beethoven' continued to be a favourite with the Beatles, who performed it on stage during their American tours in 1964.

Their live performance on the radio show *From Us To You* was included on *The Beatles Live At The BBC* CDs and a version was included on the Beatles' *Anthology 1* CDs.

Ronettes, The

A trio of singers from New York who became a popular American singing group. They comprised Estelle and Veronica 'Ronnie' Bennett and Nedra Talley. The group was discovered by Phil Spector who wrote and produced their first major hit, 'Be My Baby'. Other hits included 'Baby I Love You', 'Da Doo Ron Ron', 'Best Part Of Breaking Up' and 'Do I Love You'.

The Ronettes were among the first visitors the Beatles had at the Plaza Hotel in New York when they arrived for their first American visit in February 1964. The Ronettes also appeared with the Beatles on their last tour of America in August 1966. However, Ronnie didn't appear on the tour with them and her cousin Elaine stood in for her.

Spector married Ronnie, who later sought a career as a solo singer under the name Ronnie Spector. George Harrison and Phil Spector got together to try to find a hit for Ronnie on the Apple label in 1971. They co-produced the single 'Try Some, Buy Some', which George had written. George also co-wrote the flipside, 'Tandoori Chicken', with Phil Spector. The single was issued in Britain on Apple 33 on 16 April 1971 and in America on 19 April on Apple 1832. Unfortunately, it only reached No. 77 in the American charts. George was later to use the backing track for 'Try Some, Buy Some', which he recorded over and used on his *Living In The Material World* album.

Rory Storm & The Hurricanes

Rory Storm was one of the true legendary figures of the Mersey Beat scene. His real name was Alan Caldwell and he was an ex-cotton salesman when he first formed a skiffle group Al Caldwell's Texans. He changed the name to the Raving Texans in January 1957 and their line-up comprised Al Caldwell (guitar/vocals), Johnny Byrne (guitar/vocals), Paul Murphy (guitar/vocals), Reg Hales (washboard) and Jeff Truman (tea-chest bass). Spud Ward, former member of the Swinging Bluejeans, took over from Truman on bass guitar. The group continued as the Raving Texans until July 1959. For a short time in 1959 he changed the group's name, first to Al Storm & the Hurricanes, then Jett Storm & the Hurricanes and, finally, by the end of the year the group had become Rory Storm & the Hurricanes.

Alan had taken up the name Rory after appearing on a show with Rory Blackwell. Johnny Byrne also used the stage name Johnny

Guitar. On 13 March 1959 Rory opened his own club, the Morgue, in Broadgreen. At the time the blond-haired, 6ft 2in singer was eighteen years old. Ringo joined his band on 25 March 1959 at an appearance at the Mardi Gras Club, Mount Pleasant, and as Jett Storm & the Hurricanes they auditioned at the Liverpool Empire on 18 October for the Carroll Levis talent contest. It was during another contest earlier that year, the 6.5 Special, that Ringo and Rory first met. Ringo had left the Eddie Clayton Skiffle Group and was playing with the Darktown Skiffle Group. Rory told him he was short of a drummer and he decided to join him.

The line-up of Rory Storm & the Hurricanes was Rory Storm (vocals), Johnny Guitar (lead), Ty Brian (guitar), Lu Walters (bass/vocals) and Ringo Starr (drums). This line-up remained the same until August 1962 when Ringo joined the Beatles.

In May 1960 the group secured a summer season at Butlin's Holiday Camp in Pwllheli. The offer was for £25 per week, but it meant that the members would have to become professional. The reluctant one was Ringo Starr who was actually known by his real name of Richie Starkey. He was an apprentice at Henry Hunt's, making school climbing frames, and didn't want to go to Butlin's. Rory decided to convince him. He was good at coining stage names and said, 'You can be Ringo Starr.' Richie said, 'No', he preferred his own name, but Rory talked him into it and said he could have his own spot, 'Ringo Starrtime', in which he would sing the number 'Boys'.

They were one of Allan Williams' main choices to fulfil the Koschmider booking in Hamburg, but because they had taken up the Butlin's season, he finally offered it to the Beatles. The Butlin's gig found them performing for sixteen hours a week in the Rock & Calypso ballroom at the North Wales camp.

The Hurricanes were to team up with the Beatles in Hamburg later that year when they appeared for a season at the Kaiserkeller in October. They were billed above the Beatles and they alternated with them on the daily twelve-hour stretch which the groups had to play. So each band did 90 minutes on and 90 minutes off.

It was during this eight-week season, on Saturday 18 October 1960, that the recording session took place at the Akustik Studio when two members of the Hurricanes, Lu Walters and Ringo, recorded with John, Paul and George. At the same session Lu sang 'Fever' and 'September Song' with Ty Brian and Johnny Guitar.

During 1961 the Hurricanes' reputation in Liverpool continued to grow and they appeared on all of the major venues, including many bills which they shared with the Beatles at places such as the Cassanova Club, the Cavern, Litherland Town Hall, Lathom Hall,

Hambleton Hall and the Liverpool Jazz Society. They also had a second summer season at Butlin's, this time at Skegness in Lincolnshire, 161 miles from Liverpool. Incidentally, Cilla Black was to say, 'Rory Storm & the Hurricanes was the very first group I sang with.' When she appeared with them she sang Peggy Lee's 'Fever'. Drummer Dave Lovelady of the Dominoes has said, 'One night at St Luke's Hall was an absolute sensation. Rory Storm came in with Wally who had got the first bass in Liverpool. There was always a bass on American records, but we'd never seen one, and here was Wally with a Framus four-string bass guitar. The groups crowded round in amazement, and when they opened with 'Brand New Cadillac', this deep, booming sound was tremendous.'

On 30 December 1961 Ringo left the group to travel to Hamburg to act as drummer in Tony Sheridan's band at the Top Ten Club, attracted by the fee and the use of a car and flat. In March 1962 he returned to the Hurricanes and they toured American Forces bases in France before returning to begin their third Butlin's season.

The big shock came later that year when the Beatles asked Ringo to join them. There are various reports on how the news was conveyed to Ringo. *Mersey Beat* reported how George Harrison went along to Admiral Grove to ask Mrs Starkey if she could let Ringo know they wanted him to join the Beatles – perhaps it was this report which resulted in Pete Best fans giving George a black eye at the Cavern! Another report says that John Lennon and then Brian Epstein put a message across the Butlin camp's public address system. Johnny Guitar says that John and Paul turned up at 10 o'clock one morning and knocked on their caravan door saying they wanted Ringo to join them. Rory told them that the Hurricanes couldn't work without a drummer and they hadn't finished their season. Paul told him that Brian Epstein said they could have Pete Best. Rory went to Liverpool, but Pete Best was too upset. Rory then returned to Skegness and used relief drummers.

Ringo had let it be known that he was becoming disenchanted as a drummer and was considering a full-time job. He'd also received a letter from Kingsize Taylor in Hamburg with the offer of a job. The Dominoes' drummer Dave Lovelady was leaving and Taylor offered Ringo £20 a week. Ringo wrote to Taylor telling him he was joining the Beatles – who had offered him £25 a week.

Rory Storm & the Hurricanes never recovered from losing Ringo. They had a succession of very good drummers, including Gibson Kemp, Ainsley Dunbar, Keef Hartley and Trevor Morais, but they seemed to miss out on the nationwide boom in the Mersey sound.

In the 1961 *Mersey Beat* poll they were voted into the No. 4

position, although in the 1962 poll they had dropped to No. 19. Perhaps this was caused by their long absences from Liverpool at Butlin's, in Hamburg and at US bases in France. However, they were still regarded as one of Liverpool's top attractions and Rory was one of the biggest of the Mersey stars locally. Disc jockey Bob Wooler called him 'Mr Showmanship' and he was a favourite within the pages of *Mersey Beat* – there were photographs of him leaving hospital with nurses after breaking a limb at a gig, signing autographs for fans at the airport, leading the Mersey Beat XI soccer team, and so on. He was also known for his exuberant stage act. At the New Brighton swimming baths he stripped off to his bathing trunks during a number and climbed up the high diving board, diving off as he finished the song. At the Majestic Ballroom, Birkenhead he scaled one of the columns at the side of the stage during a number, and fell off the balcony, breaking his arm.

Rory also had a major impediment, a stutter, which was very apparent when he was conversing, but didn't seem to affect his performance on stage. He was so involved with his stage persona that he changed his name to Rory Storm by deed poll and called his house at 54 Broadgreen Road, 'Stormsville'.

Once the Mersey scene was underway nationally, A&R men rushed up to Liverpool and signed up numerous bands – but not Rory Storm & the Hurricanes. They were featured in the Associated Rediffusion Television documentary 'Beat City', and were among the groups recorded in primitive conditions by an Oriole mobile recording unit at the Rialto Ballroom – but a contract with a major recording company eluded them. Rory even approached Brian Epstein and asked him to manage them, but he refused. Later, Arthur Howes, the promoter of the Beatles shows, took over as their manager.

Then, in 1964, Rory met Epstein in the Blue Angel Club one night and Epstein agreed to record the group personally. This was a coup and they travelled down to London where Brian was to record them at IBC Studios. They recorded 'America', the number from the musical *West Side Story*. Rory said, 'We first heard this number when we were playing in Spain. Everyone seemed to be playing it. We liked it a lot and when we came back to Liverpool we did our own arrangement and added it to our repertoire. We shortened it, used some of our own words, and it goes down a bomb!'

He told *Mersey Beat*, 'At the recording session we played one number after another to Brian Epstein. He kept saying "No" until we played this and then he gave an emphatic "Yes".'

The 'B' side was the old Everly Brothers number 'Since You

Broke My Heart', which featured some painstaking guitar work –
and the final note took two hours to perfect! 'America' was released
on Parlophone R5197 on 20 December 1964, but didn't reach the
charts. Epstein only ever recorded one other band – the Rustiks.

Rory had other chances to record, but didn't take them. Ringo
had opened the door for him and said that he'd fix it for them to
record whenever they wanted to, but Rory couldn't be bothered
finding new material and seemed content with playing the rock 'n'
roll standards. Perhaps he didn't really want to make the big time.
His sister Iris said, 'He was happy to be the King of Liverpool; he
was never keen on touring, he didn't want to give up running for
the Pembroke Harriers . . . and he'd never miss a Liverpool football
match!'

For a short time they were joined by Vince Earl, former leader of
Liverpool bands such as the Zeros and the Talismen. Then, in 1967,
Ty Brian collapsed on stage and was rushed to hospital. There were
complications resulting from a recent appendicitis operation and he
died at the age of 26. The group broke up for a short time and Rory
and Johnny Guitar tried to revive it with three new members, but it
didn't work out. After that, Rory became a disc jockey in Benidorm
and Amsterdam – a strange profession for a man with a noticeable
stutter.

In 1972 he was appearing in Amsterdam when news came that
his father had died. He returned to Liverpool to console his mother,
Vi, but neither recovered from the shock. Rory was suffering from
a chest condition and took sleeping pills to ease it. On 28
September 1972 both Rory and his mother were found dead in
'Stormsville'. Their deaths remain a mystery, although Alvin
Stardust, his brother-in-law at the time, commented, 'Rory became
very ill. He had a chest condition which meant he couldn't breathe
properly. He found it difficult to sleep so he'd take his pills with a
drop of Scotch which doped him completely. At the post-mortem it
was established that he hadn't taken enough pills to kill himself . . .
It had been nothing more than a case of trying to get some kip, but
because he was so weak, his body couldn't handle it. He died in the
night and his mother found him. She must have felt that she'd lost
everything. I think she took an overdose, but I'm convinced that
Rory didn't. When you've known somebody long enough, you
know whether they're going to do it or not. The whole thing was an
accident.'

Johnny Guitar became an ambulance driver but sadly died of
motor neurone disease in August 1999 at the age of 59. Lu Walters
became a psychiatric nurse and Vince Earl a regular on the television soap opera *Brookside*.

Rosebery Street, Dingle, Liverpool L8

Site of the first professional engagement of the Quarry Men on 22 June 1957. The group were no doubt booked because one of the main organisers was Mrs Marjorie Roberts and her son Charles was a friend of the skiffle group's drummer Colin Hanton.

The occasion was the granting of Liverpool's charter by King John and the 550th Anniversary of the event was celebrated throughout Liverpool. The Quarry Men performed on the flatbed of a stationary coal lorry belonging to the resident of No. 76, who also provided the group with a microphone. The event was a day-long party during which the Quarry Men performed twice.

Charles Roberts, who also took the famous photograph of the group performing in the street, related how two black boys from the neighbouring Hatherley Street began to heckle the group and threatened to beat up John. John jumped off the back of the truck and fled into No. 84, the Roberts' house, followed by the rest of the group. Mrs Roberts provided them with refreshments while a policeman was called and he escorted the boys to the bus stop where they caught a bus home to Woolton.

John's stepsister Julia Baird, in her book *John Lennon, My Brother*, says that she attended the gig with her sister Jacqui and their mother, Julia Lennon. She mentions that the group were called Johnny & the Rainbows because they all wore different coloured shirts (although, in Charlie Roberts' photographs, Colin Hanton's drums have 'The Quarry Men' written on them). She also observed that the group weren't paid for the gig.

Rossington, Norman Arthur

An actor, born in Wavertree, Liverpool, on Christmas Eve, 1928. After working as an office boy at the Albert Dock, he joined an amateur theatrical group at the David Lewis Theatre. He later worked for the Old Vic and National Theatre before appearing as Cupcake in the popular television comedy series 'The Army Game'. He followed with appearances in over forty feature films, ranging from *Saturday Night and Sunday Morning* and *Carry On* movies to blockbusters such as *Lawrence of Arabia*.

He is the only actor to appear in films with the Beatles and Elvis Presley, featuring in *A Hard Day's Night* in 1964 and *Double Trouble* in 1966.

Writer Alun Owen specifically wrote the part of the road manager Norm for Norman, who'd appeared in Alun's play *Progress in The Park* in 1961.

Norman was also the actor who proposed the Beatles for an

Equity card, which they had to have before being allowed to appear in their debut film.

He was also one of the celebrities introduced to the audience at the northern premiere of *A Hard Day's Night* at the Odeon, Liverpool, on Friday, 10 July 1964.

In addition, Norman took Joe McGrath, director of the Peter Cook and Dudley Moore TV series 'Not Only . . . But Also', to meet the group during an appearance at Dunstable to see if John would agree to appear on the programme, reading his poetry. As a result, John and Norman appeared with Cook and Moore on the programme, filmed on Wimbledon Common, during which John and Norm read selections of John's poetry.

As a result of *A Hard Day's Night,* Norman was hired to appear in *Tobruk* and while in Hollywood he was also cast as Arthur Babcock in the Elvis film *Double Trouble.*

In 1994 he appeared in a documentary film *You Can't Do That! The Making Of A Hard Day's Night.*

He died on 21 May 1999. He was seventy years old.

Roundhouse, The, Camden, London NW1

A circular venue in Camden. On 6 November 1968 the Beatles decided that they would play some concerts there on 15 and 16 December with Mary Hopkin and Jackie Lomax. The idea was that the concerts would be filmed for a television special. Apple booked the venue between 14–23 December 1968, but the group then decided to drop the idea.

At one time, when the Beatles and the Rolling Stones considered going into business together, they were exploring the idea of turning the Roundhouse into a recording studio.

Roundup

Children's programme, produced by STV (Scottish Television) from their Glasgow studios. During their brief tour of Scotland at the beginning of 1963, the Beatles appeared live on the show on Tuesday, 8 January, performing 'Please Please Me', prior to the record's release.

Rowe, Dick

Recording manager at Decca Records who had to live with the stigma of being known as 'The Man Who Turned Down The Beatles', which was the title of his unpublished autobiography.

This was rather unfair on Rowe, who did have an ear for talent and signed up some of the biggest pop artists of the decade for his company. When George Martin turned down Tommy Steele, for example, Rowe immediately snapped him up and he became the biggest British pop hitmaker of the 1950s.

The actual person who turned down the Beatles at Decca was Mike Smith, the man who recorded them.

Unlike EMI and the other record companies, Decca decided to give the Beatles a chance by arranging a recording audition. It was Brian Epstein who tried to talk the group into not using any of their original material for this session. John wanted to perform a strong rock 'n' roll set, just like they played at the Cavern, but Brian insisted that they perform as few of their original numbers as possible and concentrate on standards such as 'Till There Was You'.

Both John and Paul were unhappy about this advice, but acceded to Brian's wishes. Had he not interfered, perhaps the outcome of the audition would have been different.

Smith had recorded both the Beatles and Brian Poole & the Tremeloes on the same day, and he chose to sign the Tremeloes. He told Rowe he liked both groups but, since he had only recently joined the A&R department, Rowe felt he could only cope with one of the groups and left the decision to Smith.

A major point was that the Tremeloes only lived a mile away from Smith, which meant that he could spend literally as much time as possible with the Tremeloes at no cost. The Beatles, on the other hand, being from Liverpool, would have added train and hotel fares to recording bills. There was also the north/south divide at the time with Londoners not really interested in anything north of Watford.

Decca was also to act generously by letting Epstein have the tapes of the recording audition for use in promoting the group.

The stigma Rowe suffered is probably the result of Brian Epstein's account, related in his autobiography, *A Cellarful of Noise*, which was taped in a single weekend. In it he accused Rowe of saying: 'Not to mince words, Mr Epstein, we don't like your boys' sound. Groups are out: four piece groups with guitars particularly are finished.'

This would be a strange attitude for Rowe to take as the very month Decca agreed to audition the Beatles he had become part of a new team spearheading the search for new talent, and he was to sign up several guitar groups who became hit artists. Rowe was later to state that he never said what Epstein accused him of saying.

Rowe actively went out in search of talent, participating in the judging of many competitions – unlike other recording managers who stayed put and made the artists come to them.

When Rowe was judging a group competition in Liverpool at the Philharmonic Hall, he was sitting next to fellow judge, George Harrison. George told him about a London band called the Rolling Stones and Rowe rushed back to London and signed them up.

Frankly, instead of being known as the man who turned down the Beatles, which is inaccurate, he should have been lauded as the man who signed up the Rolling Stones.

For the rest of the decade the groups he signed up were responsible for many major hits, but he could never escape the charge levelled at him in Epstein's book, which probably owed more to imaginative licence than the truth. History then began to be rewritten, when the alleged quote was altered to: 'Groups of guitars are on the way out, Mr Epstein – you really should stick to selling recordings in Liverpool.'

Rowe had been suffering from diabetes for some time when he passed away at the age of 64 on 6 June 1986.

Royal Albert Hall, Kensington Gore, London SW7

Superb Victorian building, erected in 1871 in honour of the Prince Consort and destined to become one of the world's most unique concert halls.

The Beatles made their Albert Hall debut on 18 April 1963 in 'Swinging Sound '63', a radio concert broadcast live from the venue and featuring fifteen artists including Del Shannon, the Springfields, Shane Fenton, Kenny Lynch, Susan Maughan, Rolf Harris, the Vernons Girls and Chris Barber's Jazzband.

The programme was produced by Terry Henebery and Ron Belchier (confirmed on page 84 of Kevin Howlett's book *The Beatles At the Beeb*), although Shane Fenton claims (in the book *Alvin Stardust Story* by George Tremlett) that the BBC producer on that occasion was Jimmy Grant. He commented that the Beatles had a row with the BBC production staff responsible for the sound equipment. He heard the group arguing with them, John saying, 'We can't play quiet', and the BBC staff men telling them to turn their amplifiers down, which they refused to do. Paul tried to placate John saying that they may have to do what they were told in case the BBC would refuse to play any of their records. John said, 'Sod the BBC', just as Jimmy Grant came on to the scene and he asked, 'Are there any problems?' John said, 'I don't know who's supposed to be producing this show – but they're trying to get us to play quietly.' Grant told him to play normally, that everything was going to be all right.

The group spent the day rehearsing at the Albert Hall for the show, which was broadcast on the Light Programme, and they performed the numbers 'Twist And Shout' and 'From Me to You'.

There was a squabble when Del Shannon's British agent insisted on top billing for his artist, demanding that Shannon go on after the Beatles and close the show, which he did.

Shannon dropped in to see the band in America on 16 August 1965, the day after their spectacular Shea Stadium concert.

Jane Asher was in the audience at the Albert Hall that evening and posed for pictures for the *Radio Times* as an enthusiastic Beatles fan. She was introduced to the group later that evening and her five-year romance with Paul began.

Also in the audience were the Rolling Stones. The Beatles had rushed off after their appearance and Brian Jones was among a group of friends who helped to carry their guitars and amps out for them. Keith Richards was later to recall how impressed Brian had been with the Beatles' vocal harmonies and he tried to get the Rolling Stones to harmonise as a result, without success. 'After seeing the Beatles and this incredible show,' said Keith, 'which was at the height of English Beatlemania before America, he was completely overawed by them.'

The Beatles' second appearance at the Albert Hall took place on 15 September 1963 when they appeared on the bill of the *Great Pop Prom*, organised by Fleetway Publications and their magazines *Valentine, Marilyn* and *Roxy* and held on behalf of the Printers' Pension Corporation. There were ten other acts on the show, including the Rolling Stones, and the affair was hosted by disc jockey Alan Freeman.

On 29 February 1968, Yoko Ono recorded the number 'AOS' on stage at the Albert Hall and John played guitar. They were to return to the venue on 18 December 1968 to give the world a taste of 'bagism'. It was during the 'Alchemical Wedding', a huge Christmas party by London's alternative/underground scene. The couple appeared on stage inside a white bag.

On Monday, 13 December 1982, the Solid Rock Foundation in association with Capital Radio presented *An Evening For Conservation* in the presence of Her Majesty The Queen and His Royal Highness Prince Philip, the Duke of Edinburgh. The proceeds of the charity presentation, which exceeded £30,000, were donated to the Royal Society for the Protection of Birds. Joan Collins and David Bellamy were the hosts while the Royal Philharmonic Orchestra and the Royal Choral Society, conducted by Louis Clark, with guest soloists Elena Duran and Honor Herrernam, performed 'The Music of the Beatles'.

Paul and Linda McCartney were in the audience and were given a standing ovation.

The programme was recorded and broadcast on Capital Radio. It was also to provide the material for a special album, issued in January 1983 by Evolution Records (SRFL 1001) entitled *The Royal Philharmonic Orchestra Plays The Beatles 20th*

Anniversary Concert. The tracks were, Side One: 'All You Need Is Love', 'A Hard Day's Night', 'I Want To Hold Your Hand', 'Here, There And Everywhere/Norwegian Wood' (featuring Elena Duran), 'Fool On The Hill' and a Beatles medley. Side Two: 'Imagine' (featuring Joan Collins), 'Blackbird', 'Mull Of Kintyre' (featuring Roy Wood and the British Caledonian Airway Pipe and Drum Band), 'Happy Xmas (War Is Over)' and a *Sgt Pepper* medley.

Royal Caribbean Steel Band, The

When Allan Williams first opened the Jacaranda Club in Slater Street, Liverpool, he turned the tiny brick cellar, with its stone floor, into a miniature club for dancing, with entertainment provided by Lord Woodbine and His All-Steel Caribbean Band. Steel bands were scarce in Britain at the time and they proved to be a popular attraction at the club.

When Lord Woodbine left the band to open a club of his own, the remaining quartet, Everett, Otto, Bones and Slim, began to call themselves the Royal Caribbean Steel Band, Williams was to comment, 'The boys were so black and the Jac basement dance floor so dark, that you couldn't see them until they smiled.'

One night Williams arrived at the club to discover that his star attraction hadn't turned up. They then wrote from Hamburg urging him to come over and book groups into the clubs there. Williams went to Hamburg with Lord Woodbine and established contact with Bruno Koschmider.

Casey Jones, leader of Cass & the Cassanovas, always maintained that he used the Jacaranda phone to make calls to Bruno Koschmider in Germany late at night, after the club had closed, and that Allan Williams answered the phone one day and took over the contacts. If this were true, it may explain how the Royal Caribbean Steel Band found themselves in the German port. Could they have answered a call from Hamburg and found they had talked themselves into a gig?

Williams urgently needed a band to fill the vacuum and he decided to book the Silver Beetles. John and Stuart in particular, were regulars at the club and he was able to book them for a series of appearances, beginning on 30 May 1960 for a relatively low fee.

Royal Hall, Ripon Road, Harrogate, Yorkshire

The Beatles only made a single appearance at this Yorkshire venue, on Friday, 8 March 1963 on the eve of their tour with Tommy Roe/Chris Montez.

Royal Hotel, The, Copenhagen, Denmark

On Thursday, 4 June 1964, the Beatles booked into this hotel. They were to appear at the K. B. Halle in the Tivoli Gardens that evening, which was opposite the hotel.

Jimmy Nicol was with the group as Ringo was ill and had to remain in hospital in England. The suite which the boys were given was the one which had been reserved for Russian Premier Nikita Khrushchev the following fortnight. When told he was sleeping in the bed which Khrushchev would be using, George quipped, 'I'll be leaving a note for him under the pillow.'

MV *Royal Iris*

A famous Mersey ferryboat which presented regular dances on board each week as it sailed up the River Mersey from the Pier Head. Independent promoters also ran events aboard and Ray McFall, owner of the Cavern Club, rented the vessel for a series of 'Riverboat Shuffles'. The Beatles were to appear on four of them.

They shared the bill twice with Acker Bilk's Paramount Jazz Band, on Friday, 25 August 1961, on a three and a quarter hour cruise down the river, and on Friday, 6 July 1962. Their third cruise on Friday, 10 August 1962, found them sharing the bill with the appropriately named Johnny Kidd & the Pirates. Their fourth and final 'Riverboat Shuffle' took place on Friday, 28 September 1962, when they topped the bill above another local Mersey Beat group, Lee Castle & the Barons.

Before being taken out of service in the late eighties, the *Royal Iris* sailed to London and held some special cruises down the Thames with entertainment provided by several original Mersey Beat bands such as Faron's Flamingoes.

Royal Lancaster Hotel, The, Bayswater Road, London W2

Setting for a party for *Magical Mystery Tour* on Thursday, 21 December 1967, which took place in the hotel's Westbourne Suite.

The entire cast of *Magical Mystery Tour* were invited, together with the staff of NEMS Enterprises and Apple. Among the 200 guests were Mike Love and Bruce Johnson of the Beach Boys, Billy J. Kramer, Peter Asher and Mike McGear.

The fancy dress party saw Cilla Black dressed as Charlie Chaplin while her boyfriend Bobby Willis appeared as a nun. Singer Lulu was dressed as a Shirley Temple-like little girl. Maureen Starkey was kitted out as an Indian princess and Ringo as a Regency buck. Paul and Jane Asher appeared as a Pearly King and Queen. George was dressed as a Cavalier and Pattie as an Eastern Princess. Cynthia wore a lilac crinoline gown and feathered hat, while John was dressed in leather as a Rocker.

The company sat down to a traditional Christmas dinner with turkey and Christmas pudding and later there was music and dancing to the Chasers, the Symbols and the Dave Bartram Quintet. Actor Robert Morley appeared as Father Christmas and further entertainment was provided by Irish folk group the McPeake Family. There was also the showing of *Magical Mystery Tour* in colour on a large screen. A welcome addition to the entertainment was a performance by the Bonzo Dog Doo Dah Band and Freddie Lennon got up to sing.

John had had too much to drink and steamed up to Pattie, ignoring George, and turned on every iota of his charm to persuade her to join him between the sheets. It was an embarrassing moment, especially for Cynthia, until Lulu strode up and gave John a telling off, after which he returned to his wife.

The Beatles also attended a party at the hotel on 17 July 1968 following the premiere of *Yellow Submarine* at the London Pavilion. The hotel had opened a discotheque called 'The Yellow Submarine', based on the animated film, and the post-premiere reception was held there. The Rank Organisation hosted the party for 200 guests from 11.00 p.m and apart from all four Beatles and Maureen, Pattie and Yoko, there were DJs Simon Dee, Tony Blackburn, Kenny Everett and Pete Brady, Twiggy, members of the Bee Gees, Ginger Baker and fan club secretary Frieda Kelly and her husband.

Royal Lido Ballroom, Central Beach, Prestatyn, Flintshire, Wales

Liverpool manager/agent Joe Flannery took over the task of booking Mersey Beat bands into the Royal Lido, the first of them being the Beatles on 24 November 1962. Other Mersey bands he booked into the venue included Lee Curtis & the All Stars (with former Beatles drummer Pete Best), Billy Kramer with the Coasters and Johnny Templar & the Hi-Cats.

The Royal Lido was officially opened by HRH the Duke of Gloucester in June 1960. It was a prestigious ballroom with a maple dance floor, run by Prestatyn Urban Council and managed by F. E. Jackson.

Prestatyn was the town in North Wales where Beatles road manager Neil Aspinall was born. His family had evacuated from the area, moving from Liverpool during the war as the seaport was particularly hard hit. A large number of Merseyside families evacuated to North Wales during the Luftwaffe blitz. Brian Epstein's family also settled temporarily in Prestatyn in 1940.

Royal Liverpool Children's Hospital, Myrtle Street, Liverpool L7

At the age of six, Ringo was rushed to the hospital after a burst appendix caused peritonitis. He'd had bad stomach pains and was taken by ambulance to the hospital where, '. . . this nurse started smashing me stomach. That's how it felt anyway. She probably just touched it.' He went into a coma for ten weeks following the operation and remained in the hospital for over a year.

When he was thirteen he returned to Myrtle Street with a lung infection caused by pleurisy, which had developed from a cold. He was later transferred to Heswall Children's Hospital. His stay in both hospitals lasted two years and he was fifteen before he was able to return to school.

It was while at the Royal Liverpool that he began playing drums with a makeshift band of fellow patients.

Royalty

The Beatles touched every strata of British society and were even popular with the Royal Family. At one time Prince Charles wrote off requesting the Beatles' autographs – and received them. Unfortunately, they weren't genuine ones, but examples of the thousands of autographs signed on their behalf by Neil Aspinall.

The group's associations with royalty first began when they appeared at the Royal Variety Show at the Prince of Wales Theatre on 4 November 1963 in the presence of the Queen Mother, Princess Margaret and Lord Snowdon. This was the occasion when John Lennon made his famous remark to the audience, 'On this next number I want you all to join in. Would those in the cheap seats clap their hands. The rest of you can rattle your jewellery.'

After the show the Beatles were presented to the Queen Mother in the Royal Lounge. She told them she'd enjoyed the show and asked them where they would be performing next. They told her, 'Slough.' 'Ah,' she said, delighted, 'that's near us.'

When she was asked to comment on the Beatles she said, 'They are so fresh and vital. I simply adore them.'

Prince Philip called them 'good chaps'. On 23 March 1964 he presented the Beatles with two Carl Allen Awards at the Empire Ballroom, Leicester Square, and chatted with John Lennon about books. Controversy was created in October 1965 when the Queen and Prince Philip were touring Canada. The headlines in the news-papers quoted the Prince as saying that the Beatles 'were on the wane'. The press made capital of this comment on the most popular phenomenon and the *London Standard* ran a poll in which five out of seven readers said that what Prince Philip had said wasn't true. In fact Prince Philip hadn't made such a statement. He'd been misquoted. He sent Brian Epstein a personal telegram in which he explained that he'd been asked about the Beatles and had replied, 'I think the Beatles are away.'

The member of the Royal Family most associated with the Beatles is Princess Margaret. On 6 July 1964 the Princess and Lord Snowdon attended the premiere of *A Hard Day's Night* at the London Pavilion. After the premiere there was a private party at the Dorchester Hotel and the Princess and Lord Snowdon dropped by. This particularly pleased Paul McCartney who introduced his father to the Princess. The Princess and her entourage seemed to be enjoying themselves when George Harrison approached Walter Shenson, the film's producer, and said, 'When are we going to eat?' Shenson told him that they couldn't possibly eat until Princess Margaret and Lord Snowdon left. 'Just be patient,' he said. After another fifteen minutes had elapsed, George walked up to the Princess and said, 'Your Highness, we really are hungry and Mr Shenson says we can't eat until you two go.' 'I see,' said the Princess. 'Well, in that case, we'd better run.'

At the Carl Allen Awards on 8 March 1965, once again held at the Empire Ballroom, Leicester Square, Princess Margaret presented a Best Group Award to Brian Epstein on behalf of the Beatles.

Princess Margaret and Lord Snowdon once again attended a Beatles premiere on 29 July 1965 when *Help!* was unveiled at the London Pavilion.

On Tuesday, 4 March 1969, Princess Margaret made an unsched-uled visit to Twickenham Film Studios to watch Ringo Starr and Peter Sellers during the filming of *The Magic Christian*. She remained on the set from 11.00 a.m. until 5.00 p.m. Other visitors to the set that day were Paul and Linda McCartney and Mary Hopkin. Paul and the Princess spent most of the afternoon in conversation together.

The Princess also attended the premiere of *The Magic Christian* at the Odeon, Kensington, on 11 December 1969. Ringo and his wife were at the premiere, as were John and Yoko – who amused the crowds as they paraded before them with a banner proclaiming 'Britain Murdered Hanratty'. Incidentally, in his books, John referred to the Princess as Priceless Margarine.

The Beatles all managed to view the inside of Buckingham Palace when they were awarded the MBE at an Investiture on 26 October 1965. Brian Epstein was not nominated for any honour, which resulted in the 5 November 1965 edition of the *Jewish Chronicle* quoting Princess Margaret as saying, 'I think the Beatles believe that MBE stands for Mister Brian Epstein.'

On 12 March 1969 Rory McEwan was throwing a Pisces party in Chelsea to which George and Pattie Harrison had been invited. That same day there was a police raid on their home, drugs were found and they were taken to the police station for questioning. Their solicitor Martin Polden got them out and they arrived at the party that evening. Princess Margaret and Lord Snowdon were there.

George went up to them and told them that they'd just been busted.

'Oh my, what a shame,' said the Princess.

'Can you help us? Can you sort of use your influence to eliminate the bad news?' George asked.

Princess Margaret seemed horrified at the suggestion. 'Oh, I don't think so,' she said.

They were then joined by Pattie's youngest sister Paula, who took a joint out of her purse and lit it. When she noticed that everyone was staring at her she thought they were annoyed because she hadn't passed it round. She held it out to Princess Margaret and said, 'Here, do you want this?'

The Princess and Lord Snowdon fled the party.

Royalty Theatre, City Road, Chester

Chester is a pleasant town across the River Mersey from Liverpool, and the Beatles appeared there on a few occasions. They only appeared in the town's main theatre, the Royalty, once. The group performed at the venue on Wednesday, 15 May 1963

Rubber Soul

The Beatles' sixth British album release showed the group developing from their rock 'n' roll roots and becoming more adventurous in their musical outlook. George Martin was to comment, 'It was the first album to present a new, growing Beatles to the world.' Paul thought up the title – a humorous reference to white artists trying their hand at soul music: American soul music was very popular in Britain when the Beatles recorded the album between October and November 1965.

It was issued on Parlophone PCS 3075 on 3 December 1965 and topped the charts less than one week after release. The tracks were,

Side One: 'Drive My Car', 'Norwegian Wood (This Bird Has Flown)', 'You Won't See Me', 'Nowhere Man', 'Think For Yourself', 'The Word', 'Michelle'. Side Two: 'What Goes On', 'Girl', 'I'm Looking Through You', 'In My Life', 'Wait', 'If I Needed Someone', 'Run For Your Life'.

The American album was issued by Capitol on ST 2442 on 6 December 1965, containing only ten of the tracks on the British release. 'Drive My Car', 'Nowhere Man', 'What Goes On' and 'If I Needed Someone' were left off and, to bring the American album up to twelve tracks, two numbers from the British *Help!* album were included, 'I've Just Seen A Face' and 'It's Only Love'.

Rudy, Ed

At the time of the Beatles' American debut, Rudy was a syndicated columnist and radio journalist. He first met Brian Epstein in New York late in 1963 through a friend, Bud Hellewell, who was promoting the non-Capitol Beatles material in the States for Epstein.

Rudy arranged to cover the Beatles' arrival and was at John F. Kennedy Airport on 7 February 1964, attending their famous first press conference in the US. He also travelled with them to Washington and Miami.

In an interview with Al Sussman and Bill King for the fan magazine *Beatlefan*, Rudy described their Miami trip: 'It was great fun. It was a happy time, magic time. We'd drive in my car, I had a station wagon and could get a lot of people in it, and there were reporters and Beatles and we'd tune in to WYNZ . . . Sometimes they tried to run away from the press, but it was nearly impossible. There was no place they could go that someone wouldn't tell us where they were. And sometimes they let some of us go along.'

Rudy also stated that he was the only reporter to join the Beatles on their summer tour of the US in 1964. He reported the events for 440 different American radio stations and issued a couple of albums containing interviews and background to the tours. The first of the albums was issued in June 1964 and reached No. 20 in the *Billboard* charts, No. 32 in *Record World* and No. 55 in *Cash Box*. Mark Wallgren, in his book *The Beatles On Record*, points out: 'He [Rudy] then ventured into a recording studio and re-recorded himself asking all the questions which had, in fact, been asked by a wide variety of reporters. The answers given by the Beatles were spliced in. The result was an entire album of Ed Rudy "interviewing" the Beatles.'

In late 1980, Rudy decided to issue *The American Tour With Ed Rudy: News Documentary No. 2*. A blurb to advertise the release read: 'This album was recorded during their American tour by the only American newsman/announcer to cover the complete tour, Ed Rudy. The Beatles call Ed Rudy "the Fifth Beatle" and after listening to these exclusive recordings, you'll know why!'

In their *Beatlefan* feature, Sussman and King quote Rudy explaining his claim, thus: 'The Beatles called me "The Fifth Beatle". It was good fun and I appreciated it and they did that because I was covering for a lot of stations. They knew that it would make me happy and it certainly did. That's not putting down Murray the K. Murray was "The Fifth Beatle" as much as anyone else. The syndicators sold to the radio stations open-end portions of the Beatles introducing "The Fifth Beatle" and on the original tape it was me, John Lennon saying, "Stay tuned for the Fifth Beatle", and then local DJs would come in and they were "The Fifth Beatle!" '

Run For Your Life

A composition which John Lennon didn't like because he had to rush it. There was pressure for John and Paul to come up with a lot of new songs for their recordings in 1965. John even admitted to taking two lines from one of his favourite Elvis Presley numbers, 'Baby Let's Play House'. The song was recorded on Tuesday, 12 October 1965, and included on the *Rubber Soul* album.

Rushworth's Music Store, Whitechapel, Liverpool L1

The largest musical instrument suppliers on Merseyside. During the sixties it was also a record store and was situated quite close to the NEMS Whitechapel branch.

In 1962 the manager of the store was musician Bob Hobbs, who contributed a column to *Mersey Beat*. Following the band's success in the *Mersey Beat* poll, Rushworth's chairman James Rushworth presented John and George with a Gibson J45 guitar each. The guitars had been flown in specially from Chicago. Unfortunately, John's guitar was stolen during their touring days.

Russell, Ethan

A British photographer who produced the shots for the *Get Back* book, included in the limited-edition boxed presentation with the album *Let It Be*.

Ethan is featured in the first volume of *The Beatles Illustrated Lyrics* with a double-page photograph of John and Yoko illustrating 'Got To Get You Into My Life'.

Rustiks, The

A group from Paignton, Devon, who won a talent contest organised by Westward Television. Brian Epstein and Decca's Dick Rowe were among the judges and when Brian presented their prize, he announced that they would be signed to NEMS Enterprises. He even produced the group's first single, 'What A Memory Can Do', issued by Decca in September 1964. The following month they appeared on the Beatles' autumn tour. When their contract lapsed, Epstein didn't renew it.

Saints, The

A traditional American number, more commonly known as 'The Saints Go Marching In', which was popularised by jazz bands. Tony Sheridan sang lead vocals on the song when the Beatles backed him at the Polydor recording session at the Friedrich Ebert Halle in Hamburg in June 1961. It was not an uncommon number for a rock 'n' roll band to play and Bill Haley & the Comets had actually reached No. 5 in the British charts with their version of the number, 'The Saints Rock 'n' Roll' in 1956. Sheridan also chose the number because it had been the signature tune for the Norwich skiffle group he'd led called the Saints.

This particular recording has been released on many singles and albums over the years, although it is generally issued as the flipside of 'My Bonnie'.

When Paul McCartney began learning to play the trumpet at the age of fourteen, it was the only number he actually managed to master before deciding to abandon the instrument. This was primarily because it develops a muscle on the lip and Paul said: 'I only got as far as learning 'The Saints Go Marching In' before I got fed up with it. It used to hurt my lip and I didn't fancy the thought of walking around like a beat-up boxer, so I decided to buy myself a guitar.'

John Lennon was to say: 'Paul had bought a trumpet and had this wild theory that he'd actually learned how to play the oldie "When The Saints Go Marching In". He just blew away as hard as he could drowning out everything we were trying to do. He thought he was doing a great job on the tune, but we didn't recognise any of it!

'We were also starting to get going on the vocal side and that upset Paul. He found that he couldn't play trumpet and sing at the same time.'

Sam Houston Coliseum, Houston, Texas

The Beatles appeared at this arena on Thursday, 19 August 1965. The Coliseum had a 12,000 capacity and both shows that day were fully booked.

When the group arrived at Houston Airport at 2.00 a.m. there were huge crowds awaiting them. The vast numbers of fans turned into a mob and swarmed round the plane as it taxied to land. The situation was potentially dangerous and the Beatles were imprisoned in the aircraft. Together with Brian Epstein the Beatles were taken off the plane by a fork-lift and the rest of their entourage managed to join them an hour later.

At the Coliseum there were no dressing-room facilities for the group and they had to rush back to their hotel between shows in an armoured van.

Saturday Club

A unique BBC radio show because it was one of the few radio shows of its time which presented current pop acts live and on record. The programme was launched in 1958 by producer Jimmy Grant and its range of music included skiffle, trad jazz, pop and country music.

The show was so popular that at its height, during the period the Beatles were recording for the programme, it had a Saturday morning audience of between 2 and 3 million listeners and was broadcast each Saturday from 10.00 a.m.–12 noon. Its co-producer was Bernie Andrews and the show's host was Brian Matthew, who conducted more BBC radio sessions with the Beatles than anyone else.

The Beatles made their 'Saturday Club' debut on 26 January 1963, two weeks after the release of 'Please Please Me', when they appeared live performing 'Some Other Guy', 'Love Me Do', 'Please Please Me', 'Keep Your Hands Off My Baby' and 'Beautiful Dreamer'. For their second appearance on 16 March 1963 they also appeared live. Usually, the programme was pre-recorded on Tuesday afternoons and evenings at a three-and-a-half-hour recording session at the BBC's Playhouse Theatre in London, during which three or four tracks were recorded for the following Saturday's show. However, on this occasion John Lennon had been suffering from a heavy cold earlier in the week, which had also caused him to miss the appearances at the Granada, Bedford; the

Rialto, York; and the Gaumont, Wolverhampton. They recorded at
the BBC's Studio 3A which was actually used for talk shows and
not really geared for recording music. The group performed 'I Saw
Her Standing There', 'Misery', 'Too Much Monkey Business', 'I'm
Talking About You', 'Please Please Me' and 'Hippy Hippy Shake'.

Their third performance was transmitted on 25 May 1963 and
they performed 'I Saw Her Standing There', 'Do You Want To
Know A Secret?', 'Boys' and 'Long Tall Sally'. On 29 June they
performed 'I Got To Find My Baby', 'Memphis Tennessee',
'Money', 'Till There Was You', 'From Me To You' and 'Roll Over
Beethoven'. On 24 August 1963 they performed 'Long Tall Sally',
'She Loves You', 'Glad All Over', 'Twist And Shout', 'You Really
Got A Hold On Me' and 'I'll Get You'. The programme on 5
October 1963 was a special fifth-birthday edition and the Beatles
sang a rendition of 'Happy Birthday Dear Saturday Club' for the
occasion, in addition to performing 'I Saw Her Standing There',
'Memphis, Tennessee', 'I'll Get You', 'She Loves You' and 'Lucille'.
Their final 'Saturday Club' appearance of 1963 was on 21
December when they performed 'All My Loving', 'This Boy', 'I
Want To Hold Your Hand', 'Till There Was You', 'Roll Over
Beethoven' and 'She Loves You'.

Their first 'Saturday Club' in 1964 was transmitted on 15
February and they performed 'All My Loving', 'Money', 'Hippy
Hippy Shake', 'I Want To Hold Your Hand', 'Roll Over Beethoven',
'Johnny B. Goode' and 'I Wanna Be Your Man'. The next transmis-
sion was on 4 April during the week they had the top five positions
in the American charts and 'Can't Buy Me Love' at No. 1 in the UK.
They performed 'Everybody's Trying To Be My Baby', 'I Call Your
Name', 'I Got A Woman', 'You Can't Do That', 'Can't Buy Me
Love', 'Sure To Fall (In Love With You)' and 'Long Tall Sally'.

The Beatles' tenth and final appearance on the show was broad-
cast on 26 December 1964 when they performed 'Rock And Roll
Music', 'I'm A Loser', 'Everybody's Trying To Be My Baby', 'I Feel
Fine', 'Kansas City/Hey! Hey! Hey!' and 'She's A Woman'.

Savile, Jimmy

One of Britain's most popular disc jockeys, who was particularly
prominent in the sixties with his trademarks of platinum blond hair
and a big cigar.

The Beatles were booked twice at a club Jimmy co-owned in
Manchester, the Three Coins, once in 1961 and another time in
1963.

Savile met the Beatles on numerous occasions and was one of the
main presenters of 'Top Of The Pops'. He was invited to host their

Christmas show at the Odeon, Hammersmith, which commenced on 24 December 1964. Apart from acting as a compere he appeared as the Abominable Snowman in their sketch 'The Search For The Abominable Snowman'.

Jimmy also hosted the 1965 film *Pop Gear*, which featured a clip of the Beatles performing the numbers 'She Loves You' and 'Twist And Shout' at the Ardwick Apollo.

On Saturday, 30 March 1984, while appearing on the popular radio series 'Desert Island Discs', Jimmy's third record choice was 'Paperback Writer' and he related a Beatles anecdote.

He mentioned that he was sitting in a dressing-room one Tuesday, ready to do a show with them, Paul was shaving and John was tying up his bootlaces. John turned to Paul and said, 'Don't forget Thursday, we're going into the studio and it's your turn to write the number.' Paul replied, 'Oh, don't worry, I'll get something done. One of my Aunties said not to write songs about love all the time.' Ringo was sitting in a chair reading a paperback. Paul looked at him and said, 'That's what I'll write a song about.'

3 Savile Row, London W1

Building which acted as the main headquarters of Apple Corps during the late 1960s. Built between 1733 and 1735, the house had once been Lady Hamilton's London residence, bought for her by Lord Nelson, who lived in nearby Bond Street. The five-storey Georgian structure had also once housed the Albany Club. The Beatles purchased the freehold of the building on 22 June 1968 for a reported £500,000. Its previous owner had been bandleader Jack Hylton who'd run his management firm there from 1956.

The Apple staff began to move into the building on 15 July 1968 and the five floors were soon astir with the task of trying to translate the Beatles' dream of a benevolent business into reality. There were executives, accountants and secretaries – even a house astrologer and a doorman!

Unfortunately, the business was beset by problems from the onset and the appearance of Allen Klein on to the scene brought mass sackings and resignations. By 1970 the top floor comprised Allen Klein's office, a press office and an office called 'the black room'. On the second floor were Neil Aspinall, Barbara Bennett and Peter Brown. On the ground floor were John and Yoko's 'Bag Productions' and the Apple Records office. In the basement, which Jack Hylton had originally turned into a projection room, was Apple Studios.

On 23 December 1968 there was an Apple Christmas Party. The memo about the event mentioned: 'In the middle of the party we will be visited by Ernest Castro and April, entertainers to the Queen and Duke of Cornwall and the late Winston Churchill, MacDonald Hobley and others. Mr Castro is a conjuror, ventriloquist and children's entertainer. April is his assistant and also his wife and she plays guitar. So the idea is that all of us at Apple will bring our children and those of us who have no children are invited to bring a couple unless they can arrange to have one of their own in the meantime.'

There were over a hundred children at the party and John and Yoko, dressed as Mother and Father Christmas, handed out gifts, aided by Mary Hopkin.

One of the most potent images of Savile Row is that of the last performance by the Beatles on the rooftop of the building, which took place on the morning of 30 January 1969. Originally, the Beatles had considered performing at the Roundhouse in mid-December and had actually booked the venue. Then they decided they'd move it to 18 January 1969, and then changed their mind again. They only decided to perform on the rooftop of the Apple building the night before; the idea had come to them when they'd taken a breath of fresh air on the roof the previous Wednesday. The event was to be filmed and they wanted a helicopter shot of the Savile roof and the crowd in the street, but found that it was illegal to fly over London. It was also too late to borrow a balloon and film the event from that.

During the morning the equipment and film gear were set up. The performance was to last for 42 minutes with the Beatles, plus Billy Preston, performing all new songs, including 'Get Back', 'Don't Let Me Down', 'I've Got A Feeling', 'The One After 909' and 'Dig A Pony'.

The performance stopped the traffic, and there were dozens of complaints about the noise. Stanley Davis, a company director whose firm was next door to Apple, said: 'I want this bloody noise stopped. It's an absolute disgrace. You can't even use your telephone, dictate a letter or have your window open.' A man called Bobby Valentine phoned the police and a police spokesman was to comment: 'We had so many complaints we sent someone round. A tremendous din was being made.'

A spokesman for Apple said: 'It was all supposed to be very hush-hush. But when you put the Beatles on top of a building in the middle of London and ask them to sing a song it is rather difficult to keep it a secret.'

The event was captured for all time and included in the film *Let It Be*.

In 1972 it was discovered that the building was physically

collapsing, which had been caused by the removal of beam supports when the basement studio had been reconditioned. Everyone moved out while the building was being refurbished, but they never moved back in again and the building was sold to the Midlands Council Workers' Pension Fund in March 1984 for £3.2 million. It then became the headquarters for the Building Societies Association.

Savile Row is a street famous for its tailors. The Beatles supported Tommy Nutter when he opened his House of Nutter at 35a Savile Row on St Valentine's Day, 1969. Nutter made the suits for John, Paul and Ringo that are featured on the *Abbey Road* sleeve, and he also made the wedding suits for John and Yoko.

Saville Theatre, The, Shaftesbury Avenue, London W1

Brian Epstein's love of the theatre had been a lifelong passion and with the wealth he was accumulating he decided to involve himself in the West End theatre world. On 5 April 1965 his company Japspic Productions Limited, of which he was controlling Director, acquired a three-year lease for the Saville Theatre from Bernard Delfont.

Brian intended to subsidise live theatre through rock concerts which he would present on Sunday evenings. The Saville dream went sour, however, and at one time he was losing over £3,000 a week on the venture. Critics pointed out that it was at the wrong end of Shaftesbury Avenue – but it was the most central of all rock concert venues.

The theatre had an Art Deco frontage and inside there was a special box reserved for Brian and the Beatles which had its own private street entrance. The gilt-painted box had upholstered settees covered in leopard-skin prints, velvet curtains, and a private bar with a refrigerator which was always stocked with the best champagne.

Brian presented the West End premiere of James Baldwin's *Amen Corner* at the theatre, but it is for the Sunday night rock concerts that the venue is most remembered.

The Beatles held a press reception there after receiving their MBE medals in 1965 and on 10 November 1967 performed before a live audience during the filming of their pop promo for 'Hello Goodbye', dressed in their *Sgt Pepper* uniforms.

The first major pop presentation was the Four Tops on 13 November 1966 and for the show Paul McCartney designed a special backcloth.

Members of the Beatles were able to enjoy watching shows there and the group joined Brian Epstein in the box on 29 January 1967 to watch *Soundarama*, a concert featuring the Who, the Jimi Hendrix Experience, the Koobas and the Thoughts. George and Pattie and Paul and Jane Asher were present at the 4 June 1967 concert which featured the Jimi Hendrix Experience, Denny Laine and his Electric String Band, Procol Harum and the Chiffons, and were impressed by Jimi's rendition of the 'Sgt Pepper's Lonely Hearts Club Band' song. Ringo Starr also went along to see the Jimi Hendrix Experience perform on 7 May 1967.

There was some controversy when Epstein presented Chuck Berry on 19 February 1967. When two fans climbed on to the stage during Berry's act, the house manager lowered the safety curtain while Berry still had two more numbers to perform. The audience rioted and were shouting up at the box where Epstein sat with Ringo and John. He sympathised with the audience's fury and sacked the house manager Michael Bullock. The National Association of Theatrical and Kine Employees threatened to strike unless he was reinstated – despite the fact that he wasn't even a member of the Union. They told Brian that his licence would be withdrawn. He said, 'If at any time my licence is withdrawn, I shall simply move the shows to another theatre.' He then presented Chuck Berry again on 26 February and, following the trouble-free concert reinstated Bullock on 4 March.

Artists who appeared at the Saville during Brian's tenancy included Del Shannon, the Canadians, Hamilton & the Movement, Edwin Starr, Garnett Mimms, Lee Dorsey, the Impressions, Geno Washington & the Ram Jam Band, Georgie Fame, Fats Domino, Gerry & the Pacemakers, the Bee Gees, Cream, Lee Dorsey, Pink Floyd, Duane Eddy & the Wild Ones, Bo Diddley, Ben E. King, the Alan Bown Set, Denny Laine & His Electric String Band, Procol Harum, the Chiffons, Manfred Mann, the New Vaudeville Band, the Zombies, the Yardbirds, the Settlers, Jeff Beck and John Mayall's Bluesbreakers.

At the time of Brian's death, Tom Jones had been approached for a series of dates and appearances had been planned for Tim Buckley, Traffic, Stevie Wonder, P. J. Proby, Alan Price and Long John Baldry.

The theatre is now a multi-screen cinema.

Savoy Ballroom, South Parade, Southsea, Portsmouth, Hampshire

The Beatles made a single appearance at this Hampshire venue on Sunday, 7 April 1963.

Savoy Truffle

A George Harrison number included on *The Beatles* double album.
George took his inspiration from the lid of a box of Mackintosh's
Good News chocolates. It had reminded him of Eric Clapton's insatiable appetite for chocolates, despite the fact that he had cavities
and they gave him toothache.

Derek Taylor helped him out with some words in the bridges of
the song. When George was having trouble with the middle eight,
Derek mentioned *You Are What You Eat,* the title of a new film by
his friend Alan Pariser.

George is heard on double tracked lead vocals and lead guitar,
with Paul on bass and Ringo on drums and tambourine. Chris
Thomas was on organ and electric piano, Art Ellefson, Danny Moss
and Derek Collins were on tenor saxes, and Ronnie Ross, Harry
Klein and Bernard George on baritone saxes. John Lennon was not
present at the recording sessions, which took place at Trident
Studios in October 1968.

Scaffold, The

Not strictly a Mersey Beat group musically as they combined music
with poetry and humour. They were part of the large cultural scene
in Liverpool in the late fifties and early sixties which was to produce
some of the leading British poets.

The members were Roger McGough, John Gorman and Mike
McGear. The group had originally considered the ridiculous name:
the Liverpool One Fat Lady All Electric Show, but settled on the
Scaffold when they formed in 1962 after appearing together at the
Merseyside Arts Festival.

Mike McGear was actually Paul McCartney's younger brother
Mike McCartney who had changed his name because he did not
want to cash in on the familial one. The group soon had their own
TV show and by 1964 had turned professional and in 1966 began
a five-year association with the Beatles' label Parlophone, with their
first record '2 Day's Monday' produced by George Martin. This
and their other novelty record 'Goodbat Nightman' didn't fare too
well. Then, in 1967, when Mike was on the phone thanking Paul
for the present of a Nikon camera, he got the idea for a number
called 'Thank U Very Much'. Paul attended the recording session
and didn't believe it would be a hit. When it reached No. 4 in the
charts, Paul called Mike to admit he'd been wrong.

The group also had chart success with 'Do You Remember', 'Lily
The Pink', and 'Gin Gan Goolie', with 'Lily The Pink' being their
biggest hit and topping the British charts.

Paul expressed his interest in recording them and he produced an album with Mike and Roger called *McGough and McGear*, which was to become a collector's item. Paul also produced Scaffold's last hit single, 'Liverpool Lou', which reached No. 7 in the charts when it was issued by Warner Brothers in 1974.

When the group split up, Mike continued to record both with other artists and solo, he wrote books, produced other acts on record and became a photographer. Roger McGough consolidated his success as one of Britain's major contemporary poets and John Gorman appeared in a number of children's television shows before retiring to France.

The group re-formed for a special tribute concert for poet Adrian Henn at Liverpool's Philharmonic Hall in March 2000.

Scala Cinema, 58 Charlotte Street, London W1

The Beatles filmed their TV performance sequence for *A Hard Day's Night* here on 31 March 1964. There were plans to film them in front of 1,200 extras, but the Film Artists Association called a strike in protest against 'unpaid labour'. A compromise was reached in which 350 youngsters were used as extras, receiving £3.15s, and a cheese lunch with a pork pie and a banana. One of them was a thirteen-year-old Phil Collins. Among the numbers the group mimed to were 'Tell Me Why', 'And I Love Her', 'I Should Have Known Better' and 'She Loves You'. The venue was completely destroyed in a fire in 1970 and modern offices were built on the site.

Scarfe, Gerald

Prominent British cartoonist with an international reputation whose caricatures are often wickedly grotesque in their representation of famous figures. Scarfe had originally created cartoons of the Beatles during the filming of *Help!* but his most famous Beatles representation was the one made for the front cover of *Time* magazine, published on 22 September 1967. For the commission Scarfe created four life-size models of the Beatles from fibreglass and papier-mâché, which were then photographed. The figures were particularly grotesque and in 1984 were featured in *The Art Of The Beatles* exhibition at Liverpool's Walker Art Gallery.

Scarfe was to marry actress Jane Asher, former girlfriend of Paul McCartney.

Scene At 6.30

Early evening programme covering events in the North-West of England, produced by Granada Television.

Granada executives had shown interest in the Beatles due to the large correspondence they received from viewers in mid-1962 and had sent representatives to watch the group on 28 July at the Cambridge Hall, Southport and on 1 August at the Cavern Club. As a result they sent a film crew to the Cavern on 22 August, led by Dick Fontaine who filmed the group performing 'Some Other Guy' and 'Kansas City/Hey! Hey! Hey!'. This particular film wasn't shown until after the Beatles had become stars, although the 'Kansas City/Hey! Hey! Hey!' sequence was lost.

However, Granada officials were sufficiently interested in the group to provide them with their television debut on 'People And Places' on 17 October and 17 December 1962.

The programme's name was changed to 'Scene At 6.30' and Johnny Hamp booked the group to appear on 16 April 1963. They made several other appearances on the show that year and were recorded on 14 August for a 19 August transmission. Their next appearance was on 18 October. A hilarious meeting between the Beatles and Liverpool comedian Ken Dodd was screened on 27 November and repeated on 27 December. When the group appeared on the programme on 20 December, they performed 'This Boy'.

Here is a transcript of the dialogue between host Gay Byrne, the Beatles and Ken Dodd:

BYRNE: 'We have always thought that it might be a good question to put to Mr Kenneth Dodd and members of the Beatles er, to what extent do they attribute their success to their hairstyles? And we'll start by asking the question now of Mr Dodd.'

DODD: 'We call it hair (*he pronounces it "hur"*) in Liverpool ... you see we always have the judy with the fair (*he pronounces it "fur"*) hair. A fellow once went into a shop in Liverpool where they sell these minks and things and he said to the girl, "Give us one of those hairy coats." She said, "I beg your pardon, sir, what fur?" He said, "For the judy, who do you think?" '

BYRNE (*to the Beatles*): 'Do you think he owes a lot of his success to his hairstyle, fellas?'

JOHN: 'No. I don't think it helped at all.'

GEORGE: 'It might have been better if he was bald.'

DODD: 'Bald! ... With the teeth and the hair, all the gimmicks, you know, I think you definitely have to have a gimmick. You've all got gimmicks, haven't you boys?'

BYRNE: 'What about the nose?'

DODD: 'The nose ...' (*he looks at Ringo and points. Everybody laughs*). 'He's a Martian! We were writing this film script for the boys ... you know the boys are making this new film and we've been writing the script and we've cast Ringo in the role of King Charles on account of the thing, you know, and he goes along to Nell Gwynne and picks her jaffas.'

BYRNE: 'Tell us more about this picture, we didn't know about this.'

DODD: 'Oh, yes, we've written the thing. I'm writing the script, yes, with Knotty Ash University . . . he's King Charles. John is a courtier and in this film he wears a long golden wig with all beautiful curls.'

JOHN (*camping it up*): 'Oh, very nice.'

DODD: '. . . And a blue velvet jacket and like, sort of knickerbockers, with lace round the bottom and buckled shoes with diamante clips on and he sort of walks round on the film set and there's a policeman standing at the side, says he'll pinch him when he comes off.'

BYRNE: 'And what's he supposed to be doing, though?'

DODD: 'Well, John, he's a peasant. He's an evil sort (*he points at George*).'

Commenting on the fact that Ken appears to have mistaken George for John, Paul and John say, 'He's Tom, Harry.'

DODD: 'Well, thingy. He's an evil smelly peasant.'

BYRNE: 'Why is he an evil smelly peasant?'

DODD: 'Come and stand where I am . . . and Paul is a jester, you see, and he's always making the King laugh. Every time he stands on his head the King laughs like anything – he wears a kilt!'

BYRNE: 'Getting back to this group, then, have you no ambitions to form a group yourself?'

DODD: 'Love to. With the boys? Kenny & the Cockroaches or Doddy & the Diddymen.'

BYRNE: 'What about yourself, would you . . .'

DODD: 'Or Ringo & the Layabouts.'

BYRNE: 'Would you not form one yourself, Ken?'

DODD: 'Yes, I'd like to. Yes, because, the only thing is, I'd have to change me name, you see. I'd have to have a name like Cliff or Rock, something earthy.'

PAUL: 'Or Cliff Dodd . . . Rock Dodd.'

DODD: 'Let's invite suggestions for an earthy name for me.'

JOHN: 'Sod!'

Schlacht, Arthur

A German publisher based in Hamburg. In 1961 he was associated with the German record label Deutsche Grammaphon. The label specialised in classical recordings but had a pop subsidiary called Polydor, whose A&R man was the German bandleader and composer Bert Kaempfert. It was Schlacht who suggested that Kaempfert join him on a visit to the Reeperbahn to see Tony Sheridan (he was also Sheridan's publisher) and the Beatles at the Top Ten Club, whom he thought Kaempfert should record. A German rock artist Tommy Kent had also been highly impressed by Sheridan and the Beatles, and he supported Schlacht in his suggestion that Kaempfert should record them. Paul McCartney wrote to some Liverpool fans, commenting: 'The other night, one of Germany's biggest rock & roll stars came into the club. Tommy Kent's his name and he said we were the best group he'd ever heard. Hope he means it.'

Schwartz, Francie

A Pennsylvanian-born, former advertising copywriter in New York, Schwartz had watched John and Paul on the 'Tonight' show inviting talented people to submit their ideas to Apple. She had written a ten-page treatment of a movie script *Poor Richard's Almanac,* based on the life of Richard Goldstein, a violinist who played outside Carnegie Hall. Originally she sent two telegrams to Paul McCartney at Apple. The first read: 'I've written a movie and I want you to write the music. Love and Peace, Francie Schwartz.' The other read: 'Arriving London April 3.' She then flew to Britain and took the treatment along to the Apple office at 95 Wigmore Street. Paul noticed the 23-year-old brunette in the reception area and made contact. She gave Paul her Notting Hill Gate address and he came to see her one Monday morning. She was to comment, 'He settled right into a chair with me on his lap. The kisses started.'

The affair began while Paul was engaged to Jane Asher, who was away touring. Paul fixed Francie up with a job at Apple assisting Derek Taylor, mainly writing press releases for the Apple artists. She was also present at some of the *White Album* sessions. By that time Paul had invited her to move into Cavendish Avenue with him. About three weeks into the arrangement, Jane turned up unexpectedly. Her tour of the provinces with the Old Vic had ended ahead of schedule.

Margot Stevens, one of the Apple Scruffs (the group of girls who hung round the Beatles' homes, offices and recording studios), spotted Jane arriving in her car and pressed the Entryphone, warning Paul of her arrival. He didn't believe her. Jane had a key, discovered what was going on and left.

Schwartz soon tired of the treatment she was receiving from Paul and decided to end the affair and wrote an expose of it in the *News*

Of The World entitled 'Memories Of An Apple Girl'. She then wrote a book called *Body Count* for Rolling Stone publishers, Straight Arrow, concerning her various love affairs. She devoted a full chapter to her short affair with Paul, whom she describes as: '. . . a little Medici prince, pampered and laid on a satin pillow at a very early age.' The book was originally published in 1972 and reprinted in 1999.

Searchers, The

Arguably, the next best Mersey Beat band to the Beatles.

The group had its origins in the Liverpool district of Bootle (from where Billy J. Kramer originated), and John McNally and Mike Prendergast were in different skiffle groups in that area. They teamed up as a duo in 1959 and were then joined by Tony Jackson. They became a quartet when drummer Norman McGarry joined them, but his period with the band was brief and Chris Crummy, a schoolfriend of Mike's, joined them.

When Buddy Holly saw the film *The Searchers*, he penned 'That'll Be The Day', which is a phrase John Wayne used throughout the film. When the group saw the John Ford western, they decided on adopting the name the Searchers for themselves. Chris changed his name to Chris Curtis and Mike became Mike Pender.

They were joined by vocalist Bill Beck, using the name Johnny Sandon, and became known as Johnny Sandon & the Searchers, building a reputation that placed them at No. 5 in the first *Mersey Beat* poll.

Johnny left the group to team up with the Remo Four and the outfit decided to remain a quartet.

John McNally was to tell broadcaster Spencer Leigh: 'One of my regrets is not having been managed by Brian Epstein. We'd have been a better band for it and he always wanted to sign us. He came to the Cavern to see us just before Johnny Sandon left and we knew that he was coming with a view to managing us. We took our gear down the steps and then went to the Grapes for a drink. That was fatal because Johnny got drunk, Tony got drunk and when we went on stage, it was chaos. Johnny pulled all the wires out. Everything went flat. We died a death and Epstein wasn't interested.'

Oddly enough, in the first issue of the magazine *Fabulous*, Brian Epstein said: 'If I could retrace my footsteps and add just one more Liverpool group to my list of recording artists, I would choose to have the Searchers on my books.'

The Searchers appeared at the Cavern on a number of bills with the Beatles, including Saturday, 23 December 1961, and on

Wednesday, 28 February and Wednesday, 4 April 1962. The group played a season at the Star Club, Hamburg, where they first met Frank Allen, guitarist with Cliff Bennett & the Rebel Rousers.

Back in Liverpool, the group was managed by Les Ackerley, a local accountant, who also had ties with the Iron Door and the Odd Spot clubs. They signed with Pye Records. Tony Hatch became their recording manager and their debut disc, 'Sweets For My Sweet', hit the top of the charts. They appeared with the Beatles on an all-Merseyside edition of 'Thank Your Lucky Stars', promoting the song. John Lennon was to say that he considered it to be the best record to come out of Liverpool.

Brian Epstein gave them an original Lennon and McCartney number to record, 'Things We Said Today'. Management complications meant they couldn't record it and the Beatles used it as the flipside of 'A Hard Day's Night'. The Searchers' next hit, 'Sugar and Spice', was penned by their recording manager, under the name Fred Nightingale. The group's third hit, 'Needles And Pins', introduced a jangly guitar sound which inspired the American band the Byrds.

The Searchers had seven further British hits: 'Don't Throw Your Love Away', 'Someday We're Gonna Love Again', 'When You Walk In The Room', 'What Have They Done To The Rain', 'Goodbye My Love', 'He's Got No Love' and 'Take Me For What I'm Worth'. Their biggest hit in America was 'Love Potion No. 9', which was not issued as a single in Britain.

With success came musical differences. Chris, who chose most of the group's songs from his collection of American discs, felt that the group should direct themselves towards slower, melodic material, while Tony wanted more rip-roaring rock numbers. Tony left and was replaced by Frank Allen. In the mid-1960s, Chris left the group and was replaced by John Blunt, whom Billy Adamson replaced in 1969.

Although their run of hits ended in the late 1960s, they received critical acclaim for two albums on the Sire label, *The Searchers* in 1979 and *Play For Today* in 1980.

Mike left the band in 1985 to form Mike Pender's Searchers and vocalist Spencer James replaced him.

By 1995 there were three groups actively performing in Britain which contained members of the original band, all performing the early hits such as 'Sweets For My Sweet' and 'Needles and Pins'. Tony Jackson had his own outfit, John McNally continued to lead the Searchers, with Frank Allen and Mike Pender's Searchers were still active. The distinctive voice remembered from early hits such as 'Sweets For My Sweet', is that of Tony Jackson.

Searchin'

A composition by Jerry Leiber and Mike Stoller which provided the Coasters with a million-selling hit in 1957. It was part of a double 'A' side with 'Youngblood', another number which the Beatles performed in their early stage act.

The Beatles were performing this song in 1958, with Paul on lead vocals, and they also played it at their Decca audition. It subsequently appeared on a number of bootleg albums of the Decca audition, prior to appearing on *The Silver Beatles*, an album issued by Audiofidelity Enterprises in Britain on 10 September 1982. Audiofidelity also issued 'Searchin'' on a three-track single, along with 'Money' and 'Till There Was You' on AFE AFSI on 29 October 1982.

Paul was to pick 'Searchin'' as one of his favourite songs on his 'Desert Island Discs' appearance on 30 January 1982. This Decca audition recording of the number was included on the Beatles' *Anthology 1* CDs.

Sefton General Hospital, Smithdown Road, Liverpool L15

When Julia Lennon was killed in a road accident in Menlove Avenue on 15 July 1958, her body was taken to Sefton General Hospital.

The 17-year-old John was at Julia's house in Blomfield Road at the time and a policeman knocked on the door to tell John Dykins and John that she had been involved in an accident. They caught a taxi to the hospital, only to be told the tragic news.

The hospital was where Julia had given birth to her daughters by Dykins, Julia and Jacqueline.

Dykins himself was also to die at Smithdown Road Hospital following a road accident in 1969.

Cynthia gave birth to Julian at the hospital on Monday, 8 April 1963. John was on tour at the time and when Julian was born the umbilical cord had wrapped itself around his neck. When John visited his wife and son at the hospital, he exclaimed, 'Who's going to be a famous little rocker like his dad, then?'

Sefton Park, Aigburth, Liverpool

One of the several Liverpool parks. It was here that a sixteen-year-old Freddie Lennon first met Julia Stanley, a girl who caught his eye as she walked past the lake. Freddie, accompanied by a friend of his, was bold enough to engage her in flattering conversation. She told him he looked silly in the new bowler hat he was wearing, so he tossed it into the lake.

For many years Mr and Mrs Sutcliffe, Stuart's parents, lived in a ground floor flat in Aigburth Drive, a road which skirted the main entrance to the park.

Photographer Dezo Hoffmann took the Beatles into Sefton Park for a photographic session in April 1963. Paul drove them all there in his Mark 1 Cortina and they noticed a cine camera among Dezo's possessions, so they asked if they could borrow it and filmed sequences of themselves in action. Dezo then began to take his photographs and had them jumping into the air for some shots. It was one of these photographs which appeared on the cover of their *Twist And Shout* EP.

Sellers, Peter

The late Peter Sellers was one of Britain's major screen comedy stars, his most memorable character being the bungling Inspector Clouseau in the *Pink Panther* films.

He first rose to fame in Britain as a member of the Goons, an anarchic radio series in which he starred with Spike Milligan, Harry Secombe and Michael Bentine.

George Martin originally recorded Sellers, producing an album called *Songs For Swinging Sellers*, which proved to be a talking point when George Martin began recording the Beatles.

Sellers appeared as a guest of the Beatles on the Granada TV special 'The Music of Lennon & McCartney' in which he dressed as Richard III and performed a cod Shakespearian rendition of 'A Hard Day's Night'. His single of the number was issued on Parlophone R 5393 and reached No. 14 in the British charts in December 1965.

Peter Sellers and Ringo Starr became close friends during the making of *The Magic Christian* and used to play practical jokes such as knotting together the belts of coats belonging to the film crew. When one of Ringo's friends visited the set he couldn't figure out why there were so many sniggers, until he discovered that a variety of objects, including match boxes and empty cigarette packets, had been taped to his back.

Sellers agreed to sell his house Brookfield to Ringo for £70,000, even though he'd recently spent £50,000 on renovating it. John Lennon wanted to buy the house and offered him £150,000, but Sellers decided to keep his word to Ringo.

While he was negotiating the sale at Brookfield, Ringo noticed a set of drums in the studio there and was told that Peter had started out on his career as a drummer. The fifteenth-century oak-beamed house in Elstead, near Guildford in Surrey, had several acres of ground, its own lake, paddocks, walled gardens and barns, a gymnasium, changing rooms, sauna and a private cinema. Ringo was later to sell it to Stephen Stills.

Michael Sellers, Peter's son, reminiscing in his book *P.S. I Love You* (Collins, 1981), mentioned that his father had once ordered a Beatle suit to be specially made for him. His father also revealed that he'd once been asked to invest in the Beatles' career before they became famous, but had decided that the £2,000 required was a sum he didn't want to risk at the time. However, he did agree to form a property development business with George Harrison, as they both had Dennis O'Brien acting as their business manager. Sellers, however, lost interest in the company because things seemed to be taking so much time, so he resigned his directorship.

Peter presented the Beatles with a Grammy Award on the Tavern set of *Help!* for a television excerpt for America and, ironically, Sellers had originally been offered the script of *Help!* but turned it down.

Sellers used to visit George Harrison at Friar Park and had been introduced to Ravi Shankar by the Beatles. He was affected by George's philosophy for a time and began to wear kaftans, practise yoga, chant, burn incense and eat macrobiotic food.

Sellers had given Ravi Shankar financial support early in their relationship and became disenchanted when, on asking if Ravi could perform a recital for some friends, was quoted a huge fee for the short evening's entertainment.

In *The Magic Christian*, Ringo portrayed Sellers' adopted son, Youngman Grand. The two of them hosted a joint party at the fashionable Les Ambassadeurs in London and John and Yoko and Paul and Linda attended, along with a host of film stars, including George Peppard, Michael Caine, Roger Moore, Richard Harris, Sean Connery, Christopher Lee, Spike Milligan and Stanley Baker. This took place on 4 May 1969 and later that month Sellers joined Ringo, George and their respective wives on the *QE2*, heading for New York.

His version of 'She Loves You', originally recorded in 1965, was finally released in 1981.

Peter Sellers died of a heart attack in May 1980.

Seltaeb

The word 'Beatles' spelt in reverse, which was used as the name of the American arm of STRAMSACT, the company which licensed Beatles merchandise in 1964.

It began when Brian Epstein asked his solicitor David Jacobs to find someone to handle the merchandising deals on behalf of the Beatles as there were too many enquiries for NEMS to cope with.

Jacobs felt that it could be dealt with by someone acting as agent for the merchandising and he decided to ask Nicholas Byrne, a young man whom he had met at parties and had surmised was young and ambitious enough to cope with such a task. Byrne decided to go into partnership with five of his friends: Lord Peregrine Eliot, Simon Miller-Munday, Mark Warman, John Fenton and Malcolm Evans. Byrne took over the title of President of the company and asked each of his friends to invest £1,000, for which they were to receive a percentage of the shares.

Jacobs apparently had no yardstick by which to judge the percentages arising from such a deal, but he also seemed to lack a basic commonsense understanding of haggling: that as a rule of thumb someone looking for a deal expects you to bargain them down and will always start by throwing into the ring a percentage far higher than they would anticipate getting, on the presumption that it will be bargained down. Byrne said his company would take 90 per cent of the fees they received from licences, and grant NEMS and the Beatles a derisory ten per cent. To Byrne's surprise, Jacobs accepted immediately.

Byrne then went to America where firms were queuing up and clamouring for a share in the Beatles market. His team of reps found hundreds of firms willing to make bids, which turned Byrne and his partners into millionaires virtually overnight. The *Wall Street Journal* estimated that Beatles merchandising would make over $50,000,000 in the States in 1964 alone, but the sales of hundreds of ranges of goods were so successful that several sources have put the estimate at twice that figure.

One company which had a licence to manufacture Beatles clothes sold over two million T-shirts in a fortnight and also had healthy profits from sales of pants, hats, beach shirts, tennis shirts and other clothing. Another firm producing Beatle wigs could hardly cope with orders of over half a million when they were going all-out to produce 15,000 per day. The Reliant Shirt Corporation, which paid Seltaeb $100,000 for a licence to manufacture Beatle T-shirts, sold more than a million in only three days.

Byrne was licensing so many products – guitar-shaped brooches, cookies, Beatle nut-crunch popsicles, stationery, candies, toys, alarm clocks, scrapbooks, plates, lunch-boxes, loose-leaf books, pillows, purses, wallets, patches, wallpaper, belts, key-rings, pencil cases, commemorative medals, coathangers, dishcloths, dolls, play balls, scarves, toothbrushes, towels, aprons, balloons and so on – that he was living a lavish lifestyle in the best hotels, buying expensive cars and availing himself of an expenses account on which he personally ran up a bill of over $100,000.

The first inkling Brian Epstein had of the momentous blunder his British lawyer had committed by literally giving away the merchandising rights came when Byrne visited him on his arrival in the States with the Beatles and gave him a cheque for almost $10,000.

Brian realised that if Byrne could afford to give him this amount Seltaeb must have already pocketed around $90,000 – and the merchandising sales were hardly underway!

In June 1964 a new agreement was reached in which NEMS were to receive 45 per cent from the deal, but things continued to go wrong. NEMS sued Byrne for refusing to return the agreed royalties and Byrne's partners also sued him for his profligacy in spending over $150,000 on personal expenses. Byrne discovered that NEMS had begun granting licences to American firms behind his back and having the fees sent directly to the company in Britain, so he in turn sued Brian for $5,000,000.

There was another mix-up when an American court upheld his claim for the staggering amount because Brian Epstein had not turned up in court. He hadn't been told! American attorney Nat Weiss eventually sorted out the problem by having a lawyer explain the mix-up to the court and he then arranged for Brian to make a settlement of less than $100,000.

Because of the publicity surrounding the various court cases, a number of major American firms cancelled their orders and almost $100,000,000 was lost in potential merchandising sales (Woolworth's and Penney's alone had intended placing orders valued at $78,000,000). The Beatles were to launch their own merchandising company. Maximum Enterprises, a few years later – but it was too late, the big merchandising boom had passed its 1964 peak.

September In The Rain

A number which Dinah Washington took to No. 23 in the American charts late in 1961. The Beatles then included it in their repertoire, where it remained throughout 1962, with Paul McCartney on lead vocals. Dinah, whose real name was Ruth Jones, was a leading American blues singer and died on 14 December 1963.

'September In The Rain' had been originally written by Al Dubin and Harry Warren in 1937 for the film *Melody For Two* and over a decade later, in 1949, provided the George Shearing Quintet with a million-seller.

It was one of the numbers the Beatles recorded during their Decca audition session.

Service House, 13 Monmouth Street, London WC2

Original London offices for the NEMS Press Division and also the Beatles Fan Club. Tony Barrow, who took up Brian Epstein's offer to head the new Press and Publicity Division of NEMS Enterprises, moved into Monmouth Street in May 1963.

He described it as: 'Consisting of two small first-floor rooms located above a dirty book shop – premises found for us by the ever-helpful Dick James who knew the place was being vacated by a man named Joe (Mr Piano) Henderson.'

Tony remained in Monmouth Street until 1964 when he moved into the Argyll Street offices of NEMS. The London office of the fan club was opened in June 1963 and Tony Barrow invented a secretary called Anne Collingham. The tasks of the fictitious fan club secretary were carried out by several office workers and the *Beatles Monthly* magazine ran a regular two-page fan club column using the name.

Sexy Sadie

John penned this song to rid himself of the frustration and bitterness he felt towards the Maharishi Mahesh Yogi, who he believed had betrayed him by his actions in Rishikesh. John had been benefiting from Transcendental Meditation and writing lots of songs during his weeks at Rishikesh. Then came the accusations that the Maharishi was making advances to one of the women in the ashram which led to John and George confronting him and John finding himself in the position of spokesman.

When John began writing the song he considered calling it 'Maharishi What Have You Done, You Made A Fool Of Everyone'. However, he was advised for legal reasons not to mention the Maharishi by name and altered the title to 'Sexy Sadie'.

The number was included on *The Beatles* double album. A version was included on the Beatles' *Anthology 3* CDs.

Sergeant Pepper's Lonely Hearts Club Band (Album)

Arguably the most influential album of popular music ever released.

When the album was untitled and recording began, it was said to have a theme of the Beatles' childhood memories of Liverpool. In December 1966, three tracks for the proposed album were recorded: 'When I'm Sixty-Four', 'Strawberry Fields Forever' and 'Penny Lane'. The last two tracks evoked the memories of Liverpool with John's 'Strawberry Fields Forever' and Paul's 'Penny Lane'. As it turned out, recording sessions were taking far longer than in the past and EMI needed a new Beatles single in February 1967. The theme of Liverpool reminiscences was then dropped.

The new theme concerned a mythical band, which led to it being called the first 'concept' album. A Beatles associate, Tony Bramwell, said that at one time the group were considering calling the album *One Down, Six To Go,* in reference to the number of albums they had committed themselves to record under a new contract. This is likely to have been just an example of Beatles humour. The name *Sgt Pepper's Lonely Hearts Club Band* was devised and the album took five months and almost 700 hours of studio time to record.

It is said that Paul McCartney thought up the original idea. He'd suggested, 'Why don't we make the whole album as though the Pepper band really existed, as though Sgt Pepper was doing the record?' Paul at one time also suggested that the Beatles wear Salvation Army type uniforms to promote Sgt Pepper, but the others talked him out of it and the costumes they wore for the promotion were made by Maurice Burman's the theatrical costumiers.

The music was so intricate, complex and innovative that it staggered other artists who had been seeking to outdo the Beatles. Even more remarkable is the fact that this *tour de force* was recorded entirely on a four-track machine. George Martin was to comment: 'Technically, it was a bit of a nightmare. If I'd had eight or sixteen-track recording facilities I could have done a much better job. I only had four tracks and I had to stretch it to the limits.'

Another innovation was to segue the tracks on the album. John Lennon said: 'It makes the whole album sound more like a continuous show. We've put everything in a sequence, which is balanced just like a programme of stuff for a concert. It should be listened to all the way through so there's no point in having a silence every few minutes.' Brian Epstein disagreed and told the Beatles' publicist Tony Barrow, 'People still want to drop the needle on to a favourite bit and play it more often than the rest of the album.'

The cover of *Sgt Pepper's Lonely Hearts Club Band* is the most famous cover of any music album and one of the most imitated images in the world.

The original idea of having a host of celebrities, living and dead, featured on the cover was, once again, Paul McCartney's.

He said, 'We want all our heroes together here. If we believe this is a very special album for us, we should have a lot of people who are special to us on the sleeve with us.'

Both EMI and Brian Epstein disagreed with Paul's idea for the sleeve as they felt it didn't give enough prominence to the Beatles themselves. In fact, Epstein hated the idea. When he was due to return to London from New York by plane, he suddenly had a premonition that the aircraft would crash and he would be killed, so he wrote a note and gave it to his attorney Nat Weiss. The note read: 'Brown paper jacket for Sgt Pepper's Lonely Hearts Club Band.'

Robert Fraser, a prominent figure in the London arts scene, was brought in to advise on the album package and welcomed Paul's idea, at the same time suggesting that another design, submitted by the Fool, would soon appear dated.

Fraser, together with sleeve designer, the artist Peter Blake, sent the Beatles a sheet of paper recommending that they write down their twelve most popular heroes from throughout history.

A number of characters originally chosen didn't actually appear on the finished design. They included Brigitte Bardot, Rene Magritte, Alfred Jarry, The Marquis de Sade, Nietzsche, Lord Buckley, Richmal Crompton and Dick Barton. Two of John Lennon's suggestions, Adolph Hitler and Jesus Christ, were vetoed as it was considered their appearance would offend people. When Sir Joseph Lockwood arrived on the set he asked for the figure of Mahatma Gandhi to be removed as he thought it would offend record buyers in India – and India was a big market for EMI. In an early layout of the set, Gandhi had been placed behind the figure of Diana Dors. There was also a figure of Bette Davis, in her Elizabeth I costume, behind Ringo and also an Albert Schweitzer.

Since there were so many living figures featured on the cover, EMI insisted that permission be obtained from each of the persons represented. This was an extremely complex and time-consuming job and Brian Epstein commissioned his former secretary Wendy Hanson to undertake the task.

A large set was assembled at photographer Michael Cooper's studio in Flood Street, Chelsea and the tableau was created by artist Peter Blake and photographed by Cooper.

As it turned out, the full cast of figures probably does not reflect the individual heroes of each member of the Beatles completely. Ringo didn't bother to make a list, a lot of John's suggestions were vetoed, George chose mostly Indian gurus and Paul was probably influenced by Fraser, who represented a number of American painters. In fact, Fraser and Blake chose a substantial number of figures on the album, and there were numerous American painters and film stars who probably had no influence on the Beatles whatsoever. There was certainly no representation of their original musical influences – Little Richard, Buddy Holly, Chuck Berry, Gene Vincent and Carl Perkins, for example. Even Paul McCartney couldn't figure out why his choice of Brigitte Bardot – the favourite of each of the Beatles in the early 1960s – wasn't included, yet Diana Dors was.

Not every figure on the *Sgt Pepper* album cover has been identified. Some figures are almost obscured by other cut-outs. The identifiable figures are:

SRI YUKTESWAR GIRI. One of four Indian gurus selected by George. Yukteswar was Sri Yogananda's guru and author of the treatise *The Holy Science,* which dealt with the underlying unity of the Bible and the Hindu scriptures.

ALEISTER CROWLEY. A British magician, specialising in the Black Arts, who was known as 'The Great Beast'. He was once the subject of a novel by W. Somerset Maugham called *The Magician.* During his life he was involved in many scandals and was referred to in the press as 'the most evil man in Britain'. He was a practitioner of 'Sex Magic' and wrote many books on the occult.

MAE WEST. The legendary film star who, during the Second World War, had a life-saving device named after her – an inflatable rubber life-jacket. Her films included *My Little Chickadee* in which she starred with W. C. Fields, who is also featured on the cover. Ringo Starr appeared with Mae in the film *Sextette* and Beatles aide Derek Taylor was once employed to handle her publicity. When first approached for permission to use her image, Mae turned down the request, stating, 'What would I be doing in a Lonely Hearts Club?' All four Beatles wrote to her, each signing the letter, and she then agreed.

LENNY BRUCE. An American comedian who gained a cult following because of his abrasive comedy routine which shocked audiences with its liberal use of four-letter words. He died of drug abuse and was the subject of a film biopic, which starred Dustin Hoffman, and a book by Albert Goldman.

KARL HEINZ STOCKHAUSEN. A contemporary German composer, born in 1928, who was noted for his use of electronic sounds.

W. C. FIELDS. He was one of Peter Blake's choices. Fields was an eccentric American screen comedian, born Clarke William Duckenfield in 1880. His films included *Never Give A Sucker An Even Break* and *My Little Chickadee.* He was the subject of a film biopic that starred Rod Steiger.

CARL GUSTAF JUNG. A prominent psychiatrist, born in Switzerland, who studied dreams, the I Ching and various esoteric subjects. His theory of 'synchronicity' intrigued Sting of Police who named one of the group's albums after it. During the 1930s Jung had a dream in which he claimed he saw the future. In the dream he was in Liverpool, which he called 'the city of light'.

EDGAR ALLAN POE. He was John Lennon's choice. Poe was an American author, creator of the modern detective novel and several classic horror tales, including *The Fall of the House of Usher* and *The Pit and the Pendulum*. He died of a weak heart in 1849, caused by excessive drinking.

FRED ASTAIRE. Hollywood's premier star of the dance musical. His films include *Top Hat* and *Funny Face*. He was featured in John Lennon's *Imagine* film.

RICHARD MERKIN. A contemporary American painter, one of several featured on the sleeve. Possibly a choice by Robert Fraser.

BINNIE BARNES was born Gertrude Maude Barnes in Finsbury, north London, on 25 March 1903, the youngest of fourteen children to a policeman and an Italian mother. She was a former flower girl who rose to fame as Catherine Howard in *The Private Life Of Henry VIII*. She moved to Los Angeles and became an American citizen, starring in numerous films including *The Last Of The Mohicans, The Adventures Of Marco Polo* and *The Three Musketeers*. She retired from the screen in 1955 with her second husband, producer Mike Francovich. Their next door neighbour was Elvis Presley. She died in July 1989, aged 86.

THE VARGAS GIRL. A pin-up by the artist Alberto Vargas.

HUNTZ HALL was a screen comedy actor who starred in dozens of Dead End Kids and Bowery Boys films in the 1930s and 1940s. He was an original member of the Dead End Kids, who also included Leo Gorcey, Gabriel Dell, Billy Halop and Bobby Jordan. Hall died in Hollywood on 1 February 1999, aged 78. Leo Gorcey was also selected to appear in the tableau and is, in fact, featured on some of the preliminary cover photographs. However, when he was approached for permission to use the cut-out, he insisted on receiving a fee of £500 for it, so his image was taken out.

SIMON RODIA. A minor folk artist who was also a sculptor and designer. In 1954 he completed the famous Watts Tower, an unusual architectural structure of pottery and cement on a steel framework.

BOB DYLAN. America's leading solo artist of the 1960s and a friend of the Beatles. His real name was Robert Zimmerman.

AUBREY BEARDSLEY. One of the most controversial artists of the Victorian age whose career was almost ruined by a scandal caused by his series of erotic drawings. He suffered from ill health from the age of six and died at the age of 25.

SIR ROBERT PEEL. A former Prime Minister of Great Britain who originally formed the Conservative Party. Born in Bury, Lancashire, in 1788, he died in 1850. Apart from repealing the Corn Laws, he established the police force in Britain, hence early policemen were nicknamed 'peelers'.

ALDOUS HUXLEY. A noted British author whose most famous work is the novel *Brave New World*. He explored the use of hallucinogenic drugs in his book *The Doors of Perception,* a non-fiction work which inspired Jim Morrison to call his group the Doors. John Lennon was very influenced by him and this is arguably one of John's choices. Huxley died in 1963.

TERRY SOUTHERN was a friend of photographer Michael Cooper and was one of Robert Fraser's choices. The American author penned *Candy* and *The Magic Christian,* both of which were filmed featuring Ringo Starr. He was 71 years old at the time of his death in 1995.

TONY CURTIS. Peter Blake's choice. He was an American film star, born in Brooklyn, who became a teen idol in the 1950s and later appeared in comedy roles. His hair style was much copied and, in Liverpool, early members of the Beatles wore the D.A. (duck's arse) hairstyle. He was one of the guest stars in Mae West's *Sextette,* in which Ringo Starr and Keith Moon also appeared.

WALLACE BERMAN. Robert Fraser's choice, another contemporary American artist, based in Los Angeles.

TOMMY HANDLEY. A Liverpool comedian who died in 1949. He became famous for his long-running radio series 'I.T.M.A. (It's That Man Again)'.

MARILYN MONROE. Paul McCartney owns a sculpture of this famous Hollywood screen star who tragically died of an overdose of sleeping pills in 1962. Although regarded as one of the screen's 'sex goddesses', she was an under-rated comedienne and her films included *Some Like It Hot* and *The Misfits*.

WILLIAM BURROUGHS. A Paul McCartney choice. An American writer, born in 1914, whose novels gained a cult following, particularly in the 1960s when several groups named themselves after the titles of his books, which included *The Soft Machine* and *Nova Express*. He died in the mid-1990s.

SRI MAHAVATARA BABAJI is another Indian guru selected by George.

RICHARD LINDNER. Robert Fraser's choice. A German-born artist who fled to America in 1941 to escape Nazi persecution. Originally a concert pianist, he took to painting the sordid low life of New York. He died in 1978.

OLIVER HARDY. Together with his screen partner, Stan Laurel, he created one of the classic film comedy duos – Laurel & Hardy. 'Trail Of the Lonesome Pine', a song from their film *Way Out West,* provided the pair with a posthumous chart hit in the 1970s. He died in 1957.

KARL HEINRICH MARX. This German-born political theorist

developed a system of social philosophy based on his experiences in London's East End. The pamphlet he co-wrote with Friedrich Engels, *The Communist Manifesto,* had a profound effect on the course of twentieth-century history.

H. G. WELLS. The British novelist who created many enduring science fiction classic novels such as *The War Of The Worlds, The Time Machine, The Invisible Man* and *The Island Of Dr Moreau.* His book *The War Of The Worlds* was adapted into a successful rock music album by Jeff Wayne.

SRI PARAMAHANSA YOGANANDA was the first great Indian master to live in the West for a long period of time. He was instrumental in introducing Indian thought and practice to America. Mahasaya Paramahansa was the author of *Autobiography Of A Yogi,* a copy of which George presented to Henry Kissinger. George also dedicated two songs on his $33\frac{1}{3}$ album to the guru, 'Dear One' and 'See Yourself'.

STUART SUTCLIFFE. The original fifth member of the Beatles who played bass guitar with the band. He remained in Hamburg after the Beatles had performed there and tragically died of a brain haemorrhage in 1962.

DYLAN THOMAS. A Welsh poet who died in New York in 1953. He was also a playwright and wrote works such as *Under Milk Wood.*

DION. Peter Blake's choice. An American teen singing idol whose hits included 'Runaround Sue' and 'The Wanderer'. He originally fronted the Belmonts, who had a major international hit with 'Teenager In Love'. He was certainly not one of the Beatles' seminal influences.

DR DAVID LIVINGSTONE. A Scottish missionary and explorer who died in Africa in 1873.

STAN LAUREL. The Lancashire-born comedian who moved to Hollywood and found fame in partnership with Oliver Hardy. He died in 1965.

GEORGE BERNARD SHAW. The Irish-born playwright whose works included *Man And Superman, Pygmalion* and *Major Barbara.* Paul McCartney appeared as the inquisitor in a school play production of Shaw's *St Joan* when he was attending the Liverpool Institute.

JULIA ADAMS. An American actress who appeared as beauty to the beast in the film *The Creature From The Black Lagoon.* She also appeared in several westerns, including *Where The River Bends, The Lawless Breed* and *The Man From The Alamo.*

MAX MILLER. A controversial British music hall comedian, born in Brixton in 1895, who was known as 'the cheeky chappie' because of his risqué comedy routine. He died in 1963.

LUCILLE BALL. A famous Hollywood comedienne. This drawing of the actress was executed by George Petty, an artist who, like Vargas, specialised in painting pin-ups.

MARLON BRANDO. A Hollywood superstar who studied the 'Method' style of acting in films such as *A Streetcar Named Desire*. His other films ranged from *Julius Caesar* to *Superman* and the controversial *Last Tango In Paris*. An apocryphal story is that a band of bikers in his film *The Wild One* inspired the name the Beatles. This is completely untrue as the film was banned in Britain until 1968 and no member of the Beatles could possibly have seen it.

TOM MIX. One of the most famous western actors of the silent screen. A former working cowhand, he became a stunt man and then a star.

OSCAR WILDE. John Lennon's choice. An Irish playwright noted for his witty epigrams. He was involved in a major scandal due to his homosexuality and served a jail sentence before dying in ignominy in Paris in 1900.

TYRONE POWER. A Hollywood leading man who appeared in many swashbuckling roles. His films included *Captain From Castile, The Eddy Duchin Story* and *Son Of Fury*. He died of a heart attack while filming *Solomon And Sheba*.

LARRY BELL. A contemporary American artist, born in Chicago in 1939. He based himself in Little Venice in California and became a leading light in the Los Angeles art world. He began to concentrate on creating glass sculptures from 1964.

JOHNNY WEISSMULLER. A prominent athlete who became the American swimming champion, winning five gold medals in the Olympics. This led to offers from Hollywood and he became the screen's most popular Tarzan.

STEPHEN CRANE. A talented American author who died from tuberculosis in 1900 at the age of 28. His novels included *The Red Badge of Courage* and *The Outcasts of Poker Flat*.

ISSY BONN. A noted British radio and music hall star of the 1940s and 1950s.

ALBERT STUBBINS. A former soccer player with Liverpool FC. This was John's choice, although he didn't know anything about him. He'd chosen him because his father had been a fan.

ALBERT EINSTEIN. The scientific genius, born in West Germany in 1879. He spent the last twenty years of his life at the Institute for Advanced Studies at Princeton University in America. He revolutionised scientific thinking with his Theory of Relativity.

H. C. (HORACE CLIFFORD) WESTERMANN. Peter Blake's choice. A noted sculptor.

SRI LAHIRI MAHASAYA. Another of George's Indian guru selections.

LEWIS CARROLL. John Lennon's choice. Born Charles Lutwidge Dodgson in Cheshire, near Liverpool, in 1832. He was a teacher who was author of such classic works as *Alice In Wonderland* and *Through The Looking Glass*. John was inspired by his works, as is evident from songs such as 'I Am The Walrus'.

T. E. (THOMAS EDWARD) LAWRENCE. He rose to fame during the First World War when he united the Arab nations and led the fight against the Turks. He became disillusioned when the British reneged on their promises to the Arabs and later enlisted anonymously in the RAF. He wrote several books including *The Seven Pillars Of Wisdom* and died in a motorcycle accident in 1935.

SONNY LISTON. Peter Blake's choice. Liston was an American boxer who became heavyweight champion of the world when he knocked out Floyd Patterson in 1962. He died alone in 1970, his body being discovered a week after his death. This is a waxwork figure which Blake bought from Madame Tussauds and still owns.

BOBBY BREEN. The lead singer with a British dance band.

MARLENE DIETRICH. The Berlin born film star whose films included *The Blue Angel, Destry Rides Again* and *Shanghai Express*. One of the Beatles' drinking haunts in Liverpool was called The Blue Angel and Marlene appeared on the same bill as the Beatles at the Royal Variety Show on 4 November 1963. She died in May 1992.

DIANA DORS. A British film actress who was touted as a screen sex star of the 1950s. She became a popular character actress in British films and TV. She died in 1984.

SHIRLEY TEMPLE. Peter Blake's choice. There are actually three images of Shirley on the cover. The Californian actress rose to fame as a child star in such films as *Wee Willie Winkie* and *The Little Princess*, and was later to become an American ambassador. She visited the Beatles in their dressing-room at the Cow Palace, San Francisco, in 1964. When initially approached about permission to use her image she insisted on hearing the record first before she gave her approval.

THE PETTY GIRL. Another image by George Petty.

The ornate drumskin in the centre of the album cover was conceived by Peter Blake and the Beatles, who commissioned a genuine fairground artist, Joseph Ephgrave, to paint it. Madame Tussauds lent a total of nine waxworks for the cover photograph – all four Beatles, Diana Dors, Lawrence of Arabia, George Bernard Shaw and Sonny Liston. The likelihood is that because Tussauds had those waxworks not on display and available for use on the tableau, Dors, Lawrence, Shaw and Liston were included on the cover and were unlikely to be part of the Beatles' individual choices.

Other interesting features on the cover include some stone statues from the gardens of individual Beatles; a garden gnome; a flower display spelling 'Beatles'; flowers in the shape of a guitar; a cloth figure of Shirley Temple; and a doll with a knitted jumper with the words 'Welcome Rolling Stones' on it.

Despite rumours, there are no marijuana plants on display – they are actually pepperonia plants.

Sgt Pepper's Lonely Hearts Club Band was also the first album to have a gatefold sleeve – and also the first to include a full set of printed lyrics. It also came with a cardboard sheet of cut-outs of a moustache, a picture card, stripes and badges.

The Beatles were photographed in front of the tableau in their Sgt Pepper uniforms with Paul holding a cor anglais, Ringo holding a trumpet, John holding a French horn and George holding a flute.

The bizarre rumour that Paul McCartney had died, which later sprang up in America in October 1969, then led to fans seeking 'clues' in the Beatles' songs and on album covers which could back up the theory. On the *Sgt Pepper* sleeve it is alleged that the hand raised above Paul's head was an Indian symbol of death and that the flowers represented a symbolic grave. In the centrefold of the album, Paul is wearing a badge with the initials OPP, which fans suggested meant 'Officially Pronounced Dead'. (A fold makes it appear as OPD.) The patch on Paul's sleeve does sport such initials, but they stand for Ontario Provincial Police. Paul was given the official patch while the Beatles were appearing in Toronto on Tuesday, 17 August 1965. Incidentally, one of the members of the security force guarding the Beatles at the time was called Sergeant Pepper.

The back cover has George, John and Ringo with a back view of Paul. Fans said that this was because someone substituted for the dead Paul. This wasn't so, as other pictures from the same session reveal that it was Paul in the photograph.

The first airing of the album on the radio took place at 5.00 p.m. on the evening of Friday, 12 May 1967, when the pirate station Radio London broadcast the tracks. Although American stations had broadcast tracks prior to this time, Radio London claimed a 'world exclusive' because they said they were the first to play the album in its entirety as 'Album of the Week'.

A special press launch for the album was held at Brian Epstein's house in Chapel Street, Mayfair, on Friday, 19 May 1967.

When EMI released the album on Parlophone PCS 7027 on Thursday, 1 June 1967, the reaction was staggering. It sold 250,000 copies in Britain during the first week and topped the half million mark within the month. It was issued in America on Capitol SMAS 2653 on Friday, 2 June 1967 with advance orders of over a million copies, and it sold over two and a half million copies there within three months. It also topped the charts all over the world. The album was No. 1 in Britain for 27 weeks and topped the charts for nineteen weeks in America, remaining in the charts there for a total of 113 weeks.

The album received four Grammy Awards during the year of release: (1) Best Album. (2) Best contemporary Album. (3) Best Album Cover. (4) Best Engineered Album. In 1977 the British Phonogram Industry announced a special award to celebrate 25 years of British music: Best British Pop Album 1952–1977. It went to *Sgt Pepper's Lonely Hearts Club Band*.

The album tracks were: Side One: 'Sgt Pepper's Lonely Hearts Club Band', 'With A Little Help From My Friends', 'Lucy In The Sky With Diamonds', 'Getting Better', 'Fixing A Hole', 'She's Leaving Home' and 'Being For The Benefit Of Mr Kite'.

Side Two: 'Within You, Without You', 'When I'm Sixty Four', 'Lovely Rita', 'Good Morning Good Morning', 'Sgt Pepper's Lonely Hearts Club Band (reprise)' and 'A Day In The Life'.

The album was eventually issued as a compact disc on Monday, 1 June 1987. It came in a luxury box presentation with an extra booklet and tracks remastered by George Martin. There were advance orders of 75,000 which immediately launched it into the No. 3 position in the British charts.

Sgt Pepper's Lonely Hearts Club Band (Song)

Paul composed this song when he was pushing forward his concept for the Beatles' ninth British album. He'd wanted a theme and also to give the appearance of a live band and felt that this song could fulfil that function, open the album and also be reprised near the end of the LP.

He had been fascinated by the colourful names of San Francisco bands such as the Electric Prunes, the Quicksilver Messenger Service and the Grateful Dead, which inspired him to come up with the name 'Sgt Pepper's Lonely Hearts Club Band'. However, there was the suggestion that he'd originally thought of 'Dr Pepper', but discovered that there was an American soft drink of that name, and another suggestion hinted that it was actually Mal Evans who had thought the name up.

Initial recording sessions began on 1 February 1967 and resumed in March when four French horns were used, played by James W. Buck, John Burden, Tony Randall and Neil Sanders.

To provide the effect of a live band, with audience sounds and applause, the Abbey Road archives were consulted and extracts from sound effects albums were used – *Volume 6: Applause and Laughter* and *Volume 28: Audience Applause and Atmosphere, Royal Albert Hall and Queen Elizabeth Hall*.

Apart from its appearance on the *Sgt Pepper* album, the track was later used on the compilation *The Beatles 1967–1970*.

When the Robert Stigwood film *Sgt Pepper's Lonely Hearts Club Band* was released, EMI decided to take advantage of the publicity surrounding it and released 'Sgt Pepper's Lonely Hearts Club Band' as a single on Parlophone R 6022 on 30 September 1978 with the tracks 'With a Little Help From My Friends' and 'A Day In The Life'. It became the first Beatles British single to fail to enter the charts. A version of the number was included on the Beatles' *Anthology 2* CDs.

Shades Of A Personality

Another project touted as the Beatles' third movie.

At the beginning of 1967 producer Walter Shenson announced to the press that the Beatles' third film would be based on a script penned by a young playwright, Owen Holder.

'Shades Of A Personality' was a tale of multiple personality and each member of the Beatles would play the same person, portraying different aspects of his personality. John would be the main character, with the other three as alternative aspects of that character. They would share the same girlfriend and the music would not be performed by the group, but would simply be used as background music on the soundtrack. In fact, only one of the Beatles would appear on the screen at any one time and there would be no mention of the Beatles in the film. Some time was set aside for the filming, but a suitable script was not available at the time and the project was eventually abandoned.

Shadows, Cliff Richard & The

Cliff Richard & the Shadows, Britain's biggest pop group, were anathema to the majority of Liverpool bands, who were rough and ready R&B and rock 'n' roll kids, who mainly eschewed the studied professionalism of the successful artists who appeared on TV and radio in Britain at the time. There were a few Liverpool outfits who tried to imitate the Shadows' style, such as the Remo Four, but they were the exception rather than the rule. Most of the working-class bands in the 'Pool held the Shadows up to ridicule, particularly because of the choreographed steps in their act.

Rory Storm dared George Harrison to write a number in the

Shadows' style – and he obliged with 'Cry For A Shadow', which the Beatles recorded in Hamburg.

Yet despite their attitude towards the Shadows, the Beatles were to alter their opinion with the appearance of Brian Epstein. While they were still in their black leather gear, he took them to the Liverpool Empire to see a Cliff Richard & the Shadows concert. He pointed out the mohair suits, the choreographed footsteps and the way they bowed at the end of their act. He convinced the Beatles that this was how they should behave if they wanted to become a major group – and they took his advice.

Hank Marvin was to say, 'He was obviously trying to impress upon John, Paul, George and Ringo that this was the way they should present themselves: in neat looking suits and dickie bows!'

Hank was probably mistaken when he included Ringo in this comment as the group had jettisoned their black leathers before he joined them.

They were soon dressed in mohair suits themselves, bowing politely at the end of their act.

The Shadows' line-up at the time comprised Cliff Richard (guitar/vocals), Hank Marvin (lead guitar), Bruce Welch (rhythm guitar) and Brian Bennett (drums). Following a gig at Lewisham Odeon on 29 March 1963 Bruce Welch invited the Beatles to a party he was holding. It was the first time that Cliff Richard and the Beatles met. They were chatting together in Welch's kitchen, then got out their guitars, with Cliff and the Shadows playing their new release 'Lucky Lips' and the Beatles singing 'From Me To You'. Cliff was puzzled after he expressed an interest in Ray Charles to hear John say, 'I used to like him until everybody else started to like him.'

They were to meet up again when both groups found themselves in Blackpool. The Shadows were appearing for a summer season at the ABC Theatre, but had Sundays off, and the Beatles were making a Sunday appearance at the venue. The Shadows invited the Beatles to a party at a bungalow Hank Marvin had rented.

Bruce was to point out, 'The great thing was the lack of animosity or jealousy between the two groups and their mutual respect, both personal and musical.'

Lennon was to comment on Cliff in *Love Me Do*, a book by Michael Braun, in which he said: 'We've always hated Cliff. He was everything we hated in pop. But when we met him we didn't mind him at all. He was very nice. Now when people ask us if he's a bit soft we say no. We still hate his records but he's really very nice.'

The Shadows were invited to Paul McCartney's 21st birthday party. Brian, Hank and Bruce travelled from Blackpool by car to meet up with Paul and Jane Asher at the Empire Theatre, Liverpool. They then travelled to Paul's Auntie Gin's house where the party was held. They were pleased to meet various Mersey artists such as the Fourmost and Billy J. Kramer and noticed how drunk John Lennon had become during the course of the evening – which led to his incident with Bob Wooler.

The Shadows enjoyed themselves. Bruce was to comment, 'In the future, though, the only brief encounters we had with the Beatles would be over a cup of tea and a sandwich at Abbey Road Studios or a quick thumbs-up and odd word of greeting at the annual *NME* poll winners' concert.'

The Shadows issued a single in November 1981 featuring a medley, which included 'Imagine' and 'Woman'.

Shakin' All Over

One of the few genuine British rock classics, penned by Frederick Heath. Freddie began his career in a skiffle band, Freddie Heath & the Nutters. He changed his name to Johnny Kidd, led a group called the Pirates and had his first hit, 'Please Don't Touch', in 1959. They reached the No. 1 spot with 'Shakin' All Over' in 1960 and the Beatles included it in their repertoire and performed it until the following year.

Kidd had several hits, including 'A Shot Of Rhythm And Blues' and 'I'll Never Get Over You', but was killed in a road accident in October 1966.

Johnny Kidd and the Pirates topped the bill above the Beatles on the *Royal Iris* cruise on Friday, 10 August 1962.

Shankar, Ravi

Noted Indian musician, born in Benares, India, on 7 April 1920. Ravi's family moved to Paris in 1931. He said, 'Paris was fantastic at that time, it was the art capital of the world, very exciting.' At the age of thirteen he began to learn to master the sitar. His guru was Baba. Ravi shaved his hair, led a very frugal existence and made himself a sitar from a completely hollow gourd, which was very fragile.

'How many hours a day did I practise?' he said. 'I started eight hours at the beginning, some points fourteen, sometimes sixteen, but mainly twelve–fourteen.'

In his book *My Music, My Life* (Jonathan Cape, 1969), Shankar mentions that what he calls the great sitar explosion happened in 1966. In June of that year he met George Harrison and Paul McCartney at the home of a mutual friend. George voiced his enthusiasm for learning to play the sitar. Says Ravi, 'I carefully explained to him that one must undergo many long years of study and practise of the basics before one can play even a single note properly. He understood all this perfectly and said he was prepared to go through the years of discipline.'

Ravi invited him to India to study, together with Pattie, and George accepted. He invited Ravi to his Esher bungalow a few days before the sitarist was leaving England and he played sitar for all four members of the Beatles. He recalled, 'I always feel inspired when I play for a small, close group and especially for musicians – no matter what tradition or country they belong to. And that evening, as I was accompanied on the tabla by Alla Rakha, I felt very happy with my music. And my little audience responded very warmly as we played.'

On Ravi's return to India he received a letter from George saying he'd be able to spend six weeks with him. They arrived at Bombay airport, George had taken Ravi's advice and cut his hair and sprouted a moustache. The couple weren't recognised at first. They registered in the Taj Mahal Hotel under a false name, but within 24 hours everyone in Bombay knew and the hotel was besieged. Ravi called a press reception to explain that George had come, not as a Beatle, but as his disciple and they needed to be left in peace. They all then went to Kashmir and Benares to begin the lessons.

Ravi commented: 'I had George practise all the correct positions of sitting and some of the basic exercises. This was the most one could do in six weeks, considering that a disciple usually spends years learning these basics.'

During his trip George met 200 of Shankar's students and also observed a religious festival near the Ganges. Of his lessons with Shankar, he commented: 'He sat down, this great master giant of a man on the sitar, and showed me scales, the first lesson.' The trip was to have a profound effect on George, who remarked: 'I went partly to learn music and partly to see and learn as much as I could about India as possible. I'd always heard stories about men in caves in the Himalayas, hundreds of years old, and people who can levitate and people who get buried under the ground for six weeks and lots of what the West would call mysticism.' George was later to involve himself in the Krsna movement.

Ravi continued to give George lessons when he was in London and also on a trip to Hollywood in 1967. The contact with the Beatles obviously popularised him in a wider context than previously. He commented: 'The Beatles scene and the sitar explosion brought me immediately into a position of immense popularity with the young people, and I now find myself adored like a movie star or young singer.'

Following the trip, George performed on sitar for his track 'Within You, Without You' on the *Sgt Pepper* album, which was made with sitar and tabla accompaniment. In 1968 George wrote 'The Inner Light' using Indian musicians and by the summer of 1969 was recording several chant numbers with London's Radha Krsna Temple.

George arranged for Ravi to sign to the Beatles' Apple label and his first release was 'Joi Bangla'/'Oh Bhaugowan' c/w 'Raga Mishra'/'Jhinjhoti', issued in August 1971. The album *Raga* was issued in December 1971. This was the soundtrack album of the film *Raga*, a documentary. In one scene, George appears as Ravi's pupil.

Other Ravi Shankar records produced by George included *In Concert 1972*, recorded live at New York's Philharmonic Hall on 8 April 1972. This featured: Ravi Shankar (sitar), Ali Akbar Khan (sarad), Alla Rakha (tabla), Ashoka Susan (tambouras). The double album was issued in America on 22 January 1973. Another album produced by George was *Shankar Family And Friends*, issued in Britain on George's own Dark Horse label in September 1974 and in America the following month.

Ravi had been most concerned about the terrible conditions in Bangladesh and considered the idea of holding a concert in order to raise money for the starving children of that unfortunate country. Initially, he had in mind a fairly modest amount of $25,000. While he was with George in California recording the soundtrack for the film *Raga*, he put the idea to George, who immediately took the situation in hand and contacted Ringo Starr and Leon Russell. Within a matter of weeks the concert had been organised, with several major musicians enthusiastic about supporting the charity event.

The concert took place before an audience of 40,000 at Madison Square Garden, New York, on 1 August 1971 and raised $243,418.50. A cheque for that amount was sent to the United Nations Children's Fund For Relief To Refugee Children Of Bangladesh on 12 December of that year. More money was raised from the film *The Concert For Bangladesh*, released the following year. Ravi opened the actual concert and performed 'Bangla Dhun'.

His album *Chants Of India* was released on Angel Records in 1997. George Harrison produced it. George had produced four previous albums for Shankar: *Raga* and *In Concert 1972* for Apple and *Shankar, Family & Friends* and *Music Festival From India* on Dark Horse.

Oliver Craske ghosted Shankar's biography *Raga Mala*, published in 1998. Commenting on the Beatles, Shankar wrote: 'I was not attracted to their voices since they mostly sang in high falsetto pitch which seems to have remained in vogue ever since. I also had trouble understanding the words they say.'

Shankar currently lives in Encinitas, California.

Shannon, Del

American singer, real name Charles Westover, born in Central Rapids, Michigan, on 30 December 1939.

It was while he was playing a Del Shannon record, probably 'Runaway', that John Lennon found a chord variation which he used in composing 'I'll Be Back', one of his numbers on the *A Hard Day's Night* album.

Shannon was very popular in Britain, where he had thirteen chart singles between 1961 and 1965. His first million-seller was the number which inspired John Lennon, 'Runaway', which was No. 1 in the American charts for five weeks and No. 1 in the British charts for four. His other hits in 1961 and 1962 included 'Hats Off To Larry', 'So Long Baby' and 'Hey Little Girl'.

It was soon after his new hit 'Little Town Flirt' in 1963 that he appeared on 'Swingin' Sound '63' at the Royal Albert Hall, London, on a bill with the Beatles on Thursday, 18 April.

This was broadcast on the Light Programme of the BBC and there was a dispute about billing. The Beatles were obviously the most popular act in Britain at the time, with their new single 'From Me To You', which they performed on the show, soon to top the charts.

However, this didn't prevent Shannon's manager insisting that his artist be given top billing. His demands that Shannon appear after the Beatles and close the show were accepted.

During the day Shannon, impressed by the Beatles, suggested to John that he could help expose their work in America if he covered one of their songs. Initially, John seemed pleased, but then he changed his mind.

Some years later Shannon told radio journalist Spencer Leigh: 'I think John had talked to Brian Epstein, who didn't want any American performer covering their songs. He wanted to invade America all by himself.'

Shannon went ahead anyway and speedily recorded their current hit, 'From Me To You', in Britain with a British backing band. The number was issued in the US on Bigtop Records 3152 on 3 June 1963 with 'Two Silhouettes' as the flip and entered the *Cashbox* charts at No. 86 on 6 July. It reached only No. 77 in the charts, but was the first Lennon and McCartney number to become an American hit.

The *Cashbox* review read: 'Shannon, who recently did chart

business with "Two Kinds Of Teardrops", can have another big one
in "From Me To You". It's an infectious, thump-a-twist version of
the tune that's currently riding in the number one slot in England –
via the Beatles' stand (available here on VJ).'

In fact, Shannon's version was issued in America exactly eight
days before Vee Jay issued the Beatles' version.

Shannon was undoubtedly one of the first Americans to appreciate their potential in the American market, and when they were
touring the States he dropped in to see them on 16 August 1965.

Shannon, also a songwriter and producer, penned the Peter &
Gordon hit 'I Go To Pieces'.

When he appeared in the Beatles' home town on a bill with
Johnny Tillotson, the two performed a duet of 'From Me To You'
on stage at the Empire Theatre.

The singer was also booked to appear at Brian Epstein's Saville
Theatre in London, on a bill with Chuck Berry. John and Ringo
attended the show on 19 February 1967.

In 1987 Shannon made some recordings with George Harrison.
Mysteriously, Shannon was found dead at his home in Santa
Clarita, California, on 8 February 1990. He had died from gunshot
wounds, said to have been self-inflicted.

Shapiro, Helen

For a short time, Britain's most successful female singer although
her span of hits lasted only from 1961–1963. Born on 28
September 1946 in London's Bethnal Green area she was discovered by songwriter John Schroeder currently working for EMI, at a
local singing school in 1961. He recommended her to EMI and she
was signed to the Columbia label. Schroeder wrote 'Don't Treat Me
Like A Child' for her and the debut record reached No. 3 in the
British charts. This was followed-up by 'You Don't Know', which
topped the British charts and became a million-seller. At the time
Helen was only fourteen and still attending Clapton Girls' School;
special permission had to be obtained for her to make radio and
television dates.

The cinema documentary series 'Look At Life' featured the
young singer and she was voted 'No. 1 Female British Singer' in
1961 and 1962. Her other hits were 'Walkin' Back To Happiness',
'Tell Me What He Said', 'Let's Talk About Love', 'Little Miss
Lonely', 'Keep Away From Other Girls', 'Queen For Tonight', 'Woe
Is Me', 'Look Who It Is' and 'Fever'.

Helen also starred in the film *It's Trad, Dad*, directed by Richard
Lester, who introduced some of the innovations into that film which
he was later to utilise in *A Hard Day's Night*.

Helen first met the Beatles on the afternoon of 2 February 1963 at the Gaumont Cinema, Bradford, which was the first date of the nationwide tour headed by the sixteen-year-old singer, on which the Beatles were making their first package tour appearance. Although a special car had been arranged to take Helen to the various cities, she preferred to travel on the tour bus. When Helen caught flu she was unable to appear at the Taunton and York gigs and was replaced by Billie Davis, whose current hit was 'Tell Him'. In her absence, Danny Williams topped the bill. Following an appearance at the ABC, Carlisle, there was an incident at the local hotel where members of the tour were asked to leave a party for Young Conservatives.

John and Paul began to write a song for Helen which they hoped she'd record in Nashville. Norrie Paramor, her A&R man, was taking her to record in the American C&W centre and had suggested that the Beatles might come up with a number for her. They wrote a number and Paul commented, 'We've called it 'Misery', but it isn't as slow as it sounds, it moves along at quite a steady pace and we think Helen will make a pretty good job of it. We've also done a number for Duffy Power, which he's going to record.' Paramor considered that the number wasn't suitable for Helen and turned it down. They were discussing it on the coach when Kenny Lynch, who was also appearing on the tour, asked them if he could record it.

In an interview with *Mersey Beat*, Helen told of how she became a big fan of the Beatles soon after they started touring together: 'John and Paul always used to be writing numbers together on the coach. I remember them playing "From Me To You" to me, and asking me what I thought of it. I told them I thought it was terrific – and I'm glad to say I was right!

'We used to have some great times together. Not many people know it, but I've been playing the banjo for about five years. I had it with me on the tour, and now and again I would join the Beatles' line-up for an impromptu session!'

Although Helen's success in the charts ended in 1963, she continued her career as a singer, developing into a fine jazz stylist and at one time later in her career, she was managed by Tony Barrow, the former Beatles publicist.

Shaw, Sandie

One of Britain's leading female singers of the sixties, who appeared with the Beatles on the American TV show 'Shindig'.

As a fan, Sandie saw the Beatles when they appeared at the Odeon, Romford on 16 June 1963. The week previously she'd sung there for free at the Saturday morning cinema show and the manager agreed to let her in backstage for the Beatles' show.

Sandie arrived with her friend Janet Llewellyn and they watched the show from the wings. As Paul passed, he kissed her on the cheek and said, 'This one's for you, la.' Sandie, at the time, was besotted by John Lennon.

In her autobiography *The World At My Feet* (Harper Collins), she recalled, 'Later, in the dressing-room, Ringo tried to put his hands up Janet's blouse, and we both marched out indignantly. It's a good job he didn't try that on with me or he would have discovered the cotton-wool padding in my otherwise empty bra.'

The second time she managed to get backstage was when the Beatles were at the Albert Hall on 15 September 1963. She phoned up the hall and said she was John's long-lost cousin Sandra – and John actually came and answered the phone, then arranged for her to come backstage.

Shea Stadium, 126th Street and Roosevelt Avenue, Flushing, Queens, New York City

A baseball stadium which was the home of the New York Mets. The Beatles' first appearance there took place on Sunday, 15 August 1965. It was the first stage show of their 1965 tour and support acts included Brenda Holloway, the King Curtis Band (introduced by New York DJ Scott Ross), Sounds Incorporated, Cannibal & the Headhunters and a troupe of disco dancers.

It was promoter Sid Bernstein's idea to use the 55,600-seater arena and the concert became the world's biggest up to that time, attracting world record box office receipts of $304,000, of which $100,000 was the Beatles' share. Due to the vast cost of staging and, in particular, the cost of security, Bernstein himself only made a profit of $6,500. The insurance from Lloyd's of London for that one concert alone cost $25,000.

There had never been a rock concert at the stadium before, apart from a minor concert with Sammy Davis Jr. This was a fundraising event for a local synagogue which drew 2,000 people.

There was an overhead blimp decorated with Beatles slogans and the boys were flown to a nearby point by helicopter (the New York authorities refused to let the helicopter take them into the stadium itself). They finished their journey in the back of a Wells Fargo security van, driven by Pete Flynn.

At the time, Bernstein had taken on management of an American band called the Rascals, who he included on the bill for the concert. He alternated the flashing sign which said, 'Please stay in your seats for an orderly concert', with 'The Rascals are coming'. A furious Brian Epstein told Bernstein to immediately stop the message else the Beatles would not perform.

Disc jockey Murray the K welcomed the crowd in 'The biggest concert ever in history' and DJ Cousin Brucie Morrow introduced Ed Sullivan, who said, 'Now. Ladies and Gentlemen, honoured by their country, decorated by their Queen and loved here in America, HERE ARE THE BEATLES!' The boys ran on stage, each shaking hands with Sullivan, and began their performance with 'Twist And Shout'. Their other numbers were 'Everybody's Trying To Be My Baby', 'Can't Buy Me Love', 'Baby's In Black', 'Act Naturally' (Ringo's solo vocal), 'A Hard Day's Night', 'Help!' and 'I'm Down'. A white estate car was ready at the side of the stage and they were speedily driven away.

The show was filmed by Sullivan Productions Inc (Ed Sullivan's company) in association with Subafilm Ltd for a fifty-minute colour television special, which was screened in Britain by the BBC on 1 March 1966.

The Beatles' final appearance at Shea Stadium took place on Tuesday, 23 August 1966, although this didn't prove as spectacular as the first, with 11,000 unsold seats. Although the seats were of a higher price than the previous year, the concert only grossed $292,000. However, the Beatles earned even more than their previous fee, receiving $189,000. In addition to there being several hundred policemen, Bernstein paid $15,000 for special patrolmen. The Beatles arrived at the stadium in a red Wells Fargo truck. It was the fourth anniversary of John and Cynthia's wedding.

She Came In Through The Bathroom Window

When the Beatles first tried to record this number at the Apple Studios on Wednesday, 22 February 1969, the studio was in such an unfinished state that it proved impossible to record there and George Martin had to make arrangements for equipment from Abbey Road to be shipped down to Savile Row. Recording of the number was tried again at Abbey Road in July and the number was included on the *Abbey Road* album.

Paul had originally composed the number with Joe Cocker in mind and Cocker actually recorded the song once the Beatles had cut their version.

The working title had been, simply, 'Bathroom Window' and it was based on a real-life experience. Some fans had broken into Paul's house, using the bathroom window, and had stolen a number of items including clothes and photographs. A version was included on the Beatles' *Anthology 3* CDs.

Sheffield

Sheffield is the largest city in Yorkshire with a population of more than half a million people and during the 1960s there was extensive redevelopment in the city centre.

All of the Beatles' appearances there took place in 1963 and 1964.

Sheffield was also the original home of Brian Epstein's mother Queenie who, at the age of eighteen, married the 29-year-old Harry Epstein at the Synagogue, Wilson Road, Sheffield 11, on 6 September 1933. Her father Louis Hyman owned the Sheffield Cabinet Company of 11 Porter Street, Sheffield S1, a company famous for their Clarendon bedroom suites. The building and the road no longer exist.

The Beatles made their Sheffield debut at the Arena Ballroom on 12 February 1963. They then appeared on concert dates at the City Hall on 2 March, 25 May and 2 November 1963, and 9 November 1964.

Sheik Of Araby, The

A vintage number penned by Harry Smith, Francis Wheeler and Ed Snyder. Various artists recorded it, including Duke Ellington and Joe Brown & the Bruvvers, but the Beatles were probably influenced by Fats Domino's 1961 recording. They performed the song in their stage act, with George Harrison on lead vocals, and recorded it during their Decca audition. The version from the Decca audition recording was included on the Beatles' *Anthology 1* CDs.

Sheila

Number written by Tommy Roe which the singer issued in May 1962. It topped the American charts for him and when it was issued in Britain it reached the No. 3 position. The Beatles immediately included it in their repertoire as a vocal spot for George and the group performed it during their December 1962 season at Hamburg, resulting in the Adrian Barber recording. The following year the group toured Britain on a bill headed by Tommy Roe and Chris Montez.

She Loves You

This number became Britain's biggest-selling record, until overtaken by sales of Paul McCartney's 'Mull of Kintyre' in 1978. It was also the Beatles' first million-seller.

John and Paul began writing the song on a coach during a British tour and completed it the same night, 26 June 1963, in a hotel room in Newcastle-upon-Tyne after their Majestic Ballroom appearance.

Paul commented, 'John and I wrote it together. I thought of it first and thought of doing it as one of those answering songs. You know, the sort of thing the American singing groups keep doing. A couple of us would sing "She Loves You" and the others would do the "yeah yeah yeah" ones. The one would be answering everything the other two sang. Then John and I agreed it was a pretty crummy idea as it stood and since we were borrowing an American thing, I suppose it was crummy. But at least we had the basic idea of writing the song. That night in Newcastle we just sat in the hotel for a few hours and wrote it.'

The group began recording the song at Abbey Road on Monday, 1 July. John and Paul had originally played the number to George Martin on acoustic guitars and he suggested that instead of going right into the first verse, they should start with the chorus of 'She loves you, yeah, yeah, yeah'. George Harrison also came up with the idea of having the sixth chord at the end of the song.

The number was released as their fourth single on Parlophone R 5055 on 23 August 1963 with 'I'll Get You' on the flip. It was also included on their tenth British EP *The Beatles Million Sellers* in 1965 and is found on the compilation albums *A Collection Of Beatles Oldies (But Goldies), The Beatles 1962–1966*, and *20 Greatest Hits*. It was also the first track on *Savile's Time Travels – 20 Golden Hits of 1963* in 1981. It was included in *The Beatles Box* and *The Beatles Collection* sets. In America the single was issued by Swan Records on 16 September 1963 on Swan 4152. It was one of five new singles which Murray The K played on the WINS radio station in New York and it came third in popularity with listeners. The record was not successful on its initial release.

The number received its first major airing when film footage of the Beatles performing it was screened on Jack Paar's networked TV show on 3 January 1964. With the huge Beatles promotion which ensued, Swan re-released the single and it immediately succeeded 'I Want To Hold Your Hand' in the No. 1 position in America, achieving the feat of being the first time that an artist had had two consecutive chart-toppers since Elvis Presley in 1956 when 'Love Me Tender' replaced 'Don't Be Cruel'/'Hound Dog' at the top of the charts. Capitol also issued it on *The Beatles Second Album* and a live version is to be found on *The Beatles At The Hollywood Bowl*.

The number was featured on numerous of their BBC radio shows – three times on 'Saturday Club', five times on 'Pop Go The Beatles' and one time each on 'Easy Beat', 'The Ken Dodd Show' and 'From Us To You'.

There have been over sixty versions by other artists, including several foreign language recordings, and artists who have recorded it have ranged from the Chipmunks and Pinky & Perky to Vanilla Fudge and the Tottenham Hotspur Football Team. Peter Sellers also recorded two versions, one in the style of Dr Strangelove, the other in the style of an Irish dentist character.

The Beatles also entered the chart with a German language version of the number, 'Sie Liebt Dich', though it only had a brief stay in the No. 97 position in Billboard.

The number was included on the CD compilation Past Masters Volume One.

Shenson, Walter

Born in San Francisco, Shenson began his career as a public relations man for Paramount and Columbia. He moved to England in the 1950s and produced The Mouse That Roared in 1959. As a result of the success of the film, Bud Ornstein hired him to direct A Hard Day's Night. United Artists had conceived the idea of a Beatles film in order to obtain soundtrack album rights of Beatles music and approached the 45-year-old Shenson because of his reputation for working on a small budget. He was able to bring in the Beatles' debut film on a budget of only $200,000. Another American expatriate Richard Lester was hired to direct. The two also made a sequel, Mouse On The Moon in 1963.

During negotiations Brian Epstein asked for £20,000 in advance and 7½ per cent of the net profits. It was later raised to £25,000 and 20 per cent of profits. However, he didn't have the foresight to negotiate anything better for the group. On the other hand, Shenson's accountant proposed a clause in the contract allowing for the Beatles' films to revert to Shenson's ownership after fifteen years. As United Artists considered the Beatles would only have a short lifespan, they agreed.

After he'd produced their second movie, Help!, Shenson had difficulty persuading the group to make a third film with him. He'd had about forty different scripts submitted, including Shades Of A Personality and A Talent For Loving, but the Beatles were no longer interested in a film career.

They resolved their contractual obligations to United Artists by filming Let It Be and Shenson received a small percentage of the profits.

The producer remained in England, making movies such as Thirty Is A Dangerous Age, Cynthia, Don't Raise The Bridge, Lower The River and Digby, The Biggest Dog In The World.

Together with his wife Gerry, he decided to return to America in 1973 after spending eighteen years in Britain. They settled in Bel-Air, California.

The rights to *A Hard Day's Night* and *Help!* reverted to him after the fifteen-year term and he was able to re-record both of them with a stereophonic soundtrack using the Dolby system. He also added a two-minute prologue to *A Hard Day's Night*. Stills from the film, allied to graphics and optical effects, were used at the beginning of the film as a background to 'I'll Cry Instead', a song which had been originally written for the movie but unused at the time of its original release.

In 1995 he produced a documentary, *The Making Of A Hard Day's Night,* hosted and with a narration by Phil Collins. In 1999 he arranged a deal with Miramax to re-release *A Hard Day's Night* in cinemas

Sheraton Motel Hotel, Macleay Street, Sydney, Australia

When the Beatles were to tour Australia, promoter Kenn Brodziak initially had difficulty finding accommodation for them in Sydney. The four leading hotels had refused to accept a booking for them due to complaints from regular patrons and Brodziak was considering placing each Beatle in a different hotel. However, Bert Dunn, who owned the relatively small Sheraton Motel Hotel, agreed to accommodate the group and their party when they arrived on 11 June 1964.

The hotel manageress was former beauty queen Margaret Walpole, who had been Miss Victoria 1950, and she took them to their penthouse, Suite 801, and introduced them to their two Spanish maids Maria Parra and Aurora Martinez.

Derek Taylor organised a press reception in the hotel's conference room at 4.30 p.m. during which one journalist asked: 'Paul, what do you expect to find in Australia?' 'Australians', he answered.

Oddly enough, Tony Sheridan was staying at the Sheraton at the same time. The Beatles' former friend from their Hamburg days was in Australia to tour with Billy Thorpe & the Aztecs and Digger Revell. However, he was ill and didn't make any attempt to contact them.

The Beatles returned to the Sheraton when they were appearing at Sydney Stadium. On 18 June a special party had been organised in honour of Paul's birthday, which had been tied up with a competition in the *Sunday Mirror* newspaper, with Derek Taylor and comedian Dave Allen among the judges who selected seventeen girls who would attend the party at the hotel. The competition required girls between the ages of sixteen and 22 to write a 50-word essay entitled 'Why I Would Like To Be A Guest At A Beatles

Birthday Party'. There were more than 10,000 entrants. The party was quite a success and lasted until 2.00 a.m.

Sheridan, Tony

Anthony Esmond O'Sheridan McGinnity was born in Norwich, Norfolk, on 21 May 1940. He took the name Tony Sheridan in 1958. He played classical violin in the school orchestra. At the age of sixteen he attended the Norwich Boys' Grammar School and stole a clarinet from the school music room and exchanged it for a guitar in a second-hand store. He was identified for the theft. In Norwich he formed a skiffle group called the Saints, comprising himself and Kenny Packwood on guitars, Taffy McKinley and Douglas Frost on tea chest basses and Andy McKinley on drums. They all ran away from home to audition at Chas McDevitt's Skiffle Cellar in Soho, London. Sheridan and Packwood decided to stay behind and join Marty Wilde's backing group. Tony then began to perform as a solo artist at the 2 I's coffee bar in Old Compton Street. He then became a member of Vince Taylor and the Playboys for a short time. During 1959 while at the 2 I's coffee bar in London he was picked by Jack Good to appear on the 'Oh, Boy!' TV show where he began backing artists such as Cherry Wainer and Vince Taylor. He made his debut as lead vocalist on the show on 18 February 1959 and appeared on seven shows. He was then booked for a spot on another Jack Good show, 'Boy Meets Girl', headlined by Gene Vincent, but was sacked for turning up late without his guitar and, as he says, 'for being a general nuisance'. TV avenues then became closed to him. At the time he'd also formed the Tony Sheridan Trio with Brian Locking on bass and Brian Bennett on drums (who were both to become members of the Shadows). They toured England during 1960 with a number of American artists, including Conway Twitty and Roy Orbison. He also appeared on the Gene Vincent/Eddie Cochran stage tour in 1960 during which he had a ten-minute spot. He was on the bill of the Gene Vincent Show, which performed at Liverpool Stadium on 3 May 1960.

He returned to playing at the 2 I's coffee club. When German club-owner Bruno Koschmider visited the 2 I's seeking groups for his Hamburg venue, Sheridan, together with Iain Hines, formed the Jets and agreed to travel to Germany.

The Jets played 50 per cent rocked-up skiffle and 50 per cent rock 'n' roll, with numbers ranging from 'Nobody's Child' to 'What'd I Say?'. Tony acquired a Martin D28 guitar by forging pop group manager Reg Calvert's name on the agreement. He was deported to Dover where he was picked up by the police and spent ten days in Brixton prison before being let off the charge.

The Jets broke up late in 1960 and Sheridan formed a new Tony Sheridan Trio, which also lasted only a short time. By the end of the year he had engaged Horst Fascher to be his manager.

In 1961 he began a year-long residency at the Top Ten Club, during which time he was backed by several outfits, including the Beatles.

When the Beatles originally arrived in Hamburg they began to drop in to see the Jets and were particularly impressed by Sheridan – and he was dubbed 'the teacher' by Liverpool bands. John Lennon, Gerry Marsden and John McNally of the Searchers were three of the Liverpool musicians who copied Tony's high-chested guitar stance on stage – and the way he played with his legs astride. The Beatles even joined the Jets for some jam sessions on their first trip.

In 1961 the Beatles backed him at the Top Ten Club. Many years later Tony was to tell journalist Alan Clayson: 'Bert Kaempfert had been trying rock 'n' roll with young Germans, but it sounded ludicrous. He was impressed by what he saw as our authenticity. It's a shame no-one taped any of the Top Ten gigs. I was doing most of the lead guitar, though if John, say, took a solo, it was halfway good because it came out of the rawness of him. George was young, inexperienced and a bit overawed by the whole thing, but very keen to learn.'

The Beatles were hired to join him for recording sessions at the Harburg Friedrich Ebert Halle from 22 May. They provided backing for him on 'My Bonnie Lies Over the Ocean', 'When The Saints Go Marching In' and 'Why'. When Sheridan saw the recording equipment he thought it very primitive and said it looked like 'A leftover relic of the British army occupation from some sort of radio station they had.' The Beatles were credited as the Beat Brothers on the record and it was a name Sheridan used for various musicians who backed him on stage and record. Over the years there were five different groups he used under the Beat Brothers name. Ringo Starr backed him in one of these from March until May 1962. Ringo left Rory Storm & the Hurricanes in Liverpool for the tempting offer of £30 a week, a flat and the use of a car. However, he walked out after three months as he couldn't stand Tony's habit of suddenly playing numbers on stage he hadn't even rehearsed with the band.

Sheridan left the Top Ten Club for a residency at the Star Club on 12 May 1962, forming the Tony Sheridan Quartet, which later changed its name to the Star Combo. When the Star Club closed in 1964 he found himself initially joining the Glasgow outfit the Bobby Patrick Big Six, then playing jazz guitar in a Reeperbahn bar.

At the time there was a flutter of interest in him due to the large sales (although no major chart placings) of some re-releases of his 1961 recordings with the Beatles. He was invited to appear as a guest star on a British tour with the Searchers and Roy Orbison and while in London he met up with the Beatles at Whaddon House to talk about old times during a break in the filming of *A Hard Day's Night*. Several months later he was in the same hotel in Australia as the Beatles, but they never met up.

Throughout the rest of his life, Sheridan was to experience momentary surges of interest in his career, but nothing ever came of the short 'revivals'.

Sheridan continued appearing and recording in Germany until 1967 when he left to entertain the troops at US bases in Vietnam for sixteen months, accompanied by singer Barbara Evans, bassist Volker Tonndorf and drummer Jimmy Doyle. A British music paper reported he had been killed there and for several years many people believed that he was dead, but he'd returned to Germany in 1969. A few years later Horst Fascher relaunched a new Star Club in Hamburg with Sheridan topping the bill and George Harrison and Ringo Starr visited him on opening night. This was another example of a revived interest in his career and at the same time Klaus Voormann had produced a new album, *World's End,* with him.

Sheridan did get on with the Beatles initially, due to their sense of humour, although he always made derogatory remarks about people from the north of England. He was one of those southerners with a stereotyped image of what he thought northerners were like. He supposedly turned anti-British in the 1970s, applying for Irish citizenship because of what was happening in Northern Ireland – although some sources say he applied for citizenship because of the generous tax concessions offered to artists and musicians there. One can appreciate he had his own strong views – after all, he supported the Vietnam War.

He moved to America for a time where there was interest in recording and promoting him, but nothing happened. Most musicians who knew him felt that Sheridan had the potential to become a major artist. Why he didn't succeed may be due to pure bad luck or perhaps to Tony's own attitude towards success.

Paul Murphy, a Liverpudlian who had been a recording manager in Hamburg during the mid-1960s, wanted to further Tony's career and promoted him in concert with the Royal Liverpool Philharmonic Orchestra in Liverpool on 5 September 1975. Tony wrote all the songs himself and the BBC recorded the event. An album of the concert was proposed, but never released.

In 1995 he teamed up with Howie Casey and Roy Young in Bournemouth to rehearse as the Beat Brothers. They attempted to enlist Pete Best as drummer, but he had his own band, so they engaged another drummer and set off for Hamburg, but it was a short-lived venture.

He currently lives with his family in Wuppertal, Germany.

She Said, She Said

A number written by John when he was under the influence of drugs. It was included as a track on the *Revolver* album.

John was to comment, 'I wrote it about an acid trip I was on in Los Angeles. It was only the second trip we'd had. We took it because we'd started hearing things about it and we wanted to know what it was all about. Peter Fonda came over to us and started saying things like, "I know what it's like to be dead, man", and we didn't really wanna know, but he kept going on and on.'

The Beatles recorded the number on Tuesday, 21 June. When they began recording, John still hadn't given the number a title, but by the time they had finished it was decided to call it 'She Said, She Said'.

She's A Woman

A Paul McCartney composition which was recorded at Abbey Road's No. 2 studio on Thursday, 8 October 1964, during the *Beatles For Sale* sessions. Paul actually wrote the song in the studio on this day and Ringo Starr used a percussion instrument called a chocalho for the first time on this track, while Paul also added piano.

It was originally considered as a Beatles 'A' side but was eventually issued as the flipside of 'I Feel Fine' in November 1964. It was also included on the *Rarities* compilation and the 1981 album *The Beatles EP Collection*. In America it was included on the *Beatles '65* album. A live version of the song can be heard on the 1977 release *The Beatles At The Hollywood Bowl*. The Beatles performed the number on their Christmas show in 1964 and on their subsequent tours. The number was included on the CD compilation *Past Masters Volume One*.

She's Leaving Home

Number composed by Paul, with a little help from John, which was featured on the *Sergeant Pepper's Lonely Hearts Club Band* album. Paul and John sing but don't perform instrumentally on this track, which featured a string backing.

Paul originally wanted George Martin to score it. He phoned

Martin but George was busy with a session with Cilla Black and told Paul he had too much work on at the time. Paul was slightly angry and asked another arranger, Mike Leander, to meet him at his Cavendish Avenue house and asked him to arrange the number.

Recording began on Friday, 17 March 1967 and the musicians included the first woman to be specially engaged to perform on a Beatles track – Sheila Bromberg on harp.

The other musicians were Eric Gruenberg (leader), Derek Jacobs, Trevor Williams, Jose Luis Garcia (violins); John Underwood, Stephen Shingles (violas); Dennis Vigay, Alan Dalziel (cellos) and Gordon Pearce (double-bass).

Although Paul asking another arranger to work on the number initially hurt George Martin, it is a poignant song and he confessed that it made him cry.

Paul was to comment: 'It's a much younger girl than "Eleanor Rigby", but the same sort of loneliness. That was a *Daily Mirror* story again: this girl left home and her father said: "We gave her everything, I don't know why she left home." But he didn't give her that much, not what she wanted when she left home.'

The story actually appeared in the 27 February 1967 issue of the *Daily Mail* under the caption 'A-Level Girl Dumps Car and Vanishes.' The story concerned Melanie Coe, a 17-year old blonde-haired pupil at Skinner's Grammar School, Stamford Hill who vanished, leaving her car outside her home, all her clothes in her wardrobe and her chequebook behind.

Her father, John Coe, commented: 'I cannot imagine why she should run away. She has everything here. She is very keen on clothes, but she left them all, even her fur coat.'

Melanie had actually run away to meet a croupier she'd met in a club and the two rented a flat in Sussex Gardens, London. Her parents tracked her down and took her home. She married at eighteen, but it only lasted a year and she moved to America when she was 21. Later she returned and settled down outside London where she began a business buying and selling antique jewellery.

By a remarkable coincidence, Melanie had won a mime competition to the TV programme 'Ready, Steady, Go!' on Friday, 4 October 1963 when the Beatles made their debut on the programme. It was Paul himself who presented her with her prize.

Paul was remarkably accurate in his depiction of what happened to the real life girl in the story. He guessed she'd run away with a man. In his song her lover was a man from the motor trade. Many people over the years assumed that this referred to Terry Doran, a friend of the Beatles, who was a car salesman. Paul says this isn't the case, that the characters were not real people.

'She's Leaving Home' was also included on the *Love Songs* and *The Beatles Ballads* compilations.

Shimmy Shimmy
Bobby Freeman took this number to No. 37 in the American charts in 1960. The Beatles included it in their repertoire the same year with John and Paul duetting on the song. The group dropped the number in 1963.

Shindig
An American television music series, produced by Jack Good, who had launched such early British TV rock 'n' roll shows as 'Oh Boy!'

Good decided to devote an entire show to British acts and began filming at the Granville Theatre, Waltham Green, Fulham, which had previously been a variety theatre, on 3 October 1964.

Among the audience of 1,000 were 150 winners of a *Beatles Monthly* magazine competition.

Acts on the bill included Sounds Incorporated, Sandie Shaw, P. J. Proby, the Karl Denver Trio and Liverpool singers Tommy Quickly and Lyn Cornell. The Beatles topped the bill and performed three numbers: 'Kansas City', 'I'm A Loser' and 'Boys'. The show was screened in America on 20 January 1965.

Shirelles, The
An American girl group formed in New Jersey in 1957, who comprised Shirley Owens, Micki Harris, Doris Coley and Beverly Owens. They made their recording debut with 'I Met Him On A Sunday' and other hits included 'Will You Love Me Tomorrow?', 'Mama Said', 'Baby It's You', 'Soldier Boy' and 'Foolish Little Girl'. The Beatles and other Mersey bands were influenced by records of American 'girl groups' and the Beatles included the Shirelles numbers 'Boys' and 'Will You Love Me Tomorrow' in their repertoire, with Pete Best singing 'Boys', while Ringo Starr also sang the same number with Rory Storm & the Hurricanes. When the Beatles came to record their debut album *Please Please Me,* Ringo provided the lead vocal on 'Boys', recording it in one take on Monday, 11 February 1963. The Beatles also recorded another Shirelles number 'Baby It's You' on the album.

The music of the Shirelles was said to have influenced Paul when he composed the number 'Hold On Tight'.

Shirley's Wild Accordion
An instrumental piece originally due to be featured in the *Magical Mystery Tour* movie. Accordionist Shirley Evans had been hired to

appear in the film and John and Paul worked out an instrumental number for her to play. They hired songwriter Mike Leander to write down the music as they hummed it to him, to enable Shirley and her partner Reg Wale to play it at the recording session.

The number was recorded at De Lane Lea studios in London on Thursday, 12 October 1967, and John Lennon officially produced the session. Ringo added some drum sounds and Paul played a maraca.

As it turned out, the track wasn't issued on record and only appeared as a piece of incidental music in the film.

Short, Don

'Beatle In Brawl – Sorry I Socked You', was the heading for a story about the Beatles on the back page of the *Daily Mirror* newspaper on 21 June 1963. It concerned the incident in which John Lennon beat up Bob Wooler at Paul's 21st birthday party and was the first Beatles story penned by Don Short, a show business journalist on the *Daily Mirror* which, at the time, had the largest circulation of any newspaper in the world.

Short was regarded as one of the most influential of journalists and was accorded VIP treatment from the Beatles camp. He was invited to special parties and events, given exclusives, and travelled extensively with the group. He is even mentioned by name in the title story in John Lennon's book *A Spaniard In The Works*: 'The honeymood was don short by a telephant . . .'

Short was to be found around the Beatles in clubs such as the Ad Lib, at parties such as the *Sgt Pepper* party at Epstein's Chapel Street home and at events such as the Bed-In at the Amsterdam Hilton. Brian Epstein often invited him for evening drinks at his home and used to personally phone him with exclusives about the Beatles. When Short managed to get the group splashed across the front page of the *Mirror*, Epstein would send him telegrams, such as: 'Great day today. The sun is shining. Congratulations on your front page lead. We will see you at lunch. Brian.'

Short maintained his special relationship with the Beatles, although his loyalty was to the *Mirror* and he wouldn't let sympathy interfere with his using a scoop, which is probably why Derek Taylor referred to him as 'A rogue's rogue but a man for a' that'.

When the Beatles were in Hollywood and took their second LSD trip at a party, John later commented, 'There was a reporter, Don Short. We were in the garden; it was only our second one [LSD trip] and we still didn't know anything about doing it in a nice place and keeping it cool.' When they saw Short they didn't know how to act.

John said, 'We were terrified waiting for him to go, and he wondered why we couldn't come over. Neil [Aspinall], who had never had acid either, had taken it and he would have to play road manager. We said, "Go get rid of Don Short," and he didn't know what to do.'

When the Beatles were planning the launch of Apple from their Wimpole Street office, John and Yoko, Paul and Neil Aspinall were in a room drinking coffee and checking the proofs of the Beatles biography when Short appeared in the doorway with his photographer.

John and Paul, both apparently horrified at the unannounced intrusion, muttered, 'Get him out.' Short said, 'Just a quick photo, boys', and his photographer clicked away. 'And what's all this big business you're getting into?' Short asked. John turned on him, 'Get out, we're not telling you anything.'

The very next day a full-page story appeared in the *Daily Mirror*, captioned 'The Big Business Beatles' and featuring a large by-line for Don Short.

A few days after John's death, a week-long series of articles on John began to appear in the *Sun* newspaper under the by-line: 'By Don Short – The man who shared his secrets'. The series was syndicated and a small excerpt entitled 'The Lighter Side Of John Lennon' was contained in the Proteus book *A Tribute To John Lennon 1940–1980*.

Short left the *Mirror* to run a literary agency providing, among other things, 'kiss-and-tell' stories to newspapers.

Shot Of Rhythm And Blues, A

A number issued as a single by one of John's favourite artists Arthur Alexander in March 1962. The Beatles immediately included it in their repertoire, with John on lead vocals, and performed it on two 'Pop Go The Beatles' and an 'Easy Beat' radio show. The number was covered by British rock 'n' roll band Johnny Kidd & the Pirates. Their recording of the number from their *Pop Goes The Beatles* radio recording was included on the *Beatles Live At The BBC* CD.

Shotton, Pete

John Lennon's closest childhood friend, whose association with John spanned thirty years. Blond-haired Pete lived in Vale Street, quite close to John's home in Menlove Avenue. The two were at the same primary school, Sunday school and also attended Quarry Bank School together. Their first major encounter took place in an expanse of ground called 'The Tip'. Shotton believed he'd found

John's weak spot – he was enraged when people called him 'Winnie' (from his middle name, Winston). When walking across the Tip, Shotton was ambushed by Lennon who pinned him to the ground and made him promise he wouldn't call him Winnie any more. Shotton swore he wouldn't and John let him go. As he walked away, Shotton turned around and shouted 'Winnie, Winnie, Winnie, Winnie, Winnie!' They stared at one another, then John grinned and they became the best of friends.

Shotton became a member of John's gang and when John formed the Quarry Men, he talked Pete into playing washboard, even though he was not particularly interested in music. One evening, at a party, John got drunk and smashed the washboard over Pete's head, bringing his career as a musician to an end.

When John went to art college, Pete became a cadet at the Police College. They kept in touch and once the Beatles had become successful, John wanted to provide funds for Pete to set himself up in business and arranged for him to receive a cheque for £2,000. His initial business failed, but in 1964 John offered to bankroll him again and Shotton found a supermarket in Hayling Island which was up for sale for around £20,000. On 18 March 1965 a new company was formed, Hayling Supermarkets Ltd, with John, George and Pete as directors. The Beatles funded the venture.

When Apple was launched, John asked him to leave the supermarket in other hands and move to London to run the Apple Boutique. This was in 1968. Unfortunately, the shop didn't do too well and John Lyndon replaced Pete, who became John's personal assistant for a short time.

Shotton last visited Lennon in the Dakota Apartments.

His years of friendship with John are documented in his book *John Lennon: In My Life*, first published in 1983 and written in collaboration with Nicholas Schaffner.

Shout

Number written and performed by the Isley Brothers and recorded by them in 1959.

The Beatles included the song in their repertoire in 1960 with John, Paul and George producing a vocal harmony interpretation of the number. In 1964 Lulu recorded the song for her debut record and reached No. 7 in the British charts with it. The *Around The Beatles* TV show recording was included on the Beatles' *Anthology 1* CDs.

Sibylla's Club, Swallow Street, London W1

A fashionable club which first opened on 23 June 1966. The night before the official opening there was a special party at the club which was attended by the Beatles. The club was financed by celebrities, among them George Harrison who had a ten per cent stake in the venture. George was made a director of Kevin Macdonald Associated Ltd, the company which operated the club.

John and George attended a private reception at Sibylla's on 1 November 1966, in aid of the band Family, and Paul often dropped into the club with Jane Asher.

Side By Side

An early evening BBC Light Programme show broadcast from 5.00 p.m.–5.30 p.m. on each Monday. Presented by John Dunn and produced by Bryant Marriott, 'Side By Side' had a resident group, the Karl Denver Trio. The Beatles made three appearances on the show and on each occasion they opened and closed the programme singing 'Side By Side' with the Karl Denver Trio. In between, each group would alternate with a song. The title number 'Side By Side' was originally composed in 1927.

The Beatles' first broadcast took place on 22 April 1963, which had been recorded at Studio One in the Piccadilly Theatre, London, on 1 April. The group performed 'I Saw Her Standing There', 'Do You Want To Know A Secret?', 'Baby It's You', 'Please Please Me', 'From Me To You' and 'Misery'.

For their second appearance on 13 May 1963, also recorded on 1 April, they performed 'From Me To You,' 'Long Tall Sally', 'A Taste Of Honey', 'Chains', 'Thank You Girl' and 'Boys'.

Their final appearance, recorded on 4 April, took place on 24 June 1963 when the group performed 'Too Much Monkey Business', 'Love Me Do', 'Boys', 'I'll Be On My Way' and 'From Me To You'.

Sie Liebt Dich

One of two tracks the Beatles recorded in the German language. EMI's German branch, Odeon, had appealed to both Brian Epstein and George Martin for the Beatles to record in the German language as their records hadn't been selling in Germany in the quantities they'd hoped. It was not an uncommon practice in the early sixties for British artists to record their latest hits in another language to boost sales in countries such as France, Germany or Spain.

The group knew a smattering of German from their Hamburg days, but were not fluent in the language and Odeon sent along a German translator to help them with the songs.

The group were currently appearing for a season at the Olympia

Theatre in Paris, so George Martin booked the EMI Pathe Studios there on Wednesday, 29 January 1964.

Martin and engineer Norman Smith were waiting in the studios for the group, but they didn't turn up at the appointed time. Martin phoned the George V Hotel and asked Neil Aspinall why they weren't there. Neil told him that they weren't going to the studio that day and a furious Martin tore across to the hotel. He arrived to find the Beatles, together with Neil and Mal, being served tea by Jane Asher. He began shouting at them and they dived for cover behind settees and curtains. They apologised and accompanied him to the studios.

'*Sie Liebt Dich*' was the German version of 'She Loves You' and they also recorded '*Komm, Gib Mir Deine Hand*'.

The only version of '*Sie Liebt Dich*' to be issued outside Germany at the time was the one issued as a single by Swan on Swan 4182 on 21 May 1964 in the US, with 'I'll Get You' on the flip. It reached No. 97 in the American charts. The track was later issued on the compilation album *Rarities* in 1978. The number was also included on the CD compilation *Past Masters Volume One*.

Silkie, The

A folk group, formed by students at Hull University. They comprised Sylvia Tatler (vocals), Mike Ramsden (guitar/vocals), Ivor Aylesbury (guitar/vocals) and Kevin Cunningham (double bass).

The group were managed by Brian Epstein and they made their recording debut in June 1965 on the Fontana label with 'Blood River' c/w 'Close The Door Gently'.

They entered the Top 30 with their second release, the Lennon/McCartney number 'You've Got To Hide Your Love Away' c/w 'City Winds', issued in October 1965 and actually produced by John Lennon with Paul McCartney on piano and George Harrison on tambourine. The track was featured on an album of the same name, released in America on 22 November 1965 on Fontana SRF 67548.

Their other releases were 'Keys To My Soul' c/w 'Leave Me To Cry', issued in February 1966, and 'Born To Be With You' c/w 'So Sorry Now', issued in June of the same year. They also issued an album in October 1965 entitled *The Silkie Sing The Songs Of Bob Dylan*.

Silver, Johnny

The name John Lennon was purported to have used during a brief period when the Silver Beetles used pseudonyms in an attempt to smarten up their image, perhaps inspired by the Larry Parnes method of creating new names for each of his discoveries, such as Johnny Gentle.

During their short tour as backing musicians to Gentle, Paul called himself Paul Ramon, George was Carl Harrison and Stu Sutcliffe adopted the name Stu Da Stael.

In the Beatles' authorised biography, Hunter Davies mentions that John denied he used the name Johnny Silver, although the other members of the group maintained that he did.

The controversy continued after the book *The Beatles: An Illustrated Record* mentioned the Johnny Silver name. John took the trouble to send authors Roy Carr and Tony Tyler a letter, together with clippings from a gig at the Neston Institute on Merseyside immediately following their Johnny Gentle tour, which seems to bear out his contention. He wrote, 'I was never . . . repeat never known as Johnny Silver. I always preferred my own name.'

Six O'Clock

A television programme produced by BBC Ulster. The Beatles taped an interview and performed a number for the programme on 8 November 1963 when they were appearing at the Ritz Cinema, Belfast. The excerpt was screened the same evening.

6.25 Show, The

The Beatles made their BBC television debut on this early evening programme. The group recorded their spot on the show at BBC's Lime Grove Studios in London on 13 April 1963 and it was broadcast on 16 April. The group performed 'From Me To You', 'Thank You Girl' and 'Please Please Me'.

Slice Of Life, A

A radio programme produced by the BBC's Home Service. John Lennon was interviewed for the show by Brian Matthew on Tuesday, 31 March 1964, discussing his recently published book *In His Own Write*. The three minute interview was transmitted on Saturday, 2 May 1964 from 4.00 – 4.30 p.m.

Slow Down

A number written and recorded by Larry Williams in 1958 and released on the same disc as 'Dizzy Miss Lizzy'. The Beatles included it in their repertoire in 1960 with John on lead vocals. The group featured the number on their 'Pop Go The Beatles' radio show on 20 August 1963 and their studio version was included on the *Long Tall Sally* EP. It was issued as a single in America on Capitol 5255 on 24 August 1964 with 'Matchbox' and reached No. 25 in the US charts. The track is also to be found on the *Rock 'n' Roll Music* and *Rarities* albums, their American album *Something New, The Beatles Box* and *The Beatles Collection sets*. A version from the live recording on *Pop Go The Beatles* radio show was included on *The Beatles Live At The BBC* CDs. The number was also included on the CD compilation *Past Masters Volume One*.

Smith, Alan

Merseyside journalist who originally worked on the *Birkenhead News*. He based himself in London and joined the *New Musical Express*, where he eventually became editor. In the early sixties he wrote for *Mersey Beat* under the pen name George Jones and interviewed the Beatles on a number of occasions on the paper's behalf. He also interviewed them regularly for the *New Musical Express*.

He'd known Derek Taylor from his days on the *Birkenhead News* and when Derek became Press Officer at Apple, Alan asked him if he could find a job for his wife. Mavis, a former ballet dancer. When Derek met her he gave her a job as his assistant in the Apple Press Office.

Alan was involved in an incident at the Apple Christmas party on 23 December 1968. A couple of Hell's Angels from San Francisco were in attendance. One of them, Frisco Pete, became impatient waiting for the food to be served up and stalked over to John and Yoko and demanded to be fed. Alan Smith tried to smooth out the situation and Frisco Pete punched him and knocked him out.

Smith, John

A leading London concert promoter who booked the Beatles on a number of concerts in 1963. His first booking of the group was on 16 February, for a gig at the Carfax Assembly Rooms, Oxford. He also booked some dates for Epstein's Mersey Beat Showcase, featuring the Beatles, beginning with the Fairfield Hall, Croydon concert on 25 April.

Smith died of cancer on 25 April 1988 at the age of 75.

Smith, Mavis

Dark-haired former dancer with the Ballet Rambert who was married to *New Musical Express* journalist Alan Smith. Mavis had given up her dancing career to work for pop PR man Les Perrin. She'd been working for Perrin for over a year when her husband began asking Derek Taylor if he could find her a position at Apple. Derek met Mavis at a London concert and a week later invited her to join the Apple Press Office.

She worked on most of the accounts, ranging from Mary Hopkin to Badfinger, but when the artists began to leave and there wasn't much to do in the Press Office, she resigned. The action resulted in a small story in the trade publication Record Retailer on 20 June 1970:

> MAVIS SMITH LEAVES APPLE
> Mavis Smith has resigned from the Apple Press Office, which she left last weekend. Assistant to Derek Taylor for the past eighteen months, she previously worked with Leslie Perrin Associates.
> In the absence of Derek Taylor, now writing a book, Mrs Smith has been running the department together with Richard DiLello, who will now assume responsibility for press matters.

Smith, Mike

In 1961 Mike Smith was a newly appointed assistant in the A&R division at Decca Records. After Brian Epstein had approached Decca asking them to sign up the Beatles, it was decided that his position as a prominent record retailer in the north warranted some attention, and Mike Smith was assigned to travel to Liverpool to see the group.

He arrived on 13 December and Brian took him out for a meal. They then went to the Cavern to watch the Beatles perform and Smith was impressed and immediately arranged for them to travel to London to take part in a record audition at Decca's West Hampstead studios on New Year's Day, 1 January 1962.

Brian and the Beatles arrived at 11.00 a.m. prompt, and Brian was peeved when Smith turned up late. The group performed fifteen numbers and Smith expressed such enthusiasm that Brian was convinced the group would receive a contract.

Tony Barrow, in his 'Disker' column in the *Liverpool Echo*, wrote: 'Decca disc Producer Mike Smith tells me that he thinks the Beatles are great. He has a continuous tape of their audition performance which runs for over thirty minutes and he is convinced that his label will be able to put the Beatles to good use. I'll be keeping you posted.' However, Smith had to consult his boss, Dick Rowe. Rowe pointed out that another group had auditioned that day, Brian Poole & the Tremeloes. He said that Decca would only sign up one of the groups and, it was said, left the decision to Smith. Presumably, Smith felt that although he considered both bands to be good, it would be more convenient to sign up the Tremeloes because they came from nearby Dagenham. Ironically, it was Dick Rowe and Mike Smith from Decca who signed up Pete Best after he left the Beatles. Mona Best travelled to London to see them with tapes of Pete's new band and Smith recorded the group's single 'I'm Gonna Knock On Your Door'. Unfortunately, the disc wasn't a success and Decca dropped the band.

Smith also recorded the Applejacks with 'Like Dreamers Do', a Lennon & McCartney number which he'd originally recorded with the Beatles at the Decca audition.

Smith, Mimi

Nee Stanley, Mary Elizabeth Smith was John Lennon's aunt, one of Julia Lennon's four sisters.

Like her other sisters, she was known by a pet name – Mimi. Mimi married a dairy farmer, George Smith, and eventually settled in Mendips, a pleasant semi-detached house in Menlove Avenue, Liverpool. She did not have any children of her own and doted on John from the moment he was born.

When John was being reared by his mother at Newcastle Road, Mimi was upset at what she regarded as his neglect by Julia and insisted that she be allowed to rear him. When Julia went to live with John Dykins, she agreed to leave John in the hands of her sister and John was five years old when he went to live in Mendips.

Mimi took her responsibilities seriously and brought John up with care, despite the times she despaired because of his rebellious nature and poor school results, although teachers always impressed upon her that John had talent as an artist. At his junior school, when handing Mimi a bunch of John's drawings, the teacher commented: 'The perspective is amazing for a boy of eleven.' George died when John was twelve and Mimi had to care for the strong-willed, stubborn boy single-handedly. He proved something of a handful and there was often friction between them.

Mimi did not entirely approve of his interest in rock 'n' roll music and attempted to dissuade him, but on realising that he was so determined, she bought him a guitar at Frank Hessy's music store for £18 when he was seventeen. She later threatened to throw the instrument into the dustbin.

It was Mimi who took the advice of Quarry Bank Headmaster Mr Pobjoy and agreed to let John have an opportunity of studying at Liverpool College of Art.

John's interest in the Beatles gained her disapproval as she felt that the group would draw him away from his studies. She went to see the group at the Cavern and didn't like them. She told John, 'The guitar's all right as a hobby, but you'll never make a living out of it.' Much later, John had the phrase engraved on a silver plaque and presented it to her.

She was particularly upset when he left the art college and was disappointed in his determination to go to Germany. He returned broke, despite his assurances to her that he would make a lot of money, and she was able to give him an 'I told you so' speech.

His days at Mendips were coming to an end and John shared flats with fellow students and then married Cynthia. While John was on the road Cynthia stayed with Mimi for a while, but, by all accounts, preferred to return to the company of her own mother.

When the Beatles' success in Britain grew, John was determined to express his gratitude to Mimi for the love and dedication she had given to him in his formative years, and he bought her a home in Poole, overlooking the harbour.

Mimi was proud to hear the news of the Beatles' MBE award and John sent his medal to her because he knew she would appreciate it. He later asked if he could borrow it from her and returned it to the Palace, much to Mimi's fury.

Mimi was 67 years old when John died. She was saddened and appalled by the various smears which cropped up about John in subsequent books and articles, and decided to speak up on his behalf, to set the record straight, in a series of articles in the *Daily Star* newspaper in February 1981. She mentioned that John had phoned her the night before he died, that he had always asked for books, rather than toys, on his birthdays; that he paid for guitar lessons at five shillings a time out of his pocket money and that he tithed a tenth of his income each year to a charity for spastic children.

An insight was given into that magic moment when John charmed the media with his comments at the Royal Variety Show. Apparently, John already had a ready wit when he attended pantomimes in Liverpool. When a fairy who was a bit older than the others appeared on the stage, the eleven-year-old John shouted out, 'She's a bit old for a fairy, isn't she?' and when the principal boy strode on to the stage, John shouted, 'Why, he's got my wellies on!'

Mimi remained in the bungalow at Harbour's Edge, 126 Panomaram Road, Sandbanks, Poole, Dorset, for the remainder of her life and died at the age of 88 on 6 December 1991, two days before the eleventh anniversary of John's murder, a tragedy from which she never recovered. Both of John's former wives, Cynthia and Yoko, were present with Mimi at the end. The funeral took place on 11 October and Yoko, Sean and Cynthia were among the mourners. Paul, George and Ringo sent wreaths. George's read, simply, 'From George Harrison and Family'; Paul's read, 'Dear Mimi, it was a great pleasure to know you in life – you were an exceptional woman and loved by many of us. God bless, Paul, Linda and children'; and Ringo's read, 'To Aunt Mimi, with our love, Ringo and Barbara'.

Smith, Norman

The Beatles' original recording engineer. Norman was born in Edmonton, north London, and was a versatile musician, playing several instruments, until he served in the RAF. He left the Air Force in 1947 and, unable to make a career as a musician, eventually began working at Abbey Road Studios in 1959 as a tape engineer.

George Martin used him for the Beatles sessions, including their first-ever EMI recording stint, and he continued as their recording engineer right through to the *Rubber Soul* sessions in December 1965. In February 1960 he joined the A&R department at EMI as a fully fledged recording manager in his own right.

John used to call him 'Normal Smith' and Paul's pet name for him was 'Two D-C's Smith', referring to the time Norman told him to turn his amplifier down by a couple of decibels.

He revealed that during the recording sessions for *Help!*, on Friday, 11 June 1965 to be precise, he almost ended up with a track on the Beatles' album. The group had been recording in studio 3 and needed to have one more song for the proposed fourteen-track album. They didn't have one and were discussing it when Smith said he had a number he'd written and the song was in his pocket. He played it to John and Paul and they agreed they'd use it for the *Help!* album.

Dick James, who was also in the studio, immediately offered him £15,000 to buy the song outright. Norman says George Martin shook his head to him, indicating he thought it wasn't enough, so Norman asked James if he could think about it over the weekend. On the Monday morning, Paul then came up to Smith and apologised to him, saying they'd forgotten to include a Ringo Starr track on the album and as they wanted one track by Ringo per album, they'd record 'Act Naturally' with him.

Norman also engineered sessions for various bands in the 1960s, including Billy J. Kramer & the Dakotas, Freddie & the Dreamers and Cliff Bennett & the Rebel Rousers. As a producer, he began with artists such as the Pink Floyd and the Pretty Things.

At the age of 49 he was to find success in his own right as a recording artist. He used the name Hurricane Smith, which was the title of a film starring Yvonne de Carlo, which he'd originally seen in 1952. He even reached No. 1 in the American charts in 1972 with 'Oh Babe, What Would You Say?'. His other hit singles included 'Don't Let It Die' and 'Who Was It?'. After several hits he moved to the English countryside to breed horses and also launched a medical equipment company in Surrey.

Smothers Brothers Comedy Hour, The

The Smothers Brothers, Tom and Dick Smothers, were a popular comedy act with their own television show networked by CBS TV. A film of the Beatles performing 'Hey Jude' was featured on their programme on 6 October 1968. Later the same month, on 13 October 1968, the Smothers Brothers featured another Beatles promo clip, this time with the group performing 'Revolution'. The tape was one which had originally been screened on the British TV show 'Top Of The Pops' on 19 September 1968.

During the same year, on 17 November, George Harrison made a special appearance on the show in a small cameo with Tom and Dick.

Tommy Smothers was one of the voices on the chorus of 'Give Peace A Chance'. When CBS TV scrapped their show, there was much sympathy in America for the pair and they attempted a comeback by appearing at the Troubadour Club in Los Angeles in March 1974. Their show was interrupted by a drunken John Lennon who continually heckled their act. The incident received worldwide publicity.

So How Come No One Loves Me?

Number composed by Felice and Boudleaux Bryant and recorded by the Everly Brothers in 1961. The Beatles included it in their repertoire the same year, with George on lead vocals. The group performed the song on their 'Pop Go The Beatles' radio show on 23 July 1963. The session from the *Pop Go The Beatles* recording was included on *The Beatles Live At The BBC* CDs

Soldier Of Love (Lay Down Your Arms)

A composition by Cason-Moon, recorded by Arthur Alexander and issued as a single in June 1962. The Beatles included it in their repertoire the same year, with John on lead vocals. The group performed the number on their BBC radio show 'Pop Go The Beatles' on 16 July 1963. A version of the number was included on *The Beatles Live At The BBC* CDs.

Some Other Guy

A Jerry Leiber, Mike Stoller, Ritchie Barrett composition, issued as a single by Ritchie Barrett in May 1962 and becoming an immediate favourite with Mersey Beat groups, providing a minor hit for the Big Three in Britain. The Beatles immediately began performing

the number and were captured playing the song on stage at the
Cavern by a Granada film crew. It was a number which other local
groups such as the Searchers also performed. John was lead vocalist
and the Beatles performed the number on their 'Saturday Club',
'The Talent Spot' and 'Easy Beat' radio appearances. A version of
the number appeared on *The Beatles Live At The BBC* CD.

Something

George Harrison's most commercially successful composition. He
wrote it on a piano during a break in the making of *The Beatles*
double album. Paul was doing overdubs, so George went into an
empty studio and composed it. It was too late to be included on *The
Beatles* album, so he gave the number to Joe Cocker.

However, he re-recorded it and twelve violas, four violins, four
cellos and one string bass were added. The number was then
featured on the *Abbey Road* album and, at the insistence of Allen
Klein, it became a single, giving George his first-ever Beatles 'A'
side. It was issued, with 'Come Together' on the flip, on 6 October
1969 in America on Apple 2654 where it reached No. 3. In Britain
it was issued on 1 October 1969 on Parlophone R 5814 where it
went to No. 5. The number was covered by Shirley Bassey, whose
version did better than the Beatles by reaching No. 4 in the British
charts.

'Something' was included on the compilation albums *The Beatles
1967–1970*, *The Best Of George Harrison*, *Love Songs* and *The
Beatles Ballads*.

George was to say, 'When I wrote it, in my mind I heard Ray
Charles singing it, and he did do it some years later.' Frank Sinatra
called it, 'The greatest love song of the past fifty years', and it was
the most popular of George's compositions with more than 150
cover versions. George's favourite version was by James Brown and
he also liked Smokey Robinson's cover of the song.

George was possibly influenced by a song written by Apple
recording artist James Taylor, which was included on Taylor's debut
Apple album *James Taylor*, issued in December 1968. The song was
called 'Something In The Way She Moves'. A version of the number
was used on the Beatles' *Anthology 3* CDs.

Something New

The third Beatles album issued by Capitol.

It is interesting to note that although United Artists' original
approach to the Beatles regarding a film was mainly because they
wanted to secure Beatles recordings on soundtrack albums, an
agreement was made between EMI and United Artists which

allowed Capitol to use material from the film soundtracks. This resulted in *Something New* including five songs from the official soundtrack of *A Hard Day's Night*, only a month after United Artists had issued their movie soundtrack.

Despite the fact that the material wasn't new, the album reached No. 2 in the *Billboard, Cash Box* and *Record World* charts. The album tracks were, Side One: 'I'll Cry Instead', 'Things We Said Today', 'Any Time At All', 'When I Get Home', 'Slow Down', 'Matchbox'. Side Two: 'Tell Me Why', 'And I Love Her', 'I'm Happy Just To Dance With You', 'If I Fell' and *'Komm, Gib Mir Deine Hand'*.

Sommerville, Brian

After serving fourteen years in the Royal Navy, where he became a Lieutenant Commander, Brian Sommerville became a press agent, initially working for the Theo Cowan company handling clients such as Peter Sellers and Judy Garland.

Sommerville was 32 years old when he first met Brian Epstein in a Liverpool pub. He was working in a public relations department at the time. The two became friends and when Epstein bought an apartment in Knightsbridge, London, he invited Sommerville around to dinner on a number of occasions, during which he suggested that they should work together.

Epstein then arranged for Beatles publicist Tony Barrow to represent Gerry & the Pacemakers, Billy J. Kramer, Cilla Black and the Fourmost while he engaged Sommerville to represent the Beatles exclusively. He quite rightly felt that the authoritative figure and commanding voice of Sommerville would be an advantage in his handling of the press. It was, and it also came in useful when Sommerville began to travel to gigs with the Beatles and was in daily contact with theatre managers and police officers who appreciated dealing with a person who projected authority.

Sommerville did not become an employee of NEMS, but set up his own company, of which Epstein was a shareholder. As exclusive press representative to the Beatles, he received £100 a month.

Because of his receding hair, the Beatles called him 'old baldie'. He says that he got on with John, Paul and Ringo, but not with George and he had the impression that George resented him. There was one reported flare-up which occurred at the George V Hotel in Paris when George told Sommerville that a journalist would have to wait an additional hour before he'd consent to an interview. When Sommerville protested, George threw an orange juice at him and Sommerville clipped him over the ear.

It was Sommerville who arranged the publicity deal with British

European Airways for which, with the Beatles sporting an inflight bag with the letters BEAtles, the group and their party would receive three weeks unlimited travel between London and Paris, which proved helpful during their Olympia season as their low fee for the gig didn't provide for air fares.

Sommerville also arranged the Beatles' unfortunate appearance at the British Embassy in Washington, via the Embassy's Naval Attaché, who was an old friend of his.

Relations between the two Brians deteriorated and Sommerville found that Epstein was jealous of anyone who became close to the Beatles and objected to a press officer making any statements on behalf of the group. He also quibbled about hotel bills and constantly embarrassed Sommerville by arguing in public.

Sommerville's term as Press Officer for the Beatles lasted ten months. The arrangement had been made on a gentleman's agreement, but Epstein now insisted on a watertight contract with some clauses which Sommerville disagreed with. They argued and Sommerville resigned. He then advertised in *The Times* newspaper: 'Ex-Beatles Publicity Manager looking for a job.' As a result he received enough clients to start his own public relations firm, representing artists such as the Kinks, the Who and Manfred Mann.

Years later he left the field of public relations and sought a career in Law, eventually becoming a stipendiary magistrate.

Songs Lennon & McCartney Gave Away, The

A British album issued on EMI NUT 18 on 13 April 1979. This was a collection of twenty tracks by eleven different artists who had recorded Lennon & McCartney numbers. Although literally hundreds of other artists had 'covered' Beatles numbers throughout the sixties, there were a number of Lennon & McCartney compositions which were either not recorded or released by the Beatles themselves. These songs were recorded by other artists between the years 1963 and 1969. The album gathered most of these numbers on this special compilation – others not included, but which could have fitted into the brief were, 'Thingumybob' by the Black Dyke Mills Band, 'Goodbye' by Mary Hopkin, 'Theme From The Family Way' by the George Martin Orchestra, 'Love In The Open Air' by the George Martin Orchestra, and 'Come And Get It' by Badfinger. In some ways, the Plastic Ono Band tracks such as 'Give Peace A Chance' and 'Cold Turkey' would have been eligible.

Strangely enough, the one odd track was the opening track, 'I'm The Greatest' by Ringo Starr. This track featured Ringo on lead guitar and drums, with John Lennon on guitar and backing vocals, George Harrison on lead, Klaus Voormann on bass and Billy

Preston on organ. It was a song which had been written by John Lennon specially for Ringo to sing on his 1973 album *Ringo*. The track listing was, Side One: 'I'm The Greatest', Ringo Starr; 'One And One Is Two', the Strangers with Mike Shannon; 'From A Window', Billy J. Kramer with the Dakotas; 'Nobody I Know', Peter & Gordon; 'Like Dreamers Do', the Applejacks; 'I'll Keep You Satisfied', Billy J. Kramer with the Dakotas; 'Love Of The Loved', Cilla Black; 'Woman', Peter & Gordon; 'Tip Of My Tongue', Tommy Quickly. Side Two: 'Hello Little Girl', the Fourmost; 'That Means A Lot', P. J. Proby; 'It's For You', Cilla Black; 'Penina', Carlos Mendes; 'Step Inside Love', Cilla Black; 'World Without Love', Peter & Gordon; 'Bad To Me', Billy J. Kramer with the Dakotas; 'I Don't Want To See You Again', Peter & Gordon; 'I'll Be On My Way', Billy J. Kramer with the Dakotas; 'Catcall', the Chris Barber Band.

The sleeve notes were penned by the Beatles' former Press Officer, Tony Barrow.

Songs, Pictures And Stories Of The Fabulous Beatles

A repackaged version of *Introducing The Beatles*, issued by Vee Jay Records on VJLP 1092 on 12 October 1964. The album reached No. 63 in the *Billboard* charts. The copies of the record still had the number 1062 and the title *Introducing The Beatles* within the new packaging which introduced a special fold-out cover with photographs and biographies. The tracks were, Side One: 'I saw Her Standing There', 'Misery', 'Anna (Go To Him)', 'Chains', 'Boys', 'Ask Me Why'. Side Two: 'Please Please Me', 'Baby It's You', 'Do You Want To Know A Secret?', 'A Taste Of Honey', 'There's A Place', 'Twist And Shout'.

Sounds Incorporated

An instrumental group, formed in Kent in 1961. They backed several visiting American artists, such as Little Richard and Gene Vincent, and first met the Beatles at the Star Club in Hamburg. They came to the attention of Brian Epstein, who signed them to a management contract in March 1964.

The group comprised Alan Holmes (flute, sax), Griff West (sax), John St John (guitar), Barrie Cameron (keyboards), Wes Hunter (bass guitar) and Tony Newman (drums).

They appeared on the Beatles' autumn tour of Britain in October and November 1964, the *Beatles Christmas Show* at the Odeon, Hammersmith and the Beatles' American tour in August 1965.

They abbreviated their name to Sounds Inc in 1967.

The group, whose signature tune was the 'William Tell Overture', appeared in the film *Live It Up*. In March 1967, three members of the group, Barrie Cameron, David Glyde and Alan Holmes, played saxophones on the 'Good Morning, Good Morning' session for the *Sgt Pepper* album.

Sour Milk Sea

John Lennon and Paul McCartney weren't the only ones who utilised the peaceful sojourn in Rishikesh to produce a number of songs. While George Harrison was relaxing at the Maharishi's ashram he also wrote some numbers, one of which was called 'Sour Milk Sea'.

For some reason he didn't put the number forth as a possible song to be recorded by the Beatles but kept it until he had the opportunity of recording an old friend, Liverpool singer Jackie Lomax, who'd been signed to the Apple label. 'Sour Milk Sea' became Jackie's solo single, which George produced, with a star-studded ensemble, which included himself and Jackie on rhythm guitars, Eric Clapton on lead guitar, Ringo Starr on drums and Nicky Hopkins on piano.

The number was one of the first four Apple singles released. It was issued in Britain on Apple 3 on 6 September 1968 and in America on Apple 1802 on 26 August, but failed to register in the charts. A major disappointment as Lomax had the potential to become a major star.

South Africa

The Beatles always refused to tour South Africa because of apartheid. Despite this, their records were hits there until 1966. On 8 August of that year, following the controversy aroused by John Lennon's quotes regarding Jesus Christ in his interview with Maureen Cleave, the South African Broadcasting Corporation (SABC) announced that it was banning the airplay of all Beatles records. A ban on the sales of Beatles records was also introduced. The ban continued until after the group split up, although it was lifted on 3 March 1971 – but only on Beatles records. The ban on John Lennon's songs and records continued.

South Today

A BBC TV magazine programme covering the Hampshire area. Reporter John Johnson taped an interview with the Beatles at the Royal Beach Hotel in Southsea on Tuesday, 12 November 1963 and it was broadcast on the programme that evening at 6.10 p.m.

Southern Sporting Club, The Corona, Birch Street, Hyde Road, Manchester

While Merseyside boasted scores of venues which promoted rock 'n' roll music, the nearby city of Manchester was noted for its cabaret clubs, venues aimed at the older audiences who drank alcohol, with middle-of-the-road music and entertainers. Brian Epstein had tried introducing the Beatles to the cabaret circuit before and tried again on 13 June 1963 with a double-booking for the evening at this cabaret club and the Palace Theatre Club in nearby Stockport.

Southern, Terry

American author who co-penned the risqué novel *Candy* with Mason Hoffenberg. It was initially considered too sexually explicit to be published in America and was originally issued in Paris by the Olympia Press. When it was eventually published in the United States it became a bestseller and was filmed, providing Ringo Starr with his first solo screen role.

Southern also wrote *The Magic Christian,* first published in 1959, which provided Ringo with his second non-Beatle film role, in which he co-starred with Peter Sellers.

Appropriately, perhaps, Ringo had the words 'Buy a Terry Southern book' included in the sleeve notes of his *Goodbye Vienna* album.

Terry Southern was also one of the many characters to be featured on the sleeve of the *Sergeant Pepper* album.

Southern scripted several films during the 1960s, the most notable of which was *Dr Strangelove,* co-written with Stanley Kubrick. Since so many copies of *Candy* were pirated, he did not become rich on the proceeds and was reputed to be suffering financial hardships at the time of his death. He died in 1995 at the age of 71.

Speakeasy Club, The, 48 Margaret Street, London W1

Fashionable members' club, part of the same group as the Revolution and Blaise's clubs. Overseer of all three was Jim Carter-Fea and manager at the Speakeasy was Roy Flynn.

The Beatles began attending the club in 1967, and it was a haunt for most of the big name British rock stars of the time and frequented by all the visiting American figures. There was live music, often by a name band, and a special restaurant section divided from the rest of the club by a glass wall.

The restaurant provided the setting on 3 July 1967 for a special party in honour of the Monkees, organised by Vic Lewis of NEMS Enterprises who had brought the Monkees to Britain.

Among the guests that night were the Monkees, *sans* Davy Jones, and the Beatles, *sans* Ringo Starr. Also present at the private function were the Who, Cream, Manfred Mann, Dusty Springfield, Lulu, Klaus Voormann, Kenny Everett, Bill and Virginia Harry and Jonathan King.

Spector, Phil

The legendary record producer who was born Philip Harvey Spector in New York on 26 December 1940. He moved to California in the early fifties with his widowed mother.

Interestingly enough, the record which inspired him to become a musician was 'Rock Island Line' by the British performer Lonnie Donegan, who was a main inspiration of the Beatles. Spector bought a guitar and performed 'Rock Island Line' in a talent contest in 1957 and the same year formed a group called the Sleepwalkers, while still at high school, with Sandy Nelson, Bruce Johnson and Kim Fowley. When they broke up at the end of 1958 Spector formed the Teddy Bears and penned the number 'To Know Him Is To Love Him', which provided them with a No. 1 hit. He moved back to New York in 1960 and by 1961 had begun to produce records of new artists he discovered and launched the Phille label. Among his hits were songs such as 'He's A Rebel', 'Zip-A-Dee-Doo-Dah', 'And Then He Kissed Me' and 'Be My Baby' by artists such as the Crystals, Bob B. Soxx & the Bluejeans and Darlene Love, all of whom are featured in his 1963 album *Phil Spector's Christmas Album*. It was during this period that he developed his famous 'wall of sound', a distinctive system of multiple recording which produced a denser sound on record.

The Beatles sought Spector's advice on the American scene and he accompanied them on their first flight to New York in February 1964. Later that year he produced a novelty single, 'I Love Ringo' c/w 'Beatle Blues' by Bonnie Jo Mason, who later became successful as Cher.

Spector produced the Righteous Brothers performing 'You've Lost That Loving Feeling', but George Martin quickly recorded Cilla Black's cover version in Britain and as she was popular there, her record overtook the Righteous Brothers in the British charts – and then Andrew Loog Oldham took out a newspaper advertisement pointing out the superiority of the Righteous Brothers version, which then overtook Cilla's record and reached the No. 1 position. During the sixties, Spector's success continued, although he was noted for his production of singles, rather than albums.

When Allen Klein was brought in to handle the Beatles' affairs, one of the problems was the mess of the 'Get Back' product, a mass of tapes which George Martin and Glyn Johns had been trying to assemble into an album. Klein suggested that Spector be put in charge of the project and allowed to assemble the tapes. John Lennon was not convinced and decided to try Spector out first on one of the Plastic Ono singles, so he had Phil produce 'Instant Karma'. The single became the first solo Beatles record to sell a million in America, reaching No. 3 in the charts – it also reached No. 5 in Britain. As the single didn't display the heavy Spector 'wall of sound', the producer was allowed to handle the 'Get Back' tapes, which were eventually released as the album *Let It Be*.

By all accounts, the Beatles were not too certain of the success of the Spector mixing on *Let It Be*, which overloaded some tracks with the 'wall of sound'. Paul McCartney, in particular, was furious with what Spector had done to his 'The Long And Winding Road'. Spector had sent each member of the Beatles an acetate of his production work on *Let It Be*, together with a long letter explaining his reasons for the changes he had made. Paul McCartney felt sick about the over-production of 'The Long And Winding Road', which he'd envisioned as a simple production and which had now been overloaded with celestial choirs and orchestral backing. Paul wrote to Allen Klein demanding that the original version of his number be used – but he was ignored. 'The Long And Winding Road' was issued in America where it became the Beatles' final No. 1 single, although it wasn't issued as a single in Britain.

George and John, on the other hand, didn't seem to have been upset by the hand of Spector on their work and George engaged him to participate in the production of his *All Things Must Pass* album. Spector also worked with Lennon on *John Lennon/Plastic Ono Band* and produced his single 'Power To The People'.

In the sixties Spector had married Ronnie Bennett of the Ronettes and, in an attempt to revive her solo recording career, produced her singing the George Harrison composition 'Try Some, Buy Some'. He also produced 'God Save Oz' by Bill Elliott and the Elastic Oz Band for Lennon.

Apple Records issued his famous Christmas album and he became A&R man for the company. His next project was the John Lennon album *Imagine*, followed by his recording of the Madison Square Garden show for *The Concert For Bangladesh* album. By this time Apple was crumbling and among the last productions he did for the company were 'Happy Christmas (War Is Over)' by John and Yoko. He also worked with John and Yoko on their *Some Time In New York City* album.

In 1973 John had decided to record an album of rock 'n' roll records which he was going to call 'Oldies But Moldies'. It was eventually released as *Rock 'n' Roll*. He arranged for Phil Spector to produce the album in Los Angeles, but the resultant sessions became chaotic and there were disagreements between the two which caused a halt in the recordings, with Spector holding on to the tapes which had been recorded. It was reported that he had been involved in a car accident at the time. Lennon found he was unable to contact Spector and when Spector eventually turned over the tapes for a reportedly large sum of money, they were found to be virtually unusable.

Later in the seventies, Spector produced artists such as Dion, Leonard Cohen and the Ramones and in 1981 co-produced Yoko Ono's album *Season Of Glass* with Yoko at New York's Hit Factory.

Speedy Prompt Delivery Service

When the Beatles returned from their first trip to Hamburg they were literally broke. Their proposed residency at the Top Ten Club could no longer take place as the venue had burnt down. Paul's father pressed him to apply for a job. 'It's time for you to get serious about life, to look for real work, to make some real money, to get off your behind.' Jim told him.

Paul went to the labour exchange and was given the job of package deliverer for the Speedy Prompt Delivery Service. He was laid off after a couple of weeks because he said he was, 'So buggered sometimes I fell asleep on the lorry when we went to places like Chester.'

Spinetti, Victor

An actor, director, writer and producer who was born in Cwm, near Ebbw Vale, Gwent. Victor was the only person, apart from the Beatles themselves, to appear in all three of their acting films: *A Hard Day's Night, Help!* and *Magical Mystery Tour*.

Spinetti's association with the Beatles began when 'The lads saw a production I was in, *Oh! What A Lovely War,* and they said, "We want you in our film!" And that was that.'

In *A Hard Day's Night* he played the neurotic director of the television show they were in. He next appeared as Professor Foot in *Help!* The Beatles then asked him to appear in *Magical Mystery Tour* as the courier Jolly Jimmy Johnson. He commented: 'They wanted me to play the courier on the bus in *Magical Mystery Tour* so I would be travelling with them all the time. But I couldn't, because I was doing a show in London, so I could only join them from London and go back there to do the show. Otherwise I would have loved to have gone on that whole trip, it would have been marvellous.

'I had to write my own script. I've got a letter from John somewhere saying, "Well, write it yourself. You know, just do your own bits." I said "OK", so I did the drill-sergeant thing that I had done in *Oh! What A Lovely War,* where I was portraying the kind of establishment figure who was telling them to get their hair cut, pull themselves together and behave like responsible people. In other words, be killers!'

He dropped in to see the Beatles recording in November 1967, ostensibly to discuss with John the new play they were doing together. The group was recording their fifth fan club record and Victor joined them during a rendition of 'Christmas Time (Is Here Again)'.

Victor produced and co-authored a special stage version of John's two books. He said: 'A girl from Detroit called Adrienne Kennedy who wrote a play which was put on at the Royal Court Theatre came to see me when I was in London doing *The Odd Couple* and asked me to be in it. And I read it and said, "Well, you know, if you are going to put this on stage you will have to do more than you have done." And I told her what I felt about the person growing up and his own reactions to family situations, schools etc. Because it's very autobiographical, the whole thing.

'And so she said, "Come and tell Ken Tynan," and I told Ken Tynan and he said, "Come and tell Laurence Olivier," and I told Laurence Olivier and he said, "My dear baby, direct it for us!" So then I said to Adrienne, "Have you had permission from John to do this, turn it into a play?" and she said, "No!".

'I said, "But you have to!" So I rang him up and asked him, and he said, "Yeah, OK. You got permission." And then he came to a rehearsal and became interested, and then we worked together on the script.

'At the rehearsal he in fact cried and said, "These were all the things that I was thinking about when I was 16," and he got involved in it and eventually we spent quite a bit of time together working on the script, writing out those little extra things that one needed for it.'

To promote the play, Victor and John appeared on the BBC 2 programme 'Release' and discussed it. A book of the play, credited to Victor, Adrienne and John was published in 1968. The production originally appeared in a single performance in December 1967, then opened as a one-act play at the Old Vic on 18 June 1968.

Victor was also to appear in a cameo role in Paul's video of 'London Town'.

Sporthallen, Hamngatan, Eskilstuna, Sweden

The Beatles made their final appearance of their short Swedish tour at this venue on Tuesday, 29 October 1963. Also on the bill were Jerry Williams, the Violents, Trio Me' Bumba, the Telstars and Mona Skarstrom.

Springfield Ballroom, Janvrin Road, St Saviour, Jersey, Channel Islands

One of the venues where the Beatles appeared during a week-long engagement on the Channel Islands, booked by the promoter John Smith. The Beatles first appeared at the venue for two nights, on 6 and 7 August 1963, and ended their Channel Islands appearances with another two-night engagement on 9 and 10 August 1963.

Stanley Abattoir Social Club, East Prescot Road, Old Swan, Liverpool L14

The social club for the staff of Stanley Abattoir, the main Liverpool slaughterhouse. The Quarry Men were booked to appear at the club for a single Saturday night dance on 16 November 1957, during which they played two sets.

Stanley Street, Liverpool L1

City centre street leading off Whitechapel which contains Frank Hessy's music store and Radio City, the independent radio station.

The street is also the home of Tommy Steele's sculpture of Eleanor Rigby.

The popular Cockney entertainer made the statue and presented it to the City of Liverpool. It was unveiled before a gathering of 300 people on Friday, 3 December 1982, and Tommy commented: 'Please enjoy her. It is my present to you and I hope you enjoy her as much as I do.'

The Eleanor Rigby statue is cleverly attached to an actual bench seat above which there is a plaque which reads:

ELEANOR RIGBY
Donated to
'All The Lonely People'
'The statue was sculpted and donated to the City of Liverpool by Tommy Steele as a tribute to the Beatles. The casting was sponsored by the *Liverpool Echo*.'

December 1982.

Star Club, The, 39 Grosse Freiheit, St Pauli, Hamburg, Germany

The club was situated in a cobbled street crammed with a bizarre mixture of clubs, pubs and tea shops, branching off from the Reeperbahn in Hamburg's notorious St Pauli district.

It was formerly the site of the Stern Kino, a cinema, and only minor conversions were made to turn it into a rock venue. Above the entrance was a huge star, the club's trademark, projecting out from the façade and illuminated at night to compete with all the other exciting neon invitations – Regina, Tabu, Salome, Spiel Casino – which lit up the street. The Grosse Freiheit also contained many captivating nighteries such as Gretel und Alfons, the beershop frequented by British bands; a club whose main feature was generously proportioned women wrestling in mud; another whose numbered tables were each fitted with an internal telephone – enabling clients to call up any of the lightly clad young hostesses disporting themselves around; a tiny tea shop run by two little old ladies; and opposite the Star Club a strip joint called the Colibri in the former premises of the Kaiserkeller, where the Beatles appeared in 1961.

Right next to the Star Club itself was a church, and the club shared its entrance with the Monica Biershop. Inside there was a large reception hall where, to the left, was a staircase leading to the Erotica Film-Night-Club on the next floor, to the rear of the Star Club balcony. This was the setting for a non-stop Cinemascope film show consisting mainly of colour movies made by club-owner Manfred Weissleder. On each side of the screen giant-sized slides of nude females flickered and changed while a real stripper performed in front of the screen. The stairs continued to the next floor which housed Manfred's office and living quarters.

The ceiling of the entrance was covered in copies of *Mersey Beat*, the Liverpool paper, and there were sets of doors leading to what were formerly the rear stalls. Through the doors was the long bar, with one of the barmaids, Bettina Derlin, displaying her own little gallery of photographs of her favourite groups.

The area which used to house the stalls had been stripped of all the cinema seats and fitted with settee-like seating and tables. On the stage was a huge backdrop depicting the Manhattan skyline.

Weissleder sent Horst Fascher and Roy Young to Liverpool in January 1962 to book the Beatles and as many other top Mersey bands as possible. Horst visited Brian Epstein at his office in Whitechapel and a contract was negotiated and signed on 22 January 1962. One of the clauses read: 'It is agreed that the band will not perform or accept other engagements in Germany from the date of this contract until the contract becomes effective.' Peter Eckhorn of Hamburg's Top Ten Club was also in Liverpool trying to book the Beatles and offered them 200 marks each per week. The

Star Club upped this to 350 marks, but by the time Epstein had completed his negotiations for their first engagement to open the club from 13 April to 31 May, Manfred had upped his offer to 2,000 deutschmarks per week: 500 for each member!

For their debut, the posters displayed in Hamburg for several weeks prior to the engagement read:

Die Not hat ein ENDE!
Die Zeit der Dorfmusik ist vorbei!
Am Freitag, dem 13 April, eroffnet
STAR CLUB
die Rock 'n' Twist Parade 1962
mit The Beatles, Tex Roberg, Roy Young,
The Graduates, The Bachelors.
Zusatzlich ab Mai: Tony Sheridan Quartet
und Gerry And The Pacemakers.
Eine Ballung der Spitzenklasse Europas
Hmb: St. Pauli, Gr. Freiheit 39.

It was most unfortunate that the tragic news of Stuart Sutcliffe's death hit the Beatles immediately they arrived in April. But they had no alternative but to begin their first season at the club. During their seven-week stint they shared billing with two of their American rock 'n' roll heroes, Little Richard and Gene Vincent. The group were required to play for four hours on one evening, with an hour's break between each set, and three hours the following evening.

Their second engagement at the Star Club took place from 1 to 14 November later in 1962 and brought them 600 marks each per week and their third and final engagement, from 18–31 December, brought them 750 marks.

During their Christmas season, Adrian Barber, former member of Liverpool band the Big Three, who had become stage manager at the Star Club, experimented with a domestic tape recorder to check out the acoustics of the club. With a single mike fixed in the right spot he found he could get good results recording the Beatles on stage, complete with the dialogue between the group and the audience, the repartee, the jokes, and even a laugh and a bit of a song from Horst Fascher.

Adrian completed his recordings on 31 December 1962, New Year's Eve. He was approached by Ted Taylor, leader of Kingsize Taylor & the Dominoes, who asked him what he was going to do with the tapes. As Adrian had only recorded them for test purposes he told Taylor he could have them.

They were forgotten for many years until a Liverpool promotion in the mid-seventies in which Taylor was appearing. He mentioned the tapes to Allan Williams, who took them to Paul Murphy of Buk Records. As a result, fifteen years after Adrian's test recording, they emerged on a double album *The Beatles Live! At The Star Club In Hamburg, Germany: 1962*.

The Star Club had a number of flats in the Grosse Freiheit which Weissleder allowed the Beatles to live in, but told them, 'I always want you should enjoy yourselves in the Star Club, but if you make shit I send you home.' There were so many Liverpool bands appearing at the club over the next two years that there were signs declaring 'Uncle Manfred's Home For Lost Scousers'.

The original club closed down in June 1964, although there have been several attempts to revive it, most notably by Horst Fascher in the early seventies. The building was destroyed by fire in the eighties.

Starkey, Jason

The second son of Ringo and Maureen Starkey, born at Queen Charlotte's Hospital, London, on 19 August 1967.

Starkey, Lee Parkin

Ringo and Maureen's only daughter, born at Queen Charlotte's Hospital, London, on 11 November 1970. The name Parkin was the reintroduction of a former Starkey family name.

In her teens Lee went to acting school, but didn't like it and left. She next tried a make-up school, but although she received her diploma, said she didn't like it either. She became co-owner of a boutique in Portobello Road. When her mother Maureen married Isaac Tigrett and moved to live in Los Angeles, Lee talked her partner Christian Paris into relocating the shop in LA and they moved their Planet Alice boutique there in 1991 when Lee was twenty. At the official opening of the boutique, situated on Melrose Avenue, Maureen and Isaac and Ringo and Barbara (who had also settled in LA) were in attendance.

The psychedelic boutique had clothes which were in the sixties style and reminiscent of clothes from the original Apple Boutique. Lee became seriously ill and underwent a major operation on her brain but, fortunately, has regained her health.

Starkey, Richard

Father of Ringo Starr, originally a Liverpool dockworker and member of a large family. He had two brothers, Billy and Georgie, and three sisters, Angie, Lily and May. He later changed jobs and began to work in a bakery where he met Elsie Gleave. They were married in 1936 and initially moved in with Richard's parents who lived in the Dingle area of Liverpool. They then moved into a small two-storey terraced house in Madryn Street in the same area. Their son Richard, named after his father (a working class tradition of the time), was born in 1940.

Although Richard senior was called Dickie, it was decided to call Richard junior Richie. Dickie Starkey left the family home when Richie was three years old. There seemed to be no acrimony and the couple were divorced.

There were only a few brief occasions when Richie saw his father again, twice when he was a young child. Dickie had remained in Liverpool and still worked at the bakery and visited his son during one of his regular hospital confinements. He also met him at the Starkey parents' home in 1962.

Dickie remarried and moved from Liverpool to another town in the north-west of England. Little was heard of him until 1980 when the *Daily Express* ran him down and wrote a story on him. Now a window cleaner, he was to say about his son: 'He's done well, the lad, and good luck to him, but he owes me nothing.' Dickie also mentioned that the only item of Beatles memorabilia that he possessed was an autographed photograph.

Starkey, Zak

The eldest son of Richard and Maureen Cox, born on 13 September 1965 at Queen Charlotte's Hospital, London.

Since their first child was a boy, Ringo had the choice of name and decided on Zak, because it was what he wished he'd been called as a youth. He commented: 'Its' a nice strong name and it can't be shortened – that was something I didn't want at all.'

Although Ringo told the press, 'I won't let Zak be a drummer', he bought him a drum kit for his ninth birthday. He gave him only one lesson, when he was ten, telling him that as he'd been self-taught, Zak should simply listen to records and play along with them. However, he did hire a piano teacher for his son.

Zak was five years old when the Beatles split, but being the son of a famous father caused problems and he had a serious drinking difficulty by the age of fifteen. For a time, Ringo kicked him out of the family home, Tittenhurst Park.

The estrangement deepened when Ringo and Maureen divorced, as Zak blamed Ringo for the break-up of the marriage.

He was married himself on 24 January 1985, at the age of 19, to 25-year-old Sarah Menikides. The wedding was kept secret, even from his parents.

When Zak and Sarah had a baby daughter, Tatia Jayne, the

father and son relationship became close once again when Ringo saw his grand-daughter for the first time. Zak said: 'The look of joy on his face is one I'll never forget.' Tatia weighed 7lb 2oz at her birth on 7 September 1985.

Zak had a degree of success in his own right as a drummer, appearing in bands such as the Next, Nightfly and Ice, spending ten years as a session musician and also playing with artists such as Roger Daltrey and Bobby Womack. His major influence was Keith Moon, who bought him a drum kit for his birthday and encouraged him to play. Zak commented: 'My old man's a good timekeeper but I've never thought of him as a great drummer.'

He joined his father in the All Starr Band on world tours in 1992 and 1995 and for a time settled in Los Angeles, sharing a house with his brother and sister.

After his mother contracted leukaemia, he donated some of his bone marrow to save her, but she died as a result of the operation in December 1994.

In 1995, Zak moved back to England with his wife and daughter and, in September 1995, formed a band called Face with Ronnie Thomas, Gary Nuttall and Danny Burton.

Starline Club, Windsor Street, Liverpool L8

Premises of a former cinema, turned into a drinking club which had an extension of licence to sell alcohol during the afternoon. For a short period in 1961 the Beatles dropped into the club following some Cavern lunchtime sessions, for additional rehearsals. They also appeared at the club for some evening sessions.

Starr, Freddie

Mersey Beat musician who eventually became one of Britain's leading comedians. Born Freddie Fowell, he made his first public appearance in 1950 and in January 1961 joined Howie Casey and the Seniors, the first Mersey band to make a record in Britain.

They auditioned for Fontana, who suggested that they record some twist numbers, and the group was to record an entire album in one afternoon. Their debut single, 'Double Twist', was penned by Freddie and Derry Wilkie and Freddie penned the title track of their album *Twist at the Top*. Because they were let down financially by promoters, Derry Wilkie left the band and they broke up soon after, in the summer of 1962.

He originally considered going to Germany and just using his first name, but discovered there was already a successful singer in Germany called Freddie. He then thought of Ringo Starr and changed his name to Freddie Starr.

Freddie led the Ventures until November 1962, when he replaced Gus Travis as lead singer with the Midnighters. They appeared second on the bill to the Beatles at the Majestic Ballroom, Birkenhead on 31 January 1963 and twice with the Beatles at the Cavern in 1963: on Wednesday, 23 January and Tuesday 19 February.

The group also recorded three singles with Joe Meek, although they all failed to make any impact in the charts. Freddie was disenchanted with the records, as they weren't the type of material which suited him, and he called them 'commercial rubbish'. The three Decca releases were 'Who Told You?', 'Baby Blue' and 'Never Cry on Someone's Shoulder'.

Freddie was due to appear in the Lionel Bart/Alun Owen musical *Maggie May*, but it fell through and he teamed up with the Delmonts, in August 1963, mainly to appear in cabaret.

He then became a solo act, performing impressions and comedy. An appearance on 'Sunday Night at the London Palladium' established him as a leading comedian and he has steered himself through a controversial but successful career as a comic ever since.

Freddie did, however, finally have a hit record as a singer with 'It's You', which reached No. 9 in the British charts in February 1974.

Starr, Ringo

Richard Starkey was born in the front room of 9 Madryn Street in Liverpool's Dingle area on 7 July 1940 to Elsie and Richard Starkey. Father and son began to be referred to as Big Richie and Little Richie, although the marriage was soon to break up and the couple were divorced in 1943 when Elsie moved to nearby 10 Admiral Grove with her son. Richie attended St Silas Infants' School where he began to suffer the first of many illnesses which seriously affected his education.

At the age of six he was taken to the Royal Children's Infirmary in Myrtle Street suffering from acute abdominal pains. A ruptured appendix was diagnosed and this led to an inflamed peritoneum and the first of several operations for the youth. He went into a coma for two months, during which there were other operations, but he finally emerged from the coma, although he remained in hospital for several further months.

He returned to St Silas where his classmates included Billy Fury and Billy Hatton, then moved on to Dingle Vale Secondary Modern.

Elsie met and married a painter and decorator from Romford called Harry Graves, whom Richie referred to as his 'step ladder'.

In 1953, at the age of thirteen, Richie caught a cold which turned into chronic pleurisy necessitating another stay at Myrtle Street hospital. The illness caused some lung complications which resulted in the youth being sent to Heswall Children's Hospital in the Wirral, where he remained until 1955.

For a time he had a job as delivery boy for British Rail, which lasted only a few months as he failed the medical. He next took on a job as barman on a ferry to New Brighton for a short time before becoming a trainee joiner at Henry Hunt and Sons, along with his next door neighbour Eddie Miles. Early in 1957 Eddie and Richie formed the Eddie Clayton Skiffle Group with three other employees from Hunt's, and they made their debut at Peel Street Labour Club. Richie's stepfather Harry bought him a secondhand drum kit and the aspiring drummer soon changed outfits and became a member of the Darktown Skiffle Group, although he also sat in with other bands. In March 1959 he made his debut with Al Caldwell's Texans at the Mardi Gras Club in Mount Pleasant and decided to join the group, who were to change their name to Rory Storm & the Hurricanes. They secured a booking at the Cavern, which was strictly a jazz club at the time, using the name the Jazzmen, but were fined ten shillings by owner Ray McFall for playing 'Whole Lotta Shakin' Goin' On', because rock 'n' roll was not allowed to be played at the club at the time.

When the Hurricanes secured a summer season from July to September, at the Butlin's holiday camp in Pwllheli, Wales, performing in the Rock & Calypso Ballroom, they encouraged Richie to pack in his job at Hunt's. Rory Storm was a showman and he insisted that Richie add some colour to his act by renaming him Ringo Starr and introducing a solo spot called 'Ringo Starrtime', during which Richie, now named Ringo, sang numbers such as 'Boys' and 'You're Sixteen'.

The Hurricanes became one of the most popular groups on Merseyside and in October 1960 topped the bill at Hamburg's Kaiserkeller club, above the Beatles. They were also paid more money than the Beatles and could afford to stay at the Seamen's Mission. It was during their trip to Hamburg that the Beatles and members of Rory Storm & the Hurricanes recorded at the Akustik Studios, with a line-up comprising John Lennon, Paul McCartney, George Harrison, Ringo Starr and Lu Walters.

On their return to Liverpool the Hurricanes soon found that the Beatles, Gerry & the Pacemakers and other groups were now booked to headline over them. At one time, Ringo considered joining the Seniors, then decided to take up an offer to be part of Tony Sheridan's backing group at the Top Ten Club in Hamburg

and joined him there in January 1962. He returned to Liverpool to
take up the drum spot with the Hurricanes once more, but began to
feel at a loose end and even considered resuming his apprenticeship
at Hunt's. He also wrote to the Chamber of Commerce in Houston,
Texas, to enquire about the possibility of emigrating. He received
the necessary forms, but couldn't be bothered filling them in. He
also contemplated marriage to his girlfriend Maureen Cox.

While the Hurricanes were appearing for yet another summer
season at Butlin's, this time in Skegness, Ringo received a letter
from Kingsize Taylor offering him twenty pounds a week if he
would join them as a replacement for Dave Lovelady, who was
leaving the group to complete his studies. Ringo agreed to join him.
Then, one day, John Lennon and Paul McCartney turned up at the
camp and offered Ringo £25 a week if he'd join them. The extra
five pounds sealed it and Ringo agreed to become a Beatle as from
August 1962.

Much has been said about the musical prowess of the individual
drummers. Pete Best was noted as a top drummer in Liverpool and
the reasons for him being sacked are more likely to be based on the
fact that John, Paul and George simply didn't want him in the band
any more, rather than the oft-touted theory that he wasn't a good
enough drummer. The reason they offered the job to Ringo is also
more likely to be because they had played with him in Hamburg
and had become friendly with him and felt he would fit in with the
band. He certainly didn't have any major reputation as a drummer
on Merseyside, as has been suggested. If anyone was reckoned to be
Liverpool's top drummer, it was Johnny Hutchinson of the Big
Three. Incidentally, Hutchinson considered Best to be an excellent
drummer and Billy Kramer was also to comment, 'I didn't think the
Beatles were any better with Ringo Starr. I never doubted his ability
as a drummer but I thought they were a lot more raw and raucous
with Pete.' Locally, fans were calling Ringo 'The luckiest man in the
world'.

At the time, Ringo had a silver streak in his hair and a beard.
These went and he adopted the Beatles-style haircut and image.
When he arrived at Abbey Road Studios to record with the group
for the first time, the same thing happened to him as had happened
to Pete Best. George Martin said he'd prefer to engage a session
drummer and the 32-year-old Andy White was hired for the
session.

Ringo was given his own solo spot with the Beatles, the chance to
sing one song, as he'd done in the 'Ringo Starrtime' spot with Rory
Storm & the Hurricanes. Ringo was also to have his own vocal
numbers on the Beatles albums. They included 'Boys' on *Please*

Please Me, 'I Wanna Be Your Man' on *With The Beatles*, 'Honey Don't' on *Beatles For Sale*, 'Act Naturally' on *Help!*, 'What Goes On' on *Rubber Soul*, 'Yellow Submarine' on *Revolver*, 'With A Little Help From My Friends' on *Sgt Pepper's Lonely Hearts Club Band*, 'Don't Pass Me By' on *The Beatles*, and 'Octopus's Garden' on *Abbey Road*. There were only a handful of songs he performed on stage between 1962 and 1966: 'Boys', 'Honey Don't', 'I Wanna Be Your Man' and 'Act Naturally'.

As it turned out, Ringo was perfect for the Beatles and at one time was the most popular member of the group with American fans. He also proved to be more of a natural actor than any other member of the group and received favourable reviews for his performance in *A Hard Day's Night*. So much so, that he was put into the central position in their second film *Help!* Over the years, Ringo appeared in more films than any other member of the band. They included *Candy* (1968); *The Magic Christian* (1969); *Blindman* (1971); *200 Motels* (1971); *Born To Boogie* (1972); *Son Of Dracula* (1972); *That'll Be The Day* (1973); *Harry And Ringo's Night Out* (1974); *Lisztomania* (1975); *Sextette* (1978); *The Last Waltz* (1978); *The Kids Are Alright* (1979); *Caveman* (1981) and *Give My Regards To Broad Street* (1984).

Ringo married his long-time girlfriend Maureen Cox on 11 February 1965 and the couple were to have three children: Zak, Jason and Lee. The pair were eventually to divorce in July 1975 and Ringo was to marry Barbara Bach, his co-star in *Caveman*, on 27 April 1981.

Following the Beatles' break-up. Ringo had an initially successful solo recording career, although this faded slightly over the years.

Ringo was also to appear in various TV shows, including his own special, 'Ringo', and a TV mini-series 'Princess Daisy', with his wife Barbara.

After a number of years out of the limelight, during which he did voice-overs for the children's TV series 'Thomas The Tank Engine' and experienced drink problems, which resulted in himself and Barbara attending a drying out clinic, he reappeared on the scene with an All-Starr Band to tour America and Japan in 1989. This proved to be so successful that he formed another All-Starr Band in 1992, which began an American and European tour in June 1992. Members comprised his son Zak, guitarists Dave Edmunds, Nils Lofgren, Todd Rundgren and Joe Walsh, saxophonist Tim Cappello, bassist Timothy B. Schmit and keyboards player Burton Cummings.

Ringo continues to record and tour with various line-ups of the All-Starr Band.

St Barnabas Church Hall, Penny Lane, Liverpool L18

A church hall where the Quarry Men appeared early in their career. The venue is now called Dovedale Towers.

St Bridget's Church, Carrog, North Wales

Church where James McCartney married his second wife Angela Lucia Williams of Northwood, Kirby, on 24 November 1964.

Jim owned a house named Afon Rho in Carrog that fronted the River Dee.

The vicar of St Bridget's at the time was the Reverend D. J. Bevan, who was one time chaplain at Walton Hospital, Liverpool, where Paul was born and his mother Mary had been nursing sister.

The vicar and his wife were personal friends of the McCartney family.

On Friday, 7 June 1968, Peter Michael McCartney, then 24 years old, married 23-year-old hairdresser Angela Fishwick at the church.

Paul, who was best man, arrived at St Bridget's in his green Aston Martin D.B.6 just before 3.00 p.m. accompanied by his fiancée, Jane Asher. He stood out from the psychedelically dressed guests by wearing a plain dark suit, white shirt and carnation. Commenting on the presence of the press as well as almost the entire population of the village, the Rev Bevan said, 'We were all sworn to secrecy but somehow it leaked out this morning.'

St James' Church Hall, Gloucester Terrace, London W2

The Beatles performed at a lunchtime audition for BBC Television at this venue on 23 November 1962.

It was an audition they failed.

St James' Swimming Baths, St James Street, Doncaster, Yorkshire

The swimming baths in this Yorkshire town were occasionally used for dances, with the pool being covered over by boards. The Beatles made a single appearance at the venue on Wednesday, 20 February 1963.

St John's Hall, Snaefell Avenue, Tuebrook, Liverpool L13

After Pete Best joined the Beatles and following their return to Liverpool after their first Hamburg season, the group were unofficially managed by Pete's mother, Mrs Mona Best, who sought work for them at various local venues, in addition to her own Casbah Club. She also promoted independently under the name Casbah Promotions and first presented the Beatles at St John's Hall on Friday, 17 February 1961. The billing read: 'The Fabulous Beatles Rock Combo. Gene Day & the Jango Beats. 3/6d.' For the engagement she paid the Beatles a fee of twenty pounds, unusually high for a local group at the time.

Following their season at the Top Ten Club, Hamburg, from 27 March–2 July, Mrs Best gave the group their first booking on their return, at this venue on 13 July 1961.

Other gigs at the hall took place on 20 July, 27 July (also on the bill were the Big Three and Cilla Black), 3 August, 10 August, 17 August (Johnny Gustafson of the Big Three performed with the Beatles on this occasion), 24 August, 31 August and 8 September 1961.

St Paul's Presbyterian Church Youth Hall, North Road, Tranmere, Birkenhead, Liverpool L42

The Beatles appeared at this venue twice. The initial gig took place on 10 February 1962 and they returned exactly a month later on Saturday, 10 March. Also on the bill of their second show at the hall were the Country Four with Brian Newman. The dance began at 7.30 p.m. and lasted until 11.30 p.m. Tickets were five shillings each.

St Peter's Parish Church, Church Road, Woolton, Liverpool L25

Site of the historic occasion on Saturday, 6 July 1957 when John Lennon and Paul McCartney met for the first time.

The event was the annual summer fete and Pete Shotton's mum had secured a booking at the event for the Quarry Men.

The leaflets advertising the event read:

Woolton Parish Church

GARDEN FETE

And

Crowning of Rose Queen

Saturday, July 6th, 1957

To be opened at 3p.m. by Dr. Thelwall Jones

Procession at 2p.m.

Liverpool Police Dogs Display

Fancy Dress Parade

Sideshows Refreshments

Band Of The Cheshire Yeomanry

The Quarry Men Skiffle Group
Adults 6d. children 3d. Or by Programme
GRAND DANCE
At 8p.m. in the Church Hall
GEORGE EDWARDS' BAND
THE QUARRY MEN SKIFFLE GROUP
Tickets 2/-

The procession through the Woolton streets saw a mixed group, with the band of the Cheshire Yeomanry leading and the Quarry Men, perched on the back of a coal merchant's lorry, bringing up the rear. There were various floats containing Boy Scouts, Girl Guides and Brownies in between, together with the thirteen-year-old Rose Queen, Sally Wright.

The Quarry Men that day featured John Lennon, Eric Griffiths, Colin Hanton, Rod Davis, Pete Shotton and Len Garry while Geoff Rhind, a schoolboy with a Box Brownie, took a photograph of them for posterity.

As Ivan Vaughan wasn't playing tea-chest bass that day he'd invited along a friend from the Liverpool Institute, Paul McCartney, who cycled to the event.

During the Quarry Men's performance they played 'Baby Let's Play House', 'Maggie May', 'Cumberland Gap', 'Railroad Bill', 'Putting On the Style' and 'Come Go With Me'.

After they'd finished playing and took their gear over to the church hall where they were performing that evening, Ivan took the fifteen-year-old Paul across to meet them.

The young lad made an impression because he showed them how to tune a guitar, which none of the band could do. He particularly impressed John with his knowledge of the lyrics of rock 'n' roll songs and even wrote out the words of 'Twenty Flight Rock' and 'Be-Bop-A-Lula' for John. To cap it all, he borrowed a guitar and began to play some Little Richard numbers, including 'Long Tall Sally' and 'Tutti Frutti'.

Years later, Paul was to recall that John's breath smelled of beer, the result of several bottles of light ale he'd bought at a local off-licence.

St Silas Primary School, Pengwern Street, Liverpool L8

Ringo attended this school, which was only a hundred yards from his house, between the years 1945–50. It was a Church of England Primary School. On his first day, the five-year-old, returning home at noon, told his mother that he didn't have to go back in the afternoon – but his mother noticed other children returning to St Silas, and she made him return. His classmates included Ronald Wycherley, who was later to find fame as Billy Fury, and Billy Hatton, who became a member of the Fourmost. At the age of seven, Ritchie suffered appendicitis, which led to peritonitis and spent a year away from the school at the Royal Children's Hospital. On his return he was placed in a class with children a year his junior.

St Thomas' Hall, Keith, Banffshire, Scotland

One of the small venues where the Silver Beetles appeared during the short tour of Scotland promoted by Larry Parnes, on which they backed Liverpool singer Johnny Gentle. The group appeared at the hall on 25 May 1960.

Step Inside Love

The third song penned by Paul McCartney which Cilla Black recorded. The others were 'Love Of The Loved' and 'It's For You'.

Paul composed the number for Cilla's 1968 television show 'Cilla', and recorded an acoustic version of the number as a demo for her. George Martin recorded the number and it was issued in Britain on Parlophone R 5674 on 8 May 1968 and in America on Bell 726 on 6 May. It reached No. 8 in the British charts but failed to make any impact in the States.

Steppin' Out

The Beatles made a single appearance on this half-hour BBC radio programme broadcast each Monday from 10.00 a.m. It was presented by Diz Disley and produced by Terry Henebery.

The group appeared on 3 June 1963 and performed 'Please Please Me', 'I Saw Her Standing There', 'Roll Over Beethoven', 'Thank You Girl' and 'From Me To You'. They also recorded 'Twist And Shout', but it was not transmitted.

Sterner, Georg

A German waiter who acted as Bruno Koschmider's interpreter when the promoter came to England looking for bands. Sterner was to return to Germany to work for Koschmider in the Kaiserkeller and Allan Williams offered to give him a lift.

Sterner had been working at the Heaven and Hell coffee bar in London and he joined the minibus containing Allan and his wife Beryl, her brother Barry Chang, Lord Woodbine and John, Paul, George, Pete and Stuart on their journey to Hamburg.

The Beatles had considered him a friend, but discovered that he was Koschmider's 'spy' and reported on them. One day when they were rehearsing at the club and had two girl fans with them, Sterner was offensive to the girls and hit one of them. Pete Best knocked him to the floor. As a result Koschmider fined Pete five pounds for hitting Sterner and also charged the others five pounds each for allowing it to happen. It was also Sterner who told Koschmider that the group were going to play at the rival Top Ten Club.

Stigwood, Robert

An Australian impresario who arrived in Britain at the onset of the sixties and initially became successful managing singers such as John Leyton and Mike Sarne. He also managed comedian Frankie Howerd and scriptwriters Ray Galton and Alan Simpson. He was to experience financial difficulties and at one point decided to liquidate his company. A few days before the liquidation he borrowed £10,000 from EMI. Sir Joseph Lockwood considered that Stigwood knew that the money would never be paid back and refused to allow EMI to do any further business with him.

Stigwood then formed the Robert Stigwood Organisation with David Shaw, a financial adviser.

Brian Epstein became acquainted with the 32-year-old impresario at a Saturday night party held at the Waldon Court flat Stigwood shared with Chris Stamp. Epstein then began a series of discussions with him regarding a merger of their two companies.

Brian told Stigwood that he was becoming disenchanted with the business, that he felt control slipping away from him. He said that the pressure was becoming too much and he wanted to retire to Spain and manage bullfighters.

Initially, Stigwood wanted to buy NEMS, but Brian ended up buying the Robert Stigwood Organisation in a deal which made Stigwood Joint Managing Director of NEMS, with Vic Lewis, while Epstein would remain as Chairman, personally looking after the Beatles and Cilla Black.

As far as Brian was concerned, Stigwood and Shaw could have the rest. Brian had been offered twenty million dollars only two years previously for his organisation (although this included the Beatles and Cilla), yet he offered Stigwood and Shaw a 51 per cent controlling interest in NEMS for only £500,000. He gave them a deadline of raising the cash by May 1967. When the date passed, there was a verbal agreement to extend the offer until September – by which time Brian had died. Although negotiations had been going on for three months, the merger was not officially announced until 13 January 1967.

The announcement surprised a number of people as Epstein had considered and rejected mergers with Bernard Delfont, Tito Burns and Danny Betesh, all of whom had a bigger reputation in the industry than Stigwood and Shaw.

Stigwood moved into NEMS' Argyll Street offices and there was immediate internecine warfare between the camps.

Vic Lewis' people didn't get on with Stigwood's, and neither did the original NEMS staff. Geoffrey Ellis commented: 'He could be an absolute bastard. The longer I stayed at NEMS, the less friendly I became with him.' Long-time members of NEMS such as Alistair Taylor found themselves being given conflicting assignments by Epstein and Stigwood and the NEMS people regarded Stigwood as an autocrat.

Among the acts which Stigwood brought under the NEMS umbrella were Cream, the Moody Blues, Jimi Hendrix, the Who, Screaming Lord Sutch, Crispian St Peters and Oscar.

When he had settled in at NEMS, a group arrived at the offices to see Brian. They were referred to Stigwood, who was now responsible for signing new acts to the company. They were called the Bee Gees and Stigwood immediately signed them. Soon, much to Brian's annoyance, he began proclaiming that they would be bigger than the Beatles. He took them to New York to launch them in America, renting a yacht for them for an all-day promotion. When Epstein heard of it, he cancelled it, saying, 'The Bee Gees can charter a yacht when they've earned a million dollars. Until then they should be out playing.'

When Epstein died, Stigwood and Shaw began to plan raising the £500,000 to buy the option on NEMS, but the Beatles told him directly that they did not wish to have anything to do with their management. Clive Epstein, who had now been appointed Chairman, also suggested that Stigwood should split from NEMS with all his artists and a substantial amount in severance pay (a figure of £25,000 has been quoted). Under the circumstances, Stigwood decided not to exercise his option, and on 8 December 1967 Stigwood and Shaw resigned their directorships.

The Bee Gees went on to become a supergroup and Stigwood's empire became hugely successful. He was to employ former NEMS staffers such as Peter Brown and he moved to America and produced the hit movie musicals *Saturday Night Fever* and *Grease*.

He also produced a number of Beatles-associated ventures. In 1974 he produced a Broadway musical *Sgt Pepper's Lonely Hearts Club Band*, in 1975 he produced the West End stage musical *John, Paul, George, Ringo and Bert* and in 1978 he produced the movie musical *Sgt Pepper's Lonely Hearts Club Band*.

Stockton Wood Road Primary School, Stockton Wood Road, Speke, Liverpool L24

A large primary school built in the Speke area of Liverpool after World War II.

It was close to where Paul McCartney and his younger brother Mike lived at the time and was the first primary school they attended. Within a short time it had taken in so many pupils that, at over 1,500, it had the largest primary school enrolment in Britain. Due to the overcrowding, caused by the post-war 'baby boom', Paul and Mike were moved to the Joseph Williams Primary School.

Stowe School, Stowe, Buckinghamshire

A British public boarding school on 750 acres of lush land in Buckinghamshire which was the site of an unusual gig for the Beatles on Thursday, 4 April 1963. It was unusual because instead of performing before an audience of screaming teenage girls, the group took the stage before an all-male audience of schoolboys who sat politely in their seats and listened quietly to the music throughout the show.

In January a boy from Liverpool, David Moores, who was a pupil at the school, wrote to Brian Epstein with a booking request. David offered a fee of £100 and Brian accepted. In his correspondence with Moores he wrote to say: 'It would be a great pleasure for the boys to appear at Stowe ... There are four Beatles, a road manager and myself ... With regard to the lighting I will arrange that with those concerned more or less immediately before the performance ... I am delighted that you are arranging a meal for us after the performance ... Is there a good hotel in the district?'

The group performed in the school's Roxburgh Hall and one of the students recorded the entire show on his domestic tape recorder.

After their performance the Beatles mingled with students in the assembly hall, then had their meal and visited the headmaster's study.

Incidentally, David Moores went on to become owner and chairman of Liverpool FC.

Strach, Doctor Walter

The man the Beatles called 'Uncle Walter'.

The Czech financial wizard worked in the offices of Bryce, Hanmer and Isherwood, a Liverpool firm of accountants who had offices in Albemarle Street, London. When Brian Epstein moved his organisation to London he appointed the firm to handle the Beatles' finances and Strach was placed in charge of their account – initially he was given the task of finding the individual group members new premises to live in during 1963.

A senior partner in the firm, Strach immediately began to sort out the Beatles' tax difficulties and formed a limited company for them in which he was Treasurer and Secretary.

'Uncle Walter' lived in Weybridge and suggested it was an ideal place for the Beatles to live. John and Ringo settled there, but George bought a bungalow in Esher and Paul preferred to live in central London.

Walter advised them on their personal investments and when the four wanted to put money into John Bloom's washing machine company he talked them out of it. In 1965 he suggested that their profits from the film *Help!* be placed into Cavalcade Productions, a Bahamian company formed by the Beatles and Walter Shenson and administered by Strach. Unfortunately, it didn't make a profit for them. When sterling was devalued in 1967 it suffered an £8,000 loss.

Incidentally, Strach also had a home in the Bahamas where he invited George and Pattie to spend a holiday in December 1964.

Stramscact

The name of the merchandising company, established in Britain late in 1963 by Nicholas Byrne and five partners to sell licences for Beatles product.

The deal, arranged by Brian Epstein's lawyer, did not prove advantageous to the Beatles and was to result in them losing what was probably the greatest merchandising opportunity of the sixties at the height of the American Beatlemania of 1964!

Merchandising was modest in Britain for Stramscact, compared to the vast profits to be made in the United States and the American arm of the company was called Seltaeb.

Strangers, The

A popular Liverpool band who were placed No. 8 in the first *Mersey Beat* popularity poll. They were also one of the groups featured on the front cover of *Mersey Beat*.

The group never made the big time and never even succeeded in cutting a record.

They appeared with the Beatles for the first time at Aintree Institute on one of the Friday night 'Battle Of The Groups!' promotions. Bob Wooler advertised the event in the Liverpool Echo:

'Beatles Vs Strangers
Referee: Bob Wooler
Never before have these two great groups appeared together.'

Both bands were to appear on further bills together on Mersey venues, but the Strangers' fame never spread outside the Merseyside area.

Lead singer Joe Fagin became a popular solo singer and reached No. 3 in the British charts in January 1984 with 'That's Livin' Alright'.

He also charted with 'Back With The Boys Again' in 1986.

Stratton Smith, Tony

A journalist and author whom Brian Epstein originally approached to ghost his biography *A Cellarful Of Noise*. Stratton spent a number of days in Holland discussing the project with Brian, but eventually turned it down.

His meetings with Epstein inspired him to become a pop group manager and in 1965 he signed up his first act – Paddy, Klaus & Gibson. This trio comprised two Liverpudlians and the Beatles' old friend from Hamburg, Klaus Voormann. They had been managed by Don Paul, former member of the vocal group the Viscounts, and Tony took up a co-management deal and immediately booked the group a residency at London's fashionable Pickwick Club.

John Lennon and George Harrison pestered Epstein into taking over the group and a reluctant Stratton Smith had to agree to the transfer. He felt that NEMS failed to develop the group.

His next signing was another Liverpool singer, Beryl Marsden, who was to appear with the Beatles on tour. Unfortunately, Beryl proved almost impossible to manage, failing to turn up to gigs and turning her back on opportunities which would have furthered her career.

Stratton Smith also spent a great deal of time and effort on the Koobas, another Liverpool band, who also appeared on tour with the Beatles. They had minor success, but eventually disbanded.

For a time Stratton Smith returned to writing, but then entered the management field again with Nice, formed Charisma Records and enjoyed tremendous success until his death from cancer in 1987. He was 53 years old.

Strawberry Fields Forever

A song which, on several occasions, John Lennon pointed out as being his best Beatles song.

Strawberry Fields is a real place, a children's community home run by the Salvation Army at Beaconsfield Road, Woolton, Liverpool L25 6LJ. It is very close to where John lived as a child and he often used to wander in Strawberry Fields and attended summer fetes in its grounds.

The home now has a special unit called Lennon Court which can accommodate four children.

In 1966 both John and Paul wrote songs about Liverpool for a proposed new album and 'Strawberry Fields Forever' was the first number written for it. That particular album project was abandoned in favour of *Sgt Pepper's Lonely Hearts Club Band* and the two Liverpool songs were issued as a single.

Recording began on Thursday, 24 November 1966, and a number of interesting recording techniques were used, including vari-speed, tapes played backwards and the ADT (Artificial Double Tracking Device).

John had originally played the number to George Martin on an acoustic guitar. A week after the original recording sessions John approached Martin and said he'd like another crack at recording it. Martin suggested including cellos and trumpets and on Thursday, 15 December, he overdubbed the instruments, with Tony Fisher, Greg Bowen, Derek Watkins and Stanley Roderick on trumpets and John Hall, Derek Simpson and Norman Jones on cellos.

Further discussions revealed that John liked the two versions and he asked Martin to join up the beginning of the first one to the end of the second one. Initially, George thought it was virtually impossible as they were in different keys and tempos, but he was able to work it out to the satisfaction of all.

The number was issued in Britain as the flipside of Paul's 'Penny Lane' on Parlophone R5570 on 17 February 1967. It reached No. 2 in the charts, but was held off the top position by Engelbert Humperdinck's 'Release Me', becoming the first Beatles single since 'Love Me Do' not to reach the top of the British charts.

It was issued in America on Capitol 5810 on 13 February 1967 with advance orders of over a million copies – and it reached No. 1 in the US charts.

The number was included on *The Beatles 1967–1970* compilation and on the *Magical Mystery Tour* album. A version of the number opened Disc Two of the Beatles' *Anthology 2* CDs.

Subscription Rooms, Stroud, Gloucestershire

The Beatles' first venture into the south of England under Epstein's management, which took place on Sunday, 31 March 1962.

The engagement was booked through the Cana Variety Agency and the group were advertised as 'Liverpool's top vocal and instrumental group – stars of Polydor Records – the sensational Beatles'. The Rebel Rousers, who had formed the previous year, were also on the same bill.

The Beatles returned to the venue for their second and final appearance there on 1 September 1962.

Suffolk Downs Racetrack, Waldemar Avenue, East Boston, Massachusetts

One of the most unusual venues the Beatles were to appear in during their 1966 tour of North America.

They appeared for one show only at the racecourse on Thursday, 18 August. The event, which was promoted by Frank Connelly Productions, began at 8.30 p.m. 25,000 people were able to watch the group from the stands. A special stage had been constructed in the centre of the track and 100 labourers had worked throughout the day and night putting in 13,000 chairs.

The Beatles performed for thirty minutes wearing forest green trousers, jackets trimmed with emerald satin buttons and labels, with chartreuse pin-striped shirts with large floppy collars.

During the final number a youth managed to get on stage and touch both John and Paul before two bodyguards grabbed him. In the audience was Joseph Kennedy, the thirteen-year-old son of Senator Robert Kennedy, accompanied by 34 friends.

Sullivan, Ed

For over a quarter of a century Ed Sullivan hosted one of America's most popular TV entertainment shows and received his biggest-ever ratings when the Beatles made their debut.

In the 1920s Sullivan was sports editor of a New York newspaper called the *Evening Graphic*. In 1930 he was given the opportunity of hosting his own radio programme, for which he received $100 a week. By 1932 he was hosting a programme for CBS called 'Ed Sullivan Entertains'. At the same time he was acting as a Broadway columnist and as MC to dinners and shows.

One of these dinners, the Harvest Moon Ball, was televised on 3 September 1947. The show was seen by Worthington Miner, the Director of Programme Developments for CBS Television, and he thought that Sullivan would be an ideal host for a TV series. It was called 'The Toast Of The Town' and made its debut on 20 June 1948.

For the next 25 years, Sullivan hosted a prime-time Sunday evening show in which his guests included senators, variety acts, sports stars, astronauts, opera singers, Hollywood actors and rock stars. His show was considered so important that many star names made their actual television debut on it, including Bob Hope, Louis Armstrong, Humphrey Bogart, Walt Disney, Clark Gable, Grace Kelly, Fred Astaire, Margot Fonteyn, James Cagney, Julie Andrews, Lena Horne, Charles Laughton and Yul Brynner.

His biggest-rating show in the fifties took place in 1956 when he booked Elvis for the programme. However, he told his cameramen to photograph Elvis only from the waist up, commenting, 'We had a lot of Lutherans, a lot of clergy and nuns in our viewing audience. It was a Sunday night show.'

On 31 October 1963, Sullivan was at London Airport. It was when the Beatles were returning from their Swedish tour and the roof of the Queens Building was packed with screaming fans. Sullivan said, 'My wife Sylvia and I were in London, at Heathrow Airport. There was the biggest crowd I've ever seen in my life! I asked someone what was going on, and he said, "The Beatles." "Who the hell are the Beatles?" I asked. But I went back to my hotel, got the name of their manager, and arranged for them to do three shows.

'When we got home, I found out that apparently Sylvia and I were the only people in the country who'd even heard of the Beatles. I was very worried. But just one week before they arrived, their song "I Wanna Hold Your Hand" became a big hit, and on the night of their first show – 9 February 1964 – they were so popular that people all over the country were having dinner parties to watch them.'

Brian Epstein arrived in New York and checked into the Regency Hotel on 11 November 1963 and met with Sullivan several times in his office at Suite 1102 in the Delmonico Hotel.

He made a deal with Bob Precht, Sullivan's son-in-law and the show's producer. The usual payment for a star for one appearance on the show was $7,500. The deal for the Beatles was for $10,000 for three shows; $3,500 each for two live shows and $3,000 for one taped show. After the deal had been done, Precht was worried because the group were unknown in America. He phoned Sullivan to tell him of his reservations but Sullivan said, 'I think they're worth the investment.'

On the show itself, Sullivan read out a telegram from Elvis, sent by Colonel Parker, and told the kids in the audience to pay respectful attention to the other performers, adding, 'And if you don't, I'll call a barber ...' After the first commercial break, Sullivan appeared again and said, 'Our city – indeed the country – has never seen anything like these four young men from Liverpool. Ladies and gentlemen, the Beatles.'

The Beatles appeared on stage for a total of thirteen and a half minutes. Ray Block, musical director for the 'Ed Sullivan Show', was to comment, 'The only thing that's different is the hair, as far as I can see. I give them a year.'

During that initial show on 9 February, they appeared on the first half performing 'All My Loving', 'Till There Was You' and 'She

Loves You' and reappeared in the second half to sing 'I Saw Her Standing There' and 'I Want To Hold Your Hand'.

Their next Sullivan appearance was telecast from the Deauville Hotel, Miami Beach, Florida, on 16 February 1963.

During the first half they performed 'She Loves You', 'This Boy', 'All My Loving' and in the second half, 'I Saw Her Standing There', 'From Me To You' and 'I Want To Hold Your Hand'.

Their third appearance was a segment they'd prerecorded before they left America and it was screened on 23 February 1964. The group performed 'Twist And Shout', 'Please Please Me' and 'I Want To Hold Your Hand'.

Their appearance on 24 May 1964 was filmed in London during the making of *A Hard Day's Night*. They were in a special segment of the show and were seen performing 'You Can't Do That'.

Their 23 February 1964 show was repeated on 23 August 1964 and their 9 February 1964 show was repeated on 20 September 1964.

The group taped another appearance before a live audience at the CBS Studios in New York on 14 August 1965 and it was broadcast on 12 September 1965. The group performed 'I Feel Fine', 'I'm Down', 'Help!', 'Yesterday', 'Act Naturally' and 'Ticket To Ride'.

On 5 June 1966 the promotional films of 'Rain' and 'Paperback Writer' were screened on the show.

On 12 February 1967 'The Ed Sullivan Show' presented the two promotional films directed by Peter Goldmann, 'Penny Lane' and 'Strawberry Fields Forever'.

Their performance of 'Hello Goodbye', which they'd filmed on stage at the Saville Theatre in London, was screened on the programme on 26 November 1967 and on 15 February 1970 there was a filmed segment of the group performing 'Two Of Us', from the filming of *Let It Be*, which had been taken from an hour-long TV special 'Salute To The Beatles'.

Following the success of the Beatles' appearances, Sullivan continued to provide a showcase for rock acts. The British stars who appeared on 'The Ed Sullivan Show' included Gerry & the Pacemakers, the Searchers, Billy J. Kramer and the Dakotas, Cilla Black, the Dave Clark Five, the Animals, the Rolling Stones, the Bachelors, Peter & Gordon, Freddie & the Dreamers and Herman's Hermits.

Despite the fact that it still had high ratings, CBS cancelled 'The Ed Sullivan Show' because they wanted to modernise their schedule and it eventually went off the air on 6 June 1971. Sullivan died on 13 October 1974.

Summertime

The famous George Gershwin standard. Several Liverpool bands played the number and various rock 'n' roll artists had turned to evergreen standards for inspiration, such as Gene Vincent with 'Over The Rainbow'. 'Summertime' had been recorded by Sam Cooke in 1957 and Ray Charles in 1958; either of the two is likely to have influenced the Beatles in their selection of the number, which was introduced into their repertoire in their Quarry Men days.

Sun King

Number penned by John and included on the *Abbey Road* album.

His original title was '*Los Paranois*', probably because of the pieces of nonsense in Spanish and Italian at the end of the song.

When the Beatles began recording the number on Thursday, 24 July 1969, the working title had been changed to 'Here Comes The Sun King', although *Abbey Road* also contains a George Harrison composition called 'Here Comes The Sun'. A variety of unusual sounds were used including cowbells.

Sunny Heights, St George's Road, Weybridge, Surrey

The estate which Ringo bought following his marriage to Maureen in 1965 on the advice of Walter Stracht. The property cost £37,000 and Ringo spent a further £40,000 on improvements and additions to the Tudor-style mansion, which had large gardens overlooking St George's Hill golf course.

Situated in the stockbroker belt of Weybridge, which became known as the 'Beatle Belt', Sunny Heights was home to the Starrs for three years. It had no swimming pool, but there was a little bar called 'The Flying Cow' and a cowboy holster presented to Ringo by Elvis Presley was displayed there.

The garage housed three cars – a Mini Cooper, a Facel Voga and a Land Rover – and in the gardens there was a playhouse in a tree.

The pets at Sunny Heights included two Airedale dogs, Daisy and Donovan, a white poodle called Tiger and nine cats!

When John Lennon eventually left for America, Ringo purchased Tittenhurst Park in Ascot from him for a reported fee of £2,000,000.

Sure To Fall (In Love With You)

A number which Carl Perkins recorded for Sun Records in January 1956.

The Quarry Men included it in their repertoire, with Paul McCartney on lead vocals and continued to perform it when they became the Beatles, until late in 1962. It is also one of the numbers the group recorded during their audition for Decca Records. A version of the number was included on *The Beatles Live At The BBC* CD.

Sutcliffe, Millie

Scots-born mother of Stuart Sutcliffe. Her husband Charles was a merchant seaman who, as a second engineer, spent a great deal of time at sea. The couple had three children, Stuart and two daughters, Joyce and Pauline.

The family moved to Liverpool and settled at 37 Aigburth Drive. Millie worked as a teacher at a local school for the blind and helped to support Stuart when he was studying at Liverpool College of Art. She had a very close relationship with her son and a strong belief in his talent as an artist.

After Stuart had left the Beatles and settled in Hamburg, she received a call from Rod Murray, who had shared a flat in Gambier Terrace with Stuart and John Lennon. He told her that he could no longer afford the premises now that the other two had left and that they hadn't paid up their share of the rent. She paid Stuart's share to Rod and hired a van to collect his belongings, including a camp bed which he'd slept on.

She said that many people were to claim that Stuart had slept in a coffin – but that was nonsense, it was definitely a camp bed. She also took with her a chest of drawers full of Lennon's clothes, which she stored for a while in Aigburth until her husband returned home from sea and threw them all out.

She was in constant touch with Stuart in Germany and began to tell her friends that she was worried because Stuart had fallen down the steps leading from the attic where he lived in Astrid Kirchherr's house. He'd struck his head and had begun to experience a series of headaches which continued to worsen, at times inducing a temporary blindness.

Prior to the fall there had been no instances of Stuart suffering from headaches and until her death in 1985, Mrs Sutcliffe was convinced that the fall down the attic steps was the cause of her son's death.

When Stuart died on 10 April Astrid sent Millie two telegrams, one saying that he was very ill, the other that he had died. However, she received them out of sequence. She flew to Hamburg and brought her son's body home to Liverpool.

Aware of how close Stuart was to John, she was surprised that

John never attended the funeral. She was even more disappointed when, after arranging for a posthumous exhibition of Stuart's work at the Walker Art Gallery in Liverpool, none of the Beatles agreed to attend. This was probably not a snub on their part as they'd booked holidays at the time.

She never heard from John again until Sunday, 8 November 1964. The Beatles were appearing at the Empire Theatre, Liverpool and Bill and Virginia Harry were backstage and suggested to John that they drop in on Millie Sutcliffe.

Together with Pete Shotton and his wife they all went up to Aigburth Drive and Millie was thrilled. She gave John a clipping of one of their first-ever write-ups, headed ' "Rock" group at Neston Institute', a book *How To Draw Horses* which John had won as a prize at school many years before and had lent to Stuart. She then took them round the rooms where Stuart's paintings were displayed and John remembered a number of them. She then invited John and Bill Harry to take their pick of any work of Stuart's they wanted. John picked a blue abstract oil painting and said, 'This will take pride of place in my living room.'

Mrs Sutcliffe decided to devote the rest of her life to promoting Stuart's work and arranged a further exhibition of his work in London. After the death of her husband, when her daughters had grown up and left home, she went to live in Sevenoaks, Kent, where she died before discovering the rising interest in her son's body of artwork.

Sutcliffe, Stuart

The original 'Fifth Beatle' was born Stuart Fergusson Victor Sutcliffe in Edinburgh on 23 June 1940. His father, Charles, was a seaman, his mother, Millie, a teacher and he had two younger sisters, Joyce and Pauline.

When the family moved to Merseyside, settling at 37 Aigburth Drive, Stuart attended Prescot Grammar School and later attended Liverpool College of Art. He immediately displayed a talent which impressed teachers and students alike, with some tutors stating that he was the most brilliant artist the college had produced.

Although on a different course, Bill Harry sought him out and they became friends. They also made friends with John Lennon, from a different class from either of them and, together with other students such as Rod Murray, they would spend a great deal of their spare time together in the local pub Ye Cracke and at student flats in the area.

Stuart was slight, small and introvert. He and Harry used to talk about literature, art, films and mystical philosophy. Popular books at the time were Colin Wilson's *The Outsider* and J. D. Salinger's *The Catcher In The Rye*. They also obtained copies of books by San Francisco Beat poets, published by the City Lights Bookshop, and copies of books from the Olympia Press in Paris. Harry was in charge of the art college film society and he mostly booked foreign films such as *L'Age d'Or* and *Un Chien Andalou*. Andrzej Wajda's films were also popular and a cult figure to some of the students was Zbigniew Cybulski. He particularly impressed Stuart, who tried to affect his look by wearing dark-tinted glasses like the star who had come to be called 'the Polish James Dean'.

In later years, Beatles biographers pointed out that Stuart tried to look like James Dean. They were wrong. He wasn't interested in Dean, the influence came from Cybulski. Stuart's knowledge of art was extensive and although his later work turned to the abstract, his initial college work was heavily under the influence of Vincent Van Gogh, the most popular artist with the students there.

At Stuart's flat in Percy Street, Harry and Stuart used to discuss the type of philosophy which seeks to explore the meaning of existence – mysticism, talking about what the future could hold and, in particular, how they could capture their own background and experience in their art. These were the sort of discussions they used to continue at Ye Cracke with John and Rod.

The college and the Liverpool Institute were one building and Paul McCartney and George Harrison were students at the Institute. During their breaks they'd frequent the college canteen or rehearse in the life rooms. John felt that his group needed a bass guitarist and he separately approached both Stuart and Rod offering them the job if they could get a bass guitar.

By this time John, Rod and Stuart were sharing a flat in Gambier Terrace. A painting by Stuart was entered into the John Moores Exhibition at the Walker Art Gallery and was bought by millionaire Moores himself, which enabled Stuart to buy a Hofner President bass guitar. But he didn't know how to play it. Another student at the college, David May, offered to teach him to play 'C'mon Everybody' if Stuart would let him measure his guitar, which would enable David to build one of his own.

As the group played at the Saturday evening dances in the college canteen, they were regarded as the college band. However, not having much money they couldn't afford a PA system. Stuart and Harry were both members of the Students' Union Committee and they proposed and seconded the motion that the Union should advance funds to the group to enable them to buy an amplifier which they could use, not only at the school dances, but wherever they played.

When Stuart joined John's group, Harry advised him against it because he applied the same dedicated enthusiasm to it that he had displayed towards his art and Harry thought that his art would suffer. John was often cruelly sarcastic to Stuart, even though he had become his closest friend, and he received general abuse from the band at this time, who didn't take him seriously. John referred to this by saying, 'We'd tell Stu he couldn't sit with us, or eat with us. We'd tell him to go away, and he did.' John and Paul generally made fun of Stuart on stage throughout his entire period with the band.

It was obvious that Stuart would never be as good a musician as he was an artist. He did, however, bring something intangible to the group, a touch of style. Stuart had an artistic sense which also displayed itself in the way he looked and how he dressed. Despite his slight stature and the fact that he was an introvert, he drew people to him: Arthur Ballard, a college tutor, used to spend a great deal of time giving him extra tuition outside college hours; Allan Williams, who ran the coffee bar the Jacaranda, which they attended, was impressed by Stuart's quiet personality, intelligence and talent. He asked him to paint a mural in the club, which he did, with the help of Rod Murray. When Williams co-promoted the Liverpool Stadium concert headlined by Gene Vincent, it was Stuart who asked him why he hadn't booked the group. Williams liked Stuart and short-listed them for the auditions to be held for Larry Parnes and Billy Fury at the Wyvern Club. At the auditions Stuart is reputed to have played with his back to Parnes causing many writers to say that this prevented the group being booked as Billy Fury's backing band. Parnes himself disputes this and says he had no objections to Stuart – it was the age and appearance of drummer Tommy Moore which put him off. The audition resulted in the band being booked to back Johnny Gentle on a tour of Scotland and Stuart chose to use the stage name Stu Da Stael in deference to a Russian artist he admired.

Stuart didn't have any real musical contribution to make to the group, and his main spotlight was when he took over on lead vocal on the Elvis Presley hit 'Love Me Tender'. Yet he gave the group an added dimension with his aura of mystery, brooding good looks and intelligence. It was Stuart who suggested that they call them-selves Beetles, although John replaced one of the 'e's' with an 'a'. It was said that Stuart had thought of the name because it was similar to that of Buddy Holly's backing group the Crickets. His mother thought it was because he was often called a Beatnik, because he wore very tight jeans, winklepickers and at one time had a goatee beard. She was also to comment at one time, 'Stuart's influence on them has been played down as if he was not a potent member of the formation. At the time I was amazed that he was going around with them and threatened to withdraw my financial support. I thought I was doing my duty, but he started buying paints rather than food. Stuart went around like an orphan of the storm. So I relented and agreed to come and see his group.

'John knew I was coming, the others didn't. Harrison spotted me and said, "Stuart, your Mum's here." They thought I'd come to create a scene. But it was a pleasant surprise. I thought their music was out of this world. Afterwards, Stuart said, "What did you think of it, mother?" I couldn't express the feeling of pleasure the music gave me.'

Millie believed that Stuart's influence on their image was an important one: the leather look, the original Beatle haircut, even the collarless suit were all a product of Stuart's influence, she claims. 'I remember when Stuart had the black leather suit and Astrid was wearing it all the time. In fact, Astrid liked it so much that Stuart hardly had a chance to wear it at all. As for the Cardin suit, Stuart had it on the very last time he came home. It was a velvet Cardin suit. He took his sister Pauline down to the Cavern to see John and the next day Pauline said to me, "Those Beatles hate Stuart, especially Paul McCartney."

'They were saying, "Oh, you're wearing your sister's suit, Stuart", mocking the suit the way they mocked his Beatle haircut. They always made Stuart out as a softie, but it was the other way around. Stuart had a strong character and in the important things John abided by what Stuart said. As for the haircut, it started when Stuart's hair was falling down and sticking out. One night Astrid had been moaning about his hair and then took him into the bathroom and cut it. He told me, "They [the Beatles] laughed at it. I defied them and kept it that way." '

In May 1960 Williams started booking the group at the Jacaranda and then offered them the opportunity of performing in Germany.

After they arrived in Hamburg and were discovered by the young Hamburg students who included Astrid Kirchherr, Stuart's days with the group were numbered. For one thing, Paul wanted him out. He wanted to take over on bass guitar himself. This led to tension between them which manifested itself in a physical fight in which the more powerful Paul grappled with Stuart on stage at the Top Ten Club, much to the delight of the customers, who thought it was part of the show. The 'Exis' were attracted more to Stuart than to any other member of the group – he had a particular charismatic appeal which drew them to him. Astrid fell in love with Stuart and she arranged for Stuart to lodge in the attic flat at her home in the Hamburg suburb of Altona.

When the Beatles returned to Liverpool in December 1961, Stuart remained in Hamburg. For a few gigs they had to get Chas Newby in as a replacement. When he left to return to college, John asked George to play bass. George refused and John asked Paul. Paul began to play his Lucky 7 upside down and backwards with piano strings on it. George wrote to Stuart: 'Come home sooner, as if we get a new bass player for the time being, it will be crumby, as he will have to learn everything. It's no good with Paul, playing bass, we've decided, that is if he had some kind of bass and amp to play on!'

Talking about Stuart, Astrid was to comment: 'If he wasn't painting, he was writing or playing the guitar. He used to spend hours writing letters to John in Liverpool. He'd put down all his feelings, all his experiences, even put in illustrations and pages of poetry. These letters used to run to twenty pages or so. And John's were just as long and deep.'

Stuart was to play some further gigs with the group when they returned to appear at the Top Ten Club in March 1961, but his days as a Beatle were drawing to a close. Paul now wanted to take over as bass guitarist and when they received an offer to back Tony Sheridan on record, he insisted that he play bass on the recordings.

Stuart had also returned to his first love, art, and had managed to secure a place at an art college in Hamburg. Two of his German friends, who were also artists, recommended that he seek a place at the State High School of Art Instruction in Hamburg. For a while he worked in Gustal Seitz's Sculpture Department until the official authority came through for him to commence work under Eduardo Paolozzi, who had arranged for Stuart to receive a grant.

When discussing Stuart in the 1967 book *Art In A City*, Paolozzi said: 'He was a very perceptive and sensitive person and very restless.' He also said: 'There is that sort of marvellously desperate thing about the whole Liverpool business now. I always felt there was a desperate thing about Stuart in his life ... I was afraid of it.'

It was around this time that his mother, Millie Sutcliffe, began telling Stuart's friends in Liverpool that she was concerned about her son because he was experiencing terrible headaches and blackouts after a fall down some stairs in Astrid's house. At Christmas 1961 he visited Liverpool with Astrid and his friends noticed how pale and ill he looked. Mike McCartney commented: 'When I met him in a jazz club when he was home on holiday a few weeks ago he said he had a feeling that something was going to happen to him when he went back to Hamburg. He was obviously worried and nervous.'

A letter from a reader in *Mersey Beat* pointed out that Stuart was no longer playing with the group and asked if the rumour were true that he'd died in Hamburg! It was a reflection of the mystique that Stuart radiated which caused people to create stories about him. There was a rumour that he slept in a coffin in Gambier Terrace – completely unfounded, just like the disputed tale that he was kicked in the head in a fight – it never happened.

Stuart announced that he was going to marry Astrid in June 1962 after he'd completed his course at college.

During his classes at college he began to suffer severe headaches and blackouts. Astrid said, 'For days at a time he would not come down from his attic studio to eat or sleep, and the headaches became violent, they seemed like fits.'

In February 1962 he was examined by a doctor, who could find nothing wrong. He fainted in class and had to be given pain killers, but although X-rays were taken, the doctors said they could find nothing wrong with him. He even suffered from temporary blindness.

On 10 April 1962 Astrid found Stuart unconscious in his bed. She called for an ambulance and while they were being driven to hospital, Stuart died in Astrid's arms. It was 4.30 p.m. He was 21 years old, Astrid was 23.

Astrid had sent two cables to Millie, who was 54 years old at the time. The first read, 'My Stuart is dying', the second, 'My Stuart is dead'. The second cable arrived before the first.

Charles Sutcliffe couldn't be contacted as he'd sailed for South America and wouldn't be in touch for a further three weeks. Twenty-year-old Joyce Sutcliffe said, 'He has a weak heart and we cannot radio his ship to tell him. He will be told when he reaches port.'

At the autopsy it was officially declared that the cause of death was 'Cerebral paralysis due to bleeding into the right ventricle of the brain.'

Astrid met the Beatles at the airport the next day to tell them the dreadful news. John burst into hysterical laughter and couldn't stop. 'It was his way of not wanting to face the truth,' said Astrid.

Millie flew to Hamburg and brought her son's body home to Liverpool. He was buried at Huyton Parish Church Cemetery in Stanley Road/Bluebell Lane, Huyton. His resting place is number 552 in the 1939 section.

His mother decided to devote her time to gain recognition for Stuart's work and a memorial exhibition was arranged at the Walker Art Gallery in Liverpool in 1964. Interest in Stuart seemed to fade away. When Millie arranged another exhibition of his work at a small gallery in London, few people attended. When his paintings were offered up for sale at a Liverpool convention in the seventies for only £40 each, there were few takers for the pieces.

Almost 25 years after his death a sudden burst of interest took flower and began to grow. *The Sunday Times* included him in a feature on 'Smart Art', mentioning how his pictures were now fashionable among collectors. His work also commanded high prices at Sotheby's Pop auctions.

In the late eighties Pauline Sutcliffe worked on a book about her brother's life and art in collaboration with Mike Evans and an exhibition of Stuart's work was launched in London and Liverpool. Granada Television broadcast a documentary of his life in Hamburg called 'Midnight's Angel', and a feature film based on his life, *Backbeat*, starred Stephen Dorff as Stuart.

The Beatles selected Stuart as one of the figures to appear on the cover of their *Sgt Pepper's Lonely Hearts Club Band* album.

Suzy Parker

Song which the Beatles recorded at Twickenham Film Studios during their filming of *Let It Be* in January 1969. They are seen performing the number in the film and the number was copyrighted in the name of all four members of the group although the song has never appeared on record.

Swan Records

An independent record label founded in Philadelphia in 1957 by Bernie Binnick and Tony Mammarella. Among their hit artists was Freddie Cannon and the label had leased his British releases to the Top Rank label, which had been acquired by EMI in 1960. When the Swan label president was in Britain at the beginning of September 1963, he asked EMI if they had a reciprocal licence for him. They asked if he'd be interested in the Beatles' latest release, 'She Loves You'.

A licence was set up and Swan released 'She Loves You' on 16 September 1963, with 'I'll Get You' on the flip. *Cashbox* reviewed the record calling 'She Loves You' 'a robust romantic rocker that the crew works over with solid sales authority' and 'I'll Get You' as 'a catchy cha-cha twist handclapper'.

It didn't sell and was soon relegated to the bargain bins. Then Capitol finally agreed to release Beatles products and issued 'I Want to Hold Your Hand'. A week after 'I Want To Hold Your Hand' entered the American charts, Swan re-released 'She Loves You', which was to sell 3 million copies in America and replace 'I Want To Hold Your Hand' at the top of the charts.

With the Beatles becoming so successful, Swan approached EMI for further Beatles material but were told that Capitol now held exclusive American rights. However, they did have a German language version of 'She Loves You', '*Sie Liebt Dich*', which Capitol had declined to release. Swan accepted it and released the record in May 1964. It reached No. 97 in the *Billboard* charts.

Sweden

The Beatles toured Sweden from 24–31 October 1963. It was their first foreign tour and the first time they had played outside Britain since their Hamburg days.

They appeared on Swedish radio and television and performed nine shows in five concerts, for which they received a reported £2,000.

There were mob scenes in Sweden where the Beatles haircut was referred to as being in a 'Hamlet style'. The group opened their brief tour at the Nya aulan in Karlastad on the 25th, followed by the Kungliga Hallen in Stockholm on the 26th, the Borashallen in Boras on the 28th and the Sporthallen, Eskilstuna, on the 29th.

The Beatles returned to Sweden on 28 and 29 July for four concerts at the Johanneshovs Isstadion in Stockholm.

Sweet Georgia Brown

One of the numbers recorded at the May 1961 recording session in Hamburg in which the Beatles were produced backing Tony Sheridan by Bert Kaempfert.

The song was composed by Ben Bernie, Maceo Pinkard and Kenneth Casey in the 1920s, but was open to contemporary interpretations and had, in fact, been recorded by the Coasters in 1957.

The American label ATCO issued it as a single on ATCO 6302 on 1 June 1964 with 'Take Out Some Insurance On Me Baby' on the flip. Although the label proclaimed 'The Beatles, featuring Tony Sheridan', it didn't chart.

Sweet Little Sixteen

Composed by Chuck Berry who had a million-seller with it in 1958. The song was included in the repertoire of the Quarry Men, with John on lead vocal. The Beatles performed the number at the Star Club and it's to be found on *The Beatles Live! At the Star Club In Hamburg: 1962* album. They also recorded it for their BBC radio show 'Pop Go The Beatles' on 23 July 1963, John also recorded 'Sweet Little Sixteen' for his *Rock 'n' Roll* album which he recorded in 1975. The 'Pop Go The Beatles' performance was used on *The Beatles Live At The BBC* CD.

Swinging Bluejeans, The

Liverpool's longest-surviving group who still perform regularly throughout the world.

When they formed in 1957 they were a skiffle band known as the Swinging Bluegenes. They had their own guest night at the Cavern Club. In June 1961, when John Carter left the band to move to Canada, the line-up was: Ray Ennis (lead guitar), Ralph Ellis (solo), Les Braid (bass) and Paul Moss (banjo).

The group began to perform a three-quarters of an hour spot every Friday, Saturday and Sunday at the Cavern and opened their Tuesday evening guest nights in 1961.

On 21 March 1961 they welcomed the Beatles to their first-ever Cavern evening spot. Other Bluegenes guest nights on which the Beatles appeared included 25 July 1961 and 28 August 1962. The Beatles also appeared on the bill with the Bluegenes, Gene Vincent and Sounds Incorporated on Sunday, 1 July 1962, which was the first Sunday at the Cavern which wasn't headlined by a jazz band.

The Bluegenes were held in high regard in Liverpool and when Bob Wooler compiled a list of Top Ten Liverpool bands in the 5 October 1961 issue of Mersey Beat, with the Beatles placed at No. 1, he qualified this by writing, 'My list of what I rate to be the ten most popular rock groups on Merseyside – excluding the Bluegenes, of course. They are beyond comparison. They are in a class of their own.'

With the growing popularity of groups and the death of the Trad Jazz boom, the group altered their name to the Swinging Bluejeans and began to play rock 'n' roll. Their line-up was: Ray Ennis (guitar), Ralph Ellis (guitar), Les Braid (bass guitar) and Norman Kuhlke (drums).

After the success of the Beatles, the Swinging Bluejeans made their recording debut with 'It's Too Late Now' c/w 'Think Of Me', released in June 1963.

They then released 'The Hippy Hippy Shake', which the Beatles voted a hit on their 'Juke Box Jury' special on 7 December 1963. It became the Bluejeans' biggest hit.

The Bluejeans' success continued for some years. They appeared in a special film for Pathe Pictorial, had their own weekly Radio Luxembourg show 'Swingtime', appeared on the Christmas 1963 edition of TV's popular 'Z Cars', performing 'Hippy Hippy Shake', 'Angie' and 'Money'. They also appeared in the film *Circularama Cavalcade* which had its London premiere on 11 March 1964.

Their current line-up is: Ray Ennis (guitar), Les Braid (bass guitar), Alan Lowell (guitar), and Ian McGee (drums). Lowell replaced Colin Manley, who died in April 1999.

Swinging Sound '63

Title of a radio special broadcast live from the Royal Albert Hall on 18 April 1963. This was one of three special radio presentations by the BBC from the Albert Hall, but the only one on which the Beatles appeared.

The programme was produced by Terry Henebery and Ron Belchier. The Beatles were second on the bill to Del Shannon and among the other artists appearing were the Springfields, Shane Fenton, Kenny Lynch, Susan Maughan, Rolf Harris, the Vernons Girls and Chris Barber's Jazzband.

The Beatles performed 'Twist And Shout' and 'From Me To You'.

Sydney Stadium, Sydney, Australia

The Beatles appeared at Sydney Stadium for six concerts on 18, 19, 20 June 1964 with two concerts a night at 6.00 p.m. and 8.00 p.m., attracting over 12,000 people – the biggest-ever audiences for a pop concert at the stadium up to that time.

One newspaper hired a technician with a decibel meter who registered 114 decibels when the Beatles appeared on stage. As a Boeing 707 registered 90–100 decibels at 2,000 feet, the newspaper headline read: 'Beatles Fans Sound Like A Jet In Flight.'

The show was compered by Alan Field and the first group on stage were the Phantoms.

They remained on stage to back Johnny Devlin and Johnny Chester. Sounds Incorporated then closed the first half and the Beatles appeared for the entire second half of each show.

The *Sydney Sun* commented, 'Wanted: one new set of drums, ear drums. Even today, more than twelve hours after the first Sydney concert, I've still got to tilt my head to hear properly. But I can't blame the Beatles, it's the fans – they sounded like a very high-pitched swarm of locusts descending on a ripening crop.' The *Sunday Mirror* said: 'Beatles have thin legs and long hair, and would be very useful in a house for cleaning cobwebs off ceilings.'

Take Good Care Of My Baby

A Gerry Goffin, Carole King number which provided Bobby Vee with an American No. 4 hit in 1961. The Beatles included it in their repertoire that year with George Harrison on lead vocals.

Take Out Some Insurance On Me Baby

Number composed by Charles Shingleton and Waldonese Hall. The song was recorded by Jimmy Reed and issued as a single in America on Vee Jay Records in April 1959. Tony Sheridan included it in his repertoire and it was one of the numbers he recorded with the Beatles in May 1961.

The song was also known as 'If You Love Me, Baby' and it was under this title that it appeared as the flipside of 'Ain't She Sweet' when it was issued in Britain on Polydor NH 52-317 on 29 May 1964. The single reached No. 24 in the *New Musical Express* charts. It was also used as the flipside of 'Sweet Georgia Brown' in America when it was issued on Atco 6302 on 1 June 1964, although the title was now back to 'Take Out Some Insurance On Me Baby'. The record failed to gain a chart placing.

It next appeared on the British album *The Beatles First* in June 1964 and has been used on various other releases.

Talent For Loving, A

A novel by Richard Condon which was originally to have been the basis for the Beatles' third film. Bud Ornstein, Head of Production for United Artists, originally suggested the property and Brian

Epstein and the Beatles all liked Condon's book. Ornstein left United Artists to set up Pickfair Films in partnership with Brian Epstein, and it was officially announced to the press that 'A Talent For Loving' would be the Beatles' new film.

The story was a Western set in the year 1871 and concerned an epic 1,400-mile horse race between the Rio Grande and Mexico City, with a sub-plot about an American who arrives in Mexico to claim his land, only to find a Mexican has claimed the same land. The biggest part was to go to Ringo, who loved the idea of being in a Western. Filming was to have begun in 1965, but it was postponed, supposedly because of potentially bad weather in Spain, where locations were to be made.

As it turned out, the Beatles hated the first draft of the script they received and became disenchanted with the project. They decided to opt out. Later in 1965, John commented, 'Walter Shenson thinks we're still considering that film, but as far as I'm concerned, it's scrapped. The original book was great, but the script they showed us turned out lousy.' Following a meeting between the Beatles and Shenson in December 1965, it was officially announced that they would no longer make the film.

A Talent For Loving was eventually made and released in 1969, with Richard Widmark, Genevieve Page, Topol and Cesar Romero.

Talent Spot, The

BBC Light Programme radio show of the early sixties which spotlighted new talent. The half-hour programme was broadcast at 5.00 p.m. each Tuesday and was produced by Brian Willey and presented by Gary Marshal.

The Beatles made their London radio debut on the show on 4 December 1962, which was recorded at the BBC Paris Studio, Regent Street, on 27 November, and they performed 'Love Me Do', 'P.S. I Love You' and 'Twist And Shout'. Their second and final appearance on the programme was transmitted on 29 January 1963, following their recording at the Paris Studio on 22 January, when they performed 'Please Please Me', 'Ask Me Why' and 'Some Other Guy'. Their version of 'Three Cool Cats' was not transmitted.

A Taste Of Honey

Composed by Ric Marlow and Bobby Scott for the play *A Taste Of Honey* in 1960, it was included in the Beatles' repertoire in 1962, with Paul on lead vocal. The group featured the song on several of their BBC radio shows including 'Here We Go', 'Side By Side', 'Easy Beat', 'The Beat Show' and two of their 'Pop Go The Beatles', shows. The group also recorded it for their *Please Please Me* album. It was one of the tracks included on their first British EP release *Twist And Shout*. In America Vee Jay issued it on the *Introducing The Beatles* and *Songs, Pictures And Stories Of The Fabulous Beatles* albums and the *Souvenir Of Their Visit To America (The Beatles)* EP while Capitol featured it on *The Early Beatles* album. It was also on *The Beatles Box* and *The Beatles Collection* sets. A radio version of the number was used on *The Beatles Live At The BBC* CD.

Taxman

A George Harrison number included on their *Revolver* album. George wrote the number following his frustration at the high taxes in Britain. It happened when he realised that if anyone actually started earning real money, then most of it would go to the government in taxes. In the song he mentions Harold Wilson and Ted Heath, who were the leaders of the Labour and Conservative parties.

One wonders if George remembered the song in July 1973 when he had to hand over a cheque for £1,000,000 to the Inland Revenue in taxes for the Bangladesh concert and album. The Beatles were plagued with tax problems and it was in an attempt to alleviate them that they formed Apple. At one point Ringo commented, 'The government's taking over 90 per cent of all our money anyway – we're left with 1/9th in the pound.' In *I. Me. Mine*, George wrote '"Taxman" was when I first realised that even though we had started earning money, we were actually giving most of it away in taxes; it was and still is typical. Why should this be so? Are we being punished for something we had forgotten to do?'

The number was recorded in April 1966 and John Lennon said, 'Many people have written in asking about how we sounded in the studio when we weren't actually recording a song. So at the beginning of "Taxman" there's a candid recording showing us just like that.' 'Taxman' was to resurface in 1976 on the *Rock 'n' Roll Music* and *The Best Of George Harrison* albums. A version was included on the Beatles' *Anthology 2* CDs.

Taylor, Alistair

The man who became known as Apple's 'Mr Fixit' originally joined the Whitechapel branch of NEMS as Brian Epstein's personal assistant. He accompanied Brian to the Cavern to see the Beatles for the first time and on 13 December 1961 was a witness to the management contract which Brian drew up for the group. However, Brian didn't sign the contract, explaining to them that it would give them the freedom to opt out if they wished – but it was signed by all four Beatles and Alistair.

Soon after, Brian offered Alistair two and a half per cent of the group, but Alistair turned him down, even though he wasn't asked to invest any money in exchange for the percentage.

Due to his wife Lesley's asthma problem, Alistair was advised to move away from Liverpool and he took a job at Pye Records in London. In 1963 he bumped into Brian, they had lunch together and Alistair was offered the job as General Manager of NEMS Enterprises at a salary of £1,000 a year.

Alistair became involved in handling many tasks for the Beatles and received the tag 'Mr Fixit' for his efforts, which ranged from attending an auction to buying an island for John Lennon to surveying a farm in Scotland for Paul.

On Sunday, 27 August 1967, Alistair received a call from Joanne Newfield, Brian's secretary, asking him to come over to Chapel Street. He rushed over and was devastated to find Brian dead in his bedroom.

When the Beatles formed Apple, John Lennon phoned Alistair to ask him to become Office Manager and during the next few years he played his 'Mr Fixit' role again. Early on, Paul had designed an advertisement for Apple and wanted Alistair to pose for the picture. It was a photograph of him wearing a suit and a bowler hat, posing as a one-man band and it was featured in a poster campaign and advertisements in the music press. The copy which Paul wrote read: 'This man has talent. One day he sang his songs to a tape recorder (borrowed from the man next door). In his neatest handwriting he wrote an explanatory note (giving his name and address) and, remembering to enclose a picture of himself, sent the tape, letter and photograph to Apple Music, 94 Baker Street, London W1. If you were thinking of doing the same thing yourself – do it now! This man now owns a Bentley!'

One day Alistair was having lunch with a client when he received a call from Peter Brown insisting he return to the office straight away. He arrived to see that Brown had been given a list of Apple personnel to be sacked and Alistair's name was top of the list. A victim of the Allen Klein-inspired wholesale sackings at Apple.

Alistair attempted to call John and Paul, but was unable to. Then he read a quote from Paul in the *Daily Mail* in which, when asked to comment on Alistair's sacking, he said, 'It isn't possible to be nice about giving someone the sack.'

He never saw any of the Beatles again and went to work in a hotel. A number of years later he was 'discovered' by a number of

Beatles fans and invited to appear at Beatle conventions to relate his stories.

His book *Yesterday: The Beatles Remembered*, which he wrote with Martin Roberts, was published by Sidgwick & Jackson in 1988. It was written in an unfortunate style as a series of letters to an imaginary pen pal called Michelle.

Taylor, Derek

A close associate of the Beatles from 1963. Derek was born in Liverpool on 7 May 1934. He became a journalist and initially worked on the *Hoylake and West Kirby Advertiser* before graduating to the *Liverpool Daily Post* and *Liverpool Echo*. In 1962 he was offered the post of showbusiness correspondent for the northern edition of the *Daily Express*, based in Manchester.

On 30 May 1963, Derek attended the Beatles' concert at the Odeon, Manchester, and his review appeared in the *Daily Express* the next day. He wrote: 'The Liverpool Sound came to Manchester last night and I thought it was magnificent . . . Indecipherable, meaningless nonsense, of course, but as beneficial as a week on a beach at the Pier Head overlooking the Mersey. The spectacle of these fresh, cheeky, sharp, young entertainers in apposition to the shiny-eyed teenage idolators is as good as a rejuvenating drug for the jaded adult.'

He next travelled to Liverpool to interview Brian Epstein, and the piece appeared in the *Daily Express* on 20 June 1963 under the banner 'Epstein, the Brain Behind the Beatles'. Then, at a preview of a BBC TV Beatles documentary, 'The Mersey Sound', Bill Harry informed him of the Beatles' seasons in Hamburg and he flew to the German city to research their experiences there, which resulted in a week-long series in the Express. By that time he came to be known at the *Express* as 'the Beatles man' and later in 1963 he interviewed them backstage at the Floral Hall, Southport, on 15 October and at the Apollo, Ardwick, on 20 November. At the time he referred to them as, 'The gay quartet of grammar-school boys.'

Together with John Buchanan, the editor of the Manchester edition of the paper, Derek travelled to Liverpool once again to see Epstein and to suggest that a Beatle should contribute a weekly article to the *Express*, ghosted by Derek. Derek told Epstein that he had George in mind because he seemed nice and pleasant to talk to. Derek had also visited all the Beatles' families and familiarised himself with their history and began a close relationship between the group and his newspaper. On 14 January 1964 he flew with them to Paris where he ghosted George's column.

When Epstein's assistant Barry Leonard had a dispute with him and left his employ, Derek wrote to Brian requesting the job, but received no reply. He decided not to pursue it. A short time later, Epstein asked Derek to visit him in Liverpool and wondered whether he could recommend someone who could ghost his biography. Derek offered his services and the two of them stayed for five days at the Imperial Hotel, Torquay, while Derek taped Brian's memoirs, which were published as *A Cellarful of Noise*. Brian then offered Derek the job as his personal assistant and he agreed to take up the post in April 1964.

In addition to becoming Epstein's personal assistant, Taylor also became his scriptwriter and he travelled with the Beatles' entourage on their world tour of Europe, the Far East and Australasia, and also their American tour of 1964. However, the adventure was to last for only five months. At the end of the tour, when the group had embarked on a social night out, Epstein accused Derek of riding in a limousine meant for him, which Taylor denied. There was an argument and he resigned and, in October, Wendy Hanson replaced him.

Derek was then offered a job as press officer by Radio KRLA in Los Angeles and moved over to California with his family in February 1965 and remained there until April 1968. He became a public relations consultant for Prestige Promotions, based on Sunset Boulevard, and his first clients were the Byrds. He was also to represent groups such as the Beach Boys and helped to organise the Monterey International Pop Festival in 1967. At the same time he was contributing a regular column called 'Hollywood Calling' to 'Disc & Music Echo', a weekly British music paper, and continued to keep in touch with the Beatles. When George Harrison went on a trip to Los Angeles he arranged to meet Derek and, while he was waiting, penned 'Blue Jay Way'. Derek had also introduced the Beatles to the work of Harry Nilsson.

When the Beatles decided to form Apple Corps, they invited Derek to join them as press officer and he returned to England with his family. He was highly active representing the Beatles once again, initially from offices at 95 Wigmore Street, then from the famous Apple building at 3 Savile Row. They were exhilarating times for him and at one point there were plans for him to write a musical about Apple with George Harrison, but the project was dropped when Derek admitted he couldn't write a script.

He departed from Apple on New Year's Day 1970 and went to work for Warner Bros Records as director of special projects. He then became involved in a number of activities involving the ex-members of the Beatles. He was perhaps closest to George and helped him to compile his book *I. Me. Mine*. Derek also became the most reliable and informative of the 'insiders' who wrote books. They have included *As Time Goes By* (Straight Arrow, 1973), *Fifty Years Adrift* (Genesis Publications, 1984) and *It Was Twenty Years Ago* (Bantam Press, 1987).

Derek died at the age of 65 at his Suffolk home following a long battle against cancer on Sunday, 7 September 1997. His wife Joan and six children, Timothy, Gerard, Abigail, Vanessa, Domenic and Annabel, survived him.

Domenic is an actor and appeared in 'EastEnders' in 1998 as Nick Holland, Cindy Beale's rich boyfriend.

Commenting on Derek, Paul McCartney was to say, 'He was a beautiful man. It is time for tears and words may come later.' There was a private funeral on Friday, 12 September, attended by Mike McCartney, Neil Aspinall, Neil Innes, Michael Palin and Jools Holland. He was working on the Beatles' *Anthology* book in the months before he died.

Taylor, James

American singer/songwriter who was discovered by Apple A&R man Peter Asher in 1968. He became one of the initial artists signed to the Apple label and when Asher began producing Taylor's debut album, Paul McCartney played bass on the track 'Carolina In My Mind'. It's interesting to note that another song on the *James Taylor* album was called 'Something In The Way She Moves', which George Harrison used as the first line of his song 'Something' the following year.

Taylor was disturbed by what he considered was Apple's lack of promotion of his records and he returned to America and left the Apple label in 1969. Peter Asher remained as his producer when Taylor signed to the Warner Brothers label. Ironically for Apple, Taylor immediately became a major hit with his first Warner Album, *Sweet Baby James*, and his million-seller single, 'Fire And Rain'. Taylor was to enjoy chart success in America throughout the seventies.

It's likely that the rot set in when Paul McCarney became angry when Jane Asher announced that their engagement was over. A furious Paul wanted Peter Asher fired but Ron Kass talked him out of it. However, from that point Asher and the artists he looked after personally didn't receive the attention from Apple that they'd previously enjoyed.

Taylor, Kingsize

Ted Taylor was to become one of Liverpool's unsung heroes. A singer with a unique voice and one of the very best of the Mersey bands, he missed out on the success of the Mersey boom, due mainly to the fact that he and his group spent much of their time based in Hamburg.

Taylor first joined a skiffle group, the James Boys, in 1956 and then teamed up with the Dominoes in 1958. By 1960 the band had changed their name to Kingsize Taylor & the Dominoes and began to build their local reputation. They made their Cavern debut on 25 January 1961, with Cilla Black joining them for the gig as one of the lead vocalists. Cilla, who was Taylor's girlfriend for a time, made several cameo appearances with the band.

The group were voted No. 6 in the first *Mersey Beat* poll and they made their Hamburg debut in 1962 and were so popular they were offered a residency. Drummer Dave Lovelady, who'd taken time off from his architectural studies from the Hamburg gig, couldn't remain, so Kingsize contacted Ringo Starr and asked if he'd be his replacement. Ringo agreed, but a few days later wrote back saying he'd received an offer from the Beatles which he'd decided to accept.

Brian Redman stepped in on drums and the group remained in Hamburg, appearing with a host of their idols, including Fats Domino, Little Richard, Jerry Lee Lewis, Joey Dee & the Starlighters and Johnny & the Hurricanes. They also provided backing for singer Davy Jones, whom the Beatles had backed in Liverpool.

Redman left the group and the Dominoes contacted Gibson Kemp, who'd replaced Ringo Starr in the Hurricanes, and the seventeen-year-old obtained a special work permit and joined them. They were recorded on stage at the Star Club by Adrian Barber, former member of the Big Three and now stage manager at the club. He recorded most of the bands who appeared there and Taylor asked him if he could have the Beatles' tapes he'd recorded. The Dominoes also made numerous records for Phillips and Polydor in Hamburg although, recording for rival labels, they changed their name to the Shakers for the Polydor releases.

The group returned from Germany in 1964 to plug their first Decca single, 'Stupidity', appeared on 'Thank Your Lucky Stars' and backed Chuck Berry on his British tour.

There were various members in the line-up of Taylor's group over the years and included saxophonist Howie Casey, Paddy Chambers of Faron's Flamingos and singer Steve Aldo.

Taylor returned to Germany in 1965, appearing in Hamburg and Frankfurt with his group Kingsize Taylor & His Band, but there were problems with gangsters involved in certain clubs, the group never got paid, they were repatriated back to Britain in 1965 where the band broke up and Taylor became a butcher.

Years later he was to dig up Adrian Barber's recordings of the Beatles and sell them.

Teatro Adriano, Rome, Italy

Venue where the Beatles appeared during their European tour in 1965. They were due to make two appearances on 27 June at 4.30 p.m. and 9.30 p.m. An extra two appearances were added for the following day, although attendances on both days didn't reach capacity. The daily newspaper *Paese Sera* noted that the cinema was not air-conditioned and commented: 'Whoever succeeds in half-filling a cinema in mid-afternoon with the temperature at 37 [98 degrees Fahrenheit] can well be satisfied.'

The gig was recorded by EMI Italy and an album *Live In Italy* was issued later in the year featuring the tracks 'Twist And Shout', 'She's A Woman', 'I'm A Loser', 'Can't Buy Me Love', 'Baby's In Black', 'I Wanna Hold Your Hand', 'A Hard Day's Night', 'Everybody's Trying To Be My Baby', 'Rock And Roll Music', 'I Feel Fine', 'Ticket To Ride' and 'Long Tall Sally'.

Unfortunately, permission hadn't been obtained from the Beatles to release this album and it had to be withdrawn two weeks after release. A thousand copies of the album had already been sold and are obviously of great interest to collectors.

EMI Italy replaced it with an album *The Beatles In Italy*, but this consisted of studio tracks which hadn't previously been available on singles in that country.

Among the celebrities who attended the concerts in Rome were actor Marcello Mastroianni and actress Ursula Andress. The Rome newspaper *Il Messaggero* wrote: 'No more than four ugly faces, four long heads of hair, four sublime idiots, four barefoot bums – but they succeeded in creating a spectacle that one can only admire.'

Technical College Hall, Borough Road, Birkenhead, Liverpool L41

A college 'over the water' from Liverpool where the Beatles were booked to appear for three consecutive Fridays in February 1962 on Fridays 9, 16 and 23.

Teddy Boy

Number penned by Paul McCartney which the Beatles began recording at Apple Studios on Friday, 24 January 1969. They continued recording the number the following Wednesday, originally intending it to be included on the 'Get Back' album, which was scrapped.

When Phil Spector was mixing the 'Get Back' tapes to produce the *Let It Be* album, 'Teddy Boy' was one of the tracks he re-mixed, although it wasn't used on the album and the Beatles' version remains unreleased.

However, Paul recorded a solo version of the number which was included on his album *McCartney*, issued on 17 April 1970.

A 'Teddy Boy' was one of the youth cults of the late fifties in Britain and was so called due to his use of a long Edwardian style jacket with velvet collar. The number finally surfaced on the Beatles' *Anthology 3* CDs.

Teenage Heaven

A number recorded by Eddie Cochran in 1959 which the Beatles included in their repertoire in 1960.

Teenager's Turn

Title of the BBC Light Programme radio show on which the Beatles made their radio debut. The show was broadcast form the Playhouse Theatre, Manchester each Thursday between 5.00 p.m. and 5.30 p.m., although it was recorded the previous day. The resident band was the Northern Dance Orchestra.

Producer Peter Pilbeam thought the name 'Beatles' was bizarre but decided to book them as a result of the audition tapes. They recorded the show on Wednesday, 7 March 1962, and it was transmitted the following day.

The group organised a coach to take them from Liverpool to Manchester in which they were joined by members of their Liverpool fan club, Mr Jim McCartney, Bill and Virginia Harry and Peter Mackey, who was then President of the Students' Union at Liverpool College of Art. Mackey had joined the coach, which departed from Mount Street, at the side of the College of Art/Liverpool Institute, hoping to confront the Beatles about the PA equipment which the Students' Union had purchased and which the Beatles had never returned. He did manage to confront John Lennon, and a non-plussed John told him he'd been skint in Hamburg and had sold it.

The shows were recorded before a live audience and *Mersey Beat* reported: 'John, Paul and George made their entrance on stage to cheers and applause, but when Pete walked on – the fans went wild! The girls screamed. In Manchester his popularity was assured by his looks alone.'

The group were mobbed as they left the theatre, but although John, Paul and George managed to reach the coach, Pete was prevented from doing so. Eventually he escaped, with his mohair suit ripped, to receive a ticking-off from Mr McCartney who accused him of trying to upstage the other members of the group.

The Beatles performed four numbers in the theatre, three of them sung by John: 'Hello Little Girl', 'Memphis Tennessee' and 'Please Mr Postman'; and one sung by Paul, 'Dream Baby'. 'Hello Little Girl' was not broadcast.

The show's presenter, Ray Peters, had the honour of being the first person to announce the Beatles on the radio.

The name 'Teenager's Turn' was dropped by the time they returned for their second broadcast on 14 June (for transmission the next day) and was then called 'Here We Go'.

Tell Me What You See
Number penned by Paul McCartney, although it is said that John aided him on the lyrics at the recording session, which took place on Thursday, 18 February 1965. Paul played electric piano on the session and the group was also to feature a South American musical instrument called a guiro. The number was included on their album *Help!* in August 1965 and on the American album *Beatles VI* in June 1965. It was later included on the *Love Songs* compilation in 1977.

Tell Me Why
Number composed by John which was included on the *A Hard Day's Night* album. The group recorded the number on Thursday, 27 February 1964, and it was also included on the British EP, *Extracts From The Film A Hard Day's Night*.

It was issued in America on United Artists' soundtrack album of the film in June 1964 and the following month turned up on Capitol's *Something New* album.

Temple, Shirley
The greatest child star of the movies. Born in California in 1928, Shirley became one of the screen's most popular stars of the thirties and was voted Top Box Office Star when she was only seven years old, and Top Female Box Office Attraction for the years 1935, 1936, 1937 and 1938.

She retired from films while in her teens and was to marry John Agar and, later, Charles Black, an aide to Richard Nixon. As Shirley Temple Black she entered politics, unsuccessfully, but later became an American Ambassador.

When the Beatles appeared at the Cow Palace, San Francisco on 19 August 1964, a sheriff's deputy spotted Temple, Black and their eight-year-old daughter Lori and escorted them backstage. The

Beatles were in a partitioned section and were reluctant to come out and meet her. Neil Aspinall had to cajole them into going to meet her 'just for a few minutes'. George, however, was adamant: he wouldn't see her. Neil took the three Beatles into the other part of the room.

Charles Black, a major local political figure, had brought his camera and wanted to take a photograph. Brian Epstein had a rule against 'celebrity photographs', but Derek Taylor decided to waive it. He went behind the partition to talk George into joining the others. George raised his voice. 'I never liked her films, don't like her, don't want to meet her or have my picture taken.'

Derek pleaded with him and eventually he emerged. Meanwhile, the corps of press photographers outside were getting very angry as they wanted a photograph of the Beatles and Shirley Temple. They began banging on the door and Derek had to placate them by telling them he'd let them have Black's roll of film which they could pool together as long as they returned it after the show. He told Black about the arrangement and, although reluctant, he agreed. The film was given to the photographers and after the show, one of them, Curt Gunther, delivered a blank roll of film to Taylor. When Taylor asked what had happened he was told that they hadn't come out. An embarrassed Taylor had to explain this to an angry Charles Black.

Two days later, photographs of Shirley, Lori and the Beatles began to appear in the newspapers. Hedda Hopper ran a story about the incident, chiding the Beatles and the photographers. Mysteriously, the film was then sent to Hopper, who was able to pass it over to the Blacks.

Tennessee
A number written and recorded by Carl Perkins in 1956. The Quarry Men included it in their repertoire, with John Lennon on lead vocals, and continued to play the number when they became the Beatles until 1961.

Terry Young Combo, The
A six-man instrumental group booked to appear on the Roy Orbison/Beatles British tour of May/June 1963. In addition to a short spot in which they played a couple of instrumentals, they provided backing for some of the solo artists, including David Macbeth and Louise Cordet.

Thank You Girl
Looking back on his early collaborations with Paul, John Lennon was to comment, 'Paul and I wrote this as a 'B'-side for one of our

first records. In the old days we used to write and write all the time, but nowadays I only do it if I'm particularly inspired.' The two of them penned the song while they were touring in 1963.

'Thank You Girl' was first issued in Britain as the flipside of 'From Me To You' in April 1963. In America, Vee Jay issued the single in May 1963, but it failed to register. Vee Jay then included the track on their *Jolly What! The Beatles and Frank Ifield On Stage* album in February 1964 and issued it as the flipside of 'Do You Want To Know A Secret? in March 1964 and the single reached No. 2 in the American charts.

In Britain it was included on *The Beatles Hits* EP in September 1963 and first appeared on an album when it was included on *Rarities*, included in *The Beatles Collection* boxed set in December 1978. The Beatles recorded the number on Tuesday, 5 March 1963, when it went under the working title 'Thank You Little Girl'. An 'Easy Beat' performance which was included on *The Beatles Live At The BBC* CDs. The number was included on the CD compilation *Past Masters Volume One*.

Thank Your Lucky Stars

First of the major networked TV pop shows of the sixties, produced by ABC TV from their Birmingham studios at Aston Road, Aston, Birmingham. As a result of arranging for the Beatles to be booked on the show, Dick James was able to secure their music publishing rights.

'Thank Your Lucky Stars' producer, Philip Jones, was a friend of James' and when Brian Epstein was in the publisher's office discussing the promotion of 'Please Please Me', James phoned Jones and asked him to book the Beatles on the show. Jones said he couldn't do that until he heard the record. James played it to him over the phone and Jones said they could appear on the programme the following Saturday.

The Beatles made their debut on the programme when they recorded 'Please Please Me' on 13 January 1963. It was transmitted on 19 January. They also performed 'Please Please Me' on 17 February for a programme broadcast on 23 February.

For their third appearance they recorded 'From Me To You' at ATV's Teddington Studios on 14 April, for transmission on 20 April. They also performed 'From Me To You' on 12 May for transmission on 18 May on a show which also featured the Countrymen, Dickie Pride, Heidi Bruhl, Peter Jay & the Jaywalkers, Shani Wallis, Al Saxon and Jimmy Young.

The 23 June recording in Birmingham was a special event – the 'All Merseyside' edition of the programme, broadcast on 29 June, and the other acts included Gerry & the Pacemakers, Billy J.

Kramer and the Dakotas, the Big Three and the Vernons Girls. The group's next appearance was on 18 August, for a 24 August transmission.

Another 'All Merseyside' edition took place on 15 December for transmission on 21 December and the group were presented with two Gold Discs during the recording. They performed 'I Want To Hold Your Hand', 'All My Loving' and 'Twist And Shout'. Other artists on the bill included Billy J. Kramer and the Dakotas, Cilla Black, Tommy Quickly, the Searchers and the Breakaways.

The Beatles appeared twice in 1964 both times recording at the Teddington studios, firstly on 11 July for transmission on 18 July and finally on 14 November for transmission on 21 November. In 1965 they made a single appearance at the Birmingham studios on 28 March for transmission on 3 April. This was their last recording for the programme.

'Thank Your Lucky Stars', like 'Ready, Steady, Go!', was a programme produced by a local television station and networked over the ITV system, but was also likely to be a victim when the TV franchise ended, and eventually a new station took over the broadcasting for the area. This happened with both 'Thank Your Lucky Stars' and 'Ready, Steady, Go!'. 'Top Of The Pops', on the other hand, was a BBC programme and therefore had its longevity guaranteed. The final programme of 'Thank Your Lucky Stars' was broadcast on 25 June 1966 when a promotional film for 'Paperback Writer' was screened.

That Means A Lot

An unreleased Beatles song mainly composed by Paul McCartney for the film *Help!* The Beatles recorded it on Saturday, 20 February, and Thursday, 30 March 1965. John Lennon was to say: 'The song is a ballad which Paul and I wrote for the film but we found we just couldn't sing it. In fact, we made a hash of it, so we thought we'd better give it to someone who could do it well.'

That someone turned out to be P. J. Proby who asked John if they could give him a song, just like they'd given one to Peter & Gordon. They gave him 'That Means A Lot'. Then he asked them for another favour – could they talk George Martin into producing it for him? They did and Proby recorded the number at Abbey Road Studios on 7 April 1965, but the record wasn't a hit for him.

The Beatles' original demo disc was included on the *Anthology 2* CD.

That's All Right Mama

The Beatles used this number as part of their repertoire from the early Quarry Men days, with Paul on lead vocal. It was originally penned by Arthur 'Big Boy' Crudup and was Elvis Presley's first record release. The Beatles performed the number on their BBC radio show 'Pop Go The Beatles' on 16 July 1963. This 'Pop Go The Beatles' performance was included on *The Beatles Live At The BBC* CDs.

There's A Devil In Her Heart

A number which was originally recorded by female vocal group the Donays on the American Brent label in August 1962. The number wasn't a hit, but it appealed to the Beatles, who included it in their stage act, with George on lead vocal.

The actual title of the Donays' version, penned by Richard B. Drapkin, was '(There's A) Devil In His Heart'.

The Beatles recorded the number and it was included on their *With The Beatles* album. The song was also to surface on the Capitol release *The Beatles Second Album*.

There's A Place

A number penned by John which was included in the Beatles' stage repertoire in 1963. It was recorded on the morning of Monday, 11 February 1963, during their marathon recording session for the *Please Please Me* album.

The evocative song was an early example of a reflective Lennon lyric and apart from the *Please Please Me* album it was used as one of the tracks on the *Twist And Shout* EP. In America it was featured on the Vee Jay albums *Introducing The Beatles, The Beatles vs The Four Seasons* and *Songs, Pictures And Stories Of The Fabulous Beatles*, and also surfaced as the flipside of the Tollie single 'Twist and Shout' in 1964. Later the same year the single was reissued in the Capitol 'Oldies' series. In 1980 it was included on Capitol's *The Beatles Rarities* album.

Things We Said Today

Number penned by Paul which the Beatles recorded in June 1964 for their *A Hard Day's Night* album. It was also issued on the EP *Extracts From A Hard Day's Night* and on the American album *Something New*.

The Beatles included the number in the repertoire of their world tour and Paul also featured it on his own 1989/1990 world tour.

Think For Yourself

One of the two George Harrison compositions featured on the *Rubber Soul* album. A song about someone he'd parted the ways with, although he said he couldn't remember who the 'someone' was.

When the Beatles recorded the number on Monday, 8 November 1965, the working title of the song was 'Won't Be There With You'. There was a fuzzbox used at the recording, an electronic device which could control distortion. This was attached to Paul's bass guitar and it was said to be the first time a bass fuzz had been used on a record.

The track was also included on the album *The Best of George Harrison*.

Thirty Days

A number written and recorded by Chuck Berry in 1955. The Beatles included it in their stage act during 1961 with John Lennon on lead vocals.

This Boy

A number penned by John on which he and Paul harmonise. They performed the song on their BBC radio appearances for 'Saturday Club' and 'From Us To You' and it was issued on the flipside of 'I Want To Hold Your Hand'.

'This Boy' was included on the *Love Songs* and *Rarities* compilations, *The Beatles Box* and *The Beatles Collection* sets, the American album *Meet The Beatles* and the American EP *4 By The Beatles*. The group also performed the number on their 'Sunday Night At The London Palladium' appearance in October 1963, on their 'Ed Sullivan Show' appearance in February 1964 and on their winter tour of America later the same year.

An instrumental version of the number, by the George Martin Orchestra, was featured in the film *A Hard Day's Night* as incidental music in the background of the scene where Ringo wanders along a towpath. Martin's instrumental version of the song was called 'Ringo's Theme' and the George Martin orchestra single was originally released in Britain on 7 August 1964 with 'And I Love Her' on the flipside, although it didn't make any impact on the charts. When it was issued in America on 31 July 1964, it rose to No. 53 in the Top 100. It was also included on Martin's Parlophone album *Off The Beatle Track* and on an EP, Music From *A Hard Day's Night*, by the George Martin Orchestra, issued on 19 February 1965. The version from the TV show 'The Morecambe & Wise Show', together with a second version from the studio recordings was included on the Beatles' *Anthology 1* CDs. The number was also included on the CD compilation *Past Masters Volume One*.

This Is Their Life
An aural documentary produced by Radio Luxembourg and originally broadcast in two parts. The first was transmitted on 10 May
1964 and the second on 17 May.

Thomas, Chris
A British record producer. At the age of 21 he was employed as an
assistant by AIR, the production company founded by George
Martin. He then worked as an assistant to Martin during most of
his 1968 recording sessions, learning the tricks of the trade. He
returned from holiday early in September to find Martin had left
him a note: 'Chris: hope you had a nice holiday. I'm off on mine
now. Make yourself available to the Beatles. Neil and Mal know
you're coming down.'
  He began to work with the Beatles on a number of tracks for
their album *The Beatles*, from 9–26 September. Although the
Beatles were virtually producing themselves by that time, John
Lennon insisted that Chris be credited as producer. The tracks he
worked on with them included 'Helter Skelter', 'Glass Onion', 'I
Will', 'Cry Baby Cry', 'Birthday', 'Piggies', 'Happiness Is A Warm
Gun' and 'What's The New Mary Jane'. He also played harpsi-
chord on 'Piggies' and keyboards on 'Savoy Truffle' and 'Long,
Long, Long'.
  It was Chris who also told them that the rock 'n' roll movie *The
Girl Can't Help It* was being given its first British TV screening on
Wednesday, 18 September and they went to see it, in between
sessions, at Paul's house in nearby Cavendish Avenue. The party
comprised all four Beatles, Yoko Ono, Pattie Harrison and Chris.
  Chris also acted as producer on Beatles recordings between
Friday, 18 April and Friday, 2 May 1969.

Three Coins Club, Fountain Street, Manchester
A club which opened in October 1961. Being situated in Fountain
Street, it took its name from the film *Three Coins In The Fountain*.
Jimmy Savile was a co-owner of the club and recalls booking the
Beatles there for the first time on a Sunday in November 1961 for a
fee of five pounds. He remembers it being a Sunday as the club only
booked live groups on Sunday evenings. The Beatles appeared for a
second time at the club on 27 January 1963.

Three Cool Cats
A Lieber/Stoller composition which provided an American hit for
the Coasters in 1959. The Quarry Men included it in their repertoire

and performed it during their audition for Decca Records on 1 January 1962, with George on lead vocal and John and Paul harmonising. A track from their Decca audition that was included on the Beatles' *Anthology 1* CDs.

Three Musketeers, The

The famous adventure by Alexandre Dumas, which has been adapted for the screen on several occasions. It was once mooted as a vehicle for the Beatles, their possible third film for United Artists. There was even talk of the Beatles' favourite film actress Brigitte Bardot appearing as Lady de Winter. Paul McCartney was later to comment, '*The Three Musketeers* came up quite early on . . . it would have been quite wildly out of character. I wonder if it had anything to do with the fact that Dick Lester ended up doing both *The Three* and *The Four Musketeers*?'

Lester made *The Three Musketeers (The Queen's Diamonds)* and *The Four Musketeers (The Revenge Of Milady)* back to back for 20th Century Fox, the first being released in 1973, more than six years after it had originally been mooted as a Beatles vehicle. Michael York portrayed d'Artagnan, Oliver Reed was Athos, Richard Chamberlain played Aramis with Frank Finlay as Porthos and Faye Dunaway as Milady de Winter.

Three Steps To Heaven

A posthumous No. 1 hit for Eddie Cochran in Britain, although it failed to reach the American charts. The Beatles included it in their repertoire in 1960 and 1961.

Ticket To Ride

One of John Lennon's favourite compositions which the Beatles recorded on Monday, 15 February 1965, shortly before leaving for the Bahamas to begin production of their second feature film.

Paul McCartney also played lead guitar on the track – a duty usually handled by George Harrison. It's one of the few Beatles tracks on which Paul plays lead, but he repeated the exercise on another *Help!* soundtrack number, 'Another Girl'.

The single was issued in Britain on Parlophone R 5265 on 9 April 1965 where it reached No. 1 in the charts. It was issued in America with advance orders of 750,000 on Capitol 5407 on 14 April 1965, where it also topped the charts. Of interest is the fact that the American label credits the song: 'From The United Artists release *Eight Arms To Hold You*'. The flipside was another John Lennon composition, 'Yes It Is'.

The Beatles performed the number on their various tours during

1965 and included it on their 'Ed Sullivan Show' appearance in September of that year.

It was also included on the *Help!* album, *A Collection Of Beatles Oldies (But Goldies)*, *The Beatles 1962–1966*, *The Beatles At The Hollywood Bowl*, *Reel Music* and *20 Greatest Hits*, and 'The Beatles Movie Medley' single. The performance featured on the radio show 'The Beatles Invite You To Take A Ticket To Ride' was included on *The Beatles Live At The BBC* CDs while one of the studio takes was used on the Beatles' *Anthology 2* CDs.

Tigrett, Maureen Cox Starkey

Maureen was born Mary Cox on 4 August 1946. A convent-educated Liverpool girl, she became a manicurist's assistant then joined Ashley Du Pre's hairdressing salon as an assistant hairdresser at the age of fifteen.

A Cavern Club regular, she once went out with Johnny 'Guitar' Byrne of Rory Storm & the Hurricanes. Ringo was drummer with the group. Three weeks after he joined the Beatles he dated Maureen. He spotted her queuing up outside the Cavern for a lunchtime session and started chatting to her, asking if she would come out with him after a Cavern gig the following night. She told him her parents insisted on her being at home by 11.50 p.m. at the latest, so they arranged to go for a day out together. They went to the park, the pictures, had some drinks in the Pink Parrot Club in Duke Street and then went to the Blue Angel Club in Seel Street.

Although Maureen became his girlfriend, she saw little of him for the first six months, due to his hectic schedule.

By late 1964, with Ringo based in London and Maureen in Liverpool, Ringo was dating Vicki Hodge, the model. On Tuesday, 1 December he was taken to University College Hospital to have his tonsils out. Maureen decided to take matters into her own hands, caught a train to London and visited Ringo in hospital, taking him some ice cream. She then spent Christmas with him and by mid-January was pregnant. During a visit to the Ad Lib Club one evening, a slightly tipsy Ringo went down on his knees at 3.00 a.m. to propose. Maureen was 18 years old and Ringo was 24.

The couple were married at Caxton Hall, Westminster, on Thursday, 11 February 1965 at a simple ceremony that took place at 8.00 a.m. – the hall had opened two hours early to avoid the expected crowds. Brian Epstein acted as best man and in attendance were Ringo's mother and stepfather, Maureen's mother and father, John and Cynthia and George Harrison, who arrived on a bicycle. Paul was on holiday at the time. The wedding breakfast took place at Brian's house and he had also arranged for the couple to have a short honeymoon at 2 Princes Crescent, Hove, Sussex, the home of the Beatles' solicitor David Jacobs.

Ringo and Maureen moved into a Montague Square flat, but when their first son Zak was born on 13 September 1965, Ringo bought a house, Sunny Heights, in Weybridge. Their second son Jason was born on 19 August 1967 and their daughter Lee on 11 November 1970.

The marriage had seemed a strong one until George and Pattie Harrison were invited to dinner one evening. Allegedly, George suddenly announced that he was madly in love with Maureen. A furious Ringo strode out, a tearful Pattie locked herself in the bathroom and a red-faced Maureen was lost for words. In the aftermath of this declaration it was rumoured that George and Maureen had a brief affair. When George was asked, 'How could you, with your best friend's wife?' he replied, 'Incest, I guess.'

The marriage never survived the scandal and the couple gradually grew apart with Ringo drinking heavily and visiting nightclubs in the company of models. Eventually, they were divorced on Thursday, 17 July 1975 with Ringo admitting to adultery with American actress Nancy Andrews.

Maureen and Ringo remained friends and Ringo was very generous, not only immediately settling £500,000 on her but later buying her a £250,000 house in Little Venice, London, and continuing with financial support for many years to come.

On Saturday, 27 May 1989, in Monte Carlo, Maureen eventually remarried. Her second husband was her long-time boyfriend, multimillionaire Isaac Tigrett, co-founder of the famous Hard Rock Café. Among the wedding guests were Cynthia Lennon, Sting and Dan Ackroyd. The couple, who had been together for fourteen years and had a child, Augusta Burton Tigrett, were married by Reverend Don Malloy, who had married Elvis and Priscilla Presley.

Maureen was diagnosed with leukaemia in April 1994. She entered the Fred Hutchinson Cancer Research Centre in Seattle, Washington, on 20 October. She was then given a bone marrow transplant, donated by her son Zak, but it was unsuccessful and she died on Friday, 30 December 1994 from complications after the transplant. She was 48 years old.

Till There Was You

Song written by Meredith Willson for the Broadway musical *The Music Man*, which starred Robert Preston. It was also made into a big budget musical feature film.

Paul particularly liked the number after hearing Peggy Lee's 1961 version, and it was included in the Beatles act in 1962. Paul sang the song during the Beatles' Decca audition and it has resurfaced on various albums of Decca tapes, including *The Complete Silver Beatles*. He also performed it on stage at the Star Club, Hamburg, and it became one of the many that Adrian Barber recorded live at that venue.

The Beatles featured it on two of their 'Pop Go The Beatles' shows, two 'Saturday Club' shows and two 'From Us To You' shows for BBC radio.

The official version was recorded for the *With The Beatles* album issued in Britain in November 1963 and it also appeared on the *Meet The Beatles* compilation, released in America in January 1964.

It was said that during the recording of 'Till There Was You', Brian Epstein was in the studio and remarked to George Martin that he thought there was a flaw in Paul's voice. John spoke into the mike, 'We'll make the records. You just go on counting the percentages.' A version was included on the Beatles' *Anthology 1* CDs.

Tim, Tiny

An American singer of novelty songs whose 1968 hit was 'Tiptoe Through The Tulips'. The Beatles sponsored his first British concert at the Royal Albert Hall that year and he also made a guest appearance on their 1968 Christmas Fan Club record. He died of heart failure after singing the song at a charity dinner in Minnesota in September 1996. He continually lied about his age, but is believed to have been at least 66 years old when he died. His ex-wife Susan Khary was to say, 'The last thing he heard was the applause.'

Tip Of My Tongue

Number penned by Paul McCartney and added to the Beatles' repertoire in 1962. The group recorded it on Monday, 26 November 1962, but George Martin considered that it wasn't suitable and it was left on the shelf. It was recorded by Brian Epstein's protégé Tommy Quickly and released in Britain on Piccadilly 7N 35137 on 30 July 1963, but failed to chart.

To Know Her Is To Love Her

A number composed by Phil Spector who thought of the title after seeing the words 'To know him was to love him' on his father's grave. He recorded it with the Teddy Bears in 1968 as 'To Know Him Is To Love Him', but the Beatles changed the 'him' to 'her' when they included it in their repertoire in 1961, with John on lead vocal. A live version of the number is to be found on *The Beatles Live! At The Star Club in Hamburg, Germany: 1962* album and they also recorded it for their 'Pop Goes The Beatles' radio show on

6 August 1963. A radio performance of the number was included on *The Beatles Live At The BBC* CDs.

Tomorrow Never Knows

The innovative closing track of *Revolver*, although it was the first number to be recorded for the album.

At the time John Lennon composed the song, Dr Timothy Leary's version of *The Egyptian Book Of The Dead* was in vogue. It was a guide for young people seeking to gain spiritual enlightenment, particularly through the use of the drug LSD. It inspired John and he utilised one line from the book in his song.

When recording began on Wednesday, 6 April 1966, John's various ideas had to be technically translated to what could actually be achieved in the studio by George Martin and Geoff Emerick. John said, 'I want to sound as though I'm the Dalai Lama singing from the highest mountain top. And yet I still want to hear the words I'm singing.' This was achieved by putting his voice through one of the Leslie speakers. John had said, 'With "Tomorrow Never Knows" I'd imagine in my head that in the background you could hear thousands of monks chanting. That was impractical of course and we did something different. I should have tried to get my original idea, the monks singing. I realise now that's what I wanted.' Amazing results were obtained by the use of tape loops and playing several machines at various speeds. To achieve some birdlike sounds, a tape loop of Paul laughing was used.

'Mark 1', the working title, was obviously not a suitable name for the number and the title actually came from a Ringo Starr remark – 'Tomorrow Never Knows', his version of 'Tomorrow Never Comes'. A version of the track was included on the Beatles' *Anthology 2* CDs.

Tonight Show, The

Major American chat show. John and Paul appeared on NBC's 'The Tonight Show' on 15 May 1968 to discuss their launch of Apple. The usual host Johnny Carson was away at the time and the duo were interviewed by former baseball player Joe Garagiola. The former Hollywood actress Tallulah Bankhead was also a guest on the show and her attitude towards John and Paul was quite antagonistic. Later, John was to comment that, 'She was pissed out of her head.'

During their discussion of Apple's philosophy, which they described as a form of 'Western Communism', Paul said, 'We always had to go to the big men on our knees and touch our forelocks and say, "Please, can we do so and so . . . ?" We're in the happy position of not needing any more money, so for the first time the bosses aren't in it for a profit. If you come to me and say, "I've had such and such a dream", I'll say to you, "Go away and do it." '

John commented, 'The aim isn't just a stack of gold teeth in the bank. We've done that bit. It's more of a trick to see if we can get artistic freedom within a business structure – to see if we can create things and sell them without charging five times their cost.'

There was an audience of eleven million watching the show that evening.

Too Bad About Sorrow

Possibly the first song John and Paul wrote together. It was included as part of the Quarry Men's repertoire in the late 1950s, but was dropped when the group changed their name to the Beatles, and the song has never been recorded.

Too Much Monkey Business

A Chuck Berry composition, originally recorded in 1956. The Beatles included it in their repertoire in 1961, with John on lead vocals. The group featured it on two 'Pop Go The Beatles' shows and also a 'Saturday Club' and a 'Side By Side' radio recording. A 1963 'Pop Goes The Beatles' track was included on the 1994 release *The Beatles Live At The BBC*.

Top Gear

A BBC Light Programme radio show which made its debut on 16 July 1964. It was a Thursday evening show transmitted from 10.00 p.m. to midnight, was presented by Brian Matthew and produced by Bernie Andrews. The Beatles made an appearance on the first show, which they recorded on 14 July at the BBC's Broadcasting House studios. The group performed 'Long Tall Sally', 'Things We Said Today', 'A Hard Day's Night', 'And I Love Her', 'I Should Have Known Better', 'If I Fell' and 'You Can't Do That'. Also on the bill were the Nashville Teens, Dusty Springfield and Carl Perkins.

Their second and final appearance took place on 26 November 1964, recorded at the Playhouse Theatre, Manchester on 17 November. The group performed 'I'm A Loser', 'Honey Don't', 'She's A Woman', 'Everybody's Trying To Be My Baby', 'I'll Follow The Sun' and 'I Feel Fine'.

Top Ten Club, 136 Reeperbahn, Hamburg, Germany

When 21-year-old Peter Eckhorn returned home from sea, his father decided to pass over the Hippodrome premises on the

Reeperbahn to him. It had previously been a topless circus. Eckhorn decided to convert the place into a rock 'n' roll club and had a stage and dance floor constructed and wooden booths, painted black, were fitted in.

With premises which could accommodate 2,000 people, Eckhorn decided to open it as the Top Ten Club in October 1960. Initially, he poached Horst Fascher from the Kaiserkeller club – and the poaching continued with the club securing Tony Sheridan & the Jets and even some barmaids and Rosa, the bierfrau from Bruno Koschmider's employ. Eckhorn also tried to book Liverpool's Derry & the Seniors, but the group were broke, disenchanted with Hamburg and approached the British Embassy to provide them with an assisted passage home.

The Beatles, still at the Kaiserkeller, began drifting to the Top Ten during their breaks. Koschmider's 'spy' George Sterner informed him of this and he began to make threats to them. They ignored him and began to get on stage to jam with the Jets – on one session the two groups performed a 70-minute version of 'What'd I Say'.

Koschmider was furious and pointed out a clause in their contract which disallowed them to play at any other venue within a 45-mile radius of the Kaiserkeller. When they ignored him he threatened to take away their protection. They didn't worry unduly about this as they had Horst Fascher's protection in the area – but another kind of 'protection' disappeared, and the police swooped on George Harrison for being under age. In the St Pauli area there was a curfew for youngsters under the age of eighteen. The Beatles received a letter from Koschmider:

I the undersigned, hereby give notice to Mr GEORGE HARRISON and to BEATLES BAND to leave on November 30th 1960.
'This notice is given to the above by order of the Public Authorities who have discovered that Mr GEORGE HARRISON is only 17 (seventeen) years of age.

The Beatles had, in fact, agreed to a residency at the Top Ten to replace the Jets. The group moved into the dormitory upstairs at the Top Ten Club, which had bunk beds and was much more comfortable than the accommodation at the Bambi Kino, even though the toilets were four floors below.

When George was deported, the Beatles then played a few sets at the Top Ten with John taking over on lead guitar, or even leaving out a lead guitar spot altogether and Paul played piano. They felt things were much better with 10 DM increase in pay per day. This didn't last for long. Paul and Pete had returned to the Bambi Kino for their gear and they were awakened from their sleep at the Top Ten 'dormitory' by the police, who put them in cells and deported them without allowing them to contact the British Embassy – for reportedly trying to set fire to the Bambi.

John returned to Liverpool several days later and Stuart Sutcliffe remained in Hamburg with Astrid Kirchherr.

The Jets were disbanding, but Eckhorn managed to get Tony Sheridan, Iain Hines and Colin Milander to stay and with Del Ward on drums and an American musician, they managed to remain for a further two months, until Eckhorn could find a replacement in the form of Gerry & the Pacemakers.

Although the Jets disbanded, Sheridan remained in Hamburg. Hines returned to England but was later to come back to the Top Ten and act as their booking manager.

Eckhorn parcelled up Pete Best's drums and had them sent to Liverpool and agreed to book the group for April 1962 if they could resolve the deportation bans.

Pete Best had been making arrangements for their return to Hamburg and on 28 March 1961 he received a letter from the West German Immigration Office granting the group a one-year concession. It read: 'We should like to point out explicitly, that this decision is a special concession of the Foreign Dept., and you are expected to refrain from any more penalties in the future, and that you are to obey the German Laws and Provisions. In this way you are given the opportunity to fulfil the engagement contracted by you with Mr Eckhorn's firm, until 14.4.1961.'

Stu kept in touch with the rest of the group and in a letter to Pete Best, he added the P.S: 'Everything has worked out fine. Paul will ring you or you ring Paul as soon as you have this. One thing I forgot to tell Paul, and that is that you both must pay Peter Eckhorn 79 DM, his cost of sending you home. The lifting of the deportation ban is only valid for one year, then you can have it reviewed. One thing they made clear, if you have any trouble with the Police, no matter how small, then you've had it forever.'

Once the Beatles had arrived and begun to play at the Top Ten on 27 March 1961, Eckhorn extended their contract twice and they played a total of fourteen weeks at the venue. They were required to play between 7.00 p.m. to 2.00 a.m. with a fifteen-minute break each hour. George Harrison commented, 'We performed like a gang of lunatics. It was all right once we got the hang of it all and it was great fun. The boss would send up cups of coffee on stage and we'd take turns to take a nip.' Paul McCartney said, 'We'd try out any sort of numbers from the Top Twenty. In a way it was marvellous, simply because we could experiment. Tired? We were dead wacked but we got great kicks out of watching the audiences, seeing the way they reacted to different gear.'

The Beatles had built their own following in Hamburg and among the regular crowd were the 'Exis' with friends such as Astrid Kirchherr and Klaus Voormann. During the early evening they had crowds of youngsters and after 10.00 p.m., when the curfew came into operation, the age group would be between eighteen and 25 years old.

While they were at the Top Ten Stuart Sutcliffe left the group. There had been confrontations with Paul, who wanted to take over the bass spot, and Stuart was becoming involved with his art studies once again. Before Stuart left, they encouraged him to write a letter to Allan Williams stating that they wouldn't be paying him any commission as they'd set up the deal with Eckhorn themselves. Williams sent a letter to them at the Top Ten dated 20 April 1961:

Dear All,

I am very distressed to hear you are contemplating not paying my commission out of your pay, as we agreed in our Contract for your engagement at the Top Ten Club.

May I remind you, seeing you are all appearing to get more than a little swollen-headed, that you would not even have smelled Hamburg if I had not made the contacts, and by Law it is illegal for any person under contract to make a contract through the first contract. I would also point out that the only reason you are there is through work that I did and if you had tried yourselves to play at the Top Ten without a bona fide contract and working through a British Government approved agency you would not be in Germany now.

Remember in your last contract under Koschmider you agreed not to play 30 weeks from terminating that contract. The only reason you managed to get out of that was, again, through myself. So far as you are concerned, he kept the contract.

So you see lads, I'm very annoyed you should welsh out of your agreed contract. If you decide not to pay I promise that I shall have you out of Germany inside two weeks through several legal ways and don't you think I'm bluffing.

I will also submit a full report of your behaviour to the Agency Members Association, of which I am a full member, and every Agent in England is a member, to protect Agents from Artistes who misbehave and welsh out on your contracts. Don't underestimate my ability to carry out what I have written . . .

My friend who has the Agency in London is bringing Ray Charles over to England in September and they plan to do a tour. I had thought of you going on tour with him, but unless you honour our agreement you can forget it. I will fix it for Rory Storm. This is no sprat, you check with your musical papers.

Look lads, I can do more for you than all the rest of Liverpool put together if I want to. Remember the others are only copying my original idea. In fact I told Ray McFall to put on Rock. So I think you are mad to try and make good with the Liverpool crowd who only want you to play for themselves.

I don't want to fall out with you but I can't abide anybody who does not honour their word or bond, and I could have sworn you were all decent lads, that is why I pushed you when nobody wanted to hear you.

Yours sincerely,
Allan.

The Beatles ignored him.

During their residency Bert Kaempfert arrived at the club with a party of people. He had been advised to listen to Tony Sheridan with a view to recording him for the Deutsche Grammophon's pop label Polydor. While there he also booked the Beatles to back him and their recordings with Sheridan were made during this trip.

After the Beatles returned to Liverpool, Sheridan continued to play at the Top Ten with different permutations of the Beat Brothers.

At one time Pete Eckhorn lured Ringo Starr away from Rory Storm & the Hurricanes with promises of a car, a flat and good weekly wages. Ringo backed Tony at the club for six months.

When Eckhorn sought to rebook the Beatles during a trip to Liverpool, he was referred to their new manager Brian Epstein. Epstein demanded 500 DM for each Beatle per week. Eckhorn offered 450. Brian wouldn't budge and eventually negotiated a deal with the new St Pauli rock venue, the Star Club.

The Top Ten continued presenting rock 'n' roll until Eckhorn's death.

Tours

The Beatles' first experience of touring began on 20 May 1960 in the town of Alloa, Scotland, when they were booked to appear as Johnny Gentle's backing group. They called themselves the Silver Beetles at the time, but were unbilled in the advertisements for the tour, which comprised seven gigs in Scotland, ending at Peterhead on 28 May. The tour was typical of the type organised by impresario Larry Parnes for his stable of acts, which included Marty Wilde, Billy Fury, Duffy Power and Dickie Pride. They were short tours of ballroom and town hall venues and the artists had to basically 'rough it', travellling in tiny vans and staying at cheap hotels. During this first tour, the group, with the exception of John, created stage names, although the Beatles weren't generally publicised and the billing read: 'Johnny Gentle and his group'.

JOHNNY GENTLE SCOTTISH TOUR, 1960

20 May	Town Hall, Alloa
21 May	Northern Meeting Ballroom, Inverness
23 May	Dalrymple Hall, Fraserburgh
25 May	St Thomas' Hall, Keith
26 May	Town Hall, Forres
27 May	Regal Ballroom, Nairn
28 May	Rescue Hall, Peterhead

The prestige tours in Britain at the time were those run by major London-based promoters such as Arthur Howes and Tito Burns. They comprised a bill topped by a star name who had a current or recent hit, supported by some lesser-known recording acts in a loose bill introduced by a compere/comedian. This type of package tour generally visited the cinema chains run by ABC, Gaumont, Granada, Odeon and Regal, and there was a particular emphasis on Sunday concert presentations. The other type of tour prevalent at the time was the ballroom tour, which visited chains such as the Rank or Mecca ballroom circuit.

At the beginning of 1963, the group were booked by the Cana Variety Agency to appear on a short Scottish tour. Although the agency had secured the Beatles at the bargain price of £42 per show, they lost money on the event because of the atrocious weather which saw the first of the shows, at the Longmore Hall, Keith, cancelled.

SCOTTISH TOUR, 1963

3 Jan	Two Red Shoes Ballroom, Elgin
4 Jan	Town Hall, Dingwall
5 Jan	Museum Hall, Bridge of Allan
6 Jan	Beach Ballroom, Aberdeen

However, the Beatles enjoyed touring at the time and John Lennon commented, 'Touring was a relief. We were beginning to feel stale and cramped. We'd get tired of one stage and be deciding to pack up when another stage would come up. We'd outlived the Hamburg stage and hated going back to Hamburg those last two times.'

Brian Epstein was determined to place the Beatles on a theatre tour. Tito Burns made enquiries about the band, but didn't follow up and Larry Parnes wouldn't agree to the modest fee asked by Epstein for his protégés, so Brian contacted Arthur Howes who, despite the group's poor reception at the 'trial' appearance at the Embassy, Peterborough, booked them to appear on the bill of the Helen Shapiro tour from 2 February–3 March 1963. Also on the bill were Danny Williams, Kenny Lynch, the Honeys, the Kestrels, the Red Price Band and compere Dave Allen. Despite various Beatle books mentioning that the group were virtually the bottom-of-the-bill act on the tour, Howes' advertisement for the tour appearing on the cover of the *New Musical Express* on 22 February 1963 has them placed second on the bill to Helen Shapiro, with their named printed bolder than the other acts.

The group were also able to travel in the tour bus with the rest of the acts, instead of in the white van which Brian Epstein had bought for Neil Aspinall to drive them to gigs in. This was the year in which travelling in a van with the equipment ended.

HELEN SHAPIRO TOUR, 1963

2 Feb	Gaumont, Bradford
5 Feb	Gaumont, Doncaster
6 Feb	Granada, Bedford
7 Feb	Regal, Kirkgate
8 Feb	ABC, Carlisle
9 Feb	Empire, Sunderland
23 Feb	Granada, Mansfield
24 Feb	Coventry Theatre, Coventry
26 Feb	Gaumont, Taunton
27 Feb	Rialto, York
28 Feb	Granada, Shrewsbury
1 March	Odeon, Southport
2 March	City Hall, Sheffield
3 March	Gaumont, Hanley

Top-of-the-bill acts were usually afforded special treatment and were generally driven to venues in private transport and not by tour coach – although Helen Shapiro preferred to travel on the bus with the rest of the company. Ringo also noticed the difference between top-of-the-bill performers and the support acts when he spotted a television in Helen's dressing-room while the rest of them had to make do with transistor radios!

Accommodation was not as rough as on their tour for Larry Parnes and they were generally booked into hotels of a comfortable standard.

During the Shapiro tour, Ringo was still feeling his way with the group and commented, 'I was still the odd one out, the new boy. But the togetherness of the tour helped a lot. It made me feel more part of a team. At first I worried about who I'd share with at our hotels, but mostly it was me in with Paul, and George with John sharing another room.'

John said, 'It really was a relief to get out of Liverpool and try something new. Back home we'd worked night after night on the same cramped stage. Bradford wasn't very far away, but at least it was different as a field. We'd all started feeling tired, jaded, tied down with the club scenes. Touring, with a different venue each night, was a real lift.'

Howes became the man who was to promote most of their British tours and their success with Helen Shapiro caused him to immediately book them on the Tommy Roe/Chris Montez tour, only six days after the Shapiro tour had closed. Once again they were given billing immediately below the bill-toppers and in larger letters than the rest of the company. The other acts on the tour were the Viscounts, Debbie Lee, the Terry Young Combo and Tony Marsh and the dates were from 9–31 March 1963.

TOMMY ROE/CHRIS MONTEZ TOUR, 1963

9 March	Granada, East Ham
10 March	Hippodrome, Birmingham
12 March	Granada, Bedford
13 March	Rialto, York
14 March	Gaumont, Wolverhampton
15 March	Colston Hall, Bristol
16 March	City Hall, Sheffield
17 March	Embassy, Peterborough
18 March	Regal, Gloucester
19 March	Regal, Cambridge
20 March	ABC, Romford
21 March	ABC, Croydon
22 March	Gaumont, Doncaster
23 March	City Hall, Newcastle-upon-Tyne
24 March	Empire, Liverpool
26 March	Granada, Mansfield
27 March	ABC, Northampton

28 March	ABC, Exeter
29 March	Odeon, Lewisham
30 March	Guildhall, Portsmouth
31 March	De Monfort Hall, Leicester

Manchester-based agency Kennedy Street Enterprises had booked the Beatles to appear on a tour supporting an American artist in May. Originally the bill-topper was to be Duane Eddy, but this didn't work out and Ben E. King and then the Four Seasons were considered. Eventually, Roy Orbison was booked to headline. However, the Beatles' popularity was now so big in Britain that the American star was asked if he would allow the Beatles to be bill-toppers. The advertising was designed in such a way that either Orbison or the Beatles could be taken as the bill-toppers, although the Beatles closed the show with a 45-minute spot. Also on the bill were Gerry & the Pacemakers, David Macbeth, Louise Cordet, Erkey Grant, Ian Crawford, the Terry Young Combo and Tony Marsh. The tour ran from 18 May–9 June 1963.

ROY ORBISON/BEATLES TOUR, 1963

18 May	Adelphi, Slough
19 May	Gaumont, Hanley
20 May	Gaumont, Southampton
22 May	Gaumont, Ipswich
23 May	Odeon, Nottingham
24 May	Granada, Walthamstow
25 May	City Hall, Sheffield
26 May	Empire, Liverpool
28 May	Gaumont, Worcester
29 May	Rialto, York
30 May	Odeon, Manchester
31 May	Odeon, Southend-on-Sea
1 June	Granada, Tooting
2 June	Hippodrome, Brighton
3 June	Granada, Woolwich
4 June	Town Hall, Birmingham
5 June	Odeon, Leeds
7 June	Odeon, Glasgow
8 June	City Hall, Newcastle-upon-Tyne
9 June	King George's Hall, Blackburn

It was during the Orbison tour that the fans started throwing jelly babies at them, due to a chance remark on television that George enjoyed the sweets. Another facet of the Beatles' tour appearances

was that female fans screamed so long and so hard throughout their
show that it became almost impossible to hear what the group
sounded like and their musical expertise on tour was never really
called upon again. The group were now so popular that they could
afford to be driven to gigs by car, usually a chauffeur-driven luxury
model as befitted their new status as celebrities and stars. It was
also the time when their freedom of movement was curtailed. No
longer able to slip out for a pint in a local pub during the long
periods in the dressing-rooms, they also found it difficult to eat out
at local restaurants near the theatres where they were appearing
and generally food had to be brought in to them, usually by Neil
Aspinall. They were now also playing for periods of 25 minutes or
half an hour, in contrast to the long stints they used to perform in
Hamburg and Liverpool.

Bill-toppers in their own right now, the Beatles next began a
mini-tour of Scotland with Mike Berry as support.

BEATLES MINI-TOUR OF SCOTLAND, 1963

5 Oct	Concert Hall, Glasgow
6 Oct	Carlton, Kirkcaldy
7 Oct	Caird Hall, Dundee

Mike Berry also accompanied the band on their short tour of
Sweden between 25 and 29 October, where there was also support
from local talent such as the Phantoms. It was the Beatles' first tour
abroad – their appearances in Hamburg had been more in the
nature of seasons at a particular club rather than a proper tour.

BEATLES TOUR OF SWEDEN, 1963

25 Oct	Nya aulan, Karlstad
26 Oct	Kungliga Hallen, Stockholm
27 Oct	Cirkus, Goteborg
28 Oct	Borashallen, Boras
29 Oct	Sporthallen, Eskilstunä

The group immediately commenced their autumn tour of Britain,
their fourth British tour that year. Among the support acts were Peter
Jay & the Jaywalkers, the Brook Brothers with the Rhythm and Blues
Quartet, the Vernons Girls, the Kestrels and compere/comedian
Frank Berry. The tour lasted from 1 November–13 December.

BEATLES AUTUMN TOUR OF BRITAIN, 1963

1 Nov	Odeon, Cheltenham
2 Nov	City Hall, Sheffield

3 Nov	Odeon, Leeds
5 Nov	Adelphi, Slough
6 Nov	ABC, Northampton
7 Nov	Adelphi, Dublin
8 Nov	Ritz, Belfast
9 Nov	Granada, East Ham
10 Nov	Hippodrome, Birmingham
13 Nov	ABC, Plymouth
14 Nov	ABC, Exeter
15 Nov	Colston Hall, Bristol
16 Nov	Winter Gardens, Bournemouth
17 Nov	Coventry Theatre, Coventry
19 Nov	Gaumont, Wolverhampton
20 Nov	ABC, Ardwick
21 Nov	ABC, Carlisle
22 Nov	Globe, Stockton-on-Tees
23 Nov	City Hall, Newcastle-upon-Tyne
24 Nov	ABC, Hull
26 Nov	Regal, Cambridge
27 Nov	Rialto, York
28 Nov	ABC, Lincoln
29 Nov	ABC, Huddersfield
30 Nov	Empire, Sunderland
1 Dec	De Montfort Hall, Leicester
3 Dec	Guildhall, Portsmouth
7 Dec	Odeon, Liverpool
8 Dec	Odeon, Lewisham
9 Dec	Odeon, Southend-on-Sea
10 Dec	Gaumont, Doncaster
11 Dec	Futurist, Scarborough
12 Dec	Odeon, Nottingham
13 Dec	Gaumont, Southampton

1963 closed and 1964 opened with the Beatles' first Christmas Show taking place at the Finsbury Park Astoria, with Cilla Black, Billy J. Kramer with the Dakotas, the Fourmost, Tommy Quickly and the Remo Four, the Barron Knights with Duke D'Mond and Rolf Harris in support. The group then appeared for a short season at the Paris Olympia from 16 January–4 February 1964, and the French proved to be the most disappointing of all foreign audiences. Noticeably different was the fact that the audiences were mainly male – and the Beatles only brought them to life when they performed some rock 'n' roll classics.

It was when the group were booked to appear in America and

their mammoth major tours before tens of thousands of fans began
that the face of touring was to be completely revolutionised.
Although those early tours of America by the Beatles seem crude by
the standards of today's spectaculars, it was the Beatles who laid
the groundwork for what was to come. As vast concerts of this type
had never been organised on such a scale before, the Beatles, more
by design than choice, had to create some new rules. A ceiling was
placed on ticket prices by Brian Epstein, contracts stipulated that
security must be provided, together with the availability of a good
hi-fi system and a sound engineer, as well as microphones and other
equipment. Even details of the size of stages was worked out in
advance. The promoters were to provide proper dressing-room
facilities but also a TV set, clean towels cots and mirrors, plus
limousines with chauffeurs. They also included a clause for the
southern states: 'Artists will not be required to perform before a
segregated audience'.

The Beatles only made two concert appearances in America in
February, at the Coliseum, Washington DC, on 11 February and at
Carnegie Hall, New York, on 12 February. Their next major tour
was the first world tour, which took place from 4 June to 29 June.
For the initial part of the tour Ringo Starr was taken ill and
drummer Jimmy Nicol deputised.

THE WORLD TOUR, 1964

4 June	Tivoli Gardens, Copenhagen, Denmark
6 June	Exhibition Hall, Blokker, Denmark
10 June	Princess Theatre, Hong Kong
12 June	Centennial Hall, Adelaide, Australia
13 June	Centennial Hall, Adelaide, Australia
15 June	Festival Hall, Melbourne, Australia
18 June	Sydney Stadium, Sydney, Australia
19 June	Sydney Stadium, Sydney, Australia
20 June	Sydney Stadium, Sydney, Australia
22 June	Town Hall, Wellington, New Zealand
23 June	Town Hall, Wellington, New Zealand
24 June	Town Hall, Auckland, New Zealand
25 June	Town Hall, Auckland, New Zealand
26 June	Town Hall, Dunedin, New Zealand
27 June	Majestic Theatre, Christchurch, New Zealand
29 June	Festival Hall, Brisbane, Australia
30 June	Festival Hall, Brisbane, Australia

On their return from Australia the group appeared at a small
number of concert venues in Britain and then made a short trip to

Sweden for two concerts before next creating history with their first tour of America, breaking audience records as they appeared at major arenas throughout the States. Their tour lasted from 19 August to 28 September 1964 and the other artists on the bill included Jackie De Shannon, the Righteous Brothers, the Bill Black Combo and the Exciters.

THE BEATLES' FIRST AMERICAN TOUR, 1964

19 Aug	Cow Palace, San Francisco
20 Aug	Convention Hall, Las Vegas
21 Aug	Coliseum, Seattle
22 Aug	Empire Stadium, Vancouver
23 Aug	Hollywood Bowl, Los Angeles
26 Aug	Red Rock Stadium, Denver
27 Aug	The Gardens, Cincinnati
28 Aug	Forest Hills Stadium, New York
30 Aug	Convention Hall, Atlantic City
2 Sep	Convention Hall, Philadelphia
3 Sep	State Fair Coliseum, Indianapolis
4 Sep	Auditorium, Milwaukee
5 Sep	International Amphitheatre, Chicago
6 Sep	Olympia Stadium, Detroit
7 Sep	Maple Leaf Gardens, Toronto
8 Sep	Forum, Montreal
11 Sep	Gator Bowl, Jacksonville
12 Sep	Boston Gardens, Boston
13 Sep	Civic Centre, Baltimore
14 Sep	Civic Arena, Pittsburgh
15 Sep	Public Auditorium, Cleveland
16 Sep	City Park Stadium, New Orleans
17 Sep	Municipal Stadium, Kansas City
18 Sep	Memorial Coliseum, Dallas
20 Sep	Paramount Theatre, New York

Their winter tour of Britain was once again promoted by Arthur Howes and began at the Gaumont, Bradford, site of the first night of their Helen Shapiro tour. Support acts were Mary Wells, the Rustiks, Michael Haslam, Sounds Incorporated and Tommy Quickly and the Remo Four. Compere was Bob Bain.

AUTUMN TOUR OF BRITAIN, 1964

9 Oct	Gaumont, Bradford
10 Oct	De Montfort Hall, Leicester
11 Oct	Odeon, Birmingham

13 Oct	ABC, Wigan
14 Oct	ABC, Manchester
15 Oct	Globe, Stockton-on-Tees
16 Oct	ABC, Hull
19 Oct	ABC, Edinburgh
20 Oct	Caird Hall, Dundee
21 Oct	Odeon, Glasgow
22 Oct	Odeon, Leeds
23 Oct	Gaumont State, Kilburn
24 Oct	Granada, Walthamstow
25 Oct	Hippodrome, Brighton
28 Oct	ABC, Exeter
29 Oct	ABC, Plymouth
30 Oct	Gaumont, Bournemouth
31 Oct	Gaumont, Ipswich
1 Nov	Astoria, Finsbury Park
2 Nov	King's Hall, Belfast
4 Nov	Ritz, Luton
5 Nov	Odeon, Nottingham
6 Nov	Gaumont, Southampton
7 Nov	Capitol, Cardiff
8 Nov	Empire, Liverpool
9 Nov	City Hall, Sheffield
10 Nov	Colston Hall, Bristol

The Beatles ended the year with *Another Beatles Christmas Show* at the Odeon, Hammersmith, London, commencing 24 December 1964 and closing on 16 January 1965 with the Yardbirds, the Mike Cotton Sound, Michael Haslam, Freddie & the Dreamers, Elkie Brooks, Sounds Incorporated, Ray Fell and Jimmy Savile in support.

The group next embarked on a two-week tour of Europe, taking in France, Italy and Spain.

EUROPEAN TOUR, 1965

20 June	Palais De Sports, Paris
22 June	Palais d'Hiver, Lyon
24 June	Velodromo, Milan
25 June	Palazzo dello Sport, Genoa
27 June	Teatro Adriano, Rome
28 June	Teatro Adriano, Rome
30 June	Palais des Fetes, Nice
2 July	Plaza de Toros de Madrid, Madrid
3 July	Plaza de Toros de Madrid, Madrid

Their next tour of America opened with the spectacular Shea Stadium appearance which, with an audience of 55,600, created a world record for a concert. Support acts on the tour were the King Curtis band, Brenda Holloway and Sounds Incorporated.

AMERICAN TOUR, 1965

15 Aug	Shea Stadium, New York
17 Aug	Maple Leaf Gardens, Toronto
18 Aug	Atlanta Stadium, Georgia
19 Aug	Sam Houston Coliseum, Houston
20 Aug	White Sox Park, Chicago
21 Aug	Metropolitan Stadium, Minneapolis
22 Aug	Memorial Coliseum, Portland
28 Aug	Balboa Stadium, San Diego
29 Aug	Hollywood Bowl, Los Angeles
30 Aug	Hollywood Bowl, Los Angeles
31 Aug	Cow Palace, San Francisco

Touring was now beginning to tell on the Beatles. Their equipment was not vast by today's standards and they appeared on stages with small Vox amplifiers, but as their music could hardly be heard through the piercing sounds of screaming fans, it didn't seem to be a problem, although the group were becoming bored. Their next tour of Britain was to be the last time they toured in the UK. They were supported by Birmingham band the Moody Blues, the Paramounts from Southampton and three Liverpool acts, the Koobas, Beryl Marsden and Steve Aldo. With only nine appearances, it became their shortest theatre tour of Britain. The group had also decided not to hold a third Christmas Show.

BRITISH TOUR, 1965

3 Dec	Odeon, Glasgow
4 Dec	City Hall, Newcastle
5 Dec	Empire, Liverpool
7 Dec	Apollo, Ardwick, Manchester
8 Dec	City Hall, Sheffield
9 Dec	Odeon, Birmingham
10 Dec	Odeon, Hammersmith
11 Dec	Astoria, Finsbury Park
12 Dec	Capitol, Cardiff

1966 was the Beatles' last year as a touring group and it also saw the virtual end of their live appearances. They appeared at the *New Musical Express* Poll Winners' Concert on 1 May which, apart from their rooftop appearance on the Apple building, was their last live show in Britain. They next embarked on a short tour of Germany and Japan, supported by Cliff Bennett & the Rebel Rousers and Peter & Gordon.

TOUR OF GERMANY AND JAPAN, 1966

24 June	Circus Krone, Munich, Germany
25 June	Grugahalle, Essen, Germany
26 June	Ernst Merck Halle, Hamburg, Germany
30 June	Budokan Hall, Tokyo, Japan
1 July	Budokan Hall, Tokyo, Japan
2 July	Budokan Hall, Tokyo, Japan
4 July	Araneta Coliseum, Manila, Philippines

The most horrific incidents in their touring career occurred in Manila where they were manhandled and jeered at following a reported snub to the country's First Lady, Imelda Marcos. On the plane home, a shaken group decided that their touring days must soon be over. This was consolidated by their final American tour which was blighted by the uproar caused over John Lennon's quotes about Christ in an interview with Maureen Cleave. The American media exploited the quotes out of context and out of all proportion, resulting in the first wave of anti-Beatles feeling that had arisen in America. The love affair between America and the Beatles seemed to have soured. A reluctant Lennon had to submit to a humiliating public apology and there was still anti-Beatle feeling in the southern states and middle-America, with various death threats. At some gigs the Beatles had to duck when they heard sharp noises, fearing them to be gunshots.

They decided that touring was no longer to be on the agenda and George Harrison sighed with relief when flying home after their final concert, saying, 'I'm not a Beatle any more.' In fact, the Beatles were about to move into the most important phase of their career, their studio years, when they were able to develop their songwriting and musical abilities inside the recording studio – to an extent they would never have been able to do if they had continued touring.

Towards the end of their career, Paul McCartney was anxious for the Beatles to take to the road again, even if it meant appearing unannounced at colleges or small venues, or booking places such as London's Roundhouse. Given time he might have persuaded Ringo and even John to embark on some further live gigs – but never George. George had made his mind up that he would never tour again with the Beatles – and that is how it was.

Their final American tour saw them with acts such as the Ronettes, the Cyrkle and the Remains in support.

FINAL AMERICAN TOUR, 1966

12 Aug	International Amphitheatre, Chicago
13 Aug	Olympia Stadium, Detroit
14 Aug	Municipal Stadium, Cleveland
15 Aug	Washington Stadium, Washington DC
16 Aug	Philadelphia Stadium, Philadelphia
17 Aug	Maple Leaf Gardens, Toronto
18 Aug	Suffolk Downs Racecourse, Boston
19 Aug	Memphis Coliseum, Memphis
20 Aug	Crosley Field, Cincinnati
21 Aug	Busch Stadium, St Louis
23 Aug	Shea Stadium, New York
24 Aug	Shea Stadium, New York
25 Aug	Seattle Coliseum, Seattle
28 Aug	Dodger Stadium, Los Angeles
30 Aug	Candlestick Park, San Francisco

Tower Ballroom, New Brighton, Wirral, Merseyside L45

One of Merseyside's largest ballroom facilities, which was able to accommodate 5,000 people. When it was originally constructed it sported the largest iron tower in Europe after the Eiffel Tower and was taller than Blackpool's famous Tower. The Tower itself was dismantled to provide metal for the war effort, but the material was never used and the Tower was never rebuilt.

George Harrison's grandfather was once a commissionaire at the ballroom.

Sam Leach was the promoter responsible for recognising the ballroom's potential as a venue for spectacular dance promotions and on 10 November 1961 he launched 'Operation Big Beat', which featured a number of Liverpool bands.

The show opened at 7.30 p.m. and the Beatles appeared at 8.00 p.m. They then fulfilled another engagement at Knotty Ash Village Hall before returning for their second Tower appearance that evening at 11.30 p.m. Tickets for the event had been sold in advance at NEMS' Whitechapel store, which was managed by Brian Epstein, who must have been aware of the event, although it pre-dated the supposed enquiry from 'Raymond Jones'. The event drew an audience of 3,000 people.

'Operation Big Beat II' took place on the evening of Friday, 24 November 1961, with the Beatles once again topping the bill. The other local groups who appeared were Rory Storm & the Hurricanes, Gerry & the Pacemakers, the Remo Four, Earl Preston

& the Tempest Tornadoes and Faron & the Flamingos. Late-night transport had to be arranged with the various local authorities as the event took place between 7.30 p.m. and 2.00 a.m. Tickets cost 6/- (30p). An added treat for the audience was the appearance of Emile Ford, who'd had several chart hits, including 'What Do You Want To Make Those Eyes At Me For' and 'Slow Boat To China'; he got up on stage and sang with Rory Storm & the Hurricanes and American singer Davy Jones, who joined the Beatles on stage and sang two numbers with them.

The Beatles returned to top the bill again on 1 December 1961 at a six-group extravaganza which attracted 2,000 people.

On 8 December 1961 Leach organised a further Tower promotion, adding South African singing star Danny Williams to the bill, whose current hit 'Moon River' was at No. 4 in the British charts. Leach also booked Davy Jones as headliner and he was once again backed by the Beatles – and they actually backed him earlier in the day at a Cavern lunchtime session.

Leach's final Tower promotion of the year took place on 15 December and featured five bands on a five-and-a-half-hour show. The Beatles topped the bill, which showed the appearance, for one night only, a former top Liverpool band Cass & the Cassanovas. When Brian Casser had originally left the group, the remaining three members continued as the Big Three. On this evening's bill Casser joined the Big Three under their old name for a special reunion performance.

The first bill of the New Year was on Friday, 12 January 1962, on an extravaganza called 'Twist Around The Tower'. Leach advertised the bill as 'The Greatest Show on Merseyside, starring that horrible hairy Monster Screaming Lord Sutch (X certificate) and his horde of Savages, with Philips recording artists Mel (King of Twist) Turner and the Bandits. Also, *Mersey Beat* Poll Winners The Beatles (After 11.30 p.m.), Rory Storm & the Hurricanes, the Strangers. We introduced the Twist to Merseyside, Now we present another lead – a sensational Twist exhibition team, Mr Twist & the Twistettes'. Bill toppers Screaming Lord Sutch & the Savages failed to turn up.

The Beatles' next Tower appearance took place on 19 January, followed by a special Pre-Panto Ball on 15 February. Panto Day was an annual event in Liverpool, organised by students at Liverpool University. They would parade around the city on huge decorated floats, dressed in costumes, collecting for local charities. On the Panto Day evening, all students who had taken part in the event were invited to a special Panto Day Ball. Leach capitalised on the publicity by putting on his bill on the eve of Panto Day, with Terry

Lightfoot and his New Orleans Jazz Band co-headlining with the Beatles. It drew an audience of 3,500 people. The Beatles then appeared at the Tower on a further Sam Leach bill the following night, 16 February. On 23 February they appeared at the ballroom twice, initially at 9.00 p.m., followed by a set at 10.45 p.m.

On 2 March they appeared at another Tower event, billed as the Mad March Rock Ball.

The Beatles' appearance on Friday, 6 April, was their last Tower appearance prior to their season at Hamburg's Star Club. The two headliners were Emile Ford & the Checkmates and the Beatles and the other bands were Gerry & the Pacemakers, Howie Casey & the Seniors, Rory Storm & the Hurricanes and the Big Three. Adding some novelty were the Original Kingtwisters.

Leach was the local promoter who had shown the foresight to gamble on promoting rock shows at the Tower. It was situated in an unfortunate location – near the promenade of a fading holiday resort on the Wirral peninsula. However, Sam had solved this problem by organising special late-night transport by bus and train to all areas of Liverpool and the Wirral. Once he'd got his system into place and had developed the Tower as a successful venue for promotion, other promoters obviously considered taking advantage of its facilities.

The next Beatles appearance there was on a promotion financed by Brian Epstein and organised and compered by Bob Wooler. It was the first of a series of planned prestige gigs by Epstein to place the Beatles on a bill with name artists. For this appearance on Thursday 21 June 1962, the bill was topped by Bruce Channel. Channel had had a massive hit with 'Hey Baby!' and he was backed by harmonica player Delbert McLinton & the Barons. The Beatles were advertised as 'Parlophone Recording Artistes and stars of the BBC's "Teenage Turn"'. Bolton group the Statesmen were next on the bill, followed by Mersey groups the Big Three and the Four Jays.

'Operation Big Beat II' on 29 June, topped by the Beatles, featured ten local bands in a five-and-a-half-hour spectacular.

The next Brian Epstein presentation at the Tower featured Joe Brown and the Bruvvers headlining over the Beatles on 27 July. The other acts on the bill were the Statesmen, the Big Three, Steve Day & the Drifters and the Four Jays.

For their appearance at the venue on 17 August, the Beatles had drummer Johnny Hutchinson sitting in with them as Pete Best had been ignominiously sacked a few days previously.

Sam Leach presented his 'Operation Big Beat V' on 14 September, another five-and-a-half-hour marathon featuring six local groups, headed by the Beatles. Later the same month the Beatles appeared at the Tower on 21 September with four other local bands – the occasion was a celebration of Rory Storm's birthday.

The next event was another five-and-a-half-hour extravaganza, this time promoted by Brian Epstein and starring Little Richard on a 12-act bill. Sam Leach had originally offered Richard £350 for a Tower Ballroom booking and looked like securing the American star until he was outbid by Epstein who paid £500 for Richard and lost money on the gig, although the Beatles' career was boosted by the prestigious appearance.

It was another NEMS Enterprises presentation and Bob Wooler production and, apart from the Beatles, Lee Curtis & the All Stars appeared with their new drummer, Pete Best. Other acts on the bill were the Big Three, Billy J. Kramer with the Coasters, the Dakotas with Pete MacLaine, the Four Jays, the Merseybeats, Rory Storm & the Hurricanes and the Undertakers. Epstein was later to produce the Hurricanes on record and was also later to sign Billy J. Kramer and team him with Manchester's Dakotas. He was also to sign the Big Three, whose drummer Johnny Hutchinson filled the stopgap when Best was sacked. Epstein considered signing the Merseybeats and eventually they became a NEMS band, and he signed the Four Jays, who became the Fourmost. Jackie Lomax, lead singer with the Undertakers, later became an Apple artist, recorded by both Paul McCartney and George Harrison.

During the course of the evening, photographer Les Chadwick took the famous picture of Little Richard and the Beatles on behalf of *Mersey Beat*, the newspaper.

On 23 November the Beatles appeared on the bill of the 12th Annual Lancashire and Cheshire Arts Ball. Also appearing were Billy J. Kramer and the Coasters, the Llew Hird Jazz Band and the Clan McCleod Pipe Band.

Their last Tower appearance during 1962 was on 7 December when they topped the bill on a line-up of seven local bands.

The Beatles' final appearance at the Tower Ballroom took place on Friday, 14 June 1963, on a special NEMS Enterprises' presentation on their 'Mersey Beat Showcase' series. The Beatles were supported by Gerry & the Pacemakers and five other groups.

The Tower was burned down in 1969, leaving only the foundations.

Town Hall, Alloa, Clackmannanshire, Scotland

Venue where the Silver Beetles made their debut with Johnny Gentle on the short Beat Ballad Show tour. The appearance took place on Friday, 20 May 1960. The group and Gentle had never played together before and had a single rehearsal, lasting only thirty minutes, prior to their performance that evening. The numbers they rehearsed were 'Poor Little Fool', 'Mary Lou', 'He'll Have To Go', 'Have I Told You Lately?' 'I Don't Know Why I Love You', 'I Need Your Love' and 'OK You Win'. The Silver Beetles also had their own spot during which they performed 'Hello Little Girl', 'The One After 909', 'Bye Bye Love', 'Tutti Frutti', 'Lucille', 'Long Tall Sally', 'Twenty Flight Rock', 'Hallelujah I Love Her So', 'Stuck On You', 'That'll Be The Day', 'Be Bop A Lula', 'Wild Cat', 'What'd I Say', 'Little Queenie' and 'Hully Gully'.

Second on the bill was Alex Harvey and his Beat Band, advertised as 'Scotland's answer to Tommy Steele', who began his set with 'Willie And The Hand Jive'. The Glaswegian was to become a friend of the Beatles during his appearances in Hamburg and later became a successful recording and concert artist in the 1970s, a career curtailed by his early death.

The other artist on the bill was a local ballad singer Bobby Rankine.

Entrance to the event was 4/-.

The Silver Beetles weren't billed on the tour as the advertisements announced 'Johnny Gentle And His Group'. They backed Gentle from 10.30 to 11.00 p.m. and then had their own hour spot, followed by Harvey.

Gentle opened the show singing 'Have I Told You Lately' and, during his performance of 'It Doesn't Matter Anymore', photographer Ken Beaton took a shot of the white-jacketed Gentle, with George at his side – the only visual record that exists of that particular tour.

Promoter Duncan McKinnon watched the show, wasn't impressed by the Silver Beetles and phoned Larry Parnes to complain about them.

Alloa itself had a population of 14,000 in 1960.

Town Hall, Queen Street, Auckland, New Zealand

The group appeared at this venue on New Zealand's North Island for four shows over a period of two nights, which drew capacity audiences of over 10,000 people. The appearances took place on Wednesday, 24 and Thursday, 25 June 1964. Initially, there was some hostility from authorities in Auckland, although the concerts were very successful and brought the group enthusiastic reviews.

Town Hall, Congreve Street, Birmingham

The Beatles appeared at this venue once, during their tour with Roy Orbison on Tuesday, 4 June 1963.

Town Hall, Dingwall, Ross and Cromarty, Scotland

The beginning of 1963 saw the Beatles undertake a brief tour of Scotland during hazardous weather conditions. One of the gigs was at the Town Hall in Dingwall where they appeared on Friday, 4 January 1963.

Town Hall, Moray Place, Dunedin, New Zealand

After appearing on the North Island of New Zealand, the Beatles flew to the South Island to appear in Dunedin and Christchurch. They appeared for two shows on the evening of Friday, 26 June 1964 at this venue with capacity audiences of 4,000.

The reception in the Town Hall was incredibly loud, although the enthusiastic audience didn't leave their seats to attempt to reach the group on stage as the raised platform was far too high. A line of policemen, their arms linked, stood between the audience and the stage and, because the linked arms inhibited their movement, some playful fans knocked off their helmets and played football with them in the aisles.

Town Hall, Market Street, Earlestown, Newton-Le-Willows, Cheshire

Venue where the Beatles made a single appearance on Friday, 30 November 1962 in 'The Big Beat Show No. 2', a promotion by the T & T Vicars Sports and Social Club. The civic building is over a hundred years old and presented dances regularly until the mid-1960s.

Town Hall, High Street, Forres, Morayshire, Scotland

The Beatles appeared here during their Beat Ballad Tour of Scotland on Thursday, 26 May 1960. The dance ran from 9.00 p.m. to 1.00 a.m., cost five shillings (25p) admittance and also featured Rikki Barnes And His All Stars and Lena and Stevie.

The impecunious Silver Beetles were staying overnight at the Royal Hotel in the town that night, but slipped away without paying the bill.

Town Hall, Town Hall Chambers, Church Road, Lydney, Gloucestershire

A single appearance at this venue in Gloucestershire for the Beatles, who performed at the venue on Friday, 31 August 1962.

Town Hall, Wellington, New Zealand

The Beatles opened their brief tour of New Zealand with four shows at this theatre in Wellington, on the North Island. The group appeared at the Town Hall on 22 and 23 June 1964 and the 2,500-seater hall was fully booked.

At the first show on Monday, 22 June, the PA system was very primitive and the sound was inadequate. Johnny Devlin had to convince the man who owned the PA system that he could turn it up without it being destroyed and it proved to be fine for the second show. There were 50 police in the hall and they kept forcing the girls back into their seats. One young man managed to scramble on stage and almost knocked Ringo off his drum stool before he was bundled away. Incidentally, Ringo sang the number 'Boys' during the New Zealand gigs, instead of 'I Wanna Be Your Man', which he sang in Australia.

Town Hall, Paul's Moss, Dodington, Whitchurch, Shropshire

The Beatles only made a single appearance at this Town Hall in Shropshire, on 19 January 1963.

Townsend, Ken

The General Manager of Abbey Road Studios in London.

He joined the Abbey Road Studios in the mid-fifties as a tape engineer and was present assisting George Martin on the Beatles' first EMI recording audition on 6 June 1962. When he was chief technical engineer he worked closely with the Beatles and credits them with creating an atmosphere of experimentation which led to a revolution in recording methods.

In an attempt to facilitate some of the Beatles' experiments in the fields of double-tracking, he invented a machine which he called ADT (Artificial Double Tracking). He was driving home one night after a Beatles session in which they had spent the entire evening double-tracking when the idea came to him to develop a system of electronically putting one vocal on to another.

John Lennon persisted in calling the machine 'Ken's Flanger', with the result that 'flanging' has become a standard technical term used in recording studios throughout the world.

Trash

A group from Glasgow, Scotland, originally known as the Pathfinders. They were discovered by Tony Meehan, ex-member of the Shadows.

They were signed to Apple and given the name White Trash by Richard Di Lello of the Press Office. This caused problems when they attempted to promote their debut single 'Road to Nowhere' because people found the name offensive, so it was shortened to Trash.

The group recorded the Beatles' medley number 'Golden Slumbers/Carry That Weight', which reached No. 35 in the British charts in September 1969. They had no further success and disbanded due to problems within the Apple company. Their album *White Trash*, although given the catalogue number SAPCOR 7, was never released.

Members of the group comprised: Ian Crawford-Clews (vocals), Fraser Watson (lead guitar), Ronald Leahy (organ), Colin Hunter-Morrison (bass guitar) and Tim Donald (drums).

Trentham Gardens Ballroom, Trentham Gardens, Trentham, Staffordshire

The Beatles only made a single appearance at this ballroom in Staffordshire, immediately following their short tour of Scotland, on 11 October 1963.

Treslong Studios

Dutch studios where the Beatles rehearsed for a television show soon after their arrival at Schiphol Airport on Friday, 5 June 1964.

The studios were situated in Hillegom, which was 26 miles from the capital, Amsterdam. Prior to their performance for the Vara Broadcasting Company, Herman Stok and Berend Boudewijn interviewed them on videotape in the bar of the studios. The interviewers asked them some rather bland questions regarding marriage, their opinion of Dutch girls, who mended their socks during their tours and such like. They then left the bar and walked into the studio where they performed before an audience.

The numbers they played were 'She Loves You', 'Twist And Shout', 'All My Loving', 'Roll Over Beethoven', 'Long Tall Sally' and 'Can't Buy Me Love'.

The videotaped show was broadcast five days later on Wednesday, 10 June.

Tribute Records

The Beatles have been the subject of scores of recordings by other artists. It is rare when a real person or a group of people themselves become the subject of a record, but in the case of the Beatles, their popularity ensured a large number of tributes, spoofs and novelty discs.

As in the case with most tribute records, few of them entered the charts. In Britain the comedienne Dora Bryan reached No. 20 in the charts with 'All I Want For Christmas Is A Beatle' in 1963 and German instrumental group D.B.M. reached No. 45 in the charts with 'Beatles Discomania' in 1977.

Among other records inspired by the Beatles are 'Lennon Quickie' by Neil Innes, 'Lennon Song' by Bert Gaunt, 'Lennon & McCartney' by John Moreland, 'Paul McCartney' by Tony Hazzard, 'Beatles Are In Town' by Norma Johnson, 'Beatle Boots' by Bruce Brand and Steven J. Hamper, 'Beatle Days' by Richard Jones and Tim Sebastian, 'Beatle Drive' by James Douglas and James Duncan, 'Beatle Express' by Heinz Kiessling, 'Beatle Woman' by J. Fish, 'Beatle Man' by Chris Laidlow, 'Beatles and the MBE' by Leroy M. Emanuel, 'Beatles Go Home' by Dick Hyman, 'Beatles Got To Go' by Lee Byron and Llewellyn Vincent, 'Beatle Bug' by Long, David, Wellbourne and Jay, 'Beatles-Go-West' by Leon Young and 'Come Back Beatles' by Lipstick.

Some of the tributes were made by well-known artists using a pseudonym. Phil Spector, for instance, produced 'I Love Ringo' by Bonnie Jo Mason, who turned out to be Cher, and Gene Cornish & the Unbeatables, who cut the album *I Wanna Be A Beatle*, later became famous as the Rascals.

Ella Fitzgerald released 'Ringo Beat' and comedian Rolf Harris came out with 'Ringo For President'. Ringo, in fact, seemed to be quite a popular subject for the tribute disc and others include: 'Treat Him Tender, Maureen (Now That Ringo Belongs To You)' by Angie and the Chicklettes, 'I Want Ringo For Christmas' by the Four Sisters, 'Ringo's Dog' by the Jack Dorsey Big Band, 'You Can't Go Far Without A Guitar Unless You're Ringo Starr' by Neil Sheppard. 'I Want to Kiss Ringo Goodbye' by Penny Valentine, 'Santa, Bring Me Ringo For Christmas' by Christine Hunter, 'Ringo' by Weekend, 'Ringo' by the Starlettes, 'Ringo' by Bob Dean, 'Ringo Part One/Part Two' by Carl & the Haircuts, 'My Ringo' by the Rainbows, 'Ringo Ringo' by Darlene Terri, 'Ringo, Dingo' coupled with 'Here Comes Ringo' by the Tributes, 'R (Is for Ringo)' by Tina Ferra, 'Ringo-Dear' by Gary Ferrier, 'Ringo Boy' by Dori Peyton, 'Ringo's Jerk' by Ron Ringo, 'Ringo's Walk' by Joey & the Classics, 'Like Ringo' by Dick Lord, 'Go Go With Ringo' by the Whippets, 'Ringo Did It' by Veronica Lee & the Moniques, 'Where Did Ringo Go?' by the Beatle Bugs, 'Ringo Comes To Town' by Chug and Doug, 'Ringo, I Want To Know Your Secret' by Pat Wynter, 'A Tribute to Ringo Starr (The Other Ringo)' by Larry Finnegan, 'Ringo For President' by the Young World Singers, 'What's Wrong With Ringo' by the BonBugs (this

girl group was later to re-emerge as the Shangri Las with a huge
hit, 'The Leader Of The Pack'), 'Bingo Ringo' by Butler Daws (the
man who provided the voice of the Huckleberry Hound character
in the cartoons – and some copies of the single were actually credited to Huckleberry Hound), 'Minuet For Ringo' by Viv Prince
(former drummer with the Pretty Things) and 'Ringo, Ringo Little
Star' by Al and Lou Marks Fisher.

John also seemed to be singled out with: 'Get Back John' by Inner
City Mission, 'John, You Went Too Far This Time' by Rainbo
(referring to John's interview in which Christ was mentioned),
'Crazy John' by Tom Paxton and 'Let John and Yoko Stay In The
USA' by the Justice Department.

Rumours of Paul's death sparked off: 'Ballad Of Paul' by the
Mystery Tour, 'St Paul' by Terry Knight, 'Brother Paul' by Billy
Shears & the All Americans and 'We're All Paul Bearers' by
Zacharias & the Tree People.

There have been various tributes which include Beatle medleys
such as 'You Can't Do That' by Harry Nilsson, 'Titles' by Barclay
James Harvest, *Eine Kleine Beatlemusik* by Fritz Spiegel and 'The
Beatles Cracker Suite' by Arthur Wilkinson and his Orchestra.

Spike Milligan issued a spoof version of 'Yellow Submarine' entitled 'Purple Aeroplane' and Peter Sellers gave thespian renditions of
'A Hard Day's Night, 'Help!' and 'She Loves You.'

The most popular Beatles single to be given the 'treatment' was 'I
Want To Hold Your Hand' and the spoofs included 'I Don't Want To
Hold Your Hand' by Rupert Holmes, 'I'll Let You Hold My Hand' by
the Bootles, 'I Want To Hold Your Hair' by the Bagels, 'I Don't Want
To Hold Your Hand' by Homer and Jethro, 'Yes, You Can Hold My
Hand' by the Beatlettes, 'I Want to Bite Your Hand' by Gene Moss,
'You Can Hold My Hand' by Lafawn Paul, 'Just Hold My Hand' by
Paul Perryman and 'Yes, You Can Hold My Hand' by the Teen Bugs.

There are many other records in this vein, including: 'We Love
You Beatles' by the Carefrees (based on the tune 'We Love You
Conrad' from the musical 'Bye Bye Birdie', it reached No. 39 in the
Billboard charts), 'The Boy With The Beatle Hair' by the Swans,
'She Loves You' by the Haircuts, 'A Beatle I Want To Be' by Sonny
Curtis, 'Bring Back The Beatles' by David Peel, 'My Beatle Haircut'
by the Twilighters, 'Beatle Fan' by Zeke Mullins, 'Beatle Baby Walk'
by the Al Martin Six, 'Beatle Song' by Dick Pillar and his Orchestra,
'To Kill A Beatle' by Johnny Garnier, 'I Ain't No Beatle' by Jerry
Foster, 'Beatles, We Want Our Girls Back' by the Defenders, 'The
Beatle Song' by the Twilighters, 'The Beatles Is Back (Yea, Yea, Yea)'
by Lenore King and Tommy Anderson, 'The Beatles Song' by the
Japanese Beatles, 'Beatle Walk' by David Hamilton, 'Beatle Crazy'

by Bill Clifton, 'The Beatles' Flying Saucer' by Ed Solomon, 'The Beatles' by the Buddies, 'Beatlemania In The USA' by the Liverpools, 'Beatle Stomp' by the Exterminators, 'Let's Bug The Beatles' by the Insects, 'Beatle Beat' by Benny & the Bedbugs, 'Letter To The Beatles' by the Four Preps, 'Little Beatle Boy' by the Angels, 'Sgt Pepper's Epitaph' by Keith Green, 'I'm Better Than The Beatles' by Jekyll & Hyde, 'The Beatles Barber' by Scott Douglas, 'The Guy With The Long Liverpool Hair' by the Outsiders, 'Saga Of The Beatles' by Johnny & the Hurricanes, 'My Boyfriend Got A Beatle Haircut' by Donna Lynn (which reached No. 83 in the *Billboard* charts), 'We Love The Beatles' by the Vernons Girls, 'Beatle Fever' by the Bedbugs, 'John, Paul, George and Ringo' by the Bulldogs, 'Beatle Fever' by Brett & Terry and 'The Beatle Dance' by Ernie Maresca.

Satirist Allan Sherman issued 'Pop Hates The Beatles', sung to the tune of 'Pop Goes The Weasel', in which a father chastises his daughter over her Beatle fervour. He also recorded another number called 'I Hate The Beatles'.

Gary Usher and Roger Christian, who produced the documentary album *The Beatles Story* in 1964, came out with a record, 'The Beetle', which was a dance number. There were several attempts to create a dance craze around the Beatles, including 'The Beatle Beat' by Benny & the Bedbugs, 'Beatle Crawl' by the Del Ricos and 'The Beatles Dance' by Tommy Bee.

The subject of Beatles novelty discs has been exhaustively researched by Charles Reinhart in his book *You Can't Do That*, published by Pierian Press in 1981.

Trident Studios, Trident House, 17 St Anne's Court, London W1

One of the numerous independent recording studios which began to spread in Britain in the late sixties. During the recording of *The Beatles* white album, the group decided to try recording at Trident, which had the advantage of an eight-track board. Unknown to them, Abbey Road had received delivery of an eight-track deck, but it was not currently in operation.

They began recording 'Hey Jude' at Trident on Wednesday, 31 July, and hired Trident on 1, 2 and 6 August 1968, before returning to Abbey Road. They were back at Trident for a six-day period from Tuesday, 1 October, during which they recorded 'Honey Pie', 'Dear Prudence', 'Savoy Truffle' and 'Martha My Dear'.

Trocadero Cinema, The, Camden Street, Liverpool L3

Once a major city centre cinema, but it suffered the fate of 95 per cent of Liverpool's cinemas – closure due to shrinking audiences of the television age.

The 'Troc' as it was affectionately called, was Julia Lennon's favourite cinema. When she and Freddie were married in 1938 they spent their honeymoon evening in the cinema and when the show ended for the night, Julia returned to her parents' home in Wavertree while Freddie went back to his lodgings.

The cinema's name was changed to the Gaumont in the 1950s and in 1964 was the setting for a reception for the film *Ferry 'Cross The Mersey*, which Gerry Marsden attended as Guest of Honour. Pat Delaney, the Cavern's famous doorman, once mimed on stage there to old Al Jolson records prior to a trailer for the film *Jolson Sings Again*.

Troy, Doris

American R&B singer who had hits such as 'It's In His Kiss' in the early sixties. After she joined Billy Preston for the recording of his first Apple album, she was signed up to Apple Records herself and her single 'Ain't That Cute' was produced by George Harrison, who also co-wrote the song with Doris. The flipside was 'Vaya Con Dios' and the single was issued in Britain on Apple 24 on 13 February 1970 and in America on Apple 1820 on 16 March.

She only recorded one album for Apple, *Doris Troy*, and there were a number of prominent musicians who performed with her on the LP, including George Harrison, Ringo Starr, Jackie Lomax, Steven Stills and Klaus Voormann. Of the numbers on the album, George arranged 'Jacob's Ladder' and co-wrote 'Gonna Get My Baby Back'. He also played guitar on 'Vaya Con Dios'. George, Ringo and Steven Stills penned the album tracks 'Give Me Joy Joy' and 'Gonna Get My Baby Back'.

Truth

British duo comprising Steve Gold and Frank Aiello. The pair were with Dick James in his office one day discussing the possibility of having a Beatles number for their third single, following two unsuccessful record releases. Their manager, Jeff, was sitting in the outer office when Paul McCartney walked in and asked him for a light. He considered this a good omen and when Truth issued 'Girl', a single taken from the *Rubber Soul* album, on 2 February 1966, it reached No. 18 in the charts, remaining in the charts for a total of five weeks, providing the group with their biggest hit.

Tuesday Rendezvous

Title of a television programme produced by Associated-Rediffusion. The Beatles appeared live on the programme on 4 December 1962, which was recorded at the company's studios in Kingsway, London, during which they promoted 'Love Me Do'.

They appeared on another live performance of the programme on 9 April 1963.

Twenty Flight Rock

A number which Eddie Cochran performed in the film *The Girl Can't Help It*. This was the film that was to influence John, Paul and George. They included the number in their repertoire.

20 Greatest Hits

EMI had originally planned to bring out an extra special album to celebrate the twentieth anniversary of the Beatles' recording career. This album was to be called *The Beatles Greatest Hits* and it would feature 26 tracks – all 22 of the Beatles' original singles, together with the additional four tracks from the double-'A' sided singles. Release was set for 11 October 1982 on EMTV 34 and the album was to be advertised on British television.

The company then changed its mind and issued a twenty-track album. This was the first of the Beatles compilation albums to feature their singles tracks only and on release it reached No. 9 in the British charts.

The sleeve was designed by Roy Kohara and Peter Shea and the inside of the gatefold sported a collage of photographs by Chuck Ames.

The tracks on the album were, Side One: 'Love Me Do', 'From Me To You', 'She Loves You', 'I Want To Hold Your Hand', 'Can't Buy Me Love', 'A Hard Day's Night', 'I Feel Fine', 'Ticket To Ride', 'Help!', 'Day Tripper', 'We Can Work It Out'. Side Two: 'Paperback Writer', 'Yellow Submarine', 'Eleanor Rigby', 'All You Need Is Love', 'Hello Goodbye', 'Lady Madonna', 'Hey Jude', 'Get Back' and 'The Ballad Of John And Yoko'.

Although maintaining the same sleeve design, the Capitol release of *20 Greatest Hits* had a different track listing. This was because the No. 1 singles in America differed slightly from the British ones – there were twenty No. 1 records in the States and only seventeen in Britain. Also, the American charts included chart entries for both sides of a single. The Capitol listing featured all twenty American No. 1 hits – all million sellers – and was issued on Capitol SV-12245 in October 1982. The tracks were, Side One: 'She Loves

You', 'Love Me Do', 'I Want To Hold Your Hand', 'Can't Buy Me Love', 'A Hard Day's Night', 'I Feel Fine', 'Eight Days A Week', 'Ticket To Ride', 'Help!', 'Yesterday', 'We Can Work It Out', 'Paperback Writer'. Side Two: 'Penny Lane', 'All You Need Is Love', 'Hello Goodbye', 'Hey Jude', 'Get Back', 'Come Together', 'Let It Be' and 'The Long And Winding Road'.

21 Club, New York City
On Saturday, 8 February 1964, Capitol Records hosted a special dinner party for the Beatles at the prestigious 21 Club. George Harrison was absent due to his throat infection and Ringo quipped to one of the waiters, 'Do you have any vintage coke?' When asked at a press conference if they had enjoyed their dinner at the club, a journalist added, 'Did they feed you on pheasant and stuff?'

'Pheasant, you're joking! I had chops and chips,' was the reply.

Twickenham Film Studios, The Barons, Twickenham, Surrey
Film facility on the outskirts of London which was used for the filming of some interior scenes in *A Hard Day's Night* and *Help!* The promotional films for 'Hey Jude' and 'Revolution' were also made here.

The Beatles began filming *Let It Be* here from 2–17 January 1969. They weren't happy with the cold atmosphere of the place and were irked that they had to film from early in the morning when they would have preferred working in the early evening. George Harrison walked out for a time on 10 January and the group then decided to abandon the Twickenham location and complete their filming at the Apple Studios in Savile Row.

Ringo was back at Twickenham studios several weeks later when he began filming *The Magic Christian* with Peter Sellers at the beginning of March. Princess Margaret visited the set on 4 March and Paul and Linda were also there at the time.

Twiggy
Born Lesley Hornby in London in September 1949, Twiggy was to become one of the leading fashion models of the Swinging Sixties. The first record she ever brought was 'Please Please Me' and she went to see the Beatles at Finsbury Park Astoria in 1963.

Once Twiggy was established as a model she sought to expand her career by becoming an actress. She and her manager, Justin De Villeneuve, thought that William Faulkner's *The Hanging Tree* would make a good film project for her and decided to approach the Beatles for backing. They met John and Paul in the Old Compton Street studio where they were editing *Magical Mystery Tour*.

Twiggy was to say: 'For me it was like meeting God. Paul was the one who was my hero; he was the one I'd stuck pictures of all over my desk at school and on my bedroom wall. At 13 it was him I'd screamed my head off for at the Finsbury Park Astoria. I was so excited to be meeting him at last, but trying to be cool. And he was lovely, just as I'd imagined, and he was the one I became most friends with. The Beatles did like the film idea, but we never managed to get it together.

However, Paul suggested they contact Ken Russell, and Twiggy was later to star in his film *The Boyfriend*.

Twiggy commented in her autobiography *Twiggy*: 'I've stayed good friends with Paul and Linda McCartney. When Linda first came over here she didn't know anyone and I felt quite sorry for her and I'd take her shopping. We became quite close.'

At one time the Beatles considered filming *Lord Of The Rings* and intended giving Twiggy a prominent role.

In 1967, Twiggy toured America on behalf of Yardley cosmetics. The master of ceremonies on her tour was Terry Knight. Twiggy thought he was a talented singer and guitarist and said, 'When we came back to England it was just the time when Paul McCartney was looking for someone to produce, and we'd earned a lot of money from the tour so we paid Terry's air fare for him and we thought to bring him over to Paul would be a nice break for him. But when he arrived here, imagine it, Paul and Linda had gone off to their Scottish hideaway and Paul had forgotten all about the meeting. So poor Terry had to wait around a few days, and then he got his flight back and that was the end of it.' Terry became a multimillionaire within two years. He took over management of Grand Funk Railroad and later sent Twiggy back the cheque for the air flight.

In 1968 there were plans for Twiggy to tour Russia and Granada Television intended making a documentary film of the trip. Unfortunately, it fell through. Twiggy said, 'Paul actually wrote a song for that trip to Russia that didn't come off – and it was "Back In The USSR", which went on *The Beatles* white album. Justin was in Mr Chow's with Paul one night having dinner, and he said "Hey, what about that song you were going to do for us when we were going to Russia?" and immediately Paul started singing it at the top of his voice.'

Twiggy, watching the talent contest 'Opportunity Knocks' on television one night, noticed Mary Hopkin singing 'Turn, Turn,

Turn'. Twiggy knew that Paul was looking for artists to promote. She said, 'It just happened that that weekend we went to see Paul at his Dad's house in Liverpool. He mentioned that he was looking for people to record and I said, "Did you see that girl on 'Opportunity Knocks?'" and Angie, his stepmother, said she'd seen it too, and we all hoped Mary would win or we wouldn't see her the next week. So we all sat down and wrote cards for her, with our names – and we got about twenty people rallied together to vote for her. She won easily. Paul watched the show, agreed she was wonderful and rang her up immediately. She didn't believe it was him on the phone! But he sent a chauffeured car down to Wales for her, and then got together to make her name.'

After making *The Boyfriend*, Twiggy sought further roles, and a film called *Gotta Sing, Gotta Dance* was planned. The name was inspired by the Gene Kelly song 'Broadway Melody', which contains the words 'Gotta Dance', and the story was set on a cruise liner in the thirties. But the film was never made. Paul wrote the title song for the film, which he never actually recorded. However, as the film project had been abandoned, Paul later used 'Gotta Sing, Gotta Dance' as the main dance spectacular in the 'James Paul McCartney' TV special.

Twin Cities' Metropolitan Stadium, Minneapolis, Minnesota

The Beatles appeared before 25,000 people at this 45,000- seater auditorium during a single evening performance on Saturday, 21 August 1965.

The group had flown in from Chicago and their press conference that day was broadcast in its entirety by a local radio station. During the press reception George was presented with a brand new guitar, which he played during the evening's performance.

Twist And Shout (EP)

The very first Beatles EP to be issued. Following the success of the Beatles' debut album and the first three singles, Parlophone decided to issue a release on the extended play format which comprised four tracks contained in a stiff picture sleeve cover.

On its release on Parlophone GEP 8882 on 2 July 1963 it reached No. 4 in the *New Musical Express* chart, the main British chart at the time, and became the very first EP ever to enter the Top Ten singles chart. It eventually sold over 800,000 copies in the UK and after slipping out of the charts after ten weeks, it reappeared in the charts for a further ten weeks. The tracks were: 'Twist And Shout',

'A Taste Of Honey', 'Do You Want To Know A Secret?' and 'There's A Place', all tracks from the *Please Please Me* album which was currently No. 1 in the album charts.

Twist And Shout (Single)

At 10.00 p.m. on the evening of Monday, 11 February 1963, the marathon recording session for the *Please Please Me* album was nearly over, but they still needed one more song to complete the album. Everyone was gathered in the Abbey Road canteen discussing it, and 'Twist And Shout', which had been an American hit for the Isley Brothers in 1962 and included in the Beatles' repertoire the same year, was suggested. It had been written by Bert Berns, using a pseudonym Bert Russell, and Phil Medley.

As they'd been recording throughout the day their throats were sore, but John took some Zubes and ripped through the number in two takes, the first being selected as the album track.

Following the release of the album on 22 March 1963, Brian Poole & the Tremeloes released a single of 'Twist And Shout' on 28 June, which reached No. 4 in the charts. This was ironic considering that Decca Records had chosen to sign the Tremeloes rather than the Beatles and that the Tremeloes had been completely unsuccessful in the charts until they decided to cover this number from the Beatles album.

The Beatles' first EP release on GEP 8882, issued on 12 July 1963, was entitled *Twist And Shout*, and it also reached No. 4. It was the highest position ever reached by an EP in the British charts up to that date. The other tracks on the EP were 'A Taste Of Honey', 'Do You Want To Know A Secret?' and 'There's A Place'.

The number was frequently featured on their BBC radio recordings and was included on four 'Pop Go The Beatles' shows, plus 'The Talent Spot', 'Swinging Sound '63', 'The Beat Show', 'Easy Beat' and 'Saturday Club'.

A live version was included on *The Beatles At The Star Club* album and a further live recording was used on their *The Beatles At the Hollywood Bowl* album in 1976. It was also issued as the flip-side of 'Back In The USSR' in June 1976 on a single to promote the release of the *Rock 'n' Roll Music* double album.

The number was also used as the powerful closing song at a number of their concert performances and they played it on their 'Sunday Night At The London Palladium' appearance in October 1963, their 'Royal Variety Show' performance in November 1963 and their 'Ed Sullivan Show' television appearance in February 1964.

The song was also included on *Rock 'n' Roll* and *The Beatles Box* and *The Beatles Collection* sets.

In America Vee Jay included it on their *Introducing The Beatles* and *Songs, Pictures And Stories Of The Fabulous Beatles* albums. Vee Jay also issued it as a single on their Tollie label with 'There's A Place' on the flip. It was issued on Tollie 9001 on 2 March 1964 where it sped up the *Billboard* charts, reached the No. 2 position and sold a million copies within three weeks. Capitol also issued it with 'There's A Place' on the flip on Capitol Starline 6061 on 11 October 1965, but it failed to chart. A version of the number was included on the Beatles' *Anthology 1* CDs.

Two Of US
A Paul McCartney composition, originally called 'On Our Way Home'. Recording of the number began on Friday, 24 January 1969, and the track was to open the *Let It Be* album.

It begins with John saying, '"I Dig A Pony" by Charles Hawtrey on the deaf aids. Phase one in which Doris gets her oats.' This is similar to remarks he made on one of the versions of 'Dig It': 'That was "Can You Dig It" by Georgie Wood, now we'd like to do "Hark The Angels Come".' (Charles Hawtrey was one of the 'Carry On' movie regulars and Georgie Wood was a midget comedian.)

The number was recorded by a New York trio called Mortimer (Guy Masson, Tony Van Benschoten and Tom Smith) and intended for release as their debut single on the Apple Records label. However, the Beatles weren't confident about the record and it was never issued. A version of the song was included on the Beatles' *Anthology 3* CDs.

Two Red Shoes Ballroom, Elgin, Morayshire, Scotland
The first date of the Beatles' second tour of Scotland on Thursday, 3 January 1963. Originally, the tour was due to open on 2 January at the Longmore Hall, Keith, Banffshire, but bad weather prevented the Beatles fulfilling the first booking and the tour had to be shortened to five days. The Scottish gigs had been booked by the Cana Variety Association in conjunction with Scottish promoter Albert Bonici. Due to the problems caused by extremely bad weather, the worst for decades, Brian Epstein offered Bonici the option of booking all future Beatles appearances in Scotland exclusively.

University College Hospital, Gower Street, London WC1

Hospital to which Ringo Starr was admitted on 3 June 1964. Earlier that day he'd been taking part in a photographic session at a studio in Barnes. He collapsed and a local doctor examined him and found him to be suffering from tonsilitis and pharyngitis.

This was on the eve of the Beatles' world tour and a replacement had to be found. The drummer who deputised while Ringo was in hospital was Jimmy Nicol, 24-year-old former member of Georgie Fame & the Blue Flames. When he was discharged on Thursday, 11 June, Ringo joked, 'Everybody was just great to me. But don't tell John, Paul or George or they'll want to be ill too.'

Ringo returned to the hospital on 1 December that year to have his tonsils removed. He held an afternoon press conference at the hospital and the operation took place the next day. During his stay, he was visited by his Liverpool girl friend, Maureen Cox, and the couple were to marry a few months later.

Ringo was offered his tonsils as a souvenir, but declined.

George entered the same hospital for a tonsilectomy on 7 February 1969 and accepted their offer of the grisly souvenir, taking the tonsils home with him in a jar.

25 Upton Green, Speke, Liverpool L24

After eighteen years on the waiting list, the Harrison family moved in 1949 to a new council estate on the outskirts of Liverpool. With a bathroom and extra bedroom, it was a much superior dwelling to Arnold Grove and on the first day there, George kept running around the room in his excitement. It was situated at the end of a circular street, with a grass field in the centre. Mrs Louise Harrison, however, particularly missed the friendliness of the Wavertree area and found the neighbours lacked the warmth of those at the previous address. Their stay here lasted exactly ten years.

Val

Surname unknown. In a 1964 interview, Paul McCartney's brother Mike said that Val was the first girl that Paul ever liked. He was at a tender age at the time and began to notice Val on the school bus, staring at her long hair. 'Then one night word came along the grapevine that Val liked him,' said Mike. 'You should have seen the way he went on! He was completely knocked out! He took Val out once or twice – to the cinema, visiting friends, that sort of thing. Then the whole affair suddenly fizzled out.'

Van Eaton, Lon and Derek

Brothers, former members of a group called Jacob's Creek, who were signed to Apple Records after submitting a demo tape in 1971. They were brought to England to record and had their album *Brother* issued by Apple in the US on 22 September 1972 and in the UK on 9 February 1973. Klaus Voormann produced the LP, although George Harrison personally produced one track, 'Sweet Music'.

When Apple mainly became a release outlet for the Beatles, the brothers moved to A&M and issued their second album *Who Do You Out Do?* in 1974. It was to be their last album for over twenty years. They did session work on Ringo's *Goodnight Vienna* album and on George's 'Dark Horse' single. Lon also appeared on *Ringo's Rotogravure*, *Ringo The 4th* and *Bad Boy*.

In the 1980s, Lon moved to Colorado with his wife Constance. Derek followed, settling in Denver, got married and left the music business.

Derek suffered a heart attack in 1994 and, to cover medical expenses, they cut an album, *Dinosaurs,* on which Ringo Starr played drums. They also issued an album *Black And White* on 9 May 1998.

Van Gelder, Dick
The late Dutch impresario who was responsible for bringing the Beatles to the Netherlands. He was 55 years old when he'd originally contacted Brian Epstein in 1963 seeking to book the band for appearances in Holland, but Brian said that they had too many commitments and the earliest they could appear would be June 1964 as part of their world tour. The contract was signed but just as the Beatles were due to fly out to Denmark on the first leg of the tour, Ringo collapsed. The Beatles finally arrived on 5 June to appear in two concerts at Blokker the next day.

Vara Broadcasting Corporation
Dutch television company which filmed the Beatles during their trip to Holland in 1964.

The group were signed to appear on the show by Joop Sims, the chief executive of the Vara Broadcasting Company. They filmed the group at the Treslong Studios, Hillegom, 25 miles outside Amsterdam on the evening of 5 June 1964, and the show was broadcast on 8 June. The group performed 'She Loves You', 'Twist And Shout', 'All My Loving', 'Roll Over Beethoven', 'Long Tall Sally' and 'Can't Buy Me Love'.

They stayed overnight at the Doelen Hotel in Oude Doelen Street in Amsterdam and later toured the red light district. In the morning they began a canal tour at 11.00 a.m. The event was covered by Vara and broadcast live on the radio, with interviewer Herman Stok covering the trip.

Vartan, Sylvie
A blonde-haired French *chanteuse* of the sixties who was married to France's rock 'n' roll idol Johnny Hallyday. Sylvie co-starred with the Beatles and Trini Lopez at the Olympia, Paris, from 16 January–4 February 1964. The predominantly male audience were as enthusiastic about the performance of the attractive young singer as they were about *Les Beatles*.

Vaughan, Ivan
A close friend of John Lennon and Paul McCartney, who lived in Vale Street in the Woolton area of Liverpool with his widowed mother. Their rear garden backed on to Mendips, where John lived

with his Aunt Mimi. They also lived close to Pete Shotton and Nigel Whally and all became a close-knit gang.

When he was six years old, Ivan went to Dovedale Primary School, as did John. Later John went to Quarry Bank School, while Ivan attended Liverpool Institute in 1952.

Ivan had the same madcap sense of humour as John and they both loved 'The Goon Show'. When John invited him to join the Quarry Men on tea-chest bass, Ivan painted 'Ive the Jive, the Ace on the Bass' on his instrument, although he alternated with Nigel Whally, until Len Garry replaced them both.

At the Institute, Ivan was in the same class as Paul (they were born on the same day).

Ivan's behaviour was eccentric, to say the least. One day when his mother wasn't home, he painted his name in letters three-foot high right across the front of the house. Pupils at the Institute had to wear regulation black shoes, but one day Ivan arrived at school having coloured his shoes with thick dollops of canary yellow paint. Another time he left off his Institute uniform and entered Quarry Bank with John. Ivan said he was a new student and was given a set of textbooks and told to join the class. When the head-master heard of it he reported the incident to the Institute head-master, who only mildly chastised the youth. Ivan also played truant quite often and would forge notes from his mother stating that he hadn't been able to attend because she couldn't afford to buy him new shoes!

Institute old boy Peter Sissons was to comment: 'John Lennon was a highly original character, but in my opinion, much of the outrageousness and unpredictability he displayed later in life came from Ivan Vaughan and not the other way round.'

One day Ivan asked Paul if he'd like to come along and watch his skiffle group play at a church fete. Paul wasn't particularly struck on the idea, but Ivan said that it would be a great place to pick up girls, so the two of them cycled along that afternoon. The date was 6 July 1957 and, after the Quarry Men's first set, Ivan took Paul into the church hall and introduced him to John.

He considered Paul to be talented and said: 'I only ever brought great fellows to meet John.'

A week later, when Paul was cycling to Ivan's house, he met Pete Shotton, who asked him if he'd like to join the group.

Over the years, Ivan kept in touch with his friends, particularly Paul and John. He was a Cambridge graduate and became a teacher and studied educational psychology.

He regularly visited them, travelled to America with them and was present at the time of the *Sgt Pepper* sessions. When Apple was launched, the Beatles suggested that Ivan and Janet, his school-teacher wife, head the proposed Apple School. Ivan was given an advance payment of £10,000, but it was decided that the idea was premature and the scheme was dropped.

Incidentally, Jan taught French and when Paul was composing 'Michelle', he asked her if she could help him write the French verses.

Sadly, during the 1970's Ivan contracted Parkinson's disease, for which there is no known cure. Deciding not to simply accept the situation, he began to battle against the disease, using himself as a guinea pig for new drugs and mercilessly knocking his limbs against solid objects when they refused to respond.

Jonathan Miller heard of his remarkable and courageous struggle and produced a documentary, simply called 'Ivan', which was transmitted on BBC2 TV on 3 December 1984 as part of the 'Horizon' series. Paul allowed his song 'Blackbird' to be played at the beginning and end of the programme free of charge. Paul invited Ivan to spend Christmas 1984 with the McCartneys at their home in Sussex and continued to keep in touch until Ivan's death.

Of the documentary, which centred on a day in his life, Ivan commented: 'I decided to make my illness my hobby. Not as something useful. Not to help thousands. Just selfishly, to find out all I could about it and its implications. I wanted to explore it, to play with it, and even to laugh about it.'

His book, *Ivan: Living with Parkinson's Disease* was published in 1986. Tragically, Ivan died in 1994. His death touched Paul so deeply that he began to write poetry for the first time since he was a child.

Vee Jay Records

An independent American label which had enjoyed success in the States with the release of some British singles – the Frank Ifield hits 'I Remember You' and 'Lovesick Blues'. In 1963 Barbara Gardener, the head of the International division of the company, arrived in London to negotiate the release of albums by Chris Barber and Alex Bradford Gospel Group.

While in London she was approached to release Beatles products in America due to the fact that Capitol had turned the opportunity down. On 21 January 1963 she signed a short-term agreement to release Beatles records in America on the Vee Jay label.

The first Beatles record to be issued was 'Please Please Me' coupled with 'Ask Me Why' on 25 February 1963. It didn't chart. They next issued 'From Me To You' coupled with 'Thank You Girl', but considered its highest placing, No. 116 in *Billboad*, to be unsuccessful. The single was also made 'Pick Of the Week' in *Cash Box* magazine.

The final Vee Jay release that year was the album *Introducing The Beatles*, which they issued on 22 July 1963. This also failed to register and Vee Jay were reputed to have turned down the opportunity of continuing issuing Beatles products and 'She Loves You' went to the Swan label. However, this was not strictly correct. A music licensing firm in New York called Trans-Global cancelled Vee Jay's right to release products on 8 August 1963 because they had not paid royalties for the first two Beatles releases. Trans-Global also informed Vee Jay that they no longer had licensing rights to the Beatles tracks for 'Love Me Do' and 'P.S. I Love You'. This caused problems for Vee Jay, who had already pressed the album *Introducing The Beatles*, which contained the two numbers. To have destroyed all the albums would have caused the company to go bankrupt, so they went ahead with the release, but did not list any of the tracks on the back cover of the album.

When the Beatles seemed set to become a major chart act, Vee Jay set about re-releasing the limited Beatles products they had and used ingenuity in issuing a string of singles and albums, beginning with the *Introducing The Beatles* album on 27 January 1964, which reached No. 2 in the *Billboard* and *Cash Box* charts and No. 1 in the *Record World* chart. Three days later, on 30 January 1964 they issued the single 'Please Please Me' c/w 'From Me To You' which reached No. 3 in all three trade charts.

Vee Jay realised that to take advantage of the limited number of Beatles tracks they had, they needed to issue them in as many different formats as possible and next issued *Jolly What! The Beatles And Frank Ifield On Stage* on 26 February 1964. This was an album comprising a number of the Frank Ifield tracks on their catalogue with four Beatles tracks. The album only reached No. 104 in the charts. For their next release they took an unusual step. EPs weren't a popular format in America and were extremely rare. Vee Jay noticed how popular EPs were in Britain and decided to release four of the *Introducing The Beatles* tracks as an EP, with a special cardboard cover, which they called *Souvenir Of Their Visit To America: The Beatles*. Initially, the EP was issued in a cardboard sleeve at $1.29 on 23 March 1964. As this was an unusual price for a record they then issued it in an ordinary paper sleeve at the usual price of a single and claimed that they sold a million copies. This is quite possible, even though the EP didn't register in any of the main charts. Since EPs weren't generally issued in America, the trade magazines may not have included the EP in their chart figures.

Using the same cover picture as the *Souvenir* EP (paintings of the heads of Ringo, George, John and Paul), they issued the single 'Do You Want To Know A Secret?' c/w 'Thank You Girl' on 23 March

1964, the same day as the EP, and the single went to No. 2 in *Billboad* and No. 3 in *Cash Box* and *Record World*.

On 10 August they issued four Beatles singles in a reissue series called 'Oldies 45', but none of them registered in the charts. They were 'Do You Want To Know A Secret?' c/w 'Thank You Girl', 'Please Please Me' c/w 'From Me To You', 'Love Me Do' c/w 'P.S. I Love You' and 'Twist and Shout' c/w 'There's A Place'.

Still utilising their tracks from *Introducing the Beatles*, they repackaged them in a double album with tracks by the Four Seasons and issued *The Beatles vs The Four Seasons* on 1 October 1964. The album only reached No. 142 in the charts. Undaunted, within two weeks Vee Jay had issued yet another repackaging of the *Introducing The Beatles* tracks called *Songs, Pictures And Stories Of The Fabulous Beatles* on 12 October 1964. This reached No. 100 in *Cash Box*, No. 79 in *Record World* and No. 63 in *Billboard*. It was the final Vee Jay release. The company had been plagued by problems since Capitol had realised the potential of the Beatles and in January 1964, EMI's music publishing company, Ardmore & Beechwood Music, attempted to obtain a court order restraining Vee Jay records from issuing 'Love Me Do' and 'P.S. I Love You' on an album. They maintained that Trans-Global, who were licensed to distribute EMI products in America, had cancelled the Vee Jay agreement on 8 August 1963 because of the non-payment of royalties due from the first two Beatles singles issued by Vee Jay. As a result, Trans-Global relinquished its rights to their tracks to EMI and they were then acquired by Capitol Records.

A restraining order was placed on Vee Jay, and its managing director Jay Lasker said that they had ceased shipping Beatles products because of it, but were to take legal action as he considered they had a five-year contract with the Beatles and they were not in default for not paying the royalties. They took out a law suit against both Capitol Records and Swan, who were also issuing Beatles products at the time. The legal representatives of both Capitol and Vee Jay decided to settle the matter between themselves, due to the complications which could arise from the legal suits. It was agreed that *Introducing The Beatles* could be reissued if the two Ardmore & Beechwood tracks were removed. Vee Jay replaced the two tracks with 'Please Please Me' and 'Ask Me Why'.

However, the legal problems didn't go away. Capitol considered that Vee Jay had violated their agreement by altering and repackaging *Introducing The Beatles* as *Songs, Pictures And Stories Of The Fabulous Beatles*. As a result, a trial without jury took place on 15 July 1964 in which Vee Jay pointed out that their 9 April 1964 licence did not mention that they could not repackage the Beatles product they had. Capitol disagreed, saying that Vee Jay had breached the agreement by presenting the album in different packaging. On 23 July, Judge Mervyn A. Aggeler announced:

'The court finds in favour of Vee Jay Records on all the issues raised in their cross-complaint.

'Vee Jay Records has the unqualified right to advertise and promote the covered masters in any cover, jacket or package which Vee Jay Records, Inc., deems appropriate.

'Vee Jay has the unqualified right to advertise, sell and promote the long playing album in the type of jacket, a copy of which is attached to Vee Jay Records complaint, marked as Exhibit C.

'Capitol Records and Beechwood Music, Inc., are permanently restrained from declaring that promotion of the long playing record *Introducing The Beatles*, in the redesigned jacket, constitutes or will constitute a breach in contracts, the Licence Agreement and Mechanical License both dated April 9 1965.'

As a result, Vee Jay were allowed to release Beatles records they had masters of in any form until 15 October 1964. After that time they no longer had the right to issue any Beatles product.

Vee Jay also had a subsdiary label called Tollie, on which they issued some Beatles singles. The first Tollie release was 'Twist And Shout' c/w 'There's A Place', issued on 2 March 1964. These tracks from the *Introducing The Beatles* album went to No. 1 in *Cash Box* and *Record World* and No. 2 in *Billboard*. The second Tollie release was 'Love Me Do' c/w 'P.S. I Love You' on Tollie 9008 on 27 April 1964, which topped all three trade charts and was a million-seller.

VEE JAY DISCOGRAPHY (IN CHRONOLOGICAL ORDER)

'Please Please Me' c/w 'Ask Me Why', Vee Jay 498, 25 February 1963.

'From Me To You' c/w 'Thank You Girl', Vee Jay 522, 27 May 1963.

Introducing The Beatles, Vee Jay 1062, 22 July 1963. Tracks: 'I Saw Her Standing There', 'Misery', 'Anna (Go To Him)', 'Chains', 'Boys', 'Love Me Do', 'P.S. I Love You', 'Baby, It's You', 'Do You Want To Know A Secret?', 'A Taste Of Honey', 'There's A Place', 'Twist And Shout'.

Introducing The Beatles, VJLP 1062, 27 January 1964. Tracks: 'I Saw Her Standing There', 'Misery', 'Anna (Go To Him)', 'Chains', 'Boys', 'Ask Me Why', 'Please Please Me', 'Baby, It's You', 'Do You Want To Know A Secret?', 'A Taste Of Honey', 'There's A Place', 'Twist And Shout'.

'Please Please Me' c/w 'From Me To You', VJ 581, 30 January 1964.

Jolly What! The Beatles And Frank Ifield On Stage, VJLP 1085, 26 February 1964. Beatles tracks: 'Please Please Me', 'From Me To You', 'Ask Me Why', 'Thank You Girl'.

'Twist And Shout', Tollie 9001, 2 March 1964.

Souvenir Of Their Visit To America: The Beatles. VJLP 1–902 Vee Jay, 23 March 1964. Tracks: 'Misery', 'A Taste Of Honey', 'Ask Me Why', 'Anna (Go To Him)'.

'Do You Want To Know A Secret?' c/w 'Thank You Girl', VJ 587 Vee Jay, 23 March 1964.

'Love Me Do' c/w 'P.S. I Love You', Tollie 9008, 27 April 1964.

'Do You Want To Know A Secret?' c/w 'Thank You Girl', OL 149 Oldies 45, 10 August 1964.

'Please Please Me' c/w 'From Me To You', OL 150 Oldies 45, 10 August 1964.

'Love Me Do' c/w 'P.S. I Love You', OL 151 Oldies 45, 10 August 1964.

'Twist And Shout' c/w 'There's A Place', OL 152 Oldies 45, 10 August 1964.

The Beatles vs The Four Seasons. VJDX 30 Vee Jay, 1 October 1964. Beatles tracks: 'I Saw Her Standing There', 'Misery', 'Anna (Go To Him)', 'Chains', 'Boys', 'Ask Me Why', 'Please Please Me', 'Baby, It's You', 'Do You Want To Know A Secret?', 'A Taste Of Honey', 'There's A Place', 'Twist And Shout'.

Songs, Pictures And Stories Of The Fabulous Beatles. VJLP 1092 Vee Jay, 12 October 1964. Beatles tracks: 'I Saw Her Standing There', 'Misery', 'Anna (Go To Him)', 'Chains', 'Boys', 'Ask Me Why', 'Please Please Me', 'Baby, It's You', 'Do You Want To Know A Secret?', 'A Taste Of Honey', 'There's A Place', 'Twist And Shout'.

Velodromo, Vigorelli
Venue situated on Via Arona in Milan, Italy where the Beatles performed two shows on 24 June 1965, the first at 4.30 p.m. the

second at 9.30 p.m. The appearances were part of their fourteen-day European tour and the first of only three Italian venues that the Beatles visited in their entire career. Despite the popularity of the group in the Italian charts, their live appearances didn't draw a fraction of the response they received in English-speaking countries and the Italian gigs didn't prove to be sell-outs.

Although there were 700 police and 400 guards to control the crowds at this open-air 22,000-seater stadium, only 7,000 people attended the afternoon show. There was a better response in the evening, with an audience of 20,000, although they still did not fill the stadium's capacity.

The repertoire was the same throughout their entire European fortnight: 'Twist And Shout', 'She's A Woman', 'I'm A Loser', 'Can't Buy Me Love', 'Baby's In Black', 'I Wanna Be Your Man', 'A Hard Day's Night', 'Everybody's Trying To Be My Baby', 'Rock And Roll Music', 'I Feel Fine', 'Ticket To Ride' and 'Long Tall Sally'.

Vernons Girls, The

The Liverpool Football Company Vernons Pools sponsored a seventy-strong girls' choir called the Vernons Girls for promotional purposes. This line-up was slimmed to a more manageable sixteen and they began to appear on television shows such as 'Oh Boy!' and recorded for Parlophone between 1958 and 1961, without success.

Various members of the vocal group split into solo and other acts, including Lynn Cornell, the Ladybirds, the Breakaways and the Two Tones.

The Breakaways appeared with the Beatles on the Little Richard Show at the Empire Theatre, Liverpool, on Sunday, 28 October 1962.

By 1962, the Vernons Girls were down to a trio comprising Maureen Kennedy, Jean Owen and Frances Lee. They signed to Decca Records and as the Vernons Girls Featuring Maureen reached No. 16 in the charts with 'Lover Please'. They also had minor hits with 'Locomotion', 'You Know What I Mean', 'Funny All Over' and 'Do The Bird'.

It was this trio who featured with the Beatles on the TV show 'Thank Your Lucky Stars' on Saturday, 20 April 1963. Later that year they also appeared on the first all-Merseyside edition of 'Thank Your Lucky Stars' on 20 June. The Vernons Girls was part of the Beatles' autumn tour of Britain between 1 November and 13 December 1963 and were included on the Pops Alive! Show at the Prince of Wales Theatre in London, when the Beatles topped the bill on Sunday, 31 May 1964.

The trio was also booked to appear on the Beatles' Associated Rediffusion Television show 'Around The Beatles', first transmitted on Wednesday, 6 May 1964.

Lynn Cornell, a blonde girl who had lived quite close to Paul McCartney, married Andy White, the drummer who recorded with the Beatles at the Parlophone 'Love Me Do' and 'P.S. I Love You' sessions. She was still a member of the Vernons Girls when they recorded 'We Love The Beatles', a novelty record which didn't make the charts, although she did have one British chart hit as a solo singer, 'Never On Sunday'.

She did have some success with the similarly titled 'We Love You Beatles' in 1964. She recorded this number as a member of the Carefrees, with another former Vernons Girl, Betty Prescott. The other members were Barbara Kay, Johnny Evans, John Stevens and Don Riddell. The single was issued in America, where it reached No. 39 in the *Billboard* charts, becoming the biggest-selling Beatles novelty single ever released. It was issued in America on London International 10614 in 1964.

As a solo singer she was booked to appear with the Beatles on the all-British edition of the American pop show 'Shindig', recorded at the Granville Theatre, Fulham Broadway, London, on 3 October 1964.

In 1990, Maggie Stredder decided to re-form the Vernons Girls as a trio, with Sheila Bruce and Penny Lightfoot. Sheila had been one of Paul McCartney's earliest girlfriends – and he'd originally broken her nose by throwing a ball into her face. At one time she was married to singer Tommy Bruce.

Vickers, Mike

A former member of Manfred Mann. He became an arranger and worked on some projects for George Martin. Martin called him to ask him to arrange the number 'All You Need Is Love'. Vickers was sent an acetate and then visited Paul's Cavendish Avenue house where he worked together on it with Paul and John. He was also to conduct the Our World Orchestra during the famous recording.

Victoria Hall, Village Road, Higher Bebington, Wirral L63

A relatively isolated venue, which is probably why very few Mersey Beat bands ever played there. The Beatles only appeared at the hall once, on Saturday, 4 August 1962.

Veilinghal Op Hoop Van Zegen, Veilingqwg, Blokker, Holland.

The Beatles only appeared in Holland once. The event took place on Saturday, 6 June 1964 on their second appearance during their 25-day world tour.

The group performed two shows at the 7,000-seater venue, which was 35 miles from Amsterdam. The group travelled in two white Cadillacs, escorted by motorcycle police. Thousands of fans lined the streets, although for the matinee show at 2.30 p.m. the hall was only half full, with an audience of approximately 1,500. This matinee had been added to the schedule at the last minute by Radio Veronica and a major reason for the low turnout was due to the fact that youngsters had to attend school on Saturdays. This was evident when the evening show was completely sold out. The Beatles had a four-and-a-half hour wait until the second show, unaware that a civic reception at a local restaurant and a tour of a Dutch village had been planned.

Introductions were made by Ben Essing and preceding the Beatles on stage were nine local acts: The Fancy Free, Karin Kent, Jack and Bill, Herman van Keeken, Wanda, Dion Mercedes and his Improvers, The Torero's and Cisca Peters.

The Beatles performed for 25 minutes and their repertoire was: 'I Saw Her Standing There', 'I Want To Hold Your Hand', 'You Can't Do That', 'All My Loving', 'She Loves You', 'Till There Was You', 'Roll Over Beethoven', 'Can't Buy Me Love', 'This Boy' and 'Long Tall Sally' and the audience sang along with the Beatles.

The Beatles took to the stage for the second show at 10.05 p.m. and were filmed for newsreels.

There were only eight support spots on the evening bill: The Hot Jumpers, Wanda, Candy Kids, John Rassel, Karin Kent, Herman van Keeken, Kwintet Dominique and Wanda.

There were 95 traffic police, 130 private guards and 120 security men present. Blokker, a small village of approximately 2,000 people, had no railway station and apart from the audience arriving by car and motorbike, there were 200 coaches – 140 fans chartered a plane from England. Several Dutch celebrities were present, including Rob de Nijs, Wim Kan and Willem van Kooten. There was also a team of researchers from the Institute for Mass Psychology in Amsterdam and the Sociological Institute of the Royal University of Utrecht, investigating this new phenomenon. Professor Groenman from Utrecht commented, 'I want to go and listen what kind of music the Beatles sing, and even more to investigate if it is music at all.'

The organisers had been paid Ft. 5.037,31 by sponsors Heineken, Honda and Joy, a soft drinks manufacturer.

Village Hall, Thingwall Road, Irby, Heswall, Wirral L61

The Beatles appeared only once at this hall in the Wirral peninsula, which also housed the Newton Dancing School. They appeared there on Friday, 7 September 1962.

Vincent, Gene

One of the Beatles' favourite rock 'n' roll stars. Soon after the Quarry Men formed they included Vincent's major hit 'Be-Bop-A-Lula' in their repertoire (Paul wrote out the words to this song for John on their first meeting). His 'Dance In The Street' was also part of their early stage act and his haunting version of 'Somewhere Over The Rainbow', which he performed on the 3 May 1960 concert at Liverpool Stadium, attended by John, Paul, George and Stuart, was also incorporated into their repertoire.

Gene Vincent's 1956 rock interpretation of 'Ain't She Sweet' was also an inspiration and John began performing it with the Quarry Men.

When the Beatles first went to Hamburg, drummer Pete Best was to observe, 'John did his best to imitate Gene Vincent, grabbing up the microphone as if he were going to lay into the audience with it.'

Vincent was born Vincent Eugene Craddock in Norfolk, Virginia, on 11 February 1935. In 1955 his leg was crushed in a motorbike accident and the callipered leg continued to pain him throughout his life. After a number of hits in America he was brought to Britain to appear on several TV shows and decided to make his home in England. He was touring with Eddie Cochran when they were both involved in a road accident in which Cochran died. Shortly afterwards, Vincent made his Liverpool Stadium appearance.

The Beatles met their idol in Hamburg in April 1962 when both acts appeared at the Star Club and they became friends. John even asked Vincent for his autograph. When later asked by Sounds Incorporated what Hamburg was like, Vincent told them. 'Oh, it's OK there. I had a nice band backing me up. They're called the Beatles.'

Gene also appeared with the Beatles at the Cavern on 1 July 1962, backed by Sounds Incorporated. Mike McCartney took a photograph of Vincent with John and Paul, in which all of them are wearing black leather jackets.

The American rock 'n' roll star appeared in Liverpool on a number of occasions and during a visit in 1964 he told *Mersey Beat*, 'I sing rock 'n' roll because the kids always seem to have liked it – anyway, the stuff the Beatles sing is just rock 'n' roll, but a bit noisier.'

Vincent died of cardiac failure in 1971.

Viscounts, The

A British male vocal group who were added to the bill of the Chris Montez/Tommy Roe Tour promoted by Arthur Howes and featuring the Beatles, in 1963. The vocal outfit had enjoyed two minor chart hits, 'Short'nin' Bread' in 1960 and 'Who Put the Bomp' in 1961.

Vollmer, Jurgen

When the Beatles began their appearances at the Kaiserkeller in 1961 they attracted three particularly enthusiastic students who became dedicated followers. The first was Klaus Voormann, and on his third visit to the club he brought along Astrid Kirchherr and Jurgen Vollmer. Fortunately, both Astrid and Jurgen were excellent photographers and have provided posterity with some brilliant photographs of the Beatles in their early years.

Although Jurgen attended the Beatles' sessions at the Kaiserkeller, he didn't take any photographs of them performing at the venue because it was so dark it would have required a flash. He didn't want to use a flash in case it attracted the attention of the 'rockers' in the audience, who were always looking for an excuse to start a fight. The majority of pictures he took were of the Beatles on stage at the Top Ten Club.

A number of the photographs were first printed in *Mersey Beat* and pictures were later to grace the pages of prestigious American magazines at the height of Beatlemania.

John Lennon actually took out a subscription to *Mersey Beat* as a present to Jurgen, and included references to Jurgen in the classified advertisements which he took out in the paper. One of them was used as the sleeve of John Lennon's *Rock 'n' Roll* album.

Jurgen was the person who actually gave John and Paul what became known as the 'Beatle cut'. During the time they watched the Beatles in Hamburg, both Klaus and Jurgen wore their hair combed slightly forward in the French style, while the Beatles had hair cuts similar to those of the 'rockers'. It was Astrid who styled Stuart's hair that way. Later, George would comb his hair forward, but would then change his mind and comb it back again.

Late in 1961, Jurgen moved from Hamburg to Paris. While he was there, John and Paul visited him. They decided they wanted their hair styled in the fashion of Jurgen, which was the way lots of young French men had their hair styled. He was to say, 'I gave both of them their first "Beatles" haircut in my hotel room on the Left Bank.'

Jurgen later moved to New York and published a number of books of his photographs, including *Nureyev In Paris, Sex Appeal* and *African Roots*.

Editions De Nesle, Paris, published a collection of his early photographs in a slim eighty-page book in 1980 entitled *Rock 'n'*

Roll Times. It included ten pages devoted to the Beatles, taken during their early Hamburg appearances. There is also a foreword by John Lennon who describes Vollmer as 'the first photographer to capture the beauty and spirit of the Beatles'.

Voormann, Klaus

Son of a prominent Berlin physician, Klaus became a student in Hamburg in 1956, studying illustration at the Meister Schile. In 1958 he began going steady with a fellow student, Astrid Kirchherr, a pale, blonde girl who was studying photography. Klaus moved into a room in the house in Altona where Astrid and her mother lived.

In October 1960, the two had an argument, which led to Klaus wandering around the city centre, first going to the cinema and then finding himself in the Grosse Freiheit in the St Pauli district.

He was attracted by sounds coming from a club called the Kaiserkeller and went inside. On stage were a rock 'n' roll band from Liverpool called Rory Storm & the Hurricanes. The student was mesmerised by the appearance of the young musicians and the exciting sound they made on stage, but he was even more impressed by the band that followed them – the Beatles.

Klaus was completely captivated by the group and stayed in the club for hours, although he didn't pluck up the courage to speak to them. Back home to told Astrid about the group and asked her to come along and see them with him. She refused.

The next evening he returned to the Kaiserkeller, this time taking along with him a record cover he'd designed for a single called 'Walk Don't Run'. When the Beatles came off stage he approached John Lennon, whom he took to be their leader. In his halting English he explained that he liked to design album covers. John just pointed Stuart out to him and told him to show his work to Stu, as he was the artist. However, nervousness overtook Klaus again and he didn't approach Stu.

On the third visit he was accompanied by Astrid and Jurgen Vollmer, another student friend, and they were all fascinated by the visual appearance of the Beatles, particularly Stu, with his dark glasses and moody look. Astrid, in particular, was immediately attracted to the bass guitarist.

The three became regular visitors to watch the group and brought along other student friends. Soon the Beatles were joining their table and chatting to them. As a result Astrid asked Klaus if he could teach her some English.

Within a short time it proved obvious that Stu and Astrid were attracted to each other. She and Klaus had been sweethearts for two years, but within a fortnight Stu and Astrid had fallen in love. It was initially embarrassing for all concerned, but Klaus accepted the situation and Stu moved into the Kirchherrs' home.

The Beatles continued to prove a major influence on Klaus' life and he decided to become a bass guitarist, just like Stu. He moved to England, where he teamed up with two Liverpool musicians, Paddy Chambers and Gibson Kemp, in a band called Paddy, Klaus & Gibson.

They were managed by Tony Stratton-Smith, an author and journalist who had become enamoured of the music scene and also managed Liverpool artists the Kubas and Beryl Marsden. Unlike Epstein, Stratton-Smith really loved and was knowledgeable about the music and had specific plans to establish Paddy, Klaus & Gibson, beginning with a residency at the prestigious Pickwick Club in London's West End, which was frequented by celebrities such as Paul McCartney and Jane Asher.

The Beatles mentioned Paddy, Klaus & Gibson to Epstein and he decided to make them a management offer. Despite Stratton-Smith's frustration, he reluctantly agreed to the management change. They signed with Epstein on 13 August 1965 and were soon to vanish into obscurity and then disband.

Arguably, they would have found success with Stratton-Smith, who went on to mastermind the success of Genesis and created the well-respected Charisma record label.

After the dissolution of the group, Klaus had the opportunity of joining one of several bands – the Hollies, John Mayall, the Moody Blues or Manfred Mann. He chose Manfred Mann, replacing Jack Bruce, and played on all the Manfred records featuring Mike D'Abo.

While in England, Klaus remained in close touch with the Beatles. Possibly remembering his first tentative approach to them in Hamburg with his design for a record sleeve, John Lennon phoned him up and gave him a free hand to design the cover of their seventh album *Revolver*. Klaus was to comment: 'John called me while they were in the studio working on the album and asked if I had any ideas that I might want to use for the cover. I did a few rough sketches that I might want to use for the cover and went to them with scribbles and showed it to them.'

His design brought Klaus a Grammy award. He was also to design the cover of George Harrison's *Wonderwall* and album covers for the Bee Gees and Jackie Lomax.

During the 1960s he married Christine Hargraves, a British actress who appeared on the popular Granada TV soap opera 'Coronation Street', and they settled in Hampstead. At one of their dinner parties, George Harrison noticed that Klaus had a pedal harmonium and started playing it, intrigued with the sounds it made. It possibly had some influence when he composed 'Within You, Without You'.

When Paul McCartney announced publicly that he was leaving the Beatles, John, George and Ringo considered replacing him with Klaus and continuing as a group using the name the Ladders.

Klaus was invited to discuss the plan with them at the Apple offices on Friday, 19 March 1971, only days after the High Court had granted Paul victory in the first round of his battle to dissolve the Beatles.

When Klaus and his wife Christine spent days at George's Friar Park mansion, the music paper *Melody Maker* ran the headline: 'New Beatles Klaus Goes Into Hiding.' On Saturday 20 March a story appeared in the *Daily Mirror* suggesting that Klaus was to be the new replacement for Paul, which was denied by Apple's then publicist Les Perrin. On Friday, 26 March, Apple issued a statement denying that John, George and Ringo were to continue as a group with the addition of Klaus.

In some ways it seemed as if Klaus had stepped into the shoes of the tragic Stuart Sutcliffe – becoming a bass guitarist, designing a Beatles album sleeve and almost becoming a Beatle himself.

Despite the collapse of plans to have Klaus become the new Beatle, he was involved in numerous solo recordings by John, George and Ringo, initially becoming a member of the Plastic Ono Band, making records with John and appearing with the group in London and Toronto.

The singles by John on which Klaus played include 'Cold Turkey', 'Instant Karma', 'Power To The People', 'God Save Us', 'Listen The Snow Is Falling' (the flipside of Happy Xmas) and 'Whatever Gets You Thru The Night'. The albums include *Plastic Ono Band – Live Peace In Toronto 1969, John Lennon/Plastic Ono Band, Imagine, Walls and Bridges* and *Rock 'n' Roll*.

The recordings that he made with George include singles such as 'My Sweet Lord' and the albums *All Things Must Pass, The Concert For Bangladesh, Living in The Material World, Dark Horse* and *Extra Texture (Read All About It)*.

With Ringo he recorded the singles 'It Don't Come Easy', 'Back Off Bugaloo' and 'Photograph', and the albums *Sentimental Journey, Ringo* (packaged with a 24-page lyric book featuring ten lithographs by Klaus which illustrated each of the songs), *Goodnight Vienna* and *Ringo's Rotogravure.*

In the 1970s, Klaus lived for a time on George Harrison's Friar Park estate, then moved to Los Angeles for eight years, playing on sessions with various artists, including Carly Simon, Billy Preston and Harry Nilsson.

He introduced Ringo to Harry Nilsson and co-composed a number with Ringo which was intended as the title song for the film *Blindman*, although it wasn't used in the final print.

Klaus also gained skill as a record producer and produced an album for Tony Sheridan called *World's End*.

In 1979, after playing in Dr John's Band, he decided to move back to Germany with his girlfriend and son (he'd split from Christine some years before). He became a record producer and one of his acts, Trio, had an international hit with 'Da Da Da' in 1984. He then decided to spend more time with his two children.

In June 1995, Klaus was among the artists contacted by Neil Aspinall regarding the design of the *Anthology* series of CD covers and video jackets, and was later commissioned to design them.

Klaus also worked for six years during the 1990s on six oil paintings and a series of sketches depicting the Beatles' early days in Hamburg. Together with Astrid Kirchherr's photographs, the paintings and drawings were published in a special limited edition called *Hamburg Days* by Genesis Publications late in 1999.

Wait

A number mainly written by Paul which was actually recorded on Thursday, 17 June 1965 during the *Help!* album sessions, but was rejected for that particular LP. It then filled a gap in the *Rubber Soul* recordings. The group called up the original tape and, by overdubbing the number with vocal harmonies and percussion, provided the track for *Rubber Soul*.

Walletjes, Amsterdam, Holland

The red light district of Amsterdam, although a place not as notorious as Hamburg's St Pauli district. The Beatles visited Walletjes on the evening of 5 June 1964.

The area is in a picturesque setting alongside the city's canals and is crowded with brothels and sex shops. The Beatles had several drinks and decided to visit some. There was a photograph taken of John crawling out of the doorway of one of the brothels on his hands and knees. Commenting on the incident in the book *Lennon Remembers*, he says: 'There are photographs of me in which I am crawling on my knees through Amsterdam while I'm coming out of a brothel or something and people are saying, "Good morning, John!" and the police escorted us to those places and all that. They didn't want a scandal.'

Walters, Lu

Lu, whose real name was Walter Eymond, was the bass guitarist/vocalist with Rory Storm & the Hurricanes, regarded as one of Liverpool's leading bands.

The bespectacled singer had been a member of the group since their formation at the end of the fifties as the Raving Texans. Their drummer was Ringo Starr.

In 1960 the Hurricanes were appearing at the Kaiserkeller in Hamburg at the same time as the Beatles. In fact, the Beatles had been appearing at the Indra Club, a smaller venue than the Kaiserkeller, but were then moved further up the Grosse Freihect where the posters proclaimed: 'Original Rock 'n' Roll Bands. RORY STORM And His HURICAN und The Beatles. England. Liverpool.'

Earlier in the month Lu had visited the Indra to watch the Beatles and took to the stage to sing several numbers with them. Allan Williams was watching the show and was so impressed with Lu's singing that he arranged for him to make a record in a local studio with the Beatles backing him.

Reputedly, Pete Best was not feeling well at the time and the Hurricanes' drummer Ringo replaced him for the session which took place at the record-your-voice booth of Akustik Studio at 57 Kirchenalle, just behind Hamburg Central Station, on Saturday 15 October 1960.

Lu, together with John, George, Paul and Ringo, recorded 'Summertime'. It was the first time the quartet who were to be known as the 'The Fab Four' played together.

After the session the Beatles asked Williams if they could record a few numbers themselves with Ringo, but without Lu. Williams, who had paid ten pounds for the session, refused to spend any more money.

Several copies of the disc were made. Williams lost his copy over a decade later when he left it behind him in a London pub.

Walton Hospital

Situated at 107 Rice Lane, Liverpool 9. Paul was born here on 18 June 1942 and, as his mother had previously been a nursing sister in the maternity ward there, she was given a private room.

Paul was due to be delivered by midwife Hilda Knite, who was senior midwife at the hospital. She said: 'Paul and Mike's mother was one of my pupils and I trained her to be a midwife. She came back to have her babies at Walton Hospital. I used to take most of the ex-staff on my small block. I remember Paul had to be delivered by a doctor because it was a tricky delivery.' Hilda was a midwife from 1936 until her retirement in 1965.

When Jim McCartney first saw his newborn son he thought that the baby looked terrible and commented: 'He had one eye open and he just squawked all the time. They held him up and he looked like a horrible piece of red meat.'

Warwick Hotel, Corner of 6th Avenue and 54th Street, New York City

The Beatles had originally resided at the Plaza Hotel when visiting New York in 1964, but had changed to the Warwick in 1965. When the Beatles arrived in New York for their third American tour, Cilla Black was appearing at the Persian Room in the Plaza Hotel and other celebrities who were staying there, such as Diana Dors, had expected the Beatles to return to the Plaza.

The group flew out from London on Friday, 13 August 1965, and were taken by limousine to the Warwick. At 2.30 p.m. they took part in a press conference in the hotel conference hall, which was attended by several hundred journalists. The reception went on for an hour: Paul was asked if he had been secretly married to Jane Asher and George was asked if he were marrying Pattie. When they were asked why they were staying at the Warwick instead of the Plaza, Ringo said, 'We can't afford those prices.' John mentioned that he'd bought his Aunt Mimi a bungalow in Poole and Ringo was presented with an antique sword and a pikestaff in celebration of his recent birthday.

During their stay at the hotel they had many visitors, including Bob Dylan, the Supremes, the Crystals and Del Shannon. Dylan introduced them to marijuana. Among the media at the hotel was Don Short of the *Daily Mirror*, music journalist Judy Sims, Chris Hutchins of the *New Musical Express, Brian Matthew* of Radio One and disc jockeys Larry Kane and Jim Stagg.

The group had a suite on the 33rd floor and hosted members of the American Fan Club who had been brought along by Bernice Young, the Fan Club President. During their stay at the hotel the Beatles were also presented with a gold record for their *Beatles VI* album.

Washington Coliseum, Washington DC

A sports stadium which became the venue for the Beatles' first live outdoor concert appearance in America on 11 February 1964. The concert had been booked by Norman Weiss of General Artists Corporation and promoted by Harry Lynn.

The group were due to fly down to Washington from New York, but there was a snowstorm. The Beatles refused to fly in a blizzard, remembering what had happened to Buddy Holly a few years earlier, so arrangements were made for them to travel down in a private train coach from Pennsylvania Station in New York to Union Station in Washington. When they arrived there were 3,000 fans at the station, but they were prevented from approaching the Beatles by the twenty-foot platform gates.

The group were rushed to the Shoreham Hotel. The entire seventh floor had been booked for the group and their entourage, but one family had refused to move out of their room. While the Beatles were at the Coliseum the assistant manager cut off the family's light, heat and water and told them there had been a power failure on the seventh floor. They agreed to be relocated to the ninth floor.

The Beatles took to the stage at 8.31 p.m., following acts such as Tommy Roe and the Chiffons. They performed from a rotating stage and the noise was so deafening that they couldn't even hear themselves perform. They were pelted by jelly beans for the first time. Unlike the soft British jelly babies, the beans were covered by a hard shell and rained down on them like bullets.

They performed 'Roll Over Beethoven', 'From Me To You', 'I Saw Her Standing There', 'This Boy', 'All My Loving', 'I Wanna Be Your Man', 'Please Please Me', 'Till There Was You', 'She Loves You', 'I Want To Hold Your Hand', 'Twist And Shout' and 'Long Tall Sally'. Immediately after they finished their act they rushed to their dressing-rooms surrounded by a phalanx of twelve policemen. A happy Ringo exclaimed, 'They could have ripped me apart and I couldn't have cared less. What an audience! I could have played for them all night.'

A camera team from CBS was present filming the concert for a special closed circuit presentation to be screened at cinemas on 14 and 15 March. The film, entitled *Live At The Washington Coliseum*, featured 'Roll Over Beethoven', 'From Me To You', 'I Saw Her Standing There', 'This Boy', 'All My Loving' and 'I Wanna Be Your Man'. The ending came part way through a version of 'Twist And Shout' because the cameraman had run out of film!

Washington DC Stadium, 2001 E Capitol Street, Washington DC

The Beatles' final tour of America was fraught with tension due to the hostile atmosphere created by the reaction to the 'Beatles are bigger than Christ' interview. Outside the stadium, dressed in full robes, stalked the Imperial Wizard of the Maryland Clan and five klansmen from Prince George's County Ku Klux Klan.

The show began at 6.00 p.m. before an audience of 32,164 fans. Other acts on the bill were the Cyrkle, the Ronettes, the Remains and Bobby Webb.

We Can Work It Out

It has been suggested that Jane Asher was once again Paul's inspiration when he wrote this song and, again, John helped him out with the song's middle section.

The number had the distinction of being the Beatles' very first double 'A' side, with 'Day Tripper', and was issued in Britain on 3 December 1965 on Parlophone R5389, leaping straight to the top of the charts. In America it came out on 6 December 1965, where it sold a million and also topped the charts.

It was included on *A Collection of Beatles Oldies (But Goldies), The Beatles 1962–1966, The Beatles Box, 20 Greatest Hits* and the American album *Yesterday And Today*.

This is also a number which has been recorded by dozens of different artists, including Dionne Warwick, George Burns, Petula Clark, Deep Purple, Humble Pie, Johnny Mathis, Melanie, Johnny Nash, Sam & Dave and Caterine Valente. Stevie Wonder had the most successful version in 1971, when his single reached No. 9 in the States and No. 22 in Britain. The Beatles performed the song on their British tour in 1965. The number was included on the CD compilation *Past Masters Volume Two*.

Wedding Album

The third of John and Yoko's albums which could be considered part of their *Unfinished Music* series.

It took eight months in the preparation, had an extremely elaborate packaging set and was issued on Apple SAPCOR 11 on 7 November 1969.

The entire first side of the album, entitled 'John And Yoko', lasted 22 minutes and 38 seconds and comprised the duo calling out each other's names in numerous ways – cajoling, laughing, shouting, pleading, whispering, crying and so on. Side Two lasted for 24 minutes and 54 seconds and was called 'Amsterdam'. This side was recorded during the 'bed-in' while John and Yoko were honeymooning at the Amsterdam Hilton. Apart from the couple talking to reporters, there were four musical items: 'John, Let's Hope For Peace', 'Goodbye Amsterdam, Goodbye', 'Bed Peace' and 'Goodnight'.

The album was packaged in a box which contained a poster of the couple's wedding, a photograph of a piece of wedding cake, a cartoon strip of the wedding by John, a strip of 'passport' pictures and various photographs by Mlle Danlau, Richard DiLello, John Kelly, Nico Koster, David Nutter and John and Yoko. The packaging was designed by John Kosh.

The record failed to enter the charts, but there was an amusing story concerning the release. Advance review copies had been sent out comprising two single-sided test discs, with a factory test whistle on the reverse of each. The *Melody Maker* reviewer, Richard Williams, mistakenly believed he'd been sent a double album to review and consequently reviewed all 'four' sides, including the two sides with the EMI factory whistle. He described the blank sides as consisting 'entirely of single tones maintained throughout, presumably produced electronically'.

John and Yoko were amused and sent him a telegram from Bombay, where they were staying, which read: 'DEAR RICHARD THANK YOU FOR YOUR FANTASTIC REVIEW ON OUR WEDDING ALBUM INCLUDING C-AND-D SIDE STOP WE ARE CONSIDERING IT FOR OUR NEXT RELEASE STOP MAYBE YOU ARE RIGHT IN SAYING THAT THEY ARE THE BEST SIDES STOP WE BOTH FEEL THAT THIS IS THE FIRST TIME A CRITIC TOPPED THE ARTIST STOP WE ARE NOT JOKING STOP LOVE AND PEACE STOP JOHN AND YOKO LENNON.'

Weedon, Bert

A celebrated British guitarist, born in London in 1960. A self-taught musician from the age of twelve, he had a string of chart entries, including 'Guitar Boogie Shuffle', 'Big Beat Boogie', 'Nashville Boogie' and 'Ginty'. His manual *Play In A Day Guide To Modern Guitar Playing* sold more than two million copies and influenced a generation of guitarists including George Harrison, Eric Clapton and Jeff Beck.

When the Beatles made their debut on the children's show 'Tuesday Rendezvous' on Tuesday, 4 December 1962, Weedon was a resident musician on the programme. The Beatles wrote a number for him – but it was allegedly lost in the post. However, the Shadows wrote a number for him, 'Mr Guitar', which became his final chart entry. Weedon was also on the bill when the Beatles appeared on the TV show 'Thank Your Lucky Stars', broadcast on Saturday, 20 April 1963.

He lives in Buckinghamshire with his wife Maggie and still tours with his one-man show.

Weiss, Nat

A former New York divorce attorney who first met Brian Epstein in 1964. A few years previously he had represented Larry Parnes when the British impresario had attempted to launch Tommy Steele in the States. Parnes recommended Weiss to Epstein and suggested that he look him up.

In fact, the two met at a party at the Plaza Hotel in New York. They got to chatting and Epstein took him on as an attorney. Gradually, Weiss turned from a divorce attorney to one specialising in musicians and promotions, and represented a number of clients including John McLaughlin, Cat Stevens, Peter Asher, James Taylor and Miles Davis.

Weiss and Epstein became friends and Weiss would meet him at the airport each time he arrived in New York. In 1965, Brian asked him if he'd be interested in artist management and Weiss said yes. Epstein said he'd help him, and Weiss discovered a group playing in an Atlantic City bar and signed them up. They were called the Rondells, but Epstein changed their name to the Cyrkle. He then suggested that he and Weiss become partners, and they formed Nemperor Artists together, and the Cyrcle were included on the Beatles' 1966 tour of America. Nemperor Artists, in fact, took over all bookings for the Beatles' 1966 American tour.

Epstein had been unhappy about the design of the *Sgt Pepper* cover and when Weiss took him to the airport Brian was convinced that the plane would crash and gave Weiss a note with the message: 'Brown paper jackets for Sgt Pepper's Lonely Hearts Club Band.'

A few months before he died, Epstein asked Weiss to become his manager.

Weiss, Norman

An executive of the prestigious American agency General Artists Corporation when the Beatles were becoming a major act in Europe. As Weiss dealt with European activities, British agent Vic Lewis called him on behalf of Brian Epstein and suggested that the time was right for the Beatles to tour America. The Beatles were appearing at the Olympia, Paris on a bill with Trini Lopez in January 1964 and Weiss, who represented Lopez, had arranged to visit him in Paris. He asked Lewis to set up a meeting with Epstein and on his arrival he tied up a deal to book the Beatles for two shows at Carnegie Hall for promoter Sid Bernstein and for them to make a live concert appearance at the Coliseum in Washington DC.

Weiss organised the Beatles' first American tour on behalf of GAC and he advised Brian Epstein that he should only accept bookings for large arenas such as stadiums and should ask for $25,000 in advance, plus a percentage of the gate receipts.

Weissleder, Manfred

Imposingly tall, blond club-owner in the St Pauli district of Hamburg. Manfred owned several strip clubs and also produced lavish nudist films that were screened at his various venues.

His entrepreneurial skills were utilised when he decided to open Hamburg's biggest rock 'n' roll venue, the Star Club, which, with the passage of time, has become Germany's equivalent of the legendary Cavern Club.

Unlike promoters such as Bruno Koschmider, who didn't particularly care about the well-being of bands, Manfred ensured that they were paid good money, installed in decent accommodation and were protected from being ripped off or mugged in the area by giving them a special Star Club badge. This little emblem served to warn off any potential attackers. When Gene Vincent complained a taxi driver had given him a hard time, Manfred took a gang of waiters to the Reeperbahn, had Vincent point out the taxi driver and turned the cab upside down in the street!

Groups were so appreciative of his approach that they dubbed the Star Club 'Manfred's Home for Wayward Scousers'.

He even bought a number of flats in the Grosse Freiheit for the bands to live in and allowed the Beatles to use the flats, telling them: 'I always want you should enjoy yourselves in the Star Club, but if you make shit I send you home.'

He took over the premises of the Stern Kino at 39 Grosse Freiheit and transformed it into a comfortable club, stripping out the cinema seats and replacing them with settee-style seating and tables. The ceiling of the entrance foyer was decorated with copies of *Mersey Beat* and the stage area had a colourful backdrop mural of the Manhattan skyline.

One of his first decisions was to appoint Horst Fascher as his assistant. He decided not only to book the best groups from Liverpool and other parts of the UK, but to nurture home-grown bands and to book the biggest names in American rock. As a result, appearing with the Mersey bands were their great heroes Little Richard, Jerry Lee Lewis, the Everly Brothers, Gene Vincent, Ray Charles, Johnnie & the Hurricanes, Bo Diddley and Joey Dee & the Starliters.

Manfred also decided to bring in the top Liverpool names such as the Beatles, the Searchers, Kingsize Taylor & the Dominoes and the Big Three.

In January 1962, a few months before the club's official opening, he sent Horst and pianist Roy Young to Liverpool to book as many top Mersey bands as possible.

The astute Manfred had also instructed Horst to make sure there was exclusivity clauses in the contracts. When Horst met and negotiated a deal with Brian Epstein for the Beatles, the contract, which was signed on 22 January 1962, contained a clause which read: 'It is agreed that the band will not perform or accept other engagements in Germany from the date of this contract until the contract becomes effective.'

Peter Eckhorn of the Top Ten Club had offered Epstein 200 marks each per week for the Beatles. Horst had upped this to 350 marks and by the time they completed the negotiations the Beatles were to receive 500 marks each per week for their first Star Club engagement, which took place from 13 April to 31 May 1962.

Manfred raised the Beatles' fees to 600 marks each per week and booked them to appear from 1 to 14 November that same year. For their third and final Star Club season from 18 to 11 December 1962, he paid them 750 marks.

Interested in building a major rock scene in Germany, he made arrangements to promote in other cities, to open further Star Club venues, to have his own Star Club record label and to publish his own rock newspaper.

He invited Bill and Virginia Harry to move to Hamburg to run a rock newspaper, but was turned down, although Harry agreed to provide a regular column for Weissleder's publication, *Star Club News*.

Manfred hired Adrian Barber, former member of the Big Three, to become the club's stage manager and had him install a sound system to enable him to record groups live on stage.

Among the local groups he encouraged were the Rattles, promoted as 'Hamburg's Beatles'.

Manfred was very conscious of the Liverpool–Hamburg relationship and encouraged it, arranging for Bill and Virginia Harry to make several trips there to report on Star Club activities. He took colour transparencies exclusively for *Mersey Beat*, had exchange trips with the Cavern – sending groups such as the Rattles to play in Liverpool – and made various trips to Merseyside with Horst Fascher and Henry Henriod. He later employed Henry as Star Club manager.

Despite its popularity, the Star Club dream didn't last and Manfred closed it down in June 1964.

Manfred died of a heart disease on 2 February 1980.

Well ... (Baby Please Don't Go)
A number recorded by the Olympics, an R&B quartet from Los Angeles, in 1958. They had two hits, but this wasn't one of them, although the Beatles included the song in their repertoire in 1960, 1961 and 1962 with John Lennon on lead vocals.

Wells, Mary
Motown singer, born in Detroit, whose hits included the 1964 No. 1 record 'My Guy'.

After 'My Guy' entered the charts, the Beatles wanted her to appear on tour with them and she was booked to join their Autumn Tour, making her debut with them on the bill at the Gaumont,

Bradford on 9 October. The tour lasted for four weeks. When it reached the Apollo, Ardwick, Manchester, Mary was interviewed backstage by Bill Harry for *Mersey Beat* and she told him, 'I first heard that I'd be touring with the Beatles in September and I thought it was wonderful. I admire them very much and as far as I'm concerned they're the best.' She added, 'I'd just love to record a number by John and Paul and I think I'll ask them about it.'

Harry talked to John Lennon that same night and John said, 'We've got a number which we think will really be suitable for her.' However, nothing transpired from it.

Mary also appeared on the television special 'Around The Beatles'. She was also to pay tribute to the Beatles when she recorded the album *Love Songs To The Beatles*, which featured the tracks: 'He Loves You', 'All My Loving', 'Please Please Me', 'Do You Want To Know A Secret?', 'Can't Buy Me Love', 'I Should Have Known Better', 'Help!', 'Eight Days A Week', 'And I Love Him', 'Ticket To Ride', 'Yesterday' and 'I Saw Him Standing There'.

Mary died in August 1992.

We Love You

A number recorded by the Rolling Stones. When the group were recording at Olympic Studios in Barnes, John Lennon and Paul McCartney dropped in to see them and ended up providing backing vocals on this song.

Bill Wyman recalled the event in his autobiography *Stone Alone* (Viking, 1990): 'We went into the Olympic Studios on 12 and 13 June [1967] to record "We Love You", produced by Andrew [Oldham]. In July John Lennon and Paul McCartney overdubbed back-up vocals as a gesture of support, and another sound-effect was added after the trial: the sound of a prison door being slammed.'

This reference was to the trial which took place after members of the Rolling Stones were arrested following a drug bust.

72 Western Avenue, Speke, Liverpool L15

The home of the McCartney family from 1947 until 1953. The house was situated on a large council estate and Mary McCartney was the local midwife.

When the family moved into the estate from their previous address in Sir Thomas White Gardens, Paul was four years old.

15 Whaddon House, William Mews, London SW1

When George and Ringo moved down to London in 1963 they lived together in Flat 7 of this residential building. Previously, they had used a small flat in Green Street. When they were unable to renew the Green Street lease they discovered that Brian Epstein had moved into Whaddon House where there was an available apartment on the next floor to him.

John, Cynthia and Julian moved to Emperor's Gate and although Paul was supposed to be sharing the flat with George and Ringo, he mainly stayed with Jane Asher's family in Wimpole Street. Brian Epstein used his private flat, situated in the Knightsbridge area, to hold several lavish parties. The Whaddon House address was the one given on Ringo's wedding certificate in February 1965 as his home, but by that time he had moved to Montague Square.

Whally, Nigel

A playfriend of John Lennon's from the age of five, Nigel lived in Vale Road, close to John's home in Menlove Avenue. He became part of the small, close-knit group of friends cultivated by John, and was nicknamed 'Whalloggs'. When Nigel started at Bluecoat Grammar School, John formed his skiffle group the Quarry Men and Nigel was appointed tea-chest player, a task he divided between himself and Ivan Vaughan. One night when two tough Woolton teddy boys Rod and Willo threatened to beat them up as they alighted from a bus, the Quarry Men fled leaving the tea-chest bass in the road. After that, Nigel became their manager and Len Garry took over on tea-chest bass.

Nigel had cards printed:

COUNTRY. WESTERN. ROCK 'N' ROLL. SKIFFLE.
THE QUARRY MEN
OPEN FOR ENGAGEMENTS.

When he left school he became an apprentice golf professional at Lee Park Golf Club. He arranged for the group to play there for free, but they got a slap-up meal and when the hat was passed round they ended up with twice as much as they'd have received for a paid booking! At the club Nigel also played golf with Dr Sytner whose son Alan had just opened the Cavern as a jazz club. He arranged for the Quarry Men to appear there and they received a booking for 7 August 1957. Paul didn't play with them on this occasion as he was on holiday. They began with the Del Vikings number 'Come Go With Me', then John launched into 'Hound Dog' and 'Blue Suede Shoes'. Sytner immediately had a note delivered to them on stage: 'Cut out the bloody Rock.'

The stint as manager didn't last very long as Paul wasn't happy about Nigel receiving an equal split with them.

On 15 July 1958 Nigel dropped around to see if John was at home in Mendips. He wasn't, but Mimi was talking to Julia Lennon at the gate. Nigel walked with Julia for about 200 yards and then continued up Menlove Avenue while she crossed the road. He heard a squeal of brakes and turned to see Julia's body tossed into the air by a car. She was killed and the off-duty policeman who was driving was sent to trial, with Nigel as a witness. The man was acquitted.

When he was eighteen Nigel left the area and he later became a golf pro at Wrotham Heath Golf Club in Borough Green, Kent.

His father was Chief Superintendent Harold Whally, head of City Police 'A' Division. The *Liverpool Echo* reported when he met John and Paul backstage after they'd become famous: 'Mr Whally first met the two Beatles when they were part of a skiffle group which his son, Nigel managed in 1957. "I used to worry about some of the clubs and places they were performing at. I told them that there was no future in that kind of thing and advised them to drop it. I told them a few times to get a haircut as well." '

What Goes On

One of the many numbers John Lennon wrote early in his career, before the Beatles achieved fame, although the number was never included in the group's stage repertoire. The band originally intended to record the song during their recording session on Tuesday, 5 March 1963, but studio time ran out. The number wasn't revived until their recording session on Thursday, 4 November 1965, by which time it had undergone a number of changes. The group were under pressure for more tracks for the *Rubber Soul* album deadline and also needed the customary Ringo Starr vocal track.

Both Paul and Ringo participated in the final structure of the song and Paul made a demo of the number as a guide to Ringo. Ringo was also given a co-composer credit, which may explain the number's slight country music feel. It was the first Beatles number on which Ringo received a songwriting credit.

'What Goes On' was included on the British *Rubber Soul* album, but was one of two numbers left off the American release. It was issued in the States as the flipside of the 'Nowhere Man' single in February 1966 and its 'B'-side placing in the American charts saw it reach No. 89, while the 'A' side reached No. 3. The song was also used on Capitol's *Yesterday . . . And Today* album.

What's Happening: The Beatles In The USA

A 53-minute film, released in 1967. The documentary was made by brothers Albert and David Maysles, who were later responsible for the Rolling Stones documentary 'Gimme Shelter'.

What's Happening followed the Beatles on their first visit to America in February 1964, covering their stay in New York, their train journey to Washington DC, their appearance on the 'Ed Sullivan Show' and several of their interviews. The two brothers had already used much of the material for a TV special they had made called 'The Beatles in New York'.

Later that year, *What's Happening: The Beatles In The USA* was also featured in an hour-long CBS TV variety show hosted by Carol Burnett, called 'The Entertainers', under the title 'The Beatles in the USA'.

What's The New Mary Jane?
A song John wrote while at the Maharishi's ashram in Rishikesh, India, in 1968. John and George were the only members of the Beatles who played on the track recorded on Wednesday, 14 August 1968 during the recordings of tracks for *The Beatles* double album. It was rejected for the album, no doubt because of the drug imagery associated with the name 'Mary Jane', a slang word referring to marijuana. John later considered releasing it as a Plastic Ono Band single and added overdubs to it on Wednesday, 26 November 1969. However, he never did get to release it. Over the years, many Beatles fans waited in anticipation of this 'unissued Beatles classic', which eventually surfaced on the *Anthology 3* CD in 1996.

What You're Doing
Number by Paul which was used for the *Beatles For Sale* album when, once again, the Beatles were under pressure to adhere to a recording schedule. They first recorded the number on Tuesday and Wednesday, 29 and 30 September 1964, but weren't satisfied with that version and re-recorded it on Monday, 26 October. Apart from the *Beatles For Sale* album, the number also appeared on the American *Beatles VI* LP.

When I Get Home
Number penned by John Lennon which was included on the *Hard Day's Night* album. The Beatles recorded the number on Tuesday, 2 June 1964, and it was also included on the American album *Something New* and the British EP *Extracts From The Album A Hard Day's Night*. The influence of some of John 's favourite American girl groups such as the Shirelles is evident.

When I'm Sixty-Four
Paul had written the song at the piano in his Forthlin Road home when he was fifteen. He was to comment, 'I think my father was around 56 at the time I wrote the song and as the age for retirement

is 65 in England I thought 64 was a nice number and it sounded better than 65.' Paul's father had just reached the age of 64 in July 1966, which may have prompted its inclusion on the *Sergeant Pepper* album.

Recording of the number began on Tuesday, 6 December 1966, and the influence of Paul's father's musical tastes is evident on it. In fact, George Martin was to say: 'I'm sure Paul had his father in his thoughts when he wrote the song. It sounds more like a Des O'Connor number than a Beatles song. It really is a typical McCartney song without the assistance of the other three. If it had been up to Lennon, the song would never have been recorded.'

It was the first *Sergeant Pepper* track to be completed and it also featured three clarinettists – Robert Burns, Henry MacKenzie and Frank Reidy.

'When I'm Sixty-Four' has been recorded by over forty different artists, including Keith Moon, Kenny Ball & His Jazzmen, Bernard Cribbins, Georgie Fame and Frankie Howerd.

Where Have You Been All My Life

A song which had been recorded by one of John Lennon's idols, Arthur Alexander, in May 1962. The number had been composed by Barry Mann and Cynthia Weil and John sang lead vocals on the number when it was included in the Beatles' stage act. They performed it at the Star Club, Hamburg, and it is one of the tracks on the Star Club double album.

Where It's At

A BBC Radio 1 programme. The Saturday, 20 May 1967 show was hosted by Chris Denning and lasted for ninety minutes from 4.00 p.m. It included a feature on *Sgt Pepper's Lonely Hearts Club Band,* which had previously been recorded by Kenny Everett in which there were excerpts from interviews with John, Paul and Ringo. All the tracks from the album, with the exception of 'A Day In The Life', which the BBC had banned, were played. The show on Saturday, 25 November 1967, which was broadcast from 2.00 p.m., was co-hosted by Kenny Everett and Chris Denning. The programme included a previously taped interview with John Lennon which lasted for eighteen minutes. All six tracks from the *Magical Mystery Tour* EP were also played during the course of the programme, including 'I Am The Walrus', which was later banned by the BBC for the use of the word 'knickers'.

While My Guitar Gently Weeps

George Harrison composition which appeared on *The Beatles* double album.

George was visiting his parents' home near Merseyside when he first began writing the number. At the time he'd been consulting the *I Ching*, the Eastern 'Book of Changes', which gave him the idea of writing a song based upon the first thing he saw when opening a book. At his parents' home he just picked a book at random, opened it and the first words he noticed were 'gently weeps'. He put the book down and began writing the song.

Recording of the number actually began on 25 July 1968, although there were to be several versions of the number, one in which George sings and plays to the accompaniment of an acoustic guitar and has added an extra verse to the song.

The version that was issued on the album contained an electric guitar solo from Eric Clapton, while George and John played acoustic guitars. The idea to include Clapton (one of George's closest friends) on the track came only a short time before the session when Eric was giving George a lift in his car. George suggested that Eric play on the track. Initially, Eric was amazed at the suggestion, because no other rock musician had been featured on a Beatles recording before, but George assured him that the number was his and he wanted Eric to play on it. Eric included his overdubs on the recording on Friday, 6 September 1968.

The track was also included on *The Beatles 1967–1970* compilation and Harrison's *The Best Of George Harrison* collection in 1976. A solo acoustic number by George was featured on the Beatles' *Anthology 3* CDs.

Whitaker, Bob

Born and reared in England, Whitaker moved to Melbourne, Australia, in 1961, initially working as a film editor for ABV2 television before becoming a photographer working on advertising, fashion and editorial assignments. In 1964, when he was 23 years old, a colleague Adman Rawings was commissioned to interview Brian Epstein during the Beatles' Australasian tour and invited Whitaker along to take the photographs. Epstein liked the pictures so much that he visited Whitaker's studio to view some more of his work. Impressed, Epstein offered him a job at NEMS back in England where he would become the company's official photographer, taking shots of all the acts, in addition to becoming NEMS' artistic director. Whitaker turned him down.

Three months later, Epstein cabled Whitaker repeating his offer and this time the photographer accepted and flew to London. He became official photographer to the Beatles from August 1964 to November 1966 and travelled extensively with them documenting their tours in America, Germany and Japan, in addition to arranging studio sessions.

In 1966, following a suggestion by John Lennon, Whitaker took the notorious 'butcher' shots, which were used in Beatles advertisements in Britain, but censored when one of the images was used in America as the cover of the *Yesterday ... And Today* album. The image of the Beatles in butchers' smocks with decapitated dolls and pieces of red meat caused panic among Capitol Records executives and the cover was replaced.

Whitaker also took the photograph that became the replacement cover, an innocuous shot of the group posing around a travelling trunk. Bob's photographs for *Revolver* were passed over in favour of the award-winning Klaus Voormann design, although a Whitaker shot was used on the back cover. Another Whitaker shot was used on the back cover of the *A Collection of Beatles Oldies* album.

Twenty-five years later a selection of Whitaker's photographs of the Beatles was published in a book, *The Unseen Beatles,* published by Collins with text by Martin Harrison.

White, Andy

A session drummer who played on the Beatles' first single. Recording manager George Martin usually brought in various Musicians' Union drummers for studio sessions, including Ron Bowden, Jimmy Nicol, Bobbie Graham, Clem Cattini and Andy White.

Martin engaged White for the session on 11 September 1962. White was 32 years old at the time and played with the Vic Lewis Orchestra. He arrived at Abbey Road at seven that evening for the three-hour session, for which he was paid £5.15.

Ringo hadn't known about the arrangement and immediately felt anxious when he arrived to discover White setting up his drums.

Ron Richards began recording the session and Martin arrived halfway through. Martin told them: 'I'm giving you a very good drummer who's probably better than Ringo Starr, and that's who's going to play the drums.'

Ringo was showing signs of depression as the recording got under way, so he was asked to participate by playing maracas on 'P.S. I Love You'.

There were two versions of the 'A' side, 'Love Me Do', completed at the session, one with Andy playing drums and Ringo playing tambourine, the other with Ringo as drummer.

Despite Martin's preference for session drummers, the version of 'Love Me Do' initially released as a single featured Ringo on drums. The version with White was included on the *Please Please Me* album, then surfaced as a single issued with a black label when it was re-pressed in April 1963.

White was married to singer Lynn Cornell, a former member of the Vernons Girls. He was later to join the BBC Radio Orchestra in Glasgow, then moved to America, where he worked with a variety of artists including Louis Armstrong, Chuck Berry, Shirley Bassey and Marlene Dietrich. By 1992 he had settled in a two-room apartment in New York where he worked as a part-time librarian and appeared as a drum sergeant for the New York Police band drummers.

White, Ron

The General Marketing Manager of EMI Records in London in 1961 when he was approached by Brian Epstein regarding the Beatles. As NEMS was a major record retailer, White agreed to meet him and Epstein played him the Polydor single 'My Bonnie', and showed him photographs of the group, suggesting that they would be an ideal band for EMI to sign. White pointed out that it was difficult to judge what the band were like from a record on which they were backing another singer, but he offered to take it round personally to all of EMI's four A&R (Artistes and Repertoire) managers and play it to them. In the meantime, Epstein arranged the Decca audition, then wrote to White on 8 December 1961. He expressed his disappointment that he hadn't heard from White and mentioned they would be seeing Decca A&R men. He wrote: 'These boys who are superb instrumentalists also produce some exciting and pulsating vocals. They play mostly their own compositions and one of the boys has written a song which I really believe to be the hottest material since "Livin' Doll".'

White's reply had actually crossed in the post and was dated 7 December. He told Epstein that he would be having the record carefully assessed by each of EMI's A&R men. White first played it to Norrie Paramor, whose artists included Cliff Richard and the Shadows and Frank Ifield. Paramor told him that they were a bit like the Shadows and as the Shadows were at the peak of their career, he didn't need a similar group. White then approached Walter Ridley who recorded artists such as Alma Cogan and Frankie Vaughan. Ridley rejected them saying he wasn't particularly interested in their sound. White then took the material to Norman Newall, who recorded artists such as Russ Conway, and he told White that he thought they sounded like the Shadows and he wouldn't like to compete with Paramor, who recorded the Shadows.

EMI's fourth A&R man, George Martin, was on holiday at the time, so White didn't offer it to him. He then replied to Epstein on 18 December, formally rejecting the band, writing, 'I am sorry that I have been so long in giving you a decision but I have now had an opportunity of playing the record to each of our Artistes Managers. Whilst we appreciate the talents of this group we feel that we have sufficient groups of this type at the present time under contract and that it would not be advisable for us to sign any further contracts of this nature at present.'

Had George Martin not been on holiday at the time he would have been approached by White and, in the light of the Beatles being rejected by his three other colleagues, the chances are that Martin would have rejected them, too. So EMI gave the Beatles the thumbs down, without even offering to audition them, while, at the same time, Decca Records was sufficiently interested to send Mike Smith up to Liverpool to see them and also to arrange for them to perform a recording audition in London. Fate would have it that although Mike Smith wanted to sign the group, Brian Poole & the Tremeloes were signed instead. In the light of this, it seems unfair that Decca has been looked upon for so many years as the recording company which turned down the Beatles when, in fact, EMI originally rejected them first.

When the white label of 'Love Me Do' was presented at the EMI meeting to decide which records were worthy of release, the majority of sales-orientated EMI executives voted it a miss. White, however, decided he would back George Martin's judgement and release the single. Then he realised the name was familiar. Considering he had formally rejected the group and then discovered that one of his A&R men had accepted them, White decided to send another letter to Epstein and wrote, 'I was nonplussed and somewhat embarrassed to see details of a contract going through for "The Beatles" especially in view of my letter to you of 18 December 1961 when I told you that our Artistes Managers did not feel we could use them.' He mentioned how pleased he was that the contract was being negotiated and added, 'My only reason for writing is to endeavour to explain what must appear to you an anomaly in our organisation. I can assure you that our Artistes Managers did hear the record but I know you will appreciate that even Artistes Managers are human and can change their mind!'

At a later stage, White was to become Managing Director of EMI Records. He died on 18 September 1989, at the age of 67, after a long illness.

Why

A number penned by Tony Sheridan in 1958 in collaboration with Bill Crompton. Its full title was 'Why (Can't You Love Me Again)'. The song was one of the numbers selected when the Beatles backed

Tony Sheridan during a recording session with Bert Kaempfert in May 1961, when they also provided the vocal harmony on the track.

Due to the success of the Beatles in Britain it was issued as one of the tracks on an EP, *My Bonnie*, released by Polydor on H21 610 on 12 July 1963. A single of the number, with 'Cry For A Shadow' on the flip, was issued in America on MGM K13227 on 27 March 1964 and it reached No. 88 on the *Billboard* chart. Its release in Britain on Polydor NH 52 275 on 28 February 1964 didn't secure a chart placing. It was also included on a Polydor compilation *Let's Do The Twist, Hully Gully, Slop, Locomotion, Monkey* on Polydor SLPHM 237 622 on 8 May 1964. It next appeared on the album *The Beatles First*, issued in June 1964 and reissued in August 1967, and on *The Early Years* compilation, issued by Contour in June 1971 (this album was issued in the States by Polydor under the title *The Beatles – Circa 1960 – In The Beginning*). It was included on the Charly Records album *The Savage Young Beatles* in 1982 and *First Movement*, issued by Phoenix in 1982.

Why Don't We Do It In The Road?

On Wednesday, 9 October 1968, Paul McCartney took engineer Ken Townsend aside and they went into Studio Three of Abbey Road and recorded this number which Paul had written. Paul sang vocals, on which there was some double-tracking, and also played guitar, piano and bass.

The following day, together with Townsend and Ringo Starr, Paul went into Studio Three again and completed the number, with Ringo overdubbing drums and including further vocals, handclaps and another bass track. This was more or less a Paul McCartney solo effort. Some years later John Lennon was to say how disappointed he was to discover that Paul had gone ahead and done the track without consulting either himself or George or asking them to participate in the recording.

The number was included on *The Beatles* white album. Paul performs solo on this alternative version of the number that was included on the Beatles' *Anthology 3* CDs.

95 Wigmore Street, London W1

Site of the first offices of the Beatles' Apple Corps company. Two office suites were rented in the building and the group and their friends and associates planned the growth of their Apple empire. During one discussion session they were interrupted by Don Short of the *Daily Mirror*, who revealed their plans in a full-page story.

Soon after moving into Wigmore Street Ringo, Maureen, Peter

Brown, Neil Aspinall and Mal Evans were locked inside the building by the caretaker.

The offices were maintained for a period of time after all the main business had been transferred to Savile Row in the autumn of 1968.

Wild Honey Pie

John, George and Ringo weren't around when Paul recorded this brief number at Abbey Road Studios on 20 August 1968. Paul sang, played guitar and bass drum and also double-tracked. At only 53 seconds in length, it is the shortest cut on *The Beatles* double album.

Paul had originally penned the song in India but had never really intended recording it. However, both Jane Asher and Pattie Harrison liked it and encouraged him to record it. He commented, 'This was just a fragment of an instrumental which we weren't sure about, but Pattie liked it very much so we decided to leave it on the album.'

Wild In The Country

The name of an Elvis Presley film. Elvis also recorded the title song which reached No. 26 in the American charts. It was penned by Hugo Peretti, Luigi Creatore and George Weiss. Pete Best performed the number when it was included in the Beatles' repertoire in 1961.

Williams, Allan

Born in the Merseyside area of Bootle, he was a Liverpool coffee bar owner when he first became acquainted with John Lennon and Stuart Sutcliffe in 1959. The two were among some art students who frequented his Jacaranda Club in Slater Street. Shortly after he'd promoted a show at the Liverpool Stadium featuring Gene Vincent and leading Merseyside groups, Sutcliffe approached him to ask him why he hadn't booked his group on the show. They were always hanging around his club and, being from the art school, Alan had had Stu work on some floats and decorations for one of his promotions and some murals in the Jacaranda.

Williams advised them to get a drummer and Brian Casser of Cass & the Cassanovas put them on to one called Tommy Moore.

Larry Parnes, who'd noticed the Liverpool bands on the Stadium show, asked Williams to arrange an audition of local bands as he was seeking a backing band for Billy Fury. Williams set up the auditions at his Wyvern Club and the Silver Beatles were among the groups auditioning, which resulted in them being booked to back Johnny Gentle on a short Scottish tour.

Williams at the time was booking groups on occasional gigs through his Jacaranda Enterprises. Following the Silver Beatles' return from Scotland he arranged for them to appear at some gigs promoted by Les Dodd in the Wirral and gave them a few bookings at the Jacaranda – and had them provide backing for a stripper at the New Cabaret Artistes Club.

He'd put Derry Wilkie & the Seniors on the Stadium show, included them in the Wyvern audition and, when their promised season backing a Parnes artist fell apart, took them to the 2 I's in London which resulted in them being the first Liverpool band to be booked in Hamburg. As a result of the Seniors' success in Hamburg, club-owner Bruno Koschmider requested other bands. Allan attempted unsuccessfully to book Rory Storm & the Hurricanes and Gerry & the Pacemakers and then finally turned to the Beatles.

As Allan was travelling to Hamburg in an attempt to talk Koschmider into giving him booking rights for other bands, he took the Beatles along with him in a hired mini-van.

His brief association with the Beatles then ended. They arranged a season at the Top Ten Club in Hamburg and refused to give him a percentage, reckoning that they'd got the booking themselves and shouldn't be required to pay an agency fee. Williams wrote to them saying: 'I will also submit a full report of your behaviour to the Agency Members Association, of which I am a full member, and every Agent in England is a member, to protect Agents from Artistes who misbehave and welsh out of agreements.'

He no longer got them any bookings and the association had lasted less than a year.

Through his Jacaranda Enterprises, Allan had set up gigs for various local groups including Derry & the Seniors, Rory Storm & the Hurricanes, Gerry & the Pacemakers and the Beatles.

However, in a book he co-wrote with journalist Bill Marshall, he claimed that he'd actually managed the Beatles, writing: 'I was the Beatles' first manager. I still have their contracts, ragged and burnt from being involved in a fire.' The contracts in question were actually just the agency contract for the Kaiserkeller booking and not management contracts – they were slightly burnt in a fire at a proposed new Liverpool club of his, the Top Ten, which burned down. His co-writer Bill Marshall admitted that the book was mostly an exaggeration, mainly written by him.

Although Allan had his part to play in their early career, and no one can deny that, he never managed the group. They were just one of several local bands he arranged bookings for. In fact, he booked Derry Wilkie & the Seniors on more gigs than the Beatles, but never claimed to be their manager – and despite putting Rory Storm & the Hurricanes into the Kaiserkeller with them being billed above the Beatles, he has never claimed to have managed them, either.

Allan's main concern was running his clubs and coffee bars, and booking local groups was merely a sideline, which came to an end at the close of 1960.

As Mark Lewisohn wrote in *The Beatles Live* in 1986: 'Williams, a stockily-built opportunist who, from May 1960 until April 1961, became the group's occasional booking agent or, as he still claims, "their first manager" (even now, more than twenty years on, the Beatles strongly dispute Williams' claims).'

However, following their return from Hamburg in November 1960, Williams was not responsible for any of their bookings again, apart from two Grosvenor Hall gigs, which had already been arranged.

Williams, Danny

Ballad singer born in Port Elizabeth, South Africa, on 7 January 1942. He made his recording debut with 'Tall a Tree' in 1959 and appeared regularly on the television show 'Drumbeat' prior to reaching No 1 in the British charts in 1961 with 'Moon River'.

On Friday, 8 December 1961, Williams, then currently at No. 4 in the charts with 'Moon River', had been appearing for a week at Liverpool's Cabaret Club. He was added to the bill of a concert at the Tower Ballroom, New Brighton, which featured the Beatles.

Williams was also on the bill of the Beatles' first British nationwide tour, which was headed by Helen Shapiro. When Helen was ill on 26 and 27 February 1964, Williams topped the bill.

The 'velvet-voiced' singer had seven British chart hits between 1961 and 1963 and a major hit in America in 1963. He didn't enter the British charts again until 1977, with 'Dancin' Easy'. He continued to record for various labels, without success, and was signed to Prestige Records in 1991.

Williams, Larry

American artist who began his career as a session pianist for Lloyd Price. He then began to record and compose a number of songs, two of which were Top Twenty hits in Ameica – 'Short Fat Fanny' and 'Bony Moronie'.

Williams was a seminal influence on the Beatles and the songs of his which they included in their repertoire were 'Bony Moronie', 'Short Fat Fanny', 'Bad Boy', 'Dizzy Miss Lizzy' and 'Slow Down'.

Williams recorded for the Specialty label in the States and issued 'Bad Boy' in January 1959. The Beatles recorded it during their *Help!*

album sessions, with John on lead vocals, and it was included on *A Collection Of Beatles' Oldies (But Goldies)*. 'Dizzy Miss Lizzy' was issued on a single by Williams in February 1958, with 'Slow Down' on the flipside. The Beatles recorded 'Dizzy Miss Lizzy', which was included on their *Help!* album, with John on lead vocals. John also sang the lead on 'Slow Down', which they included on their *Long Tall Sally* EP.

John Lennon was to record 'Bony Moronie' on his *Rock 'n' Roll* album.

Williams committed suicide on 2 January 1980.

Wilson Hall, Speke Road, Garston, Liverpool L19

The second gig for the Quarry Men in which Paul was present took place on Thursday, 7 November 1957 at this venue, which was run by promoter Charlie McBain. The line-up comprised John Lennon, Paul McCartney, Colin Hanton, Eric Griffiths and Len Garry. Nigel Whally was with them, but had to leave halfway through the night due to an asthma attack. They were each paid 50/-. Two teddy boys, Rod and Willo, were determined to beat up John. They next appeared on 7 December 1957. When the Quarry Men appeared at the hall on 6 February 1958, Paul had been trying to convince John to allow George Harrison to join the group and arranged for him to hear George play. It was a most unusual audition – George performed 'Raunchy' for them on the upper deck of a bus. George was fourteen years old at the time, although it was shortly before his fifteenth birthday, and John thought he was too young.

Garston is adjacent to Speke, where George lived at the time, and he has related how John was impressed with the guitarist of the Ed Clayton Skiffle Group, who were also on the bill. He told George that if he could play like Eddie Clayton (incidentally, Ringo was once a member of the Ed Clayton Skiffle Group), he'd let him join.

George's father Harry was chairman of the Speke Bus Depot Social Club and he booked the Quarry Men to appear at Wilson Hall on a club Christmas function on the afternoon of 1 January 1959.

Wilson Hall, which was named after Francis Wilson who built it, became a supermarket in the Lennon's chain in the 1970s and a carpet warehouse in the 1980s.

Wilson, Sir Harold

British politician, born in Yorkshire in 1916, who was elected leader of the Labour Party in 1963 and became Prime Minister in October 1964. On 14 October 1964, the eve of the election, he received a telegram from Brian Epstein which read: 'Hope your group is as much a success.'

The Beatles first met him on Thursday, 19 March 1964 when he was still leader of the opposition. The occasion was the twelfth annual luncheon of the Variety Club of Great Britain. The event took place at the Dorchester Hotel in Park Lane, London.

Wilson presented the Beatles with their award as Show Business Personalities of 1963.

When John Lennon got up to make his acceptance speech, he began, 'Mr Chief Barker . . .' He then looked at Wilson and added '. . . and Mr Dobson'. This was a typical piece of Lennon humour, obscure to the population in general as he was referring to the Liverpool firm called Barker & Dobson.

Their award was a Silver Heart, which John referred to as a 'Purple Heart'.

At the reception, Wilson commented, 'We are all proud of the creation of a new musical idiom in world communications. But I will refrain from making political capital out of the Beatles, unlike the leader of a certain political party.'

Wilson, who was the MP for the Huyton district of Liverpool, recommended the Beatles for an MBE and he also officially reopened the Cavern Club on 23 July 1966. The Beatles sent a telegram of support.

Wilson was to say that his favourite Beatles song was 'She Loves You'.

His wife Mary was to comment, 'I think they are lovely boys, and I've been dying to meet them. Harold and I are both tremendous fans of the Beatles and always listen to them and watch them on television. Harold and I met in Liverpool. Even in those days we used the word "gear", meaning fabulous or wonderful.'

George Harrison was to harangue Wilson in his song 'Taxman', released in 1964.

Wilson died on Tuesday, 23 May 1995. The following evening, Paul McCartney was one of the celebrities to pay tribute to him on ITV's *London Tonight*. He said, 'He was very canny. The last time we met him, somebody from the press tried to put a microphone in his face and tried to get us to say something indiscreet with him. But he put the microphone in his pocket and just carried on puffing away on his pipe. I liked him a lot, he seemed like a nice man.'

Wimbledon Palais, High Street, Merton, Wimbledon, London SW19

Site of 'The Beatles London Fan Club Convention' on 14 December 1963.

The South London ballroom comprised a massive shed-like

structure with a long bar at the far end. All four members of the Beatles sat in the bar area behind tables while almost 3,000 fans passed by in a long queue to shake hands. There were several commissionaires and the Beatles were also accompanied by road managers Neil Aspinall and Mal Evans, newly appointed press officer Brian Sommerville and NEMS press agent Tony Barrow.

After the hand-shaking ceremony, the Beatles went on stage and performed several numbers, including 'Twist And Shout'. Unfortunately, the management of the Palais, fearing some sort of riot (which didn't happen with the well-behaved fans), had erected a cage-like structure in front of the stage, a physical barrier between the Beatles and their fans, which tended to inhibit the performance.

57 Wimpole Street, London W1

Address which Paul used as a London base between 1963 and late 1965. It was the home of the Ashers, who bought it in 1957.

When Paul began dating Jane Asher he got to know her family and began to visit her at their home. Describing it at the time, Jane commented: 'Well, it's very, very tall. There's the ground floor and then the first, and second, the third, the fourth floor – four floors above the ground floor.'

Jane's room was on the second floor. It was a large room, which contained lots of her bits and pieces – a record player, a large collection of classical records, lots of dolls, stuffed animals and teddy bears. The sitting-room with the television was next door to Jane's room. Her younger sister Claire lived on the third floor, which also contained the bathroom. There was also a bathroom on the fourth floor where Jane's elder brother Peter had his room, a large, L-shaped bedroom. Paul's room was on the same floor, at the rear of the house, was smaller and contained a large brown wardrobe, a bed, an easy chair, a record player and a small piano. The walls were decorated with Beatles' Gold Records and two of Jean Cocteau's drawings from Opium.

Jane's mother Margaret was a music teacher and had, in the past, taught George Martin how to play the oboe. Her husband was Dr Richard Asher, who was a specialist in blood and mental diseases at Middlesex Hospital.

Margaret's music room was in the basement of the house. Paul and John used to write regularly in the music room, although Paul was to begin composing 'Yesterday' in his own room.

When Paul first began dating Jane, he'd return to his home in Liverpool. One night, on missing his last train, Jane invited him to stay the night. Margaret Asher suggested that he could regard it as his permanent home, that he could stay whenever he was in London, thus saving himself the bother of hotels.

He lived there until the latter part of 1965 when he bought his house in Cavendish Avenue.

When the house was put up for sale in 1998 it was valued at £1.7million.

Winston's Walk

One of the earliest of the John Lennon compositions, an instrumental which he introduced into the repertoire of the Quarry Men in the late fifties. It's one of the very few instrumentals John wrote and the number was a tribute to Britain's wartime leader, Winston Churchill. Winston was John's middle name, but one which he said always used to embarrass him.

Winter Gardens, Exeter Road, Bournemouth, Hampshire

Theatre in the fashionable coastal town of Bournemouth. When the Beatles appeared there on 16 November 1963, no less than three American TV news teams covered the event, in addition to reporters from *Life* magazine.

CBS News filmed at the concert and the group were interviewed in their dressing-room after the show by Josh Dansette. On 21 November 1962 CBS News, in an item narrated by correspondent Alexander Kendrick, the concert clips were shown, along with part of the Dansette interview. Excerpts were also screened in the US on 7 December on 'CBS Evening News With Walter Cronkite'.

ABC TV had screened its brief excerpt in the US on 19 November 1963 and the NBC excerpt was featured on 'The Jack Paar Show' on 3 January 1964.

Winter Gardens, Fort Crescent, Margate, Kent

Margate is a Kentish seaside town popular with holidaymakers from London. The Beatles appeared for a short season of six consecutive nights, with two performances per evening from 8–13 July 1963. The numbers they performed were 'Roll Over Beethoven', 'Thank You Girl', 'Chains', 'Please Please Me', 'A Taste Of Honey', 'I Saw Her Standing There', 'Baby It's You', 'From Me To You' and 'Twist And Shout'. The local paper, *Isle of Thanet Gazette,* slated their performances, describing their sound as 'jungle music'. While they were appearing in Margate they stayed at the Beresford Hotel in nearby Birchington-on-Sea. The hotel was demolished in the early 1970s.

Winter Gardens Ballroom, Heald Street, Garston, Liverpool L19

A ballroom in the south end of Liverpool which featured rock 'n' roll nights on Tuesday evenings. There were also talent competitions at the venue and the Quarry Men were one of the bands who appeared at the Winter Gardens during 1958.

Winters, Mike & Bernie

One of the major British television comedy duos of the sixties. The brothers eventually parted company with Mike moving permanently to America and Bernie pursuing a solo career in Britain. Sadly, they were both to contract cancer.

The Beatles appeared on a number of shows hosted by the couple, including the 'Big Night Out' series and also 'Blackpool Night Out'.

In their autobiography *Shake A Pagoda Tree*, Mike related how they were appearing at the London Palladium when Jack Murray called to see them in their dressing-room and showed Mike a magazine picture of four lads. 'They're big up North.' he said. 'Their agent has a record shop and doesn't know what to do with them. I've got them for sixteen to twenty weeks, and I can have a permanent share of their contract if I want to. Do you want to come in with me?'

Mike told him, 'I'm not gambling any more, Jack, Bernie and I are going to work on our act and try to make a go of it. Thanks all the same.'

When the duo began hosting the series 'Big Night Out', the Beatles were booked on the fifth recording session and when the two comics arrived at Didsbury one day they saw huge mobs outside the studio and asked the doorman what was happening.

'The Beatles are on the show today, sir,' he said and, of course, they remembered the mop-tops who Jack Murray had said were big up in the North.

The group wandered in an hour late for rehearsal with Jane Asher carrying Paul's guitar, and John Lennon said, 'I'm sorry we're late, sir.' Mike told him OK, but not to make it a habit as it messed everyone else about. Then, in their act Bernie did a send-up of 'She Loves You' and the lads were very appreciative. John came round with the others afterwards and said, 'Thanks very much for all the plugs you've been giving us', which Bernie and Mike thought was rather touching.

The following Thursday, they all went to see the playback of the show at ATV House in London and when they were leaving, Brian

Epstein got in the lift with Bernie, Mike and their agent, Joe Collins. Brian told them that he wanted to get his lads into London so they introduced him to Joe, who said, 'Certainly.' He fixed up two dates for the Beatles and Mike commented, 'And [he] made £10,000 in the ten seconds it took to go down two floors. Not a bad rate of pay.'

This particular story is obviously not accurately remembered as there would be no way an agent could make £10,000 out of his percentage for two bookings of the Beatles at that particular point in their career.

The special edition of 'Big Night Out' was filmed at Teddington Studios, London, on 23 February 1964. This was screened in Britain on 29 February and was also shown in America when it was networked by the New York station WOR TV on 3 October 1965. The show was repeated by WOR TV on 4 October. The numbers the Beatles performed were: 'All My Loving', 'Till There Was You', 'I Wanna Be Your Man', 'Please Mr Postman' and 'I Want To Hold Your Hand'.

Of another Beatles appearance on 'Big Night Out' in 1964, Mike commented, 'They agreed to appear on the show immediately they returned (from their sensational tour of America). They landed at Heathrow Airport one day in February and nobody had ever before witnessed such an astounding, hysterical reception. Business ground to a halt as thousands of screaming girls took over the airport building. Then the fans streamed off to Teddington to besiege the studio, screaming and chanting, "We want the Beatles ... we want the Beatles."' The fans were unaware that the boys were being brought down river by launch and Mike and Bernie welcomed them as it drew into the bank, a few yards from the back door of the studios. Mike observed, 'They were nice lads, and we got the impression they were a little bewildered by it all. At that age it must have been onerous to adjust to instant fame.'

The cameras followed the Beatles all day long, filming them rehearsing and relaxing and, from time to time, snippets were screened on TV so that people at home could see how they were getting on. It was quite unprecedented and the show was a resounding success. Mike and Bernie got on well with the group, who seemed to like the two comedians.

Bill and Virginia Harry went to visit the Beatles when they were rehearsing for 'Blackpool Night Out' at the ABC Theatre, Blackpool on 19 July 1964. Brian Epstein, Neil Aspinall and Mal Evans were there talking to Liverpool comedian Johnny Hackett. Jimmy Edwards and Frank Berry kept coming out with jokes that weren't in the script and John Lennon said, 'They'll use different jokes in the actual programme because they want to keep the musicians in the pit laughing.'

Apart from performing numbers such as 'A Hard Day's Night' and 'Long Tall Sally', the Beatles appeared in several sketches, joined by Mike and Bernie. In one, Ringo was a patient awaiting an operation and in another they were a crew of dustmen.

Bernie Winters died of cancer in May 1991.

With A Little Help From My Friends (Song)
Paul wrote this song in March 1967 in the Cavendish Avenue workroom and received a bit of help from John with the lyrics. He'd used the working title 'Bad Finger Boogie' and was later to suggest Badfinger as a name for The Iveys. The song was included on the *Sgt Pepper* album and lead vocals were sung by Ringo.

Paul commented: 'Ringo's got a great sentimental thing. He likes soul music and always has, though we didn't see that scene for a long while till he showed us. I suppose that's why we write these sort of songs for him, with sentimental things in them, like "With A Little Help From My Friends".'

Young Idea covered the song and reached No. 29 in the charts with it in July 1967, but it was the Joe Cocker version which was to top the British charts the following year, in November 1968.

The number was included on *The Beatles 1966–1970* album and Ringo sang it on his 'Ringo' TV special in 1978.

There have been approximately 100 cover versions by a variety of artists including Barbra Streisand, Count Basie, Peter Frampton, Herb Alpert and Ike & Tina Turner.

Within You, Without You
Indian-sounding song, penned by George and included on the *Sgt Pepper's Lonely Hearts Club Band* album.

The idea first came to George when he was invited to dinner at Klaus Voormann's Hampstead house. They later began to talk and George noticed a harmonium, an instrument which he'd never played before. He began to tinker on it and the idea for 'Within You, Without You' came to him then – and he completed the song when he got home.

He was the only Beatle on the session when he recorded the number on Wednesday, 15 March 1967. There were a number of Indian instruments used during the session. George himself played a swordmandel (a zither-like instrument) and a tamboura. An Indian musician acquaintance of George played the dilruba (similar to a sitar) and tabla. Other Indian instruments were played by members of the Asian Music Circle from Finchley, and Neil Aspinall played a tamboura.

'Within You, Without You' was the final song to be completed for *Sgt Pepper's Lonely Hearts Club Band* and on Monday, 3 April 1967, George Martin, who had written a score based on George's ideas, conducted a section of strings to add to it, comprising eight violins and three cellos. The violinists were Erich Gruenberg, Alan Loveday, Julien Gaillard, Paul Scherman, Ralph Elman, David Wolfsthal, Jack Rothstein and Jack Greene. The cellists were Reginald Kilbey, Allen Ford and Peter Beaven. It was rumoured that this number replaced Paul's 'Carnival Of Light' on the Beatles' *Anthology 2* CDs, allegedly to achieve some sort of balance for George in the light of the preponderance of Lennon & McCartney compositions.

With The Beatles

The group's second album, issued on Parlophone (PCS 3045) on 22 November 1963. It went straight to the top of the album charts on the day of its release, replacing 'Please Please Me', and remained in the No. 1 position for 21 weeks, with a chart life of 40 weeks. During its first week of release it also entered the singles chart at No. 16 and reached No. 11 the following week. It remained in the singles chart for seven weeks.

Its American equivalent was *Meet The Beatles*, their first album release on Capitol Records (ST 2047), issued on 20 January 1964. This excluded five of the *With The Beatles* tracks: 'Please Mr Postman', 'Roll Over Beethoven', 'You've Really Got A Hold On Me', 'Devil In Her Heart', and 'Money', and included the tracks 'I Want To Hold Your Hand' and 'I Saw Her Standing There'.

With The Beatles included eight original compositions and three Motown numbers. The album opened with two of John's compositions. 'It Won't Be Long' and 'All I've Got To Do', followed by Paul's 'All My Loving'. George Harrison penned the next track 'Don't Bother Me', which was followed by the Lennon & McCartney composition, 'Little Child'. Paul takes over on lead vocal for 'Till There Was You', a number featured in the 1957 American musical *The Music Man* and a song which the Beatles had been featuring in their stage act in Liverpool clubs.

'Please Mr Postman' is the first of the Motown covers, a former hit in America for the Marvelettes. The Chuck Berry rock classic 'Roll Over Beethoven' is sung by George and Paul takes lead vocal on the following track, a Lennon & McCartney composition, 'Hold Me Tight'. Another Motown hit, by 'Smokey' Robinson, was 'You Really Got A Hold On Me', an American hit for the Miracles.

'I Wanna Be Your Man' was penned by Paul, with a little help from John, and Ringo takes over on vocals. This is the number which the Beatles gave to the Rolling Stones to record. 'Devil In Her Heart' had been recorded in America by female vocal group the Donays as 'Devil In His Heart', but it hadn't been a hit. This was followed by 'Not A Second Time', a John Lennon composition which was described by *The Times* music critic William Mann in such intricate detail that it helped to bring further respectability to the Beatles' music.

The final song on the album was the Motown hit 'Money (That's What I Want)', which had been Barrett Strong's only US chart success.

Woman

A number which Paul McCartney wrote specially for Peter & Gordon and the fourth and last song he was to give them. It was the 'A' side of their single, issued in America in January 1966 and in Britain the following month. The flipside was 'Wrong From The Start'. The song was also the first track on the duo's album of the same name, issued in March of that year.

Paul used the pseudonym Bernard Webb when he wrote the song and that was the name credited as songwriter on the actual record in Britain, but when it entered the charts a few weeks later, Paul admitted that he'd written it but wanted to see if he could enter the charts without using the magical Lennon & McCartney name. Webb was said to be an aspiring songwriter and a student in Paris. Paul also used the pseudonym A. Smith for the single's American release.

There were three Beatles-related numbers with this same title. In 1972, Paul's brother Mike recorded a number called 'Woman' and it was also the title of John's single, issued from his *Double Fantasy* album.

Wonderwall

Wonderwall was a film for which George Harrison composed the soundtrack. He wrote the musical parts for both the British musicians and the Indian ones, and produced the album himself. He went to Bombay to record it and commented: 'It was fantastic, really. The studio's on top of the offices but there's no sound-proofing. So if you listen closely to some of the Indian tracks on the LP you can hear taxis going by. Every time the offices knocked off at 5.30 p.m. we had to stop recording because you could just hear everybody stomping down the steps. They only had a big old EMI mono machine. It was too incredible. I mixed everything as we did it. It was nice enough because you get spoiled working on eight- and sixteen-tracks.'

The *Wonderwall* soundtrack was the first album issued by Apple Corps. It was released in Britain on SAPCOR 1 on 1 November 1968 and in America on ST 3350 on 2 December 1968.

The 94-minute film was produced by Andrew Braunsberg from a screenplay by G. Cain. It was based on a story written by Gerard Brach. Jack McGowan starred as a professor who discovers he can peek into the flat of a young model, Jane Birkin, and the scenes he witnesses turn into psychedelic fantasies. The movie also starred Irene Handl and Richard Wattis and received its London premiere on 20 January 1969.

Gordon Gow, writing in *Films and Filming*, commented: 'Unless you are jaded by too prolonged an exposure to the swinging half-myth, you might enjoy the blending of bright colours and Harrison music in *Wonderwall* ... the Harrison music replaces dialogue, waxing almost vocal like a cinema organist from the silent days.'

Wonderwall Music

The first solo Beatles album venture. *Wonderwall* was a film directed by Joe Mussot and starring Jack McGowran and Jane Birkin in a colourful psychedelic fantasy in which a man spies on a model through a chink in a wall. Mussot was a friend of George Harrison's and invited the Beatle to compose the film's soundtrack.

George recorded the album in two countries. Initially he recorded in London with Liverpool band the Remo Four who comprised Colin Manley on guitar/steel guitar, Tony Ashton on piano/organ, Roy Duke on drums and Phil Rogers on bass. Other musicians included John Barham on piano/flugelhorn and Tommy Reilly on harmonica. Eric Clapton and Ringo Starr were also reported to have aided George at the sessions.

Further sessions took place in India at the EMI studios in Bombay. George hired a number of Indian musicians: Ashish Khan on sarod, Mahapurush Misra on tabla and pakavaj, Sharad and Hanuman Jadev on shanhais, Shambu-Das, Indril Bhattacharya and Shankar Ghosh on sitars, Chandra Shakher on surbahar, Shiv Kumar Shermar on santoor, S. R. Kenkare on flute, Vinaik Vora on tharshanhai and Rij Ram Desad on harmonium and tablatarang.

Wonderwall Music was issued in Britain on Apple SAPCOR 1 on 1 November 1968 and in America on Apple ST 3350 on 2 December 1968. It reached No. 49 in the American charts but didn't chart in Britain.

The front cover illustration of the album was by Bob Gill and the tracks were, Side One: 'Microbes', 'Red Lady Too', 'Tabla And Pakavaj', 'In The Park', 'Drilling A Home', 'Guru Vandana', 'Greasy Legs', 'Ski-ing', 'Gat Kirwani', 'Dream Scene'. Side Two:

'Party Secombe', 'Love Scene', 'Crying', 'Cowboy Music', 'Fantasy Sequins', 'On The Bed', 'Glass Box', 'Wonderwall To Be Here', 'Singing Om'.

Wong, Arthur

A dedicated fan of the Quarry Men skiffle group. In 1958 he made some tapes of the group peforming, as did two other fans of the band, Geraldine and Colette Davis. However, none of the recordings exist as other items were eventually taped over the Quarry Men numbers.

Woodbine, Lord

This tall Trinidad-born, Liverpool-based character is usually known by this sobriquet, although his real name is Harold Phillips. The 'Lord' is a grandiose title, self-bestowed in a West Indian fashion, and 'Woodbine' is taken from the brand of cheap cigarettes he chain-smoked at the time. He is more familiarly known as 'Woody'.

A well-known character in the Liverpool 8 district where he put his hand to everything from building and decorating, to playing in a steel band and acting as barman. He opened his own club, the New Colony Club in Berkley Street, where the Silver Beatles appeared on one or two occasions. He also ran the new Cabaret Artistes Club for Allan Williams, a shebeen where the Silver Beatles backed a stripper known as Janice.

Lord Woodbine also joined Allan Williams, his wife Beryl and her brother Barry Chang in the mini van with the Beatles on their first trip to Hamburg.

In August 1998, the British national press made some extravagant claims about Woodbine's association with the Beatles, under headings such as 'THE MAN WHO PUT THE BEAT IN THE BEATLES', but they were wildly inaccurate and complete distortions of the facts.

Wooden Heart

A number featured in Elvis Presley's 1960 film *GI Blues*. It was released as a single in Britain where it reached No. 1 and it remained in the charts for 27 weeks – the longest chart life of any Elvis single in Britain.

The number was based on a German folk song *'Muss I Denn Zum Stadtele Hinaus'* and was adapted by Bert Kaempfert, Kay Twomey, Fred Wise and Ben Weisman. A single of the number by Elvis was issued in the States in 1964 but it only 'bubbled under' the Hot Hundred at No. 107.

The Beatles included the song in their repertoire during 1961 and 1962 with Paul McCartney on lead vocals. It was a popular number at the Cavern, and also during the Beatles' Hamburg gigs due to the fact that the part of the lyrics were in the German language.

Wooler, Bob

Born in Liverpool on 19 January 1932, Bob became a clerk in the local railway dock office in 1952, immediately following his National Service. He was living in the Garston area when, in 1957, he became involved in managing a skiffle group called the Kingstrums, who came from a notorious area of Garston called 'Under The Bridge'. He once entered them in a talent contest at the Gateacre Labour Club (which was won by the Mars Bars, who later became Gerry & the Pacemakers) and recalls, 'At that Labour Club I remember the Kingstrums coming into direct competition with John Lennon's skiffle group, the Quarry Men. Because they came from posh places like Woolton and Aigburth, the Quarry Men were considered to be snobs "Under The Bridge"!' The Kingstrums disbanded in 1958 but the experience of working on the local rock 'n' roll scene convinced Bob that he was more suited to compering the shows put on at local jive hives and as a compere-cum-disc jockey he worked part-time for promoters such as Wally Hill of Peak Promotions, appearing at Holyoake Hall in Smithdown Road and similar venues. He also co-promoted his own shows at Hambleton Hall with Vic Anton.

When the Beatles arrived back from Germany with copies of their single 'My Bonnie', they gave a copy to Bob, who began playing it at Hambleton Hall, and another to Virginia Sowry at *Mersey Beat*. The story of their recording session had already been featured on the front cover of Issue No. 2.

Bob's encyclopedic knowledge of the local scene soon made him a sought-after figure by local promoters and his advice was regularly heeded. Allan Williams offered him a full-time job as compere/host at the Top Ten Club, but when it burned down eight days after the opening, Bob was without work, apart from his compering activities – which soon provided him with full-time employment when he was engaged as compere at the Cavern Club.

Bob had a particularly pungent wit and he also created what were to become known as 'Woolerisms', a range of phrases he bestowed on local music personalities. They included 'The Nemperor' for Brian Epstein, 'Mr Showmanship' for Rory Storm, 'The Panda Footed Prince of Prance' for Faron, leader of Faron's Flamingos, 'The Sheik of Shake' for Karl Terry, leader of the Cruisers, and 'The Boswell of Beat' for Bill Harry, founder of *Mersey Beat*. Epstein was so flattered with the term 'The Nemperor' that he often used the phrase himself.

There was also a lot of good-natured banter between Bob and the Beatles during the Cavern introductions and John once told the Cavern audience that Bob was his long-lost father, whom he hadn't seen for fifteen years – and they believed him!

Bill Harry invited Bob to write a column for *Mersey Beat* under the title 'The Roving I' and his contribution for the 31 August 1961 issue was full of praise for the Beatles:

Why do you think the Beatles are so popular? Many people many times have asked me this question since that fantastic night (Tuesday, 27 December 1960) at Litherland Town Hall, when the impact of the act was first felt on this side of the river. I consider myself privileged to have been associated with the launching of the group on that exciting occasion, and grateful for the opportunities of presenting them to fever-pitch audiences at practically all of the group's subsequent appearances prior to their last Hamburg trip.

Perhaps my close associations with the group's activities, both earlier this year and since their recent re-appearance on the Merseyside scene, persuades people to think that I can produce a blueprint of the Beatles Success Story. It figures, I suppose, and if, in attempting to explain the popularity of their act, the following analysis is at variance with other people's views, well that's just one of those things. The question is nevertheless thought-provoking.

Well, then how to answer it? First some obvious observations. The Beatles are the biggest thing to have hit the Liverpool rock 'n' roll set-up in years. They were, and still are, the hottest local property any Rock promoter is likely to encounter.

I think the Beatles are No. 1 because they resurrected original style rock 'n' roll music, the origins of which are to be found in American negro singers. They hit the scene when it had been emasculated by figures like Cliff Richard and sounds like those electronic wonders, the Shadows and their many imitators. Gone was the drive that inflamed the emotions. This was studio set jungle music purveyed skilfully in a chart-wise direction by arrangement with the A&R men.

The Beatles, therefore, exploded on a jaded scene. And to those people on the verge of quitting teendom – those who had experienced during their most impressionable years the impact of rhythm 'n' blues music (raw rock 'n' roll) – this was an experience, a process of regaining and reliving a style of sounds and associated feelings identifiable with their era.

Here again in the Beatles was the stuff that screams are made of. Here was the excitement – both physical and aural – that symbolised the rebellion of youth in the ennuied mid-fifties. This was the real thing. Here they were, first five and then four human dynamos generating a beat which was irresistible. Turning back the rock clock. Pounding out items for Chuck Berry, Little Richard, Carl Perkins, the Coasters and the other great etceteras of the era. Here they were, unmindful of uniformity of dress. Unkempt-like long hair. Rugged yet romantic, appealing to both sexes. With calculated naivety and an ingenuous, throw-away approach to their music. Effecting indifference to audience response and yet always saying "Thank you". Reviving interest in, and commanding, enthusiasm for numbers which had descended the charts way back. Popularising (more than any other group) flipside items – example, "Boys". Compelling attention and influencing, wittingly or unwittingly, other groups in the style, choice and presentation of songs.

Essentially a vocal act, hardly ever instrumental (at least not in this country), here they were independently-minded, playing what they liked for kicks, kudos and cash. Privileged in having gained prestige and experience from a residency at the Hamburg Top Ten Club, during the autumn and winter of last year. Musically authoritative and physically magnetic – example the mean, moody magnificence of drummer Pete Best, a sort of teenage Jeff Chandler. A remarkable variety of talented voices which song-wise sound distinctive, but when speaking, possess the same naivety of tone. Rhythmic revolutionaries. An act which from beginning to end is a succession of climaxes. A personality cult. Seemingly unambitious, yet fluctuating between the self-assured and the vulnerable. Truly a phenomenon – and also a predicament to promoters! Such are the fantastic Beatles. I don't think anything like them will happen again.

Considering the piece was published in August 1961, it is amazingly prophetic.

In Issue No. 7 of *Mersey Beat*, Bob listed his Top Ten Mersey groups:

Well here it is then, my list of what I rate to be the ten most popular rock groups on Merseyside – excluding the Bluegenes, of course, they are beyond comparison. They are in a class of their own.

1. The Beatles
2. Gerry and the Pacemakers
3. Rory Storm and the Hurricanes
4. The Remo 4
5. The Strangers
6. Johnny Sandon and the Searchers
7. Karl Terry and the Cruisers
8. Mark Peters and the Cyclones
9. Ray and the Del Renas
10. The Big Three'

In addition to his writing activities for *Mersey Beat*, Bob composed most of the copy for the advertisements placed by promoters both in *Mersey Beat* and the *Liverpool Echo*. They were concise, lively and contained many puns.

When John Lennon paid for classified advertisements in *Mersey Beat* he would place notices such as 'HEAR BOB WOOLER SING with the Beatles at Aintree Institute; and 'Hear BOB BEATLE at the Woolerstute'.

Apart from his compering duties. Bob advised groups on stage presentation, discussed their musical repertoires with them and often recommended numbers for them to learn. Bob's collection of American singles, which he carried around with him to the venues in a portable record case, led to a lot of bands playing the numbers which Bob had searched for and selected himself.

Having sacrificed the security of a steady job to compere shows at the ill-fated Top Ten, he finally found what he was looking for when he became compere at the Cavern in 1961, a job which lasted for six years. The audience loved his announcements: 'Hello, Cavern Dwellers, and welcome to the best of cellars!' During his years at the Cavern he was to introduce the Beatles on stage more times than anyone else in the world.

The fact that the Beatles looked to him for advice was indicated when they asked him to attend their meeting with Brian Epstein on Wednesday, 3 December 1961. It was half-day closing in Liverpool that day and Epstein had requested a meeting at his office in NEMS at 4.30 p.m. Bob, John, George and Pete went to a pub called the Bridge to discuss Brian prior to the meeting and arrived late. Paul was 30 minutes late. Brian was slightly irritated at their tardiness and wanted to know who Bob was. 'This is me Dad,' said John. Bob later discussed the meeting with them. He also began to meet Brian Epstein regularly and revealed to him that the group were, in fact, actively seeking a manager.

When Epstein began to promote shows on behalf of NEMS

Enterprises in order to promote the Beatles and other groups he'd signed, he used Bob's expertise to organise, promote and run events at local venues such as the Tower Ballroom, New Brighton and the Queen's Hall, Widnes.

One of the most controversial situations regarding Wooler and the Beatles occurred at Paul McCartney's 21st birthday party on 18 June 1963. One of Bob's traits was to make cutting remarks, not intended maliciously, but rather out of his fondness for word-play. He made some reference to John's recent short holiday break in Spain with Brian Epstein, obviously couched in a way to contain a double-meaning. To a Lennon who'd drunk too many beers and wasn't interested in the subtle cleverness, it was like a red rag to a bull. He leapt on to Bob and battered him to the ground, giving him a black eye, bruised ribs and torn knuckles – which Bob sustained when he'd tried to protect his face from John's foot as he was being kicked. Members of the Fourmost pulled John off and Brian drove Bob to hospital. A small news item about the incident appeared in the *Daily Mirror* and John, initially refusing to apologise, saying 'He called me a queer so I battered his bloody ribs in', eventually allowed Epstein to smooth over the incident and Bob was paid a modest settlement of £200.

A few months later, Bob announced their final appearance at the Cavern. Their phenomenal success had taken him by surprise and for once he was lost for words, announcing them simply by saying, 'It's the Beatles!'

When the Beatles moved to London, Brian employed a number of his personal friends from Liverpool, causing an exodus of Merseyside people to the London offices of NEMS, but Bob wasn't among them. He remained at the Cavern until 1967. He became Ray McFall's right-hand man, managed groups such as the Carrolls and, for a short time, was married to Beryl Adams, Brian Epstein's former secretary.

With the closing of the Cavern, Bob took on various jobs as disc jockey in the north and worked for a time as a bingo caller at the former Locarno Ballroom. In the seventies he presented an occasional promotion in Liverpool and worked on several projects with Allan Williams, primarily Beatle conventions. By the eighties he was escorting visitors to Liverpool on special Magical Mystery Tours of the Beatles' former haunts.

Woolton Village Club, Allerton Road, Woolton, Liverpool L25

A small club in the area where John Lennon lived. The Quarry Men appeared at the venue only once, on 24 January 1958, on a special

Christmas party booking, during which they played a ten-minute spot.

Word, The

A Lennon and McCartney collaboration about which John was to say, that although he and Paul worked on it together, 'It's mainly mine'. It was included on *Rubber Soul* and, as the deadline for the album was pressing, it was rush-recorded in three takes on Wednesday, 10 November 1965, with additional instruments – Paul on piano and George Martin on harmonium.

The word in question was 'love'.

Words Of Love

A Buddy Holly song which he recorded in 1957. It was a part of the early Quarry Men repertoire and originally John and George shared lead vocals on the number, although John and Paul were to take the vocal parts later on and were heard on their 'Pop Go The Beatles' show on 20 August 1963 singing it, and it is also featured on the *Beatles For Sale* album.

When they recorded the number on Sunday, 18 October 1964, at Abbey Road it was the first and only time they recorded a Buddy Holly number in a recording studio, apart from the time they performed 'Crying, Waiting, Hoping' at their Decca audition.

The number is included on their ninth British EP *Beatles For Sale (No. 2)*, and their *Love Songs* compilation and *The Beatles Collection* set. In America it was also issued on the Capitol album *Beatles VI*.

World Without Love, A

Composition, mainly written by Paul, and the first of four songs he would give to Peter and Gordon. Jane Asher was to comment, 'The song came up one night when Paul and John were round at our home. They hadn't really finished it, but Peter and Gordon were mad keen about it right away. So the boys worked on it.' However, it has also been said that Paul offered it to Billy J. Kramer, who rejected it.

The number established the duo and took them to the top of the charts in both Britain and America, with world sales passing the million mark. It was issued in Britain on Columbia DB 7225 on 28 February 1964, and in America on Capitol 5175 on 27 April 1964.

The Beatles never recorded the number and it wasn't part of their repertoire. John Lennon was particularly amused by the opening words to the song: 'Please lock me away . . .'

Wyvern Social Club, 108 Seel Street, Liverpool L1

Club where, on 10 May 1960, the Silver Beetles were among the groups auditioning for impresario Larry Parnes who was looking for a backing band for singer Billy Fury, having been impressed by the Liverpool groups performing on the bill of the Gene Vincent concert at Liverpool Stadium on 3 May. Parnes told Allan Williams he'd like a couple of Mersey groups to back his artists on tour and Williams agreed to set up the audition. Mark Forster, one of Parnes' assistants, confirmed the arrangement in a letter in which he mentioned that they'd need backing bands for Duffy Power and Johnny Gentle. He added, 'We will make arrangements for Mr Parnes to come and audition your groups to select the most suitable. He will also bring Billy Fury as Billy will want one of these four groups for his own personal use. Incidentally, the idea of Billy wanting a group from his own home-town will provide several interesting press stories and publicity tie-ups.'

Williams had asked photographer Cheniston Roland to take photographs of the audition and a pictorial record of the events that day were captured on film, showing the groups who auditioned, in sequence. They were Cass & the Cassanovas, Derry & the Seniors, Gerry & the Pacemakers, Cliff Roberts & the Rockers and the Silver Beetles. Previous reports indicated that Rory Storm & the Hurricanes were also on the bill, although Chenison's photographs disprove this. The belief that they were on the bill probably stemmed from the fact that Rory was actually at the audition – but the publicity-conscious local singer was only there to press Billy Fury into posing in a photograph with him.

The Silver Beetles' drummer Tommy Moore was late for the audition and the group began their ten-minute spot with Johnny Hutchinson of the Cassanovas sitting in. Moore arrived halfway through the spot and took over.

Billy Fury plumped for the Silver Beetles and there are conflicting stories as to why they didn't become his backing band. Williams reports that Parnes quietly asked him if he could hear the Silver Beetles perform a number without Stuart. He alleged that Stuart wasn't a very good musician and had his back turned to Parnes during the audition. When Williams asked them to play another number, but without Stu, John Lennon refused and the opportunity was lost. Parnes, however, although knowing straight away that Stuart wasn't a good bass player, alleges that he wasn't worried about him, he was more concerned about the drummer, whom he considered far too old to be a member of a rock 'n' roll band. At the time John, for instance, was nineteen, but Tommy Moore was several years older. Such an age gap was all too apparent to Parnes.

Apart from the drummer's age, he didn't dress in the same style as the other members of the group and Parnes didn't like the fact that he was not punctual. Parnes was later to say. 'The most distinctive thing I remember is that four of them had these special haircuts and wore black trousers. They stood out amongst the others in the room. Their dress impressed me tremendously. But one of them dressed differently. I liked their style and music, but I told them they needed a more powerful drummer, somebody to drive their music along.'

Although he liked the band, Parnes didn't want to cause disharmony and didn't press the matter. Williams persuaded Stuart to draw some sketches of Fury and Parnes and Lennon requested Fury's autograph. Parnes has also recalled that after the Silver Beetles had auditioned, Lennon later asked him if they could have some extra time to play some of their self-penned numbers and he gave them an extra ten minutes at the end of the afternoon. He praised them for their original material and made a note in his pad: 'Silver Beetles: Very Good; keep note for future work'.

Allan Williams was to transform the Wyvern into the Blue Angel nightclub.

Yardbirds, The

London R&B group who formed in 1963 with the line-up of Keith Relf (vocals/harmonica), Andrew Topham (lead), Chris Dreja (rhythm), Paul Samwell-Smith (bass) and Jim McCartney (drums). Topham was soon replaced by Eric Clapton and the group took over the Crawdaddy Club residency from the Rolling Stones and were one of the varioussouthern bands who made the pilgrimage up north to appear at the Cavern in Liverpool.

The group appeared on the *Beatles Christmas Show* at the Odeon, Hammersmith in 1964, during which they had a ten-minute spot. This was probably where George Harrison noticed the nineteen-year-old guitarist Clapton for the first time. The Yardbirds were also on the bill of the Beatles' final concert appearance in Britain on 1 May 1966 at the Empire Pool, Wembley.

They had a number of hits, including 'Good Morning Little Schoolgirl' and 'For Your Love' before disbanding in 1968. At that time Jimmy Page was a member of the band and formed the New Yardbirds, although he quickly changed the name to Led Zeppelin.

Ye Cracke, Rice Street, Liverpool L1

The nearest public house to Liverpool College of Art. During a college party, John went across to Cynthia Powell and asked her for a dance. Cynthia, who had a crush on John, but was too nervous to admit it, panicked and said, 'I'm awfully sorry, but I'm engaged to a fellow in Hoylake.' Annoyed, John snapped, 'I didn't ask you to marry me.' When the dance was over, John invited Cynthia to Ye

Cracke for a drink and later that evening he took her to Stu Sutcliffe's flat and they made love for the first time.

Ye Cracke was the main after-hours haunt for some of the art students. Arthur Ballard, one of the lecturers, used to tutor some of his pupils in 'The War Office', a tiny room in the pub, so named because it was where regulars used to discuss the events of the Crimean War, as they occurred.

Once, when they were standing outside the pub one lunchtime, drinks in hand, John and Cynthia spotted actor John Gregson (a Liverpool-born British film star whose most popular film was *Genevieve*). John desperately looked around for something unusual for the actor to sign. He spotted an old boot and asked Gregson to autograph it. The actor was amused by the gesture and signed it across the stitching.

Painter Adrian Henri remembered one incident at Ye Cracke where John was lying on the floor imitating swimming movements. A barmaid told him to stop and he said, 'I can't stop, or I'll drown!'

John also used to have long conversations with Stuart Sutcliffe about art and artists, with Stu filling in the background to art movements of the early twentieth century, such as the Dada school, to him.

Bill Harry and John also used to have long conversations together in their favourite seat, beneath an etching of 'The Death of Nelson'. This is where John showed Bill samples of his poetry, which led to Harry asking him to contribute written work to *Mersey Beat*. When Lennon, Sutcliffe, Rod Murray and Harry used to chat in the evenings, Harry suggested that the four of them call themselves the Dissenters and attempt to make Liverpool famous: John and his music, Stu and Rod with their painting and Harry with his writing.

Yellow Teddybears, The

A 1963 British movie in which the Beatles were offered a cameo role.

Paul McCartney was to comment:

> Very early on we said to Brian Epstein that we wanted to be in films, but it had to be something decent. Something that we wouldn't be ashamed of later by which time it's too late. Quite early on there were a few things in the offing. Some were just rough ideas for a movie, while others were ready to go into production. One serious offer came from some London people, who were making a film called *The Yellow Teddybears*. I think they wanted us to pop up in a couple of scenes to perform a song or two.

Naturally, we thought that it could be quite interesting, maybe even a bit of a laugh – just getting our four faces up there on the big screen. However, it wasn't as easy as that. In this instance, it turned out that either somebody else would write the music and we had to perform their songs or it might have been that part of the deal meant that we also had to give away the copyright of any new songs which were featured in the film. Whatever the reason, we immediately decided that was too much, so we turned that offer down and waited until something better turned up.

The low-budget film was produced and directed by Richard Hartford Davis. After the Beatles declined the offer, the film was released with music performed by singer/guitarist Malcolm Mitchell.

Also known as *Gutter Girls* or *The Thrill Seekers* in some territories, it concerned the fortunes of teenage girls attending Peterbridge Grammar School. Pupils begin to sport small yellow teddybear badges – a sign indicating they'd lost their virginity.

Yellow Submarine (Album)

The soundtrack album of *Yellow Submarine* was issued several months after the release of the actual animated film. It had been planned to issue it in December 1968. But it was finally issued in Britain on 17 January 1969 on Parlophone PCS 7070. There had been discussions about releasing a *Yellow Submarine* EP with four Beatles numbers on it, but this plan was shelved.

The problem was that the LP couldn't strictly be regarded as a new Beatles album as one half of it contained music by the George Martin Orchestra. Two of the Beatles numbers had already been available on previous releases some time before and the record buyer was left with only four new Beatles numbers.

The album became the second Beatles album not to top the British charts, reaching only the No. 2 position, although, ironically, *The Beatles* double album occupied the No.1 position.

It was issued in America on Capitol SW 153 and also reached No. 2, once again being prevented from occupying the No.1 spot by *The Beatles* double album.

The track listing was, Side One: 'Yellow Submarine', 'Only A Northern Song', 'All Together Now', 'Hey Bulldog', 'It's All Too Much'. Side Two (all tracks by the George Martin Orchestra): 'Pepperland', 'Sea of Time', 'Sea of Holes', 'Sea of Monsters', 'March of the Meanies', 'Pepperland Laid Waste' and 'Yellow Submarine in Pepperland'.

Tunes or parts of tunes heard on the film soundtrack but not
included on the soundtrack album were: 'Eleanor Rigby', an
orchestral section of 'A Day In The Life', 'When I'm Sixty-Four',
'Nowhere Man', 'Lucy In The Sky with Diamonds', 'Sgt Pepper's
Lonely Hearts Club Band', 'With A Little Help From My Friends',
'All You Need Is Love' and 'Baby You're A Rich Man'.

Yellow Submarine (Film)

The animated feature film *Yellow Submarine,* subtitled *Nothing Is
Real,* originated in the series of Beatles cartoons made by TV
Cartoons and financed by King Features.

Hungarian-born Al Brodax originally had the idea of using the
Beatles in a 'Fantasia'-like full-length cartoon in 1966. He
contacted George Dunning, a Canadian animator who had set up a
studio in London in 1957 and who had been involved in the
Beatles' cartoon series, and director Charles Jenkins. They then
hired a Czech-born artist, Heinz Edelmann, as designer.

The official screenplay credit reads: 'Written by Lee Minoff and
Al Brodax, Jack Mendelsohn and Erich Segal, from an original
story by Lee Minoff.' However, Heinz Edelmann commented:
'There was never one script. We had about twenty. Roger
McGough (of the Scaffold) was responsible for much of it. But
there were no strong opponents for the Beatles so I had to invent
the Blue Meanies.'

Liverpool poet Roger McGough was brought in to add a
Liverpool flavour to the script and says he was paid £500, but
wasn't credited – and he would have preferred the credit to the
money.

Brodax was to say: 'We derived a lot from the *Sgt Pepper* album.
We took the word "pepper", which was positive, spicy, and created
a place called Pepperland, which is full of colour and music. But in
the hills around live Blue Meanies, who hate colour, hate everything
positive.'

Brodax recalled that when he was working on the story with
Erich Segal in a flat in London's Mayfair, John and Paul would ring
up with script suggestions. Brodax recalls one particular call, made
at 3.00 a.m. from John, in which he said: 'Wouldn't it be great if
Ringo was followed down the street by a yellow submarine?' This
somewhat bizarre notion found its way into the movie's opening
scenes.

The writer who received the lion's share of press publicity was
Eric Segal – largely because he was a university professor. One
paper wrote: 'The script has been written by a Professor of Greek
and Latin at Yale, Erich Segal, and the final draft of the film script

was typed by the Dean's wife at Yale.' Brodax was responsible for adding Segal to the project's team. 'Erich and I both have the same agent, you see,' he said. 'Erich is also writing the script for a new Richard Rodgers musical. Before that he used to do a lot of translating for foreign plays, but he's never done anything like a cartoon film before.' Segal was paid $16,000 for his work on *Yellow Submarine*.

Director George Dunning told David Rider of *Films And Filming*:

> We commissioned several artists to design the Beatles . . . in an effort to find out what the design ought to be. Fred Wolf worked mainly on animation, Dennis Rich dealt with a wide range of design and Bob Balser came over from Spain initially to do character design. We took some recorded conversations of the Beatles and animated against this to get the feel of their personalities.
>
> The involvement of Heinz Edelmann was really a plot between Charlie Jenkins and myself. We met him in the spring of 1967 to look at the trial film made and discuss the project. Then I showed Edelmann's work in the German magazine *Twen* to Al Brodax, the producer, and he was happy that Edelmann should be brought in.
>
> Edelmann was delighted to be exploring this new medium. After two weeks he presented me with four drawings and that was enough – we knew we had a worthwhile film. Next, a two-minute pilot film was made in colour with some of George Harrison's sitar music on the soundtrack. Charlie Jenkins provided some sequences using his polarisation technique, which was followed by characters in backgrounds using some *Sgt Pepper* music.
>
> Bob Balsar and Jack Stokes, as animation directors, did approximately half each, Eddie Radage did one sequence, Charlie Jenkins took charge of 'Eleanor Rigby', 'Northern Song', 'It's All Too Much' and some other parts. Heinz Edelmann controlled the overall design, developed the characters and initiated the Blue Meanies where he pointed out that what was needed in the film was an enemy. This idea consolidated the film and gave it a strong plot.

There were many different approaches and styles used in the making of *Yellow Submarine,* one of which was rotoscoping, a method devised in the 1930s by Walt Disney Studios. This is a procedure where a live-action sequence is filmed, then traced over, painted, and made to appear like animation. This technique was subsequently used in the animated version of *Lord Of The Rings*.

To match the movie's range of styles and techniques, an array of eccentric or fantastic characters were introduced, such as Jeremy Hilary Boob, PhD, the Nowhere Man, who describes himself as a 'brilliant young physicist, classicist, botanist, essayist, satirist and artist'. Lee Minoff said this character was based on director Jonathan Miller, who'd directed Minoff's play *Come Live With Me* on Broadway. Comedian Dick Emery provided the character's voice.

There were also the Hidden Persuaders, gangster-style figures with outsize boots that open to reveal guns; Jack the Nipper, who had hands like shark's teeth; the Apple Bonkers, tall, top-hatted blue-faced men who drop giant apples on to their victims' heads; the terrible Flying Glove, a jet-propelled hand; the Butterfly Stomper; the Snapping Turtle Turks; and the Blue Meanies themselves, yellow-toothed, red-lipped creatures with black masks, Mickey Mouse-type ears, large boots and woolly blue bodies.

All together, there were 40 animators and 140 technical artists who produced half-a-million cells.

The Beatles were initially unenthusiastic about the venture, merely regarding it as a way of completing their United Artists film deal. This was indicated by their attitude to the movie's soundtrack. They provided four new songs but, as George Martin pointed out, in the case of 'Hey Bulldog': 'John said "We don't really need this in our album. Let's just give them that one."'

Incidentally, the 'Hey Bulldog' sequence was deleted from the American print of *Yellow Submarine*.

A popular, but untrue myth, is that as the London Symphony Orchestra were recording the soundtrack in EMI Studios in the early hours of the morning, Brodax told the group that another song was needed. George Harrison spent a couple of hours writing, then came up with the number 'Northern Song', saying to Brodax, 'Here, Al, it's only a northern song.'

The third original number was 'Altogether Now', the fourth was 'It's All Too Much'. The other Beatles numbers used were 'Yellow Submarine', 'Eleanor Rigby', a shortened version of 'A Day In The Life', 'When I'm Sixty-Four', 'Lucy In the Sky With Diamonds', 'Sgt Pepper's Lonely Hearts Club Band' and 'All You Need Is Love'.

George Martin was musical director for the film. He composed 'Pepperland', 'Sea Of Holes', 'Sea Of Monsters', 'March Of The Meanies', 'Pepperland Laid Waste' and 'Yellow Submarine In Pepperland' which, performed by the LSO, took up one half of the soundtrack album.

The group also made a brief appearance at the end of the movie when they invite an international audience to join them in song. For the rest of the film, actors dubbed the voices of the individual Beatles. John Clive was the voice of John, Geoff Hughes was Paul and Paul Angelis, Ringo. Originally, a youth called Peter Batten was hired to provide the voice of George. Although hundreds of actors had been auditioned for the vocal parts, the production team was in a pub one day and heard a voice, which sounded like George Harrison. It proved to be Batten and they hired him. However, he proved to be an army deserter and eventually the military police arrested him. Paul Angelis then had to complete the vocals, imitating Batten imitating George. Angelis also took the part of the Chief Blue Meanie, Dick Emery provided the voices of Hilary Boob, the Lord Mayor and Max, and Lance Percival that of Old Fred.

Clive, who had formerly compered local bands in Liverpool, became involved in a number of films, including *The Italian Job* and *Revenge Of The Pink Panther*. He was also to comment about Brodax's attitude towards the voice-overs. 'He said to us: "You're going to have to change the voices to be more American." We said: "No way are we doing that. We are going to stay as close to the Beatles as we can." We really argued it and put our jobs on the line.'

Actor Angelis continued to appear in both TV and film roles in productions such as *For Your Eyes Only* and *The Grimleys*. Geoff Hughes, a former member of Mersey Beat group the Travellers, is a popular TV character appearing as Eddie Yates in 'Coronation Street' and with roles in 'Keeping up Appearances' and as Twiggy in 'The Royle Family'.

The synopsis of the plot is as follows:

Once upon a time – or maybe twice – there was a place called Pepperland. On a peaceful day in this happy kingdom, a concert by Sgt Pepper's Lonely Hearts Club Band is interrupted by an anti-musical missile attack from the Blue Meanies. The chief Blue Meanie, his assistant Max, and their 99-numbered henchmen turn their splotch guns on the docile Pepperland populace, determined to rid the world of music, happiness and love ('A world without music is a Blue world!').

Old Fred, conductor of the Band, flees to the Lord Mayor, who puts him into the Yellow submarine for a last-minute escape. The sub surfaces in Liverpool where Ringo wanders aimlessly in boredom. The sub, radar-like, follows Ringo to his house. Fred enters Ringo's house, explains the situation and enlists his aid. They proceed to round up the others. John materialises out of a Frankenstein creature-like figure, Paul is found playing classical music, and George appears out of a haze of transcendental meditation. Armed with a battery of puns and four new songs, the Beatles board the Yellow Submarine and head for Pepperland. They are detoured through the Seas of Time, Science, Monsters, Consumer Products, Nowhere, Phrenology, Green and Holes.

They undergo time warps, chase Lucy through her 'sky of diamonds', climb clocks and soup cans, become ancient and infantile, molecularised, actually 'disappear up their own existence' and almost drown in the avalanche of apples, among other adventures.

Characters they encounter on their mad 'Modyssey' include the US Cavalry, Father Mackenzie, assorted monsters (including a vacuum-flask monster), Cowboys, Indians, King Kong and several unidentifiable 'things'. Ringo takes a liking to the super-intellectual Boob (a poetic personification of the 'Nowhere Man') and takes him along on the trip: in the sea of Green he is captured by a giant blue hand.

A Pepper-powered sneeze propels the Beatles through the Sea of holes into occupied Pepperland, which has been almost completely drained of colour. The Lord Mayor is astonished at the resemblance between the Beatles and the original Sgt Pepper Band. Disguised as Apple Bonkers, they infiltrate the musical instrument compound. Then it's Beatles versus Meanies, with guitars against splotch guns, the ferocious Flying Glove, the Butterfly Stompers, the Hidden Persuaders with guns in their shoes, the snapping Turtle Turks with their mouths in their bellies and the Count Down Clown with his nose-cone nose. A battle is waged to the tune of All You Need Is Love and love becomes the overwhelming power. A surprise ending carries the fantastic fracas right into the theatre.

The film was premiered at the London Pavilion on Wednesday, 17 July 1968. Apart from the Beatles, other celebrities who attended included Donovan, Sandie Shaw, P. J. Proby, Mick Jagger, Twiggy, Simon Dee, Tony Blackburn and Alan Price.

Hans Edelmann called the film: 'The first example of non-commercial, commercial entertainment.'

In his book *Full Length Animated Feature Films*, Bruno Edena commented: 'This production had the same explosive effect in the field of full-length animation that only *Hellzapoppin* had in the traditional cinema – getting far away from logical narrative structure. It is very close in atmosphere to the spirit of Lewis Carroll.

'The film is a masterpiece and it has opened up new and undreamed of horizons for animation. It bears seeing several times for its content to be fully appreciated, and it has given such an impetus to the full-length animated film and inspired the imagination of many film-makers, and original pieces of work are now being produced on animation benches all over the world.'

The critics seemed equally impressed. The *Daily Telegraph* commented: 'Not since Disney's *Snow White* or *Make Mine Music* has a full-length animated film cartoon come upon us with such surprising skill and charm and freshness as this little epic . . .

'It is more of a Beatles film than any of their others, partly because they do not come on themselves but also because the medium of a colour cartoon gives its creators closer control over every effect.

'The Beatles' spirit is here, if not in the flesh, their good-natured gusto, their kindly curiosity, their sympathy with their fellow men and their lack of pretentiousness are all summed up here with gaiety.'

The *Evening Standard* film critic, Alexander Walker, wrote: '*Yellow Submarine* is the key film of the Beatles' era. It's a trip through the contemporary mythology that the quartet from Merseyside has helped create. It's a pop voyage – "modyssey" is the word, I suppose – that sails under the psychedelic colours of Carnaby Street to the turned-on music of *Sgt Pepper's Lonely Hearts Club Band*. It combines sensory stimulation with the art of the now in a way that will appeal to teenage ravers and Tate Gallery-goers alike.

'Its inventiveness never flags. The influence of artists like Alan Aldridge and Andy Warhol is perceptible, but never plagiarised. And the richest bit of sociological cartooning owes more to writers like Marshall McLuhan and Vance Packard – I mean the regiment of Blue Meanies with their hidden arsenal of peremptory arrows and disembodied fists beating the Pepperland proles into stupefied obedience.'

The correspondent for *Variety*, the American showbusiness magazine, wrote, 'Unlike Disney, the film makes no concession to sentiment or the cuddly. The characters are motley, matter-of-fact, grotesque and tend to be harsh and angular and are introduced for their shock effects rather than any winsome qualities. They are modern pop art and surrealistic and eschew charm and determination.'

Unfortunately, *Yellow Submarine* was not given the chance to be the financial success in Britain that it might have been. Exactly three weeks after the London premiere, Judith Simonds, writing in the

Daily Express, reported that the spokesman for Rank had said: 'Attendances at the London Pavilion where the film opened on 17 July, didn't come up to expectations. As a result the film will not get a full release. We have some two hundred cinemas throughout the country and about half will show the film.'

Peter Brown of Apple commented: 'We are all puzzled. It's been doing capacity business at the London Pavilion, so we don't understand Rank's reaction.' Charles Berman of United Artists stated: 'We have done tremendous business during the three weeks *Yellow Submarine* has been at the London Pavilion.'

The published box office receipts for the Pavilion proved that United Artists and Apple had been right and Rank wrong. It had been doing capacity business, taking in £7,000 per week. But the damage had been done and Rank's decision to withdraw the film from more than two-thirds of their cinemas drastically affected its potential box-office income in Britain.

United Artists, with proof that the Pavilion receipts were very good, stated how annoyed and astonished they were by Rank's decision. Rank had to answer and stated: 'We have played it at 12 theatres outside London. On those results, which have been rather disappointing, a number of theatre bookings for the film have been taken out. This is because the film is obviously not appealing to some people whom one might expect it to.'

In America, where it opened a few months later, it was a great success, doing the same amount of business as the other major box-office hit at the time, *Funny Girl*.

During 1978, *Yellow Submarine* was revived at three film festivals: Locarno (where it received a special mention), San Francisco and Cambridge.

MGM Home Entertainment issued *Yellow Submarine* on videocassette and DVD on 14 September 1999. It had a new digitally renovated picture, a remixed soundtrack with 5.1 Dolby surround sound and the animated song 'Hey Bulldog'. The video and DVD were released simultaneously with the CD.

The film was restored at Pacific Ocean Post Studio in Santa Monica, California. Each track was fully remixed and digitally restored in 5.1 sensurround at Abbey Road Studios under the direction of Allan Rouse, with recording manager Geoff Emerick.

The DVD was available in the original widescreen format. It also included the short feature *The Mod Odyssey;* the original theatrical trailer; an audio commentary track; a music-only track highlighting tbe film's score; an eight-page booklet packed with inside information; behind the scenes photos taken during the making of the film; video and audio interviews with Paul Angelis, John Clive, David

Livesey, Erich Segal, Jack Stokes, Heinz Edelmann, Millicent McMillan and three storyboard sequences including two that were not featured in the film: Battle of the Monsters, Sea of Monsters and Pepperland.

Yellow Submarine Songtrack

The original 1969 soundtrack album only had six Beatles songs alongside an instrumental score by the George Martin Orchestra. The new *Yellow Submarine Songtrack* (as it was now called) was issued on CD on 14 September 1999 in a remixed soundtrack with 5.1 Dolby surround sound. The fifteen tracks in 5.1 surround were mixed and recorded by EMI senior recording engineer Peter Cobbin.

The soundtrack made its debut in the *Billboard* chart at No. 15 with a bullet.

On the re-release, Paul McCartney was to comment: 'When people bought the *Yellow Submarine* soundtrack the first time around, our fans were probably a little disappointed that all the orchestral soundtrack music was on there. Without doing the George Martin soundtrack an injustice, I think it's great that finally you can buy all the songs that were in the movie. I think it's a good idea to call it a songtrack as opposed to a soundtrack, because it lets you know you're getting the songs.'

Yellow Submarine (Single)

Paul originally came up with the idea of writing a children's song in 1966. For some reason, there was talk that 'Yellow Submarine' had some allusions to drugs, which was untrue.

Paul commented, 'I knew it would get connotations, but it really was a children's song. I just loved the idea of kids singing it. With "Yellow Submarine" the whole idea was "If someday I came across some kids singing it, that will be it", so it's got to be very easy – there isn't a single big word. Kids will understand it easier than adults . . . There's some stuff in Greece like icing sugar – you eat it. It's like a sweet and you drop it into water. It's called submarine, we had it on holiday.'

The number provided Ringo with his first vocal on the 'A' side of a Beatles single. When asked if there was any reference to drugs in the lyrics, he said, 'Nothing at all. It's simply a children's song with no hidden meanings. Many people have interpreted it to be a war song, that eventually all the world would be living in yellow submarines. That's not the case.'

John Lennon and Donovan were said to have aided Paul with some of the lyrics. The recording began at Abbey Road Studios on

Thursday, 26 May 1966, and Wednesday, 1 June, was the day when a number of special effects and a chorus were added. Among the helpers in the studio that day adding to the chorus and effects were Mal Evans and Neil Aspinall, Rolling Stone Brian Jones, Marianne Faithfull, Pattie Harrison, George Martin and members of the Abbey Road staff and engineers, including Geoff Emerick, John Skinner and Terry Condon. John Lennon blew bubbles through a straw in a bucket of water and there was a 30-second introduction speech by Ringo which was cut from the final release.

It became the Beatles' second double-'A' sided single and was issued in Britain on Parlophone 5493 on 5 August 1966 where it reached No. 1 in the charts. Capitol issued it in America on Capitol 5715 on 8 August 1966 where it reached No. 2 in the charts. The single reached No. 1 in various countries around the world, including Australia, Canada, Germany, Holland, Norway, New Zealand and Sweden.

It was also included as a track on their new album *Revolver*, issued on the same day. Later that year it was included on the December 1966 compilation *A Collection Of Beatles Oldies (But Goldies)* and was also to be featured on the *Yellow Submarine* soundtrack album in January 1969, *The Beatles 1962–1966* compilation in April 1973 and the *Reel Music* compilation in March 1982. A version of the song with a spoken intro by Ringo was included on the Beatles' *Anthology 2* CDs.

Yer Blues

John Lennon's parody of the British Blues boom of the 1960s, recorded in August 1968 mainly in a small annexe next to the control room of Abbey Road's Studio Two. John had originally penned the number at Rishikesh and the Beatles' rendition of the song was included on *The Beatles* double album.

In 1968 he performed the number on the ill-fated 'The Rolling Stones Rock 'n' Roll Circus', a television project which didn't see the light of day until it was released as a video in 1998.

John also performed it with the Plastic Ono Band at the Toronto Rock And Roll Revival Concert in 1969.

Yes It Is

A number penned by John at the beginning of 1965. He wanted a three-part vocal harmony effect similar to 'This Boy'. It was recorded on Tuesday, 16 February 1965, and George Harrison was to use a guitar tone-pedal on a Beatles record for the first time. The song was issued on the flipside of 'Ticket To Ride' in April 1965. A version was included on the Beatles' *Anthology 2* CDs. The number was also included on the CD compilation *Past Masters Volume One*.

Yesterday (EP)

The Beatles' eleventh British extended player, and the first EP to feature a different lead singer on each of the four tracks. It was issued on Parlophone GEP 8948 on 4 March 1966 and the tracks were: 'Yesterday', 'Act Naturally', 'You Like Me Too Much' and 'It's Only Love'.

Yesterday (Single)

Arguably, Paul McCartney's most famous Beatles song. It first appeared on the *Help!* soundtrack in August 1965 and was the title track on a 1966 EP. It resurfaced later in 1966 on *A Collection of Beatles Oldies (But Goldies)* and on the 1973 album *The Beatles 1962–1966*. It was finally released as a single in Britain on 8 March 1976 on Apple R6013 with 'I Should Have Known Better' on the flip. It was included on the 1977 *Love Songs* album and on the 1980 album *The Beatles Ballads* and *The Beatles Box*. In America it was issued as a single on Capitol 5498 on 13 September 1965 with 'Act Naturally' on the flip. It also appeared on the 1966 American album *Yesterday And Today*.

For such a classic love ballad, it had a very unromantic working title – 'Scrambled Eggs' is what Paul called the number during the first few days of the song's gestation period. He'd woken up one morning with the tune in his head and immediately began to put it down on the piano. He first played it to George Martin at the George V Hotel in Paris, while it was still under the working title 'Scrambled Eggs', and said he'd wanted a single word title. He mentioned he'd thought of 'Yesterday', but considered it might be too corny. Martin persuaded him it wasn't.

The recording took place on Monday, 14 June 1965, and it turned out to be something of a solo job as Paul's vocals were only accompanied by a guitar and a string quartet. John, George and Ringo don't appear on the track and it was George Martin's idea to include a classic string quartet – a first for a Beatles record. The musicians comprised Tony Gilbert and Sidney Sax on violins, Francisco Gabarro on cello and Kenneth Essex on viola.

Paul commented, 'First of all, I was just playing it through for everyone, saying: "How do you like this song?" I played it just on my acoustic and sang it and the rest of the Beatles said, "That's it, love it." So George Martin and I got together and sort of cooked up this idea. I wanted just a small string accompaniment and he said, "Well, how about your actual string quartet?" I said, "Great, it sounds great." We sat down at the piano and cooked that one up. I was so proud of it, I felt it was an original tune, it didn't copy off anything and it was a big tune, it was all there and nothing repeated. I got made fun of because of it, a bit. I remember George saying, "Blimey, he's always talking about 'Yesterday', you'd think he was Beethoven or somebody." But it's the one, I reckon that it's the most complete thing I've ever written.'

Paul has been quoted as saying that 'Yesterday' is his favourite self-penned number and he has continued to use it in his solo years, performing it on both the Wings' world tour in 1975–1976 and the British tour in 1977. It is also included on the *Wings Over America* album.

At one time Paul offered it to singer Chris Farlowe. He also offered it to Billy J. Kramer. Kramer had approached Paul in Blackpool and asked him if he had a song suitable to record. Paul played him 'Yesterday', but Billy said the song wasn't what he was looking for.

As it turned out, it became one of the most recorded songs of all time and within seven years of its release there were 1,186 separate versions of the number on record.

A million-seller within ten days of release in the States, it received the 1966 Ivor Novello Award in Britain as the Outstanding Song of the Year and in America it was the most performed pop song for eight consecutive years, from 1965–1973.

Among the artists who have recorded 'Yesterday' on disc are Cilla Black, Pat Boone, Nat King Cole, Perry Como, Marianne Faithfull, Tom Jones, Otis Redding, Smokey Robinson & the Miracles and Frank Sinatra. In 1976 'Yesterday' was issued as a single in Britain for the first time and reached No. 8 in the UK chart. Two versions of the number were also included on the *Anthology 2* CDs.

In January 2000 it was announced that 'Yesterday' had been the most-played, British-written song of the century in America – the only number by a British writer to have been aired more than seven million times on TV and radio since its release.

Yesterday And Today

An American album issued on Capitol ST 2553 on 29 June 1966. Capitol Records were eager to rush out another Beatles album and compiled one containing tracks from the British albums *Help!*, *Rubber Soul* and *Revolver* which hadn't been used on the American releases of those albums. They obtained an additional three tracks from EMI which hadn't been available in the US, and decided on the title because 'Yesterday' was one of the featured tracks.

However, the album was to cause a great deal of controversy. In Britain the Beatles had posed for a photograph, taken by Robert Whitaker, in which they were dressed in white smocks. As props they had the heads and torsos of dolls and pieces of red meat, which were placed on their laps and shoulders. The picture had been used in full-page advertisements in the British musical press advertising 'Paperback Writer'. It also featured as a front-page colour cover in the music paper *Disc* on 11 June 1966.

This was the photograph originally used for the cover of *Yesterday And Today*. Advance copies went out to DJs and the media and an immediate controversy was aroused. Phone calls of complaint poured into the offices of Capitol Records and an emergency meeting was held.

The picture had aroused no great alarm in Britain, just as Maureen Cleave's article in which John talked about the Beatles and Christ aroused no opposition in Britain – yet the new album cover, which became known as the 'butcher' cover (because the picture was likened to the Beatles wearing butchers' smocks and being in an abattoir), was greeted with horror in some quarters in America.

Capitol apologised to the media and decided to withdraw it and engaged Capitol staff to spend a weekend replacing the 750,000 covers with a different picture – a bland shot of the group posing around a travelling trunk. They also had to destroy promotional material which had already been printed and the entire exercise cost them $200,000. Most employees just threw away the old sleeve and replaced it with the new one. In a number of instances, employees pasted the new cover over the old one – years later, when fans found they were able to peel off the top layer to reveal the original 'butcher' cover, the 'butcher' sleeves became collectors' items worth hundreds of dollars.

The Beatles were perplexed by the American reaction and John Lennon said that the original cover was: '. . . as relevant as Vietnam'.

At one time it was suggested that the Beatles had devised the photograph deliberately as a comment on the way Capitol 'butchered' their American albums. This was because Capitol issued less tracks on American releases than their British equivalents, allowing Capitol to build up extra tracks which could provide material for additional LPs.

The album reached No. 1 in the American charts, but Capitol said that *Yesterday And Today* was the first and only Beatles album to lose money – because of the costs associated with altering the cover and replacing the promotional material.

The tracks were, Side One: 'Drive My Car', 'I'm Only Sleeping' 'Nowhere Man', 'Doctor Robert', 'Yesterday', 'Act Naturally'. Side Two: 'And Your Bird Can Sing', 'If I Needed Someone', 'We Can Work It Out', 'What Goes On', 'Day Tripper'.

YMCA, Birkenhead Road, Hoylake, Wirral LA7

Charles Trantor was the organiser responsible for booking acts into the venue and had been an eager *Mersey Beat* reader and keen to book the Beatles. Despite this, when he eventually managed to engage the band he advertised them as 'the Beetles'.

Pete Best had been in charge of booking the group and Trantor first wrote to him on Saturday, 19 August 1961:

> Dear Mr Best,
>
> Will you let me have your terms for the services of the Beetles to play at Hoylake YMCA from 8.00 p.m. until 11.00 p.m., and if you are available on Friday, the 8th, Sept. next.
>
> As I am going away from home in two days time, I would appreciate it if you could let me have this information by return. You can get me on the phone at the above no. on Monday or Tuesday mornings.
>
> We have other dates, but this is the present urgent one as I wish to fix it before going away.

Trantor was so keen to book the group that he travelled to Pete Best's house in West Derby to offer him £30 for the single appearance.

No arrangements were made for the Beatles to appear there on the September 8 date as they had already been booked to play at St John's Hall in Tuebrook. However, the group made a single appearance at the venue on 24 February 1962, although they were not very well received by the audience and were booed off stage. By that time Brian Epstein was managing the group.

Yolland, Peter

The man who staged the two *Beatles Christmas Shows*.

Yolland had just completed a series of Intermediate French for Schools TV programmes when he was approached in October 1963 to produce the first *Beatles Christmas Show*. Yolland had produced pantomimes in provincial cities for the previous eight years and he received a phone call from agent Joe Collins who asked him whether he would be prepared to produce a show with the Beatles. He accepted the assignment, although he only had six weeks before the show was to open. He was commissioned to devise, produce and direct the

Christmas show and stage it at the Finsbury Park Astoria in London. He immediately hired TV designer Andrew Drummond to design the sets and worked out that rather than simply present a series of pop acts, he would link the Beatles throughout the show by a series of sketches. He worked on a silent movie sketch and set off to the Hippodrome, Birmingham on 10 November, accompanied by a recording engineer to record the Beatles reading their dialogue, which was to be played over the sound system. The shows were a tremendous success with over 100,000 viewing them. They ran from Christmas Eve 1963 to 11 January 1964. As a result Yolland was hired to produce another *Beatles Christmas Show* the following year at the Odeon, Hammersmith, in addition to producing a similar show for Gerry & the Pacemakers called *Gerry's Christmas Cracker*.

Plans for a third *Beatles Christmas Show* were shelved.

You Can't Do That

Number penned by John which the group recorded on 25 February 1964 as the flipside of 'Can't Buy Me Love'. It was also included as a track on the *A Hard Day's Night* album and the group performed it on their 'Saturday Club' and 'From Us To You' radio recordings. George Harrison played a twelve-string guitar on record for the first time on the number. He'd bought the guitar for $900 while in America and observed that it gave an extra depth to a group sound. Apart from their usual instruments, Paul played cowbells and Ringo played bongos.

'You Can't Do That' is also to be found on the *Rock 'n' Roll Music* compilation, the American *The Beatles Second Album* and *The Beatles Collection* set. They also performed it on the 'Ed Sullivan Show' and on their summer tour of America in 1964. A version was included on the Beatles' *Anthology 1* CDs.

You Don't Understand Me

A number recorded by San Franciscan singer Bobby Freeman in 1960 and immediately included in the Beatles' repertoire, with John Lennon on lead vocal. The Beatles also performed Freeman's minor American hit (it reached No. 37 in the charts) 'Shimmy Shimmy' at the same time.

You Know My Name (Look Up The Number)

John wanted Apple Records to release this single, with 'What's The New Mary Jane' on the flip as a 7 in single in December 1969 on Apple APPLES 1002 under the Plastic Ono Band title, but Apple wouldn't agree.

This was possibly because the two tracks were actually Beatles recordings and not attributable to the Plastic Ono Band. The Beatles had originally recorded backing tracks to 'You Know My Name' on Wednesday, 17 May and Wednesday, 7 June 1967, and Paul had once said it was his favourite Beatles track. John and Paul added vocals on Wednesday, 30 April 1969.

John completed work on these two tracks on Wednesday, 26 November 1969, and Apple had actually issued a press release announcing that the Plastic Ono Band single would be issued on 5 December. However, internal pressure in Apple, possibly from other members of the Beatles, resulted in the release being cancelled.

'You Know My Name' was then issued as a Beatles track on the flipside of the 'Let It Be' single in 1970. 'What's The New Mary Jane' remained in the vaults for a quarter of a century and one of the mixes finally appeared on *Anthology 3*. The number was included on the CD compilation *Past Masters Volume Two*.

You Like Me Too Much

A George Harrison composition recorded on Wednesday 17 February 1965. George Martin plays a Steinway Grand piano on the track. The number first surfaced on the American album *Beatles VI*, issued in June 1965, and next appeared on the *Help!* album in August 1965. The following year it was included on the *Yesterday* EP in March

You Never Give Me Your Money

Song penned by Paul and included on the 1969 album *Abbey Road*. The financial crisis at Apple was the inspiration for this number, about which George Harrison commented: 'It's very ironical in a way because you know, we've all got a big house and a car and an office but to actually get the money that you've earned is virtually impossible, it's like, illegal to earn money, well, not to earn it, it's illegal to keep the money you earn. "You never give me your money, you only give me your funny papers", you know that's what we get, bits of paper saying how much is earned and what this and that is, but you never actually get it in pounds, shillings and pence. But I think it's another one of life's little problems that you never actually solve.'

Recording of the number actually began at Olympic Sound Studios on Tuesday, 6 May 1969, and continued during July of that year at Abbey Road.

Young Blood

A Lieber/Stoller/Doc Pomus composition originally recorded by the Coasters in 1957, it was added to the Beatles' repertoire in 1959 with George performing it on stage. When the group recorded it for their 'Pop Go The Beatles' radio show on 11 June 1963, Paul sang lead vocals. A version was included on *The Beatles Live At The BBC* CD.

Young, Muriel

Female TV presenter and disc jockey, born in County Durham in 1931, who became the first woman announcer on commercial television when she made her debut on Granada TV in 1955. Muriel then went on to host a number of pop shows such as '5 o'Clock Club' and Arthur Muckslow of EMI invited her to be the presenter of the taped shows sponsored by EMI records for Radio Luxembourg. In 1961 she began to host a show called 'Monday Spectacular' from EMI House in Manchester Square before an audience of 100 people. Later she presented an EMI show from the building called 'Dance Party' and was also host on 'Friday Spectacular'.

When the Beatles appeared on 'Friday Spectacular' to promote 'Please Please Me', Muriel began to announce, 'And when I tell you that their names are John, Paul, George and Ringo . . . ' and was then completely drowned in applause and screams.

Muriel was to say 'The Beatles changed everything. Before them I used to do all my announcing in cocktail frocks and things, but after the Beatles you could wear any casual outfit you wanted. They got rid of all the stuffiness and many, many years of dressing up. And of course after them, groups like the Hollies and the Animals arrived, and you looked absolutely potty in those formal clothes, completely wrong.'

Young, Roy

Musician, born in London, who began appearing on British TV shows such as 'Oh Boy' and 'Drumbeat', making his recording debut on Fontana in 1959 before appearing in Germany in 1961. He took over a month-long residency at the Top Ten Club, immediately following the Beatles' first season there, and had his contract extended to five months. He then teamed up with Tony Sheridan in the Beat Brothers and, for a short period, their drummer was Ringo Starr. He was then signed to a three-year-contract as a solo artist at the Star Club and joined Horst Fascher on his trip to England to book the Beatles for the club. He often joined the Beatles on stage during their Star Club appearances.

In a 1996 interview with writer Hans Olof Gottfridsson, Roy claimed that Brian Epstein offered him the opportunity of joining the Beatles. He said: 'I did various performances with the Beatles.

One night at the end of one of the shows, as I was leaving the stage, Brian Epstein approached me with an offer to go back to England with the four lads, as he would call them, to procure a record contract. As much as I would have loved to have done so at that time, I had to decline his offer as I was still under a three-year contract with the Star Club.'

Roy was later to join Cliff Bennett & the Rebel Rousers and in 1969 formed his own outfit, the Roy Young Band. He currently lives in the United States.

You Really Got A Hold On Me

A number penned by William 'Smokey' Robinson, which provided the Miracles with their second million-selling single following its release on 19 November 1962. It reached No. 8 in the US charts. 'You Really Got A Hold On Me' was included in the Beatles' repertoire the following year with John on lead vocal, although he shares lead vocal with George on the version they recorded for the *With The Beatles* album. The number was the first track of the new album to be recorded and, when they were in the studio on Thursday, 18 July 1963, they also cut another Tamla Motown number, 'Money (That's What I Want)'.

'You Really Got A Hold On Me' was included on the Capitol release *The Beatles Second Album* and is part of *The Beatles Collection* set.

The group performed the number on four of their 'Pop Go The Beatles' radio shows, with John on lead vocal, and they performed the number in the *Let It Be* film, with Billy Preston playing organ. The group also recorded the song during their 'Saturday Club' appearance on 30 July 1963 and that version appeared on their *The Beatles Live At The BBC* CD in November 1994.

You're Going To Lose That Girl

A number written by John Lennon in an attempt to capture the spirit of the sound of one of his favourite girl groups, the Shirelles. The Beatles recorded the number on Friday, 19 February 1965.

It was composed for the film *Help!* and appears on the British and American soundtrack albums. It is also included on the 1977 compilation *Love Songs*. It is often wrongly called 'You're Gonna Lose That Girl'.

Your Feet's Too Big

Song composed by Ada Benson and Fred Fisher, which the Beatles included in their repertoire in 1961, with Paul on lead vocal. The song was originally popularised by Fats Waller in 1939, but it's likely that the Beatles included it in their repertoire after hearing the Chubby Checker release in 1961. The Beatles performed it in Hamburg and it's to be found on *The Beatles Live! At The Star Club In Hamburg, Germany: 1962* album.

Your Mother Should Know

A Paul McCartney composition in which he tried to capture some of the spirit of songs from the 1930s. He even mentions in the number: 'a song that was a hit before your mother was born'.

'Your Mother Should Know' was recorded at Chappell Recording Studios at 52 Maddox Street, London W1, on Tuesday and Wednesday 22 and 23 August 1967, due to the fact that the Abbey Road Studios were fully booked at the time.

It was also the last recording sessions undertaken by the Beatles prior to Brian Epstein's death and he actually popped into the Chappell studios on the Wednesday to hear the playbacks of the song. A few days later he was dead.

Further recordings of the song were made at Abbey Road, but Paul decided to use the version recorded at the Chappell Studios. The track appeared on the British *Magical Mystery Tour* sound-track package of two EPs in December 1967, on the American album *Magical Mystery Tour* issued by Capitol in November 1967 and on the British released *Magical Mystery Tour* album issued in November 1976. Take 27 from the original recording sessions was included on the Beatles' *Anthology 2* CDs.

Your True Love

A number written and recorded by Carl Perkins in 1957. The Quarry Men included it in their act with George Harrison on lead vocals and continued to perform it on stage when they became the Beatles.

You've Got To Hide Your Love Away

Written by John at his home, Kenwood. He commented, 'This was written in my Dylan days for the film *Help!* When I was a teenager I used to write poetry, but was always trying to hide my real feelings . . . and it's one of those that you sort of sing sadly to yourself.'

John started to sing 'Here I stand, head in hand . . . ' then began to think about his emotions and decided he'd try to express himself like he'd done in this early writings.

The number was included on the *Help!* soundtrack, released in August 1965. It was also included on *The Beatles 1962–1966* compilation, the 1977 compilation *Love Songs*, the 1978 *The Beatles Collection*, the 1980 *The Beatles Ballads* and Reel Music in 1982.

Brian Epstein arranged for it to be recorded by Silkie, a folk group he managed who were composed of ex-students from Hull University. Their single was jointly produced by John and Paul with Paul playing guitar and George on tambourine. The Silkie single entered the *New Musical Express* chart for one week at No. 29. A version appeared on the Beatles' *Anthology 2* CD.

You Win Again

A country-style number written and recorded by the legendary Hank Williams in 1952. Jerry Lee Lewis recorded the song in 1958 and it was included in both the Quarry Men's and the Beatles' repertoires, with John Lennon on lead vocals.

You Won't See Me

A number penned by Paul, which was featured on the *Rubber Soul* album, issued in December 1965. It was one of three songs needed to complete the album and was recorded during an extremely lengthy recording session on Thursday, 11 November 1965. The song was also included on the Beatles' twelfth British EP *Nowhere Man*, issued in July 1966.

Zappa, Frank

Baltimore-born rock musician of some notoriety. He formed the
group the Mothers of Invention and although *Sgt Pepper's Lonely
Hearts Club Band* is regarded as rock music's first 'concept' album,
the claim has also been made of the Mothers of Invention's debut
double album *Freak Out*, issued the previous year in August 1966.
In fact, Paul McCartney once cited *Freak Out* as a key inspiration
for *Sgt Pepper*. *Freak Out* was one of the first albums to blend
popular music with classical arrangements and its theme was a
social commentary on contemporary America.

Frank was preparing an album to be called 'Our Man In
Nirvana' in 1967, but with the release of *Sgt Pepper* he scrapped
the plans, instead coming up with *We're Only In It For The
Money*. This was in reference to the Beatles making money out of
their new psychedelic/hippy image. During a break in the
recording of the album, Zappa and the Mothers visited Britain to
appear at the Albert Hall and during the trip Zappa phoned Paul
McCartney to ask permission to parody the *Sgt Pepper* album.
Paul referred him to the Beatles management office because: 'He
kept talking about "product", so it sounded like a business
matter.' Paul was not amused by the Zappa album project, which
caused the LP to be delayed for a few months. Zappa hired a
graphic artist, Calvin Schenkel, to make a parody of the sleeve in
which the Sgt Pepper military uniforms became dresses for trans-
vestites, with Zappa appearing in drag surrounded by a host of
characters who included the Phantom Of The Opera and Liberace.

The flowers of the *Pepper* sleeve were represented here by carrots and water melons.

In September 1967, Zappa came to the defence of John Lennon in an interview in the British music paper *Disc & Music Echo*, voicing his opinion that John was correct in his statement about the Beatles being more popular than Jesus in an interview with Maureen Cleave.

On 6 June 1971 when Zappa and the Mothers were appearing on a series of concerts at the Fillmore East, the last act to be booked at Bill Graham's famous rock venue which was closing down, John and Yoko joined him on stage. The concert was recorded and Zappa had intended using some of the tracks on his forthcoming album *Fillmore East*. Allen Klein refused to do a deal, so Zappa let him have the tapes. They turned up on John's double album *Sometime In New York City* and the illustration on the inner sleeve was a parody of Zappa's *Fillmore East* cover. John and Yoko had recorded four numbers with Zappa: 'Well . . . Baby Please Don't Go', 'Jamrag', 'Scumbag' and 'Au'. 'Scumbag' was a number jointly written by John, Yoko and Frank.

In 1971 Frank also teamed up with Ringo Starr after asking him to appear in his film *200 Motels*. Ringo took on the roles of both Larry the Dwarf and Frank Zappa. When Zappa's bass guitarist Jeff Simmons left the group, Frank intended replacing him in the film with Wilfred Brambell, who'd appeared as Paul's grandfather in *A Hard Day's Night*. He couldn't get him and used Ringo's chauffeur Martin Lickert instead.

Zappa died from a terminal illness in December 1993.

Zapple

An experimental record label from Apple which was launched on 9 May 1969 with two albums, John and Yoko's *Unfinished Music No. 2: Life With The Lions,* which was issued on Zapple 01, and George Harrison's experiments with a moog synthesizer called *Electronic Sound* on Zapple 02.

Paul McCartney had originally designed a cover for the series of Zapple albums, which featured a large, apple-shaped cut-out on the front with a picture printed on the inner sleeve. But this was later dropped.

John and Yoko's *Unfinished Music No.1: Two Virgins,* released prior to the launch of the Zapple label, was issued on Apple, as was the November 1969 LP *The Wedding Album*. The label was launched on 3 February 1969. Jim Mahoney & Association, a public relations company based in Los Angeles, issued the following release:

Beatles to introduce Zapple, new label and recording concept on May 1. The label will be called Zapple and will emphasise a series of 'spoken word' albums and some music releases of a more wide-ranging and esoteric nature. Price of the Zapple albums will generally be $1.98 or $4.98 depending on the type of release.

Zapple will be a division of Apple Records, which is headed by Ron Kass, who is also chief executive for all Apple music activities. Supervising the Zapple program will be Barry Miles, a British writer-intellectual in his late 20s.

The first three releases on the Zapple label are now being pressed and include:

1. A new John Lennon–Yoko Ono album entitled *Unfinished Music No.2 – Life With The Lions*;
2. A George Harrison composed-produced electronic music album which was recorded with a Moog;
3. A spoken-word album recorded by poet-writer Richard Brautigan.

Other well-known writer-poets already committed to Zapple releases include: Laurence Ferlinghetti – America's best selling 'serious' poet; poet-playwright Michael McClure; veteran literary figures Kenneth Patchen and Charles Olson and poet essayist Allen Ginsberg. Additionally, Zapple will release one of the late Lenny Bruce's last concerts as an album.

It is the hope of Apple Corps Ltd, that the new label will help pioneer a new area for the recording industry equivalent to what the paperback revolution did to book publishing.

The company is now studying new market ideas for the label, which hopes to eventually retail in outlets where paperback books and magazines are sold. University and college outlets will also be emphasised in Zapple's distribution plans.

Discussions are now in progress with several world figures as well as leaders in the various arts and sciences to record their works and thoughts for the label. The Beatles plan to tape several discussion sessions amongst themselves as an album release – probably for the fall. It is assumed that Zapple will have little difficulty attracting those people who might not normally record albums because of the general educational tone of the project.

Plans were set in motion to record *Listening To Richard Brautigan* as a third release on Zapple 03, to be issued in Britain on 23 May 1969. The album mainly consisted of author Brautigan reading excerpts from his works, such as *Trout Fishing In America, Revenge Of The Lawn, The Pill Versus The Springhill Mining Disaster* and *The Telephone Door That Leads Eventually To Some Love Poems*.

In the wake of Allen Klein's appearance at Apple, the Zapple label was abandoned before contracts could be exchanged on the Brautigan album and Zapple never released it. The album did appear a year later when Capitol issued it on their Harvest label on Harvest ST-4224 on 21 September 1970.

Brautigan was to write an introduction to a paperback book *The Beatles' Illustrated Lyrics* in 1975. He died in 1984, a suspected suicide.

With the presence of Klein at the helm of Apple, Zapple itself was scrapped after the first two releases, both of which failed to make the charts.

Zec, Donald

At the time of the Beatles' rise to national fame in Britain, the *Daily Mirror* was the newspaper with the world's largest circulation and its main showbusiness writer was Donald Zec.

Zec had conducted interviews with a range of world-famous stars, including Marilyn Monroe, at his home at 28 Maitland Court, Lancaster Terrace, London.

The Melody Maker, a music publication owned by the Mirror group, was due to announce that the Beatles had topped their readers' poll and Zec was commissioned to write a feature on them.

He first attended their concert at the Odeon, Dunstable Road, Luton, on 6 September 1963. Then he invited the group to his home for the interview, which appeared on Tuesday, 10 September under the heading 'Four Frenzied Little Lord Fauntleroys Who are Making £5,000 Every Week'.

The earnings were exaggerated, as the group wasn't pocketing that amount of money at the time. Zec also referred to their hair as being 'A stone-age hair style'. Such a large feature in the newspaper was a major boost to their career in Britain.

Zodiac Coffee Club, Duke Street, Liverpool L1

Small, narrow basement coffee club near Liverpool city centre where Cilla White (later known as Cilla Black) used to work part-time behind the counter and where she met her future husband Bobby Willis. Various members of the local scene used to frequent the premises and on one night there was a lengthy jam session with different members of local bands, including the Beatles, Gerry & the Pacemakers, the Big Three and Rory Storm & the Hurricanes.

The club only had one door which acted as both entrance and exit and the Beatles and several other musicians were under siege there one night when a local gang attempted to break down the door and attack the customers.